W9-CHS-121

How Toys Work

Levers

Siân Smith

Heinemann
LIBRARY

Chicago, Illinois

www.capstonepub.com
Visit our website to find out more information about Heinemann-Raintree books.

To order:
☎ Phone 800-747-4992
💻 Visit www.capstonepub.com to browse our catalog and order online.

© 2012 Heinemann Library
an imprint of Capstone Global Library, LLC
Chicago, Illinois

All rights reserved. No part of this publication may be reproduced or transmitted in any form or by any means, electronic or mechanical, including photocopying, recording, taping, or any information storage and retrieval system, without permission in writing from the publisher.

Edited by Dan Nunn, Rebecca Rissman, and Sian Smith
Designed by Joanna Hinton-Malivoire
Picture research by Mica Brancic
Production by Victoria Fitzgerald

Originated by Capstone Global Library Ltd
Printed and bound in China by South China Printing Company Ltd

16 15 14 13 12
10 9 8 7 6 5 4 3 2 1

Library of Congress Cataloging-in-Publication Data
Smith, Siân.
  Levers / Siân Smith.
      p. cm.—(How toys work)
  Includes bibliographical references and index.
  ISBN 978-1-4329-6579-2 (hb)—ISBN 978-1-4329-6586-0 (pb)
1. Levers—Juvenile literature. 2. Toys—Juvenile literature. I. Title.
TJ147.S633 2013
  621.8—dc23   2011041303

Acknowledgments
The author and publisher are grateful to the following for permission to reproduce copyright material: Alamy pp. 14, 17 (© Finnbarr Webster); © Capstone Global Library Ltd pp.7, 20, 21 (Lord and Leverett); 5, 6, 8, 9, 10, 11, 13, 18, 19, 22c, 23 top (Karon Dubke); iStockphoto pp.16, 23 bottom (© Sergey Lavrentev); Shutterstock pp.4 (© Peteri), 4 bottom left (© Elena Schweitzer), 4 top left (© Jiri Hera), 4 top right (© Adi), 12 (© axle71), 15 (© Warren Goldswain), 22a (© Foong Kok Leong), 22b (© Barnaby Chambers); 22d (© Perseo Medusa).

Cover photograph of a boy and a girl on a seesaw reproduced with permission of Shutterstock (© Warren Goldswain). Back cover photograph of a game reproduced with permission of © Capstone Publishers (Karon Dubke).

We would like to thank David Harrison, Nancy Harris, Dee Reid, and Diana Bentley for their assistance in the preparation of this book.

Every effort has been made to contact copyright holders of material reproduced in this book. Any omissions will be rectified in subsequent printings if notice is given to the publisher.

All the Internet addresses (URLs) given in this book were valid at the time of going to press. However, due to the dynamic nature of the Internet, some addresses may have changed, or sites may have changed or ceased to exist since publication. While the author and publisher regret any inconvenience this may cause readers, no responsibility for any such changes can be accepted by either the author or the publisher.

Contents

Different Toys

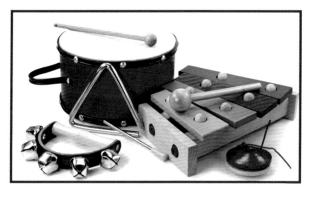 

There are many different kinds
of toys.

Toys work in different ways.

Levers

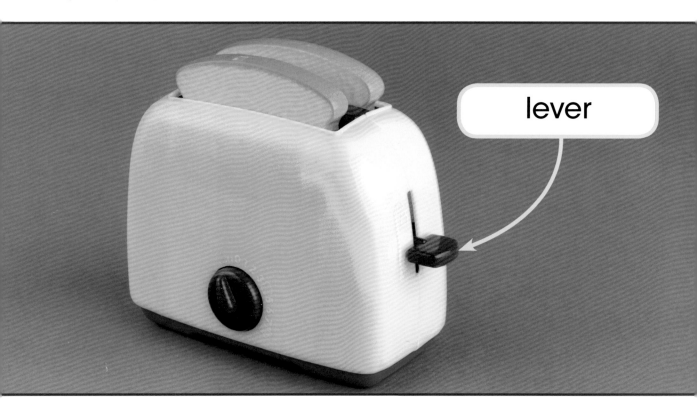

lever

Some toys use levers to work.

lever

A lever can be a hard stick or bar.

A lever can make things easy
to move.

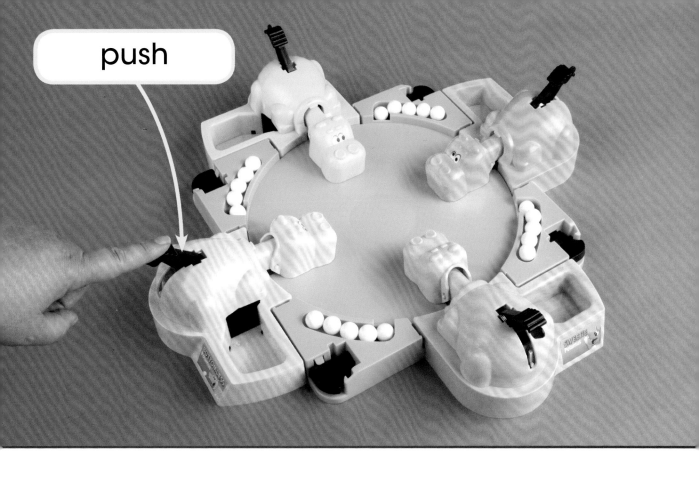

push

We push or pull a lever.

pivot

The lever turns at a place called
a pivot.

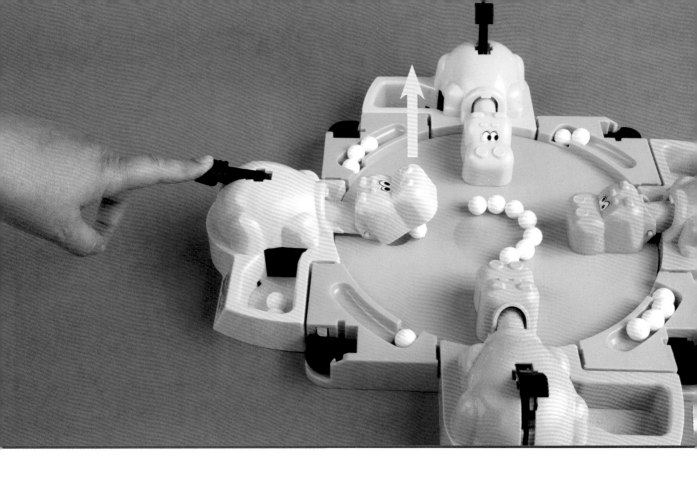

The lever makes something move.

More Toys with Levers

A toy shovel is a type of lever.

Your hand turns the shovel to lift
up sand.

A seesaw is a type of lever.

pivot

A seesaw turns in the middle.

When we sit on one end, we push
it down.

This pushes the other end up.

lever

This digger uses a lever.

shovel

You pull the lever to move the shovel.

lever

This toy uses a lever.

You push the lever to move
the arms.

Quiz

(a)

(b)

(c)

(d)

Which one of these toys uses a lever to work?

22

Answer on page 24

Picture Glossary

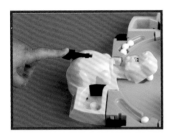

lever a lever is used to make something move. Many levers are shaped like bars or rods.

pivot name given to the place where something turns

Index

Answer to question on page 22: Toy c uses a lever to work.

Notes for Parents and Teachers

Introduction

Show the children a collection of toys. One or more of the toys should have a lever mechanism. Ask the children if they can spot the toy with the lever. Do they know what a lever is and what it does?

More information about levers

Explain that a lever is a tool we use that helps us to make something move. Levers also make it easier for us to lift or move heavy things. Many levers are shaped like a stick or bar. You push or pull a lever at one end, and it makes something move in the middle or at the other end of the lever. Demonstrate a lever in action. Explain that the place where a lever turns is called a pivot. (It is also called a fulcrum.)

Follow-up activities

Encourage the children to look around their homes to find one example of a lever. Ask them to draw this or bring it in so that these examples can be shared. For more advanced work on simple machines, children can work with an adult to discuss and play the games at: www.edheads.org/activities/simple-machines.

Annual Conference Series   1995

SIGGRAPH 95
Conference Proceedings
August 6 - 11, 1995
Edited by Robert Cook
Panels Chair Leo Hourvitz

A publication of ACM SIGGRAPH
Production Editor Stephen N. Spencer

*Sponsored by the Association for
Computing Machinery's Special
Interest Group on Computer Graphics*

COMPUTER GRAPHICS

PROCEEDINGS

The Association for Computing Machinery, Inc.

1515 Broadway, 17th Floor
New York, NY 10036

Copyright © 1995 by the Association for Computing Machinery, Inc. (ACM). Permission to make digital or hard copies of part of all of this work for personal or classroom use is granted without fee provided that copies are not made or distributed for profit or commercial advantage and that copies bear this notice and the full citation on the first page. Copyrights for components of this work owned by others than ACM must be honored. Abstracting with credit is permitted. To copy otherwise, to republish, to post on servers, or to redistribute to lists, requires prior specific permission and/or a fee. Request permission to republish from: Publications Dept., ACM, Inc. Fax +1 (212) 869-0481 or E-mail *permissions@acm.org*.

For other copying of articles that carry a code at the bottom of the first or last page or screen display, copying is permitted provided that the per-copy fee indicated in the code is paid through the Copyright Clearance enter, 222 Rosewood Drive, Danvers, MA 01923.

Sample Citation Information:
...Proceedings of SIGGRAPH 95 (Los Angeles, CA, August 6–11, 1995). In *Computer Graphics* Proceedings, Annual Conference Series, 1995, ACM SIGGRAPH, pp. xx–yy.

Orders from nonmembers of ACM placed within the United States should be directed to:

Addison-Wesley Publishing Company
Order Department
Jacob Way
Reading, MA 01867
    Tel: 1-800-447-2226

Addison-Wesley will pay postage and handling on orders accompanied by check. Credit card orders may be placed by mail or by calling the Addison-Wesley Order Department at the number above. Followup inquiries should be directed at the same number. Please include the Addison-Wesley ISBN number with your order:
    A-W Softcover Proceedings and
    CD-ROM Package ISBN:
    0-201-84776-0

Orders from nonmembers of ACM placed from outside the United States should be addressed as noted below.

Europe/Middle East:
Addison-Wesley Publishing Group
Concertgebouwplein 25
1071 LM Amsterdam
The Netherlands
    Tel: +31 20 6717296
    Fax: +31 20 6645334

Germany/Austria/Switzerland:
Addison-Wesley Verlag Deutschland GmbH
Hildachstraße 15d
Wachsbleiche 7-12
53111 Bonn
Germany
    Tel: +49 228 98 515 0
    Fax: +49 228 98 515 99

United Kingdom/Africa:
Addison-Wesley Publishers Ltd.
Finchampstead Road
Wokingham, Berkshire RG11 2NZ
United Kingdom
    Tel: +44 734 794000
    Fax: +44 734 794035

Asia:
Addison-Wesley Singapore Pte. Ltd.
15 Beach Road
#05-02/09/10 Beach Centre
Singapore 0718
    Tel: +65 339 7503
    Fax: +65 339 9709

Japan:
Addison-Wesley Publishers Japan Ltd.
Nichibo Building
1-2-2 Sarugakucho
Chiyoda-ku, Tokyo 101
Japan
    Tel: +81 33 2914581
    Fax: +81 33 2914592

Australia/New Zealand:
Addison-Wesley Publishers Pty. Ltd.
6 Byfield Street
North Ryde, N.S.W. 2113
Australia
    Tel: +61 2 878 5411
    Fax: +61 2 878 5830

Latin America:
Addison Wesley Iberoamericana S.A.
Boulevard de las Cataratas #3
Colonia Jardines del Pedregal
Delegacion Alvaro Obregon
01900 Mexico D.F.
    Tel: +52 5 660 2695
    Fax: +52 5 660 4930

Canada:
Addison-Wesley Publishing (Canada) Ltd.
26 Prince Andrew Place
Don Mills, Ontario M3C 2T8 Canada
    Tel: 416-447-5101
    Fax: 416-443-0948

Orders from ACM Members:

A limited number of copies are available at the ACM member discount. Send order with payment in U.S. dollars to:

ACM Order Department
P.O. Box 12114
Church Street Station
New York, NY 10257

OR, for information on accepted European currencies and exchange rates, contact:

ACM European Service Center
Avenue Marcel Thiry 204
1200 Brussels
Belgium
    Tel: +32 2 774 9602
    Fax: +32 2 774 9690
    Email: *acm_europe@acm.org*

Credit card orders from U.S. and Canada:
    1-800-342-6626
Credit card orders may also be placed by mail.

Credit card orders from the New York metropolitan area and outside the U.S.:
    +1 212-626-0500

Single-copy orders placed by fax:
    +1 212-944-1318

Electronic mail inquiries may be directed to *acmhelp@acm.org*.

Please include your ACM member number and the ACM order number with your order:

    ACM Order Number: 428950
    ACM ISBN: 0-89791-701-4

Contents

Papers Sessions, Thursday, August 10, 1995

Papers Sessions, Friday, August 11, 1995

Panel Sessions, Wednesday, August 9, 1995

Panel Sessions, Thursday, August 10, 1995

Panel Sessions, Friday, August 11, 1995

Preface

Welcome to SIGGRAPH 95, the 22nd annual ACM Conference on Computer Graphics and Interactive Techniques. These proceedings contain the papers that were presented during the Technical Program of the conference, which was held in Los Angeles, California on August 9-11, 1995.

The SIGGRAPH proceedings are unlike any other conference proceedings; they are unique in that they contain much of the very best research in the field. The reviewing process is rigorous and very selective, ensuring that the papers are of the highest caliber and that the proceedings continue to be a prestigious place to publish.

This year there were a record 257 papers submitted. The sheer volume of these submissions was overwhelming; if stacked on top of each another, they would have been over 30 feet high. Of these, we accepted 56 papers, 1 paper shy of last year's record. The growing international character of SIGGRAPH was also evident: 42% of the submitted papers were from outside the United States, representing 20 countries on 5 continents. And 20 of the accepted papers had at least one international author.

I am pleased that we were able to be more generous with the page limits than in previous years. Although we couldn't accommodate every request, in most cases we were able to allow the authors an extra couple of pages in which to describe their work. Unfortunately, the large number of papers we accepted means that once again we had some parallel paper sessions at the conference. I elected to have these parallel sessions rather than accept fewer papers or give the authors less time for their presentations.

I wish that everyone could see the review process at work. For years, I have been impressed with the effort given to making this process professional and fair. Though mistakes are certainly made from time to time, there is a tremendous amount of integrity and virtually no politics. The emphasis is exactly where it should be: on finding the best papers.

Here's a snapshot of how the reviewing process worked this year. First, I selected the Papers Committee. It consisted of 25 of the leading researchers in the field, 7 of whom had never been on the Papers Committee before. Then I spent two days with Ed Catmull and Holly Rushmeier (the SIGGRAPH 92 and 96 Papers Chairs) assigning each paper to 2 committee members, one of whom was designated the senior reviewer. The committee members had been asked to rate themselves in more than 50 different areas of expertise to help assure that the papers went to qualified reviewers. Each committee member ended up with an average of 22 papers, half as senior reviewer.

The senior reviewers were responsible for finding at least three additional reviewers from at least two additional institutions for each paper. There were a total of 370 of these additional reviewers. I continued the blind reviewing process introduced last year: the authors were asked to remove their names and all identifying information from the papers, so that the reviewers who were not on the Papers Committee would not know their identities.

The Papers Committee then met in Monterey, California on March 18-19, 1995 to discuss the papers. As each paper was discussed, anyone connected with any of the institutions the authors represented in a paper left the room during the discussion and the identities of the members of the committee who reviewed that paper were hidden from them. This ensured a free discussion and protected the anonymity of the reviewers.

Computer graphics is a broad and inclusive field. Many other fields have had their roots in computer graphics, including computer-human interaction, multimedia, and virtual reality. Because of this, the committee made an extra effort to be generous to work in new areas.

My thanks go first and foremost to the members of the papers committee. I am often impressed by the people I meet at SIGGRAPH because of their intelligence, creativity, integrity, and generous spirit. In no place is this more evident than on the Papers Committee. Serving on this committee involves a staggering amount of work. I am grateful that so many of the best people in the field are willing to devote so much of their limited time to helping ensure the continued quality of these proceedings.

I am grateful to Andrew Glassner, the SIGGRAPH 94 Papers Chair, for giving me a first hand look at the process last year. I would also like to thank Al Barr, Leona Caffey, Ed Catmull, Mary Anne Cook, Steve Cunningham, John Dill, Brenda Dreier, Brian Herzog, Betsy Johnsmiller, Sharon Kaiser, Jim Kajiya, Peter Meechan, Deborah Peifer, Holly Rushmeier, Stephen Spencer, and Cindy Stark for all of their help and support.

Every year I look forward to the SIGGRAPH proceedings to see what new and surprising advances have been made in the previous year. This year there is a great mixture of papers that represent both brand new directions as well as papers that go further that ever before in directions that are well known. I hope you will find them as exciting as I do.

– Robert Cook

1995 ACM SIGGRAPH Awards

Computer Graphics Achievement Award

Kurt Akeley

The SIGGRAPH achievement award is presented to Kurt Akeley in recognition of his contributions to the architecture, design, and realization of high performance 3D graphics hardware systems. These architectures define not only his company, but provide the high-performance 3D graphics facilities that enable scientists, engineers, animators, and other users to visualize, create, and dream in new ways.

Kurt Akeley received a B.E.E. from the University of Delaware in 1980, and an M.S.E.E. from Stanford in 1982. That year he was a member, with previous Achievement Awardee Jim Clark, of the founding team of Silicon Graphics, Incorporated. He has been a key technical contributor since then with primary design responsibility for most of the high-end graphics architectures in SGI's product history. Kurt developed the frame buffers and processor subsystems for the early IRIS series products, and many of the CAD tools used to design these and other products. He was instrumental in developing the graphics systems for the Power Series and Onyx systems, including the GTX, the VGX, and the RealityEngine. He also led the design and documentation of the OpenGL graphics software specification, which is now supported by Silicon Graphics and many other workstation and personal computer vendors.

Clearly he is a hardware wizard, but one who also has a deep understanding of software and especially the critical interaction between hardware and software. Currently, as Vice President and Chief Engineer at SGI, he is responsible for the specification of extensions to the OpenGL graphics software interface. He has received eight patents and has others pending.

In addition to his design contributions, Kurt has published papers about those architectures, and about graphics architectures in general. These publications are seminal contributions for the graphics community around the world. It is practically impossible for a paper describing new ideas in graphics architecture to omit, as background, essential references to Kurt Akeley's contributions. In addition, at the annual SIGGRAPH conferences Kurt's courses on graphics architectures and graphics programming have educated legions of professionals in our industry. He also contributes on the panels and program committees. In 1984 his colleagues at Silicon Graphics recognized his contributions by selecting him as the first overall "Spirit of SGI" award winner. He received the 1993 Distinguished Alumnus award from the Department of Electrical Engineering of the University of Delaware, and was given a University of Delaware Presidential Citation for Outstanding Achievement in 1995.

In short, through his tangible achievements Kurt Akeley has enabled a unique industry, and has enriched the lives of many thousands of users who are now able to break new ground in their own fields because of the power his inventions provide. Therefore, SIGGRAPH is pleased to present the SIGGRAPH Achievement Award to Kurt Akeley.

Publications

Kurt Akeley and Tom Jermoluk, "High-Performance Polygon Rendering," SIGGRAPH '88 Conference Proceedings, pp. 239-246.

Kurt Akeley, "The Silicon Graphics 4D/240GTX Superworkstation," IEEE Computer Graphics and Applications, July 1989, pp. 71-83.

Paul Haeberli and Kurt Akeley, "The Accumulation Buffer: Hardware Support for High-Quality Rendering," SIGGRAPH '90 Conference Proceedings, pp. 309-318.

Mark Segal and Kurt Akeley, "The OpenGL Graphics System: A Specification," Silicon Graphics, Inc., 1992.

Kurt Akeley, "RealityEngine Graphics," SIGGRAPH '93 Conference Proceedings, pp. 109-116.

Previous award winners
1994	Kenneth E. Torrance
1993	Pat Hanrahan
1992	Henry Fuchs
1991	James T. Kajiya
1990	Richard Shoup and Alvy Ray Smith
1989	John Warnock
1988	Alan H. Barr
1987	Robert Cook
1986	Turner Whitted
1985	Loren Carpenter
1984	James H. Clark
1983	James F. Blinn

1995 ACM SIGGRAPH Awards

Steven A. Coons Award for Outstanding Creative Contributions to Computer Graphics

Jose Luis Encarnação

The 1995 Steven A. Coons Award is presented to Dr. Jose Luis Encarnação for leadership in applied research using computer graphics for a broad range of industrial and medical applications, in international graphics standards and in computer graphics education.

His work in computer graphics began at the Technical University of Berlin in 1967 when he was also associated with the Heinrich Hertz Institute. In the period 1972-75 he was at the University of Saarbrücken. In 1975 he became Professor at the Technical University of Darmstadt, an appointment he holds today.

His earliest work involved development of basic algorithms such as hidden-line elimination and hardware for matrix manipulations (4 by 4). The Encarnação Scan-Grid Hidden Surface algorithm was particularly appropriate for surface representations used in CAD applications for car body design. It was during this period he became concerned with graphics systems applied to computer aided design—early evidence of his long-term commitment to technology transfer between academia and industry, a hallmark of the German and European technical communities.

His efforts in standards are consistent with that commitment. Starting in 1970, Encarnação lead successful efforts at Standardization in Computer Graphics in Germany. He convened experts from all over Germany and involved many from the group of researchers he had assembled in Darmstadt. He has been especially active in DIN and ISO standards, and was a primary contributor to the GKS graphics standard. He participated in the celebrated meetings at the Chateau Seillac in 1976 that led to the Proposed Core Standard put forth by SIGGRAPH. Recognizing at that time the need for a practical 2D system, he spearheaded the effort to produce the Graphical Kernel System, GKS, an extensive elaboration of an early version of the 3D Core proposals. Subsequently, under Encarnação's direction, Günter Pfaff et al developed a GKS implementation at Darmstadt that became the leading commercial product of its kind and remains in use in German CAD and other graphics application systems.

As a professor specializing in computer graphics for more than twenty years, Dr. Encarnação has been the advisor for more than forty Ph.D. students, many of whom have themselves attained professorial positions. To ensure the stability of Computer Graphics in academic computer science and in industry he initially established the Interactive Graphics Research Group (THD-GRIS) in 1975 at the Technical University of Darmstadt. In 1984 he also founded, and became chairman of the board, of the Computer Graphics Center (ZGDV). In addition to the main laboratory in Darmstadt, it now has associated laboratories in Rostock and in

Portugal. In 1987 he became the director of the Fraunhofer Institute for Computer Graphics in Darmstadt. At the request of the government, he aided in the re-unification task by establishing a Fraunhofer Graphics Laboratory in Rostock. These institutes are staffed by computer graphics professionals, more than a hundred in Darmstadt alone, and provide a home for many more students pursuing study and research in computer graphics and its applications.

An early example of successful technology transfer accomplished by these important and valued institutes is the GRADAS system developed in 1975 for AEG. The GRADAS systems was used by the Deutsche Bundespost for more than 15 years for interactive archiving, handling and editing of communications (telephone) drawings. A more recent example is the TRITON system developed for the Deutsche Wetterdienst (weather bureau) for visualizing and presenting weather forecast on TV and now in use by six European TV-channels. The latest contribution is an ISDN-based medical teleconsultation system, KAMEDIN, now being very successfully deployed by the German Telekom.

In 1980 Encarnação was the driving force behind founding EUROGRAPHICS, the eminent forum for graphics researchers and practitioners in the greater European community. Not only did he spearhead its formation, but he devoted considerable energy as its first chairman to sustaining it through its early and formative years.

He is the author of more than one hundred journal articles as well as eight text books. In particular, his book on computer aided design was one of the earliest to apply a systems approach for describing CAD. It was translated into four languages. Revised and extended in a second edition, it remains one of the few books that presents a coherent and unified approach to a theoretical underpinning for computer aided design.

Encarnação serves on several editorial boards, including *Computer Graphics and Applications*, *The Visual Computer*, and *Computer-Aided Design*, and is Editor-in-Chief of *Computers & Graphics*.

There are many ways Dr. Encarnação has inspired and influenced both the German and broader European computer graphics communities. He has worked effectively to infuse computer graphics into the international community, forging ties with universities, institutes and industry around the world, including Brazil, China, Japan, Mexico, Portugal, Spain, and the USA. He has received prizes and been awarded honorary degrees in recognition of these achievements.

Dr. Encarnação has been a tireless worker and supporter of computer graphics both as a key enabling technology and as a critical academic discipline within the field of computer science. His vision, insight, and energies have successfully sustained his devotion to academic excellence while providing critical liaison with industrial and standardization efforts. In recognition of these accomplishments and contributions to Computer Graphics, SIGGRAPH is pleased to present Dr. Jose Luis Encarnação the Steven Anson Coons Award.

References

Encarnação, J. and E.G. Schlechtendahl. "Computer Aided Design: fundamentals and system architectures." Springer Verlag, 1983. A second edition with R. Lindner was published in 1990.

Encarnação, J., G. Enderle, K. Kansy, G. Nees, E.G. Schlechtendahl, J. Weiss and P. Wisskirchen. "The workstation concept of GKS and the resulting conceptual differences to the GSPC core system." Computer Graphics 14(3), 226-230 (1980).

Encarnação, J. "Computer Graphics, Eine Einfuhrung in die Programmierung und Anwendung von graphischen Systemen." Oldenbourg, Munich, 1975. Two revised editions with W. Straßer will be followed by a fourth edition in 1995.

Encarnação, J., W. Giloi, J. Saniter, W. Straßer and K Waldschmidt. Programmierungs- und geraetetechnische Realisierung einer 4x4 Matrix fuer Koordinatentransformationen auf Computer-Bildschirmgeraeten; Elektron. Rechenanlagen 15, 5, 1972.

Encarnação, J., P. Bono, M. Encarnação and W. Herzner, "PC Graphics with GKS," Hanser Verlag (1987) and Prentice Hall (1990)

Previous award winners
1993	Edwin E. Catmull
1991	Andries van Dam
1989	David C. Evans
1987	Donald P. Greenberg
1985	Pierre Bézier
1983	Ivan E. Sutherland

Geometry Compression

Michael Deering

Sun Microsystems[†]

ABSTRACT

This paper introduces the concept of Geometry Compression, allowing 3D triangle data to be represented with a factor of 6 to 10 times fewer bits than conventional techniques, with only slight losses in object quality. The technique is amenable to rapid decompression in both software and hardware implementations; if 3D rendering hardware contains a geometry decompression unit, application geometry can be stored in memory in compressed format. Geometry is first represented as a generalized triangle mesh, a data structure that allows each instance of a vertex in a linear stream to specify an average of two triangles. Then a variable length compression is applied to individual positions, colors, and normals. Delta compression followed by a modified Huffman compression is used for positions and colors; a novel table-based approach is used for normals. The table allows any useful normal to be represented by an 18-bit index, many normals can be represented with index deltas of 8 bits or less. Geometry compression is a general space-time trade-off, and offers advantages at every level of the memory/interconnect hierarchy: less storage space is needed on disk, less transmission time is needed on networks.

CR Categories and Subject Descriptors: I.3.1 [Computer Graphics]: Hardware Architecture; I.3.3 [Computer Graphics]: Picture/ Image Generation *Display algorithms*; I.3.7 [Computer Graphics]: Three Dimensional Graphics and Realism.

Additional Keywords and Phrases: 3D graphics hardware, compression, geometry compression.

1 INTRODUCTION

Modern 3D computer graphics makes extensive use of geometry to describe 3D objects. Many graphics techniques are available for such use. Complex smooth surfaces can be succinctly represented by high level abstractions such as trimmed NURBS. Detailed surface geometry can many times be rendered by use of texture maps. But as realism is added, more and more raw geometry is required, usually in the form of triangles. Position, color, and normal components of these

[†]2550 Garcia Avenue, UMPK14-202
Mountain View, CA 94043-1100
michael.deering@Eng.Sun.COM (415) 786-6325

Permission to make digital/hard copy of part or all of this work for personal or classroom use is granted without fee provided that copies are not made or distributed for profit or commercial advantage, the copyright notice, the title of the publication and its date appear, and notice is given that copying is by permission of ACM, Inc. To copy otherwise, to republish, to post on servers, or to redistribute to lists, requires prior specific permission and/or a fee.

triangles are typically represented as floating point numbers; an isolated triangle can take on the order of 100 bytes or more of storage to describe. To maximize detail while minimizing the number of triangles, triangle re-tessellation techniques can be employed. The techniques described in the current paper are complementary: for a fixed number of triangles, minimize the total bit-size of the representation, subject to quality (and implementation) trade-offs.

While many techniques exist for (lossy and lossless) compression of 2D pixel images, and at least one exists for 2D geometry [2], no corresponding techniques have previously been available for compression of 3D triangles. This paper describes a viable algorithm for Geometry Compression, which furthermore is suitable for implementation in real-time hardware. The availability of a decompression unit within rendering hardware means that geometry can be stored and transmitted entirely in compressed format. This addresses one of the main bottlenecks in current graphics accelerators: input bandwidth. It also greatly increases the amount of geometry that can be cached in main memory. In distributed networked applications, compression can help make shared VR display environments feasible, by greatly reducing transmission time. Even low-end video games are going true 3D with a vengeance, but without compression even CD-ROMs are limited to a few tens of millions of triangles total storage.

The technique described here can achieve (lossy) compression ratios of between 6 and 10 to 1, depending on the original representation format and the final quality level desired. The compression proceeds in four stages. The first is the conversion of triangle data into a generalized triangle mesh form. The second is the quantization of individual positions, colors, and normals. Quantization of normals includes a novel translation to non-rectilinear representation. In the third stage the quantized values are delta encoded between neighbors. The final stage performs a Huffman tag-based variable-length encoding of these deltas. Decompression is the reverse of this process; the decompressed stream of triangle data is then passed to a traditional rendering pipeline, where it is processed in full floating point accuracy.

2 REPRESENTATION OF GEOMETRY

Today, most major MCAD and many animation modeling packages allow the use of CSG (constructive solid geometry) and free-form NURBS in the construction and representation of geometry. The resulting trimmed polynomial surfaces are a high-level representation of regions of smooth surfaces. However for hardware rendering, these surfaces are typically pre-tessellated in software into triangles prior to transmission to the rendering hardware, *even on hardware that supports some form of hardware NURBS rendering*. Furthermore, much of the advantage of the NURBS representation of geometry is for tasks other than real-time rendering. These non-rendering tasks include representation for machining, physical analysis (for example, simulation of turbulence flow), and interchange. Also, accurately representing the trimming curves for NURBS is quite data intensive; as a compression technique, trimmed NURBS can be not much more compact than pre-tessellated triangles, at least at typical rendering tessellation densities. Finally, not all objects are compactly represented by NURBS; outside the mechanical engineering world of automobile hoods and jet turbine blades, the entertainment world of tiger's teeth and tennis shoes do not have large, smooth areas where NURB representations would have any advantage. Thus while NURBS will continue to be appropriate in many cases in the modeling world, compressed triangles will be far more compact for many classes of application objects.

For many years photorealistic batch rendering has made extensive use of texture map techniques (color texture maps, normal bump maps, displacement maps) to compactly represent fine geometric detail. With texture mapping support starting to appear in rendering hardware, real-time renders can also apply these techniques. Texture mapping works quite well for large objects in the far background: clouds in the sky, buildings in the distance. At closer distances, textures work best for 3D objects that are mostly flat: billboards, paintings, carpets, marble walls, etc. But for nearby objects that are not flat, there is a noticeable loss of quality. One technique is the "signboard", where the textured polygon always swivels to face the observer. But this technique falls short: when viewed in stereo, especially head-tracked virtual reality stereo, nearby textures are plainly perceived as flat. Here even a lower detail but fully three dimensional polygonal representation of a nearby object is much more realistic. Thus geometry compression and texture mapping are complementary techniques; each is more appropriate for a different portion of a scene. What is important to note is that geometry compression achieves the *same or better* representation density as texture mapping. In the limit they are the same thing; in the Reyes rendering architecture [1] deformation mapped texels are converted into micro-polygons before being rendered.

Since the very early days of 3D raster computer graphics, polyhedral representation of geometry has been supported. Specified typically as a list of vertices, edges, and faces, arbitrary geometry can be expressed. These representations, such as winged-edge data structures (cf. [6]), were as much designed to support editing of the geometry as display. Nowadays vestiges of these representations live on as interchange formats (for example, Wavefront OBJ). While theoretically compact, some of the compaction is given up for readability by use of ASCII representation of the data in interchange files. Also, few of these formats are set up to be directly passed to rendering hardware as drawing instructions. Another historical vestige is the support of n-sided polygons in such formats. While early rendering hardware could accept such general primitives, nearly all of today's (very much faster) hardware mandates that all polygon geometry be reduced to triangles before being submitted to hardware. Polygons with more than three sides cannot in general be guaranteed to be either planar or convex. If quadrilaterals are accepted as rendering primitives, the fine print somewhere indicates that they will be (arbitrarily) split into a pair of triangles before rendering. In keeping with this modern reality, we restrict geometry to be compressed to triangles.

Modern graphics languages specify binary formats for the representation of collections of 3D triangles, usually as arrays of vertex data structures. PHIGS PLUS, PEX, XGL, and proposed extensions to OpenGL are of this form. These formats define the storage space taken by executable geometry today.

Triangles can be isolated or chained in "zig-zag" or "star" strips. IrisGL, XGL, and PEX 5.2 define a form of generalized triangle strip that can switch from a zig-zag to star-like vertex chaining on a vertex by vertex basis (at the expense of an extra header word per vertex in XGL

and PEX). In addition, a restart code allows multiple disconnected strips of triangles to be specified within one array of vertices. In these languages, all vertex components (positions, colors, normals) may be specified by 32-bit single precession IEEE floating point numbers, or 64-bit double precision numbers. XGL, IrisGL, and OpenGL also have some 32-bit integer support. IrisGL and OpenGL support input of vertex position components as 16-bit integers; normals and colors can be any of these as well as 8-bit components.

As will be seen, positions, colors, and normals can be quantized to significantly fewer than 32 bits (single precision IEEE floating point), with little loss in visual quality. Indeed, such bit-shaving can be utilized in commercial 3D graphics hardware, so long as supported by appropriate numerical analysis (cf. [3][4]).

3 GENERALIZED TRIANGLE MESH

The first stage of geometry compression is to convert triangle data into an efficient linear strip form: the *generalized triangle mesh*. This is a near-optimal representation of triangle data, given fixed storage.

The existing concept of a generalized triangle strip structure allows for compact representation of geometry while maintaining a linear data structure. That is, the geometry can be extracted by a single monotonic scan over the vertex array data structure. This is very important for pipelined hardware implementations, a data format that requires random access back to main memory during processing is very problematic.

However, by confining itself to linear strips, the generalized triangle strip format leaves a potential factor of two (in space) on the table. Consider the geometry in figure 1. While it can be represented by one triangle strip, many of the interior vertices appear twice in the strip. This is inherent in any approach wishing to avoid references to old data. Some systems have tried using a simple regular mesh buffer to support re-use of old vertices, but there is a problem with this in practice: in general, geometry does not come in a perfectly regular rectangular mesh structure.

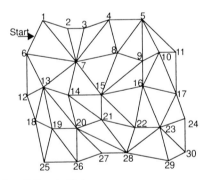

Generalized Triangle Strip:
R6, O1, O7, O2, O3, M4, M8, O5, O9, O10, M11, M17, M16, M9, O15, O8, O7, M14, O13, M6, O12, M18, M19, M20, M14, O21, O15, O22, O16, O23, O17, O24, M30, M29, M28, M22, O21, M20, M27, O26, M19, O25, O18

Generalized Triangle Mesh:
R6p, O1, O7p, O2, O3, M4, M8p, O5, O9p, O10, M11, M17p, M16p, M-3, O15p, O-5, O6, M14p, O13p, M-9, O12, M18p, M19p, M20p, M-5, O21p, O-7, O22p, O-9, O23, O-10, O-7, M30, M29, M28, M-1, O-2, M-3, M27, O26, M-4, O25, O-5

Legend:
First letter: R = Restart, O = Replace Oldest, M = Replace Mi
Trailing "p" = push into mesh buffer
Number is vertex number, -number is mesh buffer reference where -1 is most recent pushed vertex.

Figure 1. Generalized Triangle Mesh

The generalized technique employed by geometry compression addresses this problem. Old vertices are *explicitly* pushed into a queue, and then explicitly referenced in the future when the old vertex is desired again. This fine control supports irregular meshes of nearly any shape. Any viable technique must recognize that storage is finite; thus the maximum queue length is fixed at 16, requiring a 4-bit index. We refer to this queue as the *mesh buffer*. The combination of generalized triangle strips and mesh buffer references is referred to as a *generalized triangle mesh*.

The fixed mesh buffer size requires all tessellators/re-strippers for compressed geometry to break up any runs longer than 16 unique references. Since geometry compression is not meant to be programmed directly at the user level, but rather by sophisticated tessellators/re-formatters, this is not too onerous a restriction. Sixteen old vertices allows up to 94% of the redundant geometry to avoid being re-specified.

Figure 1 also contains an example of a general mesh buffer representation of the surface geometry.

The language of geometry compression supports the four vertex replacement codes of generalized triangle strips (replace oldest, replace middle, restart clockwise, and restart counterclockwise), and adds another bit in each vertex header to indicate if this vertex should be pushed into the mesh buffer or not. The mesh buffer reference command has a 4-bit field to indicate which old vertex should be re-referenced, along with the 2-bit vertex replacement code. Mesh buffer reference commands do *not* contain a mesh buffer push bit; old vertices can only be recycled once.

Geometry rarely is comprised purely of positional data; generally a normal and/or color are also specified per vertex. Therefore, mesh buffer entries contain storage for all associated per-vertex information (specifically including normal and color). For maximum space efficiency, when a vertex is specified in the data stream, (per vertex) normal and/or color information should be directly bundled with the position information. This bundling is controlled by two state bits: *bundle normals with vertices* (bnv), and *bundle colors with vertices* (bcv). When a vertex is pushed into the mesh buffer, these bits control if its bundled normal and/or color are pushed as well. During a mesh buffer reference command, this process is reversed; the two bits specify if a normal and/or color should be inherited from the mesh buffer storage, or inherited from the *current normal* or *current color*. There are explicit commands for setting these two current values. An important exception to this rule occurs when an explicit "set current normal" command is followed by a mesh buffer reference, with the bnv state bit active. In this case, the former overrides the mesh buffer normal. This allows compact representation of hard edges in surface geometry. The analogous semantics are also defined for colors, allowing compact representation of hard edges in textures.

Two additional state bits control the interpretation of normals and colors when the stream of vertices is turned into triangles. The *replicate normals over triangle* (rnt) bit indicates that the normal in the final vertex that completes a triangle should be replicated over the entire triangle. The *replicate colors over triangle* (rct) bit is defined analogously.

4 COMPRESSION OF XYZ POSITIONS

The 8-bit exponent of 32-bit IEEE floating-point numbers allows positions literally to span the known universe: from a scale of 15 billion light years, down to the radius of sub-atomic particles. However for any given tessellated object, the exponent is really specified just once by the current modeling matrix; within a given modeling space, the object geometry is effectively described with only the 24-bit fixed-point mantissa. Visually, in many cases far fewer bits are needed; thus the language of geometry compression supports variable quantization of position data down to as little a one bit. The question then is what is the maximum number of bits that should be supported? Based on empirical visual tests we have done, as well as silicon im-

plementation considerations, we decided to limit our implementation to support of at most 16 bits of precision per component of position.

We still assume that the position and scale of the local modeling spaces are specified by full 32-bit or 64-bit floating-point coordinates. If sufficient numerical care is taken, multiple such modeling spaces can be stitched together without cracks, forming seamless geometry coordinate systems with much greater than 16-bit positional precision.

Most geometry is local, so within the 16-bit (or less) modeling space (of each object), the delta difference between one vertex and the next in the generalized mesh buffer stream is very likely to b less than 16 bits in significance. Indeed one can histogram the bit length of neighboring position deltas in a batch of geometry, and based upon this histogram assign a variable length code to compactly represent the vertices. The typical coding used in many other similar situations is customized Huffman code; this is the case for geometry compression. The details of the coding of position deltas are postponed until section 7, where they can be discussed in the context of color and normal delta coding as well.

5 COMPRESSION OF RGB COLORS

We treat colors similar to positions, but with a smaller maximum accuracy. Thus rgbα color data is first quantized to 12-bit unsigned fraction components. These are absolute linear reflectivity values, with 1.0 representing 100% reflectivity. An additional parameter allows color data effectively to be quantized to any amount less than 12 bits, i.e. the colors can all be within a 5-5-5 rgb color space. (The α field is optional, controlled by the *color alpha present* (cap) state bit.) Note that this decision does *not* necessarily cause mock banding on the final rendered image; individual pixel colors are still interpolated between these quantized vertex colors, and also are subject to lighting.

After considerable debate, it was decided to use the same delta coding for color components as is used for positions. Compression of color data is where geometry compression and traditional image compression face the most similar problem. However, many of the more advanced techniques for image compression were rejected for geometry color compression because of the difference in focus.

Image compression (for example, JPEG [7]) makes several assumptions about the viewing of the decompressed data that *cannot* be made for geometry compression. In image compression, it is known a priori that the pixels appear in a perfectly rectangular array, and that when viewed, each pixel subtends a narrow range of visual angles. In geometry compression, one has almost no idea what the relationship between the viewer and the rasterized geometry will be.

In image compression, it is known that the spatial frequency on the viewer's eyes of the displayed pixels is likely higher than the human visual system's color acuity. This is why colors are usually converted to yuv space (cf. [6]), so that the uv color components can be represented at a lower spatial frequency than the y (intensity) component. Usually the digital bits representing the sub-sampled uv components are split up among two or more pixels. Geometry compression can't take advantage of this because the display scale of the geometry relative to the viewer's eye is not fixed. Also, given that compressed triangle vertices are connected to 4 - 8 or more other vertices in the generalized triangle mesh, there is no consistent way of sharing "half" the color information across vertices.

Similar arguments apply for the more sophisticated transforms used in traditional image compression, such as the discrete cosine transform. These transforms assume a regular (rectangular) sampling of pixel values, and require a large amount of random access during decompression.

Another traditional approach avoided was pseudo-color look-up tables. Any such look-up table would have to have a (fixed) maximum size, and yet still is a very expensive resource for real-time processing. While pseudo-color indices would result in a slightly higher compression ratio for certain scenes, it was felt that the rgb model is more general and considerably less expensive.

Finally, the rgb values are represented as linear reflectance values. In theory, if all the effects of lighting are known ahead of time, a bit or two could have been shaved off the representation if the rgb components had been represented in a nonlinear, or perceptually linear (sometime referred to as gamma corrected) space. However, in general, the effects of lighting are not predictable, and considerable hardware resources would have had to be expended to convert from nonlinear to linear light on the fly.

6 COMPRESSION OF NORMALS

Probably the most innovative concept in geometry compression is the method of compressing surface normals. Traditionally 96-bit normals (three 32-bit IEEE floating-point numbers) are used in calculations to determine 8-bit color intensities. 96 bits of information theoretically could be used to represent 2^{96} different normals, spread evenly over the surface of a unit sphere. This is a normal every 2^{-46} radians in any direction. Such angles are so exact that spreading out angles evenly in every direction from earth you could point out any rock on Mars with sub-centimeter accuracy.

But for normalized normals, the exponent bits are effectively unused. Given the constraint $|N| = 1$, at least one of N_x, N_y, or N_z, *must* be in the range of 0.5 to 1.0. During rendering, this normal will be transformed by a composite modeling orientation matrix T: $N' = N \cdot T$.

Assuming the typical implementation in which lighting is performed in world coordinates, the view transform is not involved in the processing of normals. If the normals have been pre-normalized, then to avoid redundant re-normalization of the normals, the composite modeling transformation matrix T is typically pre-normalized to divide out any scale changes, and thus:

$$T_{0,0}{}^2 + T_{1,0}{}^2 + T_{2,0}{}^2 = 1, \text{ etc.}$$

During the normal transformation, floating-point arithmetic hardware effectively truncates all additive arguments to the accuracy of the largest component. The result is that for a normalized normal, being transformed by a scale preserving modeling orientation matrix, in all but a few special cases, the numerical accuracy of the transformed normal value is reduced to no more than 24-bit fixed-point accuracy.

Even 24-bit normal components are still much higher in angular accuracy than the (repaired) Hubble space telescope. Indeed, in some systems, 16-bit normal components are used. In [3] 9-bit normal components were successfully used. After empirical tests, it was determined that an angular density of 0.01 radians between normals gave results that were not visually distinguishable from finer representations. This works out to about 100,000 normals distributed over the unit sphere. In rectilinear space, these normals still require high accuracy of representation; we chose to use 16-bit components including one sign and one guard bit.

This still requires 48 bits to represent a normal. But since we are only interested in 100,000 specific normals, in theory a single 17-bit index could denote any of these normals. The next section shows how it is possible to take advantage of this observation.

Normal as Indices

The most obvious hardware implementation to convert an index of a normal on the unit sphere back into a N_x N_y N_z value, is by table look-up. The problem is the size of the table. Fortunately, there are several symmetry tricks that can be applied to vastly reduce the size

of the table (by a factor of 48). (In [5], effectively the same symmetries are applied to compress processed voxel data.)

First, the unit sphere is symmetrical in the eight quadrants by sign bits. In other words, if we let three of the normal representation bits be the three sign bits of the xyz components of the normal, then we only need to find a way to represent one eighth of the unit sphere.

Second, each octant of the unit sphere can be split up into six identical pieces, by folding about the planes $x = y$, $x = z$, and $y = z$. (See Figure 2.) The six possible sextants are encoded with another three bits. Now only 1/48 of the sphere remains to be represented.

This reduces the 100,000 entry look-up table in size by a factor of 48, requiring only about 2,000 entries, small enough to fit into an on-chip ROM look-up table. This table needs 11 address bits to index into it, so including our previous two 3-bit fields, the result is a grand total of 17 bits for all three normal components.

Representing a finite set of unit normals is equivalent to positioning points on the surface of the unit sphere. While no perfectly equal angular density distribution exists for large numbers of points, many near-optimal distributions exist. Thus in theory one of these with the same sort of 48-way symmetry described above could be used for the decompression look-up table. However, several additional constraints mandate a different choice of encoding:

1) We desire a scalable density distribution. This is one in which zeroing more and more of the low order address bits to the table still results in fairly even density of normals on the unit sphere. Otherwise a different look-up table for every encoding density would be required.

2) We desire a delta-encodable distribution. Statistically, adjacent vertices in geometry will have normals that are nearby on the surface of the unit sphere. Nearby locations on the 2D space of the unit-sphere surface are most succinctly encoded by a 2D offset. We desire a distribution where such a metric exists.

3) Finally, while the computational cost of the normal encoding process is not too important, in general, distributions with lower encoding costs are preferred.

For all these reasons, we decided to utilize a regular grid in the angular space within one sextant as our distribution. Thus rather than a monolithic 11-bit index, all normals within a sextant are *much* more conveniently represented as two 6-bit orthogonal angular addresses, revising our grand total to 18-bits. Just as for positions and colors, if more quantization of normals is acceptable, then these 6-bit indices can be reduced to fewer bits, and thus absolute normals can be represented using anywhere from 18 to as few as 6 bits. But as will be seen, we can delta encode this space, further reducing the number of bits required for high quality representation of normals.

Normal Encoding Parameterization

Points on a unit radius sphere are parameterized by two angles, θ and ϕ, using spherical coordinates. θ is the angle about the y axis;

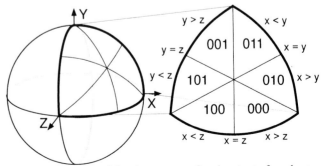

Figure 2. Encoding of the six sextants of each octant of a sphere.

ϕ is the longitudinal angle from the y=0 plane. The mapping between rectangular and spherical coordinates is:

$$x = \cos\theta \cdot \cos\phi \qquad y = \sin\phi \qquad z = \sin\theta \cdot \cos\phi \quad (1)$$

Points on the sphere are folded first by octant, and then by sort order of xyz into one of six sextants. All the table encoding takes place in the positive octant, in the region bounded by the half spaces:

$$x \geq z \qquad z \geq y \qquad y \geq 0$$

This triangular-shaped patch runs from 0 to $\pi/4$ radians in θ, and from 0 to as much as 0.615479709 radians in ϕ: ϕ_{max}.

Quantized angles are represented by two n-bit integers $\hat{\theta}_n$ and $\hat{\phi}_n$, where n is in the range of 0 to 6. For a given n, the relationship between these indices θ and ϕ is

$$\theta(\hat{\theta}_n) = \operatorname{asin}\tan\left(\phi_{max} \cdot (n - \hat{\theta}_n)/2^n\right)$$
$$\phi(\hat{\phi}_n) = \phi_{max} \cdot \hat{\phi}_n/2^n \qquad (2)$$

These two equations show how values of $\hat{\theta}_n$ and $\hat{\phi}_n$ can be converted to spherical coordinates θ and ϕ, which in turn can be converted to rectilinear normal coordinate components via equation 1.

To reverse the process, e.g. to encode a given normal N into $\hat{\theta}_n$ and $\hat{\phi}_n$, one cannot just invert equation 2. Instead, the N must be first folded into the canonical octant and sextant, resulting in N'. Then N' must be dotted with all quantized normals in the sextant. For a fixed n, the values of $\hat{\theta}_n$ and $\hat{\phi}_n$ that result in the largest (nearest unity) dot product define the proper encoding of N.

Now the complete bit format of absolute normals can be given. The uppermost three bits specify the octant, the next three bits the sextant, and finally two n-bit fields specify $\hat{\theta}_n$ and $\hat{\phi}_n$. The 3-bit sextant field takes on one of six values, the binary codes for which are shown in figure 2.

This discussion has ignored some details. In particular, the three normals at the corners of the canonical patch are multiply represented (6, 8, and 12 times). By employing the two unused values of the sextant field, these normals can be uniquely encoded as 26 special normals.

This representation of normals is amenable to delta encoding, at least within a sextant. (With some additional work, this can be extended to sextants that share a common edge.) The delta code between two normals is simply the difference in $\hat{\theta}_n$ and $\hat{\phi}_n$: $\Delta\hat{\theta}_n$ and $\Delta\hat{\phi}_n$.

7 COMPRESSION TAGS

There are many techniques known for minimally representing variable-length bit fields (cf. [7]). For geometry compression, we have chosen a variation of the conventional Huffman technique.

The Huffman compression algorithm takes in a set of symbols to be represented, along with frequency of occurrence statistics (histograms) of those symbols. From this, variable length, uniquely identifiable bit patterns are generated that allow these symbols to be represented with a near-minimum total number of bits, assuming that symbols do occur at the frequencies specified.

Many compression techniques, including JPEG [7], create unique symbols as tags to indicate the length of a variable-length data-field that follows. This data field is typically a specific-length delta value. Thus the final binary stream consists of (self-describing length) variable length tag symbols, each immediately followed by a data field whose length is associated with that unique tag symbol.

The binary format for geometry compression uses this technique to represent position, normal, and color data fields. For geometry compression, these <tag, data> fields are immediately preceded by (a more conventional computer instruction set) op-code field. These fields, plus potential additional operand bits, are referred to as *geometry instructions* (see figure 3).

Traditionally, each value to be compressed is assigned its own associated label, e.g. an xyz delta position would be represented by three tag-value pairs. However, the delta xyz values are *not* uncorrelated, and we can get both a denser and simpler representation by taking advantage of this fact. In general, the xyz deltas statistically point equally in all directions in space. This means that if the number of bits to represent the largest of these deltas is n, then statistically the other two delta values require an average of n-1.4 bits for their representation. Thus we made the decision to use a *single* field-length tag to indicate the bit length of Δx, Δy, *and* Δz. This also means that we cannot take advantage of another Huffman technique that saves somewhat less than one more bit per component, but our bit savings by not having to specify two additional tag fields (for Δy and Δz) outweigh this. A single tag field also means that a hardware decompression engine can decompress all three fields in parallel, if desired.

Similar arguments hold for deltas of rgbα values, and so here also a single field-length tag indicates the bit-length of the r, g, b, and α (if present) fields.

Both absolute and delta normals are also parameterized by a single value (n), which can be specified by a single tag.

We chose to limit the length of the Huffman tag field to the relatively small value of six bits. This was done to facilitate high-speed low-cost hardware implementations. A 64-entry tag look-up table allows decoding of tags in one clock cycle. Three such tables exist: one each for positions, normals, and colors. The tables contain the length of the tag field, the length of the data field(s), a data normalization coefficient, and an absolute/relative bit.

One additional complication was required to enable reasonable hardware implementations. As will be seen in the next section, all instruction are broken up into an eight-bit header, and a variable length body. Sufficient information is present in the header to determine the length of the body. But in order to give the hardware time to process the header information, the header of one instruction must be placed in the stream *before the body of the previous instruction*. Thus the sequence ... B0 H1B1 H2B2 H3 ... has to be encoded:

... H1 B0 H2 B1 H3 B2 ... .

8 GEOMETRY COMPRESSION INSTRUCTIONS

All of the pieces come together in the geometry compression instruction set, seen in figure 3.

The **Vertex** command specifies a Huffman compressed delta encoded position, as well as possibly a normal and/or color, depending on bundling bits (bnv and bcv). Two additional bits specify a vertex replacement code (rep); another bit controls mesh buffer pushing of this vertex (mbp).

The **Normal** command specifies a new current normal; the **Color** command a new current color. Both also use Huffman encoding of delta values.

The **Set State** instruction updates the five state bits: rnt, rct, bnv, bcv, and cap.

The **Mesh Buffer Reference** command allows any of the sixteen most recently pushed vertices (and associated normals and/or colors) to be referenced as the next vertex. A 2-bit vertex replacement code is also specified.

The **Set Table** command sets entries in one of the three Huffman decoding tables (Position, Normal, or Color) to the entry value specified.

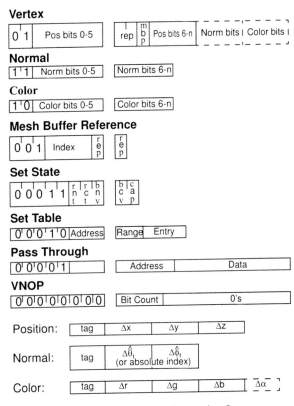

Vertex

Normal

Color

Mesh Buffer Reference

Set State

Set Table

Pass Through

VNOP

Position:

Normal:

Color:

Figure 3. Geometry Compression Instruction Set

The **Pass Through** command allows additional graphics state not controlled directly by geometry compression to be updated in-line.

The **VNOP** (Variable length no-op) command allows fields within the bit stream to be aligned to 32-bit word boundaries, so that aligned fields can be patched at run-time.

9 RESULTS

The results are presented in figure 5 a-l and table 1. Figures 5 a-g are of the same base object (a triceratops), but with different quantization thresholds on positions and normals. Figure 5a is the original full floating-point representation: 96-bit positions, and 96-bit normals, which we denote by P96/N96. Figure 5b and 5c show the effects of purely positional quantization: P36/N96 and P24/N96, respectively. Figures 5d and 5e show only normal quantization: P96/N18 and P96/N12. Figures 5f and 5g show combined quantization: P48/N18 and P30/N36.

Figures 5 h-l show only the quantized results: for a galleon (P30/N12), a Dodge Viper (P36/N14), two views of a '57 Chevy (P33/N13), and an insect (P39/N15).

Without zooming into the object, positional quantization much above 24-bits has virtually no significant visible effect. As the normal quantization is reduced, the positions of specular highlights on the surfaces are offset slightly, but it is not visually apparent that these changes are reductions in quality, at least above 12 bits per normal. Note that the quantization parameters were photographed with the objects: otherwise even the author was not able to distinguish between the original and most compressed versions.

Compression (and other) statistics on these objects are summarized in table 1. The final column shows the compression ratios achieved over existing executable geometry formats. While the total byte count of the compressed geometry is an unambiguous number (and shown in the penultimate column), to state a compression ratio, some assumptions

must be made about the object's uncompressed executable representation. We assumed optimized generalized triangle strips, with both positions and normals represented by floating-point values. This is how the "original size" column was calculated. To see the effect of pure 16-bit fixed point simple strip representation, we also show the byte count for this mode of OpenGL (the average strip length went way down, in the range of 2-3). Because few if any commercial products take advantage of generalized triangle strips, the potential memory space savings are considerably understated by the numbers in the table.

The earlier columns in the table break down the bit usage by component: just position tag/data, just normal tag/data, and everything else (overhead). The "quant" columns show the quantization thresholds. All results in table 1 are (measured) actual compression, with one exception. Because our software compressor does not yet implement a full meshifying algorithm, we present estimated mesh buffer results in parentheses (always next to actual results). This estimate assumes a 42% hit ratio in the mesh buffer.

While certainly there is statistical variation between objects (with respect to compression ratios), we have noted some general trends. When compressing using the highest quality setting of the quantization knobs (P48/N18), the compression ratios are typically about 6. When most objects start showing visible quantization artifacts, the ratios are nearly 10.

10 GEOMETRY COMPRESSION SOFTWARE

So far the focus has been on the justification and description of the geometry compression format. This section addresses some of the issues that arise when actually performing the compression; the next section addresses issues related to hardware and software implementation of decompression.

An important measure for any form of compression is the ratio of the time required for compression relative to decompression. Several otherwise promising techniques for image compression have failed in the marketplace because they require several thousand times more time to compress than to decompress. It is acceptable for off-line image compression to take 60X more time than decompression, but not too much more; for real-time video conferencing the ratio should be 1.

Geometry compression *does not* have this real-time requirement. Even if geometry is being constructed on the fly, most techniques for creating geometry (such as CSG) take orders of magnitude more time than displaying geometry. Also, unlike the continuous images found in movies, in most applications of geometry compression a compressed 3D object will be displayed for many sequential frames before being discarded. If the 3D object needs to be animated, this is typically done with modeling matrices. Indeed for a CD-based game, it is quite likely that an object will be decompressed billions of times by customers, while compressed only once by the authoring company.

Like some other compression systems, geometry compression algorithms can have a compression-time vs. compression-ratio knob. Thus for a given target level of quality, the more time allowed for compression, the better the compression ratio that can be achieved by a geometry compression system. There is a corresponding knob for quality of the resulting compressed 3D object. The lower the quality knob, the better the compression ratio achieved.

We have found an esthetic judgment involved in geometry compression, based upon our experiences with the system so far. Some 3D objects start to look bad when the target quantization of normals and/or positions is reduced even a little, others are visually unchanged even with a large amount of quantization. Sometimes the compression does cause visible artifacts, but may only make the object look different, not necessarily lower in quality. Indeed in one case an elephant started looking better (more wrinkled skin) the more we quantized his normals! The point is that there is also a subjective component to geometry compression. In any highly compressed case, the original artist or modeling person that created the 3D object should also pass (interactive) judgment on the visual result of the compression. He or She alone can really say if the compressed object has captured the spirit of the original intent in creating the model.

But once a model has been created *and* compressed, it can be put into a library, to be used as 3D clip-art at the system level.

Below is an outline of the geometry compression algorithm:

1. Input explicit bag of triangles to be compressed, along with quantization thresholds for positions, normals, and colors.

2. Topologically analyze connectivity, mark hard edges in normals and/or color.

3. Create vertex traversal order & mesh buffer references.

4. Histogram position, normal, and color deltas.

5. Assign variable length Huffman tag codes for deltas, based on histograms, separately for positions, normals, colors.

6. Generate binary output stream by first outputting Huffman table initializations, then traversing the vertices in order, outputting appropriate tag and delta for all values.

Implementation status: a compressor of Wavefront OBJ format has been implemented. It supports compression of positions and normals, and creates full generalized triangle strips, but does not yet implement a full meshifying algorithm. The geometry compression format supports many more sophisticated compression opportunities than our existing compressor utilizes. We hope in the future to explore variable precision geometry, and fine structured updates of the compression tables. Eventually modelers should generate compressed geometry directly; our current compressor spends a lot of time figuring out geometric details that the tessellator already knew. The current (un-optimized) software can compress ~3K tris/sec.

11 GEOMETRY DECOMPRESSION HARDWARE

While many of the techniques employed by geometry compression are universal, some of the details were specifically designed to allow-cost, high-speed hardware implementations. A geometry compression format designed purely for software decompression would, of course, be a little different.

The features that make the geometry compression instruction set amenable to hardware implementation include: one pass sequential processing, limited local storage requirements, tag look-up rather than usual Hamming bit-sequential processing, and most arithmetic is comprised of shifts, adds, and look-ups.

Below is an outline of the geometry decompression algorithm:

1. Fetch the rest of the next instruction, and the first 8 bits of the instruction after that.

2. Using the tag table, expand any compressed value fields to full precision.

3a.If values are relative, add to current value; otherwise replace.

3b.If mesh buffer reference, access old values.

3c.If other command, do housekeeping.

4. If normal, pass index through ROM table to obtain full N_x N_y N_z values.

5. Output values in generalized triangle strip form to next stage.

Implementation status: a software decompressor has been implemented, and successfully decompresses compressed geometry, at a rate of ~10K triangles/second. Hardware designs are in progress, a simplified block diagram can be seen in figure 4.

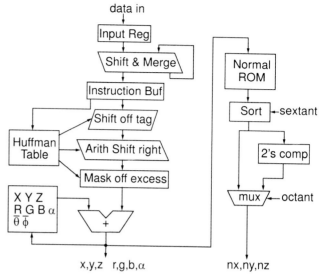

Figure 4. Decompression hardware block diagram (simplified).

12 CONCLUSIONS

A new technique for (lossy) compression of 3D geometric data has been presented. Compression ratios of 6 to 10 to one are achievable with little loss in displayed object quality. The technique has been designed for the constraints of low cost inclusion into real-time 3D rendering hardware, but is also of use in pure software implementations.

ACKNOWLEDGEMENTS

The author would like to thank Aaron Wynn for his work on the hardware and the meshifier, Michael Cox for help with the writing, Scott Nelson for comments on the paper and help with figures 1 & 2, and Viewpoint DataLabs for the 3D objects used in figure 5.

REFERENCES

1. Cook, Robert, L. Carpenter, and E. Catmull. The Reyes Image Rendering Architecture. Proceedings of SIGGRAPH '87 (Anaheim, CA, July 27-31, 1987). In *Computer Graphics* 21, 4 (july 1987), 95-102.

2. Danskin, John. *Compressing the X Graphics Protocol*, Ph.D. Thesis, Princeton University, 1994.

3. Deering, Michael, S. Winner, B. Schediwy, C. Duffy and N. Hunt. The Triangle Processor and Normal Vector Shader: A VLSI system for High Performance Graphics. Proceedings of SIGGRAPH '88 (Atlanta, GA, Aug 1-5, 1988). In *Computer Graphics* 22, 4 (July 1988), 21-30.

4. Deering, Michael, and S. Nelson. Leo: A System for Cost Effective Shaded 3D Graphics. Proceedings of SIGGRAPH '93 (Anaheim, California, August 1-6, 1993). In *Computer Graphics* (August 1993), 101-108.

5. Durkin, James, and J. Hughes. *Nonpolygonal Isosurface Rendering for Large Volume Datasets*. Proceedings of Visualization '94, IEEE, 293-300.

6. Foley, James, A. van Dam, S. Feiner and J Hughes. *Computer Graphics: Principles and Practice*, 2nd ed., Addison-Wesley, 1990.

7. Pennebaker, William, and J. Mitchell. *JPEG Still Image Compression Standard*, Van Nostrand Reinhold, 1993.

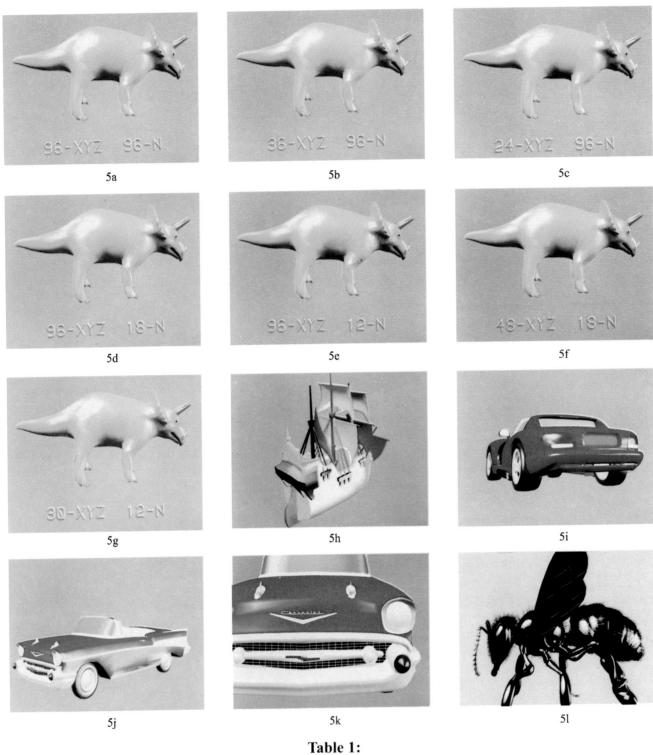

5a   5b   5c

5d   5e   5f

5g   5h   5i

5j   5k   5l

Table 1:

object name	#Δ's	Δstrip length	overhead/ vertex	xyz quant	bits/ xyz	norm quant	bits/ norm	bits/tri	original size (bytes)	OpenGL 16-bit comp	compressed size (bytes)	compression ratio
triceratops	6,039	15.9	8.2	48	35.8	18	16.9	61.3 (41.2)	179,704	151,032	46,237 (31,038)	3.9X (5.8X)
triceratops	6,039	15.9	8.2	30	17.8	12	11.0	36.0 (26.5)	179,704	151,032	27,141 (19,959)	6.7X (9.1X)
galleon	5,118	12.2	8.2	30	22.0	12	11.0	41.3 (29.7)	155,064	105,936	26,358 (18,954)	5.9X (8.2X)
viper	58,203	23.8	8.2	36	20.1	14	10.9	37.5 (27.2)	1,698,116	1,248,492	272,130 (197,525)	6.3X (8.6X)
57chevy	31,762	12.9	8.2	33	17.3	13	10.9	35.8 (26.4)	958,160	565,152	141,830 (104,691)	6.8X (9.2X)
insect	229,313	3.3	8.7	39	26.3	15	12.8	58.7 (40.9)	8,383,788	5,463,444	1,680,421 (1,170,237)	5.0X (7.2X)

Polygon-Assisted JPEG and MPEG Compression of Synthetic Images

Marc Levoy
Computer Science Department
Stanford University

Abstract

Recent advances in realtime image compression and decompression hardware make it possible for a high-performance graphics engine to operate as a rendering server in a networked environment. If the client is a low-end workstation or set-top box, then the rendering task can be split across the two devices. In this paper, we explore one strategy for doing this. For each frame, the server generates a high-quality rendering and a low-quality rendering, subtracts the two, and sends the difference in compressed form. The client generates a matching low quality rendering, adds the decompressed difference image, and displays the composite. Within this paradigm, there is wide latitude to choose what constitutes a high-quality versus low-quality rendering. We have experimented with textured versus untextured surfaces, fine versus coarse tessellation of curved surfaces, Phong versus Gouraud interpolated shading, and antialiased versus nonantialiased edges. In all cases, our polygon-assisted compression looks subjectively better for a fixed network bandwidth than compressing and sending the high-quality rendering. We describe a software simulation that uses JPEG and MPEG-1 compression, and we show results for a variety of scenes.

CR Categories: I.4.2 [Computer Graphics]: Compression — *Approximate methods* I.3.2 [Computer Graphics]: Graphics Systems — *Distributed/network graphics*

Additional keywords: client-server graphics, JPEG, MPEG, polygon-assisted compression

1. Introduction

In this era of open systems, it is common for multiple graphics engines that are software compatible but have greatly differing performance to reside on the same network. A research group might have a dozen low-end workstations on desktops and one high-performance workstation in a centralized laboratory. Future multi-user video games may have hundreds of set-top boxes connected by cable or phone lines to a centralized game server. Recent advances in realtime image compression and decompression hardware make it possible for the high-performance machine to operate as a rendering server for the low-end machines. This can be accomplished straightforwardly by rendering on the server, then compressing and transmitting an image stream to the client. The client decompresses and displays the image stream in a window distinct from its own frame buffer.

Unfortunately, the standards for compressing images and video - mainly JPEG [Wallace91] and MPEG [Le Gall91] - were developed for use on natural scenes, and they are not well suited

for compressing synthetic images. In particular, they perform poorly at the edges of objects and in smoothly shaded areas.

In this paper, we consider an alternative solution that partitions the rendering task between client and server. We use the server to render those features that cannot be rendered in real time on the client - typically textures and complex shading. These are compressed using JPEG or MPEG and sent to the client. We use the client to render those features that compress poorly using JPEG or MPEG - typically edges and smooth shading. The two renderings are combined in the client for display on its screen. The resulting image is subjectively better for the same bandwidth than can be obtained using JPEG or MPEG alone. Alternatively, we can produce an image of comparable quality using less bandwidth.

The remainder of the paper is organized as follows. In section 2, we give an overview of our solution, and we suggest typical hardware realizations. In section 3, we describe a software simulator we have built to test our idea, and we discuss several implementation issues. In section 4, we explore ways to partition the rendering task between client and server. Some partitionings work well, and some do not, as we shall see. In sections 5 and 6, we discuss related work, limitations, and extensions.

2. Client-server relationship

Figure 1 shows the flow of data in our proposed client-server system. The hardware consists of a high-performance workstation (henceforth called the server), a low-performance workstation (henceforth called the client), and a network. To produce each frame of synthetic imagery, these two machines perform the following three steps:

(1) On the server, compute a high-quality and low-quality rendering of the scene using one of the partitioning strategies described in section 4.

(2) Subtract the two renderings, apply lossy compression to the difference image, and send it to the client.

(3) On the client, decompress the difference image, compute a low-quality rendering that matches the low-quality rendering computed on the server, add the two images, and display the resulting composite image.

Depending on the partitioning strategy, there may be two geometric models describing the scene or one model with two rendering options. The low-quality model may reside on both machines, or it may be transmitted from server to client (or client to server) for each frame. If the model resides on both machines, this can be implemented using display lists or two cooperating copies of the application program. The latter solution is commonly used in networked visual simulation applications.

To provide interactive performance, the server in such a system would normally be a graphics workstation with hardware-accelerated rendering. The client might be a lower-end hardware-accelerated workstation, or it might be a PC performing rendering in software, or it might be a set-top box utilizing a

Address: Center for Integrated Systems   Email: levoy@cs.stanford.edu
        Stanford University   Web: http://www-graphics.stanford.edu
        Stanford, CA 94305-4070

Permission to make digital/hard copy of part or all of this work for personal or classroom use is granted without fee provided that copies are not made or distributed for profit or commercial advantage, the copyright notice, the title of the publication and its date appear, and notice is given that copying is by permission of ACM, Inc. To copy otherwise, to republish, to post on servers, or to redistribute to lists, requires prior specific permission and/or a fee.

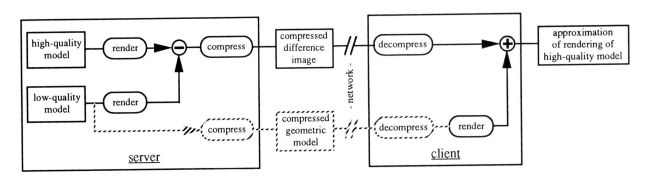

Figure 1: Flow of data in proposed client-server rendering system. High and low-quality renderings may differ in shading, geometric detail, or other aspects. Transmission of the low-quality geometric model is optional, so it is drawn dashed in the figure.

combination of software and hardware. Differencing and compression on the server, and decompression and addition on the client, would most likely be performed in hardware, although real-time software implementations are also beginning to appear.

One important caveat regarding the selection of client and server is that there are often slight differences in pixel values between equivalent-quality renderings computed by high-performance and low-performance machines, even if manufactured by the same vendor. If both renderings are antialiased, these differences are likely to be small. Nevertheless, they may adversely affect the reconstruction in step three.

3. Software simulation

Since no commercially available workstation yet offers both high-performance rendering and real-time compression/decompression, we have built a software simulation. Rendering is performed using the REYES rendering system [Cook87] or the SoftImage Creative Environment, and compression is performed using the Independent JPEG Group's codec [Lane] or the Berkeley MPEG-1 codec [Rowe].

Images in our simulations are represented as 24-bit RGB pixels with two exceptions. First, the codecs performs compression in YCrCb using 4:1:1 subsampling - 4 pixels of Y to 1 each of Cr and Cb. Second, pixels in the difference image D are computed from pixels in the high and low quality images H and L using the formula $D = 127+(H-L)/2$. This formula maps zero-difference pixels to gray and maps positive and negative differences to lighter and darker colors, respectively (see figure 2c). Following this division by 2, features in the difference image are represented by pixel excursions (from the mean) half as large as corresponding features in the high-quality rendering. To prevent these features from being quantized twice as severely during compression, we adjust the quantization tables to compensate. The effect is to match the feature degradation (and code size) that would have resulted had we not divided the difference pixels by 2.

Our experiments using the JPEG codec are presented in figures 2 through 5. Selected statistics for figures 2 and 3 are summarized in table I. The table gives statistics for image-based compression, for polygon-assisted compression using resident geometric models, and for polygon-assisted compression using a transmitted low-quality model.

Whenever a model is transmitted, it should be compressed. We have not implemented compression of geometric models, and little research has been done on the subject, but we can estimate the performance of a simple lossless scheme as follows. We assume a polygon mesh, which contains on average one vertex per polygon. In our application, vertices can be transformed from object space to screen space prior to transmission, after which a two-byte fixed point representation suffices for each coordinate. Thus, we need 10 bytes per vertex (6 bytes for XYZ + 4 bytes for RGBA). One can then difference the coordinates and colors of successive vertices and encode the differences using Huffman or arithmetic coding. If successive vertices are spatially adjacent as they would be in a mesh, this technique should perform well. Danskin has used a similar method to compress sequences of mouse events in X, obtaining 3:1 compression [Danskin94]. We thus estimate that each polygon in a compressed model requires 3.3 bytes.

To help us understand the performance of polygon-assisted compression, we have computed the entropies of the high-quality renderings and difference images. As expected, the latter consistently have less entropy than the former. We have also computed the root mean square errors in the polygon-assisted compressions and image-based compressions, relative in each case to the high-quality renderings. Unfortunately, root mean square error is a poor measure of subjective image quality. In our opinion, the only meaningful way to evaluate the performance of our method is to look at the images.

We have also computed several animations using motion JPEG and MPEG-1. Our conclusions match those for still images: polygon-assisted compression yields subjectively better imagery than image-based compression for the same bandwidth. MPEG-1 looks better than motion JPEG even at higher compression rates due to its use of motion compensation, but neither looks as good as polygon-assisted compression. Unfortunately, still images or analog videotape recordings do not capture the full quality difference, which is only evident by looking at a workstation screen.

4. Partitioning strategies

Image-based compression (e.g. JPEG) of synthetic images fails most severely at the silhouette edges of objects and in smoothly shaded areas. What these two features have in common is spatial coherence. In other words, they both exhibit relatively large-scale structure. In choosing how to partition a synthetic image into a polygon rendering and a compressed difference image, we should therefore strive to incorporate into the rendering as much of the coherent structure of the synthetic image as possible. In the following paragraphs, we describe three partitioning strategies - two that work well and one that does not.

4.1. Textured versus untextured surfaces

High-end graphics workstations (such as the Silicon Graphics RealityEngine) are typically optimized for the display of textured surfaces, while low-end workstations (such as the Silicon Graphics Indy) are typically optimized for the display of untextured surfaces. Given these capabilities, the most obvious way to partition rendering between a high-end server and a low-end client is to omit surface texture on the client.

To demonstrate this, we consider a room composed of flat surfaces that exhibit smooth shading and texture (see figure 2). The model contains 1131 polygons with a fixed color at each vertex. This color was calculated using a hierarchical radiosity algorithm that approximates the diffuse interreflection among textured surfaces [Gershbein94]. The high-quality rendering (figure 2a) employs antialiasing, Gouraud-interpolated shading, and texturing. The low-quality rendering (figure 2b) employs antialiasing and Gouraud-interpolated shading but no texturing. The difference between the two renderings is shown in figure 2c.[†]

Figures 2d through 2g show image-based compression of the high-quality rendering using varying JPEG quality factors. Figures 2h through 2k show polygon-assisted compression using quality factors selected to match as closely as possible the code sizes in figures 2d through 2g, assuming that the geometric model resides on both machines. The quality factors, code sizes, and compression rates are given below each image. Figures 2l and 2m (on the next page of figures) give one more pair, enlarged so that details may be seen. The statistics for these two figures also appear in table I.

In every case, polygon-assisted compression is superior to image-based compression. There are two distinct reasons for this:

- The polygon-assisted rendering contains undegraded edges and smoothly shaded areas - precisely those features that fare poorly in JPEG compression.
- The difference image contains less information than the high-quality rendering, so it can be compressed using a higher JPEG quality factor without increasing code size - even higher than is required to compensate for the division by 2 in the difference image representation. Thus, texture features, which are present only in the difference image, fare better using our method.

As an alternative to comparing images at matching code sizes, we can compare the code sizes of images of equal quality. Unfortunately, such comparisons are difficult because the degradations of the two methods are different - polygon-assisted compression always produces perfect edges and smooth shading, while JPEG never does. If one allows that figure 2j generated using polygon-assisted compression is comparable in quality to figure 2d generated using image-based compression, then our method gives an additional 3x compression for this scene.

Table I also estimates the number of bytes required to generate figure 2m if the model is transmitted from server to client using the lossless compression method proposed in section 3. This size (13529 bytes) lies between the code sizes of figures 2e and 2f. Even in this case, polygon-assisted compression is superior in image quality to image-based compression, both in terms of its edges and smooth shading and in terms of the JPEG quality factor used to transmit the texture information.

[†]If rendered on a Silicon Graphics RealityEngine, both renderings can be performed - and the difference image computed - in a single pass through the data by remicrocoding the fragment generators.

4.2. Fine versus coarse tessellation of curved surfaces

Many algorithms for displaying curved surfaces operate by subdividing (tessellating) each surface into a mesh of small polygons. The shading applied at each polygon vertex is typically expensive - possibly including a sophisticated reflection model and texture, but the shading across a polygon is typically simple - constant or linearly interpolated. This suggests a partitioning strategy in which the client renders a surface using a coarse tessellation, and the server renders the surface twice - once using a coarse tessellation and once using a fine tessellation.

To demonstrate this, we consider a bowling pin modeled as a bicubic patch mesh (see figure 3). The geometry and surface properties are modeled in the RenderMan scene description language [Hanrahan90]. Using the REYES rendering system [Cook87], we tessellate the patch mesh twice, generating two micropolygon models with associated vertex colors.

Figure 3d shows image-based compression of the high-quality rendering using a JPEG quality factor of 15. Figure 3e shows polygon-based compression using a quality factor selected to match the code size in figure 3d, assuming that the low-quality model resides on both machines. Again, the superiority of polygon-assisted compression over image-based compression is evident, particularly along edges and in smoothly shaded areas.

4.3. Antialiased Phong-shaded versus nonantialiased Gouraud-shaded

We now demonstrate a partitioning strategy that does not work well. Our model is an extruded letter defined using a few large polygons (see figure 4) and rendered using SoftImage. The high-quality rendering uses texturing, antialiasing, Phong lighting, and Phong interpolated shading. (Although Phong shading is not supported on current high-performance workstations, it can be approximated using an environmental reflectance map.) The low-quality rendering uses Phong lighting and Gouraud interpolated shading, but no texturing or antialiasing.

Although polygon-assisted compression is still superior to image-based compression, the difference is less pronounced than in the previous demonstrations. The most obvious artifact in figure 4j is that the edges are not well antialiased. Subtracting a jagged edge (figure 4g) from an antialiased edge (figure 4f) yields an edge-like structure in the difference image (figure 4h). This structure fares poorly during JPEG compression, leaving the edge jagged in the reconstruction. This degradation will also occur to edges in textures in section 4.1, but in most applications important edges are modeled as geometry, not as texture.

The other disturbing artifact in figure 4j is a blockiness on the face of the letter. The Phong-shaded (figure 4f) and Gouraud-shaded (figure 4g) pixels on the face are similar in color, but they do not match exactly. These small differences are lost during compression, leading to the appearance of 8x8 block artifacts. These artifacts can be reduced somewhat through the application of post-processing techniques [Luo94].

For comparison, figure 5 shows a more successful partitioning of the same scene. In this case, the high and low-quality renderings differ only by the omission of texture. This partitioning is less practical, however, because it requires antialiasing on the client. An alternative partitioning would omit antialiasing on both server and client. In this case, edges would have jaggies, but these jaggies would not be compounded by JPEG artifacts.

	Room	Pin
A. High-quality rendering	fig2a	fig3a
number of polygons	1131	75,467
number of pixels	512 x 512	320 x 800
entropy (bits/pixel)	5.8	3.0
B. Low-quality rendering	fig 2b	fig 3b
number of polygons	1131	3153
C. Difference image	fig 2c	fig 3c
entropy (bits/pixel)	3.0	1.3
D. Image-based compression	fig 2l	fig 3d
JPEG quality factor	15	15
JPEG code size (bytes/frame)	9836	6030
compression ratio	80:1	127:1
error versus uncompressed (rms)	6.1	4.1
E. Polygon-assisted compression		
(resident model)	fig 2m	fig 3e
JPEG quality factor	41	55
JPEG code size (bytes/frame)	9759	5955
compression ratio	81:1	129:1
error versus uncompressed (rms)	7.5	2.9
F. Polygon-assisted compression		
(transmitted model)		
JPEG code size (from above)	9759	5955
Model size (est. bytes/frame)	3770	10510
Total size	13529	16465
compression ratio	58:1	47:1

Table I: Image-based compression versus polygon-assisted compression, compared for the scenes pictured in figures 2 and 3. In D, we select a quality factor that gives 20 frames per second while requiring 2 Mbs or less of network bandwidth. In E, we select a quality factor that matches as closely as possible the code size obtained in D, assuming that the low-quality geometric model resides on both client and server. In F, we estimate the number of bytes required to generate D assuming that a losslessly compressed low-quality model is transmitted from server to client.

5. Related work

The problem presented in this paper is a special case of two general problems: compression of geometric models and compression of synthetic images. Although these two problems have been recognized for a long time, interest in them has risen recently due to the growing synergy between digital video, computer graphics, and networking technologies.

Schemes for compressing geometric models can be categorized as lossy or lossless. Lossy schemes can be further subdivided into methods that simplify the geometry and methods that represent the full geometry using a quantized representation. Geometric simplification methods include hand-generation of hierarchical models [Clark76], automatic decimation of polygon meshes [Hoppe93], and 3D scan conversion of geometry into multiresolution voxel arrays [Wang94]. A good survey of these methods is given in [Heckbert94]. Quantized representations is largely an unexplored area; a notable exception is [Deering95] in these proceedings. Lossless compression of geometric models is also largely unexplored. The prospect of a consumer market for downloadable video games, in which the model is a significant fraction of the total game size, makes this an attractive area for future research.

Schemes for compressing synthetic images can be categorized according to the role played by the underlying geometric model. In the present paper, the model is used to partition the synthetic image into a set of polygons and a difference image. Alternatively, the model could be used to locally adapt the quantization table in a block-based compression scheme to match the characteristics of commonly occurring blocks. Adaptation could be based on block content hints from the model or importance hints from the application program. Although there is a large literature on adaptive quantization, we know of no results that incorporate information from a 3D graphics pipeline. This seems like a fruitful area for future research. Another possibility is to augment a transform coding scheme by adding basis functions that directly represent edges and bilinearly interpolated shading. The screen axis aligned rectangles of Intel's DVI PLV standard offer some of this [Luther91]. The present paper can be viewed as a generalization of this scheme to unconstrained overlapping triangles.

For animation sequences, a geometric model can be used to derive optical flow - the interframe movement of each pixel in an image. Optical flow can in turn be used to compute block motion vectors [Wallach94] or block image warps [Agrawala95]. Flow can also be used to implement non-blocked predictive coding of closely spaced views [Guenter93] or to derive an image morph that interpolates between widely spaced views [Chen93]. Among these, only [Guenter93] is lossless.

Textures and volumes provide another opportunity for combining compression and image synthesis. A lossless compression scheme for volumes based on DPCM and Huffman coding is described in [Fowler94]. Lossy schemes include vector quantization [Ning93], multidimensional trees [Wilhelms94], differences of Gaussians wavelets [Muraki94] and Haar and Daubechies wavelets [Westermann94]. Also related are algorithms for applying texture manipulation operators (such as magnifying or minifying) directly to JPEG representations of textures [Smith94].

6. Conclusions

We have described a method for using a high-performance graphics workstation as a rendering server for a low-performance workstation, and we have explored several strategies for partitioning the rendering task between client and server. Our method improves image quality over compressing and transmitting a single rendering because it removes from the transmitted image those features that compress poorly - mainly edges and smooth shading. These are instead rendered locally on the client.

Our method has several limitations. First, it will require a careful implementation to avoid excessive latency. Second, it requires either storing the low-quality geometric model on both machines or transmitting it for each frame. The former solution requires some memory in the client. The later solution depends on our ability to compress the model. Some geometric models will not compress well, and complex models will always be too large to transmit. Third, our method is most useful on scenes of moderate image complexity. For synthetic scenes whose complexity approximates that of natural scenes, our method will convey little or no advantage. Finally, our method is most useful at high compression rates (more than 25:1). If the network can support transmission of the high-quality rendering at a low compression rate, both MPEG and motion JPEG perform well enough for most interactive tasks.

Extensions to our work include investigating the compression of geometric models, employing an alternative coding technique such as wavelet-based compression, and exploring the use of polygon-assisted compression as a file format for archiving, (non-realtime) image transmission, and printing. In addition, a quantitative model of compression error that reliably captures subjective image quality is sorely needed.

Regarding the longevity of our method, while it is true that low-end machines are getting more powerful each year, there will always be a high-end machine that costs more money and delivers more performance. Thus, although the partitionings described in this paper may become obsolete, there will probably always be partitionings for which our method provides an advantage. In a similar vein, an assumption underlying our method is that compression, transmission, and decompression taken together are less expensive than rendering the original model locally on the client. Although the computational expense of compressing a pixel using transform-based coding is largely independent of image content and will probably remain constant for the forseeable future, the cost of rendering that pixel will rise as image synthesis methods become more sophisticated. This points toward a continuing niche for our method.

7. Acknowledgements

Discussions with Anoop Gupta, Pat Hanrahan, David Heeger, and Navin Chaddha were useful during this project. The suggestions of one reviewer were particularly insightful, and I have attempted to incorporate them into my revised manuscript. The possibility of remicrocoding the RealityEngine was suggested to me by Brian Cabral of Silicon Graphics. The radiosity model was provided by Reid Gershbein, and the the bowling pin model was taken from Steve Upstill's RenderMan Companion. This research was supported by the NSF under contract CCR-9157767.

8. References

[Agrawala95] Agrawala, M., Beers, A.C., Chaddha, N., "Model-based Motion Estimation for Synthetic Animations." Submitted for publication.

[Chen93] Chen, S.E., Williams, L., "View Interpolation for Image Synthesis," *Proc. SIGGRAPH '93* (Anaheim, California, August 1-6, 1993). In Computer Graphics Proceedings, Annual Conference Series, 1993, ACM SIGGRAPH, pp. 279-288.

[Clark76] Clark, J.H., "Hierarchical Geometric Models for Visible Surface Algorithms," *CACM*, Vol. 19, No. 10, October, 1976, pp. 547-554.

[Cook87] Cook, R., Carpenter, L, Catmull, E., "The REYES Image Rendering Architecture," *Computer Graphics (Proc. Siggraph)*, Vol. 21, No. 4, July, 1987, pp. 95-102.

[Danskin94] Danskin, J., "Higher Bandwidth X," *Proc. Multimedia '94* (San Francisco, October 15-20, 1994), ACM, pp. 89-96.

[Deering95] Deering, M., "Geometry Compression," Proc. SIGGRAPH '95 (Los Angeles, California, August 7-11, 1995), In *Computer Graphics* Proceedings, Annual Conference Series, 1995, ACM SIGGRAPH.

[Fowler94] Fowler, J.E., Yagel, R., "Lossless Compression of Volume Data," *Proc. 1994 Symposium on Volume Visualization*, A. Kaufman and W. Krueger eds., ACM, pp. 43-50.

[Gershbein94] Gershbein, R., Schroeder, P., Hanrahan, P., "Textures and Radiosity: Controlling Emission and Reflection with Texture Maps," Proc. SIGGRAPH '94 (Orlando, Florida, July 24-29, 1994). In *Computer Graphics* Proceedings, Annual Conference Series, 1994, ACM SIG-

GRAPH, pp. 51-58.

[Guenter93] Guenter, B.K., Yun, H.C., Mersereau, R.M., "Motion Compensated Compression of Computer Animation Frames," *Proc. SIGGRAPH '93* (Anaheim, California, August 1-6, 1993). In Computer Graphics Proceedings, Annual Conference Series, 1993, ACM SIGGRAPH, pp. 297-304.

[Hanrahan90] Hanrahan, P., Lawson, J., "A Language for Shading and Lighting Calculations," *Computer Graphics (Proc. Siggraph)*, Vol. 24, No. 4, August, 1990, pp. 289-298.

[Heckbert94] Heckbert, P., Garland, M., "Multiresolution Modeling for Fast Rendering," *Proc. Graphics Interface '94* (May 18-20, 1994, Banff, Alberta), Canadian Information Processing Society, pp. 43-50.

[Hoppe93] Hoppe, H. DeRose, T., Duchamp, T., McDonald, J., Stuetzle, W., "Mesh Optimization," *Proc. SIGGRAPH '93* (Anaheim, California, August 1-6, 1993). In Computer Graphics Proceedings, Annual Conference Series, 1993, ACM SIGGRAPH, pp. 19-26.

[Lane] Lane, T., *Independent JPEG Group Software Codec*, Version 4, Internet distribution, URL ftp://ftp.uu.net/graphics/jpeg.

[Le Gall91] Le Gall, D., "MPEG: A Video Compression Standard for Multimedia Applications," *CACM*, Vol. 34, No. 4, April, 1991, pp. 46-58.

[Luo94] Luo, J., et al., "A New Method for Block Effect Removal in Low Bit-Rate Image Compression," *Proc. ICASSP '94*, pp. V-341-344.

[Luther91] Luther, A.C., *Digital Video in the PC Environment*, 2nd edition, McGraw-Hill Book Company, New York, 1991.

[Muraki94] Muraki, S., "Multiscale 3D Edge Representation of Volume Data by a DOG Wavelet," *Proc. 1994 Symposium on Volume Visualization*, A. Kaufman and W. Krueger eds., ACM, pp. 35-42.

[Ning93] Ning, P., Hesselink, L., "Fast Volume Rendering of Compressed Data," *Proc. Visualization '93*, G. Nielson and D. Bergeron ed., IEEE, October, 1993, pp. 11-18.

[Rowe] Rowe, L.A., Gong, K., Patel, K., Wallach, D., *MPEG-1 Video Software Encoder*, Version 1.3, Internet distribution, URL ftp://mm-ftp.cs.berkeley.edu/pub/multimedia/mpeg.

[Smith94] Smith, B.C., "Fast Software Processing of Motion JPEG Video," *Proc. Multimedia '94* (San Francisco, October 15-20, 1994), ACM, pp. 77-88.

[Wallace91] Wallace, G., "The JPEG Still Picture Compression Standard," *CACM*, Vol. 34, No. 4, April, 1991, pp. 30-44.

[Wallach94] Wallach, D.S., Kunapalli, S., Cohen, M.F., "Accelerated MPEG Compression of Dynamic Polygonal Scenes," Proc. SIGGRAPH '94 (Orlando, Florida, July 24-29, 1994), In *Computer Graphics* Proceedings, Annual Conference Series, 1994, ACM SIGGRAPH, pp. 193-197.

[Wang94] Wang, S.W., Kaufman, A.E., "Volume Sampled Voxelization of Geometric Primitives," *IEEE Computer Graphics and Applications*, Vol. 14, No. 5, September, 1994, pp. 26-32.

[Westermann94] Westermann, R., "A Multiresolution Framework for Volume Rendering," *Proc. 1994 Symposium on Volume Visualization*, A. Kaufman and W. Krueger eds., ACM, pp. 51-58.

[Wilhelms94] Wilhelms, J., Van Gelder, A., "Multi-Dimensional Trees for Controlled Volume Rendering and Compression," *Proc. 1994 Symposium on Volume Visualization*, A. Kaufman and W. Krueger eds., ACM, pp. 27-34.

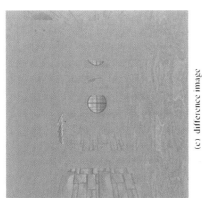
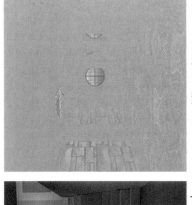

Figure 2: Comparison of image-based compression and polygon-assisted compression. The model is a room with illumination computed using a hierarchical radiosity algorithm. Figures d through g = JPEG of fig a. Figures h through k = fig b + JPEG of c (Figures l and m are on the next page.)

(a) high-quality rendering: 1131 textured antialiased Gouraud-shaded polygons

(b) low-quality rendering: 1131 untextured antialiased Gouraud-shaded polygons

(c) difference image

(d) q = 80, code = 32723 bytes, rate = 24:1
(e) q = 40, code = 17109 bytes, rate = 46:1
(f) q = 20, code = 11509 bytes, rate = 68:1
(g) q = 10, code = 8022 bytes, rate = 98:1
(d) through (g): image-based compression

(h) q = 92, code = 31862 bytes, rate = 25:1
(i) q = 77, code = 17463 bytes, rate = 45:1
(j) q = 55, code = 11580 bytes, rate = 68:1
(k) q = 29, code = 8065 bytes, rate = 98:1
(h) through (k): polygon-assisted compression

(m) polygon-assisted compression. q = 41. code = 9759 bytes. rate = 81:1

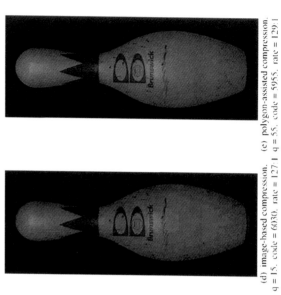

(e) polygon-assisted compression. q = 55. code = 5955. rate = 129:1

(d) image-based compression. q = 15. code = 6030. rate = 127:1

(c) difference image

Figure 3: Comparison for a different partitioning: fine versus coarse tessellation of a curved surface. The model is a bowling pin defined as a bicubic patch mesh.

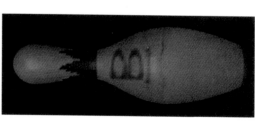

(b) low-quality rendering: 3153 untextured antialiased Gouraud-shaded polygons

(a) high-quality rendering: 75,467 untextured antialiased flat-shaded polygons

(l) image-based compression. q = 15. code = 9836 bytes. rate = 80:1

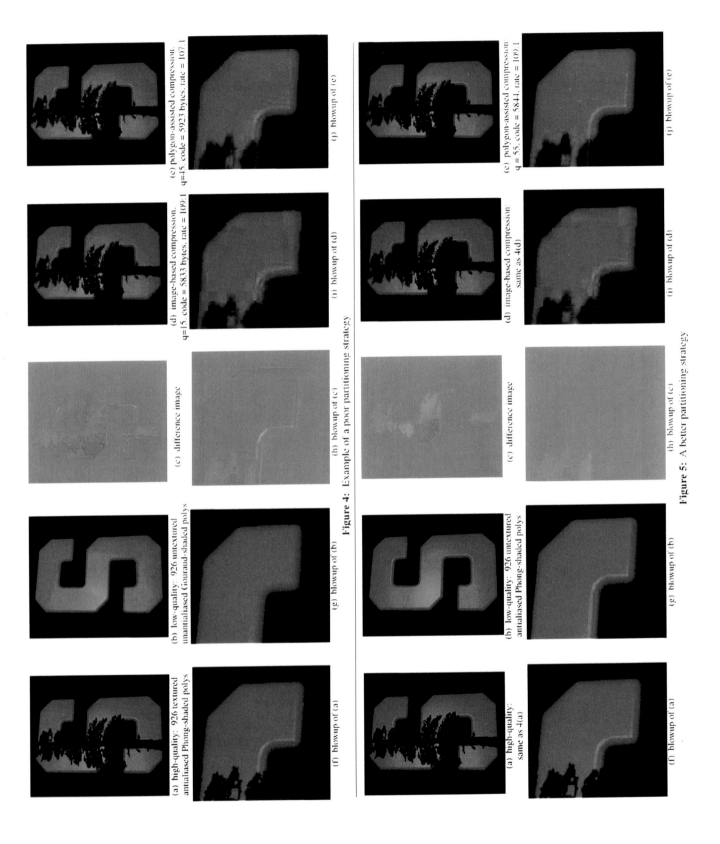

(a) high-quality: 926 textured antialiased Phong-shaded polys

(b) low-quality: 926 untextured unantialiased Gouraud-shaded polys

(c) difference image

(d) image-based compression. q=15, code = 5833 bytes, rate = 109:1

(e) polygon-assisted compression. q=45, code = 5923 bytes, rate = 107:1

(f) blowup of (a)

(g) blowup of (b)

(h) blowup of (c)

(i) blowup of (d)

(j) blowup of (e)

Figure 4: Example of a poor partitioning strategy

(a) high-quality: same as 4(a)

(b) low-quality: 926 untextured antialiased Phong-shaded polys

(c) difference image

(d) image-based compression: same as 4(d)

(e) polygon-assisted compression. q = 55, code = 5844, rate = 109:1

(f) blowup of (a)

(g) blowup of (b)

(h) blowup of (c)

(i) blowup of (d)

(j) blowup of (e)

Figure 5: A better partitioning strategy

QuickTime® VR – An Image-Based Approach to Virtual Environment Navigation

Shenchang Eric Chen

Apple Computer, Inc.

ABSTRACT

Traditionally, virtual reality systems use 3D computer graphics to model and render virtual environments in real-time. This approach usually requires laborious modeling and expensive special purpose rendering hardware. The rendering quality and scene complexity are often limited because of the real-time constraint. This paper presents a new approach which uses 360-degree cylindrical panoramic images to compose a virtual environment. The panoramic image is digitally warped on-the-fly to simulate camera panning and zooming. The panoramic images can be created with computer rendering, specialized panoramic cameras or by "stitching" together overlapping photographs taken with a regular camera. Walking in a space is currently accomplished by "hopping" to different panoramic points. The image-based approach has been used in the commercial product QuickTime VR, a virtual reality extension to Apple Computer's QuickTime digital multimedia framework. The paper describes the architecture, the file format, the authoring process and the interactive players of the VR system. In addition to panoramic viewing, the system includes viewing of an object from different directions and hit-testing through orientation-independent hot spots.

CR Categories and Subject Descriptors: I.3.3 [Computer Graphics]: Picture/Image Generation– Viewing algorithms; I.4.3 [Image Processing]: Enhancement– Geometric correction, Registration.
Additional Keywords: image warping, image registration, virtual reality, real-time display, view interpolation, environment maps, panoramic images.

1   INTRODUCTION

A key component in most virtual reality systems is the ability to perform a walkthrough of a virtual environment from different viewing positions and orientations. The walkthrough requires the synthesis of the virtual environment and the simulation of a virtual camera moving in the environment with up to six degrees of freedom. The synthesis and navigation are usually accomplished with one of the following two methods.

1.1 3D Modeling and Rendering

Traditionally, a virtual environment is synthesized as a collection of 3D geometrical entities. The geometrical entities are rendered in real-time, often with the help of special purpose 3D rendering engines, to provide an interactive walkthrough experience.

Permission to make digital/hard copy of part or all of this work for personal or classroom use is granted without fee provided that copies are not made or distributed for profit or commercial advantage, the copyright notice, the title of the publication and its date appear, and notice is given that copying is by permission of ACM, Inc. To copy otherwise, to republish, to post on servers, or to redistribute to lists, requires prior specific permission and/or a fee.

The 3D modeling and rendering approach has three main problems. First, creating the geometrical entities is a laborious manual process. Second, because the walkthrough needs to be performed in real-time, the rendering engine usually places a limit on scene complexity and rendering quality. Third, the need for a special purpose rendering engine has limited the availability of virtual reality for most people since the necessary hardware is not widely available.

Despite the rapid advance of computer graphics software and hardware in the past, most virtual reality systems still face the above problems. The 3D modeling process will continue to be a very human-intensive operation in the near future. The real-time rendering problem will remain since there is really no upper bound on rendering quality òr scene complexity. Special-purpose 3D rendering accelerators are still not ubiquitous and are by no means standard equipment among personal computer users.

1.2 Branching Movies

Another approach to synthesize and navigate in virtual environments, which has been used extensively in the video game industry, is branching movies. Multiple movie segments depicting spatial navigation paths are connected together at selected branch points. The user is allowed to move on to a different path only at these branching points. This approach usually uses photography or computer rendering to create the movies. A computer-driven analog or digital video player is used for interactive playback. An early example of this approach is the movie-map [1], in which the streets of the city of Aspen were filmed at 10-foot intervals. At playback time, two videodisc players were used to retrieve corresponding views to simulate the effects of walking on the streets. The use of digital videos for exploration was introduced with the Digital Video Interactive technology [2]. The DVI demonstration allowed a user to wander around the Mayan ruins of Palenque using digital video playback from an optical disk. A "Virtual Museum" based on computer rendered images and CD-ROM was described in [3]. In this example, at selected points in the museum, a 360-degree panning movie was rendered to let the user look around. Walking from one of the points to another was simulated with a bi-directional transition movie, which contained a frame for each step in both directions along the path connecting the two points.

An obvious problem with the branching movie approach is its limited navigability and interaction. It also requires a large amount of storage space for all the possible movies. However, this method solves the problems mentioned in the 3D approach. The movie approach does not require 3D modeling and rendering for existing scenes; it can use photographs or movies instead. Even for computer synthesized scenes, the movie-based approach decouples rendering from interactive playback. The movie-based approach allows rendering to be performed at the highest quality with the greatest complexity without affecting the playback performance. It can also use inexpensive and common video devices for playback.

1.3 Objectives

Because of the inadequacy of the existing methods, we decided to explore a new approach for the creation and navigation of virtual environments. Specifically, we wanted to develop a new system which met the following objectives:

First, the system should playback at interactive speed on most personal computers available today without hardware acceleration. We did not want the system to rely on special input or output devices, such as data gloves or head-mount displays, although we did not preclude their use.

Second, the system should accommodate both real and synthetic scenes. Real-world scenes contain enormously rich details often difficult to model and render with a computer. We wanted the system to be able to use real-world scenery directly without going through computer modeling and rendering.

Third, the system should be able to display high quality images independent of scene complexity. Many virtual reality systems often compromise by displaying low quality images and/or simplified environments in order to meet the real-time display constraint. We wanted our system's display speed to be independent of the rendering quality and scene complexity.

1.4 Overview

This paper presents an image-based system for virtual environment navigation based on the above objectives. The system uses real-time image processing to generate 3D perspective viewing effects. The approach presented is similar to the movie-based approach and shares the same advantages. It differs in that the movies are replaced with "orientation-independent" images and the movie player is replaced with a real-time image processor. The images that we currently use are cylindrical panoramas. The panoramas are orientation-independent because each of the images contains all the information needed to look around in 360 degrees. A number of these images can be connected to form a walkthrough sequence. The use of orientation-independent images allows a greater degree of freedom in interactive viewing and navigation. These images are also more concise and easier to create than movies.

We discuss work related to our approach in Section 2. Section 3 presents the simulation of camera motions with the image-based approach. In Section 4, we describe QuickTime VR, the first commercial product using the image-based method. Section 5 briefly outlines some applications of the image-based approach and is followed by conclusions and future directions.

2. RELATED WORK

The movie-based approach requires every displayable view to be created and stored in the authoring stage. In the movie-map [1] [4], four cameras are used to shoot the views at every point, thereby, giving the user the ability to pan to the left and right at every point. The Virtual Museum stores 45 views for each 360-degree pan movie [3]. This results in smooth panning motion but at the cost of more storage space and frame creation time.

The navigable movie [5] is another example of the movie-based approach. Unlike the movie-map or the Virtual Museum, which only have the panning motion in one direction, the navigable movie offers two-dimensional rotation. An object is photographed with a camera pointing at the object's center and orbiting in both the longitude and the latitude directions at roughly 10-degree increments. This process results in hundreds of frames corresponding to all the available viewing directions. The frames are stored in a two-dimensional array which are indexed by two rotational parameters in interactive playback. When displaying the object against a static background, the effect is the same as rotating the object. Panning to look at a scene is accomplished in the same way. The frames in this case represent views of the scene in different view orientations.

If only the view direction is changing and the viewpoint is stationary, as in the case of pivoting a camera about its nodal point (i.e. the optical center of projection), all the frames from the pan motion can be mapped to a canonical projection. This projection is termed an environment map, which can be regarded as an orientation-independent view of the scene. Once an environment map is generated, any arbitrary view of the scene, as long as the viewpoint does not move, can be computed by a reprojection of the environment map to the new view plane.

The environment map was initially used in computer graphics to simplify the computations of specular reflections on a shiny object from a distant scene [6], [7], [8]. The scene is first projected onto an environment map centered at the object. The map is indexed by the specular reflection directions to compute the reflection on the object. Since the scene is far away, the location difference between the object center and the surface reflection point can be ignored.

Various types of environment maps have been used for interactive visualization of virtual environments. In the movie-map, anamorphic images were optically or electronically processed to obtain 360-degree viewing [1], [9]. A project called "Navigation" used a grid of panoramas for sailing simulation [10]. Real-time reprojection of environment maps was used to visualize surrounding scenes and to create interactive walkthrough [11], [12]. A hardware method for environment map look-up was implemented for a virtual reality system [13].

While rendering an environment map is trivial with a computer, creating it from photographic images requires extra work. Greene and Heckbert described a technique of compositing multiple image streams with known camera positions into a fish-eye view [14]. Automatic registration can be used to composite multiple source images into an image with enhanced field of view [15], [16], [17].

When the viewpoint starts moving and some objects are nearby, as in the case of orbiting a camera around an object, the frames can no longer be mapped to a canonical projection. The movement of the viewpoint causes "disparity" between different views of the same object. The disparity is a result of depth change in the image space when the viewpoint moves (pivoting a camera about its nodal point does not cause depth change). Because of the disparity, a single environment map is insufficient to accommodate all the views. The movie-based approach simply stores all the frames. The view interpolation method presented by Chen and Williams [18] stores only a few key frames and synthesizes the missing frames on-the-fly by interpolation. However, this method requires additional information, such as a depth buffer and camera parameters, for each of the key frames. Automatic or semi-automatic methods have been developed for registering and interpolating images with unknown depth and camera information [16], [19], [20].

3. IMAGE-BASED RENDERING

The image-based approach presented in this paper addresses the simulation of a virtual camera's motions in photographic or computer synthesized spaces. The camera's motions have six degrees of freedom. The degrees of freedom are grouped in three classes. First, the three rotational degrees of freedom, termed "camera rotation", refer to rotating the camera's view direction while keeping the viewpoint stationary. This class of motions can be accomplished with the reprojection of an environment map and image rotation. Second, orbiting a camera about an object while keeping the view direction centered at the object is termed "object rotation" because it is equivalent to rotating the object. This type of motion requires the movement of the viewpoint and can not be achieved with an environment map. Third, free motion of the camera in a space, termed "camera movement", requires the change of both the viewpoint and the viewing direction and has all six degrees of freedom. In addition to the above motions, changing the camera's field-of-view, termed "camera zooming", can be accomplished through multiple resolution image zooming.

Without loss of generality, the environment is assumed to be static in the following discussions. However, one can generalize this method to include motions via the use of time-varying environment maps, such as environment map movies or 360-degree movies.

3.1 Camera Rotation

A camera has three rotational degrees of freedom: pitch (pivoting about a horizontal axis), yaw (pivoting about a vertical axis) and roll (rotating about an axis normal to the view plane). Camera rolling can be achieved trivially with an image rotation. Pitch and yaw can be accomplished by the reprojection of an environment map.

An environment map is a projection of a scene onto a simple shape. Typically, this shape is a cube [8] or a sphere [6], [7]. Reprojecting an environment map to create a novel view is dependent on the type of the environment map. For a cubic environment map, the reprojection is merely displaying the visible regions of six texture mapped squares in the view plane. For a spherical environment map, non-linear image warping needs to be performed. Figure 1 shows the reprojection of the two environment maps.

If a complete 360 degree panning is not required, other types of environment maps such as cylindrical, fish-eye or wide-angled planar maps can be used. A cylindrical map allows 360-degree panning horizontally and less than 180-degree panning vertically. A fish-eye or hemi-spherical map allows 180-degree panning in both directions. A planar map allows less than 180-degree panning in both directions.

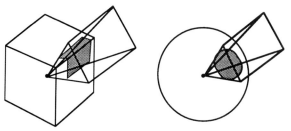

Figure 1. Reprojecting a cubic and a spherical environment map.

3.2 Object Rotation

As mentioned earlier, orbiting the camera around an object, equivalent to rotating the object about its center, can not be accomplished simply with an environment map. One way of solving this problem is the navigable movie approach. The movie contains frames which correspond to all the allowable orientations of an object. For an object with full 360-degree rotation in one direction and 140 degrees in another direction at 10 degree increments, the movie requires 504 frames. If we store the frames at 256 by 256 pixel resolution, each frame is around 10K bytes after compression. The entire movie consumes roughly 5 MB of storage space. This amount of space is large but not impractical given the current capacity of approximately 650 MB per CD-ROM.

The view interpolation approach [18] needs to store only a few key views of an object. The new views are interpolated on-the-fly from the key views, which also means the rotation angle can be arbitrary.

3.3 Camera Movement

A camera moving freely in a scene involves the change of viewpoint and view direction. The view direction change can be accomplished with the use of an environment map. The viewpoint change is more difficult to achieve.

A simple solution to viewpoint change is to constrain the camera's movement to only particular locations where environment maps are available. For a linear camera movement, such as walking down a hallway, environment maps can be created for points along the path at some small intervals. The cost of storing the environment maps is roughly six times the cost of storing a normal walkthrough movie if a cubic map is used. The resulting effects are like looking out of a window from a moving train. The movement path is fixed but the passenger is free to look around. Environment map movies are similar to some special format movies such as Omnimax® (180 degree fish-eye) or CircleVision (360-degree cylindrical) movies, in which a wider than normal field-of-view is recorded. The observer can control the viewing direction during the playback time.

For traversing in a 2D or 3D space, environment maps can be arranged to form a 2D or 3D lattice. Viewpoints in space are simply quantized to the nearest grid point to approximate the motion (figure 2). However, this approach requires a larger number of environment maps to be stored in order to obtain smooth motion. A more desirable approach may be the view interpolation method [18] or the approximate visibility method [12], which generates new views from a coarse grid of environment maps. Instead of constraining the movement to the grid points, the nearby environment maps are interpolated to generate a smooth path.

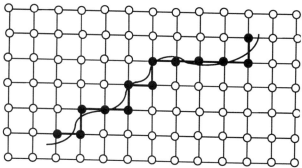

Figure 2. An unconstrained camera path and an approximated path along the grid lines.

3.4 Camera Zooming

Changing the camera's field of view is equivalent to zooming in and out in the image space. However, using image magnification to zoom in does not provide more detail. Zooming out through image reduction may create aliasing artifacts as the sampling rate falls below the Nyquist limit. One solution is multiple resolution image zooming. A pyramidal or quadtree-like structure is created for each image to provide different levels of resolution. The proper level of resolution is selected on-the-fly based on the zooming factor. To achieve the best quality in continuous zooming, the two levels which bound the current zooming factor can be interpolated, similar to the use of mip-maps for anti-aliasing in texture mapping [21].

In order to avoid loading the entire high resolution image in memory while zooming in, the image can be segmented so that the memory requirement is independent of the zoom factor. As the zoom factor increases, a smaller percentage of a larger image is visible. Conversely, a larger percentage of a lower resolution image needs to be displayed. Therefore, the number of pixels required of the source image is roughly constant and is only related to the number of pixels displayed. One way of segmenting the image is dividing the multiple levels of image into tiles of the same size. The higher resolution images yield more tiles and vice versa. In this way, when the zooming factor changes, only a fixed number of tiles need to be visited.

The different levels of resolution do not need to come from the same image. The detailed image could be from a different image to achieve effects like the "infinite zoom" [22], [23].

4. QUICKTIME VR

The image-based approach has been implemented in a commercial product called QuickTime VR, built on top of Apple Computer's QuickTime digital multimedia framework. The current implementation includes continuous camera panning and zooming, jumping to selected points and object rotation using frame indexing.

Currently, QuickTime VR uses cylindrical environment maps or panoramic images to accomplish camera rotation. The choice of a cylindrical map over other types is based on a number of factors. It is easier to capture a cylindrical panorama than other types of environment maps. One can use commercially available panoramic cameras which have a rotating vertical slit. We have also developed a tool which automatically "stitches" together a set of overlapping photographs (see 4.3.1.2) to create a seamless panorama. The cylindrical map only curves in one direction, which makes it efficient to perform image warping.

QuickTime VR includes an interactive environment which uses a software-based real-time image processing engine for navigating in space and an authoring environment for creating VR movies. The interactive environment is implemented as an operating system component that can be accessed by any QuickTime 2.0 compliant application program. The interactive environment comprises two types of players. The panoramic movie player allows the user to pan, zoom and navigate in a scene. It also includes a "hot spot" picking capability. Hot spots are regions in an image that allow for user interaction. The object movie player allows the user to rotate an object or view the object from different viewing directions. The players run on most Macintosh® and Windows™ platforms. The panoramic authoring environment consists of a suite of tools to perform panoramic image stitching, hot spot marking, linking, dicing and compression. The object movies are created with a motion-controllable camera.

The following sections briefly describe the movie format, the players and the process of making the movies.

4.1 The Movie Format

QuickTime VR currently includes two different types of movies: panoramic and object.

4.1.1 The Panoramic Movie

Conventional QuickTime movies are one-dimensional compressed sequences indexed by time. Each QuickTime movie may have multiple tracks. Each track can store a type of linear media, such as audio, video, text, etc. Each track type may have its own player to decode the information in the track. The tracks, which usually run parallel in time, are played synchronously with a common time scale. QuickTime allows new types of tracks and players to be added to extend its capabilities. Refer to [24] and [25] for a detailed description of the QuickTime architecture.

Panoramic movies are multi-dimensional event-driven spatially-oriented movies. A panoramic movie permits a user to pan, zoom and move in a space interactively. In order to retrofit panoramic movies into the existing linear movie framework, a new panoramic track type was added. The panoramic track stores all the linking and additional information associated with a panoramic movie. The actual panoramic images are stored in a regular QuickTime video track to take advantage of the existing video processing capabilities.

An example of a panoramic movie file is shown in figure 3. The panoramic track is divided into three nodes. Each node corresponds to a point in a space. A node contains information about itself and links to other nodes. The linking of the nodes form a directed graph, as shown in the figure. In this example, Node 2 is connected to Node 1 and Node 3, which has a link to an external event. The external event allows custom actions to be attached to a node.

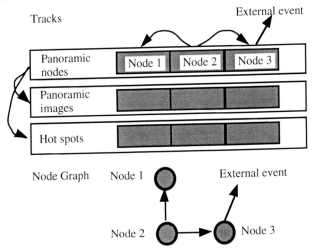

Figure 3. A panoramic movie layout and its corresponding node graph.

The nodes are stored in three tracks: one panoramic track and two video tracks. The panoramic track holds the graph information and pointers to the other two tracks. The first video track holds the panoramic images for the nodes. The second video track holds the hot spot images and is optional. The hot spots are used to identify regions of the panoramic image for activating appropriate links. All three tracks have the same length and the same time scale. The player uses the starting time value of each node to find the node's corresponding panoramic and hot spot images in the other two tracks.

The hot spot track is similar to the hit test track in the Virtual Museum [3]. The hot spots are used to activate events or navigation. The hot spots image encodes the hot spot id numbers as colors. However, unlike the Virtual Museum where a hot spot needs to exist for every view of the same object, the hot spot image is stored in panoramic form and is thereby orientation-independent. The hot spot image goes through the same image warping process as the panoramic image. Therefore, the hot spots will stay with the objects they attach to no matter how the camera pans or zooms.

The panoramic and the hot spot images are typically diced into smaller frames when stored in the video tracks for more efficient memory usage (see 4.2.1 for detail). The frames are usually compressed without inter-frame compression (e.g., frame differencing). Unlike linear video, the panoramic movie does not have an a priori order for accessing the frames. The image and hot spot video tracks are disabled so that a regular QuickTime movie would not attempt to display them as linear videos. Because the panoramic track is the only one enabled, the panoramic player is called upon to traverse the contents of the movie at playback time.

The track layout does not need to be the same as the physical layout of the data on a storage medium. Typically, the tracks should be interleaved when written to a slow medium, such as a CD-ROM, to minimize the seek time.

4.1.2 The Object Movie

An object movie typically contains a two-dimensional array of frames. Each frame corresponds to a viewing direction. The movie has more than two dimensions if multiple frames are stored for each direction. The additional frames allow the object to have time-varying behavior (see 4.2.2). Currently, each direction is assumed to have the same number of frames.

The object frames are stored in a regular video track. Additional information, such as the number of frames per direction and the numbers of rows and columns, is stored with the movie header. The frames are organized to minimize the seek time when rotating the object horizontally. As in the panoramic movies, there is no inter-frame compression for the frames since the order of rotation is not known in advance. However, inter-frame compression may be used for the multiple frames within each viewing direction.

4.2 The Interactive Environment

The interactive environment currently consists of two types of players: the panoramic player and the object player.

4.2.1 The Panoramic Player

The panoramic player allows the user to perform continuous panning in the vertical and the horizontal directions. Because the panoramic image has less than 180 degrees vertical field-of-view, the player does not permit looking all the way up or down. Rotating about the viewing direction is not currently supported. The player performs continuous zooming through image magnification and reduction as mentioned previously. If multiple levels of resolution are available, the player may choose the right level based on the current memory usage, CPU performance, disk speed and other factors. Multiple level zooming is not currently implemented in QuickTime VR.

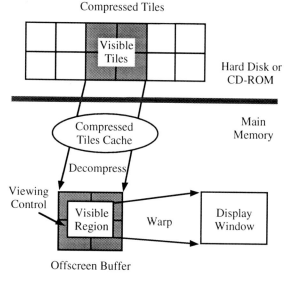

Figure 4. Panoramic display process.

The panoramic player allows the user to control the view orientation and displays a perspectively correct view by warping a panoramic image. Figure 4 shows the panoramic display process. The panoramic images are usually compressed

and stored on a hard disk or a CD-ROM. The compressed image needs to be decompressed to an offscreen buffer first. The offscreen buffer is generally smaller than the full panorama because only a fraction of the panorama is visible at any time. As mentioned previously, the panoramic image is diced into tiles. Only the tiles overlapping the current view orientation are decompressed to the offscreen buffer. The visible region on the offscreen buffer is then warped to display a correct perspective view. As long as the region moves inside the offscreen buffer, no additional decompression is necessary. To minimize the disk access, the most recent tiles may be cached in the main memory once they are read. The player also performs pre-paging to read in adjacent tiles while it is idle to minimize the delay in interactive panning.

The image warp, which reprojects sections of the cylindrical image onto a planar view, is computed in real-time using a software-based two-pass algorithm [26]. An example of the warp is shown in figure 5, where the region enclosed by the yellow box in the panoramic image is warped to create a perspective view below.

The performance of the player varies depending on many factors such as the platform, the color mode, the panning mode and the window sizes. The player is currently optimized for display in 16-bit color mode. Some performance figures for different processors are given below. These figures indicate the number of updates per second in a 640x400-pixel window in 16-bit color mode. Because the warping is performed with a two-pass algorithm, panning in 1D is faster than full 2D panning. Note that the Windows version has a different implementation for writing to display which may affect the performance.

Processor	1D Panning	2D Panning
PowerPC601/80	29.5	11.6
MC68040/40	12.3	5.4
Pentium/90	11.4	7.5
486/33	5.9	3.6

The player can perform image warping at different levels of quality. The lower quality settings perform less filtering and the images are more jagged but are faster. To achieve the best balance between quality and performance, the player automatically adjusts the quality level to maintain a constant update rate. When the user is panning, the player switches to lower quality to keep up with the user. When the user stops, the player updates the image in higher quality.

Moving in space is currently accomplished by jumping to points where panoramic images are attached. In order to preserve continuity of motion, the view direction needs to be maintained when jumping to an adjacent location. The panoramas are linked together by matching their orientation manually in the authoring stage (see 4.3.1.4). Figure 6 shows a sequence of images generated from panoramas spaced 5 feet apart.

The default user interface for navigation uses a combination of a 2D mouse and a keyboard. When the cursor moves over a window, its shape changes to reflect the permissible action at the current cursor location. The permissible actions include: continuous panning in 2D; continuous zooming in and out (controlled by a keyboard); moving to a different node; and activating a hot spot. Clicking on the mouse initiates the corresponding actions. Holding down and dragging the mouse performs continuous panning. The panning speed is controlled by the distance relative to the mouse click position.

In addition to interactive control, navigation can be placed under the control of a script. A HyperCard® external command and a Windows DLL have been written to drive the player. Any application compatible with the external command or DLL can control the playback with a script. A C run-time library interface will be available for direct control from a program.

4.2.2 The Object Player

While the panoramic player is designed to look around a space from the inside, the object player is used to view an object from the outside. The object player is based on the navigable movie approach. It uses a two-dimensional array of frames to accommodate object rotation. The object frames are created with a constant color background to facilitate compositing onto other backgrounds. The object player allows the user to grab the object using a mouse and rotate it with a virtual sphere-like interface [27]. The object can be rotated in two directions corresponding to orbiting the camera in the longitude and the latitude directions.

If there is more than one frame stored for each direction, the multiple frames are looped continuously while the object is being rotated. The looping enables the object to have cyclic time varying behavior (e.g. a flickering candle or streaming waterfall).

4.3 The Authoring Environment

The authoring environment includes tools to make panoramic movies and object movies.

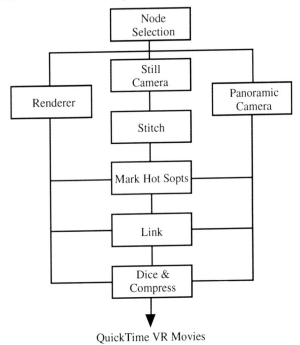

Figure 7. The panoramic movie authoring process.

4.3.1 Panoramic Movie Making

A panoramic movie is created in five steps. First, nodes are selected in a space to generate panoramas. Second, the panoramas are created with computer rendering, panoramic photography or "stitching" a mosaic of overlapping photographs. Third, if there are any hot spots on the panorama, a hot spot image is constructed by marking regions of the panorama with pseudo colors corresponding to the hot spot identifiers. Alternatively, the hot spots can be generated with computer rendering [28], [3]. Fourth, if more than one panoramic node is needed, the panoramas are linked together by manually registering their viewing directions. Finally, the panoramic images and the hot spot images are diced and compressed to create a panoramic movie. The authoring process is illustrated in figure 7.

4.3.1.1 Node Selection

The nodes should be selected to maintain visual consistency when moving from one to another. The distance between two adjacent nodes is related to the size of the virtual environment and the distance to the nearby objects. Empirically we have found that a 5-10 foot spacing to be adequate with most interior spaces. The spacing can be significantly increased with exterior scenes.

4.3.1.2 Stitching

The purpose of stitching is to create a seamless panoramic image from a set of overlapping pictures. The pictures are taken with a camera as it rotates about its vertical axis in one direction only. The camera pans at roughly equal, but not exact, increments. The camera is mounted on a tripod and centered at its nodal point with minimal tilting and rolling. The camera is usually mounted sideways to obtain the maximum vertical field-of-view. The setup of the camera is illustrated in figure 8. The scene is assumed to be static although some distant object motion may be acceptable.

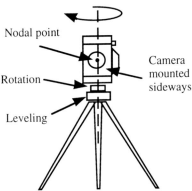

Figure 8. Camera setup for taking overlapping pictures.

The stitcher uses a correlation-based image registration algorithm to match and blend adjacent pictures. The adjacent pictures need to have some overlap for the stitcher to work properly. The amount of overlap may vary depending on the image features in the overlapping regions. In practice, a 50% overlap seems to work best because the adjacent pictures may have very different brightness levels. Having a large overlap allows the stitcher to more easily smooth out the intensity variation.

The success rate of the automatic stitching depends on the input pictures. For a typical stitching session, about 8 out of 10 panoramas can be stitched automatically, assuming each panorama is made from 12 pictures. The remaining 2 panoramas requires some manual intervention. The factors which contribute to automatic stitching failure include, but are not limited to, missing pictures, extreme intensity change, insufficient image features, improper camera mounting, significant object motion and film scanning errors.

In addition to being able to use a regular 35 mm camera, the ability to use multiple pictures, and hence different exposure settings, to compose a panorama has another advantage. It enables one to capture a scene with a very wide intensity range, such as during a sunset. A normal panoramic camera captures the entire 360 degrees with a constant exposure setting. Since film usually has a narrower dynamic range than the real world does, the resultant panorama may have areas under or over exposed. The stitcher allows the exposure setting to be specifically tailored for each direction. Therefore, it may create a more balanced panorama in extreme lighting conditions.

Although one can use other devices, such as video or digital cameras for capturing, using still film results in high resolution images even when displayed at full screen on a monitor. The film can be digitized and stored on Kodak's PhotoCD. Each PhotoCD contains around 100 pictures with 5 resolutions each. A typical panorama is stitched with the middle resolution pictures (i.e., 768 x 512 pixels) and the resulting panorama is around 2500 x 768 pixels for pictures taken with a 15 mm lens. This resolution is enough for a full screen display with a moderate zoom angle. The stitcher takes around 5 minutes to automatically stitch a 12-picture panorama on a PowerPC 601/80 MHz processor, including reading the pictures from the PhotoCD and some post processing. An example of a panoramic image stitched automatically is shown in figure 9.

4.3.1.3 Hot Spot Marking

Hot spots identify regions of a panoramic image for interactions, such as navigation or activating actions. Currently, the hot spots are stored in 8-bit images, which limit the number of unique hot spots to 256 per image. One way of creating a hot spot image is by painting pseudo colors over the top of a panoramic image. Computer renderers may generate the hot spot image directly.

The hot spot image does not need to have the same resolution as the panoramic image. The resolution of the hot spot image is related to the precision of picking. A very low resolution hot spot image may be used if high accuracy of picking is not required.

4.3.1.4 Linking

The linking process connects and registers view orientation between adjacent panoramic nodes. The links are directional and each node may have any number of links. Each link may be attached to a hot spot so that the user may activate the link by clicking on the hot spot.

Currently, the linking is performed by manually registering the source and destination view orientations using a graphical linker. The main goal of the registration is to maintain visual consistency when moving from one node to another.

4.3.1.5 Dicing and Compression

The panoramic and hot spot images are diced before being compressed and stored in a movie. The tile size should be optimized for both data loading and offscreen buffer size. A large number of tiles increases the overhead associated with loading and decompressing the tiles. A small number of tiles requires a large offscreen buffer and reduces title paging efficiency. We have found that dicing a panoramic image of 2500x768 pixels into 24 vertical stripes provides an optimal balance between data loading and tile paging. Dicing the panorama into vertical stripes also minimizes the seek time involved when loading the tiles from a CD-ROM during panning.

A panorama of the above resolution can be compressed to around 500 KB with a modest 10 to 1 compression ratio using the Cinepak compressor, which is based on vector quantization and provides a good quality vs. speed balance. Other compressors may be used as well for different quality and speed tradeoffs. The small disk footprint for each panorama means that a CD-ROM with over 600 MB capacity can hold more than 1,000 panoramas. The capacity will only increase as higher density CD-ROMs and better compression methods become available.

The hot spot image is compressed with a lossless 8-bit compressor. The lossless compression is necessary to ensure the correctness of the hot spot id numbers. Since the hot spots usually occupy large contiguous regions, the compressed size is typically only a few kilo-bytes per image.

4.3.2 Object Movie Making

Making an object movie requires photographing the object from different viewing directions. To provide a smooth object

rotation, the camera needs to point at the object's center while orbiting around it at constant increments. While this requirement can be easily met in computer generated objects, photographing a physical object in this way is very challenging unless a special device is built.

Currently, we use a device, called the "object maker," to accomplish this task. The object maker uses a computer to control two stepper motors. The computer-controlled motors orbit a video camera in two directions by fixing its view direction at the center of the object. The video camera is connected to a frame digitizer inside the computer, which synchronizes frame grabbing with camera rotation. The object is supported by a nearly invisible base and surrounded by a black curtain to provide a uniform background. The camera can rotate close to 180 degrees vertically and 360 degrees horizontally. The camera typically moves at 10-degree increments in each direction. The entire process may run automatically and takes around 1 hour to capture an object completely.

If multiple frames are needed for each direction, the object may be captured in several passes, with each pass capturing a full rotation of the object in a fixed state. The multi-pass capture requires that the camera rotation be repeatable and the object motion be controllable. In the case of candle light flickering, the multiple frames may need to be captured successively before the camera moves on to the next direction.

5. APPLICATIONS

The panoramic viewing technology can be applied to applications which require the exploration of real or imaginary scenes. Some example applications include virtual travel, real estate property inspection, architecture visualizations, virtual museums, virtual shopping and virtual reality games.

An example of panoramic movie application is the commercial CD-ROM title: Star Trek/The Next Generation®– Interactive Technical Manual. This title lets the user navigate in the Starship Enterprise using panoramic movies. Several thousand still photographs were shot to create more than two hundred panoramic images, which cover most areas in the starship. In addition, many object movies were created from the props in the set.

The object movie can be applied to visualize a scientific or engineering simulation. Most simulations require lengthy computations on sophisticated computers. The simulation results can be computed for all the possible view orientations and stored as an object movie which can be inspected by anyone with a personal computer.

Time-varying environment maps may be used to include motions in a scene. An example of time-varying environment maps has been generated using time-lapse photography. A camera was fixed at the same location and took a panoramic picture every 30 minutes during a whole day. The resulting movie shows the time passage while the user is freely looking around.

Another use of the orientation-independent movie is in interactive TV. A movie can be broadcast in a 360-degree format, perhaps using multiple channels. Each TV viewer can freely control the camera angle locally while watching the movie. A similar idea called "electronic panning camera" has been demonstrated for video conferencing applications [29].

Although most applications generated with the image-based approach are likely to be CD-ROM based in the near future because of CD-ROM's large storage capacity, the variable-resolution files make the approach practical for network transmission. A low-resolution panoramic movie takes up less than 100 KB per node and provides 360-degree panning in a

320x240-pixel window with reasonable quality. As network speeds improve and better compression technologies become available, on-line navigation of panoramic spaces may become more common in the near future. One can use the same spatial navigation metaphor to browse an informational space. The ability to attach information to some spatial representations may make it easier to become familiar with an intricate information space.

6. CONCLUSIONS AND FUTURE DIRECTIONS

The image-based method makes use of environment maps, in particular cylindrical panoramic images, to compose a scene. The environment maps are orientation-independent images, which allow the user to look around in arbitrary view directions through the use of real-time image processing. Multiple environment maps can be linked together to define a scene. The user may move in the scene by jumping through the maps. The method may be extended to include motions with time-varying environment maps. In addition, the method makes use of a two-dimensional array of frames to view an object from different directions.

The image-based method also provides a solution to the levels of detail problem in most 3D virtual reality display systems. Ideally, an object should be displayed in less detail when it is farther away and in more detail when it is close to the observer. However, automatically changing the level of detail is very difficult for most polygon based objects. In practice, the same object is usually modeled at different detail levels and the appropriate one is chosen for display based on some viewing criteria and system performance [30], [31]. This approach is costly as multiple versions of the objects need to be created and stored. Since one can not predict how an object will be displayed in advance, it is difficult to store enough levels to include all possible viewing conditions.

The image-based method automatically provides the appropriate level of detail. The images are views of a scene from a range of locations. As the viewpoint moves from one location to another within the range, the image associated with the new location is retrieved. In this way, the scene is always displayed at the appropriate level of detail.

This method is the underlying technology for QuickTime VR, a system for creating and interacting with virtual environments. The system meets most of the objectives that we described in the introduction. The playback environment supports most computers and does not require special hardware. It uses images as a common representation and can therefore accommodate both real and imaginary scenes. The display speed is independent of scene complexity and rendering quality. The making of the Star Trek title in a rather short time frame (less than 2 months for generating all the panoramic movies of the Enterprise) has demonstrated the system's relative ease in creating a complex environment.

The method's chief limitations are the requirements that the scene be static and the movement be confined to particular points. The first limitation may be eased somewhat with the use of time-varying environment maps. The environment maps may have motions in some local regions, such as opening a door. The motion may be triggered by an event or continuously looping. Because the motions are mostly confined to some local regions, the motion frames can be compressed efficiently with inter-frame compression.

Another solution to the static environment constraint is the combination of image warping and 3D rendering. Since most backgrounds are static, they can be generated efficiently from environment maps. The objects which are time-varying or event driven can be rendered on-the-fly using 3D rendering. The rendered objects are composited onto the map-generated background in real-time using layering, alpha masking or z-buffering. Usually, the number of interactive objects which need to be rendered in real-time is small, therefore, even a software based 3D renderer may be enough for the task.

Being able to move freely in a photographic scene is more difficult. For computer rendered scenes, the view interpolation method may be a solution. The method requires depth and camera information for automatic image registration. This information is not easily obtainable from photographic scenes.

Another constraint with the current panoramic player is its limitation in looking straight up or down due to the use of cylindrical panoramic images. This limitation can be removed if other types of environment maps, such as cubic or spherical maps, are used. However, capturing a cubic or a spherical map photographically may be more difficult than a cylindrical one.

The current player does not require any additional input and output devices other than those commonly available on personal computers. However, input devices with more than two degrees of freedom may be useful since the navigation is more than two-dimensional. Similarly, immersive stereo displays combined with 3D sounds may enhance the experience of navigation.

One of the ultimate goals of virtual reality will be achieved when one can not discern what is real from what is virtual. With the ability to use photographs of real scenes for virtual navigation, we may be one step closer.

7. ACKNOWLEDGMENTS

The author is grateful to the entire QuickTime VR team for their tremendous efforts on which this paper is based. Specifically, the author would like to acknowledge the following individuals: Eric Zarakov, for his managerial support and making QuickTime VR a reality; Ian Small, for his contributions to the engineering of the QuickTime VR product; Ken Doyle, for his QuickTime integration work; Michael Chen, for his work on user interface, the object maker and the object player; Ken Turkowski, for code optimization and PowerPC porting help; Richard Mander, for user interface design and study; and Ted Casey, for content and production support. The assistance from the QuickTime team, especially Jim Nitchal's help on code optimization, is also appreciated. Dan O'Sullivan and Mitch Yawitz's early work on navigable movies contributed to the development of the object movie.

Most of the work reported on in this paper began in the Computer Graphics program of the Advanced Technology Group at Apple Computer, Inc. The panoramic player was inspired by work from Gavin Miller. Ned Greene and Lance Williams contributed ideas related to environment mapping and view interpolation. Frank Crow's encouragement and support throughout were critical in keeping the research going. The author's interns, Lili Cheng, Chase Garfinkle and Patrick Teo, helped in shaping up the project into its current state.

The images in figure 6 are extracted from the "Apple Company Store in QuickTime VR" CD. The Great Wall photographs in figure 9 were taken with the assistance of Helen Tahn, Zen Jing and Professor En-Hua Wu. Thanks go to Vicki de Mey for proofreading the paper.

REFERENCES

[1] Lippman, A. Movie Maps: An Application of the Optical Videodisc to Computer Graphics. Computer Graphics(Proc. SIGGRAPH'80), 32-43.

[2] Ripley, D. G. DVI–a Digital Multimedia Technology.

Communications of the ACM. 32(7):811-822. 1989.

[3] Miller, G., E. Hoffert, S. E. Chen, E. Patterson, D. Blackketter, S. Rubin, S. A. Applin, D. Yim, J. Hanan. The Virtual Museum: Interactive 3D Navigation of a Multimedia Database. The Journal of Visualization and Computer Animation, (3): 183-197, 1992.

[4] Mohl, R. Cognitive Space in the Interactive Movie Map: an Investigation of Spatial Learning in the Virtual Environments. MIT Doctoral Thesis, 1981.

[5] Apple Computer, Inc. QuickTime, Version 1.5 for Developers CD. 1992.

[6] Blinn, J. F. and M. E. Newell. Texture and Reflection in Computer Generated Images. Communications of the ACM, 19(10):542-547. October 1976.

[7] Hall, R. Hybrid Techniques for Rapid Image Synthesis. in Whitted, T. and R. Cook, eds. Image Rendering Tricks, Course Notes 16 for SIGGRAPH'86. August 1986.

[8] Greene, N. Environment Mapping and Other Applications of World Projections. Computer Graphics and Applications, 6(11):21-29. November 1986.

[9] Yelick, S. Anamorphic Image Processing. B.S. Thesis. Department of Electrical Engineering and Computer Science. May, 1980.

[10] Hodges, M and R. Sasnett. Multimedia Computing– Case Studies from MIT Project Athena. 89-102. Addison-Wesley. 1993.

[11] Miller, G. and S. E. Chen. Real-Time Display of Surroundings using Environment Maps. Technical Report No. 44, 1993, Apple Computer, Inc.

[12] Greene, N and M. Kass. Approximating Visibility with Environment Maps. Technical Report No. 41. Apple Computer, Inc.

[13] Regan, M. and R. Pose. Priority Rendering with a Virtual Reality Address Recalculation Pipeline. Computer Graphics (Proc. SIGGRAPH'94), 155-162.

[14] Greene, N. Creating Raster Ominmax Images from Multiple Perspective Views using the Elliptical Weighted Average Filter. IEEE Computer Graphics and Applications. 6(6):21-27, June, 1986.

[15] Irani, M. and S. Peleg. Improving Resolution by Image Registration. Graphical Models and Image Processing. (3), May, 1991.

[16] Szeliski, R. Image Mosaicing for Tele-Reality Applications. DEC Cambridge Research Lab Technical Report, CRL 94/2. May, 1994.

[17] Mann, S. and R. W. Picard. Virtual Bellows: Constructing High Quality Stills from Video. Proceedings of ICIP-94. 363-367. November, 1994.

[18] Chen, S. E. and L. Williams. View Interpolation for Image Synthesis. Computer Graphics(Proc. SIGGRAPH'93), 279-288.

[19] Cheng, N. L. View Reconstruction form Uncalibrated Cameras for Three-Dimensional Scenes. Master's Thesis, Department of Electrical Engineering and Computer Sciences, U. C. Berkeley. 1995.

[20] Laveau, S. and O. Faugeras. 3-D Scene Representation as a Collection of Images and Fundamental Matrices. INRIA, Technical Report No. 2205, February, 1994.

[21] Williams, L. Pyramidal Parametrics. Computer Graphics(Proc. SIGGRAPH'83), 1-11.

[22] Berman, D. R., J. T. Bartell and D. H. Salesin. Multiresolution Painting and Compositing. Computer Graphics (Proc. SIGGRAPH'94), 85-90.

[23] Perlin, K. and D. Fox. Pad: An Alternative Approach to the Computer Interface. Computer Graphics (Proc. SIGGRAPH'93), 57-72.

[24] Hoffert, E., L. Mighdoll, M. Kreuger, M. Mills, J. Cohen, et al. QuickTime: an Extensible Standard for Digital Multimedia. Proceedings of the IEEE Computer Conference (CompCon'92), February 1992.

[25] Apple Computer, Inc. Inside Macintosh: QuickTime. Addison-Wesley. 1993.

[26] Chen, S. E. and G. S. P. Miller. Cylindrical to planar image mapping using scanline coherence. United States Patent number 5,396,583. Mar. 7, 1995.

[27] Chen, M. A Study in Interactive 3-D Rotation Using 2-D Control Devices. Computer Graphics (Proc. SIGGRAPH'88), 121-130.

[28] Weghorst, H., G. Hooper and D. Greenberg. Improved Computational Methods for Ray Tracing. ACM Transactions on Graphics. 3(1):52-69. 1986.

[29] 'Electronic Panning' Device Opens Viewing Range. Digital Media: A Seybold Report. 2(3):13-14. August, 1992.

[30] Clark, J. H. Hierarchical Geometric Models for Visible Surface Algorithms. Communications of the ACM, (19)10:547-554. October, 1976

[31] Funkhouser, T. A. and C. H. Séquin. Adaptive Display Algorithm for Interactive Frame Rates During Visualization of Complex Virtual Environments. Computer Graphics(Proc. SIGGRAPH'93), 247-254.

Figure 6. A walkthrough sequence created from a set of panoramas spaced 5 feet apart.

Figure 5. A perspective view created from warping a region enclosed by the yellow box in the panoramic image.

Figure 9. A stitched panoramic image and some of the photographs the image stitched from.

Plenoptic Modeling:
An Image-Based Rendering System

Leonard McMillan[†] and Gary Bishop[‡]

Department of Computer Science
University of North Carolina at Chapel Hill

ABSTRACT

Image-based rendering is a powerful new approach for generating real-time photorealistic computer graphics. It can provide convincing animations without an explicit geometric representation. We use the "plenoptic function" of Adelson and Bergen to provide a concise problem statement for image-based rendering paradigms, such as morphing and view interpolation. The plenoptic function is a parameterized function for describing everything that is visible from a given point in space. We present an image-based rendering system based on sampling, reconstructing, and resampling the plenoptic function. In addition, we introduce a novel visible surface algorithm and a geometric invariant for cylindrical projections that is equivalent to the epipolar constraint defined for planar projections.

CR Descriptors: I.3.3 [**Computer Graphics**]: Picture/Image Generation– *display algorithms*, *viewing algorithms*; I.3.7 [**Computer Graphics**]: Three-Dimensional Graphics and Realism– *hidden line/ surface removal*; I.4.3 [**Image Processing**]: Enhancement– *registration*; I.4.7 [**Image Processing**]: Feature Measurement– *projections*; I.4.8 [**Image Processing**]: Scene Analysis.

1. INTRODUCTION

In recent years there has been increased interest, within the computer graphics community, in image-based rendering systems. These systems are fundamentally different from traditional geometry-based rendering systems. In image-based systems the underlying data representation (i.e model) is composed of a set of photometric observations, whereas geometry-based systems use either mathematical descriptions of the boundary regions separating scene elements (B-rep) or discretely sampled space functions (volumetric).

The evolution of image-based rendering systems can be traced through at least three different research fields. In photogrammetry the initial problems of camera calibration, two-dimensional image registration, and photometrics have progressed toward the determination of three-dimensional models. Likewise, in computer vision, problems such as robot navigation, image discrimination, and image understanding have naturally led in the same direction. In computer graphics, the progression toward image-based rendering systems

[†‡]CB 3175 Sitterson Hall, Chapel Hill, NC 27599
[†] (919) 962-1797   mcmillan@cs.unc.edu   http://www.cs.unc.edu/~mcmillan
[‡] (919) 962-1886   gb@cs.unc.edu   http://www.cs.unc.edu/~gb

Permission to make digital/hard copy of part or all of this work for personal or classroom use is granted without fee provided that copies are not made or distributed for profit or commercial advantage, the copyright notice, the title of the publication and its date appear, and notice is given that copying is by permission of ACM, Inc. To copy otherwise, to republish, to post on servers, or to redistribute to lists, requires prior specific permission and/or a fee.

was initially motivated by the desire to increase the visual realism of the approximate geometric descriptions by mapping images onto their surface (texture mapping) [7], [12]. Next, images were used to approximate global illumination effects (environment mapping) [5], and, most recently, we have seen systems where the images themselves constitute the significant aspects of the scene's description [8].

Another reason for considering image-based rendering systems in computer graphics is that acquisition of realistic surface models is a difficult problem. While geometry-based rendering technology has made significant strides towards achieving photorealism, creating accurate models is still nearly as difficult as it was ten years ago. Technological advances in three-dimensional scanning provide some promise in model building. However, they also verify our worst suspicions— the geometry of the real-world is exceedingly complex. Ironically, the primary subjective measure of image quality used by proponents of geometric rendering systems is the degree with which the resulting images are indistinguishable from photographs.

One liability of image-based rendering systems is the lack of a consistent framework within which to judge the validity of the results. Fundamentally, this arises from the absence of a clear problem definition. Geometry-based rendering, on the other hand, has a solid foundation; it uses analytic and projective geometry to describe the world's shape and physics to describe the world's surface properties and the light's interaction with those surfaces.

This paper presents a consistent framework for the evaluation of image-based rendering systems, and gives a concise problem definition. We then evaluate previous image-based rendering methods within this new framework. Finally, we present our own image-based rendering methodology and results from our prototype implementation.

2. THE PLENOPTIC FUNCTION

Adelson and Bergen [1] assigned the name *plenoptic* function (from the latin root *plenus*, meaning complete or full, and *optic* pertaining to vision) to the pencil of rays visible from any point in space, at any time, and over any range of wavelengths. They used this function to develop a taxonomy for evaluating models of low-level vision. The plenoptic function describes all of the radiant energy that can be perceived from the point of view of the observer rather than the point of view of the source. They postulate

> "... all the basic visual measurements can be considered
> to characterize local change along one or two dimensions
> of a single function that describes the structure of the
> information in the light impinging on an observer."

Adelson and Bergen further formalized this functional description by providing a parameter space over which the plenoptic function is valid, as shown in Figure 1. Imagine an idealized eye which we are free to place at any point in space (V_x, V_y, V_z). From there we can select any of the viewable rays by choosing an azimuth and elevation angle

(θ,ϕ) as well as a band of wavelengths, λ, which we wish to consider.

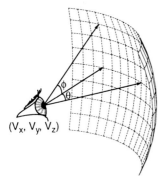

FIGURE 1. The plenoptic function describes all of the image information visible from a particular viewing position.

In the case of a dynamic scene, we can additionally choose the time, t, at which we wish to evaluate the function. This results in the following form for the plenoptic function:

$$p = P(\theta, \phi, \lambda, V_x, V_y, V_z, t) \qquad (1)$$

In computer graphics terminology, the plenoptic function describes the set of all possible environment maps for a given scene. For the purposes of visualization, one can consider the plenoptic function as a scene representation. In order to generate a view from a given point in a particular direction we would need to merely plug in appropriate values for (V_x, V_y, V_z) and select from a range of (θ,ϕ) for some constant t.

We define a complete sample of the plenoptic function as a full spherical map for a given viewpoint and time value, and an incomplete sample as some solid angle subset of this spherical map.

Within this framework we can state the following problem definition for image-based rendering. *Given a set of discrete samples (complete or incomplete) from the plenoptic function, the goal of image-based rendering is to generate a continuous representation of that function.* This problem statement provides for many avenues of exploration, such as how to optimally select sample points and how to best reconstruct a continuous function from these samples.

3. PREVIOUS WORK

3.1 Movie-Maps
The Movie-Map system by Lippman [17] is one of the earliest attempts at constructing an image-based rendering system. In Movie-Maps, incomplete plenoptic samples are stored on interactive video laser disks. They are accessed randomly, primarily by a change in viewpoint; however, the system can also accommodate panning, tilting, or zooming about a fixed viewing position. We can characterize Lippman's plenoptic reconstruction technique as a nearest-neighbor interpolation because, when given a set of input parameters $(V_x, V_y, V_z, \theta, \phi, t)$, the Movie-Map system can select the nearest partial sample. The Movie-Map form of image-based rendering can also be interpreted as a table-based evaluation of the plenoptic function. This interpretation reflects the database structure common to most image-based systems.

3.2 Image Morphing
Image morphing is a very popular image-based rendering technique [4], [28]. Generally, morphing is considered to occur between two images. We can think of these images as endpoints along some path through time and/or space. In this interpretation, morphing becomes a method for reconstructing partial samples of the continuous plenoptic function along this path. In addition to photometric data, morphing uses additional information describing the image flow field. This information is usually hand crafted by an animator. At first

glance, this type of augmentation might seem to place it outside of the plenoptic function's domain. However, several authors in the field of computer vision have shown that this type of image flow information is equivalent to changes in the local intensity due to infinitesimal perturbations of the plenoptic function's independent variables [20], [13]. This local derivative behavior can be related to the intensity gradient via applications of the chain rule. In fact, morphing makes an even stronger assumption that the flow information is constant along the entire path, thus amounting to a locally linear approximation. Also, a blending function is often used to combine both reference images after being partially flowed from their initial configurations to a given point on the path. This blending function is usually some linear combination of the two images based on what percentage of the path's length has been traversed. Thus, morphing is a plenoptic reconstruction method which interpolates between samples and uses local derivative information to construct approximations.

3.3 View Interpolation
Chen's and Williams' [8] view interpolation employs incomplete plenoptic samples and image flow fields to reconstruct arbitrary viewpoints with some constraints on gaze angle. The reconstruction process uses information about the local neighborhood of a sample. Chen and Williams point out and suggest a solution for one of the key problems of image-based rendering— determining the visible surfaces. Chen and Williams chose to presort the quadtree compressed flow-field in a back-to-front order according to its (geometric) z-value. This approach works well when all of the partial sample images share a common gaze direction, and the synthesized viewpoints are restricted to stay within 90 degrees of this gaze angle.

An image flow field alone allows for many ambiguous visibility solutions, unless we restrict ourselves to flow fields that do not fold, such as rubber-sheet local spline warps or thin-plate global spline warps. This problem must be considered in any general-purpose image-based rendering system, and ideally, it should be done without transporting the image into the geometric-rendering domain.

Establishing flow fields for a view interpolation system can also be problematic. Chen and Williams used pre-rendered synthetic images to determine flow fields from the z-values. In general, accurate flow field information between two samples can only be established for points that are mutually visible to both samples. This points out a shortcoming in the use of partial samples, because reference images seldom have a 100% overlap.

Like morphing, view interpolation uses photometric information as well as local derivative information in its reconstruction process. This locally linear approximation is nicely exploited to approximate perspective depth effects, and Chen and Williams show it to be correct for lateral motions relative to the gaze direction. View interpolation, however, adds a nonlinearity by allowing the visibility process to determine the blending function between reference frames in a closest-take-all (a.k.a. winner-take-all) fashion.

3.4 Laveau and Faugeras
Laveau and Faugeras [15] have taken advantage of the fact that the epipolar geometries between images restrict the image flow field in such a way that it can be parameterized by a single disparity value and a fundamental matrix which represents the epipolar relationship. They also provide a two-dimensional raytracing-like solution to the visibility problem which does not require an underlying geometric description. Their method does, however, require establishing correspondences for each image point along the ray's path. The Laveau and Faugeras system also uses partial plenoptic samples, and results are shown only for overlapping regions between views.

Laveau and Faugeras also discuss the combination of information from several views but primarily in terms of resolving visibility. By relating the reference views and the desired views by the homogenous transformations between their projections, Laveau and Faugeras can compute exact perspective depth solutions. The reconstruction process again takes advantage of both image data and local derivative information to reconstruct the plenoptic function.

3.5 Regan and Pose

Regan and Pose [23] describe a hybrid system in which plenoptic samples are generated on the fly by a geometry-based rendering system at available rendering rates, while interactive rendering is provided by the image-based subsystem. At any instant, a user interacts with a single plenoptic sample. This allows the user to make unconstrained changes in the gaze angle about the sample point. Regan and Pose also discuss local reconstruction approximations due to changes in the viewing position. These approximations amount to treating the objects in the scene as being placed at infinity, resulting in a loss of the kinetic depth effect. These partial updates can be combined with the approximation values.

4. PLENOPTIC MODELING

We claim that all image-based rendering approaches can be cast as attempts to reconstruct the plenoptic function from a sample set of that function. We believe that there are significant insights to be gleaned from this characterization. In this section, we propose our prototype system in light of this plenoptic function framework.

We call our image-based rendering approach Plenoptic Modeling. Like other image-based rendering systems, the scene description is given by a series of reference images. These reference images are subsequently warped and combined to form representations of the scene from arbitrary viewpoints. The warping function is defined by image flow field information that can either be supplied as an input or derived from the reference images.

Our discussion of the plenoptic modeling image-based rendering system is broken down into four sections. First, we discuss the representation of the plenoptic samples. Next, we discuss their acquisition. The third section covers the determination of image flow fields, if required. And, finally, we describe how to reconstruct the plenoptic function from these sample images.

4.1 Plenoptic Sample Representation

The most natural surface for projecting a complete plenoptic sample is a unit sphere centered about the viewing position. One difficulty of spherical projections, however, is the lack of a representation that is suitable for storage on a computer. This is particularly difficult if a uniform (i.e. equal area) discrete sampling is required. This difficulty is reflected in the various distortions which arise in planar projections of world maps in cartography. Those uniform mappings which do exist are generally ill-suited for systematic access as a data structure. Furthermore, those which do map to a plane with consistent neighborhood relationships are generally quite distorted and, therefore, non-uniform.

A set of six planar projections in the form of a cube has been suggested by Greene [10] as an efficient representation for environment maps. While this representation can be easily stored and accessed by a computer, it provides significant problems relating to acquisition, alignment, and registration when used with real, non-computer-generated images. The orthogonal orientation of the cube faces requires precise camera positioning. The wide, 90 degree field-of-view of each face requires expensive lens systems to avoid optical distortion. Also, the planar mapping does not represent a uniform sampling, but instead, is considerably oversampled in the edges and corners. However, the greatest difficulty of a cube-oriented planar projection set is describing the behavior of the image flow fields across the boundaries between faces and at corners. This is not an issue when the six planar projections are used solely as an environment map, but it adds a considerable overhead when it is used for image analysis.

We have chosen to use a cylindrical projection as the plenoptic sample representation. One advantage of a cylinder is that it can be easily unrolled into a simple planar map. The surface is without boundaries in the azimuth direction, which simplifies correspondence searches required to establish image flow fields. One short-coming of a projection on a finite cylindrical surface is the boundary conditions introduced at the top and bottom. We have chosen not to employ end caps on our projections, which has the problem of limiting the vertical field of view within the environment.

4.2 Acquiring Cylindrical Projections

A significant advantage of a cylindrical projection is the simplicity of acquisition. The only acquisition equipment required is a video camera and a tripod capable of continuous panning. Ideally, the camera's panning motion would be around the exact optical center of the camera. In practice, in a scene where all objects are relatively far from the tripod's rotational center, a slight misalignment offset can be tolerated.

Any two planar perspective projections of a scene which share a common viewpoint are related by a two-dimensional homogenous transform:

$$
\begin{bmatrix} u \\ v \\ w \end{bmatrix} = \begin{bmatrix} a_{11} & a_{12} & a_{13} \\ a_{21} & a_{22} & a_{23} \\ a_{31} & a_{32} & a_{33} \end{bmatrix} \begin{bmatrix} x \\ y \\ 1 \end{bmatrix} \tag{2}
$$

$$
x' = \frac{u}{w} \qquad y' = \frac{v}{w}
$$

where x and y represent the pixel coordinates of an image I, and x' and y' are their corresponding coordinates in a second image I'. This well known result has been reported by several authors [12], [28], [22]. The images resulting from typical camera motions, such as pan, tilt, roll, and zoom, can all be related in this fashion. When creating a cylindrical projection, we will only need to consider panning camera motions. For convenience we define the camera's local coordinate system such that the panning takes place entirely in the x-z plane.

In order to reproject an individual image into a cylindrical projection, we must first determine a model for the camera's projection or, equivalently, the appropriate homogenous transforms. Many different techniques have been developed for inferring the homogenous transformation between images sharing common centers of projection. The most common technique [12] involves establishing four corresponding points across each image pair. The resulting transforms provide a mapping of pixels from the planar projection of the first image to the planar projection of the second. Several images could be composited in this fashion by first determining the transform which maps the Nth image to image N-1. These transforms can be catenated to form a mapping of each image to the plane of the first. This approach, in effect, avoids direct determination of an entire camera model by performing all mappings between different instances of the same camera. Other techniques for deriving these homogeneous transformations without specific point correspondences have also been described [22], [25].

The set of homogenous transforms, H_i, can be decomposed into two parts which will allow for arbitrary reprojections in a manner similar to [11]. These two parts include an intrinsic transform, S, which is determined entirely by camera properties, and an extrinsic transform, R_i, which is determined by the rotation around the camera's center of projection:

$$
\bar{u} = H_i \bar{x} = S^{-1} R_i S \bar{x} \tag{3}
$$

This decomposition decouples the projection and rotational components of the homogeneous transform. By an appropriate choice of coordinate systems and by limiting the camera's motion to panning, the extrinsic transform component is constrained to a function of a single parameter rotation matrix describing the pan.

$$
R_y = \begin{bmatrix} \cos\theta & 0 & \sin\theta \\ 0 & 1 & 0 \\ -\sin\theta & 0 & \cos\theta \end{bmatrix} \tag{4}
$$

Since the intrinsic component's properties are invariant over all of the images, the decomposition problem can be broken into two parts: the determination of the extrinsic rotation component, R_i, followed by the determination of an intrinsic projection component, S. The first step in our method determines estimates for the extrinsic panning angle between each image pair of the panning sequence. This is accomplished by using a linear approximation to an infinitesimal rotation by the angle θ. This linear approximation results from substituting $1 + O(\theta^2)$ for the cosine terms and $\theta + O(\theta^3)$ for the sine terms of the rotation matrix. This infinitesimal perturbation has been shown by [14] to reduce to the following approximate equations:

$$x' = x - f\theta - \frac{\theta (x - C_x)^2}{f} + O(\theta^2)$$
$$y' = y - \frac{\theta (x - C_x)(y - C_y)}{f} + O(\theta^2) \qquad (5)$$

where f is the apparent focal length of the camera measured in pixels, and (C_x, C_y) is the pixel coordinate of the intersection of the optical axis with the image plane. (C_x, C_y) is initially estimated to be at the center pixel of the image plane. A better estimate for (C_x, C_y) is found during the intrinsic matrix solution.

These equations show that small panning rotations can be approximated by translations for pixels near the image's center. We require that some part of each image in the sequence must be visible in the successive image, and that some part of the final image must be visible in the first image of the sequence. The first stage of the cylindrical registration process attempts to register the image set by computing the optimal translation in x which maximizes the normalized correlation within a region about the center third of the screen. This is first computed at a pixel resolution, then refined on a 0.1 subpixel grid, using a Catmull-Rom interpolation spline to compute subpixel intensities. Once these translations, t_i, are computed, Newton's method is used to convert them to estimates of rotation angles and the focal length, using the following equation:

$$2\pi - \sum_{i=1}^{N} atan\left(\frac{t_i}{f}\right) = 0 \qquad (6)$$

where N is the number of images comprising the sequence. This usually converges in as few as five iterations, depending on the original estimate for f. This first phase determines an estimate for the relative rotational angles between each of the images (our extrinsic parameters) and the initial focal length estimate measured in pixels (one of the intrinsic parameters).

The second stage of the registration process determines the S, or structural matrix, which describes various camera properties such as the tilt and roll angles which are assumed to remain constant over the group of images. The following model is used:

$$S = \Omega_x \Omega_z P \qquad (7)$$

where P is the projection matrix:

$$P = \begin{bmatrix} 1 & \sigma & -C_x \\ 0 & \rho & -C_y \\ 0 & 0 & f \end{bmatrix} \qquad (8)$$

and (C_x, C_y) is the estimated center of the viewplane as described previously, σ is a skew parameter representing the deviation of the sampling grid from a rectilinear grid, ρ determines the sampling grid's aspect ratio, and f is the focal length in pixels as determined from the first alignment stage.

The remaining terms, Ω_x and Ω_z, describe the combined effects of camera orientation and deviations of the viewplane's orientation from perpendicular to the optical axis. Ideally, the viewplane would be normal to the optical axis, but manufacturing tolerances allow these numbers to vary slightly [27].

$$\Omega_x = \begin{bmatrix} 1 & 0 & 0 \\ 0 & \cos\omega_x & -\sin\omega_x \\ 0 & \sin\omega_x & \cos\omega_x \end{bmatrix} \qquad (9)$$

$$\Omega_z = \begin{bmatrix} \cos\omega_z & -\sin\omega_z & 0 \\ \sin\omega_z & \cos\omega_z & 0 \\ 0 & 0 & 1 \end{bmatrix} \qquad (10)$$

In addition, the ω_z term is indistinguishable from the camera's roll angle and, thus, represents both the image sensor's and the camera's rotation. Likewise, ω_x is combined with an implicit parameter, ϕ, that represents the relative tilt of the camera's optical axis out of the panning plane. If ϕ is zero, the images are all tangent to a cylinder and for a nonzero ϕ the projections are tangent to a cone.

This gives six unknown parameters, $(C_x, C_y, \sigma, \rho, \omega_x, \omega_z)$, to be determined in the second stage of the registration process. Notice that, when combined with the θ_i and f parameters determined in the first stage, we have a total of eight parameters for each image, which is consistent with the number of free parameters in a general homogeneous matrix.

The structural matrix, S, is determined by minimizing the following error function:

$$\text{error}(C_x, C_y, \sigma, \rho, \omega_x, \omega_z) = \sum_{i=1}^{n} 1 - \text{Correlation}(I_{i-1}, S^{-1}R_{y_i}SI_i) \qquad (11)$$

where I_{i-1} and I_i represent the center third of the pixels from images i-1 and i respectively. Using Powell's multivariable minimization method [23] with the following initial values for our six parameters,

$$C_x = \frac{\text{image width}}{2} \qquad C_y = \frac{\text{image height}}{2}$$
$$\sigma = 0 \qquad \rho = 1 \qquad \omega_x = 0 \qquad \omega_z = 0 \qquad (12)$$

the solution typically converges in about six iterations. At this point we will have a new estimate for (C_x, C_y) which can be fed back into stage one, and the entire process can be repeated.

The registration process results in a single camera model, $S(C_x, C_y, \sigma, \rho, \omega_x, \omega_z, f)$, and a set of the relative rotations, θ_i, between each of the sampled images. Using these parameters, we can compose mapping functions from any image in the sequence to any other image as follows:

$$I'_i = S^{-1}R_{y_{i+1}}R_{y_{i+2}}R_{y_{i+3}}\ldots R_{y_j}SI_j \qquad (13)$$

We can also reproject images onto arbitrary surfaces by modifying S. Since each image pixel determines the equation of a ray from the center-of-projection, the reprojection process merely involves intersecting these rays with the projection manifold.

4.3 Determining Image Flow Fields

Given two or more cylindrical projections from different positions within a static scene, we can determine the relative positions of centers-of-projection and establish geometric constraints across all potential reprojections. These positions can only be computed to a scale factor. An intuitive argument for this is that from a set of images alone, one cannot determine if the observer is looking at a model or a full-sized scene. This implies that at least one measurement is required to establish a scale factor. The measurement may be taken either between features that are mutually visible within images, or the distance between the acquired image's camera positions can be used. Both techniques have been used with little difference in results.

To establish the relative relationships between any pair of cylindrical projections, the user specifies a set of corresponding points that are visible from both views. These points can be treated as rays in space with the following form:

$$\bar{x}_a(\theta, v) = \bar{C}_a + t\bar{D}_a(\theta, v) \qquad \bar{D}_a(\theta, v) = \begin{bmatrix} \cos{(\phi_a - \theta)} \\ \sin{(\phi_a - \theta)} \\ k_a \left(C_{v_a} - v \right) \end{bmatrix} \quad (14)$$

where $\bar{C}_a = (A_x, A_y, A_z)$ is the unknown position of the cylinder's center of projection, ϕ_a is the rotational offset which aligns the angular orientation of the cylinders to a common frame, k_a is a scale factor which determines the vertical field-of-view, and C_{v_a} is the scanline where the center of projection would project onto the scene (i.e. the line of zero elevation, like the equator of a spherical map).

A pair of tiepoints, one from each image, establishes a pair of rays which ideally intersect at the point in space identified by the tiepoint. In general, however, these rays are skewed. Therefore, we use the point that is simultaneously closest to both rays as an estimate of the point's position, $\bar{p}$, as determined by the following derivation.

$$\bar{p}(\theta_a, v_a, \theta_b, v_b) = \frac{\bar{x}_a - \bar{x}_b}{2} \qquad (15)$$

where (θ_a, v_a) and (θ_b, v_b) are the tiepoint coordinates on cylinders A and B respectively. The two points, $\bar{x}_a$ and $\bar{x}_b$, are given by

$$\bar{x}_a = \bar{C}_a + t\bar{D}_a(\theta_a, v_a)$$
$$\bar{x}_b = \bar{C}_b + s\bar{D}_b(\theta_b, v_b) \qquad (16)$$

where

$$t = \frac{\text{Det}\left[\bar{C}_a - \bar{C}_b, \bar{D}_b(\theta_b, v_b), \bar{D}_a(\theta_a, v_a) \times \bar{D}_b(\theta_b, v_b)\right]}{\left|\bar{D}_a(\theta_a, v_a) \times \bar{D}_b(\theta_b, v_b)\right|^2}$$

$$s = \frac{\text{Det}\left[\bar{C}_b - \bar{C}_a, \bar{D}_a(\theta_a, v_a), \bar{D}_a(\theta_a, v_a) \times \bar{D}_b(\theta_b, v_b)\right]}{\left|\bar{D}_a(\theta_a, v_a) \times \bar{D}_b(\theta_b, v_b)\right|^2} \qquad (17)$$

This allows us to pose the problem of finding a cylinder's position as a minimization problem. For each pair of cylinders we have two sets of six unknowns, $[(A_x, A_y, A_z, \phi_a, k_a, C_{va}), (B_x, B_y, B_z, \phi_b, k_b, C_{vb})]$. In general, we have good estimates for the k and C_v terms, since these values are found by the registration phase. The position of the cylinders is determined by minimizing the distance between these skewed rays. We also choose to assign a penalty for shrinking the vertical height of the cylinder in order to bring points closer together. This penalty could be eliminated by accepting either the k or C_v values given by the registration.

We have tested this approach using from 12 to 500 tiepoints, and have found that it converges to a solution in as few as ten iterations of Powell's method. Since no correlation step is required, this process is considerably faster than the minimization step required to determine the structural matrix, S.

The use of a cylindrical projection introduces significant geometric constraints on where a point viewed in one projection might appear in a second. We can capitalize on these restrictions when we wish to automatically identify corresponding points across cylinders. While an initial set of 100 to 500 tiepoints might be established by hand, this process is far too tedious to establish a mapping for the entire cylinder. Next, we present a geometric constraint for cylindrical projections that determines the possible positions of a point given its position in some other cylinder. This constraint plays the same role that the epipolar geometries [18], [9], used in the computer vision community for depth-from-stereo computations, play for planar projections.

First, we will present an intuitive argument for the existence of such an invariant. Consider yourself at the center of a cylindrical projection. Every point on the cylinder around you corresponds to a ray in space as given by the cylindrical epipolar geometry equation. When one of the rays is observed from a second cylinder, its path projects to a curve which appears to begin at the point corresponding to the origin of the first cylinder, and it is constrained to pass through

the point's image on the second cylinder.

This same argument could obviously have been made for a planar projection. And, since two points are identified (the virtual image of the camera in the second projection along with the corresponding point) and, because a planar projection preserve lines, a unique, so called epipolar line is defined. This is the basis for an epipolar geometry, which identifies pairs of lines in two planar projections such that if a point falls upon one line in the first image, it is constrained to fall on the corresponding line in the second image. The existence of this invariant reduces the search for corresponding points from an $\mathbf{O}(N^2)$ problem to $\mathbf{O}(N)$.

Cylindrical projections, however, do not preserve lines. In general, lines map to quadratic parametric curves on the surface of a cylinder. Surprisingly, we can completely specify the form of the curve with no more information than was needed in the planar case.

The paths of these curves are uniquely determined sinusoids. This *cylindrical epipolar geometry* is established by the following equation.

$$v(\theta) = \frac{N_x \cos{(\phi_a - \theta)} + N_y \sin{(\phi_a - \theta)}}{N_z k_a} + C_{v_a} \qquad (18)$$

where

$$\bar{N} = (\bar{C}_b - \bar{C}_a) \times \bar{D}_a(\theta_a, v_a) \qquad (19)$$

This formula gives a concise expression for the curve formed by the projection of a ray across the surface of a cylinder, where the ray is specified by its position on some other cylinder.

This cylindrical epipolar relationship can be used to establish image flow fields using standard computer vision methods. We have used correlation methods [9], a simulated annealing-like relaxation method [3], and the method of differences [20] to compute stereo disparities between cylinder pairs. Each method has its strengths and weaknesses. We refer the reader to the references for further details.

4.4 Plenoptic Function Reconstruction

Our image-based rendering system takes as input cylindrically projected panoramic reference images along with scalar disparity images relating each cylinder pair. This information is used to automatically generate image warps that map reference images to arbitrary cylindrical or planar views that are capable of describing both occlusion and perspective effects.

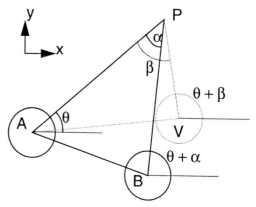

FIGURE 2. Diagram showing the transfer of the known disparity values between cylinders A and B to a new viewing position V.

We begin with a description of cylindrical-to-cylindrical mappings. Each angular disparity value, α, of the disparity images, can be readily converted into an image flow vector field, $(\theta + \alpha, v(\theta + \alpha))$ using the epipolar relation given by Equation 18 for each position on the cylinder, (θ, v). We can transfer disparity values from the known cylindrical pair to a new cylindrical projection in an arbitrary position, as in Figure 2, using the following equations.

$$a = (B_x - V_x) \cos (\phi_A - \theta) + (B_y - V_y) \sin (\phi_A - \theta)$$

$$b = (B_y - A_y) \cos (\phi_A - \theta) - (B_x - A_x) \sin (\phi_A - \theta)$$

$$c = (V_y - A_y) \cos (\phi_A - \theta) - (V_x - A_x) \sin (\phi_A - \theta) \qquad (20)$$

$$\cot (\beta(\theta, v)) = \frac{a + b \cot (\alpha(\theta, v))}{c}$$

By precomputing $[\cos (\phi_i - \theta), \sin (\phi_i - \theta)]$ for each column of the cylindrical reference image and storing $\cot (\alpha)$ in place of the disparity image, this transfer operation can be computed at interactive speeds.

Typically, once the disparity images have been transferred to their target, the cylindrical projection would be reprojected as a planar image for viewing. This reprojection can be combined with the disparity transfer to give a single image warp that performs both operations. To accomplish this, a new intermediate quantity, δ, called the *generalized angular disparity* is defined as follows:

$$d = (B_x - A_x) \cos (\phi_A - \theta) + (B_y - A_y) \sin (\phi_A - \theta)$$

$$\delta(\theta, v) = \frac{1}{d + b \cot (\alpha(\theta, v))} \qquad (21)$$

This scalar function is the cylindrical equivalent to the classical stereo disparity. Finally, a composite image warp from a given reference image to any arbitrary planar projection can be defined as

$$x(\theta, v) = \frac{\bar{r} \cdot D_A(\theta, v) + k_r \delta(\theta, v)}{\bar{n} \cdot D_A(\theta, v) + k_n \delta(\theta, v)}$$

$$y(\theta, v) = \frac{\bar{s} \cdot D_A(\theta, v) + k_s \delta(\theta, v)}{\bar{n} \cdot D_A(\theta, v) + k_n \delta(\theta, v)} \qquad (22)$$

where

$$\bar{r} = \bar{v} \times \bar{o} \qquad k_r = \bar{r} \cdot (\bar{C}_a - V)$$

$$\bar{s} = \bar{o} \times \bar{u} \qquad k_s = \bar{s} \cdot (\bar{C}_a - V) \qquad (23)$$

$$\bar{n} = \bar{u} \times \bar{v} \qquad k_n = \bar{n} \cdot (\bar{C}_a - V)$$

and the vectors $\bar{p}$, $\bar{o}$, $\bar{n}$ and $\bar{v}$ are defined by the desired view as shown in Figure 3.

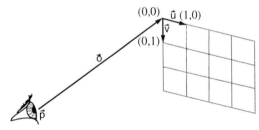

FIGURE 3. The center-of-projection, $\bar{p}$, a vector to the origin, $\bar{o}$, and two spanning vectors ($\bar{u}$ and $\bar{v}$) uniquely determine the planar projection.

In the case where $\delta(\theta, v) = constant$, the image warp defined by Equation 22, reduces to a simple reprojection of the cylindrical image to a desired planar view. The perturbation introduced by allowing $\delta(\theta, v)$ to vary over the image allows arbitrary shape and occlusions to be represented.

Potentially, both the cylinder transfer and image warping approaches are many-to-one mappings. For this reason we must consider visibility. The following simple algorithm can be used to determine an enumeration of the cylindrical mesh which guarantees a proper back-to-front ordering, (See Appendix). We project the desired viewing position onto the reference cylinder being warped and partition the cylinder into four toroidal sheets. The sheet boundaries are defined by the θ and v coordinates of two points, as shown in Figure 4. One point is defined by the intersection of the cylinder

with the vector from the origin through the eye's position. The other is the intersection with the vector from the eye through the origin.

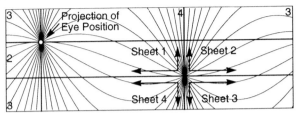

FIGURE 4. A back-to-front ordering of the image flow field can be established by projecting the eye's position onto the cylinder's surface and dividing it into four toroidal sheets.

Next, we enumerate each sheet such that the projected image of the desired viewpoint is the last point drawn. This simple partitioning and enumeration provides a back-to-front ordering for use by a painter's style rendering algorithm. This hidden-surface algorithm is a generalization of Anderson's [2] visible line algorithm to arbitrary projected grid surfaces. Additional details can be found in [21].

At this point, the plenoptic samples can be warped to their new position according to the image flow field. In general, these new pixel positions lie on an irregular grid, thus requiring some sort of reconstruction and resampling. We use a forward-mapping [28] reconstruction approach in the spirit of [27] in our prototype. This involves computing the projected kernel's size based on the current disparity value and the derivatives along the epipolar curves.

While the visibility method properly handles mesh folds, we still must consider the tears (or excessive stretching) produced by the exposure of previously occluded image regions. In view interpolation [8] a simple "distinguished color" heuristic is used based on the screen space projection of the neighboring pixel on the same scanline. This approach approximates stretching for small regions of occlusion, where the occluder still abuts the occluded region. And, for large exposed occluded regions, it tends to interpolate between the boundaries of the occluded region. These exposure events can be handled more robustly by combining, on a pixel-by-pixel basis, the results of multiple image warps according to the smallest-sized reconstruction kernel.

5. RESULTS

We collected a series of images using a video camcorder on a leveled tripod in the front yard of one of the author's home. Accurate leveling is not strictly necessary for the method to work. When the data were collected, no attempt was made to pan the camera at a uniform angular velocity. The autofocus and autoiris features of the camera were disabled, in order to maintain a constant focal length during the collection process. The frames were then digitized at a rate of approximately 5 frames per second to a resolution of 320 by 240 pixels. An example of three sequential frames are shown below.

Immediately after the collection of the first data set, the process was repeated at a second point approximately 60 inches from the first. The two image sequences were then separately registered using the methods described in Section 4.2. The images were reprojected onto the surface of a cylinder with a resolution of 3600 by 300 pixels. The results are shown in Figures 5a and 5b. The operating room scene, in Figure 5c, was also constructed using these same methods.

Next, the epipolar geometry was computed by specifying 12 tiepoints on the front of the house. Additional tiepoints were gradually added to establish an initial disparity image for use by the simulated

FIGURE 5. Cylindrical images a and b are panoramic views separated by approximately 60 inches. Image c is a panoramic view of an operating room. In image d, several epipolar curves are superimposed onto cylindrical image a.

annealing and method of differences stereo-correspondence routines. As these tiepoints were added, we also refined the epipolar geometry and cylinder position estimates. The change in cylinder position, however, was very slight. In Figure 5d, we show a cylindrical image with several epipolar curves superimposed. Notice how the curves all intersect at the alternate camera's virtual image and vanishing point.

After the disparity images are computed, they can be interactively warped to new viewing positions. The following four images show various reconstructions. When used interactively, the warped images provide a convincing kinetic depth effect.

6. CONCLUSIONS

The plenoptic function provides a consistent framework for image-based rendering systems. The various image-based methods, such as morphing and view interpolation, are characterized by the different ways they implement the three key steps of sampling, reconstructing, and resampling the plenoptic function.

We have described our approach to each of these steps. Our method for sampling the plenoptic function can be done with equipment that is commonly available, and it results in cylindrical samples about a point. All the necessary parameters are automatically estimated from a sequence of images resulting from panning a video camera through a full circle.

Reconstructing the function from these samples requires estimating the optic flow of points when the view point is translated. Though this problem can be very difficult, as evidenced by thirty years of computer vision and photogrammetry research, it is greatly simplified when the samples are relatively close together. This is because there is little change in the image between samples (which makes the estimation easier), and because the viewer is never far from

a sample (which makes accurate estimation less important).

Resampling the plenoptic function and reconstructing a planar projection are the key steps for display of images from arbitrary viewpoints. Our methods allow efficient determination of visibility and real-time display of visually rich environments on conventional workstations without special purpose graphics acceleration.

The plenoptic approach to modeling and display will provide robust and high-fidelity models of environments based entirely on a set of reference projections. The degree of realism will be determined by the resolution of the reference images rather than the number of primitives used in describing the scene. Finally, the difficulty of producing realistic models of real environments will be greatly reduced by replacing geometry with images.

ACKNOWLEDGMENTS

We are indebted to the following individuals for their contributions and suggestions on this work: Henry Fuchs, Andrei State, Kevin Arthur, Donna McMillan, and all the members of the UNC/UPenn collaborative telepresence-research group.

This research is supported in part by Advanced Research Projects Agency contract no. DABT63-93-C-0048, NSF Cooperative Agreement no. ASC-8920219, Advanced Research Projects Agency order no. A410, and National Science Foundation grant no. MIP-9306208. Approved by ARPA for public release - distribution unlimited.

REFERENCES

[1] Adelson, E. H., and J. R. Bergen, *"The Plenoptic Function and the Elements of Early Vision,"* **Computational Models of Visual Processing**, Chapter 1, Edited by Michael Landy and J. Anthony Movshon. The MIT Press, Cambridge, Mass. 1991.

[2] Anderson, D., *"Hidden Line Elimination in Projected Grid Surfaces,"* **ACM Transactions on Graphics**, October 1982.

[3] Barnard, S.T. "A Stochastic Approach to Stereo Vision," SRI International, Technical Note 373, April 4, 1986.

[4] Beier, T. and S. Neely, *"Feature-Based Image Metamorphosis,"* **Computer Graphics** (SIGGRAPH'92 Proceedings), Vol. 26, No. 2, pp. 35-42, July 1992.

[5] Blinn, J. F. and M. E. Newell, *"Texture and Reflection in Computer Generated Images,"* **Communications of the ACM**, vol. 19, no. 10, pp. 542-547, October 1976.

[6] Bolles, R. C., H. H. Baker, and D. H. Marimont, *"Epipolar-Plane Image Analysis: An Approach to Determining Structure from Motion,"* **International Journal of Computer Vision**, Vol. 1, 1987.

[7] Catmull, E., *"A Subdivision Algorithm for Computer Display of Curved Surfaces"* (Ph. D. Thesis), Department of Computer Sci-

ence, University of Utah, Tech. Report UTEC-CSc-74-133, December 1974.

[8] Chen, S. E. and L. Williams. *"View Interpolation for Image Synthesis,"* **Computer Graphics** (SIGGRAPH'93 Proceedings), pp. 279-288, July 1993.

[9] Faugeras, O., **Three-dimensional Computer Vision: A Geometric Viewpoint**, The MIT Press, Cambridge, Massachusetts, 1993.

[10] Greene, N., *"Environment Mapping and Other Applications of World Projections,"* **IEEE Computer Graphics and Applications**, November 1986.

[11] Hartley, R.I., *"Self-Calibration from Multiple Views with a Rotating Camera,"* **Proceedings of the European Conference on Computer Vision**, May 1994.

[12] Heckbert, P. S., *"Fundamentals of Texture Mapping and Image Warping,"* Masters Thesis, Dept. of EECS, UCB, Technical Report No. UCB/CSD 89/516, June 1989.

[13] Horn, B., and B.G. Schunck, *"Determining Optical Flow,"* **Artificial Intelligence**, Vol. 17, 1981.

[14] Kanatani, K., *"Transformation of Optical Flow by Camera Rotation,"* **IEEE Transactions on Pattern Analysis and Machine Intelligence**, Vol. 10, No. 2, March 1988.

[15] Laveau, S. and O. Faugeras, *"3-D Scene Representation as a Collection of Images and Fundamental Matrices,"* INRIA, Technical Report No. 2205, February, 1994.

[16] Lenz, R. K. and R. Y. Tsai, *"Techniques for Calibration of the Scale Factor and Image Center for High Accuracy 3D Machine Vision Metrology,"* **Proceedings of IEEE International Conference on Robotics and Automation**, March 31 - April 3, 1987.

[17] Lippman, A., *"Movie-Maps: An Application of the Optical Videodisc to Computer Graphics,"* **SIGGRAPH '80 Proceedings**, 1980.

[18] Longuet-Higgins, H. C., *"A Computer Algorithm for Reconstructing a Scene from Two Projections,"* **Nature**, Vol. 293, September 1981.

[19] Longuet-Higgins, H. C., *"The Reconstruction of a Scene From Two Projections - Configurations That Defeat the 8-Point Algorithm,"* **Proceedings of the First IEEE Conference on Artificial Intelligence Applications**, Dec 1984.

[20] Lucas, B., and T. Kanade, *"An Iterative Image Registration Technique with an Application to Stereo Vision,"* **Proceedings of the Seventh International Joint Conference on Artificial Intelligence**, Vancouver, 1981.

[21] McMillan, Leonard, *"A List-Priority Rendering Algorithm for Redisplaying Projected Surfaces,"* Department of Computer Science, UNC, Technical Report TR95-005, 1995.

[22] Mann, S. and R. W. Picard, *"Virtual Bellows: Constructing High Quality Stills from Video,"* **Proceedings of the First IEEE International Conference on Image Processing**, November 1994.

[23] Press, W. H., B. P. Flannery, S. A. Teukolsky, and W. T. Vetterling, **Numerical Recipes in C**, Cambridge University Press, Cambridge, Massachusetts, pp. 309-317, 1988.

[24] Regan, M., and R. Pose, *"Priority Rendering with a Virtual Reality Address Recalculation Pipeline,"* **SIGGRAPH'94 Proceedings**, 1994.

[25] Szeliski, R., *"Image Mosaicing for Tele-Reality Applications,"* **DEC and Cambridge Research Lab Technical Report**, CRL 94/2, May 1994.

[26] Tomasi, C., and T. Kanade, *"Shape and Motion from Image Streams: a Factorization Method; Full Report on the Orthographic Case,"* Technical Report, CMU-CS-92-104, Carnegie Mellon University, March 1992.

[27] Tsai, R. Y., *"A Versatile Camera Calibration Technique for High Accuracy 3D Machine Vision Metrology Using Off-the-Shelf TV Cameras and Lenses,"* **IEEE Journal of Robotics and Automation**, Vol. RA-3, No. 4, August 1987.

[28] Westover, L. A., *"Footprint Evaluation for Volume Rendering,"* **SIGGRAPH'90 Proceedings**, August 1990.

[29] Wolberg, G., **Digital Image Warping**, IEEE Computer Society Press, Los Alamitos, CA, 1990.

APPENDIX

We will show how occlusion compatible mappings can be determined on local spherical frames embedded within a global cartesian frame, W. The projected visibility algorithm for cylindrical surfaces given in the paper can be derived by reducing it to this spherical case.

First, consider an isolated topological multiplicity on the projective mapping from S_i to S_j, as shown below

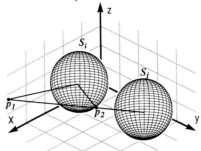

Theorem 1: In the generic case, the points of a topological multiplicity induced by a mapping from S_i to S_j, and the two frame origins are coplanar.

Proof: The points of the topological multiplicity are colinear with the origin of S_j since they share angular coordinates. A second line segment connects the local frame origins, S_i and S_j. In general, these two lines are distinct and thus they define a plane in three space.

Thus, a single affine transformation, $\mathbf{A}$, of W can accomplish the following results.

- Translate S_i to the origin
- Rotate S_j to lie on the x-axis
- Rotate the line along the multiplicity into the xy-plane
- Scale the system so that S_j has the coordinate (1,0,0).

With this transformation we can consider the multiplicity entirely within the xy-plane, as shown in the following figure.

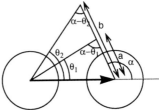

Theorem 2: If $\cos\theta_1 > \cos\theta_2$ and $(\theta_1, \theta_2, \alpha) \in [0, \pi]$ then $a < b$.

Proof: The length of sides a and b can be computed in terms of the angles θ_1, θ_2 and α using the law of sines as follows.

$$\frac{a}{\sin\theta_1} = \frac{1}{\sin(\alpha-\theta_1)} \qquad \frac{b}{\sin\theta_2} = \frac{1}{\sin(\alpha-\theta_2)}$$

$$\frac{a}{b} = \frac{\sin\alpha\cot\theta_2 - \cos\alpha}{\sin\alpha\cot\theta_1 - \cos\alpha}$$

if $\cos\theta_1 > \cos\theta_2$ then $\cot\theta_1 > \cot\theta_2$, thus $a < b$

Thus, an occlusion compatible mapping, can be determined by enumerating the topological mesh defined on AS_i in an order of increasing $\cos\theta$, while allowing later mesh facets to overwrite previous ones. This mapping is occlusion compatible since, by Theorem 2, greater range values will always proceed lesser values at all multiplicities. Notice, that this mapping procedure only considers the changes in the local frame's world coordinates, and makes no use of the range information itself.

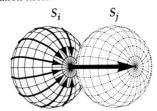

Multi-Level Direction of Autonomous Creatures
for Real-Time Virtual Environments

Bruce M. Blumberg and Tinsley A. Galyean*
MIT Media Lab

ABSTRACT

There have been several recent efforts to build behavior-based autonomous creatures. While competent autonomous action is highly desirable, there is an important need to integrate autonomy with "directability". In this paper we discuss the problem of building autonomous animated creatures for interactive virtual environments which are also capable of being directed at multiple levels. We present an approach to control which allows an external entity to "direct" an autonomous creature at the motivational level, the task level, and the direct motor level. We also detail a layered architecture and a general behavioral model for perception and action-selection which incorporates explicit support for multi-level direction. These ideas have been implemented and used to develop several autonomous animated creatures.

1. INTRODUCTION

Since Reynold's seminal paper in 1987, there have been a number of impressive papers on the use of behavioral models to generate computer animation. The motivation behind this work is that as the complexity of the creature's interactions with its environment and other creatures increases, there is an need to "endow" the creatures with the ability to perform autonomous activity. Such creatures are, in effect, autonomous agents with their own perceptual, behavioral, and motor systems. Typically, authors have focused on behavioral models for a specific kind of creature in a given environment, and implemented a limited set of behaviors. There are examples of locomotion [2, 5, 7, 14, 16], flocking [18], grasping [9], and lifting [2]. Tu and Terzopoulos's Fish [20] represent one of the most impressive examples of this approach.

Advances in behavioral animation are critically important to the development of creatures for use in interactive virtual environments. Research in autonomous robots [4, 8, 12] supports the need to couple real-time action with dynamic and unpredictable environments. Their insights only serve to strengthen the argument for autonomous animated creatures.

Pure autonomy, perhaps, should not be the ultimate goal. Imagine making an interactive virtual "Lassie" experience for children. Suppose the autonomous animated character playing Lassie did a fine job as a autonomous dog, but for whatever reason was ignoring the child. Or suppose, you wanted the child to focus on some

aspect of the environment which was important to the story, but Lassie was distracting her. In both cases, you would want to be able to provide external control, in real-time, to the autonomous Lassie. For example, by increasing its "motivation to play", it would be more likely to engage in play. Alternatively, Lassie might be told to "go over to that tree and lie down" so as to be less distracting.

Thus, there is a need to understand how to build animated characters for interactive virtual environments which are not only capable of competent autonomous action but also capable of responding to external control. We call this quality "directability." This is the fundamental problem addressed in this paper.

This paper makes 3 primary contributions to the body of literature regarding animated autonomous characters. Specifically, we describe:

- An approach to control which allows an external entity to "direct" a virtual character at a number of different levels.
- A general behavioral model for perception and action-selection in autonomous animated creatures but which also supports external control.
- A layered architecture which supports extensibility, reusability and multiple levels of direction.

An experimental toolkit which incorporates these ideas has been successfully used to build a number of creatures: a virtual dog used in an interactive virtual environment, and several creatures used in an interactive story telling environment.

The remainder of the paper is organized as follows. In section 2 we present a more detailed problem statement and summarize the key contributions of our approach. In section 3 we present an overview of the general architecture. In sections 4, 5 and 6 we discuss the motor, sensory and behavior systems in more depth. In section 7 we discuss how directability is integrated into our architecture. Finally, in section 8 we discuss some aspects of our implementation and give examples of its use.

2. PROBLEM STATEMENT

An autonomous agent is a software system with a set of goals which it tries to satisfy in a complex and dynamic environment. It is autonomous in the sense that it has mechanisms for sensing and interacting with its environment, and for deciding what actions to take so as to best achieve its goals[12]. In the case of an autonomous animated creature, these mechanisms correspond to a set of sensors, a motor system and associated geometry, and lastly a behavior system. In our terminology, a creature is an animate object capable of goal-directed and time-varying behavior.

Deciding on the "right" action or set of actions is complicated by a number of factors. For example, due to the problems inherent in sensing and perception, a creature's perception of its world is likely to be incomplete at best, and completely erroneous at worst.

*MIT Media Lab, 20 Ames St., Cambridge MA, 02139.
bruce/tag@media.mit.edu

Permission to make digital/hard copy of part or all of this work for personal or classroom use is granted without fee provided that copies are not made or distributed for profit or commercial advantage, the copyright notice, the title of the publication and its date appear, and notice is given that copying is by permission of ACM, Inc. To copy otherwise, to republish, to post on servers, or to redistribute to lists, requires prior specific permission and/or a fee.

There may be competing goals which work at cross-purposes (e.g. moving toward food may move the creature away from water). This can lead to dithering in which the creature oscillates among competing activities. On the other hand, an important goal may be un-obtainable, and pursuit of that goal may prevent the satisfaction of lower priority, but attainable goals. External opportunities need to be weighed against internal needs in order to provide just the right level of opportunistic behavior. Actions may be unavailable or unreliable. To successfully produce competent autonomous action over extended periods of time, the Behavior System must provide solutions to these problems, as well as others.

However, as mentioned earlier, strict autonomy is not the goal. We need, in addition, to direct the creature at a number of different levels. Three levels of input, (motivational, task, and direct) are outlined in Figure 1. Additionally, commands at the direct level need to be able to take three imperative forms:

- Do it, independent of the Behavior System.
- Do it, if the Behavior System doesn't object.
- Suggest how an action should be performed, should the Behavior System wish to perform that action.

Thus, the behavior and motor systems must be designed and implemented in such a way that it is possible to support these levels and types of direction at run-time.

Building autonomous animated creatures is inherently an iterative process. This is particularly true since we are in the early phases of understanding how to build them. Ideally, a common approach should be taken for the specification of geometry through to behavior so that a developer need only learn a single framework. Lastly, an embedded interpreter is required to facilitate testing, as well as run-time direction.

2.1 Multiple Levels of Control

We provide an approach to control which allows an external entity to "direct" an autonomous animated creature at a number of different levels. These levels are detailed in Figure 1. By providing

Motivational Level	Task Level	Direct Level
just do the right thing	do THIS the right way	do what I tell you
"you are hungry"	"go to that tree"	"wag your tail"

Figure 1: Here we articulate three levels at which a creature can be directed. At the highest level the creature would be influenced by changing its current motivation and relying on it to react to this change. If you tell it to be hungry it will go off looking for food. At the task level you give it a high level directive and you expect it to carry out this command in a reasonable manner (for example walking around a building instead of through it.) At the lowest level you want to give a creature a command that directly changes its geometry.

the ability to "direct" the creature at multiple levels the animator or developer can choose the appropriate level of control for a given situation. Both Badler and Zeltzer have proposed similar decomposition of control [2, 23].

2.2 A General Behavior Model

We propose a distributed behavioral model, inspired by work in Ethology and autonomous robot research, for perception and action-selection in autonomous animated creatures but which also supports external control. The contributions of this model include:

- A general model of action-selection which provides greater control over temporal patterns of behavior than previously described approaches have offered.
- A natural and general way to model the effect of external stimuli and internal motivation.
- An approach in which multiple behaviors may suggest actions to be performed and preferences for how the

actions are to be executed, while still maintaining the advantages of a winner-take-all architecture.
- An implementation which supports motivational and task level direction at run-time.

We also describe a robotics inspired approach to low-level autonomous navigation in which creatures rely on a form of synthetic vision to perform navigation and obstacle avoidance.

2.3 A Layered Architecture

A 5-layered architecture for autonomous animated creatures is described. Several important abstraction barriers are provided by the architecture:

- One between the Behavior System and the Motor Skills, which allows certain behaviors (e.g. "move-toward") to be independent of the Motor Skills which perform the desired action (e.g. "drive" vs. "walk") in a given creature.
- One between the Motor Skills and geometry which serves as both an abstraction barrier and a resource manager.

The result is an architecture which encourages re-usability and extensibility, while providing the necessary foundation to support autonomous action with interactive direction.

3. ARCHITECTURE

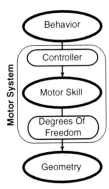

Figure 2: Block diagram of a creature's architecture. The basic structure consists of the three basic parts (Geometry, Motor Skills and Behavior) with two layers of abstraction between these parts (Controller, and Degrees of Freedom).

Figure 2 shows the basic architecture for a creature. The geometry provides the shapes and transforms that are manipulated over time for animation. The Motor Skills provide atomic motion elements which manipulate the geometry in order to produce coordinated motion. "Walking" or "Wagging the tail" are examples of Motor Skills. Motor Skills manipulate the geometry with no knowledge of the environment or state of a creature, other than that needed to execute the skill. At the top rests the Behavior System of a creature. This element is responsible for deciding what to do, given its goals and sensory input and triggering the correct Motor Skills to achieve the current task or goal. In addition to these three parts, there are two layers of insulation, the controller and the degrees of freedom (DOFs), which are important to making this architecture generalizable and extensible.

Behaviors implement high level capabilities such as, "find food and eat", or "sit down and shake", as well as low level capabilities such as "move to" or "avoid obstacle" by issuing the appropriate motor commands (i.e "forward", "left", "sit", etc.) to the controller. Some behaviors may be implemented in a creature-independent way. For example, the same "move to" behavior may be applicable to any creature with basic locomotive skills (e.g. forward, left, right,...) although each may use different Motor Skills to perform the required action. It is the controller which provides this common interface to the Motor Skills by mapping a generic command ("forward") into the correct motor skill(s) and parameters for a given creature. In this way, the same behavior may be used by more than one type of creature.

Figure 3 shows the sources of input to the creature. Sensors are

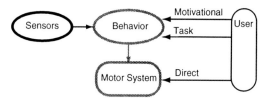

Figure 3: There are two sources of input to a creature. First are sensors associated with the creature. These sensors are used by the Behavior System to enable both task level and autonomous behavior. The other source of input is from the user (or application using the creature.) This input can happen at multiple levels, ranging from simply adjusting a creature's current motivational state to directly turning a motor skill on or off.

elements of a creature which the creature uses to interrogate the environment for relevant information. The creature may also take additional input from the user or the application using the creature. These directives can enter the creature's computational model at the three different levels.

4. MOTOR SYSTEM

We use the term "motor system" to refer to the three layers that lie between the Behavior System and the geometry, Figure 2. These parts include the Motor Skills in the center, and the abstraction and interface barriers on either side of the Motor Skills. Together these three layers of the architecture provide the mapping from motor commands to changes in the geometry over time.

The motor system is designed to meet the following 5 important criteria:

- Act as an abstraction barrier between high-level commands (e.g. "forward") and the creature specific implementation (e.g. "walking").
- Support multiple imperative forms for commands.
- Provide a generic set of commands which all creatures can perform.
- Minimize the amount of "house-keeping" required of the Behavior System.
- Provides resource management so as to support coherent, concurrent motion.

Within these three layers of the motor system, the controller provides the high level abstraction barrier and the support of multiple imperative forms. Motor skills can be inherited allowing basic skills to be shared amongst creatures. Also, Motor Skills are designed to minimize the "house-keeping" that an external user or Behavior System must do. It is the degree of freedom abstraction barrier that serves as the resource manager.

4.1 Degrees of Freedom (DOFs)

Degrees of Freedom (DOFs) are "knobs" that can be used to modify the underlying geometry. They are the mechanism by which creatures are repositioned and reshaped. For example, DOFs might be used to wag the tail, move a joint, or reposition an entire leg. DOFs serve 2 important functions:

- Resource management. Provides a locking mechanism so that competing Motor Skills do not conflict.
- An abstraction barrier. Utilizes interpolators to re-map simple input values (0 to 1) to more complex motion.

The resource management system is a simple one. Each DOF can be locked by a motor skill, restricting it by anyone else until unlocked. This locking provides a mechanism for insuring coherent, concurrent motion. As long as two or more Motor Skills do not conflict for DOFs they are free to run concurrently. Alternatively, if a motor skill requests DOFs that are already locked it will be informed it cannot run currently.

When functioning as an abstraction barrier a DOF provides a mechanism to map a simple input value (often a number between 0 and 1) to another space via interpolators and inverse kinematics such as in, Figure 4. It is this abstraction that allows a motor skill

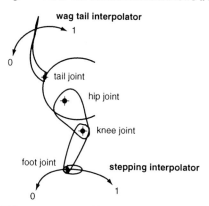

Figure 4: DOFs in a creature can provide interfaces to the geometry at several different levels. For example, joints (and therefore the associated transformations) can be directly controlled or indirectly as is the case with this leg. Here inverse kinematics is used to move the foot. An additional level of abstraction can be added by using interpolators. The interpolator on the leg provides a "one knob" interface for the motor skill. By giving a number between 0 and 1 the motor skill can set the location of the leg along one stepping cycle. Likewise the tail can be wagged with only one number.

to position a leg along a stepping cycle via one number. Note that when a high level DOF (the stepping DOF in this example) is locked the lower level DOFs it utilizes (the leg joints) are in turn locked.

4.2 Motor Skills

A motor skill utilizes one or more DOFs to produce coordinated movement. Walking, turning, or lower head are all examples of Motor Skills. A motor skill can produce complicated motion, and the DOFs' locking mechanism insures that competing Motor Skills are not active at the same time. In addition, Motor Skills present an extremely simple interface to upper layers of the architecture. A motor skill can be requested to turned on, or to turn off. In either case, arguments may be passed as part of the request.

Motor skills rely heavily on degrees of freedom to do their work. Each motor skill declares which DOFs it needs in order to perform its task. It can only become active if all of these DOFs are unlocked. Once active, a motor skill adjusts all the necessary DOFs with each time-step to produce coordinated animation.

Most Motor Skills are "spring-loaded." This means that if they have not been requested to turn on during an update cycle, they begin to move their DOFs back toward some neutral position and turn off within a few time-steps. The advantage of this approach is that a behavior, which turns on a skill, need not be concerned with turning it off at the correct time. The skill will turn itself off, thereby reducing the amount of "bookkeeping." Because Motor Skills are "spring-loaded" the Behavior System is required to specify which skills are to be active with each time-step. This may seem like a burden but it is consistent with a reactive behavior system which re-evaluates what actions it should perform during every update cycle. It should also be noted that this spring-loaded feature can be turned off, to facilitate sources of direction other than the Behavior System.

There are a number of basic Motor Skills which all creatures inherit, such as ones for setting the position or heading of the creature.

4.3 Controller

The controller is a simple but significant layer in the architecture which serves an important function as an abstraction barrier between the Behavior System and the underlying Motor Skills. The primary job of the controller is to map commands such as "forward", "turn", "halt", "look at" etc. into calls to turn on or turn off the appropriate motor skill(s). Thus, "forward" may result in the "walk" motor skill being turned on in the dog but the "move" motor skill in the case of the car. This is an important function because it allows the Behavior System or application to use one set of commands across a potentially wide-range of creatures, and lets the motor system of each creature to interpret them differently but appropriately.

The controller accepts commands in the form of a data structure called a motor command block. This data structure specifies the command and any arguments. In addition, a motor command block can store return arguments, allowing functions that inquire about the state of a creature (its position, its velocity) to be treated by the same mechanism as all other commands. A command block can be issued to the controller as one of three imperative forms: primary command - to be executed immediately; secondary - to be queued at a lower priority; and as a meta command - suggesting how another command should be run, Figure 5. These different impera-

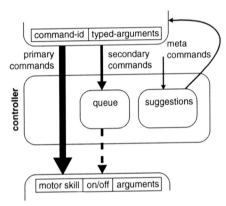

Figure 5: An incoming command is represented in a motor command block consisting of a command id and an optional list of typed arguments. If these arguments are not supplied then defaults stored in the controller are used. Any given command will turn on or off one or more Motor Skills, while also providing any necessary arguments. Commands take two levels of importance. Primary commands are executed right away, while secondary commands are queued. These queued commands are executed at the end of each time cycle, and only if the necessary resources (DOFS) are available. It is expected that these secondary commands will be used for suggested but not imperative actions. The last type of input into the controller is in the form of a meta-command. These commands are stored as suggestion of how to execute a command. For example, "if you are going to walk I suggest that you walk slowly." These are only stored in the controller and it is the responsibility of the calling application (or user) to use or ignore a suggestion.

tive forms are used extensively by the Behavior System (see section 6.6). They allow multiple behaviors to simultaneously express their preferences for motor actions.

5. SENSING

There are at least three types of sensing available to autonomous animated creatures:
- Real-world sensing using real-world "noisy" sensors.
- "Direct" sensing via direct interrogation of other virtual creatures and objects.
- "Synthetic Vision" in which the creature utilizes vision techniques to extract useful information from an image rendered from their viewpoint.

While it is important to support all three types of sensing, we have found synthetic vision to be particularly useful for low-level navigation and obstacle avoidance. Several researchers, including Renault [17], Reynolds[18], and Latombe[10] have suggested similar approaches.

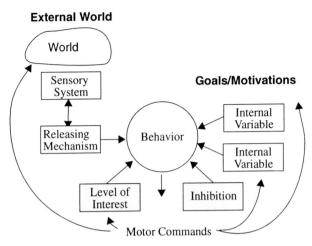

Figure 6:The purpose of a Behavior is to evaluate the appropriateness of the behavior, given external stimulus and internal motivations, and if appropriate issue motor commands. Releasing Mechanisms act as filters or detectors which identify significant objects or events from sensory input, and which output a value which corresponds to the strength of the sensory input. Motivations or goals are represented via Internal Variables which output values which represents the strength of the motivation. A Behavior combines the values of the Releasing Mechanisms and Internal Variables on which it depends and that represents the value of the Behavior before Level of Interest and Inhibition from other Behaviors. Level of Interest is used to model boredom or behavior-specific fatigue. Behaviors must compete with other behaviors for control of the creature, and do so using Inhibition (see text for details).There are a variety of explicit and implicit feedback mechanisms.

5.1 Synthetic Vision For Navigation

Horswill [8] points out that while "vision" in general is a very hard problem, there are many tasks for which it is possible to use what he calls "light-weight" vision. That is, by factoring in the characteristics of the robot's interaction with the environment and by tailoring the vision task to the specific requirements of a given behavioral task, one can often simplify the problem. As a result, vision techniques developed for autonomous robots tend to be computationally cheap, easy to implement, and reasonably robust.

Synthetic vision makes sense for a number of reasons. First, it may be the simplest and fastest way to extract useful information from the environment (e.g. using vision for low-level obstacle avoidance and navigation versus a purely analytical solution). This may be particularly true if one can take advantage of the rendering hardware. Moreover, synthetic vision techniques will probably scale better than analytical techniques in complex environments. Finally, this approach makes the creature less dependent on the implementation of its environment because it does not rely on other creatures and objects to respond to particular queries.

Our approach is simple. The scene is rendered from the creature's eye view and the resulting image is used to generate a potential field from the creature's perspective (this is done in an approach similar to that of Horswill). Subsequently, a gradient field is calculated, and this is used to derive a bearing away from areas of high potential. Following Arkin [1], some behaviors within the Behavior System represent their pattern of activity as a potential fields as well (for example, moveto). These potential fields are combined with the field generated by the vision sensor to arrive at a compromise trajectory.

This sensor is a simple example of using a technique borrowed from robotics. It was simple to implement, works well in practice, and is general enough to allow our virtual dog to wander around in new environments without modification.

6. BEHAVIOR SYSTEM

The purpose of the Behavior System is to send the "right" set of control signals to the motor system at every time-step. That is, it must weigh the potentially competing goals of the creature, assess the state of its environment, and choose the set of actions which make the "most sense" at that instant in time. More generally, it provides the creature with a set of high-level behaviors of which it is capable of performing autonomously in a potentially unpredictable environment. Indeed, it is this ability to perform competently in the absence of external control which makes high level motivational or behavioral control possible.

Action-selection has been a topic of some interest among Ethologists and Computer Scientists alike, and a number of algorithms have been proposed [3, 4, 12, 19-22]. Earlier work [3], presented a computational model of action-selection which draws heavily on ideas from Ethology. The algorithm presented below is derived from this work but incorporates a number of important new features. The interested reader may consult [3] for the ethological justification for the algorithm. The remainder of this section describes the major components of the Behavior System, and how it decides to "do the right thing"

6.1 Behaviors

While we have spoken of a Behavior System as a monolithic entity, it is in fact a distributed system composed of a loosely hierarchical network of "self-interested, goal-directed entities" called Behaviors. The granularity of a Behavior's goal may vary from very general (e.g. "reduce hunger") to very specific (e.g. "chew food"). The major components of an individual Behavior are shown in Figure 6. This model of a distributed collection of goal-directed entities is consistent with ethological models as well as recent theories of the mind [15].

Behaviors compete for control of the creature on the basis of a value which is re-calculated on every update cycle for each Behavior. The value of a Behavior may be high because the Behavior satisfies an important need of the creature (e.g. its Internal Variables have a high value). Or it may be high because the Behavior's goal is easily achievable given the Behavior's perception of its environment (e.g. its Releasing Mechanisms have a high value).

Behaviors influence the system in several ways: by issuing motor commands which change the creature's relationship to its environment, by modifying the value of Internal Variables, by inhibiting other Behaviors, or by issuing suggestions which influence the motor commands issued by other Behaviors.

Behaviors are distinguished from Motor Skills in two ways. First, a Behavior is goal-directed whereas a Motor Skill is not. For example, "Walking" in our model is a Motor Skill. "Moving toward an object of interest" is a Behavior. Second, a Behavior decides when it should become active, whereas a Motor Skill runs when something else decides it should be active. Typically, Behaviors rely on Motor Skills to perform the actions necessary to accomplish the Behavior's goals.

6.2 Releasing Mechanisms and Pronomes

Behaviors rely on objects called "Releasing Mechanisms" to filter sensory input and identify objects and/or events which are relevant to the Behavior, either because they are important to achieving the Behavior's goal, or because their presence determines the salience of the Behavior given the creature's immediate environment. Releasing Mechanisms output a continuous value which typically depends on whether the stimuli was found, on its distance and perhaps on some measure of its quality. This is important because by representing the output of a Releasing Mechanism as a continuous quantity, the output may be easily combined with the strength of internal motivations which are also represented as continuous values. This in turn allows the creature to display the kind of behavior one finds in nature where a weak stimulus (e.g. day-old pizza) but a strong motivation (e.g. very hungry) may result in the same behavior as a strong stimulus (e.g. chocolate cake) but weak motivation (e.g. full stomach).

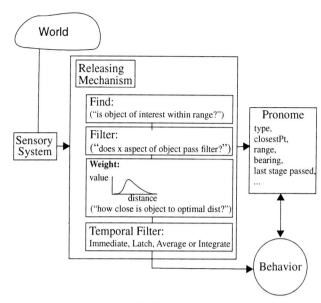

Figure 7: Releasing Mechanisms identify significant objects or events from sensory input and output a value which represents the strength of the stimulus. By varying the allowed maximum for a given Releasing Mechanism, a Behavior can be made more or less sensitive to the presence of whatever input causes the Releasing Mechanism to have a non-zero value. A Releasing Mechanism has 4 phases (Find, Filter, Weight and Temporal Filtering), as indicated above, each of which is implemented by callbacks. Releasing Mechanisms can often share the same generic callback for a given phase. Temporal Filtering is provided to deal with potentially noisy data.

While Releasing Mechanisms may be looking for very different objects and events, they typically have a common structure. This is described in more detail in Figure 7. The importance of this is that it is possible to share functionality across Releasing Mechanisms.

In addition to transducing a value from sensory input, a Releasing Mechanism also fills in a data structure available to the Behavior called a Pronome [15]. The Pronome acts like a pronoun in English: The use of Pronomes makes it possible for the Behavior to be written in terms of "it", where "it" is defined by the Behavior's Pronome. Thus, a "stopNearAndDo" Behavior can be implemented without reference to the kind of object it is stopping near. Pronomes may be shared among behaviors, thus allowing the construction of a generic "find and do" hierarchy. While the motivation for Pronomes comes from theories of mind [15] as opposed to ethology, they make sense in an ethological context as well. In any event, the use of Pronomes greatly facilitates the integration of external control, and simplifies the construction of behavior networks by providing a level of abstraction.

6.3 Internal Variables

Internal Variables are used to model internal state. Like Releasing Mechanisms, Internal Variables express their value as a continuous value. This value can change over time based on autonomous growth and damping rates. In addition, Behaviors can potentially modify the value of an Internal Variable as a result of their activity.

Both Releasing Mechanisms and Internal Variables may be shared by multiple Behaviors.

6.4 Behavior Groups

Behaviors are organized into groups of mutually inhibiting behaviors called Behavior Groups as shown in Figure 8. While we find a loose hierarchical structure useful this is not a requirement (i.e. all the Behaviors can be in a single Behavior Group). Behavior Groups are important because they localize the interaction among Behaviors which facilitates adding new Behaviors.

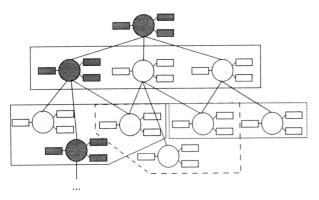

Figure 8: Behaviors are organized into groups of mutually inhibiting Behaviors called Behavior Groups. These Behavior Groups are in turn organized in a loose hierarchical fashion. Behavior Groups at the upper levels of the hierarchy contain general types of behaviors (e.g. "engage-in-feeding") which are largely driven by motivational considerations, whereas lower levels contain more specific behaviors (e.g. "pounce" or "chew") which are driven more by immediate sensory input. The arbitration mechanism built into the algorithm insures that only one Behavior in a given Behavior Group will have a non-zero value after inhibition. This Behavior is then active, and may either issue primary motor commands, or activate the Behavior Group which contains its children Behaviors (e.g. "search-for-food", "sniff", "chew" might be the children of "engage-in-feeding"). The dark gray behaviors represent the path of active Behaviors on a given tick. Behaviors which lose to the primary Behavior in a given Behavior Group may nonetheless influence the resulting actions of the creature by issuing either secondary or meta-commands.

6.5 Inhibition and Level of Interest

A creature has only limited resources to apply to satisfying its needs (e.g. it can only walk in one direction at a time), and thus there needs to be some mechanism to arbitrate among the competing Behaviors. Moreover, once a creature is committed to satisfying a goal, it makes sense for it to continue pursuing that goal unless something significantly more important comes along.

We rely on a phenomena known as the "avalanche effect" [15] to both arbitrate among Behaviors in a Behavior Group and to provide the right amount of persistence. This is done via mutual inhibition. Specifically, a given Behavior A will inhibit a Behavior B by a gain I_{AB} times Behavior A's value. By (a) restricting the inhibitory gains to be greater than 1, (b) by clamping the value of a Behavior to be 0 or greater, and (c) requiring that all Behaviors inhibit each other, the "avalanche effect" insures that once the system has settled, only one Behavior in a Behavior Group will have a non-zero value. This model of inhibition was first proposed, in an ethological context by Ludlow [11], but see Minsky as well.

This model provides a robust mechanism for winner-take-all arbitration. It also provides a way of controlling the relative persistence of Behaviors via the use of inhibitory gains. When the gains are low, the system will tend to dither among different behaviors. When the gains are high, the system will show more persistence.

The use of high inhibitory gains can, however, result in pathological behavior in which the creature pursues a single, but unattainable goal, to the detriment of less important, but achievable ones. Ludlow addressed this problem by suggesting that a level of interest be associated with every Behavior. It is allowed to vary between 0 and 1 and it has a multiplicative effect on the Behavior's value.When Behavior is active the level of interest decreases which in turn reduces the value of the Behavior regardless of its intrinsic value. Eventually, this will allow another Behavior to become active (this is known as time-sharing in the ethological literature). When the behavior is no longer active, its level of interest rises.

Inhibitory gains and level of interest provide the designer with a good deal of control over the temporal aspects of behavior. This is an important contribution of this algorithm.

6.6 Use of Primary, Secondary and Meta-commands

Being active means that a Behavior or one if its children has top priority to issue motor commands. However, it is extremely important that less important Behaviors (i.e. those which have lost the competition for control) still be able to express their preferences for actions. This is done by allowing Behaviors which lose to issue suggestions in the form of secondary and meta-commands as described earlier. These suggestions are posted prior to the winning Behavior taking its action, so it can utilize the suggestions as it sees fit.

For example, a dog may have a behavior which alters the dog's characteristics so as to reflect its emotional state. Thus, the behavior may issue secondary commands for posture as well as for the desired ear, tail and mouth position, and use a meta-command for the desired gait. The use of a meta-command for gait reflects the fact that the behavior may not know whether the dog should go forward or not. However, it does know how it wants the dog to move, should another behavior decide that moving makes sense.

Despite the use of secondary and meta-commands, the winning behavior still has ultimate say over what actions get performed while it is active. It can over-rule a secondary command by removing it from the queue or by executing a Motor Skill which grabs a DOF needed by a given secondary command. In the case of meta-commands, the winning behavior can choose to ignore the meta-command, in which case it has no effect.

6.7 The Algorithm

The action-selection algorithm is described below. The actual equations are provided in appendix A.

On each update cycle:

(1) All Internal Variables update their value based on their previous value, growth and damping rates, and any feedback effects.

(2) Starting at the top-level Behavior Group, the Behaviors within it compete to become active. This is done as follows:

(3) The Releasing Mechanisms of each Behavior update their value based on the current sensory input. This value is then summed with that of the Behavior's Internal Variables and the result is multiplied by its Level Of Interest. This is repeated for all Behaviors in the group.

(4) For each Behavior in the group, the inhibition due to other Behaviors in the group is calculated and subtracted from the Behavior's pre-inhibition value and clamped to 0 or greater.

(5) If after step (4) more than one Behavior has a non-zero value then step (4) is repeated (using the post-inhibition values as the basis) until this condition is met. The Behavior with a non-zero value is the active Behavior for the group.

(6) All Behaviors in the group which are not active are given a chance to issue secondary or meta-commands. This is done by executing a suggestion callback associated with the Behavior.

(7) If the active Behavior has a Behavior Group as a child (i.e. it is not a Behavior at the leaf of the tree), then that Behavior Group is made the current Behavior Group and the process is repeated starting at step (3). Otherwise, the Behavior is given a chance to issue primary motor commands via the execution of a callback associated with the Behavior.

7. INTEGRATION OF DIRECTABILITY

Having described the Behavior and Motor Systems we are now in a position to describe how external control is integrated into this architecture. This is done in a number of ways.

First, motivational control is provided via named access to the Internal Variables which represent the motivations or goals of the Behavior System. By adjusting the value of a given motivational variable, the creature can be made more or less likely to engage in Behaviors which depend on that variable.

Second, all the constituent parts of a Behavior are also accessible at run-time, and this provides another mechanism for exerting behavioral control. For example, by changing the type of object for which the Releasing Mechanism is looking, the target of a given Behavior can easily be altered (e.g. "fire hydrants" versus "user's pants leg"). In addition, a Behavior may be made more or less opportunistic by adjusting the maximum allowed "strength" of its Releasing Mechanisms. A Behavior can be made in-active by setting its level of interest to zero.

Third, the Behavior System is structured so that action-selection can be initiated at any node in the system. This allows an external entity to force execution of a particular part or branch of the Behavior System, regardless of motivational and sensory factors which might otherwise favor execution of other parts of it. Since branches often correspond to task-level collections of Behaviors, this provides a form of task-level control.

Forth, it is easy to provide "imaginary" sensory input which in turn may trigger certain behaviors on the part of the creature. For example, objects may be added to the world which are only visible to a specific creature.The advantage of this technique is that it does not require the external entity to know anything about the internal structure of the creature's Behavior System.

The mechanisms described above for controlling the Behavior System naturally support both prescriptive and proscriptive control. For example, by adjusting the level of a motivational variable which drives a given branch of the Behavior System, the director is expressing a weighted preference for or against the execution of that behavior or group of behaviors.

The multiple imperative forms supported by the Motor Controller allow the director to express weighted preferences directly at the motor level. For example, at one extreme, the director may "shut off" the Behavior System and issue motor commands directly to the creature. Alternatively, the Behavior System can be running, and the director may issue persistent secondary or meta-commands which have the effect of modifying or augmenting the output of the Behavior System. For example, the external entity might issue a secondary command to "wag tail". Unless this was explicitly over-ruled by a Behavior in the Behavior System, this would result in the Dog wagging its tail. External meta-commands may also take the form of spatial potential field maps which can be combined with potential field maps generated from sensory data to effectively attract or repel the creature from parts of its environment.

8. IMPLEMENTATION

These ideas have been implemented as part of an object-oriented architecture and toolkit for building and controlling autonomous animated creatures. This toolkit is based on Open Inventor 2.0. Most of the components from which one builds a creature, including all of the components of the Behavior System, and the action-selection algorithm itself are derived from Inventor classes.This allows us to define most, of a creature and its Behavior System via a text file using the Inventor file format. This is important for rapid prototyping and quick-turnaround, as well as to facilitate the use of models generated via industry-standard modelers. We also make extensive use of Inventor's ability to provide named access to field variables at run-time. This is important for integration of external control. Callbacks are used to implement most of the custom functionality associated with specific Releasing Mechanisms and Behaviors. This coupled with extensive parameterization reduces the need to create new subclasses. Lastly, an embedded Tcl interpreter is provided for interactive run-time control.

We have developed several creatures using this tool kit. For the Alive project [13], we have developed "Silas T. Dog" an autonomous animated dog which interacts with a user in a 3D virtual world in a believable manner. Silas responds to a dozen or so gestures and postures of the user, and responds appropriately (e.g. if the user bends over and holds out her hand, Silas moves toward the

outstretched hand and eventually sits and shakes his paw). The dog always looks at its current object of interest (head, hand, etc.), and when it is sad or happy, its tail, ears and head move appropriately. Silas has a number of internal motivations which he is constantly trying to satisfy. For example, if his desire to fetch is high, and the user has not played ball with him, he will find a ball and drop it at the person's feet. Similarly, he will periodically take a break to get a drink of water, or satisfy other biological functions.

Silas represents roughly 3000 lines of C++ code, of which, 2000 lines are for implementing his 24 dog specific Motor Skills. He responds to 70 motor commands. His Behavior System is comprised of roughly 40 Behaviors, 11 Behavior Groups, 40 Releasing Mechanisms and 8 Internal Variables. Silas runs at 15Hz on a Onyx Reality Engine with rendering and sensing time (i.e. the second render for his synthetic vision) comprising most of the update time. The evaluation of the Behavior System itself typically takes less than 6-8 milliseconds.

We have also developed a number of creatures which are used in the context of an interactive story system [6]. This system features a computational director which provides "direction" to the creatures so as to meet the requirements of the story. For example, at the beginning of the story, a dog hops out of a car and wanders around. If the user, who is wearing a head-mounted display, does not pay attention to the dog, the director will send the dog over to the user. If the user still does not pay attention, the director effectively tells the dog: "the user's leg is a fine replacement for a hydrant, and you really have to...". The resulting behavior on the part of the dog usually captures the user's attention.

Figure 9: Silas and his half brother Lucky.

9. CONCLUSION

Autonomy and directability are not mutually exclusive. We have detailed an architecture and a general behavioral model for perception and action-selection which can function autonomously while accepting direction at multiple levels. This multi-level direction allows a user to direct at whatever level of detail is desirable. In addition, this blend of autonomy and direction is demonstrated with several creatures within the context of two applications.

Acknowledgments

The authors would like to thank Professors Pattie Maes, Alex P. Pentland and Glorianna Davenport for their support of our work. Thanks go, as well, to the entire ALIVE team for their help. In particular, thanks to Bradley Rhodes for suggesting the use of pronomes. We would also like to thank Taylor Galyean and Marilyn Feldmeier for their work modeling the setting and "Lucky." This work was funded in part by Sega North America and the Television of Tomorrow Consortium.

Appendix A.

Behavior Update Equation:

$$v_{it} = Max\left[\left(li_{it} \cdot Combine(\sum_k rm_{ki}, \sum_j iv_{jt}) - \sum_m n_{mi} \cdot v_{mt}\right), 0\right]$$

Where at time t for Behavior i, v_{it} is its value; li_{it} is the level of interest; rm_{kt} and iv_{jt} are the values of Releasing Mechanism k, and Internal Variable j, where k and j range over the Releasing Mechanisms and Internal Variables relevant to Behavior i; n_{mi} (n>1) is the Inhibitory Gain that Behavior m applies against Behavior i; v_{mt} is the value of Behavior m, where m ranges over the other Behaviors in the current Behavior Group. *Combine()* is the function used to combine the values of the Releasing Mechanisms and Internal Variables for Behavior i (i.e addition or multiplication).

Internal Variable Update Equations:

$$iv_{it} = (iv_{i(t-1)} \cdot damp_i) + growth_i - \sum_k effects_{kit}$$

Where at time t for Internal Variable i, iv_{it} is its value; $iv_{i(t-1)}$ is its value on the previous time step; $damp_i$ and $growth_i$ are damping rates and growth rates associated with Internal Variable i; and $effects_{kit}$ are the adjustments to its value due to the activity of Behavior k, where k ranges over the Behaviors which directly effect its value when active.

$$effects_{kit} = (modifyGain_{ki} \cdot v_{k(t-1)})$$

Where $effects_{kit}$ is the effect of Behavior k on Internal Variable i at time t; $modifyGain_{ki}$ is the gain used by Behavior k against Internal Variable i and $v_{k(t-1)}$ is the value of Behavior k in the preceding time step.

Level of Interest Update Equation:

$$li_{it} = Clamp(((li_{i(t-1)} \cdot damp_i) + growth_i - (v_{i(t-1)} \cdot bRate_i)), 0, 1)$$

Where li_{it} is the Level Of Interest of Behavior i at time t, and $bRate_i$ is the boredom rate for Behavior i. Clamp(x,y,z) clamps x to be between y and z. Note Level Of Interest is just a special case of an Internal Variable.

Releasing Mechanism Update Equation:

$$rm_{it} = Clamp(TemporalFilter(t, rm_{i(t-1)}, Find(s_{it}, dMin_i, dMax_i) \cdot Filter(s_{it}) \cdot Weight(s_{it}, dOpt_i)), min_i, max_i)$$

Where rm_{it} is the value of Releasing Mechanism i at time t; s_{it} is the relevant sensory input for i; $dMin_i$ and $dMax_i$ are minimum and maximum distances associated with it; *Find()* returns 1 or 0 if the object of interest is found within s_{it} and within $dMin_i$ to $dMax_i$; *Filter()* returns 1 or 0 if the object of interest matches some additional criteria; *Weight()* weights the strength of the stimulus based on some metric such as optimal distance $dOpt_i$; *TemporalFilter()* applies a filtering function (latch, average, integration, or immediate) over some period t; and *Clamp()* clamps the resulting value to the range min_i to max_i.

REFERENCES

1. Arkin, R.C., Integrating Behavioral, Perceptual, and World Knowledge in Reactive Navigation, in *Designing Autonomous Agents*, P. Maes, Editor. 1990, MIT Press, Cambridge, pp.105-122.
2. Badler, N.I., C. Phillips, and B.L. Webber, *Simulating Humans: Computer Graphics, Animation, and Control*. 1993, Oxford University Press, New York.
3. Blumberg, B. Action-Selection in Hamsterdam: Lessons from Ethology. in *Third International Conference on the Simulation of Adaptive Behavior*. Brighton, England,1994, MIT Press. pp.108-117.
4. Brooks, R., A Robust Layered Control System for a Mobile Robot. 1986. *IEEE Journal of Robotics and Automation* RA-2.pp. 14-23.
5. Bruderlin, Armin and Thomas W. Calvert. Dynamic Animation of Human Walking. Proceedings of SIGGRAPH 89 (Boston, MA, July 31-August 4, 1989). In *Computer Graphics* 23, 3 (July 1989), 233-242.
6. Galyean, T. A. *Narrative Guidance of Interactivity*, Ph.D. Dissertation, Massachusetts Institute of Technology, 1995.
7. Girard, Michael and A. A. Maciejewski. Computational Modeling for the Computer Animation of Legged Figures. Proceedings of SIGGRAPH 85 (San Francisco, CA, July 22-26, 1985). In *Computer Graphics* 19, 263-270.
8. Horswill, I. A Simple, Cheap, and Robust Visual Navigation System. in *Second International Conference on the Simulation of Adaptive Behavior*. Honolulu, HI, 1993. MIT Press, pp.129-137.
9. Koga, Yoshihito, Koichi Kondo, James Kuffner, and Jean-Claude Latombe. Planning Motion with Intentions. Proceedings of SIGGRAPH 94 (Orlando, FL, July 24-29, 1994). In *Computer Graphics* Proceedings, Annual Conference Series, 1994, ACM, SIGGRAPH, pp. 395-408.
10. Latombe, J. C., *Robot Motion Planning*. 1991, Kluwer Academic Publishers, Boston.
11. Ludlow, A., The Evolution and Simulation of a Decision Maker, in *Analysis of Motivational Processes*, F.T.&.T. Halliday, Editor. 1980, Academic Press, London.
12. Maes, P., Situated Agents Can Have Goals. *Journal for Robotics and Autonomous Systems* 6(1&2), 1990, pp. 49-70.
13. Maes, P., T. Darrell, and B. Blumberg. The ALIVE System: Full-body Interaction with Autonomous Agents. in *Proceedings of Computer Animation'95 Conference*, Switzerland, April 1995, IEEE Press, pp. 11-18.
14. McKenna, Michael and David Zeltzer. Dynamic Simulation of Autonomous Legged Locomotion. Proceedings of SIGGRAPH 90 (Dallas, TX, August 6-10, 1990). In *Computer Graphics* 24, 4 (August 1990), pp.29-38.
15. Minsky, M., *The Society of Mind*. 1988, Simon & Schuster, New York.
16. Raibert, Marc H. and Jessica K. Hodgins. Animation of Dynamic Legged Locomotion. Proceedings of SIGGRAPH 91 (Las Vegas, NV, July 28-August 2, 1991). In Computer Graphics 25, 4 (July 1991), 349–358
17. Renault, O., N. Magnenat-Thalmann, D. Thalmann. A vision-based approach to behavioral animation. *The Journal of Visualization and Computer Animation* 1(1),1990, pp.18-21.
18. Reynolds, Craig W. Flocks, Herds, and Schools: A Distributed Behavioral Model. Proceedings of SIGGRAPH 87 (Anaheim, CA, July 27-31, 1987). In Computer Graphics 21, 4 (July 19987), 25-34.
19. Tinbergen, N., *The Study of Instinct*. 1950, Clarendon press, Oxford.
20. Tu, Xiaoyuan and Demetri Terzopoulos. Artificial Fishes: Physics, Locomotion, Perception, Behavior. Proceedings of SIGGRAPH 94 (Orlando, FL, July 24-29, 1994). In *Computer Graphics* Proceedings, Annual Conference Series, 1994, ACM, SIGGRAPH, pp. 43-50.
21. Tyrrell, T. The Use of Hierarchies for Action Selection, in *Second International Conference on the Simulation of Adaptive Behavior*. 1993. MIT Press, pp.138-147.
22. Wilhelms J., R. Skinner. A 'Notion' for Interactive Behavioral Animation Control. *IEEE Computer Graphics and Applications* 10(3) May 1990, pp. 14-22.
23. David Zeltzer, Task Level Graphical Simulation: Abstraction, Representation and Control, in *Making Them Move*. Ed. Badler, N., Barsky, B., and Zeltzer D. 1991, Morgan Kaufmann Publishers, Inc.

Realistic Modeling for Facial Animation

Yuencheng Lee[1], Demetri Terzopoulos[1], and Keith Waters[2]

University of Toronto[1] and Digital Equipment Corporation[2]

Abstract

A major unsolved problem in computer graphics is the construction and animation of realistic human facial models. Traditionally, facial models have been built painstakingly by manual digitization and animated by ad hoc parametrically controlled facial mesh deformations or kinematic approximation of muscle actions. Fortunately, animators are now able to digitize facial geometries through the use of scanning range sensors and animate them through the dynamic simulation of facial tissues and muscles. However, these techniques require considerable user input to construct facial models of individuals suitable for animation. In this paper, we present a methodology for automating this challenging task. Starting with a structured facial mesh, we develop algorithms that automatically construct functional models of the heads of human subjects from laser-scanned range and reflectance data. These algorithms automatically insert contractile muscles at anatomically correct positions within a dynamic skin model and root them in an estimated skull structure with a hinged jaw. They also synthesize functional eyes, eyelids, teeth, and a neck and fit them to the final model. The constructed face may be animated via muscle actuations. In this way, we create the most authentic and functional facial models of individuals available to date and demonstrate their use in facial animation.

CR Categories: I.3.5 [**Computer Graphics**]: Physically based modeling; I.3.7 [**Computer Graphics**]: Animation.

Additional Keywords: Physics-based Facial Modeling, Facial Animation, RGB/Range Scanners, Feature-Based Facial Adaptation, Texture Mapping, Discrete Deformable Models.

1 Introduction

Two decades have passed since Parke's pioneering work in animating faces [13]. In the span of time, significant effort has been devoted to the development of computational models of the human face for applications in such diverse areas as entertainment, low bandwidth teleconferencing, surgical facial planning, and virtual reality. However, the task of accurately modeling the expressive human face by computer remains a major challenge.

Traditionally, computer facial animation follows three basic procedures: (1) design a 3D facial mesh, (2) digitize the 3D mesh, and (3) animate the 3D mesh in a controlled fashion to simulate facial actions.

In procedure (1), it is desirable to have a refined topological mesh that captures the facial geometry. Often this entails digitizing

[1]Department of Computer Science, 10 King's College Road, Toronto, ON, Canada, M5S 1A4. {vlee | dt}@cs.toronto.edu

[2]Cambridge Research Lab., One Kendall Square, Cambridge, MA 02139. waters@crl.dec.com

Permission to make digital/hard copy of part or all of this work for personal or classroom use is granted without fee provided that copies are not made or distributed for profit or commercial advantage, the copyright notice, the title of the publication and its date appear, and notice is given that copying is by permission of ACM, Inc. To copy otherwise, to republish, to post on servers, or to redistribute to lists, requires prior specific permission and/or a fee.

as many nodes as possible. Care must be taken not to oversample the surface because there is a trade-off between the number of nodes and the computational cost of the model. Consequently, meshes developed to date capture the salient features of the face with as few nodes as possible (see [17, 14, 21, 9, 23] for several different mesh designs).

In procedure (2), a general 3D digitization technique uses photogrammetry of several images of the face taken from different angles. A common technique is to place markers on the face that can be seen from two or more cameras. An alternative technique is to manually digitize a plaster cast of the face using manual 3D digitization devices such as orthogonal magnetic fields sound captors [9], or one to two photographs [9, 7, 1]. More recently, automated laser range finders can digitize on the order of 10^5 3D points from a solid object such as a person's head and shoulders in just a few seconds [23].

In procedure (3), an animator must decide which mesh nodes to articulate and how much they should be displaced in order to produce a specific facial expression. Various approaches have been proposed for deforming a facial mesh to produce facial expressions; for example, parameterized models [14, 15], control-point models [12, 7], kinematic muscle models [21, 9], a texture-map-assembly model [25], a spline model [11], feature-tracking models [24, 16], a finite element model [6], and dynamic muscle models [17, 20, 8, 3].

1.1 Our Approach

The goal of our work is to automate the challenging task of creating realistic facial models of individuals suitable for animation. We develop an algorithm that begins with cylindrical range and reflectance data acquired by a Cyberware scanner and automatically constructs an efficient and fully functional model of the subject's head, as shown in Plate 1. The algorithm is applicable to various individuals (Plate 2 shows the raw scans of several individuals). It proceeds in two steps:

In step 1, the algorithm adapts a well-structured face mesh from [21] to the range and reflectance data acquired by scanning the subject, thereby capturing the shape of the subject's face. This approach has significant advantages because it avoids repeated manual modification of control parameters to compensate for geometric variations in the facial features from person to person. More specifically, it allows the automatic placement of facial muscles and enables the use of a single control process across different facial models.

The generic face mesh is adapted automatically through an image analysis technique that searches for salient local minima and maxima in the range image of the subject. The search is directed according to the known relative positions of the nose, eyes, chin, ears, and other facial features with respect to the generic mesh. Facial muscle emergence and attachment points are also known relative to the generic mesh and are adapted automatically as the mesh is conformed to the scanned data.

In step 2, the algorithm elaborates the geometric model constructed in step 1 into a functional, physics-based model of the subject's face which is capable of facial expression, as shown in the lower portion of Plate 1.

We follow the physics-based facial modeling approach proposed by Terzopoulos and Waters [20]. Its basic features are that it animates facial expressions by contracting synthetic muscles embedded in an anatomically motivated model of skin composed of three spring-mass layers. The physical simulation propagates the muscle forces through the physics-based synthetic skin thereby deforming the skin to produce facial expressions. Among the advantages of the physics-based approach are that it greatly enhances the degree of realism over purely geometric facial modeling approaches, while reducing the amount of work that must be done by the animator. It can be computationally efficient. It is also amenable to improvement, with an increase in computational expense, through the use of more sophisticated biomechanical models and more accurate numerical simulation methods.

We propose a more accurate biomechanical model for facial animation compared to previous models. We develop a new biomechanical facial skin model which is simpler and better than the one proposed in [20]. Furthermore, we argue that the skull is an important biomechanical structure with regard to facial expression [22]. To date, the skin-skull interface has been underemphasized in facial animation despite its importance in the vicinity of the articulate jaw; therefore we improve upon previous facial models by developing an algorithm to estimate the skull structure from the acquired range data, and prevent the synthesized facial skin from penetrating the skull.

Finally, our algorithm includes an articulated neck and synthesizes subsidiary organs, including eyes, eyelids, and teeth, which cannot be adequately imaged or resolved in the scanned data, but which are nonetheless crucial for realistic facial animation.

2 Generic Face Mesh and Mesh Adaptation

The first step of our approach to constructing functional facial models of individuals is to scan a subject using a Cyberware Color Digitizer™. The scanner rotates 360 degrees around the subject, who sits motionless on a stool as a laser stripe is projected onto the head and shoulders. Once the scan is complete, the device has acquired two registered images of the subject: a range image (Figure 1) — a topographic map that records the distance from the sensor to points on the facial surface, and a reflectance (RGB) image (Figure 2) — which registers the color of the surface at those points. The images are in cylindrical coordinates, with longitude (0–360) degrees along the x axis and vertical height along the y axis. The resolution of the images is typically 512×256 pixels (cf. Plate 1)

The remainder of this section describes an algorithm which reduces the acquired geometric and photometric data to an efficient geometric model of the subject's head. The algorithm is a two-part process which repairs defects in the acquired images and conforms a generic facial mesh to the processed images using a feature-based matching scheme. The resulting mesh captures the facial geometry as a polygonal surface that can be texture mapped with the full resolution reflectance image, thereby maintaining a realistic facsimile of the subject's face.

2.1 Image Processing

One of the problems of range data digitization is illustrated in Figure 1(a). In the hair area, in the chin area, nostril area, and even in the pupils, laser beams tend to disperse and the sensor observes no range value for these corresponding 3D surface points. We must correct for missing range and texture information.

We use a *relaxation method* to interpolate the range data. In particular, we apply a membrane interpolation method described in [18]. The relaxation interpolates values for the missing points so as to bring them into successively closer agreement with surrounding points by repeatedly indexing nearest neighbor values. Intuitively, it stretches an elastic membrane over the gaps in the surface. The images interpolated through relaxation are shown in Figure 1(b) and

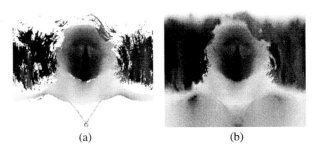

(a)   (b)

Figure 1: (a) Range data of "Grace" from a Cyberware scanner. (b) Recovered plain data.

illustrate improvements in the hair area and chin area. Relaxation works effectively when the range surface is smooth, and particularly in the case of human head range data, the smoothness requirement of the solutions is satisfied quite effectively.

Figure 2(a) shows two 512×256 reflectance (RGB) texture maps as monochrome images. Each reflectance value represents the surface color of the object in cylindrical coordinates with corresponding longitude (0–360 degrees) and latitude. Like range images, the acquired reflectance images are lacking color information at certain points. This situation is especially obvious in the hair area and the shoulder area (see Figure 2(a)). We employ the membrane relaxation approach to interpolate the texture image by repeated averaging of neighboring known colors. The original texture image in Figure 2(a) can be compared with the interpolated texture image in Figure 2(b).

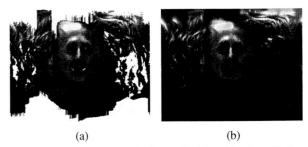

(a)   (b)

Figure 2: (a) Texture data of "George" with void points displayed in white and (b) texture image interpolated using relaxation method.

The method is somewhat problematic in the hair area where range variations may be large and there is a relatively high percentage of missing surface points. A thin-plate relaxation algorithm [18] may be more effective in these regions because it would fill in the larger gaps with less "flattening" than a membrane [10].

Although the head structure in the cylindrical laser range data is distorted along the longitudinal direction, important features such as the slope changes of the nose, forehead, chin, and the contours of the mouth, eyes, and nose are still discernible. In order to locate the contours of those facial features for use in adaptation (see below), we use a modified Laplacian operator (applied to the discrete image through local pixel differencing) to detect edges from the range map shown in Figure 3(a) and produce the field function in Fig. 3(b). For details about the operator, see [8]. The field function highlights important features of interest. For example, the local maxima of the modified Laplacian reveals the boundaries of the lips, eyes, and chin.

2.2 Generic Face Mesh and Mesh Adaptation

The next step is to reduce the large arrays of data acquired by the scanner into a parsimonious geometric model of the face that can eventually be animated efficiently. Motivated by the adaptive meshing techniques [19] that were employed in [23], we significantly

(a)   (b)

Figure 3: (a) Original range map. (b) Modified Laplacian field function of (a).

improved the technique by adapting a generic face mesh to the data. Figure 4 shows the planar generic mesh which we obtain through a cylindrical projection of the 3D face mesh from [21]. One of the advantages of the generic mesh is that it has well-defined features which form the basis for accurate feature based adaptation to the scanned data and automatic scaling and positioning of facial muscles as the mesh is deformed to fit the images. Another advantage is that it automatically produces an efficient triangulation, with finer triangles over the highly curved and/or highly articulate regions of the face, such as the eyes and mouth, and larger triangles elsewhere.

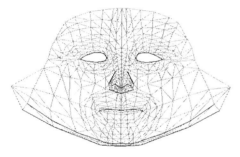

Figure 4: Facial portion of generic mesh in 2D cylindrical coordinates. Dark lines are features for adaptation.

We label all facial feature nodes in the generic face prior to the adaptation step. The feature nodes include eye contours, nose contours, mouth contours, and chin contours.

For any specific range image and its positive Laplacian field function (Figure 3), the generic mesh adaptation procedure performs the following steps to locate feature points in the range data (see [8] for details):

Mesh Adaptation Procedures

1. Locate nose tip
2. Locate chin tip
3. Locate mouth contour
4. Locate chin contour
5. Locate ears
6. Locate eyes
7. Activate spring forces
8. Adapt hair mesh
9. Adapt body mesh
10. Store texture coordinates

Once the mesh has been fitted by the above feature based matching technique (see Plate 3), the algorithm samples the range image at the location of the nodes of the face mesh to capture the facial geometry, as is illustrated in Figure 5.

The node positions also provide texture map coordinates that are used to map the full resolution color image onto the triangles (see Plate 3).

2.3 Estimation of Relaxed Face Model

Ideally, the subject's face should be in a neutral, relaxed expression when he or she is being scanned. However, the scanned woman in

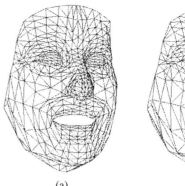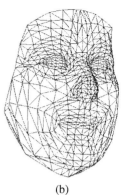

(a)   (b)

Figure 5: (a) Generic geometric model conformed to Cyberware scan of "Heidi". (b) Same as (a). Note that "Heidi's" mouth is now closed, subsequent to estimation of the relaxed face geometry.

the "Heidi" dataset is smiling and her mouth is open (see Plate 2). We have made our algorithm tolerant of these situations. To construct a functional model, it is important to first estimate the relaxed geometry. That is, we must infer what the "Heidi" subject would look like had her face been in a relaxed pose while she was being scanned. We therefore estimate the range values of the closed mouth contour from the range values of the open mouth contour by the following steps:

1. Perform adaptation procedures in Sec. 2.2 without step 3.
2. Store nodal longitude/latitude into adapted face model.
3. Perform lip adaptation in step 3 in sec. 2.2
4. Store nodal range values into adapted face model.

As a result, the final reconstructed face model in Figure 5(b) will have a relaxed mouth because the longitude and latitude recorded is the default shape of our closed mouth model (see Figure 4). Moreover, the shape of the final reconstructed face is still faithful to the head data because the range value at each facial nodal point is obtained correctly after the lip adaptation procedure has been performed. Relaxing the face shown in Figure 5(a) results in the image in Figure 5(b) (with eyelids inserted — see below).

3 The Dynamic Skin and Muscle Model

This section describes how our system proceeds with the construction of a fully functional model of the subject's face from the facial mesh produced by the adaptation algorithm described in the previous section. To this end, we automatically create a dynamic model of facial tissue, estimate a skull surface, and insert the major muscles of facial expression into the model. The following sections describe each of these components. We also describe our high-performance parallel, numerical simulation of the dynamic facial tissue model.

3.1 Layered Synthetic Tissue Model

The skull is covered by deformable tissue which has five distinct layers [4]. Four layers—epidermis, dermis, sub-cutaneous connective tissue, and fascia—comprise the skin, and the fifth consists of the muscles of facial expression. Following [20], and in accordance with the structure of real skin [5], we have designed a new, synthetic tissue model (Figure 6(a)).

The tissue model is composed of triangular prism elements (see Figure 6(a)) which match the triangles in the adapted facial mesh. The epidermal surface is defined by nodes 1, 2, and 3, which are connected by epidermal springs. The epidermis nodes are also connected by dermal-fatty layer springs to nodes 4, 5, and 6, which define the fascia surface. Fascia nodes are interconnected by fascia

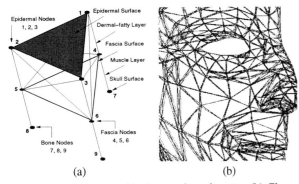

(a)   (b)

Figure 6: (a) Triangular skin tissue prism element. (b) Close-up view of right side of an individual with conformed elements.

springs. They are also connected by muscle layer springs to skull surface nodes 7, 8, 9.

Figure 9(b) shows 684 such skin elements assembled into an extended skin patch. Several synthetic muscles are embedded into the muscle layer of the skin patch and the figure shows the skin deformation due to muscle contraction. Muscles are fixed in an estimated bony subsurface at their point of emergence and are attached to fascia nodes as they run through several tissue elements. Figure 6(b) shows a close-up view of the right half of the facial tissue model adapted to an individual's face which consists of 432 elements.

3.2   Discrete Deformable Models (DDMs)

A discrete deformable model has a node-spring-node structure, which is a uniaxial finite element. The data structure for the node consists of the nodal mass m_i, position $x_i(t) = [x_i(t), y_i(t), z_i(t)]'$, velocity $v_i = dx_i/dt$, acceleration $a_i = d^2x_i/dt^2$, and net nodal forces $f_i^n(t)$. The data structure for the spring in this DDM consists of pointers to the head node i and the tail node j which the spring interconnects, the natural or rest length l_k of the spring, and the spring stiffness c_k.

3.3   Tissue Model Spring Forces

By assembling the discrete deformable model according to histological knowledge of skin (see Figure 6(a)), we are able to construct an anatomically consistent, albeit simplified, tissue model. Figure 6(b) shows a close-up view of the tissue model around its eye and nose parts of a face which is automatically assembled by following the above approach.

- The force spring j exerts on node i is

$$g_j = c_j(l_j - l_j^r)s_j$$

  - each layer has its own stress-strain relationship c_j and the dermal-fatty layer uses biphasic springs (non-constant c_j) [20]
  - l_j^r and $l_j = ||x_j - x_i||$ are the rest and current lengths for spring j
  - $s_j = (x_j - x_i)/l_j$ is the spring direction vector for spring j

3.4   Linear Muscle Forces

The muscles of facial expression, or the muscular plate, spreads out below the facial tissue. The facial musculature is attached to the skin tissue by short elastic tendons at many places in the fascia, but is fixed to the facial skeleton only at a few points. Contractions of the facial muscles cause movement of the facial tissue. We model

28 of the primary facial muscles, including the zygomatic major and minor, frontalis, nasii, corrugator, mentalis, buccinator, and angulii depressor groups. Plate 4 illustrates the effects of automatic scaling and positioning of facial muscle vectors as the generic mesh adapts to different faces.

To better emulate the facial muscle attachments to the fascia layer in our model, a group of fascia nodes situated along the muscle path—i.e., within a predetermined distance from a central muscle vector, in accordance with the muscle width—experience forces from the contraction of the muscle. The face construction algorithm determines the nodes affected by each muscle in a precomputation step.

To apply muscle forces to the fascia nodes, we calculate a force for each node by multiplying the muscle vector with a force length scaling factor and a force width scaling factor (see Figure 7(a)). Function Θ_1 (Figure 8(a)) scales the muscle force according to the length ratio $\varepsilon_{j,i}$, while Θ_2 (Figure 8(b)) scales it according to the width $\omega_{j,i}$ at node i of muscle j:

$$\varepsilon_{j,i} = ((m_j^F - x_i) \cdot m_j)/(||m_j^A - m_j^F||)$$
$$\omega_{j,i} = ||p_i - (p_i \cdot n_j)n_j||$$

- The force muscle j exerts on node i is

$$f_i^j = \Theta_1(\varepsilon_{j,i})\Theta_2(\omega_{j,i})m_j$$

  - Θ_1 scales the force according to the distance ratio $\varepsilon_{j,i}$, where $\varepsilon_{j,i} = \rho_{j,i}/d_j$, with d_j the muscle j length.
  - Θ_2 scales the force according to the width ratio $\omega_{j,i}/w_j$, with w_j the muscle j width.
  - m_j is the normalized muscle vector for muscle j

Note that the muscle force is scaled to zero at the root of the muscle fiber in the bone and reaches its full strength near the end of the muscle fiber. Figure 9(b) shows an example of the effect of muscle forces applied to a synthetic skin patch.

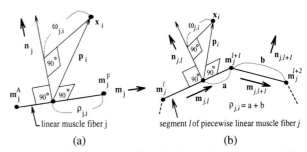

(a)   (b)

Figure 7: (a) Linear muscle fiber. (b) Piecewise linear muscle fiber.

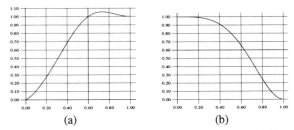

(a)   (b)

Figure 8: (a) Muscle force scaling function Θ_1 wrt $\varepsilon_{j,i}$, (b) Muscle force scaling function Θ_2 wrt $\omega_{j,i}/w_j$

3.5   Piecewise Linear Muscle Forces

In addition to using linear muscle fibers in section 3.4 to simulate sheet facial muscles like the frontalis and the zygomatics, we also model sphincter muscles, such as the orbicularis oris circling the mouth, by generalizing the linear muscle fibers to be piecewise linear and allowing them to attach to fascia at each end of the segments. Figure 7(b) illustrates two segments of an N-segment piecewise linear muscle j showing three nodes $\mathbf{m}_j^l$, $\mathbf{m}_j^{l+1}$, and $\mathbf{m}_j^{l+2}$. The unit vectors $\mathbf{m}_{j,l}$, $\mathbf{m}_{j,l+1}$ and $\mathbf{n}_{j,l}$, $\mathbf{n}_{j,l+1}$ are parallel and normal to the segments, respectively. The figure indicates fascia node i at $\mathbf{x}_i$, as well as the distance $\rho_{j,i} = a + b$, the width $\omega_{j,i}$, and the perpendicular vector $\mathbf{p}_i$ from fascia node i to the nearest segment of the muscle. The length ratio $\varepsilon_{j,i}$ for fascia node i in muscle fiber j is

$$\varepsilon_{j,i} = \frac{(\mathbf{m}_j^{l+1} - \mathbf{x}_i) \cdot \mathbf{m}_{j,l} + \sum_{k=l+1}^{N} \| \mathbf{m}_j^{k+1} - \mathbf{m}_j^k \|}{\sum_{k=1}^{N} \| \mathbf{m}_j^{k+1} - \mathbf{m}_j^k \|}$$

The width $\omega_{j,i}$ calculation is the same as for linear muscles. The remaining muscle force computations are the same as in section 3.4. Plate 4 shows all the linear muscles and the piecewise linear sphincter muscles around the mouth.

3.6 Volume Preservation Forces

In order to faithfully exhibit the incompressibility [2] of real human skin in our model, a volume constraint force based on the change of volume (see Figure 9(a)) and displacements of nodes is calculated and applied to nodes. In Figure 9(b) the expected effect of volume preservation is demonstrated. For example, near the origin of the muscle fiber, the epidermal skin is bulging out, and near the end of the muscle fiber, the epidermal skin is depressed.

- The volume preservation force element e exerts on nodes i in element e is

$$\mathbf{q}_i^e = k_1(V^e - \tilde{V}^e)\mathbf{n}_i^e + k_2(\mathbf{p}_i^e - \tilde{\mathbf{p}}_i^e)$$

  - $\tilde{V}^e$ and V^e are the rest and current volumes for e
  - $\mathbf{n}_i^e$ is the epidermal normal for epidermal node i
  - $\tilde{\mathbf{p}}_i^e$ and $\mathbf{p}_i^e$ are the rest and current nodal coordinates for node i with respect to the center of mass of e
  - k_1, k_2 are force scaling constants

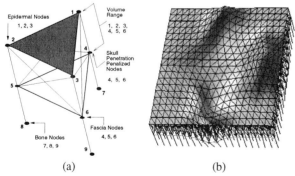

(a)   (b)

Figure 9: (a) Volume preservation and skull nonpenetration element. (b) Assembled layered tissue elements under multiple muscle forces.

3.7 Skull Penetration Constraint Forces

Because of the underlying impenetrable skull of a human head, the facial tissue during a facial expression will slide over the underlying bony structure. With this in mind, for each individual's face model reconstructed from the laser range data, we estimate the skull surface normals to be the surface normals in the range data image. The skull is then computed as an offset surface. To prevent nodes from penetrating the estimated skull (see Figure 9(a)), we apply a skull non-penetration constraint to cancel out the force component on the fascia node which points into the skull; therefore, the resulting force will make the nodes slide over the skull.

- The force to penalize fascia node i during motion is:

$$\mathbf{s}_i = \begin{cases} -(\mathbf{f}_i^n \cdot \mathbf{n}_i)\mathbf{n}_i & \text{when } \mathbf{f}_i^n \cdot \mathbf{n}_i < 0 \\ 0 & \text{otherwise} \end{cases}$$

  - $\mathbf{f}_i^n$ is the net force on fascia node i
  - $\mathbf{n}_i$ is the nodal normal of node i

3.8 Equations of Motion for Tissue Model

Newton's law of motion governs the response of the tissue model to forces. This leads to a system of coupled second order ODEs that relate the node positions, velocities, and accelerations to the nodal forces. The equation for node i is

$$m_i \frac{d^2\mathbf{x}_i}{dt^2} + \gamma_i \frac{d\mathbf{x}_i}{dt} + \tilde{\mathbf{g}}_i + \tilde{\mathbf{q}}_i + \tilde{\mathbf{s}}_i + \tilde{\mathbf{h}}_i = \tilde{\mathbf{f}}_i$$

  - m_i is the nodal mass,
  - γ_i is the damping coefficient,
  - $\tilde{\mathbf{g}}_i$ is the total spring force at node i,
  - $\tilde{\mathbf{q}}_i$ is the total volume preservation force at node i,
  - $\tilde{\mathbf{s}}_i$ is the total skull penetration force at node i,
  - $\tilde{\mathbf{h}}_i$ is the total nodal restoration force at node i,
  - $\tilde{\mathbf{f}}_i$ is the total applied muscle force at node i,

3.9 Numerical Simulation

The solution to the above system of ODEs is approximated by using the well-known, explicit Euler method. At each iteration, the nodal acceleration at time t is computed by dividing the net force by nodal mass. The nodal velocity is then calculated by integrating once, and another integration is done to compute the nodal positions at the next time step $t + \Delta t$, as follows:

$$\begin{aligned} \mathbf{a}_i^t &= \frac{1}{m_i}(\tilde{\mathbf{f}}_i^t - \gamma_i \mathbf{v}_i^t - \tilde{\mathbf{g}}_i^t - \tilde{\mathbf{q}}_i^t - \tilde{\mathbf{s}}_i^t - \tilde{\mathbf{h}}_i^t) \\ \mathbf{v}_i^{t+\Delta t} &= \mathbf{v}_i^t + \Delta t \mathbf{a}_i^t \\ \mathbf{x}_i^{t+\Delta t} &= \mathbf{x}_i^t + \Delta t \mathbf{v}_i^{t+\Delta t} \end{aligned}$$

3.10 Default Parameters

The default parameters for the physical/numerical simulation and the spring stiffness values of different layers are as follows:

Mass (m)	Time step (Δt)	Damping (γ)
0.5	0.01	30

	Epid	Derm-fat 1	Derm-fat 2	Fascia	Muscle
c	60	30	70	80	10

3.11 Parallel Processing for Facial Animation

The explicit Euler method allows us to easily carry out the numerical simulation of the dynamic skin/muscle model in parallel. This is because at each time step all the calculations are based on the results from the previous time step. Therefore, parallelization is achieved by evenly distributing calculations at each time step to all available processors. This parallel approach increases the animation speed to allow us to simulate facial expressions at interactive rates on our Silicon Graphics multiprocessor workstation.

4 Geometry Models for Other Head Components

To complete our physics-based face model, additional geometric models are combined along with the skin/muscle/skull models developed in the previous section. These include the eyes, eyelids, teeth, neck, hair, and bust (Figure 10). See Plate 5 for an example of a complete model.

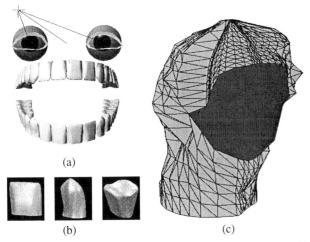

Figure 10: (a) Geometric models of eyes, eyelids, and teeth (b) Incisor, canine, and molar teeth. (c) hair and neck.

4.1 Eyes

Eyes are constructed from spheres with adjustable irises and adjustable pupils (Figure 10(a)). The eyes are automatically scaled to fit the facial model and are positioned into it. The eyes rotate kinematically in a coordinated fashion so that they will always converge on a specified fixation point in three-dimensional space that defines the field of view. Through a simple illumination computation, the eyes can automatically dilate and contract the pupil size in accordance with the amount of light entering the eye.

4.2 Eyelids

The eyelids are polygonal models which can blink kinematically during animation (see Figure 10(a)). Note that the eyelids are open in Figure 10(a).

If the subject is scanned with open eyes, the sensor will not observe the eyelid texture. An eyelid texture is synthesized by a relaxation based interpolation algorithm similar to the one described in section 2.1. The relaxation algorithm interpolates a suitable eyelid texture from the immediately surrounding texture map. Figure 11 shows the results of the eyelid texture interpolation.

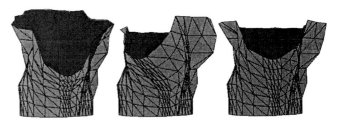

Figure 11: (a) Face texture image with adapted mesh before eyelid texture synthesis (b) after eyelid texture synthesis.

4.3 Teeth

We have constructed a full set of generic teeth based on dental images. Each tooth is a NURBS surfaces of degree 2. Three different teeth shapes, the incisor, canine, and molar, are modeled (Figure 10(b)). We use different orientations and scalings of these basic shapes to model the full set of upper and lower teeth shown in Figure 10(a). The dentures are automatically scaled to fit in length, curvature, etc., and are positioned behind the mouth of the facial model.

4.4 Hair, Neck, and Bust Geometry

The hair and bust are both rigid polygonal models (see Figure 10(c)). They are modeled from the range data directly, by extending the

facial mesh in a predetermined fashion to the boundaries of the range and reflectance data, and sampling the images as before.

The neck can be twisted, bent and rotated with three degrees of freedom. See Figure 12 for illustrations of the possible neck articulations.

Figure 12: articulation of neck.

5 Animation Examples

Plate 1 illustrates several examples of animating the physics-based face model after conformation to the "Heidi" scanned data (see Plate 2).

- The *surprise* expression results from contraction of the outer frontalis, major frontalis, inner frontalis, zygomatics major, zygomatics minor, depressor labii, and mentalis, and rotation of the jaw.
- The *anger* expression results from contraction of the corrugator, lateral corrugator, levator labii, levator labii nasi, anguli depressor, depressor labii, and mentalis.
- The *quizzical look* results from an asymmetric contraction of the major frontalis, outer frontalis, corrugator, lateral corrugator, levator labii, and buccinator.
- The *sadness* expression results from a contraction of the inner frontalis, corrugator, lateral corrugator, anguli depressor, and depressor labii.

Plate 6 demonstrates the performance of our face model construction algorithm on two male individuals ("Giovanni" and "Mick"). Note that the algorithm is tolerant of some amount of facial hair.

Plate 7 shows a third individual "George." Note the image at the lower left, which shows two additional expression effects—cheek puffing, and lip puckering—that combine to simulate the vigorous blowing of air through the lips. The cheek puffing was created by applying outwardly directed radial forces to "inflate" the deformable cheeks. The puckered lips were created by applying radial pursing forces and forward protruding forces to simulate the action of the orbicularis oris sphincter muscle which circles the mouth.

Finally, Plate 8 shows several frames from a two-minute animation "*Bureaucrat Too*" (a second-generation version of the 1990 "*Bureaucrat*" which was animated using the generic facial model in [20]). Here "George" tries to read landmark papers on facial modeling and deformable models in the SIGGRAPH '87 proceedings, only to realize that he doesn't yet have a brain!

6 Conclusion and Future Work

The human face consists of a biological tissue layer with nonlinear deformation properties, a muscle layer knit together under the skin, and an impenetrable skull structure beneath the muscle layer. We have presented a physics-based model of the face which takes all of these structures into account. Furthermore, we have demonstrated a new technique for automatically constructing face models of this sort and conforming them to individuals by exploiting high-resolution laser scanner data. The conformation process is carried out by a feature matching algorithm based on a reusable generic mesh. The conformation process, efficiently captures facial geometry and photometry, positions and scales facial muscles, and also estimates the skull structure over which the new synthetic facial tissue model can slide. Our facial modeling approach achieves an unprecedented level of realism and fidelity to any specific individual. It also achieves a good compromise between the complete emulation of the complex biomechanical structures and functionality of the human face and real-time simulation performance on state-of-the-art computer graphics and animation hardware.

Although we formulate the synthetic facial skin as a layered tissue model, our work does not yet exploit knowledge of the variable thickness of the layers in different areas of the face. This issue will in all likelihood be addressed in the future by incorporating additional input data about the subject acquired using noninvasive medical scanners such as CT or MR.

Acknowledgments

The authors thank Lisa White and Jim Randall for developing the piecewise linear muscle model used to model the mouth. Range/RGB facial data were provided courtesy of Cyberware, Inc., Monterey, CA. The first two authors thank the Natural Science and Engineering Research Council of Canada for financial support. DT is a fellow of the Canadian Institute for Advanced Research.

References

[1] T. Akimoto, Y. Suenaga, and R. Wallace. Automatic creation of 3D facial models. *IEEE Computer Graphics and Applications*, 13(5):16–22, September 1993.

[2] James Doyle and James Philips. *Manual on Experimental Stress Analysis*. Society for Experimental Mechanics, fifth edition, 1989.

[3] Irfan A. Essa. *Visual Interpretation of Facial Expressions using Dynamic Modeling*. PhD thesis, MIT, 1994.

[4] Frick and Hans. *Human Anatomy*, volume 1. Thieme Medical Publishers, Stuttgart, 1991.

[5] H. Gray. *Anatomy of the Human Body*. Lea & Febiber, Philadelphia, PA, 29th edition, 1985.

[6] Brian Guenter. A system for simulating human facial expression. In *State of the Art in Computer Animation*, pages 191–202. Springer-Verlag, 1992.

[7] T. Kurihara and K. Arai. A transformation method for modeling and animation of the human face from photographs. In *State of the Art in Computer Animation*, pages 45–57. Springer-Verlag, 1991.

[8] Y.C. Lee, D. Terzopoulos, and K. Waters. Constructing physics-based facial models of individuals. In *Proceedings of Graphics Interface '93*, pages 1–8, Toronto, May 1993.

[9] N. Magneneat-Thalmann, H. Minh, M. Angelis, and D. Thalmann. Design, transformation and animation of human faces. *Visual Computer*, 5:32–39, 1989.

[10] D. Metaxas and E. Milios. Reconstruction of a color image from nonuniformly distributed sparse and noisy data. *Computer Vision, Graphics, and Image Processing*, 54(2):103–111, March 1992.

[11] M. Nahas, H. Hutric, M. Rioux, and J. Domey. Facial image synthesis using skin texture recording. *Visual Computer*, 6(6):337–343, 1990.

[12] M. Oka, K. Tsutsui, A. Ohba, Y. Kurauchi, and T. Tago. Real-time manipulation of texture-mapped surfaces. In *SIGGRAPH 21*, pages 181–188. ACM Computer Graphics, 1987.

[13] F. Parke. Computer generated animation of faces. In *ACM National Conference*, pages 451–457. ACM, 1972.

[14] F. Parke. Parameterized models for facial animation. *IEEE Computer Graphics and Applications*, 2(9):61–68, November 1982.

[15] F. Parke. Parameterized models for facial animation revisited. In *SIGGRAPH Facial Animation Tutorial Notes*, pages 43–56. ACM SIGGRAPH, 1989.

[16] Elizabeth C. Patterson, Peter C. Litwinowicz, and N. Greene. Facial animation by spatial mapping. In *State of the Art in Computer Animation*, pages 31–44. Springer-Verlag, 1991.

[17] S. Platt and N. Badler. Animating facial expression. *Computer Graphics*, 15(3):245–252, August 1981.

[18] D. Terzopoulos. The computation of visible-surface representations. *IEEE Transactions on Pattern Analysis and Machine Intelligence*, PAMI-10(4):417–438, 1988.

[19] D. Terzopoulos and M. Vasilescu. Sampling and reconstruction with adaptive meshes. In *Proceedings of Computer Vision and Pattern Recognition Conference*, pages 70–75. IEEE, June 1991.

[20] D. Terzopoulos and K. Waters. Physically-based facial modeling, analysis, and animation. *Visualization and Computer Animation*, 1:73–80, 1990.

[21] K. Waters. A muscle model for animating three-dimensional facial expression. *Computer Graphics*, 22(4):17–24, 1987.

[22] K. Waters. A physcial model of facial tissue and muscle articulation derived from computer tomography data. In *Visualization in Biomedical Computing*, pages 574–583. SPIE, Vol. 1808, 1992.

[23] K. Waters and D. Terzopoulos. Modeling and animating faces using scanned data. *Visualization and Computer Animation*, 2:123–128, 1991.

[24] L. Williams. Performance-driven facial animation. In *SIGGRAPH 24*, pages 235–242. ACM Computer Graphics, 1990.

[25] J. Yau and N. Duffy. 3-D facial animation using image samples. In *New Trends in Computer Graphics*, pages 64–73. Springer-Verlag, 1988.

Plate 1: Objective. *Input*: Range map in 3D and texture map (top). *Output*: Functional face model for animation.

Plate 2: Raw 512×256 digitized data for Heidi (top left), George (top right), Giovanni (bottom left), Mick (bottom right).

Plate 3: Adapted face mesh overlaying texture map and Laplacian filtered range map of Heidi.

Plate 6: Animation examples of Giovanni and Mick.

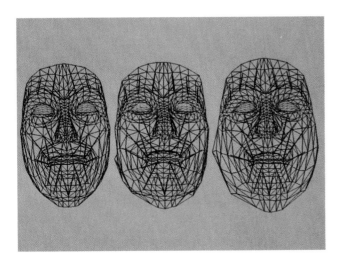

Plate 4: Muscle fiber vector embedded in generic face model and two adapted faces of Heidi and George.

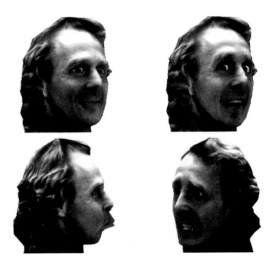

Plate 7: Animation example of George.

Plate 5: Complete, functional head model of Heidi with physics-based face and geometric eyes, teeth, hair, neck, and shoulders (in Monument Valley).

Plate 8: George in four scenes from "*Bureaucrat Too*".

Automated Learning of Muscle-Actuated Locomotion Through Control Abstraction

Radek Grzeszczuk and Demetri Terzopoulos

Department of Computer Science, University of Toronto [1]

Keywords: *learning, locomotion, control, artificial life, physics-based modeling*

Abstract: *We present a learning technique that automatically synthesizes realistic locomotion for the animation of physics-based models of animals. The method is especially suitable for animals with highly flexible, many-degree-of-freedom bodies and a considerable number of internal muscle actuators, such as snakes and fish. The multilevel learning process first performs repeated locomotion trials in search of actuator control functions that produce efficient locomotion, presuming virtually nothing about the form of these functions. Applying a short-time Fourier analysis, the learning process then abstracts control functions that produce effective locomotion into a compact representation which makes explicit the natural quasi-periodicities and coordination of the muscle actions. The artificial animals can finally put into practice the compact, efficient controllers that they have learned. Their locomotion learning abilities enable them to accomplish higher-level tasks specified by the animator while guided by sensory perception of their virtual world; e.g., locomotion to a visible target. We demonstrate physics-based animation of learned locomotion in dynamic models of land snakes, fishes, and even marine mammals that have trained themselves to perform "SeaWorld" stunts.*

1 Introduction

The animation of animals in motion is an alluring but difficult problem. With the advent of visually realistic models of humans and lower animals, even small imperfections in the locomotion patterns can be objectionable. The most promising approach to achieving a satisfactory level of authenticity is to develop physically realistic artificial animals that employ internal actuators, or muscles, to closely approximate the movements of natural animal bodies. As these animal models become increasingly complex, however, animators can no longer be expected to control them manually. Sophisticated models must eventually assume the responsibility for their own sensorimotor control. Like real animals, they should be capable of learning to control themselves.

This paper addresses a natural question: Is it possible for a physics-based, muscle-actuated model of an animal to learn from first principles how to control its muscles in order to locomote in a natural fashion? Unlike prior work on motion synthesis, we target state-of-the-art animate models of at least the level of realism and complexity of the snakes and worms of Miller [8] or the fish of Tu and Terzopoulos [17]. In both of these cases, the muscle controllers

[1] 10 King's College Road, Toronto, Ontario, Canada, M5S 1A4
    E-mail: {radek|dt}@cs.toronto.edu

Permission to make digital/hard copy of part or all of this work for personal or classroom use is granted without fee provided that copies are not made or distributed for profit or commercial advantage, the copyright notice, the title of the publication and its date appear, and notice is given that copying is by permission of ACM, Inc. To copy otherwise, to republish, to post on servers, or to redistribute to lists, requires prior specific permission and/or a fee.

© 1995   ACM-0-89791-701-4/95/008 $3.50

that produce locomotion were carefully hand crafted using knowledge gleaned from the biomechanics literature [7] and long hours of experimentation. Our goal in this paper is to devise algorithms that can provide such animal models the ability to learn how to locomote automatically, in a way that is inspired by the remarkable ability of real animals to acquire locomotion skills through action and perception.

At the foundation of our approach lies the notion that natural locomotion patterns are energetically efficient. This allows us to formalize the problem of learning realistic locomotion as one of optimizing a class of objective functionals, for which there are various solution techniques. We formulate a bottom-up, multilevel strategy for learning muscle controllers. At the early stages of the learning process, the animate model has no *a priori* knowledge about how to locomote. It is as if the animal had a fully functional body, but no motor control center in its "brain". Through practice—repeated locomotion trials with different muscle actions—the animal learns how to locomote with increasing effectiveness, by remembering actions that improve its motor skills as measured by the objective functional. Repeated improvements eventually produce life-like locomotion.

When basic locomotive skill is achieved, the animate models abstract the low-level muscle control functions that they have learned and train themselves to perform some specific higher-level motor tasks. The learning algorithm abstracts detailed muscle control functions into a highly compact representation. The representation now emphasizes the natural quasi-periodicities of effective muscle actions and makes explicit the coordination among multiple muscles that has led to effective locomotion. Finally, the artificial animals can put into practice the compact, efficient controllers that they have learned in order to accomplish the sorts of tasks that animators would have them do.

We are particularly interested in realistic motion synthesis for three dimensional models of animals that are highly deformable and can move continuously within their virtual worlds. Plates 1–5 show frames from animations of animal models that we have created, which have learned to locomote and perform interesting motor tasks automatically. We use spring-mass systems to construct our models, following the work of [8, 17]. This results in biomechanical models with numerous degrees of freedom and many parameters to control. The reader should peruse [8, 17] to become familiar with the details of the models.

An example will serve to illustrate the challenges of controlling highly deformable body models: Fig. 1 illustrates a biomechanical model of a Sonoral coral snake [4] that we use in one of our animations (Plate 1). The body consists of 10 segments. Each segment has two pairs of longitudinal muscle springs that are under the active control of the snake's brain. All other springs are passive dynamic elements that maintain the structural integrity of the body. The snake can actuate its body by varying the rest lengths of the 40 muscle springs over time. To simplify matters slightly, paired muscles on either side in each segment are actuated synchronously, and this yields a total of 20 actuators. Clearly, it is counterproductive to provide the animator direct control over so many actuators. Instead, we would like the snake to train itself to control its body. We will

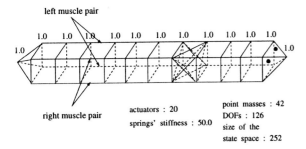

left muscle pair

1.0 1.0 1.0 1.0 1.0 1.0 1.0 1.0 1.0 1.0
1.0   1.0

right muscle pair

actuators : 20
springs' stiffness : 50.0

point masses : 42
DOFs : 126
size of the
state space : 252

Figure 1: *The snake biomechanical model consists of nodal masses (points) and springs (lines). It has twenty independent actuators (muscle springs): ten on the left side of the body and ten on the right side. Each actuator comprises a pair of synchronous muscles. The numbers along the body indicate nodal masses in cross sectional planes. The cross-springs, shown in only one segment, maintain the structural integrity of the body.*

develop algorithms that will enable its brain to exercise its body until it discovers the actuator coordination needed to achieve efficient serpentine locomotion. The snake will monitor the progress of the learning cycle using an objective functional that incorporates sensory feedback about its actions.

An advantage of our approach from the point of view of the animator is its generality. In principle, it is applicable to all animate models motivated by internal muscles, whether highly deformable, or articulate. In this paper, we demonstrate its power using 4 different, highly deformable animal body models in varied media—terra firma, water, and air (see Appendix A). Another advantage is that the approach allows us to equip our models with sensors that enable them to perceive their environment. Sensory perception is modeled through the objective functional to be optimized. The sensory contribution to the objective functional represents the animal's perception of the degree to which its goal has been achieved. Making the artificial animal perceptually aware allows it to handle tasks that depend on dynamic events in the environment and gives the animator a potent tool with which to control the model.

1.1 Related Work

The issue of control is central to physics-based animation research. Optimal control methods formulate the control problem in terms of an objective functional which must be minimized over a time interval, subject to the differential equations of motion of the physical model [1]. The "spacetime constraints" method [19] has attracted a certain following (e.g., [3]), but it is problematic because, in principle, it treats physics as a penalty constraint (that can be "stretched like a spring") and, in practice, the need to symbolically differentiate the equations of motion renders it impractical for all but the simplest physical models.

We pursue a different approach toward locomotion control that is suitable for complex physical models. The approach is inspired by the "direct dynamics" technique which was described in the control literature by Goh and Teo [5] and earlier references cited therein. Direct dynamics prescribes a generate-and-test strategy that optimizes a control objective functional through repeated forward dynamic simulation and motion evaluation.

The direct dynamics technique was developed further to control articulated musculoskeletal models in [10] and it has seen application in the mainstream graphics literature to the control of planar articulated figures [18, 9]. Pandy *et al.* [10] search the model actuator space for optimal controllers, but they do not perform global optimization. Van de Panne and Fiume [18] use simulated annealing for global optimization. Their models are equipped with simple sensors that probe the environment and use the sensory information to influence control decisions. Ngo and Marks' [9] stimulus-response

control algorithm presents a similar approach. They apply the genetic algorithm to find optimal controllers. The genetic algorithm is also used in the recent work of Sims [15]. Risdale [14] reports an early effort at controller synthesis for articulated figures from training examples using neural networks.

A characteristic of prior methods that tends to limit them to relatively simple planar models with few actuators is that they attempt to tackle the control problem at only a single level of abstraction. Typically, they deal with the control problem at an abstract level, say, in terms of a small number of controller network weights [18, 15] or whole body motions [9]. We advocate a multilevel controller learning technique that can handle complex models even though it seeks, based on first principles, optimal muscle actuation functions in a very concrete representation that makes the weakest possible assumptions. Thus the learning process is bootstrapped essentially from scratch. Earlier versions of our work were presented in [6, 16].

1.2 Overview

We describe our multilevel learning technique in the following two sections. Section 2 presents the strategy for learning low level controllers. Low level control learning is time consuming because of the high dimensionality of the search space. It is therefore prudent to reuse controllers. To this end, Section 3 presents the strategy for abstracting high level controllers. The abstraction step dramatically reduces dimensionality, stores the reduced description in the animal's memory, and permits the control problems to be defined in terms of higher level motor goals. This approach leads naturally to reusable solutions. We search for good low level control solutions for a set of simple tasks and use them as building blocks to achieve higher level goals. Section 4 presents a thorough experimental evaluation of our learning approach and more results.

2 Learning Low Level Control

Our low-level learning technique repeatedly generates a controller, applies it to drive a short-time forward simulation of the dynamic body model, and measures its effectiveness at producing locomotion using an objective functional. Typically, this low-level motor learning cycle is lengthy (as it can be in real animals, such as humans). However, it is simple and ultimately quite effective.

2.1 Biomechanical Models, Muscles, Actuators, Controllers

The *biomechanical models* that we employ are constructed of nodal masses and springs, as is detailed in Appendix A. Their dynamics is specified by the Lagrangian equations of motion

$$m_i \ddot{\mathbf{x}}_i + \gamma_i \dot{\mathbf{x}}_i + \sum_{j \in N_i} \mathbf{f}_{ij}^s = \mathbf{f}_i \qquad (1)$$

where node i has mass m_i, position $\mathbf{x}_i(t) = [x_i(t), y_i(t), z_i(t)]$, velocity $\dot{\mathbf{x}}$, and damping factor γ_i, and where $\mathbf{f}_i$ is an external force. Spring S_{ij}, which connects node i to neighboring nodes $j \in N_i$, exerts the force $\mathbf{f}_{ij}^s(t) = -(c_{ij}e_{ij} + \gamma_{ij}\dot{e}_{ij})\mathbf{r}_{ij}/\|\mathbf{r}_{ij}\|$ on node i (and it exerts the force $-\mathbf{f}_{ij}^s$ on node j), where c_{ij} is the elastic constant, γ_{ij} is the damping constant, and $e_{ij}(t) = \|\mathbf{r}_{ij}\| - l_{ij}$ is the deformation of the spring with separation vector $\mathbf{r}_{ij}(t) = \mathbf{x}_j - \mathbf{x}_i$. The natural length of the spring is l_{ij}.

Some of the springs in the biomechanical model play the role of contractile *muscles*. Muscles contract as their natural length l_{ij} decreases under the autonomous control of the motor center of the artificial animal's brain [17]. To dynamically contract a muscle, the brain must supply an *activation function* $a(t)$ to the muscle. This continuous time function has range $[0, 1]$, with 0 corresponding to a fully relaxed muscle of length l_{ij}^r and 1 to a fully contracted muscle of length l_{ij}^c. More specifically, for a muscle spring, $l_{ij} = al_{ij}^c + (1 - a)l_{ij}^r$.

Typically, individual muscles form muscle groups, called *actuators*, that are activated in unison. Referring to Fig. 1 for example, the 40 muscles in the snake model are grouped pairwise in each segment to form 10 left actuators and 10 right actuators. Each actuator i is activated by a scalar *actuation function* $u_i(t)$, whose range is again normalized to $[0, 1]$. The actuation function transforms straightforwardly into activation functions for each muscle in the actuator. Thus, to control the snake's body we must specify the actuation functions $\mathbf{u}(t) = [u_1(t), \ldots, u_i(t), \ldots, u_N(t)]'$, where $N = 20$.

The continuous vector-valued function of time $\mathbf{u}(t)$ is called the *controller* and its job is to produce locomotion. Controllers may be stored within the artificial animal's motor control center.

2.2 Objective Functional

A continuous *objective functional E* provides a quantitative measure of the progress of the locomotion learning process. The functional is the weighted sum of a term E_u that evaluates the controller $\mathbf{u}(t)$ and a term E_v that evaluates the motion $\mathbf{v}(t)$ that the controller produces in a time interval $t_0 \leq t \leq t_1$, with smaller values of E indicating better controllers $\mathbf{u}$. Mathematically,

$$E(\mathbf{u}(t)) = \int_{t_0}^{t_1} (\mu_1 E_u(\mathbf{u}(t)) + \mu_2 E_v(\mathbf{v}(t)))\, dt, \qquad (2)$$

where μ_1 and μ_2 are scalar weights. Fig. 2 illustrates this schematically.

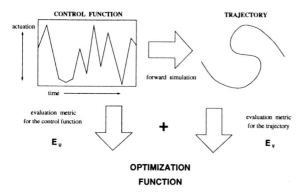

Figure 2: *The objective function guiding the optimization is a weighted sum of terms that evaluate the trajectory and the control function.*

It is important to note that the complexity of our models precludes the closed-form evaluation of E. As the figure indicates, to compute E, the artificial animal must first engage $\mathbf{u}(t)$ to produce a motion $\mathbf{v}(t)$ with its body (in order to evaluate term E_v). This is done through forward simulation of the biomechanical model over the time interval $t_0 \leq t \leq t_1$ using the controller $\mathbf{u}(t)$.

We may want to promote a preference for controllers with certain qualities via the controller evaluation term E_u. For example, we can guide the optimization of E by discouraging large, rapid fluctuations of $\mathbf{u}$, since chaotic actuations are usually energy inefficient. We encourage lower amplitude, smoother controllers through the function

$$E_u = \frac{1}{2}\left(\nu_1 \left|\frac{d\mathbf{u}}{dt}\right|^2 + \nu_2 \left|\frac{d^2\mathbf{u}}{dt^2}\right|^2\right), \qquad (3)$$

with weighting factors ν_1 and ν_2. The two component terms in (3) are potential energy densities of linear and cubic variational splines in time, respectively. The former penalizes actuation amplitudes, while the latter penalizes actuation variation.

The distinction between good and bad control functions also depends on the goals that the animal must accomplish. In our learning experiments we used trajectory criteria E_v such as the final distance to the goal, the deviation from a desired speed, etc. These and other criteria will be discussed shortly in conjunction with specific experiments.

2.3 Time and Frequency Domain Discrete Controllers

To solve the low level control problem, we must optimize the objective functional (2). This cannot be done analytically. We convert this continuous optimal control problem to an algebraic parameter optimization problem [5] by parameterizing the controller through discretization using basis functions. Mathematically, we express

$$u_i(t) = \sum_{j=1}^{M} u_i^j B^j(t), \qquad (4)$$

where the u_i^j are scalar parameters and the $B^j(t)$, $1 \leq j \leq M$ are (vector-valued) temporal basis functions. There are two qualitatively different choices of basis functions—local and global.

In the local discretization, the parameters u_i^j are nodal variables and the $B^j(t)$ can be spline basis functions. The simplest case is when the u_i^j are evenly distributed in the time interval and the $B^j(t)$ are tent functions centered on the nodes with support extending to nearest neighbor nodes, so that $\mathbf{u}(t)$ is the linear interpolation of the nodal variables (Fig. 3, top). Smoother B-splines can be used in a similar fashion. Since the nodal parameters are naturally ordered in a time sequence, we will refer to locally discretized controllers as *time domain controllers*.

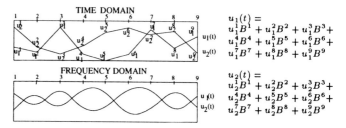

Figure 3: *Simple time domain controller (top) with two control functions $u_1(t)$ and $u_2(t)$. Each function is a piecewise linear polynomial generated by 9 control points. Simple frequency domain controller (bottom) with two control functions, each a sum of 9 sinusoidal basis functions $B^j(t) = \cos(\omega^j t + \phi^j)$.*

In the global discretization, the support of the $B^j(t)$ covers the entire temporal domain $t_0 \leq t \leq t_1$. A standard choice is sinusoidal basis functions $B^j(t) = \cos(\omega^j t + \phi^j)$ where ω^j is the angular frequency and ϕ^j is the phase, and the parameters u_i^j are amplitudes (Fig. 3, bottom). We will refer to controllers discretized globally using sinusoidal bases of different frequencies and phases as *frequency domain controllers*.

The time domain and frequency domain representations offer different benefits and drawbacks. The time domain controller yields a faster low-level learning rate. This issue is discussed in detail in Section 4.1. The frequency domain controller, on the other hand, does not require a change of basis during the abstraction process described in Section 3. It can also sometimes be extended arbitrarily in time since it favors periodicity.

2.4 Optimization of the Discrete Objective Function

Since $\mathbf{u}(t)$ has N basis functions, the discretized controller is represented using NM parameters. Substituting (4), into the continuous objective functional (2), we approximate it by the discrete *objective function* $E([u_1^1, \ldots, u_N^M]')$.

Learning low level control amounts to using an optimization algorithm to iteratively update the parameters of a time domain or frequency domain controller so as to maximize the discrete objective function and produce increasingly better locomotion. We have used both simulated annealing and the simplex method to optimize the objective function. The reader should refer to a text such as [12] for details about these optimization methods.

Simulated annealing has three features that make it particularly suitable for our application. First, it is applicable to problems with a large number of variables yielding search spaces large enough to make exhaustive search prohibitive. Second, it does not require gradient information about the objective function. Analytic gradients are not directly attainable in our situation since evaluating E requires a forward dynamic simulation of the animal. Third, it avoids getting trapped in local suboptima of E. In fact, given a sufficiently slow annealing schedule, it will find a global optimum of the objective functional. Robustness against local suboptima can be important in obtaining control functions that produce realistic motion. The benefit of using the simplex method over simulated annealing in some cases is its faster convergence rate. On the other hand, since it is a local optimization technique, strictly speaking, it can be applied successfully only to the class of optimization problems in which the topography of E is globally convex. Section 4.1 will describe in more detail the advantages and pitfalls of both methods when applied to the low level learning problem.

All of the biomechanical models described in Appendix A have demonstrated the ability to learn effective low level time domain locomotion controllers. Plates 1, 2, and 3 show frames from animations with controllers that have been learned by the snake, ray, and shark models, which produce natural and effective locomotion. Plate 3 illustrates a race among four sharks that have learned for different durations. The shark that is furthest from the camera has learned how to locomote for the shortest period of time, which yields muscle control functions that are essentially random and achieve negligible locomotion. Sharks closer to the camera have learned for progressively longer periods of time. The closest shark, which locomotes the best wins the race.

3 Abstracting High Level Control

It is time consuming to learn a good solution for a low level controller because of the high dimensionality of the problem (large NM), the lack of gradient information to accelerate the optimization of the objective functional, and the presence of suboptimal traps that must be avoided. Consequently, it is costly to produce animation by perpetually generating new controllers. The learning procedure must be able to abstract compact higher level controllers from the low level controllers that have been learned, retain the abstracted controllers, and apply them to future locomotion tasks.

The process of abstraction takes the form of a dimensionality reducing change of representation. More specifically, it seeks to compress the many parameters of the discrete controllers to a compact form in terms of a handful of basis functions. Natural, steady-state locomotion patterns tend to be quasi-periodic and they can be abstracted very effectively without substantial loss. The natural choice, therefore, is to represent abstracted controllers using the global sinusoidal basis functions discussed earlier. For the frequency domain controller, the dimensionality reduction is achieved trivially by retaining all basis functions whose amplitudes u_i^j exceed a low threshold and suppressing those below threshold. This results in a small set of significant basis functions with associated amplitudes that constitute the abstracted controller. To abstract a time domain controller, we apply the fast Fourier transform (FFT) [12] to the parameters of the time domain controller and then suppress the below-threshold amplitudes.

3.1 Using Abstracted Controllers

Typically, our artificial animals are put through a "basic training" regimen of primitive motor tasks that it must learn, such as locomoting at different speeds and executing turns of different radii. They learn effective low level controllers for each task and retain compact representations of these controllers through controller abstraction. The animals subsequently put the abstractions that they have learned into practice to accomplish higher level tasks, such as target tracking or leaping through the air. To this end, abstracted controllers are concatenated in sequence, with each controller slightly overlapping the next. To eliminate discontinuities, temporally adjacent controllers are smoothly blended together by linearly fading and summing them over a small, fixed region of overlap, approximately 5% of each controller (Fig. 4).

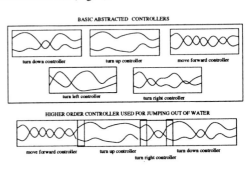

Figure 4: *Higher level controller for jumping out of water is constructed from a set of abstracted basic controllers.*

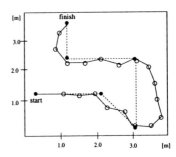

Figure 5: *The solid curve indicates the path of the fish tracking the goal. Black dots mark consecutive positions of the goal and white dots mark the starting point of a new controller.*

Currently we use abstracted controllers in two ways. In one scenario, the animated model has learned a repertoire of abstracted controllers that it applies in a greedy fashion to navigate in the direction of a target. It modifies its locomotion strategy periodically by invoking the abstracted controller that gives it the greatest immediate gain over the subsequent time interval. For example, Fig. 5 shows a path generated by the shark model using this method as it is presented with a series of targets. The shark has learned six basic abstracted controllers to accomplish this task: do-nothing, go-straight, sharp-turn-left, sharp-turn-right, wide-turn-left, and wide-turn-right. It then discovered how to sequence these controllers, and for what durations to apply them in order to locomote to successive targets indicated by black dots. The circles on the path in Fig. 5 indicate positions where the shark reevaluated its current strategy. Changes in the path's direction indicate that the shark has switched to a different controller which provides a bigger immediate gain. Plate 4 shows rendered frames from the locomotion animation with the targets rendered as red buoys. This method is inexpensive and can be made to work in real time. Unfortunately, the greedy strategy is bound to fail on a problem that requires careful planning.

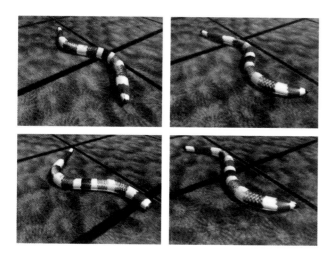

Plate 1: *Locomotion pattern learned by the artificial snake.*

Plate 4: *Target tracking using abstracted controllers (see text).*

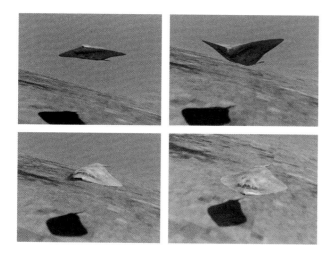

Plate 2: *Locomotion pattern learned by the artificial ray.*

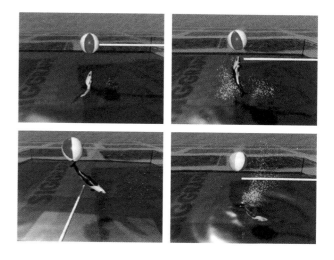

Plate 5: *SeaWorld tricks learned by the artificial dolphin.*

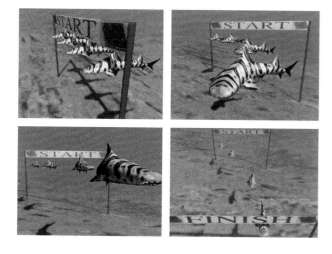

Plate 3: *Shark race illustrates the progress of learning (see text).*

The second method overcomes the limitations of the greedy strategy by learning composite abstracted controllers that accomplish complex locomotion tasks. Consider the spectacular stunts performed by marine mammals that elicit applause at theme parks like "SeaWorld". We can treat a leap through the air as a complex task that can be achieved using simpler tasks; e.g., diving deep beneath a suitable leap point, surfacing vigorously to gain momentum, maintaining balance during the ballistic flight through the air, and splashing down dramatically with a belly flop.

We have developed an automatic learning technique that constructs a macro jump controller of this sort as an optimized sequence of basic abstracted controllers. The optimization process is, in principle, similar to the one in low level learning. It uses simulated annealing for optimization, but rather than optimizing over nodal parameters or frequency parameters, it optimizes over the selection, ordering, and duration of abstracted controllers. Thus the animal model applying this method learns effective macro controllers of the type shown at the bottom of Fig. 4 by optimizing over a learned repertoire of basic abstracted controllers illustrated at the top of the figure.

3.2 Composing Macro Controllers

We first train the artificial dolphin so that it learns controllers for 5 basic motor tasks: turn-down, turn-up, turn-left, turn-right, and move-forward. We then give it the task of performing a stunt like the one described above and the dolphin discovers a combination of controllers that accomplishes the stunt. In particular, it discovers that it must build up momentum by thrusting from deep in the virtual pool of water up towards the surface and exploit this momentum to leap out of the water. Plate 5(a) shows a frame as the dolphin exits the water. The dolphin can also learn to perform tricks while in the air. Plate 5(b) shows it using its nose to bounce a large beach-ball off a support. The dolphin can learn to control the angular momentum of its body while exiting the water and while in ballistic flight so. that it can perform aerial spins and somersaults. Plate 5(c) shows it in the midst of a somersault in which it has just bounced the ball with its tail instead of its nose. Plate 5(d) shows the dolphin right after splashdown. In this instance it has made a dramatic bellyflop splash. By discovering controllers that enable it to control its body in these complex ways, the dolphin can amuse and entertain the animator, who would be hard pressed to design similar controllers by hand for a physics-based model with as many control parameters as the dolphin model has.

To train the dolphin to perform a variety of stunts we introduced additional "style" terms into the objective function that afford extra control on the animal's trajectory in the air. For example, a simple jump was learned by optimizing over the maximum height at some point in time. In order to train the dolphin to jump a hurdle, we introduced a term to control its orientation as it clears the hurdle—at the apex of its trajectory, it should be in a horizontal orientation and it should face downward upon reentry. The somersault controller was discovered by adding a term that encouraged maximum angular velocity of the body in flight. We can maximize or minimize the area of the animal's body that hits the water upon reentry for crowd-drenching splashes or for high scores from the judges for a clean dive.

Different style terms can, in principle, be added indefinitely to the control function. The only limitation seems to be the increasing complexity of the optimization. We have noted that although it can produce some interesting results, simulated annealing is not especially well suited to this kind of optimization problem. We suspect that this is due to the combinatorial nature of the problem and the fact that simulated annealing does not take advantage of partial solutions that it finds along the way, but instead starts with a new set of parameters at every iteration of the optimization process. Unfortunately, at a high level of abstraction sometimes even small changes in the set of parameters produce drastically different trajectories. Genetic algorithms may perform better on such problems.

4 Additional Experiments and Results

This section presents a more thorough experimental study of our approach and reports additional results.

4.1 Performance of the Optimizers

Fig. 6(a) compares the performance of the simplex method and simulated annealing in seeking optimal time and frequency domain controllers for the shark model given the task of locomoting to a specified goal location; i.e., $E_v = ||\mathbf{d}_g||^2$, where $\mathbf{d}_g$ is the separation vector between the nose node of the shark and the goal point. The term E_u (3) in the objective functional (2) was disabled for these tests ($\mu_2 = 0$). For simplicity, the 4 muscles in each segment were grouped into a single actuator ($N = 3$ actuators total), with the left muscle pair receiving contraction signals that are exactly out of phase with the right muscle pair. A time interval was discretized using $M = 15$ parameters; hence, the dimensionality of the search space was $NM = 45$.

Both methods converge to good time domain controllers. The simplex method yields a final objective functional value of $E_o = 0.49$ after approximately 500 iterations. Simulated annealing finds a slightly better solution, $E_o = 0.42$, but only after 3500 iterations. For frequency domain controllers, the results differ substantially. Simulated annealing performs almost as well as for the time domain controller, yielding an objective function value of $E_o = 0.52$ after 3500 iterations.[2] However, the simplex method does much worse— it fails to get below $E_o = 0.65$.

Fig. 6(b–c) compares the convergence for simulated annealing on both types of controllers. The results are better for the objective function represented in the time domain (Fig. 6(b)) than for the frequency domain representation (Fig. 6(c)). For the time domain representation we need approximately 700 iterations to get very close to the global minimum. The number of iterations for the frequency domain representation is much greater.

The above results suggest that it is much harder to optimize the objective using frequency domain controllers. To understand why, we plotted E against pairs of randomly chosen parameters u_i^j (labeled x and y in the plots), using both time and frequency domain representations. We stepped the selected parameters through a range of values while keeping the other parameters constant and evaluated the objective function repeatedly to obtain a 3D surface plot (each repetition required a forward simulation of the locomotion). The plot in Fig. 7(a) reveals the simple convex topography of E for time domain controllers, while the plot in Fig. 7(b) reveals the much more irregular, nonconvex topography of E for frequency domain controllers.

Evidently, small changes in the local basis functions of the time domain controller produce small, well-behaved changes in the value of the objective function. By contrast, small changes in the global basis functions of the frequency domain controller produce relatively larger, more irregular changes in the value of the objective function.

The many local minima in the topography of the objective function associated with the frequency domain controller lead to failure of the simplex method and they present more of a challenge to simulated annealing. The convex structure of the objective function associated with the time domain controller allows both annealing and simplex to converge very quickly. Moreover, they often yield better time domain controllers than frequency domain controllers. We conclude that the time domain controller representation is a worthwhile one.

4.2 Influencing Controllers via the Objective Functional

In Section 2.2 we discussed how the term E_u in (2) that evaluates controllers allows us to influence the motion. For example, we can discourage chaotic motions. This section investigates the effect of different E_u terms in more detail. Again, we employ the shark with the same goal E_v as in the previous section.

Fig. 8(a) shows the results obtained with the time domain representation for $\nu_2 = 0$, hence the discrete term $E_u = \nu_1/2h^2(u_i^{j+1} - u_i^j)^2$, where h is the timestep between nodal parameters. The objective function was evaluated for $\nu_1 = 0.0, 0.1, 0.2$ (top to bottom). As the value of ν_1 increases, both the amplitude and the frequency

---

[2] We start the simulated annealing procedure at the temperature $T_0 = 0.5$. The annealing schedule is $T_{i+1} = \alpha T_i$ where $0 \leq \alpha \leq 1$. Usually $\alpha = 0.9$, but Fig. 6(b–c) shows the results obtained with different schedules. The maximum number of steps before the temperature drop is $10NM$ and the minimum number of accepted perturbations before the temperature drop is NM For $N = 15$ it takes about one hour on an SGI Indigo workstation to get a solution for each control function. At each step the values of all parameters are perturbed randomly. The perturbation is bounded by 10% of the range of admissible values. So, for example, if the maximum contraction of the muscle is 20% of its relaxed length, each perturbation will be at most 2%. The bound on the perturbation remains fixed over the annealing process. This yields much faster convergence than if we decreased the magnitude of the perturbation with temperature.

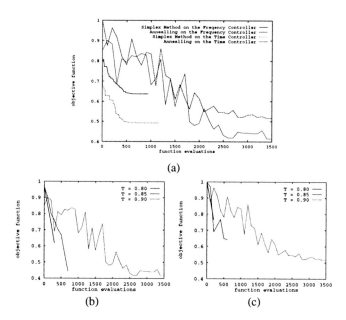

(a)

(b)   (c)

Figure 6: *(a) Performance comparison of the simplex method and of simulated annealing. Convergence rate of simulated annealing on the time domain controller (b) and on the frequency controller (c) with cooling rates:* $T_0 = 0.8$, $T_1 = 0.85$, *and* $T_2 = 0.9$.

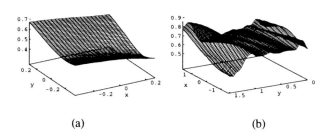

(a)   (b)

Figure 7: *Topography of objective function (in 2 dimensions) of time domain representation (a) and frequency domain representation (b).*

of the learned actuation functions drop and the shark learns locomotion controllers that result in less energy expenditure. Fig. 8(b) shows the results obtained with $\nu_1 = 0$, hence the discrete term $E_u = \nu_2/2h^4(u_i^{j+1} - 2u_i^j + u_i^{j-1})^2$ with $\nu_2 = 0.0, 0.002, 0.006$ (top to bottom). As the value of μ increases, the amplitude of the learned actuation functions remains constant and only the frequency decreases.

4.3 Abstracted Learning Results

Next, we report results for the shark and the snake in abstracting learned time domain controllers for straight locomotion and left turns. Right turn controllers were obtained by swapping signals sent to left and right actuators.

To obtain good abstracted controllers for the shark, it was sufficient for both straight motion and left turn to retain the single dominant mode of the FFT. Fig. 9(a) shows learned controllers for the shark swimming straight. In this experiment, the left and right muscle pairs in each segment constitute independent actuators, but note how the animal has learned to actuate its left muscles approximately out of phase with those on the right side. The posterior segment muscles contract with roughly half the frequency of the other muscles and the muscles on either side of the body are activated in sequence with a slight phase shift. For the swim left

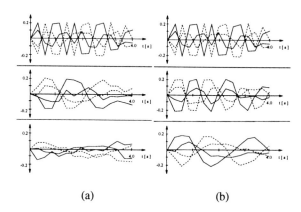

(a)   (b)

Figure 8: *Influence of* E_u *on controller: (a)* $\nu_2 = 0$; *(b)* $\nu_1 = 0$.

sequence (Fig. 9(b)) the posterior and anterior segment muscles on the right side of the body are essentially unused, while all the muscles on the left side of the body move approximately in phase.

It suffices to use two primary modes of the Fourier transform to get an effective abstracted controller for the turning snake. For straight locomotion (Fig. 9(c)) it is difficult to interpret the time domain actuation functions. However, if we look at the learned abstracted controller for straight locomotion, we can clearly see that the main modes have the same frequency, but their phase is shifted slightly, as expected. When a real snake turns, it first coils itself in the direction of the turn then switches back to its normal serpentine mode of locomotion. This pattern is revealed in the automatically learned turn controller shown in Fig. 9(d). First, all the muscles on the right side of the body relax and all the muscles on the left side contract. Then they resume their action for straight serpentine locomotion.

A   Biomechanical Model Structure and Simulation

Animals such as snakes, worms, fishes, and marine mammals, with highly flexible bodies are well suited to mechanical modeling using spring-mass systems. All of our animal body models consist of an internal biomechanical model with contractile muscles coupled to an external, texture-mapped, NURBS surface display model.

Fig. 1 shows the spring-mass system for the coral snake (*Micruroides euryxanthus*), which is similar to the one in [8]. Plate 1 shows the display model. The muscle springs can contract to 30% of their relaxed length. The body mass is distributed evenly among all nodes.

Fig. 10 shows the spring-mass system for the Leopard shark (*Triakis semifasciata*) [2], which is similar to the fish model in [17]. Plates 3 and 4 show the display model. The 4 posterior muscles can contract to 10% of their relaxed length; the 8 other muscles to 20%. The figure specifies the nodal mass distribution.

We model a Heaviside's dolphin (*Cephalorhynchus heavisidii*) [11] (Plate 5 shows the display model) straightforwardly by turning the shark spring-mass system on its side, such that the muscles serve as caudal (tail) fin elevator and depressors. We equip the dolphin with functional pectoral fins that allow it to roll, pitch, and yaw in the water (see [17] for details about fins).

Fig. 11 shows the spring-mass system for the Kuhl's stingray (*Dasyatis kuhlii*) [13]. Plate 2 shows the display model. Four left and 4 right elevator muscles and an equal number of depressor muscles are capable of flexing the wings by contracting to 20% of their relaxed length. Mass is distributed evenly among all the nodes.

To model snake locomotion, we use directional friction against the ground which generates reaction forces that move the body forward, as described in [8]. To model marine animal locomotion, we compute hydrodynamic reaction forces acting on each of the

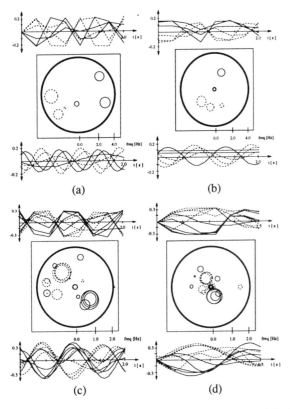

(a)   (b)

(c)   (d)

Figure 9: *Learned controller for the swim straight (a) and the left turn (b) for the shark. Learned controller for the straight motion (c) and the left turn (d) for the snake. For each part: (top) learned time domain controller (dotted lines indicate actuator functions for left side of body, solid lines indicate actuator functions for right side); (center) primary modes of controller FFT (radius of circles indicates mode amplitudes, radial distances from center of surrounding circle indicate frequencies, angular positions within surrounding circle indicate phases); (bottom) abstracted controller obtained by retaining primary modes.*

model's faces, as described in [17]. These forces produce external nodal forces f_i in the equations of motion (1).

We use a stable, efficient semi-implicit Euler method [12] to numerically integrate these ODEs. It is implicit in the internal forces on the lhs of (1) and explicit in the external forces f_i.

Acknowledgments

We thank Xiaoyuan Tu, who developed the original fish biomechanical model, for her software and cooperation, and Geoffrey Hinton for valuable discussions. This work was made possible by a grant from the Natural Sciences and Engineering Research Council of Canada. DT is a fellow of the Canadian Institute for Advanced Research.

References

[1] L. S. Brotman and A. N. Netravali. Motion interpolation by optimal control. Proc. ACM SIGGRAPH, 22(4):309–407, 1988.

[2] J. I. Castro. *The Sharks of North American Waters*. Texas Unviersity Press, 1983.

[3] M. F. Cohen. Interactive spacetime control for animation. Proc. ACM SIGGRAPH, 26(2):293–301, 1992.

[4] C. H. Ernst. *Venomous Reptiles of North America*. Smithsonian Institution Press, 1992.

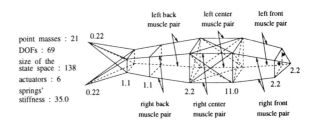

Figure 10: *The shark biomechanical model has six actuators consisting of a pair of muscles that share the same activation function. The numbers along the body indicate the mass of each point in the corresponding cross sectional plane. The cross-springs that maintain the structural integrity of the body are indicated in one of the segments only.*

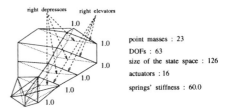

Figure 11: *The ray biomechanical model has four sets of actuators: left and right depressors and left and right elevators. The numbers along the body indicate the mass of each point in the corresponding cross sectional plane. The cross-springs that maintain the structural integrity of the body are indicated in one of the segments only.*

[5] C. J. Goh and K. L. Teo. Control parameterization: A unified approach to optimal control problems with general constraints. *Automatica*, 24:3–18, 1988.

[6] R. Grzeszczuk. Automated learning of muscle based locomotion through control abstraction. Master's thesis, Dept. of Comp. Sci., Univ. of Toronto, Toronto, ON, January 1994.

[7] R. McNeill Alexander. *Exploring Biomechanics: Animals in Motion*. Scientific American Library, New York, 1992.

[8] G.S.P. Miller. The motion dynamics of snakes and worms. Proc. ACM SIGGRAPH, 22(4):169–177, 1988.

[9] J. T. Ngo and J. Marks. Spacetime constraints revisited. Proc. ACM SIGGRAPH, 27(2):343–351, 1993.

[10] M. G. Pandy, F. C. Anderson, and D. G. Hull. A parameter optimization approach for the optimal control of large-scale musculoskeletal systems. *Transactions of the ASME*, 114(450), November 1992.

[11] Best P.B. and Abernethy R. B. Heaviside's dolphin. In *Handbook of Marine Mammals*, volume 5, pages 289–310. Academic Press, 1994.

[12] W. H. Press, B. Flannery, et al. *Numerical Recipes: The Art of Scientific Computing, Second Edition*. Cambridge University Press, 1992.

[13] J. E. Rendal, Allen G. R., and Steene R. C. *Fishes of the Great Barrier Reef and Coral Sea*. Univ. of Hawaii Press, Honolulu, HI, 1990.

[14] G. Risdale. Connectionist modeling of skill dynamics. *Journal of Visualization and Computer Animation*, 1(2):66–72, 1990.

[15] K. Sims. Evolving virtual creatures. Proc. ACM SIGGRAPH, pages 15–22, 1994.

[16] D. Terzopoulos, X. Tu, and R. Grzeszczuk. Artificial fishes: Autonomous locomotion, perception, behavior, and learning in a simulated physical world. *Artificial Life*, 1(4):327–351, 1994.

[17] X. Tu and D. Terzopoulos. Artificial fishes: Physics, locomotion, perception, behavior. Proc. ACM SIGGRAPH, pages 43–50, 1994.

[18] M. van de Panne and E. Fiume. Sensor-actuator networks. Proc. ACM SIGGRAPH, 27(2):335–343, 1993.

[19] A. Witkin and M. Kass. Spacetime constraints. Proc. ACM SIGGRAPH, 22(4):159–167, 1988.

Animating Human Athletics

Jessica K. Hodgins   Wayne L. Wooten

David C. Brogan   James F. O'Brien

College of Computing, Georgia Institute of Technology

ABSTRACT

This paper describes algorithms for the animation of men and women performing three dynamic athletic behaviors: running, bicycling, and vaulting. We animate these behaviors using control algorithms that cause a physically realistic model to perform the desired maneuver. For example, control algorithms allow the simulated humans to maintain balance while moving their arms, to run or bicycle at a variety of speeds, and to perform a handspring vault. Algorithms for group behaviors allow a number of simulated bicyclists to ride as a group while avoiding simple patterns of obstacles. We add secondary motion to the animations with spring-mass simulations of clothing driven by the rigid-body motion of the simulated human. For each simulation, we compare the computed motion to that of humans performing similar maneuvers both qualitatively through the comparison of real and simulated video images and quantitatively through the comparison of simulated and biomechanical data.

Key Words and Phrases: computer animation, human motion, motion control, dynamic simulation, physically realistic modeling.

INTRODUCTION

People are skilled at perceiving the subtle details of human motion. We can, for example, often identify friends by the style of their walk when they are still too far away to be recognizable otherwise. If synthesized human motion is to be compelling, we must create actors for computer animations and virtual environments that appear realistic when they move. Realistic human motion has several components: the kinematics and dynamics of the figure must be physically correct and the control algorithms must make the figure perform in ways that appear natural. We are interested in the last of these: the design of control strategies for natural-looking human motion.

In particular, this paper describes algorithms that allow a rigid-body model of a man or woman to stand, run, and turn at a variety of speeds, to ride a bicycle on hills and around obstacles, and to perform a gymnastic vault. Figure 1 shows two examples of the animated behaviors. The rigid-body models of the man and woman

College of Computing, Georgia Institute of Technology, Atlanta, GA 30332-0280. [jkh|wlw|dbrogan|obrienj]@cc.gatech.edu

Permission to make digital/hard copy of part or all of this work for personal or classroom use is granted without fee provided that copies are not made or distributed for profit or commercial advantage, the copyright notice, the title of the publication and its date appear, and notice is given that copying is by permission of ACM, Inc. To copy otherwise, to republish, to post on servers, or to redistribute to lists, requires prior specific permission and/or a fee.

Figure 1: Images of a runner on the track in the 1996 Olympic Stadium and a gymnast performing a handspring vault in the Georgia Dome.

are realistic in that their mass and inertia properties are derived from data in the biomechanics literature and the degrees of freedom of the joints are chosen so that each behavior can be completed in a natural-looking fashion.

Although the behaviors are very different in character, the control algorithms are built from a common toolbox: state machines are used to enforce a correspondence between the phase of the behavior and the active control laws, synergies are used to cause several degrees of freedom to act with a single purpose, limbs without required actions in a particular state are used to reduce disturbances to the system, inverse kinematics is used to compute the joint angles that would cause a foot or hand to reach a desired location, and the low-level control is performed with proportional-derivative control laws.

We have chosen to animate running, bicycling, and vaulting because each behavior contains a significant dynamic component. For these behaviors, the dynamics of the model constrain the motion and limit the space that must be searched to find control laws for natural-looking motion. This property is most evident in the gymnastic vault. The gymnast is airborne for much of the maneuver, and the control algorithms can influence the internal motion of the joints but not the angular momentum of the system as a whole. The runner, on the other hand, is in contact with the ground much of the time and the joint torques computed by the control algorithms directly control many of the details of the motion. Because the dynamics do not provide as many constraints on the motion, much more effort went into tuning the motion of the runner to look natural than into tuning the motion of the gymnast.

Computer animations and interactive virtual environments require a source of human motion. The approach used here, dynamic simulation coupled with control algorithms, is only one of several options. An alternative choice, motion capture, is now widely available in commercial software. The difficulty of designing control algorithms has prevented the value of simulation from being demonstrated for systems with internal sources of energy, such as humans. However, simulation has several potential advantages over motion capture. Given robust control algorithms, simulated motion can easily be computed to produce similar but different motions while maintaining physical realism (running at 4 m/s rather than 6 m/s for example). Real-time simulations also allow the motion of an animated character to be truly interactive, an important property for virtual environments in which the actor must move realistically in response to changes in the environment and in response to the actions of the user. And finally, when the source of motion is dynamic simulation we have the opportunity to use multiple levels of simulation to generate either secondary motion such as the movement of clothing and hair or high-level motion such as obstacle avoidance and group behaviors.

BACKGROUND

Research in three fields is relevant to the problem of animating human motion: robotics, biomechanics, and computer graphics. Researchers in robotics have explored control techniques for legged robots that walk, run, balance, and perform gymnastic maneuvers. While no robot has been built with a complexity similar to that of the human body, control strategies for simpler machines provide basic principles that can be used to design control strategies for humanlike models.

Raibert and his colleagues built and controlled a series of dynamic running machines, ranging from a planar machine with one telescoping leg to three-dimensional machines that ran on two or four legs. These machines walked, jumped, changed gait, climbed stairs, and performed gymnastic maneuvers ([14–16], [26–28]). The control algorithms for human running described in this paper build on these control algorithms by extending them for systems with many more controlled degrees of freedom and more stringent requirements on the style of the motion.

Biomechanics provides the data and hypotheses about human motion required to ensure that the computed motion resembles that of a human performing similar maneuvers. The biomechanics literature contains motion capture data, force plate data, and muscle activation records for many human behaviors. These data were used to tune the control algorithms for running, bicycling, and balancing. Cavagna presents energy curves for walking and running as well as studies of energy usage during locomotion[8]. McMahon provides graphs of stance duration, flight duration, and step length as a function of forward speed[21]. Gregor surveys biomechanical studies of bicyclists[13]. Takei presents biomechanical data of elite female gymnasts performing a handspring vault and relates the data to the scores that the gymnasts received in competition[33].

Many researchers in computer graphics have explored the difficult problems inherent in animating human motion. The Jack system developed at the University of Pennsylvania contains kinematic and dynamic models of humans based on biomechanical data[1]. It allows the interactive positioning of the body and has several built-in behaviors including balance, reaching and grasping, and walking and running behaviors that use generalizations of motion capture data[18].

Bruderlin and Calvert used a simplified dynamic model and control algorithms to generate the motions of a walking human[6]. The leg model included a telescoping leg with two degrees of freedom for the stance phase and a compound pendulum model for the swing phase. A foot, upper body, and arms were added to the model kinematically, and were made to move in an oscillatory pattern similar to that observed in humans. Pai programmed a walking behavior for a dynamic model of a human torso and legs in a high-level fashion by describing a set of time-varying constraints, such as, "maintain ground clearance during leg swing," "lift and put down a foot," "keep the torso vertical," and "support the torso with the stance leg" [25].

None of these approaches to generating motion for animation are automatic because each new behavior requires additional work on the part of the researcher. In recent years, the field has seen the development of a number of techniques for automatically generating motion for new behaviors and new creatures. Witkin and Kass[38], Cohen[10], and Brotman and Netravali[5] treat the problem of automatically generating motion as a trajectory optimization problem. Another approach finds a control algorithm instead of a desired trajectory ([37], [36], [23], [31], and [32]). In contrast, the control algorithms described in this paper were designed by hand, using a toolbox of control techniques, our physical intuition about the behaviors, observations of humans performing the tasks, and biomechanical data. While automatic techniques would be preferable to hand design, automatic techniques have not yet been developed that can find solutions for systems with the number of controlled degrees of freedom needed for a plausible model of the human body. Furthermore, although the motion generated by automatic techniques is appealing, much of it does not appear natural in the sense of resembling the motion of a biological system. We do not yet know whether this discrepancy is because only relatively simple models have been used or because of the constraints and optimization criteria that were chosen.

DYNAMIC BEHAVIORS

The motion of each behavior described in this paper is computed using dynamic simulation. Each simulation contains the equations of motion for a rigid-body model of a human and environment (ground, bicycle, and vault), control algorithms for balancing, running, bicycling, or vaulting, a graphical image for viewing the motion, and a user interface for changing the parameters of the simulation. The user is provided with limited high-level control of the animation. For example, the desired velocity and facing direction for the bicyclist and runner are selected by the user. During each simulation time step, the control algorithm computes desired positions and velocities for each joint based on the state of the system, the requirements of the task and input from the user. Proportional-derivative servos compute joint torques based on the desired and actual value of each joint. The equations of motion of the system are integrated forward in time taking into account the internal joint torques and the external forces and torques from interactions with the ground plane or other objects. The details of the human model and the control algorithm for each behavior are described below.

Human Models

The human models we used to animate the dynamic behaviors were constructed from rigid links connected by rotary joints with one, two or three degrees of freedom. The dynamic models were derived from the graphical models shown in figure 2 by computing the mass and moment of inertia of each body part using algorithms for computing the moment of inertia of a polygonal object of uniform density[20] and density data measured from cadavers[11]. We also verified that the model could perform maneuvers that rely on the parameters of the dynamic system using data from Frohlich[12].

The controlled degrees of freedom of the model are shown in figure 2. Each internal joint of the model has a very simple muscle model, a torque source, that allows the control algorithms to apply

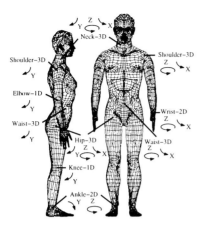

Figure 2: The controlled degrees of freedom of the human model. The gymnast represented in the figure has 15 body segments and a total of 30 controlled degrees of freedom. The runner has 17 body segments and 30 controlled degrees of freedom (two-part feet with a one degree of freedom joint at the ball of the foot and only one degree of freedom at the ankle), The bicyclist has 15 body segments and 22 controlled degrees of freedom (only one degree of freedom at the neck, hips, and ankles). The directions of the arrows indicates the positive direction of rotation for each degree of freedom. The polygonal models were purchased from Viewpoint Datalabs.

a torque between the two links that form the joint. The equations of motion for each system were generated using a commercially available package[30]. The points of contact between the feet and the ground, the bicycle wheels and the ground, and the gymnast's hands and the vault are modeled using constraints. The errors for the constraints are the relative accelerations, velocities, and positions of one body with respect to the other. The constraints are stabilized using Baumgarte stabilization[2].

Running

Running is a cyclic behavior in which the legs swing fore and aft and provide support for the body in alternation. Because the legs perform different functions during the phases of the locomotion cycle, the muscles are used for different control actions at different times in the cycle. When the foot of the simulated runner is on the ground, the ankle, knee, and hip provide support and balance. During the flight phase, a leg is swung forward in preparation for the next touchdown. These distinct phases and corresponding changes in control actions make a state machine a natural tool for selecting the control actions that should be active at a particular time. The state machine and transition events used for the simulation of running are shown in figure 3.

To interact with the animation of the runner, the user specifies desired values for the magnitude of the velocity on the ground plane and the facing direction. The control laws for each state compute joint torques that move the velocity and facing direction toward these desired values while maintaining balance. The animated runner can run at speeds between 2.5 m/s and 5 m/s and runs along a user-defined path.

We call the leg that is on the ground or actively being positioned for touchdown the *active leg*. The other leg is called the *idle leg*. During flight, the active leg is swung forward in anticipation of touchdown. Using the degrees of freedom of the leg in a synergistic fashion, the foot is positioned at touchdown to correct for errors in forward speed and to maintain balance. Forward speed is controlled by placing the average point of support during stance underneath the hip and taking into account the change in contact point from heel to metatarsus during stance. At touchdown, the desired distance from

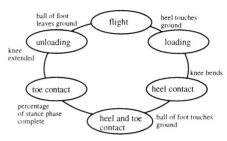

Figure 3: A state machine is used to determine the control actions that should be active for running given the current state of the system. The transition events are computed for the active leg. At liftoff the active and idle legs switch roles. The states correspond to the points of contact on the ground: flight, heel contact, heel and toe contact, and toe contact. The other two states, loading and unloading, are of very short duration and ensure that the foot is firmly planted on the ground or free of the ground before the control actions for stance or flight are invoked.

the hip to the heel projected onto the ground plane is

$$x_{hh} = 1/2(t_s\dot{x} - \cos(\theta)l_f) + k(\dot{x} - \dot{x}_d) \quad (1)$$
$$y_{hh} = 1/2(t_s\dot{y} - \sin(\theta)l_f) + k(\dot{y} - \dot{y}_d) \quad (2)$$

where t_s is an estimate of the period of time that the foot will be in contact with the ground (based on the previous stance duration), $\dot{x}$ and $\dot{y}$ are the velocities of the runner on the plane, $\dot{x}_d$ and $\dot{y}_d$ are the desired velocities, θ is the facing direction of the runner, l_f is the distance from the heel to the ball of the foot, and k is a gain for the correction of errors in speed. The length of the leg at touchdown is fixed and is used to calculate the vertical distance from the hip to the heel, z_{hh}. The disturbances caused by the impact of touchdown can be reduced by decreasing the relative speed between the foot and the ground at touchdown. This technique is called *ground speed matching* in the biomechanical literature. In this control system, ground speed matching is accomplished by swinging the hip further forward in the direction of travel during flight and moving it back just before touchdown.

The equations for x_{hh}, y_{hh}, and z_{hh}, and the inverse kinematics of the leg are used to compute the desired knee and hip angles at touchdown for the active leg. The angle of the ankle is chosen so that the toe will not touch the ground at the same time as the heel at the beginning of stance.

During stance, the knee acts as a passive spring to store the kinetic energy that the system had at touchdown. The majority of the vertical thrust is provided by the ankle joint. During the first part of stance, *heel contact*, the toe moves toward the ground because the contact point on the heel is behind the ankle joint. Contact of the ball of the foot triggers the transition from *heel contact* to *heel and toe contact*. The transition from *heel and toe contact* to *toe contact* occurs when the time since touchdown is equal to a percentage of the expected stance duration (30-50% depending on forward speed). After the transition, the ankle joint is extended, causing the heel to lift off the ground and adding energy to the system for the next flight phase.

Throughout stance, proportional-derivative servos are used to compute torques for the hip joint of the stance leg that will cause the attitude of the body (roll, pitch, and yaw) to move toward the desired values. The desired angle for roll is zero except during turning when the body leans into the curve. The desired angle for pitch is inclined slightly forward, and the desired angle for yaw is set by the user or the higher-level control algorithms for grouping behaviors and obstacle avoidance.

The idle leg plays an important role in locomotion by reducing disturbances to the body attitude caused by the active leg as it swings

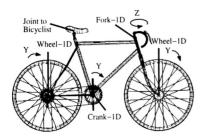

Figure 4: The four degrees of freedom of the bicycle model. The direction of the arrows indicates the positive direction of rotation for each degree of freedom. The polygonal model is a modification of a model purchased from Viewpoint Datalabs.

forward and in toward the centerline in preparation for touchdown. The idle leg is shortened so that the toe does not stub the ground, and the hip angles mirror the motion of the active leg to reduce the net torque on the body:

$$\alpha_{x_d} = \alpha_{x_{lo}} - (\beta_{x_d} - \beta_{x_{lo}}) \qquad (3)$$
$$\alpha_{y_d} = \alpha_{y_{lo}} - (\beta_{y_d} - \beta_{y_{lo}}) \qquad (4)$$

where α_{x_d} and α_{y_d} are the desired rotations of the idle hip with respect to the pelvis, $\alpha_{x_{lo}}$ and $\alpha_{y_{lo}}$ are the rotation of the idle hip at the previous liftoff, β_{x_d} and β_{y_d} are the desired position of the active hip, and $\beta_{x_{lo}}$ and $\beta_{y_{lo}}$ are the position of the active hip at the previous liftoff. The mirroring action of the idle leg is modified by the restriction that the legs should not collide as they pass each other during stance.

The shoulder joint swings the arms fore and aft in a motion that is synchronized with the motion of the legs:

$$\gamma_{y_d} = k\alpha_y + \gamma_0 \qquad (5)$$

where γ_{y_d} is the desired fore/aft angle for the shoulder, k is a scaling factor, α_y is the fore-aft hip angle for the leg on the opposite side of the body, and γ_0 is an offset. The other two degrees of freedom in the shoulder (x and z) and the elbows also follow a cyclic pattern with the same period as γ_{y_d}. The motion of the upper body is important in running because the counter oscillation of the arms reduces the yaw oscillation of the body caused by the swinging of the legs. However, the details of the motion of the upper body are not constrained by the dynamics of the task and amateur athletes use many different styles of arm motion when they run. Observations of human runners were used to tune the oscillations of the arms to produce a natural-looking gait.

The control laws compute desired values for each joint and proportional-derivative servos are used to control the position of all joints. For each internal joint the control equation is

$$\tau = k(\theta_d - \theta) + k_v(\dot{\theta}_d - \dot{\theta}) \qquad (6)$$

The desired values used in the proportional-derivative servos are computed as trajectories from the current value of the joint to the desired value computed by the control laws. Eliminating large step changes in the errors used in the proportional-derivative servos smoothes the simulated motion.

Bicycling

The bicyclist controls the facing direction and speed of the bicycle by applying forces to the handlebars and pedals with his hands and feet. The rider is attached to the bicycle by a pivot joint between the bicycle seat and the pelvis (figure 4). Spring and damper systems connect the hands to the handlebars, the feet to the

pedals, and the crank to the rear wheel. The connecting springs are two-sided and the bicyclist is able to pull up on the pedals as if the bicycle were equipped with toe-clips and a fixed gear (no freewheel). The connection between the crank and the rear wheel includes an adjustable gear ratio. The bicycle wheels have a rolling resistance proportional to the velocity.

The control algorithm adjusts the velocity of the bicycle by using the legs to produce a torque at the crank. The desired torque at the crank is

$$\tau_{\mathrm{crank}} = k(v - v_d) \qquad (7)$$

where k is a gain, v is the magnitude of the bicyclist's velocity, and v_d is the desired velocity. The force applied by each leg depends on the angle of the crank because we assume that the legs are most effective at pushing downwards. For example, the front leg can generate a positive torque and the rear leg can generate a negative torque when the crank is horizontal. To compensate for the crank position, the desired forces for the legs are scaled by a weighting function between zero and one that depends on the crank position, θ_{crank}:

$$w = \frac{\sin(\theta_{\mathrm{crank}}) + 1}{2}. \qquad (8)$$

θ_{crank} is zero when the crank is vertical and the right foot is higher than the left. If $\tau_{\mathrm{crank}} > 0$, the force on the pedal that the legs should produce is

$$f_l = \frac{w\tau_{\mathrm{crank}}}{l} \qquad (9)$$
$$f_r = \frac{(1 - w)\tau_{\mathrm{crank}}}{l} \qquad (10)$$

where f_l and f_r are the desired forces from the left and right legs respectively, and l is the length of a crank arm. If τ_{crank} is less than zero, then the equations for the left and right leg are switched. An inverse kinematic model of the legs is used to compute hip and knee torques that will produce the desired pedal forces.

To steer the bicycle and control the facing direction, the control algorithm computes a desired angle for the fork based on the errors in roll and yaw:

$$\theta_{\mathrm{fork}} = -k_\alpha(\alpha - \alpha_d) - k_{\dot{\alpha}}\dot{\alpha} + k_\beta(\beta - \beta_d) + k_{\dot{\beta}}\dot{\beta} \qquad (11)$$

where α, α_d, and $\dot{\alpha}$ are the roll angle, desired roll, and roll velocity and β, β_d, and $\dot{\beta}$ are the yaw angle, desired yaw, and yaw velocity. k_α, $k_{\dot{\alpha}}$, k_β, and $k_{\dot{\beta}}$ are gains. The desired yaw angle is set by the user or high-level control algorithms; the desired roll angle is zero. Inverse kinematics is used to compute the shoulder and elbow angles that will position the hands on the handlebars with a fork angle of θ_{fork}. Proportional-derivative servos move the shoulder and elbow joints toward those angles.

These control laws leave the motion of several of the joints of the bicyclist unspecified. The wrists and the waist are held at a nearly constant angle with proportional-derivative controllers. The ankle joints are controlled to match data recorded from human subjects[9].

Vaulting and Balancing

To perform a vault, the gymnast uses a spring board to launch herself toward the vaulting horse, pushes off the horse with her hands, and lands on her feet on the other side of the horse. The vault described here, a handspring vault, is one in which the gymnast performs a full somersault over the horse while keeping her body extended in a layout position. This vault is structured by a state machine with six states: hurdle step, board contact, first flight, horse contact, second flight, and landing. The animation of the handspring vault begins during the flight phase preceding the touchdown on the springboard.

The initial conditions were estimated from video footage (forward velocity is 6.75 m/s and the height of the center of mass is 0.9 m).

The simulated gymnast lands on a spring board that deflects based on a linear spring and damper model. When the springboard reaches maximum deflection, the control system extends the knees, pushing on the springboard and adds energy to the system. As the springboard rebounds, it launches the gymnast into the air and the first flight state begins. Using a technique called *blocking*, the control system positions the hips forward before touchdown on the springboard so that much of the horizontal velocity at touchdown is transformed into rotational and vertical velocity at liftoff.

During the first flight state, the control system prepares to put the gymnast's hands on the horse by positioning her shoulders on the line between the shoulders and the desired hand position on the vault:

$$\gamma_{y_d} = \lambda_y - \phi \qquad (12)$$

where γ_{y_d} is the desired shoulder angle relative to the body, λ_y is the angle between vertical and a vector from the shoulder to the desired hand position on the vault, and ϕ is the pitch angle of the body (with respect to vertical). Because the shoulders are moving toward the vault during flight, this control law performs ground speed matching between the hands and the horse. The wrists are controlled to cause the hands to hit the horse palm down and parallel to the surface of the horse.

During the next state, the gymnast's hands contact the vault and the arms are held straight. No torque is applied at the shoulder or the wrist and the angular and forward velocity of the gymnast carries her over the horse as she performs the handspring. When the hands leave the vault, the second flight phase begins.

During the second flight state, the control system maintains a layout position with the feet spread slightly to give a larger area of support at touchdown. When the feet hit the ground, the control system must remove the horizontal and rotational energy from the somersault and establish an upright, balanced position. The knees and waist are bent to absorb energy. Vaulters land on soft, 4 cm thick mats that help to reduce their kinetic energy. In our simulation, the behavior of the mat is approximated by reducing the stiffness of the ground. When the simulated gymnast's center of mass passes over the center of the polygon formed by the feet, a balance controller is activated. After the gymnast is balanced, the control system straightens the knees and hips to cause the gymnast to stand up.

The balance controller not only allows the gymnast to stand up after a landing but also compensates for disturbances resulting from the motion of other parts of the body while she is standing. For example, if the gymnast bends forward, the ankles are servoed to move the center of mass of the gymnast backwards. The balance controller also allows the simulated gymnast throw her arms back in a gesture of success after the vault and to take a bow.

HIGHER-LEVEL BEHAVIORS

The control algorithms provide the animator with control over the velocity and facing direction of the runner and bicyclist. However, choreographing an animation with many bicyclists or runners would be difficult because the animator must ensure that they do not run into each other while moving as a group and avoiding obstacles. Building on Reynolds[29], we implemented an algorithm that allows bicyclists to move as a group and to avoid simple configurations of obstacles on the terrain. The performance of the algorithm for a simulation of a bike race on a hill is shown in figure 5.

In contrast to most previous implementations of algorithms for group behaviors, we use this algorithm to control a group where the members have significant dynamics. The problem of controlling these individuals more closely resembles that faced by

biological systems because each individual has limited acceleration, velocity, and turning radius. Furthermore, the control algorithms for bicycling are inexact, resulting both in transient and steady-state errors in the control of velocity and facing direction.

The algorithm for group behaviors computes a desired position for each individual by averaging the location and velocity of its visible neighbors, a desired group velocity, and a desired position with respect to the visible obstacles. The details of this computation are presented in Brogan and Hodgins[4]. This desired position is then used as an input to the control algorithm for the bicyclist. The desired position is known only to the individual bicyclist and his navigational intent is communicated to the other cyclists only through their observation of his actions.

The desired position for the bicycle that is computed by the algorithm for group behaviors is used to compute a desired velocity and facing direction:

$$v_d = k_p e + k_v(v_{gl} - v) \qquad (13)$$

where v_d is the desired velocity in the plane, v is the actual velocity, e is the error between the current position of the bicyclist and the desired position, k_p is the proportional gain on position, k_v is the proportional gain on velocity, and v_{gl} is the group's global desired velocity (specified by the user).

SECONDARY MOTIONS

While we are often not consciously aware of secondary motions, they can add greatly to the perceived realism of an animated scene. This property is well known to traditional animators, and much of the work in creating believable hand animation focuses on animating the motion of objects other than the primary actors. This effect can be duplicated in computer animation by identifying the objects in the environment that should exhibit passive secondary behavior and including a simulation suitable for modeling that type of behavior. In some cases, the simulated motion of the passive secondary objects can be driven by the rigid body motion of the primary actors. As examples of this approach, we have simulated sweatpants and splashing water. The behavior of the sweatpants is computed by using the motion of the simulated runner to drive a passive system that approximates the behavior of cloth. Similarly, the motion of splashing water is driven by the motion of a platform diver when it impacts the water ([24] and [35]). Ideally, all objects that do not have active control could be implemented in this fashion. Unfortunately, computational resources and an incomplete understanding of physical processes restrict the size and types of the passive systems that we are able to simulate.

Several methods for physically based animation of cloth have been described in the literature ([7], [22], [3], and [34]). Carignan[7] implemented a system that uses the motion of a kinematic human walker developed by Laurent[19] to drive the action of the cloth. Our approach is similar to that described by Terzopoulos and Fleischer[34]. We use an elastic model to define the properties of the cloth. Collisions are detected using a hierarchical object grouping algorithm and resolved using inverse dynamics to compute reaction forces. Although our cloth model is not significantly different from previous methods, our approach of using dynamically correct rigid body motion to drive the passive system results in an animated scene where all the motion is governed by a consistent set of physically based rules.

DISCUSSION

This paper presents algorithms that allow an animator to generate motion for several dynamic behaviors. Animations of platform diving, unicycle riding and pumping a swing have been described

Figure 5: Images of an athlete wearing sweat pants running on a quarter mile track in the 1996 Olympic Stadium, a gymnast performing a handspring vault in the Georgia Dome, a bicyclist avoiding a jogger, a group of bicyclists riding around a corner during a race, a group of runners crossing the finish line, and a comparison between a simulated and a human runner on a treadmill. In each case, the spacing of the images in time is equal with the stadium runner at intervals of 0.066 s, the gymnast at 0.5 s, the single bicyclist at 1.0 s, the group of bicyclists at 0.33 s, the group of runners at 0.5 s and the composite of the simulated and human runner at 0.066 s.

elsewhere ([35], [17]). Taken together with previous work, these dynamic behaviors represent a growing library. While these behaviors do not represent all of human motion or even of human athletic endeavors, an animation package with ten times this many behaviors would have sufficient functionality to be interesting to students and perhaps even to professional animators.

Several open questions remain before the value of simulation as a source of motion for animation and virtual environments can be conclusively demonstrated:

How can we make it easier to generate control algorithms for a new behavior? This paper partially addresses that question by presenting a toolbox of techniques that can be used to construct the control algorithms for a set of diverse behaviors. However, developing sufficient physical intuition about a new behavior to construct a robust control algorithm remains time consuming. We hope that these examples represent a growing understanding of the strategies that are useful in controlling simulations of human motion and that this understanding will lead to the development of more automatic techniques.

What can we do to reduce the number of new behaviors that need to be developed? One idea that has been explored by researchers in the domain of motion capture and keyframing is to perform transitions between behaviors in an automatic or semiautomatic fashion. Such transitions may be much more amenable to automatic design than the design of entire control algorithms for dynamic simulations.

What rules can we add to the system to improve the naturalness of the motion? The techniques presented here are most effective for behaviors with a significant dynamic component because the dynamics constrain the number of ways in which the task can be accomplished. When the gross characteristics of the motion are not constrained by the dynamics of the system, the task can be completed successfully but in a way that appears unnatural. For example, the simulated runner can run while holding his arms fixed at his sides, but an animation of that motion would be amusing rather than realistic. Humans are strong enough and dextrous enough that simple arm movements such as picking up a coffee cup can be completed in many different ways. In contrast, only good athletes can perform a handspring vault and the variations seen in their performances are relatively small. When the dynamics do not significantly constrain the task, the control algorithms must be carefully designed and tuned to produce motion that appears natural while matching the key features of the behavior when performed by a human. The tuning process might be aided by data from psychophysical experiments that would provide additional constraints for the motion.

Can human motion be simulated interactively? To be truly interactive, the motion of synthetic actors in virtual environments must be computed in real time (simulation time must be less than wall clock time). Our implementation of the bicyclist runs ten times slower than real time on a Silicon Graphics Indigo^2 Computer with an R4400 processor. We anticipate that with improved dynamic simulation techniques, and the continued increase in workstation speed, a three-dimensional human simulation will run in real time within a few years.

A related question is whether the behaviors are robust enough for the synthetic actors to interact in a natural fashion with unpredictable human users. The runner can run at a variety of speeds and change direction, but abrupt changes in velocity or facing direction will cause him to fall down. The planning or reactive response algorithms that lie between the locomotion control algorithms and the perceptual model of the simulated environment will have to take in account the limitations of the dynamic system and control system.

One goal of this research is to demonstrate that dynamic simulation of rigid-body models can be used to generate natural-looking motion. Figure 5 shows a side-by-side comparison of video

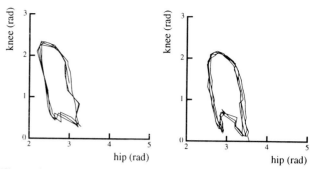

Figure 6: A phase plot of the hip and knee angles seen in the simulated runner (left) and measured in human subjects (right). The simulated motion is qualitatively similar to the measured data.

Variables	Human			Simulation
	Mean	Min	Max	
Mass (kg)	47.96	35.5	64.0	64.3
Height (m)	1.55	1.39	1.66	1.64
Board contact (s)	0.137	0.11	0.15	0.105
First flight (s)	0.235	0.14	0.30	0.156
Horse contact (s)	0.245	0.19	0.30	0.265
Second flight (s)	0.639	0.50	0.78	0.632
Horizontal velocity (m/s)				
Board touchdown	6.75	5.92	7.25	6.75
Board liftoff	4.61	3.97	5.26	4.01
Horse touchdown	4.61	3.97	5.26	4.01
Horse liftoff	3.11	2.48	3.83	2.83
Vertical velocity (m/s)				
Board touchdown	-1.15	-1.54	-.71	-1.13
Board liftoff	3.34	2.98	3.87	3.81
Horse touchdown	1.26	0.74	2.39	2.13
Horse liftoff	1.46	0.56	2.47	1.10
Aver. vertical force (N)				
Board contact	2175	1396	2792	5075
Horse contact	521	309	752	957

Table 1: Comparison of velocities, contact times, and forces for a simulated vaulter and human data measured by Takei. The human data was averaged from 24 subjects. The simulated data was taken from a single trial.

footage of a human runner and images of the simulated runner. This comparison represents one form of evaluation of our success in generating natural-looking motion. Figure 6 shows biomechanical data for running and represents another form of validation. Table 1 compares data from female gymnasts[33] and data from the vault simulation.

From the perspective of computer graphics, the final test would be a form of the Turing Test. If simulated data and motion capture data were represented using the same graphical model, would the audience occasionally choose the simulated data as the more natural motion? The user may find it easy to identify the motion source because motion capture data often has noise and registration problems with limbs that appear to change length and feet that slide on the ground. Simulated motion also has characteristic flaws, for example, the cyclic motion of the runner is repetitive allowing the eye to catch oscillations in the motion that are not visible in the motion of the human runner.

The animations described in this paper and a Turing test comparison with motion capture data can be seen on the WWW at **http://www.cc.gatech.edu/gvu/animation/Animation.html**

ACKNOWLEDGMENTS

The authors would like to thank Debbie Carlson and Ron Metoyer for their help in developing our simulation and rendering environment, Jeremy Heiner and Tom Meyer for their modeling expertise, Amy Opalak for digitizing the motion of the bicyclist, John Snyder and the User Interface and Graphics Research group at Microsoft for allowing the use of their collision detection system, and the CAD Systems Department at the Atlanta Committee for the Olympic Games for allowing us to use models of the Olympic venues. This project was supported in part by NSF NYI Grant No. IRI-9457621, by Mitsubishi Electric Research Laboratory, and by a Packard Fellowship. Wayne Wooten was supported by a Intel Foundation Graduate Fellowship.

REFERENCES

[1] Badler, N. I., Phillips, C. B., Webber, B. L. 1993. *Simulating Humans.* Oxford: Oxford University Press.

[2] Baumgarte, J. 1972. Stabilization of Constraints and Integrals of Motion in Dynamical Systems. *Computer Methods in Applied Mechanics and Engineering* 1:1–16.

[3] Breen, D. E., House, D. H., Wozny, M. J., 1994. Predicting the Drape of Woven Cloth Using Interacting Particles. *Proceedings of SIGGRAPH*, 365–372.

[4] Brogan, D. C., Hodgins J. K. 1995. Group Behaviors for Systems with Significant Dynamics. To appear in *IEEE/RSJ International Conference on Intelligent Robot and Systems.*

[5] Brotman, J. S., Netravali, A. N. 1988. Motion Interpolation by Optimal Control. *Proceedings of SIGGRAPH*, 309–315.

[6] Bruderlin, A., Calvert, T. W. 1989. Goal-Directed, Dynamic Animation of Human Walking. *Proceedings of SIGGRAPH*, 233–242.

[7] Carignan, M., Yang, Y., Magnenat-Thalmann, N., Thalmann, D. 1992. Dressing Animated Synthetic Actors with Complex Deformable Clothes. *Proceedings of SIGGRAPH*, 99–104.

[8] Cavagna, G. A., Thys, H., Zamboni, A. 1976. The Sources of External Work in Level Walking and Running. *Journal of Physiology* 262:639–657.

[9] Cavanagh, P., Sanderson, D. 1986. The Biomechanics of Cycling: Studies of the Pedaling Mechanics of Elite Pursuit Riders. In *Science of Cycling*, Edmund R. Burke (ed), Human Kinetics: Champaign, Ill.

[10] Cohen, M. F. 1992. Interactive Spacetime Control for Animation. *Proceedings of SIGGRAPH*, 293–302.

[11] Dempster, W. T., Gaughran, G. R. L. 1965. Properties of Body Segments based on Size and Weight. *American Journal of Anatomy* 120: 33–54.

[12] Frohlich, C. 1979. Do springboard divers violate angular momentum conservation? *American Journal of Physics* 47:583–592.

[13] Gregor, R. J., Broker, J. P., Ryan, M. M. 1991. Biomechanics of Cycling *Exercise and Sport Science Reviews* Williams & Wilkins, Philadelphia, John Holloszy (ed), 19:127–169.

[14] Hodgins, J. K. 1991. Biped Gait Transitions. In *Proceedings of the IEEE International Conference on Robotics and Automation*, 2092–2097.

[15] Hodgins, J., Raibert, M. H. 1990. Biped Gymnastics. *International Journal of Robotics Research* 9(2):115–132.

[16] Hodgins, J. K., Raibert, M. H. 1991. Adjusting Step Length for Rough Terrain Locomotion. *IEEE Transactions on Robotics and Automation* 7(3): 289–298.

[17] Hodgins, J. K., Sweeney, P. K, Lawrence, D. G. 1992. Generating Natural-looking Motion for Computer Animation. *Proceedings of Graphics Interface '92*, 265–272.

[18] Ko, H., Badler, N. I. 1993. Straight-line Walking Animation based on Kinematic Generalization that Preserves the Original Characteristics. In *Proceedings of Graphics Interface '93.*

[19] Laurent, B., Ronan, B., Magnenat-Thalmann, N. 1992. An Interactive Tool for the Design of Human Free-Walking Trajectories. In *Proceedings of Computer Animation '92*, 87–104.

[20] Lien, S., Kajiya, J. T. 1984. A Symbolic Method for Calculating the Integral Properties of Arbitrary Nonconvex Polyhedra. *IEEE Computer Graphics and Applications* 4(5):35–41.

[21] McMahon, T. A. 1984. *Muscles, Reflexes, and Locomotion.* Princeton: Princeton University Press.

[22] Magnenat-Thalmann, N. 1994. Tailoring Clothes for Virtual Actors, *Interacting with Virtual Environments*, Edited by MacDonald, L., and Vince, J., John Wiley & Sons, 205–216.

[23] Ngo, J. T., Marks, J. 1993. Spacetime Constraints Revisited. *Proceedings of SIGGRAPH*, 343–350.

[24] O'Brien, J. F., Hodgins, J. K., 1995, Dynamic Simulation of Splashing Fluids. *Proceedings of Computer Animation '95*, 198–205.

[25] Pai, D. 1990. Programming Anthropoid Walking: Control and Simulation. Cornell Computer Science Tech Report TR 90-1178.

[26] Playter, R. R., Raibert, M. H. 1992. Control of a Biped Somersault in 3D. In *Proceedings of the IEEE International Conference on Robotics and Automation*, 582–589.

[27] Raibert, M. H. 1986. *Legged Robots That Balance.* Cambridge: MIT Press.

[28] Raibert, M. H., Hodgins, J. K. 1991. Animation of Dynamic Legged Locomotion. *Proceedings of SIGGRAPH*, 349–356.

[29] Reynolds, C. W. 1987. Flocks, Herds, and Schools: A Distributed Behavioral Model. *Proceedings of SIGGRAPH*, 25–34.

[30] Rosenthal, D. E., Sherman, M. A. 1986. High Performance Multibody Simulations Via Symbolic Equation Manipulation and Kane's Method. *Journal of Astronautical Sciences* 34(3):223–239.

[31] Sims, K. 1994. Evolving Virtual Creatures. *Proceedings of SIGGRAPH*, 15–22.

[32] Sims, K. 1994. Evolving 3D Morphology and Behavior by Competition. *Artificial Life IV*, 28–39.

[33] Takei, Y. 1990. Techniques Used by Elite Women Gymnasts Performing the Handspring Vault at the 1987 Pan American Games. *International Journal of Sport Biomechanics* 6:29-55.

[34] Terzopoulos, D., Fleischer, K. 1988. Modeling Inelastic Deformation: Viscoelasticity, Plasticity, Fracture. *Proceedings of SIGGRAPH*, 269–278.

[35] Wooten, W., Hodgins, J. K. 1995. Simulation of Human Diving. To appear in *Proceedings of Graphics Interface '95.*

[36] van de Panne M., Fiume, E. 1993. Sensor-Actuator Networks. *Proceedings of SIGGRAPH*, 335–342.

[37] van de Panne M., Fiume, E., Vranesic, Z. 1990. Reusable Motion Synthesis Using State-Space Controllers. *Proceedings of SIGGRAPH*, 225–234.

[38] Witkin, A., Kass, M. 1988. Spacetime Constraints. *Proceedings of SIGGRAPH*, 159–168.

TicTacToon: A Paperless System for Professional 2D Animation

Jean-Daniel Fekete*   Érick Bizouarn   Éric Cournarie   Thierry Galas   Frédéric Taillefer

2001 S.A.
2, rue de la Renaissance, F92184 ANTONY Cedex

*LRI, CNRS URA 410, Bâtiment 490
Université de Paris-Sud, F91405 ORSAY Cedex

Abstract

TicTacToon is a system for professional 2D animation studios that replaces the traditional paper-based production process. TicTac-Toon is the first animation system to use vector-based sketching and painting: it uses an original method to transform a pen trajectory with varying pressure into a stroke of varying thickness, in real-time. TicTacToon provides resolution independence, a virtually infinite number of layers, the ability to dynamically manage perspective and sophisticated support for reuse of drawings. Other innovations include replacement of the rostrum model with a 3D model and integration into the overall 2D animation production process.

TicTacToon is in daily use by 2D animation studios for a wide range of productions, from commercials to television series and even a feature film. The user interface enables professionals to sketch and draw as they do on paper. Over 100 professional animators have used the system over a period of two years and most need less than an hour before beginning productive work. TicTac-Toon eliminates most tedious tasks and frees professional animators for more creative work.

Keywords: 2D animation, vector-based sketching, cel animation

1 Introduction

The field of professional 2D animation has not profited much from advances in computer-assisted animation. Most professional studios still animate by hand, using a process that has changed little since the 1950's. In striking contrast to related fields such as commercials, art and 3D animation, 2D animation studios use computers in a supporting rather than a central role. Walt Disney Feature Animation [28] is the exception; they have been using a computer-assisted system since 1987. The key issues identified by Edwin Catmull [9] 17 years ago remain issues today.

Why are computer graphics tools so difficult to apply to 2D animation? It is not enough to simply solve technical problems. The studio must also be convinced. Today's creation process is essentially a production line, in which a studio of 50 to 300 people work together to produce tens of thousands of drawings for a single feature film or television episode. Everyone has a specified role and follows detailed procedures to move from one stage to the next. Any

This work was supported by the French Centre National de la Ciné-matographie and by the Media Program of the European Union.

Permission to make digital/hard copy of part or all of this work for personal or classroom use is granted without fee provided that copies are not made or distributed for profit or commercial advantage, the copyright notice, the title of the publication and its date appear, and notice is given that copying is by permission of ACM, Inc. To copy otherwise, to republish, to post on servers, or to redistribute to lists, requires prior specific permission and/or a fee.

attempt to computerize the traditional set of tasks must take into account overhead costs in both time and quality.

This paper begins by describing the animation process, to illustrate the problems faced by 2D animation studios. We then examine other solutions, partial or global, that have already been proposed. We then describe TicTacToon and evaluate it based on how well it addresses specific technical issues, handles user interface concerns and fits within the social organization of an animation studio.

1.1 The Traditional Animation Process

Figure 1 shows the traditional animation process. Most steps involve an *exposure sheet*, which lists all the frames in a scene. Each line includes the phoneme pronounced by each character and the order and position in which the camera will shoot the figures and the background.

Each scene requires a set of stages, of which only the background can be painted in parallel with the animation stages (from key-frame to paint). The stages include:

Story Board: Splits script into *scenes* with dialog and music.

Sound Track: Records dialog and music in prototype form.

Sound Detection: Fills the dialog column of an *exposure sheet.*

Layout: Manages the drawing of backgrounds and main character positions, with specifications for camera movement and other animation characteristics.

Background Painting: Paints the background according to the layout.

Key Frame Animation: Draws extreme positions of characters as specified by the layout. Provides instructions for the *in-betweeners.*

In-Betweening: Draws the missing frames according to the key-frame animator's instructions.

Cleaning: Cleans up the drawings to achieve final quality of the strokes.

Paint: Photocopies the clean drawings onto acetate celluloid (cels) and paints zones with water color.

Check: Verifies animation and backgrounds according to the layout and approves for shooting.

Record: Shoots frame-by-frame on film or video, using a *rostrum* (explained later).

2 State of the Art

Robertson's [27] survey of commercial computer graphics systems identifies two main types of animation systems: *Ink and Paint* and *Automated In-Betweening*. In both cases, all artwork is drawn on paper and later digitized and managed by the computer after the cleaning stage (Figures 1(a) and 1(b)).

2.1 Ink and Paint Systems

Ink and Paint systems perform the following steps, starting from scanned images of each animated character:

- Remove noise from images.

- Close gaps between strokes to prepare for paint.

- Paint using seed-fill.

- Compose images of characters and backgrounds, applying zoom, rotation and pans as in a *rostrum*.

- Record on film or video.

2.2 Automated In-Betweening Systems

Automated In-Betweening systems begin with a scanned key frame and perform the following steps:

- Clean and vectorize, sometimes using semi-automatic methods.

- Match pairs of drawings or match drawings to a template (see below).

- Paint, if colors are not part of the template.

- Interpolate in-betweens according to an exposure sheet.

- Render and compose images of characters and backgrounds, applying zoom, rotation and pans as in a *rostrum*.

- Record on film or video.

- Put in database for reuse.

2.3 Technical Issues

Catmull [9] and, more recently, Durand [10] discuss several technical issues to address in order to provide an effective system. We review some of them here.

2.3.1 Input of drawings

All commercial systems involve scanning drawings. Ink and Paint systems — like PEGS [34] and Toonz [21] — must scan every drawing whereas Automated In-Betweening systems — like Animo [7] — need only scan the key drawings. Catmull mentions tablets as a possible solution, but Durand argues that, "as sophisticated as they may be at this time, [they] could not offer the same versatility as traditional tools."

Toonz and PEGS scan drawings at a multiple of the final resolution to avoid jaggies. PEGS can optionally micro-vectorize scanned animations. The Animo system provides tools for automatic tracing from the scanned key drawing. In all cases, an operator is required for checking the results.

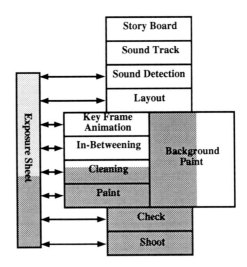

(a) The Ink and Paint Process

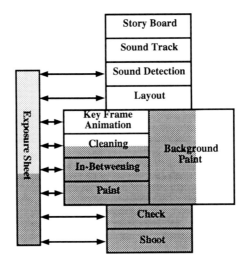

(b) The Automated In-Betweening Process

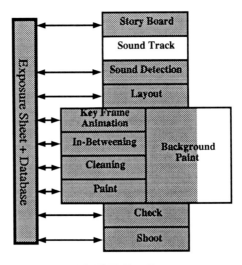

(c) The TicTacToon Process

Figure 1: Work flow of the different stages in animation Work done on computers is marked with a dark background

2.3.2 Automated In-Betweening

The two main classes of Automated In-Betweening systems are based on templates [6, 7] or explicit correspondence [31]. In template-based systems, a designer creates a template for each character. Animators must then restrict the character's movements according to the template. An operator must then specify the correspondence between each key frame and the template. Explicit correspondence systems use two key drawings and generate in-betweens on a curve-by-curve basis. An operator is also required to specify the correspondence between the curves on the two key drawings. Sometimes, a zero-length curve must be created when a new detail appears or disappears between them.

2.3.3 Animation Painting

Ink and Paint systems use an area flooding algorithm [19]. All systems optimize the painting when successive drawings of a character contain zones that are mostly aligned and have the same color.

Automated In-Betweening systems associate graphic attributes with zones during the specification of correspondence.

2.3.4 Construction of Image Layers

Ink and Paint systems only manipulate pixel images. They support transforms to the geometry (pan, zoom, rotate), as well as to the color intensity, as described in [35]. In addition, all the commercial systems can apply special effects — specified in the software exposure sheet — to layers (color transforms, blur, transparency, etc.)

Vector-based systems use a variant of the scan-line algorithm [13, pages 92–99] to transform their graphical structure into a pixel image. For graphical attributes, flat colors and constant transparency are simple to implement. Automated In-Betweening systems such as [7] can also use textures and shading on animated characters since they can maintain space coherence.

2.3.5 Composition of Image Layers

Ink and Paint systems compose the layers using the alpha-blending arithmetic [24]. Vector-based systems can choose to compose layers at the pixel level or manage the composition during scan-conversion [8]. Commercial products provide no information about this point.

For recording, all current computer-assisted systems use the rostrum model to specify the way images are composed, positioned and turned relative to the camera. A rostrum includes a camera, a set of movable transparent trays holding the cels and a background area (Figure 2). The camera axis is always perpendicular to the layers of cels, but can be panned, moved forward or back, and zoomed in or out. Cels can also be moved or rotated on the trays.

The rostrum model makes managing an animation's perspective difficult. The animator must use traditional techniques for drawing perspective and translate it into the physical movement of the different layers of the rostrum. The computer system can only check if the calculation was correct and help to fix errors. Although Levoy [18] has proposed using a 3D editor, no commercial system has implemented one.

2.3.6 Other Computer Tools

Studios are not hostile to computer systems. They already use computer tools to assist them in stages such as storyboarding, sound detection, and layout. However, the data they produce must be re-entered into the process by hand.

Storyboards can be fine-tuned with an editing system (e.g. [2]) by mixing rough images with a sound track. The resulting storyboard must then be re-entered by hand.

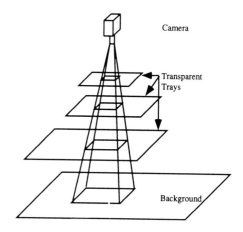

Figure 2: A Rostrum.

Sound Detection can be performed automatically by transforming the sound track into a list of phonemes which are then be transcribed by hand onto an exposure sheet.

Complicated layouts can be created with a 3D program, live action or rotoscoping. However, these cannot be integrated: the layout is printed on paper and used as in a traditional layout.

Animation can be checked with pencil tests. The animators record several drawings on a computer and play the animation in real time. Each drawing must be input with a scanner or camera and a subset of the exposure sheet must be typed in. Although computers have been available at this stage for some time, they are not always efficient. Animators must usually wait for the equipment, so they tend to draw more in-betweens than necessary. They later remove them, after checking the action on the pencil test machine.

3 Animation with TicTacToon

TicTacToon is designed to support a paperless 2D animation production line. To be successful, we had to solve a number of technical problems, provide a user interface that enhances the existing skills of professional animators and take into account the existing organizational structure of today's animation studios. This section describes the overall system and how it addresses each issue.

3.1 System Overview

TicTacToon structures the stages of the production line into a set of tasks. A workstation is assigned to a specific stage and individual tasks are performed within rooms [3] listed below:

- Lobby
- Storyboard/Database
- Layout
- Exposure Sheet
- Sketching/Animation

- Paint
- Render/Record
- Scan
- Electronic Mail

Figure 1(c) shows that TicTacToon supports all stages of production, except sound track recording. Major features include:

- a paperless process to avoid changing media,
- resolution independence to use real perspective and to enable reuse of drawings at any zoom level,

- a user interface that replicates the tools used by animators on paper, and

- a 3D model to replace the rostrum model.

These features eliminate many tedious tasks and increase productivity. TicTacToon also provides innovative solutions to the following problems:

- drawing directly on a computer system,

- painting on a vector-based system, and

- providing an environment acceptable to traditional animators without too much training.

TicTacToon runs on Digital Alpha AXP workstations using the X Window System [29] and a modified version of the InterViews toolkit [20, 11]. TicTacToon does not require any special graphic hardware; it interacts with the digitizer using the X Input Extension protocol [12].

3.2 Technical Issues

The design of TicTacToon poses several technical problems. This section describes how TicTacToon handles sketching, painting and rendering. Sketching is vector-based and painting uses planar maps and a gap-closing technique.

3.2.1 Vector-based sketching

Vector-based sketching poses two main problems: finding fast-enough algorithms and making a user interface suited to the animator's work. Three steps are involved: providing graphical feedback as the user draws, vectorizing the curve when the pen goes up, and redrawing the curve in place of the traced feedback. Users should not notice the last two steps.

The tablet sends an event every time the pen's state is modified. The state contains a pressure level, ranging from 64 to 512, depending on the digitizer, and X and Y coordinates, with a precision of 0.002 inches. The surface is 18"x12". Current digitizers can send up to 200 events per second if the user moves quickly enough.

TicTacToon uses the brush/stroke model described in [26]. A *brush* can be any convex shape and is defined by a Bézier path [1]. A *stroke* is a line drawn with a brush; the width is modulated by the amount of pressure applied to the pen. Pen pressure is normalized between 0 (no pressure) and 1 (full pressure). The brush shape is scaled according to the pen pressure and a linear modulation function. This function is defined by two scaling factors for pressures 0 and 1. If the factors are equal, the result is a fixed-width pen. In general, though, the scale factors are 0 for pressure 0 and 1 for pressure 1.

To compute the strokes, we use a variant of a fast curve fitting algorithm developed by Thierry Pudet. Compared to Plass [23], Schneider [30] and more recently Gonczarowski [16], this algorithm tries to optimize the fitting time rather than the number of Bézier segments that fit a set of sampled points.

Least Squares Curve Fitting Previous curve fitting algorithms start with the samples, a tolerance parameter and perform the following steps:

1. Filter the samples to reduce noise.

2. Find corners or other singular points.

3. Define an initial parameterization for the samples.

4. Perform a least-squares curve fitting.

5. If the distance between the curve and the samples greatly exceeds the tolerance, split the samples in two parts, apply step 3 to both parts and connect the resulting segments.

6. If the distance between the curve and the samples exceeds the tolerance, change the parameterization and restart at 4.

7. Otherwise, output the segment.

In step 5, two more operations should be performed when splitting the samples: the splitting point should be chosen carefully and the resulting fitted curves should connect smoothly, i.e. the derivative at the splitting point should be evaluated and the least-squares fit should be constrained to maintain the direction of the derivatives at the connecting ends.

Step 5 is the bottleneck for this algorithm. Splitting the samples at the point of maximum distance to the computed curve, as in [30, 16], is computationally expensive, since the distance must be computed for every sample. Yet, this step, together with step 6, is essential for minimizing the number of segments.

Pudet avoids steps 6 and thus avoids computing the distance from the fitted curve to each sample point. Step 5 becomes:

5. If the distance between the curve and *any sample point* exceeds the tolerance, split the samples in two parts *at the middle*, apply step 3 to both parts and connect the resulting segments.

6. Otherwise, output the segment.

If the algorithm were used to fit cubic Bézier segments, it would produce too many small segments. Instead, Pudet fits quintic Bézier segments, which have more freedom than cubic and tend to fit more samples without re-parameterization.

Variable Width Stroke Pudet's algorithm performs a second curve fitting for the outline of the stroke. Our variation improves feedback by eliminating this second fitting. We recompute the curve's envelope when it is redrawn and cache it to avoid further recomputation. We draw the envelope of each curve by generating a single polygon for the whole outline of the curve's stroke. We have optimized the most common brush shapes, e.g., circles and ellipses.

In order to make pressure information independent of the stroke's geometry, we define a *stroke profile* that maps a number between 0 and 1 (the normalized curvilinear index or NCI) to the pressure at that point. For example, the NCI for a point halfway along the stroke would be .5. This technique speeds computation of the envelope polygon and lets the stroke trajectory be modified while still keeping pressure information.

Another problem is noise: even the best digitizers suffer from both electronic interference and mechanical vibration. We apply a simple low pass filter to the samples. The fitting in itself filters the data, enabling the system to track the original gesture more accurately.

In summary, curve fitting transforms the input samples into a list of quintic Bézier segments and a stroke profile. Benefits include resolution independence (i.e., smooth curves at all zoom levels), compact representation of the pen's trajectory and filtering of the original stroke.

We have tested the vector-based sketching technique with professional animators for two years. This software requires a workstation with a fast FPU to achieve good performance; we used Digital AXP machines. The results have been very promising. The only problem reported involved performance when sketching and simultaneously running another program that loads the machine.

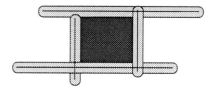

Figure 3: A zone looks closed but is actually open at the upper left corner.

We can envision a pathological case: drawing a very long stroke without releasing the pen. However, we found that this rarely occurs in practice. Animators only do it when cleaning a drawing and they still take more time to start a new stroke than for TicTacToon to draw the previous one.

3.2.2 Painting with planar maps and gap closing

A drawing consists of a list of strokes. In order to paint it, we must define a set of zones from these strokes, i.e. compute the topology of the drawing. We use the MapKernel library [14] to compute the planar topology defined by a set of Bézier paths. This topology is incrementally modified when adding or removing edges and also supports hit detection. The set of zones is extracted from the planar map as a new set of Bézier paths.

To compute the planar map, TicTacToon uses the central path rather than the outlines of each stroke, which halves the planar map's size. This allows later modifications of the brush strokes, e.g., when reusing a character. However, using central paths causes a problem: a zone that appears closed may actually be open. Even if the edges of the strokes intersect, the central paths may not (see Figure 3).

We use the algorithm we described in [15] that corrects this problem and finds the other small gaps that are always present in real drawings. Gaps are closed by adding invisible lines and changing the topology maintained by the MapKernel. This step takes several seconds and is usually run in the background to avoid making painters wait for the operation to finish. Once the gaps have been closed, a painter simply selects a color and points to the relevant zones. Painted zones are inserted at the beginning of the drawing's display list as one graphical element. This element consists of a grouped list of background zones, described as Bézier paths with a fill color. Since painted zones are rendered differently, as discussed below, this element is given a special tag.

3.2.3 Rendering

We use a painter's algorithm to render each graphic primitive into an image buffer which is then composed into the final image using alpha-blending arithmetic.

Our **graphical primitives** are very similar to PostScript [1], with the following differences:

- Instead of cubic Bézier paths, we support Bézier curves up to the 7th degree, though we only use quintics, cubics, quadratics and lines.

- Pixel images can have an alpha channel.

- Colors have an alpha component.

- We use a brush shape and a stroke profile to modulate the stroke width.

- Variations of attributes along and/or across the paths are supported, thus providing shading facilities (see Figure 5). We

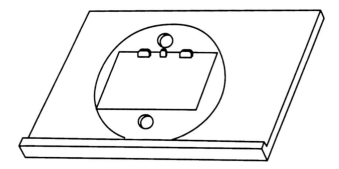

Figure 4: A Lightbox used by animators.

call them *annotations*. For now, they apply to color and transparency. An intuitive interface is available to generate such annotations.

The rendering algorithm proceeds by breaking down the strokes into elementary shaded polygons and scan-convert them.

First, the central Bézier path is discretized into line segments and normals are computed. Then, if the path only has a pressure profile, the stroke outline is generated and scan-converted. Otherwise, if there is an annotation along the path, attribute values are computed for each vertex of the discretized path and the stroke is split into 4-sided shaded polygons. When there is an annotation across the path, each polygon must be sliced into smaller pieces.

The polygons are then scan-converted into the image buffer. After the last polygon has been processed, the image buffer is merged with the final image.

The image buffer is used for applying special effects such as blur. It also helps to alleviate one current limitation of the alpha-blending arithmetic, which assumes that the area of a pixel covered by a polygon is randomly distributed over that pixel. Since the paths produced by the paint program are contiguous and never overlap, if two polygons overlap the same pixel, the total area covered is the sum of each area, which violates the assumption. Our algorithm renders all the components of such structured graphics into the same image buffer and merges pixel values by adding each color/alpha component (the "PLUS" operator of [24]). The image buffer is then overlaid on the final image, using the regular "OVER" operator.

3.3 User Interface Issues

Animators usually spend eight hours a day drawing, so it is critical to make the user interface both comfortable and easy to use. We observed animators at work in order to understand their needs and then iteratively designed the system, responding to their feedback about a series of prototypes.

This section describes how traditional animators work and then presents various aspects of TicTacToon's user interface, emphasizing tools that support sketching and the layout module.

Traditional animators work on a *Lightbox* (Figure 4). The disk is a sheet of translucent plastic that can be turned, using finger holes at the top and bottom. A strip light behind the disk lights up all layers of tracing paper at once.

Paper sheets are punched and inserted into peg bars, usually on top of the disk. The holes act as a reference and are used to accurately position the animations. Animators can work comfortably with this setup all day long.

3.3.1 Animation and Sketching Tools

TicTacToon's Animation Editor performs or enhances the following functions of a lightbox:

- stacking drawings,

- turning the light on or off, for stacks as well as individual drawings,

- changing the position of underlying drawings without actually modifying the drawings themselves,

- quickly flipping between successive sketches to find and check the best stroke position for a movement, and

- zooming, panning and turning the viewport.

TicTacToon provides a set of tools to support sketching, flipping among sketches and turning the viewpoint.

Sketching: Animators begin drawing in-betweens by stacking the initial and final key drawings. They put a new sheet of paper on the lightbox, turn it on, and sketch an in-between, according to the key-frame animator's instructions. They regularly check their drawings by turning off the light. The in-between animator must sometimes superimpose different parts of key drawings. For example, if a character jumps and his arm also moves, the movement of the arm may be seen more easily by superimposing the arms of the two key drawings.

Translated into TicTacToon actions, an animator creates a new drawing, drags the two key drawings, drops them into position, and begins sketching with the digitizer pen. Different parts of the key drawing can also be superimposed on the current drawing.

Flipping: Animators flip between sketches to check that their animations are correct. This requires manual dexterity, since they place the drawings between their fingers, and limits them to four or five drawings. They must also flip non-sequentially, since drawings are stacked as key 1, key 2 and in-betweens, rather than key 1, in-betweens and key 2.

TicTacToon can flip any number of drawings in any order. To create the impression of movement, it is important to switch between drawings in less than 5 milliseconds to maintain retinal persistency. We cannot guarantee this redraw speed since complex vector-based drawings can take an unbounded amount of time to draw. This is not a problem for most animators, but those who use a large number of strokes must check their animations with the pencil test module instead of flipping. Alternatively, we could cache the drawings as Pixmaps.

Turning the drawing: The human hand has mechanical constraints that limit its precision in some positions [33]. Animators can turn the disk to find the most comfortable and accurate drawing position. Most animators draw with the right hand and use the left for turning the drawing and turning the lightbox on and off.

TicTacToon also lets animators draw with one hand while looking at the drawing on the screen. Special function keys are assigned to the keyboard so that the other hand need not move to perform the following functions: undo/redo, flip up/flip down, turn the viewport, and reset the viewport.

Partial Editing of Strokes: We provide almost unlimited undo/redo. Animators make very few mistakes and would rather erase and redraw a stroke than twiddle with curve parts. We removed tools that enabled them to manipulate the Bézier curves because they were distracting and never used constructively. We may reconsider this decision if new paradigms for re-editing strokes prove successful (e.g., [4]).

Graphical feedback from the pen: We have experimented with several devices to provide feedback under the tracing pen. A ball-point pen can be inserted into some cordless digitizers. If the animator places a sheet of paper on the digitizer, it is possible to draw with both the pen and the computer. However, animators do not like the feel of ball-point pens, which are too soft compared to their usual pencils. Moreover, they cannot "undo" a stroke on paper.

We have also tried a cordless digitizer on an LCD screen. With current hardware, a distance of several millimeters separates the pen surface from the LCD screen. This produces a parallax error, similar to that observed with touch-sensitive screens [25]. It is difficult for animators to continue their strokes because they often miss the expected starting position.

Animators prefer to draw on a flat surface and look at the drawing on the screen. One animator gave a compelling argument as to why he preferred this approach. After three months of uninterrupted work using TicTacToon, he tried using paper again. He told us that he found it very annoying because his hand was always hiding some part of the drawing.

3.3.2 The Layout Module

The Layout supports the whole animation process. It provides two views: the exposure sheet and a 3D view (Figure 8). The exposure sheet presents the logical structure of an animation: which characters and backgrounds are present in a specific frame. The 3D view presents the graphical structure: the position of characters and backgrounds and the trajectory they follow.

Unlike traditional animation, which provides only a static specification of a scene, TicTacToon begins with a playable version of each scene, using rough drawings. A layout animator can reuse animations or backgrounds from a database and can check camera movements and synchronize them with character movements. A copy of the layout specification is handed off to subsequent stages, which replace rough drawings with new work. Animators can check their drawings at any time, to ensure that they conform to the layout and that the action works. The layout stage can also check that work has been done correctly.

Unlike the traditional rostrum model, TicTacToon positions animations in a 3D world, in a way similar to Levoy [18]. However, the camera axis is always kept perpendicular to the drawings. This model acts like a theater background designed to be seen from only one perspective. As in 3D systems, the characters and camera are assigned a general trajectory in 3D space. Since they can't turn around the X or Y axis, they use 2D instead of 3D general transforms. This model automatically maintains perspective and the correct stacking order.

The columns of a traditional exposure sheet relate directly to the levels of a rostrum. The columns in TicTacToon's exposure sheet contain one character or a character part. An animation can be seen as a list of successive drawings or grouped into a cycle, which is a repeatable list of consecutive drawings. For example, a walking character is usually defined with a cycle of 8 drawings. TicTacToon exposure sheets handle cycles as structured objects that can be placed on a trajectory and tuned precisely. Prototype walks can be stored for most characters and reused as the basis for all their walks. Television serials only define actions for a few specific angles: 0, 30°, 60°, 90° and the symmetricals. Storing reusable walks (and runs) saves time for both the layout and other animators.

The Layout stage can check complex camera movements on prototypes and precisely tune the movement of each character. Animators can modify prototype walks, as when a wounded character limps, and save time by reusing parts of the prototype walk.

As in traditional animation, story boards consist of a set of small sketches of important actions in a scene with an associated script, including dialog, music, and intentions. Figure 6 shows a Story Board designed with TicTacToon.

Traditional animation uses only eight mouth shapes (Figure 7). We have developed a mouth shape detection program that avoids using phoneme recognition and is speaker and language independent. The success rate is around 90%, with errors only at the transitions. Mouth shapes can be edited, played and corrected and the result is directly inserted in the sound column of the exposure sheet.

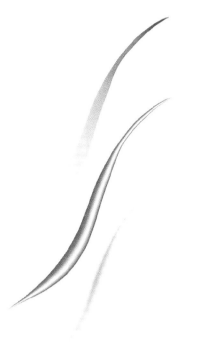

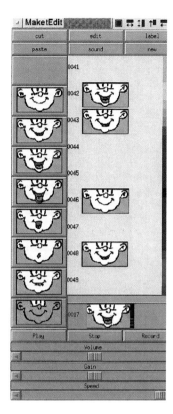

Figure 5: Rendering effects on strokes.

Figure 6: The story board module.

Figure 7: The Voice Detection module.

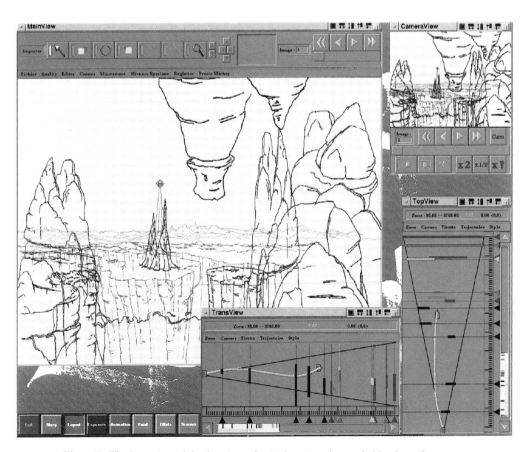

Figure 8: The Layout module showing a front view, top view and side view of a scene.

Over 100 professional animators in several studios have used TicTacToon over the past two years. So far, more than 90% were able to immediately switch from paper to TicTacToon. The unsuccessful animators included some who refused to try it, some who were afraid of computers in general and some who had difficulties with specific aspects of the user interface. Animators have been the strongest supporters of TicTacToon and some have convinced their studios to adopt it. This is in strong contradiction with Durand in [10].

We addressed an early criticism of the digitizer's pen and replaced it with a model that was both pressure sensitive and rigid. The other major criticism is the digitizer's surface which is too slippy for some and too soft for others. We find similar kinds of individual preferences about pencil hardness and paper quality. Although most animators adapt to the digitizer's surface after about a month, we are still investigating possible improvements.

3.4 Social organization of the work

To succeed, an animation system must provide more than useful technical features and a good user interface; it must also fit within the existing work context of an animation studio. Both formal and informal communication are essential for the smooth running of a studio. Since animators express themselves with cartoons as well as words, we provide a metamail compliant mailer [5] with TicTac-Toon. We receive mail messages from production sites all over the world, including formal (bug reports, request for information) and informal (jokes, tricks and caricatures), illustrating the same range of communication as would be found in a traditional animation studio.

TicTacToon supports a number of operations that help manage the production line. Animators exchange their work via exposure sheets and a distributed database. They also use electronic mail to notify the necessary people when their work is ready to be processed and get feedback about their own work. We do not want the studio staff to have to become system operators. TicTacToon does not require prior computer skills and we have hidden operating system commands such as copying directories and naming files.

TicTacToon is designed to enhance the animation process, not just raise productivity. As 3D production studios increase the scope of their work, we expect that they will require the same level of organizational support needed by today's 2D studios.

4 Discussion

Current tools to support animation have both advantages and disadvantages over traditional techniques. This section examines the advantages and disadvantages of two types of computer tools, Ink and Paint systems and Automated In-Betweening systems, and then discusses the relative advantages and disadvantages of TicTacToon.

4.1 Ink and Paint Systems

4.1.1 Advantages

Speed up painting: Hand painting is the most tedious task in traditional animation: using a computer can speed up the process by a factor of 5 [34]. The average speed is 100 drawings per day depending upon the number of zones per drawing and the number of colors being used. In traditional animation, a maximum of 40 drawings can be painted per day, with an average of 20.

Remove limits on the number of layers: Computers can also handle more than the five composition layers found in traditional animation, which is limited by the opacity of acetate celluloid.

Simplify shooting: A virtual rostrum is easier to use than a real rostrum.

Allow images from other sources: Highest quality backgrounds are still hand-painted and scanned in. However, images from other sources — like paint programs, rendering programs or digitized live action — can also be imported.

4.1.2 Disadvantages

Increase the cleaning time: Films require huge numbers of drawings, in the order of tens of thousands. Computer systems can add manual actions to traditional work and machine processing time can be slow. For example, Ink and Paint systems require cleaner drawings than traditional animation does. Animators must spend extra time cleaning to avoid having the computer spend more time filtering, which increases the cost of the hand-cleaning stage.

Consume large resources: Reuses, though possible, are only made by large studios. With the exception of backgrounds, most images are usually removed from disk after recording. Pixel images require a lot of storage, especially if the final format is 35mm film. The technology required to manage such images remains expensive and without a planned long term production (over two years), the extra storage and network cost is not guaranteed to be balanced by the increase in productivity. Some systems address this by vectorizing the images after the cleaning stage [34], most others don't [21, 22].

Add medium change costs: Finally, several marginal costs result from the transition between paper and computer:

- A special staff is required to scan and check drawings.

- The exposure sheet must be typed into the system.

- Information is not usually propagated back from the computer to the paper world. Since artists do not receive feedback, some problems recur.

The overhead of transferring between paper and computer accounts for a minimum of 10% for a well-organized process to 25% or more for less well-organized processes [17] in the final cost.

4.2 Automated In-Betweening Systems

4.2.1 Advantages

Reduce the number of hand-drawn in-betweens: Computer-assisted In-betweening is designed to reduce the number of hand-drawn in-betweens and increase reuse of animation. Once a drawing has been vectorized and the correspondence specified, an animation can be tuned precisely. Some actions can be reused at different tempos which also decreases the number of hand-drawn drawings.

Allow procedural rendering: Since zones and edges composing successive key drawings are matched, the interpolation process can automatically maintain space coherence between procedurally computed attributes used for rendering. For example, the checked texture of a character's shirt will be correctly animated when he moves his arms. Unlike with traditional animation, many special effects can be animated automatically.

Like Ink and Paint Systems, Automated In-Betweening Systems allow an unlimited number of layers, an easier shooting and access to images from other sources. Painting takes a small portion of the key frame matching process.

4.2.2 Disadvantages

Change the nature of in-betweening and limit its complexity: Crafting an animation with an Automated In-Betweening system is slow: We have found that inputing and tuning simple in-betweens take about the same time as drawing them by hand. Even with recent advances in algorithms, it remains difficult to match a drawing to a

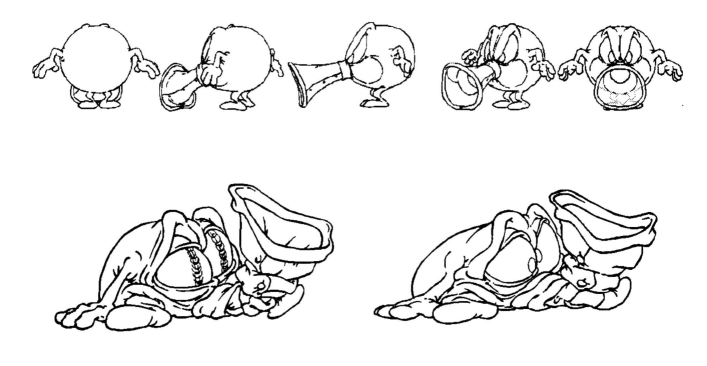

Figure 9: Model of the Klaxon character and two key drawings very distorted from the model.

template or two successive drawings to each other. Template-based systems require key drawings to conform to the model. (Figure 9 illustrates how much key frames can differ from the model.) Explicit correspondence systems must match each key drawing to the previous and next drawings. In both cases, the animation is restricted to fairly standard drawings; matching unusual images is very time-consuming.

Traditional animators use a special notation on the key frames to specify the rhythm of the animation. Automated In-Betweening systems make it difficult to control this rhythm, which lowers the quality of the animation. Generating automated in-betweens is time-consuming and transforms the animator's work from drawing images to removing and tuning the *slowing in* and *slowing out* of an action. Tuning in-betweens requires a cross of skills from a traditional animator and a computer graphist who can precisely manipulate Bézier curve handles. Few such animators exist.

Require a skill in modeling: Template-based systems require both 3D modeling as well as traditional animation skills. Crafting a good model is expensive and must be taken into account when estimating the cost of the production. Given this cost, these systems are only cost-effective for productions with few characters.

Does not provide as much reuse as expected: Animations are less reusable than might be expected. Reuse must be planned at the storyboard stage, which is not integrated with the computer part of the process. All these problems contribute to the perception by animation studios that computer assisted in-between programs produce poor quality animation.

Moreover, like Ink and Paint systems, they also add medium change costs.

4.3 TicTacToon

4.3.1 Advantages

Avoids medium change costs: With TicTacToon, all stages of the work are performed on computer (see Figure 10), with one workstation being allocated to a specific stage. This avoids the cost of transferring from paper to computer.

Offers resolution independence: Vector-based backgrounds provide both resolution independence and more importantly, an alpha channel. We also integrate pixel-based images, which can be made with a paint program or scanned in.

Allows reuses: TicTacToon animations are vector-based (Bézier-based) and require 20KB to 100KB per character. We provide a database system to manage and qualify animations.

Distributes information in a playable form: Each stage has access to all information, from the earliest written scenario to the database of reusable images. Animators can test scenes at any time, to clarify the author's intent. Paper need not be carried from place to place, risking loss or damage and animators can spend more time at their desks drawing.

Provides interactive tools to increase animator's productivity: TicTacToon provides a number of features that support high quality animation. Compared to Automated In-Betweening systems, animators spend more time on art work and can check their work interactively. The animations themselves can be much more complicated, sometimes containing hundreds of layers. Scenes can be played and checked before even starting character animation and background painting. As with traditional animation, TicTacToon permits varying width strokes.

Animators using TicTacToon can work up to 30% faster than with traditional animation. If we also include cut and paste and reuse of existing images, the savings are even greater.

TicTacToon share all the advantages of Ink and Paint systems.

Painting speed is roughly the same. By improving the rostrum model, it further simplifies the shooting of complex scenes, using hundreds of layers. Also, TicTacToon accepts scanned backgrounds and provides tools to manage them, including cut overlays (chroma key), assembly of background parts, and correct/adjust colorimetry. These tools are the most tedious to use and implement.

Pixel-based backgrounds can be made device-independent by scanning them at high resolution (we recommend 400 to 600 dpi). Although this requires more storage, the relative number of backgrounds is small (in the thousands) compared to the number of animated drawings.

4.3.2 Disadvantages

Changes the nature of layout: Some traditional layout animators reported problems using the layout program. They are more familiar with the rostrum model than the 3D model and have learned how to "cheat" with perspective. However, layout animators who work with special effects had no problems.

Does not allow fast enough flipping for some animators: Animators who use a large number of strokes can find the redraw latency too slow when flipping between animations. These animators must use the pencil test module to check their animation. Some animators would like an in-betweening module for simple animations (see the section on Future Work).

Does not change the nature of painting: Painting is still tedious, although we have tuned the user interface to be as simple as possible. The current interface is much faster, but keeps the painter so busy clicking the mouse to paint and using the keyboard to change the drawing that the job seems much more painful. The studios hire a non-skilled person to perform this task. We would like to avoid this gap in skill since it has important economic and social implications.

Limits the quality of vector-based backgrounds: Vector-based backgrounds does not yet achieve the level of quality of pixel based images made by the best paint programs or scanning.

5 Future work

We are enhancing TicTacToon in the following ways:

Speed up the painting process: We would like to handle cleaning and painting in the same stage. This would require automatically finding the color of a zone, either from a template or from a previously painted cel.

Support some procedural rendering: We already allow more graphical effects than used on traditional character animation. However, we are working on adding procedural rendering like computed texture for strokes and 3D effects.

Optimize rendering: Currently, a single frame can take from a few seconds to several minutes to compute. Many optimizations can be performed, including those described by Wallace [35] and Shantsis [32]. Others are more specific to vector-based drawings, such as caching rendered images for later reuse. However, since an image recorder takes 30 seconds to shoot a frame on a 35mm film, it is only important to increase rendering speed when images take more than 30 seconds.

Implement Computer-Assisted In-Betweening: Animators usually ask for assistance when in-betweening objects such as bouncing balls, falling snow, and air bubbles in water. We are working on a special module for this.

Connect with a 3D system: We are currently working on inferring 3D features from 2D drawings.

6 Conclusion

TicTacToon is a system for professional 2D animation studios that replaces the traditional paper-based production process. It provides a practical solution to the problem of converting from analog to digital 2D animation.

TicTacToon is the first animation system to use vector-based sketching and painting. Other innovations include replacing the rostrum model with a constrained 3D model and integration of the system into the overall 2D animation production process. TicTacToon eliminates most tedious tasks, freeing animators for more creative work. We believe that TicTacToon can be the first of a new generation of tools to support digital animation.

Acknowledgments

This work has been done in collaboration with the former Paris Research Laboratory of Digital. Thanks to Michel Gangnet, Henry Gouraud, Thierry Pudet, Jean-Manuel Van Thong for their support and their work on MapKernel and Fitlib. At 2001, thanks to Jean-Louis Moser, Olivier Arnaud and Gregory Denis for their work on TicTacToon. Wendy Mackay and Michel Beaudouin-Lafon provided support and advice for the writing of this article, Wendy rewrote most of it into readable English. Digital has been supporting our work from the beginning, with special thanks to Jacques Lefaucheux.

References

[1] Adobe Systems Incorporated. *PostScript Language Reference Manual*. Addison-Wesley, Reading, MA, USA, second edition, 1990.

[2] Adobe Systems Incorporated, 1585 Charleston Road, P. O. Box 7900, Mountain View, CA 94039-7900, USA, Tel: (415) 961-4400. *Adobe Premiere 1.0 User Guide*, 1993.

[3] D. Austin Henderson, Jr. and Stuart K. Card. Rooms: The Use of Multiple Virtual Workspaces to Reduce Space Contention in a Window-Based Graphical User Interface. *TOGS*, 5(3):211–243, 1986.

[4] Thomas Baudel. A Mark-Based Interaction Paradigm for Free-Hand Drawing. In *Proceedings of the ACM SIGGRAPH Symposium on User Interface Software and Technology*, Marina del Rey, 1994. ACM.

[5] Nathaniel S. Borenstein and Ned Freed. MIME (Multipurpose Internet Mail Extension): Mechanism for Specifying and Describing the Format of Internet Message Bodies. Request for Comments: 1341, June 1992.

[6] N. Burtnyk and M. Wein. Interactive Skeleton Techniques for Enhancing Motion Dynamics in Key Frame Animation. *Communications of the ACM*, 19:564–569, 1976.

[7] Cambridge Animation. *The Animo System*.

[8] Edwin E. Catmull. A hidden-surface algorithm with anti-aliasing. *Computer Graphics (SIGGRAPH '78 Proceedings)*, 12(3):6–11, August 1978.

[9] Edwin E. Catmull. The problems of computer-assisted animation. *Computer Graphics (SIGGRAPH '78 Proceedings)*, 12(3):348–353, August 1978.

[10] Charles X. Durand. The "TOON" project: requirements for a computerized 2D animation system. *Computers and Graphics*, 15(2):285–293, 1991.

[11] Jean-Daniel Fekete. A Multi-Layer Graphic Model for Building Interactive Graphical Applications. In *Proceedings of Graphics Interface '92*, pages 294–300, May 1992.

[12] Paula Ferguson. The X11 Input Extension: Reference Pages. *The X Resource*, 4(1):195–270, December 1992.

[13] James D. Foley, Andries van Dam, Steven K. Feiner, and John F. Hughes. *Fundamentals of Interactive Computer Graphics*. Addison-Wesley Publishing Company, second edition, 1990.

[14] Michel Gangnet, Jean-Claude Hervé, Thierry Pudet, and Jean-Manuel Van Thong. Incremental Computation of Planar Maps. In Jeffrey Lane, editor, *Computer Graphics (SIGGRAPH '89 Proceedings)*, volume 23, pages 345–354, July 1989.

[15] Michel Gangnet, Jean-Manuel Van Thong, and Jean-Daniel Fekete. Automated Gap Closing for Freehand Drawing. [Technical Sketch] SIGGRAPH'94, Orlando, 1994.

[16] Jakob Gonczarowski. A Fast Approach to Auto-tracing (with Parametric Cubics). In Robert A. Morris and Jacques André, editors, *Raster Imaging and Digital Typography II— Papers from the second RIDT meeting, held in Boston, Oct. 14–16, 1991*, pages 1–15, New York, 1991. Cambridge University Press.

[17] Claude Huhardeaux. The Label 35 System. Personal Communication, 1989.

[18] Mark Levoy. A Color Animation System Based on the Multiplane Technique. In *Computer Graphics (SIGGRAPH '77 Proceedings)*, volume 11, pages 65–71, Summer 1977.

[19] Mark Levoy. Area Flooding Algorithms. In *Two-Dimensional Computer Animation, Course Notes 9 for SIGGRAPH 82*. ACM Press, New York, NY 10036, USA, July 1982.

[20] Mark A. Linton, John M. Vlissides, and Paul R. Calder. Composing user interfaces with InterViews. *IEEE Computer*, 22(2):8–22, February 1989.

[21] Microsoft Corporation. SoftImage Toonz Feature Summary. Part No. 098-58493, One Microsoft Way, Redmond, WA 98052-6399, 1995.

[22] Bill Perkins. The Creative Toonz System. Personal Communication, 1994.

[23] Michael Plass and Maureen Stone. Curve Fitting with Piecewise Parametric Cubics. *Computer Graphics (SIGGRAPH '83 Proceedings)*, 17(3):229–239, July 1983.

[24] Thomas Porter and Tom Duff. Compositing Digital Images. In Hank Christiansen, editor, *Computer Graphics (SIGGRAPH '84 Proceedings)*, volume 18, pages 253–259, July 1984.

[25] Richard L. Potter, Linda J. Weldon, and Ben Shneiderman. Improving the Accuracy of Touch Screens: an Experimental Evaluation of Three Strategies. In *Proceedings of ACM CHI '88 Conference on Human Factors in Computing Systems*, pages 27–32, Washington, DC, 1988.

[26] Thierry Pudet. Real Time Fitting of Hand-Sketched Pressure Brushstrokes. In *Eurographics'94. Proceedings of the European Computer Graphics Conference and Exhibition*, Amsterdam, Netherlands, 1994. North-Holland.

[27] Barbara Robertson. Digital Toons. *Computer Graphics World*, pages 40–46, July 1994.

[28] Barbara Robertson. Disney Lets CAPS Out of the Bag. *Computer Graphics World*, pages 58–64, July 1994.

[29] Robert W. Scheifler and Jim Gettys. The X Window System. *ACM Transactions on Graphics*, 5(2):79–109, 1986.

[30] Philip J. Schneider. An Algorithm for Automatically Fitting Digitized Curves. In Andrew S. Glassner, editor, *Graphics Gems I*, pages 612–626, 797–807. Academic Press, 1990.

[31] Thomas W. Sederberg, Peisheng Gao, Guojin Wang, and Hong Mu. 2D Shape Blending: An Intrinsic Solution to the Vertex Path Problem. In James T. Kajiya, editor, *Computer Graphics (SIGGRAPH '93 Proceedings)*, volume 27, pages 15–18, August 1993.

[32] Michael A. Shantsis. A Model for Efficient and Flexible Image Computing. In Andrew Glassner, editor, *Proceedings of SIGGRAPH '94 (Orlando, Florida, July 24–29, 1994)*, Computer Graphics Proceedings, Annual Conference Series, pages 147–154. ACM SIGGRAPH, ACM Press, July 1994.

[33] Peter Van Sommers. *Drawing and Cognition*. Cambridge University Press, Cambridge, 1984.

[34] Jean-Michel Spiner. *PEGS Technical Description V1.00*, 1994.

[35] Bruce A. Wallace. Merging and transformation of raster images for cartoon animation. *Computer Graphics (SIGGRAPH '81 Proceedings)*, 15(3):253–262, August 1981.

(a) Rough drawing.

(b) Clean drawing.

(c) The cleaned animation sequence.

(d) Painted drawing.

(e) Final scene.

Figure 10: A character at different stages in the TicTacToon system

Fourier Principles for Emotion-based Human Figure Animation

Munetoshi Unuma   Ken Anjyo   Ryozo Takeuchi

Hitachi Research Laboratory†

Hitachi, Ltd.

Abstract

This paper describes the method for modeling human figure locomotions with emotions. Fourier expansions of experimental data of actual human behaviors serve as a basis from which the method can interpolate or extrapolate the human locomotions. This means, for instance, that transition from a walk to a run is smoothly and realistically performed by the method. Moreover an individual's character or mood, appearing during the human behaviors, is also extracted by the method. For example, the method gets "briskness" from the experimental data for a "normal" walk and a "brisk" walk. Then the "brisk" run is generated by the method, using another Fourier expansion of the measured data of running. The superposition of these human behaviors is shown as an efficient technique for generating rich variations of human locomotions. In addition, step-length, speed, and hip position during the locomotions are also modeled, and then interactively controlled to get a desired animation.

CR Categories and Subject Descriptors: I.3.3 [**Computer Graphics**]: Picture/Image Generation; I.3.7 [**Computer Graphics**]: Three-dimensional Graphics and Realism, Animation; I.6.3 [**Simulation and Modeling**]: Applications

Additional Keywords and Phrases: Human figure animation, Fourier analysis, Emotion

1. Introduction

Human or more generally articulated figure animations have been seen in a variety of application fields including advertising, entertainment, education, and simulation. The primary research goal now to further the animations is providing a system which allows animators to easily and interactively design and get desired movements. Many approaches to this goal are available, including key-framing[8], physics or robotics based methods [1, 3, 6, 11], and space-time control [5]. However many open problems remain and the required reality or complexity of the human animation may be rather different according to its application.

† 7-1-1 Omika Hitachi Ibaraki 319-12 Japan
{unuma, anjyo, takeuchi}@hrl.hitachi.co.jp

Permission to make digital/hard copy of part or all of this work for personal or classroom use is granted without fee provided that copies are not made or distributed for profit or commercial advantage, the copyright notice, the title of the publication and its date appear, and notice is given that copying is by permission of ACM, Inc. To copy otherwise, to republish, to post on servers, or to redistribute to lists, requires prior specific permission and/or a fee.

In a general system for articulated figure animations, an articulated body is modeled with a hierarchy of rotational joints each of which may have up to three degrees of freedom. Moreover, motion control of the model is also hierarchically prescribed, such as script-based specifications at the highest level of control and key-framing for joint angles control at the lowest. By the use of higher level control, the system should reduce the user's load of direct specifications for the desired movement [7, 9]. This heavy task would be reducible by introducing into the system a knowledge database about the variety of movements. A basic problem is then how to get and construct the database, which is particularly crucial for describing human behaviors. In other words the problem is how to *model* the behaviors, since we cannot measure all kinds of human behaviors in advance. We also note that human behavior is usually affected by an individual's emotion or character (to some extent), which must therefore be modeled.

In this paper we consider the problem of how to model human behaviors with emotions for the purpose of advertising or entertainment use. Therefore the solution of the problem should allow interactive and real-time control, while providing variations of movements, including cartoon-like exaggerations or expressions. The database of the human behaviors should then be concise and small enough for quick response and for needing limited storage in the computer's memory. In existing methods to tackle the problem, dynamic simulation [3, 11] or procedural models [2, 4] often have been used. However, dynamic simulation techniques require experiments (usually off-line) from the animator to get the desired result, whereas procedural approaches employ trial and error steps for suitable choice of the parameters involved. These inconveniences may occur particularly when animating individualized behaviors (such as with mood, characters or emotions). This is mainly because the existing methods do not directly deal with "emotion" or "mood" appearing with the human behavior. For instance, in making a "brisk" walk with a physics-based approach, if the animator wants to change the degree of briskness of the human model, then he has to adjust the parameters which are physically meaningful but do not directly prescribe nuances of emotion or mood.

The method we propose in this paper is for making "emotion-based" human animations. Characteristics of human behaviors are extracted in the method simply from the empirical data of actual human movements, without any physics-based simulations. Based on the Fourier series expansion of the original measured data, a functional model is defined for generating a rich variation of movements, far from the original. A prototype of the functional model was originally introduced in our former work [10], where the prototype was used only for describing the emotional aspect of human locomotions through the Fourier analysis and synthesis. In making a human figure animation, however, we must treat not only the emotional aspect but also the kinematic aspect. Therefore the functional model in this paper is further extended to provide intuitive parameters for simultaneously controlling emotional and kinematic human locomotions, where the kinematic control, for example, prescribe speed and step-length of the human figure model. In addition real-time and interactive control is performed with the functional model and this consequently provides wider variations of human figure animations than previous approaches.

2. Functional Models for Human Locomotions

2.1 Preparation

We first prepare a skeleton model represented with a hierarchical structure of rotational joints. The number of joints of the model and the degrees of freedom depend largely on the desired reality or quality. In this paper we employ a relatively simple model with nineteen joints which are hierarchically defined in Fig. 1. As shown in Fig. 2, each joint then has three degrees of freedom for rotation around x, y and z axes in the local coordinate system at each joint, where the y-axis is in the same direction as the stick direction of the previous joint.

Now we assume that the rotational joint angles Θ^m_x, Θ^m_y and Θ^m_z at the m-th joint are measured for all the joints except when m = 8 and 9, with a motion capturing system. The eighth and ninth joint angles' data are not used in our method (see Fig.1(a)), since tiptoe's landing is treated differently than other parts of the body (see **3.1**). The obtained data set of the m-th joint is then of a form like $\{(\Theta^m_x(i\Delta t), \Theta^m_y(i\Delta t), \Theta^m_z(i\Delta t)) \mid i = 1, 2, ..., n\}$, where Δt denotes the time interval specified in measuring with the capturing system, and $m \neq 8$ or 9. In addition, we assume that the obtained data set represents an (almost) periodic behavior, such as walking and running.

2.2 Rescaled Fourier Functional Model

Based on the discrete data of the m-th joint angle, let us first construct a functional model with continuous parameter of t, which represents the periodic behavior of the joint angle. In general, however, the period of the functional model is rather hard to estimate from the measured data of the joint angle, since the original data may be "noisy". Then we employ the Fourier

series expansion (approximation) of the joint angle as the functional model. For simplicity, hereafter, $\Theta_m(t)$ denotes $\Theta^m_x(t)$, $\Theta^m_y(t)$, or $\Theta^m_z(t)$. The period of $\Theta_m(t)$ for each m is originally the same value T_Θ, and the Fourier coefficients are obtained with the sample values $\Theta_m(t_p)$, $t_p \in [-T_\Theta/2, T_\Theta/2]$. In practice, however, we can estimate these coefficients, based on the sample values in a larger interval. After rescaling time parameter t, we may suppose that the period of $\Theta_m(t)$ is normalized to be 2π. Thus we have the following expressions, which we call a *rescaled Fourier functional model*:

$$\Theta_m(t) = A_{m\,0} + \Sigma_{n \geq 1} A_{m\,n} \sin(n\,t + \phi_{m\,n}). \qquad (1)$$

Similarly, based on the discrete sample data of the joint angles for another periodic behavior, we have

$$\Pi_m(t) = B_{m\,0} + \Sigma_{n \geq 1} B_{m\,n} \sin(n\,t + \psi_{m\,n}). \qquad (2)$$

We use, again by rescaling, $\Pi_m(t)$ as described in (2), whereas the original period of $\Pi_m(t)$ may be different from that of Θ_m.

As explained later, the effect of "rescaling" in the above functional models occurs typically when we make a transition animation between two different locomotions, such as "from walking to running".

2.3 Interpolation, Extrapolation, and Transition

We show, in this section, how the rescaled Fourier functional models are effectively used in making variations of human behaviors.

Let us consider the following function of two variables s and t:

$$\Xi_m(s,t) = \{(1-s)A_{m\,0} + sB_{m\,0}\} +$$
$$\Sigma_{n \geq 1}\{(1-s)A_{m\,0} + sB_{m\,0}\}\sin\{n\,t + (1-s)\phi_{m\,n} + s\psi_{m\,n}\}. \quad (3)$$

In (3), if we suppose that $0 \leq s \leq 1$, Ξ_m is then an interpolant

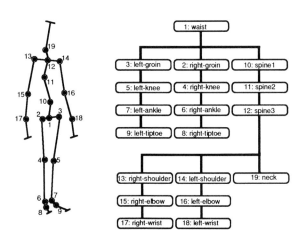

(a) Rotational joints considered.　　(b) Connection of human joints.

Figure 1. Skeleton model used.

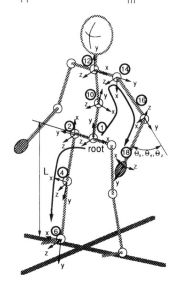

Figure 2. Local coordinate system of the model.

between Θ_m and Π_m in the mathematical sense that, as s varies from 0 to 1, Ξ_m continuously changes from Θ_m to Π_m. Moreover, in the context of human animations, we see that Ξ_m not only interpolates Θ_m and Π_m, but also extrapolates them. This means that the animations obtained from Ξ_m still provide realistically human movements as the interpolant, while expressing exaggerated behaviors as the extrapolant.

Fig. 3 shows an example: $\Theta_m(t)$ (= $\Xi_m(0, t)$) represents a "normal" walk (Fig.3(a)) and $\Pi_m(t)$ (= $\Xi_m(1, t)$) shows a "depressed" or "tired" walk (Fig.3(b)). If $0 < s < 1$, we see "a little tired" walk (Fig.3(c)). If $s > 1$, then we see that the degree of being "tired" is amplified (Fig.3(d)). On the other hand, if s becomes less than 0, the model looks rather brisk (Fig.3(e)). A smooth transition from walk to run is also obtained, if we get $\Pi_m(t)$ from the measured data of a run, with $\Theta_m(t)$ being the above walk function. The interpolant $\Xi_m(s, t)$ ($0 < s < 1$) then gives the smooth transition.

These examples illustrate well the rescaling effect involved in a rescaled Fourier functional model. For example, if we want to make the transition animation from walking to running by a traditional method, a skilled animator is required to consider many parameters, such as, speed, step, or one locomotion cycle. In particular the original data sets $\{\Theta_m(t)\}$ and $\{\Pi_m(t)\}$ have to be carefully synchronized. This means, for instance, that the arms must reach their furthest swinging position at the same time in both data sets, before making the transition animation. Once we get the "rescaled" Fourier expressions as described in (1) and (2), the synchronization of the data sets are automatically made and the desired animation is easily obtained. Finally we also note that the number of sine functions (n in (1) - (3)) is rather small (our experiments show that n is usually 3, and 7 at most). This implies that human locomotions are characterized with the small number of Fourier coefficients and phases in the Fourier functional model.

We have used $\Xi_m(s, t)$ in (3) as an inter/extrapolant and for making a transition animation, based on the two different measured data. In this case parameter s travels in the frequency-phase domain. An alternative of $\Xi_m(s, t)$ may be defined as $(1-s)\Theta_m(t) + \Pi_m(t)$, where s moves in the joint angle (time) domain. In both cases similar variations of human behaviors may be synthesized as long as we employ the rescaled Fourier functional models.

3. Fourier Characterizations for Human Animation

3.1 Step-Constraints Parameters

Next we see that the rescaled Fourier functional model is endowed with the "step-constraints" parameters, which control kinematic aspects of human locomotions: step length, speed, hip position, etc. In the following, italics denote parameters' names appearing on the screen of the prototyping editor (see **3.3**).

Step: The step length is specified in the Fourier domain by adjusting the spectrum component. For example, when using $\Theta_m(t)$ in (1), replace $A_{m\,n}$ by $step A_{m\,n}$. Then *step* is controlled. If *step* becomes larger, the step length is longer (Fig. 4).

Speed: Time-interval *speed*(= $\Delta\tau$) can be independently specified. Based on the discrete values $\{\Theta_m(k\Delta\tau)\}_k$, the human animation is made. If *speed* tends to 0, then the human model smoothly stops walking.

In particular we note that the above parameter *step* is easily introduced, because of the (rescaled) Fourier expressions of a measured data set.

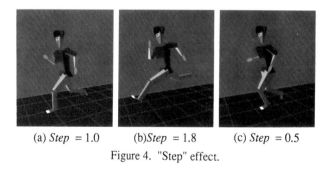

(a) *Step* = 1.0   (b)*Step* = 1.8   (c) *Step* = 0.5

Figure 4. "Step" effect.

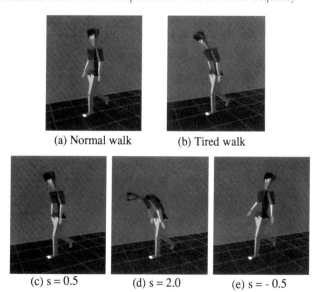

(a) Normal walk   (b) Tired walk

(c) s = 0.5   (d) s = 2.0   (e) s = - 0.5

Figure 3. Interpolation and extrapolation of "tired" walk (a) and (b) are obtained directly from the measured data sets, while (c) - (e) are by the method.

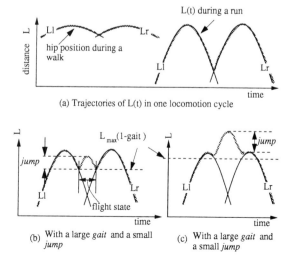

(a) Trajectories of L(t) in one locomotion cycle

(b) With a large *gait* and a small *jump*   (c) With a large *gait* and a small *jump*

Figure 5. Definition of hip position.

The next two parameters, *gait* and *jump*, relate to the hip position. To explain them, we must consider a human walking for a moment. Since one foot is always on the ground during the walk, we may assume that the following function L (t) is equal to the hip position L_{Walk} (t):

$$L(t) = max(L_l(t), L_r(t)). \qquad (4)$$

where $L_l(t)$ or $L_r(t)$ means the vertical length of the left or right groin from the ground, respectively. Since locomotion is a periodic activity with a basic pattern of one locomotion stride, we need to observe only one step of the locomotion, as shown in Fig.5(a). Then we consider the case of running, in which L (t) is shown like Fig.5(a), and it does not express the hip position anymore. A run actually involves a flight state. Therefore, to define the hip position L_{Run} (t) in the running case using L (t), we introduce the following parameters:

Gait: The parameter prescribes the time of the flight state, taking values from 0 to 1. At every frame during the animation, the normalized value N(t) is compared with the value of *gait*, where $N(t) = \{L_{max} - L(t)\}/L_{max}$ and $L_{max} = max_t\{L(t)\}$. If $gait \geq N(t)$, then we set L_{Run} (t) = L(t). Otherwise we define

$$L_{Run}(t) = L(t) + jump \sqrt{L_{max}(1- gait) - L(t)}, \qquad (5)$$

where *jump* is another parameter described next.
Intuitively, if *gait* becomes larger, the running movement looks more like a walk (Fig.6).

Jump: This controls the height during the flight. Figs.5(b) and (c), for example, show typical cases. If *jump* is much larger 1.0, the flight state is rather exaggerated.

(a) *gait* = 0.06   (b) *gait* = 0.5

Figure 6. "Gait" effect.

3.2 Superposition of Human Behaviors

In section **2.3**, we showed experimentally that the rescaled Fourier functional models successfully provide smooth transition of two different (measured) human movements. More generally, in this section, *superposition* of the functional models is used as an efficient technique for making emotion-based human figure animations.

Let $\{\Phi^1_m(t)\}$ and $\{\Phi^2_m(t)\}$ be the rescaled Fourier functional models of two different measured data sets:

$$\Phi^1_m(t) = A^1_{m0} + \Sigma A^1_{mn} \sin(nt + \phi^1_{mn}). \qquad (6\text{-}1)$$
$$n \geq 1$$

$$\Phi^2_m(t) = A^2_{m0} + \Sigma A^2_{mn} \sin(nt + \phi^2_{mn}). \qquad (6\text{-}2)$$
$$n \geq 1$$

Then we consider the following differences of the above Fourier coefficients:

$$A^{12}_{mn} = A^1_{mn} - A^2_{mn}. \qquad (7\text{-}1)$$

$$\phi^{12}_{mn} = \phi^1_{mn} - \phi^2_{mn}. \qquad (7\text{-}2)$$

The pairs $\{(A^{12}_{mn}, \phi^{12}_{mn})\}_n$ (n = 0, 1, 2, ...) are called the *Fourier characteristics* of the two measured data sets. As mentioned earlier, we may assume n is in practice rather small. Therefore it is believed that the Fourier characteristics provide a small and concise database of human behaviors. For example we can have the Fourier characteristics of "briskness", which are obtained from the two rescaled Fourier functional models of a normal walk and a "brisk" walk.

Associated with these Fourier characteristics, we can define the *Fourier characteristic function* as

$$\Psi_m(t) = A^{12}_{m0} + \Sigma A^{12}_{mn} \sin(nt + \phi^{12}_{mn}). \qquad (8)$$
$$n \geq 1$$

The superposition of human behaviors by our method is then stated as:

Suppose that we have the Fourier characteristic function $\Psi_m(t)$ in (8), and that we have another measured data set with its rescaled Fourier functional model Π_m (t) in (2). Then, Ψ_m and Π_m give a rich variation of human behaviors through linear interpolation, extrapolation, and transition, if Ψ_m and Π_m express mutually meaningful human behaviors.

Fig. 7 shows examples of this technique. In this case Π_m (t) in the above statement expresses the running data for Fig. 7(a), while the Fourier characteristic function $\Psi_m(t)$ describes "briskness" which is extracted from the data of a walk and of a "brisk" walk. Then we get a "brisk" run as shown in Fig. 7(b), where we employ $\Xi_m(s, t)$ in (3) for linear transition. Similarly we have a "tired" or "depressed" run from the data of a run and "tiredness" in Fig. 7(c). In this way our experimental results assert that the superposition works well.

(b) a "brisk" run

(a) a run

(c) a "tired" run

Figure 7. Superposition of human behaviors - "briskness" and "tiredness" are extracted from the measured data sets of walking.

Formally, if we assume that $\Phi^2{}_m(t)$ in (8) is identically zero, the techniques described in section **2.3** can be regarded as a special case of the superposition technique. In such a case, the rescaled Fourier functional model of a measured data set simply equals its Fourier characteristic function.

3.3 Results and Discussion

The demonstration editor in Fig.8 is used for real-time previewing. The method runs in almost real-time (about 10 frames per second) on a R4000 workstation. The step-constraints parameters and the Fourier characteristics, such as of briskness, tiredness, or a run, are therefore interactively specified with the editor.

Figs. 9 and 10 show examples of the effects of these parameters and characteristics. We note that consistency of the parameters and characteristics observed in Fig. 9 is also derived from the rescaled Fourier functional models. The two still images in Fig. 10 are taken from an animation example, featuring the "TV robo". Combined with additional stage effects, such as a flash in Fig. 10(a), the proposed method succeeded in making the TV robo perform well on the bright and dark side of life. An additional feature of the rescaled Fourier functional model is demonstrated with Fig. 10(b), where a shivering walk is made. This is easily achieved by adding randomized higher frequency terms to the Fourier functional model. Adding noise as higher frequency terms to a rescaled Fourier functional model is useful for such dramatization. We also note that the generated animations show a wider variation than existing physics-based or procedural approaches.

Currently the proposed method is not invertible. This means that the transition from running to walking by the method is unnatural, while the realistic transition from walking to running is made by the method. This problem must be addressed. The very limitation of the superposition technique in **3.2** will be clarified under more explicit formulation.

4. Conclusion

Based on the experimental data set of a few different human movements, the proposed method allows human movements to be interactively designed and generated in a wider variety. The key idea in the method is the use of Fourier series expansions of the measured data sets. Then smooth interpolation, extrapolation, and transition between different types of movements were made. In addition mood or characteristics of the human behaviors, such as "tiredness", and "briskness", were successfully extracted by the method.

A promising direction of future research involves extensions of the method in order to describe non-periodic human behaviors and to model a crowd or throng of people. In addition, the integration of the proposed method and dynamics techniques will be indispensable for further applications.

Acknowledgements

We would like to thank Yoshihiro Uehara of Nippon Television Network Corp. (NTV) for his generous support and encouragement, and Yoshinori Sugano of NTV and Shigeru Yamada of NTV Art Center Corp. for their production help. We are also grateful to Shinya Tanifuji and Motomi Odamura for their support of the publication of this research. Additional thanks go to Carol Kikuchi and Masa Tani for their comments and suggestions.

References

[1] Badler, N., Phillips C., and Webber, B.L. *Simulating Humans.* Oxford University Press 1993.

[2] Boulic, R., Magnenat-Thalmann, N., and Thalmann, D. A Global Human Walking Model with Real-time Kinematic Personification. *The Visual Computer.* 6, 344-358, 1990.

[3] Bruderlin, A. and Calvert, T.W. Goal-directed, Dynamic Animation of Human Walking. Proceedings of SIGGRAPH 89 (Boston, Massachusetts, July 31- August 4, 1989). In *Computer Graphics,* 23, 3 (July 1989), 233-242.

[4] Bruderlin, A., Teo, C.G. and Calvert, T.W. Procedural Movement for Articulated Figure Animation. *Computers & Graphics.* 18, 453- 461, 1994.

[5] Cohen, M.F. Interactive Spacetime Control for Animation. Proceedings of SIGGRAPH 92 (Chicago, Illinois, July 26-31, 1992). In *Computer Graphics,* 26, 2 (July 1992), 293-302.

[6] Girard, M. and Maciejewski, A.A. Computational Modeling for Computer Generation of Legged Figures. Proceedings of SIGGRAPH 85 (San Francisco, California, July 23-27, 1985). In *Computer Graphics,* 19, 3 (July 1985), 263-270.

[7] Koga, Y., Kondo, K., Kuffner, J. and Latombe, J-C. Planning Motions with Intentions. Proceedings of SIGGRAPH 94 (Orlando, Florida, July 24- 29, 1994). In *Computer Graphics* Proceedings, Annual Conference Series, 1994. ACM SIGGRAPH, pp. 395-408, 1994.

[8] van de Panne, M. and Fiume, E. Sensor-Actuator Networks. Proceedings of SIGGRAPH 93 (Anaheim, California, August 1- 6, 1993). In *Computer Graphics* Proceedings, Annual Conference Series, 1993. ACM SIGGRAPH, pp. 335-342, 1993.

[9] Sturman, D. Interactive Keyframe Animation of 3-D Articulated Models. *Graphics Interface '86, Tutorial on Computer Animation.* 1986.

[10] Unuma, M., and Takeuchi, R. Generation of Human Motion with Emotion. Proceedings of Computer Animation '91, pp. 77 - 88, 1991.

[11] Wilhelms, J. Using Dynamic Analysis for Realistic Animation of Articulated Bodies. *IEEE Computer Graphics and Applications* 7, 12-27, 1987.

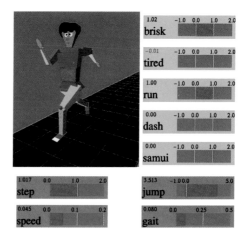

Figure 8. Demonstration editor.

(a) $run = 1.0$; $jump = 5.0$

(b) $run = 1.0$, $brisk = 1.37$; $step = 1.8$, $gait = 0.5$

(c) $run = 1.0$, $brisk = 1.37$; $step = 1.8$, $gait = 0.06$

Figure 9. Emotion-based running examples with step-constraints.

(b) "Shade"

Figure 10. Stills from animation example.
(Courtesy NTV Corp.)

Motion Signal Processing

Armin Bruderlin[1]
Simon Fraser University

Lance Williams[2]
Apple Computer, Inc.

Abstract

Techniques from the image and signal processing domain can be successfully applied to designing, modifying, and adapting animated motion. For this purpose, we introduce multiresolution motion filtering, multitarget motion interpolation with dynamic time-warping, waveshaping and motion displacement mapping. The techniques are well-suited for reuse and adaptation of existing motion data such as joint angles, joint coordinates or higher level motion parameters of articulated figures with many degrees of freedom. Existing motions can be modified and combined interactively and at a higher level of abstraction than conventional systems support. This general approach is thus complementary to keyframing, motion capture, and procedural animation.

Keywords: human animation, motion control, digital signal processing.

1 Introduction

Motion control of articulated figures such as humans has been a challenging task in computer animation. Using traditional keyframing [27], it is relatively straightforward to define and modify the motion of rigid objects through translational and rotational trajectory curves. However, manipulating and coordinating the limbs of an articulated figure via keyframes or the spline curves they define is a complex task that draws on highly developed human skills. More general, global control of the character of an animated motion would be useful in fine-tuning keyframed sequences. Such global control would make predefined sequences more useful, and libraries of animated motion more valuable.

Much of the recent research in motion control of articulated figures has been directed towards reducing the amount of motion specification to simplify the task of the animator. The idea is to build some knowledge about motion and the articulated structure into the system so that it can execute certain aspects of movement autonomously. This has lead to the development of higher level control schemes [5, 6, 15, 22, 33] where the knowledge is frequently specified in terms of rules, and physically-based modeling techniques [8, 12, 18, 30, 31] in which knowledge is embedded in the equations of motion, constraints and possibly an optimization expression. Both approaches often suffer from lack of interactiv-

ity: they don't always produce the motion which the animator had in mind, and complex models have a slow interactive cycle. To increase the expressive power of such models, more control parameters can be introduced. Once again, higher-level editing tools for the trajectories of such control parameters would ease animators' burdens and generalize their results.

An alternative method to obtain movements of articulated figures is performance animation where the motion is captured from live subjects. Although a variety of technologies have been developed to fairly reliably measure performance data [19], the computer graphics literature makes scant mention of editing techniques for recorded motion. In the absence of effective editing tools, a recorded movement that is not quite "right" requires the whole data capture process to be repeated.

Because of the complexity of articulated movements and the limitations of current motion control systems as outlined above, we believe that it is desirable to develop tools that make it easy to reuse and adapt existing motion data. For this purpose, we adopt techniques from the image and signal processing domain which provide new and useful ways to edit, modify, blend and align motion parameters of articulated figures. These techniques represent a pragmatic approach to signal processing by providing analytic solutions at interactive speeds, and lend themselves to higher level control by acting on several or all degrees of freedom of an articulated figure at the same time.

In this paper, we treat a motion parameter as a sampled signal. A signal contains the values at each frame[1] for a particular degree of freedom. These values could come from evaluating a spline curve in a keyframing system, or be derived from the tracked markers in a motion capture system. In animating articulated figures we are often concerned with signals defining joint angles or positions of joints, but the signal-processing techniques we have implemented also apply to higher level parameters like the trajectory of an end-effector or the varying speed of a walking sequence.

In Section 2, we present the method of multiresolution filtering and its application to parameters of motion. Section 3 discusses multitarget interpolation, while pinpointing a severe problem of this technique when used for motion blending — the absence of an automatic alignment or registration of movements. A solution to this problem is given based on the principle of dynamic time-warping. Section 4 introduces waveshaping as a rapid nonlinear signal modification method useful for tasks such as mapping joint limits of articulated figures. Section 5 concludes the editing techniques we have developed with motion displacement mapping, an extremely general tool which permits editing of densely-sampled motion data with the ease of keyframing. Each of these sections provides illustrative examples. Finally, conclusions are given in section 6.

[1]School of Computing Science, Simon Fraser University, Burnaby, B.C. V5A 1S6, Canada, (armin@cs.sfu.ca).

[2]Apple Computer, Inc., 1 Infinite Loop, MS 301-3J, Cupertino, CA 95014, USA, (amberinca@aol.com).

Permission to make digital/hard copy of part or all of this work for personal or classroom use is granted without fee provided that copies are not made or distributed for profit or commercial advantage, the copyright notice, the title of the publication and its date appear, and notice is given that copying is by permission of ACM, Inc. To copy otherwise, to republish, to post on servers, or to redistribute to lists, requires prior specific permission and/or a fee.

[1]Sampled signals have values defined at regular intervals which, in a good animation system, should be completely decoupled from the nominal "frame rate" of the final product. We will speak of "frames" at the sample rate without intending any loss of generality.

© 1995   ACM-0-89791-701-4/95/008 $3.50

2 Multiresolution Filtering

In the motion capture realm, most systems have provision for non-linear impulse-noise removal filters (Tukey filters) as well as linear smoothing filters for noise reduction in digitized data. There has been less published discussion of the use of signal processing operations to edit or modify captured motion for creative purposes. The "lag, drag, and wiggle" recursive filters in Inkwell [17] represent more relevant previous work in the application of signal processing to keyframed 2D animated motion. These filters were used to stylize motion by invoking linear systems behavior without a more structured physical model, and permitted lively animated effects without unduly taxing the animator. In another related approach, Unuma et al. [28] apply Fourier transformations to data on human walking for animation purposes. Based on frequency analysis of the joint angles, a basic 'walking' factor and a 'qualitative' factor like "brisk" or "fast" are extracted. These factors are then used to generate new movements by interpolation and extrapolation in the frequency domain, such that now a walk can be changed continuously from normal to brisk walking.

"Multiresolution filtering" describes a range of digital filter-bank techniques which typically pass a signal through a cascade of lowpass filters to produce a set of short-time bandpass or lowpass signal components. By applying filtering recursively to the output of successive filter bank stages, and downsampling lowpass components as appropriate, these filter banks can be quite efficient; they can produce short-time spectra at roughly the same $n \log(n)$ expense as the Fast Fourier Transform.

The method of multiresolution filtering has been extensively exercised by Burt et al. [4, 20] as an image representation method advantageous for certain kinds of operations, such as seamless merging of image mosaics and intra-image interpolation (noise removal). It has also been applied to temporal dissolves between images [26]. Images may be stored as lowpass (Gaussian) or bandpass (Laplacian) pyramids of spatial filterbands, where each level represents a different octave band of spatial frequencies. Operations like merging two images are then performed band-by-band before reconstructing the image by adding up the resulting bands. In this way, the fine detail of an image corresponding to the higher frequencies can be treated separately from the coarse image features encoded by the low frequencies.

In the currently popular wavelet parlance [7], Burt's Gaussian pyramid is a multiresolution analysis in terms of a cubic B-spline scaling function. The corresponding Laplacian pyramid is simply a bandpass counterpart, where each successively higher level of detail has an interpolated copy of the level beneath subtracted from it. The Laplacian pyramid can be computed directly in this way, or via a modified wavelet transform. Burt's method is more efficient for signals of more than one dimension [29]. As a general observation, for synthesis and modification (as well as many analysis tasks for computer vision), oversampled filter banks like Burt's are more useful than strict subband decompositions (where the number of coefficients does not exceed the number of samples in the original signal). A direct contrast is in the way small translations of an image are projected: sparse decompositions change radically with small offsets of the input image, whereas the Burt pyramids change smoothly. The reduction in coefficients attendant on a subband filterbank may speed numerical solution of some problems; a recent effort in the animation domain is the wavelet formulation of spacetime interpolation for physically- based keyframing by Liu et al. [18]. They did not use the the frequency decomposition to provide direct manipulation of motion, and we believe Burt's method is more appropriate for this purpose.

The first step in applying Burt's multiresolution analysis is to obtain the lowpass pyramid by successively convolving the image with a B-spline filter kernel (e.g. 5×5), while the image is subsampled by a factor of 2 at each iteration (as shown at the left of Figure 1, where G_0 is the original image). This process is repeated until the image size is reduced to one pixel, which is the average intensity, or DC value. The bandpass pyramid is then calculated by repeatedly differencing 2 successive lowpass images, with the subtrahend image being expanded first in each case (right of Figure 1, where L_0 is the highest frequency band). The image can be reconstructed without manipulation by adding up all the bandpass bands plus the DC. The same procedure can be performed on two or more images at the same time, whereby operations like merging are executed band by band before reconstructing the final result.

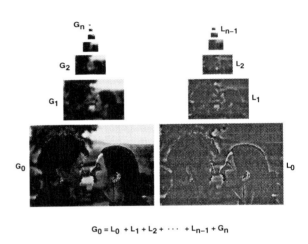

$$G_0 = L_0 + L_1 + L_2 + \cdots + L_{n-1} + G_n$$

Figure 1: Left: lowpass pyramid; right: bandpass pyramid.

2.1 Motion Multiresolution Filtering

The principles of image multiresolution filtering are now applied to motion parameters of an articulated figure, motivated by the following intuition: low frequencies contain general, gross motion patterns, whereas high frequencies contain detail, subtleties, and (in the case of digitized motion) most of the noise. Each motion parameter is treated as a one-dimensional signal from which the lowpass (G) and bandpass (L) levels are calculated. An example is illustrated in Figure 2 based on the signal of the sagittal knee angle of two walking cycles generated with GAITOR [2].

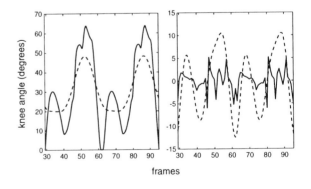

Figure 2: Left: lowpass G_0 (solid) and G_3 (dashed; B-spline kernel of width 5); right: bandpass L_0 (solid) and L_2 (dashed) of the sagittal knee angle for two walking cycles.

2.1.1 Filtering Algorithm

The length m (number of frames) of each signal determines how many frequency bands (fb) are being computed:

$$\text{let } 2^n \leq m \leq 2^{n+1}, \text{ then } fb = n.$$

Instead of constructing a pyramid of lowpass and bandpass sequences where each successive sequence is reduced by a factor of two, alternatively the sequences are kept the same length and the filter kernel (w) is expanded at each level by inserting zeros between the values of the filter kernel (a, b, c below) [3]. For example, with a kernel of width 5,

$$
\begin{aligned}
w_1 &= [c \ b \ a \ b \ c], \\
w_2 &= [c \ 0 \ b \ 0 \ a \ 0 \ b \ 0 \ c], \\
w_3 &= [c \ 0 \ 0 \ 0 \ b \ 0 \ 0 \ 0 \ a \ 0 \ 0 \ 0 \ b \ 0 \ 0 \ 0 \ c], \text{etc.},
\end{aligned}
$$

where $a = 3/8$, $b = 1/4$ and $c = 1/16$. Since we are dealing with signals rather than images, the storage penalty compared to a true pyramid is not as significant ($fb \times i$ versus $4/3 \times i$, where $i =$ number of data points in original signal), while reconstruction is faster since the signal does not have to be expanded at each level. We now state the motion multiresolution algorithm in detail. Steps 1 to 5 are performed simultaneously for each motion parameter signal:

1. calculate lowpass sequence of all fb signals ($0 \leq k < fb$) by successively convolving the signal with the expanded kernels, where G_0 is the original motion signal and G_{fb} is the DC:

$$G_{k+1} = w_{k+1} \times G_k;$$

This can be calculated efficiently by keeping the kernel constant and skipping signal data points (i ranges over all data points of a signal)[2]:

$$G_{k+1}(i) = \sum_{m=-2}^{2} w_1(m) \, G_k(i + 2^k m);$$

2. obtain the bandpass filter bands ($0 \leq k < fb$):

$$L_k = G_k - G_{k+1};$$

3. adjust gains for each band and multiply L_k's by their current gain values (see example below).

4. blend bands of different motions (optional, see multitarget interpolation below).

5. reconstruct motion signal:

$$G_0 = G_{fb} + \sum_{k=0}^{fb-1} L_k.$$

---

[2]We implemented several treatments of the boundary of the signal, that is when $i + 2^k m$ lies outside the domain of the signal. The two most promising approaches have proved to be reflecting the signal, and keeping the signal values constant (i.e. equal to the first/last data point) outside its boundaries.

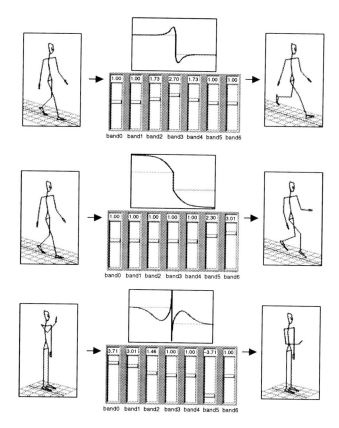

Figure 3: Adjusting gains of bands for joint angles; top: increasing middle frequencies; middle: increasing low frequencies; bottom: using negative gain value.

2.1.2 Examples

An application of motion multiresolution filtering is illustrated in Figure 3. Displayed like an equalizer in an audio amplifier, this is a kind of graphic equalizer for motion, where the amplitude (gain) of each frequency band can be individually adjusted via a slider before summing all the bands together again to obtain the final motion. A step function shows the range and effect of changing frequency gains. We applied this approach successfully to the joint angles (70 degrees of freedom) of a human figure. The same frequency band gains were used for all degrees of freedom. In the example illustrated at the top of Figure 3, increasing the middle frequencies (bands 2, 3, 4) of a walking sequence resulted in a smoothed but exaggerated walk. By contrast, increasing the high frequency band (band 0) added a nervous twitch to the movement (not shown in Figure 3), whereas increasing the low frequencies (bands 5, 6) generated an attenuated, constrained walk with reduced joint movement (Figure 3 middle). Note that the gains do not have to lie in the interval [0, 1]. This is shown at the bottom of Figure 3, where band 5 is negative for a motion-captured sequence of a figure knocking at the door, resulting in exaggerated anticipation and follow-through for the knock. We also applied the same filtering to the joint positions (147 degrees of freedom) of a human figure. Increasing the gains for the middle frequency bands of a walking sequence produced a slight scaling effect of the end effectors, and resulted in a squash-and-stretch cartoon walk (Figure 4).

From the examples, it becomes apparent that some constraints such as joint limits or non-intersection with the floor can be violated in the filtering process. Our motion-editing philosophy is to employ constraints or optimization after the general character of the motion has been defined (see displacement mapping in section 5 below; or a

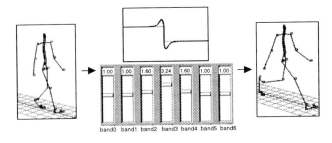

Figure 4: Adjusting gains of bands for joint positions.

more general optimization method [13]). Whereas being trapped in local minima is the bane of global optimization for most problems, animated motion is a good example of an underconstrained problem where the closest solution to the animator's original specification is likely the best. Of course, many animators disdain consistent physics, which is another good reason to decouple motion editing from constraint satisfaction.

Finally, we suggest that a multiresolution approach could also be quite useful in defining motion sequences, rather than simply modifying them. Much like an artist creating a picture blocks out the background first with a big brush, then adds more and more detail with finer and finer brushes, a generic motion pattern could be defined first by low frequencies, and then "finetuned" by adding in higher frequency refinements[3].

3 Multitarget Interpolation

Multitarget interpolation refers to a process widely used in computer animation to blend between different models. The technique was originally applied in facial animation [1, 21]. We might have a detailed model of a happy face, which corresponds parametrically to similar models of a sad face, quizzical face, angry face, etc. The control parameters to the model might be high level (like "raise left eyebrow by 0.7"), very high level (like "be happy"), or they might simply be the coordinates of the points on a surface mesh defining the shape of part of the face. By blending the corresponding parameters of the different models to varying degrees, we can control the expression of the face.

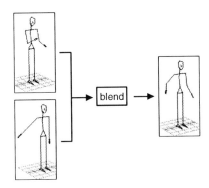

Figure 5: Example of multitarget motion interpolation.

3.1 Multitarget Motion Interpolation

We can apply the same technique to motion. Now we might have a happy walk, a sad walk, angry walk, etc., that can be blended freely to provide a new result. Figure 5 shows an example of blending two

[3]Personal communication, Ken Perlin, New York University, 1994.

different motions of a human figure, a drumming sequence and a "swaying arm sideways" sequence. In this case, the blend is linear, i.e. add 0.4 of the drum and 0.6 of the arm-sway. In general, the blend can be animated by "following" any trajectory in time. Guo et al. [11] give a good discussion of this approach which they term parametric frame space interpolation. Our approach generalizes on theirs in that the motion parameters such as joint angles to be blended are completely decoupled from one another, and have no implicit range limits. Each component of an arbitrary ensemble of input parameters can have an independent blending coefficient assigned to it.

As indicated in step (4) of the multiresolution algorithm above, we can mix multitarget interpolation and multiresolution filtering to blend the frequency bands of two or more movements separately. This is illustrated in Figure 6 for the same two motions (a drum and an arm-sway) as in Figure 5. Adjusting the gains of each band for each motion and then blending the bands provides finer control while generating visually much more pleasing and convincing motion.

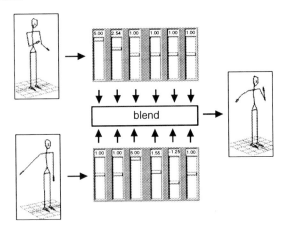

Figure 6: Multitarget interpolation between frequency bands.

However, there is a potential problem when applying multitarget interpolation to motion which relates to the notion of parametric correspondence as stated above: for all our face models to "correspond parametrically" implies that the parameters of each of the models has a similar effect, so that if a parameter raises the left eyebrow of face number one, a corresponding parameter raises the left eyebrow in face number two. If our parameters are simply surface coordinates, it means that the points on each surface correspond, so if the point at U, V coordinates $U1, V1$ is at the tip of the left eyebrow, the point at the same coordinates in any other face will also be at the tip of the left eyebrow.

In motion, parametric correspondence means much the same thing, except that now a correspondence with respect to time is required. If we are blending walk cycles, the steps must coincide so that the feet strike the ground at the same time for corresponding parameter values. If the sad walk is at a slower pace than the happy walk, and we simply blend them together without first establishing a correspondence between the steps, the blend will be a curious dance of uncoordinated motions, and the feet will no longer strike the ground at regular intervals; indeed, they are no longer guaranteed to strike the ground at all (see Figure 7). Thus, multitarget motion interpolation must include both a distortion (remapping a function in time) and a blend (interpolating among different mapped values). In the visual domain a transformation like this is termed a "morph."

Another example is illustrated in Figure 8; here the motion sequences of two human figures waving at different rates and intensities (a "neutral" and a "pronounced" wave) were first blended without timewarping. This resulted in a new wave with undesirable

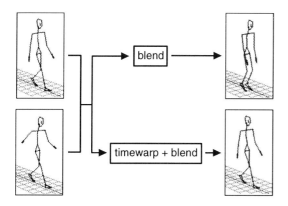

Figure 7: Blending two walks without (top) and with (bottom) correspondence in time.

secondary waving movements superimposed. After timewarping the neutral to the pronounced wave, the blend produced the neutral wave at the pronounced rate. In the following section we describe an automatic method for establishing correspondence between signals to make multitarget motion interpolation meaningful and useful.

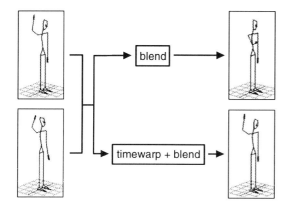

Figure 8: Blending two waves without (top) and with (bottom) correspondence in time.

3.2 Dynamic Timewarping

The field of speech recognition has long relied on a nonlinear signal matching procedure called "dynamic timewarping" to compare templates (for phonemes, syllables or words) with input utterances [9]. Apart from being subject to the usual random error, each acoustic input signal also shows variations in speed from one portion to another with respect to the template signal. The timewarp procedure identifies a combination of expansion and compression which can best "warp" the two signals together.

In our case, timewarping is applied in the discrete time domain to register the corresponding motion parameter signals such as joint angles. In Figures 7 and 8, the timewarping was done simultaneously for all 70 rotational degrees of freedom of the human figure for the duration of the movement sequences. If we have a military march and a drunken stagger, two new gaits can immediately be defined from the timewarp alone: the military march at the drunken pace, and the drunken stagger at the military pace. Figure 9 shows an example for one degree of freedom (knee angle) for the two walks warped in Figure 7. However, we are not limited to these two extreme warps, but may freely interpolate between the mappings of the two walks, and between the amplitudes of the signals through these mappings independently.

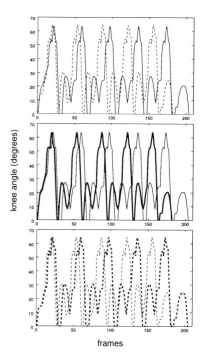

Figure 9: Top: sagittal knee angles curves of two walks; middle: bold = solid curve warped to match dashed; bottom: bold dashed = dashed curve warped to match solid.

3.2.1 Timewarp Algorithm

The problem can be decomposed and solved in two steps: finding the optimal sample correspondences between the two signals, and applying the warp. The vertex correspondence problem is defined as finding the globally optimal correspondence between the vertices (samples) of the two signals: to each vertex of one signal, assign (at least) a vertex in the other signal such that a global cost function measuring the "difference" of the two signals is minimized. In this sense, the problem is related to contour triangulation [10] and shape blending [24], and is solved by dynamic programming optimization techniques. The solution space can be represented as a two-dimensional grid, where each node corresponds to one possible vertex assignment (see Figure 10). The optimal vertex correspondence solution is illustrated in the grid by a path from $(0, 0)$ to $(9, 9)$. In general, there are $O(n^n/n!)$ such possible paths[4].

When applying timewarping to recognition, the best fit to a canon of signals is computed; no subsequent use is made of a warped signal. The algorithms which perform the warp typically do so by forming a discrete, point-sampled correspondence [9]. For synthetic purposes, more continuous transformations and cost functions are appropriate [32, 25]. We adopted Sederberg's shape blending algorithm [24] which guarantees a globally optimal solution by visiting every node in the grid once ($O(n^2)$ with constant amount of work per node). Upon reaching node (n, n), the optimal solution is recovered by backtracking through the graph. Sederberg's "physically-based" approach measures the difference in "shape" of the two signals by calculating how much work it takes to deform one signal into the other. The cost function consists of the sum of local stretching and bending work terms, the former involving two, the latter three adjacent vertices of each signal. Intuitively, the larger the difference in distance between two adjacent vertices of

---

[4]This holds for the vertex correspondence problem, where we favor a diagonal move in the graph over a south-followed-by-east-move or an east-followed-by-a-south-move. For contour triangulation [10], where diagonal moves are denied, the complexity is $O((2n)!/(n!n!))$.

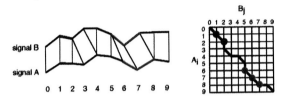

Figure 10: Vertex correspondence problem and cost functions.

one signal and the two vertices of the other (given by two adjacent nodes in the graph), the bigger the cost. Similarly, the larger the difference in angles between three adjacent vertices of one signal and the three vertices of the other (given by three adjacent nodes in the graph), the bigger the cost (for details, see [24]; an illustration is given in Figure 10). One additional check was introduced to make sure that we are really comparing corresponding angles in the two signals: if the middle of the three vertices used to calculate the angle is a local minimum in one signal and a local maximum in the other signal, then one of the angles (α) is inverted before calculating the cost term ($\alpha = 360 \deg - \alpha$).

The second part of the problem is to apply the warp given the optimal vertex correspondences. As in speech recognition [9], three cases are distinguished: substitution, deletion and insertion. This is indicated in the optimal path by a diagonal, horizontal and vertical line, respectively, between two nodes. For the following explanations, we assume that signal B is warped into A as shown in Figure 11, and the warped signal is denoted by B_w. Then if B_j and A_i are related by a substitution it follows that $B_{w_i} = B_j$. In case of a deletion, where multiple samples of B, $(B_j, B_{j+1}, \ldots, B_{j+k})$, correspond to one A_i, $B_{w_i} = \text{mean}(B_j, B_{j+1}, \ldots, B_{j+k})$. Finally, an insertion implies that one sample of B, B_j, maps to multiple samples of A, $(A_i, A_{i+1}, \ldots, A_{i+k})$. In this case, the values for $B_{w_i}, B_{w_{i+1}}, \ldots, B_{w_{i+k}}$ are determined by calculating a cubic B-spline distribution around the original value B_j.

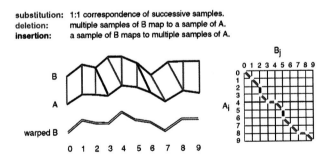

Figure 11: Application of timewarp (warp B into A).

4 Waveshaping

The transformations discussed so far are operations on the time history of a signal. Operations which are evaluated at each point in the signal without reference to its past or future trajectory are occasionally termed *point processes*. Such operations include scaling or offsetting the signal, but are more generally described as a functional composition. Familiar uses of functional composition in graphics include gamma correction and color-lookup, as well as tabular warping functions for images.

"Digital waveshaping" is the term applied to functional composition in computer sound synthesis. In this domain, a normalized input signal x (e.g. scaled to the range from -1 to $+1$) is directed through a discrete *shaping* function f (or waveshaping table) to synthesize steady-state or time-varying harmonic sound spectra. Although waveshaping is in general a nonlinear operation, its effects when applied to an input sine wave can be easily characterized [16]. In practical terms, if f is defined as the identity function $f(x) = x$, the signal will pass through unchanged. If f is slightly changed, say, to having a subtle bump near 0, then the signal x will be altered in that it will have slightly positive values where, and around where, it was zero before, thus x has now some bumps as well. If f is defined as a partial cycle of a cosine function going from minimum to maximum over the $[-1, +1]$ range, the values of x will be exaggerated in the middle and attenuated at the extremes. If f is a step function, x will be quantized to two values.

4.1 Motion Waveshaping

An example of how this idea can be adopted for animation is illustrated in Figure 12. Here the default identity shaping function has been modified to limit the joint angles for a motion sequence of an articulated figure waving. In the figure, "hard" limits are imposed: values of x greater than a limit value simply map to that value. An alternative is a "soft" limit: as values exceed the limit, they are mapped to values that gradually approach it. The implementation of our shaping function is based on interpolating cubic splines [14]; a user can add, delete and drag control points to define the function and then apply it to all or some degrees of freedom of an articulated figure.

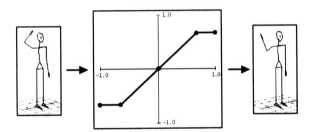

Figure 12: Capping of joint angles via a shape function.

Another application of waveshaping is to map the shape of input motions to a "characteristic" function. The shaping function in Figure 13 applied to the motion-captured data of a human figure sitting and drinking introduced extra undulations to the original monotonic reaching motion. In this way, it is possible to build up a library of shaping functions which will permit rapid experimentation with different styles of movement.

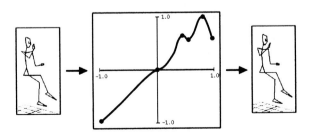

Figure 13: Adding undulations to motion via waveshaping.

5 Motion Displacement Mapping

Displacement mapping provides a means to change the shape of a signal locally through a displacement map while maintaining continuity and preserving the global shape of the signal. To alter a movement, the animator just changes the pose of an articulated figure at a few keyframes. A spline curve is then fitted through these displacements for each degree of freedom involved, and added to the original movement to obtain new, smoothly modified motion. The basic approach is illustrated in Figure 14. Step 1 is to define the desired displacements (indicated by the three vertical arrows) with respect to the motion signal; in step 2, the system then fits an interpolating cubic spline [14] through the values of the displacements (note that the first and last data points are always displacement points). The user can then adjust the spline parameters in step 3 before the system calculates the displaced motion satisfying the displacement points (step 4).

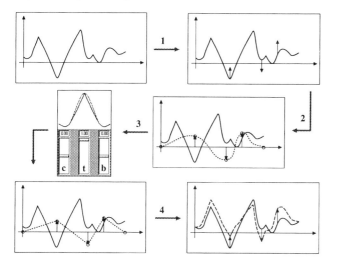

Figure 14: Steps in displacement mapping.

The displacement process can be applied iteratively until a desired result is achieved. Since the operation is cheap, a fast feedback loop is guaranteed. In the top part of Figure 15, we took the output of a multiresolution filtering operation on joint angles of a human walking figure, where some of the joint limits were violated and the feet did not make consistent contact with the ground, and read it into LifeForms [5], a system to animate articulated figures. There we adjusted some of the joints and translated the figure at a few keyframes for which displacement curves were quickly generated and applied to the motion of the figure as described above. To refine the resulting motion, a second loop was executed; a frame of the final result is shown on the top right of Figure 15. The same technique was used in modifying the rotoscoped motion of a human figure sitting and drinking (Figure 15, middle). Here, three out of the 600 motion-captured frames were modified to include some additional gestures of the arms and legs. In Figure 15, bottom, the joint angles for the arm and neck of a motion-captured knocking-at-a-door-sequence were changed for one frame via motion displacement mapping to obtain a knock at a higher impact point.

6 Conclusions

In this paper we have assembled a simple library of signal processing techniques applicable to animated motion. A prototype system has been implemented in the programming language C using the

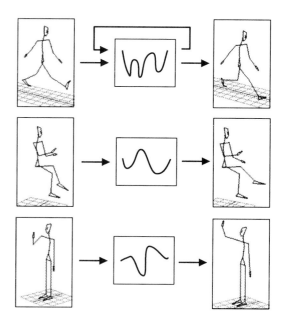

Figure 15: Examples of applying displacement curves.

Khoros application development environment [23]. The immediate goals of our motion-editing experiments have been fulfilled: the motion signal processing techniques provide a rapid interactive loop, and facilitate reuse and adaptation of motion data. By automating some aspects of motion editing such as time-registration of signals or increasing the middle frequencies for several degrees of freedom at the same time, these techniques lend themselves to higher level motion control and can serve as building blocks for high-level motion processing.

Of all the techniques introduced here, perhaps motion displacement mapping will prove to be the most useful; it provides a means by which a basic movement such as grasping an object from one place on a table can be easily modified to grasping an object anywhere else on the table. This allows simple and straightforward modification of motion-capture data through a standard keyframing interface. Timewarping as a non-linear method to speed up or slow down motion is useful in blending different movements. It could also play an important role in synchronizing various movements in an animation as well as in synchronizing animation with sound. Multiresolution filtering has been demonstrated as an easy tool to change the quality of a motion. Waveshaping represents a simple but efficient way to introduce subtle effects to all or some degrees of freedom. As the use of motion capture is becoming increasingly popular and libraries of motions are increasingly available, providing alternate methods for modifying and tweaking movement for reuse can be of great value to animators.

We believe that a wide range of animation tasks can be addressed with these techniques at a high level which is complimentary to and extends conventional spline tweaking tools:

- blending of motions is straightforward by using multitarget interpolation with automatic time registration of movements. This is a convenient way to build up more complex motions from elementary ones. For more fine-control, the frequency bands can first be computed for each motion before blending band-by-band while adjusting the frequency gains.

- concatenating motions is another practical application of multitarget interpolation, giving the user control over blending interval (transition zone) and blending coefficient. Multiresolution can be applied to concatenate band-by-band.

- capping of joint angles is a task easily accomplished by wave-shaping. This tool is also well suited to apply user-defined undulations to all or some degrees of freedom to make a "bland" motion more expressive.

- some animation tasks which can be achieved with multiresolution analysis include "toning down" a motion by increasing the low frequency gains, "exaggerating" a movement by increasing the middle frequencies, producing a "nervous twitch" by increasing the higher frequencies, and generating "anticipation and follow-through" by assigning negative gain values. Because of immediate feedback, the user can quickly experiment with different combinations of gain values for specific movement qualities.

- editing of motion-captured data is very desirable yet very tedious in current systems. As mentioned above, displacement mapping provides an interface through which the animator can conveniently change such data at a few selected "keyframes" while preserving the distinctive "signature" of the captured motion.

References

[1] BERGERON, P., AND LACHAPELLE, P. Controlling facial expressions and body movements in the computer-generated animated short: Tony de Peltrie. In *Computer Graphics (SIGGRAPH '85), Course Notes: Techniques for Animating Characters* (July 1985).

[2] BRUDERLIN, A., AND CALVERT, T. Interactive animation of personalized human locomotion. In *Graphics Interface '93, Proceedings* (May 1993), pp. 17–23.

[3] BURT, P. Multiresolution method for image merging. In *Computer Graphics (SIGGRAPH '86), Course Notes: Advanced Image Processing* (August 1986).

[4] BURT, P., AND ADELSON, E. A multiresolution spline with application to image merging. *ACM Transactions on Graphics 2*, 4 (October 1983), 217–236.

[5] CALVERT, T., BRUDERLIN, A., DILL, J., SCHIPHORST, T., AND WELMAN, C. Desktop animation of multiple human figures. *IEEE Computer Graphics & Applications 13*, 3 (1993), 18–26.

[6] CASSELL, J. ET AL. Animated conversation: Rule-based generation of facial expression, gesture & spoken intonation for multiple conversational agents. In *Computer Graphics (SIGGRAPH '94 Proceedings)* (July 1994), pp. 413–420.

[7] CHUI, C. K. *An Introduction to Wavelets, Series: Wavelet Analysis and its Applications*. Academic Press, Inc., 1992.

[8] COHEN, M. Interactive spacetime control for animation. In *Computer Graphics (SIGGRAPH '92 Proceedings)* (July 1992), vol. 26, pp. 293–302.

[9] DEMORI, R., AND PROBST, D. *Handbook of Pattern Recognition and Image Processing*. Academic Press, 1986, ch. Computer Recognition of Speech.

[10] FUCHS, H., KEDEM, Z., AND USELTON, S. Optimal surface reconstruction from planar contours. *Communications of the ACM 10*, 10 (1977), 693–702.

[11] GUO, S., ROBERGE, J., AND GRACE, T. Controlling movement using parametric frame space interpolation. In *Computer Animation '93, Proceedings* (1993), pp. 216–227.

[12] ISAACS, P., AND COHEN, M. Controlling dynamic simulation with kinematic constraints, behavior functions and inverse dynamics. In *Computer Graphics (SIGGRAPH '87 Proceedings)* (1987), vol. 21, pp. 215–224.

[13] KASS, M. Condor: Constraint-based dataflow. In *Computer Graphics (SIGGRAPH '92 Proceedings)* (1992), vol. 26, pp. 321–330.

[14] KOCHANEK, D., AND BARTELS, R. Interpolating splines with local tension, continuity and bias control. In *Computer Graphics (SIGGRAPH '84 Proceedings)* (1984), vol. 18, pp. 33–41.

[15] KOGA, Y., KONDO, K., KUFFNER, J., AND LATOMBE, J.-C. Planning motions with intentions. In *Computer Graphics (SIGGRAPH '94 Proceedings)* (July 1994), pp. 395–408.

[16] LEBRUN, M. Digital waveshaping synthesis. *Journal of the Audio Engineering Society 27*, 4 (1979), 250–266.

[17] LITWINOWICZ, P. Inkwell: A 2 1/2–D animation system. In *Computer Graphics (SIGGRAPH '91 Proceedings)* (1991), vol. 25, pp. 113–122.

[18] LIU, Z., GORTLER, S., AND COHEN, M. Hierarchical spacetime control. In *Computer Graphics (SIGGRAPH '94 Proceedings)* (July 1994), pp. 35–42.

[19] MEYER, K., APPLEWHITE, H., AND BIOCCA, F. A survey of posission trackers. *Presence: Teleoperators and Virtual Environments 1*, 2 (Spring 1992), 173–200.

[20] ODGEN, J., ADELSON, E., BERGEB, J., AND BURT, P. Pyramid-based computer graphics. *RCA Engineer 30*, 5 (1985), 4–15.

[21] PARKE, F. ET AL. State of the art in facial animation. In *Computer Graphics (SIGGRAPH '90), Course Notes* (August 1990).

[22] PHILLIPS, C., AND BADLER, N. Interactive behaviors for bipedal articulated figures. In *Computer Graphics (SIGGRAPH '91 Proceedings)* (1991), vol. 25, pp. 359–362.

[23] RASURE, J., AND KUBICA, S. The Khoros application development environment. Tech. rep., Khoral Research, Inc., 4212 Courtney NE, Albuquerque, NM, 87108, USA, 1993.

[24] SEDERBERG, T., AND GREENWOOD, E. A physically-based approach to 2–D shape blending. In *Computer Graphics (SIGGRAPH '92 Proceedings)* (1992), vol. 26, pp. 26–34.

[25] SERRA, B., AND BERTHOLD, M. Subpixel contour matching using continuous dynamic programming. *IEEE Computer Vision and Pattern Recognition* (1994), 202–207.

[26] STEIN, C., AND HITCHNER, H. The multiresolution dissolve. *SMPTE Journal* (December 1988), 977–984.

[27] STURMAN, D. A discussion on the development of motion control systems. In *Graphics Interface '86, Tutorial on Computer Animation* (1986).

[28] UNUMA, M., AND TAKEUCHI, R. Generation of human motion with emotion. In *Computer Animation '93, Proceedings* (1993), pp. 77–88.

[29] VELHO, L. *Piecewise Descriptions of Implicit Surfaces and Solids*. PhD thesis, University of Toronto, Computer Science, 1994.

[30] WILHELMS, J. Virya–a motion control editor for kinematic and dynamic aniamtion. In *Graphics Interface '86, Proceedings* (1986), pp. 141–146.

[31] WITKIN, A., AND KASS, M. Spacetime constraints. In *Computer Graphics (SIGGRAPH '88 Proceedings)* (1988), vol. 22, pp. 159–168.

[32] WITKIN, A., TERZOPOULUS, D., AND KASS, M. Signal matching through scale space. *International Journal of Computer Vision* (1987), 133–144.

[33] ZELTZER, D. Towards an integrated view of 3–D computer character animation. In *Graphics Interface '85, Proceedings* (1985), pp. 105–115.

Motion Warping

Andrew Witkin and Zoran Popović

Computer Science Department
Carnegie Mellon University
Pittsburgh, PA 15213

Keywords—animation, motion capture

Abstract

We describe a simple technique for editing captured or keyframed animation based on warping of the motion parameter curves. The animator interactively defines a set of keyframe-like constraints which are used to derive a smooth deformation that preserves the fine structure of the original motion. Motion clips are combined by overlapping and blending of the parameter curves. We show that whole families of realistic motions can be derived from a single captured motion sequence using only a few keyframes to specify the motion warp. Our technique makes it feasible to create libraries of reusable "clip motion."

1   Introduction

Systems for real-time 3-D motion capture have recently become commercially available. These systems hold promise as a means of producing highly realistic human figure animation with more ease and efficiency than traditional techniques afford. Motion capture can be used to create custom animation, or to create libraries of reusable clip-motion. Clip-motion libraries could facilitate conventional animation, or serve as databases for on-the-fly assembly of animation in interactive systems.

The ability to edit captured motion is vitally important. Custom animation must be tweaked or adjusted to eliminate artifacts, to achieve an accurate spatial and temporal match to the computer generated environment, or to overcome the spatial constraints of motion capture studios. To reuse clip motion we must to be able to freely alter the geometry (e.g. to fit a canned walk onto uneven terrain, to retarget a reaching motion, or to compensate for geometric variations from model to model) and the timing (for speed control, synchronization, etc.) and we also need to be able to perform seamless transitions, e.g. from a walk to a run, or from sitting to standing to walking. To be useful, editing should be much easier than animating from scratch, and should preserve the quality and naturalness of the original motion.

Motion capture yields an unstructured representation—a sequence of sampled positions for each degree of freedom, or through pre-processing using inverse kinematics, sequences of joint angle

values. Editing this kind of iconic description poses a problem analogous to that of editing a bitmapped image or a sampled hand-drawn curve (see figure 1.)

One approach to editing is to fit curves to the raw data, producing a keyframe-like description than can be modified by editing the curve's control points. The drawback of this approach is that the fit curve is liable to need at least as many control points as would have been needed to keyframe the motion manually. To make a global change to the motion would require all or most of the control points to be adjusted, losing much of motion capture's advantage over hand animation.

An alternative is to edit by transforming the iconic description, in a manner analogous to image morphing [1]. This is the approach we take here. We hypothesize that much of the "aliveness" of captured motion, distinguishing it from most keyframe animation, resides in the high-frequency details, and that these details can survive smooth transformations perceptually intact, provided the transformations are not too extreme.

The methodology we propose is similar to that of conventional keyframing, in that the animator interactively modifies the pose at selected frames. In fact, we are able to use a standard keyframe animation system as an interactive front end. However, we take the keyframes as constraints on a smooth deformation to be applied to the captured motion curves. The deformation satisfies the keyframe constraints while preserving the fine details of the original motion. This simple technique allows a whole family of realistic motions to be created from a single prototype using just a handful of keyframes to control the motion warp. Although inspired by the need to manipulate captured motion, the techniques we describe are applicable to keyframed motion as well. The main contribution of the paper is to introduce motion warping as a means of editing captured motion and to demonstrate that even very complex motions such as a human walk or a tennis swing can be radically reshaped using just a few keyframes without losing their realistic appearance.

To create transitions between clips, we perform motion blends using a technique similar to that described in [7]: the motions to be joined are overlapped, with one or more critical correspondence points identified. The combined motion is generated by time-warping the constituent motions to align the correspondence points, then blending using time-dependent weights.

The remainder of the paper is organized as follows: in the next section, we briefly describe related work. Section 3 describes the details of our warping and blending methods. In Section 4 we describe our implementation and results. We conclude with a brief discussion of the method's advantages and limitations, and directions for further work.

The authors' address is Computer Science Department, Carnegie Mellon University, 5000 Forbes Ave., Pittsburgh PA 15213. Andrew Witkin's email address is aw@cs.cmu.edu. Zoran Popović's email address is zoran@cs.cmu.edu.

Permission to make digital/hard copy of part or all of this work for personal or classroom use is granted without fee provided that copies are not made or distributed for profit or commercial advantage, the copyright notice, the title of the publication and its date appear, and notice is given that copying is by permission of ACM, Inc. To copy otherwise, to republish, to post on servers, or to redistribute to lists, requires prior specific permission and/or a fee.

2   Background

Keyframe animation is usually edited by adding, deleting, and modifying keyframes, the same process used to create the animation initially. Consequently, motion editing has seldom been treated as a distinct topic. State-of-the-art animation systems such as

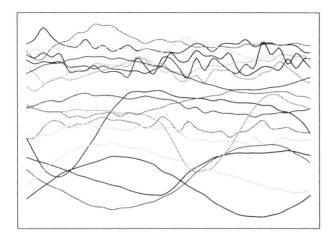

Figure 1: Some of the captured motion curves of human walking.

SOFTIMAGE™, Alias™, and Wavefront™ do provide simple motion editing tools (e.g. curve fitting, global scaling and translation). A motion editing system described in [2] provides a variety of tools for manipulating keyframes, and for frame-by-frame "repair" to enforce constraints. Commercial motion capture services possess proprietary editing tools which, to the best of our knowledge, employ curve fitting and control-point adjustment rather than deformation. As noted in the preceding section, this approach is not well suited to large-scale transformations.

As we have pointed out, a fair analogy can be drawn between our approach and image morphing [1], in that geometric deformations are being applied to iconic data. Litwinovicz and Williams [6] perform motion transformations to map motion tracking data onto image morphing control points. A few researchers have proposed function fitting [5], or motion curve filtering [9] to reduce data volume. In a similar vein, Finkelstein and Salesin's multiresolution curve fitting technique [3] might also be adapted to motion editing: modification of coarse-scale components would allow large-scale changes. However, it appears that the method would have to be significantly extended to handle multiple keyframe constraints.

Several motion blending techniques have been reported previously [7, 4, 2], although they do not appear to have been applied to captured motion data. The blending technique used here most closely resembles that of Perlin [7]. In his system, procedural motions are are concatenated using eased blending curves, using noise functions to add high frequency "texture" to the motion. Blending is also used to create hybrid motions. Perlin mentions the possibility of applying his techniques to captured data.

3   Warping

Articulated objects such as human figures are usually represented as rotation hierarchies parameterized by a whole-body translation, a whole-body rotation, and a set of joint angles. Motion is described by a set of *motion curves* each giving the value of one of the model's parameters as a function of time.

We wish to derive new motion curves based on a set of sparse keyframe-like constraints that are interactively specified by the animator. Subject to the constraints, the new curves should be similar to the originals in the sense that fine details of the motion are preserved.

We warp each motion curve independently, so we can consider just a single curve $\theta(t)$. As in conventional keyframing, the constraints include a set of (θ_i, t_i) pairs each giving the value that θ must assume at the specified time. In addition, we allow a set of

(t'_j, t_j) pairs acting as *time warp* constraints, each giving the time t'_j to which the value originally associated with time t_j should be displaced.

The warped motion curve $\theta'(t')$ is defined by two functions, $\theta'(t) = f(\theta, t)$, and $t = g(t')$. We map from t' to t rather than the other way around because this is the direction in which we will need to go: given an actual frame time, g tells us where to go in the untimewarped motion curve to fetch θ'. [1]

Constructing a suitable timewarp function is straightforward: we need a smooth well-behaved function $g(t')$ that interpolates the timewarp constraints, satisfying $t_j = g(t'_j)$, $\forall j$. Just about any interpolating spline would do; we chose the Cardinal spline [8]. Notice that g need not be monotonic: a negative slope means that time is reversed, which is sometimes desirable. A potential problem is that spline overshoot could induce unwanted time reversals. We have not found this to be a problem in practice with Cardinal splines, although it might be more of an issue if C2 splines were used.

We warp the values using a transformation of the form $\theta'(t) = a(t)\theta(t) + b(t)$, where $a(t)$ and $b(t)$ are scaling and offset functions respectively. The two functions must satisfy $\theta'_i(t_i) = a(t_i)\theta(t_i) + b(t_i)$, $\forall i$. A problem is that the values of a and b are not uniquely determined at the constraint points: we must somehow decide what mixture of scale and offset to use. After considering various schemes, we found that allowing the user to select manually whether to scale or shift works best. When scaling has been selected, we hold $b(t_i)$ constant as the user modifies a keyframe, obtaining $a(t_i) = (\theta'_i(t_i) - b(t_i))/\theta(t_i)$, and when shifting has been selected we hold $a(t_i)$ constant and solve for $b(t_i)$. Frequently, no scaling is desired, for instance to translate or rotate an entire motion. Scaling of joint angles is useful for exaggeration, in which case the offset function can be used to set the zero-point around which scaling takes place. Once the values of $a(t_i)$ and $b(t_i)$ are obtained $a(t)$ and $b(t)$ can be constructed straightforwardly using an interpolating spline, as for the time warp.

To concatenate motion clips with blending we overlap an interval at the end of the first clip with an interval at the beginning of the second, and progressively blending from the first clip to the second over the course of the overlap interval. To accomplish a seamless transition, one or both segments must generally be warped to bring them into reasonable alignment. If the intervals to overlap are of unequal duration they must be time warped as well. The blend is a straightforward weighted sum of the two motion curves as described in [7]: $\theta_{blend}(t) = w(t)\theta_1(t) + (1 - w(t))\theta_2(t)$, where $\theta_1(t)$ and $\theta_2(t)$ are the motion curves being blended and $w(t)$ is a normalized slow-in/slow-out weight function.

4   Results

Our implementation uses SOFTIMAGE/Creative Environment™ as a front end. From the animator's standpoint, setting up a motion warp is no different than creating ordinary keyframes: the animator selects a frame to be a key, then poses the model interactively. (The user must also specify whether the scaling or offset is being adjusted—offset is the default.) Time warp constraints can be imposed by sliding keyframe markers on a time line, or by entering times directly. There is nothing to preclude timewarping each motion curve independently, but thus far we have restricted ourselves to a single, global timewarp function.

All of the warped clips we have created required between one and five motion-warping keyframes to create, far fewer in each case than would be required to specify even a highly simplified version of the motion by direct keyframing. We have derived a large set of clip

---

[1] We could easily allow t' to depend on θ as well as t, letting f and g perform an arbitrary deformation of the (θ, t) plane but this does not appear to be useful.

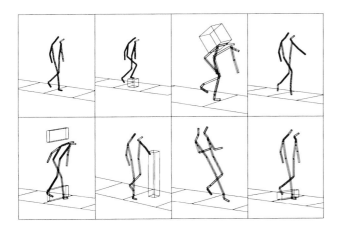

Figure 2: A frame from the original walking sequence, and the corresponding frames from a number of warped sequences. Clockwise from upper left: The original sequence; stepping onto a block; carrying a heavy weight; walking on tiptoe; bending through a doorway; stepping around a post; trucking; stepping over an obstacle

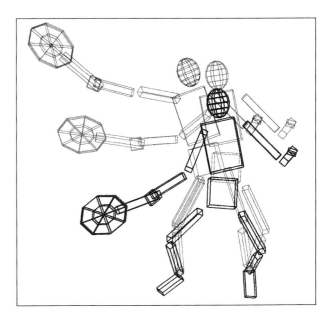

Figure 3: A frame from a captured motion sequence of a tennis forehand shot (green), and the corresponding frames from two warped sequences (red and blue.) Only a single keyframe at the moment of impact was required to produce the warped sequences.

motions from a basic captured walking sequence. The derived motions include: bending down to step through a low doorway; stepping over a low obstacle; stepping onto and down from a higher obstacle; walking around a still higher obstacle; climbing stairs; walking with a limp; a stooped walk; a "trucking" gait, and a "sneaky" walk. Figure 2 shows frames from these sequences. Figures 4 and 5 illustrate the "low doorway" in detail: figure 4 shows the original and warped motion curves for the left and right hip joints, and figure 5 shows selected frames from the original and warped sequences.

One application of motion warping is on-the-fly motion synthesis for virtual environments or games. We explored this idea by warping captured motion clips of a tennis player performing backhand, forehand, and overhead shots. Frames from several forehand shots are shown in figure 3. We found that we could produce realistic tennis shots over a wide range of ball trajectories by manually choosing the most appropriate motion clip, and setting a single key placing the racket on the ball at the desired moment of impact. The next step will be to automate clip selection and keyframing, possibly with blending between the stored clips, to create a parameterized tennis player.

We have also used motion warping to edit a clip created by conventional keyframing: we warped a straight-line cyclic walk of a bipedal creature into an animation where the same creature traverses an irregular series of stepping stones. The same effect could have been acheived by modifying all of the original keyframes, instead of warping. However, many more keys were used to specify the motion initially than were required to warp it.

5 Conclusion

We have described a simple technique for editing of captured or keyframed motion by warping and blending. We demonstrated that a wide range of new realistic motions can be created by warping and joining captured motion clips, using only a few motion-warping keyframes to modify the prototype motions, and using simple blending to join overlapping motion clips.

A key advantage of motion warping is that it fits well into the familiar keyframe animation paradigm, allowing a wide range of existing tools, techniques, and skills to be brought to bear. On the other hand, motion warping shares some limitations of standard keyframing, for example the difficulty of enforcing geometric constraints between keys. We believe that constraint techniques applicable to

conventional keyframing can be applied to motion warping as well.

A further limitation is that motion warping is a purely geometric technique, not based on any deep understand of the motion's structure. Consequently, as with analogous image morphing techniques, extreme warps are prone to look distorted and unnatural. A physically based technique in the spirit of [10] might overcome this limitation.

Acknowledgements

We thank Softimage, Inc. and BioVision, Inc. for access to motion capture data. This research was supported in part by a Science and Technology Center Grant from the National Science Foundation, #BIR-8920118, by the Engineering Design Research Center, an NSF Engineering Research Center at Carnegie Mellon University, by the Phillips Laboratory, Air Force Material Command, USAF, under cooperative agreement number F29601-93-2-0001, by Apple Computer, Inc, and by an equipment grant from Silicon Graphics, Inc.

References

[1] T. Beier and S. Neely. Feature-based image metamorphosis. In Edwin E. Catmull, editor, *Computer Graphics (SIGGRAPH '92 Proceedings)*, volume 26, pages 35–42, July 1992.

[2] R. Boulic, Zhiyong Huang, N.M. Thalmann, and D. Thalmann. Goal-oriented design and correction of articulated figure motion with the track system. *Computers and Graphics (UK)*, 18:443–52, July-Aug. 1994.

[3] A. Finkelstein and D. H. Salesin. Multiresolution curves. In *Computer Graphics (SIGGRAPH '94 Proceedings)*, volume 28, pages 261–268, July 1994.

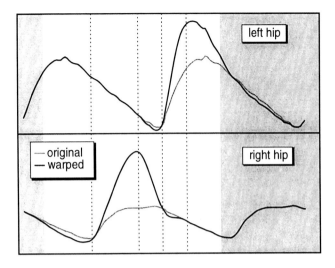

Figure 4: Original and warped motion curves for left and right hip joints. The unshaded portion matches figure 5. Vertical lines denote motion warping keyframes.

[4] S. Guo, J. Robergé, and T. Grace. Controlling movement using parametric frame space interpolation. In *Proceedings of Computer Animation '93*, pages 216–227, 1993.

[5] H. Ko and N. I. Badler. Straight line walking animation based on kinematic generalization that preserves the original characteristics. In *Proceedings Graphics Interface '93*, pages 9–16, May 1993.

[6] P. Litwinowicz and L. Williams. Animating images with drawings. In *Computer Graphics (SIGGRAPH '94 Proceedings)*, pages 409–12, July 1994.

[7] K. Perlin. Real time responsive animation with personality. *IEEE Transactions on Visualization and Computer Graphics*, 1(1), March 1995.

[8] I. J. Schoenberg. Cardinal spline interpolation. *CBMS (Conf. Board of the Mathematical Sciences)*, 12, 1973.

[9] M. Unuma and R. Takeuchi. Generation of human walking motion with emotion for computer animation. *Trans. Inst. Electron. Inf. Commun. Eng. D-II (Japan)*, J76D-II:1822–31, Aug. 1993.

[10] A. Witkin and M. Kass. Spacetime constraints. In *Computer Graphics (SIGGRAPH '88 Proceedings)*, volume 22, pages 159–168, August 1988.

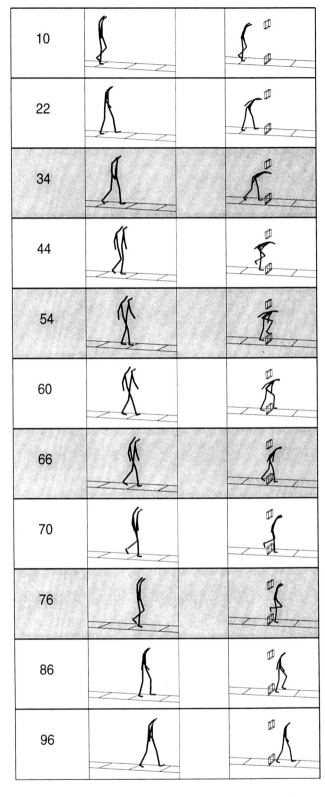

Figure 5: Selected frames from an original and warped motion sequence. Time runs from top to bottom. On each row are shown the frame number, the original frame, and the warped frame. The four shaded rows correspond to motion warping keyframes.

Automatic Reconstruction of Surfaces and Scalar Fields from 3D Scans[1][2]

Chandrajit L. Bajaj[3]   Fausto Bernardini[3][4]   Guoliang Xu[5]

Department of Computer Sciences
Purdue University

ABSTRACT

We present an efficient and uniform approach for the automatic reconstruction of surfaces of CAD (computer aided design) models and scalar fields defined on them, from an unorganized collection of scanned point data. A possible application is the rapid computer model reconstruction of an existing part or prototype from a three dimensional (3D) points scan of its surface. Color, texture or some scalar material property of the physical part, define natural scalar fields over the surface of the CAD model.

Our reconstruction algorithm does not impose any convexity or differentiability restrictions on the surface of the original physical part or the scalar field function, except that it assumes that there is a sufficient sampling of the input point data to unambiguously reconstruct the CAD model. Compared to earlier methods our algorithm has the advantages of simplicity, efficiency and uniformity (both CAD model and scalar field reconstruction). The simplicity and efficiency of our approach is based on several novel uses of appropriate sub-structures (alpha shapes) of a three-dimensional Delaunay Triangulation, its dual the three-dimensional Voronoi diagram, and dual uses of trivariate Bernstein-Bézier forms. The boundary of the CAD model is modeled using implicit cubic Bernstein-Bézier patches, while the scalar field is reconstructed with functional cubic Bernstein-Bézier patches.

CR Categories and Subject Descriptors: I.3.5 [Computer Graphics]: Computational Geometry and Object Modeling; J.6 [Computer-Aided Engineering]: Computer-Aided Design.

Additional keywords: Geometric modeling, shape recovery, range data analysis, algebraic surfaces, triangulations, alpha-shapes.

[1] This work has been supported in part by NSF grant CCR 92-22467, AFOSR grant F49620-94-1-0080, ONR grant N00014-94-1-0370 and ARO grant DAAH04-95-1-0008.

[2] See also
http://www.cs.purdue.edu/research/shastra/shastra.html

[3] Department of Computer Sciences, Purdue University, West Lafayette, IN 47907-1398 USA. Email: {bajaj, fxb}@cs.purdue.edu

[4] Additional partial support from CNR, Italy

[5] Computing Center, Academia Sinica, P. O. Box 2719, Beijing, 100080, P. R. China. Email: xuguo@cs.purdue.edu

Permission to make digital/hard copy of part or all of this work for personal or classroom use is granted without fee provided that copies are not made or distributed for profit or commercial advantage, the copyright notice, the title of the publication and its date appear, and notice is given that copying is by permission of ACM, Inc. To copy otherwise, to republish, to post on servers, or to redistribute to lists, requires prior specific permission and/or a fee.

© 1995   ACM-0-89791-701-4/95/008 $3.50

INTRODUCTION

In this paper we present an approach for the reconstruction of a surface, and scalar fields defined over it, from scattered data points. The points are assumed sampled from the surface of a 3D object, and the sampling is assumed to be *dense* and *uniform* (these terms will be given a more precise meaning later in the paper).

Laser range scanners are able to produce a dense sampling, usually organized in a rectangular grid, of an object surface. Some models also allow to measure the RGB components of the color (i.e. three scalar fields) at each sampled point. When the object has a simple shape, this grid of points can be a sufficient representation. However, objects with a more complex geometry, e.g. objects with holes, handles, pockets, cannot be scanned in a single pass, and the various scans are not easy to merge [42]. Other applications, for example recovering the shape of a bone from contour data extracted from a CT scan, require reconstruction of a surface from data points organized in slices. The approach of considering the input points as *unorganized* has the advantage of generating cross-derivatives by a uniform treatment of all spatial directions.

The reconstruction problem we are considering may be formally stated as follows:

Let an unorganized collection of points $P = \{(x_i, y_i, z_i)\} \subset \mathbf{R}^3$ and associated values $W = \{w_i\} \subset \mathbf{R}^1, i = 1 \ldots n$, be given. The points P are assumed sampled from a domain D in $\mathbf{R}^3$ (the boundary of a three-dimensional object) while the values W are assumed sampled from some scalar function F on the domain D.

Construct a C^1 smooth piecewise polynomial surface S^D : $f^D(x, y, z) = 0$ and a C^1 smooth piecewise polynomial function (surface-on-surface) S^F : $f^F(x, y, z)$ on some domain that contains P such that, for $i = 1 \ldots n$:

(a) $|f^D(x_i, y_i, z_i)| < \varepsilon^D$

(b) $|f^F(x_i, y_i, z_i) - w_i| < \varepsilon^F$

where ε^D and ε^F are user-defined approximation parameters. The user can also choose the degree of the Bernstein-Bézier polynomial patches used in the approximation.

Additionally, generate different visualizations of the domain surface S^D and the surface-on-surface S^F.

In this paper we reconstruct the C^1 smooth domain S^D using a piecewise algebraic surface (the zero contour of a C^1 trivariate piecewise polynomial function). The surface is constituted by barycentric implicit Bernstein-Bézier patches, which are guaranteed to be single-sheeted within each tetrahedron. We have also developed a method similar to the one described here, but based on tensor-product Bernstein-Bézier patches [5].

Some researchers have focused on reconstructing a piecewise-linear representation of the unknown surface D [38, 25, 13, 30, 43]. These papers provide a very nice survey of both the varied nature of applications and past approaches.

Related prior work [2, 6, 7, 15, 16, 27, 28, 35, 33] of fitting with smooth implicit surface patches, minimally all require an input surface triangulation of the data points. The surface fitting paper of [32] is similar to ours in that it only assumes a sufficiently dense set of input data points but differs from our approach in the adaptive nature of refinement, in time efficiency and in the degree of the implicit surface patches used. The authors propose either a C^0 reconstruction algorithm based on an adaptive tetrahedral decomposition, or a scheme that uses tri-quadratic (degree six) tensor product implicit surface patches with a Powell-Sabin type split to achieve C^1 continuity.

Our scheme effectively utilizes the incremental Delaunay triangulation for a more adaptive fit; the dual Voronoi diagram for efficient point location in signed distance computations and degree three implicit surface patches. Furthermore, in the same time it also computes a C^1 smooth approximation S^F of the sampled scalar function.

A different, three-step solution is described in papers [30, 31, 29]. In the first phase, a triangular mesh that approximates the data points is created. In a second phase, the mesh is optimized with respect to the number of triangles and the distance from the data points. A third step constructs a smooth surface from the mesh.

If the surface S^D is given, the problem of constructing the scalar function S^F is known as surface interpolation on a surface, and arises in several application areas, e.g. in modeling and visualizing the rain fall on the earth, the pressure on the wing of an airplane or the temperature on the surface of a human body. Note that the trivariate scalar function S^F is a two dimensional surface in $\mathbf{R}^4$ since its domain is the two dimensional surface S^D (and not all of $\mathbf{R}^3$). The problem is relatively recent and was posed as an open question by Barnhill [9]. A number of methods have been developed since then for its solution (for surveys see [10, 26, 37, 34]). Most of the proposed approaches interpolate scattered data over planar or spherical domain surfaces. In [12] and [35], the domain surface is generalized to a convex surface and a topological genus zero surface, respectively. Pottmann [39] presents a method which does not possess similar restrictions on the domain surface but requires it to be at least C^2 differentiable. In [11] the C^2 restriction is dropped, however the interpolation surface is constructed by transfinite interpolation using non-polynomials. A similar non-polynomial transfinite interpolant construction is used in [36], while the interpolation scheme in [41] requires at least C^4 continuity. Another approach, based on interpolation with cubic (for C^1) or quintic (for C^2) polynomials, is described in [8].

1 OVERVIEW OF THE ALGORITHM

Our algorithm consists of the following three phases:

1. **Preprocessing:** Preprocess the data points so that a *signed-distance* function is defined and efficiently computable. I.e., given a query point q, the function must return the approximate distance of the point from the domain surface S^D, with a positive sign if q lies outside the object, and a negative sign otherwise. We use α-shapes [21] to compute a piecewise linear approximation of the domain S^D, from which the approximated signed distance is computed. Details on this part are given in Section 2.

2. **Approximation:** Incrementally decompose the space into tetrahedra. For each tetrahedron τ that contains a portion of the domain D, compute Bernstein-Bézier trivariate implicit approximants f_τ^D and f_τ^F for both the domain D and the field F, based on data points and on the signed-distance function described above. Then compute the errors of the approximants for the given data points, and repeat the process, refining at each step the decomposition, until the errors meet the specified requirements. The use of a global signed-distance function in the computation of the coefficients of each patch guarantees C^0 continuity of the reconstructed surfaces. We use an incremental 3D Delaunay triangulation scheme together with a suitable point-insertion scheme to avoid badly-shaped tetrahedra in the spatial decomposition. This part of the algorithm is further detailed in Section 3.

3. **Smoothing:** Use a Clough-Tocher 12-way split to make the reconstructed surfaces C^1-smooth. See Section 4 for details.

Our domain surface S^D and surface-on-surface S^F reconstruction scheme does not impose any convexity or differentiability restrictions on the original domain surface D or function F, except that it assumes that there is a sufficient sampling of the input point data to unambiguously reconstruct the domain surface D. While it is difficult to precisely bound the required sampling density, we address this issue in Section 2.4 and characterize the required sampling density in terms of an α-shape (subgraph of a Delaunay triangulation of the points) which matches the topology of the original (unknown) sampled surface D. Compared to the above methods our algorithm thus has the following advantages:

1. It unifies the reconstruction of the domain surface D and the scalar function F defined on the domain surface;

2. It is adaptive and approximates large dense data sets with a relatively small number of C^1 smooth patches.

Outline of the paper: The rest of our paper is as follows. In Sections 2, 3 and 4 we present a detailed description of Phases 1, 2 and 3 of the reconstruction algorithm as outlined above. In Section 5 we illustrate all the phases of the algorithm with the aid of a simple 2D example. In Section 6 we show some examples of reconstructed surfaces and surface-on-surfaces, and discuss possible directions of future investigation.

More details on the algorithm and additional examples can be found in [4].

2 PHASE 1: PREPROCESSING AND THE SIGNED-DISTANCE FUNCTION

As we mentioned in Section 1, our algorithm relies on the computation of the signed-distance $\delta(q)$ of a query point q from the domain surface D. The absolute value of $\delta(q)$ is defined as the Euclidean minimal distance of the point q from the domain surface D, while its sign is arbitrarily defined to be positive when q lies outside the object whose boundary is D, and negative otherwise.

In our implementation of the algorithm, we use α-shapes to compute a piecewise linear approximation L^D of the domain D, and make use of the associated data-structures (3D Delaunay triangulation and Voronoi diagram) to efficiently locate q w.r.t. the object and compute the associated signed-distance. An alternative method for computing an approximated signed-distance function, based on propagation of normals, is described in [30].

Before describing the actual signed-distance computation, we briefly review some concepts and results from Computational Geometry used in the algorithm. The style of this presentation is informal. The reader can refer to the papers in the references for more details.

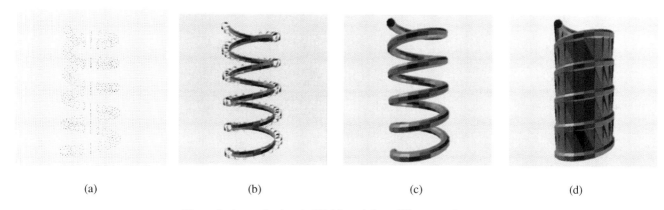

(a)   (b)   (c)   (d)

Figure 1: A set of points in 3D (a), and three different α-shapes.

2.1 Delaunay Triangulations

Given a set P of points in $\mathbf{R}^3$ one can build a tetrahedralization of the convex hull of P, that is, a partition of $conv(P)$ into tetrahedra, in such a way that the circumscribing sphere of each tetrahedron τ does not contain any other point of P than the vertices of τ. Such a tetrahedralization is called a (3D) Delaunay triangulation and, under non degeneracy assumptions (no three points on a line, etc.) it is unique. Many different techniques have been proposed for the computation of Delaunay triangulations (see [19, 40, 18]). For our purposes, an incremental approach is particularly well-suited, as it can be used in both the preprocessing phase and the incremental refining of the adaptive, approximating triangulation (see Section 3).

The algorithm we use is the randomized, incremental, flipping-based algorithm proposed in [22], with heed paid to robustness issues due to finite precision calculations [18]. At the beginning the triangulation is initialized as a single tetrahedron, with vertices "at infinity", that contains all points of P. At each step a point from P is inserted as a new vertex in the triangulation, the tetrahedron in which p lies is split and the Delaunay property is re-established by "flipping" tetrahedra.

This algorithm uses a data structure, called the history DAG, that maintains the collection of discarded tetrahedra. The DAG is used to locate the tetrahedron in which the point to be inserted lies. When a tetrahedron is split or groups of tetrahedra are flipped, they become internal nodes of the DAG while the newly created tetrahedra become their children in the DAG. To locate a point, one starts at the root of the DAG (the single tetrahedron of the initial triangulation) and follows links down to a leaf.

It is possible to build the Delaunay triangulation of a set of n points in $\mathbf{R}^d$ in $O(n \log n + n^{\lceil d/2 \rceil})$ expected time. The second term in this expression is of the same order as the maximum number of possible simplices. In practice, the running time of the algorithm (for $d = 2, 3$) is much better than this theoretic bound (the actual running time depends on the distribution of points).

2.2 Voronoi Diagrams

Voronoi diagrams are well known tools in computational geometry (see [3] for a survey). They provide an efficient solution to the *Post Office Problem*, that is an answer to the query: what is the closest point $p \in P$ to a given point q? Voronoi diagrams are related to Delaunay triangulations by duality. It is easy to build a Voronoi diagram once one has the corresponding triangulation, and vice-versa. A Voronoi diagram is a partition of the space into convex cells. There is a cell for each point of $p \in P$, and the cell of a point p is the set of points that are closer to p than to any other point of P. So, all one has to do to answer the closest-point query is to locate the cell the query point lies in. Efficient point-location data structures can be built on top of the Voronoi diagram. Using the randomized approach described in [14], one builds the point-location data-structure (called an *RPO-tree*, for Randomized Post Office tree) on top of the Voronoi diagram in $O(n^{2+\epsilon})$ expected time, for any fixed $\epsilon > 0$, and is then able to answer the closest-point query in $O(\log n)$ expected time. The data structure requires $O(n^{2+\epsilon})$ space in the worst case. We use the *RPO-tree* data structure for our point location and signed-distance computations.

2.3 α-Shapes

Given the Delaunay triangulation $\mathcal{T}$ of a point set P, regarded as a simplicial complex, one can assign to each simplex $\sigma \in \mathcal{T}$ (vertices, edges, triangles and tetrahedra) a *size* defined in the following way. Let Θ_σ be the smallest sphere whose boundary contains all vertices of σ. Then the *size* of σ will be defined to be equal to the square of the radius of Θ_σ, and σ will be said to be *conflict-free* if Θ_σ does not contain any point of P other than the vertices of σ.

The subcomplex Σ_α of simplices $\sigma \in \mathcal{T}$ with either one of the following properties:

(a) The size of σ is less than α and σ is conflict-free

(b) σ is a face of τ and $\tau \in \Sigma_\alpha$,

is called the α-shape of P.

α-Shapes have been introduced in the plane in [20] and then extended to the three-dimensional space in [21].

One can intuitively think of an α-shape as the subcomplex of $\mathcal{T}$ obtained in the following way: imagine that a ball-shaped eraser, whose radius is $\sqrt{\alpha}$, is moved in the space, assuming all possible positions such that no point of P lies in the eraser. The eraser removes all simplices it can pass through, but not those whose size is smaller than α. The remaining simplices (together with all their faces) form the α-shape for that value of the parameter α. Two extreme cases are the 0-shape, which reduces to the collection of points P, and the ∞-shape, that coincides with the convex-hull of P. Notice that there exists only a finite number of different α-shapes. The collection of all possible α-shapes of P is called the *family* of α-shapes of P (see Figure 1), and can be computed in time proportional to the number of simplices in $\mathcal{T}$. We use the α-shape computation for our generating an initial piecewise linear approximation L^D of the domain surface D (see Section 2.4).

2.4 Signed-Distance Computation

Obviously the domain surface D is unknown, so we need to build some suitable approximation of it to classify points as either internal or external to the object being reconstructed, and to compute a distance from it.

In the preprocessing phase the Delaunay triangulation of the set of input points P is computed, and then the Voronoi diagram and the family of α-shapes of P are constructed. During the process, the history DAG and the RPO-tree data structures are built to allow a fast location of the tetrahedron and Voronoi cell a query point q lies in. Note that all these data structures are intimately related.

Tetrahedra in the Delaunay triangulation are classified as either internal or external (and assigned a corresponding sign) based on a particular α-shape chosen as a "good" linear approximation L^D to the surface to be reconstructed. The computation of the signed-distance is then reduced to locating the query point q in both the Delaunay triangulation, to decide its sign $s = \pm1$, and in the Voronoi diagram, to find the closest point $p \in P$. The approximated signed-distance $s \cdot |pq|$ is then returned.

A difficulty in the process outlined above is the choice of a suitable value for α. We assume that the input data is dense enough so that there exists an α such that the α-shape approximates the object with the same topology as the original unknown surface D. In our current scheme a suitable α is selected interactively. The boundary of the selected α-shape must possess the following properties:

(a) It does not contain any singular (i.e. isolated) vertex;

(b) There are no "missing" edges, i.e. there can be missing triangles in the boundary, but if two adjacent triangles are missing, their common edge must be in the α-shape.

These properties make a slightly weaker condition than requiring that there exist an α-shape that correctly approximates the object *and* that has a *complete* boundary. In our experience it is sometime difficult to find an α value such that these stronger conditions are satisfied, even for "reasonably dense" samplings.

When an α-shape with the above properties is determined, it is easy to distinguish between internal and external tetrahedra in the underlying triangulation $\mathcal{T}$. One does a breadth first search on the dual graph of $\mathcal{T}$, starting with a tetrahedron that is known to be external (e.g. one that has a vertex at infinity) and continuing with adjacent tetrahedra. These tetrahedra are marked as external (positive sign) and put in a queue for further processing. When one hits a tetrahedron τ belonging to Σ_α, τ is marked as internal and not enqueued. The same happens when, visiting an adjacent tetrahedron τ of a positive tetrahedron σ, one finds that the common face (or all three edges of the common face) belongs to Σ_α. This means that going from σ to τ one crosses the boundary, so τ is marked as internal (negative sign) and not enqueued.

When the data points are not very dense or uniform, the error caused by using the approximated distance computation described above can be too large. In these cases, it is possible to improve the error by returning the distance of the query point from L^D, instead of P.

3 PHASE 2: INCREMENTAL REFINEMENT AND APPROXIMATION

In Phase 2 of the algorithm a 3D Delaunay triangulation $\mathcal{T}$ is initialized and incrementally refined, and C^0-continuous piecewise-polynomial functions (approximants) f^D and f^F are generated.

For each tetrahedron $\tau \in \mathcal{T}$ that contains a portion of D we compute two Bernstein-Bézier trivariate polynomials f_τ^D and f_τ^F, to approximate the part of domain surface and scalar field contained

in τ, respectively. The coefficients of the polynomials are computed using data points within τ and the signed-distance function described in Section 2.4.

After computing the two polynomials, the errors of the approximants are estimated and, if one or both the errors are too large, the current triangulation $\mathcal{T}$ is refined, until the errors are within the given bounds. The triangulation refinement is done by adding at each step a new point to split the tetrahedron with the maximum error, and using the incremental Delaunay triangulation algorithm to update the triangulation.

Before describing in further details the computation of the approximating functions, we recall some facts and terminology related to Bernstein-Bézier trivariate forms.

3.1 Bernstein-Bézier (BB) Form

Let p_1, p_2, p_3, $p_4 \in \mathbf{R}^3$ be affine independent. Then the tetrahedron τ with vertices p_1, p_2, p_3, and p_4, is $\tau = [p_1p_2p_3p_4]$. For any $p = \sum_{i=1}^{4} \alpha_i p_i \in \tau$, $\alpha = (\alpha_1, \alpha_2, \alpha_3, \alpha_4)^T$ is the barycentric coordinate of p. Let $p = (x, y, z)^T$, $p_i = (x_i, y_i, z_i)^T$. Then the barycentric coordinates relate to the Cartesian coordinates via the following relation

$$
\begin{bmatrix} x \\ y \\ z \\ 1 \end{bmatrix} = \begin{bmatrix} x_1 & x_2 & x_3 & x_4 \\ y_1 & y_2 & y_3 & y_4 \\ z_1 & z_2 & z_3 & z_4 \\ 1 & 1 & 1 & 1 \end{bmatrix} \begin{bmatrix} \alpha_1 \\ \alpha_2 \\ \alpha_3 \\ \alpha_4 \end{bmatrix} \quad (1)
$$

Any polynomial $f(p)$ of degree n can be expressed as a Bernstein-Bézier (BB) form over τ as

$$
f(p) = \sum_{|\lambda|=n} b_\lambda\, B_\lambda^n(\alpha), \quad \lambda \in \mathcal{Z}_+^4
$$

where

$$
B_\lambda^n(\alpha) = \frac{n!}{\lambda_1!\lambda_2!\lambda_3!\lambda_4!}\, \alpha_1^{\lambda_1}\alpha_2^{\lambda_2}\alpha_3^{\lambda_3}\alpha_4^{\lambda_4}
$$

is a Bernstein polynomial, $|\lambda| = \sum_{i=1}^{4} \lambda_i$ with $\lambda = (\lambda_1, \lambda_2, \lambda_3, \lambda_4)^T$, $\alpha = (\alpha_1, \alpha_2, \alpha_3, \alpha_4)^T$ is the barycentric coordinate of p, $b_\lambda = b_{\lambda_1\lambda_2\lambda_3\lambda_4}$ (as a subscript, we simply write $\lambda_1\lambda_2\lambda_3\lambda_4$ for $(\lambda_1, \lambda_2, \lambda_3, \lambda_4)^T$) are called Bézier ordinates, and $\mathcal{Z}_+^4$ stands for the set of all four dimensional vectors with nonnegative integer components.

The points

$$
p_\lambda = \frac{\lambda_1}{n}p_1 + \frac{\lambda_2}{n}p_2 + \frac{\lambda_3}{n}p_3 + \frac{\lambda_4}{n}p_4, \quad |\lambda| = n
$$

are called the *regular points* of τ. The points $(p_\lambda, b_\lambda) \in \mathbf{R}^4$ are called *Bézier points* and their piecewise linear interpolation *Bézier net*.

The following lemma gives necessary and sufficient conditions for continuity.

Lemma 3.1 ([24]). *Let $f(p) = \sum_{|\lambda|=n} a_\lambda B_\lambda^n(\alpha)$ and $g(p) = \sum_{|\lambda|=n} b_\lambda B_\lambda^n(\alpha)$ be two polynomials defined on two tetrahedra $[p_1p_2p_3p_4]$ and $[p_1'p_2p_3p_4]$, respectively. Then*

(i) *f and g are C^0 continuous at the common face $[p_2p_3p_4]$ if and only if*

$$
a_\lambda = b_\lambda, \quad \text{for all } \lambda = 0\lambda_2\lambda_3\lambda_4, \ |\lambda| = n \quad (2)
$$

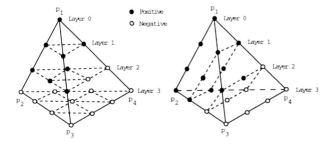

Figure 2: The layers of Bézier ordinates in a tetrahedron. (left) Three-sided patch. (right) Four-sided patch.

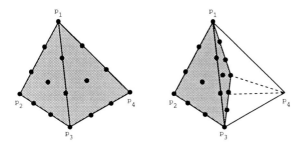

Figure 3: The splitting of a tetrahedron (right) into four sub-tetrahedra (left). Only one of the resulting sub-tetrahedra is shown.

(ii) *f and g are C^1 continuous at the common face $[p_2p_3p_4]$ if and only if (2) holds and, for all $\lambda = 0\lambda_2\lambda_3\lambda_4$, $|\lambda| = n - 1$,*

$$b_{\lambda+e_1} = \beta_1 a_{\lambda+e_1} + \beta_2 a_{\lambda+e_2} + \beta_3 a_{\lambda+e_3} + \beta_4 a_{\lambda+e_4} \quad (3)$$

where $\beta = (\beta_1, \beta_2, \beta_3, \beta_4)^T$ is defined by the following relation

$$p_1' = \beta_1 p_1 + \beta_2 p_2 + \beta_3 p_3 + \beta_4 p_4, \quad |\beta| = 1$$

The relation (3) will be called coplanar condition.

The following Lemmas give sufficient conditions for a patch to be *single-sheeted* (see [6] for proofs and further details).

Lemma 3.2 *Let $\tau = [p_1p_2p_3p_4]$. The regular points of τ can be thought of as organized in triangular layers, that we can number from 0 to n going from p_1 to the opposite face $[p_2p_3p_4]$ (see Figure 2). If the Bézier ordinates are all positive (negative) on layers $0, \ldots, k - 1$ and all negative (positive) on layers $k + 1, \ldots, n$ $(0 < k < n)$, then the patch is single-sheeted (i.e., any line through p_1 and $p \in [p_2p_3p_4]$ intersects the patch only once).*

Lemma 3.3 *Let $\tau = [p_1p_2p_3p_4]$. The regular points of τ can be thought of as organized in quadrilateral layers, that we can number from 0 to n going from edge $[p_1p_2]$ to the opposite edge $[p_3p_4]$ (see Figure 2). If the Bézier ordinates are all positive (negative) on layers $0, \ldots, k - 1$ and all negative (positive) on layers $k+1, \ldots, n$ $(0 < k < n)$, then the patch is single-sheeted (i.e., any line through $p \in [p_1p_2]$ and $q \in [p_3p_4]$ intersects the patch only once).*

In the Lemmas above, the Bézier ordinates on layer k can have any sign. Patches satisfying the conditions of Lemma 3.2 will be called *three-sided*; those satisfying the conditions of Lemma 3.3 will be called *four-sided*.

3.2 Outline of Phase 2 of the Algorithm

We are now ready to present in details the steps required to compute the approximant functions f^D and f^F.

1. Build an initial bounding tetrahedron τ, such that $P \subset \tau$. Set $T = \{\tau\}$ and V = vertices of τ. Mark τ as *new*.

2. For each *new* tetrahedron $\tau \in T$, compute the signed-distance at all its regular points p_λ. If the values of $\delta(p_\lambda)$, $|\delta| = n$, do not satisfy either Lemma 3.2 or Lemma 3.3, then set $\vartheta_\tau^D = \vartheta_\tau^F = \infty$. Otherwise, compute local approximants

$$f_\tau^D(p) = \sum_{|\lambda|=n} b_\lambda^D B_\lambda^n(\alpha) \quad (4)$$

$$f_\tau^F(p) = \sum_{|\lambda|=n} b_\lambda^F B_\lambda^n(\alpha) \quad (5)$$

for the domain surface D and scalar field F as follows:

For the domain approximant, the coefficients b_λ^D are computed by first interpolating the computed values of the signed-distance function:

$$f_\tau^D(p_\lambda) = \delta(p_\lambda), \quad |\lambda| = n \quad (6)$$

The tetrahedron τ is then split into four sub-tetrahedra $\tau_1 \ldots \tau_4$ (see Figure 3) by joining the baricenter of τ with its four vertices (τ_k is the sub-tetrahedron opposite to vertex p_k). The regular points on the faces of the sub-tetrahedra coincide with those of the original tetrahedron τ. For these points we use the coefficients computed from (6). Notice that on the shared face of two adjacent tetrahedra these coefficients will coincide, as f^D, restricted to that face, interpolates the signed distance at a number of points equal to the number of its coefficients. All interior coefficients of the sub-tetrahedra are computed by solving the least squares problem

$$\begin{cases} f_{\tau_k}^D(p_i) = 0, & p_i \in P \cap \tau_k, k = 1 \ldots 4 \\ f_{\tau_k}^D(p_\lambda) = \delta(p_\lambda), & |\lambda| = n, \lambda_k \neq 0, k = 1 \ldots 4 \end{cases}$$
$$(7)$$

where we use the values of the signed-distance at regular points (of each sub-tetrahedron τ_k) in addition to the data points contained in τ. The signed-distance data helps in avoiding multiple sheets in the approximating patch.

For the scalar field approximant we compute a least squares approximation of the field values at data points within τ:

$$f_\tau^D(p_i) = w_i, \quad p_i \in P \cap \tau \quad (8)$$

Notice that the field approximant is not globally continuous. Continuity will be achieved by averaging and interpolating values of the approximant at the vertices V of T in a subsequent phase, described in Section 4.

3. If the coefficients computed in the step above do not satisfy the conditions of either Lemma 3.2 or Lemma 3.3, set $\vartheta_\tau^D = \vartheta_\tau^F = \infty$. Otherwise, compute the approximation error for both functions:

$$\vartheta_\tau^D = \frac{\sqrt{\sum_{k=1}^4 \sum_{p_i \in P \cap \tau} f_\tau^D(p_i)^2}}{\text{Card}(P \cap \tau)}$$

$$\vartheta_\tau^F = \frac{\sqrt{\sum_{p_i \in P \cap \tau} (f_\tau^F(p_i) - w_i)^2}}{\text{Card}(P \cap \tau)}$$

(if $\tau \cap P = \emptyset$, then set $\vartheta_\tau^D = 0$ and $\vartheta_\tau^F = 0$), and keep track of the following two quantities:

$$\vartheta_{\sigma'}^D = \max_{\tau \in T}\{\vartheta_\tau^D\}$$

and

$$\vartheta_{\sigma''}^F = \max_{\tau \in T}\{\vartheta_\tau^F\}$$

4. If both $\vartheta_{\sigma'}^D < \varepsilon^D$ and $\vartheta_{\sigma''}^F < \varepsilon^F$ then the algorithm stops the incremental refinement phase and begins the smoothing phase. Otherwise, either σ' or σ'' is selected for further refinement (according to a user-definable strategy. E.g.: choose always σ' first, assigning priority to the surface, as variations of the scalar field F generally correspond to variations of the surface). The circumcenter q of the selected tetrahedron is computed and added to the set V of vertices of the triangulation, q is inserted in T and T is updated with splits and flippings to accommodate the new vertex and restore the Delaunay property (adding the center of the circumscribing sphere of σ is utilizing the empty sphere property of Delaunay triangulations and in general yields good aspect ratio tetrahedra in the final triangulation [17]). At the same time the subset $P \cap \tau$ of points that lie within each modified tetrahedron τ is updated. This is done by considering the points originally within the modified simplex, and reclassifying them with respect to the splitting/flipping planes.

Then mark all split/flipped tetrahedra as *old* and all newly created ones as *new* and go back to step 2.

4   PHASE 3: ACHIEVING C^1 CONTINUITY VIA A 3D CLOUGH-TOCHER SCHEME

The functions $f^D(p)$ and $f^F(p)$ computed in phase 2 of the algorithm are not C^1 continuous. To achieve C^1 continuity, we apply a subdivision scheme to the tetrahedra of T, and compute C^1-smooth Bernstein-Bézier patches on the refined triangulation.

We base our trivariate scheme on the n-dimensional Clough-Tocher scheme given by Worsey and Farin [44, 23]. In this scheme, one computes for each vertex in the original triangulation an average of the values of the functions f^D and f^F and their gradients, for all patches that share that vertex (the surface approximant is already C^0, so only the gradient needs to be averaged). In addition, the average gradient at the middle point of each edge is computed. Each tetrahedron is then split into twelve sub-tetrahedra by inserting the incenter of each tetrahedron and a point on each face (the point on the face shared by two adjacent tetrahedra must be collinear with their incenters [44]), and joining these points with the original vertices. A cubic trivariate polynomial is built on each sub-tetrahedron. The coefficients of the twelve resulting patches are computed based on the value of the function at each vertex, the average gradient at vertices and mid-edge points, and the continuity constraint. The resulting patches are C^1 continuous and interpolate the averaged values and gradient of the functions.

Another trivariate Clough-Tocher scheme (see [1]) splits each tetrahedron into four sub-tetrahedra. However the interpolants in each sub-tetrahedra are now of quintic degree and furthermore require C^2 data at the vertices of the main tetrahedron. Since our data at the vertices of the tetrahedral mesh comes from the averaging of locally computed low degree interpolants, the higher order derivatives tend to be un-reliable in general. We therefore prefer to use the lower degree cubic scheme that uses only first order derivatives at the vertices.

An alternative approach to build a C^1 interpolant with cubic patches has been presented in [8], and its application to our method is described in [4].

5   A SIMPLE 2D EXAMPLE

We present in this section an example of the three phases of the algorithm. For presentation purposes, the steps are illustrated with the aid of a 2D example. The method is in fact perfectly suited for being applied in 2D reconstruction, and we chose to describe it only for the 3D case to keep the notation simple and because the most interesting applications arise from the study of fields on the surface of 3D objects. Restricting ourselves to a bi-dimensional example allows us to illustrate the various steps with pictures which we believe are more easily understood. The generalization of the techniques involved should be clear from the text.

In the following we refer to Figures 4(a)–(n). Figure (a) shows the sample points $P \in \mathbf{R}^2$. Figure (b) shows the associated function values W. The computed Delaunay triangulation and associated Voronoi diagram are depicted in Figure (c). These data structures will be used for fast point location in signed-distance computation. The chosen α-shape is shown in Figure (d). Four steps of the approximation phase are illustrated in Figures (e) though (i). Notice the adaptive subdivision of the plane. The implicit Bernstein-Bézier patches are shown in red. Empty triangles are light-blue and those containing a patch are grey. These triangles lie on the zero plane, so their intersection with the patches form the implicit curve $f^D = 0$. Figures (l) and (m) show the final reconstructed C^1 implicit patches, after Clough-Tocher subdivision, for both the domain and the scalar field. The zero contour of f^D is finally shown in Figure (n).

6   EXAMPLES AND CONCLUSIONS

Some examples of reconstruction of 3D objects and associated scalar fields are presented in this Section.

The data for the human femur in Figure 5, 9223 points, comes from contouring of a CT scan. The algorithm does not use the fact that the data is arranged in slices. The reconstructed C^1 surface is made by 400 cubic patches. The reconstruction algorithm took about 10 minutes on a SGI Indigo[2].

The engine in Figure 6 has been reconstructed from a data set containing 9800 points. The number of patches generated in the approximation phase is 382, with an error equal to 1/100 of the size of the object. Each patch is of degree 3, and is therefore defined by 20 coefficients. At the same time, an approximate C^1 scalar field (pressure form a simulated experiment) over the surface has also been computed. Several techniques can be used to visualize this surface-on-surface data. In Figure 6(c) we show iso-pressure regions. With the *normal projection* method, each point p on the domain surface S^D is projected in the direction normal to S^D, to a distance proportional to the value $f^F(p)$ of the field at that point. The projected surface is visible in transparency in Figure 6(d), with iso-contours of the pressure projected on it.

The data for the head of Spock is a subsampling (about 10^4 points have been used) of scan data obtained with a laser 3D digitizer. The reconstructed surface is constituted by 1100 cubic patches.

REFERENCES

[1] ALFELD, P. A trivariate clough-tocher scheme for tetrahedral data. *Computer Aided Geometric Design 1* (1984), 169–181.

[2] ALFELD, P. Scattered data interpolation in three or more variables. In *Mathematical Methods in Computer Aided Geometric Design*, T. Lyche and L. Schumaker, Eds. Academic Press, Boston, 1989, pp. 1–34.

[3] AURENHAMMER, F. Power diagrams: properties, algorithms and applications. *SIAM J. Comput. 16* (1987), 78–96.

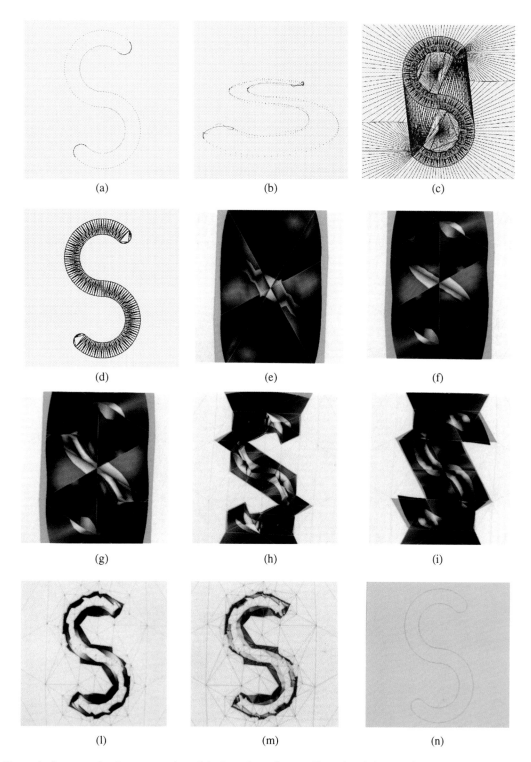

Figure 4: An example of reconstruction of the boundary of a two-dimensional shape and an associated scalar field.

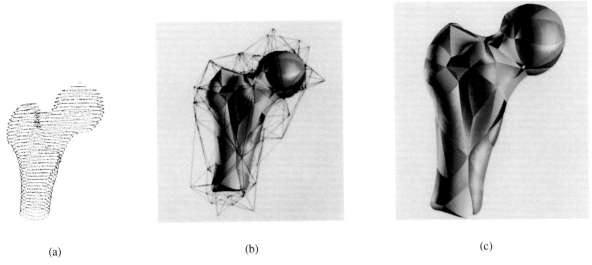

Figure 5: (a) Data set for the upper part of a human femur. Data from a CT scan. (b) Final decomposition (wireframe). (c) Reconstructed object.

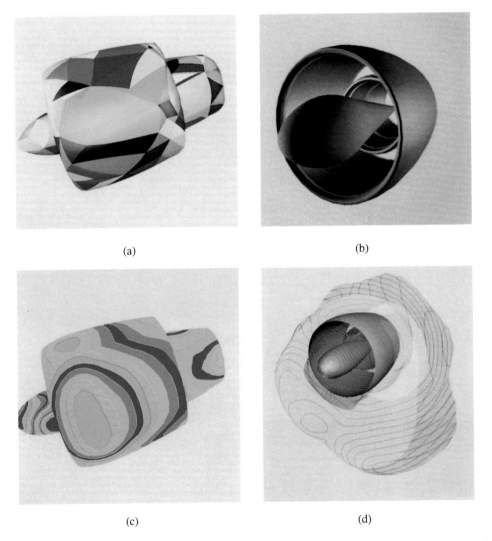

Figure 6: A jet engine. (a) C^0 reconstructed domain. Patches are visible in different colors. (b) Reconstructed domain (after C^1 smoothing). (c) Iso-pressure contours and regions of a surface-on-surface pressure function displayed on the surface of the jet engine. (d) The reconstructed engine surface and visualization of the pressure surface function surrounding the jet engine using the normal projection method.

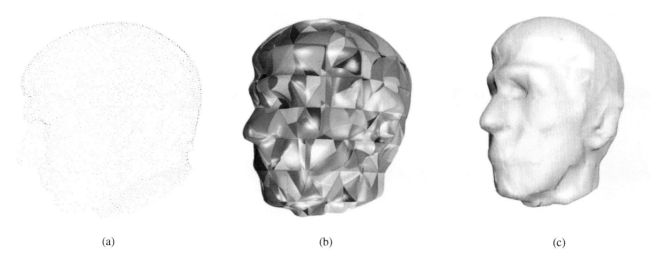

(a)   (b)   (c)

Figure 7: (a) A set of dense, scattered, noisy data points. (b) and (c) C^1 smooth reconstructed surface. In (b) patches have been randomly colored.

[4] BAJAJ, C., BERNARDINI, F., AND XU, G. Reconstruction of surfaces and surfaces-on-surfaces from unorganized weighted points. Computer Science Technical Report CSD-TR-94-001, Purdue University, 1994.

[5] BAJAJ, C., BERNARDINI, F., AND XU, G. Adaptive reconstruction of surfaces and scalar fields from dense scattered trivariate data. Computer Science Technical Report CSD-TR-95-028, Purdue University, 1995.

[6] BAJAJ, C., CHEN, J., AND XU, G. Modeling with cubic A-patches. ACM Transactions on Graphics (1995). To Appear.

[7] BAJAJ, C., AND IHM, I. C^1 smoothing of polyhedra with implicit algebraic splines. Computer Graphics 26, 2 (July 1992), 79–88. Proceedings of SIGGRAPH 92.

[8] BAJAJ, C., AND XU, G. Modeling scattered function data on curved surfaces. In Fundamentals of Computer Graphics, Z. T. J. Chen, N. Thalmann and D. Thalmann, Eds. Beijing, China, 1994, pp. 19–29.

[9] BARNHILL, R. E. Surfaces in computer aided geometric design: A survey with new results. Computer Aided Geometric Design 2 (1985), 1–17.

[10] BARNHILL, R. E., AND FOLEY, T. A. Methods for constructing surfaces on surfaces. In Geometric Modeling: Methods and their Applications, G. Farin, Ed. Springer, Berlin, 1991, pp. 1–15.

[11] BARNHILL, R. E., OPITZ, K., AND POTTMANN, H. Fat surfaces: a trivariate approach to triangle-based interpolation on surfaces. Computer Aided Geometric Design 9 (1992), 365–378.

[12] BARNHILL, R. E., PIPER, B. R., AND RESCORLA, K. L. Interpolation to arbitrary data on a surface. In Geometric Modeling, G. Farin, Ed. SIAM, Philadelphia, 1987, pp. 281–289.

[13] BOISSONAT, J. D. Geometric structures for three-dimensional shape representation. ACM Transactions on Graphics 3, 4 (Oct. 1984), 266–286.

[14] CLARKSON, K. L. A randomized algorithm for closest-point queries. SIAM J. Comput. 17 (1988), 830–847.

[15] DAHMEN, W. Smooth piecewise quadratic surfaces. In Mathematical Methods in Computer Aided Geometric Design, T. Ly-

che and L. Schumaker, Eds. Academic Press, Boston, 1989, pp. 181–193.

[16] DAHMEN, W., AND THAMM-SCHAAR, T.-M. Cubicoids: modeling and visualization. Computer Aided Geometric Design 10 (1993), 93–108.

[17] DEY, T. K., BAJAJ, C. L., AND SUGIHARA, K. On good triangulations in three dimensions. Internat. J. Comput. Geom. Appl. 2, 1 (1992), 75–95.

[18] DEY, T. K., SUGIHARA, K., AND BAJAJ, C. L. Delaunay triangulations in three dimensions with finite precision arithmetic. Comput. Aided Geom. Design 9 (1992), 457–470.

[19] EDELSBRUNNER, H. Algorithms in Combinatorial Geometry, vol. 10 of EATCS Monographs on Theoretical Computer Science. Springer-Verlag, Heidelberg, West Germany, 1987.

[20] EDELSBRUNNER, H., KIRKPATRICK, D., AND SEIDEL, R. On the shape of a set of points in the plane. IEEE Trans. on Information Theory 29, 4 (1983), 551–559.

[21] EDELSBRUNNER, H., AND MUCKE, E. P. Three-dimensional alpha shapes. ACM Transactions on Graphics 13, 1 (Jan. 1994), 43–72.

[22] EDELSBRUNNER, H., AND SHAH, N. R. Incremental topological flipping works for regular triangulations. In Proc. 8th Annu. ACM Sympos. Comput. Geom. (1992), pp. 43–52.

[23] FARIN, G. Triangular Bernstein-Bézier patches. Computer Aided Geometric Design 3 (1986), 83–127.

[24] FARIN, G. Curves and Surfaces for Computer Aided Geometric Design: A Practical Guide. Academic Press, 1990.

[25] FAUGERAS, O. D., HEBERT, M., MUSSI, P., AND BOISSONNAT, J. D. Polyhedral approximation of 3-D objects without holes. Computer Vision, Graphics and Image Processing 25 (1984), 169–183.

[26] FRANKE, R. Recent advances in the approximation of surfaces from scattered data. In Multivariate Approximation, C.K.Chui, L.L.Schumaker, and F.I.Utreras, Eds. Academic Press, New York, 1987, pp. 275–335.

[27] GUO, B. Surface generation using implicit cubics. In Scientific Visualizaton of Physical Phenomena, N. M. Patrikalakis, Ed. Springer-Verlag, Tokyo, 1991, pp. 485–530.

[28] GUO, B. Non-splitting macro patches for implicit cubic spline surfaces. *Computer Graphics Forum 12*, 3 (1993), 434–445.

[29] HOPPE, H., DeROSE, T., DUCHAMP, T., HALSTEAD, M., JIN, H., McDONALD, J., SCHWITZER, J., AND STUELZLE, W. Piecewise smooth surface reconstruction. In *Computer Graphics Proceedings* (1994), Annual Conference Series. Proceedings of SIGGRAPH 94, ACM SIGGRAPH, pp. 295–302.

[30] HOPPE, H., DeROSE, T., DUCHAMP, T., McDONALD, J., AND STUELZLE, W. Surface reconstruction from unorganized points. *Computer Graphics 26*, 2 (July 1992), 71–78. Proceedings of SIGGRAPH 92.

[31] HOPPE, H., DeROSE, T., DUCHAMP, T., McDONALD, J., AND STUELZLE, W. Mesh optimization. In *Computer Graphics Proceedings* (1993), Annual Conference Series. Proceedings of SIGGRAPH 93, ACM SIGGRAPH, pp. 19–26.

[32] MOORE, D., AND WARREN, J. Approximation of dense scattered data using algebraic surfaces. In *Proceedings of the 24th annual Hawaii International Conference on System Sciences* (1991), V. Milutinovic and B. D. Shriver, Eds., vol. 1.

[33] NIELSON, G. M. Modeling and visualizing volumetric and surface-on-surface data. In *Focus on Scientific Visualization*, H. Hagen, H. Muller, and G. M. Nielson, Eds. Springer, 1992, pp. 219–274.

[34] NIELSON, G. M. Scattered data modeling. *IEEE Computer Graphics & Applications 13* (1993), 60–70.

[35] NIELSON, G. M., FOLEY, T., LANE, D., FRANKE, R., AND HAGEN, H. Interpolation of scattered data on closed surfaces. *Computer Aided Geometric Design 7*, 4 (1990), 303–312.

[36] NIELSON, G. M., FOLEY, T. A., HAMANN, B., AND LANE, D. Visualizing and modeling scattered multivariate data. *IEEE Computer Graphics & Applications 11*, 3 (May 1991), 47–55.

[37] NIELSON, G. M., AND FRANKE, R. Scattered data interpolation and applications: A tutorial and survey. In *Geometric Modeling: Methods and Their Applications*, H. Hagen and D. Roller, Eds. Springer, 1990, pp. 131–160.

[38] O'ROURKE, J. Polyhedra of minimal area as 3D object models. In *Proc. of the International Joint Conference on Artificial Intelligence* (1981), pp. 664–666.

[39] POTTMANN, H. Interpolation on surfaces using minimum norm networks. *Computer Aided Geometric Design 9* (1992), 51–67.

[40] PREPARATA, F. P., AND SHAMOS, M. I. *Computational Geometry: an Introduction.* Springer-Verlag, New York, NY, 1985.

[41] RESCORLA, K. C^1 trivariate polynomial interpolation. *Computer Aided Geometric Design 4* (1987), 237–244.

[42] TURK, G., AND LEVOY, M. Zippered polygonal meshes from range images. In *Computer Graphics Proceedings* (1994), Annual Conference Series. Proceedings of SIGGRAPH 94, ACM SIGGRAPH, pp. 311–318.

[43] VELTKAMP, R. C. 3D computational morphology. *Computer Graphics Forum 12*, 3 (1993), 115–127.

[44] WORSEY, A., AND FARIN, G. An n-dimensional clough-tocher interpolant. *Constructive Approximation 3*, 2 (1987), 99–110.

Creation and Rendering of Realistic Trees

Jason Weber[1]
Teletronics International, Inc.

Joseph Penn[2]
Army Research Laboratory

*"From such small beginnings - a mere grain of dust,
as it were - do mighty trees take their rise."*
Henry David Thoreau from "Faith in a Seed"

ABSTRACT

Recent advances in computer graphics have produced images approaching the elusive goal of photorealism. Since many natural objects are so complex and detailed, they are often not rendered with convincing fidelity due to the difficulties in succinctly defining and efficiently rendering their geometry. With the increased demand of future simulation and virtual reality applications, the production of realistic natural-looking background objects will become increasingly more important.

We present a model to create and render trees. Our emphasis is on the overall geometrical structure of the tree and not a strict adherence to botanical principles. Since the model must be utilized by general users, it does not require any knowledge beyond the principles of basic geometry. We also explain a method to seamlessly degrade the tree geometry at long ranges to optimize the drawing of large quantities of trees in forested areas.

1 INTRODUCTION

Historically, much of the effort in computer graphics has been directed toward rendering precisely defined geometrical shapes such as manufactured objects whose geometry must be clear-cut and well-defined. CAD tools that are often used to design these objects can also be used to specify the geometrical properties in terms of simpler surfaces or solid geometric primitives. The complexity of many objects is generally low enough to allow complex lighting and ray-tracing computations that approach photorealism.

Natural objects offer a more profound challenge. A hillside may contain hundreds of trees, billions of grass blades, and countless rocks, pebbles, and ground variations. Each tree may easily be characterized by hundreds of thousands of leaves and thousands of branches, branchlets, and stems oriented in complex directions. A complex landscape could require an unimaginable large number of polygons to define every minute facet. As a result, complex natural backgrounds containing vegetation are often neglected in high quality image generation and scene simulation because of the difficulty of properly defining and rendering them in a reasonable time. Emphasis is placed on the buildings, vehicles, and assorted manufactured objects that are often the focus of the dominant action in a scene. Because of speed requirements, two-dimensional texture-mapped trees drawn as rotating billboards are common today in many real-time applications, but their appearance can be objectionable. This is especially evident when a viewer is in motion. See [ROHL94] for examples of 2D trees. As simulations become more realistic, the deficiencies in the background objects become more apparent.

We present a model to create and render trees. In designing this model, we have set guidelines focused on the requirements of scene simulation. The foremost requirement is the appropriate level of resolution and quality. For items to appear realistic in a dynamic simulation, the viewer must get the proper sense of rotational as well as translational motion when passing or circling objects.

Realism also depends on the accuracy of textural effects due to leaves and branches within the tree shadowing each other at various times of the day. Therefore, all trees must be three-dimensional. Fortunately, as background objects, trees would rarely be taller than 5 to 20 percent of screen height. Therefore, fine details such as leaf curvature and vein structure are not important. But, a tree's branch structure must be very accurate at this resolution. Leaves do not completely conceal the underlying branches of dormant or sparsely foliated trees.

The model must be capable of creating a wide variety of actual tree types and related vegetation such as shrubs, bushes, and palms, as well as cacti and even large grasses. Shrubs, for example, can be easily simulated with the model since they really only differ from trees in that they are usually shorter and have multiple trunks originating directly from the ground [REIL91]. The model must be able to handle random parameters so that a very large number of structural variations can be generated from the design specifications of a particular tree species. It should also implement time-dependent oscillations due to wind and other perturbations.

Use of the model must be understandable by a common user with only a general knowledge of basic geometry, such as directly observable angles and lengths. This excludes the use of any model parameters requiring understanding of difficult principles such as differential equations. Likewise, the model must be stable and easy to use. User-entered free-form equations could easily cause unpredictable behavior. Aspects of the model that may be difficult to control should be isolated from the user and be represented by intuitive parameters. However, the model should not be constrained in a way that interferes with the user's freedom of design.

The specification for the tree must be compact and be able to recreate and render the tree geometry efficiently. This includes the ability to degrade geometry to low resolution at long ranges, where increased speed is necessary to render large forested areas. Any degradation must use negligible overhead and be seamless, even in dynamic simulations where ranges to trees are continuously changing.

This model was designed to successfully meet these criteria. We demonstrate the tree model in our natural environment scene generator. We have developed a compact but varied library of specification files for generating trees that are used in simulating a wide variety of landscapes.

The following section briefly discusses other tree models. The third section gives an overview of our observations of trees. The fourth section goes into the specific details and equations explaining how our parameters are used to create the geometric description. The fifth section explains our method of drawing optimally-degraded instances of the trees at longer ranges. The sixth section is a very short description of our project and how we use the trees in our application. An appendix includes a listing of our parameters and four sample tree specifications.

2 PREVIOUS MODELS

We will make some comparisons and contrasts to other tree models here and throughout the paper. We cannot fully explain the previous work in this space and will direct the reader to definitive references.

Honda introduced a model using parameters to define the skeleton of a tree [HOND71]. He clearly illustrated the difference between the monopodial and dichotomous branching. In dichotomous branching, the branches tend to split apart in different directions from the original. Monopodial branching tends to act similarly except that one branch continues inline from the original. Honda assumes that monopodial branching is a special case concerning structures that are parallel to the line of gravity.

Lindenmayer introduced a string rewriting system [LIND68] for cellular interaction commonly called the L-system. This is later applied to plants and trees and is extensively described in his book with Prusinkiewicz [PRUS90] which describes the system with a few extensions, such as allowing for context-sensitivity and random variations. Basically, the string starts with a seed of a single character. A set of rules defines how to substitute characters during an iteration of rewriting. Presumably, any one character may be converted into several characters. This process is continued iteratively and the string grows. After a designated number of iterations, these strings can be interpreted as geometric commands. Rules can be selected to produce the monopodial or dichotomous branching, as desired.

Aono and Kunii stated that the L-system was not capable of producing complex three-dimensional patterns of branching [AONO84]. They demonstrated their models which also introduced interesting features such as attraction, inhibition, and statistical variations of angles. They made a

---

1 weber@teleport.com, now employed at Dynamics Research Corporation
2 joseph@belvior-arl-irisgt.army.mil

0-89791-701-4/95/008

detailed evaluation of the arrangement of branches or leaves on a parent stem. Prusinkiewicz and Lindenmayer's book, printed later, argued that Aono and Kunii's rejection of the L-system was no longer justified based on their recent improvements.

Oppenheimer used fractals to form trees. He used parameters such as branching angle, branch-to-parent size ratio, stem taper rates, helical twist, and branches per stem segment. These specifications resemble our approach. The Oppenheimer model, however, following the fractal theory of self-similarity, uses the same specifications for every recursive level. He introduces random variations to alleviate some of the self-similarity [OPPE86]. We believe the self-similarity of fractals to be an unnecessary constraint that limits models to a relatively small number of basic trees. Oppenheimer's images appear to be influenced by Bloomenthal whose paper concentrated on the quality of the surface geometry assuming that a reasonable tree skeleton exists [BLOO85]. Bloomenthal splined between points on the skeleton and used a ramiform to represent branch splitting. He also used a bark texture map created from a digitized x-ray of a plaster cast. However, such detail is only useful when the tree is viewed at very close ranges.

Reeves and Blau created trees and grasses by utilizing a particle system [REEV85]. They primarily emphasized the forest environment instead of concentrating on the structural detail of individual plants. In addition, they decided to focus more on the visual results than the specific details of actual botanical data. For our application, we followed similar guidelines.

De Reffye et al. have had impressive results with a strict botanical model [REFF88]. Their system models growth to a certain age using probabilities of death, pause, ramification, and reiteration. They admit that it takes a considerable knowledge of both botany and of their model to create images with great fidelity to nature.

Since all the models strive to achieve the same result, realistic trees, they will all have some characteristics in common. Although our model does not draw from any of the previous models, comparisons will be made for the benefit of the reader.

3 APPROACH / OVERVIEW

We visualize the structure of a tree as a primary trunk consisting of a variably curved structure similar to a cone. In some trees, this single structure may split multiple times along its length, forming additional similarly curved structures which can likewise split along their length [CHND88]. This is how we visualize dichotomous branching. The attributes of these "clones" closely match that of the remaining length of their twin, except that they are generated using different random seeds. After splitting, some will tend to curve more to compensate for the directional change caused by the splitting angle.

Monopodial or "child" branches are formed from the trunk and any existing clones. These branches can have entirely different attributes from their "parents". Many attributes, such as length, are defined relative to the corresponding attribute of their parents. For example, a child branch's length is specified as a fraction of its parent's length. These branches, themselves, can have sub-branches and so on. For the resolution requirements of simulation, these levels of recursion can be generally be limited to three or four. It is important to point out that nearly all of the other models consider each branching, whether monopodial or dichotomous, to be discrete levels. They often require nine or ten of these levels. While this is primarily convention, it will be significant in optimized rendering (Section 5). Also, branch level control can assist in designing a tree. We usually begin by deactivating the rendering of all levels but the first (the trunk). Once the trunk's appearance is acceptable, we activate and design the second level, and so on, ascending degrees of complexity to the third and fourth levels. This allows us to view the general shape and structure of the tree without the visual confusion and performance loss due to drawing minor branches and leaves. In many cases, foliated trees can be drawn reasonably well in a final rendering without displaying any of the minor branches.

Specific trees appear to form particular shapes [CHND88,CHAN82]. These shapes are usually the result of the lengths of the primary branches according to their position on the trunk of the tree, e.g., a conically shaped tree has larger main branches near the base of the trunk. Alternatively, it is sometimes easier to define the general shape of the crown by envisioning an invisible envelope around the tree which inhibits growth of branches. In addition, many trees have branches that show a preference to curve towards a vertical direction, either up or down, presumably responding to the competing influences of light and gravity.

Cross-sectional variations can be particularly noticeable in the trunk. The scale of the cross-section does not necessarily taper linearly as with a perfect cone. Some cacti can even have periodic scaling in addition to simple random variations. The radial distance about any particular cross-section can also vary randomly and/or periodically. In addition, the radius of the trunk clearly flares at the base of the many trees.

Wind causes complex oscillatory motion throughout the tree that varies in amplitude and frequency determined by the length and thickness of the trunk and branches.

These are the characteristics we have observed and incorporated into our model. We model enough of the significant effects that a great variety of trees and related objects can be incorporated into any simulation that requires natural environments. Plate 1 shows twenty-four trees rendered with the model.

4 TREE CREATION

The appendix lists most of the parameters currently used by our tree model. It will be used for reference throughout this paper. For the benefit of readers who wish to experiment with the demo program, the intuitive multi-character variable names used in the parameter files will also be used in the equations throughout this paper. We should stress that many of these parameters have standard botanical names which we have neglected. We are not trying to create a new convention, but merely attempting to clarify the meanings of the parameters using simple geometric names recognized by our potential end users. Many of the parameters are repeated for each level of recursion to permit greater control and flexibility. Additional parameters, mostly dealing with seasonal color and lighting properties, are not listed and will not be discussed. The parameters are referred to in the text by name and appear as bold italic, as in *Shape*. Where necessary, parameters are prefixed by a number that distinguishes similar parameters at different levels of recursion. Generalized parameters can appear in the text with an *n* prefix, such as *nTaper* referring to *0Taper*, *1Taper*, *2Taper* and *3Taper*. This refers non-specifically to any of the like parameters. Many parameters are followed by a variation parameter with the same name and a '*V*' suffix, such as *nLength* and *nLengthV*. The variations are usually positive numbers indicating the magnitude of variation about the previous parameter. However, since a few special trees, like palms, require exceptions to common trends [REIL91], some parameters use the negative sign as a flag to activate a special mode. All angular parameters are specified in degrees. Likewise, angles in the equations are in degrees, unless otherwise stated. Except where noted, our equations describe structures based on our physical observations and research in tree reference manuals (see References).

Additionally, four trees parameter lists are given for comparison in Appendix. These specifications were designed using photographs in tree reference manuals. These trees, Quaking Aspen, Black Tupelo, Weeping Willow, and California Black Oak, can be seen in Plates 1q, 2, 5, and 1a, respectively. As trees vary widely and can be hard to identify even by experts [SYMO58], these specific definitions could be used to represent many different species of trees. Figure 1 is a diagram demonstrating some of the parameters. It does not show a complete tree, but rather exaggerates certain components to clarify their construction.

4.1 The Curved Stem

Our model is based on two elements, the stem and the leaf. We will use the generic term "stem" to refer to the trunk or branches at any level of recursion. The unit stem is a narrow near-conical tube whose relative z-axis is coincident with its central axis. Note that each stem has it own relative coordinate system. For a main branch whose z-axis points out perpendicularly to the trunk's z-axis, the branch's y-axis points up toward the sky and its x-axis points parallel to the ground surface, according to the right-hand rule. The tube of a stem at a recursive level *n* is divided into a number of near-cylindrical segments defined by *nCurveRes*. Each segment is stored as a nearly-circular cross-section. These cross-sections are later connected together to draw a triangular mesh. If *nCurveBack* is zero, the z-axis of each segment on the stem is rotated away from z-axis of the previous segment by (*nCurve/nCurveRes*) degrees about its x-axis. If *nCurveBack* is non-zero, each of the segments in the first half of the stem is rotated (*nCurve/(nCurveRes/2)*) degrees and each in the second half is rotated (*nCurveBack/(nCurveRes/2)*) degrees. This two part curve allows for simple S-shaped stems. In either case, a random rotation of magnitude (*nCurveV/nCurveRes*) is also added for each segment. A special mode is used when *nCurveV* is negative. In that case, the stem is formed as a helix. The declination angle is specified by the magnitude of *nCurveVary*.

4.2 Stem Splits

A stem generally extends out to the periphery of the tree, potentially splitting off cloned stems along its length. A cloned stem is considered at the same recursive level as its twin and inherits all of its properties. The frequency of splitting is defined by *nSegSplits*. This is the number of new clones added for each segment along the stem and is usually between 0 and 1, with 1 referring to a dichotomous split on every segment. A value of 2 would indicate a ternary split. There is no pre-determined limit to the number of splits per segment; but, since each clone can also generate its own clones at the next segment, the resulting number of stems can easily reach undesirable levels. For instance, with a *nCurveRes* of 5 and *nSegSplits* of 2, one stem will eventually split off into 81 separate clones: $(nSegSplits+1)^{nCurveRes-1}=3^4$. Note in the top center diagram in Figure 1 where a tree has *0SegSplits* of 1 and *0CurveRes* of 3. The resulting splitting results in a trunk with four total stems: $(1+1)^{3-1} = 4$. There is an additional parameter *nBaseSplits* that specifies the equivalent of *nSegSplits* at the end of the first segment of the trunk. This allows for an independent number of splits at the base of the tree, thus permitting trees that seem to have multiple trunks with few further splitting tendencies. Fractional values of *nSegSplits* will cause additional splits to be evenly distributed throughout all segments of all stems in that particular level of recursion. For example, an *nSegSplits* of 1.2 will form one clone on 80% of the level *n* segments and two clones on 20% of the segments. Note that this yields an average number of 1.2 splits per segment. Using random numbers simplistically to distribute the fractional part of *nSegSplits* is unacceptable because when, by chance, several consecutive segments all get the extra split, they can form an unnaturally large number of stems in close proximity on part of the tree. To evenly distribute the splits, we use a technique similar to Floyd-Steinburg Error Diffusion [FLOY76]. For each recursive level, a global value holds an "error value" initialized to 0.0. Each time *nSegSplits* is used, this error is added to create a $\text{SegSplits}_{\text{effective}}$ which is rounded to the nearest integer. The difference ($\text{SegSplits}_{\text{effective}}$-*nSegSplits*) is subtracted from the error. So, if a value is rounded up, it is more likely that the next value will be rounded down (and vice versa).

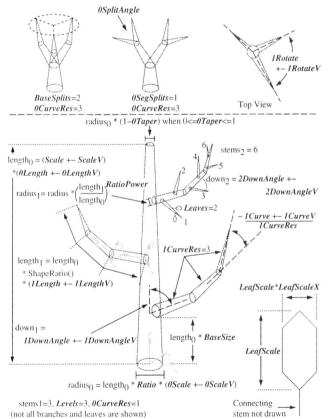

stems1=3, *Levels*=3, *0CurveRes*=1
(not all branches and leaves are shown)

Figure 1: Tree Diagram

If there are any clones, then the z-axes of the stem and its clones each rotate away from the z-axis of the previous segment by

$$\text{angle}_{\text{split}} = (nSplitAngle \pm nSplitAngleV) - \text{declination}$$

limited to a minimum of 0, where the "declination" angle (defined here as the angle of a stem from the tree's positive z-axis) can be found by taking the inverse cosine of the z component of a unit z vector passed through the current matrix transformation of the relative coordinate system. The first clone continues the original mesh and cannot rotate around the z-axis or it would twist the mesh (i.e., if one rotated one of the circular faces on a cylinder about the longitudinal axis, the resulting section of geometry would render as a hourglass shape). This $\text{angle}_{\text{split}}$ is later distributed over the

remaining segments in the reverse direction so that the stem will tend to return to its originally intended direction. This compensation prevents overspreading due to large numbers of stem splits. The extent that any level of stems spreads out can be easily controlled using the curve parameters.

A stem and its clones are also spread apart by rotating them about an axis that is parallel to the z-axis of the tree. This parallel axis of rotation intersects at the point where the split occurred. Note that they are not rotated about the relative z-axis of the stem as this would disturb the proper orientation of the relative x and y axes. In the normal case of a single clone, the original stem (which is continued after its clone is created) is rotated about the parallel axis by an angle of magnitude:

$$[\ 20 + 0.75 * (30 + |\ \text{declination-90}\ |) * \text{RANDOM}_{0\ \text{to}\ 1}^2\ ]$$

The sign of this angle is random as well. This equation diverges two nearly-horizontal branches by 20 to 50 degrees about the parallel axis, but allows near-vertical branches to spread up to 140 degrees. Excessive rotation for a near-horizontal branch could cause a very unnatural effect.

4.3 Stem Children

One could theoretically build a tree just from clones, but the variety of trees you could produce would be greatly limited. The even distribution that makes the splits controllable also makes the shape formed from the resulting stems and clones very uniform. Also, many trees do not exhibit a clear splitting nature and have branches that grow from other branches in a spiral or nearly coplanar manner. For this, we can spawn children, which are considered one recursive level below their parents. Although a child can have entirely different attributes from its parent, some of these attributes are defined relative to its parent's equivalents. Note that the other models generally only allow each tree to be dichotomous, monopodial, or somewhere in between. Honda recognized a problem with excessive branching and sought to resolve it with branch interactions and unequal flow rates [HOND81]. Since our clones and children allow for dichotomous and monopodial branching simultaneously, we rarely encounter this problem. Also, since our parameters can address the character of an entire stem and not just its segment-to-segment nature, we allow users to make changes on a level they can more easily understand and visualize. *nBranches* defines the maximum number of child sub-stems that a particular level of stems can create over the length of all of its segments. The actual number of children from any stem might be less than this maximum. The number of successive child stems (really "grandchildren") is computed as

$$\text{stems} = \text{stems}_{\text{max}} * (0.2 + 0.8 * (\text{length}_{\text{child}}/\text{length}_{\text{parent}})\ /\text{length}_{\text{child,max}})$$

for the first level of branches, and

$$\text{stems} = \text{stems}_{\text{max}} * (1.0 - 0.5 * \text{offset}_{\text{child}}/\text{length}_{\text{parent}})$$

for further levels of branches, where $\text{offset}_{\text{child}}$ is the position in meters of the child along the parent's length (from the base). Any stem that has been cloned or is, itself, a clone reduces its propensity to form clones by half. Given a normalized position "ratio" from 0.0 to 1.0, a function ShapeRatio(shape, ratio) uses various pre-defined relations:

Shape	Result	
0 (conical)	0.2 + 0.8 * ratio	
1 (spherical)	0.2 + 0.8 * sin(π * ratio)	
2 (hemispherical)	0.2 + 0.8 * sin(0.5 * π * ratio)	
3 (cylindrical)	1.0	
4 (tapered cylindrical)	0.5 + 0.5 * ratio	
5 (flame)	ratio/0.7	ratio≤0.7
	(1.0 - ratio)/0.3	ratio>0.7
6 (inverse conical)	1.0 - 0.8 * ratio	
7 (tend flame)	0.5 + 0.5 * ratio/0.7	ratio≤0.7
	0.5 + 0.5 * (1.0 - ratio)/0.3	ratio>0.7
8 (envelope)	*use pruning envelope (see Section 4.6)*	

Generally, the **Shape** parameter is used as the index to this table of curves. These shapes correspond to generic shapes defined in the botanical tree texts, previously referenced.

The maximum relative length ($\text{length}_{\text{child,max}}$) of any recursive level of stems is *nLength±nLengthV* which is defined as a fraction of its parent's specific length. For example, a child with $\text{length}_{\text{child,max}}$ of 0.3 and a 10 meter long parent could reach a maximum length of about 3 meters. A length is computed by

$$\text{length}_{\text{child}} = \text{length}_{\text{trunk}} * \text{length}_{\text{child,max}} *$$
$$\text{ShapeRatio}(\ \textit{Shape}, (\text{length}_{\text{trunk}}-\text{offset}_{\text{child}})/(\text{length}_{\text{trunk}}-\text{length}_{\text{base}}))$$

for the first level of branches and

$$\text{length}_{\text{child}} = \text{length}_{\text{child,max}} * (\text{length}_{\text{parent}} - 0.6 * \text{offset}_{\text{child}})$$

for further levels of branches, where $length_{base}$ is the fractional bare area at the base of the tree calculated as (***BaseSize****$scale_{tree}$) and $scale_{tree}$ defined as (***Scale***±***ScaleV***) in meters . The trunk has no parent, so its length is defined by

$$length_{trunk} = (\ \textbf{\textit{0Length}} \pm \textbf{\textit{0LengthV}}\ )*scale_{tree}$$

If ***nDownAngleV*** is positive, the z-axis of a child rotates away from the z-axis of its parent about the x-axis at an angle of (***nDownAngle***±***nDownAngleV***). However, if ***nDownAngleV*** is negative, the variation is distributed along the height of the tree by

$$downangle_{child} = \textbf{\textit{nDownAngle}} \pm [\ \textbf{\textit{nDownAngleV}} *$$
$$(\ 1 - 2 * \text{ShapeRatio}(\ 0, (length_{parent} - offset_{child})\ /$$
$$(length_{parent} - length_{base})\ )\ )\ ]$$

This can be used to linearly change the down angle based on the position of the child along its parent, as with the Black Tupelo's main branches seen in Plate 2b. Note how they are angled upward near the crown of the tree and angled downward near the bottom. If ***nRotate*** is positive, each child formed along the parent is placed in a helical distribution by rotating about the z axis of its parent relative to the previous child by the angle (***nRotate***±***nRotateV***). In the special case where ***nRotate*** is negative, each child is rotated about its parent's z-axis relative to its parent's y-axis by the angle (180+***nRotate***±***nRotateV***) on alternating sides of the parent branch. This allows for a nearly coplanar child stem distribution. Since the y-axis of any stem with a small downangle points back toward its parent, the planar distribution from such a stem is aligned with that parent. This makes it easy to design trees where sub-branches tend to spawn parallel to the ground surface. This effect is most obvious in the tree shown in Plate 1v.

Aono and Kunii go into detail about the proper divergence and branching angle [AONO84]. These correspond to our rotation and down angles, respectively. They note the Schimper-Braun law which states that this divergence angle is a fraction of 360 degrees based on a Fibonacci sequence of 1/2, 1/3, 2/5, 3/8, ... , resulting in possible angles of 180, 120, 144, 135, and so on. Our results show that any number near 140 degrees works well in most situations. Aono and Kunii also note that the branching angle (our down angle) appears to be smaller for branches that form later as the tree matures. De Reffye attributes this to gravity affecting the increased mass of older branches and simulates the effect including elastic curvature using Young's modulus [REFF88]. The change in the branching angle can result in large angles at the base of the tree and smaller angles along the height of the tree. We implement this linearly with the negative ***nDownAngleV*** as noted above. However, Aono and Kunii state that changing their model to implement this effect does not add much realism. We find the effect, as implemented in our model, to be very substantial, especially in dormant or sparsely foliated trees.

4.4 Stem Radius

For all levels except the trunk, the radius at the base of a stem is defined as a function of the radius of its parent stem. The trunk's radius is proportional to the scale of the entire tree.

$radius_{trunk} = length_{trunk} * \textbf{\textit{Ratio}} * \textbf{\textit{0Scale}}$		trunk
$radius_{child} = radius_{parent} * (\ length_{child} / length_{parent}\ )^{RatioPower}$		branches

The maximum radius of a stem is explicitly limited to the radius of the parent at the point from which it was spawned. The radius of the stem can be tapered along its length. In the simplest form, this can be used to render the stem as a bent cone. However, there are other variations that allow for other cases according to the following chart:

nTaper	Effect
0	Non-tapering cylinder
1	Taper to a point (cone)
2	Taper to a spherical end
3	Periodic tapering (concatenated spheres)

Any fractional value from 0 to 3 is permitted to allow adjustment for a desired effect. The periodic tapering can be seen in the cactus of Plate 1(L) which has an ***0Taper*** of 2.2. For a normalized position Z from 0 to 1 along the length of a stem, the following equations compute $radius_Z$, the tapered radius in meters:

unit_taper = ***nTaper***	$0 \leq \textbf{\textit{nTaper}} < 1$
unit_taper = 2 - ***nTaper***	$1 \leq \textbf{\textit{nTaper}} < 2$
unit_taper = 0	$2 \leq \textbf{\textit{nTaper}} < 3$
$taper_Z = radius_{stem} * (\ 1 - \text{unit\_taper} * Z\ )$	(purely tapered radius)

and when $0 \leq \textbf{\textit{nTaper}} < 1$

$$radius_Z = taper_Z$$

or when $1 \leq \textbf{\textit{nTaper}} \leq 3$

$$Z_2 = (\ 1 - Z\ ) * length_{stem}$$

depth = 1	(***nTaper*** < 2) OR (Z_2 < $taper_Z$)
depth = ***nTAPER*** - 2	otherwise
$Z_3 = Z_2$	***nTaper*** < 2
$Z_3 = \|Z_2 - 2 * taper_Z * \text{integer}(\ Z_2 / (2 * taper_Z) + 0.5\ )\|$	otherwise
$radius_Z = taper_Z$	(***nTaper***<2) AND ($Z_3 \geq taper_Z$)

$$radius_Z = (1 - depth) * taper_Z +$$
$$depth * \text{sqrt}(\ taper_Z^2 - (Z_3 - taper_Z)^2\ ) \qquad \text{otherwise}$$

where 'depth' is a scaling factor used for the periodic tapering. This periodic tapering is useful for some cacti, where annual growth can accumulate in segments [HAUS91]. Similarly, it can be used as a rough approximation of the scales on palm trees.

In addition to tapering, the trunk may also vary its radius by other means. Flaring creates an exponential expansion near the base of the trunk. At the unit position Z from 0 to 1 along the length of a stem, the following $flare_Z$ scales the $radius_Z$ computed above.

$$y = 1 - 8 * Z$$
$$flare_Z = \textbf{\textit{Flare}} * (\ 100^y - 1\ ) / 100 + 1$$

where the value of y is limited to a minimum of zero. Note that this equation scales the radius by a minimum of 1 and a maximum of about (1 + ***Flare***).

The trunk can also have an irregular non-circular cross-section. This can be very apparent in the large supporting "knees" of cypress trees [REIL91]. These variations are also clearly present on some cacti, which can have pronounced ribs or ridges [HAUS91]. ***Lobes*** specifies the number of peaks in the radial distance about the perimeter. Even numbers can cause obvious symmetry, so odd numbers such as 3, 5, and 7 are preferred. The ***LobeDepth*** specifies the magnitude of the variations as a fraction of the radius as follows:

$$lobe_Z = 1.0 + \textbf{\textit{LobeDepth}} * \sin (\ \textbf{\textit{Lobes}} * angle\ )$$

given a specific "angle" from the x-axis about the z-axis. Note that a ***LobeDepth*** of zero effectively turns lobing off. The $lobe_Z$ value cumulatively scales $radius_Z$ as did $flare_Z$. Finally, a simple scaling factor (***0Scale***±***0ScaleV***) can also be applied to the trunk.

Bloomenthal modeled this flaring and lobing using an "equipotential curve surrounding the points of intersection of the tree skeleton with the plane of the contour" [BLOO85], essentially the blended circumference of several circles moving further away from the center of the trunk near the base of the tree.

4.5 Leaves

The recursive proliferation of children is limited by ***Levels***. This specifies the maximum level of stems that will be created starting from 0 for the trunk, usually to 3 or 4. If ***Leaves*** is non-zero, then leaves are used as the last level of recursion. The leaves use the ***nDownAngle***, ***nDownAngleV***, ***nRotate***, and ***nRotateV*** from the that level of recursion. Any leaves or stems beyond level 3 will simply use the parameters of level 3. Our most common configuration is to set ***Levels*** to 3 and ***Leaves*** to a non-zero value which would give you the following levels of recursion: trunk (0), branches (1), sub-branches (2), and leaves (3). Some trees, such as the weeping willow, require sub-sub-branches as well. ***Leaves*** specifies the density in the same manner as ***nBranches*** did for stems. As with stems, the actual density used is also dependent upon other factors such as the length of the parent branch relative to the maximum length for the parent's level. Given that the leaves are at the second level of recursion or further, the following density is used:

$$\text{leaves\_per\_branch} = \textbf{\textit{Leaves}} *$$
$$\text{ShapeRatio}(\ 4\ \textit{(tapered)}, offset_{child}/length_{parent}\ ) * quality$$

given a quality factor supplied by the parent program that is usually near 1. This quality factor is also used to scale the leaves to maintain consistent coverage. This distribution of leaves has the natural effect of preferentially placing leaves near the outside of the tree. For a negative value of ***Leaves***, a special mode is used in which the leaves are placed in a fan at the end of the parent stem, as with some palm fronds. The angle over which the leaves fan out is specified by ***nRotate***. Note that when in fan mode, ***nRotate*** is not needed for its original purpose. A negative value can also be applied to ***nBranches*** with similar results, but we have not yet modeled any trees requiring this attribute. We realize that these negative flags can become a bit confusing, but they are only used in a few special cases. Many users will never need them.

Leaves can assume many different shapes [CHND88]. We allow for a few common geometries of leaves based on *LeafShape*. This parameter is used as an index to a list of pre-defined leaf shapes, such as oval, triangle, 3-lobe oak, 3-lobe maple, 5-lobe maple, any 3 leaflets. Each shape can be sized and scaled. For optimum coverage versus computational expense, the oval leaves are most commonly used. The pre-defined leaf geometries are stored with unit width and length. They are scaled as they are used to create the tree geometry. The length of the leaves, in meters, is determined by [*LeafScale* / sqrt(quality)]. The width, in meters, is determined by [*LeafScale**LeafScaleX / sqrt(quality)].

4.6 Pruning

Pruning is used to force a tree to fit inside a specific envelope. We originally avoided such a feature since we felt that the shape of a tree should proceed from its underlying structure, not from the use of artificial boundaries. We now concede that under the influence of certain environmental conditions or to control an "uncooperative" tree, pruning can be very useful. Prusinkiewicz demonstrates pruning applied to the L-system model [PRUS94]. Essentially, growth of branches is blocked by the edge of the envelope boundary. Since the L-system progressively grows connecting nodes, the model can simply hinder growth near a boundary. Our model must approach the problem differently. Since our stems often reach from the trunk to the tree's outer edges simply chopping off the ends of the offending branches,will make the tree's appearance suffer. While this may be the effect from some actual physical pruning, we would rather use pruning as a tool to influence the shape of a tree through the underlying structure. To do this, every stem must adjust its length to fit inside the envelope. Each stem must "know this new length" before it spawns any children since each child's length is dependent on its parent's length. Generally, the child branches are recursively spawned during the formation of the parent's segment from which they grow. This is necessary since the child must use a geometric transformation relative to the transformation of that segment. At that point, the ultimate extent of the parent is not known, so there must first be a non-recursive probing pass for each stem to measure and rescale its length and then a fully-recursive second pass to actually form the geometry and spawn the children. Note that the probing must also that each of the stem's clones fits. If any stem or clone punctures the boundary, its length can be iteratively reduced and re-probed until it fits.

While the model is capable of using any arbitrary envelope such as the topiary dinosaur in Prusinkiewicz's paper, the general user should be more comfortable with an easily selected simple envelope. Figure 2 shows a pruning envelope.

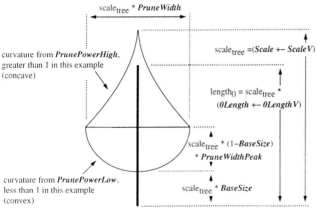

Figure 2: Pruning Diagram

The envelope covers a pseudo-ellipsoidal shape with a top at $scale_{tree}$ and bottom at (*BaseSize**$scale_{tree}$) in meters. The maximum width of the envelope is (*PruneWidth**$scale_{tree}$) in meters. This maximum width occurs at a position along the tree's z-axis as specified by *PruneWidthPeak*. This peak is defined as the distance from the bottom of the envelope as a fraction of the total height of the envelope. A *PruneWidthPeak* of 0.5 would center the peak as with a standard ellipsoid. The curvature of the envelope can also be independently controlled above and below the peak using *PrunePowerHigh* and *PrunePowerLow*, respectively. A power of 1 gives a linear envelope from *PruneWidth* to 0 over the distance from *PruneWidthPeak* to the top or bottom of the envelope. A power of 2 gives a rounded concave envelope, while a power of 0.5 gives a rounded convex

envelope. To determine whether a given transformed point (x,y,z) is inside the envelope, the boolean 'inside' is computed as:

$$r = sqrt (x^2 + y^2 + z^2)$$

$$ratio = (scale_{tree} - z) / (scale_{tree} *(1\text{-}\textit{BaseSize}))$$

$$inside = [r / scale_{tree} < \textit{PruneWidth} *$$

$$ShapeRatio(8 \textit{ (envelope)}, ratio)]$$

where ShapeRatio(8, ratio) is defined as

$$[ratio / (1 - \textit{PruneWidthPeak})]^{\textit{PrunePowerHigh}}$$

when ratio < 1 - *PruneWidthPeak*, or

$$[(1 - ratio) / (1 - \textit{PruneWidthPeak})]^{\textit{PrunePowerLow}}$$

when ratio ≥ 1 - *PruneWidthPeak*. ShapeRatio(8, ratio) always returns 0 when ratio is not in the range of 0 to 1. The *Shape* parameter can use this index of 8 for a custom shape even if pruning is not turned on. This allows the user to define a shape not covered by the predefined shapes. If *Shape* is 8 and pruning is on, the tree will tend to match the customized shape even before pruning takes place. This may cause some strongly curved stems to fall short of the envelope's edge.

The effects of pruning can be diminished by using the *PruneRatio*. This defines a weighted average between the unpruned original length and the completely pruned length. A *PruneRatio* of 1 activates full pruning while a *PruneRatio* of 0.0 effectively turns pruning off. Thus with values between 0 and 1, partial pruning can be utilized to avoid artificially smooth boundaries. Plate 7 demonstrates the use of the pruning envelope to control the weeping willow.

4.7 Wind Sway

We model stem bending as the deflection of an elastic rod with a circular cross-section fixed on one end. This rod has a uniformly distributed force applied to it. The solution of this is a classic problem of mechanics where applying the Myosotis method yields useful solutions for the deflection [HART77]. We then consider this rod as a kind of pendulum [HALL88]. The entire system is then modeled as the superposition of coupled oscillators whose periods and phase angles differ so that the paths of points on a stem are very complex Lissajous figures [ALON70]. These results confirm our general observation that light to moderate winds induce trees to move so that branches sway at various directions and rates of oscillations. We currently model the oscillatory effects observed for light to moderate winds only.

In our model, tree movement is simulated by introducing time-variant curvature changes to the stem segments. This effect is added to the structural curvature introduced by *nCurve* and *nCurveBack* causing rotations between segments about both x and y axes. With wind speeds varying from $wind_{speed}$ to ($wind_{speed}$+ $wind_{gust}$), the sway angles $sway_x$ and $sway_y$ at unit position Z from 0 to 1 of a segment along the length of a stem are computed at any "time" (in seconds) using:

$a_0 = 4 * length_{stem} (1 - Z) / radius_Z$	(degrees)
$a_1 = wind_{speed} / 50 * a_0$	(degrees)
$a_2 = wind_{gust} / 50 * a_0 + a_1/2$	(degrees)
$b_x = sway\_offset_x + radius_{stem} / length_{stem} * time/15$	(radians)
$b_y = sway\_offset_y + radius_{stem} / length_{stem} * time/15$	(radians)
$sway_x = [a_1 * sin(b_x) + a_2 * sin (0.7 * b_x)] / nCurveRes$	(degrees)
$sway_y = [a_1 * sin(b_y) + a_2 * sin (0.7 * b_y)] / nCurveRes$	(degrees)

The angles $sway\_offset_x$ and $sway\_offset_y$ are randomly selected for each stem in the tree. When the wind sway is activated, each tree geometry description must be reformed for each frame in an animation to adapt to the new angles. By using the same random seed, a specific tree will always have the same basic geometry, perturbed only by the wind-activated curvature variations. The angles $sway_x$ and $sway_y$ cause rotations between segments about the x and y axes, respectively.

4.8 Vertical Attraction

With even hemispherical illumination (sky shine), tree shoots grow upwards because they are negatively geotropic and positively phototropic. An upward growth tendency is usually a subtle effect and can be implemented using the declination and orientation of each segment in each stem. For sub-branches and beyond, this curving effect is used in addition to the other curvature effects. The trunk and main branches do not use these functions since any such effect can be more easily controlled through the previous curve parameters. The *AttractionUp* parameter specifies the upward tendency. Zero denotes no effect and negative numbers cause downward drooping as in the Weeping Willow. A magnitude of one results in a tendency of each stem to curve just enough so that its last segment points in a vertical direction. Higher magnitudes cause stems to curve toward the vertical much sooner. Very high magnitudes such as 10 may result in snaking oscillations due to over-correction. This is not necessarily an undesirable result since branches on some trees exhibit a distinctly sinusoidal shape characteristic. Once the effects of *nCurve* are introduced to a segment, curve_up$_{segment}$ is computed for each segment as

$$\text{declination} = \cos^{-1}(\text{transform\_z}_z) \qquad \text{(radians)}$$
$$\text{orientation} = \cos^{-1}(\text{transform\_y}_z) \qquad \text{(radians)}$$

$$\text{curve\_up}_{segment} = \textit{AttractionUp} * \text{declination} *$$
$$\cos (\text{orientation}) / \textit{nCurveRes} \qquad \text{(radians)}$$

where transform_z$_z$ is the z component of a unit z vector passed through the current viewing transformation and transform_y$_z$ is the z component of a unit y vector passed through the current viewing transformation. This curve_up$_{segment}$ is added to the segment's curvature.

4.9 Leaf Orientation

Left alone, the modeled leaves will generally assume seemingly random orientations. However, in reality, leaves are oriented to face upwards and outwards, presumably to optimize the available direct (sun) and scattered (sky) light. We can use the declination and orientation of each leaf to rotate them toward the light. The necessary rotations are computed based on the current viewing transformation and are applied prior to creating the leaf into the geometric description. The effect, fractionally controlled by "bend", is applied by obtaining the leaf's position (leaf$_x$, leaf$_y$, leaf$_z$) and normal (leaf$_{nx}$, leaf$_{ny}$, leaf$_{nz}$) in tree coordinates from the current transform matrix, then computing the current and desired angles:

$$\text{theta}_{position} = \text{atan}_2 (\text{leaf}_y, \text{leaf}_x)$$
$$\text{theta}_{bend} = \text{theta}_{position} - \text{atan}_2 (\text{leaf}_{ny}, \text{leaf}_{nx})$$

then computing the change:

$$\text{rotate}_z (\text{bend} * \text{theta}_{bend})$$

then recomputing declination, orientation, and normal vector using new transform:

$$\text{phi}_{bend} = \text{atan}_2 (\text{sqrt}(\text{leaf}_{nx}^2 + \text{leaf}_{ny}^2), \text{leaf}_{nz})$$
$$\text{rotate}_z (-\text{orientation})$$
$$\text{rotate}_x (\text{bend} * \text{phi}_{bend})$$
$$\text{rotate}_z (\text{orientation})$$

Plate 6 shows the bending effect applied to a Sassafras tree. The modified leaf orientations greatly increase the diffusive reflections from the tree. The increased variations improve the overall appearance.

5 DEGRADATION AT RANGE

A tree generated with our algorithm may have on the order of 5000 to 100,000 facets. The detail can be increased automatically for even higher resolution images, such as the Weeping Willow in Plate 3 boosted to over 1 million facets. Currently, a high-end graphics workstation may be capable of only about 50,000 facets in real time. The high resolution of the trees is necessary to have an accurate representation at close ranges of 10 to 50 meters or in equivalent magnified views of greater ranges, as in narrow fields-of-view. However, at long ranges, such as 1000 meters, a much lower resolution tree could be rendered faster with little or no loss in apparent quality.

At first thought, it may seem useful to form multiple geometric descriptions of the same tree at different "levels of detail". At longer ranges, progressively lower resolution geometric descriptions would be used. This approach has two problems. First, each instance of a tree consumes resources. An average tree's geometric description may use about 1Mb of RAM. Also, it may require 1 to 10 seconds to form the data. These numbers become much more significant when multiplied by, perhaps, 100 instances. While this could be managed, a more critical second problem arises with the quantization of the resolution. In a still picture, the changes between resolutions would not be very apparent since the variably resolved trees appear as different trees. However, in a dynamic simulation, specific trees would switch from one resolution to the next. This would result in wide "resolution waves" flowing through forest canopies. This is unacceptable for realistic simulation.

A method is needed that uses a single geometric description and renders it at an optimal resolution for any range. The changes between the differently resolved geometries must be very fine, preferably corresponding with removal or modification of each facet one at a time. There should be

negligible overhead (CPU and RAM) involved with this reinterpretation of the specified geometry.

Since the trees are not arbitrary objects, we can fit a range-degradation algorithm to their expected geometry. Each tree geometry is organized into four discrete geometric descriptions: 3 stem levels and the leaves. Any stems beyond the third level are grouped with the third level. The deeper levels of stems are rarely visible at long ranges and are often obscured by the leaves. Oppenheimer recognized that he could use polygonal tubes for large-scale details and vectors (lines) for the smaller details [OPPE86]. He warns that artifacts can occur if the "cutover" level is not deep enough. He also states that many small branches can be rendered as triangular tubes. Our method of rendering makes similar approximations for efficiency.

To most efficiently use the CPU and memory, our technique does not convert the geometry, it merely re-interprets it. With progressively increasing ranges, a tree will re-interpret stem meshes as lines and leaf polygons as points. With longer ranges, some individual stems and leaves will disappear altogether. The specific geometry at any range can be rendered properly by altering limits and increments in the loops that draw the data. Although we speak of removing items one by one, we do not actually mark or delete them. We merely change the loop parameters that scan the stored geometry so that items are skipped. Any number of arbitrarily-ranged trees can be drawn in any order. The time and space overhead required to compute and hold these boundary limits is negligible. A 100,000 facet tree geometry may be rendered at 2 kilometers as about 30 lines and 1000 points. This allows vast expanses of trees to be drawn very quickly. A viewer can then move close to any of these trees and see them at their full resolution.

Since the items in each geometric description are ordered in the same manner as they were created, they generally start from the bottom of the tree and work up. The items are not randomly organized; therefore, we cannot simply remove objects one at a time in order from the top or bottom of the list. This could cause the top of the tree to be heavily degraded while the bottom remained unchanged, or vice versa. Instead, we group the items of a type of geometry into groups of a small size which we will call "masses". The number of elements per mass is determined by an appropriate "mass_size". We use a mass_size of 16 for all the stems and 4 for the leaves. Curve fitting equations give a value between 0 and mass_size. To explain, we will use the general term "primitive" to refer non-specifically to polygons, lines, or points and the general term "item" to refer non-specifically to leaves, trunk, branches, or sub-branches. The total number of elements in the geometric description of any item is given as "total_number$_{item}$". Of this, we wish to draw a certain fraction of these items using a specific primitive. The portion to be drawn is specified by the non-integer "number$_{primitive,item}$", which is between 0 and mass_size$_{primitive,item}$. For example, a mass_size$_{lines,1}$ of 16 divides up main branch lines into masses of 16. A number$_{lines,1}$ of 5 says that for every 16 cross-sections of recursion level 1, there should be lines connecting the first five. Fractional numbers will draw an additional item for a percentage of the masses. If there were 160 main-branch cross-sections (10 masses) and number$_{lines,1}$ of 5.3, then the first 3 masses would show 6 of 16 lines and the last 7 masses would show 5 of 16 lines. A loop to draw the reduced portion of the item using a specific primitive would be:

```
int_number_primitive,item = integer( number_primitive,item )
masses_primitive,item = total_number_item / mass_size_primitive,item
change_primitive,item = masses_primitive,item *
                ( number_primitive,item - int_number_primitive,item )
for mass = 0 to masses_primitive,item
    {
    start = mass * mass_size_primitive,item
    end = start + int_number_primitive,item

    if mass < change_primitive,item
        end = end + 1

    for index = start to end
        draw_primitive,item( index )
    }
```

To compute the necessary number$_{primitive,item}$, we need to first convert the range to a calibrated scale. This adjusts for the current image size and vertical field of view. A modified range value, r$_2$, is computed as:

$$r_2 = \text{range} * 1000 / \text{height}_{image} * \text{Field\_Of\_View}_y / 60$$

This compensates for the effect of a telephoto lens that causes a tree to appear to be much closer.

The following equations outline how number$_{primitive,item}$ is computed for different levels at different ranges. First, we use the general quality factor supplied by the parent program (usually between 0 and 1) to determine some general scaling factors:

s = quality / 2   tree is evergreen, or in summer and fall
s = quality   otherwise
d = 100   in spring
d = 200   otherwise

Then, we compute the polygons, lines, and points needed for each display item as follows.

Level 0 Stems (trunk)

	$r_2 < 100$	don't draw trunk lines (can appear as seam)
$100 <$	r_2	draw all trunk lines

	$r_2 < 300$	$number_{polygons,0} = mass\_size_{polygons,0}$
$300 <$	$r_2 < 800$	$number_{polygons,0} = mass\_size_{polygons,0} * [1.5 - r_2/600]$
$800 <$	r_2	don't draw trunk polygons at all

Level 1 Stems (main branches)

	$r_2 < 200s$	$number_{polygons,1} = mass\_size_{polygons,1} * [1.5 - r_2/600]$
		(bounded 0 to $mass\_size_{polygons,1}$)
		$number_{lines,1} = mass\_size_{lines,1}$
$200s <$	$r_2 < 2000s$	don't draw polys
		$number_{lines,1} = mass\_size_{lines,1} *$
		$[\ 2.2 - 1.2\ (r_2/200s)^{0.3}\ ]$
$2000s <$	r_2	draw nothing for main branches

Level 2 Stems (other branches)

	$r_2 < 50s$	$number_{polygons,2} = mass\_size_{polygons,2}$
		$number_{lines,2} = mass\_size_{lines,2}$
$50s <$	$r_2 < 100s$	$number_{polygons,2} = mass\_size_{polygons,2} * [\ 2 - r_2/50s\ ]$
		$number_{lines,2} = mass\_size_{lines,2}$
$100s <$	$r_2 < 500s$	don't draw polys
		$number_{lines,2} = mass\_size_{lines,2} * [\ 2 - (r_2/100s)^{0.5}\ ]$
$500s <$	r_2	draw nothing for secondary branches

Leaves

	$r_2 < d/4$	$number_{polygons,3} = mass\_size_{polys,3}$
		$number_{points,3} = mass\_size_{points,3}$
$d/4$	$r_2 < d$	$number_{polygons,3} = mass\_size_{polys,3} *$
		$[\ 4/3 - r_2\ /\ (3d/4)\ ]$
		$number_{points,3} = mass\_size_{points,3}$
$d <$	r_2	$number_{polygons,3} = 0$
		$number_{points,3} = mass\_size_{points,3} * [\ 1.5 - r_2\ /\ 2d\ ]$
		(minimum of 1)

The effects of these equations can be seen in Table 2 which summarizes the total number of triangles, lines, and points. Triangles refer to elements of the triangular meshes which comprise the polygons.

Item	5m	30m	60m	120m	240m	600m	1200m
Level 0 Triangles	1440	1440	1440	1440	1440	760	0
Level 0 Lines	0	0	0	36	36	36	36
Level 1 Triangles	960	960	960	0	0	0	0
Level 1 Lines	240	240	240	223	153	35	0
Level 2 Triangles	17736	14580	0	0	0	0	0
Level 2 Lines	5912	5912	5363	2648	0	0	0
Leaf Triangles	53248	53248	49800	28200	0	0	0
Leaf Points	13312	13312	13312	13312	11944	1664	1664

Table 2: Number of elements drawn at specific ranges in summer on Quaking Aspen

Plate 4 shows the Quaking Aspen rendered at the ranges listed in Table 2, excluding 5 meters, progressively zoomed by powers of two.

6 APPLICATION

Our project involves the development of software to produce accurate and realistic high resolution imagery in both the visible and infrared spectrums. The emphasis is on positioning vehicles in the context of natural environments for studies of detection and recognition by both humans and machines. The backgrounds and vehicles must be of equally high fidelity to alleviate any bias in the testing.

The software utilizes readily available elevation maps and creates synthetically-generated shading variations for numerous natural effects. Readily available feature maps are usually at a poor resolution and often only describe trees as deciduous, coniferous, neither, or both. This is inadequate for our needs. We create our own feature maps from any available information such as scenario data (meteorological, topographical, vegetative type and placement, etc.), satellite imagery, and photographs, both aerial and at ground level. We describe vegetation using a 16-bit raster feature map where 14 bits specify 14 trees or related objects (not mutually-exclusive), and 2 bits specify 3 types of grass (mutually-exclusive). Any of the 14 trees (from a larger list) and 3 grass types can be selected differently for any specific scene. For any one of the 14 selected trees, any number of variations can be specified. These variations use the same parameter file, but are generated from a different random seed. During rendering, these variations of a tree type are spread randomly over positions where the appropriate bit for that tree is set in the vegetation feature map. This can prevent large forests of similar tree types from appearing too uniform and self-similar. Other feature maps are used for soils, rocks, waterways, and roadways. Currently, we generally resolve elevation and features maps at 1 or 2 meters per sample. The grass resembles that of Reeves and Blau's particle grass [REEV85]. In our case, the grass is drawn as curved lines composed of Gouraud-shaded segments.

Shadowing within the trees is produced using a standard shadow map technique [FOLE92]. The shadow map can be used to mark which geometric components (polygons, lines, points) will be shadowed before rendering takes place. This technique is only valid if each rendered instance of each specific geometric description has the same rotational orientation about its z-axis. Otherwise, the shadows would be rotated with the tree. This restriction is usually acceptable since each tree selected can have multiple variations, each of which can be randomly scaled for each instance.

Plate 3 shows various images of a visual simulation from different points of view. Plate 3f was made from an altered scenario with higher tree density. A moderate haze was applied to the image in Plate 3b.

7 CONCLUSION

We have introduced a model based on geometrical observables to create and render three-dimensional trees for simulating natural scenery. A wide variety of complex realistic tree structures can be generated quickly using a small number of parameters. The resulting images appear quite similar to images of real botanical trees. We have demonstrated the efficient use of the model with our synthetic scene generator.

We explained a range degradation methodology to smoothly degrade the tree geometry at long ranges. This is used to optimize the drawing of large quantities of trees in forested areas.

Our attention in designing the model was focused on allowing a general user to create trees that generally match images from books or photographs. The user needs no knowledge of botany or complex mathematical principles, only a basic understanding of geometry. We concentrated on the general structural appearance of a tree instead of the biological and biophysical principles that produced its structure.

Currently, the rendering of our trees at close range is not quite fast enough to meet the needs of real time simulation. A high end graphics workstation may only be able to draw one very close tree or a few dozen long range trees in real time. However, newer hardware will inevitably bring higher performance. In the near future, tree models such as this will be important in many areas of computer graphics.

ACKNOWLEDGEMENTS

All images were created with the CREATION software developed by Teletronics and the Modeling Simulation Branch of the US Army Research Laboratory.

Thanks to the US Army Research Lab who supported this project and helped with this paper, specifically Teresa Kipp, John Ho (retired), Gertrude Kornfeld (retired), Hung Nguyen, E. "Glenn" Dockery, Michael Lander, Janice Colby, and Giap Huynh, and also Dickson Fang and Scott Hawley of Teletronics. Thanks also to Dynamics Research Corporation.

REFERENCES

[ALON70] M. Alonso, E. Finn. *Physics*. Addison-Wesley, Reading, Massachusetts, 1970, pp. 160-166.

[AONO84] M. Aono, T. Kunii. Botanical Tree Image Generation. *IEEE Computer Graphics and Applications*. May, 1984, pp.10-34, Volume 4, No.5.

[BLOO85] J. Bloomenthal. Modeling the Mighty Maple. Proceedings of SIGGRAPH '85 (San Francisco, California, July 22-26, 1985). In *Computer Graphics* Proceedings, Annual Conference Series, 1985, ACM SIGGRAPH, pp. 305-311.

[CHND88] P. Chandler, A. Cook, G. DeWolf, G Jones, K Widin. *Taylor's Guide to Trees*. Houghton Mifflin Company, Boston, 1988.

[CHAN82] F. Chan, F. Ching, W Collins, M. Evans, W. Flemer, J. Ford, F. Galle, R Harris, R. Korbobo, F. Lang, F. Mackaness, B. Mulligan, R. Ticknor. *Trees*. The American Horticultural Society, Mount Vernon, Virginia, 1982.

[COLL74] G. Collingwood, W. Brush. *Knowing Your Trees*. The American Forestry Association, Washington, DC., 1974.

[FOLE92] J. Foley, A. vanDam, S. Feiner, J. Hughes. *Computer Graphics, Principles and Practice*, Second Edition. Addison-Wesley, Reading, Massachusetts, 1992.

[FLOY76] R. Floyd, L. Steinburg. An Adaptive Algorithm for Spatial Grey Scale, *Proceedings SID*. 1976, pp. 75-77.

[HALL88] D. Halliday, R, Resnick. *Fundamentals of Physics*, 3rd Ed. J. Wiley & Sons, New York, 1988, pp. 306-322.

[HAUS91] E. Haustein. *The Cactus Handbook*. Hamlin, London, 1991.

[HART77] J. Den Hartog. *Strength of Materials*. Dover, Mineola, 1977, pp. 79-88.

[HOND71] H. Honda. Description of the Form of Trees by the Parameters of the Tree-like Body: Effects of the Branching Angle and the Branch Length on the Shape of the Tree-like Body. *Journal of Theoretical Biology*. 1971, pp. 331-338.

[HOND81] H. Honda, P. Tomlinson, J. Fisher. Computer Simulation of Branch Interaction and Regulation by Unequal Flow Rates in Botanical Trees. *American Journal of Botany*. 1981, pp. 569-585.

[LIND68] A. Lindenmayer. Mathematical Models for Cellular Interactions in Development, I&II. *Journal of Theoretical Biology*. 1968, pp. 280-315.

[OPPE86] P. Oppenheimer. Real Time Design and Animation of Fractal Plants and Trees. Proceedings of SIGGRAPH '86 (Dallas, Texas, August 18-22, 1986). In *Computer Graphics* Proceedings, Annual Conference Series, 1986, ACM SIGGRAPH, pp. 55-64.

[PAGE93] J. Page. *Planet Earth: Forest*. Time-Life Books, Alexandria, Virginia, 1983.

[PRUS90] P. Prusinkiewicz, A. Lindenmayer. *The Algorithmic Beauty of Plants*. Springer-Verlag, New York, 1990.

[PRUS94] P. Prusinkiewicz, M. James, R. Měch. Synthetic Topiary. Proceedings of SIGGRAPH '94 (Orlando, Florida, July 24-29, 1994). In *Computer Graphics* Proceedings, Annual Conference Series, 1994, ACM SIGGRAPH, pp. 351-358.

[REEV85] W. Reeves. Approximate and Probabilistic Algorithms for Shading and Rendering Structured Particle Systems. Proceedings of SIGGRAPH '85 (San Francisco, California, July 22-26, 1985). In *Computer Graphics* Proceedings, Annual Conference Series, 1985, ACM SIGGRAPH, pp. 313-322.

[REFF88] P. de Reffye, C. Edelin, J. Françon, M. Jaeger, C. Puech. Plant models faithful to botanical structure and development. Proceedings of SIGGRAPH 88 (Atlanta, Georgia, August 1-5, 1988). In *Computer Graphics* Proceedings, Annual Conference Series, 1988, ACM SIGGRAPH, pp. 151-158.

[REIL91] A. Reilly. *The Secrets of Trees*. Gallery Books, New York, 1991.

[ROHL94] J. Rohlf, J. Helman.. IRIS Performer: A High Performance Multiprocessing Toolkit for Real-Time 3D Graphics. Proceedings of SIGGRAPH '94 (Orlando, Florida, July 24-29, 1994). In *Computer Graphics* Proceedings, Annual Conference Series, 1994, ACM SIGGRAPH, pp. 381-394, specifically Figures 14 and 17 on page 394.

[SYMO58] G. Symonds. *The Tree Identification Book*. William Morrow & Company, New York, 1958.

[TOOT84] E. Tootill, S. Blackmore. *The Facts on File Dictionary of Botany*. Market House Books LTD, Aylesbury, UK, 1984, p.155.

APPENDIX: Parameter List

Parameter	Description	Quaking Aspen	Black Tupelo	Weeping Willow	CA Black Oak
Shape	general tree shape id	7	4	3	2
BaseSize	fractional branchless area at tree base	0.4	0.2	0.05	0.05
Scale,ScaleV,ZScale,ZScaleV	size and scaling of tree	13, 3, 1, 0	23, 5, 1, 0	15, 5, 1, 0	10, 10, 1, 0
Levels	levels of recursion	3	4	4	3
Ratio,RatioPower	radius/length ratio, reduction	0.015, 1.2	0.015, 1.3	0.03, 2	0.018, 1.3
Lobes,LobeDepth	sinusoidal cross-section variation	5, 0.07	3, 0.1	9, 0.03	5, 0.1
Flare	exponential expansion at base of tree	0.6	1	0.75	1.2
0Scale,0ScaleV	extra trunk scaling	1, 0	1, 0	1, 0	1, 0
0Length,0LengthV, 0Taper	fractional trunk, cross-section scaling	1, 0, 1	1, 0, 1.1	0.8, 0, 1	1, 0, 0.95
0BaseSplits	stem splits at base of trunk	0	0	2	2
0SegSplits,0SplitAngle,0SplitAngleV	stems splits & angle per segment	0, 0, 0	0, 0, 0	0.1, 3, 0	0.4, 10, 0
0CurveRes,0Curve,0CurveBack,0CurveV	curvature resolution and angles	3, 0, 0, 20	10, 0, 0, 40	8, 0, 20, 120	8, 0, 0, 90
1DownAngle,1DownAngleV	main branch: angle from trunk	60, -50	60, -40	20, 10	30, -30
1Rotate,1RotateV,1Branches	spiraling angle, # of branches	140, 0, 50	140, 0, 50	-120, 30, 25	80, 0, 40
1Length,1LengthV, 1Taper	relative length, cross-section scaling	0.3, 0, 1	0.3, 0.05, 1	0.5, 0.1, 1	0.8, 0.1, 1
1SegSplits,1SplitAngle,1SplitAngleV	stem splits per segment	0, 0, 0	0, 0, 0	0.2, 30, 10	0.2, 10, 10
1CurveRes,1Curve,1CurveBack,1CurveV	curvature resolution and angles	5, -40, 0, 50	10, 0, 0, 90	16, 40, 80, 90	10, 40, -70, 150
2DownAngle,2DownAngleV	secondary branch: angle from parent	45, 10	30, 10	30, 10	45, 10
2Rotate,2RotateV,2Branches	spiraling angle, # of branches	140, 0, 30	140, 0, 25	-120, 30, 10	140, 0, 120
2Length,2LengthV, 2Taper	relative length, cross-section scaling	0.6, 0, 1	0.6, 0.1, 1	1.5, 0, 1	0.2, 0.05, 1
2SegSplits,2SplitAngle,2SplitAngleV	stem splits per segment	0, 0, 0	0, 0, 0	0.2, 45, 20	0.1, 10, 10
2CurveRes,2Curve,2CurveBack,2CurveV	curvature resolution and angles	3, -40, 0, 75	10, -10, 0, 150	12, 0, 0, 0	3, 0, 0, -30
3DownAngle,3DownAangleV	tertiary branch: angle from parent	45, 10	45, 10	20, 10	45, 10
3Rotate,3RotateV,3Branches	spiraling angle, # of branches	77, 0, 10	140, 0, 12	140, 0, 300	140, 0, 0
3Length,3LengthV, 3Taper	relative length, cross-section scaling	0, 0, 1	0.4, 0, 1	0.1, 0, 1	0.4, 0, 1
3SegSplits,3SplitAngle,3SplitAngleV	stem splits per segment	0, 0, 0	0, 0, 0	0, 0, 0	0, 0, 0
3CurveRes,3Curve,3CurveBack,3CurveV	curvature resolution and angles	1, 0, 0, 0	1, 0, 0, 0	1, 0, 0, 0	1, 0, 0, 0
Leaves,LeafShape	number of leaves per parent, shape id	25, 0	6, 0	15, 0	25, 0
LeafScale,LeafScaleX	leaf length, relative x scale	0.17, 1	0.3, 0.5	0.12, 0.2	0.12, 0.66
AttractionUp	upward growth tendency	0.5	0.5,	-3	0.8
PruneRatio	fractional effect of pruning	0	0	1	0
PruneWidth,PruneWidthPeak	width, position of envelope peak	0.5, 0.5	0.5, 0.5	0.4, 0.6	0.5, 0.5
PrunePowerLow,PrunePowerHigh	curvature of envelope	0.5, 0.5	0.5, 0.5	0.001, 0.5	0.5, 0.5

Plate 2: Black Tupelo,
(a) with leaves (b) without leaves

Plate 1: (a,b) Black Oak,   (c,d) Sassafras,
     (e,f)   Swamp Oak,   (g)   Cottonwood, (h) Tamarack,
     (i,j)   Lombardy Poplar, (k)   Queen Palm, (l) cactus,
     (m,n) Rock Elm,   (o)   Black Spruce, (p) Austrian Pine,
     (q,r) Quaking Aspen, (s)   Balsam Fir,   (t) White Cedar,
     (u)   Bamboo, (v) *generic*, (w) Jack Pine,   (x) Longleaf Pine

Plate 4: Range Degradation

Plate 3: Scene from (a) Northeast, (b) Northwest, (c,d) South, (e) Overhead; and (f) with Modifications   Plate 5: Weeping Willow

Plate 6: Sassafras with leaves (a) unmodified, (b) re−oriented

Plate 7: Weeping Willow: (a) unpruned, (b) pruned

Depicting Fire and Other Gaseous Phenomena
Using Diffusion Processes

Jos Stam

Eugene Fiume

Department of Computer Science, University of Toronto[1]

Abstract

Developing a visually convincing model of fire, smoke, and other gaseous phenomena is among the most difficult and attractive problems in computer graphics. We have created new methods of animating a wide range of gaseous phenomena, including the particularly subtle problem of modelling "wispy" smoke and steam, using far fewer primitives than before. One significant innovation is the reformulation and solution of the advection-diffusion equation for densities composed of "warped blobs". These blobs more accurately model the distortions that gases undergo when advected by wind fields. We also introduce a simple model for the flame of a fire and its spread. Lastly, we present an efficient formulation and implementation of global illumination in the presence of gases and fire. Our models are specifically designed to permit a significant degree of user control over the evolution of gaseous phenomena.

Keywords: fire, smoke, gaseous phenomena, diffusion, advection, warped blobbies, light transport, multiple scattering, particle systems, turbulence.

1 Introduction

The interplay of light with gases, aerosols and dust spans across the most visually delicate and the most explosive of natural phenomena. The depiction of these phenomena has been of great interest to computer graphics for over a decade, and their application to computer animation is clear.

Any graphical model of a gaseous phenomenon must have three components: a representation of the gas, a model for its spatiotemporal behaviour, and an illumination model to determine its appearance. Graphical models for gaseous phenomena have fallen into two classes. Models from one class combine the representation of the gas and its motion into a solid texture, animating the gas by varying parameters of the texture [14, 7]. Obtaining convincing motion with this approach becomes difficult because of the non-physical nature of the parameters and the cost associated with visualizing the solid texture. These parameters can be related, however, to a statistical model of turbulence [20].

We prefer the alternative approach, which keeps the three components intact, and animates the gas using wind fields. The earliest

[1]10 King's College Circle, Toronto, Ontario, Canada, M5S 1A4
E-mail: {stam|elf}@dgp.toronto.edu

Permission to make digital/hard copy of part or all of this work for personal or classroom use is granted without fee provided that copies are not made or distributed for profit or commercial advantage, the copyright notice, the title of the publication and its date appear, and notice is given that copying is by permission of ACM, Inc. To copy otherwise, to republish, to post on servers, or to redistribute to lists, requires prior specific permission and/or a fee.

related work in computer graphics is by Reeves [17], in which particle systems were used to evoke a variety of visual effects, including fire. Recent work has focussed on the depiction of specific phenomena such as steam, mist, clouds or fire (e.g., [24, 4]). In these models, a wind field both advects (i.e., displaces) and diffuses "blobs" of density over time. Thus an immediate benefit is that the motion of a gas can be seen in real-time. However, the regular shape of the blobs often makes the gas look artificial. In this work, we improve the blob model by nonuniformly modifying the shape of the field over time. The field is warped by the surrounding wind field in a manner consistent with a real blob of gas (see Figure 8). The corresponding results are more convincing, using an order of magnitude fewer particles than our previous work [24].

The rendering of gases has been an active area of computer graphics research since the seminal work of Blinn [2]. Most, if not all, of the algorithms first sample the density and the optical properties of the gas on a grid and then solve for illumination. In a first pass, the effects of multiple scattering are resolved. Depending on the scattering distribution functions employed, different possibilities arise. For isotropic or constant scattering, a zonal radiosity-style method can be employed [18]. For arbitrary scattering, researchers have used a spherical harmonics expansion [10], a discretization of the angles [11] or brute-force ray-tracing [1]. These approximations are known respectively as the P_N method, discrete ordinates and Monte-Carlo simulation in the radiative transfer literature [6]. Once the effects of multiple scattering are computed, a final image is obtained by voxel-traversal algorithms [7, 19, 12]. However, the grid approximation has two deficiencies: the grid is memory intensive for complicated gas geometries, and it introduces sampling artifacts that are evident in animation. The appearance of artifacts can be alleviated by prefiltering the data on the grid prior to voxel traversal rendering [21], at the cost of diminished visual detail.

In view of these limitations, we have developed a new rendering algorithm which is an extension of the ray-tracing progressive refinement solution for radiosity [25]. Specifically, shooting operations both to and from gaseous blobs are derived. In addition, we use a diffusion approximation to resolve the effects of multiple scattering. Once the scattered intensity is resolved, it can be integrated to yield images of the gas from arbitrary viewpoints using an efficient blob tracer [24]. Our algorithm has been designed to capture the essential visual features of gaseous phenomena as efficiently as possible.

We are fascinated with the depiction of fire. The general phenomenon of fire and combustion "in spite of their fundamental importance and practical applications, are far from being fully understood. This is due, above all, to their interdisciplinary character and great complexity" [5]. Perhaps because of this, there has been little actual progress in visual models for fire. A simple laminar flame was texture mapped onto a flame-like implicit primitive and then volume-traced by Inakage [8]. Recently, two groups of researchers have worked on the problem of the spread of fire.[1] Perry and Picard apply a velocity spread model from combustion science to propagate their flames [15]. On the other hand, Chiba et al. compute the exchange of heat between objects by projecting the environment onto a plane [4]. The spread of the flame is a function of both the temperature and the concentration of fuel. In this paper, we present a similar model in three dimensions for the creation, extinguishing and spread of fire. The spread of the fire is entirely controlled by the amount of fuel available, the geometry of the environment and the initial conditions (i.e., where we light the match). Although our model relies on physical equations, it should not be confused with a physically accurate simulation of fire. Indeed, the latter is still an active area of research in combustion science. This paper focuses on producing convincing physically-motivated depictions of the motion and appearance of fire.

The structure of the paper is as follows. In the next section, we discuss the general methodology we use to model gaseous phenomena. In Section 3 we introduce diffusion equations for the evolution of the density, temperature and diffuse intensity of gases. In Section 4 an efficient solution to the diffusion equations is derived using "warped" blobs. In Section 5 we outline our solution to the intensity field. Then, in Section 6 we advance our simple flame model, discussing the results in Section 7. Finally, in Section 8 we discuss our conclusions, pointing towards future research.

2 Overview of the Method

A gas is described by physical quantities that vary as a function of space and time. These quantities include the density of gas particles, and the surrounding velocity and temperature fields. Generally, the relationships governing these quantities are strongly coupled and are known as the Navier-Stokes equations. For example, the temperature field introduces gradients in the velocity field, but the velocity field advects and diffuses the temperature field. With reacting gases such as fire, additional equations are needed to account for the underlying chemical reactions. The full physical simulation of this set of equations is prohibitively expensive. Their nonlinear nature and the wide range of scales required would severely strain computational speed and memory available on even the most powerful computers. Even if such a simulation were available, it would be of limited interest to computer graphics, because of the user's inability to control the phenomenon. Certain effects would not be achievable. The degree of user control must be balanced against the need for the turbulent behaviour of a gas. Turbulence is difficult to model without an underlying physical or statistical model driving it.

In our model, an animator governs the behaviour of a gas by specifying a wind field. The animator manages the global motion of the gas by using smooth fields, and controls the small scale behaviour by modifying the statistical parameters and scale of a turbulent wind field as in [24]. The latter field adds complexity to the motion. In addition, we assume that the motion field is incompressible so that its density ρ_f is constant. Once the wind field is given, we employ an advection-diffusion type equation to compute the evolution of both the density field and the temperature field. Diffusion type equations are employed for two reasons. First, they capture the main characteristics of many transport phenomena. Second, they are simple enough to be understood by an animator with a limited knowledge of physics. Indeed, most of us are familiar with diffusion processes since they are ubiquitous in everyday life (e.g., milk dissolving in a coffee cup). Given a user-specified wind field $\mathbf{u}(\mathbf{x}, t)$, the evolution over time of a scalar field $\theta(\mathbf{x}, t)$ is

assumed to be governed by the following diffusion process:

$$\frac{D\theta}{Dt} = \kappa_\theta \nabla^2 \theta + S_\theta - L_\theta,$$

where $D\theta/Dt = \partial\theta/\partial t + \mathbf{u} \cdot \nabla\theta$ is the *total derivative* giving the variation over time of the field θ on a particle advected by the wind field $\mathbf{u}$. Apart from the wind field, the evolution is characterized by a diffusion coefficient κ_θ, sources S_θ and sinks L_θ. For rapidly evolving phenomena such as the propagation of light, only the *steady state* $D\theta/Dt = 0$ of this equation is considered.

By approximating the scalar field by a set of fuzzy particles, a user is able to visualize the effect of the wind field in real-time on a graphics workstation. Finally, when the user is satisfied with a particular behaviour, the fuzzy particles can be rendered by a global illumination algorithm for high-quality animations.

3 Diffusion Processes

3.1 Density and Temperature

The main physical characteristics of a gas are described by its density ρ, its temperature T, its velocity $\mathbf{u}$ and its radiative properties.[2] The evolution of the density is given by a diffusion equation. The diffusion coefficient in this case models the mixing caused by the small scales of the turbulence not modelled by our wind fields [24]. The sink term is modelled as simple decay over time at a constant rate: $L = \alpha\rho$. The source is either specified by a user or is related to a simple model of chemical reactions (see Section 6). A similar equation for the evolution of the temperature is reached by assuming that the kinetic energy is negligible compared to the heat released by the gas, and that buoyancy and pressure fluctuations are small [5]:

$$c_p \rho_f \frac{DT}{Dt} = \kappa_T \nabla^2 T + S_T - L_T.$$

Often, this reduced equation is utilized in theoretical investigations of the propagation of flames [3]. It is too simple to yield physically accurate simulations. However, we employ this equation because it captures some essential features of the flame. The specific heat at constant pressure c_p characterizes the efficiency of the fluid to release heat. The density of the fluid ρ_f is supposed to be constant, since our wind fields are incompressible[3]. The exact form of the source, sink and absorption terms depend on the type of gas. We explore this specifically in the case of fire in Section 6.

3.2 Intensity Field

A gas modifies the intensity field of light $I_\lambda(\mathbf{x}, \mathbf{s})$ by scattering, absorption and emission. The emission of a gas in local thermodynamic equilibrium is proportional to *black-body emission* [6]:

$$Q_\lambda = E_\lambda B_\lambda(T) = E_\lambda \frac{2h}{\lambda^5 c} \left[\exp\left(\frac{hc}{\lambda kT}\right) - 1 \right]^{-1},$$

where E_λ models the contribution of each wavelength λ to the the emission, h is Planck's constant, k is Boltzmann's constant and c is the speed of light. The total emission over all frequencies is proportional to the fourth power of the temperature:

$$\int_0^\infty B_\lambda(T)\, d\lambda = \sigma_{SB} T^4, \tag{1}$$

---

[1]This is of course in the context of computer graphics. There is an enormous literature on fire in various areas, including forestry, chemistry, and physics.

[2]To shorten the notation, explicit dependence of the fields on all its variables is not always included.

[3]The density ρ_f of the fluid should not be confused with the density of microscopic particles ρ advected and diffused by the fluid.

where σ_{SB} is Stefan-Boltzmann's constant. In order to shorten the notations somewhat, we drop the explicit dependence on wavelength from the following radiative properties. The scattering properties of a gas are characterized by its *albedo* Ω and its *phase function* $p(\mathbf{s}, \mathbf{s}')$. The albedo gives the fraction of light that is scattered versus that which is absorbed. The phase function models the spherical distribution of the scattered light. Although various distributions exist for different types of gases, we assume that the following reduced description is sufficient

$$p(\mathbf{s} \cdot \mathbf{s}') = 1 + \bar{\mu}\, \mathbf{s} \cdot \mathbf{s}'. \tag{2}$$

where $\bar{\mu} = 3/4\pi \int_{-1}^{+1} \mu p(\mu) d\mu$ is the *first moment* of the phase function and characterizes the anisotropy of the scattering. Values of $\bar{\mu}$ near $+1$ indicate a preference for forward scattering. Values near -1 indicate predominantly backward scattering. A direct consequence of the simple distribution is that the scattered intensity depends only weakly on its angular variable:

$$\mathcal{S}\{I(\mathbf{x}, \mathbf{s})\} = \frac{1}{4\pi} \int_{4\pi} p(\mathbf{s} \cdot \mathbf{s}') I(\mathbf{s}')\, d\mathbf{s}' = I^0(\mathbf{x}) + \frac{\bar{\mu}}{3} \mathbf{I}^1(\mathbf{x}) \cdot \mathbf{s}. \tag{3}$$

where I^0 and $\mathbf{I}^1$ are known as the *average intensity* and *average flux* respectively. These two functions actually correspond to the first four coefficients of the intensity field into a spherical harmonics basis. In fact, the derivations outlined in this paper can be generalized to higher-order expansions[22].

The number of interactions per unit length of the light field with the gas is proportional to the density of the gas and is equal to $\sigma_t \rho$, where σ_t is called the *extinction cross-section*.

The gas diminishes the intensity of light traveling along a ray $\mathbf{x}_u = \mathbf{x}_0 - u\mathbf{s}$ by absorption and outscatter, and increases the intensity through self-emission and inscatter. The intensity reaching a point $\mathbf{x}_0$ along a direction $\mathbf{s}$ is then equal to two contributions. The first is a portion of the intensity leaving the point of intersection $\mathbf{x}_b$ of the ray with a background surface. The second contribution is the light created within the gas:

$$I(\mathbf{x}, \mathbf{s}) = I^{out}(\mathbf{x}_b)\tau(0, b) + \int_0^b \sigma_t \rho(\mathbf{x}_u)\tau(0, u)J(\mathbf{x}_u, \mathbf{s})ds. \tag{4}$$

where $\tau(v, w) = \exp(-\int_v^w \sigma_t \rho(\mathbf{x}_u)du)$ is the *transparency*, and the *source intensity* is the sum of single-scattering, multiple scattering and self-emission:

$$J = J_s + J_d + (1 - \Omega)Q, \tag{5}$$

The *single-scattering intensity* J_s accounts for the first scatter of the incident intensity I_i entering the gas: $J_s = \Omega\mathcal{S}\{I_i\}$. The *diffuse intensity* J_d on the other hand, is entirely created within the gas through the phenomenon of multiple scattering. Since we have restricted ourselves to simple scattering distributions, the diffuse intensity in fact satisfies a diffusion equation (see Appendix A). This is a well known approximation in transport theory and is valid when the number of interactions of light with the gas is high, specifically when the dimensionless number $\sigma_t \rho l_0$ is high, where l_0 is a length characterizing the scales involved. For atmospheric scattering the approximation is usually considered to be valid when the density is higher than 0.01 [9].

4 Blob Solution of Diffusion Equations

Diffusion equations can be solved numerically using stable finite difference schemes [16]. In this case, the solution is sampled on a grid. Hence, the method can only resolve scales that are bigger than the grid spacing. These values, then, are interpolated to yield

a "smoothed" version of the exact solution. Unfortunately, for three-dimensional problems grid-based schemes are intractable, because of memory limitations. Consequently, we develop an alternative method of solution by generalizing the above smoothing process. Generally, the approximate solution can be represented as the convolution of the exact solution with a *smoothing kernel* $W_\sigma(r)$:

$$\theta_\sigma(\mathbf{x}, t) = \int W_\sigma(|\mathbf{x} - \mathbf{x}'|)\theta(\mathbf{x}', t)\, d\mathbf{x}',$$

where the σ corresponds to the grid spacing. The smoothing kernel is normalized and tends towards a delta distribution as $\sigma \to 0$. The latter two conditions are required such that the exact solution is recovered when the grid spacing goes to zero. Because the smoothing kernel depends solely on distance, the approximation is of order two [13]. Therefore, the field θ can always be replaced by its smoothed equivalent to within the order of accuracy of the smoothing process itself, e.g.,

$$(\theta\gamma)_\sigma = \theta_\sigma \gamma_\sigma + O(\sigma^2). \tag{6}$$

Instead of a grid, we consider a set of samples $\{\mathbf{x}_k(t)\}_{k=1}^N$ evolving over time. By assigning a mass $m_k(t)$ to each sample, we represent the density as $\rho(\mathbf{x}, t) = \sum_{k=1}^N m_k(t)\delta(\mathbf{x} - \mathbf{x}_k(t))$. Then, a smoothed approximation of the density field is given by:

$$\rho_\sigma(\mathbf{x}, t) = \sum_{k=1}^N m_k(t)W_\sigma(|\mathbf{x} - \mathbf{x}_k(t)|),$$

i.e., the density is a superposition of *blobs* centred at the sample locations. This representation induces one for other fields using Eq. 6, i.e., $(\rho\theta)_\sigma = \rho_\sigma\theta_\sigma$. Hence,

$$\theta_\sigma(\mathbf{x}, t) = \frac{1}{\rho_\sigma(\mathbf{x}, t)} \sum_{k=1}^N m_k(t)\theta_k(t)W_\sigma(|\mathbf{x} - \mathbf{x}_k(t)|),$$

where $\theta_k(t) = \theta(\mathbf{x}_k(t), t)$.

An approximate solution to the diffusion equation is obtained naturally when the samples move along the wind field. Because this equation is linear, it is enough that each blob satisfies it. A sufficient (and convenient) condition for each blob k to satisfy the diffusion equation is that the smoothing kernel is a Gaussian:

$$W_{\sigma_k(t)}(r) = \frac{1}{(2\pi)^{3/2}\sigma_k^3(t)} \exp\left(-\frac{r^2}{2\sigma_k^2(t)}\right),$$

with standard deviation proportional to $\sqrt{\kappa_\theta t}$. The diffusion then expands the size of the blobs over time. The sink term is satisfied if the coefficients $\theta_k(t)$ satisfy

$$\frac{d}{dt}\theta_k(t) = -L_\theta(\mathbf{x}_k(t), t).$$

We use the source term of the density to generate new blobs at each time step of the simulation. From the source term, we can define a probability density distribution for each time t:

$$\varphi_\rho(\mathbf{x}, t) = S_\rho(\mathbf{x}, t) \left/ \left(\int S_\rho(\mathbf{x}', t)\, d\mathbf{x}'\right)\right..$$

Quite often, the source term is constant on a given domain, and the density distribution is uniform. The location $\mathbf{x}_k$ of the new blob hence is determined by generating a random point from this distribution. The initial mass of each blob is a function of the

Figure 1: Blob Warping

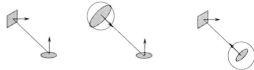

Figure 2: Patch to Patch   Blob to Patch   Patch to Blob

number N_0 of new blobs per time step and of the initial size σ_0 of each blob:

$$m_k = (2\pi)^{3/2}\sigma_0^3/N_0 S_\rho(\mathbf{x}_k, t)\Delta t,$$

where Δt is the time step. The animator determines the number of new blobs and the initial size.

The preceding procedure is a generalization of our blob solution for the evolution of a density distribution in a moving fluid [24]. However, after a large amount of diffusion, that is, with sufficient simulation time, the increasing variance causes the spherical shape for each blob to become apparent. Real gases, and especially fire, are poorly approximated by a superposition of spherical blobs, with the exception perhaps of very billowy smoke. The problem is due to the fact that as the blobs get bigger, the "shape" of the actual distribution is not uniform but is in fact advected by the velocity field (see Figure 1). To account for this nonuniformity, we shall more accurately track the shape of each blob as the advection of a regular blob over a fixed time t_0. To achieve this, we could take samples in the blob at some time $t - t_0$ and then trace each sample over an interval t_0 through the wind field. However, this introduces sampling artifacts. A better approach is to backtrace from the warped blob toward the initial blob (see Figure 1). For each point $\mathbf{x}$, there corresponds a point $\mathbf{x}^{-1}$ obtained by tracing the point back through the wind field for a time t_0:

$$\mathbf{x}^{-1} = \mathbf{x} - \int_t^{t-t_0} \mathbf{u}(\mathbf{x}(t'), t') \, dt'. \qquad (7)$$

To include this warping in our simulations, we replace the smoothing kernel by one evaluated at the backtraced points:

$$W_{\sigma_k(t)}(|\mathbf{x} - \mathbf{x}_k(t)|) \longrightarrow W_{\sigma_k(t)-\eta t_0}\left(|\mathbf{x}^{-1} - \mathbf{x}_k^{-1}(t)|\right),$$

where η is a factor accounting for the spread of the blob due to advective effects; it is a function of the magnitude and scale of the wind field at the point $\mathbf{x}$. In our implementation, it is a user-specified constant. The extra cost of the blob-warping method is the evaluation of the above integral, which can be achieved by a simple Eulerian scheme.

5   Resolving the Intensity Field

As in the density and temperature fields, we represent the source intensity into a superposition of blobs:

$$J(\mathbf{x}, \mathbf{s}) = \frac{1}{\rho(\mathbf{x})} \sum_{k=1}^{N} m_k J_k(\mathbf{s}) W_\sigma(|\mathbf{x} - \mathbf{x}_k|).$$

The angular variation of each coefficient in this expansion is determined by the shape of the phase function and is therefore (see Eq. 3):

$$J_k(\mathbf{s}) = J_k^0 + \mathbf{J}_k^1 \cdot \mathbf{s}.$$

These coefficients are computed by utilizing an extension of the shooting algorithm used in diffuse environments [25]. The surfaces of the environment are first discretized into an ensemble of patches. At each step of the algorithm, the outgoing intensity I^{out} from one

patch is shot into the environment and is collected at the other patches of the environment. We extend this work by including shooting operations from a patch to the blobs and conversely, from a blob to the patches. In addition, we develop shooting operations from non-physical lights, such as directional sources, to the blobs. These shooting operations resolve the single scattering intensity. The diffuse intensity is obtained by solving Eq. 11. A summary of the algorithm is given next.

> Set source intensity to emission: $J = (1 - \Omega)Q$.
> Collect intensity from light sources: $J \leftarrow J + \Omega S\{I_{lights}\}$.
> do
>> Shoot from patches to other patches.
>> Collect intensity from patches: $J \leftarrow J + \Omega S\{I_{patches}\}$.
>> Compute diffuse intensity: J_d.
>> Add to source intensity: $J \leftarrow J + J_d$.
>> Shoot source intensity to the patches.
> Until *converged*

This algorithm is similar to the one presented in [11].

5.1   Shooting Operations

To derive our shooting operations, we consider the basic interchange of intensity between a surface area A_2 and an area dA_1 separated by a distance d_{12} along a direction $\mathbf{s}_{12}$:

$$I_{12}^{in} = I_2^{out} F_{12}, \qquad (8)$$

where F_{12} is the form factor between the two surfaces. When A_2 is a disk, the form factor can be approximated by [25]:

$$F_{12} = \frac{A_2}{A_2 + d_{12}^2}(\mathbf{n}_1 \cdot \mathbf{s}_{12})(-\mathbf{n}_2 \cdot \mathbf{s}_{12}),$$

where $\mathbf{n}_1$ and $\mathbf{n}_2$ denote the normals at A_2 and dA_1, respectively. The contribution of the intensity leaving A_2 to the outgoing intensity I_1^{out} is then given by $I_1^{out} = r_1 I_{12}^{in}$, where r_1 is the reflectance of the receiving patch.

A single shooting operation from a patch to a blob is a special case of Eq. 8, since an infinitesimal receiving surface at the centre of the blob can always be aligned along $\mathbf{s}_{12}$, i.e., $\mathbf{n}_1 \cdot \mathbf{s}_{12} = 1$. The contribution to the source intensity at the blob is then

$$J_{12}(\mathbf{s}) = I_2^{out} F_{12} \Omega(1 + \bar{\mu}\, \mathbf{s} \cdot \mathbf{s}_{12}).$$

Therefore, the first two coefficients in the angular expansion of the source intensity are updated as

$$J_1^0 \leftarrow J_1^0 + \Omega I_2^{out} F_{12} \quad \text{and} \quad \mathbf{J}_1^1 \leftarrow \mathbf{J}_1^1 + \Omega \bar{\mu} I_2^{out} F_{12}\, \mathbf{s}_{12}.$$

Similarly, the shooting operation from a blob to a patch is achieved by considering a disk of area $A(\sigma) = 2\pi\sigma^2$ at the centre of the blob aligned with the direction $\mathbf{s}_{12}$, i.e., $-\mathbf{n}_2 \cdot \mathbf{s}_{12} = 1$. The outgoing intensity at the patch then is equal to

$$I_1^{out} \leftarrow I_1^{out} + r_1 J_2(\mathbf{s}_{12}) F_{12}. \qquad (9)$$

This step can be sped up by constructing a hierarchical tree-data structure of the blobs [24]. Instead of shooting from a single blob, we shoot from the centre of mass of each blob cluster.

Figure 3: Inverse Warp of the Ray

We have also included shooting operations from non-physical light sources to the blobs, since these lights are extremely useful in creating many visual effects. The contribution of a directional light source of intensity I^0_{dir} and direction $\mathbf{s}_0$ is achieved by:

$$J_1(\mathbf{s}) \leftarrow J_1(\mathbf{s}) + I^0_{dir}\Omega(1 + \bar{\mu}\,\mathbf{s}\cdot\mathbf{s}_0).$$

The shooting operations from point lights and spotlights can be derived likewise.

Shadowing by surfaces is included in these calculations by multiplying each form factor by an occlusion term. Similarly, partial shadowing caused by the gas is included by multiplying the form factor by the transparency between the shooting and receiving elements. Aliasing can be avoided by shooting from a subdivision of the shooting blob/patch [25].

We could derive similar shooting operations between blobs. However, since usually there is a large overlap of blobs, the disk form factor is not accurate. Also, in the case of many blobs, these shooting operations become very expensive. Instead, we solve for the first two coefficients in the angular expansion of the source intensity using the diffusion approximation (see Eq. 11).

5.2 Multiple Scattering

When the blob representation of the diffuse intensity is inserted into the diffusion equation (Eq. 11) we get the following equation:

$$\sum_{k=1}^{N} m_k J^0_{d,k}\left(\nabla\kappa_d(\mathbf{x})\nabla W_k(\mathbf{x}) - \alpha_d(\mathbf{x})W_k(\mathbf{x})\right) + S_d(\mathbf{x}) = 0,$$

where $W_k(\mathbf{x}) = W_{\sigma_k}(|\mathbf{x} - \mathbf{x}_k|)/\rho(\mathbf{x})$. By setting $\mathbf{x} = \mathbf{x}_l$, for $l = 1,\ldots,N$ we get a system of N-linear equations for the unknowns $J^0_{d,k}$ which can be solved using an LU-decomposition for example [16]. Once we compute a solution, the coefficients of the source intensity are updated:

$$J^0_k \leftarrow J^0_k + J^0_{d,k}\ \text{ and }\ \mathbf{J}^1_k \leftarrow \mathbf{J}^1_k + \mathbf{J}^1_d(\mathbf{x}_k),$$

where $\mathbf{J}^1_d$ is given by Eq. 12. This method is in fact equivalent to a finite-element solution for the diffusion equation. When the gas does not intersect any surfaces, the boundary conditions are naturally satisfied by the blob representation. For more details about the method and the boundary conditions, see [23].

5.3 Integrating the Transport Equation

Once an approximation of the source intensity is computed, the intensity field at any point in the environment is obtained by integrating the scattering equation along a ray (Eq. 4). By truncating the domain of the blobs, we reduce the number of blobs intersecting a particular ray. These intersections define a partition of the ray into disjoint intervals $[u_j, u_{j+1}]$, with $j = 0,\ldots,M-1$ [24]. To take into account the warping of the blob, we transform each interval backwards as illustrated in Figure 3. The density on each interval is approximated by its value at the point $\mathbf{z}^{-1}_j$ calculated by backwarping the midpoint $\mathbf{z}_j = (\mathbf{x}_{u_j} + \mathbf{x}_{u_{j+1}})/2$ of the interval:

$$\rho_j = \sum_k m_k W_{\sigma_k}\left(|\mathbf{z}^{-1}_j - \mathbf{x}^{-1}_k|\right),$$

where the sum is over the blobs which overlap the j-th interval. Consequently, both the transparency and the source intensity on each interval are approximated by:

$$\tau_j \approx \exp(-\sigma_t(u_{j+1} - u_j)\rho_j)\ \text{ and }$$
$$J_j(\mathbf{s}) \approx 1/\rho_j \sum_k m_k J_k(\mathbf{s})W_{\sigma_k}\left(|\mathbf{z}^{-1}_j - \mathbf{x}^{-1}_k|\right),$$

respectively. The evaluation of the integral can be performed by traversing the intervals from front to back:

for all rays in ray-trace tree do
    $I = 0$
    $\tau_{tot} = 1$
    for $j = 0,\ldots,M-1$ do
        $I \leftarrow I + \tau_{tot}(1 - \tau_j)J_j(\mathbf{s})$
        $\tau_{tot} \leftarrow \tau_{tot}\tau_j$
        if $\tau_{tot} <$EPS then exit
    end for
    $I \leftarrow I + \tau_{tot}I^{out}(\mathbf{x}_b)$
end for

6 A Simple Fire Model

Flames result from the combustion of fuels and oxidizers. As the molecules of these compounds meet at a sufficiently high temperature, a chemical reaction becomes possible. The resultant burning compounds are called the *flame*. We are not interested in a complete physical model for this reaction, but rather with those mechanisms essential to a good visual representation. In particular, we shall derive simple but effective models for the evolution of density fields giving the concentration of flames, smoke, and fuel. Flames and smoke can be subsequently rendered. We first describe the source and sink terms appearing in the diffusion equations for the density of the fuel, flame and smoke.

Given the density ρ_{fuel} of the fuel and its temperature T_{fuel} at a given point, the rate of production of the flame density ρ_{flame} is given by the *Arrhenius formula*. Assuming a constant concentration of oxidants [3],

$$S_{\rho,\text{flame}} = L_{\rho,\text{fuel}} = \nu_a \exp\left(-\frac{T_a}{T_{\text{fuel}}}\right)\rho_{\text{fuel}}. \qquad (10)$$

T_a is the *activation temperature*, which is directly related to the energy E_a released during the reaction by $T_a = E_a/R$, where R is the universal gas constant. The term ν_a is a "frequency", depending on the exact nature of the combustibles, characterizing the rate of the reaction.

Most naturally occurring fires create smoke particles as the flame cools down. To our knowledge, no definite analytical models of this exist. To model the creation of a density of smoke ρ_{smoke}, we use an equation similar to that used to produce burning fuel:

$$S_{\rho,\text{smoke}} = \nu_b \exp\left(-\frac{T_{\text{flame}}}{T_s}\right)\rho_{\text{flame}},$$

where T_s is the temperature below which smoke particles start to form, and ν_b is another material-dependent constant.

The initial temperature of the flame is related to the heat released during the reaction modelled by Eq. 10. The source term appearing in the diffusion equation for its evolution is then $S_{T,\text{flame}} = c_p S_{\rho,\text{flame}} T_a$. The temperature of the flame decreases mainly through radiating heat. Since emission dominates in flames, the loss of heat is equal to the contributions of the radiation from all angles and all wavelengths:

$$L_{T,\text{flame}} = \int_0^\infty \int_{4\pi} \sigma_{t,\lambda}\rho Q_\lambda(T)\,d\mathbf{s}\,d\lambda = 4\pi\rho\alpha_{\text{flame}}\sigma_{SB}T^4,$$

where the *average absorption cross-section* is defined by

$$\alpha_{\text{flame}} = \frac{\int_0^\infty \sigma_{t,\lambda} E_\lambda B_\lambda(T)\, d\lambda}{\int_0^\infty B_\lambda(T)\, d\lambda} = \frac{1}{\sigma_{SB} T^4} \int_0^\infty \sigma_{t,\lambda} Q_\lambda\, d\lambda,$$

Notice that we have used Eq. 1.

The temperature of the fuel rises because of radiated heat from nearby flames. The source term for the temperature of the fuel is then the fraction of this radiation which is incident upon the fuel. This is similar to a shooting operation from a flame blob to a patch (solid fuel) or to a blob (liquid fuel) (see Eq. 9):

$$S_{T,\text{fuel}} = \rho_{\text{fuel}} \alpha_{\text{fuel}} F_{12} \sigma_{SB} T_{\text{flame}}^4,$$

where α_{fuel} is the average absorption cross-section of the fuel. To achieve real-time simulation, we only shoot from a couple of blob-clusters. The loss of temperature due to radiation is similar to the loss term for the temperature of the flame:

$$L_{T,\text{fuel}} = 2\pi \rho_{\text{fuel}} \alpha_{\text{fuel}} \sigma_{SB} T^4,$$

6.1 Implementation

We have implemented the fire model for a fuel map defined on solid objects. This corresponds to non-burning objects coated with a flammable substance. Note that we do not model the change in geometry caused by the burning process. The user specifies the fuel density as a texture map and assigns burning properties (such as the specific heat) to each object. This is analogous to attributing reflection properties to an object in a renderer. To begin a fire simulation, the user metaphorically strikes a match by indicating the origin(s) of combustion, and the simulation commences. The flame model simulation is summarized in the following algorithm.

```
for each time frame do
    for each solid object in the scene do
        Update temperature of the object
        Generate flame blobs and update fuel map
    end
    for all flame blobs do
        Update temperature and density
        Generate smoke blobs
        Move and diffuse
    end
    for all smoke blobs do
        Update density
        Move and diffuse
    end
end
```

The temperature of the fuel is updated using a Crank-Nicholson finite difference scheme, since the domain of the fuel texture map is two-dimensional and there is no advection [16]. Typical resolutions for our simulations were 20×20. The evolution of the temperature and the density of the flame was performed using our blob method. We computed the evolution of the density of the smoke likewise. We allowed an animator to explore the parameter space by mapping the various physical quantities of the model into a graphical interface.

7 Results

We have developed an interactive implementation of the above models. As in [24], the user specifies wind fields and the effects of turbulence and the scale of the wind fields on blobs can be immediately visualized. Various parameters (such as field positioning, scaling, and magnitude) can be modulated in real time.

Figure 4 illustrates a spread simulation. The simulation is synchronized to the passage of real time so that an accurate evolution of the simulation can be subsequently rendered. Figure 5 gives one frame of a fire scene. As described above, a smoke density can also be produced. Rendered smoke can be seen at four stages in Figure 6. Each frame rendered at video resolution took approximately 20 minutes of CPU time on an SGI Indigo 2 with a R4000 processor. This includes rendering smoke and fire, the illumination caused by fire, shadowing and self-shadowing, using roughly 1000 blobs.

Other nuances of our models can be gleaned from different renderings of steam densities. Figure 7 illustrates the effect of multiple scattering at different albedos, with one image having only single scattering performed. A constant phase function was employed, and the images in this figure contain approximately 150 blobs. Solving for the diffuse intensity required one LU-decomposition, which took approximately one second of CPU time. Figure 10 shows four frames from an animation of an observer flying around a backlit cloud with predominantly forward scattering ($\bar{\mu} = 0.75$).

Figure 8(left) depicts the use of unwarped spherical blobs that are allowed to expand uniformly in all directions. At right, we see a much more convincing depiction in which the blobs are themselves warped due to advection. The cost of warping is directly related to solving Equation 7. Ten steps of an Euler integration proved adequate. In practice, then, the rendering time only increased by a factor 10.

Figure 9 illustrates a more "artistic" use of our fire/smoke model.

8 Conclusions and Future Work

We have presented a general model for the representation, animation, and illumination of gaseous phenomena, paying particular attention to a model for fire. While the mathematics characterizing these phenomena is technically complicated, their implementation is efficient, and a nonexpert user can control the evolution of complex gaseous phenomena, such as multiple fires with turbulent smoke and steam swirls.

An issue for further work is *ease* of control over these phenomena. We stated at the outset that the user's control is largely based on the prior specification of turbulent wind fields. For modelling purposes, this is quite appropriate for interactive simulations involving steam. However, the fire model has a large set of interdependent parameters which are not necessarily easy to manipulate. Thus getting the fire to look "just right" can be problematic.

In many cases, such as in the creation of heat fields, it is quite feasible to generate wind fields dynamically. Here, wind fields can be specialized to a one or more blobs, giving them additional buoyancy, for example.

Also, we would like to model the automatic destruction of objects while burning. We are contemplating the use of more accurate models for the reaction causing the flame, so that we can model explosions more effectively.

Acknowledgements

The financial support of the Natural Sciences and Engineering Research Council of Canada and of the Information Technology Research Centre of Ontario is gratefully acknowledged. The helpful suggestions of the referees are greatly appreciated.

A   Diffusion Approximation

The diffusion approximation for diffuse intensity is given by [6]

$$\nabla \kappa_d(\mathbf{x}) \nabla J_d^0(\mathbf{x}) - \alpha_d(\mathbf{x}) J_d^0(\mathbf{x}) + S_d(\mathbf{x}) = 0, \qquad (11)$$

where

$$
\begin{aligned}
\kappa_d(\mathbf{x}) &= \left((1 - \Omega\bar{\mu}/3)\sigma_t\rho(\mathbf{x})\right)^{-1}, \\
\alpha_d(\mathbf{x}) &= (1 - \Omega)\sigma_t\rho(\mathbf{x}) \ \text{and} \\
S_d(\mathbf{x}) &= \sigma_t\rho(\mathbf{x}) \left(J_s^0(\mathbf{x}) - \kappa_d(\mathbf{x})\nabla \cdot \mathbf{J}_s^1(\mathbf{x}) + Q(\mathbf{x})\right).
\end{aligned}
$$

The directional coefficient in the angular expansion is proportional to the gradient of J_d^0:

$$\mathbf{J}_d^1(\mathbf{x}) = \kappa_d(\mathbf{x})(-\nabla J_d^0(\mathbf{x}) + \sigma_t\rho(\mathbf{x})\mathbf{J}_s^1(\mathbf{x})). \qquad (12)$$

For the exact form of the boundary condition see [23], for example.

References

[1] P. Blasi, B. Le Saec, and C. Schlick. "A Rendering Algorithm for Discrete Volume Density Objects". *Computer Graphics Forum*, 12(3):201–210, 1993.

[2] J. F. Blinn. "Light Reflection Functions for Simulation of Clouds and Dusty Surfaces". *ACM Computer Graphics (SIGGRAPH '82)*, 16(3):21–29, July 1982.

[3] J. D. Buckmaster, editor. *Frontiers in Applied Mathematics. The Mathematics of Combustion*. SIAM, Philadelphia, 1985.

[4] N. Chiba, K. Muraoka, H. Takahashi, and M. Miura. "Two-dimensional Visual Simulation of Flames, Smoke and the Spread of Fire". *The Journal of Visualization and Computer Animation*, 5:37–53, 1994.

[5] J. Chomiak. *Combustion. A Study in Theory, Fact and Application*. Abacus Press/Gordon and Breach Science Publishers, New York, 1990.

[6] J. J. Duderstadt and W. R. Martin. *Transport Theory*. John Wiley and Sons, New York, 1979.

[7] D. S. Ebert and R. E. Parent. "Rendering and Animation of Gaseous Phenomena by Combining Fast Volume and Scanline A-buffer Techniques". *ACM Computer Graphics (SIGGRAPH '90)*, 24(4):357–366, August 1990.

[8] M. Inakage. "A Simple Model of Flames". In *Proceedings of Computer Graphics International 89*, pages 71–81. Springer-Verlag, 1989.

[9] A. Ishimaru. *VOLUME 1. Wave Propagation and Scattering in Random Media. Single Scattering and Transport Theory*. Academic Press, New York, 1978.

[10] J. T. Kajiya and B. P. von Herzen. "Ray Tracing Volume Densities". *ACM Computer Graphics (SIGGRAPH '84)*, 18(3):165–174, July 1984.

[11] E. Languénou, K.Bouatouch, and M.Chelle. Global illumination in presence of participating media with general properties. In *Proceedings of the 5th Eurographics Workshop on Rendering*, pages 69–85, Darmstadt, Germany, June 1994.

[12] M. Levoy. "Efficient Ray Tracing of Volume Data". *ACM Transactions on Computer Graphics*, 9(3):245–261, July 1990.

[13] J. J. Monaghan. "Why Particle Methods Work". *SIAM Journal of Scientific and Statistical Computing*, 3(4):422–433, December 1982.

[14] K. Perlin. "An Image Synthesizer". *ACM Computer Graphics (SIGGRAPH '85)*, 19(3):287–296, July 1985.

[15] C. H. Perry and R. W. Picard. "Synthesizing Flames and their Spread". *SIGGRAPH'94 Technical Sketches Notes*, July 1994.

[16] W. H. Press, B. P. Flannery, S. A. Teukolsky, and W. T. Vetterling. *Numerical Recipes in C. The Art of Scientific Computing*. Cambridge University Press, Cambridge, 1988.

[17] W. T. Reeves. "Particle Systems. A Technique for Modeling a Class of Fuzzy Objects". *ACM Computer Graphics (SIGGRAPH '83)*, 17(3):359–376, July 1983.

[18] H. E. Rushmeier and K. E. Torrance. "The Zonal Method for Calculating Light Intensities in the Presence of a Participating Medium". *ACM Computer Graphics (SIGGRAPH '87)*, 21(4):293–302, July 1987.

[19] G. Sakas. "Fast Rendering of Arbitrary Distributed Volume Densities". In F. H. Post and W. Barth, editors, *Proceedings of EUROGRAPHICS '90*, pages 519–530. Elsevier Science Publishers B.V. (North-Holland), September 1990.

[20] G. Sakas. "Modeling and Animating Turbulent Gaseous Phenomena Using Spectral Synthesis". *The Visual Computer*, 9:200–212, 1993.

[21] G. Sakas and M. Gerth. "Sampling and Anti-Aliasing of Discrete 3-D Volume Density Textures". In F. H. Post and W. Barth, editors, *Proceedings of EUROGRAPHICS '91*, pages 87–102. Elsevier Science Publishers B.V. (North-Holland), September 1991.

[22] J. Stam. Forthcoming Ph.D. thesis, Department of Computer Science, University of Toronto, 1995.

[23] J. Stam. "Multiple Scattering as a Diffusion Process". In *Proceedings of the 6th Eurographics Workshop on Rendering*, Dublin, Ireland, June 1995.

[24] J. Stam and E. Fiume. "Turbulent Wind Fields for Gaseous Phenomena". In *Proceedings of SIGGRAPH '93*, pages 369–376. Addison-Wesley Publishing Company, August 1993.

[25] J. R. Wallace, K. E. Elmquist, and E. A. Haines. "A Ray Tracing Algorithm for Progressive Radiosity". *ACM Computer Graphics (SIGGRAPH '89)*, 23(3):315–324, July 1989.

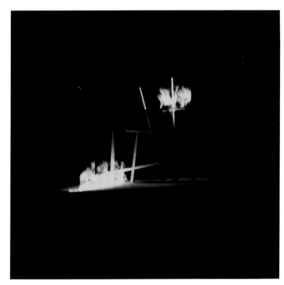

Figure 4: Spread of fire

Figure 5: A smokeless rendered fire image.

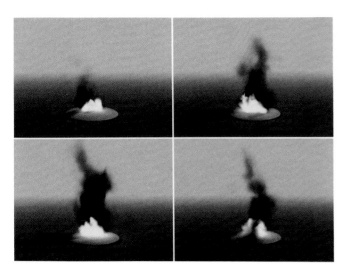

Figure 6: Bonfire with smoke.

Figure 9: Multi-coloured Fire

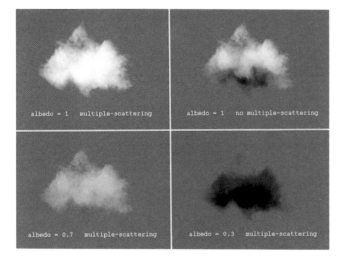

Figure 7: Effect of multiple/single scattering with varying albedo.

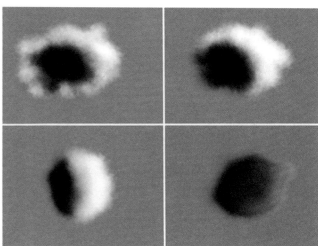

Figure 10: Backlit cloud with anisotropic forward scattering.

Figure 8:   Spherical blobs vs. warped blobs

Versatile and Efficient Techniques
for Simulating Cloth and Other Deformable Objects

Pascal VOLINO (*), Martin COURCHESNE (**) (*)
and   Nadia Magnenat THALMANN (*) (**)

ABSTRACT

We are presenting techniques for simulating the motion and the deformation of cloth, fabrics or, more generally, deformable surfaces. Our main goal is to be able to simulate any kind of surface without imposing restrictions on shape or geometrical environment. In particular, we are considering difficult situations with respect to deformations and collisions, like wrinkled fabric falling on the ground. Thus, we have enhanced existing algorithms in order to cope with any possible situation. A mechanical model has been implemented to deal with any irregular triangular meshes, handle high deformations despite rough discretisation, and cope with complex interacting collisions. Thus, it should deal efficiently with situations where nonlinearities and discontinuities are really non marginal. Collision detection has also been improved to efficiently detect self-collisions, and also to correctly consider collision orientations despite the lack of surface orientation information from preset geometrical contexts, using consistency checking and correction. We illustrate these features through simulation examples.

Keywords: deformable surfaces, collision detection, collision response, mechanical simulation, animation.

1 - INTRODUCTION

Many efforts have already been made to represent the natural motion of deformable objects under relatively simple contact constraints with the environment and restricted deformation situations. But real life situations provide a wide range of complexities, such as crumpling when an object falls to the ground, high deformations, wrinkling and friction when for example a synthetic actor puts on a cloth. Previous work has emphasized the precision of the mechanical model and the realism of the deformations while restricting animation contexts. However, to create scenarios with wrinkle and crumple situations where the deformations are ruled by lots of bendings and collisions, we need an efficient model able to deal with high deformations despite rough triangulation, where friction and collision are handled in a robust way. In addition, the model should not restrict simulated objects to particular situations shapes, therefore allowing objects to be composed of both regular and irregular meshes.

Previously, collision detection was often handled in very simple ways, subject to geometrical optimizations made possible by the simplicity of the situation (for example, some parts of the garment colliding with some parts of the body). The response was directed by simple geometrical considerations (vertex-to-triangle repulsion and friction, inside-outside orientation). But if we consider very general wrinkling situations, collision detection becomes a very difficult and time consuming task, because the lack of geometrical context prevents the use of optimizations. It also becomes difficult maintaining orientation consistency between the detected collisions.

Our main goal is to develop a very versatile and robust mechanical model, that is specially designed to rapidly and easily simulate deformable surface motion in any situation. It will be associated with a powerful and general collision detection and handling system that does not require any predefined context for efficiently and accurately computing collisions and self-collisions.

Remaining as general as possible, the model should be directly applicable to any object such as complex garments formed by several panels stacked on several layers or, more generally, any other kind of surface not necessarily discretised into uniform triangulation.

2 - PREVIOUS WORK

Previous works on deformable object animation using physically based models have permitted animation of cloth-like objects in many kinds of situations. Weil [35] pioneered cloth animation using an approximated model based on relaxation of the surface. Haumann et al. produced animations with flags or leaves moving in the wind, or curtains blowing in a breeze [16]. Kunii and Gotoda used a hybrid model incorporating physical and geometrical techniques to model garment wrinkles [18]. Aono simulated wrinkle propagation on a handkerchief using an elastic

(*)   **MIRAlab, C.U.I., University of Geneva**
24, Rue du Général Dufour   1211 Genève - Switzerland
Tel: (41)22 705 7763   Fax: (41)22 705 7780
E-mail: pascal@cui.unige.ch   thalmann@uni2a.unige.ch

(**)   **H.E.C., University of Montreal**
5255, Av. Décelles   H3T-IU6 Montreal - Canada
E-mail: martin@athos.miralab.hec.ca

0-89791-701-4/95/008

model [2]. Terzopoulos and Fleischer developed a general elastic model and applied it to a wide range of objects including cloth [28] [29]. Interaction of clothes with synthetic actors in motion [19] [10] [39] marked the beginning of a new era in cloth animation in more complex situations. However, there were still a number of restrictions on the simulation conditions on the geometrical structure and the mechanical situations, imposed by the simulation model or the collision detection.

Deformable objects may be represented by different geometrical models, Triangular grids are most common, but polynomial surfaces [37] [4] and particle systems [6] are also used for solutions to specific mechanical simulations. Yelling nice and accurate deformations, they constrain both the initial shape and the allowed deformations. Each model requires different techniques for modeling complex objects such as panels-and-seaming for cloth objects [39]. Furthermore, global mechanical models such as finite elements and finite difference are not suitable for situations involving constraints and nonlinearities as non-marginal situations all over the surfaces. These situations happen when modeling the highly nonlinear deformations required for wrinkles and crumples [11], and when there are numerous collisions and much friction.

For coping with these mentioned situations, we provide a model resulting directly from the integration of Newton's motion equation. It allows us to efficiently and accurately integrate the effects caused by nonlinearities and collisions, and provides a small and efficiently computed adaptive time step, the best way for handling numerous discontinuities. We also remove modeling constraints by allowing simulation of any kind of non regular triangular meshes.

Collision detection and response has been used mainly for stopping cloth from penetrating the body and, more marginally, for preventing self-collisions between different parts of the cloth. The first time-consuming problem was to extract the possible colliding elements from the whole set of elements composing the cloth and the body surfaces. Many techniques have been developed, based on different ideas and adapted for various surface representations. For example, mathematical algorithms have been developed for situations where the surfaces are represented by curved patches or parametrical surfaces, as described in [3], [4], [31], [13], [27]. In the case of representing surfaces by a huge set of flat polygons, techniques based on rasterisation [26] or the tracking of the closest distance on the convex hull [22], [20] have been developed. Unfortunately, these techniques are not well suited for efficient detection on deformable surface animations, as they require either expensive z-buffer rendering or constructing the convex hull of the objects at each frame.

Closer to meeting our requirements are algorithms based on voxelisation or hierarchical octree subdivisions, as described in [39]. They are quite simple and efficient, but require a heavy data structure update at each frame. Hierarchical groupings for bounding-box tests have also been developed [33], [34], which are very efficient for handling a huge number of surface elements, but not well suited for surface self-collision detection.

We propose an efficient algorithm for detecting collisions, especially self-collisions on animated discretised surfaces [32]. It takes advantage of adjacency between the elements of a hierachisation, built once during preprocessing, for selectively performing collision tests using a very simple surface curvature criteria.

Besides being detected, collisions have to be handled in an accurate way for collision response. With cloth animation, this problem was relatively simple as long as the only situation considered was having the cloth already and constantly worn by the body [39]. Thus, a simple vertex-to-triangle interference using some proximity criteria could be considered. Furthermore, as the geometrical situation was quite constant and collision existed mainly when the cloth penetrated the body and wrinkles penetrated each other, the considered surfaces being already "oriented". Simple geometrical considerations could determine that a vertex had crossed, or was at the correct side of a polygon.

Unfortunately, as we are now considering very general and non-restrictive situations where any surface can collide with any other, considering what and how elements are colliding becomes a nontrivial problem for obtaining correct collision response. Difficulties arise when considering the lack of preset orientation information among the surfaces. This leads us to consider techniques for tracking collision orientation, as well as techniques which cope with and correct any orientation inconsistencies that may arise.

3 - THE MECHANICAL MODEL

The main idea of our model is to integrate Newton's motion equation in a direct way to keep quickly evaluated time steps small and very frequent collision detection. More sophisticated and time consuming models based on global minimizations or Lagrangian dynamics formulations allowing higher time step would represent a waste of time. Thus, discontinuous responses such as collisions will be handled in an accurate way. Furthermore, this direct formulation allows us easy and precise inclusion of any nonlinear mechanical behavior. With such a model, we can also act directly on the position and speed of the elements, and thus avoid handling collisions through strong repulsion forces that perturb the simulation.

The animated deformable object is represented as a particle system by sets of vertices forming irregular triangles, thus allowing surfaces of any shape to be easily modeled and simulated.

3.1 - Description of the physical object

The object is considered to be isotropic and of constant thickness. Elastic properties of the object are mainly described by the standard parameters [23] that are:

E   the Young modulus

ν the Poisson coefficient

ρ the density

T   the thickness

Rough discretisation, however, alters the behavior of the surface. In particular, heterogeneous triangulations are "rigidifying" the whole surface, preventing easy buckling. These effects have to be corrected through tuning and adjustments of the mechanical parameters. In particular, textile easily buckles into double curvature, but buckle formation requires a change of area that increases with the size of the discretised elements [8]. To facilitate buckle formation on roughly discretised objects without loosing textile stretching stiffness, we use a variable Young modulus for reducing the stretching stiffness for compression and small extension.

3.2 - The motion equation

Using Newton's second law F=ma, the motion equation consists of a pair of coupled first-order differential equations for position and velocity. The system of equations is resolved using the second order (midpoint method) of the Euler-Cromer method [15].

The constraints implied in deformable object motion are divided in two categories:

* Continuous constraints including internal and some external ones such as wind and gravity.

* Discontinuous constraints resulting from collisions with other objects.

Discontinuous constraints induce instantaneous change in the state of the object. Considering the collision frequency, the interruption of the simulation every time a collision occurs would take much computation. Rather than considering complicated methods for solving differential equations with discontinuities [7] which may not be efficient for very complex collision situations, we prefer handling collisions separately.

The problem of solving the differential equations has been simplified considerably using a two phase process, similarly to House et al. [17]:

a - Considering only the continuous constraints, differential equations are solved using a time step that ensures mechanical stability for every vertices, computed from the acceleration of the vertices versus the length of their connected edges. However, we do not recompute acceleration at each step for vertices which do not require such a small time step.

b - Then, collisions are detected and discontinuous constraints are handled, through direct correction of position and speed complying momentum transfer laws.

3.3 - Internal strains

Internal strains are either in-plane, from planar extension and shearing, or out-of-plane, from bending and twisting. Considering the irregularity of the triangle mesh, the force evaluation should be independent from the size and shape of the triangles.

* Elastic and shearing strain

A triangle is considered as a thin flat object in a plane stress situation. Each edge of the triangle is taken as a strain gauge giving strain measurement on the cloth surface (fig. 1). A set of three measurements, called "strain rosette" [30], is enough for completely evaluating the strain. The unit elongations given by each edge at an angle θ_i are related using: [25]

$$\varepsilon_{\theta_i} = \varepsilon_u \cos^2\theta_i + \varepsilon_v \sin^2\theta_i + 2\gamma_{uv} \sin\theta_i \cos\theta_i \qquad (1)$$

We compute the unit elongations (ε_u, ε_v) and shear (γ_{uv}) in an arbitrary, conveniently defined (u,v) coordinate system. Then, the Hook law for a uniform isotropic material [30] directly gives the stress components:

$$\sigma_{u,v} = \frac{E}{1-v^2}[\varepsilon_{u,v} + v\varepsilon_{v,u}] \qquad \tau_{uv} = G\gamma_{uv} = \frac{E}{2(1+v)}\gamma_{uv} \qquad (2)(3)$$

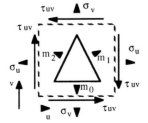

Fig. 1 : Stress evaluation in a triangle

The stress components on a triangle are convert into in-plane forces along its edges. The force applied on the edge j of the triangle i is:

$$\mathbf{F}_i^j = T L_j [\mathbf{m_j} \cdot \mathbf{u} \, \sigma_u - \mathbf{m_j} \cdot \mathbf{v} \, \tau_{uv}]\mathbf{u} + [\mathbf{m_j} \cdot \mathbf{v} \, \sigma_v + \mathbf{m_j} \cdot \mathbf{u} \, \tau_{uv}]\mathbf{v}' \qquad (4)$$

where $\mathbf{m_j}$ is a unit vector perpendicular to the edge j in the triangle plane. This force is then equally distributed on the two extremity vertices.

* Bending strain

Curvature force are very weak compared to in-plane forces. As we intend to consider high deformation, the force evaluation must consider the possible case where the radius of curvature is less than the size of the triangles.

The edge between two triangles is used as a hinge for curvature manifestation (fig. 2a) providing information on single curvature only. It is known from the Mohr circle that it is always possible to decompose any twist strain into a combination of pure bending strains [8]. Considering the arbitrary orientation of the edges, even if we have no control on them, twist strain is taken into account via the additive property of curvature.

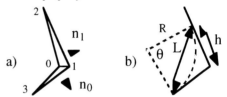

Fig. 2 : Curvature evaluation.

Using the angle between the normals (fig. 2a), we look for the maximum curvature radius (R) for which the corresponding arc fits inside the triangles. Referring to fig. 2b, h is less than or equal to the height of the triangles and L is greater than h*a, with a<1. This adaptation will allow R to reach values smaller than the size of the triangles. The local curvature (K) is the inverse of R.

To prevent K and the bending force from reaching infinity, we limit K to a maximal value. If the angle continues to grow, a specific high bending constraint handling will be performed.

The associated momentum in width units is:

$$M = D'DK = E D' \frac{T^3}{12(1-v^2)} K \qquad (5)$$

where D, the flexural rigidity, is associated with D' an the extra parameter which is needed to allow fine tuning of bending strain. Using D'=1 would be appropriated for continuous solid sheets but would not reflect the real comportment of textile [1]. The material is still isotropic. The force corresponding to M is obtained using the triangle dimensions and normal.

3.4 - Time effect

Textile material is not purely elastic and its response to stress depends on its straining history. Several phenomena, some of which are described in [23] and [21], yield time effects that appear as recovery behavior, creep, stress relaxation of stress, etc.

Integral and analytical theories aim to describe mathematically the macroscopic behavior of material. Since permanent or semi-permanent damage is closely related to the quality and straining history of fiber and textile's structure, an exact representation of them is impossible. Rather than trying to idealize the behavior with complex equations, we developed a simple empirical equation to model the consequences.

Basically, pure elastic behavior for a deformation "x(t)-x(0)" of an element at a time t is described by Hook's law:

$$F(t) = k (x(t) - x(0)) \qquad (6)$$

which is added a linear viscoelastic response according to Newton's law:

$$F_v(t) = \gamma_x \frac{(x(t) - x(t\text{-}dt))}{dt} \qquad (7)$$

where k and γ_x are elasticity and viscosity constants.

When deformation exceeds a given ratio, we switch from the viscoelastic behavior described above to a plastic behavior for which the equilibrium x(0) is moved to a new value, modeling permanent deformation. A relaxation time has also been defined, defining how fast the equilibrium evolves back to its original value, as soon as the deforming constraints are released.

3.5 - Collision management

We correct the non-constrained simulation by detecting and taking the collision effects into account.

Rather than computing "collision forces" through inverse kinematics from the momentum conservation law [10], we directly integrate the constraints by position and speed corrections on the concerned vertices accordingly to momentum conservation. Thus, we avoid dealing with high reaction forces that alter the mechanical simulation.

For instance, if a collision is detected between two elements, we compute the new positions of these elements that satisfy both the collision geometrical constraints and the mass center invariance. If some elements are implied into several collisions, we iterate the process until all the constraints are satisfied. Then, the speed of the elements is evaluated accordingly to momentum conservation, using perfectly inelastic collision for the normal speed along the collision plane, and coulombian friction for the tangential speed.

This technique ensures very fast collision response computation, each collision being handled independently and by avoiding high reaction forces. However, robustness is required for the collision detection algorithm, to maintain consistency in complex interdependent collisions situations where the collision response may not be able to solve completely all the constraints.

3.6 - Stability control

As we are dealing with nonlinear models put into widely varying conditions, some situations (for example, deformation caused by collisions) might lead to numerical instability. Once we detect increasing instability by monitoring local mechanical energy variations, we artificially distribute kinetic energy through momentum transfers in the neighborhood of the concerned elements. This transfer accelerates the propagation and the fairing of the perturbation. This technique increases the global robustness of the system for difficult conditions.

4 - COLLISION DETECTION AND HANDLING

For dealing with complex collision situations such as crumpling, we need efficient collision and self-collision detection, as well as a robust collision handling. We are now discussing these two aspects.

4.1 - Fast self-collision detection

Collision and particularly self-collision detection is often the bottleneck of simulation applications in terms of calculation time, because of the scene complexity that involves a huge number of geometrical tests for determining which elements are colliding.

In our case, the problem is complicated further because we are handling discretised surfaces that may contain thousands of polygons. We also are considering general situations where we cannot make any hypotheses about region proximities. Finally, we have to efficiently detect self-collisions within the surfaces. This prevents the use of standard bounding box algorithms because potentially colliding regions of a surface are always touching each other by adjacency.

We have developed a very efficient algorithm for handling this situation [32]. This algorithm is based on hierarchisation and takes advantage of the adjacency which, combined with a surface curvature criteria, let us skip large regular regions from the self-collision detection. We then get a collision evaluation time that is roughly proportional to the number of colliding elements, and independent of the total number of elements that compose our deforming surfaces.

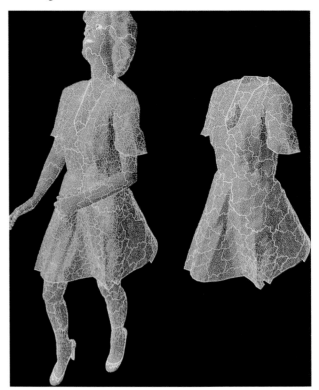

Fig. 3 : Hierarchical collision and self-collision detection on cloth. Less than 5% of the detection time is spent for self-collisions.

4.2 - Handling different kinds of collisions

Once the possible colliding triangles of our surfaces are located, we extract different types of geometrical collisions:

* Proximities

They are represented by couples of elements that are closer than a threshold distance. That may be triangle-to-vertex, edge-to-edge, and more marginally edge-to-vertex and vertex-to-vertex proximities. They illustrate collision interaction. They are used for computing collision response.

Interferences

They are represented by edges-triangle couples that are crossing each other. They illustrate situations where two surfaces are interpenetrating. They reveal inconsistent collision situations that have to be corrected.

4.3 - Collision consistency

Collision response implies the correction of position and velocity to prevent contact and crossing. However, this problem cannot be efficiently resolved in complicated situations such as interaction between multiple collisions. It may occasionally happen that some vertices move to "the wrong side" of a colliding surface, a situation with which the collision response must cope.

Usually, the "right side" of a vertex from a triangle is determined by "inside-outside" orientation assumptions for the surfaces, made possible for some simple collision situations or geometrical contexts (for example, the vertices of the cloth have to be pushed outside the body, and colliding wrinkles have the same surface orientation). However, as we intend to simulate cloth or any other deformable surface in any situation, such orientation information is not available, and we cannot deduce from vertex-triangle proximity at which side of the triangle the vertex should be.

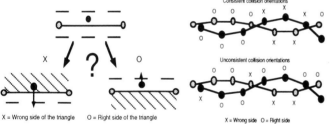

X = Wrong side of the triangle   O = Right side of the triangle

X = Wrong side   O = Right side

Fig. 4 : Orientation ambiguity and collision consistency.

Our contribution has been to create algorithms able to correctly orient the detected collisions so as to correct any wrong situation. We use a combination of techniques described below.

* Remnant proximities

As we said, vertices may marginally cross the colliding surfaces, but the response must return them to the correct side, even if they are temporarily out of the scope of the collision detection.

For solving this problem, a proximity will be kept in memory for a certain time after its last detection, even when the concerned elements move far away from each other. During this time, the proximity will be geometrically updated with respect to the displacements of the objects. If this collision then gets detected again, its orientation is still known according to its "history".

* Cinematical tracking

For each newly detected proximity, we compute the relative movement of the concerned elements, and we can know whether a crossing has happened just before detection or not. If not, the elements are still at right side of each other.

* Consistency checking and correction

Even using the previously mentioned techniques, it is always possible that some collisions get incorrect orientation due to inaccurate response. This occurs mainly in complicated cases that lead to geometrically incorrect situations, and therefore erroneous detection.

Our algorithm should not be perturbed by such false situations, and should be able to correct the wrong collision orientations, whenever they happen.

Usually a contact region between two surfaces is represented by several collisions. The elements concerned by this group of collisions define "collision regions" on both surfaces. Our main

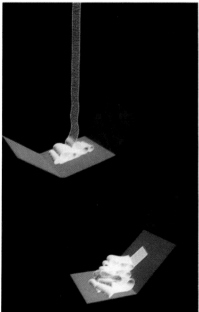

Fig. 5 : Complex collisions (calc time : 5 hrs)

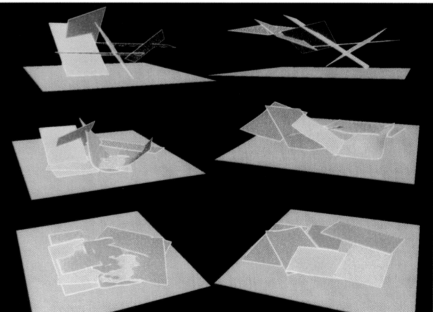

Fig. 6 : Falling without, and with collision consistency correction

idea is to ensure global consistency of the collision behavior within and between these regions.

Regions are efficiently computed by neighborhood walking and labelling through all detected collisions. We update incrementally the regions as the surfaces are moving through the detected collisions.

For a consistent collision situation between two surfaces:

* The collision orientation should remain constant within the collision regions of the two surfaces, so that the whole collision group behave consistently.

* The two regions should be oriented accordingly, so that the surfaces are repulsing each other if they are at the correct side of each other, or attracting if they are not.

For determining the region orientation, we use a statistical evaluation of all the collision orientations within the region, according to their reliability (whether they have been deduced from remnance or tracking). We then force all the collisions of the region to the same orientation.

Using this process whenever any inconsistency has been detected (using edge-to-triangle interference), we can efficiently correct the situation by forcing every detected collision to behave accordingly to the majority's choice.

4.4 - Incremental collision detection

In situations where large surfaces collide but where the deformations and relative movements remain small, and when the overall geometrical configuration remains constant, recomputing proximities which have simply evolved in position is meaningless.

We provide some incremental algorithms that will update the existing proximities between each animation step, using some quick geometric computations for each of them, instead of using the whole global detection computation.

Depending of the situation, different actions are provided:

* The proximity direction and distance is recomputed according to the displacement of the concerned elements.

* The proximity may evolve through neighboring elements (sliding).

* The proximity is forgotten (or remnant) when the concerned elements are not in the detection range.

* Some new proximities may appear from the neighboring elements of existing collisions.

We could imagine using exclusively incremental detection in situations involving only sliding of two permanently colliding surfaces, thus permitting very fast evaluation computation. However, new collision "zones" on topologically variable situations will not be detected. A good compromise is to alternate incremental detection with full detection, according to the simulation conditions.

5 - RESULTS

The mechanical simulation and collision detection algorithms have been implemented in the C language on Silicon Graphics workstations. An animation system has been designed to handle moving objects coming from various animation sources (fixed and frame-by-frame animated objects, objects transformed by mathematical transformations, and of course objects animated by mechanical simulation) that interact with the other objects.

Any object may be subjected to mechanical simulation (provided it is discretised into a triangular mesh). A cloth object is imported directly from existing panel design software, and is assembled using the same mechanical software. Once this process is finished and the cloth becomes a single object, it may be handled as any other mechanical object.

We have used this animation system for testing our algorithms. Mainly, the following tests have been performed.

5.1 - Mechanical properties

We have simulated sets of objects with different mechanical data which illustrate the different mechanical properties that can be handled:

In order to simulate some "exceptional" conditions where our cloth, or any kind of other object, is subject to variable interaction that will cause much random wrinkling and deformation, we put our objects in a rotating cylinder that animates them the same way a drying machine would.

The dryer is primarily a test which validates the efficiency and the robustness of the collision detection algorithm. Any kind of collision configuration may occur, and interaction between different collisions is high. Secondly, it is a good test for the validation of the mechanical model under the high deformations caused by collisions between deforming objects, as well as for collision response and friction. It also verifies the numerical stability of the model.

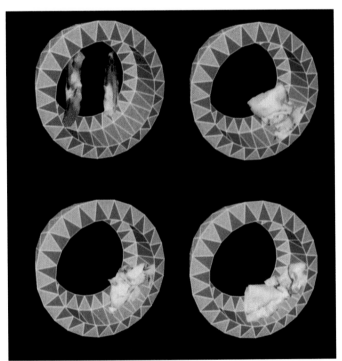

Fig. 7 : Crumpling garments in the dryer
Calc time : 8 hrs for 1 min animation.

5.2 - Cloth assembly and simulation

To define cloth objects, we use existing software for designing 2D panels, as described in [36]. The cloth is assembled according to its seaming borders by a 3D mechanical simulation where "elastics" provide forces to join the seaming lines together.

We have considerably improved the seaming process by using well-tuned viscoelastic forces, which also simulate transversal viscosity and damping for directing the panel borders straight to the destination.

Once the seaming lines are close enough, we engage a "hard" seam by topologically merging together the corresponding vertices and edges to obtain a single surface. As there is no constraint with respect to the discretisation of our surfaces, we can imagine building any kind of object using this process.

Designed this way, a cloth object is handled in the simulation system the same way as any other mechanical object. There are no constraints according to the geometrical context (the cloth may not be worn by a body). We have complete freedom to decide how to manipulate this object.

6 - CONCLUSION AND FUTURE WORK

We have developed an efficient set of techniques that allows us to simulate any kind of deformable surface in various mechanical situations. Our main contribution was to design algorithms that could handle very general, context-free situations: First by implementing a robust process for mechanical simulation that can cope with difficult situations involving high deformations and numerous collisions, and secondly by linking it to a powerful collision detection system that, in addition to good performance for collision and self-collision detection, is able to deal with the lack of geometrical context for correctly orienting collision response.

Our main idea was to keep the system, which was basically designed for cloth simulation, as general and versatile as possible, by not restricting simulations to special contexts, or objects to certain shapes.

Besides providing performance and robustness improvements, this powerful tool can be used to build applications involving garments in some very particular situations, like grasping and folding. Because of the versatility of the simulation algorithm, we can further imagine not only simulating the cloth worn by the body, but also trying to realistically reproduce an actor grasping his/her clothes and dressing himself/herself.

ACKNOWLEDGMENTS

This work is supported by the Swiss National Research Foundation and the European ESPRIT HUMANOID2 project. Thanks to all the people that have contributed to it, and particularly to Jean-Claude Mousally for his assistance in preparing some illustrations and Hans-Martin Werner for reviewing the English text.

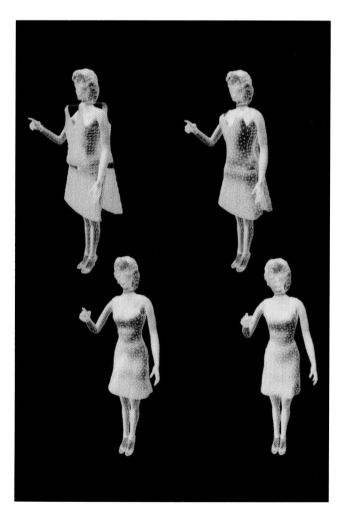

Fig. 8 : Seaming garment panels around tho body (calc time : 10 min)

Fig. 9 : Calc time : 5 hrs for 15 sec animation

BIBLIOGRAPHY

[1] : **J. Amirbayat, J.W.S. Hearle,** *"The Complex Buckling of Flexible Sheet Material - Part1 : Theoretical Approach"*, Int. J. Mech. Sci., 28(6), pp 339-358, 1986.

[2] : **M. Aono,** *"A Wrinkle Propagation Model for Cloth"*, Computer Graphics International Proc., Springer-Verlag, 1990.

[3] : **D. Baraff,** *"Curved Surfaces and Coherence for Non-Penetrating Rigid Body Simulation"*, Computer Graphics (proc. SIGGRAPH'90), 24(4), pp 19-28, 1990.

[4] : **D. Baraff, A. Witkin,** *"Dynamic Simulation of Non-Penetrating Flexible Bodies"*, Computer Graphics (proc. SIGGRAPH'92), 26(2), pp 303-308, 1992.

[5] : **D. Baraff, A. Witkin,** *"Global Methods for Simulating Flexible Bodies"*, Computer Animation Proc., Springer-Verlag, pp 1-12, 1994.

[6] : **D.E. Breen, D.H. House, M.J. Wozny,** *"Predicting the Drape of Woven Cloth using Interacting Particles"*, Computer Graphics (proc. SIGGRAPH'94), .28(4), pp 365-372, 1994.

[7] : **R.Barzel,** *"Physically-Based Modeling for Computer Graphics"*, Academic Press, 1992.

[8] : **C. R. Calladine,** *"Theory of Shell Structures"*, Cambridge University Press, 1983.

[9] : **J.F. Canny, D. Manocha,** *"A new approach for Surface Intersection"*, International journal of Computational Geometry and Applications, 1(4), pp 491-516, 1991.

[10] : **M. Carignan, Y. Yang, N. Magnenat Thalmann, D. Thalmann,** *"Dressing Animated Synthetic Actors with Complex Deformable Clothes"*, Computer Graphics (proc. SIGGRAPH'92), 26(2), pp 99-104, 1992.

[11] : **E. F. Denby,** *"The Deformation of Fabrics during Wrinkling - A Theoretical Approach"*, Textile Reserch Journal, Landcaster PA., 46, pp 667-670, 1976.

[12] : **S.G. Dhande, P.V.M. Rao, S. Tavakkoli, C.L. Moore,** *"Geometric Modeling of Draped Fabric Surfaces"*, IFIP Trans. Graphics Design and Visualisation, North Holland, pp 349-356, 1993.

[13] : **T. Duff,** *"Interval Arithmetic and Recursive Subdivision for Implicit Functions and Constructive Solid Geometry"*, Computer Graphics (proc. SIGGRAPH'92), 26(2), pp 131-138, 1992.

[14] : **K.L. Gay, L. Ling, M. Damodaran,** *"A Quasi-Steady Force Model for Animating Cloth Motion"*, IFIP Trans. Graphics Design and Visualisation, North Holland, pp 357-363, 1993.

[15] : **H. Gould, J. Tobochnik,** *"An introduction to computer simulation methods: Applications to physical systems"*, Reading Mass., Addison-Wesley, 1988.

[16] : **D.R. Haumann, R.E. Parent,** *"The Behavioral Test-Bed: Obtaining Complex Behavior With Simple Rules"*, The Visual Computer, Springer-Verlag, 4, pp 332-347, 1988.

[17] : **D. E. Breen, D. H. House, P. H. Getto,** *"A Physically-based Particle Models of woven cloth"*, The Visual Computer, 8(5-6), Springer-Verlag, Heidelberg, pp 264-277, 1992.

[18] : **T.L. Kunii, H.Gotoda,** *"Modeling and Animation of Garment Wrinkle Formation processes"*, Computer Animation Proc., Springer-Verlag, pp 131-146, 1990.

[19] : **B. Lafleur, N. Magnenat Thalmann, D. Thalmann,** *"Cloth Animation with Self-Collision Detection"*, Proc. of the IFIP conference on Modeling in Computer Graphics (proc. SIGGRAPH'91), Springer, pp 179-187, 1991.

[20] : **M.C. Lin, D. Manocha,** *"Interference Detection between Curved Objects for Computer Animation"*, Computer.Animation Proc., Springer-Verlag, pp 43-55, 1993.

[21] : **A.H. Manich, M.D. De Castellar,** *"Elastic Recovery of Polyester Staple Fiber Rotor Spun Yarn"*, Textile Research Journal, Landcaster PA., 62, pp 196-199, 1992.

[22] : **M. Moore, J. Wilhelms,** *"Collision Detection and Response for Computer Animation"*, Computer Graphics (proc. SIGGRAPH'88), 22(4), pp 289-298, 1988.

[23] : **W.E. Morton, J.W.S. Hearle,** *"Physical properties of textile fibers"*, Manchester and London, The textile institute, Butterworths, 1962.

[24] : **L.F. Palazzi, D.R. Forsey,** *"A Multilevel Approach to Surface Response in Dynamically Deformable Models"*, Computer Animation Proc., Springer-Verlag, pp 21-30, 1994.

[25] : **D. Rosenthal,** *"Resistance and Deformation of Solid Media"*, N-Y, Pergamon Press, 1974.

[26] : **M. Shinya, M.C. Forgue,** *"Interference Detection through Rasterisation"*, The journal of Visualisation and Computer Animation, J. Wiley & Sons, 4(2), pp 132-134, 1991.

[27] : **J.M. Snyder, A.R. Woodbury, K. Fleisher, B. Currin, A.H. Barr,** *"Interval Methods for Multi-Point Collisions between Time-Dependant Curved Surfaces"*, Computer Graphics annual series, pp 321-334, 1993.

[28] : **D. Terzopoulos, J.C. Platt, H. Bar,** *"Elastically Deformable Models"*, Computer Graphics (proc. SIGGRAPH'87), 21, pp 205-214, 1987.

[29] : **D. Terzopoulos, K. Fleischer,** *"Modeling Inelastic Deformation: Viscoelasticity, Plasticity, Fracture"*, Computer Graphics (proc. SIGGRAPH'88), 22, pp 269-278, 1988.

[30] : **S. Timoshenko, J. N. Goodier,** *"Theory of Elasticity"*, 3rd ed., N-Y, McGraw-Hill, 1970.

[31] : **B. Von Herzen, A.H. Barr, H.R. Zatz,** *"Geometric Collisions for Time-Dependant Parametric Surfaces"*, Computer Graphics (proc. SIGGRAPH'90), 24(4), pp 39-48, 1990.

[32] : **P. Volino, N. Magnenat Thalmann,** *"Efficient Self-Collision Detection on Smoothly Discretised Surface Animations using Geometrical Shape Regularity"*, Computer Graphics Forum (EuroGraphics Proc.), 13(3), pp 155-166, 1994.

[33] : **R.C. Webb, M.A. Gigante,** *"Using Dynamic Bounding Volume Hierarchies to improve Efficiency of Rigid Body Simulations"*, Computer Graphics International Proc., Springer-Verlag, pp 825-841, 1992.

[34] : **R.C. Webb, M.A. Gigante,** *"Distributed, Multi-Person, Physically-Based Interaction in Virtual Worlds"*, Computer Graphics International Proc., Springer-Verlag, pp 41-48, 1993.

[35] : **J. Weil,** *"The synthesis of Cloth Objects"*, Computer Graphics (proc. SIGGRAPH'86), 4, pp 49-54, 1986.

[36] : **H.M. Werner, N. Magnenat Thalmann, D. Thalmann,** *"User Interface for Fashion Design"*, Graphics Design and Visualisation, IFIP Trans. North Holland, pp 197-204, 1993.

[37] : **A. Witkin, W. Welch,** *"Fast Animation and Control of Non-Rigid Structures"*, Computer Graphics (proc. SIGGRAPH'90), 24, pp 243-252, 1990.

[38] : **F. Yamaguchi,** *"An Unified Approach to Interference Problems using a Triangle Processor"*, Computer Graphics (proc. SIGGRAPH'85), 19, pp 141-149, 1985.

[39] : **Y. Yang, N. Magnenat Thalmann,** *"An Improved Algorithm for Collision Detection in Cloth Animation with Human Body"*, Computer Graphics and Applications (Pacific Graphics Proc.), World Scientific Publishing, 1, pp 237-251, 1993.

[40] : **M. Zyda, D. Pratt, W. Osborne, J. Monahan,** *"Real-Time Collision Detection and Response"*, The journal of visualisation and Computer Animation, 4(1), J. Wiley & Sons, pp 13-24, 1993.

Feature-based Control of Visibility Error:
A Multi-resolution Clustering Algorithm
for Global Illumination

François Sillion[1]   *George Drettakis*[2]

[1]CNRS   [2]ERCIM-INRIA
*i*MAGIS
B.P. 53, 38041 Grenoble Cedex 9, France.

Abstract

In this paper we introduce a new approach to controlling error in hierarchical clustering algorithms for radiosity. The new method ensures that just enough work is done to meet the user's quality criteria. To this end the importance of traditionally ignored visibility error is identified, and the concept of *features* is introduced as a way to evaluate the quality of an image. A methodology to evaluate error based on features is presented, which leads to the development of a *multi-resolution visibility* algorithm. An algorithm to construct a suitable hierarchy for clustering and multi-resolution visibility is also proposed. Results of the implementation show that the multi-resolution approach has the potential of providing significant computational savings depending on the choice of feature size the user is interested in.   They also illustrate the relevance of the feature-based error analysis. The proposed algorithms are well suited to the development of interactive lighting simulation systems since they allow more user control. Two additional mechanisms to control the quality of a simulation are presented: The evaluation of internal visibility in a cluster produces more accurate solutions for a given error bound; a progressive multi-gridding approach is introduced for hierarchical radiosity, allowing continuous refinement of a solution in an interactive session.

Keywords: Visibility error, Clustering, Feature-based error metric, Multi-resolution visibility, Hierarchical radiosity, Progressive multi-gridding, Global Illumination.

1 Introduction

Modern global illumination algorithms allow the precise simulation of interreflection effects, penumbrae caused by extended light sources, and subtle shading variations caused by complex reflectance properties [2, 15]. Lighting simulation systems operate under very tight and often contradictory constraints: users typically require guaranteed and easily controllable precision levels, with maximum speed for interactive design. An important goal of rendering research is thus to enable the user to reduce the solution error where such reduction is deemed desirable, while at the same time limiting the time spent to achieve this reduction.

---

*i*MAGIS is a joint research project of CNRS, INRIA, INPG and UJF. Email: [Francois.Sillion|George.Drettakis]@imag.fr.

Permission to make digital/hard copy of part or all of this work for personal or classroom use is granted without fee provided that copies are not made or distributed for profit or commercial advantage, the copyright notice, the title of the publication and its date appear, and notice is given that copying is by permission of ACM, Inc. To copy otherwise, to republish, to post on servers, or to redistribute to lists, requires prior specific permission and/or a fee.

Unfortunately, the algorithmic complexity of radiosity methods (quadratic in the number of objects) in effect impairs their use for scenes containing more than a few thousands objects, while Monte-Carlo methods are unable to provide low and medium-quality solutions without too much noise. Therefore means must be found to focus the effort on the most important parts of the calculation.

This paper presents new algorithms and criteria that together allow very fine and efficient user control of the perceived quality of a solution. This is accomplished by first acknowledging the importance of *visibility error*, and using the concept of *features* to evaluate the quality of a solution. This leads to the introduction of *multi-resolution visibility*, which allows precise control of the quality vs. time tradeoff. Additional mechanisms are then discussed to control the quality of a simulation in a working system.

Previous work: error-driven computation and visibility

The introduction of the hierarchical radiosity algorithm [5] was a major step towards the design of practical lighting simulation systems. First, it reduces the overall resource requirements for a given solution. Second, it uses a surface subdivision criterion as an explicit control mechanism. This criterion embodies the priorities used to guide the simulation, as it directs the computational effort to "areas of interest", introducing a natural tool for error estimation.

Hierarchical radiosity (HR) remains quadratic in the number of input objects (since each pair of objects must be linked before hierarchical subdivision begins), and therefore is not suited to large collections of small objects. *Clustering*, the operation of grouping objects together into composite objects that can interact, provides a means to eliminate the quadratic complexity term. Such clustering can be performed manually [11, 7] or automatically [16, 13].

Historically, subdivision criteria for HR first consisted of simple bounds on either the form factor or the exchange of radiosity between two surface patches [5], under the assumption that the error incurred is proportional to the magnitude of the transfer. Using the concept of importance these bounds can be made dependent on the user's interest for each region [17]. However such bounds tend to be quite conservative and thus produce unnecessary subdivision [6].

Recent work has attempted to characterize possible sources of error in global illumination [1], and establish error bounds on radiosity solutions [8]. These error bounds can then be used in the subdivision criterion of a hierarchical algorithm. Since the estimation of the error is decoupled from that of the actual transfer, subdivision can be avoided in regions where significant transfers take place without much error, resulting in better focus of the computational expense.

Existing error controls however typically ignore visibility as a possible source of error, or simply increase the error estimate by a constant factor in situations of partial visibility. Trivial bounds of 0 (total occlusion) and 1 (total visibility) are often used. While these bounds are always valid, their use results in unnecessary work being done to narrow down other error bounds by increasing the subdivision. Global visibility algorithms can be used to exploit the structure of architectural scenes and produce guaranteed visibility information [18], but they are not suited to large collections of independent objects. For exchanges between surfaces, *discontinuity meshing* also provides explicit visibility information, and indeed considerably improves the efficiency of HR [10]. However for Monte-Carlo or clustering approaches it is either impossible or impractical to calculate analytic visibility and error bounds must be used. For exchanges between clusters, an approximate visibility estimate can be derived using equivalent volume extinction properties [13], but the error introduced in the process has not yet been analyzed.

Visibility error is admittedly difficult to evaluate, since the computation of visibility itself is a costly process. Still, controlling this source of error is imperative since the quality of shadows plays a significant role in determining the user's perception of image quality. In complex environments where clustering is most useful, a dominant part of computation time is spent in visibility calculations involving small, geometrically complex objects. Resulting visibility variations produce fine detail shadows, which may be of little interest to the user, or may be lost in the implicit averaging over a surface patch.

Paper overview

The preceding discussion has shown that a key issue in designing efficient lighting simulation systems is to provide adequate control mechanisms to ensure that just enough work is done to meet the user's quality criteria. It appears that control of visibility error has not yet been attempted, despite its great potential for tightening global bounds and reducing computation costs. The goal of this paper is twofold: first, a new approach to visibility error estimation is proposed, based on *features*, that legitimates the use of a *multi-resolution visibility* algorithm. Second, quality control mechanisms are discussed for interactive simulation systems development.

We begin in Section 2 with the introduction of features to evaluate image quality, and show why existing error metrics are incapable of determining when a given level of detail is satisfactorily represented. A simple metric is then proposed to illustrate how to take into account the user's interest in a minimal *feature size*. This leads to Section 3 where we explain how to compute *multi-resolution visibility* information using a spatial hierarchy augmented with equivalent *extinction* properties. Selection of a hierarchical level for visibility computation can then be based on the resulting feature size on the receiver. In this paper an application to clustering algorithms is discussed, but multi-resolution visibility is equally promising for Monte Carlo techniques. The construction of a suitable hierarchy is discussed in Section 4. In Section 5 we show that the multi-resolution visibility algorithm successfully generates images (currently for isotropic clusters) in which only selected features sizes are accurately represented, resulting in computational savings. Section 6 presents more quality controls for clustering algorithms, specifically intra-cluster visibility determination in linear time and progressive multi-gridding. We conclude in Section 7.

2   Feature-Based Error Analysis

To a large extent the quality of an image is judged based on how well features of different sizes are represented. It is not easy to characterize what constitutes an illumination feature. For the purposes of this paper, we will consider image features to be the connected regions of varying illumination related to shadows (regions in umbra or penumbra).

2.1 L^p metrics are inadequate for "feature detection"

A major difficulty for accurate lighting simulation is that in general the exact solution is not known at the time of computation. Thus the estimation of the error in a proposed approximation is particularly difficult, and must rely on the computation of error bounds for all algorithmic operations. Even in the case where an exact solution is available, it is not a simple task to define the quality of a given approximation. This is done by choosing a particular error metric to quantify the distance between an approximate solution and the true solution. A "good" metric should therefore convey a sense of the user's requirements. A central observation in this paper is that when simulating a complex scene, the user is typically interested in capturing illumination variations down to a certain scale. Very small details are not as important, or at least not in all areas of the scene. We strive to define a control mechanism that will avoid any work that would only generate such small details.

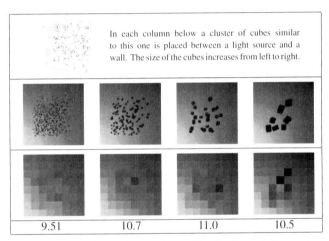

In each column below a cluster of cubes similar to this one is placed between a light source and a wall. The size of the cubes increases from left to right.

| 9.51 | 10.7 | 11.0 | 10.5 |

Figure 1: Comparison of approximate illumination solutions using different clusters. Top: reference images (illumination of the wall). Middle: approximate images using a coarse mesh. Bottom: L^2 error norms. Note that the four images have similar L^2 error values, and all hide some illumination information. However the varying size of the missing features cannot be discovered.

Figure 1 illustrates the issue by showing shadows cast on a wall by four different groups of objects. Four approximate images, all computed using the same mesh size, are shown below the "exact" images. Consider a user who is interested in shadows of a specific size, e.g. those of the image on the extreme right, but is satisfied by the averaging of the smaller, detailed shadows on the left[1]. The user thus does not wish more work to be done for the detail shadows, but wishes to have a more accurate representation at the larger scale. The subdivision criterion used in a HR algorithm for instance should be capable of halting the subdivision for the left-hand group, while ordering further computation for the group on the right. Thus an error measure should distinguish between the four cases.

Traditional error metrics are incapable of making such a distinction. As an example consider the commonly used family of error metrics expressing the distance between a reference function f and an approximate function $\widehat{f}$ as the L^p norm

$$\|\widehat{f} - f\|_p = \left(\int |\widehat{f}(x) - f(x)|^p dx \right)^{\frac{1}{p}}$$

---

[1] Perhaps a more realistic example would be a situation where a user is viewing an office scene from the doorway, and in which accurate shadows for chairs and desks are important, but averaged, low quality shadows from details such as pens on a desk are satisfactory.

L^p norms simply add error contributions from all points on a surface (or in an image), and do not take into account higher-level properties of the radiance distributions, such as the size and shape of illumination features. This is illustrated by the similar values obtained for the four groups in Figure 1. Appendix A shows that in fact for a point light source the L^1 or L^2 error introduced by averaging all visibility variations depends only on the average visibility, and not on the size or shape of the shadows.

2.2 A proposal for an error metric based on feature size

Our hypothesis is that illumination features (shadows or bright areas) are important only as far as they have a significant visual impact. Therefore it is possible to define a *feature size* on a receiving surface, and decide that features smaller than that size are "unimportant": their absence should not contribute to the error.

In the remainder of the paper we refer to the radiosity function over a surface as an "image". This terminology should not mask the important fact that the entire discussion takes place in three-dimensional object space. In order to demonstrate the relevance of the feature-based approach, we assume for now that we have access to all the information in a reference solution. The multi-resolution visibility technique of Section 3 will show how the ideas developed here can still be used in the absence of such a reference.

A simple error metric based on features is defined by segmenting the image f into two components by means of a *feature mask* $\mathcal{F}^s(f, x)$: a binary function that equals one at points x that belong to a "feature" (of size greater than s) of function f. Computation of feature masks from the reference solution is described in the next section. For points in the mask region we compute an L^p norm of the difference between the approximate function and the reference function. For points outside the feature mask, we are content with an average value (since features present there are smaller than s). Thus in our current implementation we compute average values at each point, for both the approximate and reference functions, using a box filter of size s around the point of interest, and compute an L^p norm of the difference between the averages.

The feature-based error metric (FBEM) is summarized by the following formula, where $\overline{f^s}$ represents the filtered version of f:

$$\|\widehat{f} - f\|_p^s = \left(\int |\overline{\widehat{f^s}}(x) - \overline{f^s}(x)|^p \left[1 - \mathcal{F}^s(f, x)\right] dx \right.$$

$$\left. + \int |\widehat{f}(x) - f(x)|^p \mathcal{F}^s(f, x) dx \right)^{\frac{1}{p}} \quad (1)$$

2.3 Examples

Table 1 shows the FBEM values computed for the four groups of Figure 1 and different values of the minimum feature size s. The object-space size of typical shadows in these images is respectively 11, 16.5, 22 and 31. For small s values, all FBEM values are high since the metric is equivalent to an L^2 metric in the limit of $s = 0$. As s increases, FBEM values decrease more rapidly for the groups containing smaller objects, as expected. There appears to be a residual error of about 3 due to the mesh size used for the approximate solutions.

Assume the user is interested in clearly seeing features of size 30 or greater, while being content with an average for all features smaller that this size. The extreme right-hand image of Figure 1 requires more work since the FBEM value for $s = 30$ is high. The approximation for the other three images is deemed satisfactory since the error is low.

Thus, using the FBEM presented above, it is possible to reveal the presence of features greater than a given threshold in the approx-

Feature size:				
5	14.76	16.34	17.25	17.31
16	9.37	12.24	15.76	15.80
24	4.78	6.50	9.06	14.74
30	4.23	3.16	6.90	13.37
40	3.65	2.33	3.35	6.94

Table 1: Feature-based error metric (FBEM) for the four approximate images of Figure 1 and five different feature sizes. The four measures are equivalent for small feature sizes, and decrease at different rates as a function of s. Images are shown again for clarity.

imate images, opening the way for selective subdivision based on the user's minimum feature size of interest. Of course this could not be used *as is* in a subdivision criterion for HR, since it uses a reference solution, but it is useful for *a posteriori* validation of control mechanisms.

2.4 Computation of feature masks

According to the definition of features given above, computing a feature mask amounts to identifying connected regions of "significant" size. Mathematical morphology provides tools to isolate features based on their size [12]. Consider a binary image, representing for example the characteristic function of an object. We define the action of an *Erosion* operator as follows: all points outside the object (white) are untouched. All points inside the object that have a neighbor outside become white. All other points remain black. An *Expansion* operator is defined similarly by including in the objects all outside points that have a neighbor in the object. Figure 2 shows a reference image and images obtained after a number of erosions (top) or expansions (middle).

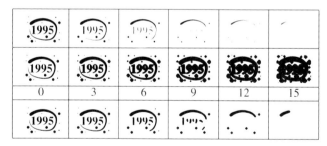

Figure 2: Effect of repeated applications of the erosion (top), expansion (middle) and combined erosions/expansion (bottom) operations on a binary image. The reference image appears in the left column, and the number of applications of the operators increases from left to right. For the bottom row we apply n erosions followed by n expansions.

Clearly an object of diameter $2d$ will disappear after d erosions are applied in sequence. Thus applying a sequence of n erosions followed by n expansions will successfully eliminate all small regions, but keep larger regions (slightly modifying their shape in the process). This process is illustrated in the bottom row of Figure 2.

Computing the effect of the erosion operator on a binary image is straightforward using bitwise operations: the result is the logical OR of the image and the four translated copies of itself (by one pixel) in the $+x$, $-x$, $+y$ and $-y$ directions. For the expansion operator the logical operator AND is used.

In our examples, the original binary image is computed by recording all areas of the receiver that have a partial or occluded view of the light source. This expensive operation was performed only once during the creation of the reference image. Feature masks are computed by applying the proper number ($p/2$ for a feature size of p) of successive erosions and expansions to eliminate unwanted features. Figure 3 shows some feature masks for the four groups used above.

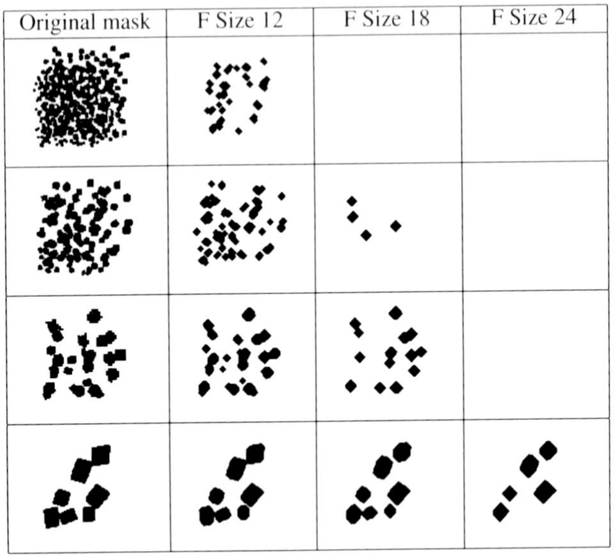

Original mask	F Size 12	F Size 18	F Size 24

Figure 3: Some feature masks for the images in Figure 1.

3 A Multi-resolution Visibility Algorithm

In the previous section we presented the concept of a *feature size* and introduced an error metric which permits the evaluation of image quality determined by how well illumination features are represented. We now use these fundamental concepts to develop a *multi-resolution* (MR) visibility algorithm. With this algorithm, expensive high quality visibility calculations are only performed when they are expected to help in the accurate representation of features deemed "interesting" by the user.

Hierarchical spatial subdivision structures are often used in the calculation of global illumination algorithms, in particular when form-factor estimation is performed with ray-tracing [19, 4, 5, etc.]. In radiosity clustering algorithms the hierarchy of clusters is also used for radiometric calculations, by letting clusters represent their contents for some energy transfers [13, 16]. The following *multi-resolution visibility* algorithm naturally extends previous clustering approaches by allowing clusters to also represent their contents in some visibility calculations. If a specific feature size s has been chosen, it is unnecessary to consider the contents of a cluster for visibility if these contents will produce features smaller than s.

3.1 Approximate visibility computation between clusters using an extinction model

Let us assume that we have grouped all objects in the scene into a hierarchy of clusters. Approximate visibility calculations can be performed using an analogy between clusters and absorbing volumes [13]. The approximation (asymptotically exact for homogeneous isotropic clusters when the size of the objects goes to zero) consists of associating an *extinction coefficient* κ with each cluster. The transmittance function between two points P and Q in the scene is

then given by

$$
\begin{aligned}
T(P, Q) &= e^{-\int_{PQ} \kappa(u)du} \\
&= e^{-\sum_{i \in \mathcal{C}(PQ)} \kappa_i l_i}
\end{aligned}
$$

where $\mathcal{C}(PQ)$ is the set of clusters traversed by the ray joining P and Q, κ_i is the extinction coefficient of cluster i, and l_i is the length traveled inside cluster i by the ray.

Extinction coefficients express the probability that a random ray is intercepted in the cluster, and are computed as

$$
\kappa_i = \frac{\sum_j A_j}{4V_i}
$$

where the area of all surface patches contained in cluster i is summed and divided by the cluster's volume. Since a surface contributes to the extinction of only one cluster, the attenuation due to overlapping clusters is correctly obtained by adding their extinction contributions.

3.2 Multi-Resolution Visibility

In the rest of this section we consider the emitter-blocker-receiver configuration shown in Figure 4, which consists of two surfaces, the emitter E and the receiver R, in two-dimensions. This restriction is for presentation purposes only and is removed later.

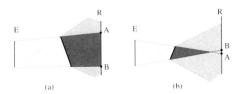

Figure 4: Definition of shadow features created by a blocker. (a) The umbra region is unbounded since the blocker is larger than the emitter: there is always an umbral region on the receiver. (b) For some positions of the blocker the receiver has no umbral region.

If a blocker (which for now we also consider to be a surface) is placed between the emitter and the receiver, *umbra* and *penumbra* regions are created in space. Depending on the position of the blocker, there may or may not be an umbral region on the receiver. (Figure 4). Given the definition discussed above the size of the umbral zone on the receiver –AB in Figure 4(a)–, if it exists, is the *feature size*.

The blocker may actually be a hierarchical representation of a collection of objects (a *cluster*) as pictured in Figure 5(a). In this case, at each level of the hierarchy an extinction coefficient is stored allowing the approximate calculation of the attenuation of a ray if it passes through the cluster, as described previously.

Multi-resolution visibility can be performed by avoiding the descent into the hierarchy after a certain level. When the required conditions are met the extinction coefficient is used instead, thus avoiding the intersection of the ray with all the descendants of this cluster. Evidently, the effect is that visibility is no longer exact, but an average estimation of transmittance. It is here that a large potential gain in computation time can be achieved. In scenes where the small detail objects (e.g., models of phones, keyboards, small objects on a desk etc.), comprise the largest part of the geometric complexity, the intersection with these objects can quickly become the overwhelming expense of visibility (and overall) computation. By considering the higher level clusters for visibility computation instead of the numerous contents, when such a choice is dictated by the chosen feature size, this expense can be completely avoided.

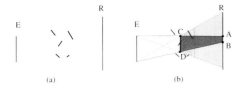

Figure 5: Visibility estimation through a cluster. (a) the blocker is a hierarchy of clusters. (b) an "equivalent blocker" is used to estimate the maximum feature size on the receiver.

Recall the discussion in Section 2 in which the user wishes to accurately represent all features of size greater than s on the receiver. To achieve this, all that is required is to descend sufficiently far into the hierarchy so that the large shadows are accurately calculated, while performing the approximate calculation for small, detail shadows.

To facilitate such a choice each cluster is augmented with a description of the maximum blocker size $BSIZE$ of its contents (we give a precise definition of this in the following section). It then suffices to place a fictitious blocker of size $BSIZE$, at the center of the actual cluster $-C'D'$ in Figure 5(b). The descent in the cluster hierarchy can be terminated if the projected umbral region of the fictitious blocker (AB in Figure 5) is smaller than the chosen feature size s.

Contiguous regions which let light traverse must also be considered as feature creators since a feature can be considered "negative" (umbra in a bright region), or "positive" (lit areas inside a dark region). We thus extend our definition of features from Section 2 by defining $BSIZE$ to be the maximum of the connected regions of light or shadow. This is consistent with the symmetric expression of visibility error with respect to umbra and light presented in Appendix A.

3.3 Characterization of a Cluster for MR Visibility

All that is required in order to apply the preceding algorithm is the determination of $BSIZE$ for each cluster. The restriction to two-dimensions is now lifted, and the treatment for three-dimensional clusters is described. For now clusters are assumed to contain objects placed so that the cluster density can be considered isotropic, and thus does not depend on the direction of incidence of a ray.

The goal is to determine a representative size for a blocking cluster, which will allow the calculation of the maximum feature size given a specific emitter-receiver configuration. At first glance it may seem natural to take $BSIZE$ to be the size of the largest object contained in the cluster. However there is one important consideration: it is the *connected region* of shadow on the receiver which we wish to consider. Furthermore, as discussed above, the regions of light potentially blocked by the contents of the cluster *and* the regions of light which pass through must be considered separately.

A preprocessing step is performed to calculate $BSIZE$ for all clusters in the hierarchy. For each cluster, all the contained objects are orthographically projected into a binary image. This operation is performed for a given cluster and a given direction, resulting in a *view-independent* characterization. The consequence of the isotropic cluster assumption is that a single orthographic projection is sufficient. For non-isotropic clusters the $BSIZE$ parameter is a function of the direction of interest. A simple solution in that case would be to interpolate from a number of sampled directions. Our current research focuses on more efficient representations for such directional information [14].

The erosion and expansion operators from Section 2.4 are then used to compute the maximum sizes for blockers and free regions

inside a cluster. Erosions (respectively expansions) are computed until all objects have disappeared (respectively until all free space has disappeared). The *number* of erosion or expansion operations defines the value of $BSIZE$ for the blocked and free regions respectively. In our implementation we do the projections, erosions and expansions using Graphics hardware.

4 A Hierarchical Structure for Clustering and Multi-Resolution Visibility

Previous automatic clustering approaches have used spatial data structures developed for ray-tracing (hierarchical bounding boxes [3] were used in [16], while in [13] a K-D tree was used). In this section we show that given the calculation of average visibility based on extinction coefficients in the manner of [13], it is beneficial to develop a special-purpose hierarchical data structure, such that the resulting clusters have properties suitable for cluster-based hierarchical radiosity and multi-resolution visibility.

By definition, clusters are constructed to *represent* as accurately as possible the collection of objects they contain. By introducing computation of visibility using extinction coefficients and also multi-resolution visibility, apart from the representation of energy transfer of the contained objects as a whole, the clusters also need to correctly represent the transmission properties of the collection of contained objects.

These two modes of representation place different constraints on the cluster hierarchy. From the point of view of energy exchanges, good clusters allow tight bracketing of radiance or visibility functions (thus surfaces with similar orientation that do not shadow each other are preferred). From the point of view of visibility approximation, good clusters are ones for which the extinction property is plausible (thus homogeneous isotropic clusters are preferred). Given these constraints, we have identified two key properties for clusters: (a) *proximity* and (b) *homogeneity* of the contained objects. Maintaining proximity is a natural way to group objects when the cluster is used to represent radiative transfers. Also, for multi-resolution computation it is important that objects contained in a cluster are close so that the averaging performed does not introduce unacceptable artifacts. Homogeneity here means that we want a cluster to group objects of similar size, and is crucial for the resulting quality of the average visibility computation.

As a simple measure of proximity, we use the percentage of empty space resulting from a clustering operation (i.e., the addition of an object or a cluster to another cluster). Thus we prefer clusters in which the empty space is minimized.

To efficiently group objects of similar size we use a hierarchy of n levels of uniform grids. We start with level 0, which is a single voxel the size of the bounding box of the scene and then at each level i we create a grid which is subdivided into 2^i voxels along each axis. We then insert each object into the level for which its bounding box fits the voxel size.

Once these grids have been constructed, we start at the lowest level n, containing the smallest objects. We group the objects entirely contained in each voxel, by attempting to minimize the empty space, in accordance to the proximity criterion described above. In addition, objects which are very small compared to the grid size are grouped into an appropriate cluster, even if the resulting cluster is largely empty. Once all the voxels of a level have been treated, we attempt to add the objects not entirely contained in a single voxel at this level to the clusters already constructed, again using the same criteria. We then insert the clusters created to the grid of the level immediately above, and iterate.

Once the cluster hierarchy has been created, the data structure is augmented with average transmission behavior by propagating the average extinction values up the hierarchical structure as in [13].

When multi-resolution visibility is used, the $BSIZE$ estimation is also performed for each cluster in the hierarchy in the manner described in Section 3.

Figure 6 presents results obtained with the new hierarchy using first a surface visibility algorithm similar to that of [16], and then the average visibility proposed in [13]. The scene consists of 5380 polygons. It is interesting to observe the significant time gain achievable by the average visibility algorithm given a suitable hierarchy (we observe a factor of 4), while approximate shadows are preserved.

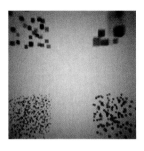

3D view of test scene.   Reference sol. (2069 s).

Figure 7: Reference image used in the error comparisons.

Surface vis: 1 216 s.   Volume vis: 376 s.

Figure 6: Timings (in seconds) using the new hierarchy construction. Throughout the paper all timing information was obtained on an Indigo R4000 computer.

Constructing a suitable hierarchy for cluster-based hierarchical radiosity with extinction and multi-resolution visibility is a difficult problem. The results indicate that the first solution presented here, based on proximity and homogeneity, results in the construction of hierarchies well suited to approximate and multi-resolution visibility calculations.

5 Results of multi-resolution visibility

We have implemented the hierarchy construction, the calculation of $BSIZE$ and the multi-resolution visibility algorithm in a hierarchical radiosity clustering testbed.

To evaluate the results of the multi-resolution visibility approach we have computed images of test environments using different values for the feature sizes of interest s on a receiver.

The first test scene is shown in Figure 7 (left). It contains the four clusters used in Section 2 and a light source (in yellow). The right-hand image is the illumination obtained on the back wall and serves as a reference image. For all these images visibility was always computed solely using extinction properties (thus we do not attempt to characterize the error introduced by averaged transmission visibility itself).

Figure 8 shows four images, where the desired feature size parameter (see Section 2.2) is changed. For each image the computation time in seconds is given. A very low error threshold was used to ensure that the mesh density was maximal for all images. Thus the decrease in computation time as the desired feature size becomes larger measures the speedup in the visibility calculation.

We next show that multi-resolution visibility is consistent with the feature-based error metric (FBEM) from Section 2.2, by computing the FBEM for the images described above. Although the four clusters have been grouped in a single image for simplicity, we apply the error metric only on the region of the image corresponding to each cluster, to obtain an FBEM value for each of the four groups.

For the four images, we show for each cluster the value of L^2 error norm (back row) and the value of the FBEM for a feature size s equal to that used in the MR Visibility algorithm. We note that

as we increase s the L^2 norm for all clusters increases, as more and more averaging is being performed. Still the increase appears later for larger objects, as expected. The FBEM values are always of similar magnitude, despite the fact that very different levels of averaging are being used in different clusters in a given image. This shows that the multi-resolution visibility algorithm accomplishes its purpose: given a desired feature size, it ensures that the corresponding FBEM remains low while allowing time gains.

Figure 9 shows that even greater speedups can be achieved when a medium error threshold allows MR visibility to reduce the amount of subdivision. The explicit incorporation of MR visibility in refinement criteria is a promising path for further acceleration.

6 Control of Image Quality for Clustering

Recent algorithms separate the computation of high-quality images into two phases: a coarse quality global illumination calculation is first performed using elaborate algorithms such as discontinuity meshing or clustering in a *global pass*. A view-dependent, potentially very expensive *local pass* follows [9, 16]. This local pass is typically a ray-casting operation: at each pixel the energy from all the links is collected, allowing the calculation of high-quality shadows. The cost of this local pass is often many times larger than that of the light-transfer calculation using clusters. In essence this pass may eradicate all computation time benefit achieved by using the clusters in the first place, and exclude any possibility for interactivity with quality and error control.

In contrast, we maintain a "progressive refinement" philosophy, by providing explicit quality controls, allowing computational cost to be focused on desired characteristics of the resulting image. The first component of this approach is the multi-resolution visibility presented above. This technique, coupled with the use of *importance* [17] to assign appropriate feature sizes to different objects could plausibly replace the global/local pass approach while affording more interactivity. We present next two supplementary quality controls: first, the correct treatment of intra-cluster visibility and second, progressive multi-gridding permitting rapid interactive response for hierarchical radiosity.

6.1 Intra-cluster visibility

Previous clustering algorithms compute a bound on energy transfer that ignores visibility (bound of 1 on the visibility error), both between the two clusters but also in the distribution of light on each side [16, 13]. This potentially results in light leaks at the scale of the cluster. This behavior is not only visually displeasing but also flawed: since bounds are computed on irradiance values, that irradiance is distributed to many surfaces which should be shadowed,

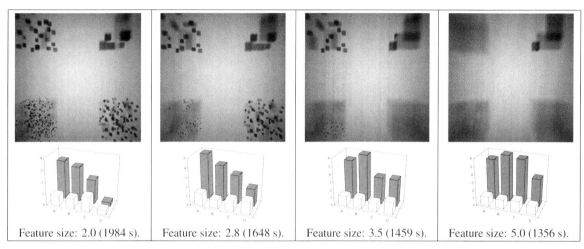

| Feature size: 2.0 (1984 s). | Feature size: 2.8 (1648 s). | Feature size: 3.5 (1459 s). | Feature size: 5.0 (1356 s). |

Figure 8: Results for the multiresolution visibility algorithm.

Figure 9: Increasing the desired feature size reduces both the amount of subdivision and the cost of visibility computations. (left) Fsize = 0, $621s$. (middle) Fsize = 4, $245s$. (right) Fsize = 8, $148s$. Tree courtesy of CIRAD, modelled with 7967 polygons using AMAP.

thereby creating energy.

If visibility information inside the cluster with respect to a source cluster can be computed (with some approximation) in time linear in the number of contained objects, the overall time and space complexity of $O(s \log s)$ for clustering is not modified [16].

We propose the use of an item buffer to quickly evaluate this visibility. The cluster's contents are projected in the direction of the light source using a z-buffer to determine visible surfaces from that direction. By counting instances of an item number in the buffer we obtain an estimate of the projected area of each patch visible from the direction of the source. This is used as the projected area in kernel calculations when computing energy bounds. Note that the resolution of the item-buffer can be adapted to the contents of each cluster, provided we know the size of the smallest object in each cluster. Thus the aliasing problems inherent to the item-buffer approach can be reduced. The same technique is also used at the other end of a link, to evaluate the energy leaving a cluster.

Figure 10: Results of introducing intra-cluster visibility.

In the images of Figure 10 we present an example where a link (shown in purple) has been created from the light source to a cluster of books. Ignoring intra-cluster visibility (left) results in the creation of energy since all books are fully illuminated. Using the visibility buffer to modulate the energy distribution (right), energy is preserved while improving the appearance of the image.

6.2 Progressive multi-gridding

In hierarchical radiosity algorithms subdivision is controlled by an error threshold on individual interactions. A global bound on error is difficult to determine and it is consequently difficult for the user to choose an error threshold so as to achieve a certain quality. The problem is exacerbated with clustering, since the subdivision of links is amortized with time, and thus successive iterations may become much more expensive as the allowed error decreases. This sharp and unpredictable increase in iteration time may then destroy interactivity.

As a remedy we develop a *progressive multi-gridding* approach. By analyzing the distribution of error bounds on the links created, we can predict how many of these links would survive a given decrease in the error threshold, and thus estimate the time required for a subsequent iteration with the new error threshold. In a manner more intuitive to the user the amount of computation can be specified (in the form of a maximum number of links to refine) and the system proceeds to deduce the new threshold to use for hierarchical refinement.

This analysis can be performed at a marginal cost by recording a histogram of the distribution of error bounds computed. Specifically, the interval between 0 and the current error threshold ε is divided into a number of bins, each associated with a counter. Every time a link is created (or left unchanged) during the hierarchical subdivision procedure, we increment the counter for the bin corresponding to the link's error bound. At the start of the next progressive multi-gridding iteration, the new error threshold is chosen such that the sum of all counter for bins with higher error levels is less than a user-specified limit k. This effectively chooses an error threshold such that at most k links are refined. This multi-gridding algorithm does not accelerate the computation but guarantees a continuous update of the simulation.

7 Conclusions

Important advances towards the goal of providing interactive systems capable of treating very complex environments have been made by hierarchical radiosity and clustering algorithms. Nonetheless several important shortcomings of previous approaches were identified in this paper: (a) visibility error is typically ignored, (b) traditional error metrics do not allow the user to specify a desired level of detail and (c) progressive refinement of the simulation is difficult to achieve.

In this paper we introduced a new approach to error estimation based on illumination *features*, which allows the user to choose a level of detail relevant to a given simulation. The quality of a solution then relates to how well features of the user-determined size have been represented.

The principles introduced by the feature-based analysis were used to develop a *multi-resolution visibility algorithm*. The hierarchy constructed for clustering contains transmission information as in [13] and is further augmented with an estimate of the largest equivalent blocker size from its contents. This information is used to limit the cost of visibility calculations. An algorithm which efficiently constructs a suitable hierarchy was also presented. The results of the implementation for isotropic environments show significant computational speedup using MR visibility when the user does not require the accurate representation of small features.

Two additional quality control mechanisms were introduced: *intra-cluster visibility* which corrects potential light-transfer error suffered by previous clustering algorithms, and *progressive multigridding* which is essential for interactive clustering systems.

We believe that the introduction of feature-based error and quality evaluation is an important step which will lead to significant acceleration of global illumination algorithms. Multi-resolution visibility is an example of such an achievement.

In future work the extension of our approach to non-isotropic environments must be completely developed. Promising first results in representing directional information for clustering have been obtained [14]. We have not yet addressed the analysis of error caused by the use of extinction coefficients and the effect of visibility correlations between clusters and their contents. Research in these areas is extremely important for the development of reliable quality controls. It will be interesting to observe the results of the application of our approach to Monte Carlo methods. A more in-depth study of feature-based error metrics must be performed. Finally better algorithms for hierarchy construction should be investigated.

8 Acknowledgements

George Drettakis was hosted successively by INRIA (Grenoble, France), UPC (Barcelona, Spain) and GMD (St. Augustin, Germany) as an ERCIM postdoctoral fellow, and was financed in part by the Commission of the European Communities. Pat Hanrahan provided parts of the hierarchical radiosity code; Jean-Daniel Boissonnat suggested the use of erosion/expansion operations. The scene in Figure 6 was assembled using pieces of the Berkeley Soda Hall model; thanks to Seth Teller and all members of the UC Berkeley walkthrough group.

References

[1] James Arvo, Kenneth Torrance, and Brian Smits. A framework for the analysis of error in global illumination algorithms. In *Computer Graphics Proceedings, Annual Conference Series:* SIGGRAPH '94 (Orlando, FL), pages 75–84, 1994.

[2] Michael F. Cohen and John R. Wallace. *Radiosity and Realistic Image Synthesis.* Academic Press, Boston, 1993.

[3] J. Goldsmith and J. Salmon. Automatic creation of object hierarchies for ray tracing. *IEEE Computer Graphics and Applications*, 7(5):14–20, May 1987.

[4] Eric A. Haines. Shaft culling for efficient ray-traced radiosity. In P. Brunet and F.W. Jansen, editors, *Photorealistic Rendering in Computer Graphics*, pages 122–138. Springer Verlag, 1993. Proceedings of the Second Eurographics Workshop on Rendering (Barcelona, Spain, May 1991).

[5] Pat Hanrahan, David Saltzman, and Larry Aupperle. A rapid hierarchical radiosity algorithm. *Computer Graphics*, 25(4):197–206, August 1991. Proceedings SIGGRAPH '91 in Las Vegas.

[6] Nicolas Holzschuch, François Sillion, and George Drettakis. An efficient progressive refinement strategy for hierarchical radiosity. In *Fifth Eurographics Workshop on Rendering*, Darmstadt, Germany, June 1994.

[7] Arjan J. F. Kok. Grouping of patches in progressive radiosity. In *Proceedings of Fourth Eurographics Workshop on Rendering*, pages 221–231. Eurographics, June 1993. Technical Report EG 93 RW.

[8] Dani Lischinski, Brian Smits, and Donald P. Greenberg. Bounds and error estimates for radiosity. In *Computer Graphics Proceedings, Annual Conference Series:* SIGGRAPH '94 (Orlando, FL), pages 67–74, July 1994.

[9] Dani Lischinski, Filippo Tampieri, and Donald P. Greenberg. Discontinuity meshing for accurate radiosity. *IEEE Computer Graphics and Applications*, 12(6):25–39, November 1992.

[10] Dani Lischinski, Filippo Tampieri, and Donald P. Greenberg. Combining hierarchical radiosity and discontinuity meshing. In *Computer Graphics Proceedings, Annual Conference Series:* SIGGRAPH '93 (Anaheim, CA), pages 199–208, August 1993.

[11] Holly Rushmeier, Charles Patterson, and Aravindan Veerasamy. Geometric simplification for indirect illumination calculations. In *Proceedings Graphics Interface '93*. Morgan Kaufmann, 1993.

[12] J. Serra. *Image analysis and mathematical morphology : 1.* Academic Press, London, 1982.

[13] François Sillion. A unified hierarchical algorithm for global illumination with scattering volumes and object clusters. *to appear in IEEE Transactions on Visualization and Computer Graphics*, 1(3), September 1995. (a preliminary version appeared in the fifth Eurographics workshop on rendering, Darmstadt, Germany, June 1994).

[14] François Sillion, George Drettakis, and Cyril Soler. A clustering algorithm for radiance calculation in general environments. In *Sixth Eurographics Workshop on Rendering*, Dublin, Ireland, June 1995.

[15] François Sillion and Claude Puech. *Radiosity and Global Illumination.* Morgan Kaufmann publishers, San Francisco, 1994.

[16] Brian Smits, James Arvo, and Donald P. Greenberg. A clustering algorithm for radiosity in complex environments. In *Computer Graphics Proceedings, Annual Conference Series:* SIGGRAPH '94 (Orlando, FL), pages 435–442, July 1994.

[17] Brian E. Smits, James R. Arvo, and David H. Salesin. An importance-driven radiosity algorithm. *Computer Graphics*, 26(4):273–282, July 1992. Proceedings of SIGGRAPH '92 in Chicago.

[18] Seth J. Teller and Patrick M. Hanrahan. Global visibility algorithms for illumination computations. In *Computer Graphics Proceedings, Annual Conference Series:* SIGGRAPH '93 (Anaheim, CA), pages 239–246, August 1993.

[19] John R. Wallace, Kells A. Elmquist, and Eric A. Haines. A ray tracing algorithm for progressive radiosity. *Computer Graphics*, 23(3):315–324, July 1989. Proceedings SIGGRAPH '89 in Boston.

A Visibility error using L^1 and L^2 norms

Consider a patch P illuminated by a point source at point y. To quantify the visibility error on the receiver patch, we compute the L^1 and L^2 norms of the difference between the visibility function $v(x, y)$ defined for $x \in P$, and its average value $\bar{v}$ over patch P. If P^+ is the region of patch P that receives light, $\bar{v}$ is equal to the ratio of the areas of P^+ and P. Separating the integrals into one over P^+ and one over $(P - P^+)$, we find

$$\|v - \bar{v}\|_1 = 2\bar{v}(1 - \bar{v}) \tag{2}$$

and similarly for the L^2 norm

$$\|v - \bar{v}\|_2 = \sqrt{\bar{v}(1 - \bar{v})} \tag{3}$$

Note that both estimates only depend on the average visibility across patch P, not on the distribution of the visibility function. Also note the dependency in $\bar{v}(1 - \bar{v})$, yielding a small error for either almost complete occlusion or almost complete visibility.

Live Paint:

Painting with Procedural Multiscale Textures

Ken Perlin
Media Research Laboratory
Courant Institute of Mathematical Sciences – New York University

Luiz Velho
IMPA – Instituto de Matemática Pura e Aplicada

Abstract

We present actively procedural multiresolution paint textures. Texture elements may be linearly combined to create complex composite textures that continue to refine themselves when viewed at successively greater magnification. Actively procedural textures constitute a powerful drawing tool that can be used in a multiresolution paint system. They provide a mechanism to generate an infinite amount of detail with a simple and compact representation. We give several examples of procedural textures and show how to create different painting effects with them.

1 Introduction

The introduction of multiresolution paint systems is a recent development in the field of computer graphics, [10], [1], [5], [12]. In this type of system, the user can view and modify an image at any desired resolution. This is possible because the internal image representation supports multiple levels of detail.

In multiresolution paint systems it is possible to make modifications at different image magnifications. The user can quickly make coarse changes over large areas of the picture, as well as fine and precise changes over small areas. Although this capability provides a great degree of control over the painting process, it is the painting tool that ultimately determines what goes into the picture. For this reason, it is necessary to develop tools that can take full advantage of multiresolution paint systems.

Standard painting tools are designed to operate at fixed resolution and, therefore, can generate only a certain amount of image detail, commensurate with resolution. When the user wants to create fine detail over a large area of the image, s/he must paint at a high magnification level. This task is time consuming, even if a multiresolution paint system is used.

The power of multiresolution paint systems is enhanced if painting tools are able to exploit the underlying multiresolution image representation by operating at multiple levels of detail. In this way, when the user wants to paint a complex pattern over a large area of the picture, s/he can perform the operation at a coarse level very quickly and still create as much detail as desired.

In this paper, we develop a framework for the design and implementation of multiresolution painting tools. This framework is based on general procedural textures defined over both spatial and scale domains. These procedures are executed at multiple resolution levels in order to add texture details to the picture. Basic texture elements can be linearly combined to create complex composite textured brushes. This framework fits naturally into the context of multiresolution paint systems.

The structure of this paper is as follows: Section 2 reviews the principles of multiresolution paint systems; Section 3 gives a general overview of multiresolution textures; Section 4 shows where texture is invoked in the system; Section 5 explains how the texture refinement method works; Section 6 illustrates the system in action with examples and pretty pictures; Section 7 discusses the use of images in our framework; and Section 8 concludes with final remarks and a discussion of future work.

2 Multiresolution Paint Systems

A multiresolution paint system allows the user to view and modify an image at multiple resolution levels.

The painting process consists of a cycle in which the following tasks are repeatedly executed:

$$\text{modify image at level } x$$
$$\text{move up or down a level}$$

For this, the system must support:

- Multiresolution Image Representation;

- Painting and Compositing at Multiple Levels.

We can classify multiresolution paint systems with respect to the way they implement the image data structure and the operations mentioned above.

2.1 Multiresolution Image Representations

There are two basic ways to represent an image at multiple resolutions: with a *lowpass* pyramid or with a *bandpass* pyramid.

---

[1] Courant Institute of Mathematical Sciences, New York University, 719 Broadway 12th Floor, New York, NY, 10003. **perlin@cs.nyu.edu**

[2] IMPA – Instituto de Matemática Pura e Aplicada, Estrada Dona Castorina 110, Rio de Janeiro, RJ, Brazil, 22460-320. **lvelho@visgraf.impa.br**

Permission to make digital/hard copy of part or all of this work for personal or classroom use is granted without fee provided that copies are not made or distributed for profit or commercial advantage, the copyright notice, the title of the publication and its date appear, and notice is given that copying is by permission of ACM, Inc. To copy otherwise, to republish, to post on servers, or to redistribute to lists, requires prior specific permission and/or a fee.

© 1995   ACM-0-89791-701-4/95/008 $3.50

A lowpass pyramid consists of multiple copies of the image at different resolutions, [11]. In Figure 1(a) we show an example of a lowpass pyramid with 4 levels.

A bandpass pyramid consists of a coarse resolution version of the image, together with a sequence of image details that are required to produce finer resolution versions of the image from coarse versions, [2]. The bandpass pyramid can be constructed by taking differences between consecutive levels of the lowpass pyramid. In Figure 1(b) we show an example of a bandpass pyramid with 4 levels. The images in the bandpass pyramid may contain negative values. For this reason, the figure shows zero values as middle gray.

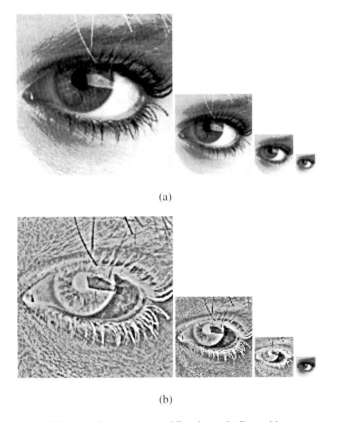

(a)

(b)

Figure 1: Lowpass (a) and Bandpass (b) Pyramids

Note that the lowpass pyramid is a redundant representation since the same information is present at all levels of the pyramid. The bandpass pyramid, on the other hand, is not redundant because it keeps only the information necessary to go from coarse to fine resolution levels.

A Wavelet pyramid is a kind of bandpass pyramid which discriminates image details along the horizontal, vertical and diagonal directions, [6].

2.2 Multiresolution Painting and Compositing

There are two main ways in which image operations can be incorporated into a multiresolution paint system: by re-execution or by lazy evaluation.

If the system allows the image to be represented at arbitrarily high resolutions, then it is not possible to perform image operations at all levels simultaneously during the interaction cycle. Multiresolution paint systems generally deal with this as follows: while the user is painting, the system only updates the currently visible level. Changes to the image are cached, to be propagated to other

resolution levels at a later time. What distinguishes different implementations of image operations is the strategy used to postpone the propagation of changes.

If a re-execution strategy is used, changes are cached as prescriptions for redrawing. When the user moves to another level of detail, all cached operations are re-executed at that level.

If a lazy evaluation strategy is used, modifications to the image are iteratively propagated through the image pyramid when the user magnifies the view to successively more detailed levels. Changes that will affect higher resolutions are evaluated only when the user first magnifies the view sufficiently to see these resolutions.

2.3 Classification of Multiresolution Paint Systems

The multiresolution image data structures and operations described above have a direct correspondence with one another. Accordingly, there are two types of multiresolution paint systems:

I – Lowpass pyramid + Re-execution strategy

II – Bandpass pyramid + Lazy evaluation strategy

Examples of type *I* systems are Live Picture [5] and XRes [12]. Examples of type *II* systems are the Haar wavelet [1] and the B-spline wavelet [10] paint programs.

The general idea of multiresolution painting tools applies equally well to painting systems of types *I* and *II*. Although in this paper we will emphasize implementation techniques that are more suited to systems of type *II*, the same techniques could be used with proper changes in systems of type *I*.

3 Multiresolution Textures

In this section we introduce the concept of multiscale textures and discuss how they are implemented.

3.1 Motivation

Let us say that a user of a paint system wishes to paint with a "rock" generating brush. After painting, the user should subsequently be able to zoom in and continue to see ever finer details of the rock texture.

Alternatively, if the user paints with a "checkerboard" brush, then no matter how far s/he zooms into the checkerboard texture, the boundaries between the white and black squares should always remain sharp.

Let us now suppose that the user paints some rock, then zooms in a bit and paints some translucent checkerboard over the rock. As the user zooms in, arbitrarily small rock details should still be visible behind the checkerboard, but attenuated. Both of the composited textures should continue to reveal more high frequency detail as the user's view zooms in.

The user should, for example, be able to paint with a brush which consists of one part checkerboard and two parts rock, or in fact to freely mix any such texture elements.

In this manner, the user should be able to paint with and to composite many different layers of procedural texture, with the expectation that all visible layers will appear in the proper proportion at all levels of detail.

3.2 How to do this

In order to implement this behavior we have developed a model for multiscale painted texture that allows procedural textures to be combined additively.

The key insight is that texture must be added in two distinct ways:

(1) Whenever the user paints a texture, the system must display that texture's initial appearance.

(2) As the user successively magnifies the view, the system must continue to add detail to the painted texture.

It is the responsibility of the texture procedure to perform these two functions.

To make this all happen properly and efficiently, we need two tools: Procedural Bandpass Pyramids and Procedural Ink.

3.3 Procedural Bandpass Pyramids

To do sharpening properly, we use procedural bandpass pyramids. First let us briefly review bandpass image pyramids. Each level of a bandpass pyramid gives the difference in detail between successive submagnifications of an image. Consider an image of resolution $2^n \times 2^n$. If we want to view this image at a resolution of $2^{n-1} \times 2^{n-1}$, we can blur it using a smoothing filter and then decimate. If the image is then blown up again with a good interpolation filter, it will appear blurry. Information has been lost. We must add a correction to each pixel of this blurry image in order to recreate the original image. This correction is itself a $2^n \times 2^n$ image containing the image details that were lost.

If we apply the same process to the decimated image, recursively, we can create a sequence of such detail images with descending resolutions: $2^n \times 2^n, 2^{n-1} \times 2^{n-1}, \ldots 2 \times 2$. This sequence of images constitutes a bandpass pyramid [2].

Once we have its bandpass pyramid, we can reconstitute an image at any submagnification. Beginning with a single pixel, we magnify and add the 2×2 bandpass image, then repeat with the 4×4 bandpass image, and so on. The pixels of the $2^k \times 2^k$ image of a bandpass pyramid are called "level-k bandpass coefficients".

A multiresolution paint system can show an image at various scales. Bandpass coefficients make up the difference between the less detailed view that is visible when the image is small, and the more detailed image that is available after magnifying by two. If we look at it this way, we can see that as we continue to magnify the user's view of a texture, our texture procedure should correspondingly add in the next level of bandpass coefficients, so that the texture will always have sharp detail.

Images are finite. At some point a multiresolution paint system will magnify the view beyond any stored image's resolution. For levels beyond this, the image simply becomes blurrier, since it can contribute no more bandpass coefficients. In other words, the image's bandpass pyramid is of finite depth.

But procedural textures are not so restricted. We can define a "procedural" bandpass pyramid which given a type, and values for x, y, and $level$, returns the difference in a texture's appearance when viewed at successive magnifications. Procedural bandpass pyramids can be of infinite depth.

Here is a simple example. It is well known that the appearance of rock can be synthesized by $1/f$ noise [9]. The difference in this texture's appearance between successive magnifications is just the addition of attenuated random noise at the higher magnification. A procedure that simulates a bandpass pyramid with this behavior is quite simple to define:

$$\text{add\_texture}(\text{ROCK}, x, y, level) := \frac{\text{pseudorandom}(x, y, level)}{2^{level/2}}$$

where the pseudorandom function is implemented by the same permutation method used to choose pseudorandom gradients from Z^3 for the Noise function [9].

The tricky aspect of this process is that we need to sharpen each painted texture only the first time that the view is magnified to a new level of greatest detail. For example, if the user paints a texture,

then zooms in and out a few times, we do not want to add bandpass coefficients to the texture again and again. The result would be incorrect. For this reason, texture propagation is controlled by procedural "ink".

3.4 Procedural Ink

In the sections that follow, we will use the phrase "texture instance" to refer to a primitive texture component. Some examples are: rock of a particular scale, a checkerboard of a certain size, sawtooth stripes of a particular width, or a source image texture painted on at a certain scale. We build all textures as combinations of texture instances.

Procedural ink is texture in latent state. We represent it as a vector of amplitudes; each element of the ink vector modulates the amplitude of one texture instance. The first ink channel is reserved for $ink.alpha$ – the attenuation of the ink vector itself. All elements of the ink vector will be attenuated by this $ink.alpha$.

Textures are mixed by compositing and layering ink vectors. The resulting composite ink vector is then used to control a texture generator procedure. Here is a key point: Because all elements of an ink vector are premultiplied by $ink.alpha$, we can mix textures simply by adding various ink vectors.

As noted above, we want to do sharpening only the first time that a viewer magnifies a painted area to a new view. In order to accomplish this we need a form of lazy evaluation. This is where the ink comes in. Ink controls when the texture gets sharpened. The key property of ink is that it flows downhill – toward levels of ever greater detail. As ink flows down, it causes the system to refine those texture instances which the ink modulates.

More precisely, each element of the ink vector is used to scale the bandpass coefficients that must be added in order to sharpen one texture instance.

Ink is only used for texture refinement at the moment that it first enters a view level. This will happen only in one case: when there is ink at the current view, and then the user magnifies the view. At this time, the used ink leaves the coarser level, and pools at the more detailed level, waiting for the user to further magnify the view.

Note that there can be considerable delay between the time that a texture is painted and the time that this lazy-evaluation sharpening occurs. For example, the user might paint at some level, then *decrease* the magnification, zooming out to paint something somewhere else. Meanwhile, the ink is still sitting at the former level. When the user later returns to that view and magnifies, only then will the ink continue its downward journey.

4 Where Texture is called

Texture is called in two places: once as the user interactively paints, and again when the view is magnified, in order to add bandpass coefficients.

4.1 Texturing during painting

When the user paints at a sample using *drawing_ink*, and with opacity *drawing_alpha*, then the *color*, *alpha* and *ink* at the sample are modified as follows:

(1) $color := \text{texture}(drawing\_ink) \text{ OVER}_{drawing\_alpha} \, color$

(2) $alpha := 1.0 \text{ OVER}_{drawing\_alpha} \, alpha$

(3) $ink := drawing\_ink \text{ OVER}_{drawing\_alpha} \, ink$

where "b OVER_t a" denotes linear interpolation $a + t(b - a)$, *texture* is a compound procedural texture as defined in subsection 5.2, and *ink* is a prescription for evaluating the procedural texture.

This is the point where the ink is first injected into the system, and where the first, coarse view of the texture is painted. Note that the new color is merged directly into the sample. There is no need to explicitly store back-to-front layers.

4.2 Texture refinement during magnification

Texture is also invoked when the user increases the magnification level of the view. As the user's view changes from a coarser level to a more detailed level, ink flows down to this new level, so that more texture detail can be induced.

When the view is magnified from a coarser to a more detailed level, we need to propagate both *color* and *ink* to the new level. To describe this process, we define:

- *detail*: the portion of a sample's color at the more detailed level that was too finely detailed to be visible at the coarser level. This quantity is generated by the multiresolution paint system at the moment that magnification was reduced. If this is the first time that we have ever visited the more detailed level, then this quantity will be zero. In our implementation, this quantity is computed from B-spline wavelets.

- *coarse*: a magnified view of what is currently visible at the coarser level.

- *new_ink*: a magnified view of the new ink from all coarser levels which now needs to flow down to this more detailed level.

Let us first review the magnification procedure in a multiresolution paint system that uses lazy evaluation, but that does not support procedural texture. In such a system, *ink* is just a vector of [*red, green, blue, alpha*].

Let us consider the situation where the user has painted with *new_ink* at some coarser level *after* the last time s/he had visited the next more detailed level. Now the user wants to magnify the view. Because the system has lazy evaluation, this *new_ink* will not yet be incorporated into the more detailed level. To incorporate this *new_ink*, we do the following steps at the more detailed level:

(1) *color* := *coarse* + (1 - *new_ink.alpha*) * *detail*

(2) *ink* := *new_ink* OVER$_{new\_ink.alpha}$ *ink*

Notice that we do not do an OVER operation in step (1). This is because the *coarse* value already incorporates all *new_ink* that has been painted at all coarser levels. Only the detail is out of date.

After this, we erase (i.e. set to zero) all the ink at the coarse level that has flowed to the more detailed level. The general effect is that as the user's view is progressively magnified, *ink* at coarser levels continually "flows down" to more detailed levels. As it does so, its appearance becomes progressively blurrier.

To support procedural texture, we need only to add a term to step (1):

(1) *color* := *coarse* + texture(*new_ink*)
                + (1 - *new_ink.alpha*) * *detail*

Note that all elements of *new_ink* are already attenuated by *new_ink.alpha*. The result is that all added texture is attenuated by *new_ink.alpha*. That is why we simply add texture, instead of overlaying it on top of the detail.

Now as the ink flows down, it is continually refined.

5 From Ink to Texture

Texture comes in different "types". Each type requires a different refinement method.

In the following sections, we describe how texture is combined, show various texture procedures, and give some examples.

5.1 Types and Instances

As described above, a procedural texture is built up by adding bandpass coefficients to each texture instance modulated by the ink vector, at successive levels of detail.

The "type" of a texture instance identifies the method that is used for adding bandpass coefficients at each level. The method chosen will determine the general look of the texture.

Each texture instance is identified by:

- its type

- its base magnification level (equal to the view level at which the user painted the texture).

A unique element of the ink vector is allocated to each texture instance, the first time that instance is painted. This ink element contains the amplitude that will be used to scale the bandpass coefficients as that texture instance is refined.

5.2 Adding Texture

All texture instances are combined linearly. The texture procedure simply loops through the ink vector and sums the contribution from each instance i:

$$\sum_i amplitude_i \ * \ \text{add\_texture}(type_i, x, y, level - base\_level_i)$$

Note that this arrangement allows us to linearly combine different ink vectors. As any ink element is attenuated, the detail values added to its corresponding texture instance will be equally attenuated.

5.3 Some Examples of Texture Types

For each type of texture, there is a corresponding procedural bandpass pyramid; a function that computes how much detail must be added into that texture at each level. We now describe the procedural bandpass pyramid used to construct various specific types of texture. Each type is specified in **Boldface**, followed by its refinement method.

The variable *dlevel* below refers to the difference between the current level and the texture instance's base magnification level. Note that *dlevel* = 0 when the first coarse texture is painted, and that *dlevel* > 0 whenever the texture is subsequently sharpened.

White:
     if *dlevel* = 0 then 1 else 0

Rock:
     pseudorandom($x,y,dlevel$) / $2^{dlevel/2}$

Stripes:
     sqr_wave(x) / $(dlevel + 0.4)^{0.1}$

Sawtooth:
     saw_wave(x) / $(dlevel + 1)^{0.14}$

Squares:
     sqr_wave(x) * sqr_wave(y) / $(dlevel + 0.1)^{0.14}$

where sqr_wave and saw_wave are defined as follows:

```
square_wave(x)
    if i = 0 or i = n/2-1 then 1
    else if i = n/2 or i = n-1 then -1 else 0

saw_wave(x)
    if i = 0 then 1 else if i = n-1 then -1 else 0
```

with $n := 2^{dlevel+1}$ and $i := x \bmod n$.

In practice each of the above power curves is computed only once, and then stored in a table, which is subsequently indexed by *dlevel*. These particular power curves depend on the B-spline reconstruction kernel that we use, [10]. A system with a different reconstruction kernel would require different curves.

White is handled as a special case, since White texture requires no sharpening. For this reason, in practice we modulate all White texture instances in one element of *drawing_ink*. We change the amplitude of this element each time the user lightens or darkens the brush.

6 Examples

In this section we give some examples of the procedural multiresolution textures and their use. First we show some examples of magnifying and compositing textures. Then we present a more advanced example: creating an entire multiresolution terrain model by painting with procedural textures.

6.1 Simple Examples

Figure 2(a) shows the name of a beautiful city written with a sawtooth generating brush. Figure 2(b) is a magnified view into the dot above the letter "i". Figure 2(c) is magnified even further. Each image is four times the magnification of the previous image. We note that the intensity ramps in the horizontal direction are piecewise linear.

Figure 3 shows successive magnifications of a translucent blending of three active textures: rock, squares, and horizontal stripes. Note how in Figure 3(c) the squares texture smoothly blends into the stripes texture.

Figure 4 shows the effect of a smoothing brush. This brush simply averages neighboring values in the image, and blends the result with White ink. The White ink element modulates brightness; the alpha ink element modulates opacity. The most important effect of this brush is that it locally reduces or eliminates texture sharpening. Figure 4(a) shows rock texture. Figure 4(b) shows an "X" drawn over this with a smoothing brush. Figure 4(c) is a magnified view into just below the central cross of the "X".

6.2 Advanced Example: A Terrain Model

Terrain modeling is an important application where fractal images may be used to describe elevation data [3], [4]. This example exploits the expressiveness of procedural textures in a system that combines interactive painting with 3D visualization.

Figure 5 shows a terrain being interactively modeled in the system. On the right, the user sees an interactive height field view of the intensity image. First we will describe this interaction tool, and then we will discuss the example in Figure 5.

The user sees a perspective view of intensity, as a height field mesh. The mesh is rendered back to front, so no Z buffer is required. The brightness at each location on this mesh is composed of a weighted sum of that location's height and directional derivatives. The user can interactively pan and tilt this view with the mouse.

In order to maintain interactivity on platforms that do not have polygon transformation hardware, we use progressive refinement. The user can change the view and see the results in real time over a coarse mesh approximation. Then while the user goes back to painting, the terrain model gradually increases to full resolution over several seconds, as a background activity. Any further changes to the view during this time will interrupt the refinement process and start it again.

In figure 5(a) we see a height field created by magnifying the view into a squiggle drawn with a rock texture. In figure 5(b) we

have drawn a new rock texture instance as a wavy horizontal across the image. In the height field view, this appears as a mountainous ridge across the terrain. We also have drawn with a dark erasing brush near the bottom of the image to simulate the flat terrain of a river.

In figure 5(c) we magnify the view into the bay that appeared in the lower left of figure 5(b). Then, we sprinkle some individual bright squares near the river. In the height field view these appear as tall buildings. Note that the edges of these buildings will be perfectly sharp, no matter how close we get.

In this same figure, we have also used a transparent brush to paint some squares generating texture at several scales, in order to simulate a large cityscape. This can be seen at the left edge of the image. As we paint, the opacity of the brush controls the height of the buildings at the brush. The more time we spend over any area, the taller the buildings grow.

This entire process took less than a minute of painting.

7 Using Images

In this section we discuss how images can be used to complement our framework for multiresolution procedural textures.

7.1 Images as Procedural Brushes

In addition to using textures that are strictly procedural, we can use a multiresolution image as a texture source [7]. This enables many useful paint operations and provides a way to seamlessly incorporate multiresolution images into the system.

A multiresolution source image is represented internally by a bandpass pyramid, ie. a coarse image at the base resolution level and a sequence of detail images for the other levels.

The corresponding data structure is:

- size of the base image ($n \times m$)

- number of levels of the bandpass pyramid

- bandpass pyramid

The encapsulation of images in a procedural brush is done by associating a source image with a texture instance. When the user selects a source image to paint, a new texture is instantiated: an index of the ink vector is allocated, a reference from this index to the data structure representing the selected image is established, and the base level is set to the current resolution level.

An image texture is similar to a procedural texture with the exception that the values are copied from its bandpass pyramid instead of being generated algorithmically. The operation is divided in two parts: at the base level pixels are copied from the base image onto the canvas; when the user changes level and the image needs to be refined, the bandpass coefficients are added.

Before using a source image as a procedural brush, we need first to construct a bandpass pyramid for it. For this purpose, we employ a modified version of the wavelet transform engine used in the system. This can be done as an independent operation by a program that builds a library of source image brushes or as a built-in operation of the paint system to create a source image brush from any rectangular region of the canvas.

Source images can be replicated by the procedural brush to cover a larger region of the canvas by using a rectangular tiling arrangement. Image replication has to be taken into account in the construction of the bandpass pyramid. If we wish the texture to tile the source image, then we must employ "toroidal" end conditions when building the pyramid, with both horizontal and vertical wraparound.

7.2 Synthesizing Textures from Image Samples

The design of procedural textures usually requires some kind of programming [9]. A powerful alternative to this way of creating procedural textures is the automatic generation of a procedural bandpass pyramid from a sample image of the texture.

For this, we need a mechanism to predict the coefficients of the next level of the pyramid based on the current ones. In some cases, the prediction rules are very simple. For example, in the case of perfectly sharp edges and fractals the coefficients are multiples of each other as shown in subsection 5.3.

In the general case, the mappings between coefficients at different levels are inherently non-linear and multi-modal. We are currently investigating a technique to generate these mappings from a statistical analysis of a sample texture. This technique is similar to the one used for image compression in [8]. The method is based on a vector quantization of the bandpass pyramid and a subsequent analysis of the correlation between the codes generated by the vector quantizer. This analysis allows us to build a prediction table for each code in a codebook, which gives a mapping from coarser to more detailed bandpass coefficients. The texture procedure then uses the prediction tables to generate new bandpass coefficients during refinement.

8 Conclusions

In this paper we have introduced the concept of actively procedural multiresolution paint textures. These are live picture elements that continue to refine themselves when viewed at magnifications greater than the one at which they were originally painted.

8.1 Summary

We presented a framework to implement these active textures and incorporate them as procedural brushes into a multiresolution paint system.

We have described a simple way to linearly combine primitive texture elements in order to create complex composite textures. We have explained how to use source images in procedural brushes. We have discussed how to automatically generate multiresolution procedural textures from an image sample of the texture. We have given several examples of the use of our framework in a multiresolution paint system.

In conclusion, active procedural texture constitutes a powerful new painting tool to more fully exploit the power of multiresolution paint systems.

8.2 Future Work

Future work should go in several main directions:

- Enhancing the capabilities of the current framework;

- Adding more texture generators of interest;

- Developing an environment for the design of procedural textures;

- Investigating extrapolation techniques to generate missing image details.

The current framework could be enhanced by incorporating the notion of layers and interpreted code, as in [9], to combine texture instances in arbitrary ways. This capability would allow the generation of arbitrarily complex infinite resolution textures from simple primitives and operators.

We also plan to build up a family of texture generators for simulating terrains of architectural interest. This would include treetops, shrubbery, the appearance of rows of houses – including slanted roofs and chimneys and even roof texture – and so on. The idea is that an Architect could work up a sketch of a landscaping, or cluster of dwellings, or a city, using broad strokes – perhaps just to play with the feel of how various arrangements would look.

From a production standpoint, it would be good to have a complete environment for designing multiresolution procedural textures. This would include programming, testing and debugging facilities that can work together with the paint system.

A final area of investigation is the use of techniques for analyzing the correlation between levels of the bandpass pyramid described in Section 3 in order to perform extrapolation of coarse resolution images when detail information is not available.

Acknowledgements

The authors wish to thank Lance Williams for fruitful discussions and for pointing out the work of [8]. Many thanks also to Stephane Mallat for several valuable suggestions. Special thanks to Karl Sims for inspiring comments on multiscale noise.

This work was partially supported by grants from MCT/CNPq – Conselho Nacional de Desenvolvimento Científico e Tecnológico and from the National Science Foundation.

REFERENCES

[1] Deborah Berman, Jason Bartell, and David Salesin. Multiresolution painting and compositing. *Computer Graphics, Annual Conference Series (SIGGRAPH '94 Proceedings)*, pages 85–90, 1994.

[2] Peter J. Burt. The laplacian pyramid as a compact image code. *IEEE Transactions on Communications*, 31:532–540, April 1983.

[3] Alain Fournier, Don Fussell, and Loren Carpenter. Computer rendering of stochastic models. *Communications of the ACM*, 25(6):371–384, June 1982.

[4] John Peter Lewis. Texture synthesis for digital painting. *Computer Graphics (SIGGRAPH '84 Proceedings)*, 18(3):245–252, July 1984.

[5] Lively pictures. *Byte Magazine*, 20(1):171–174, 1995. Live Picture – Product Review.

[6] Stephane Mallat. Multifrequency channel decompositions of images and wavelet models. *IEEE Trans. on Acoust. Signal Speech Process.*, 37(12):2091–2110, 1989.

[7] Joan M. Ogden, Edward H. Adelson, J.R. Bergen, and Peter J. Burt. Pyramid-based computer graphics. *RCA Engineer*, 30(5):4–13, September–October 1985.

[8] Alex Pentland and Bradley Horowitz. A practical approach to fractal-based image compression. In *Proceedings of Data Compression Conference*, pages 176–185, held in Snowbird, UT, 1991. IEEE Computer Society Press.

[9] Ken Perlin. An image synthesizer. *Computer Graphics (SIGGRAPH '85 Proceedings)*, 19(3):287–293, 1985.

[10] Ken Perlin and Luiz Velho. A wavelet representation for unbounded resolution painting. Technical report, New York University, New York, 1992.

[11] Lance Williams. Pyramidal parametrics. *Computer Graphics (SIGGRAPH '83 Proceedings)*, 17(3):1–11, July 1983.

[12] Xres, the alternative to photoshop? *Mac Format Magazine*, 23, pages 72–74, 1995. XRes – Graphics Software Review.

(a)

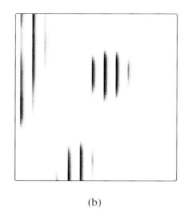
(b)

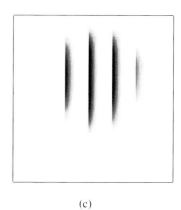
(c)

Figure 2: Sawtooth Texture

(a)

(b)

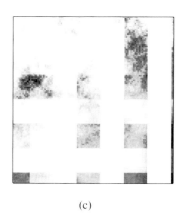
(c)

Figure 3: Blending of rock, squares, and horizontal stripes

(a)

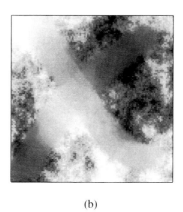
(b)

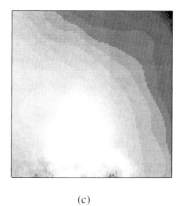
(c)

Figure 4: The effect of a smoothing brush

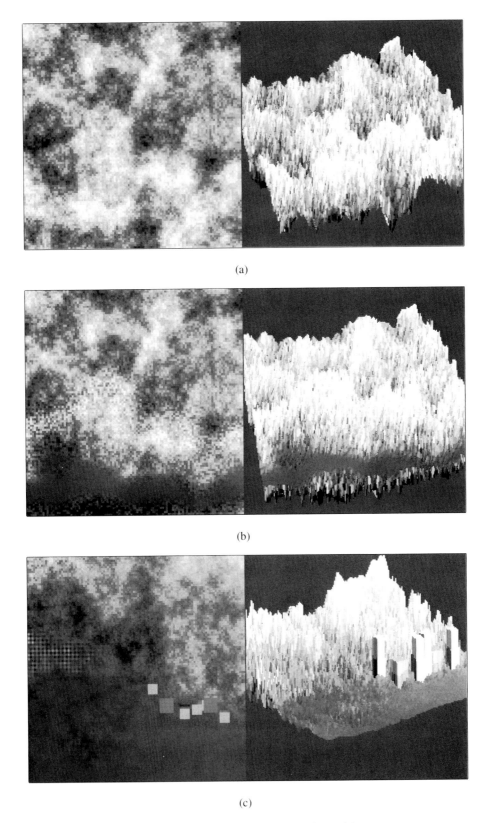

(a)

(b)

(c)

Figure 5: Interactive design of a terrain model

Spherical Wavelets:
Efficiently Representing Functions on the Sphere

Peter Schröder[*][†]   Wim Sweldens[*][‡]

University of South Carolina

Abstract

Wavelets have proven to be powerful bases for use in numerical analysis and signal processing. Their power lies in the fact that they only require a small number of coefficients to represent general functions and large data sets accurately. This allows compression and efficient computations. Classical constructions have been limited to simple domains such as intervals and rectangles. In this paper we present a wavelet construction for scalar functions defined on the sphere. We show how biorthogonal wavelets with custom properties can be constructed with the *lifting scheme*. The bases are extremely easy to implement and allow *fully adaptive subdivisions*. We give examples of functions defined on the sphere, such as topographic data, bidirectional reflection distribution functions, and illumination, and show how they can be efficiently represented with spherical wavelets.

CR Categories and Subject Descriptors: I.3.0 [Computer Graphics]: *General*; G.1.0 [Numerical Analysis]: *General – Numerical Algorithms*; G.1.1 *Interpolation – Smoothing*; G.1.2 *Approximation – Nonlinear Approximation*.

Additional Key Words and Phrases: wavelets, sphere.

1 Introduction

1.1 Wavelets

Over the last decade wavelets have become an exceedingly powerful and flexible tool for computations and data reduction. They offer both theoretical characterization of smoothness, insights into the structure of functions and operators, and practical numerical tools which lead to faster computational algorithms. Examples of their use in computer graphics include surface and volume illumination computations [16, 29], curve and surface modeling [17], and animation [18] among others. Given the high computational demands and the quest for speed in computer graphics, the increasing exploitation of wavelets comes as no surprise.

While computer graphics applications can benefit greatly from wavelets, these applications also provide new challenges to the underlying wavelet technology. One such challenge is the construction of wavelets on general domains as they appear in graphics applications.

Classically, wavelet constructions have been employed on infinite domains (such as the real line $\mathbf{R}$ and plane $\mathbf{R}^2$). Since most practical computations are confined to finite domains a number of boundary constructions have also been developed [5]. However,

[*]Department of Mathematics.

[†]Department of Computer Science.

[‡]Department of Computer Science, Katholieke Universiteit Leuven, Belgium.

Permission to make digital/hard copy of part or all of this work for personal or classroom use is granted without fee provided that copies are not made or distributed for profit or commercial advantage, the copyright notice, the title of the publication and its date appear, and notice is given that copying is by permission of ACM, Inc. To copy otherwise, to republish, to post on servers, or to redistribute to lists, requires prior specific permission and/or a fee.

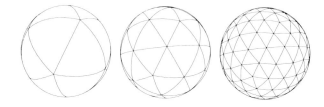

Figure 1: *The geodesic sphere construction starting with the icosahedron on the left (subdivision level 0) and the next 2 subdivision levels.*

wavelet type constructions for more general manifolds have only recently been attempted and are still in their infancy.

Our work is inspired by the ground breaking work of Lounsbery *et al.*[20, 19] (hereafter referred to as LDW). While their primary goal was to efficiently represent *surfaces* themselves we examine the case of efficiently representing *functions defined on a surface*, and in particular the case of the sphere.

Although the sphere appears to be a simple manifold, techniques from $\mathbf{R}^2$ do not easily extend to the sphere. Wavelets are no exception. The first construction of wavelets on the sphere was introduced by Dahlke *et al.*[6] using a tensor product basis where one factor is an exponential spline. To our knowledge a computer implementation of this basis does not exist at this moment. A continuous wavelet transform and its semi-discretization were proposed in [13]. Both these approaches make use of a (φ, θ) parameterization of the sphere. This is the main difference with our method, which is parameterization independent.

Aside from being of theoretical interest, a wavelet construction for the sphere leading to efficient algorithms, has practical applications since many computational problems are naturally stated on the sphere. Examples from computer graphics include: manipulation and display of earth and planetary data such as topography and remote sensing imagery, simulation and modeling of bidirectional reflection distribution functions, illumination algorithms, and the modeling and processing of directional information such as environment maps and view spheres.

In this paper we describe a simple technique for constructing biorthogonal wavelets on the sphere with customized properties. The construction is an incidence of a fairly general scheme referred to as the *lifting scheme* [27, 28].

The outline of the paper is as follows. We first give a brief review of applications and previous work in computer graphics involving functions on the sphere. This is followed by a discussion of wavelets on the sphere. In Section 3 we explain the basic machinery of lifting and the fast wavelet transform. After a section on implementation, we report on simulations and conclude with a discussion and suggestions for further research.

1.2 Representing Functions on the Sphere

Geographical information systems have long had a need to represent sampled data on the sphere. A number of basic data structures originated here. Dutton [10] proposed the use of a geodesic sphere

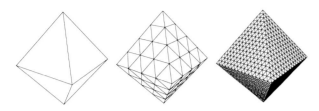

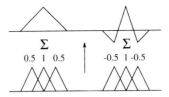

Figure 3: *A simple example of refinement on the line. The basis functions at the top can be expressed as linear combinations of the refined functions at the bottom.*

Figure 2: *Recursive subdivision of the octahedral base shape as used by LDW for spherelike surfaces. Level 0 is shown on the left followed by levels 2 and 4.*

construction to model planetary relief, see Figure 1 for a picture of the underlying subdivision. More recently, Fekete [12] described the use of such a structure for rendering and managing spherical geographic data. By using hierarchical subdivision data structures these workers naturally built sparse adaptive representations. There also exist many non-hierarchical interpolation methods on the sphere (for an overview see [22]).

An important example from computer graphics concerns the representation of functions defined over a set of directions. Perhaps the most notable in this category are bidirectional reflectance distribution functions (BRDFs) and radiance. The BRDF, $f_r(\vec{\omega}_i, \vec{x}, \vec{\omega}_o)$, describes the relationship at a point $\vec{x}$ on a surface between incoming radiance from direction $\vec{\omega}_i$ and outgoing radiance in direction $\vec{\omega}_o$. It can be described using spherical harmonics, the natural extension of Fourier basis functions to the sphere, see e.g. [30]. These basis functions are globally supported and suffer from some of the same difficulties as Fourier representations on the line such as ringing. To our knowledge, no fast (FFT like) algorithm is available for spherical harmonics. Westin *et al.* [30] used spherical harmonics to model BRDFs derived from Monte Carlo simulations of micro geometry. Noting some of the disadvantages of spherical harmonics, Gondek *et al.*[15] used a geodesic sphere subdivision construction [10, 12] in a similar context.

The result of illumination computations, the radiance $L(\vec{x}, \vec{\omega})$, is a function which is defined over all surfaces and all directions. For example, Sillion *et al.* [26] used spherical harmonics to model the directional distribution of radiance. As in the case of BRDF representations, the disadvantages of using spherical harmonics to represent radiance are due to the global support and high cost of evaluation. Similarly no locally controlled level of detail can be used.

In finite element based illuminations computations wavelets have proven to be powerful bases, see e.g. [24, 3]. By either reparameterizing directions over the set of visible surfaces [24], or mapping them to the unit square [3], wavelets defined on standard domains (rectangular patches) were used.

Mapping classical wavelets on some parameter domain onto the sphere by use of a parameterization provides one avenue to construct wavelets on the sphere. However, this approach suffers from distortions and difficulties due to the fact that no globally smooth parameterization of the sphere exists. The resulting wavelets are in some sense "contaminated" by the parameterization. We will examine the difficulties due to an underlying parameterization, as opposed to an *intrinsic* construction, when we discuss our construction.

We first give a simple example relating the compression of *surfaces* to the compression of functions defined *on surfaces*.

1.3 An Example

LDW constructs wavelets for surfaces of arbitrary topological type which are parameterized over a polyhedral base complex. For the case of the sphere they employed an octahedral subdivision domain

(see Figure 2). In this framework a given goal surface such as the earth is parameterized over an octahedron whose triangular faces are successively subdivided into four smaller triangles. Each vertex can now be displaced radially to the limit surface. The resulting sequence of surfaces then represents the multiple levels of detail representation of the final surface.

As pointed out by LDW compressing surfaces is closely related to compressing functions *on surfaces*. Consider the case of the unit sphere and the function $f(s) = f(\theta, \varphi) = \cos^2 \theta$ with $s \in S^2$. We can think of the graph of this function as a surface over the sphere whose height (displaced along the normal) is the value of the function f. Hence an algorithm which can compress surfaces can also compress the graph of a scalar function defined over some surface.

At this point the domain over which the compression is defined becomes crucial. Suppose we want to use the octahedron O. Define the projection $T : O \longrightarrow S^2$, $s = T(p) = p/\|p\|$. We then have $\tilde{f}(p) = f(T(p))$ with $p \in O$. Compressing $f(s)$ with wavelets on the sphere is now equivalent to compressing $\tilde{f}(p)$ with wavelets defined on the octahedron. While f is simply a quadratic function over the sphere, $\tilde{f}$ is considerably more complicated. For example a basis over the sphere which can represent quadratics exactly (see Section 3.4) will trivially represent f. The same basis over the octahedron will only be able to *approximate* $\tilde{f}$.

This example shows the importance of incorporating the underlying surface correctly for any construction which attempts to efficiently represent functions defined *on that surface*. In case of compression of surfaces themselves one has to assume some canonical domain. In LDW this domain was taken to be a polyhedron.

By limiting our program to functions defined on a fixed surface (sphere) we can custom tailor the wavelets to it and get more efficiency. This is one of the main points in which we depart from the construction in LDW.

2 Wavelets on the Sphere

2.1 Second Generation Wavelets

Wavelets are basis functions which represent a given function at multiple levels of detail. Due to their local support in both space and frequency, they are suited for sparse approximations of functions. Locality in space follows from their compact support, while locality in frequency follows from their smoothness (decay towards high frequencies) and vanishing moments (decay towards low frequencies). Fast $O(n)$ algorithms exist to calculate wavelet coefficients, making the use of wavelets efficient for many computational problems.

In the classic wavelet setting, i.e., on the real line, wavelets are defined as the dyadic translates and dilates of one particular, fixed function. They are typically built with the aid of a *scaling function*. Scaling functions and wavelets both satisfy refinement relations (or two scale relations). This means that a scaling function or wavelet at a certain level of resolution (j) can be written as a linear combination of scaling basis functions *of the same shape but scaled* at one level finer (level $j + 1$), see Figure 3 for an example.

The basic philosophy behind *second generation wavelets* is to build wavelets with all desirable properties (localization, fast transform) adapted to much more general settings than the real line, e.g.,

Functions	
$\varphi_{j,k}, \; k \in \mathcal{K}(j)$	primal scaling functions
$\tilde{\varphi}_{j,k}, \; k \in \mathcal{K}(j)$	dual scaling functions
$\psi_{j,m}, \; m \in \mathcal{M}(j)$	primal wavelets
$\tilde{\psi}_{j,m}, \; m \in \mathcal{M}(j)$	dual wavelets
Biorthogonality relationships	
$\langle \varphi_{j,k}, \tilde{\varphi}_{j,k'} \rangle = \delta_{k,k'}$	$\varphi_{j,k}$ and $\tilde{\varphi}_{j,k'}$ are biorthogonal
$\langle \psi_{j,m}, \tilde{\psi}_{j',m'} \rangle = \delta_{m,m'} \delta_{j,j'}$	$\psi_{j,m}$ and $\tilde{\psi}_{j',m'}$ are biorthogonal
$\langle \varphi_{j,k}, \tilde{\psi}_{j,m} \rangle = 0$	$V_j \perp \tilde{W}_j$
$\langle \psi_{j,m}, \tilde{\varphi}_{j,k} \rangle = 0$	$W_j \perp \tilde{V}_j$
Vanishing moment relations	
$\tilde{\psi}_{j,m}$ has N vanishing moments	$\varphi_{j,k}$ reprod. polyn. degree $< N$
$\psi_{j,m}$ has $\tilde{N}$ vanishing moments	$\tilde{\varphi}_{j,k}$ reprod. polyn. degree $< \tilde{N}$
Refinement relations	
$\varphi_{j,k} = \sum_{l \in \mathcal{K}(j+1)} h_{j,k,l}\, \varphi_{j+1,l}$	scaling function refinement eq.
$\tilde{\varphi}_{j,k} = \sum_{l \in \mathcal{K}(j+1)} \tilde{h}_{j,k,l}\, \tilde{\varphi}_{j+1,l}$	dual scaling function refinement eq.
$\psi_{j,m} = \sum_{l \in \mathcal{K}(j+1)} g_{j,m,l}\, \varphi_{j+1,l}$	wavelet refinement equation
$\tilde{\psi}_{j,m} = \sum_{l \in \mathcal{K}(j+1)} \tilde{g}_{j,m,l}\, \tilde{\varphi}_{j+1,l}$	dual wavelet refinement equation
$V_j = \text{clos span}\{\varphi_{j,k} \mid k \in \mathcal{K}(j)\}$	with V_0 the coarsest space
$W_j = \text{clos span}\{\psi_{j,m} \mid m \in \mathcal{M}(j)\}$	with W_0 the coarsest space
$V_j \oplus W_j = V_{j+1}$	wavelets encode difference between
	levels of approximation
Wavelet transforms	
$\lambda_{j,k} = \langle f, \tilde{\varphi}_{j,k} \rangle$	scaling function coefficient
$\gamma_{j,m} = \langle f, \tilde{\psi}_{j,m} \rangle$	wavelet coefficient
Forward Wavelet Transform (Analysis)	
$\lambda_{j,k} = \sum_{l \in \mathcal{K}(j)} \tilde{h}_{j,k,l}\, \lambda_{j+1,l}$	scaling function coeff., fine to coarse
$\gamma_{j,m} = \sum_{l \in \mathcal{M}(j)} \tilde{g}_{j,m,l}\, \lambda_{j+1,l}$	wavelet coeff., fine to coarse
Inverse Wavelet Transform (Synthesis)	
$\lambda_{j+1,l} = \sum_{k \in \mathcal{K}(j)} h_{j,k,l}\, \lambda_{j,k}$ $+ \sum_{m \in \mathcal{M}(j)} g_{j,m,l}\, \gamma_{j,m}$	scaling function coeff., coarse to fine

Table 1: *Quick reference to the notation and some basic relationships for the case of second generation biorthogonal wavelets.*

wavelets on manifolds. In order to consider wavelets on a surface, we need a construction of wavelets which are *adapted to a measure* on the surface. In the case of the real line (and classical constructions) the measure is dx, the usual translation invariant (Haar) Lebesgue measure. For a sphere we will denote the usual area measure by $d\omega$. Adaptive constructions rely on the realization that translation and dilation are not fundamental to obtain the wavelets with the desired properties. The notion that a basis function can be written as a finite linear combination of basis functions at a finer, more subdivided level, is maintained and forms the key behind the fast transform. The main difference with the classical wavelets is that the filter coefficients of second generation wavelets are not the same throughout, but can change locally to reflect the changing (non translation invariant) nature of the surface and its measure.

Classical wavelets and the corresponding filters are constructed with the aid of the Fourier transform. The underlying reason is that translation and dilation become algebraic operations after Fourier transform. In the setting of second generation wavelets, translation and dilation can no longer be used, and the Fourier transform thus becomes worthless as a construction tool. An alternative construction is provided by the lifting scheme.

2.2 Multiresolution Analysis

We first introduce multiresolution analysis and wavelets and set some notation. For more mathematical detail the reader is referred to [9]. All relationships are summarized in Table 1.

Consider the function space $L_2 = L_2(S^2, d\omega)$, i.e., all functions of finite energy defined over S^2. We define a multiresolution analysis as a sequence of closed subspaces $V_j \subset L_2$, with $j \geq 0$, so that

I $V_j \subset V_{j+1}$, (finer spaces have higher index)

II $\bigcup_{j \geq 0} V_j$ is dense in L_2,

III for each j, scaling functions $\varphi_{j,k}$ with $k \in \mathcal{K}(j)$ exist so that $\{\varphi_{j,k} \mid k \in \mathcal{K}(j)\}$ is a Riesz basis[1] of V_j.

Think of $\mathcal{K}(j)$ as a general index set where we assume that $\mathcal{K}(j) \subset \mathcal{K}(j+1)$. In the case of the real line we can take $\mathcal{K}(j) = 2^{-j}\mathbf{Z}$, while for an interval we might have $\mathcal{K}(j) = \{0, 2^{-j}, \ldots, 1-2^{-j}\}$. Note that, unlike the case of a classical multiresolution analysis, the scaling functions need not be translates or dilates of one particular function. Property (I) implies that for every scaling function $\varphi_{j,k}$, coefficients $\{h_{j,k,l}\}$ exist so that

$$\varphi_{j,k} = \sum_l h_{j,k,l}\, \varphi_{j+1,l}. \tag{1}$$

The $h_{j,k,l}$ are defined for $j \geq 0$, $k \in \mathcal{K}(j)$, and $l \in \mathcal{K}(j+1)$. Each scaling function satisfies a different refinement relation. In the classical case we have $h_{j,k,l} = h_{l-2k}$, i.e., the sequences $h_{j,k,l}$ are independent of scale and position.

Each multiresolution analysis is accompanied by a dual multiresolution analysis consisting of nested spaces $\tilde{V}_j$ with bases given by dual scaling functions $\tilde{\varphi}_{j,k}$, which are biorthogonal to the scaling functions:

$$\langle \varphi_{j,k}, \tilde{\varphi}_{j,k'} \rangle = \delta_{k,k'} \; \text{ for } \; k, k' \in \mathcal{K}(j),$$

where $\langle f, g \rangle = \int f\, g\, d\omega$ is the inner product on the sphere. The dual scaling functions satisfy refinement relations with coefficients $\{\tilde{h}_{j,k,l}\}$.

In case scaling functions and dual scaling functions coincide, ($\varphi_{j,k} = \tilde{\varphi}_{j,k}$ for all j and k) the scaling functions form an *orthogonal* basis. In case the multiresolution analysis and the dual multiresolution analysis coincide ($V_j = \tilde{V}_j$ for all j but not necessarily $\varphi_{j,k} = \tilde{\varphi}_{j,k}$) the scaling functions are *semi-orthogonal*. Orthogonality or semi-orthogonality sometimes imply globally supported basis functions, which has obvious practical disadvantages. We will assume neither and always work in the most general biorthogonal setting (neither the multiresolution analyses nor the scaling functions coincide), introduced for classical wavelets in [4].

One of the crucial steps when building a multiresolution analysis is the construction of the wavelets. They encode the difference between two successive levels of representation, i.e., they form a basis for the spaces W_j where $V_j \oplus W_j = V_{j+1}$. Consider the set of functions $\{\psi_{j,m} \mid j \geq 0, m \in \mathcal{M}(j)\}$, where $\mathcal{M}(j) \subset \mathcal{K}(j+1)$ is again an index set. If

1. the set is a Riesz basis for $L_2(S^2)$,
2. the set $\{\psi_{j,m} \mid m \in \mathcal{M}(j)\}$ is the Riesz basis of W_j,

we say that the $\psi_{j,m}$ define a spherical wavelet basis. Since $W_j \subset V_{j+1}$, we have

$$\psi_{j,m} = \sum_l g_{j,m,l}\, \varphi_{j+1,l} \; \text{ for } \; m \in \mathcal{M}(j). \tag{2}$$

An important property of wavelets is that they have vanishing moments. The wavelets $\psi_{j,m}$ have $\tilde{N}$ vanishing moments if $\tilde{N}$ independent polynomials $P_i, 0 \leq i < \tilde{N}$ exist so that

$$\langle \psi_{j,m}, P_i \rangle = 0,$$

for all $j \geq 0, m \in \mathcal{M}(j)$. Here the polynomials P_i are defined as the restriction to the sphere of polynomials on $\mathbf{R}^3$. Note that independent polynomials on $\mathbf{R}^3$ can become dependent after restriction to the sphere, e.g., $\{1, x^2, y^2, z^2\}$.

---

[1] A Riesz basis of some Hilbert space is a countable subset $\{f_k\}$ so that every element f of the space can be written uniquely as $f = \sum_k c_k\, f_k$, and positive constants A and B exist with $A \|f\|^2 \leq \sum_k |c_k|^2 \leq B \|f\|^2$.

For a given set of wavelets we have dual basis functions $\tilde{\psi}_{j,m}$ which are biorthogonal to the wavelets, or $\langle \psi_{j,m}, \tilde{\psi}_{j',m'} \rangle = \delta_{m,m'} \delta_{j,j'}$ for $j, j' \geqslant 0$, $m \in \mathcal{M}(j)$, $m' \in \mathcal{M}(j')$. This implies $\langle \tilde{\psi}_{j,m}, \varphi_{j,k} \rangle = \langle \tilde{\varphi}_{j,k}, \psi_{j,m} \rangle = 0$ for $m \in \mathcal{M}(j)$ and $k \in \mathcal{K}(j)$, and for $f \in \mathrm{L}_2$ we can write the expansion

$$f = \sum_{j,m} \langle \tilde{\psi}_{j,m}, f \rangle \, \psi_{j,m} = \sum_{j,m} \gamma_{j,m} \, \psi_{j,m} \qquad (3)$$

Given all of the above relationships we can also write the scaling functions $\varphi_{j+1,l}$ as a linear combination of *coarser* scaling functions and wavelets using the dual sequences (cf. Eqs. (1,2))

$$\varphi_{j+1,l} = \sum_k \tilde{h}_{j,k,l} \, \varphi_{j,k} + \sum_m \tilde{g}_{j,m,l} \, \psi_{j,m}.$$

If not stated otherwise summation indices are understood to run over $k \in \mathcal{K}(j)$, $l \in \mathcal{K}(j+1)$, and $m \in \mathcal{M}(j)$.

Given the set of scaling function coefficients of a function f, $\{\lambda_{n,k} = \langle f, \tilde{\varphi}_{j,k} \rangle \mid k \in \mathcal{K}(n)\}$ where n is some finest resolution level, the fast wavelet transform recursively calculates the $\{\gamma_{j,m} \mid 0 \leqslant j < n, \, m \in \mathcal{M}(j)\}$, and $\{\lambda_{0,k} \mid k \in \mathcal{K}(0)\}$, i.e., the coarser approximations to the underlying function. One step in the fast wavelet transform computes the coefficients at a coarser level (j) from the coefficients at a finer level $(j+1)$

$$\lambda_{j,k} = \sum_l \tilde{h}_{j,k,l} \, \lambda_{j+1,l} \text{ and } \gamma_{j,m} = \sum_l \tilde{g}_{j,m,l} \, \lambda_{j+1,l}.$$

A single step in the inverse transform takes the coefficients at the coarser levels and reconstructs coefficients at a finer level

$$\lambda_{j+1,l} = \sum_k h_{j,k,l} \, \lambda_{j,k} + \sum_m g_{j,m,l} \, \gamma_{j,m}.$$

3 Wavelet Construction and Transform

We first discuss the *lifting scheme* [27, 28]. After the introducing of the algebra we consider two important families of wavelet bases, interpolating and generalized Haar. At the end of this section we give a concrete example which shows how the properties of a given wavelet basis can be improved by lifting it and lead to better compression.

Lifting allows us to build our bases in a fully biorthogonal framework. This ensures that all bases are of finite (and small) support and the resulting filters are small and easy to derive. As we will see it is also straightforward to incorporate custom constraints into the resulting wavelets.

3.1 The Lifting Scheme

The whole idea of the lifting scheme is to start from one basic multiresolution analysis, which can be simple or even trivial, and construct a new, more performant one, i.e., the basis functions are smoother or the wavelets have more vanishing moments. In case the basic filters are finite we will have lifted filters which are also finite.

We will denote coefficients of the original multiresolution analysis with an extra superscript ^{o} (from old or original), starting with the filters $h^o_{j,k,l}$, $\tilde{h}^o_{j,k,l}$, $g^o_{j,k,l}$, and $\tilde{g}^o_{j,k,l}$. The *lifting scheme* now states that a new set of filters can be found as

$$h_{j,k,l} = h^o_{j,k,l}, \qquad g_{j,m,l} = g^o_{j,m,l} - \sum_k s_{j,k,m} \, h_{j,k,l},$$
$$\tilde{g}^o_{j,m,l} = \tilde{g}_{j,m,l}, \qquad \tilde{h}_{j,k,l} = \tilde{h}^o_{j,k,l} + \sum_m s_{j,k,m} \, \tilde{g}_{j,m,l},$$

and that, for any choice of $\{s_{j,k,m}\}$, the new filters will automatically be biorthogonal, and thus lead to an invertible transform. The scaling functions $\varphi_{j,l}$ are the same in the original and lifted multiresolution analysis, while the dual scaling function and primal wavelet change. They now satisfy refinement relations

$$\psi_{j,m} = \sum_l g^o_{j,m,l} \, \varphi_{j+1,l} - \sum_k s_{j,k,m} \, \varphi_{j,k} \qquad (4)$$
$$\tilde{\varphi}_{j,k} = \sum_l \tilde{h}^o_{j,k,l} \, \tilde{\varphi}_{j+1,l} + \sum_m s_{j,k,m} \, \tilde{\psi}_{j,m}.$$

Note that the dual wavelet has also changed since it is a linear combination (with the old coefficients $\tilde{g}^o$) of a now changed dual

scaling function. Equation (4) is the key to finding the $\{s_{j,k,m} \mid k\}$ coefficients. Since the scaling functions are the same as in the original multiresolution analysis, the only unknowns on the right hand side are the $s_{j,k,m}$. We can choose them freely to enforce some desired property on the wavelets $\psi_{j,m}$. For example, in case we want the wavelet to have vanishing moments, the condition that the integral of a wavelet multiplied with a certain polynomial P_i is zero can now be written as

$$0 = \sum_l g^o_{j,m,l} \langle \varphi_{j+1,l}, P_i \rangle - \sum_k s_{j,k,m} \langle \varphi_{j,k}, P_i \rangle.$$

For a fixed j and m, this is a linear equation in the unknowns $\{s_{j,k,m} \mid k\}$. If we choose the number of unknown coefficients $s_{j,k,m}$ equal to the number of equations N, we need to solve a linear system for each j and m of size $N \times N$. A priori we do not know if this linear system can always be solved. We will come back to this later.

The fast wavelet transform after lifting can be written as

$$\gamma_{j,m} = \sum_l \tilde{g}^o_{j,m,l} \, \lambda_{j+1,l}$$
$$\lambda_{j,k} = \sum_l \tilde{h}^o_{j,k,l} \, \lambda_{j+1,l} + \sum_m s_{j,k,m} \, \gamma_{j,m},$$

i.e., as a sequence of two steps. First the old dual high and low pass filters. Next the update of the old scaling function coefficients with the wavelet coefficients using the $\{s_{j,k,m} \mid k\}$. The inverse transform becomes

$$\lambda_{j+1,l} = \sum_k h^o_{j,k,l} \left(\lambda_{j,k} - \sum_m s_{j,k,m} \, \gamma_{j,m} \right) + \sum_m g^o_{j,m,l} \, \gamma_{j,m}.$$

Instead of writing everything as a sequence of two steps involving $\{s_{j,k,m} \mid k\}$ we could have formed the new filters h and $\tilde{g}$ first and then applied those in a single step. Structuring the new filters as two stages, however, simplifies the implementation considerably and is also more efficient.

Remarks:

1. The multiple index notation might look confusing at first sight, but its power lies in the fact that it immediately corresponds to the data structure of the implementation. The whole transform can also be written as one giant sparse matrix multiplication, but this would obscure the implementation ease of the lifting scheme.

2. Note how the inverse transform has a simple structure directly related to the forward transform. Essentially the inverse transform subtracts exactly the same linear combination of wavelet coefficients from $\lambda_{j,k}$ as was added in the forward transform.

3. It is also possible to keep the dual scaling function fixed and put the conditions on the dual wavelet. The machinery is exactly the same provided one switches primals and duals and thus toggles the tildes in the equations. We refer to this as the *dual lifting scheme*, which employs coefficients $\tilde{s}_{j,k,m}$. It allows us to improve the performance of the dual wavelet. Typically, the number of vanishing moments of the dual wavelet is important to achieve compression. Also, the lifting scheme and the dual lifting scheme can be alternated to bootstrap one's way up to a desired multiresolution analysis (cakewalk construction).

4. The construction in LDW can be seen as a special case of the lifting scheme. They use the degrees of freedom to achieve pseudo-orthogonality (i.e., orthogonality between scaling function and wavelets of one level within a small neighborhood) starting from an interpolating wavelet. The lifting scheme is more general in the sense that it uses a fully biorthogonal setting and that it can start from any multiresolution analysis with finite filters. The pseudo-orthogonalization requires the solution of linear systems which are of the size of the neighborhood (typically 24 by 24). Since many wavelets may in fact be the same caching of matrix computations is possible.

5. After finishing this work, the authors learned that a similar construction was obtained independently by Dahmen and collaborators. We refer to the original papers [2, 8] for details.

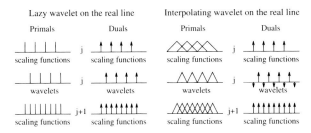

Figure 4: *For the Lazy wavelet all primals are Kronecker functions (1 at the origin, 0 otherwise), while all duals are unit pulses (Dirac distributions). Going from a finer to a coarser scale is achieved by subsampling with the missing samples giving the wavelet spaces* ($\mathcal{K}(j) = 2^{-j}\mathbf{Z}$, $\mathcal{M}(j) = 2^{-j}(\mathbf{Z}+1/2)$, *and* $x_{j,k} = k$). *The well known linear B-splines as primal scaling and wavelet functions with Diracs as duals can be reached with dual lifting* ($\tilde{s}_{j,k,m} = 1/2\,\delta_{k-2^{-j-1},m} + 1/2\,\delta_{k+2^{-j-1},m}$), *resulting in* $\tilde{\varphi}_{j,k} = \delta(\cdot - k)$ *and* $\tilde{\psi}_{j,m} = -1/2\,\delta(\cdot - m - 2^{-j-1}) + \delta(\cdot - m) - 1/2\,\delta(\cdot - m + 2^{-j-1})$.

6. Evidently, the lifting scheme is only useful in case one has an initial set of biorthogonal filters. In the following sections we will discuss two such sets.

3.2 Fast Lifted Wavelet Transform

Before describing the particulars of our bases we give the general structure of all transforms. Forward (analysis) and inverse (synthesis) transforms are always performed level wise. The former begins at the finest level and goes to the root while the latter starts at the root and descends to the leaf level. `AnalysisI` computes the unlifted wavelet coefficients at the parent level while `AnalysisII` performs the lifting if the basis is lifted otherwise it is empty. Similarly, `SynthesisI` performs the inverse lifting, if any, while `SynthesisII` computes the scaling function coefficients at the child level.

```
Analysis
    For level = leaflevel to rootlevel
        AnalysisI(level)
        AnalysisII(level)
Synthesis
    For level = rootlevel to leaflevel
        SynthesisI(level)
        SynthesisII(level)
```

The transforms come in two major groups: (A) Lifted from the Lazy wavelet: this involves interpolating scaling functions and a vertex based transform; (B) Lifted from the Haar wavelet: this involves a face based transform. We next discuss these in detail.

3.3 Interpolating Scaling Functions

We first give a trivial example of a wavelet transform: the Lazy wavelet [27, 28]. The Lazy wavelet transform is an orthogonal transform that essentially does not compute anything. However, it is fundamental as it is connected with interpolating scaling functions. The filters of the Lazy fast wavelet transform are given as

$$h^o_{j,k,l} = \tilde{h}^o_{j,k,l} = \delta_{k,l} \text{ and } g^o_{j,m,l} = \tilde{g}^o_{j,m,l} = \delta_{m,l}.$$

Consequently, the transform does not compute anything, it only subsamples the coefficients. Figure 4 (left) illustrates this idea for the case of the real line.

Scaling functions $\{\varphi_{j,k} \mid j \geqslant 0, k \in \mathcal{K}(j)\}$ are called *interpolating* if a set of points $\{x_{j,k} \mid j \geqslant 0, k \in \mathcal{K}(j)\}$ with

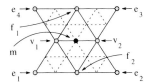

Figure 5: *Neighbors used in our bases. Members of the index sets used in the transforms are shown in the diagram* ($m \in \mathcal{M}(j)$, $\{v_1, v_2, f_1, f_2, e_1, e_2, e_3, e_4\} = \mathcal{K}_m$).

$x_{j,k} = x_{j+1,k}$ exists, so that

$$\forall k, k' \in \mathcal{K}(j): \quad \varphi_{j,k}(x_{j,k'}) = \delta_{k,k'}.$$

An example for such functions on the real line is shown on the right side of Figure 4. In case of interpolating scaling functions, we can always take the dual scaling functions to be Dirac distributions, $\tilde{\varphi}_{j,k}(x) = \delta(x - x_{j,k})$, which are immediately biorthogonal (see the dual scaling functions on the right of Figure 4). This leads to trivial inner products with the duals, namely evaluation of the function at the points $x_{j,k}$.

The set of filters resulting from interpolating scaling functions and Diracs as their formal dual, can be seen as a *dual lifting of the Lazy wavelet*. This implies that $h_{j,k,k'} = \delta_{k,k'}$, $h_{j,k,m} = \tilde{s}_{j,k,m}$, $\tilde{g}_{j,m,k} = -\tilde{s}_{j,k,m}$, $\tilde{g}_{j,m,m'} = \delta_{m,m'}$. The wavelets are given by $\psi_{j,m} = \varphi_{j+1,m}$ and the dual wavelets by

$$\tilde{\psi}_{j,m} = \delta(\cdot - x_{j+1,m}) - \sum_k \tilde{s}_{j,k,m}\,\delta(\cdot - x_{j,k}).$$

The linear B-spline (right side of Figure 4) can be seen to be the dual lifting of the Lazy wavelet. Since we applied dual lifting the primal wavelet does not yet have a vanishing moment.

Below we present other choices for the filter coefficients $h_{j,k,m}$. Typically one can choose the $\tilde{s}_{j,k,m}$ to insure that $\tilde{\psi}_{j,m}$ has vanishing moments (this will lead to the Quadratic scheme), or that $\varphi_{j,k}$ is smooth (this will lead to the Butterfly scheme).

At this point we have an interpolating multiresolution analysis, which was dually lifted from the Lazy wavelet. A disadvantage of this multiresolution analysis is that the functions cannot provide Riesz bases for L$_2$. The dual functions do not even belong to L$_2$. This is related to the fact that the wavelet does not have a vanishing integral since it coincides with a scaling function. Consequently, unconditional convergence of the expansion (3) is not guaranteed. One can now apply the primal lifting scheme to try to overcome this drawback by ensuring that the primal wavelet has at least 1 vanishing moment. Note that this is only a necessary and not a sufficient condition. This yields

$$\tilde{h}_{j,k,l} = \delta_{k,l} + \sum_m s_{j,k,m}\,\tilde{g}_{j,m,l}$$
$$g_{j,m,l} = \delta_{m,l} - \sum_k s_{j,k,m}\,h_{j,k,l}.$$

The resulting wavelet can be written as

$$\psi_{j,m} = \varphi_{j+1,m} - \sum_k s_{j,k,m}\,\varphi_{j,k}. \tag{5}$$

In the situation in Figure 4 setting $s_{j,k,m} = 1/4\,\delta_{m,k+2^{-j-1}} + 1/4\,\delta_{m,k-2^{-j-1}}$ results in $\psi_{j,m}$ having a vanishing integral. This choice leads us to the well known $(2,2)$ biorthogonal wavelet of [4].

3.4 Vertex Bases

Up to this point we have treated all index sets involved in the various filters as abstract sets. We now make these index sets more concrete. In order to facilitate our description we consider all index sets as defined locally around a given site $x_{j+1,m}$. A diagram is given in Figure 5. The index of a given site is denoted $m \in \mathcal{M}(j)$ and all the neighboring vertices ($x_{j,k}$ with $k \in \mathcal{K}(j)$) needed in the transform have indices v, f, and e respectively. To give some more intuition to these index sets recall wavelets on the real line as in Figure 4. In that case the set $\mathcal{K}(0) \ni l$ would consist of all integers, while $\mathcal{M}(-1) \ni m$ would contain the odd and $\mathcal{K}(-1) \ni k$ the even integers. For vertex based schemes we may think of the sites $m \in \mathcal{M}(j)$ as always living on the midpoint of some parent edge (these being the "odd" indices), while the endpoints of a given edge form the "even" indices ($k \in \mathcal{K}(j)$), and their union $l \in \mathcal{K}(j) \cup \mathcal{M}(j) = \mathcal{K}(j+1)$ gives the set of all indices. For each m the filters only range over some small neighborhood. We will refer to the elements in these neighborhoods by a local naming scheme (see Figure 5), $k \in \mathcal{K}_m \subset \mathcal{K}(j)$. For example, the site m lies in between the elements of $\mathcal{K}_m = \{v_1, v_2\}$.

For all vertex bases the unlifted scaling coefficients are simply subsampled during analysis and upsampled during synthesis, while the wavelet coefficients involve some computation.

AnalysisI(j):

$\forall k \in \mathcal{K}(j): \qquad \lambda_{j,k} := \lambda_{j+1,k}$

$\forall m \in \mathcal{M}(j): \qquad \gamma_{j,m} := \lambda_{j+1,m} - \sum_{k \in \mathcal{K}_m} \tilde{s}_{j,k,m} \lambda_{j,k}$

SynthesisII(j):

$\forall k \in \mathcal{K}(j): \qquad \lambda_{j+1,k} := \lambda_{j,k}$

$\forall m \in \mathcal{M}(j): \qquad \lambda_{j+1,m} := \gamma_{j,m} + \sum_{k \in \mathcal{K}_m} \tilde{s}_{j,k,m} \lambda_{j,k}$

We now give the details of the wavelet coefficient computations.

Lazy: As mentioned above the Lazy wavelet does nothing but subsampling. The resulting analysis and synthesis steps then become

$$\gamma_{j,m} := \lambda_{j+1,m} \quad \text{and} \quad \lambda_{j+1,m} := \gamma_{j,m}.$$

respectively. The corresponding stencil encompasses no neighbors, i.e., the sums over $\tilde{s}_{j,k,m}$ are empty.

Linear: This basic interpolatory form uses the stencil $k \in \mathcal{K} = \{v_1, v_2\}$ (see Figure 5) for analysis and synthesis

$$\gamma_{j,m} := \lambda_{j+1,m} - 1/2(\lambda_{j+1,v_1} + \lambda_{j+1,v_2})$$
$$\lambda_{j+1,m} := \gamma_{j,m} + 1/2(\lambda_{j,v_1} + \lambda_{j,v_2}),$$

respectively. Note that this stencil does properly account for the geometry provided that the m sites at level $j+1$ have equal geodetic distance from the $\{v_1, v_2\}$ sites on their parent edge. Here $\tilde{s}_{j,v_1,m} = \tilde{s}_{j,v_2,m} = 1/2$.

Quadratic: The stencil for this basis is given by $\mathcal{K}_m = \{v_1, v_2, f_1, f_2\}$ (see Figure 5) and exploits the degrees of freedom implied to kill the functions x^2, y^2, and z^2 (and by implication the constant function [1]). Using the coordinates of the neighbors of the involved sites a small linear system results

$$\begin{pmatrix} 1 & 1 & 1 & 1 \\ x^2_{j,v_1} & x^2_{j,v_2} & x^2_{j,f_1} & x^2_{j,f_2} \\ y^2_{j,v_1} & y^2_{j,v_2} & y^2_{j,f_1} & y^2_{j,f_2} \\ z^2_{j,v_1} & z^2_{j,v_2} & z^2_{j,f_1} & z^2_{j,f_2} \end{pmatrix} \begin{pmatrix} \tilde{s}_{j,v_1,m} \\ \tilde{s}_{j,v_2,m} \\ \tilde{s}_{j,f_1,m} \\ \tilde{s}_{j,f_2,m} \end{pmatrix} = \begin{pmatrix} 1 \\ x^2_{j+1,m} \\ y^2_{j+1,m} \\ z^2_{j+1,m} \end{pmatrix}$$

Since $x^2 + y^2 + z^2 = 1$ this system is singular (but solvable) and the answer is chosen so as to minimize the l_2 norm of the resulting filter coefficients. Note that this is an instance of dual lifting with effective filters $\tilde{s}_{j,k,m} = h_{j,k,m} = -\tilde{g}_{j,m,k}$.

Butterfly: This is the only basis which uses other than immediate neighbors (all the sites $\mathcal{K}_m$ denoted in Figure 5). Here $\tilde{s}_{v_1} = \tilde{s}_{v_2} = 1/2$, $\tilde{s}_{f_1} = \tilde{s}_{f_2} = 1/8$, and $\tilde{s}_{e_1} = \tilde{s}_{e_2} = \tilde{s}_{e_3} = \tilde{s}_{e_4} = -1/16$. It is inspired by a subdivision scheme of Dyn et al. [11] for the construction of smooth surfaces.

3.5 Lifting Vertex Bases

All of the above bases, Lazy, Linear, Quadratic, and Butterfly can be lifted. In this section we use lifting to assure that the wavelet has at least one vanishing moment. It does not improve the ability of the dual wavelet to annihilate more functions. Consequently the ability

of the bases to compress is not increased, but smaller error results when using them for compression (see the example in Section 3.8 and the results in Section 5). We propose wavelets of the form

$$\psi_{j,m} = \varphi_{j+1,m} - s_{j,v_1,m} \varphi_{j,v_1} - s_{j,v_2,m} \varphi_{j,v_2}. \tag{6}$$

In words, we define the wavelet at the midpoint of an edge as a linear combination of the scaling function at the midpoint ($j+1, m$) and two scaling functions on the *coarser level* at the two endpoints of the parent edge ($j, v_{1,2}$). The weights $s_{j,k,m}$ are chosen so that the resulting wavelet has a vanishing integral

$$s_{j,k,m} = I_{j+1,m}/2\,I_{j,k} \quad \text{with} \quad I_{j,k} = \int_{\mathbb{S}^2} \varphi_{j,k}\, d\omega\,.$$

During analysis lifting is a second phase (at each level j) after the $\gamma_{j,m}$ computation, while during synthesis it is a first step followed by the regular synthesis step (Linear, Quadratic, or Butterfly as given above). The simplicity of the expressions demonstrates the power of the lifting scheme. Any of the previous vertex basis wavelets can be lifted *with the same expression*. The integrals $I_{j,k}$ can be approximated on the finest level and then recursively computed on the coarser levels (using the refinement relations).

AnalysisII(j):

$\forall m \in \mathcal{M}(j): \begin{cases} \lambda_{j,v_1} \mathrel{+}= s_{j,v_1,m}\, \gamma_{j,m} \\ \lambda_{j,v_2} \mathrel{+}= s_{j,v_2,m}\, \gamma_{j,m} \end{cases}$

SynthesisI(j):

$\forall m \in \mathcal{M}(j): \begin{cases} \lambda_{j,v_1} \mathrel{-}= s_{j,v_1,m}\, \gamma_{j,m} \\ \lambda_{j,v_2} \mathrel{-}= s_{j,v_2,m}\, \gamma_{j,m} \end{cases}$

For the interpolating case in the previous section, the scaling function coefficients at each level are simply samples of the function to be expanded (inner products with the $\tilde{\varphi}_{n,k}$). In the lifted case the coefficients are defined as the inner product of the function to be expanded with the (new) dual scaling function. This dual scaling

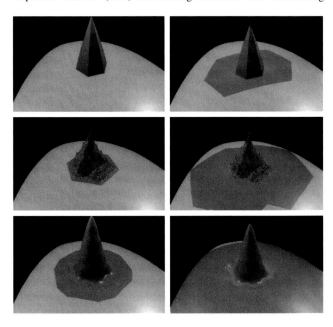

Figure 6: *Images of the graphs of all vertex based wavelets. On the left is the scaling function (or unlifted wavelet) while the right shows the lifted wavelet with 1 vanishing moment. From top to bottom: Linear, Quadratic, and Butterfly. Positive values are mapped to a linear red scale while negative values are shown in blue. The gray area shows the support.*

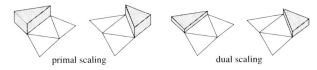

primal scaling   dual scaling

Figure 7: *Example Haar scaling functions on a triangular subdivision. On the left are primal functions each of height 1. On the right are the biorthogonal duals each of height $\alpha(T_i)^{-1}$. Disjoint bases have inner product of 0 while overlapping (coincident supports) lead to an inner product of 1. (For the sphere all triangles are spherical triangles.)*

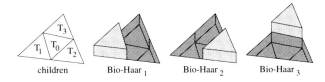

children   Bio-Haar $_1$ Bio-Haar $_2$ Bio-Haar $_3$

Figure 8: *The Bio-Haar wavelets. Note that the heights of the functions are not drawn to scale.*

function is only defined as the limit function of a non-stationary subdivision scheme. The inner products at the finest level therefore need to be approximated with a quadrature formula, i.e., a linear combination of function samples. In our implementation we use a simple one point quadrature formula at the finest level.

Figure 6 shows images of the graphs of all the vertex based ψ functions for the interpolating and lifted case.

3.6 The Generalized Haar Wavelets and Face Bases

Consider spherical triangles resulting from a geodesic sphere construction $T_{j,k} \subset \mathrm{S}^2$ with $k \in \mathcal{K}(j)$ (note that the face based $\mathcal{K}(j)$ are not identical to the vertex based $\mathcal{K}(j)$ defined earlier). They satisfy the following properties:

1. $\mathrm{S}^2 = \bigcup_{k \in \mathcal{K}(j)} T_{j,k}$ and this union is disjoint, i.e., the $T_{j,k}$ provide a simple cover of S^2 for every j,
2. for every j and k, $T_{j,k}$ can be written as the union of 4 "child" triangles $T_{j+1,l}$.

Let $\alpha(T_{j,k})$ be the spherical area of a triangle and define the scaling functions and dual scaling functions as

$$\varphi_{j,k} = \chi_{T_{j,k}} \quad \text{and} \quad \tilde{\varphi}_{j,k} = \alpha(T_{j,k})^{-1} \chi_{T_{j,k}}.$$

Here χ_T is the function whose value is 1 for $x \in T$ and 0 otherwise. The fact that the scaling function and dual scaling function are biorthogonal follows immediately from their disjoint support (see Figure 7). Define the $V_j \subset \mathrm{L}_2$ as

$$V_j = \mathrm{clos\ span}\{\varphi_{j,k} \mid k \in \mathcal{K}(j)\}.$$

The spaces V_j then generate a multiresolution analysis of $\mathrm{L}_2(\mathrm{S}^2)$.

Now fix a triangle $T_{j,*}$. For the construction of the generalized Haar wavelets, we only need to consider the set of children $T_{j+1,l=0,1,2,3}$ of $T_{j,*}$. We call these bases the Bio-Haar functions (see Figure 8). The wavelets ($m = 1, 2, 3$) are chosen as

$$\psi_{j,m} = 2(\varphi_{j+1,m} - I_{j+1,m}/I_{j+1,0} \; \varphi_{j+1,0}),$$

so that their integral vanishes. A set of semi-orthogonal dual wavelets is then given by

$$\tilde{\psi}_{j,m} = 1/2(\tilde{\varphi}_{j+1,m} - \tilde{\varphi}_{j,*}).$$

These bases are inspired by the construction of *orthogonal* Haar wavelets for general measures, see [14, 21] where it is shown that the Haar wavelets form an unconditional basis.

The Bio-Haar wavelets have only 1 vanishing moment, but using the dual lifting scheme, we can build a new multiresolution

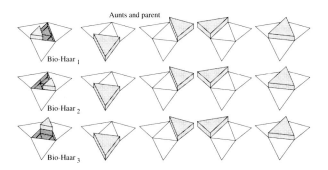

Aunts and parent

Bio-Haar $_1$

Bio-Haar $_2$

Bio-Haar $_3$

Figure 9: *Illustration of the dual lifting of the dual Bio-Haar wavelets. New dual wavelets can be constructed by taking linear combinations of the original dual Bio-Haar wavelets and parent level dual scaling functions. Each such linear combination is signified by a row. Solving for the necessary weights $\tilde{s}_{j,k,m}$ requires the solution to a small matrix problem whose right hand side encodes the desired constraints.*

analysis, in which the dual wavelet has more vanishing moments. Let $T_{j,k=4,5,6}$ be the neighboring triangles of $T_{j,*}$ (at level j), and $\mathcal{K}_m = \{*, 4, 5, 6\}$. The new dual wavelets are

$$\tilde{\psi}_{j,m} = 1/2(\tilde{\varphi}_{j+1,m} - \tilde{\varphi}_{j,*}) - \sum_{k \in \mathcal{K}_m} \tilde{s}_{j,k,m} \tilde{\varphi}_{j,k}.$$

Note that this is a special case of Equation (4). The coefficients $\tilde{s}_{j,k,m}$ can now be chosen so that $\tilde{\psi}_{j,m}$ has vanishing moments. Figure 9 illustrates this idea. In the left column are the three dual Bio-Haar wavelets created before. The following four columns show the dual scaling functions over the parent and aunt triangles $T_{j,k=*,4,5,6}$. Each row signifies one of the linear combinations.

Similarly to the Quadratic vertex basis we construct dually lifted Bio-Haar wavelets which kill the functions x^2, y^2, z^2, and thus 1. This leads to the equations

$$\sum_{k \in \mathcal{K}_m} \tilde{s}_{j,k,m} \langle \tilde{\varphi}_{j,k}, P \rangle = 1/2 \langle \tilde{\varphi}_{j+1,m} - \tilde{\varphi}_{j,*}, P \rangle$$

with $P = x^2, y^2, z^2, 1$. The result is a 4×4 singular (but solvable) matrix problem for each $m = 1, 2, 3$. The unknowns are the $\tilde{s}_{j,k,m}$ with $k = *, 4, 5, 6$ and the entries of the linear system are moments of dual scaling functions. These can be computed recursively from the leaf level during analysis.

The Bio-Haar and lifted Bio-Haar transforms compute the scaling function coefficient during analysis at the parent triangle as a function of the scaling function coefficients at the children and possibly the scaling function coefficients at the neighbors of the parent triangle (in the lifted case). The three wavelet coefficients of the parent level are stored with the children T_1, T_2, and T_3 for convenience in the implementation. During synthesis the scaling function coefficient at the parent and the wavelet coefficients stored at children T_1, T_2, and T_3 are used to compute scaling function coefficients at the 4 children.

As before, lifting is a second step during analysis and modifies the wavelet coefficients. During synthesis lifting is a first step before the inverse Bio-Haar transform is calculated.

```
AnalysisII(j):

    ∀ m ∈ M(j):   γ_{j,m}  -=  ∑_{k∈K_m} s̃_{j,k,m} λ_{j,k}

SynthesisI(j):

    ∀ m ∈ M(j):   γ_{j,m}  +=  ∑_{k∈K_m} s̃_{j,k,m} λ_{j,k}
```

3.7 Basis Properties

The lifting scheme provides us with the filter coefficients needed in the implementation of the fast wavelet transform. To find the basis functions and dual basis functions that are associated with them, we use the *cascade algorithm*. To synthesize a scaling function φ_{j_0,k_0} one simply initializes the coefficient $\lambda_{j_0,k} = \delta_{k,k_0}$. The inverse wavelet transform starting from level j_0 with all wavelet coefficients $\gamma_{j,m}$ with $j \geqslant j_0$ set to zero then results in $\lambda_{j,k}$ coefficients which converge to function values of φ_{j_0,k_0} as $j \to \infty$. In case the cascade algorithm converges in L_2 for both primal and dual scaling functions, biorthogonal filters (as given by the lifting scheme) imply biorthogonal basis functions.

One of the fundamental questions is how properties, such as convergence of the cascade algorithm, Riesz bounds, and smoothness, can be related back to properties of the filter sequences. This is a very hard question and at this moment no general answer is available to our knowledge. We thus have no mathematical proof that the wavelets constructed form an unconditional basis except in the case of the Haar wavelets. A recent result addressing these questions was obtained by Dahmen [7]. In particular, it is shown there which properties in addition to biorthogonality are needed to assure stable bases. Whether this result can be applied to the bases constructed here needs to be studied in the future.

Regarding smoothness, we have some partial results. It is easy to see that the Haar wavelets are not continuous and that the Linear wavelets are. The original Butterfly subdivision scheme is guaranteed to yield a C^1 limit function provided the connectivity of the vertices is at least 4. The modified Butterfly scheme that we use on the sphere, will also give C^1 limit functions, provided a locally smooth (C^1) map from the spherical triangulation to a planar triangulation exists. Unfortunately, the geodesic subdivision we use here does not have this property. However, the resulting functions appear visually smooth (see Figure 6). We are currently working on new spherical triangulations which have the property that the Butterfly scheme yields a globally C^1 function.

In principle, one can choose either the tetrahedron, octahedron, or icosahedron to start the geodesic sphere construction. Each of them has a particular number of triangles on each level, and therefore one of them might be more suited for a particular application or platform. The octahedron is the best choice in case of functions defined on the hemisphere (cfr. BRDF). The icosahedron will lead to the least area imbalance of triangles on each level and thus to (visually) smoother basis functions.

3.8 An Example

We argued at the beginning of this section that a given wavelet basis can be made more performant by lifting. In the section on interpolating bases we pointed out that a wavelet basis with Diracs for duals and a primal wavelet, which does not have 1 vanishing moment, unconditional convergence of the resulting series expansions cannot be insured anymore. We now give an example on the sphere which illustrates the numerical consequences of lifting.

Consider the function $f(s) = \sqrt{|s_x|}$ for $s = (s_x, s_y, s_z) \in S^2$. This function is everywhere smooth except on the great circle $s_x = 0$, where its derivative has a discontinuity. Since it is largely smooth but for a singularity at 0, it is ideally suited to exhibit problems in bases whose primal wavelet does not have a vanishing moment. Figure 10 shows the relative l_1 error as a function of the number of coefficients used in the synthesis stage. In order to satisfy the same error threshold the lifted basis requires only approximately $1/3$ the number of coefficients compared to the unlifted basis.

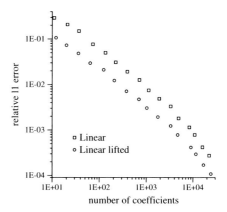

Figure 10:   *Relative l_1 error as a function of the number of coefficients for the example function $f(s) = \sqrt{|s_x|}$ and (lifted) Linear wavelets. With the same number of coefficients the error is smaller by a factor of 3 or conversely a given error can be achieved with about $1/3$ the number of coefficients if the lifted basis is used.*

4   Implementation

We have implemented all the described bases in an interactive application running on an SGI Irix workstation. The basic data structure is a forest of triangle quadtrees [10]. The root level starts with 4 (tetrahedron), 8 (octahedron), or 20 (icosahedron) spherical triangles. These are recursively subdivided into 4 child triangles each. Naming edges after their opposite vertex, and children after the vertex they retain (the central child becomes T_0) leads to a consistent naming scheme throughout the entire hierarchy. Neighbor finding is a simple $O(1)$ (expected cost) function using bit operations on edge and triangle names to guide pointer traversal [10]. A vertex is allocated once and any level which contains it carries pointers to it. Each vertex carries a single λ and γ slot for vertex bases, while face bases carry a single λ and γ slot per spherical triangle. Our actual implementation carries other data such as surface normals and colors used for display, function values for error computations, and copies of all γ and λ values to facilitate experimentation. These are not necessary in a production system however.

Using a recursive data structure is more memory intensive (due to the pointer overhead) than a flat, array based representation of all coefficients as was used by LDW. However, using a recursive data structure enables the use of adaptive subdivision and results in simple recursive procedures for analysis and synthesis and a subdivision oracle. For interactive applications it is straightforward to select a level for display appropriate to the available graphics performance (polygons per second).

In the following subsections we address particular issues in the implementation.

4.1   Restricted Quadtrees

In order to support lifted bases and those which require stencils that encompass some neighborhood the quadtrees produced need to satisfy a restriction criterion. For the Linear vertex bases (lifted and unlifted) and the Bio-Haar basis no restriction is required. For Quadratic and lifted Bio-Haar bases no neighbor of a given face may be off by more than 1 subdivision level (every child needs a proper set of "aunts"). For the Butterfly basis a two-neighborhood must not be off by more than 1 subdivision level. These requirements are easily enforced during the recursive subdivision. The fact that we only need "aunts" (as opposed to "sisters") for the lifting scheme allows us to have wavelets on *adaptively subdivided* hierarchies. This is a crucial departure from previous constructions, e.g., tree

Basis	Analysis	Synthesis	Lifted Basis	Analysis	Synthesis
Linear	3.59	3.55	Linear	5.85	5.83
Quadratic	21.79	21.00	Quadratic	24.62	24.68
Butterfly	8.43	8.42	Butterfly	10.64	10.62
Bio-Haar	4.31	6.09	Bio-Haar	42.43	36.08

Table 2: *Representative timings for wavelet transforms beginning with 4 spherical triangles and expanding to level 9 (2^{20} faces and $2^{19} + 2$ vertices). All timings are given in seconds and measured on an SGI R4400 running at 150MHz. The initial setup time (allocating and initializing all data structures) took 100 seconds.*

wavelets employed by Gortler et al.[16] who also needed to support adaptive subdivision.

4.2 Boundaries

In the case of a hemisphere (top 4 spherical triangles of an octahedral subdivision), which is important for BRDF functions, the issues associated with the boundary need to be addressed. Lifting of vertex bases is unchanged, but the Quadratic and Butterfly schemes (as well as the lifted Bio-Haar bases) need neighbors, which may not exist at the boundary. This can be addressed by simply using another, further neighbor instead of the missing neighbor (across the boundary edge) to solve the associated matrix problem. It implicitly corresponds to adapting filter coefficients close to the boundary as done in interval constructions, see e.g. [5]. This construction automatically preserves the vanishing moment property even at the boundary. In the implementation of the Butterfly basis, we took a different approach and chose in our implementation to simply reflect any missing faces along the boundary.

4.3 Oracle

One of the main components in any wavelet based approximation is the oracle. The function of the oracle is to determine which coefficients are important and need to be retained for a reconstruction which is to meet some error criterion. Our system can be driven in two modes. The first selects a deepest level to which to expand all quadtrees. The storage requirements for this approach grow exponentially in the depth of the tree. For example our implementation cannot go deeper than 7 levels (starting from the tetrahedron) on a 32MB Indy class machine without paging. Creating full trees, however, allows for the examination of *all* coefficients throughout the hierarchies to in effect implement a perfect oracle. The second mode builds sparse trees based on a *deep refinement* oracle. In this oracle quadtrees are built depth first exploring the expansion to some (possibly very deep) finest level. On the way out of the recursion a local `AnalysisI` is performed and any subtrees whose wavelet coefficients are all below a user supplied threshold are deallocated. Once the sparse tree is built the restriction criterion is enforced and the (possibly lifted) analysis is run level wise.

The time complexity of this oracle is still exponential in the depth of the tree, but the storage requirements are proportional to the output size. With extra knowledge about the underlying function more powerful oracles can be built whose time complexity is proportional to the output size as well.

4.4 Transform Cost

The cost of a wavelet transform is proportional to the total number of coefficients, which grows by a factor of 4 for every level. For example, 9 levels of subdivision starting from 4 spherical triangles result in 2^{20} coefficients (each of λ and γ) for face bases and $2^{19} + 2$ (each of λ and γ) for vertex bases. The cost of analysis and synthesis is proportional to the number of basis functions, while the constant of proportionality is a function of the stencil size.

Table 2 summarizes timings of wavelet transforms for all the new bases. The initial setup took 100 seconds and includes allocation and initialization of all data structures and evaluation of the $\lambda_{9,k}$. Since the latter is highly dependent on the evaluation cost of the function to be expanded we used the constant function 1 for these timings. None of the matrices which arise in the Quadratic, and Bio-Haar bases (lifted and unlifted) was cached, thus the cost of solving the associated 4×4 matrices with a column pivoted QR (for Quadratic and lifted Bio-Haar) was incurred both during analysis and synthesis. If one is willing to cache the results of the matrix solutions this cost could be amortized over multiple transforms.

We make three main observations about the timings: (A) Lifting of vertex bases adds only a small extra cost, which is almost entirely due to the extra recursions; (B) the cost of the Butterfly basis is only approximately twice the cost of the Linear basis even though the stencil is much larger; (C) solving the 4×4 systems implied by Quadratic and lifted Bio-Haar bases increases the cost by a factor of approximately 5 over the linear case (note that there are twice as many coefficients for face bases as for vertex bases).

While the total cost of an entire transform is proportional to the number of basis functions, evaluating the resulting expansion at a point is proportional to the depth (log of the number of basis functions) of the tree times a constant dependent on the stencil size. The latter provides a great advantage over such bases as spherical harmonics whose evaluation cost at a single point is proportional to the total number of bases used.

5   Results

In this section we report on experiments with the compression of a planetary topographic data set, a BRDF function, and illumination of an anisotropic glossy sphere.

Most of these experiments involved some form of coefficient thresholding (in the oracle). In all cases this was performed as follows. Since all our bases are normalized with respect to the L_∞ norm, L_2 thresholding against some user supplied threshold ϵ becomes

$$\text{if } |\gamma_{j,m}| \sqrt{\text{supp}(\psi_{j,m})} < \epsilon, \, \gamma_{j,m} := 0.$$

Furthermore ϵ is scaled by $(\max(f) - \min(f))$ for the given function f to make thresholding independent of the scale of f.

5.1   Compression of Topographic Data

In this series of experiments we computed wavelet expansions of topographic data over the entire earth. This function can be thought of as both a surface, and as a scalar valued function giving height (depth) for each point on a sphere. The original data, ETOPO5 from the National Oceanic and Atmospheric Administration gives the elevation (depth) of the earth from sea level in meters at a resolution of 5 arc minutes at the equator. Due to the large size of this data set we first resampled it to 10 arc minutes resolution. All expansions were performed starting from the tetrahedron followed by subdivision to level 9.

Figure 11 shows the results of these experiments (left and middle). After computing the coefficients of the respective expansions at the finest level of the subdivision an analysis was performed. After this step all wavelet coefficients below a given threshold were zeroed and the function was reconstructed. The thresholds were successively set to 2^{-i} for $i = 0, \ldots, 17$ resulting in the number of coefficients and relative l_1 error plotted (left graph). The error was computed with a numerical quadrature one level below the finest subdivision to insure an accurate error estimation. The results are plotted for all vertex and face bases (Linear, Quadratic, Butterfly, Bio-Haar, lifted and unlifted). We also computed l_2 and l_∞ error norms and the resulting graphs (not shown) are essentially identical

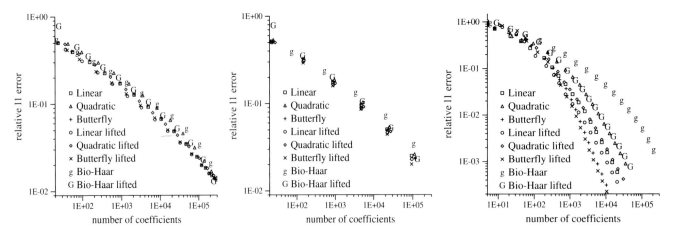

Figure 11: *Relative l_1 error as a function of the number of coefficients used during the reconstruction of the earth topographic data set (left and middle) and BRDF function (right). The six vertex bases and two face bases perform essentially the same for the earth. On the left with full expansion of the quadtrees to level 9 and thresholding. In the middle the results of the deep refinement oracle to level 10 with only a sparse tree construction. The curves are identical validating the refinement strategy. On the right the results of deep refinement to level 9 for the BRDF. Here the individual bases are clearly distinguished.*

(although the l_∞ error stays initially high before falling off due to deep canyon features). The plot reaches to about one quarter of all coefficients. The observed regime is linear as one would expect from the bases used.

The most striking observation about these error graphs is the fact that all bases perform similar. This is due to the fact that the underlying function is non-smooth. Consequently smoother bases do not perform any better than less performant ones. However, when drawing pictures of highly compressed versions of the data set the smoother bases produce visually better pictures (see Figure 12). Depending on the allowed error the compression can be quite dramatic. For example, 7 200 coefficients are sufficient to reach 7% error, while 119 000 are required to reach 2% error.

In a second set of experiments we used the deep refinement oracle (see Section 4.3) to explore the wavelet expansion to 10 levels (potentially quadrupling the number of coefficients) with successively smaller thresholds, once again plotting the resulting error in the middle graph of Figure 11. The error as a function of coefficients used is the same as the relationship found by the perfect oracle. This validates our deep refinement oracle strategy. Memory requirements of this approach are drastically reduced. For example, using a threshold of 2^{-9} during oracle driven refinement to level 10 resulted in 4 616 coefficients and consumed a total of 27MB (including 10MB for the original data set). Lowering the threshold to 2^{-10} yielded 10 287 coefficients and required 43MB (using the lifted Butterfly basis in both cases).

Finally Figure 12 shows some of the resulting adaptive data sets rendered with RenderMan using the Butterfly basis and a pseudo coloring, which maps elevation onto a piecewise linear color scale. Total runtime for oracle driven analysis and synthesis was 10 minutes on an SGI R4400 at 150MHz.

5.1.1 Comparison with LDW

The earth data set allows for a limited comparison of our results with those of LDW. They also compressed the ETOPO5 data set using pseudo orthogonalized (over a 2 neighborhood) Linear wavelets defined over the octahedron. They subdivide to 9 levels (on a 128MB machine) which corresponds to twice as many coefficients as we used (on a 180MB machine), suggesting a storage overhead of about 3 in our implementation. It is hard to compare the quality of the bases without knowing the exact basis used or the errors in the compressed reconstruction. However, LDW report the number of coefficients selected for a given threshold (741 for

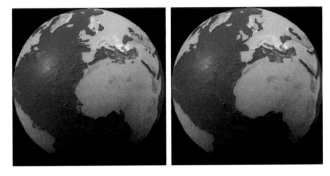

Figure 12: *Two views of the earth data set with 15 000 and 190 000 coefficients respectively using the Butterfly basis with l_1 errors of 0.05 and 0.01 respectively. In the image on the left coastal regions are rather smoothed since they contain little height variation (England and the Netherlands are merged and the Baltic sea is desertificated). However, such spiky features as the Cape Verde Islands off the coast of Africa are clearly preserved.*

0.02, 15 101 for 0.002, and 138 321 for 0.0005). Depending on the basis used we generally select fewer coefficients (6 000 − 15 000 for 0.002 and 28 000 − 65 000 for 0.0005). As timings they give 588 seconds (on a 100 MHz R4000) for analysis which is significantly longer than our smoothest basis (lifted Butterfly). Their reconstruction time ranges from 75 (741 coefficients) to 1 230 (138 058 coefficients) seconds which is also significantly longer than our times (see Table 2). We hypothesize that the timing and storage differences are largely due to their use of flat array based data structures. These do not require as much memory, but they are more compute intensive in the sparse polygonal reconstruction phase.

5.2 BRDF Compression

In this series of experiments we explore the potential for efficiently representing BRDF functions with spherical wavelets. BRDF functions can arise from measurements, simulation, or theoretical models. Depending on the intended application different models may be preferable. Expanding BRDF functions in terms of locally supported hierarchical functions is particularly useful for wavelet based finite element illumination algorithms. It also has obvious applications for simulation derived BRDF functions such as those of Westin et al. [30] and Gondek et al. [15].

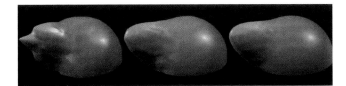

Figure 13: *Graphs of adaptive oracle driven approximations of the Schlick BRDF with 19, 73, and 203 coefficients respectively (left to right), using the lifted Butterfly basis. The associated thresholds were 2^{-3}, 2^{-6}, and 2^{-9} respectively, resulting in relative l_1 errors of 0.35, 0.065, and 0.015 respectively.*

The domain of a complete BRDF is a hemisphere times a hemisphere. In our experiments we consider only a fixed incoming direction and expand the resulting function over all outgoing directions (single hemisphere). To facilitate the computation of errors we used the BRDF model proposed by Schlick [23]. It is a simple Padé approximant to a micro facet model with geometric shadowing, a microfacet distribution function, but no Fresnel term. It has roughness ($r \in [0, 1]$, where 0 is Dirac mirror reflection and 1 perfectly diffuse) and anisotropy ($p \in [0, 1]$, where 0 is Dirac style anisotropy, and 1 perfect isotropy) parameters. To improve the numerical properties of the BRDF we followed the suggestion of Westin *et al.* [30] and expanded $\cos \theta_o f_r(\vec{\omega}_i, 0, \cdot)$.

In the experiments we used all 8 bases but specialized to the hemisphere. The parameters were $\theta_i = \pi/3$, $r = 0.05$, and $p = 1$. The results are summarized in Figure 11 (rightmost graph). It shows the relative l_1 error as a function of the number of coefficients used. This time we can clearly see how the various bases differentiate themselves in terms of their ability to represent the function within some error bound with a given budget of coefficients. We make several observations

- all lifted bases perform better than their unlifted versions, confirming our assertion that lifted bases are more performant;

- increasing smoothness in the bases (Butterfly) is more important than increasing the number of vanishing moments (Quadratic);

- dual lifting to increase dual vanishing moments increases compression ability dramatically (Bio-Haar and lifted Bio-Haar);

- overall the face based schemes do not perform as well as the vertex based schemes.

Figure 13 shows images of the graphs of some of the expansions. These used the lifted Butterfly basis with an adaptive refinement oracle which explored the expansion to level 9 (i.e., it examined 2^{19} coefficients). The final number of coefficients and associated relative l_1 errors were (left to right) 19 coefficients ($l_1 = 0.35$), 73 coefficients ($l_1 = 0.065$), and 203 coefficients ($l_1 = 0.015$). Total runtime was 170 seconds on an SGI R4400 at 150MHz.

5.3 Illumination

To explore the potential of these bases for global illumination algorithms we performed a simple simulation computing the radiance over a glossy, anisotropic sphere due to two area light sources. We emphasize that this is not a solution involving any multiple reflections, but it serves as a simple example to show the potential of these bases for hierarchical illumination algorithms. It also serves as an example of applying a finite element approach to a curved object (sphere) without polygonalizing it.

Figure 14 shows the results of this simulation. We used the lifted Butterfly basis and the BRDF model of Schlick with $r = 0.05$, $p = 0.05$, and an additive diffuse component of 0.005. Two area light sources illuminate the red sphere. Note the fine detail in the pinched off region in the center of the "hot" spot and also at the

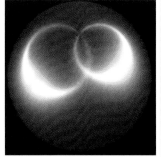 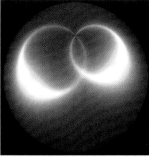

Figure 14: *Results of an illumination simulation using the lifted Butterfly basis. A red, glossy, anisotropic sphere is illuminated by 2 area light sources. Left: solution with 2 000 coefficients ($l_1 = 0.017$). Right: solution with 5 000 coefficients ($l_1 = 0.0035$)*

north pole where all "grooves" converge.

6 Conclusions and Future Directions

In this paper we have introduced two new families of wavelets on the sphere. One family is based on interpolating scaling functions and one on the generalized Haar wavelets. They employ a generalization of multiresolution analysis to arbitrary surfaces and can be derived in a straightforward manner from the trivial multiresolution analysis with the lifting scheme. The resulting algorithms are simple and efficient. We reported on the application of these bases to the compression of earth data sets, BRDF functions and illumination computations and showed their potential for these applications. We found that

- for smooth functions the lifted bases perform significantly better than the unlifted bases;

- increasing the dual vanishing moments leads to better compression;

- smoother bases, even with only one vanishing moment, tend to perform better for smooth functions;

- our constructions allow non-equally subdivided triangulations of the sphere.

We believe that many applications can benefit from these wavelet bases. For example, using their localization properties a number of spherical image processing algorithms, such as local smoothing and enhancement, can be realized in a straightforward and efficient way [25].

While we limited our examination to the sphere, the construction presented here can be applied to other surfaces. In the case of the sphere enforcing vanishing *polynomial* moments was natural because of their connection with spherical harmonics. In the case of a general, potentially non-smooth (Lipschitz) surface, polynomial moments do not necessarily make much sense. Therefore, one might want to work with local maps from the surface to the tangent plane and enforce vanishing moment conditions in this plane.

Future research includes

- the generalization to arbitrary surfaces,

- the incorporation of smoother (C^2) subdivision schemes as recently introduced by Dyn *et al.* (personal communication, 1995),

- the use of these bases in applications such as the solution of differential and integral equations on the sphere as needed in, e.g., illumination or climate modeling.

Acknowledgments

The first author was supported by DEPSCoR Grant (DoD-ONR) N00014-94-1-1163. The second author was supported by NSF EPSCoR Grant EHR 9108772 and DARPA Grant AFOSR F49620-93-1-0083. He is also Senior Research Assistant of the National Fund of Scientific Research Belgium (NFWO). Other support came from Pixar Inc. We would also like to thank Princeton University and the GMD, Germany, for generous access to computing resources. Help with geometric data structures was provided by David Dobkin. Finally, the comments of the referees were very helpful in revising the paper.

References

[1] ALFELD, P., NEAMTU, M., AND SCHUMAKER, L. L. Bernstein-Bézier polynomials on circles, sphere, and sphere-like surfaces. Preprint.

[2] CARNICER, J. M., DAHMEN, W., AND PEÑA, J. M. Local decompositions of refinable spaces. Tech. rep., Insitut für Geometrie und angewandte Mathematik, RWTH Aachen, 1994.

[3] CHRISTENSEN, P. H., STOLLNITZ, E. J., SALESIN, D. H., AND DEROSE, T. D. Wavelet Radiance. In *Proceedings of the 5th Eurographics Workshop on Rendering*, 287–302, June 1994.

[4] COHEN, A., DAUBECHIES, I., AND FEAUVEAU, J. Biorthogonal bases of compactly supported wavelets. *Comm. Pure Appl. Math. 45* (1992), 485–560.

[5] COHEN, A., DAUBECHIES, I., JAWERTH, B., AND VIAL, P. Multiresolution analysis, wavelets and fast algorithms on an interval. *C. R. Acad. Sci. Paris Sér. I Math. I*, 316 (1993), 417–421.

[6] DAHLKE, S., DAHMEN, W., SCHMITT, E., AND WEINREICH, I. Multiresolution analysis and wavelets on S^2 and S^3. Tech. Rep. 104, Institut für Geometrie und angewandte Mathematik, RWTH Aachen, 1994.

[7] DAHMEN, W. Stability of multiscale transformations. Tech. rep., Institut für Geometrie und angewandte Mathematik, RWTH Aachen, 1994.

[8] DAHMEN, W., PRÖSSDORF, S., AND SCHNEIDER, R. Multiscale methods for pseudo-differential equations on smooth manifolds. In *Conference on Wavelets: Theory, Algorithms, and Applications*, C. K. C. et al., Ed. Academic Press, San Diego, CA, 1994, pp. 385–424.

[9] DAUBECHIES, I. *Ten Lectures on Wavelets*. CBMS-NSF Regional Conf. Series in Appl. Math., Vol. 61. Society for Industrial and Applied Mathematics, Philadelphia, PA, 1992.

[10] DUTTON, G. Locational Properties of Quaternary Triangular Meshes. In *Proceedings of the Fourth International Symposium on Spatial Data Handling*, 901–910, July 1990.

[11] DYN, N., LEVIN, D., AND GREGORY, J. A Butterfly Subdivision Scheme for Surface Interpolation with Tension Control. *Transactions on Graphics 9*, 2 (April 1990), 160–169.

[12] FEKETE, G. Rendering and Managing Spherical Data with Sphere Quadtrees. In *Proceedings of Visualization 90*, 1990.

[13] FREEDEN, W., AND WINDHEUSER, U. Spherical Wavelet Transform and its Discretization. Tech. Rep. 125, Universität Kaiserslautern, Fachbereich Mathematik, 1994.

[14] GIRARDI, M., AND SWELDENS, W. A new class of unbalanced Haar wavelets that form an unconditional basis for L_p on general measure spaces. Tech. Rep. 1995:2, Industrial Mathematics Initiative, Department of Mathematics, University of South Carolina, 1995. (ftp://ftp.math.scarolina.edu/pub/imi_95/imi95_2.ps).

[15] GONDEK, J. S., MEYER, G. W., AND NEWMAN, J. G. Wavelength Dependent Reflectance Functions. In *Computer Graphics* Proceedings, Annual Conference Series, 213–220, 1994.

[16] GORTLER, S., SCHRÖDER, P., COHEN, M., AND HANRAHAN, P. Wavelet Radiosity. In *Computer Graphics* Proceedings, Annual Conference Series, 221–230, August 1993.

[17] GORTLER, S. J., AND COHEN, M. F. Hierarchical and Variational Geometric Modeling with Wavelets. In *Proceedings Symposium on Interactive 3D Graphics*, 35–42, April 1995.

[18] LIU, Z., GORTLER, S. J., AND COHEN, M. F. Hierarchical Spacetime Control. *Computer Graphics* Proceedings, Annual Conference Series, 35–42, July 1994.

[19] LOUNSBERY, M. *Multiresolution Analysis for Surfaces of Arbitrary Topological Type*. PhD thesis, University of Washington, 1994.

[20] LOUNSBERY, M., DEROSE, T. D., AND WARREN, J. Multiresolution Surfaces of Arbitrary Topological Type. Department of Computer Science and Engineering 93-10-05, University of Washington, October 1993. Updated version available as 93-10-05b, January, 1994.

[21] MITREA, M. *Singular integrals, Hardy spaces and Clifford wavelets*. No. 1575 in Lecture Notes in Math. 1994.

[22] NIELSON, G. M. Scattered Data Modeling. *IEEE Computer Graphics and Applications 13*, 1 (January 1993), 60–70.

[23] SCHLICK, C. A customizable reflectance model for everyday rendering. In *Fourth Eurographics Workshop on Rendering*, 73–83, June 1993.

[24] SCHRÖDER, P., AND HANRAHAN, P. Wavelet Methods for Radiance Computations. In *Proceedings 5th Eurographics Workshop on Rendering*, June 1994.

[25] SCHRÖDER, P., AND SWELDENS, W. Spherical wavelets: Texture processing. Tech. Rep. 1995:4, Industrial Mathematics Initiative, Department of Mathematics, University of South Carolina, 1995. (ftp://ftp.math.scarolina.edu/pub/imi_95/imi95_4.ps).

[26] SILLION, F. X., ARVO, J. R., WESTIN, S. H., AND GREENBERG, D. P. A global illumination solution for general reflectance distributions. *Computer Graphics (SIGGRAPH '91 Proceedings)*, Vol. 25, No. 4, pp. 187–196, July 1991.

[27] SWELDENS, W. The lifting scheme: A construction of second generation wavelets. Department of Mathematics, University of South Carolina.

[28] SWELDENS, W. The lifting scheme: A custom-design construction of biorthogonal wavelets. Tech. Rep. 1994:7, Industrial Mathematics Initiative, Department of Mathematics, University of South Carolina, 1994. (ftp://ftp.math.scarolina.edu/pub/imi_94/imi94_7.ps).

[29] WESTERMAN, R. A Multiresolution Framework for Volume Rendering. In *Proceedings ACM Workshop on Volume Visualization*, 51–58, October 1994.

[30] WESTIN, S. H., ARVO, J. R., AND TORRANCE, K. E. Predicting reflectance functions from complex surfaces. *Computer Graphics (SIGGRAPH '92 Proceedings)*, Vol. 26, No. 2, pp. 255–264, July 1992.

Multiresolution Analysis of Arbitrary Meshes

Matthias Eck*   Tony DeRose*   Tom Duchamp*
Hugues Hoppe†   Michael Lounsbery‡   Werner Stuetzle*

*University of Washington, Seattle, WA   †Microsoft Research, Redmond, WA   ‡Alias Research, Seattle, WA

Abstract

In computer graphics and geometric modeling, shapes are often represented by triangular meshes. With the advent of laser scanning systems, meshes of extreme complexity are rapidly becoming commonplace. Such meshes are notoriously expensive to store, transmit, render, and are awkward to edit. Multiresolution analysis offers a simple, unified, and theoretically sound approach to dealing with these problems. Lounsbery *et al.* have recently developed a technique for creating multiresolution representations for a restricted class of meshes with *subdivision connectivity*. Unfortunately, meshes encountered in practice typically do not meet this requirement. In this paper we present a method for overcoming the subdivision connectivity restriction, meaning that completely arbitrary meshes can now be converted to multiresolution form. The method is based on the approximation of an arbitrary initial mesh M by a mesh M^J that has subdivision connectivity and is guaranteed to be within a specified tolerance.

The key ingredient of our algorithm is the construction of a parametrization of M over a simple domain. We expect this parametrization to be of use in other contexts, such as texture mapping or the approximation of complex meshes by NURBS patches.

CR Categories and Subject Descriptors: I.3.5 [Computer Graphics]: Computational Geometry and Object Modeling. - surfaces and object representations; J.6 [Computer-Aided Engineering]: Computer-Aided Design (CAD); G.1.2 [Approximation]: Spline Approximation.

Additional Keywords: Geometric modeling, subdivision surfaces, wavelets.

1 Introduction

In computer graphics and geometric modeling, shapes are often represented by triangular meshes. With the advent of laser scanning systems, meshes of extreme complexity are rapidly becoming commonplace. The objects shown in Color Plates 1(k) and 2(g) for instance, consist of 69,473 and 103,713 triangles, respectively. Such meshes are notoriously expensive to store, transmit, and render. They are also awkward to edit, as many vertices typically must be moved to make a change of substantial spatial extent.

Multiresolution analysis offers a promising new approach for addressing these difficulties in a simple, unified, and theoretically sound way. A multiresolution representation of a mesh, as recently developed by Lounsbery *et al.* [11], consists of a simple base mesh (Color Plate 1(e)) together with a sequence of local correction terms,

called *wavelet coefficients*, capturing the detail present in the object at various resolutions. Color Plates 1(g)–(h) show a sequence of intermediate resolution models incorporating an increasing number of wavelets.

Multiresolution mesh representations are particularly convenient for a number of applications, including:

- *Compression/simplification*: A multiresolution mesh can be compressed by removing small wavelet coefficients. Moreover, the threshold for removal can be chosen such that the resulting approximation is guaranteed to be within a specified error tolerance of the original mesh. A number of examples are shown in the color plates.

- *Progressive display and transmission*: An attractive method for displaying a complex object is to begin with a low resolution version that can be quickly rendered, and then progressively improve the display as more detail is obtained from disk or over a network. Using a multiresolution representation, this is simply achieved by first displaying the base mesh, and then progressively adding the contributions of wavelet coefficients in order of decreasing magnitude.

- *Level-of-detail control*: High performance rendering systems often use a level-of-detail hierarchy, that is, a sequence of approximations at various levels-of-detail. The crudest approximations are used when the viewer is far from the object, while higher detail versions are substituted as the viewer approaches. Multiresolution representations naturally support this type of display by adding successively smaller wavelet coefficients as the viewer approaches the object, and by removing them as the viewer recedes. Moreover, the coefficients can be added smoothly, thereby avoiding the visual discontinuities encountered when switching between approximations of different resolution. This use of multiresolution representations is illustrated in Color Plates 1(k) and 1(l).

- *Multiresolution editing*: Editing at various scales can proceed along the lines developed by Finkelstein and Salesin [4] by ordering coefficients according to their support, that is, by the spatial extent of their influence. Color Plates 2(e) and 2(f) show edits of a mesh at low and high levels of detail.

Although the multiresolution analysis of Lounsbery *et al.* [11] can be applied to meshes of arbitrary topological type, it has a serious shortcoming: it is restricted to meshes with *subdivision connectivity*, that is, to meshes obtained from a simple base mesh by recursive 4-to-1 splitting (see Figure 1). Figure 6(a) shows an example of a mesh with subdivision connectivity — it results from recursively splitting the faces of an octahedron four times. Unfortunately, few of the meshes encountered in practice have this restricted structure.

Permission to make digital/hard copy of part or all of this work for personal or classroom use is granted without fee provided that copies are not made or distributed for profit or commercial advantage, the copyright notice, the title of the publication and its date appear, and notice is given that copying is by permission of ACM, Inc. To copy otherwise, to republish, to post on servers, or to redistribute to lists, requires prior specific permission and/or a fee.

In this paper we present a method for overcoming the subdivision connectivity restriction, meaning that completely arbitrary meshes can now be converted to multiresolution form. Our approach is to develop an algorithm for approximating an arbitrary mesh M (as in Color Plate 1(a)), which might not have subdivision connectivity, by a mesh M^J that does (as in Color Plate 1(f)), and is guaranteed to be within a prescribed tolerance ϵ_1 of M. We refer to this process as *remeshing*, and we call M^J the *remesh*.

Multiresolution analysis of an arbitrary mesh M thus proceeds in two steps: we first use remeshing to approximate M by a mesh M^J with subdivision connectivity, and then use the method of Lounsbery *et al.* to convert M^J to multiresolution representation. (Although we cannot reproduce here all the results of Lounsbery *et al.* [11], we have included a brief summary in Appendix A.)

The key ingredient of the remeshing procedure — and the principal technical contribution of the paper — is the construction of a parametrization of M over a *base complex K^0* possessing a small number of faces. We then sample the parametrization to produce the remesh. Considerable care is taken to create a parametrization and a sampling pattern so that the resulting remesh can be well approximated with relatively few wavelet coefficients.

The construction of parametrizations for complex shapes over simple domains is a fundamental problem that occurs in numerous applications, including texture mapping, and the approximation of meshes by NURBS patches. We therefore expect that our parametrization algorithm will have uses outside of remeshing.

The remainder of the paper is organized as follows. In Section 2, we describe the relationship between our work and previously published methods. In Section 3, we give a high level overview of the major steps of the remeshing algorithm. The details of the algorithm are presented in Sections 4-7. In Section 8, we apply our method to meshes of varying complexity, and give examples of compression, level-of-detail control, and editing. We close with conclusions and future work in Section 9.

2   Related Work

The difficulty of dealing with complicated shapes is evidenced by the extensive recent research on the topic.

The problems of compression/simplification and level-of-detail control have been addressed by Turk [20], Schroeder *et al.* [19], Hoppe *et al.* [8], Rossignac and Borrel [16], and Varsney [22]. Our approach differs from these methods in three principal respects. First, it provides guaranteed error bounds, whereas the approaches of Turk, Schroeder *et al.*, and Hoppe *et al.* do not. Second, it produces a single compact representation from which a continuous family of lower resolution approximations can be quickly and easily constructed, whereas the previous methods generate a discrete set of models of varying complexity. (We should note, however, that Turk, and Rossignac/Borrel, and Varsney present methods for interpolating between models.) Third, our representation can be simply and conveniently edited at multiple scales, whereas it is hard to imagine how one would achieve similar results using the previous approaches.

The editing of complex shapes was a central motivation for the introduction of hierarchical B-splines by Forsey and Bartels [6]. Forsey and Bartels [5] and Forsey and Wang [7] have subsequently developed methods for fitting hierarchical B-splines to meshes topologically equivalent to a disk. Finkelstein and Salesin [4] have demonstrated how wavelet representations of B-spline curves and tensor product surfaces can be used to achieve similar benefits. The main advantage of our method is its ability to deal with shapes of arbitrary topological type.

The problem of parametrizing meshes has recently been con-

sidered by Maillot *et al.* [12] in the context of texture mapping. However, the parametrizations they construct are not useful for our purpose: their surface tiles are not triangular, and their local parametrizations do not fit together continuously. Additionally, our local parametrizations, based on the well-established theory of harmonic maps, are simpler to compute than the ones used by Maillot *et al.*, and seem to produce parametrizations of comparable quality (see Section 4).

Finally, the technique of Schröder and Sweldens [18] could be used in place of Lounsbery *et al.* for multiresolution analysis of the remesh.

3   Overview of Remeshing

The basic idea of remeshing is to construct a parametrization of M over a suitably determined domain mesh K^0. This parametrization is then resampled to produce a mesh M^J that has subdivision connectivity and is of the same topological type as M.

Our remeshing algorithm consists of three steps, as illustrated in Color Plates 1(a)-1(h):

1. *Partitioning:* Partition M into a number of triangular regions $T_1, ..., T_r$, as shown in Color Plate 1(d). We want the number r of regions to be small, because the lowest complexity approximation we can construct has r faces, as shown in Color Plate 1(e). Basic tools used in partitioning are harmonic maps, maps that preserve as much of the metric structure (lengths, angles, etc.) of M as possible. Harmonic maps are described in Section 4. A detailed description of our partitioning algorithm is given in Section 5.

   Identifying each of the m vertices or *nodes* of the triangulation $T_1, ..., T_r$ with a canonical basis vector of $\mathbf{R}^m$ defines a mesh in $\mathbf{R}^m$, called the *base complex*, with a face corresponding to each of the r triangular regions. This mesh serves as the domain of the parametrization constructed in the next step.

2. *Parametrization:* For each region T_i of M construct a (local) parametrization $\rho_i : F_i \rightarrow T_i$ over the corresponding face F_i of the base complex K^0. The local parametrizations are made to fit together continuously, meaning that collectively they define a globally continuous parametrization $\rho : K^0 \rightarrow M$. We want the coordinate functions of the parametrization to vary as little as possible since such functions have multiresolution approximations with few significant wavelet coefficients, leading to high compression ratios. Harmonic maps in a sense minimize distortion and therefore are particularly well suited for this purpose. A description of the parametrization step is presented in Section 6.

3. *Resampling:* Perform J recursive 4-to-1 splits on each of the faces of K^0 (see Figure 1). This results in a triangulation K^J of K^0 with subdivision connectivity. The remesh M^J, as shown in Color Plate 1(f), is obtained by mapping the vertices of K^J into $\mathbf{R}^3$ using the parametrization ρ, and constructing an interpolating mesh in the obvious way; M^J therefore has vertices lying on M, and has subdivision connectivity.

   The resampling step is described more fully in Section 7, and it is shown that J can be determined so that M^J and M differ by no more than a specified remeshing tolerance ϵ_1.

4   Harmonic maps

A crucial building block of our remeshing algorithm is a method for constructing a parametrization of a (topological) disk $D \subset M$ over a convex polygonal region $P \subset \mathbf{R}^2$. This method is used in two places: in the construction of the triangulation $T_1, \ldots, T_r$ of

(a) (b) (c)

Figure 1: 4-to-1 splitting of a triangular face: (a) the initial face; (b) after one 4-to-1 split; (c) after two 4-to-1 splits.

M (see Section 5), and in the parametrization of M over the base complex K^0 (see Section 6). We want this parametrization to have small distortion; for example, if D is (close to) planar, we want the parametrization to be (close to) linear. Because the region may be geometrically complex (see, for example, Figure 2), some distortion is usually inevitable.

While it is not clear in general how to find a parametrization ρ with small distortion, there is a closely related and well-studied problem that has a unique solution: Fix a homeomorphism g between the boundary of D and the boundary of the polygonal region P; then there is a unique *harmonic map* $h : D \rightarrow P$ that agrees with g on the boundary of D and minimizes *metric dispersion* (see Eells and Sampson [3], pages 114–115, and the survey article by Eells and Lemaire[2]). Metric dispersion is a measure of the extent to which a map stretches regions of small diameter in D. It is thus a measure of metric distortion.

In addition to minimizing metric distortion, the harmonic map h has a number of important properties: (i) It is infinitely differentiable on each face of D; (ii) it is an embedding [17]; and (iii) it is independent of the triangulation of D. Because $h : D \rightarrow P$ is an embedding, the inverse h^{-1} is a parametrization of D over P. We will return below to the issues of choosing the boundary map g and of computing approximations to h.

The dispersion minimizing property of harmonic maps is illustrated in Figure 2, which shows a piecewise linear approximation of a harmonic map from a geometrically complex region onto a polygon. The relatively dense regions of the polygon correspond to the ears and nose of the cat. Notice that the aspect ratios of triangles tend to be preserved. Notice also that the map introduces a certain amount of area compression. This is inevitable because the region has a large area relative to its circumference, and consequently any embedding must introduce some distortion in edge lengths. The harmonic map tends to minimize such distortion while maintaining the embedding property and attempting to preserve aspect ratios of triangles.

Harmonic maps can be visualized as follows. Imagine D to be composed of elastic, triangular rubber sheets sewn together along their edges. Stretch the boundary of D over the boundary of the polygon P according to the map g. The harmonic map minimizes the total energy $E_{harm}[h]$ of this configuration of rubber sheets.

Rather than constructing the harmonic map directly, we compute a piecewise linear approximation. Assume that n vertices $v_1, \ldots, v_n$, called *corners*, have been selected on the boundary ∂D of D (see Figure 2), and (for technical reasons) assume that the degree of each of the remaining boundary vertices is at least 3.

We choose the polygon P by mapping the corners of D onto the vertices of an n-gon in $\mathbf{R}^2$. The vertices of the n-gon are positioned on a circle such that the sides subtend angles proportional to the arc lengths of the boundary segments of D joining the corresponding corners. We then define g to be the piecewise linear map that sends the corners of ∂D to the vertices of P, and is a homothety (i.e. an isometry up to a constant factor) between each boundary segment of D and the corresponding side of P (Figure 2).

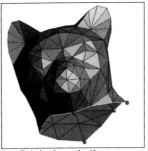 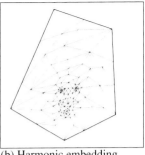

(a) Original mesh tile (b) Harmonic embedding

Figure 2: The harmonic map for the head of a cat. The neck of the cat is mapped onto the boundary of the polygon. The "corner" vertices (thoses sent to vertices of the polygon) are indicated by small balls.

Now suppose that h is any piecewise linear map that agrees with g on the boundary. It is therefore uniquely determined by its values $h(i)$ at the vertices of D. By explicitly integrating the functional E_{harm} over each face, one finds that E_{harm} can be reinterpreted as the energy of a configuration of springs with one spring placed along each edge of D:

$$E_{harm}[h] = 1/2 \sum_{\{i,j\} \in \text{Edges}(D)} \kappa_{i,j} \|h(i) - h(j)\|^2, \qquad (1)$$

where the spring constants $\kappa_{i,j}$ are computed as follows: For each edge $\{i, j\}$, let $\mathrm{L}_{i,j}$ denote its length as measured in the initial mesh D, and for each face $\{i, j, k\}$, let $\text{Area}_{i,j,k}$ denote its area, again as measured in D. Each interior edge $\{i, j\}$ is incident to two faces, say $\{i, j, k_1\}$ and $\{i, j, k_2\}$. Then

$$\kappa_{i,j} = \left(\mathrm{L}_{i,k_1}^2 + \mathrm{L}_{j,k_1}^2 - \mathrm{L}_{i,j}^2 \right) / \text{Area}_{i,j,k_1} + \left(\mathrm{L}_{i,k_2}^2 + \mathrm{L}_{j,k_2}^2 - \mathrm{L}_{i,j}^2 \right) / \text{Area}_{i,j,k_2}$$

The formula for spring constants associated to boundary edges has only one term.

Although the spring constants $\kappa_{i,j}$ can assume negative values, the function (1) is positive definite, and its unique minimum can be found by solving a sparse linear least-squares problem for the values $h(i)$. In contrast to the harmonic map itself, its piecewise linear approximation is not always an embedding. In our experience, this problem occurs extremely rarely (3 times in the roughly 1000 harmonic maps we computed). In these cases we use uniform spring constants.

For the remainder of this paper we refer to the unique piecewise linear function minimizing (1) as a harmonic map, although strictly speaking it is only an approximation.

Others have developed similar approaches to embedding disk-like regions. One such approach, described by Kent *et al.* [9], is also based on minimizing the energy of a network of springs. They choose spring constants to be either all equal or inversely proportional to edge lengths. Maillot *et al.* [12] introduced another functional, also based on elasticity theory.

Figure 3 illustrates the behavior of the various embedding schemes in a simple example where the region D (see Figure 3(a)) is a triangulation of a planar polygon P and $g : \partial D \rightarrow \partial P$ is the identity. The harmonic map (Figure 3(b)) is the identity map and therefore has no metric distortion. The method of Kent *et al.* with either choice of spring constants produces considerable metric distortion (Figure 3(c) and (d)).

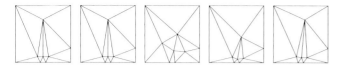

Figure 3: Comparison of various "spring embeddings". From left to right: (a) Original mesh; (b) Harmonic map and embedding of Maillot *et al.* with $\alpha = 1$; (c) $\kappa_{i,j} = 1$; (d) $\kappa_{i,j} = 1/L_{i,j}$; (e) Embedding of Maillot *et al.* with $\alpha = 1/2$.

The mathematical properties of the functional proposed by Maillot *et al.* are not entirely clear. In particular, the smooth theory to which it is an approximation does not yield planar embeddings of geometrically complex regions. This led them to introduce a user-specified tuning parameter α. In the example of Figure 3, the choice $\alpha = 1$ also produces the identity map, whereas the choice $\alpha = 1/2$ leads to small distortion (see Figure 3(e)). The method of Maillot *et al.* appears produce results whose quality is comparable to ours (for appropriately chosen α). However, their method requires non-linear optimization, whereas our method requires only the solution of a sparse linear least-squares problem.

5 Partitioning

Our partitioning scheme is based on the concepts of Voronoi diagrams and Delaunay triangulations. Let us first see how these concepts could be used to partition a dense triangulation of a planar region into a small number of large triangles. We could begin by selecting a set of relatively uniformly distributed vertices of the dense triangulation, and then compute the Delaunay triangulation for the selected vertices. One method for computing the Delaunay triangulation for a set of sites in the plane is to first construct the Voronoi diagram. Its polyhedral dual is the Delaunay triangulation if Voronoi tiles meet three at a corner.

By analogy, our approach is to first partition the faces of M into a set of Voronoi-like tiles τ_i using a discrete approximation of the Voronoi diagram as described in Section 5.1. Unlike typical uses of Voronoi diagrams, we do not know the sites *a priori* — they are determined dynamically as the Voronoi diagram is constructed.

We then construct the dual to the Voronoi diagram, resulting in a Delaunay-like partition of M into triangular regions T_i, as described in Section 5.2.

5.1 Constructing the Voronoi diagram

As mentioned above, we use a discrete version of the Voronoi diagram to partition M into a set of Voronoi-like tiles. An efficient algorithm for constructing true Voronoi diagrams on the surface of a mesh has been developed by Mount [15], but it is rather difficult to implement, and is unnecessary for our purposes.

We first describe an algorithm for computing tiles $\tau_1, ..., \tau_s$ given a set of sites logically positioned at the centroids of the *site faces* $S = \{f_1, ..., f_s\}$. We then present an algorithm for selecting a set S of site faces for which the induced Voronoi diagram is dual to a triangulation. The results of applying the Voronoi algorithm is shown in Color Plate 1(b).

Constructing the Voronoi diagram for a given set of site faces
A Voronoi tile τ_i consists of all faces for which the closest site face is f_i. Our measure of distance between faces is an approximation of geodesic distance over the surface. It is defined by constructing a dual graph to the mesh: the nodes of the graph correspond to faces of M, and the edges of the graph connect nodes corresponding to adjacent faces. We set the cost of edges in this dual graph to be the distance between centroids of the corresponding faces. The distance between two faces is defined as length of the shortest path in this dual graph.

Constructing the Voronoi diagram is a multi-source shortest path problem in the dual graph, which we solve using a variant of Dijkstra's algorithm [1]. The algorithm simultaneously grows the Voronoi tiles from their site faces until they cover M.

Selecting the site faces In this section we describe an algorithm for selecting a set S of site faces such that the induced Voronoi diagram, computed as above, is dual to a triangulation. Although our algorithm for selecting such site faces can be applied to any mesh M, let us assume for the moment that M does not possess boundaries. With this assumption, the Voronoi diagram must satisfy the following conditions to be dual to a triangulation:

1. tiles must be homeomorphic to disks;

2. no pair of tiles may share more than one *cut* (a cut is a contiguous set of edges of M along which a pair of tiles touch);

3. no more than three tiles can meet at any vertex.

The algorithm begins by initializing S with a single randomly chosen site face. In the outer loop we then incrementally add faces to S until the induced tiling satisfies conditions (1) through (3) above.

In the inner loop (tile growth), tiles associated with the faces in S are grown until either they cover M, in which case tile growth terminates, or until condition (1) is violated. Violation of condition (1) can be detected by examining only the neighborhood of the most recently added face. If condition (1) is violated, this face is added to S and tile growth is resumed.

When tile growth is complete, conditions (2) and (3) are checked. If condition (2) is violated, a face along one of the offending shared cuts is selected as a new site face. If condition (3) is violated, one of the faces adjacent to the offending vertex is selected as a site. If all adjacent faces already are sites, the Voronoi algorithm fails. This has never happened in any of the examples we have run. If it were to happen, we would simply use the original mesh as the base mesh.

To accommodate boundaries, we introduce a single *fictitious* Voronoi tile, logically outside of M, that touches each of the boundaries of M. Conditions (1) through (3) can then be applied without change. To ensure that the Delaunay-like triangulation covers M, we require that boundary tiles (those adjacent to the fictitious tile) have sites on the boundary of M. This issue is addressed again in the next section. To achieve this requirement, the algorithm adds a new boundary site face whenever an interior tile touches a boundary. As before, when tile growth stops, conditions (2) and (3) are checked, and if violated, appropriate new sites are added.

It sometimes happens that tiles have adjacent short cuts, a situation that leads to Delaunay-like triangles with poor aspect ratios, and hence to poor compression rates. We therefore add to the list of conditions one that disallows such tiles. Adjacent cuts of a tile are deemed short if the sum of their lengths is less than 10% of the length of the boundary of the tile. When an offending pair of cuts is found, one of the faces they share is added as a new site.

Properties of the Voronoi algorithm The time complexity of the Voronoi algorithm depends on the number s of sites that are needed, for which there is no general formula. For a fixed set of s sites, the Voronoi tiles can be constructed using an s-source version of Dijkstra's algorithm. Like the ordinary single source Dijkstra algorithm, the s-source version can be implemented efficiently ($O(n \log n)$ time) using a priority queue, where the priority of a face is the distance to the nearest site.

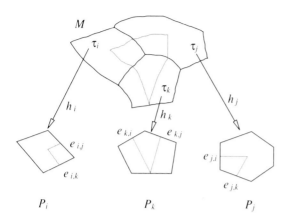

Figure 4: Construction of initial Delaunay paths on M.

Naively rerunning Dijkstra's algorithm from scratch each time a new site face is added would require $O(s\,n\log n)$ time. However, the algorithm can be sped up significantly by incrementally updating the priority queue as new sites are added to S.

Finally, because our site selection algorithm uses a greedy search, it cannot be expected to produce a minimal set of sites.

5.2 Constructing the Delaunay triangulation

The partition of M into Voronoi tiles obtained in the previous section has the property that its dual graph consists of 3-sided faces. However, mapping these 3-sided faces onto the surface is a nontrivial problem. The obvious approach of connecting pairs of Voronoi sites by the shortest paths on the surface — as is done in constructing the Delaunay triangulation in the plane — is not guaranteed to produce a valid triangulation for arbitrary manifolds since the resulting paths can cross. Moreover, finding the shortest paths between two points on a mesh is itself a difficult problem [14]. Our alternative uses harmonic maps twice: once to produce an initial Delaunay triangulation, and then again to improve the triangulation by straightening its edges.

Constructing an initial Delaunay triangulation. The first step is to compute the harmonic map h_i that carries each Voronoi tile τ_i into an appropriate planar polygon P_i, as described in Section 4. The inverse of h_i provides a parametrization of τ_i over P_i which we use to construct paths lying on M.

Let τ_i and τ_j denote two adjacent interior Voronoi tiles as illustrated in Figure 4. The path of the initial Delaunay triangulation joining these tiles is constructed as follows: the cut shared by the tiles is mapped to an edge $e_{i,j}$ of P_i by the harmonic map h_i; similarly, the cut is mapped to an edge $e_{j,i}$ of P_j by h_j (see Figure 4). We construct a line $L_{i,j}$ from the centroid of P_i to the midpoint of $e_{i,j}$, and a line $L_{j,i}$ from the centroid of P_j to the midpoint of $e_{j,i}$. The path is formed by mapping these lines onto M using the inverse harmonic maps. That is, the path is obtained by joining $h_i^{-1}(L_{i,j})$ and $h_j^{-1}(L_{j,i})$.[1]

The construction of a path between an interior tile τ_i and a boundary tile τ_k is slightly different, as indicated in Figure 4. In order for the Delaunay triangulation to cover M, it is necessary to construct paths from the boundary. (The site selection algorithm of Section 5.1 was designed with this goal in mind in that it guarantees

---

[1]Note that this path does not connect the site faces as one might expect. We have found that the method described here produces more uniform triangulations than were obtained by connecting site faces.

that boundary tiles have site faces on the boundary.) We therefore select a boundary vertex v_k of the site face f_k, and construct $L_{k,i}$ as the line from $h_k(v_k)$ to the midpoint of $e_{k,i}$. The line $L_{i,k}$ is constructed as before from the centroid of P_i to the midpoint of $e_{i,k}$.

Finally, two adjacent boundary tiles τ_k and τ_ℓ are connected by the path along the boundary between v_k and v_ℓ.

The edges of the paths thus constructed are generally not edges of M. For convenience in constructing the parametrizations of Section 6, we refine M to include the path edges.

Straightening the Delaunay edges. The edges of the initial Delaunay triangles constructed in the first step can have kinks where they cross the border between two Voronoi tiles (see Color Plate 1(c)). To straighten a Delaunay edge, we construct a second harmonic map from the union of the two Delaunay triangles adjacent to the edge into a planar quadrilateral, as described in Section 4. We then replace the edge by the image of the corresponding diagonal of the quadrilateral under the inverse harmonic map. This straightening step is applied to all Delaunay edges in an arbitrary order, resulting in a final triangulation $T_1,...,T_r$. Color Plate 1(d) shows the result of straightening the edges in Color Plate 1(c).

6 Parametrization

Identifying each of the m vertices or *nodes* of the triangulation $T_1,...,T_r$ with a canonical basis vector of $\mathbf{R}^m$ defines the base complex $K^0 \subset \mathbf{R}^m$, with a face corresponding to each of the r triangular regions. The goal of this section is to construct a continuous parametrization $\rho : K^0 \to M$ of the initial mesh over K^0. We map each triangle T_i onto a triangular region of the plane, again using harmonic maps described in Section 4. We then affinely map the triangular region onto the corresponding face F_i of the base complex. The composition of the two maps is an embedding, and therefore its inverse ρ_i defines a parametrization of T_i over F_i. By construction, the maps ρ_i agree on shared boundaries, and thus the ρ_i collectively define a continuous parametrization ρ of M over K^0.

7 Resampling

In this section, we describe a method for producing a mesh M^J with subdivision connectivity from the parametrization $\rho : K^0 \to M$ constructed in Section 6. We also show how to determine the subdivision level J so that M^J and M differ by no more than a specified remeshing tolerance ϵ_1.

For a given value of J, we first produce a triangulation K^J of K^0 by performing J recursive 4-to-1 splits of the faces of K^0. We then approximate ρ by a function ρ^J defined as the piecewise linear interpolant to ρ on K^J; that is, ρ^J is such that $\rho^J(\mathbf{x}_i^J) = \rho(\mathbf{x}_i^J)$, where the points $\mathbf{x}_i^J$ (called *knots*) denote the vertices of K^J.

The simplest strategy for performing a 4-to-1 split of a face is to position the split points at midpoints of edges, as illustrated in Figure 1. We refer to this process as *parametrically uniform resampling* since the faces of K^J are of equal size. Alternatively, we could attempt to place the knots so that the images of triangles of K^J, that is, the triangles of the remesh M^J, are of equal size. We refer to this as *geometrically uniform resampling*.

As one of our fundamental objectives is high compression rate, we evaluate the performance of a resampling strategy by the number of wavelet coefficients needed for a given compression tolerance ϵ_2. This number is governed by at least two competing factors:

1. As mentioned in Section 3, the coordinate functions of ρ should be as slowly varying as possible; this is largely achieved by the distortion minimizing property of the harmonic map parametrizations.

ϵ_2	Geom. Uniform	Hybrid	Param. Uniform
0.5%	(2679) [5422]	(1768) [3562]	(2224) [4502]
1.0%	(1100) [2180]	(795) [1591]	(1044) [2079]
2.0%	(416) [809]	(385) [758]	(455) [881]
5.0%	(112) [223]	(130) [245]	(143) [302]

Table 1: Performance of the three sampling strategies on the cat model. Parentheses denote the number of significant wavelet coefficients; square brackets denote the number of triangles. All examples were run using $\epsilon_1 = 1.0\%$. Errors are measured as a percentage of the object's diameter.

2. The triangles of M^J should be of roughly uniform size. Lounsbery *et al.* define wavelets so that the magnitude of a wavelet coefficient is a measure of the "unweighted" least-squares error that would be incurred if the coefficient were set to zero. By unweighted we mean that deviations on large triangles of M^J are counted no more heavily than deviations on small triangles. If M^J has triangles of roughly uniform size, magnitudes of wavelet coefficients are better measures of geometric error.

The strategy that has performed best in our experiments is a hybrid strategy using geometrically uniform sampling in the first few splitting steps (the first three steps in all our examples), and parametrically uniform sampling in subsequent steps. Intuitively, this strategy does a reasonable job of uniformly distributing the triangles on a coarse scale, while still remaining faithful to the harmonic parametrization on smaller scales.

This intuition is supported by numerical results. Our tests have shown that hybrid resampling typically results in wavelet expansions with fewer significant coefficients than either parametrically uniform or geometrically uniform resampling. Moreover, the number of subdivisions J necessary to satisfy a remeshing tolerance ϵ_1 is often smaller and hence the remesh is often faster to compute and requires less storage. Table 1 presents the results of an experiment for the cat mesh (shown in Color Plate 2(d)) for various wavelet compression tolerances ϵ_2. Notice that hybrid resampling is particularly advantageous for small tolerances.

7.1 Geometrically uniform resampling

The task of determining new knots $\mathbf{x}_i^j \in K^0$ so that the triangles generated are roughly uniform in size is an optimization problem whose solution we approximate using the following recursive greedy algorithm.

In the parametrically uniform resampling process the knot $\mathbf{x}_i^j$ at level j is simply computed as midpoint of the edge of the two (neighboring) knots $\mathbf{x}_{n_1(i)}^{j-1}$ and $\mathbf{x}_{n_2(i)}^{j-1}$ at level $j-1$. Instead of performing uniform subdivision, we define

$$\mathbf{x}_i^j = (1 - \lambda_i^j) \cdot \mathbf{x}_{n_1(i)}^{j-1} + \lambda_i^j \cdot \mathbf{x}_{n_2(i)}^{j-1} \quad \text{with} \quad \lambda_i^j \in (0,1),$$

where the splitting parameter λ_i^j is determined as follows: Split the two faces adjacent to the edge from $\mathbf{x}_{n_1(i)}^{j-1}$ to $\mathbf{x}_{n_2(i)}^{j-1}$, as illustrated in Figure 5. Our goal is to find λ_i^j so that the regions $R_i^j = \triangle_{i,1}^j \cup \triangle_{i,3}^j$ and $S_i^j = \triangle_{i,2}^j \cup \triangle_{i,4}^j$ map to regions of equal area on M.

In the current implementation we have simplified the area computations by using a discrete approximation: We scatter a roughly uniform collection of points on the faces of M, then map these sample points back to K^0 using ρ^{-1} (ρ^{-1} is the harmonic map, so it is already known). We then use binary search to compute the parameter λ_i^j so that the number of sampled points in the regions R_i^j and

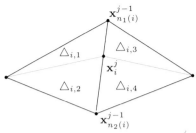

Figure 5: Computing the new knot $\mathbf{x}_i^j$

S_i^j are nearly equal.

7.2 Bounding the remeshing error

In this section we describe how to determine J such that the remesh M^J and the initial mesh M deviate by no more than a remeshing tolerance ϵ_1 in an L^∞ sense. That is, we seek to find the smallest J such that

$$\max_{\mathbf{x} \in K^0} \|\rho(\mathbf{x}) - \rho^J(\mathbf{x})\| \le \epsilon_1.$$

Our strategy for determining J will be to perform successive steps of 4-to-1 splitting until the error bound is satisfied.

To bound the error for a given value of J, let $E(\mathbf{x}) := \rho(\mathbf{x}) - \rho^J(\mathbf{x})$ denote the (vector-valued) error function. First, note that the preimages of the triangles of M under ρ form a partition π of K^0, and that ρ is a linear function on each triangle of π. Next, recall that ρ^J is linear within each of the triangles of the partition K^J of K^0. Thus, $E(\mathbf{x})$, the difference between the two, is linear within each cell of the union partition $\pi^J = \pi \cup K^J$. The squared norm of $E(\mathbf{x})$ is therefore quadratic and convex up over each cell of π^J, and so must achieve is maximum value at a vertex of π^J.

The L^∞ error for a given value of J can therefore easily be determined by evaluating $E(\mathbf{x})$ at the vertices of π^J. Using a local marching technique such as the one in Kent *et al.* [9], these vertices can be found in time proportional to the total number of vertices in π and K^J.

8 Results

Color Plates 1 and 2 illustrate the steps of the algorithm and present examples of its applications.

Color Plate 1(a)-1(h) demonstrate the complete process of multiresolution analysis for a mesh of genus 3. We first partition the original mesh of Color Plate 1(a) into Voronoi-like tiles shown in Color Plate 1(b). We then construct the initial Delaunay-like triangulation (Color Plate 1(c)), and straighten its edges (Color Plate 1(d)). The Delaunay triangles define a simple base complex that serves as the domain for the parametrization of the mesh. Resampling this parametrization using the hybrid strategy described in Section 7 with a remeshing tolerance of $\epsilon_1 = 0.75$ % required $J = 4$ subdivision steps and produced the remesh shown in Color Plate 1(f) consisting of 17,920 triangles. The lowest resolution approximation, shown in Color Plate 1(e), is a piecewise linear embedding of the base complex. Color Plates 1(g) and 1(h) show more detailed approximations using, respectively, 366 and 2,614 faces.

Table 2 summarizes the remeshing process for a variety of other meshes. (All computing times were measured on a SGI Onyx Reality Engine 2 with 256MB of memory.) Note that the number of Voronoi tiles is influenced more by the geometry of the model than by the number of faces of M.

Approximating the dinosaur and the phone with low tolerances would require high subdivision levels. This is due to the presence

object	# faces of M	# Voronoi tiles τ_i	# Delaunay triangles T_i	remesh. tol. ϵ_1	subdiv. level J	time mins
holes3	11,776	31	70	0.5 %	4	4.6
bunny	69,473	88	162	0.5 %	5	33.5
cat	698	7	9	1.0 %	6	0.8
dino	103,713	117	229	1.0 %	5	39.3
phone	165,896	69	132	2.5 %	5	346.6

Table 2: Summary of results of the remeshing algorithm

Color Plate	object	# faces of M^J	compr. tol. ϵ_2	# wavelet coeff.	# faces	time mins
1(g)	holes3	17,920	4.0 %	179	366	0.9
1(h)	holes3	17,920	0.5 %	1,298	2,614	1.0
2(a)	bunny	165,888	0.07 %	18,636	37,598	4.5
2(b)	bunny	165,888	0.7 %	2,268	4,639	3.7
2(c)	bunny	165,888	1.5 %	952	1,921	3.5
2(i)	dino	234,496	0.5 %	2,329	4,725	5.0
2(l)	phone	135,168	0.1 %	7,920	16,451	3.3

Table 3: Summary of results of the algorithm of Lounsbery *et al.*

of jagged boundaries which can only be well approximated using a large number of subdivisions.

Computing times are strongly dependent on the ratio of the number of faces of M to the number of Delaunay triangles, since the bottleneck of the algorithm, the harmonic map computation, requires solving sparse least-squares problems whose time complexity is proportional to the square of the number of vertices in the triangles.

Table 3 summarizes the results of wavelet compression applied to remeshed models. Each line of the table gives the number of faces of the remesh, the compression tolerance ϵ_2 used in the wavelet compression method described in Appendix A.2, the number of wavelet coefficients, the number of faces of the resulting approximation, and the time required for filterbank analysis and synthesis. The total deviation between the compressed model and the original is bounded by $\epsilon = \epsilon_1 + \epsilon_2$, the sum of the remeshing tolerance and the compression tolerance. Note that for storage and transmission purposes, the relevant performance measure is the number of wavelet coefficients rather than the number of faces, since only the wavelet coefficients (and their indices) have to be stored or transmitted.

Color Plates 1(k)-1(l) illustrate level-of-detail control. The original model (Color Plates 1(f) and 1(k)) was created from laser range data using the mesh zippering algorithm of Turk and Levoy [21]. Color Plates 1(k) and 1(l) show views of the original model and of lower resolution approximations from three different distances. Color Plates 2(a)-2(c) are close-ups of the approximations in Color Plate 2(l). Note the enormous reduction in the number of triangles when the multiresolution approximations are viewed from afar.

Color Plates 2(d)-(f) illustrate *multiresolution editing*. Color Plate 2(e) shows a large-scale modification caused by changing a wavelet coefficient at the coarsest level, whereas Color Plate 2(f) corresponds to changing two coefficients at an intermediate level-of-detail.

Color Plates 2(g)-(l) show the application of remeshing and multiresolution analysis to two additional meshes.

9 Conclusion

We have described an algorithm for solving the remeshing problem, that is, the problem of approximating an arbitrary mesh by a mesh

with subdivision connectivity. Combined with the previous work of Lounsbery *et al.*, our remeshing algorithm allows multiresolution analysis to be applied to arbitrary meshes. Multiresolution representations support efficient storage, rendering, transmission, and editing of complex meshes in a simple, unified, and theoretically sound way.

We have applied our remeshing algorithm and multiresolution analysis to complicated meshes consisting of more than 100,000 triangles. Examples of compression, level-of-detail rendering, and editing are shown in the Color Plates.

The key ingredient of our remeshing procedure — and the principal technical contribution of the paper — is the construction of a continuous parametrization of an arbitrary mesh over a simple domain mesh. Parametrizing complex shapes over simple domains is a fundamental problem in numerous applications, including texture mapping and the approximation of meshes by NURBS patches. We therefore expect that our parametrization algorithm will have uses outside of multiresolution analysis. We intend to explore these uses in future work.

Acknowledgments

This work was supported in part by a postdoctoral fellowship for the lead author (Eck) from the German Research Foundation (DFG), Alias Research Inc., Microsoft Corp., and the National Science Foundation under grants CCR-8957323, DMS-9103002, and DMS-9402734. We are grateful to Marc Levoy and his students at Stanford University for providing the bunny, dinosaur, and phone models.

References

[1] A. Aho, J.E. Hopcroft, and J.D. Ullman. *Data structures and algorithms.* Addison-Wesley, Reading, Mass., 1983.

[2] J. Eells and L. Lemaire. Another report on harmonic maps. *Bull. London Math. Soc.*, 20:385–524, 1988.

[3] J. Eells and J.H. Sampson. Harmonic mappings of Riemannian manifolds. *Amer. J. Math.*, 86:109–160, 1964.

[4] Adam Finkelstein and David Salesin. Multiresolution curves. *Computer Graphics (SIGGRAPH '94 Proceedings)*, 28(3):261–268, July 1994.

[5] D. Forsey and R. Bartels. Hierarchical B-spline fitting. *ACM Transactions on Graphics.* To appear.

[6] D. Forsey and R. Bartels. Hierarchical B-spline refinement. *Computer Graphics*, 22(4):205–212, 1988.

[7] David Forsey and Lifeng Wang. Multi-resolution surface approximation for animation. In *Proceedings of Graphics Interface*, 1993.

[8] H. Hoppe, T. DeRose, T. Duchamp, J. McDonald, and W. Stuetzle. Mesh optimization. *Computer Graphics (SIGGRAPH '93 Proceedings)*, pages 19–26, August 1993.

[9] James R. Kent, Wayne E. Carlson, and Richard E. Parent. Shape transformation for polyhedral objects. *Computer Graphics (SIGGRAPH '92 Proceedings)*, 26(2):47–54, July 1992.

[10] J. Michael Lounsbery. *Multiresolution Analysis for Surfaces of Arbitrary Topological Type.* PhD thesis, Department of Computer Science and Engineering, University of Washington, September 1994. Available as ftp://cs.washington.edu/pub/graphics/LounsPhd.ps.Z.

[11] Michael Lounsbery, Tony DeRose, and Joe Warren. Multiresolution analysis for surfaces of arbitrary topological type. Submitted for publication. Preliminary version available as Technical Report 93-10-05b, Department of Computer Science and Engineering, University of Washington, January, 1994. Also available as ftp://cs.washington.edu/pub/graphics/TR931005b.ps.Z.

[12] J. Maillot, H. Yahia, and A. Verroust. Interactive texture mapping. *Computer Graphics (SIGGRAPH '93 Proceedings)*, 27(3):27–34, August 1993.

[13] Stephane Mallat. A theory for multiresolution signal decomposition: The wavelet representation. *IEEE Transactions on Pattern Analysis and Machine Intelligence*, 11(7):674–693, July 1989.

[14] J.S. Mitchell, D.M. Mount, and C.H. Papadimitriou. The discrete geodesic problem. *SIAM Journal of Computing*, 16(4):647–668, 1987.

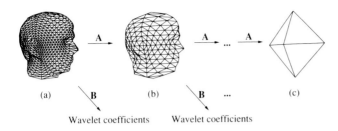

Figure 6: Decomposition of a mesh.

[15] David M. Mount. Voronoi diagrams on the surface of a polyhedron. Department of Computer Science CAR-TR-121, CS-TR-1496, University of Maryland, May 1985.

[16] J. Rossignac and P. Borrel. Multi-resolution 3D approximations for rendering. In B. Falcidieno and T.L. Kunii, editors, *Modeling in Computer Graphics*, pages 455–465. Springer-Verlag, June-July 1993.

[17] Richard Schoen and Shing-Tung Yau. Univalent harmonic maps between surfaces. *Inventiones math.*, 44:265–278, 1978.

[18] P. Schröder and W. Sweldens. Spherical wavelets: Efficiently representing functions on the sphere. *Computer Graphics, (SIGGRAPH '95 Proceedings)*, 1995.

[19] William Schroeder, Jonathan Zarge, and William Lorensen. Decimation of triangle meshes. *Computer Graphics (SIGGRAPH '92 Proceedings)*, 26(2):65–70, July 1992.

[20] Greg Turk. Re-tiling polygonal surfaces. *Computer Graphics (SIGGRAPH '92 Proceedings)*, 26(2):55–64, July 1992.

[21] Greg Turk and Marc Levoy. Zippered polygon meshes from range images. *Computer Graphics (SIGGRAPH '94 Proceedings)*, 28(3):311–318, July 1994.

[22] Amitabh Varshney. *Hierarchical Geometric Approximations*. PhD thesis, Department of Computer Science, University of North Carolina at Chapel Hill, 1994.

A Multiresolution Analysis of Subdivision Meshes

As mentioned in Section 1, the main idea of multiresolution analysis is to decompose a function into a low resolution part and a set of correction or "detail" terms at increasing resolutions. Multiresolution analysis was first formalized by Mallat [13] for functions defined on $\mathbf{R}^n$. Lounsbery [10] and Lounsbery *et al.* [11] have recently extended the notion of multiresolution analysis to functions defined on base complexes of arbitrary topological type. Their results can be used to construct multiresolution representations of meshes with subdivision connectivity. The purpose of this appendix is to summarize their basic results and algorithms at a high level.

A.1 Background

The two basic ingredients of multiresolution analysis are a sequence of nested linear function spaces and an inner product. Lounsbery *et al.* use a sequence of spaces $V^0 \subset V^1 \subset \cdots$ associated with the base complex. To describe meshes, the approximation spaces V^j consist of piecewise linear functions; specifically, V^j is the space of continuous piecewise linear functions over a partition K^j of K^0 created by performing j recursive steps of 4-to-1 splitting to the faces of K^0, as shown in Figure 1. As j increases, the triangulation K^j becomes more dense, and so the functions in V^j are better able to model arbitrary continuous functions on K^0. The inner product used by Lounsbery *et al.* is the standard inner product defined as

$$\langle f, g \rangle := \int_{\mathbf{x} \in K^0} f(\mathbf{x}) g(\mathbf{x}) d\mathbf{x}$$

where $d\mathbf{x}$ is the differential area of K^0 embedded in $\mathbf{R}^m$, so that all faces have unit area.

The inner product is used to define the following orthogonal complement spaces, also called *wavelet spaces*,

$$W^j := \{ f \in V^{j+1} \mid \langle f, g \rangle = 0 \quad \forall g \in V^j \}.$$

Intuitively, W^j captures the detail that is missed when a function in V^{j+1} is approximated by a function in V^j.

Basis functions for V^j are called *scaling functions*. In the piecewise linear case, particularly simple scaling functions for V^j are the "hat functions" on K^j: the i-th hat function $\phi_i^j \in V^j$ is the unique function in V^j that is one at $\mathbf{x}_i^j$ and zero at all other knots of K^j.

A *wavelet* $\psi_i^k(\mathbf{x})$ is a basis function for one of the wavelet spaces W^k. Lounsbery *et al.* [11] give constructions for wavelet bases on arbitrary base complexes K^0. A *wavelet basis* for V^j consists of a basis for V^0 together with bases for the wavelet spaces $W^0, ..., W^{j-1}$.

The parametrization $\rho^J \in V^J$ for V^j can be expanded in the hat function basis as

$$\rho^J(\mathbf{x}) = \sum_i v_i^J \phi_i^J, \qquad \mathbf{x} \in K^0 \qquad (2)$$

where v_i^J denote the vertex positions of M^J. A *multiresolution representation* of ρ^J refers to its expansion in a wavelet basis

$$\rho^J(\mathbf{x}) = \sum_i v_i^0 \phi_i^0(\mathbf{x}) + \sum_{j=0}^{J-1} \sum_i w_i^j \psi_i^j(\mathbf{x}), \qquad \mathbf{x} \in K^0, \quad (3)$$

where w_i^j denote the wavelet coefficients.

An algorithm known as *filterbank analysis* can be used to convert between the hat function expansion and the multiresolution representation. The geometric interpretation of filterbank analysis is shown in Figure 6. The full detail model, described by $\rho^J(\mathbf{x})$ is successively decomposed into a lower resolution approximation together with a collection of coefficients that multiply the wavelets. The result is a simple base mesh together with wavelet coefficients at various levels of detail. The operators $\mathbf{A}$ and $\mathbf{B}$ in Figure 6 refer to sparse matrices whose entries are given by Lounsbery *et al..* The filterbank analysis has an inverse process called filterbank synthesis that recovers the full resolution model from its multiresolution representation.

A.2 L^∞ Wavelet compression

The L^∞ error caused by wavelet compression is the L^∞ norm of the difference function $\delta(\mathbf{x}) = \rho^J(\mathbf{x}) - \tilde{\rho}^J(\mathbf{x})$, where $\tilde{\rho}^J(\mathbf{x})$ denotes the compressed approximation to $\rho^J(\mathbf{x})$. This difference function is simply the sum of the wavelet terms that have been removed from $\rho^J(\mathbf{x})$. Since $\delta(\mathbf{x})$ is a piecewise linear function on K^J, its L^∞ norm can be determined as in Section 7.2 by recording its values at the vertices of K^J.

Compression in principle proceeds by considering the wavelet coefficients in order of increasing magnitude. A coefficient is removed if doing so does not cause the L^∞ norm of $\delta(\mathbf{x})$ to exceed ϵ_2. If removal of a coefficient would violate the error tolerance, the coefficient is retained and the next coefficient is examined. The procedure terminates when all coefficients have been considered for removal. The examples presented in this paper have used a conservative approximation to this approach where a bound on the L^∞ norm of $\delta(\mathbf{x})$ is maintained, rather than maintaining $\delta(\mathbf{x})$ itself; we plan to implement the principled approach in the near future.

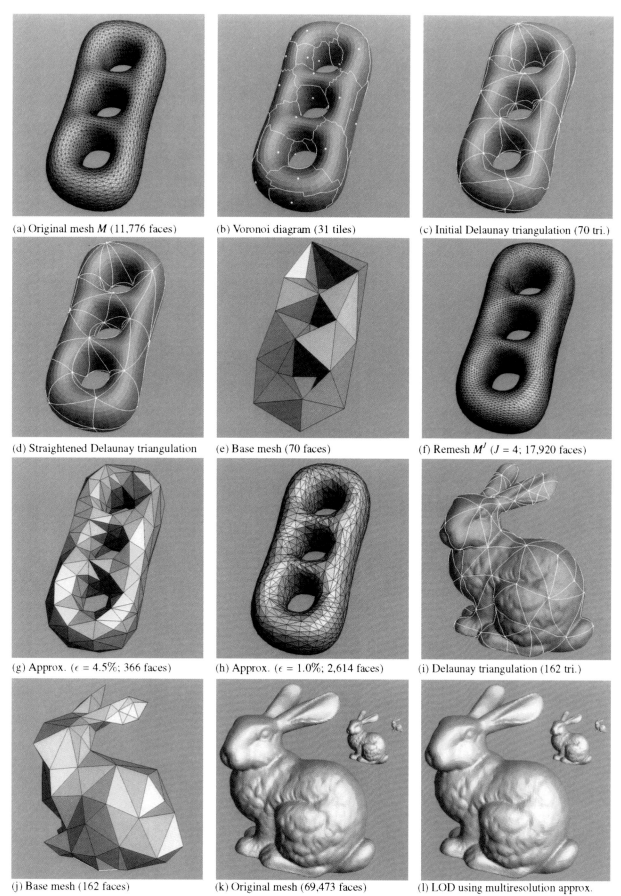

(a) Original mesh M (11,776 faces)

(b) Voronoi diagram (31 tiles)

(c) Initial Delaunay triangulation (70 tri.)

(d) Straightened Delaunay triangulation

(e) Base mesh (70 faces)

(f) Remesh M^J ($J = 4$; 17,920 faces)

(g) Approx. ($\epsilon = 4.5\%$; 366 faces)

(h) Approx. ($\epsilon = 1.0\%$; 2,614 faces)

(i) Delaunay triangulation (162 tri.)

(j) Base mesh (162 faces)

(k) Original mesh (69,473 faces)

(l) LOD using multiresolution approx.

Color Plate 1: (a-g) Example of partition, parameterization, resampling, and approximation of a mesh using multiresolution analysis; (h-k) Level-of-detail approximations of a dense mesh.

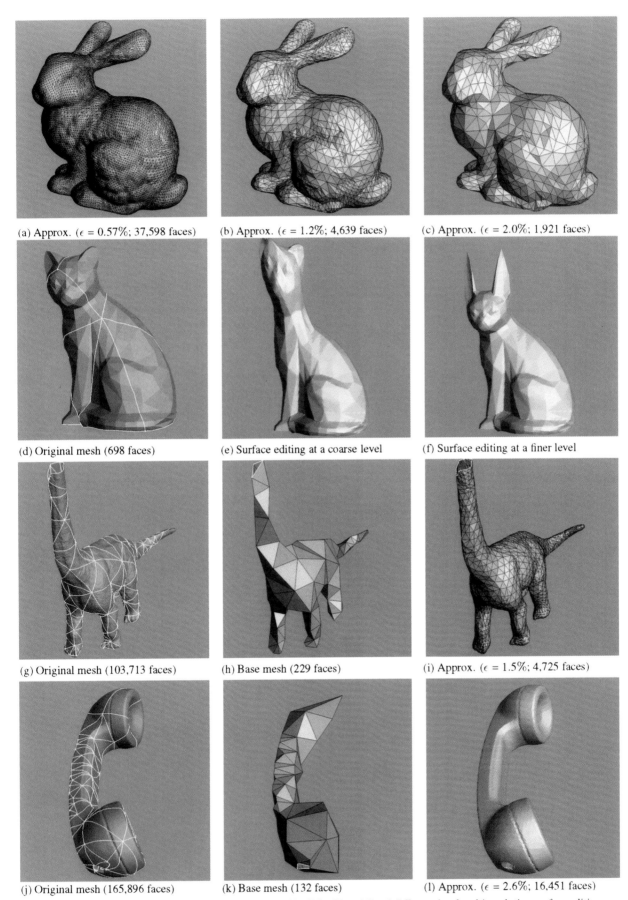

(a) Approx. ($\epsilon = 0.57\%$; 37,598 faces)   (b) Approx. ($\epsilon = 1.2\%$; 4,639 faces)   (c) Approx. ($\epsilon = 2.0\%$; 1,921 faces)

(d) Original mesh (698 faces)   (e) Surface editing at a coarse level   (f) Surface editing at a finer level

(g) Original mesh (103,713 faces)   (h) Base mesh (229 faces)   (i) Approx. ($\epsilon = 1.5\%$; 4,725 faces)

(j) Original mesh (165,896 faces)   (k) Base mesh (132 faces)   (l) Approx. ($\epsilon = 2.6\%$; 16,451 faces)

Color Plate 2: (a-c) Multiresolution approximations used in Color Plate 1(l); (d-f) Example of multiresolution surface editing; (g-l) More results of multiresolution surface approximation.

Image Snapping

Michael Gleicher

Advanced Technology Group
Apple Computer, Inc.

ABSTRACT

Cursor snapping is a standard method for providing precise pointing in direct manipulation graphical interfaces. In this paper, we introduce *image snapping*, a variant of cursor snapping that works in image-based programs such as paint systems. Image snapping moves the cursor location to nearby features in the image, such as edges. It is implemented by using gradient descent on blurred versions of feature maps made from the images. Interaction techniques using cursor snapping for image segmentation and curve tracing are presented

CR Descriptors: I.4.3 [Image Processing]: image processing software. I.3.6 [Computer Graphics]: interaction techniques.

1. INTRODUCTION

Cursor snapping is a standard method for providing precise pointing in direct manipulation graphical interfaces. Since its introduction in Sutherland's Sketchpad [30], variants of snapping have been employed by almost all object-oriented drawing, modeling and CAD applications. In this paper, we present *image snapping,* a technique that extends cursor snapping to image-based applications such as paint systems.

Image snapping retains the basic idea of traditional cursor snapping: the cursor follows the motion of the pointing device, but snaps to interesting locations that are nearby. With image snapping, features such as edges or locations of a specific color can serve as snapping targets, as shown in Figure 1.

For traditional snapping in an object-oriented drawing application we have a list of objects that provide features to snap to. To provide snapping in images, a system might apply image understanding techniques to build an analytical, object-oriented model. Such an approach is typically impractical because of the complexity of image understanding. Instead, we use image processing techniques to determine likely targets on a per-pixel basis. Image snapping searches the image made from these probabilities, called the feature map, for targets near the pointer.

1 Infinite Loop M/S 301-3J, Cupertino, CA 95014
gleicher@apple.com

Permission to make digital/hard copy of part or all of this work for personal or classroom use is granted without fee provided that copies are not made or distributed for profit or commercial advantage, the copyright notice, the title of the publication and its date appear, and notice is given that copying is by permission of ACM, Inc. To copy otherwise, to republish, to post on servers, or to redistribute to lists, requires prior specific permission and/or a fee.

This paper presents the methods for realizing image snapping. After an introduction to cursor snapping, we present techniques for searching an image for features. The task of identifying features is discussed with particular attention to edge detection. We then examine how cursor snapping applies to higher level tasks in image-based applications.

2. PRECISE POINTING IN DIRECT MANIPULATION

Almost all object-oriented drawing, modelling and CAD programs provide some technique to aid the user with precise positioning. Bier [3] surveys approaches to this problem. Techniques aim to give the user the required precision, yet maintain the dynamic and free feel of direct manipulation. The most successful methods enhance direct manipulation positioning by guiding the position of the cursor from which drawing operations are carried out. In such schemes, the position of the software cursor is decoupled from the the screen location specified by the hardware pointing device, which we call the pointer. The cursor follows the pointer, but snaps to nearby locations of interest. Most snapping interfaces, with the exception of Venolia's 3D system [33], move the cursor discontinuously: when the cursor gets within range, it jumps to its target.

A common cursor positioning aid is the fixed grid. While easy to implement and use, it permits only operations that are grid-aligned. Grids could be used in an image editing program; however, to obtain precision with respect to features in an initial image, the features would have to be aligned with the grid. This is especially impractical when the images are acquired from the real world.

Other snapping variants are scene sensitive, that is, the position of the cursor depends on the contents of the drawing or image. When the pointer comes within snapping range of an object, the object's "gravitational attraction" draws the cursor to its surface. Such methods were introduced in Sketchpad [30], where they were dubbed "gravity." Gravity was developed further in the snap-dragging work of Bier [3][4]. Many popular drawing applications provide object snapping. It can provide precision greater than the resolution of the input device since snap targets are computed analytically. Snapping also can facilitate reference to objects. Users can point near to objects, rather than being forced to point exactly on top of them.

Snapping systems often provide the user with feedback of the cursor location and snapping state. The user can see the target of a drawing operation before it occurs, and correct for bad snaps by moving the cursor or overriding snapping. Snapping with proper feedback tells the user what locations can be snapped to. Hudson [17] suggests many applications of snap feedback.

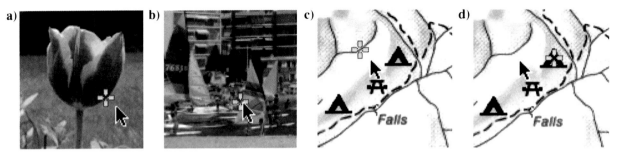

Figure 1: Examples of Image Snapping. Image snapping attracts the cursor to image features such as object edges (**a** and **b**), pixels of a specific color (blue pixels in **c**), or the centers of particular shapes found with template matching (campground symbols in **d**). The cursor state and pointer position are both always shown.

2.1 Implementing Snapping

The central piece of a snapping implementation is the function that computes the position of the cursor given the position of the pointer. In a traditional snapping implementation, this cursor function has arguments of the pointer position and the scene objects. The basic implementation of a cursor function iterates over the objects, finding the location on each that is closest to the cursor. The closest result is returned. Complications arise from the need to cull objects for better performance and computing the points that might be snap targets.

Computing snap points requires finding the point on each object that is closest to the pointer. Sutherland is "intentionally vague" [30,p.30] in describing how to do this for a line and circle, noting that each new object type requires a new method. Defining this method for more complex objects, such as curves, can be difficult. If a snapping implementation is to support snapping to object intersections, the cursor function must compute the intersection of any pair of objects, increasing the difficulty of adding new object types.

Gleicher [11] presents a generalized approach to implementing snapping using numerical constraint solving. The cursor is considered as a free floating point that minimizes its distance to the pointer location, as if it were connected by a damped spring. Each object has an implicit function that measures the distance of a point to the object, so that f(x,y)=0 defines the object's edge. When the cursor is close to an object, it is snapped to the object by treating the implicit function as a constraint on the cursor position. Intersections of objects are handled by solving multiple constraints simultaneously. The constraint snapping the cursor to an object is removed if the spring connecting the cursor to the pointer must pull too hard. We can think of generalized snapping as a physical process: the cursor is a ball that we position by pushing it around on a surface. Objects are grooves in the surface. If the ball comes close to a groove, it will fall in. If we push the ball gently, or in a direction that allows it to stay in the groove, it will roll within the groove. If we push harder, the ball will come out of the groove.

3. IMPLEMENTING IMAGE SNAPPING

The image snapping algorithm must compute the following: given the location of the pointing device, return the precise position of where the user is most likely to be pointing. We assume that positions correspond to positions in the image, that is, that the transformation from screen coordinates to image coordinates has already been applied.

The image snapping function searches a feature map for snap targets near the pointer. We postpone discussion of how to obtain the feature map until Section 4. For now, we imagine that some oracle will tell us if each pixel is part of a feature. This will not, in general, be a binary (thresholded) result. Varying values can indicate probabilities and varying amounts of feature in the image region represented by the pixel. We prefer to avoid thresholding the fea-

ture maps as it allows for anti-aliasing and also because picking a proper threshold to reject improbable pixels can be difficult to do statically (see [27] for a discussion).

We use the convention that in the image map, a maximum value indicates the absence of a feature and a minimum value indicates the most certain features. We can think of such an image map as a height field where the image features are canyons.

To search for a feature near the pointer location, we could start at the pointer location and spiral outward, stopping when either a feature pixel had been found, or when the spiral had gotten so large that anything it were to find would be out of snapping range. If the snapping radius is small, the number of pixels that need to be examined is manageable. If not, fast algorithms for computing Euclidean distance maps [9][20] can pre-compute the nearest non-zero pixel in the feature map for each pixel in the image. Such an approach to image snapping has several drawbacks:

1. It has no methods of rejecting noise;

2. It uses a preset stopping criteria, globally thresholding the feature map;

3. There is no way to trade off certainty and size for distance;

4. It stops at the first feature it finds. Another, possibly better, feature, might be equidistant, or just slightly farther away. Also, it will stop at the boundary of feature regions, rather than seeking the "best" location on the feature.

In cases where the feature map is binary, uncluttered, and assumed to be perfect, computing a map of nearest pixels using a Euclidean distance map algorithm provides a simple method for implementing image snapping. Typically, we prefer to use local stopping criteria rather than global thresholding, and perform some operation that allows the algorithm to take an entire neighborhood into account at once. The use of local extrema to define features has a long tradition, see Maxwell[23] and Cayley[7] for example, and is a commonly used in edge detection, such as [25] and [6].

We therefore, suggest a different process: follow the image map gradients to a nearby image feature point. Basically, we view the feature map as a height field, drop a ball at the pointer position, and watch it roll down hill. If the ball reaches a satisfactory feature, we have found a point to snap to. Since the downhill direction is given by the gradient (actually, the negative of the gradient), such a search is easy to implement. This method is known as steepest descent [10][28]. Issues that make steepest descent unattractive for standard numerical problems do not apply to our task of finding minima in the feature map: we are only interested in problems where we have good starting points, the discrete nature of the image provides a natural step size and accuracy bound, and the small step size and direction-based stopping criteria, discussed later, avoid troubling oscillations.

3.1 Computing Gradients and Blurring

Texts, such as Pratt[27] and Nalwa[26], contain more complete discussions of the methods for measuring gradients in images. We review the basics here. Although an image is a continuous function over a region of the plane, in practice we only have a sampled representation. Therefore, to compute derivatives, we must use discrete approximations. The simplest method is to merely look at the adjacent pixels:

$$\frac{\partial}{\partial x} f(x, y) = f(x + 1, y) - f(x, y)$$ (EQ 1)

$$\frac{\partial}{\partial y} f(x, y) = f(x, y + 1) - f(x, y)$$

Other methods look at more pixels in order to better estimate the gradient. A common measure called the Sobel operator averages the finite differences in different directions, examining a 3x3 region around the point to be evaluated. In matrix notation, the Sobel operators are:

$$S_y = \frac{1}{4} \begin{bmatrix} -1 & -2 & -1 \\ 0 & 0 & 0 \\ 1 & 2 & 1 \end{bmatrix}, \quad S_x = \frac{1}{4} \begin{bmatrix} -1 & 0 & 1 \\ -2 & 0 & 2 \\ -1 & 0 & 1 \end{bmatrix}$$ (EQ 2)

where S_x is the operator for the gradient in the x direction, and S_y is the operator for the y direction. Our implementation always computes image gradients using the Sobel operators.

On a raw feature map, image gradients provide little information for snapping. A feature can only influence a point one pixel away, there is no provision for noise suppression, and no mechanism for trading off certainty and size for distance. Also, because we know nothing about the smoothness of the image function, there is no reason to believe that the steepest direction is most likely to lead us to the nearest, or darkest, edge. These problems are illustrated in the example of a 1D image shown in Figure 2.

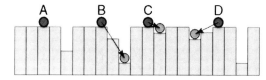

Figure 2: Cursor snapping in a 1 dimensional image shown as a height field. 4 starting points are shown. Each is given the opportunity to roll down hill. Point A does not roll anywhere since there is no gradient at its pixel. Point B correctly rolls downhill into the deep canyon. Points C and D roll down into the shallow canyons, although there are deeper ones nearby.

In short, image snapping at pixel scale [19][35], is ineffective. Abrupt changes, or high frequencies, in feature mask intensities make it impossible to sense features that are far away. Blurring the feature map to examine it at greater scale is essential for image snapping. Torre and Poggio[32] provide an alternate motivation: without blurring, evaluating gradients is an ill-posed problem.

Blurring is a standard image processing operation; most image processing texts such as Pratt[27] contain full discussions. Briefly, blurring is accomplished by taking a weighted average of the neighborhood around each pixel. Writing the weights as a matrix gives a kernel that can be convolved with the image to produce the image of averages. Linear filters are described by these kernel matrices. Larger kernels typically cause blurrier images. From the standpoint of image snapping, the larger the kernel, the larger the

neighborhood over which an image feature has influence on the cursor.

Our implementation uses B-Spline basis low-pass filter kernels created by successively convolving a 2x2 box by itself[15][16]. Such filters approximate Gaussian kernels.

Blurring the feature map has many benefits. Foremost, it allows the effects of a larger neighborhood to be felt at a given pixel. The high frequencies in images are often noise, so blurring can help cancel these effects. While these high frequencies might represent fine details in an image, too many small details can cause clutter. Also, blurring can add useful detail within the features. For example, thick line features get stripes down their center, large points get dots at their centers, and intersections are emphasized. These effects are illustrated in Figure 3 and Figure 4.

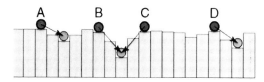

Figure 3: Cursor snapping in a blurred 1D image. A 3 pixel blurring operation has been applied to the image of Figure 2. In this case, each of the starting points snaps into a nearby deep canyon.

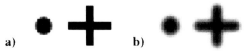

Figure 4: Blurring a simple image shows how blurring emphasizes the centers of points, lines, and intersections. The darkest points in image **b**) are centers of the circle and cross.

The benefits of blurring can be a problem. The larger area of attention can be problematic in cluttered scenes. The high frequencies in an image may not be noise, but rather, might be important features. The effect of features "migrating," for example to the center of a wide line, may not be desired.

There is a trade-off in selecting how much blurring should be used for image snapping. A large amount of blurring allows the cursor to snap from larger distances and better reject noise at the expense of the ability to resolve fine detail.

As the blur factors grow larger, issues in how to represent the feature maps arise. While a large blur allows a feature to affect a position many pixels away, the amount of this effect can be very small. We use floating point numbers to represent feature maps; however, there is still an issue with noise rejection when the system is made sensitive enough to accommodate these very small values. We use a threshold to remove extremely small values.

3.2 Searching the Feature Map

Gradients in the feature map indicate which direction a search should proceed in order to find the best feature point. The magnitude provides little information on how to search, so we ignore it for searching. The search process moves a pixel at a time beginning with the mouse position. At each step, we evaluate the gradient of the blurred feature map to determine which direction to move the search to one of the pixel's 8-connected neighbors. This quantization of the gradient direction means that we will not necessarily find the nearest point on the feature. We continue the process until it either moves too far from the initial starting point, meaning that there is no feature within the snapping radius, or when the search has found the best feature that it expects to find, e.g. a local extremum.

Local extrema are identified as places where the gradient vanishes [10]. Basically, when there is no downhill direction from a particular location, that location must be a minimum. Because of sampling, this criterion is not sufficient for image snapping. Local minima can actually occur between pixels. In such cases, the gradients of neighboring pixels will point at one another, as shown in Figure 5. We therefore add the additional stopping criterion that if the gradient changes direction too much between steps, a feature has been found. By placing limits on the range of directions allowed in a search, we can avoid looping and cycling. Our algorithm defines this search range from the initial step direction.

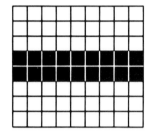 

Figure 5: A 2-pixel wide feature. The left shows a 2 pixel wide feature. The right shows this feature blurred, with arrows denoting the gradient direction. Notice that the local minima is in the center of the feature, between the pixels.

Another issue in defining a stopping criterion is that within features the gradient is not zero. That is, within a feature, some points are more "featureful" than others. Without the direction change criterion of the last paragraph, the cursor might make a turn when it reached an edge, to search along the edge for a slightly darker spot. Dragging along a feature edge would cause the cursor to jump from one point to another. If some feature point, such as an intersection or corner, is sufficiently more featureful, its "gravitational attraction" will pull the cursor in as it approaches the feature.

Notice that our stopping criterion for a search is very different than performing a thresholding on the feature map. Rather than basing the decision on the value of the feature point alone, we use information about the neighborhood around the point, as well as the particular search.

A different problem occurs when we begin our search on a feature. Because we have no static criteria to classify a pixel as a feature or not, there is no simple way to distinguish between locations that are exactly on features and locations that are too far away from features. To perform such a classification, when we encounter a starting point which does not provide a gradient direction to search in, we check to see if neighboring pixels point towards this location before discarding it as a non-target.

3.3 Sub-pixel Positioning

When a local minima occurs between pixels, the direction change stopping criterion stops the search after the search has gone too far. In such a case, we know that the real stopping point lies between the last two pixels examined in the search. We can use the gradients at these two points to better estimate where in between the centers of these two pixels the real stopping point would be.

Given the gradients at the last two pixels of the search, the real stopping point would be the place along the line between the two pixels at which the projection of the gradient vector onto the search direction reaches a zero value. To estimate this location, we compute the projection of the two gradients onto the inter-pixel line,

and approximate its change by assuming a linear transition. If the zero crossing is in-between the pixels, it is used as the sub-pixel location. This sub-pixel method only adds precision along the direction of search, so it is mainly useful for finding the centers of edges as shown in Figure 6 and Figure 7. Interpolating 4 neighboring gradients, as done for the precise edge detector of [22], might better localize points but has not been tried in our implementation.

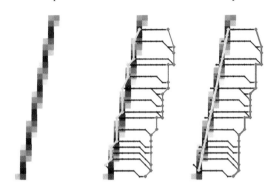

Figure 6: Snapping to a single pixel wide, anti-aliased line. The green line represents the path of the mouse, the magenta lines the search paths. In the center, the yellow line shows the pixel-aligned stopping positions. On the right, it shows the snap positions computed to sub-pixel accuracy. Notice that the points always lie on the line between the last two search points.

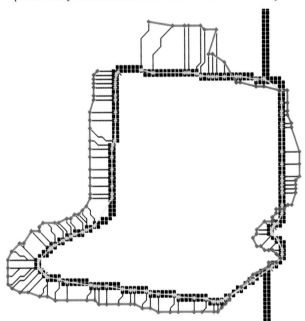

Figure 7: Snapping to the centers of the 2-pixel wide lines created by the simple edge detector applied to the segmentation image of Figure 8. Colors are explained in Figure 6.

The utility of sub-pixel positioning is not limited to cases where the feature detector is capable of localizing the features to this greater accuracy and the application can make use of the precision. In other cases, it adds important consistency when snapping to wide features. Consider image snapping without sub-pixel positioning on the example of Figure 5. If the search begins above the line, the stopping point will be on the bottom of the line, while if the search begins below the line, it will stop on the top. This means that if the user crosses the line while dragging the cursor along the feature, zig-zagging will occur. Sub-pixel positioning avoids this: starting from either side of the edge would lead to the same stopping point. Even if the sub-pixel position is rounded to the nearest pixel, consistency can be achieved.

3.4 Achieving Large Snap-Radii

Section 3.1 describes a trade-off in selecting the amount of blurring to apply to the feature map. To avoid losing the locality and fine detail of the features, we might prefer to use small amounts of blurring, especially when we have confidence in the map. The problem with small blurs in such cases is that the snapping radius is very small. In this section, we consider how we can achieve large snapping radii while still maintaining the features of small blurs.

We begin by blurring the feature map by a small amount (we typically use 3x3 or 5x5 kernels) and assume that when close to a feature, this blur provides good performance. This creates a small region around features that have gradient information pointing towards them. A simple thresholding criteria is possible: if the gradient has sufficient magnitude to determine a meaningful search direction, it will guide us to a good feature. If not, we need to use an alternate method to decide which direction to direct the search. As the search proceeds and nears a feature, it can use the small-blur gradients when they are available. We implement two methods for determining search directions for long snaps.

One way to enhance the snapping radius is to use different amounts of blurring. Such a technique is known as a multi-scale method, and is often used in computer vision, see [26, pp. 92-96] for a brief survey.

A simple multi-scale image snapping technique would create a very blurry version of the feature map in addition to the slightly blurred one. If no gradient is found for a given point in the small blur version, the larger blur version is checked. Unfortunately, this simple scheme will not work because the jumps in amount of blur will create discontinuities in the gradient field. At first, the search will proceed towards the best feature in the blurry image. As it gets close and switches to the less-blurry image, the feature will migrate differently causing a change in the search direction. Methods in computer vision typically address this by using a continuum of blurs [19][35]. For image snapping, we approximate these methods by using multiple blurs so that the changes among them are more gradual than jumping between a large and small blur. Computing and storing multiple blurred images is made practical by the use of an image pyramid [5][34] and interpolation.

Altering image snapping to use a multi-scale method is straightforward. We alter gradient evaluation so that if a zero value is produced at a point, evaluation looks at higher levels of the pyramid until a non-zero gradient is found. There are still discrete jumps between levels, and therefore discontinuities. These small jumps do not seem to be a problem in practice.

An alternate approach uses the distance map techniques of Section 3. Rather than building a map to the nearest feature, we create a map that stores the nearest point that has a gradient. Image snapping is trivially modified to begin by consulting the map to find the location for starting a search. Such a scheme still uses local properties to determine features and uses thresholding to determine where there is sufficient information to begin a search.

Our prototype implements both the multi-scale and distance mapping approaches to extending snap-radii. Computing the pyramid and distance map are approximately equivalent in computation time. We are able to mix the two approaches, for example to use 2 levels of the image pyramid coupled with the distance map. The advantages of the map method are that it can travel long distances quickly because it initially teleports rather than searches, it has no issues with small values, and does not require level interpolation on the pyramid. Pyramid methods may be preferable because the larger blurs reduce noise and clutter in the open spaces and allow

for controlling the trade-off between distance and certainty. Pyramid methods may be easier to update incrementally, but we have not implemented this yet.

In uncluttered images, pyramids and distance maps both work well for extending the snap radius. In cluttered images, larger snap-radii may be problematic for any image snapping method because it becomes less clear which feature is the desired target.

3.5 Hysteresis

In pictures that are cluttered, i.e. where there are many features close to together as in Figure 1b, snapping may be difficult as the algorithm may not select the features that the user desires. Traditional snapping combats clutter with techniques that select features on criteria other than simple closeness. For example, cycling [3][12] allows the user to select among features within the snapping radius. Such a method relies on the ability to tell different features apart, which is easy in a traditional, object-oriented, snapping implementation. To use such a method in image snapping would require somehow grouping pixels into individual features, which is not possible without image understanding.

Hysteresis in snapping gives the cursor function a preference to stay snapped to the same object. This helps prevent the cursor from jumping around annoyingly. When multiple objects are found to be within the cursor radius, the last object snapped to is given preference, rather than simply selecting the closest. Hysteresis is extremely important when tracing features, which will be discussed in Section 5.2. Figure 10 provides an example of where hysteresis would avoid a problem for the user.

As described, cursor snapping does not provide any form of hysteresis. Each snap operation is independent of past and future operations. Like cycling, lack of object structures to snap to makes adding hysteresis difficult. Returning to the previously snapped point is not the same: we would like the cursor to follow smoothly along edges. To fake hysteresis, image snapping can use the heuristic that nearby feature points are likely to be on the same object.

We have created a technique that attempts to lock the cursor onto its current feature. When locking is enabled by depressing a modifier key, subsequent mouse motions pull the cursor along the locked feature. The technique is called cursor pulling because it pulls the cursor from its previous position, rather than starting searches from the pointer location.

Cursor pulling is inspired by generalized snapping that was reviewed in Section 2.1. Like generalized snapping, when the cursor is locked, we consider it "in a groove." The positioning method switches from one that finds grooves to one that pulls the cursor along in the groove from its previous position. We displace the cursor a small amount towards the pointer and start the descent process from this point. The basic idea is that by starting at points near a point on a particular object, we are more likely to end up at another point on the same object.

The difficult decision in implementing cursor pulling is how far to displace the cursor before beginning the descent. The farther away from its initial starting point, the more likely it will end up farther away from this point, and the less likely it will return to the same object. On the other hand, if we start too close, the cursor is likely to return to the initial position. Rather than making a fixed decision, we displace the cursor back as little as possible. To implement this, we displace the cursor one pixel towards the pointer, and execute the descent process. If the cursor returns to its previous location, then we did not displace it enough, so we try again from slightly further away. We continue the process until either we find a position that descends to an acceptable location, or we give up the search because we have either gotten too far away from the original point, or have found a distance at which the cursor doesn't snap to anything. In the event that we fail to find a new location, we return the cursor to its previous location.

We enhance locking by adding the heuristic that between two points on a feature should be only other feature pixels. We add a test that looks at the pixels along the line between the previous and current snap positions. If any of these pixels clearly do not qualify as feature pixels, we return the cursor to its previously snapped position. This technique requires a static threshold for pixels that are clearly not part of a feature. It also often causes the cursor to get stuck when there is a small break in a feature that is being traced.

As we pull the cursor along a feature, it typically moves more slowly than the pointer. The user often waits for it to "catch up" over long distances. Sometimes, the cursor will stick in places where moving towards the pointer does not lead to new positions. In such cases, the mouse can be moved to coax the cursor along.

4. FEATURE IDENTIFICATION

We now consider the problem of creating the feature map. Determining which pixels the user is more likely to want to snap to consists of two problems: determining what types of features are likely to be of interest, and determining what pixels are part of these features. The first part is often application specific. For example, we might want to snap to spots of a certain color or to bright or dark areas of the image. For some applications, we might want to manually create the feature map, attracting the cursor to features that an author can identify.

Object edges serve as a generally useful set of features to snap to. The ability to snap to edges mimics the typical snap targets of traditional snapping and is desirable for many applications. The difficulty in using edge detection stems from the fact that we are interested in *perceived* edges. Without the ability to identify objects, determining what is an object edge can be difficult. Edge detection is not always difficult. For example, if we have an image that is a line drawing or has been segmented into different objects (see Figures 7 and 8), accurately identifying edges is easy. Unfortunately, such segmentations are not always available, in fact, generating them is a motivating application (see Section 5.3).

Edge detection is a common problem in image processing and computer vision. Most textbooks in either field, for example Pratt's image processing text [27] or Nalwa's vision text [26], contain surveys. Use of better edge detectors will improve the performance of image snapping. For image snapping, good edge detectors are characterized by locality, noise rejection, and sensitivity. While these criteria are similar to those typically desired for vision applications, the fact that we can handle grayscale and thick lines leads to some differences from the criteria defined by Canny [6]. In particular, his goal to have a single pixel wide response for each edge is less important for image snapping.

We have experimented with a variety of edge detectors for use in image snapping. Simple edge detection operators, such as the magnitude of the gradient, often work well. More sophisticated operators, such as Marr-Hildreth[25] or Canny[6] offer better locality and noise rejection, however, they have the less desirable property of "thinning" the edges. Non-local techniques that attempt to link edge pixels together to raise certainty about the edges, such as Hough transforms[27], edge relaxation[2] or morphological methods[27] may further improve edge detector performance for image snapping.

As shown in Section 3.3, image snapping can locate features to sub-pixel precision. Using this precision requires features that are localized to sub-pixel accuracy. Examples of edge detectors that provide such accuracy exist in the literature, such as [22] and [31].

We have experimented with a scheme that enlarges an image with interpolation, detects edges, then reduces the image back to its original size. However, most of our sub-pixel experiments have been performed on synthetic images.

Another type of feature detector is a template matcher [27] that computes the likelihood that a pixel is the center of a particular shape. Using a template matcher output with image snapping produces a method similar to numerical search-based tracking [21] where the matches and gradients have been pre-computed. Because we are typically interested in extreme points, not smoothly sliding along edges, we allow much higher tolerances on angle changes. Effective use of a template matcher typically requires using thresholding. Our primary experiments have used template matching to help a user point at symbols on a map, for example to identify campsites in a park. Although the example in Figure 1d is synthetically generated, we have had good results on scanned maps.

5. INTERACTION IN APPLICATIONS

In this section, we look at some common tasks in image editing applications and examine how image snapping applies. Automating image editing tasks is difficult without image understanding. Cursor snapping can provide precision for more manual approaches.

Our implementation provides continuous feedback of the cursor position and a modifier key to disable snapping at any time. Feedback always shows the cursor location and whether or not it is snapped, in addition to the pointer location. If the cursor is incorrectly snapped, holding down a modifier key causes it to return to the pointer location.

5.1 Point Positioning

Often, a user needs to indicate the position of a point to an application where precision is important, for example, identifying correspondence points for image morphs, finding coordinates of particular features, measuring distances between points, or indicating locations on a map. Drawing operations that use discrete points, such as rubber-band drawing of lines, are also enhanced by cursor snapping.

5.2 Curve Tracing

In an object oriented drawing program, the cursor position is only used at discrete events. For example, when we draw a line segment or rectangle by rubber banding only the initial and final positions of the dragging operation are important. This means that if the cursor makes an incorrect snap during the drag, the user can correct the error without it ever being recorded.

In image-based applications, an important class of operations does use the cursor path. Brushing, penciling, and lassoing are examples of such techniques. Having snapping during these continuous dragging operations can be extremely valuable for tracing feature curves, for example to circle objects. Because the path of the cursor is recorded (and is important), errors made by the snapping algorithm can be problematic. An example is shown in Figure 10.

Even with feature locking techniques, as in Section 3.5, bad transient snaps are unavoidable. Curve tracing with snapping can be made workable through the addition of some simple interaction techniques. First, it is crucial to provide feedback of the snapping state to the user so that errors can be recognized immediately. Second, methods for backing up in the midst of a drawing operation must be provided. One interaction technique for this is to have the user back up over the curve to erase previous drawn portions. Another technique uses a modifier key that switches curve drawing into "backup" mode. While the key is depressed, moving the cursor permits specifying points along the curve. This method does

Figure 8: This piece of a panoramic image of a store (left) contains images that have particular behaviors when clicked on. To do this, an item buffer (right) stores a segmentation image identifying objects. This segmentation was not created using image snapping, but was used to create the edges in Figure 7. With the background objects (large rectangles) repainted white and the foreground objects (computers) repainted black, the segmentation can serve as a feature map for image snapping, attracting the cursor to computers. Images Copyright Apple Computer Inc, 1994.

a)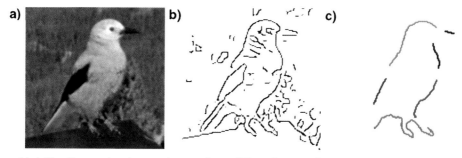b) c)

Figure 9: Lassoing a bird. The Canny edge detector (output shown (**b**)) performs well on some parts of the image, but not on others. Image snapping is used to trace the outline where meaningful snapping is easy (**c**). Other sections of the curve can be drawn manually and combined into a single lasso outline.

use a modifier key, however, it has the advantage that it allows the user to interactively find the point in the path that they want to roll back to.

5.2.1 Comparison with snakes

Curve tracing is an important enough task that techniques have been developed to help automate it. One approach is to fit deformable models to the image. A successful technique for this is the snake of Kass, Witkin and Terzopoulos [18]. The user places a snake curve near a feature and it automatically locks on to the feature. A numerical optimization moves the entire curve, both attracting it to features and keeping its shape smooth. Snake implementations allow the user to interactively pull on the snake as it progresses. Snakes have a wide variety of uses beyond assisting users in tracing curves.

A snake is an active object that seeks image features after it has been dropped on the image. Snakes provide a more highly automated process for tracing curves than image snapping, at the expense of user control. Where image snapping enhances the familiar drawing process, snakes provide a new type of active object that the user can place, watch settle, then hopefully coax into having the correct shape. Snakes address the issue of editing a curve after it has been placed, which simply drawing with image snapping does not.

Our system allows snakes and image snapping to be mixed: image snapping is used for drawing curves that can be turned into snakes for editing. This combination is useful as the snapping feedback can show the user what features the snake is likely to grab when activated. Our initial experiences show that this combination can be frustrating as the snake's internal forces rip it from a carefully placed initial curve. Improvements in the snake implementation may alleviate this problem. The issue does emphasize the difference in the use of active and passive objects as interface elements.

5.3 Image Segmentation

Another common task in image editing applications is identifying related regions of an image, known as segmenting it. Some of the many uses of segmentation that we have considered include identifying objects to cut them from their backgrounds, making mattes, and creating hit maps for interactive multimedia [8][24], as shown in Figure 8.

There is a large literature on automatically segmenting images, for example see [14] for a survey. Some of these techniques can be used to become semi-automatic interaction techniques, like Smith's tint fill [29] or the "Magic Wand" in Adobe Photoshop [1]. A more natural, but very manual, method for identifying a segment is lassoing, where a user traces around the edge of the region. Lassoing is a use of curve tracing, and is similarly enhanced by image snapping.

Lassoing objects can be a tedious task. Cursor snapping can facilitate it by freeing the user from having to precisely position the lasso. To further ease the task, our system allows the user to connect multiple curve segments to create a closed curve, eliminating the need to create the entire lasso in one motion. An example is shown in Figure 9.

Figure 10: Circling the wheel. The counter-clockwise path of the pointer is shown in magenta, the path of the cursor in cyan. If the user is not careful, lack of hysteresis can cause bad snaps during circling, as seen on the left. The center shows a more careful tracing. The right shows an alternate interaction technique: the user specifies discrete points through which a curve will be fitted.

6. CONCLUSIONS

Creating interaction techniques that help automate image editing tasks is difficult because of the challenges in understanding the content of images. Even operations that are trivial for users, such as seeing edges, can be difficult to perform in a robust and accurate fashion. This can lead to frustrating interfaces as the system fails to see things that are obvious to a user. It also suggests a partnership where visual processing is performed by the user, rather than attempting to develop fully automated solutions. Avoiding tedium and providing precision are issues in such manual interfaces. Image snapping attempts to address these issues by facilitating precise pointing at features in the image.

The difficulty of identifying features means that image snapping is not perfect. Uncertainties in edge detection lead to noise in the feature maps and "blotching" along feature edges. We are exploring the use of better feature detectors and more sophisticated image processing techniques to reduce these problems, enhance the quality of interactions, and improve the range of images on which the techniques can be applied. The methods are unlikely to ever be perfect, therefore it is important to design interaction that accommodates this unreliability. Dealing with cluttered images is particularly challenging.

Image snapping brings a familiar feature of drawing programs to image editing. However, the interactions in image editing more often use the paths drawn by the cursor than discrete positions at snap points. As discussed in Section 5.2, cursor snapping does not apply as well to paths as to discrete points. Deficiencies in image snapping, such as the lack of hysteresis and imperfect feature identification, become more serious when tracing paths. This suggests the importance of developing new interaction techniques that will work better with image snapping. Figure 10 shows an example where an alternative interface avoids path tracing. This particular example exploits the fact that the system knows the user is identifying an ellipse. The multiple click interface is also useful when the positioning must be completely manual because the edge detector fails completely (for example trying to circle the tire).

Presently, we are exploring image snapping inside of a prototype image editing application. However, since the inputs and outputs of the methods are standard, it is possible to construct a general purpose implementation. For example, an implementation at the window system level could intercept the mouse positions and look at the frame buffer directly. Such an implementation might construct and blur feature maps on the fly.

Our prototype implementation provides a testbed for exploring image snapping. Performing gradient descent on blurred feature maps creates precise pointing in images. We are exploring a variety of sources of features, including a number of edge detectors. Standard image editing interaction techniques are enhanced with a familiar method for providing precision, although new interaction techniques should better address image snapping's shortcomings.

ACKNOWLEDGMENTS

Lance Williams' encouragement and help with image processing were instrumental in the development of Image Snapping. Bruce Horn and Steve Rubin helped with Macintosh hacking. Heung-Yeung Shum, Pete Litwinowicz and Demetri Terzopoulos donated example code. Eric Chen and Ted Casey provided panoramic test images and scanning help. Bruce Horn, Frank Crow, Gavin Miller, Ken Turkowski, Heung-Yeung Shum, and Mike Kelley proofread drafts of this paper.

REFERENCES

[1]   Adobe Systems, Inc. Photoshop™ 3.0. Computer Program, 1994.

[2]   Ballard, D and Brown, C. *Computer Vision.* Prentice-Hall, 1982.

[3]   Bier, E. Snap-Dragging: Interactive Geometric Design in Two and Three Dimensions. Ph.D. Thesis, University of California, Berkeley, 1989. Also as Xerox PARC report EDL-89-2.

[4]   Bier, E and Stone, M. Snap-dragging. Proceedings of SIGGRAPH 86.Computer Graphics (20) 4: 233-240, 1986.

[5]   Burt, P and Adelson, E. A Multiresolution Spline With Application to Image Mosaics. *ACM Transactions on Graphics* (2) 4:217-236, October 1983.

[6]   Canny, J. A Computational Approach to Edge Detection. *IEEE Transactions on Pattern Analysis and Machine Intelligence* (PAMI-8) 6:679-698, 1986.

[7]   Cayley, A. On Contour and Slope Lines. *London, Edinburgh, and Dublin Philosophical Magazine and Journal of Science,* (18) 4:264-269, 1859.

[8]   Chen, SE. An Image-Based Approach to Virtual Reality. Proceedings of SIGGRAPH 95. In *Computer Graphics* Proceedings, August 1995. This volume.

[9]   Danielson, P. Euclidean Distance Mapping. *Computer Graphics Image Processing* (14) 3:227-248, November, 1980.

[10] Fletcher, R. *Practical Methods of Optimization.* John Wiley and Sons, 1987.

[11] Gleicher, M. A Differential Approach to Graphical Manipulation. Ph.D. Thesis, Carnegie Mellon University, 1994.

[12] Gleicher, M and Witkin, A. Drawing with constraints. *The Visual Computer* (11) 1, 1995.

[13] Gonzales, R and Wintz, P. *Digital Image Processing,* second edition. Addison-Wesley, 1987.

[14] Haralick, R and Shapiro, L. Survey: Image Segmentation Techniques. *Computer Vision, Graphics, and Image Proc.* (29) 100-132, 1985.

[15] Heckbert, P. Filtering by Repeated Integration. Proceedings of SIGGRAPH 86.Computer Graphics (20) 4:315-321.

[16] Hou, H, and Andrews, H. Cubic Splines for Image Interpolation and Digital Filtering. *IEEE Transactions on Acoustics, Speech and Signal Processing* (ASSP-26) 6:508-517, 1978.

[17] Hudson, S. Adaptive semantic snapping - a technique for feedback at the lexical level. In Proceedings CHI '90, pages 65-70, 1990.

[18] Kass, M, Witkin A, and Terzopoulos, D. Snakes: Active Contour Models. *Intern Journal of Computer Vision* (1) 4:321-331, 1988.

[19] Koenderink, J. The Structure of Images. *Biological Cybernetics* (50): 363-370, 1984.

[20] Leymarie, F and Levine, M. Fast Raster Scan Propagation on the Discrete Rectangular Lattice. *Computer Graphics, Vision, Image Processing: Image Understanding* (55) 1: 84-94, 1992.

[21] Lucas, B and Kanade, T. An Iterative Image Registration Technique with an Application to Stereo Vision. *Proceedings 7th IJCAI 1981,* pages 674-679, August 1981.

[22] MacViar-Whelan, P and Binford T. Intensity Discontinuity Location to Subpixel Precision. *Proceedings 7th IJCAI 1981,* pages 752-754, August 1981.

[23] Maxwell, J. On Hills and Dales. *London, Edinburgh, and Dublin Philosophical Magazine and Journal of Science,* (40) 269:421-427, 1870.

[24] Miller, G and et. al. The Virtual Museum: Interactive 3D Exploration of a Multimedia Database. *Journal of Visualization and Computer Animation* (3) 183-197, 1992.

[25] Marr, D and Hildreth, E. Theory of Edge Detection. *Proc. Royal Society of London* (207) 187-217, 1980.

[26] Nalwa, V. *A Guided Tour of Computer Vision.* Addison-Wesley, 1993.

[27] Pratt, W. *Digital Image Processing,* 2nd ed. J Wiley and Sons, 1990.

[28] Press, W, Flannery, B, Teukolsky, S, and Vettering, W. *Numerical Recipes in C.* Cambridge University Press, 1986.

[29] Smith, AR. Tint Fill. Proceedings of SIGGRAPH 79. *Computer Graphics* (13) 2:276-283.

[30] Sutherland, I. Sketchpad: A Man Machine Graphical Communication System. Ph.D. Thesis, Massachusetts Institute of Technology, 1963.

[31] Tabatabai, A and Mitchell, O. Edge Location to Subpixel Values in Digital Imagery. *IEEE Transactions on Pattern Analysis and Machine Intelligence* (PAMI-6) 2:188-201, March 1984.

[32] Torre, V and Poggio, T. On Edge Detection. *IEEE Transactions on Pattern Analysis and Machine Intelligence* (PAMI-8) 2:147-163, 1986.

[33] Venolia., D. Facile 3D Manipulation. In Proceedings INTERCHI '93, pages 31-36, 1993

[34] Williams, L. Pyramidal Parametrics. Proceedings of SIGGRAPH 83. *Computer Graphics* (17) 3:1-11.

[35] Witkin, A. Scale Space Filtering. In Alex Pentland, ed., *From Pixels to Predicates.* Ablex, 1984. Reprinted from Proceedings of IJCAI '83.

Intelligent Scissors for Image Composition

Eric N. Mortensen[1]   William A. Barrett[2]

Brigham Young University

Abstract

We present a new, interactive tool called *Intelligent Scissors* which we use for image segmentation and composition. Fully automated segmentation is an unsolved problem, while manual tracing is inaccurate and laboriously unacceptable. However, Intelligent Scissors allow objects within digital images to be extracted quickly and accurately using simple gesture motions with a mouse. When the gestured mouse position comes in proximity to an object edge, a *live-wire boundary* "snaps" to, and wraps around the object of interest.

Live-wire boundary detection formulates discrete dynamic programming (DP) as a two-dimensional graph searching problem. DP provides mathematically optimal boundaries while greatly reducing sensitivity to local noise or other intervening structures. Robustness is further enhanced with *on-the-fly training* which causes the boundary to adhere to the specific type of edge currently being followed, rather than simply the strongest edge in the neighborhood. *Boundary cooling* automatically freezes unchanging segments and automates input of additional seed points. Cooling also allows the user to be much more free with the gesture path, thereby increasing the efficiency and finesse with which boundaries can be extracted.

Extracted objects can be scaled, rotated, and composited using live-wire masks and *spatial frequency equivalencing*. Frequency equivalencing is performed by applying a Butterworth filter which matches the lowest frequency spectra to all other image components. Intelligent Scissors allow creation of convincing compositions from existing images while dramatically increasing the speed and precision with which objects can be extracted.

1. Introduction

Digital image composition has recently received much attention for special effects in movies and in a variety of desktop applications. In movies, image composition, combined with other digital manipulation techniques, has also been used to realistically blend old film into a new script. The goal of image composition is to combine objects or regions from various still photographs or movie frames to create a seamless, believable, image or image sequence which appears convincing and real. Fig. 9(d) shows a believable composition created by combining objects extracted from three images, Fig. 9(a-c). These objects were digitally extracted and combined in a few minutes using a new, interactive tool called *Intelligent Scissors*.

When using existing images, objects of interest must be extracted and segmented from a surrounding background of unpredictable complexity. Manual segmentation is tedious and time consuming, lacking in precision, and impractical when applied to long image

sequences. Further, due to the wide variety of image types and content, most current computer based segmentation techniques are slow, inaccurate, and require significant user input to initialize or control the segmentation process.

This paper describes a new, interactive, digital image segmentation tool called "Intelligent Scissors" which allows rapid object extraction from arbitrarily complex backgrounds. Intelligent Scissors boundary detection formulates discrete dynamic programming (DP) as a two-dimensional graph searching problem. Presented as part of this tool are *boundary cooling* and *on-the-fly training*, which reduce user input and dynamically adapt the tool to specific types of edges. Finally, we present *live-wire masking* and *spatial frequency equivalencing* for convincing image compositions.

2. Background

Digital image segmentation techniques are used to extract image components from their surrounding natural background. However, currently available computer based segmentation tools are typically primitive and often offer little more advantage than manual tracing.

Region based magic wands, provided in many desktop applications, use an interactively selected seed point to "grow" a region by adding adjacent neighboring pixels. Since this type of region growing does not provide interactive visual feedback, resulting region boundaries must usually be edited or modified.

Other popular boundary definition methods use active contours or snakes[1, 5, 8, 15] to improve a manually entered rough approximation. After being initialized with a rough boundary approximation, snakes iteratively adjust the boundary points in parallel in an attempt to minimize an energy functional and achieve an optimal boundary. The energy functional is a combination of internal forces, such as boundary curvature, and external forces, like image gradient magnitude. Snakes can track frame-to-frame boundary motion provided the boundary hasn't moved drastically. However, active contours follow a pattern of initialization followed by energy minimization; as a result, the user does not know what the final boundary will look like when the rough approximation is input. If the resulting boundary is not satisfactory, the process must be repeated or the boundary must be manually edited. We provide a detailed comparison of snakes and Intelligent Scissors in section 3.6.

Another class of image segmentation techniques use a graph searching formulation of DP (or similar concepts) to find globally optimal boundaries [2, 4, 10, 11, 14]. These techniques differ from snakes in that boundary points are generated in a stage-wise optimal cost fashion whereas snakes iteratively minimize an energy functional for all points on a contour in parallel (giving the appearance of wiggling). However, like snakes, these graph searching techniques typically require a boundary template--in the form of a manually entered rough approximation, a figure of merit, etc.--which is used to impose directional sampling and/or searching constraints. This limits these techniques to a boundary search with one degree of freedom within a window about the two-dimensional boundary template. Thus, boundary extraction using previous graph searching techniques is non-interactive (beyond template specification), losing the benefits of further human guidance and expertise.

[1] enm@cs.byu.edu, Dept. of Comp. Sci., BYU, Provo, UT 84602 (801)378-7605
[2] barrett@cs.byu.edu, Dept. of Comp. Sci., BYU, Provo, UT 84602 (801)378-7430

Permission to make digital/hard copy of part or all of this work for personal or classroom use is granted without fee provided that copies are not made or distributed for profit or commercial advantage, the copyright notice, the title of the publication and its date appear, and notice is given that copying is by permission of ACM, Inc. To copy otherwise, to republish, to post on servers, or to redistribute to lists, requires prior specific permission and/or a fee.

© 1995   ACM-0-89791-701-4/95/008 $3.50

The most important difference between previous boundary finding techniques and Intelligent Scissors presented here lies not in the boundary defining criteria per se, but in the *method* of interaction. Namely, previous methods exhibit a pattern of boundary approximation followed by boundary refinement, whereas Intelligent Scissors allow the user to *interactively select* the most suitable boundary from a set of *all* optimal boundaries emanating from a seed point. In addition, previous approaches do not incorporate on-the-fly training or cooling, and are not as computationally efficient. Finally, it appears that the problem of automated matching of spatial frequencies for digital image composition has not been addressed previously.

3. Intelligent Scissors

Boundary definition via dynamic programming can be formulated as a graph searching problem [10] where the goal is to find the optimal path between a start node and a set of goal nodes. As applied to image boundary finding, the graph search consists of finding the globally optimal path from a start pixel to a goal pixel--in particular, pixels represent nodes and edges are created between each pixel and its 8 neighbors. For this paper, optimality is defined as the minimum cumulative cost path from a start pixel to a goal pixel where the cumulative cost of a path is the sum of the local edge (or link) costs on the path.

3.1. Local Costs

Since a minimum cost path should correspond to an image component boundary, pixels (or more accurately, links between neighboring pixels) that exhibit strong edge features should have low local costs and vice-versa. Thus, local component costs are created from the various edge features:

Image Feature	Formulation
Laplacian Zero-Crossing	f_Z
Gradient Magnitude	f_G
Gradient Direction	f_D

The local costs are computed as a weighted sum of these component functionals. Letting $l(p,q)$ represents the local cost on the directed link from pixel p to a neighboring pixel q, the local cost function is

$$l(p,q) = \omega_Z \cdot f_Z(q) + \omega_D \cdot f_D(p,q) + \omega_G \cdot f_G(q) \qquad (1)$$

where each ω is the weight of the corresponding feature function. (Empirically, weights of $\omega_Z = 0.43$, $\omega_D = 0.43$, and $\omega_G = 0.14$ seem to work well in a wide range of images.)

The laplacian zero-crossing is a binary edge feature used for edge localization [7, 9]. Convolution of an image with a laplacian kernel approximates the 2nd partial derivative of the image. The laplacian image zero-crossing corresponds to points of maximal (or minimal) gradient magnitude. Thus, laplacian zero-crossings represent "good" edge properties and should therefore have a low local cost. If $I_L(q)$ is the laplacian of an image I at pixel q, then

$$f_Z(q) = \begin{cases} 0; & \text{if } I_L(q) = 0 \\ 1; & \text{if } I_L(q) \neq 0 \end{cases} \qquad (2)$$

However, application of a discrete laplacian kernel to a digital image produces very few zero-valued pixels. Rather, a zero-crossing is represented by two neighboring pixels that change from positive to negative. Of the two pixels, the one closest to zero is used to represent the zero-crossing. The resulting feature cost contains single-pixel wide cost "canyons" used for boundary localization.

Since the laplacian zero-crossing creates a binary feature, $f_Z(q)$ does not distinguish between strong, high gradient edges and weak, low gradient edges. However, gradient magnitude provides a direct correlation between edge strength and local cost. If I_x and I_y represent the partials of an image I in x and y respectively, then the gradient magnitude G is approximated with

$$G = \sqrt{I_x^2 + I_y^2}.$$

The gradient is scaled and inverted so high gradients produce low costs and vice-versa. Thus, the gradient component function is

$$f_G = \frac{\max(G) - G}{\max(G)} = 1 - \frac{G}{\max(G)} \qquad (3)$$

giving an inverse linear ramp function. Finally, gradient magnitude costs are scaled by Euclidean distance. To keep the resulting maximum gradient at unity, $f_G(q)$ is scaled by 1 if q is a diagonal neighbor to p and by $1/\sqrt{2}$ if q is a horizontal or vertical neighbor.

The gradient direction adds a smoothness constraint to the boundary by associating a high cost for sharp changes in boundary direction. The gradient direction is the unit vector defined by I_x and I_y. Letting $D(p)$ be the unit vector perpendicular (rotated 90 degrees clockwise) to the gradient direction at point p (i.e., for $D(p) = (I_y(p), -I_x(p))$), the formulation of the gradient direction feature cost is

$$f_D(p,q) = \frac{1}{\pi} \{ \cos[d_p(p,q)]^{-1} + \cos[d_q(p,q)]^{-1} \} \qquad (4)$$

where

$$d_p(p,q) = D'(p) \cdot L(p,q)$$
$$d_q(p,q) = L(p,q) \cdot D'(q)$$

are vector dot products and

$$L(p,q) = \begin{cases} q - p; & \text{if } D'(p) \cdot (q-p) \geq 0 \\ p - q; & \text{if } D'(p) \cdot (q-p) < 0 \end{cases} \qquad (5)$$

is the bidirectional link or edge vector between pixels p and q. Links are either horizontal, vertical, or diagonal (relative to the position of q in p's neighborhood) and point such that the dot product of $D(p)$ and $L(p, q)$ is positive, as noted in (5). The neighborhood link direction associates a high cost to an edge or link between two pixels that have similar gradient directions but are perpendicular, or near perpendicular, to the link between them. Therefore, the direction feature cost is low when the gradient direction of the two pixels are similar to each other and the link between them.

3.2. Two-Dimensional Dynamic Programming

As mentioned, dynamic programming can be formulated as a directed graph search for an optimal path. This paper utilizes an optimal graph search similar to that presented by Dijkstra [6] and extended by Nilsson [13]; further, this technique builds on and extends previous boundary tracking methods in 4 important ways:

1. It imposes no directional sampling or searching constraints.

2. It utilizes a new set of edge features and costs: laplacian zero-crossing, multiple gradient kernels.

3. The active list is sorted with an $O(N)$ sort for N nodes/pixels.

4. No a priori goal nodes/pixels are specified.

First, formulation of boundary finding as a 2-D graph search eliminates the directed sampling and searching restrictions of previous implementations, thereby allowing boundaries of arbitrary complexity to be extracted. Second, the edge features used here are more robust and comprehensive than previous implementations: we maximize over different gradient kernels sizes to encompass the various edge types and scales while simultaneously attempting to balance edge detail with noise suppression [7], and we use the laplacian zero-crossing for boundary localization and fine detail livewire "snapping". Third, the discrete, bounded nature of the local edge costs permit the use of a specialized sorting algorithm that inserts points into a sorted list (called the active list) in constant time. Fourth, the live-wire tool is free to define a goal pixel interactively, at any "free" point in the image, after minimum cost paths are computed to **all** pixels. The latter happens fast enough that the free point almost always falls within an expanding cost wavefront and interactivity is not impeded.

The Live-Wire 2-D dynamic programming (DP) graph search algorithm is as follows:

Algorithm: Live-Wire 2-D DP graph search.

```
Input:
    s              {Start (or seed) pixel.}
    l(q,r)         {Local cost function for link between pixels q and r.}

Data Structures:
    L              {List of active pixels sorted by total cost (initially empty).}
    N(q)           {Neighborhood set of q (contains 8 neighbors of pixel).}
    e(q)           {Boolean function indicating if q has been expanded/processed.}
    g(q)           {Total cost function from seed point to q.}

Output:
    p              {Pointers from each pixel indicating the minimum cost path.}

Algorithm:
    g(s)←0;  L←s;           {Initialize active list with zero cost seed pixel.}
    while L≠∅ do begin       {While still points to expand:}
      q←min(L);             {Remove minimum cost pixel q from active list.}
      e(q)←TRUE;            {Mark q as expanded (i.e., processed).}
      for each r∈N(q) such that not e(r) do begin
        g_tmp←g(q)+l(q,r);                {Compute total cost to neighbor.}
        if r∈L and g_tmp<g(r) then        {Remove higher cost neighbor's }
          r←L;                            { from list.}
        if r∉L then begin                 {If neighbor not on list,}
          g(r)←g_tmp;                     { assign neighbor's total cost, }
          p(r)←q;                         { set (or reset) back pointer, }
          L←r;                            { and place on (or return to) }
        end                               { active list.}
      end
    end
end
```

Notice that since the active list is sorted, when a new, lower cumulative cost is computed for a pixel already on the list then that point must be removed from the list in order to be added back to the list with the new lower cost. Similar to adding a point to the sorted list, this operation is also performed in constant time.

Figure 1 demonstrates the use of the 2-D DP graph search algorithm to create a minimum cumulative cost path map (with corresponding optimal path pointers). Figure 1(a) is the initial local cost map with the seed point circled. For simplicity of demonstration the local costs in this example are pixel based rather than link based and can be thought of as representing the gradient magnitude cost feature. Figure 1(b) shows a portion of the cumulative cost and pointer map after expanding the seed point (with a cumulative cost of zero). Notice how the diagonal local costs have been scaled by Euclidean distance (consistent with the gradient magnitude cost feature described previously). Though complicating the example, weighing by Euclidean distance is necessary to demonstrate that the cumulative costs to points currently on the active list can change if even lower cumulative costs are computed from as yet unexpanded neighbors. This is demonstrated in Figure 1(c) where two points

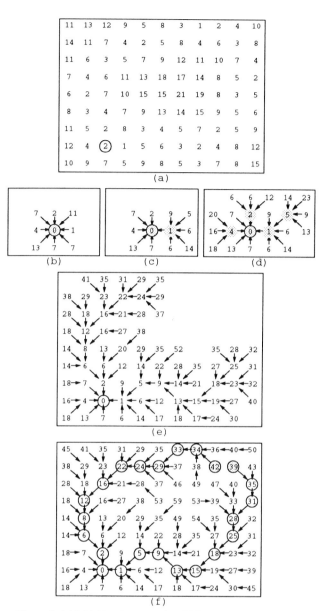

Figure 1: *(a) Initial local cost matrix. (b) Seed point (shaded) expanded. (c) 2 points (shaded) expanded. (d) 5 points (shaded) expanded. (e) 47 points expanded. (f) Finished total cost and path matrix with two of many paths (free points shaded) indicated.*

have now been expanded--the seed point and the next lowest cumulative cost point on the active list. Notice how the points diagonal to the seed point have changed cumulative cost and direction pointers. The Euclidean weighting between the seed and diagonal points makes them more costly than non-diagonal paths. Figures 1(d), 1(e), and 1(f) show the cumulative cost/direction pointer map at various stages of completion. Note how the algorithm produces a "wavefront" of active points emanating from the initial start point, called the seed point, and that the wavefront grows out faster where there are lower costs.

3.3. Interactive "Live-Wire" Segmentation Tool

Once the optimal path pointers are generated, a desired boundary segment can be chosen dynamically via a "free" point. Interactive movement of the free point by the mouse cursor causes the boundary to behave like a live-wire as it adapts to the new minimum cost path by following the optimal path pointers from the free point back

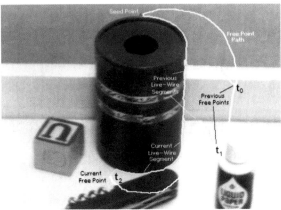

Figure 2: *Image demonstrating how the live-wire segment adapts and snaps to an object boundary as the free point moves (via cursor movement). The path of the free point is shown in white. Live-wire segments from previous free point positions (t_0, t_1, and t_2) are shown in green.*

to the seed point. By constraining the seed point and free points to lie near a given edge, the user is able to interactively "snap" and "wrap" the live-wire boundary around the object of interest. Figure 2 demonstrates how a live-wire boundary segment adapts to changes in the free point (cursor position) by latching onto more and more of an object boundary. Specifically, note the live-wire segments corresponding to user-specified free point positions at times t_0, t_1, and t_2. Although Fig. 2 only shows live-wire segments for three discrete time instances, live-wire segments are actually updated dynamically and interactively (on-the-fly) with each movement of the free point.

When movement of the free point causes the boundary to digress from the desired object edge, interactive input of a new seed point prior to the point of departure reinitiates the 2-D DP boundary detection. This causes potential paths to be recomputed from the new seed point while effectively "tieing off" the boundary computed up to the new seed point.

Note again that optimal paths are computed from the seed point to *all* points in the image (since the 2-D DP graph search produces a minimum cost spanning tree of the image [6]). Thus, by selecting a free point with the mouse cursor, the interactive live-wire tool is simply selecting an optimal boundary segment from a large collection of optimal paths.

Since each pixel (or free point) defines only one optimal path to a seed point, a minimum of two seed points must be placed to ensure a closed object boundary. The path map from the first seed point of every object is maintained during the course of an object's boundary definition to provide a closing boundary path from the free point. The closing boundary segment from the free point to the first seed point expedites boundary closure.

Placing seed points directly on an object's edge is often difficult and tedious. If a seed point is not localized to an object edge then spikes results on the segmented boundary at those seed points (since

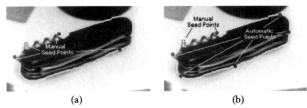

(a)	(b)

Figure 3: *Comparison of live-wire without (a) and with (b) cooling. Withot cooling (a), all seed points must be placed manually on the object edge. With cooling (b), seed points are generated automatically as the live-wire segment freezes.*

(a)

(b)

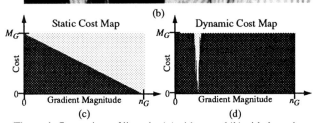
(c)   (d)

Figure 4: *Comparison of live-wire (a) without and (b) with dynamic training. (a) Without training, the live-wire segment snaps to nearby strong edges. (b) With training, it favors edges with similar characteristics as those just learned. (c) The static gradient magnitude cost map shows that without training, high gradients are favored since they map to low costs. However, with training, the dynamic cost map (d) favors gradients similar to those sampled from the previous boundary segment.*

the boundary is forced to pass through the seed points). To facilitate seed point placement, a cursor snap is available which forces the mouse pointer to the maximum gradient magnitude pixel within a user specified neighborhood. The neighborhood can be anywhere from 1×1 (resulting in no cursor snap) to 15×15 (where the cursor can snap as much as 7 pixels in both x and y). Thus, as the mouse cursor is moved by the user, it snaps or jumps to a neighborhood pixel representing a "good" static edge point.

3.4. Path Cooling

Generating closed boundaries around objects of interest can require as few as two seed points (for reasons given previously). Simple objects typically require two to five seed points but complex objects may require many more. Even with cursor snap, manual placement of seed points can be tedious and often requires a large portion of the overall boundary definition time.

Automatic seed point generation relieves the user from precise manual placement of seed points by automatically selecting a pixel on the current active boundary segment to be a new seed point. Selection is based on "path cooling" which in turn relies on path coalescence. Though a single minimum cost path exists from each pixel to a given seed point, many paths "coalesce" and share portions of their optimal path with paths from other pixels. Due to Bellman's Principle of Optimality [3], if any two optimal paths from two distinct pixels share a common point or pixel, then the two paths are identical from that pixel back to the seed point. This is particularly noticeable if the seed point is placed near an object edge and the free point is moved away from the seed point but remains in the vicinity of the object edge. Though a new optimal path is selected and displayed every time the mouse cursor moves, the paths are typically identical near the seed point and object edges and only change local to the free point. As the free point moves farther and farther away from the seed point, the portion of the active live-wire boundary segment that does not change becomes longer. New seed points generated at the end of a stable segment (i.e., that has not changed recently). Stability is measured by time (in milliseconds) on the active boundary and path coalescence (number of time the path has been redrawn from distinct free points).

This measure of stability provides the live-wire segment with a sense of "cooling". The longer a pixel is on a stable section of the live-wire boundary, the cooler it becomes until it eventually freezes and automatically produces a new seed point.

Figure 3 illustrates the benefit of path cooling. In Fig. 3(a), the user must place each seed point manually on the object boundary. However, with cooling (Fig. 3(b)), only the first seed point (and last free point) need to be specified manually; the other seed points were generated automatically via cooling.

3.5. Interactive Dynamic Training

On occasion, a section of the desired object boundary may have a weak gradient magnitude relative to a nearby strong gradient edge. Since the nearby strong edge has a relatively lower cost, the live-wire segment snaps to the strong edge rather than the desired weaker edge. This can be seen in Fig. 4(a). The desired boundary is the woman's (Harriet's) cheek. However, since part of it is so close to the high contrast shoulder of the man (Ozzie), the live-wire snaps to the shoulder.

Training allows dynamic adaptation of the cost function based on a sample boundary segment. Training exploits an object's boundary segment that is already considered to be good and is performed dynamically as part of the boundary segmentation process. As a result, trained features are updated interactively as an object boundary is being defined. On-the-fly training eliminates the need for a separate training phase and allows the trained feature cost functions to adapt *within* the object being segmented as well as between objects in the image. Fig. 4(b) demonstrates how a trained live-wire segment latches onto the edge that is similar to the previous training segment rather that the nearby stronger edge.

To facilitate training and trained cost computation, a gradient magnitude feature map or image is precomputed by scaling the minimized gradient magnitude image, G', into an integer range of size n_G (i.e., from 0 to $n_G - 1$). The actual feature cost is determined by mapping these feature values through a look-up table which contains the scaled (weighted) cost for each value. Fig 4(c) illustrates edge cost based on gradient magnitude without training. Note that with training (Fig. 4(d)) edge cost plummets for gradients that are specific to the object of interest's edges.

Selection of a "good" boundary segment for training is made interactively using the live-wire tool. To allow training to adapt to slow (or smooth) changes in edge characteristics, the trained gradient magnitude cost function is based only on the most recent or

closest portion of the current defined object boundary. A training length, t, specifies how many of the most recent boundary pixels are used to generate the training statistics. A monotonically decreasing weight function (either linearly or Gaussian based) determines the contribution from each of the closest t pixels. This permits adaptive training with local dependence to prevent trained feature from being too subject to old edge characteristics. The closest pixel (i.e., the current active boundary segment endpoint) gets a weight of 1 and the point that is t pixels away, along the boundary from the current active endpoint, gets a minimal weight (which can be determined by the user). The training algorithm samples the precomputed feature maps along the closest t pixels of the edge segment and increments the feature histogram element by the corresponding pixel weight to generate a histogram for each feature involved in training.

After sampling and smoothing, each feature histogram is then scaled and inverted (by subtracting the scaled histogram values from its maximum value) to create the feature cost map needed to convert feature values to trained cost functions.

Since training is based on learned edge characteristics from the most recent portion of an object's boundary, training is most effective for those objects with edge properties that are relatively consistent along the object boundary (or, if changing, at least change smoothly enough for the training algorithm to adapt). In fact, training can be counter-productive for objects with sudden and/or dramatic changes in edge features. However, training can be turned on and off interactively throughout the definition of an object boundary so that it can be used (if needed) in a section of the boundary with similar edge characteristics and then turned off before a drastic change occurs.

3.6 Comparison with Snakes

Due to the recent popularity of snakes and other active contours models and since the interactive boundary wrapping of the live-wire may seem similar to the "wiggling" of snakes, we highlight what we feel are the similarities and their corresponding differences between snakes and Intelligent Scissors.

Similarities (compare with corresponding differences below):

1. The gradient magnitude cost in Intelligent Scissors is similar to the edge energy functional used in snakes.

2. Both methods employ a smoothing term to minimize the effects of noise in the boundary.

3. Snakes and live-wire boundaries are both attracted towards strong edge features.

4. Both techniques attempt to find globally optimal boundaries to try to overcome the effects of noise and edge dropout.

5. Snakes and Intelligent Scissors both require interaction as part of the boundary segmentation process.

Differences (compare with corresponding similarities above):

1. The laplacian zero-crossing binary cost feature seems to have not been used previously in active contours models[1] (or DP boundary tracking methods for that matter).

2. The active contour smoothing term is internal (i.e., based on the contour's point positions) whereas the smoothing term for live-wire boundaries is computed from external image gradient directions[2(next page)].

---

1. Kass et al. [8] did use a squared laplacian energy functional to show the relationship of scale-space continuation to the Mar-Hildreth edge detection theory. However, the squared laplacian does not represent a binary condition, nor could it since the variational calculus minimization used in [8] required that all functionals be differentiable.

3. Snakes are typically attracted to edge features only within the gravity of an edge's gradient energy valley whereas the live-wire boundary can snap to strong edge features from arbitrary distances (since the 2-D DP's search window is the entire image).

4. Snakes are globally optimal over the entire contour whereas live-wire boundaries are piece-wise optimal (i.e., optimal between seed points). We feel this creates a desirable balance between global optimality and local control. This piece-wise optimality also allows for path cooling and intra-object on-the-fly training.

5. Finally, snakes refine (and interactively "nudge" by placing springs, etc.) a single rough boundary approximation where the live-wire tool interactively *selects* an optimal boundary segment from potentially *all* possible minimum cost paths.

Interactive optimal 2-D path selection is what makes Intelligent Scissors work and is the key difference between Intelligent Scissors and all previous techniques. Snakes are interactively initialized with an approximate boundary contour (often require several manually placed points); this single contour is then iteratively adjusted in an attempt to minimize an energy functional. The live-wire tool, on the other hand, is interactively initialized with just a single seed point and it then generates, at interactive speeds, all possible optimal paths from the seed point to *every* other point in the image; thus, allowing the user to interactively select the desired optimal boundary segment. As a result, Intelligent Scissors typically require less time and effort to segment an object than it takes to manually input an initial approximation to the object boundary.

Actually, the live-wire tool is much more similar to previous stage-wise optimal boundary tracking approaches than it is to snakes--since Intelligent Scissors were developed as an interactive 2-D extension to previous optimal edge tracking methods rather than an improvement on active contours.

4. Image Composition with Intelligent Scissors

As mentioned, composition artists need an intelligent, interactive tool to facilitate image component boundary definition. Since Intelligent Scissors can quickly segment object from an image, it serves as a tool for cut and paste operations. After object boundaries have been extracted, object can be copied from the image and placed into a buffer (i.e., clipboard) for future processing and placement into another image, or the same image if desired.

The cut object can be transformed--i.e., rotated, scaled, and translated, (RST)--before combination with the destination image. This is done using an interactive graphical tool with "handles" for RST control. The tool specifies a 2-D RST transformation matrix, *M*. The source image is then bilinearly interpolated through the matrix to paste the cut object into the destination image.

Image composition often requires blending an object from one image into another image such that the cut-out object is not in the foreground. This requires the composition artist to "slip" the cut-out object behind some scene components while leaving it in front of other components. This operation can again be performed using the live-wire tool to create a composition mask[1]. Scene components can be cut out of an image to create a mask such that any additions or changes to the scene will not affect masked pixels.

4.1. Edge Filtering

As described, live-wire boundaries are limited by the pixel reso-

lution of the image. This may produce jaggies along object boundaries in a resulting composition. However, subpixel accuracy can be obtained by exploiting the signed output of the laplacian operator. That is, the position of the object edge can be estimated to subpixel accuracy by using a (linearly) weighted combination of the laplacian pixel values on either side of the zero-crossings.

Since the live-wire boundary will not always correspond to a zero-crossing, jaggies can also be reduced by appropriate edge filtering, similar to anti-aliasing. Edge filtering is also desirable because real world images are acquired using finite image detectors and, as a result, pixels on or near an object boundary share information (i.e., color) from the object and the background.

One approach to edge filtering is to perform a local post-smoothing of the image around the pasted object boundary. However, this does not account for the fact that the edge pixels of the cut object very likely contain some background information from the original image. This is most noticeable when an object is composited into a scene with a different background color than the object's original background color. A more general solution would determine how much of each edge pixel corresponds to the actual object color and weight them accordingly when combining into another image.

4.2. Spatial Frequency and Contrast Matching

Once the object of interest has been segmented from the surrounding background we can scale it, rotate it, color it, or paste it onto another (destination) image. When pasting, it is desirable to perform image composition "seamlessly" in order to make it believable. That is, we should not be able to detect where the paste occurred. However, the source and the destination images will often have differing spatial frequencies or contrast due to differences in focus or lighting when the images were acquired. Thus, equivalencing of spatial frequencies and normalization of contrast is sometimes desirable in order to produce a convincing composition.

Equivalencing of spatial frequencies is performed by matching the spectral content of the cut piece and the destination image in the vicinity where it is to be pasted. Convincing composition often requires the spectra of the object and the destination image to match. This is accomplished by low-pass filtering the spectrum with the higher frequency content to match that of the other. The spectrum with the higher frequency content is determined by parameter fitting of a Butterworth low-pass filter (BLPF) to both spectra. Parameters corresponding to the spectrum with the lower frequency content are used to low-pass filter the spectrum of the other image.

The BLPF $B(u, v, d_0, n)$ is given by

$$B(u, v, d_0, n) = \frac{1}{1 + \left[\frac{\sqrt{u^2 + v^2}}{d_0}\right]^{2n}}$$

where d_0 is the distance of the cutoff frequency from the origin and n is the filter order.

Equivalencing of spatial frequencies is performed by first computing the fourier transforms, $S(u, v)$ and $I(u, v)$ of the source image $S(x, y)$ and the destination image $I(x, y)$. We then compute the log power spectra $s(u, v)$ and $i(u, v)$:

$$s(u, v) = \log [S(u, v)]^2$$

$$i(u, v) = \log [I(u, v)]^2$$

By varying the two parameters d_0 and n, a least squares fit can be used to create a normalized Butterworth filter $B(u, v, d_0', n')$ (where

2. Admittedly, the gradient direction cost used in Intelligent Scissors is more susceptible to noise in areas of low contrast (since it computes a smoothness cost based only on two points and one link). However, it is possible to extend the gradient direction term to include 3 pixels and 2 links without significant loss of computational efficiency.

1. Similar in concept to an optical mask used in motion picture special effects.

d_0' and n' are the fit parameters) matched to the spatial frequency characteristics of $i(u, v)$. If $i(u, v)$ demonstrates lower spatial frequency content than $s(u, v)$, the spatial frequencies between the two images can be equivalenced by fitting $B(u, v, d_0', n')$ to $s(u, v)$. The equivalenced result using the inverse Fourier transform

$$S'(x, y) = F^{-1}[B(u, v, d_0', n') \cdot S(u, v)]$$

is then pasted onto $I(x, y)$. Prior to pasting, the colors in the source image are scaled to the range of $I(x, y)$ to account for differences in contrast.

5. Results

Figures 5, 6, and 7 show the boundaries defined using Intelligent Scissors on a variety of image types. Fig. 5 is an artificial test image that exhibits gaussian edge blurring and point noise typical of some imaging hardware. Fig. 6 is the desktop scene used in Figures 2 and 3. Fig. 7 (a CT image of a lumbar spine) demonstrates the live-wire's application to medical imaging. The boundary definition times (of a trained user) for each displayed object boundary is given in the caption of each respective figure.

Figure 8 graphically compares the live-wire boundary definition times and boundary accuracy with manual tracing. These results show the average time and accuracy from a study where 8 untrained users[1] were asked to define the boundaries of five objects (the two objects in Fig. 5, the paper clip holder and pocket knife in Fig. 6, and the outer boundary of the spinal vertebrae in Fig. 7).

Figures 9(a-c) demonstrates Intelligent Scissors application to color images and show the boundaries defined using Intelligent Scissors for the image composition in Fig. 9(d). Objects were scaled, rotated, and (in the case of Fig. 9(a)) flipped to produce the final composition in Fig. 9(d). Note also that live-wire masking was performed on some of the foreground (grass).

Preprocessing requires 36 convolutions for color images (from 3×3, 5×5, 7×7, and 9×9 kernels), a gradient orientation calculation, a maximum gradient neighborhood search, and creation of a local

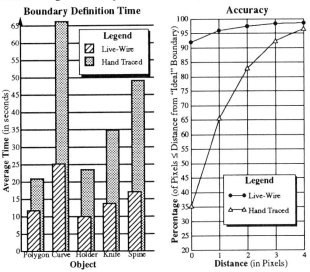

Figure 8: *Average timing and accuracy comparison between manually traced and live-wire boundaries for 8 users. Boundary times are for individual objects where accuracy measurements are over all objects.*

cost map. For color images, we maximize feature values over the three color bands rather than averaging.

Previously, dynamic programming approaches to boundary detection were typically computationally expensive. However, by formulating DP as a graph search and restricting the local costs to integer values within a range, the 2-D DP algorithm can take advantage of an $O(N)$ sort for N points. As mentioned, adding points to the sorted active list and removing points from it requires constant time. As a result, the algorithm's computational complexity for N image pixels is $O(N)$. This can be seen by examining the algorithm in a worst case situation. As a pixel is removed from the active list, it is expanded by computing the cumulative cost to all of its neighbors that have not already been expanded. In the worst case, a pixel has its cumulative cost computed by all of its 8 neighbors, resulting in $8N$ cumulative cost computations for N pixels. Obviously, not every point can be expanded after all of its neighbors have. Except for the seed point, every point that has a cumulative cost must have at least one neighboring point that has already been expanded. Thus the cumulative cost is not recomputed for those neighbors. In short, it can be shown that at most only $4N$ cumulative cost computations are performed, resulting in an $O(N)$ algorithm.

6. Conclusions and Future Work

Intelligent Scissors provide an accurate and efficient interactive tool for object extraction and image composition. In fact, and in sharp contrast to tedious manual boundary definition, object extraction using the live-wire is almost as much fun as the final result (the composition). Intelligent Scissors are intuitive to use and can be applied to existing black and white or color images of arbitrary complexity. There are many rich extensions of this work, including: (1) making use of the weighted zero-crossings in the Laplacian to perform subpixel edge filtering and anti-aliasing, (2) use of multiple layered (multiplane) masks, (3) making spatial frequency equivalencing locally adaptive, (4) varying the light source over the object using directional gradient shading (artificial or borrowed) to provide consistent lighting in the composition, and, most importantly (5) extension of the 2-D DP graph search and application of the live-wire snap and training tools to moving objects and moving, multiplane masks for composition of image sequences.

References

[1] A. A. Amini, T. E. Weymouth, and R. C. Jain, "Using Dynamic Programming for Solving Variational Problems in Vision," *IEEE Transactions on Pattern Analysis and Machine Intelligence*, vol. 12, no. 2, pp. 855-866, Sept. 1990.

[2] D. H. Ballard, and C. M. Brown, *Computer Vision.* Englewood Cliffs, NJ: Prentice Hall, 1982.

[3] R. Bellman and S. Dreyfus, *Applied Dynamic Programming*. Princeton, NJ: Princeton University Press, 1962.

[4] Y. P. Chien and K. S. Fu, "A Decision Function Method for Boundary Detection," *Computer Graphics and Image Processing*, vol. 3, no. 2, pp. 125-140, June 1974.

[5] D. Daneels, et al., "Interactive Outlining: An Improved Approach Using Active Contours," in *SPIE Proceedings of Storage and Retrieval for Image and Video Databases*, vol 1908, pp. 226-233, Feb. 1993.

[6] E. W. Dijkstra, "A Note on Two Problems in Connexion with Graphs," *Numerische Mathematik*, vol. 1, pp. 269-270, 1959.

[7] M. M. Fleck, "Multiple Widths Yield Reliable Finite Differences," *IEEE Transactions on Pattern Analysis and Machine Intelligence*, vol. 14, no. 4, pp. 412-429, April 1992.

[8] M. Kass, A. Witkin, and D. Terzopoulos, "Snakes: Active

---

1. Each user spent a few minutes becoming familiar with the live-wire tool as well as a manual tracing tool and then were asked to define the boundary of 5 objects Each boundary was defined multiple times by each user with both Intelligent Scissors and manual tracing (to also measure intra- and inter-user reproducibility--not shown).

Figure 5: *Test image exhibiting edge blurring and point noise. Boundary definition times--polygon: 4.3 sec and curve: 8.3 sec.*

Figure 6: *Desktop scene. Boundary definition times--block: 2.4 sec; paper clip holder: 3.6 sec; pocket knife: 4.6 sec; liqud paper bottle: 5.1 sec; and spoon: 9.8 sec.*

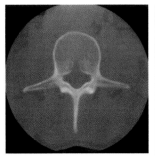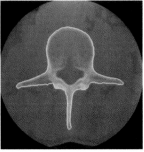

Figure 7: *Spinal vertebrae. Boundary definition time--5.9 sec.*

Contour Models," in *Proceedings of the First International Conference on Computer Vision*, London, England, pp. 259-68, June 1987.

[9] D. Marr and E. Hildreth, "A Theory of Edge Detection," in *Proceedings of the Royal Society of London--Series B: Biological Sciences*, vol. 207, no. 1167, pp. 187-217, Feb. 1980.

[10] A. Martelli, "An Application of Heuristic Search Methods to Edge and Contour Detection," *Communications of the ACM*, vol. 19, no. 2, pp. 73-83, Feb. 1976.

[11] U. Montanari, "On the Optimal Detection of Curves in Noisy Pictures," *Communications of the ACM*, vol. 14, no. 5, pp. 335-45, May 1971.

[12] E. N. Mortensen, B. S. Morse, W. A. Barrett, and J. K. Udupa, "Adaptive Boundary Dectection Using 'Live-Wire' Two-Dimensional Dynamic Programming," in *IEEE Proceedings of Computers in Cardiology*, pp. 635-638, Oct. 1992.

[13] N. J. Nilsson, *Principles of Artificial Intelligence*. Palo Alto, CA: Tioga, 1980.

[14] D. L. Pope, D. L. Parker, D. E. Gustafson, and P. D. Clayton, "Dynamic Search Algorithms in Left Ventricular Border Recognition and Analysis of Coronary Arteries," in *IEEE Proceedings of Computers in Cardiology*, pp. 71-75, Sept. 1984.

[15] D. J. Williams and M. Shah, "A Fast Algorithm for Active Contours and Curvature Estimation," *CVGIP: Image Understanding*, vol. 55, no. 1, pp. 14-26, Jan. 1992.

(a)

(b)

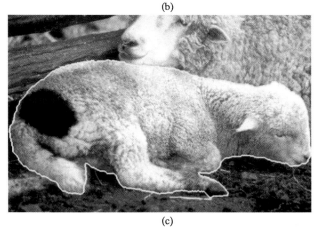

(c)

(d)

Figure 9: *Images used in a composition. (a-c) Live-wire boundaries used for segmentation. (d) Final composition: "Millennium."*

Interactive Physically-Based Manipulation
of Discrete/Continuous Models

Mikako Harada
Department of Architecture

Andrew Witkin
Department of Computer Science

David Baraff
Robotics Institute

Carnegie Mellon University
Pittsburgh, PA 15213

Abstract

Physically-based modeling has been used in the past to support a variety of interactive modeling tasks including free-form surface design, mechanism design, constrained drawing, and interactive camera control. In these systems, the user interacts with the model by exerting virtual forces, to which the system responds subject to the active constraints. In the past, this kind of interaction has been applicable only to models that are governed by continuous parameters. In this paper we present an extension to mixed continuous/discrete models, emphasizing constrained layout problems that arise in architecture and other domains. When the object being dragged is blocked from further motion by geometric constraints, a local discrete search is triggered, during which transformations such as swapping of adjacent objects may be performed. The result of the search is a "nearby" state in which the target object has been moved in the indicated direction and in which all constraints are satisfied. The transition to this state is portrayed using simple but effective animated visual effects. Following the transition, continuous dragging is resumed. The resulting seamless transitions between discrete and continuous manipulation allow the user to easily explore the mixed design space just by dragging objects. We demonstrate the method in application to architectural floor plan design, circuit board layout, art analysis, and page layout.

Keywords—Interactive techniques, physically-based modeling, grammars.

1 Introduction

Physically-based modeling has been a topic of interest in computer graphics for some time. A particular area of interest has been the use of physical simulation or related optimization techniques as a means of geometric interaction, allowing users to directly manipulate simulated objects subject to constraints. This approach has been applied to animation, image analysis, drawing, free-form surface modeling, mechanical design, and interactive molecular simulation [29, 28, 30, 5, 31, 33, 27].

Author's affiliations: Mikako Harada, (mh3i@andrew.cmu.edu), Department of Architecture; Andrew Witkin, (aw@cs.cmu.edu), Department of Computer Science; David Baraff, (baraff@cs.cmu.edu), Robotics Institute. Carnegie Mellon University, Pittsburgh PA 15213.

Permission to make digital/hard copy of part or all of this work for personal or classroom use is granted without fee provided that copies are not made or distributed for profit or commercial advantage, the copyright notice, the title of the publication and its date appear, and notice is given that copying is by permission of ACM, Inc. To copy otherwise, to republish, to post on servers, or to redistribute to lists, requires prior specific permission and/or a fee.

Despite its successes, this approach has been subject to the severe limitation that it only supports manipulation of systems governed by continuous variables. Neither discrete operations such as the addition, deletion, or replacement of parts nor discrete changes in object shapes or spatial relationships can be accommodated at all within the physically-based manipulation framework. This is an unfortunate limitation because a great many problems of interest involve both continuous and discrete parameters. An important class of such problems are layout or arrangement problems in which a collection of objects are to be placed and reshaped subject to constraints that prevent interpenetration, require adjacency, bound dimensions, etc. Such problems arise in architecture for floor planning and furniture layout, in mechanical and electromechanical design, and even in fine art.

We would like to extend the physically-based interaction paradigm to encompass the exploration of this kind of continuous/discrete problem space. We envision systems in which objects respond continuously to the user's pushing and dragging actions in a physical or quasi-physical manner, until they "hit a wall" imposed by some constraint. They then spontaneously undergo some discrete rearrangement or other transformation that does what the user asked (essentially, moving the dragged or pushed object point in the indicated direction) with the least perceived disruption in the overall arrangement. The change should occur rapidly enough to maintain interactivity, and should be visually portrayed in a fashion that the user can clearly understand.

For example, in laying out a floor plan there are many degrees of freedom as well as many constraints. Rooms may not overlap. A residential plan must include a living room, some number of bedrooms, etc. The dining room should adjoin the kitchen. Rooms have minimum dimensions or areas. Typically, all but bathrooms must adjoin an exterior wall or courtyard wall. The whole house must fit within some pre-specified envelope. Within these constraints, the size, shape, and arrangement of rooms is free to vary. Some rooms (e.g. a library or den) might be optional. Although plans may be judged objectively by criteria such as cost, subjective aesthetic criteria also play a large role, so the problem cannot be reduced to one of "black box" mixed-integer combinatorial optimization. (And such problems are, as a general rule, *NP*-hard.)

If the basic arrangement is fixed, it is a straightforward matter using existing physical manipulation techniques to push and pull on walls, adjusting dimensions within the size or area constraints. The new ingredient we want to add is this: when a wall is pushed to one of its constraint limits, the system should find a re-arrangement, (e.g. swapping the living room to the other side of the dining room) that allows the wall on which the user pushes to continue to move in the indicated direction. The disruption to the rest of the plan should be minimal, and it should be immediately clear to the user what happened.

For any particular instance of this class of problem, we are given a model whose state is given by a set of continuous and discrete (integer or boolean) variables, with a graphical representation that depends on state, and a set of equality or inequality constraint functions that likewise depend on state. Our approach to the problem handles continuous and discrete changes separately, although transitions between the two modes are seamless and transparent to the user. The user's dragging motions are treated as a "force" to be applied to the model's continuous parameters subject to the constraints. As long as this applied force is not entirely cancelled by constraint forces, the discrete variables remain frozen, and our method is just like that used in previous physical manipulation systems.

When the constraint forces cancel the user's applied force, the model is "stuck." We then search for a new state of the discrete variables. The main contribution of this paper lies in this area. We begin with a problem-specific search space that is defined by a set of transformations on the discrete variables. The form of these transformations depends on the structure of the models. The idea is to define this set of transformations to do a reasonable job of capturing perceptual similarity, so that each single transformation makes a perceptually small change to the arrangement of objects. In the domains on which we have experimented, constructing the transformations has not been difficult; we have done very well with simple operations such as swaps and moves. The set of transformations gives us a new space in which we may perform shallow searches. The search is limited to transformations that directly influence the element being dragged by the user, and is also subject to a depth limit. Subject to these restrictions, we look for a state that does the best job of moving whatever was grabbed by the user in the desired direction. To portray the transition to this new state we use simple animation tricks that provide smooth motion cues for the user.

This combination of discrete and continuous mechanisms provides seamless, pleasing interactions. The discrete search is hidden from the user. In the case of swapping rooms in a floor plan, the user's experience is something like this: we grab one wall of the living room, pulling toward the opposing wall, which is shared with the dining room. The living room shrinks until it reaches its minimum width. If we continue to pull strongly on the wall, the living room "pops" through to the other side of the dining room, with a brief interpenetration. Most of the rest of the plan is undisturbed, but the kitchen, which is constrained to be adjacent to the dining room, has swapped places as well.

The remainder of the paper is organized as follows: in the next section, we discuss the background of physical manipulation methods, as well as the relevant architecture background of shape grammars. In the following section we review the math and algorithms of continuous constrained manipulation. We then describe the discrete portion in detail. Next, we present results in architecture, board layout, page layout, and grammar-based analysis exploration of paintings. We conclude with discussion and directions for future work.

2 Background

An active research area in architecture involves the use of *Shape Grammars* as a means of formally capturing architectural style. Despite considerable evidence that such grammars are capable of representing styles, it has not previously been clear how they could actually be used to interactively explore design spaces or create designs. A main motivation of our work has been to develop means of interacting with shape grammars through direct geometric manipulation. The first portion of this section reviews prior work on shape grammars for architecture.

Embedded in the discrete problem of searching grammar-based design spaces is a problem of exploring a continuous design space by varying sizes, positions, etc. within the design constraints. Our approach to this sub-problem closely follows previous work in the

use of physically-based methods for interactive manipulation. The second portion of this section reviews this prior work.

2.1 Shape Grammars in Architecture

Shape grammars were first introduced to architecture by Stiny and Gips in the 1970's [25, 24]. Since then, shape grammars have been used theoretically to describe the historical style of architectural designs [26, 7, 17] and to specify new forms [15]. Shape grammars are appealing to architecture researchers because they are visual, and because they offer a formal mechanism for capturing the previously vague and ambiguous notion of "style."

The basic idea of shape grammars is to define a set of rewrite rules that operate on geometric models by replacing, re-arranging or modifying elements. The grammar serves to implicitly define a set of geometric models, i.e. all those that can be derived by some legal sequence of rule applications. The hope is that relatively simple rule sets can be devised that capture some aspect of architectural style, for example, generating designs for all and only Queen Anne Houses [13].

Several computer programs have been developed based on the theoretical foundation of shape grammars.[1] These systems have been used to demonstrate grammars representing floor plan layouts [8], framing structures [21], and a class of building designs [13].

Interacting with grammar-based systems has been problematic. The only means of exploring the discrete space of designs defined by a grammar has been sequential manual rule selection by the user, with, in some systems, the ability to edit an existing derivation. This mode of editing can be frustrating and extremely difficult, because the relation between a rule and its geometric effect can be obscure, particularly for rules that occur early in the sequence. We believe that the formalism of shape grammars would be far more useful if the architect could explore the space by directly manipulating the grammar's geometric output rather than the sequence of rules that produced it.

A further issue has been that these systems do not handle continuous dimensional variations (the flip side of the problem we have faced in physically-based manipulation.) A few applications allow grammars to include continuous parameters, with some user control over parameter values [21]. However, the problem of solving simultaneously for parameter values that satisfy constraints has been finessed. No existing grammar-based system allows the user to directly manipulate designs to produce geometric variations. Existing physically-based techniques, on the other hand, appear to be ideally suited to supporting such direct manipulation.

2.2 Physically-Based Modeling for Graphical Interaction

Interactive physical simulations have been used as a technique for interaction with a variety of graphical models. In computer vision and image analysis, quasi-physical active contour models known as *snakes* are widely used for interactive edge finding and tracking [14]. Snakes are essentially simulated springy "wires" that are attracted to edge features in images, and simultaneously subjected to manipulation forces imposed by the user.

The use of constrained dynamics simulations for interactive geometric modeling was described by Witkin *et al.* [32]. Flexible-surface simulations for interactive computer vision and free-form surface modeling are areas that have also been extensively investigated [29, 28, 30, 5, 31, 33]. Constrained dynamics simulations

---

[1]Shape grammars in their original form could not be implemented directly, due to problems of ambiguity. Several additional formalisms were introduced on which system implementations were based [4, 13]. Henceforth we use "shape grammar" in the broader sense of these extended geometric grammars.

have also been used to support drawing applications [11] and for interactive camera control for animation [10]. Surles [27] describes a system for interactive molecular simulations. Interactive simulations that include contact constraints were described by Baraff [3]; the continuous simulation techniques in this paper most closely follow that work.

3 Continuous Manipulation

During any interval of time in which the discrete variables of the model stay fixed, the model is represented simply as a continuous function of state $\mathbf{q}(t)$, where $\mathbf{q}(t) \in \mathbb{R}^n$ is a vector of the model's n continuous variables. Over such an interval, the model may be subject to some constraints: that is, we may require the model to satisfy the conditions

$$
\begin{aligned}
C_1(\mathbf{q}(t)) &\geq 0 \\
C_2(\mathbf{q}(t)) &\geq 0 \\
&\vdots \\
C_m(\mathbf{q}(t)) &\geq 0
\end{aligned}
\tag{1}
$$

where each function C_i is a scalar function of state, $\mathbf{q}$. The evolution of this type of constrained system over time exactly parallels work on physical simulation of impenetrable objects [2]; accordingly, we cast the continuous manipulation of our models as a problem in constrained physical simulation.

Assuming that the model's initial state $\mathbf{q}(t_0)$ satisfies $C_i(\mathbf{q}(t_0)) \geq 0$ for $1 \leq i \leq m$, the model evolves from time t_0 according to the first-order differential equation

$$
\dot{\mathbf{q}}(t) = \frac{d}{dt}\mathbf{q}(t) = \mathbf{M}^{-1}\mathbf{F}(t)
\tag{2}
$$

where $\mathbf{F}(t) \in \mathbb{R}^n$ is the "force" acting on the model at time t and $\mathbf{M}$ is an $n \times n$ diagonal "mass" matrix. By adjusting entries in $\mathbf{M}$, state variables can be "heavier" or "lighter" (that is, harder or easier to change). Aside from user preferences, the matrix $\mathbf{M}$ is needed to properly scale the problem in the case when two or more of the state variables have vastly different scale/ranges from each other. The force $\mathbf{F}(t)$ has the form

$$
\mathbf{F}(t) = \mathbf{F}_a(t) + \mathbf{F}_c(t)
$$

where $\mathbf{F}_a(t)$ represents the force applied by the user to alter the model, and $\mathbf{F}_c(t)$ represents a constraint force that is introduced so that the conditions of equation (1) can be maintained.

To allow the model to be manipulated with as little interference as possible, we seek a constraint force $\mathbf{F}_c(t)$ that interferes with the user's applied force as little as possible. Treating our manipulation problem as a physical problem, we choose $\mathbf{F}_c(t)$ to be a workless, compressive constraint force [19]. At any particular time t, such a constraint force depends on the applied force $\mathbf{F}_a(t)$ and the set of *active* constraints. A constraint C_i is said to be active at time t if $C_i(\mathbf{q}(t)) = 0$. The workless, compressive constraint forces we seek have the form

$$
\mathbf{F}_c(t) = \frac{\partial C_1(\mathbf{q}(t))}{\partial \mathbf{q}} f_1 + \cdots + \frac{\partial C_m(\mathbf{q}(t))}{\partial \mathbf{q}} f_m
$$

where the scalar variables f_i are all nonnegative and f_i is zero if the ith constraint is not active.

Suppose at time t only k of the m constraints on the model are active; without loss of generality, let $C_1(\mathbf{q}(t)) = C_2(\mathbf{q}(t)) = \cdots = C_k(\mathbf{q}(t)) = 0$. Only the k active constraints have an effect on the

model's motion at time t; in particular, if k is zero the system is (momentarily) completely unconstrained in its motion. Let $\mathbf{C}(\mathbf{q}(t)) \in \mathbb{R}^k$ be defined as the vector-collection of these k active constraints,

$$
\mathbf{C}(\mathbf{q}(t)) =
\begin{pmatrix}
C_1(\mathbf{q}(t)) \\
C_2(\mathbf{q}(t)) \\
\vdots \\
C_k(\mathbf{q}(t))
\end{pmatrix},
$$

and let the $n \times k$ matrix $\mathbf{J}$ be defined by

$$
\mathbf{J}^T = \frac{\partial \mathbf{C}(\mathbf{q}(t))}{\partial \mathbf{q}}.
$$

Using this notation, $\mathbf{F}_c(t)$ has the form $\mathbf{F}_c(t) = \mathbf{J}^T\mathbf{f}$ where the vector $\mathbf{f} = (f_1, f_2, \ldots, f_k)$ satisfies $\mathbf{f} \geq \mathbf{0}$ (with $\mathbf{0}$ a k-vector of zeros). To prevent the active constraints from decreasing past zero, we require that $\dot{\mathbf{C}}(\mathbf{q}(t)) \geq \mathbf{0}$. Using the chain rule, this yields

$$
\dot{\mathbf{C}}(\mathbf{q}(t)) = \frac{\partial \mathbf{C}(\mathbf{q}(t))}{\partial \mathbf{q}}^T \dot{\mathbf{q}}(t) = \mathbf{J}\dot{\mathbf{q}}(t) \geq \mathbf{0}.
\tag{3}
$$

Since $\dot{\mathbf{q}}(t) = \mathbf{M}^{-1}\mathbf{F}(t)$ and

$$
\mathbf{F}(t) = \mathbf{F}_a(t) + \mathbf{F}_c(t) = \mathbf{F}_a(t) + \mathbf{J}^T\mathbf{f},
$$

we can rewrite equation (3) as

$$
\mathbf{J}\mathbf{M}^{-1}\mathbf{J}^T\mathbf{f} + \mathbf{J}\mathbf{F}_a(t) \geq \mathbf{0}.
\tag{4}
$$

For the constraint force to be workless, we require not only that $\mathbf{f}$ be nonnegative and satisfy equation (4), but also that the ith component of $\mathbf{f}$ be zero if $\dot{C}_i(\mathbf{q}(t)) > 0$. This last condition prevents the constraint force from gratuitously changing $\mathbf{q}(t)$ so that an active constraint becomes inactive. Baraff [2] discusses the implementation of a fast, efficient algorithm for computing a vector $\mathbf{f}$ which satisfies all of these conditions; our system computes $\mathbf{f}$ using the described implementation.

Once $\mathbf{f}$ is computed for a given t, the constraint force and thus the total force $\mathbf{F}(t)$ acting on the system is known. Standard numerical methods are then used to integrate the system $\dot{\mathbf{q}}(t) = \mathbf{M}^{-1}\mathbf{F}(t)$ forward in time. Since constraint forces only prevent currently active constraints from being violated, and since numerical integration techniques take discrete steps from time t to time $t + \Delta t$, a constraint j that is inactive at time t may occasionally be violated at time $t + \Delta t$ (i.e. $C_j(\mathbf{q}(t + \Delta t))$ may be negative). In this case, we employ standard root finding techniques to evolve the system forward to the time t_c between t and $t + \Delta t$ at which $C_j(\mathbf{q}(t_c))$ becomes zero. The jth constraint then becomes an active constraint at this time, and a more accurate projection of $\mathbf{q}(t + \Delta t)$ can be computed. The process is the same as the collision-resolution processes employed in physical simulation systems [1].

4 Discrete Manipulation

We wish to extend the paradigm of continuous physically-based interaction to allow the state of the system to undergo discrete structural change in response to the user's actions. Although such discontinuous behavior is inherently non-physical we want to retain the spirit of continuous physical interaction, letting the user operate on the design simply by dragging objects subject to whatever constraints are in force.

In a continuous system, when the user drags an object into a wall or other constraint-imposed "dead end," the object simply halts. Instead, if the user continues to pull, we want the system to seek some discrete change that permits the object to move further in the indicated direction.

Finding such a change is a search problem. Of the discrete space of alternative states, we must find a new state that satisfies several criteria:

- The new state must match our interpretation of the user's intent. In the case of simple dragging, this means that the element being dragged must be displaced in the direction indicated by the user.

- The new state should be consistent with all problem constraints, although it turns out we will want to briefly portray illegal intermediate states as a visual cue.

- The change should not surprise the user. Rather than an involved global rearrangement, we want the change to be simple, local, and easily grasped. Ideally, we want the user to perceive some sort of direct mechanical connection between his or her action and the resulting change, as if, for example, normally impenetrable rigid objects were allowed momentarily to squeeze past or pop through each other.

- If several otherwise equivalent alternatives are found, we may wish to choose the one that rates best according to a problem-specific objective function.

- We must find the new state quickly enough to maintain interactivity, which rules out a large-scale combinatorial search.

We approach the problem by creating a set of domain-specific transformations that map states in the discrete space into other states. We use these to structure a local search and to define a metric intended to capture perceptual similarity, with distance to a new state defined by the number of transformations required to reach it. In practice, this means that we want transformations that make small, local changes, such as swapping two adjacent elements.

The user actions that triggered the search provide information that can be used to limit it, for instance, considering only those transformations that directly influence the element being dragged. In addition, to maintain interactivity, we limit the depth of the search to at most a few levels. Subject to these restrictions we seek the closest state that satisfies the user's intent subject to the design constraints, possibly weighting the similarity of the old and new states against the absolute merit of the new one as defined by the design objective function. In the subsections that follows, we describe the method in detail.

4.1 Triggering a Local Search

In our system, continuous manipulation is the main mode of interaction. The search for a discrete change is triggered automatically when continuous manipulation "hits a wall" in the sense that no further continuous change can be made in response to the force $\mathbf{F}_a$ applied by the user. Specifically, the discrete search is activated when the following conditions apply:

- there are user-applied forces ($\mathbf{F}_a \neq \mathbf{0}$),

- the applied forces do no work ($\mathbf{F}_a^T \dot{\mathbf{q}} \approx 0$),

- the applied forces are large enough to signal the direction of user action ($\|\mathbf{F}_a\| \geq k$, where k is the smallest force needed to activate discrete manipulation), and

- the configuration is not identical to that preceding the most recently performed search.

The last condition is added to avoid "thrashing" after a local discrete search fails. If these conditions are met, we initiate a local search, using the object being pulled by the user and the direction in which it is pulled to limit the search.

Although the choice of transformations is problem-specific, we generally want transformation rules that make minimal, local changes so that nearby states will appear globally similar to the original. Additional criteria are that the transformations should tend to yield nearby states that are consistent with the topological and geometric constraints, and steerable in the sense that we can directly limit the search to states that are consistent with the user's intent.

We limit the search to operations that move the target element in the desired direction, and also place an absolute limit on the depth of the search to maintain interactivity. Each candidate state is tested against the constraints and objective functions. An example of a set of transformation rules is described in the next section.

4.2 Constraints and Objectives

In addition to the "user's intent" constraint which has already been built into the search, we must consider topological and geometric constraints that are part of the problem specification. We also have two sorts of objective function: a relative one, measuring distance from the old state to a candidate new state, and an absolute one measuring the goodness of the overall design. We take a weighted sum of the two, choosing the best solution that satisfies the constraints. If no legal state is found within the depth limit of the search we remain at the old state. In this last case, the user's experience is that the object being pulled "can't go that away," in which case he or she is free to try something else.

To satisfy the constraints, we consider topological constraints first, such as adjacency requirements. If a candidate state meets all the topological constraints, we then perform a numerical constraint solution in an effort to meet the applicable continuous geometric constraints, using a general purpose continuous constrained optimization program [9]. Since we are making incremental changes, the previous geometric parameter values generally give good initial estimates for finding a new state that satisfies the constraints.

Of the states that satisfy the topological and geometric constraints, we choose the best one as measured by a compound objective function. This objective function has discrete and continuous parts as well. We let the "closeness" of the new state to the old depend on continuous geometric measures of the change, as well as on the integer-valued transformation distance between them. We could use an additional objective function to modify the search, either a persistent objective function that measures the "goodness" of the design, or a temporary one that measures the degree to which the change matches what the user asked for, or both.

After a new state is chosen, the numerical values obtained by optimization become the initial continuous parameter values for the new state. We then return to the continuous manipulation phase.

4.3 Visualizing Discrete Changes

Although we are trying to make the smallest possible discrete changes, any abrupt change to the displayed state of the model tends to be confusing. We have found that the addition of some simple visual cues is of great help to the user in understanding the discrete changes. Instead of switching directly to the new state we smoothly animate the transition, using highlighting and icons to help direct the viewer's attention. With some tuning of the appearance and timing of these visual effects we have been able to produce seamless transitions between the continuous and discrete modes of interaction, with the subjective impression that the discrete change, like the continuous one, takes place in direct mechanical response to the user's action.

5 Implementation Examples and Results

We have built an interactive system that implements the discrete and continuous manipulation techniques described in this paper. Our initial experiments have centered on a class of layout problems known as *floor planning* problems. The floor planning problem is also known as the *rectangular packing* or *rectangular dissection* problem.

The floor planning problem, in general, is to arrange a given number of rectangles within a larger rectangular space so that the space is completely filled, without any overlap between boxes.[2] Each rectangle may have lower-bound and upper-bound constraints on its dimensions and area. There may also be structural constraints between rectangles, such as adjacency constraints. The goal of floor-planning problems varies with the application, but often involves an optimization subject to the constraints, and may also involve aesthetic or other subjective criteria. Floor planning problems have long been investigated [12] and are of particular interest in architecture [22, 6, 8] and VLSI design [34, 20, 35]. In this section, we describe the implementation of a system for attacking this class of floor layout problem interactively. After showing examples, we describe the results of our experiments.

5.1 Implementation of a Floor Planning Program

Our representation for floor planning problems is based on rectangular dissection. We begin with a single rectangular region, then recursively subdivide regions, either horizontally or vertically, into two or more sub-regions.[3] Each dissection structure can be defined by a *subregion tree* in which nonterminal nodes represent either horizontal or vertical subdivisions, and leaf nodes represent the final rectangles that comprise the dissection. Kundu [18] gives a detailed description of subregion trees. A rectangular dissection and its subregion tree are shown in figure 1a. The chief advantage of this representation is that it guarantees a non-overlapping arrangement of boxes, with no empty space. In addition, the subregion tree allows us to easily extract adjacency relationships between rectangles.

The structure of the subregion tree defines the topology of the dissection. Additional information is required to define the rectangles' dimensions. In the root node we store the absolute height and width of the bounding rectangle. In each other node we store a dimensionless value r that defines its height or width as a fraction of the enclosing rectangle's height or width. If V is a vertical subdivision node with dimensions $[x, y]$ and children $R_1, R_2 \ldots, R_n$, then the dimensions of rectangle R_i are $[r_i x, y]$, where r_i is the value stored in R_i, and similarly for horizontal subdivisions. The dimensions of any rectangle, and the derivatives of its dimensions, are easily evaluated by recursively descending the tree. We enforce the constraint that $r > 0$ for all nodes, and that $\sum_i r_i = 1$ for each set of sibling nodes.

Our current system implements constraints that place upper and lower bounds on width, height, area, and aspect ratio, as well as rectangle adjacency constraints. Additional geometric constraints are easily added, since we only need to add code to compute $C(\mathbf{q})$ and $\partial C(\mathbf{q})/\partial \mathbf{q}$ to handle a new type of constraint.

In addition to constraint forces, it is sometimes desirable to add default values or "preferences" to a model. For example, a given rectangle may have a desired size, area, or aspect ratio, which the system should try to achieve unless blocked by constraints. Such preferences are easily implemented by adding penalty forces to the

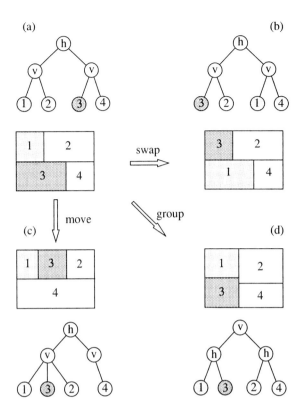

Figure 1: Rectangular dissections, subregion trees, and transformations. (a) A dissection and its subregion tree. (b–d) Transformations on (a).

model. Penalty forces are obtained by negatively scaling the gradient of the squared difference between the actual state and the desired one. Penalty forces act like springs that pull objects toward the desired configuration. They are subordinate to the hard constraints, but compete with each other. The strength of each penalty force is controlled by a user-assigned weight. During continuous manipulation, penalty forces are added to the manipulation force supplied by the user to form the total applied force, $\mathbf{F}_a(t)$. As described in section 3, a constraint force $\mathbf{F}_c(t)$ is then computed which maintains the dimensional constraints. As long as constraints do not prevent a particular preferred motion of the model, or there are not multiple contradictory preferences, the system will gradually enforce the desired preferences, while still strictly maintaining the dimensional constraints of the system.

To support discrete floor plan manipulations we have defined four transformations that operate on subregion trees: move, swap, group, and rotate. The first three of these are illustrated in figure 1.

- The *move* transformation takes as its arguments a node to be moved, the new node under which it should be placed, and an integer giving its position in the list of siblings at the new location. The target node is moved to the new location. If it is a nonterminal node, the subtree under it moves as well.

- The *swap* transformation takes as arguments two nodes, and exchanges their positions in the subregion tree, equivalent to two move operations.

- The *group* transformation takes as arguments two nodes, which must be spatially adjacent. The subregion tree is rearranged to make the nodes become siblings in the subregion tree. We use this operation when four subregions meet at or

[2]Non-overlapping, no-unused-space arrangements are sometimes called "tightly packed." If we allow unused spaces, the problem becomes a "loosely packed" problem. As we see in our examples, loosely packed problems are a subset of tightly packed problems.

[3]We define a vertical subdivision to be one that introduces a vertical boundary, and a horizontal subdivision, a horizontal boundary. Thus the rectangles created by a horizontal subdivision are one above the other.

Figure 2: Architectural room layout. (top) The user pulls on the dining room, and a discrete change occurs. (middle) Two intermediate frames from the resulting animated transition. (bottom) The new configuration.

near one point to change the order of subdivisions (i.e., from vertical first and horizontal second to horizontal first and vertical second, or vice versa).

- The *rotate* transformation takes a single node as its argument. It does not change the structure of the subregion tree. Rather, it swaps the x and y values of the minimum and maximum dimensions assigned to the corresponding rectangle. This operation is only applicable to leaf nodes.

The search space for discrete changes is the set of subregion trees generated by applying sequences of these transformations to the original tree. We are interested in interactive manipulation rather than large-scale combinatorial optimization. To maintain interactivity we must restrict the search to a very small number of alternative states. We limit the search in two ways. First, we consider only transformations that operate on nodes which are directly involved with the rectangle or edge being dragged by the user. Second, we limit the depth of the search: in the examples presented here we consider only transformation sequences of length two or less.

For each new discrete state we consider, it is generally necessary to adjust the continuous parameters to satisfy the geometric constraints if possible, and to obtain a local optimum of whatever objective function is attached to the model. To perform the continuous constrained optimization we use a general purpose optimization package called NPSOL [9] to compute a new state vector $\mathbf{q}$. The NPSOL package optimizes smooth nonlinear functions subject to both linear and nonlinear constraints. We have considered several objective functions for the new state vector $\mathbf{q}$, including objective functions that seek to keep rectangular areas close to a desired size, functions that try to minimize the change in $\mathbf{q}$ from its prior value, and objective functions which minimize the total area of the rectangular dissection. Like constraints, new types of objective functions are easily added by supplying code which evaluates an objective function's value and gradient for a particular state $\mathbf{q}$.

5.2 Examples

Within the class of floor planning problems, we show examples from four domains: architectural room layout, circuit board layout, page layout, and stylistic analysis of abstract painting.

Architectural Room Layout

A primary motivation of our research has been to build a system for architectural layout planning. In our architectural examples, rooms or functional areas are modeled as rectangles. The sides of the rectangles are the walls surrounding a room. In addition to the constraints to set bounds on the lengths and areas of each room, and the overall floorspace occupied by the rooms, adjacency constraints can be defined between some rooms. For example, we might specify that a kitchen must remain adjacent to the dining room, while an entranceway must always be adjacent to an exterior wall of the layout.

Using the system, the user can pull on either a wall or the center of a room to change the position and size of a room. Constraints or preferences can be used to prevent rooms from becoming overly narrow during this manipulation. The user can also add constraints to fix walls in place and prevent them from moving from their current position. When the user pulls on an interior wall, the exterior walls of the layout remain fixed. When the user pulls on an exterior wall, the entire layout is scaled.

During manipulation, constraints are visually indicated. For example, if a room's width has reached its lower bound, a bright line is drawn horizontally across the room, to indicate that no more horizontal compaction of the room is possible. Even if the user continues pulling in the same direction, the constraint forces prevent

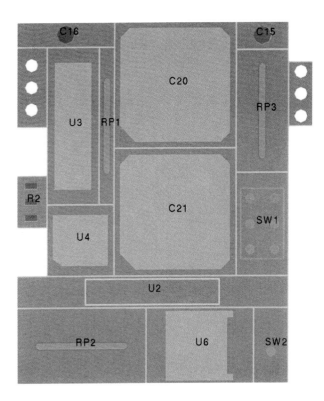

Figure 3: Circuit board layout.

the room's width from further decreasing. Similarly, a room whose area cannot be increased or decreased is bordered with a bright line to inform the user that the area of the room is currently bounded. When all progress is blocked by the constraints, a sufficiently hard pull on a blocked component of the layout activates a search for a discrete change. After the system finishes the search, a transition between the current state and the new state is shown as an "animation"; rooms fly from the current state to the new state (using simple linear interpolation).

For a proposed discrete change, the objective function on the state $\mathbf{q}$ is the difference of the desired total area of the house, and the total area occupied by the house in state $\mathbf{q}$. Two examples of architectural layout are shown; the first example shows a house with 14 rooms, while the second example has 24 rooms (21 actual rooms plus 3 extra rectangular areas to produce indentations, yielding a nonrectangular exterior shape for the house). A sample layout for the second house is shown in figure 2.

Circuit Board Layout

PC board layout is a heavily investigated application area of floor planning. In this context, the goal is to arrange a set of circuit modules on a board while minimizing the total interconnecting wire length. The objective of this problem sounds much clearer than the architectural examples. However, there are many flexible parameters that the designer must consider. The design process involves the selection of a representative among many alternatives. As an example, in designing a board layout for a wearable computer, the primary objective is to make the computer wearable; i.e., it must be small, and comfortable to carry around. The designer's concern then shifts to interface issues, such as the position of switch, the position of a strip, and the balance of weight.

We have taken a sample board layout from a design team working on a wearable computer. We have chosen an objective function that

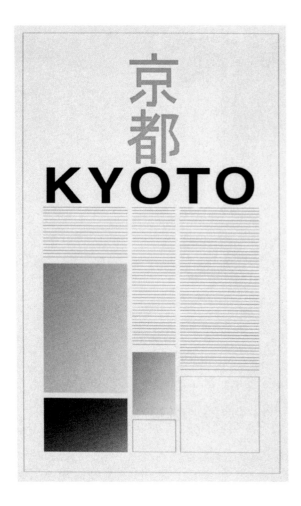

Figure 4: Page layout.

Figure 5: De Stijl style art.

seeks to minimize the total area occupied by the circuit board. The basic interactions for the board layout are the same as in the architectural examples. We have added some icons to make it easier for users to recognize each module. Additionally, rotational transformations are part of the allowable set of transformations during discrete search. A sample configuration of the circuit board is shown in figure 3.

Page Layout

Another potential application area of our approach is in graphic design for posters, covers and page layout. Figure 4 shows a sample image of typographic design, in which headlines, picture areas, and text areas are considered. In this example we apply aspect-ratio constraints to headlines and pictures, and area as well as dimension constraints to text blocks.

Analysis of Abstract Painting

Constraints are known to be one of the essential elements in defining an artistic style. In the rich combinatorial space of design, an artist's method of selective search through that space is thought to be a key element of style [23]. Our last example focuses on images from abstract painting. This example is taken from Knight [16], who has analyzed stylistic changes in the paintings by De Stijl artists. The purpose of this example is to show the usefulness of exploratory manipulation as a tool to study "styles." Knight studied artists' paint-

ings over periods of time. Dividing them into several stages, she defined generative grammars for each stage of each artist. Our example is based on her analysis on the first stage (1945–50) of Frits Glarner's work.

Primary elements of Glarner's stage I paintings are rectangular divisions; oblique divisions in each rectangle; and grey, black, white, and primary colors (red, yellow, and blue). The constraints in Glarner's work are characterized as follows:

1. The oblique division is angled slightly from 90 degrees.

2. The placement of the oblique is near the edge of a rectangle, forming a wedge shaped "strip."

3. For each rectangular division, the larger wedge is grey or white, and the narrower wedge is grey, black, white or a primary color.

4. The rectangular divisions appear regular.

5. Among six combinatorially possible relationships between two obliquely divided rectangles, only three are used.

Currently, our system is limited to the constraints listed above. Whatever changes a user makes, continuous or discrete, the image keeps the original style, as defined by the constraints. In future work, we would want to let the user easily impose new stylistic constraints if they encounter transformations which are not consistent with the desired style. Conversely, if the constraints prevent us from seeing a legal instance, we may wish to modify or delete some of the constraints. According to the work by Knight, for example, a modification to the second constraint above is one of the changes needed to go on to the next stage of Glarner's work. A sample piece of artwork in the De Stijl style generated by our system is shown in figure 5.

5.3 Results

Overall, our initial experiments in continuous and discrete manipulation have been successful. The system runs at a pleasingly interactive speed on the examples discussed. Continuous and discrete manipulations are integrated seamlessly. The usefulness of direct continuous manipulation was expected. We were gratified to find that continuous manipulation, combined with a variety of continuous constraints, yielded a powerful and simple style of manipulation. In particular, the complexity of interrelated constraints generated continuous movements of the layout that were far too complicated for the user to have formulated on their own.

The feeling when discrete changes are made is much the same: the user is freed from the burden of remembering and maintaining a large and complicated set of constraints. The work so far definitely encourages us to try more changes in the system. The conditions which activate and set the direction of discrete search work well. The set of transformations we implemented seemed trivial at first, but we found that they were powerful enough to generate many alternate solutions. Although the system makes structural changes relatively quickly, the evaluation of each possible alternative slows down as we work with more complex objective functions. The visualization of discrete changes using an interpolating animation is very effective in helping the user to understand what discrete changes have occurred. Without this visualization, users hardly recognize when and where changes have occurred.

6 Conclusion

In this paper, we have introduced a new technique for interaction with discrete/continuous geometric models, allowing users to explore problem spaces having both continuous and discrete parameters. The user can continuously manipulate an object as long as the given constraints are satisfied. When a point is reached at which no further continuous movement in the desired direction is possible, a slightly stronger pull on the mouse triggers a discrete change. This change is based on a rapid, behind-the-scenes local search, constrained by the user's pulling action. A small number of transformation rules are defined to perform actual changes. Alternatives are compared in terms of goodness of the overall design and the magnitude of the change from the previous state, subject to continuous and discrete constraints. The best among the alternatives becomes the new state.

Our approach is most useful for discrete/continuous exploration problems which are not governed by a cut-and-dried objective function, but involve aesthetic or other subjective judgements as well, and that therefore cannot be solved by conventional combinatorial optimization methods.

We have implemented a system that demonstrates seamlessly integrated continuous and discrete manipulation. We have applied the technique to planar layout problems in architecture, PC board layout, page layout, and analysis of art.

Our plans for additional work focus on ways to improve performance, and on applications to a broader class of models and problem domains. From a performance standpoint, the discrete evaluation phase is the largest bottleneck, even though the discrete search is local and limited. We currently call an external nonlinear constrained optimization package at each discrete evaluation; it may be that we can enhance performance by writing custom numerics code, or by using heuristics to further prune the search. Our current system is limited to axis-aligned rectangles; we have been able to handle somewhat more general shapes, such as L-shapes, as constrained sets of rectangles. We intend to move to much more general shapes and shape grammars.

We are currently investigating scheduling problems as a an additional application area. For example, in a resource allocation problem, resources are usually limited in quantity, and can be discrete, such as humans and machines. The activities in a project have constraints on sequential order (discrete) and completion time (continuous). We believe that our methods will carry over directly to scheduling projects such as those that arise in construction project management.

Another direction for future work is the extension of our system to 3D models. A first step is to handle floor plans for multi-story houses, which can be treated as a set of 2-D plans which are linked by constraints. For instance, locations of stairways and structural walls must be consistent.

Acknowledgements

This research was supported in part by a Science and Technology Center Grant (#BIR-8920118) and a Research Initiation Award (#CCR-9308353) from the National Science Foundation, by the Engineering Design Research Center, an NSF Engineering Research Center at Carnegie Mellon University, by the Phillips Laboratory, Air Force Material Command, USAF, under cooperative agreement number F29601-93-2-0001, by Apple Computer, Inc, and by an equipment grant from Silicon Graphics, Inc.

References

[1] David Baraff. Analytical methods for dynamic simulation of non-penetrating rigid bodies. *Computer Graphics (Proc. SIGGRAPH)*, 23:223–232, 1989.

[2] David Baraff. Fast contact force computation for nonpenetrating rigid bodies. *Computer Graphics (Proc. SIGGRAPH)*, 28:23–34, 1994.

[3] David Baraff. Interactive simulation of solid rigid bodies. *IEEE Computer Graphics and Applications*, 15:63–75, 1995.

[4] Christopher Carlson. Structure grammars and their application to design. Technical Report EDRC–01–09–89, Engineering Design Research Center, Carnegie Mellon University, Pittsburgh, PA, 1989.

[5] George Celniker and Dave Gossard. Deformable curve and surface finite-elements for free-form shape design. *Computer Graphics*, 25(4), July 1991. Proceedings SIGGRAPH '91.

[6] Ulrich Flemming. Wall representations of rectangular dissections and their use in automated space allocation. *Environment and Planning B: Planning and Design*, 5:215–232, 1978.

[7] Ulrich Flemming. More than the sum of parts: the grammar of Queen Anne houses. *Environment and Planning B: Planning and Design*, 14:323–350, 1987.

[8] Ulrich Flemming and Robert F. Coyne. A design system with multiple abstraction capabilities. In *Avignon '90: Tools, Techniques & Applications*, volume 1, pages 107–122. EC2, 1990.

[9] Philip E. Gill, Walter Murray, Michael A. Saunders, and Margaret H. Wright. User's guide for NPSOL (version 4.0): A fortran package for nonlinear programming. Technical Report SOL 86-2, Stanford University, Stanford, California, 1986.

[10] Michael Gleicher and Andrew Witkin. Through-the-lens camera control. *Computer Graphics*, 26, 1992. Proc. Siggraph '92.

[11] Michael Gleicher and Andrew Witkin. Drawing with constraints. *The Visual Computer*, 1994.

[12] John Grason. *Methods for the computer-implemented solution of a class of "floor plan"*. PhD thesis, Department of Electrical Engineering, Carnegie Mellon University, 1970.

[13] Jeff Heisserman. *Generative geometric design and boundary solid grammars*. PhD thesis, Department of Architecture, Carnegie Mellon University, 1991.

[14] Michael Kass, Andrew Witkin, and Demetri Terzopoulos. Snakes: Active contour models. *Int. J. of Computer Vision*, 1(4), 1987.

[15] Terry W. Knight. Designing with grammars. In Gerhard N. Schmitt, editor, *CAAD Futures '91 Proceedings*, pages 19–34, 1991.

[16] T.W. Knight. Transformations of De Stijl art: the paintings of Georges Vantongerloo and Fritz Glarner. *Environment and Planning B: Planning and Design*, 16:51–98, 1989.

[17] H. Koning and J. Eizenberg. The language of the prairie: Frank Lloyd Wright's prairie houses. *Environment and Planning B: Planning and Design*, 8:295–323, 1981.

[18] Sukhamay Kundu. The equivalence of the subregion representation and the wall representation for a certain class of rectangular dissections. *Communications of the ACM*, 31(6):752–763, 1988.

[19] Cornelius Lanczos. *The Variational Principles of Mechanics*. Dover Publications, Inc., 1970.

[20] David P. LaPotin. Mason: A global floor-planning approach for VLSI design. Technical Report IBMC–11657, IBM T.J. Watson Research Center, Yorktown Heights, NY 10598, January 1986.

[21] William J. Mitchell, Robin S. Ligget, Spiro N. Pollalis, and Milton Tan. Integrating shape grammars and design analysis. In *CAAD futures '91 proceedings*, pages 1–18, 1991.

[22] W.J. Mitchell, J.P. Steadman, and Robin S. Ligget. Synthesis and optimization of small rectangular floor plans. *Environment and Planning B: Planning and Design*, 3(1):37–70, 1976.

[23] Herbert A. Simon. Style in design. In Charles M. Eastman, editor, *Spatial Synthesis in Computer-Aided Building Design*, chapter 9, pages 287–309. Applied Science Publishers LTD, Ripple Road, Barking, Essex, England, 1975.

[24] G. Stiny. Introduction to shape and shape grammars. *Environment and Planning B: Planning and Design*, 7(3):343–351, 1980.

[25] G. Stiny and J. Gips. Shape grammars and the generative specification of painting and sculpture. *Information Processing*, pages 1460–1465, 1972.

[26] G. Stiny and W.J. Mitchell. The Palladian grammar. *Environment and Planning B: Planning and Design*, 5(1):5–18, 1978.

[27] Mark C. Surles. An algorithm with linear complexity for interactive, physically-based modeling of large proteins. In Edwin E. Catmull, editor, *Computer Graphics (SIGGRAPH '92 Proceedings)*, volume 26, pages 221–230, July 1992.

[28] Demetri Terzopoulos, Andrew Witkin, and Michael Kass. Energy constraints on deformable models: recovering shape and non-rigid motion. In *Proc. AAAI-87*, Seattle, 1987.

[29] Demetri Terzopoulos, Andrew Witkin, and Michael Kass. Symmetry-seeking models for 3D object reconstruction. *International Journal of Computer Vision*, 3(1), 1987.

[30] Jeffrey A. Thingvold and Elaine Cohen. Physical modeling with B-spline surfaces for interactive design and animation. *Computer Graphics*, 24(2):129–138, March 1990.

[31] William Welch and Andrew Witkin. Variational surface modeling. *Computer Graphics*, 26, 1992. Proc. Siggraph '92.

[32] Andrew Witkin, Michael Gleicher, and William Welch. Interactive dynamics. *Computer Graphics*, 24(2):11–21, March 1990. Proc. 1990 Symposium on 3-D Interactive Graphics.

[33] Andrew Witkin and William Welch. Fast animation and control of non-rigid structures. *Computer Graphics*, 24(4):243–252, July 1990. Proc. Siggraph '90.

[34] D.F. Wong, H.W. Leong, and C.L. Liu. *Simulated Annealing for VLSI Design*. Kluwer Academic Publishers, 101 Philip Drive, Assinippi Park, Norwell, Massachusetts 02061, 1988.

[35] Lin S. Woo, C.K. Wong, and D.T. Tang. Pioneer: a macro-based floor-planning design system. *VLSI System Design*, pages 32–43, August 1986.

An Interactive Tool for Placing Curved Surfaces without Interpenetration

John M. Snyder[†]
Microsoft Corporation

Abstract

We present a surface representation and a set of algorithms that allow interactive placement of curved parametric objects without interpenetration. Using these algorithms, a modeler can place an object within or on top of other objects, find a stable placement for it, and slide it into new stable placements. Novel algorithms are presented to track points of contact between bodies, detect new points of contact, and delete vanishing contacts. Interactive speeds are maintained even when the moving body touches several bodies at many contact points.

We describe a new algorithm that quickly brings a body into a stable configuration with respect to a set of external forces, subject to the constraint that it not penetrate a set of fixed bodies. This algorithm is made possible by sacrificing the requirement that a body behave physically over time. Intuitive control is still achieved by making incremental, "pseudo-physical" changes to the body's placement, while enforcing the non-interpenetration constraint after each change.

CR Categories and Subject Descriptors: I.3.5 [Computer Graphics]: Computational Geometry and Object Modeling.

Key Words: object placement/assembly, collision detection, contact point.

1 Introduction

Geometric modeling can be dissected into two tasks: creating models for a set of "parts" or basic objects, and then assembling these parts into virtual combinations. For example, to model an automobile engine, one can first create a set of parts including the engine block, pistons, nuts, and bolts, and then assemble these into an engine. While the vast majority of work in geometric modeling has focused on the part-creation task, part-assembly is nonetheless an important and difficult problem. Parts can often be modeled independently, perhaps by different people; assembling them means having to deal explicitly with relationships between all the parts together, such as the constraint that no solid object penetrate another. Increasingly in research systems, a part is modeled not as a static geometric object, but as a high-level parameterized model such as an elastic sheet with given initial geometry and material properties [WITK87,META92]. This increases the complexity of the part-assembly task, which must compute model parameters from spatial relationships between the various parts (for example, the shape of the tablecloth after it is dropped on the table).

This paper focuses on a subset of the part-assembly problem: interactive placement of rigid, solid, curved objects into physically plausible configurations (Figure 1). Parts in this context are rigid bodies parameterized by a rigid motion in 3D (i.e., a rotation and translation). The goal is to arrive at a statically balanced configuration of solids near a user-specified initial configuration. Examples include placing a spoon in a cereal bowl or filling it with cereal, placing a phone receiver on its hook, putting ice cubes in a

[†] 1 Microsoft Way, Redmond WA 98052.
johnsny@microsoft.com

Permission to make digital/hard copy of part or all of this work for personal or classroom use is granted without fee provided that copies are not made or distributed for profit or commercial advantage, the copyright notice, the title of the publication and its date appear, and notice is given that copying is by permission of ACM, Inc. To copy otherwise, to republish, to post on servers, or to redistribute to lists, requires prior specific permission and/or a fee.

 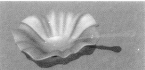

Figure 1: The Placement Problem – The algorithms described here allow, for example, repositioning of a bowl and spoon in an arbitrary configuration (left) to produce a configuration with the spoon resting stably in the bowl and the bowl resting stably on the floor (right). Points of contact computed by the algorithm are shown in yellow; the spoon is rendered transparently to make these visible.

glass, modeling a pile of fruit, and fitting oddly shaped objects into a rigid box. Many applications exist for a tool that performs such interactive placement: modeling of static virtual environments, interactive fitting/packing of 3D shapes, games (e.g. virtual 3D puzzles), and keyframe animation for physically plausible but still controllable motions.

Even this restricted problem is difficult without special tools. Traditionally, an object is placed by directly tying a graphics input device such as a mouse, trackball, or set of dials to its orientation and translation parameters. Users verify by eye that objects do not interpenetrate and are physically balanced. Because curved objects resting on each other can have many points of contact, modeling a configuration like the one in Figure 1 can take many minutes of tedious interaction: one portion of the spoon is satisfactorily placed only after some other part begins interpenetrating or pulls away. Traditional methods also provide no help in reaching a stable configuration.

To assist the user in the placement task, one option is to take advantage of the substantial work done in computer animation to make objects move physically. These techniques can be used for the placement problem by simulating through time until stability is achieved; that is, the objects stop moving. Unfortunately, none of these techniques is suitable for interactive placement of curved, non-convex, parametric shapes; the kind of shapes that many commercial modelers can produce. Most approaches restrict the kinds of shapes that can be simulated [MOOR88,BARA90,SCLA91, see SNYD93 for a survey of these restrictions]; another approach that handles general parametric surfaces is too slow for interactive applications [SNYD93]. An additional disadvantage is that physical behavior over time can actually hinder the placement problem. A physical card house can fall flat when we place the next card; a spoon dropped into a bowl accelerates, bounces, and can end up far from where we wanted it.

However, the placement problem is concerned with quick production of a desired configuration of objects, not with how they arrived there. We seek an approach that arrives at a stable state from some arbitrary state, making changes that are intuitive and controllable, but not necessarily physically accurate. To make the approach fast, we deviate from accurate physical simulation in several ways:

1. Bodies have no velocity. In fact there is no explicit notion of time in the system at all. Instead, a body is moved through a series of discrete states, each of which obeys the non-interpenetration constraint.

2. While forces and torques are solved for at each state, they aren't the real forces that a dynamic body would experience instantaneously. They are chosen to speed convergence of the body to a "nearby" stable placement, and are called *pseudo-forces* and *pseudo-torques*.

3. The exact time when contact point transitions occur (e.g., vanishing contacts) is not calculated. Instead, transitions are made after each discrete step.

4. Small, non-physical adjustments are made to an active body's position and orientation in order to preserve the non-interpenetration constraint.

5. Only one body at a time, the *active* body, can move. As it moves, it interacts with other bodies which remain fixed and are treated as infinitely massive. The user can change which body is currently active in order to move bodies sequentially into position.

As is implied in some of the above choices, the approach presented here is a limited solution to the general placement problem of rigid bodies – a very difficult problem for curved surfaces. Although the sequence of intermediate states does not correspond to a real motion of the object, the final state does represent a stable configuration according to static force balance laws, assuming immovable non-active bodies. The algorithm thus handles the common case of placing a single object on or within another that is essentially fixed, like a teapot on a table or a spoon in a bowl. Force balance is only maintained for the active body; the force it imparts to the rest of the world is ignored. The algorithm therefore can not automatically produce physically balanced heaps of multiple bodies. However, visually plausible heaps can still be modeled "from the ground up". A sequence of bodies is added to the accumulated heap; after a body reaches a stable state, it remains in that position as additional bodies are added (this technique was used to make Figures 12, 14, 15, and 16). Automatic maintenance of the non-interpenetration constraint and the ability to place the next object stably at least provide useful tools in such a modeling task.

The approach trades off robustness in order to achieve interactivity, as compared to an approach like [SNYD93]. Problems can happen when an object contacts another at a curve or surface, where one object is concave in this contact region (e.g., a torus on a cone).[1] Such configurations can still be produced, but sometimes require user intervention (see Section 6 for further discussion). As in [BARA94], our algorithms make use of heuristics for which a formal justification is lacking, but which seem to work in practice. The main example involves converting collisions on polygonal approximations to collisions on analytic surfaces using numerical iteration. We have not found selection criteria for the approximation that provide a theoretical guarantee for convergence of this iteration. In practice though, heuristic selection of the approximation gives a workable solution.

The placement algorithm described in this paper shares characteristics with optimization methods used previously [WITK87,BARZ88,GLEI92], but specializes these methods to the problem of interactive placement. The main difficulty with direct application of such methods involves handling discontinuities in the energy functional that arise from collisions. This paper explains how to slide downhill efficiently in the presence of collisions without resorting to a full-blown and very slow physical simulation. Essentially, the main contribution of this paper is a description of which physical characteristics to sacrifice in order to get good performance, and which to keep in order to get intuitive control. Several specific elements of the approach are new: we use a new surface representation that employs both polygonal and parametric representations, a new algorithm for fast tracking, creation, and deletion of contact points, and a new method that quickly converges to a stable, non-interpenetrating placement for a single body starting from some arbitrary non-interpenetrating state and subject to a set of external forces.

2   Summary

An object is placed near its desired position such that it does not touch any other objects. This is called a *noninterfering* state. Interactive collision detection, described in Section 3, makes it easy for the user to select a noninterfering initial state. In the simplest mode of interaction, the user lets the body stabilize under the influence of a gravitational pseudo-force. The body is automatically moved through a series of discrete states, each of which obeys the non-interpenetration constraint, until a stable state is reached. An independent pseudo-force calculation is made at each state transition: external pseudo-forces are computed, components balanced by contact pseudo-forces are subtracted away, and the residual is applied to produce an incremental change in the body's position. Contact points are

---

[1] Note that the problem arises only when the object is concave *at the contact region*. Concave objects that contact at isolated points or are concave only away from the region of contact are handled without difficulty.

```
place body in a noninterfering initial state
loop
    check for tracked point transitions
    compute pseudo-forces at each contact point, and on body
    update active body's placement using ε (solution step)
    adjust tracked points for new placement
        if unable, ε ← ε/2 and start loop again (loop failure)
    while new polygonal collision exists and collisions < N_simultaneous
        if unable to convert collision to a contact point then
            ε ← ε/2 and start loop again (loop failure)
        else
            add tracked point
        endif
    endwhile
    if collisions were successfully added, restore old value of ε
    if objective function increases, ε ← ε/2 (loop failure)
    if loop was completed successfully, increase ε by ε ← max(λε, ε_max)
    render current state
    complete user interaction requests: interrupt, undo, direct repositioning,
        force or parameter change, etc.
until stable
```

Figure 2: Automatic Placement Algorithm: This algorithm produces a series of placements of the body that never violate the non-interpenetration condition and converge to a stable state – a state in which contact forces balance user-specified external forces such as gravity.

relocated where the body now touches other bodies; the body's position and orientation may also be slightly adjusted to preserve all contacts. The relevant algorithms are described fully in Sections 4 and 5. The result of the algorithm is the final position of the active body and a list of contact points. The complete algorithm is outlined in Figure 2.

The sequence of state transitions generated by the automatic placement algorithm can be interrupted at any point. The user can "undo" a portion of the sequence and change the forces acting upon the body in order to reach different resting states. In addition to turning gravity on or off, the user can apply external pseudo-forces to nudge the object in any direction or make it attach to specified points on other objects. Alternatively, the body can be manually positioned relative to its current state,[2] and the automatic placement algorithm resumed from the new position. As in the case of selecting an initial state for the body, the user must choose a noninterfering state from which to resume automatic placement.

2.1   Surface Representation

A *body* is a rigidly movable solid object that interacts with other bodies. It is represented as a set of *patches*, each of which is an analytic parametric surface, whose union contains the boundary of the body. Each patch is defined so that its surface normal points toward the exterior of the body.[3]

In choosing a representation for patches, we were faced with the problem that polygonal collision detection is extremely efficient, but can't be used alone to find accurate collisions between smooth surfaces. We therefore use a hybrid representation: a polygonal approximation is used to detect new points of contact that arise between bodies, and a functional description is used to adjust these points so that they lie on the actual curved surface, and to track them as they move.

The polygonal description is a mesh of triangles with (u, v) parametric coordinates per vertex. Each vertex lies on the analytic surface. The location of a collision can then be approximated by finding two intersecting triangles and, for each triangle, barycentrically interpolating the parametric coordinates at each vertex to obtain the (u, v) coordinate at the point of intersection. The two points are used as starting points in an iterative method (multidimensional Newton-Raphson) which produces contact points on the actual surfaces. The polygonal approximation is also used during manual positioning to determine whether a body is in a noninterfering state. When interference is detected, the body is made transparent and a small dot displayed at a point of intersection. The calculations take place at interactive

---

[2] In the prototype system, the active body is moved by turning a series of 6 dials which represent translation and rotation around the coordinate axes.

[3] Although the system does not currently support open bodies, the changes required are straightforward. Contact points must record whether they are on surfaces, edges, or vertices. The systems of equations used in tracking must then make use of this information. Alternatively, surface boundaries can be handled by placing thin tubes around edges and spheres around vertices.

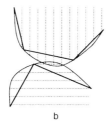

a   b

Figure 3: Collision Inconsistencies for Analytic Surfaces vs. Polygonal Approximations: (a) shows a collision between polygons but not surfaces, (b) shows a collision between surfaces but not polygons.

rates as the user moves the body. Finally, the polygonal approximation is used to select a body or a point on a body, using a ray casting algorithm as in [KAY86].

Functional descriptions for parametric surfaces are created with a symbolic language, as described in [SNYD92]. It is also possible to develop special purpose code for classes of parametric surfaces such as bicubic patches. Evaluation of surface points and derivatives up to second order is required.

Handling Inconsistencies

Since analytic surfaces are approximated by triangles for collision detection, two sorts of errors can occur as shown in Figure 3. When one of the objects is concave, a collision can happen between polygonal approximations but not the analytic surfaces (Figure 3a). This is detected by a failure in the numerical iteration to move the contact point onto the analytic surfaces (see Section 4.3) and ignored.[4] A collision between analytic surfaces can also be missed with the polygonal approximations (Figure 3b). There are three cases for what then happens: the surfaces can continue to interpenetrate until the polygonal approximations eventually collide, they can "tunnel" through each other, or they can reach a stable state in this situation. The first case is the typical one and causes no problem since the collision is eventually found. Users can ignore tunneling since the objects no longer violate the non-interpenetration condition, or undo tunneled placement states and restart the algorithm with a smaller ϵ (solution step) parameter, making it more likely a polygonal collision will be detected. The third case reduces the accuracy of the final placement: the objects violate the non-interpenetration condition by a distance bounded by the approximation errors of the two meshes. A conservative test for noninterpenetration can be developed using polygonal approximations for offset surfaces where the mesh is known to enclose the analytic surface.

Why not just use polygons?

There are three advantages of employing an analytic description of curved surfaces. First, much better accuracy can be achieved. The location of a surface is computed where it rests on points mathematically on the surface rather than on faces or edges of a faceted approximation. This can be important for CAD applications, or cases in which the camera is close to the resulting model. More accuracy is also achieved in reaching a stable state; meta-stable configurations that rest on facets are avoided.

Second, using the smooth surface makes it easier to incrementally change a body's state while enforcing the non-interpenetration condition. When one curved body can continuously slide over the surface of another, many states are unreachable when a polygonal approximation is used. Consider a cylinder approximated as an extruded regular polygon of n sides resting lengthwise on a flat plane. Only n discrete rotations of this cylinder around its axis are stable (where it rests on one of the extruded edges of the regular polygon); the real cylinder is stable for any such rotation.

Third, faster convergence to stability can be achieved. The analytic surfaces provide the exact normal vector at points of contact unavailable with a polygonal approximation. Using these normals in a force balance computation, we can move the surface a significant amount between steps. The size of the step used with a purely polygonal approximation would necessarily be tied to the size of polygonal facets in the neighborhood of

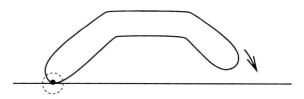

Figure 4: Spheres of neglect: A sphere is placed around current contact points within which collisions are disregarded, so that only new contact points are found.

the contact: an accurate approximation with many polygons would require a large number of steps.

3 Detecting Collisions Quickly

Our method for detecting collisions between triangulated bodies is similar to that presented in [GARC94], with several differences that tailor the algorithm to the interactive placement problem. See that reference for a detailed description of the collision detection problem.

We approximate each body with a set of triangles organized in an object-partitioning bounding box hierarchy as in [KAY86]. At the terminal nodes of the hierarchy are the triangles, each of which is marked with a (body,patch) identifier. Each node of the tree contains a bounding box in the form $(x_{min}, x_{max}, y_{min}, y_{max}, z_{min}, z_{max})$, and a list of child nodes, or information for a triangle in the case of a terminal node. Nodes can also contain information specifying a rigid motion for the subtree. In this case, the node's bounding box is in the post-transformed space; each of its child nodes store bounding boxes in local (pre-transformed) space. Bounding boxes are dynamically transformed during traversal of the hierarchy (see Section 3.2).

A similar hierarchy is then constructed for the set of bodies in the system (the *world*). The world is maintained by incrementally adjusting the active body's position in it; this is easier in an object partitioning hierarchy than in a spatial hierarchy. When a body moves, a transformation at a single node must be changed and bounding box changes propagated up the tree; the object's hierarchy remains unchanged.[5] Because a body's hierarchy is constructed just once, we can afford to use substantial computation organizing its triangles in a hierarchy that is efficient for collision detection. This processing is done before interaction begins (see Section 3.1).

Two forms of collision detection are required for interactive placement. Simple collision detection computes whether an object interferes with any other objects, and is used in choosing a noninterfering state from which to begin or resume convergence to stability. A second form of collision detection is used to compute whether a body already in contact with other bodies intersects at any additional points. To do this, we define *spheres of neglect* around the current contact points, as in [SNYD93]. During traversal, potential collisions within the spheres of neglect are discarded; the algorithm thus locates new collision points (Figure 4). The radius for each sphere is a small value determined by the distance the contact point moves from polygonal approximation to analytic surface during the contact creation process (Section 4.3). This is done because contact points are tracked on analytic surfaces but are used to discard polygonal collisions. Note that spheres of neglect are used only to ignore polygonal collisions; they do not effect contact point tracking or force calculations.

3.1 Constructing the Bounding Box Hierarchy

To construct a bounding box hierarchy for a body, we apply the recursive algorithm maketree to the flat list of triangles comprising it:

```
maketree(L)

    partition L into set of n lists L_i
    create root node R
    for each i, insert maketree(L_i) as child of R
    return R
```

---

[4] As will be discussed further in Section 4.3, such a collision is not really ignored, but is initialized as an extremal point: a point where surfaces are close but not in contact. Extremal points are tracked along with contact points. An extremal point is deleted if the separation distance increases, or is converted to a contact point if the distance becomes ≤ 0.

[5] We note that lazy evaluation of bounding box changes improves efficiency in the general case. When a transformation changes, the appropriate node's dirty flag is set and propagated up the tree until the root or a node previously marked dirty is reached. At collision time, a dirty node's transformation is updated using a callback function, and its bounding box updated as the union of its children (which must be recursively updated if marked dirty). This sort of lazy evaluation avoids needless union-of-bounding-box computations as child nodes are sequentially marked dirty. A node's bounding box and transformation is updated exactly once, no matter how many of its children have changed. Of course, these subtleties are unimportant when only a single body is moved.

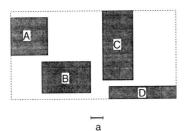

a

Figure 5: Object partitioning by gap finding: The bounding boxes around four objects (A, B, C, D) have a gap, a, when projected onto the horizontal axis. Partitioning around this gap yields the two lists (A, B) and (C, D). Note that the objects have no gap when projected onto the vertical axis.

At each invocation of maketree, the bounding box for the result node R is taken as the union of the bounding boxes of its child nodes.

The heart of the construction process is the partitioning of a list of nodes L into sublists L_i. Grouping nodes that are close together greatly improves culling during collision detection. We have used the following heuristic: the bounding boxes of each list element are projected into each of the three coordinate axes to form three lists of intervals. These lists are sorted in increasing order of interval lower bound, and then are searched for gaps (see Figure 5). We partition the list into two by using the coordinate axis that generates the gap of greatest width. All elements whose projected interval is less than the gap center are placed in one list, the rest in the other. If no gaps exist, which happens fairly frequently, we partition around the center of the containing interval. The projection axis is chosen as the coordinate axis for which the standard deviation of interval centers is greatest. This kind of partitioning gives us a branching ratio $n = 2$ in the resulting hierarchy; other branching ratios are possible by partitioning along multiple axes. We have not tried other branching ratios.

3.2 Traversing the Bounding Box Hierarchy

Collision detection is computed by traversing the bounding box hierarchy of a pair of nodes to be collided, N_A and N_B. In our system, the active body is collided against the world, although the algorithm described here can compute collisions between any two collections of bodies or within a single collection.

Pairs of nodes from the two hierarchies are examined in depth-first order according to the following basic algorithm:

```
traversetrees(N_A, N_B)
    initialize stack of active pairs with (N_A, N_B)
    while stack is nonempty
        pop off next pair (A, B)
        loop through child nodes of A and B: (A_i, B_j)
            if (A_i, B_j) collide
                if both are triangles, record collision
                else push pair onto active list
```

Associated with each pair of nodes on the active stack is a transformation which transforms the second element of the pair into the coordinate system of the first. This transformation is updated whenever child nodes are inserted that contain transformations. Relatively few of these nodes are encountered during traversal since bodies typically contain hundreds or thousands of triangles, all of which are moved by changing one node's transformation.

Three types of collision computations occur: bounding box vs. bounding box, bounding box vs. triangle, and triangle vs. triangle. If both nodes are nonterminal, a bounding box vs. bounding box collision is done by transforming the bounding box of the second object to the coordinate system of the first, and testing whether the two bounds overlap. If only one is nonterminal, a bounding box/triangle collision test is done, again in the coordinate system of the first object. Otherwise, a test for the intersection of two triangles is done. When two triangles collide, the location of the collision and pointers to the two triangles are recorded.[6]

Several changes to the basic algorithm are needed. The first is to cull nodes based on a list of spheres of neglect. To do this, we test the intersection of the bounding boxes of A and B to see whether it is entirely inside some sphere

---

[6]The algorithm currently records an arbitrary point of intersection between the two triangles.

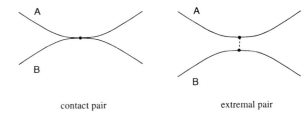

contact pair   extremal pair

Figure 6: Types of interface points: Two non-interpenetrating bodies in close proximity, A and B, can have two types of interface points. On the left, the bodies are in tangent contact at a contact pair. On the right, the bodies are slightly apart; the pair of points at minimal distance is the extremal pair.

of neglect. If so, we discard the pair. We also discard a collision between triangles if it lies within any sphere of neglect. The second change improves performance: when one node's bounding box is small with respect to the other, we do not subdivide it into its children, but compare it unsubdivided with the children of the bigger node. In our experiments, this sped up the algorithm up by factors of 2-10, the larger number attained when a very small object is collided against a much larger one.

4 Computing Points of Contact

As in [SNYD93], places where bodies interact are handled using a finite set of points even when the region of contact forms a curve or surface. In [SNYD93], points were uniformly distributed over the contact region; the approach here creates only enough points to prevent interpenetration and reach a stable state. These points are called *interface points* and consist of a pair of points on two bodies. Interface points are tracked (incrementally updated) as the body moves from state to state using numerical iteration. During collision detection, a sphere of neglect is placed around each interface point to avoid detecting collisions already being handled. We therefore store, for each interface point, a (u, v) parametric coordinate pair, a pair of (body,patch) identifiers for the surfaces in contact, and a radius for the sphere of neglect.

Two types of interface points are used: *contact pairs* and *extremal pairs*, shown in Figure 6. Bodies actually touch at contact pairs. Forces that balance external forces such as gravity are applied at the contact pairs. These forces are only applied to push objects away from interpenetrating, not to "glue" objects together. When such a gluing force is obtained, it is not applied but instead causes the contact pair to transition to an extremal pair.

Extremal pairs are points on a pair of bodies at minimal distance. The bodies do not contact in a neighborhood around the extremal pair. Forces are not applied at extremal pairs. Extremal pairs allow interface points to vanish gradually. When a gluing contact force is detected, the contact pair is converted to an extremal pair, allowing the two bodies to separate. Contact can quickly be resumed if the separation distance becomes negative. Extremal pairs are deleted when the separation distance becomes large enough.

4.1 Tracking Contacts

After the active body is moved, the automatic placement algorithm must track the interface points from their previous positions. The following two-phase tracking algorithm yields excellent numerical stability. The first phase, called the *conditioning phase*, is not necessary from a theoretical perspective, but makes the resulting system easier to solve in the next phase.[7] In this phase, each interface point, represented as a pair of (u, v) parametric locations, is independently adjusted to satisfy the extremal point conditions using numerical iteration (the equations are described in Section 4.4). The initial condition for this iteration is the parametric location of the interface point before the body was moved.

In the second phase, called the *contact adjustment phase*, we adjust both the body's rigid motion parameters and the locations of all the interface pairs to preserve the contact or extremal conditions. Numerical iteration takes place to simultaneously satisfy the extremal or contact conditions for all interface points. Initial conditions for this iteration are the body's current placement, and the parametric locations of the interface points after the conditioning phase. Note that the second phase may slightly alter the body's placement in order to satisfy the contact point conditions.

---

[7]We are able to move bodies much more between states and still maintain the contact conditions with the use of the conditioning phase.

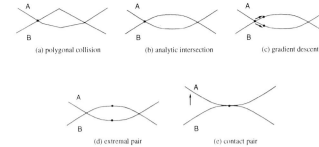

Figure 7: Steps in converting a polyhedral collision into a contact point.

When the numerical iteration in either tracking phase fails, the placement algorithm tries a smaller move of the active body from its last correct state (Figure 2).

4.2 Detecting Contact Transitions

Before a body is moved, the placement algorithm checks for transitions of contact points. When a transition is detected, the interface point is either deleted in the case of a vanishing transition, or switched between contact and extremal. The following transitions (with their conditions for occurrence) are detected:

1. *extremal-to-contact* – separation distance between bodies becomes negative

2. *contact-to-extremal* – contact force attracts rather than repels the bodies

3. *extremal vanishes* –

   - separation distance exceeds threshold
   - conditioning phase iteration fails
   - point becomes too close to another interface point
   - point falls off parametric domain of its patch

4. *contact vanishes* –

   - point becomes too close to another interface point
   - point falls off parametric domain of its patch

The user can optionally disable contact-to-extremal transitions to assure that the active body will stay in contact as it's moved. This effectively makes the selected contacts "sticky".

4.3 Creating Contacts

The automatic placement algorithm converts collision points on polygonal bodies to contact points on analytic parametric surfaces. A series of steps, illustrated in Figure 7, is performed, each of which uses the results of the previous step as the initial condition in a numerical iteration:

1. Interpolate the polygonal collision point to yield a pair of parametric points (u_1, v_1, u_2, v_2). The (body,patch) identifier for each of the intersecting triangles allows retrieval of the appropriate surface functions used in the following steps (Figure 7a).

2. Iterate onto the analytic intersection (Figure 7b).

3. Do a few steps of gradient descent to nudge the pair toward the points of maximal penetration (Figure 7c). This is necessary so that the next step iterates in the right direction (i.e., toward maximal penetration rather than maximal separation). The objective function is defined in Section 4.4, Equation 2.

4. Iterate onto the extremal pair (Figure 7d). This is a conditioning step exactly like the conditioning phase of tracking.

5. Iterate onto a contact pair (Figure 7e). In this step, the active body's position parameters and the locations of all interface points are adjusted. Equations for all interface points must be satisfied simultaneously, since the active body's placement affects the contact conditions of the previous interface points.

Steps 2, 4, and 5 involve numerical iteration which can fail. A failure in Step 2 may occur because the polygonal approximations intersect but the analytic surfaces do not (refer to Figure 3a). If failure occurs, we try iterating onto an extremal pair. If this succeeds, and the resulting separation distance (defined in Section 4.4) is positive, the interface point is added as an extremal pair rather than a contact pair. This allows the polygonal collision to be ignored during the next collision detection query. If a failure in Step 4 occurs, we disregard what amounts to a conditioning step, and go on to step 5. A failure elsewhere, or after taking the above measures, results in a collision failure and causes the placement algorithm to try a smaller solution step in its next iteration. After a successful contact point creation, the sphere of neglect radius is determined by the distance the point moved from Step 1 to Step 5. A collision failure is returned if this distance exceeds a user-settable threshold.

4.4 Contact Point Iteration

Interface point tracking and contact point creation both use multidimensional Newton iteration on a system of equations (see [PRES86] for a complete description).[8] Given a system of nonlinear equations $F(x) = 0$ and a point near the solution, x_0, a successive approximation to the true solution is achieved by solving the linear system of equations

$$0 = F(x_0) + \frac{\partial F}{\partial x}(x_0)(x_1 - x_0) \qquad (1)$$

where $\partial F / \partial x$ is the Jacobian of F. We solve the above linear system using the singular value decomposition (or SVD, see [PRES86]), which allows non-square systems to be solved and is numerically robust.[9] The process is then repeated to improve the approximation, yielding a sequence of iterates x_i. The iteration fails if $F(x_i)$ does not get closer to 0 or a maximum number of iterations is exceeded without yielding a point sufficiently close (in the residual sense) to a solution.

It only remains to describe the relevant systems of equations (F from Equation 1), and their parameters, x, for each iterative procedure. In the following, we have two points each on a rigidly movable surface $S_i(Q_i, X_i, u_i, v_i)$, $i = 1, 2$, where Q_i is a rotation in 3D[10] and X_i is a translation in 3D:

$$S_i(Q_i, X_i, u_i, v_i) \equiv Q_i \, s_i(u_i, v_i) + X_i$$

$s_i(u_i, v_i)$ represents the surface in its local coordinate system. There are three systems of equations used in the above Newton iteration:

1. intersection [iteration over (u_1, v_1, u_2, v_2)]:

$$S_1 - S_2 = 0$$

The pair of parametric points is moved to become a true intersection of the bodies, used in Step 2 of the contact point creation sequence. Note that this is a non-square system of equations: 3 equations in 4 variables, which is handled using SVD-augmented Newton iteration.

2. extremal [iteration over (u_1, v_1, u_2, v_2)]:

$$\begin{aligned} (S_1 - S_2) \times N_1 &= 0 \\ N_1 + N_2 &= 0 \end{aligned}$$

where N_1 and N_2 are the outward-pointing unit normals of the two surfaces. These conditions imply that the distance between the point pair is a local extremum (the vector between the points is in the direction of one surface's normal, and the two normals are anti-parallel). If the bodies are separated by a small distance, the iteration will cause the two points to become the points of minimum distance between the two surfaces. If the bodies interpenetrate, the iteration will cause the two to become the points of furthest penetration. This iteration is used in tracking and in Step 4 of the contact point creation sequence.

---

[8] We use the numerical package LAPACK to compute the SVD.

[9] To solve the linear system $Ax = b$, the SVD of matrix A is first computed. This yields three matrices whose product is A, $A = UDV^T$, where U and V are orthonormal, and D is a diagonal matrix. An ill-conditioned system is adjusted by setting to 0 those elements for which $D_i / D_{max} < \delta$, where D_{max} is the largest diagonal element. We then compute $x = VD^{-1}U^T$ taking into account the rank of D, since some elements have been set to 0. The result is a numerically robust solution that minimizes the solution, $||x||$, if solutions exist, and minimizes the residual, $||Mx - b||$, if not.

[10] We use a unit quaternion, $Q = (q_1, q_2, q_3, q_4)$, to represent this rotation. The coordinate system origin is at the center of mass of the body.

3. contact [iteration over $(Q_1, X_1, u_1, v_1, u_2, v_2)$]

$$S_1 - S_2 = 0$$
$$N_1 + N_2 = 0$$

We change the position and orientation of the first body as well as the parametric location of the point of contact in order to achieve a true contact point where the surfaces touch and are tangent. This iteration is used in tracking and in Step 5 of the contact point creation sequence.

Note that the position and orientation of the second body (Q_2, X_2) is held constant for all systems of equations.

Contact point creation also involves gradient descent iteration in Step 3. The objective function whose gradient is descended, the *signed separation distance function* G, is given by

$$G \equiv (S_2 - S_1) \cdot N_1 \tag{2}$$

If the bodies don't touch, this function is positive within a neighborhood of the points of maximal separation. If the bodies interpenetrate, the function is negative inside the region of interpenetration.

5 Converging to a Stable Configuration

Convergence to a stable state is achieved by the application of pseudo-forces that cause an incremental change in the position of the active body. Using force-like quantities accomplishes two things: it leads to changes in object placement that the user can predict, and it provides much faster convergence to stable placement than other update rules.[11] Pseudo-forces differ from physical forces because they are solved for statically and do not accelerate the object but are applied directly to update the object's position (see Section 5.3).

Three kinds of pseudo-forces are used: *external*, which represent gravity and user-specified "nudges", *contact*, which are applied at contact pairs to balance the external forces as much as possible, and *residual*, which represent the resulting force (external - contact) applied to adjust the body's position. The body is considered to be at rest and automatic placement halted when the residual force is sufficiently small.

It sometimes happens that exact force balance can not be achieved.[12] We therefore use a second criterion to determine stability: the *psuedo potential energy objective*. The placement algorithm tries to minimize the energy objective: a state that increases the objective is rejected. When gravity is the sole external force, the energy objective is simply the height of the center of mass of the active body. The placement algorithm thus drops the object as far as possible. When the change in energy objective is sufficiently small, the automatic placement algorithm is terminated.[13] Other forces have different objectives, discussed in Section 5.1. The total energy objective is the sum of the energy objectives for all external psuedo-forces.

5.1 Computing External Pseudo-Forces

The user can apply combinations of three types of external pseudo-forces to the active body: *gravity*, *local*, and *connection* forces (Figure 8). Pseudo-forces from these three categories can be added or deleted at any time during automatic placement to position the active body. For each external pseudo-force, the algorithm computes three quantities: a force (F) and torque (T) on the body, and an objective term (E). These are summed to produce the total force, torque, and objective.

In the following, the current location of the active body is represented by the rotation/translation pair (Q, X), as in Section 4.4. Force parameters in capital letters are in world coordinates; noncapitalized parameters are in body coordinates. External pseudo-forces always have unit length; the amount

  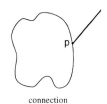

gravity   local   connection

Figure 8: Types of external pseudo-forces.

of movement is determined by the solution step (ϵ from Figure 2). Lengt measurements are scaled relative to the radius of the smallest enclosin sphere around the active object, R.

A gravity pseudo-force is applied at the body's center of mass in a give direction D (e.g., $D = (0, 0, -1)$). It thus produces no torque, and tends t translate the body along the D direction. The force, torque, and objectiv terms for this pseudo-force are given by:

$$F_{\text{gravity}} \equiv D$$
$$T_{\text{gravity}} \equiv 0$$
$$E_{\text{gravity}} \equiv -(D \cdot X)/R$$

A local pseudo-force is applied at a given point on the active body, p, i some direction d in its local coordinate system. It allows the user to pus and pull on the body. The force, torque, and objective terms are:

$$F_{\text{local}} \equiv Qd$$
$$T_{\text{local}} \equiv (Qp)/R \times F_{\text{local}}$$
$$E_{\text{local}} \equiv 0$$

To specify a local pseudo-force, the user picks a point p on the active bod and specifies a "push" or "pull" force. A push force assigns to d the negativ of the unit normal vector at p; a pull force assigns it the unnegated norma vector. The user can also directly control the direction with a 3D widget. Note that the objective term for a local pseudo-force is 0. In fact, the use typically turns off objective function processing when using local pseudo-forces, so that objects can be moved freely against gravity or other external forces without causing a loop failure when the objective function increases (refer to Figure 2).[14]

A connection pseudo-force is applied at a local point on the body, p in order to connect that point to a given point in world space P. The force, torque, and objective terms are:

$$F_{\text{connect}} \equiv \frac{P - (Qp + X)}{\|P - (Qp + X)\|}$$
$$T_{\text{connect}} \equiv (Qp)/R \times F_{\text{connect}}$$
$$E_{\text{connect}} \equiv \|P - (Qp + X)\|/R$$

5.2 Solving for Contact and Residual Pseudo-Forces

Let the total external pseudo-force and pseudo-torque on the body be given by F_e and T_e. The contact pseudo-forces are given by n scalars f_i where n represents the number of contact pairs. The direction of these forces is given by N_i where N_i is a unit vector representing the negative of the normal vector on the active body at the point of contact. To find the f_i's, we solve the linear system of force balance equations given by:

$$\sum_{i=1}^{n} f_i N_i = F_e$$

$$\sum_{i=1}^{n} f_i (p_i \times N_i) = T_e$$

where p_i is the vector from the body's center of mass to the contact point. This system has no solution if the the body isn't in a balanced state. We solve using SVD to obtain a solution which minimizes the L^2 norm of the residual.

---

[11] For example, to stabilize an object under the influence of gravity, the first update rule we tried was to translate the body down in z (direct gradient descent). Iteration was then done to satisfy the interface point conditions, which typically moves the body back up in z. In many experiments this algorithm was more than 10 times slower then the one proposed, which balances gravity with an approximation to the contact forces.

[12] For example, consider dropping a torus onto a flat ground plane such that the contact region in the resting state forms a circle. The approach advocated here will create a number of contact points whose configuration depends on the polygonal approximation used for the torus. It can easily happen that two contact points arise that do not form an exact diameter of the circle of contact. Any assignment of contact forces at these points will therefore produce a residual torque (note that the contact forces point up, normal to the plane).

[13] Using the torus/plane example, this termination criterion guarantees that the torus comes to rest in a stable state as soon as more than one contact point is generated. This is because it can no longer move in z; the energy objective remains unchanged, triggering the termination condition.

[14] In a typical placement scenario, the user first lets a body drop under the influence of gravity. When it is stable, objective function processing is turned off and local pseudo-forces are used to slide the contacting body where it's desired. Then local pseudo-forces can be deleted and objective processing re-enabled to reach a truly stable placement.

While the contact forces produced in this way are a coarse approximation, unstable objects still fall over much as they might in the real world.

To solve for the residual pseudo-force and pseudo-torque, F_r and T_r, we subtract the sum of the previously computed contact forces from the external pseudo-forces and pseudo-torques:

$$F_r \equiv F_e - \sum_{i=1}^{n} f_i N_i$$

$$T_r \equiv T_e - \sum_{i=1}^{n} f_i (p_i \times N_i)$$

The termination criterion $\|F_r\| < \delta, \|T_r\| < \delta$ stops the body when it is balanced with respect to purely normal contact forces. Note that this criterion implies the body is *physically* stable, since a static force balance has been achieved.

The user may also want to stop the body when it is stable with respect to frictional forces.[15] To do this, we compute a frictional pseudo-force and pseudo-torque residual, F_f and T_f, by first solving the frictional force balance problem

$$\sum_{i=1}^{n} f_i^U U_i + f_i^V V_i = F_r$$

$$\sum_{i=1}^{n} f_i^U (p_i \times U_i) + f_i^V (p_i \times V_i) = T_r$$

where U_i and V_i are independent tangent vectors at each contact point, and f_i^U and f_i^V are the $2n$ frictional forces along these directions to be solved for. This problem is solved using SVD and the resulting minimal L^2 solution subtracted from F_r and T_r respectively to yield the new residual F_f, T_f. This approximation to the frictional force and torque is simpler, and less physical, than used in [BARA94].

When allowing friction forces in the termination criteria, we make the additional constraint that the magnitude of the frictional pseudo-force at each contact must be less than a fixed ratio of the magnitude of the normal pseudo-force (Coulomb model of friction).[16] The final pseudo-force and pseudo-torque applied to the active body, F_N and T_N, is given by

$$F_N \equiv (1 - \alpha)F_r - \alpha F_f$$

$$T_N \equiv (1 - \alpha)T_r - \alpha F_f$$

where α is a user-specified constant related to the amount of friction desired.

5.3 Updating Body Placement

The active body's position is updated by rotating through a small angle θ in radians around an axis A and translating through a small displacement Δ. The total amount of change is governed by the scale-invariant parameter ϵ – the maximum distance to move the active body in one step, relative to the radius of its smallest enclosing sphere, R. Actual values for the update parameters are obtained from the rigid body equations of motion assuming the body was at rest before applying forces, which implies that the linear and angular velocities of the body are 0.

We first scale the pseudo-forces and pseudo-torques to be applied, F_N and T_N, by the sum of their lengths so that roughly the same amount of change happens at each step:

$$\hat{F}_N \equiv \frac{F_N}{\|F_N\| + \|T_N\|}$$

$$\hat{T}_N \equiv \frac{T_N}{\|F_N\| + \|T_N\|}$$

Since for small ϵ, $\sin(\epsilon) \approx \epsilon$, normalizing by $\|F_N\| + \|T_N\|$ implies that the amount of movement of a point on the active body's enclosing sphere due to both rotation and translation, scaled by $1/R$, will be roughly ϵ.

experiment	time	iterations
torus on cone	9.89	13
block into goblet	8.0	25
goblet sideways on ground	6.34	28
knot on ground	3.86	12
jack on ground	6.6	36
bumpy sphere on ground	3.43	14
torus on ground	10.72	37
cone on ground	16.15	23
teapot on ground	6.89	20
lid on teapot	51.23	29
straw in glass	14.03	40
ice cube in glass	13.78	39
44th ball in bowl	6.58	9
bumpy sphere on cone	21.26	50
apple on ground	3.1	12

Figure 9: Results for Various Experiments. Each experiment was run until the placement algorithm terminated. Time is clock time in seconds on a SGI Indigo Extreme 2 workstation (R4400 150MHz processor). Iteration counts are the number of main loops, including failure loops, from the placement algorithm in Figure 2.

We then derive the linear and angular accelerations from the normalized force and torque. The linear acceleration, a, is given by

$$a \equiv \hat{F}_N$$

assuming the body has unit mass. The derivative of the angular velocity, $\dot{\omega}$, (under the at-rest assumption) is given by

$$\dot{\omega} \equiv I^{-1} \hat{T}_N$$

where I is the inertia tensor of the body in world coordinates.[17]

A differential update is obtained through direct use of the linear and angular accelerations, scaled by ϵ, to yield

$$\Delta \equiv \epsilon R a$$
$$\theta \equiv \epsilon \|\dot{\omega}\|$$
$$A \equiv \frac{\dot{\omega}}{\|\dot{\omega}\|}$$

This provides a "memoryless" change to the body placement, akin to simulation in an extremely viscous fluid. Note that Δ is scaled by R since it is a length parameter in world coordinates. As before, the body state is encoded by a quaternion/vector pair (Q, X). After moving by ϵ, the new body state, (Q', X'), is given by

$$Q' \equiv (\sin(\theta/2), \cos(\theta/2)A) \cdot Q$$
$$X' \equiv X + \Delta$$

where $\cdot$ denotes quaternion multiplication.

6 Results

Figure 9 shows performance results for some simple experiments. In these experiments, time per iteration on an SGI Indigo Extreme 2 workstation varied from 0.1 seconds to several seconds. A few tens of iterations are typically necessary to stabilize an object from a nearby placement. Proportionally more iterations are required when an object must traverse a circuitous route over many bodies and contacts. The majority of the computation time (more than 90% excluding rendering) is consumed by collision detection and numerical iteration involved in contact point creation and tracking.

Figure 1 and Figures 10-16 show some results of the placement algorithm. The placement tool allows the user to replicate the active body, making it easy to place multiple instances like the ice cubes or balls in Figures 14 and 15. Parameter values used in both the performance experiments and the modeling examples were $\lambda = 1.33$, $N_{\text{simultaneous}} = 3$, $\alpha = 0$, and $\epsilon_{\text{max}} = 0.05$. The recovery parameter, λ from Figure 2, was chosen so that the solution step size recovers somewhat more slowly than it is refined.[18] Using $N_{\text{simultaneous}} = 3$ handles the vast majority of simultaneous collisions,

---

[15]This allows a body to lean on others even though external forces are unbalanced by purely normal contact forces.

[16]Note that an assignment of friction forces that produces a very small residual and does not violate the Coulomb constraint may exist, yet we may not find it. To find such a friction force assignment would require solving a quadratic optimization problem. In practice, we frequently find an acceptable force assignment with this simple method. The user can also stop the system at any time manually.

[17]The inverse of the inertia tensor I^{-1} in world coordinates is equal to $Q I_b^{-1} Q^{-1}$ where Q is the rotation of the body, and I_b^{-1} is the inertia tensor in body coordinates. I_b is appropriately scaled so that the body has unit mass. Note that an accurate inertia tensor is often not required for computer graphics applications in which only the appearance of stability matters. The identity tensor often suffices.

[18]Recall from Figure 2 that ϵ is halved if a loop failure occurs.

but when regions of contact form curves or surfaces, allows the algorithm to check for stability without distributing points over the entire contact manifold. The value ϵ_{max} = 0.05 is a good compromise between speed of convergence and predictability of movement. User setting of ϵ_{max} is sometimes useful to increase the speed of convergence or progress more slowly through a portion of the optimization in which there is an undesirably large change in the body's placement.

Polygonal tessellations of surfaces were computed by uniform sampling in parameter space. The sampling density was typically chosen so that the surfaces appeared mostly free of polygonal artifacts when viewed from distances convenient for modeling. For example, the sphere used in the test of Figure 15 was tessellated using a 41×21 mesh, the bowl with a 81×121 mesh. We have reason to believe that the algorithm functions over a wide range of mesh accuracy. In one experiment, a knot-like shape was repeatedly dropped from the same position on a plane, using successively coarser uniformly sampled polygonal meshes. A stable placement involving three contact points was achieved using meshes containing from 9600 triangles to 56 triangles. Time to convergence varied for these experiments varied from 7.27 seconds to 6.12 seconds. Below 56 triangles (mesh size 15×5), the mesh was too poor an approximation to allow convergence of polygonal collisions to analytic contacts. A reasonable deterministic heuristic for tessellation would be to bound a measure of the approximation error such as maximum length of deviation; we have not investigated such a heuristic.

The placement algorithm has been surprisingly robust in our experiments: almost all modeling tasks in the figures were performed without interrupting the algorithm and without changing parameters from their default values. Occasional problems do occur. The algorithm can get "stuck" when it is not able to convert a polygonal collision to a contact point, so that ϵ goes to 0. This happened in certain experiments when dropping a torus over a cone and the lid over the teapot. Both situations involve bodies that form a curve of contact at the stable configuration, where one body is concave at the contact. The problem occurs after one contact has been created. As the body approaches the stable state, additional polygonal collisions are found and converted to analytic contact points. The iteration often moves the contact point a significant distance over the surface, violating the maximum distance threshold. If the distance threshold is increased, the large radius of neglect for the point may cause missed collisions. If the radius of neglect is manually decreased, too many polygonal collisions can be computed, slowing the algorithm to a crawl.

With additional intervention though, modeling tasks can still be performed in these situations. When the problem occurs, the user can interrupt the placement algorithm. Increasing the distance threshold parameter and then resuming often solves the problem, though the user must watch out for missed collisions. Collision detection can also be temporarily disabled after interruption and convergence attempted with the current contacts. Again, missed collisions are a possibility. Since the problems often occur very near to the stable position, a third strategy is to interactively reposition the object slightly from its stuck position and try again. If the problem is not corrected or results in missed collisions, the user can undo the bad states and try different strategies. The desired placement is usually achieved after two or three attempts. Such measures, although clearly not ideal, may not be intolerable in an interactive modeling environment.

As might be expected, the algorithm also suffers from convergence to meta-stable placements. For example, when a sphere is dropped onto another precisely underneath, the algorithm converges with the sphere balanced on top. This is easily remedied by interactively giving the sphere a nudge (by applying a local force for one step) and resuming.

7   Conclusion

Placing curved objects in physically plausible configurations has always been a difficult task for modeling systems, but one that can add much visual richness. This paper describes a new tool for interactive placement of non-interpenetrating curved objects that makes this task easier and more accurate. Two ideas make such a tool practical. The first is the use of a hybrid surface representation. A polygonal approximation allows quick detection of contacts that arise; a functional description converts these using numerical iteration to accurate points where the analytic surfaces touch. The second idea is to reach stability using an optimization technique that passes through a discrete series of states, based on a simple static force balance law

rather than a dynamic simulation. This paper describes a way of moving a body toward a stable state which is predictable and fast.

A number of areas for extending this work remain. Handling multiple active bodies is a straightforward extension. A slightly more general contact force solver is needed; the collision detection and interface point tracking algorithms described here require no modification. We believe such an extension would be practical in an interactive setting only for a limited number of active bodies. For example, simultaneously manipulating all 44 balls from the model in Figure 15, including well over a hundred tracked contact points, does not seem practical for the near future. Nevertheless, the extension would be useful for placement of mechanical linkages containing a few curved parts. Handling interactions between rigid and flexible bodies may also be possible. Another problem we have only begun to investigate is placement from an interfering initial state to allow a tool that can extricate a penetrating body. Finally, we are investigating ways to automatically handle the problem case discussed in Section 6 without resorting to user intervention.

Acknowledgements

I wish to thank Al Barr for getting me interested in this topic, and for his many insights into physical simulation. I also owe thanks to Jim Kajiya for many helpful discussions about the role of physical simulation in object assembly. James O'Brien wrote most of the collision detection code. Michael Cohen provided an extremely valuable critical read of the document as did Jim Kajiya. Brian Guenter afforded much useful advice. I also acknowledge Bena Currin, Adam Woodbury, Kurt Fleischer, and the other members of Caltech's graphics group for geometric models used in this work and for helpful early discussions. This work wold not have been possible without the support of Microsoft, especially my manager Dan Ling.

References

[BARA90]   Baraff, David, "Curved Surfaces and Coherence for Non-penetrating Rigid Body Simulation," Computer Graphics, 24(4), pp. 19-28, August 1990.

[BARA91]   Baraff, David, "Coping with Friction for Non-penetrating Rigid Body Simulation," Computer Graphics, 25(4), pp. 31-39, July 1991.

[BARA94]   Baraff, David, "Fast Contact Force Computation for Nonpenetrating Rigid Bodies," Computer Graphics, 28(2), pp. 23-42, July 1994.

[BARZ88]   Barzel, Ronen, and A. Barr, "A Modeling System Based On Dynamic Constraints," Computer Graphics, 22(4), pp. 179-188, August 1988.

[GARC94]   Garcia-Alonso, Alejandro, N. Serrano, and J. Flaquer, "Solving the Collision Detection Problem," IEEE Computer Graphics and Applications, pp. 36-43, May 1994.

[KAY86]   Kay, Tim, and K. Kajiya, "Ray Tracing Complex Scenes," Computer Graphics, 20(4), pp. 269-278, August 1986.

[GLEI92]   Gleicher, Michael, and A. Witkin, "Through-the-Lens Camera Control," Computer Graphics, 26(2), pp. 331-340, July 1992.

[META92]   Metaxas, Dimitri, and D. Terzopoulos, "Dynamic Deformation of Solid Primitives with Constraints," Computer Graphics, 26(2), pp. 309-312, July 1992.

[MOOR88]   Moore, M. and Wilhelms, J., "Collision Detection and Response for Computer Animation," Computer Graphics, 22(4), pp. 289-298, August 1988.

[PRES86]   Press, W. H., B. P. Flannery, S. A. Teukolsky, and W. T. Vetterling, Numerical Recipes, Cambridge University Press, Cambridge, England, 1986.

[SCLA91]   Sclaroff, Stan, and A. Pentland, "Generalized Implicit Functions for Computer Graphics," Computer Graphics, 25(4), pp. 247-250, July 1991.

[SNYD92]   Snyder, John, and J. Kajiya, "Generative Modeling: A Symbolic System for Geometric Modeling," Computer Graphics, 26(2), pp. 369-378, July 1992.

[SNYD93]   Snyder, John, A. Woodbury, K. Fleischer, B. Currin, and A. Barr, "Interval Methods for Multi-point Collisions between Time-Dependent Curved Surfaces", Computer Graphics, 27(2), pp. 321-334, Aug. 1993.

[WITK87]   Witkin, Andrew, K. Fleischer, and A. Barr, "Energy Constraints on Parameterized Models," Computer Graphics, 21(4), pp. 225-232, July 1987.

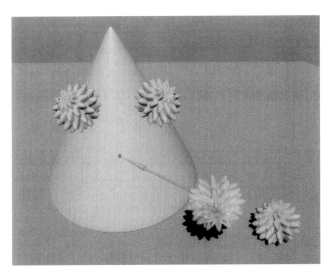
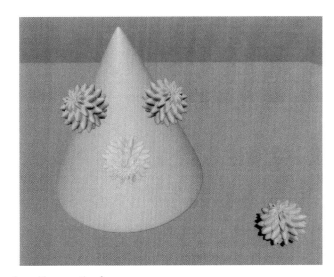

Figure 10: Sticking bodies together with connection forces.

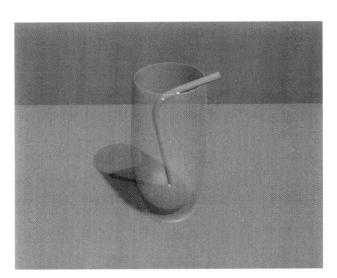
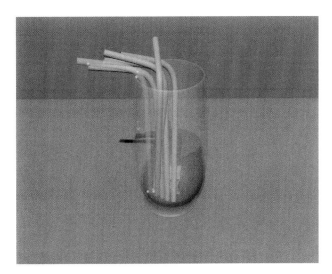

Figure 11: Dropping straws into a glass.

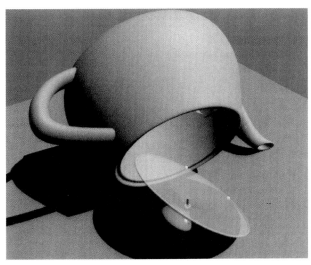

Figure 12: Cluttered scene.

Figure 13: Fallen teapot.

Figure 14: Ice in a glass.

Figure 15: 44 balls in a bowl.

Figure 16: Still life with fruit.

Artistic Screening

Victor Ostromoukhov, Roger D. Hersch

Ecole Polytechnique Fédérale de Lausanne (EPFL), Switzerland

Abstract

Artistic screening is a new image reproduction technique incorporating freely created artistic screen elements for generating halftones. Fixed predefined dot contours associated with given intensity levels determine the screen dot shape's growing behavior. Screen dot contours associated with each intensity level are obtained by interpolation between the fixed predefined dot contours. A user-defined mapping transforms screen elements from screen element definition space to screen element rendition space. This mapping can be tuned to produce various effects such as dilatations, contractions and non-linear deformations of the screen element grid. Discrete screen elements associated with all desired intensity levels are obtained by rasterizing the interpolated screen dot shapes in the screen element rendition space. Since both the image to be reproduced and the screen shapes can be designed independently, the design freedom offered to artists is very great. The interaction between the image to be reproduced and the screen shapes enables the creation of graphic designs of high artistic quality. Artistic screening is particularly well suited for the reproduction of images on large posters. When looked at from a short distance, the poster's screening layer may deliver its own message. Furthermore, thanks to artistic screening, both full size and microscopic letters can be incorporated into the image reproduction process. In order to avoid counterfeiting, banknotes may comprise grayscale images with intensity levels produced by microletters of varying size and shape.

Keywords

Image reproduction, graphic design, halftoning, artistic screening, microlettering

1 Introduction

Halftoning and screening techniques are aimed at giving the impression of variable intensity levels by varying the respective surfaces of white and black within a small area. Traditional techniques use repetitive screen elements, which pave the plane and within which screen dot surfaces define either white or black parts [16]. As long as the screen element period is small, or equivalently, the screen

EPFL/LSP CH-1015 Lausanne, Switzerland
victor@di.epfl.ch, hersch@di.epfl.ch
http://diwww.epfl.ch/w3lsp/screenart.html

Permission to make digital/hard copy of part or all of this work for personal or classroom use is granted without fee provided that copies are not made or distributed for profit or commercial advantage, the copyright notice, the title of the publication and its date appear, and notice is given that copying is by permission of ACM, Inc. To copy otherwise, to republish, to post on servers, or to redistribute to lists, requires prior specific permission and/or a fee.

Figure 1: Escher's *Sky and Water* woodcut (reproduced with permission, ©1995 M.C. Escher, Cordon Art, Baarn, Holland).

frequency is high (for example 150 screen elements per inch), distinct screen elements cannot be perceived by the human eye from a normal viewing distance [10]. However, in order to achieve such high screen frequencies, resolutions above 2400 dpi are required. With office printers, respectively photocomposers, having resolutions between 240 and 800 dpi, respectively between 1200 and 2400 dpi, halftoning or screening effects cannot be completely hidden. This explains why so much effort has been invested in developing halftoning techniques which reduce the impact of halftoning artifacts as much as possible [6].

We would like to take a different approach. Instead of looking at the halftoning layer as a pure functional layer producing undesired *artifacts*, we propose a new screening technique which enables the shape of screen dots to be tuned. By creating artistic screens which may take any desired shape, screening effects, which up to now were considered to be undesirable, are tuned to convey additional information for artistic purposes.

The approach we follow is somewhat related to the *pen and ink illustration techniques* where pen strokes are used for sketching illustrations, at the same time creating texture and intensities. While computer-aided pen and ink illustration systems [17] aim to offer the same flexibility as traditional pen-based stroking, artistic screening, as presented in this contribution, is a new computer-based image reproduction technique, which opens a new design space for artistic realizations.

For artistic screening, we extend the dynamics of screen dot

Figure 2: Mosaic tilework faces walls surrounding the courtyard of the Attarine Medeza, Fez (Courtesy of R. and S. Michaud, Rapho).

Figure 3: Thoulthi classical calligraphy by Majed Al Zouhdi (Courtesy of H. Massoudy, [8]).

shapes by using more sophisticated artistic shapes as screen dots. We would like to have full control over the evolution of the artistic screen dot shape and at the same time offer a halftoning method which is competitive with regard to conventional high-resolution clustered-dot screening. We have sought our inspiration in the work of medieval artists [1], who after having tiled the plane with repetitive polygonal patterns, created beautiful ornaments in each of the separate tiles (Fig. 2). Escher [12] further developed this technique by letting shapes circumscribed by a regular tile smoothly grow into one another (Fig. 1). The present work is also related to the decorative motives found in Islamic art which incorporate beautiful calligraphic work with letter shapes well-distributed over a given geometric surface (Fig. 3).

Previous attempts to develop screen dots having non-standard shapes were aimed at improving the tone reproduction behavior at mid-tones [9]. Elliptic screen dots for example, have an improved tone reproduction behavior due to the fact that at the transition between 45% and 55% intensity, at first only two neighbouring dots touch each other and only after a certain increase of intensity does the screen dot touch all its four neighbours (Fig. 4).

State of the art techniques for generating screen dot shapes are based on dither threshold arrays which determine the dot growing behavior. Since the dither threshold levels associated with the dither cells of a dither threshold array specify at which intensity the corresponding binary screen element pixels are to be turned on, the so generated screen dot shapes have the property of overlapping one another.

In order to generate screen dots of any shape, which need not overlap one another and which may have self-intersecting contours, we propose a new way of synthesizing screen dot shapes. We define the evolution of screen dot contours over the entire intensity range by interpolating over a set of predefined fixed dot contours which define the screen dot shape at a set of fixed intensity levels. Once the evolving shape of the halftone dot boundary is defined exactly for every discrete intensity level, the screen elements associated with each intensity level are rasterized by filling their associated screen dot contours (Section 3).

After having generated the screen elements, digital screening proceeds with the halftoning process described in more detail in Section 2. This halftoning process distinguishes itself from previous halftoning methods described in the literature [7] by the fact that the screen elements associated with every intensity level are precomputed and that no comparisons between original gray levels and dither threshold levels are necessary at image generation time. Furthermore, it ensures smooth transitions of the artistic halftone pattern in regions of high intensity gradients by applying bi-linear

interpolation between source image pixels.

The results obtained with artistic screening (Section 5) demonstrate that contour-based generation of halftone screens effectively provides a new layer of information. We show how this layer of information can be used to convey artistic and cultural elements related to the content of the reproduced images. Since there is no limitation to the size of the halftone screen elements, they can be made as large as the image itself. The introduced mapping (Section 4) between screen element definition space and screen element rendition space enables the production of highly desirable, smooth deformations of screen dots, without affecting the image content. In addition to their nice visual properties, geometric transformations of screen element shapes are of high interest for creating microscopic letters for security purposes, for example on banknotes.

Since artistic screening relies on the evolution of dot shapes at continuous intensity levels and since it allows building large screens (superscreens) containing arrays of screen subshapes, it is also able to produce traditional halftone screen dots having those frequencies and orientations which are required for traditional colour reproduction. Artistic screening may therefore also be used at high resolution as an alternative to current exact-angle clustered-dot screening techniques [2].

2 The halftoning process

Classical clustered-dot halftoning techniques rely on ordered dither threshold arrays. A dither threshold array is conceived as a discrete tile paving the output pixel plane. A dither threshold level is associated with each elementary cell of the dither threshold array. The succession of dither threshold levels specifies the dot shape growing

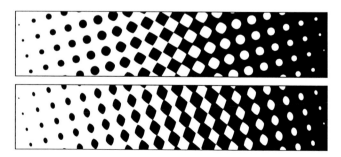

Figure 4: Traditional screen dot shapes, above with round and below with elliptic screen dots, produced by the artistic screening software package.

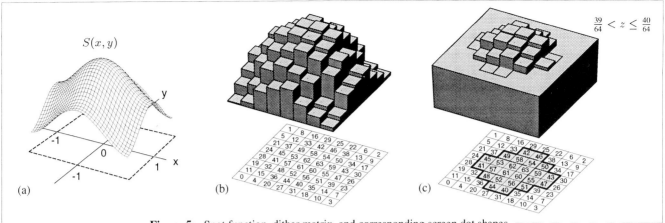

Figure 5: Spot function, dither matrix, and corresponding screen dot shapes.

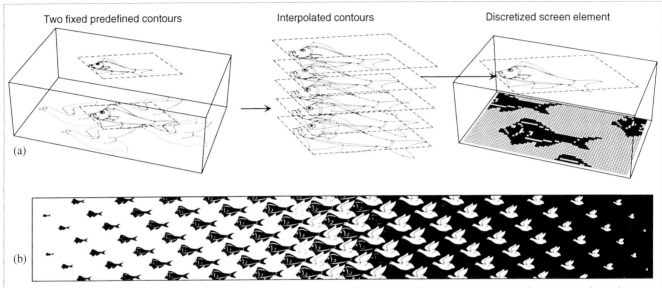

Figure 6: Artistic screening with a screen dot pattern inspired by Escher reproduced on an image representing a grayscale wedge.

behavior at increasing intensity levels (see Fig. 5). Dither threshold levels can either be specified manually or algorithmically [16]. Previous algorithmic approaches for generating discrete dither arrays are based on *spot functions* [2]. A spot function $z = S(x, y)$ defines the dither threshold levels for a dither element tile defined in a normalized coordinate space ($-1 \leq x, y < 1$).

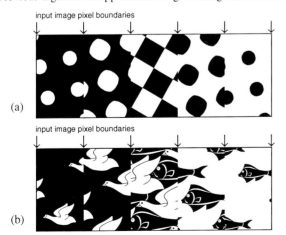

Figure 7: Effect of rapid intensity transitions on (a) standard clustered-dot screen elements and (b) artistic screen elements (enlarged).

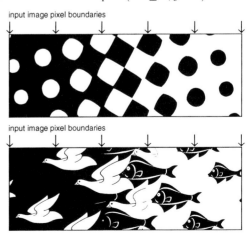

Figure 8: Rapid intensity transitions smoothed out by bi-linear interpolation of source image pixels at halftoning time on (a) standard clustered-dot screen elements and (b) artistic screen elements (enlarged).

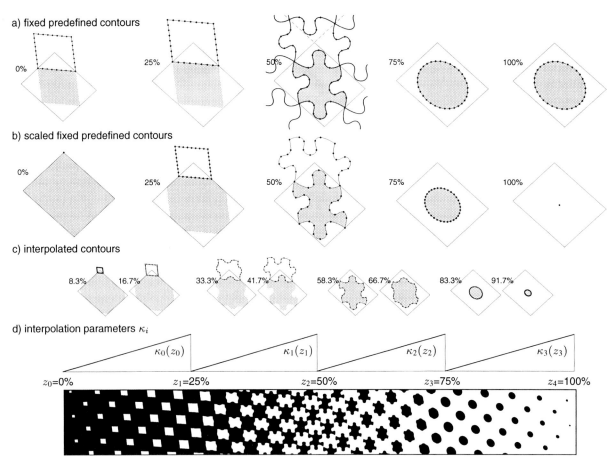

a) fixed predefined contours

b) scaled fixed predefined contours

c) interpolated contours

d) interpolation parameters κ_i

Figure 9: Simple dot shape obtained by blending between a set of fixed contours.

By discretizing this spot function, i.e, by computing its elevation at the coordinates of the centers of individual screen cells, and by numbering successive intersection points according to their elevations (Fig. 5b), one obtains the dither threshold array used for the halftoning process. The comparisons between given source image pixel intensity levels z and dither threshold levels determine the surface of a screen dot. For example, the dot shape associated with an input intensity level of 40/64 is obtained by activating all screen element pixels with threshold values 40 or greater (Fig. 5c).

With a given dither threshold array, the classical halftoning process consists of scanning the output bitmap, for each output pixel, finding its corresponding locations both in the dither array and in the grayscale input image, comparing corresponding input image pixel intensity values to dither array threshold levels and accordingly writing pixels of one of two possible ouput intensity levels to the output image bitmap.

Since artistic screening is not based on dither matrices, we precompute the screen elements (halftone patterns) representing each of the considered intensity levels. The halftoning process associated with artistic screening consists of scanning the output bitmap, and for each binary output pixel, finding its corresponding locations both in the grayscale input image and in the screen element tile. The input image intensity value determines which of the precomputed screen elements is to be accessed in order to copy its bit value into the current output bitmap location (Fig. 6a). This process may be accelerated by executing the same operations with several binary output pixels at a time [9].

In standard clustered-dot screening, due to the comparison between source pixel intensity values and dither threshold values, rapid transitions within a single halftone screen element are possible (Fig. 7a). They ensure that rapid intensity transitions occur-

ring in the original image are preserved in the halftoned image. With artistic screen elements however, rapid transitions may introduce unacceptable distortions in the screen dot shape (Fig. 7b). Smoother transitions are obtained by computing for each output bitmap pixel the corresponding interpolated gray intensity value at the corresponding location in the source image pixmap (bi-linear interpolation). Smoother intensity variations will be associated with output bitmap neighbourhoods, which will in turn smooth out the transitions within single artistic screen elements (Fig. 8). If the original image is scanned at high resolution (300 dpi and higher), undesired sharp intensity transitions may be avoided by applying to it a low-pass filter. There is a trade-off between the continuity of the halftone dot shapes and the faithful reproduction of sharp transitions.

3 Contour-based generation of discrete screen elements

Spot functions $S(x, y)$ generating simple screen dot shapes can be described easily. More complicated spot functions for generating shapes such as the dot shapes described in Fig. 6 are impossible to generate, since they cannot be described as single valued functions.

In order to generate complicated dot shapes capable of representing known subjects (birds, fishes) or objects (letter shapes), we define the evolving screen dot shape by a description of its contours. For this purpose, we introduce fixed predefined screen dot contours which are associated with specific intensity levels. Shape blending techniques [14] are used to interpolate between those predefined screen dot contours at all other intensity levels.

The fixed predefined contours, defined in a screen element def-

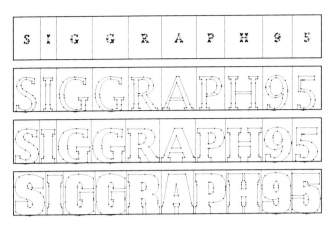

Figure 11: Screen tile containing subscreen shapes made of individual characters, at different intensity levels.

inition space, are designed by a graphist using a shape drafting software package such as Adobe Illustrator. The graphist defines his contours in the screen element definition coordinate space of his preference. Figure 9a shows a set of fixed predefined contours defining the evolution of a screen dot shape.

For ease of implementation, we assume that each fixed contour has the same number of distinct contour parts and that the contour parts of the interpolated contours are obtained by blending between corresponding fixed contour parts. Curved contour parts may be described by polynomial splines. For convenience, we use a cubic Bézier spline given by its control polygon to define each curved contour part. In order to simplify the interpolation process, we also assume that each straight line contour part is also defined by a Bézier control polygon having its vertices aligned on the given straight line segment. The arrangement of contour parts in each of the fixed predefined contours governs the interpolation process (Fig. 9).

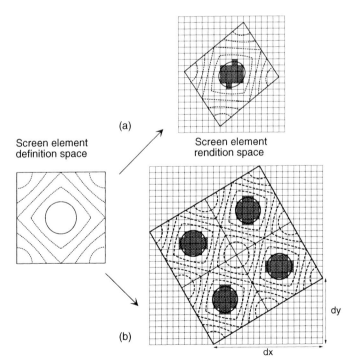

Screen element
definition space

Screen element
rendition space

(a)

(b)

dy

dx

Figure 10: Transformation between screen element definition and rendition space (a) applied to a small screen tile and (b) applied to a large screen tile (super screen) made of repetitive subscreen elements.

In order to control the speed at which the interpolated contour parts move from one fixed contour to the next, we introduce interpolation parameters $\kappa_i(z)$ varying between 0 and 1 (Fig. 9d). The coordinates of a control point $\vec{P}$ at intensity z interpolated between two fixed contour control points $\vec{P}_i$ and $\vec{P}_{i+1}$ associated with the extremities of intensity range $[z_i, z_{i+1}]$ is given by

$$\vec{P}(z) - \vec{P}_0 = (1 - \kappa_i(z))(\vec{P}_i - \vec{P}_0) + \kappa_i(z)(\vec{P}_{i+1} - \vec{P}_0) \quad (1)$$

where $\vec{P}_0$ represents the screen element origin.

Parameters $\kappa_i(z)$ are mapped to the range of intensity levels $[z_i, z_{i+1}]$ by interactively defining the curves $\kappa_i(z)$ in the same way as gamma correction curves are defined in well known grayscale halftoning packages (Adobe Photoshop for example). Figure 9 shows the full intensity range, fixed predefined and intermediate contours as well as their associated interpolation parameters.

In the range between intensity level $z_0 = 0$ and intensity level z_1 associated with the first fixed contour, the only operation which takes place is scaling. We therefore assume that the contour at level z_0 is a fixed contour of infinitely small size and that it has the same number of control points as the one at level z_1.

The tone reproduction behavior of a given printing process depends heavily on the dot gain, i.e. to what extent the printed dot has a larger surface than expected due to printer toner or ink spread properties. For a given printing process, the tone reproduction behavior depends on the shape of the printed dot. When increasing the darkness (or, equivalently, decreasing the intensity) at light and mid-tones, the relative printed surface increase is larger for dots having a higher contour to surface ratio. Since the fixed contours defining the artistic screen dot shape may have any contour to surface ratio, the surface growth of the printed dot for a given intensity difference may vary considerably at different intensity levels. We can therefore use interpolation parameters $\kappa_i(z)$ as local gamma correction factors [4].

If the created screen element is required to have a similar shape growing behavior in the light and in the dark tones, one may first design the fixed screen dot contours in the light tones and then in the dark tones. Taking into account the plane tiling behavior of a single screen element, the fixed contours associated with intensity levels, $z \leq 0.5$ are drawn at a location whose center is translated by half a period in each direction from the original screen element center. The fixed contour parts located on the three quadrants outside the original screen element boundary are copied back into the original screen element (see Fig. 9a, 50% intensity).

A single fixed contour associated with an intensity level equal to or close to $z = 0.5$ delimits the white growing region and the black growing region.

Once all fixed contours have been designed in the screen element definition space, and the table of blending parameters is initalized

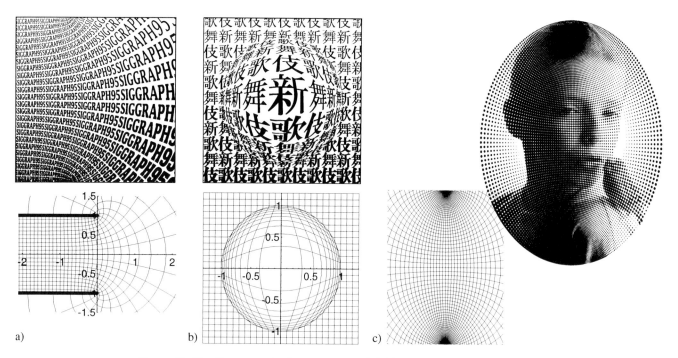

a)   b)   c)

Figure 12: Non-linear mapping between screen definition and screen rendition plane.

with values $\kappa_i(z)$, one merely needs to define the corresponding screen element boundaries in the screen element rendition space, e.g. in the space associated with the output bitmap. The transformation between screen element definition space and screen element rendition space enables the fixed predefined screen dot contours to be defined independently of the orientation and size of the final screen elements (Fig. 10). This transformation provides the basis both for screen element morphing (see Section 4) and for the generation of screen elements having exact screen angles, as required by traditional colour reproduction techniques [19].

A square screen element defined by its supporting cathets dx and dy (Fig. 10b) whose desired orientation is given by angle α can be approximated by an angle $\alpha' = \arctan(\frac{dy}{dx})$ as closely as required by increasing integer values dx and dy. The screen element's subdivision into a certain number of replicated subscreen dot shapes defines its screen frequency. In the screen element definition space, all subscreen dot shapes are identical. In the screen element rendition space however, rasterized discrete subscreen elements differ slightly one from another due to the different phase locations of their respective continuous contours (Fig. 10b). At high resolution, the so obtained exact angle screen elements are equivalent to the super-screening methods known in the field of colour reproduction [2], [13]. They have the advantage of offering the potential for colour reproduction with specifically designed screen shapes.

Once the fixed predefined contour parts have been transformed from screen element definition to rendition space, the discrete screen elements may be generated for each discrete intensity level. For reproducing 256 intensity levels, the intensity interval between $z = 0$ and $z = 1$ is divided by 255 and intermediate screen dot contours are successively generated at intensity levels $z = 0, z = 1/255, .., z = 255/255$. At each discrete intensity, the screen dot contours are rasterized by applying well known shape rasterization techniques [4]. In the case of self-intersecting dot contours or dot contours having at a single intensity level multiple intersecting contours, care must be taken to use a scan-conversion and filling algorithm supporting the non-zero winding number rule and generating non-overlapping complementary discrete shapes [5]. Furthermore, the filling algorithm must be able to fill shapes becoming smaller and smaller until they disappear [6]. Figure 6 shows the

result with an artistic screen dot shape inspired by Escher's drawing (Fig. 1a), reproduced on a grayscale wedge. Small details, such as the wings of the bird, progressively fade out as the bird's shape size decreases.

4 Screen Morphing

Since screen tiles can be as large as desired, they can be conceived so as to cover either the whole or a significant part of the surface of the destination halftoned image. Such large screen tiles are divided into elementary subscreen shapes which may contain either identical or different shapes. For microlettering applications, each elementary subscreen shape may contain a different letter shape (Fig. 11).

By defining the mapping from screen element definition space to screen element rendition space as a non-linear transformation, smooth, highly esthetic spatial variations of the subscreen shapes can be attained. For example, conformal mappings [14] [3] transform a rectangular grid of screen element sub-shapes into the subshapes of a deformed grid following electro-magnetic field lines (Fig. 12a). In that example, the conformal mapping is $w = k(1 + z + e^z)$, where k is a real scaling factor, z represents complex points $z = x + iy$ lying in the original (x, y) plane and $w = u + iv$ the corresponding complex points lying in the destination (u, v) plane.

Alternatively, if one would like to enlarge a few screen subshapes at the expense of their surrounding subshapes, one may define a circle of unit radius within which a geometric transformation maps the original rectangular grid into a highly deformed grid (Fig. 12b). A possible transformation is one that keeps the angle and modifies the distance of points from the center of the circle (fisheye transformation). With the center of the circle as the origin of the coordinate system, the mapping expressed in polar coordinates is the following:

$$\theta' = \theta; \quad r' = \begin{cases} \frac{m * \frac{r}{1-r}}{1 + m * \frac{r}{1-r}} & \text{if } r < 1 \\ r & \text{otherwise} \end{cases} \quad (2)$$

where m is a magnifying factor.

Figure 13: View of the Ibn Tulun Mosque, Cairo (Courtesy of R. and S. Michaud, Rapho).

5 High-quality artistic screening

In high-quality graphic applications, the shapes of artistic screen dots may be used as a vector for conveying additional information. This new layer of information may incorporate shapes which are related to the image. When reproduced in poster form, the screen elements of the screening layer will become sufficiently large to produce the desired visual effect.

In Figure 13, we show an example of a mosque rendered by screen dots made of calligraphic arabic letter shapes and oriental polygonal patterns. This screening layer adds a touch of islamic culture to the reproduced image.

The next example (Fig. 14) shows a poster displaying a scene inspired from the well-known Kabuki theater shows. Such a poster could be used for example to advertise a Kabuki theatre performance. The beautiful Kanji letter shapes can be seen close up whereas the full poster can only be perceived from a certain viewing distance. These two different views complement one another and each contributes towards transmitting the message to the public.

In the last example, we show that artistic screening can bring new solutions for avoiding desktop counterfeiting [15]. Since 1990, the US treasury protects banknotes by using microprinting techniques for generating letters having a size of approximatively 150 μm in order to avoid reproduction by photocopy or scanners (Fig. 15). In Figure 16, we show that by using artistic screening techniques, microletters of the type shown in Figure 11 can be incorporated into the grayscale image. Furthermore, due to the conformal mapping function $w = tg(z)$ between screen element definition and rendition spaces (Fig. 12c), a non-repetitive screen is created which cannot be scanned easily without producing Moiré effects.

6 Conclusions

We have presented a new halftoning technique, where screen elements are composed of artistic screen dot shapes, themselves created by skilled graphists. Fixed predefined dot contours associated with given intensity levels determine the screen dot shape's growing behavior. Screen dot contours associated with each intensity level are obtained by interpolation between the fixed predefined dot contours. User-defined mappings transform screen elements from screen element definition space to screen element rendition space. These mappings can be tuned to produce various effects such as dilations, contractions and non-linear deformations of the subscreen element grid. By choosing an appropriate mapping, images can be rendered while ensuring a highly esthetic behavior of their screening layer.

Since artistic screening uses precomputed screen elements, its performance at image halftoning time is similar to that of other dithering algorithms. The time required for precomputing the screen elements associated with every intensity level depends on the size of the screen element tile. Limited size repetitive screen elements such as those used in Figures 13 and 14 can be generated quickly (few minutes). On the other hand, very large screen elements morphed over the output image may require considerable computing power and time. Therefore, libraries of precomputed screen elements should be created. With such libraries, artistic screening can be made nearly as efficient as conventional halftoning.

Artistic screening can be seen as a new image reproduction technique incorporating freely created artistic screen elements used for generating halftones. Since both the image to be reproduced and the screen shapes can be designed independently, the design freedom offered to artists is very great. In the examples of sections 4 and 5, we have shown that one may reproduce simple images with complicated screen elements morphed over the destination halftone image, real images with beautiful but repetitive screen shapes or

Figure 14: *Kabuki actor*, by Toshusai Sharaku. Scene inspired from the Japanese Kabuki theater. The word Kabuki, 新歌舞伎 *shin-ka-bu-ki*, is used for creating the Kanji screen dot shape (Courtesy of the British Museum).

real images with complicated and morphed screen shapes.

Artistic screening enables both full size and microscopic letters to be incorporated into the image reproduction process. For example, next-generation banknotes may incorporate grayscale images with intensity levels produced by microletters of varying size and shape.

Currently, artistic screening is made possible by creating screen shapes with existing shape outlining tools and feeding them as input to the artistic screening software package. In the near future, we intend to add specific screen shape creation and morphing tools

in order to simplify the design of the fixed predefined screen dot contours and the specification of the transformation between screen element definition and screen element rendition space.

Thanks to these novel computer-based screening techniques, artistic screening may become an important graphic design tool. It may have a considerable impact on future graphic designs.

Figure 15: Microletters on current ten dollar notes.

Figure 16: Design of a banknote incorporating microletters as screen dot shapes.

7 Acknowledgements

We would like to thank Nicolas Rudaz for having developed the QuickTime animation illustrating the basic concepts of Artistic Screening (see SIGGRAPH'95 Proceedings on CD-ROM). We are grateful to H. Massoudy, Bella O., the British Museum, Rapho Press Agency, Paris and Cordon Art, Baarn, Holland for having kindly accepted to give us the permission to reproduce their originals.

REFERENCES

[1] K. Critchlow, *Islamic Patterns,* Thames & Hudson, 1989.

[2] P. Fink, *PostScript Screening: Adobe Accurate Screens,* Mountain View, Ca., Adobe Press, 1992.

[3] E. Fiume, A. Fournier, V. Canale, "Conformal Texture Mapping", *Eurographics'87,* North-Holland, 1987, 53–64

[4] J. Foley, A. van Dam, S. Feiner, J. Hughes, *Computer Graphics: Principles and Practice,* Addison-Wesley, Reading, Mass., 1990.

[5] R.D. Hersch, "Fill and Clip of Arbitrary Shapes", in *New Trends in Animation and Visualization,* (D. Thalmann, N. Magnenat-Thalmann, Eds.), J. Wiley & Sons, 1991, 3–12.

[6] R.D. Hersch, "Font Rasterization: the State of the Art", in *Visual and Technical Aspects of Type,* (R.D. Hersch, Ed.), Cambridge University Press, 1993, 78–109.

[7] Peter R. Jones, "Evolution of halftoning technology in the United States patent literature", *Journal of Electronic Imaging*, Vol. 3, No. 3, 1994, 257–275.

[8] H. Massoudi, *Calligraphie arabe vivante,* Flammarion, Paris, 1981.

[9] R.K. Molla, *Electronic Color Separation,* Montgomery, W.V., R.K. Printing and Publishing, 1988.

[10] M. Morgan, R.D. Hersch, V. Ostromoukhov, "Hardware Acceleration of Halftoning", Proceedings SID International Symposium, Anaheim, May 1993, published in SID 93 Digest, Vol XXIV, 151–154.

[11] L.A. Olzak, J.P. Thomas, "Seeing Spatial Patterns", in *Handbook of Perception and Human Performance,* (K.R. Boff, L. Kaufman, J.P. Thomas, Eds.), John Wiley & Sons, Vol. 1, 1986, 7.1–7.57.

[12] D. Schattschneider, *Visions of Symmetry, Note, Books, Periodic Drawings and Related Works of M.S. Escher,* W.H. Freeman and Company, New York, 1990.

[13] S.N. Schiller, D.E. Knuth, Method of controlling dot size in digital halftoning with multi-cell threshold arrays, US Patent 5305118, issued on April 19, 1994.

[14] R. Schinziger, P.A.A. Laura, *Conformal Mappings: Methods and Applications,* Elsevier, 1991.

[15] T.W. Sederberg, E. Greenwood, "A Physically Based Approach to 2-D Shape Blending" SIGGRAPH'92, *ACM Computer Graphics,* 26(2), 1992, 25–34.

[16] G. Stix, "Making money, desktop counterfeiting may keep the feds hopping", *Scientific American*, March 1994, 81–83.

[17] R. Ulichney, *Digital Halftoning,* MIT Press, 1987.

[18] G. Winkenbach, D.H. Salesin, "Computer-Generated Pen-and-Ink Illustration" Proceedings SIGGRAPH'94, *Computer Graphics, Annual Conference Series*, 1994, 91–100.

[19] J.A.C. Yule, *Principles of Color Reproduction*, John Wiley & Sons, New York, 1967.

Figure 17: The vignette shown in Fig. 16, enlarged 4 times.

Pyramid-Based Texture Analysis/Synthesis

David J. Heeger*
Stanford University

James R. Bergen†
SRI David Sarnoff Research Center

Abstract

This paper describes a method for synthesizing images that match the texture appearance of a given digitized sample. This synthesis is completely automatic and requires only the "target" texture as input. It allows generation of as much texture as desired so that any object can be covered. It can be used to produce solid textures for creating textured 3-d objects without the distortions inherent in texture mapping. It can also be used to synthesize texture mixtures, images that look a bit like each of several digitized samples. The approach is based on a model of human texture perception, and has potential to be a practically useful tool for graphics applications.

1 Introduction

Computer renderings of objects with surface texture are more interesting and realistic than those without texture. Texture mapping [15] is a technique for adding the appearance of surface detail by wrapping or projecting a digitized texture image onto a surface. Digitized textures can be obtained from a variety of sources, e.g., cropped from a photoCD image, but the resulting texture chip may not have the desired size or shape. To cover a large object you may need to repeat the texture; this can lead to unacceptable artifacts either in the form of visible seams, visible repetition, or both.

Texture mapping suffers from an additional fundamental problem: often there is no natural map from the (planar) texture image to the geometry/topology of the surface, so the texture may be distorted unnaturally when mapped. There are some partial solutions to this distortion problem [15] but there is no universal solution for mapping an image onto an arbitrarily shaped surface.

An alternative to texture mapping is to create (paint) textures by hand directly onto the 3-d surface model [14], but this process is both very labor intensive and requires considerable artistic skill.

Another alternative is to use computer-synthesized textures so that as much texture can be generated as needed. Furthermore, some of the synthesis techniques produce textures that tile seamlessly.

Using synthetic textures, the distortion problem has been solved in two different ways. First, some techniques work by synthesizing texture directly on the object surface (e.g., [31]). The second solution is to use *solid textures* [19, 23, 24]. A solid texture is a 3-d array of color values. A point on the surface of an object is colored by the value of the solid texture at the corresponding 3-d point. Solid texturing can be a very natural solution to the distortion problem:

there is no distortion because there is no mapping. However, existing techniques for synthesizing solid textures can be quite cumbersome. One must learn how to tweak the parameters or procedures of the texture synthesizer to get a desired effect.

This paper presents a technique for synthesizing an image (or solid texture) that matches the appearance of a given texture sample. The key advantage of this technique is that it works entirely from the example texture, requiring no additional information or adjustment. The technique starts with a digitized image and analyzes it to compute a number of texture parameter values. Those parameter values are then used to synthesize a new image (of any size) that looks (in its color and texture properties) like the original. The analysis phase is inherently two-dimensional since the input digitized images are 2-d. The synthesis phase, however, may be either two- or three-dimensional. For the 3-d case, the output is a solid texture such that planar slices through the solid look like the original scanned image. In either case, the (2-d or 3-d) texture is synthesized so that it tiles seamlessly.

2 Texture Models

Textures have often been classified into two categories, deterministic textures and stochastic textures. A deterministic texture is characterized by a set of primitives and a placement rule (e.g., a tile floor). A stochastic texture, on the other hand, does not have easily identifiable primitives (e.g., granite, bark, sand). Many real-world textures have some mixture of these two characteristics (e.g. woven fabric, woodgrain, plowed fields).

Much of the previous work on texture analysis and synthesis can be classified according to what type of texture model was used. Some of the successful texture models include reaction-diffusion [31, 34], frequency domain [17], fractal [9, 18], and statistical/random field [1, 6, 8, 10, 12, 13, 21, 26] models. Some (e.g., [10]) have used hybrid models that include a deterministic (or periodic) component and a stochastic component. In spite of all this work, scanned images and hand-drawn textures are still the principle source of texture maps in computer graphics.

This paper focuses on the synthesis of stochastic textures. Our approach is motivated by research on human texture perception. Current theories of texture discrimination are based on the fact that two textures are often difficult to discriminate when they produce a similar distribution of responses in a bank of (orientation and spatial-frequency selective) linear filters [2, 3, 7, 16, 20, 32]. The method described here, therefore, synthesizes textures by matching distributions (or histograms) of filter outputs. This approach depends on the principle (not entirely correct as we shall see) that all of the spatial information characterizing a texture image can be captured in the first order statistics of an appropriately chosen set of linear filter outputs. Nevertheless, this model (though incomplete) captures an interesting set of texture properties.

*Department of Psychology, Stanford University, Stanford, CA 94305. heeger@white.stanford.edu http://white.stanford.edu

†SRI David Sarnoff Research Center, Princeton, NJ 08544. jrb@sarnoff.com

Permission to make digital/hard copy of part or all of this work for personal or classroom use is granted without fee provided that copies are not made or distributed for profit or commercial advantage, the copyright notice, the title of the publication and its date appear, and notice is given that copying is by permission of ACM, Inc. To copy otherwise, to republish, to post on servers, or to redistribute to lists, requires prior specific permission and/or a fee.

Computational efficiency is one of the advantages of this approach compared with many of the previous texture analysis/synthesis systems. The algorithm involves a sequence of simple image processing operations: convolution, subsampling, upsampling, histograming, and nonlinear transformations using small lookup tables. These operations are fast, simple to implement, and amenable to special purpose hardware implementations (e.g., using DSP chips).

3 Pyramid Texture Matching

The pyramid-based texture analysis/synthesis technique starts with an input (digitized) texture image and a noise image (typically uniform white noise). The algorithm modifies the noise to make it look like the input texture (figures 2, 3, 4). It does this by making use of an invertible image representation known as an *image pyramid*, along with a function, match-histogram, that matches the histograms of two images. We will present examples using two types of pyramids: the Laplacian pyramid (a radially symmetric transform) and the steerable pyramid (an oriented transform).

3.1 Image Pyramids

A linear image transform represents an image as a weighted sum of *basis* functions. That is, the image, $I(x, y)$, is represented as a sum over an indexed collection of functions, $g_i(x, y)$:

$$I(x, y) = \sum_i y_i g_i(x, y),$$

where y_i are the transform coefficients. These coefficients are computed from the signal by projecting onto a set of *projection* functions, $h_i(x, y)$:

$$y_i = \sum_{x,y} h_i(x, y) I(x, y).$$

For example, the basis functions of the Fourier transform are sinusoids and cosinusoids of various spatial frequencies. The projection functions of the Fourier transform are also (co-)sinusoids.

In many image processing applications, an image is decomposed into a set of subbands, and the information withing each subband is processed more or less independently of that in the other subbands. The subbands are computed by convolving the image with a bank of linear filters. Each of the projection functions is a translated (or shifted) copy of one of the convolution kernels (see [28] for an introduction to subband transforms and image pyramids).

An *image pyramid* is a particular type of subband transform. The defining characteristic of an image pyramid is that the basis/projection functions are translated and dilated copies of one another (translated and dilated by a factor or 2^j for some integer j). The subbands are computed by convolving and subsampling. For each successive value of j, the subsampling factor is increased by a factor of 2. This yields a set of subband images of different sizes (hence the name image pyramid) that correspond to different frequency bands.

In an independent context, mathematicians developed a form of continuous function representation called *wavelets* (see [30] for an introduction to wavelets), that are very closely related to image pyramids. Both wavelets and pyramids can be implemented in an efficient recursive manner, as described next.

Laplacian Pyramid. The Laplacian pyramid [4, 5, 22] is computed using two basic operations: reduce and expand. The reduce operation applies a low-pass filter and then subsamples by a factor of two in each dimension. The expand operation upsamples by a factor of two (padding with zeros in between pixels) and

then applies the same low-pass filter. A commonly used low-pass filter kernel (applied separably to the rows and columns of an image) is: $\frac{1}{16}(1, 4, 6, 4, 1)$.

One complete level of the pyramid consists of two images, l^0 (a low-pass image), and b^0 (a high-pass image), that are computed as follows:

```
l0 = Reduce(im)
b0 = im - Expand(l0),
```

where im is the original input image. Note that the original image can be trivially reconstructed from l^0 and b^0:

```
reconstructed-im = b0 + Expand(l0).
```

The next level of the pyramid is constructed by applying the same set of operations to the l^0 image, yielding two new images, l^1 and b^1. The full pyramid is constructed (via the make-pyramid function) by successively splitting the low-pass image l^i into two new images, l^{i+1} (a new low-pass image) and b^{i+1} (a new band-pass image).

The combined effect of the recursive low-pass filtering and sub/upsampling operations yields a subband transform whose basis functions are (approximately) Gaussian functions. In other words, the transform represents an image as a sum of shifted, scaled, and dilated (approximately) Gaussian functions. The projection functions of this transform are (approximately) Laplacian-of-Gaussian (mexican-hat) functions, hence the name Laplacian pyramid. Note that the pyramid is *not* computed by convolving the image directly with the projection functions. The recursive application of the reduce and expand operations yields the same result, but much more efficiently.

In the end, we get a collection of pyramid subband images consisting of several bandpass images and one leftover lowpass image. These images have different sizes because of the subsampling operations; the smaller images correspond to the lower spatial frequency bands (coarser scales). Note that the original image can always be recovered from the pyramid representation (via the collapse-pyramid function) by inverting the sequence of operations, as exemplified above.

Steerable Pyramid. Textures that have oriented or elongated structures are not captured by the Laplacian pyramid analysis because its basis functions are (approximately) radially symmetric.

To synthesize anisotropic textures, we adopt the steerable pyramid transform [25, 29]. Like the Laplacian pyramid, this transform decomposes the image into several spatial frequency bands. In addition, it further divides each frequency band into a set of orientation bands.

The steerable pyramid was used to create all of the images in this paper. The Laplacian pyramid was used (in addition to the steerable pyramid, see Section 4) for synthesizing the solid textures shown in figure 5.

Figure 1(a) shows the analysis/synthesis representation of the steerable pyramid transform. The left-hand side of the diagram is the analysis part (make-pyramid) and the right hand side is the synthesis part (collapse-pyramid). The circles in between represent the decomposed subband images. The transform begins with a high-pass/low-pass split using a low-pass filter with a radially symmetric frequency response; the high-pass band corresponds to the four corners of the spatial frequency domain. Each successive level of the pyramid is constructed from the previous level's low-pass band by a applying a bank of band-pass filters and a low-pass filter.

The orientation decomposition at each level of the pyramid is "steerable" [11], that is, the response of a filter tuned to any orientation can be obtained through a linear combination of the responses

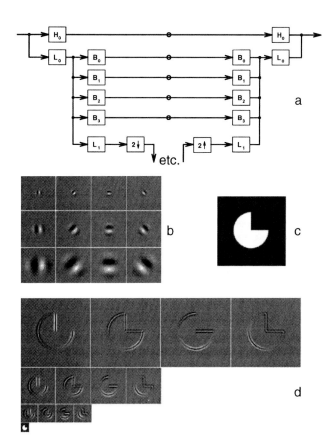

Figure 1: (a) System diagram for the first level of the steerable pyramid. Boxes represent filtering and subsampling operations: H_0 is a high-pass filter, L_0 and L_i are low-pass filters, and B_i are oriented bandpass filters. Circles in the middle represent the decomposed subbands. Successive levels of the pyramid are computed by applying the B_i and L_1 filtering and subsampling operations recursively (represented by "etc." at the bottom). (b) Several basis/projection functions of the steerable pyramid. Note that these are *not* the B_i filters, although the B_i filters do look similar to the top row of basis/projection functions. (c) Input image. (d) Steerable pyramid subband images for this input image.

of the four basis filters computed at the same location. The steerability property is important because it implies that the pyramid representation is locally rotation-invariant.

The steerable pyramid, unlike most discrete wavelet transforms used in image compression algorithms, is non-orthogonal and over-complete; the number of pixels in the pyramid is much greater than the number of pixels in the input image (note that only the low-pass band is subsampled). This is done to minimize the amount of aliasing within each subband. Avoiding aliasing is critical because the pyramid-based texture analysis/synthesis algorithm treats each subband independently.

The steerable pyramid is self-inverting; the filters on the synthesis side of the system diagram are the same as those on the analysis side of the diagram. This allows the reconstruction (synthesis side) to be efficiently computed despite the non-orthogonality.

Although the steerable pyramid filter kernels are nonseparable, any nonseparable filter can be approximated (often quite well) by a sum of several separable filter kernels [25]. Using these separable filter approximations would further increase the computational efficiency.

A C code implementation of the steerable pyramid is available at `http://www.cis.upenn.edu/~eero/home.html`.

Psychophysical and physiological experiments suggest that image information is represented in visual cortex by orientation and spatial-frequency selective filters. The steerable pyramid captures some of the oriented structure of images similar to the way this information is represented in the human visual system. Thus, textures synthesized with the steerable pyramid look noticeably better than those synthesized with the Laplacian pyramid or some other non-oriented representation. Other than the choice of pyramid, the algorithm is exactly the same.

3.2 Histogram Matching

Histogram matching is a generalization of histogram equalization. The algorithm takes an input image and coerces it via a pair of lookup tables to have a particular histogram. The two lookup tables are: (1) the cumulative distribution function (cdf) of one image, and (2) the inverse cumulative distribution function (inverse cdf) of the other image. An image's histogram is computed by choosing a bin-size (we typically use 256 bins), counting the number of pixels that fall into each bin, and dividing by the total number of pixels. An image's cdf is computed from its histogram simply by accumulating successive bin counts.

The cdf is a lookup table that maps from the interval [0,256] to the interval [0,1]. The inverse cdf is a lookup table that maps back from [0,1] to [0,256]. It is constructed by resampling (with linear interpolation) the cdf so that its samples are evenly spaced on the [0,1] interval.

These two lookup tables are used by the `match-histogram` function to modify an image (`im1`) to have the same histogram as another image (`im2`):

```
Match-histogram (im1,im2)
  im1-cdf = Make-cdf(im1)
  im2-cdf = Make-cdf(im2)
  inv-im2-cdf = Make-inverse-lookup-table(im2-cdf)
  Loop for each pixel do
      im1[pixel] =
        Lookup(inv-im2-cdf,
              Lookup(im1-cdf,im1[pixel]))
```

3.3 Texture Matching

The `match-texture` function modifies an input `noise` image so that it looks like an input `texture` image. First, match the histogram of the noise image to the input texture. Second, make pyramids from both the (modified) noise and texture images. Third, loop through the two pyramid data structures and match the histograms of each of the corresponding pyramid subbands. Fourth, collapse the (histogram-matched) noise pyramid to generate a preliminary version of the synthetic texture. Matching the histograms of the pyramid subbands modifies the histogram of the collapsed image. In order to get *both* the pixel and pyramid histograms to match we iterate, rematching the histograms of the images, and then rematching the histograms of the pyramid subbands.

```
Match-texture(noise,texture)
  Match-Histogram (noise,texture)
  analysis-pyr = Make-Pyramid (texture)
  Loop for several iterations do
    synthesis-pyr = Make-Pyramid (noise)
    Loop for a-band in subbands of analysis-pyr
        for s-band in subbands of synthesis-pyr
        do
        Match-Histogram (s-band,a-band)
    noise = Collapse-Pyramid (synthesis-pyr)
    Match-Histogram (noise,texture)
```

Whenever an iterative scheme of this sort is used there is a concern about convergence. In the current case we have not formally investigated the convergence properties of the iteration, but our experience is that it always converges. However, stopping the algorithm after several (5 or so) iterations is critical. As is the case with nearly all discrete filters, there are tradeoffs in the design of the steerable pyramid filters (e.g., filter size versus reconstruction accuracy). Since the filters are not perfect, iterating too many times introduces artifacts due to reconstruction error.

The core of the algorithm is histogram matching which is a spatially local operation. How does this spatially local operation reproduce the spatial characteristics of textures? The primary reason is that histogram matching is done on a representation that has intrinsic spatial structure. A *local* modification of a value in one of the pyramid subbands produces a *spatially correlated* change in the reconstructed image. In other words, matching the *pointwise* statistics of the pyramid representation does match some of the *spatial* statistics of the reconstructed image. Clearly, only spatial relationships that are represented by the pyramid basis functions can be captured in this way so the choice of basis functions is critical. As mentioned above, the steerable pyramid basis functions are a reasonably good model of the human visual system's image representation.

If we had a complete model of human texture perception then we could presumably synthesize perfect texture matches. By analogy, our understanding of the wavelength encoding of light in the retina allows us to match the color appearance of (nearly) any color image with only three colored lights (e.g., using an RGB monitor). Lights can be distinguished only if their spectral compositions differ in such a way as to produce distinct responses in the three photoreceptor classes. Likewise, textures can be distinguished only if their spatial structures differ in such a way as to produce distinct responses in the human visual system.

3.4 Edge Handling

Proper edge handling in the convolution operations is important. For the synthesis pyramid, use circular convolution. In other words, for an image $I(x, y)$ of size NxN, define: $I(x, y) \equiv I(x \bmod N, y \bmod N)$. Given that the synthesis starts with a random noise image, circular convolution guarantees that the resulting synthetic texture will tile seamlessly.

For the analysis pyramid, on the other hand, circular convolution would typically result in spuriously large filter responses at the image borders. This would, in turn, introduce artifacts in the synthesized texture. A reasonable border handler for the analysis pyramid is to pad the image with a reflected copy of itself. Reflecting at the border usually avoids spurious responses (except for obliquely oriented textures).

3.5 Color

The RGB components of a typical texture image are *not* independent of one another. Simply applying the algorithm to R, G, and B separately would yield color artifacts in the synthesized texture.

Instead, color textures are analyzed by first transforming the RGB values into a different color space. The basic algorithm is applied to each transformed color band independently producing three synthetic textures. These three textures are then transformed back into the RGB color space giving the final synthetic color texture.

The color-space transformation must be chosen to decorrelate the color bands of the input texture image. This transformation is computed from the input image in two steps. The first step is to subtract the mean color from each pixel. That is, subtract the average of the red values from the red value at each pixel, and likewise for the green and blue bands. The resulting color values can be plotted as points in a three-dimensional color space. The resulting 3-d cloud of points is typically elongated in some direction, but the elongated direction is typically not aligned with the axes of the color space.

The second step in the decorrelating color transform rotates the cloud so that its principle axes align with the axes of the new color space. The transform can be expressed as a matrix multiplication, $\mathbf{y} = \mathbf{M}\mathbf{x}$, where $\mathbf{x}$ is the RGB color (after subtracting the mean) of a particular pixel, $\mathbf{y}$ is the transformed color, and $\mathbf{M}$ is a 3x3 matrix.

The decorrelating transform $\mathbf{M}$ is computed from the covariance matrix $\mathbf{C}$ using the singular-value-decomposition (SVD). Let $\mathbf{D}$ be a 3xN matrix whose columns are the (mean-subtracted) RGB values of each pixel. The covariance matrix is: $\mathbf{C} = \mathbf{D}\mathbf{D}^t$, where $\mathbf{D}^t$ means the transpose of $\mathbf{D}$. The SVD algorithm algorithm decomposes the covariance matrix into the product of three components, $\mathbf{C} = \mathbf{U}\mathbf{S}^2\mathbf{U}^t$. Here, $\mathbf{U}$ is an orthonormal matrix and $\mathbf{S}^2$ is a diagonal matrix. These matrices ($\mathbf{C}$, $\mathbf{U}$ and $\mathbf{S}^2$) are each 3x3, so the SVD can be computed quickly. The decorrelating transform is: $\mathbf{M} = \mathbf{S}^{-1}\mathbf{U}^t$, where $\mathbf{S}$ is a diagonal matrix obtained by taking the square-root of the elements of $\mathbf{S}^2$.

After applying this color transform, the covariance of the transformed color values is the identity matrix. Note that the transformed color values are: $\mathbf{M}\mathbf{D} = \mathbf{S}^{-1}\mathbf{U}^t\mathbf{U}\mathbf{S}\mathbf{V}^t = \mathbf{V}^t$. It follows that the covariance of the transformed color values is: $\mathbf{V}^t\mathbf{V} = \mathbf{I}$.

The color transform is inverted after synthesizing the three texture images in the transformed color space. First, multiply the synthetic texture's color values at each pixel by $\mathbf{M}^{-1}$. This produces three new images (color bands) transformed back into the (mean subtracted) RGB color space. Then, add the corresponding mean values (the means that were subtracted from the original input texture) to each of these color bands.

4 Solid Textures

Pyramid-based texture analysis/synthesis can also be used to make isotropic 3-d solid textures. We start with an input image and a block of 3-d noise. The algorithm coerces the noise so that any slice through the block looks like the input image.

The solid texture synthesis algorithm is identical to that described above, except for the choice of pyramid: use a 2-d Laplacian pyramid for analysis and a 3-d Laplacian pyramid for synthesis. As usual, match the histograms of the corresponding subbands. Note that since the Laplacian pyramid is constructed using separable convolutions, it extends trivially to three-dimensions.

We have obtained better looking results using a combination of Laplacian and steerable pyramids. On the analysis side, construct a 2-d Laplacian pyramid and a 2-d steerable pyramid. On the synthesis side, construct a 3-d Laplacian pyramid and construct steerable pyramids from all two-dimensional (x-y, x-z, and y-z) slices of the solid. Match the histograms of the 3-d (synthesis) Laplacian pyramid to the corresponding histograms of the 2-d (analysis) Laplacian pyramid. Match the histograms of each of the many synthesis steerable pyramids to the corresponding histograms of the analysis steerable pyramid. Collapsing the synthesis pyramids gives four solids (one from the 3-d Laplacian pyramid and one from each set of steerable pyramids) that are averaged together. Some examples are shown in figure 5.

5 Texture Mixtures

Figure 6 shows some *texture mixtures* that were synthesized by choosing the color palette (decorrelating color transform) from one image and the pattern (pyramid subband statistics) from a second image.

One can imagine a number of other ways to mix/combine textures to synthesize an image that looks a bit like each of the inputs: apply `match-texture` to a second image rather than noise, combine the high frequencies of one texture with the low frequencies of another, combine two or more textures by averaging their pyramid histograms, etc.

6 Limitations and Extensions

The approach presented in this paper, like other texture synthesis techniques, has its limitations. The analysis captures some but not all of the perceptually relevant structure of natural textures. Hence, this approach should be considered one of many tools for texturing objects in computer graphics.

It is critical that the input image be a *homogeneous* texture. Figure 7 shows two input textures (cropped from different areas of the same photoCD image) and two corresponding synthetic textures. When the input is inhomogeneous (due to an intensity gradient, contrast gradient, perspective distortion, etc.) then the synthesized texture has a blotchy appearance.

The approach also fails on quasi-periodic textures and on random mosaic textures (figure 8). Although the results look interesting, they do not particularly resemble the inputs. We have had some success synthesizing quasi-periodic textures using a hybrid scheme (e.g., like [10]) that combines a periodic texture model with the pyramid decomposition. Methods that are specifically designed to capture long range statistical correlation [26] have also been successful with textures of this type. The issue with random mosaic textures is mainly one of scale. If the repeated micro-patterns are small enough, then the pyramid analysis/synthesis scheme works well (e.g., see the ivy example in figure 3).

Figure 9 shows more examples of failures. There are two aspects of these images that the pyramid texture model misses. First, these textures are locally oriented but the dominant orientation is different in different parts of the image. In a sense, they are inhomogeneous with respect to orientation. Second, they contain extended, fine structure (correlations of high frequency content over large distances). The pyramid scheme captures correlations of low frequency content over large distances, but it captures correlations of high frequency content only over very short distances.

There is no general way to construct an anisotropic solid texture from a 2-d sample. However, there are several options including: (1) constructing a solid texture as the outer product of a 2-d anisotropic color texture image and a 1-d (monochrome) signal; (2) composing (adding, multiplying, etc.) several solid textures as Peachy [23] did; (3) starting with an isotropic solid, and introducing anisotropy procedurally, like Perlin's marble [24] and Lewis' woodgrain [19]; (4) starting with an isotropic solid, and using a paint program to introduce anisotropic "touch-ups".

Image pyramids and multi-scale image representations of one sort or another are the most often used data structures for antialiased texture mapping (e.g., Renderman, Silicon Graphics Iris GL, General Electric and E&S realtime flight simulators, and reference [33]). Pyramid-based texture synthesis, therefore, can be naturally integrated into an antialiased texture mapping system.

Finally, it may be possible to write an interactive tool for texture synthesis, with a slider for each parameter in the pyramid representation. In our current implementation, each subband histogram is encoded with 256 bins. However the subband histograms of many "natural" images have a characteristic shape [27], suggesting that a very small number of parameters may be sufficient.

7 Conclusion

This paper presents a technique for created a two- or three-dimensional (solid) texture array that looks like a digitized texture image. The advantage of this approach is its simplicity; you do not have to be an artist and you do not have to understand a complex texture synthesis model/procedure. You just crop a textured region from a digitized image and run a program to produce as much of that texture as you want.

Acknowledgements: The teapot images were rendered using Rayshade. Many of the source texture images were cropped from photoCDs distributed by Pixar and Corel. Special thanks to Eero Simoncelli for designing the filters for the steerable pyramid, to Patrick Teo for writing a solid texturing extension to Rayshade, to Alex Sherstinsky for suggesting the solid texturing application, to Marc Levoy for his help and encouragement, and to Charlie Chubb and Mike Landy for stimulating discussions. Supported by an NIMH grant (MH50228), an NSF grant (IRI9320017), and an Alfred P. Sloan Research Fellowship to DJH.

References

[1] BENNIS, C., AND GAGALOWICZ, A. 2-D Macroscopic Texture Synthesis. *Computer Graphics Forum 8* (1989), 291–300.

[2] BERGEN, J. R. Theories of Visual Texture Perception. In *Spatial Vision*, D. Regan, Ed. CRC Press, 1991, pp. 114–133.

[3] BERGEN, J. R., AND ADELSON, E. H. Early Vision and Texture Perception. *Nature 333* (1988), 363–367.

[4] BURT, P. Fast Filter Transforms for Image Processing. *Computer Graphics and Image Processing 16* (1981), 20–51.

[5] BURT, P. J., AND ADELSON, E. H. A Multiresolution Spline with Application to Image Mosaics. *ACM Transactions on Graphics 2* (1983), 217–236.

[6] CHELLAPPA, R., AND KASHYAP, R. L. Texture Synthesis Using 2-D Noncausal Autoregressive Models. *IEEE Transactions on Acoustics, Speech, and Signal Processing 33* (1985), 194–203.

[7] CHUBB, C., AND LANDY, M. S. Orthogonal Distribution Analysis: A New Approach to the Study of Texture Perception. In *Computational Models of Visual Processing*, M. S. Landy and J. A. Movshon, Eds. MIT Press, Cambridge, MA, 1991, pp. 291–301.

[8] CROSS, G. C., AND JAIN, A. K. Markov Random Field Texture Models. *IEEE Transactions on Pattern Analysis and Machine Intelligence 5* (1983), 25–39.

[9] FOURNIER, A., FUSSEL, D., AND CARPENTER, L. Computer Rendering of Stochastic Models. *Communications of the ACM 25* (1982), 371–384.

[10] FRANCOS, J. M., MEIRI, A. Z., AND PORAT, B. A Unified Texture Model Based on a 2D Wold-Like Decomposition. *IEEE Transactions on Signal Processing 41* (1993), 2665–2678.

[11] FREEMAN, W. T., AND ADELSON, E. H. The Design and Use of Steerable Filters. *IEEE Transactions on Pattern Analysis and Machine Intelligence 13* (1991), 891–906.

[12] GAGALOWICZ, A. Texture Modelling Applications. *The Visual Computer 3* (1987), 186–200.

[13] GAGALOWICZ, A., AND MA, S. D. Sequential Synthesis of Natural Textures. *Computer Vision, Graphics, and Image Processing 30* (1985), 289–315.

[14] HANRAHAN, P., AND HAEBERLI, P. Direct WYSIWYG Painting and Texturing of 3D Shapes. Proceedings of SIGGRAPH 90. In *Computer Graphics* (1990), vol. 24, ACM SIGGRAPH, pp. 215–223.

[15] HECKBERT, P. S. Survey of Texture Mapping. *IEEE Computer Graphics and Applications 6* (1986), 56–67.

[16] LANDY, M. S., AND BERGEN, J. R. Texture Segregation and Orientation Gradient. *Vision Research 31* (1991), 679–691.

[17] LEWIS, J. P. Texture Synthesis for Digital Painting. Proceedings of SIGGRAPH 84. In *Computer Graphics* (1984), vol. 18, ACM SIGGRAPH, pp. 245–252.

[18] LEWIS, J. P. Generalized Stochastic Subdivision. *ACM Transactions on Graphics 6* (1987), 167–190.

[19] LEWIS, J. P. Algorithms for Solid Noise Synthesis. Proceedings of SIGGRAPH 89. In *Computer Graphics* (1989), vol. 23, ACM SIGGRAPH, pp. 263–270.

[20] MALIK, J., AND PERONA, P. Preattentive Texture Discrimination with Early Vision Mechanisms. *Journal of the Optical Society of America A 7* (1990), 923–931.

[21] MALZBENDER, T., AND SPACH, S. A Context Sensitive Texture Nib. In *Communicating with Virtual Worlds*, N. M. Thalmann and D. Thalmann, Eds. Springer-Verlag, New York, 1993, pp. 151–163.

[22] OGDEN, J. M., ADELSON, E. H., BERGEN, J. R., AND BURT, P. J. Pyramid-Based Computer Graphics. *RCA Engineer 30* (1985), 4–15.

[23] PEACHY, D. R. Solid Texturing of Complex Surfaces. Proceedings of SIGGRAPH 85. In *Computer Graphics* (1985), vol. 19, ACM SIGGRAPH, pp. 279–286.

[24] PERLIN, K. An Image Synthesizer. Proceedings of SIGGRAPH 85. In *Computer Graphics* (1985), vol. 19, ACM SIGGRAPH, pp. 287–296.

[25] PERONA, P. Deformable Kernels for Early Vision. *IEEE Transactions on Pattern Analysis and Machine Intelligence* (1995). To appear May 1995.

[26] POPAT, K., AND PICARD, R. W. Novel Cluster-Based Probability Model for Texture Synthesis, Classification, and Compression. In *Proceedings of SPIE Visual Communications and Image Processing* (1993), pp. 756–768.

[27] RUDERMAN, D. L., AND BIALEK, W. Statistics of Natural Images: Scaling in the Woods. *Physical Review Letters 73* (1994), 814–817.

[28] SIMONCELLI, E. P., AND ADELSON, E. H. Subband Transforms. In *Subband Image Coding*, J. W. Woods, Ed. Kluwer Academic Publishers, Norwell, MA, 1990.

[29] SIMONCELLI, E. P., FREEMAN, W. T., ADELSON, E. H., AND HEEGER, D. J. Shiftable Multi-Scale Transforms. *IEEE Transactions on Information Theory, Special Issue on Wavelets 38* (1992), 587–607.

[30] STRANG, G. Wavelets and Dilation Equations: A Brief Introduction. *SIAM Review 31* (1989), 614–627.

[31] TURK, G. Generating Textures on Arbitrary Surfaces Using Reaction-Diffusion. Proceedings of SIGGRAPH 91. In *Computer Graphics* (1991), vol. 25, ACM SIGGRAPH, pp. 289–298.

[32] TURNER, M. R. Texture Discrimination by Gabor Functions. *Biological Cybernetics 55* (1986), 71–82.

[33] WILLIAMS, L. Pyramidal Parametrics. Proceedings of SIGGRAPH 83. In *Computer Graphics* (1983), vol. 17, ACM SIGGRAPH, pp. 1–11.

[34] WITKIN, A., AND KASS, M. Reaction-Diffusion Textures. Proceedings of SIGGRAPH 91. In *Computer Graphics* (1991), vol. 25, ACM SIGGRAPH, pp. 299–308.

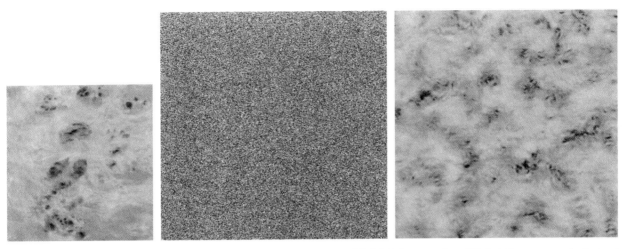

Figure 2: (Left) Input digitized sample texture: burled mappa wood. (Middle) Input noise. (Right) Output synthetic texture that matches the appearance of the digitized sample. Note that the synthesized texture is larger than the digitized sample; our approach allows generation of as much texture as desired. In addition, the synthetic textures tile seamlessly.

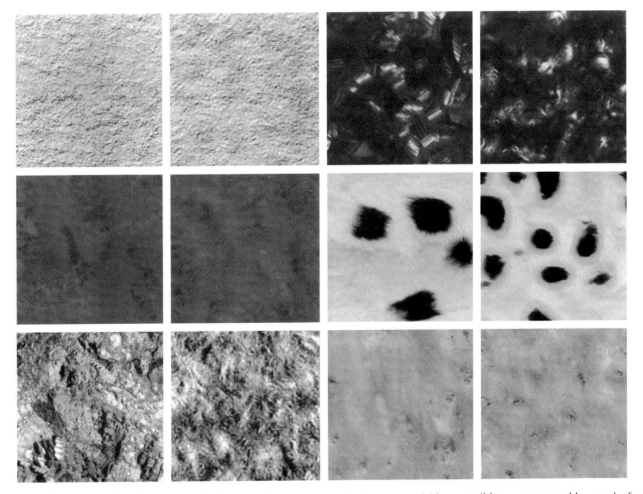

Figure 3: In each pair left image is original and right image is synthetic: stucco, iridescent ribbon, green marble, panda fur, slag stone, figured yew wood.

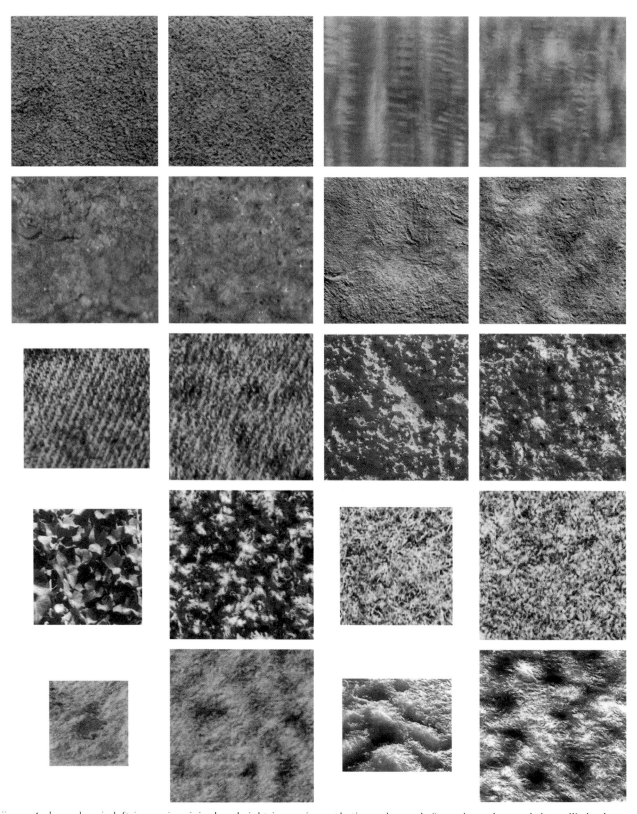

Figure 4: In each pair left image is original and right image is synthetic: red gravel, figured sepele wood, brocolli, bark paper, denim, pink wall, ivy, grass, sand, surf.

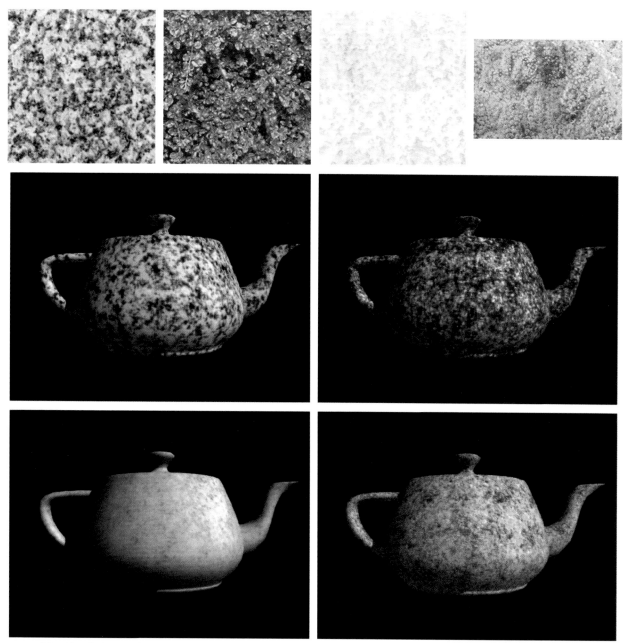

Figure 5: (Top Row) Original digitized sample textures: red granite, berry bush, figured maple, yellow coral. (Bottom Rows) Synthetic solid textured teapots.

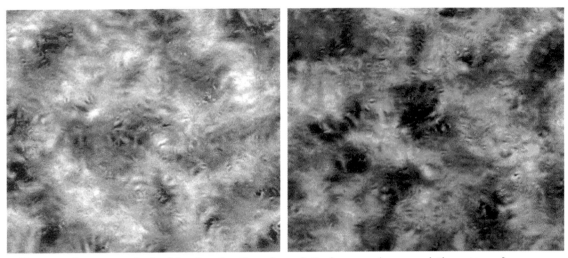

Figure 6: Texture mixtures synthesized by choosing the color palette from one image and the pattern from a second image.

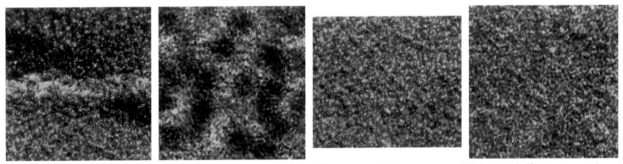

Figure 7: (Left pair) Inhomogoneous input texture produces blotchy synthetic texture. (Right pair) Homogenous input.

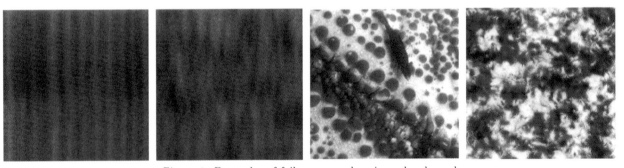

Figure 8: Examples of failures: wood grain and red coral.

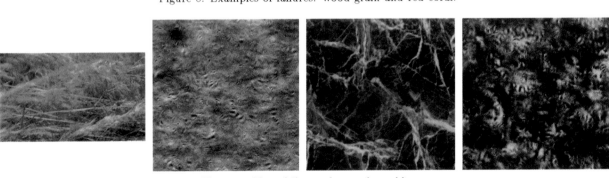

Figure 9: More failures: hay and marble.

Cellular Texture Generation

Kurt W. Fleischer
David H. Laidlaw
Bena L. Currin
Alan H. Barr

California Institute of Technology
Pasadena, CA 91125

email: {kurt, dhl, bena, barr}@druggist.gg.caltech.edu

Abstract

We propose an approach for modeling surface details such as scales, feathers, or thorns. These types of *cellular textures* require a representation with more detail than texture-mapping but are inconvenient to model with hand-crafted geometry.

We generate patterns of geometric elements using a biologically-motivated cellular development simulation together with a constraint to keep the cells on a surface. The surface may be defined by an implicit function, a volume dataset, or a polygonal mesh. Our simulation combines and extends previous work in developmental models and constrained particle systems.

Key Words: particle systems, developmental models, data amplification, constraints, texture mapping, bump mapping, displacement mapping

1 Introduction

For several years computer graphics researchers and practitioners have been grappling with the problem of creating and displaying surfaces having an organic appearance. Texture maps, bump maps, and related methods often attain the *appearance* of detailed geometry without actually creating it. These techniques do not suffice, however, when the viewpoint is close enough that the three-dimensional (3-D) geometric structure of a surface texture is apparent.

We are interested in making images of surfaces covered with interacting geometric elements, such as scales, feathers, thorns, and fur. We model these elements as small 3-D cells constrained to lie on a surface. The cells interact to form *cellular textures*: surface textures with 3-D geometry, orientation, and color. Our approach combines properties of particle systems, developmental models, and reaction-diffusion methods into one system. Figure 7 shows an example combining all of these approaches.

There are a few challenges in making images of these types of materials:

- The geometry is often too pronounced for using texture- or bump-maps.

Figure 1: Thorny Head: Both flat and thorn-shaped cells are constrained to lie on a surface defined by a polygonal dataset of a human head. Flat cells are used in the neck and chest regions, while thorn-shaped cells are used on the head. The orientation of each thorn approaches that of its neighbors, leading to a continuous field of thorns that sweeps across the head. The size of the thorns is related to the level of detail of the model; smaller thorns are placed on smaller features.

- It is often difficult to map appropriate texture coordinates onto the global geometry and topology.
- The placement, orientation, coloration, and shape of the individual elements may depend on:
    - neighboring elements,
    - surface characteristics such as local curvature, or
    - global phenomena such as sunlight.

Permission to make digital/hard copy of part or all of this work for personal or classroom use is granted without fee provided that copies are not made or distributed for profit or commercial advantage, the copyright notice, the title of the publication and its date appear, and notice is given that copying is by permission of ACM, Inc. To copy otherwise, to republish, to post on servers, or to redistribute to lists, requires prior specific permission and/or a fee.

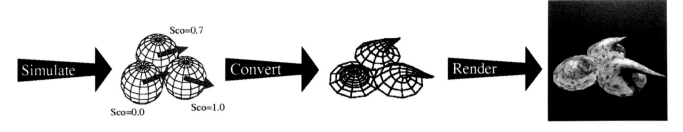

Figure 2: The cellular particle simulator computes the locations, orientations, and other values associated with the cells. This information is converted to geometry and appearance parameters, which is then passed to a renderer to create the image. Note that the cell orientations (red arrows) become the orientations of the thorns. Using a geometric modeler, we created a geometric object that changes shape from a bump to a thorn based on a single parameter [31]. We use the cell state variable S_{c0} to control this parameter (Section 4).

Because of the potentially complicated interdependencies of the elements, it is difficult to create either geometric or textural models of such objects by hand. So we turn to automatic data-amplification techniques, which are similar to the structured particle systems used to generate models of plants [26, 30].

Developmental Approach   For generating organic patterns, it is natural to consider a biologically-based simulation. In previous work [8], we developed a biological developmental model to simulate and study patterns generated by the motions and interactions of discrete cells (Figure 3). These artificial cells move about, grow, and divide in a simulated petri dish, the *extracellular environment*. The extracellular environment can contain physical barriers, diffusing chemicals, gravity, etc. The ability to form a variety of interesting patterns with the system has prompted us to explore its application to geometric texture generation (Figure 1).

The textures we model are formed from many interacting geometric elements. Actual fur, scales, and thorns may be formed from single cells or multiple cells [19]. In either case, we assume that the texture patterns arise from the interactions of discrete elements capable of movement and orientation change, and model each of these elements as one cell. The patterns are formed as the cells experience physical processes of collision, adhesion, and other local interactions.

Software Structure   The approach advocated by this paper is to automatically grow cellular textures by simulating discrete cells on surfaces. We then convert the resulting cellular information into model geometry and coloration, which is rendered. The images of this paper were generated using oriented, spherical cells, which are converted into thorns, scales, and other shapes for rendering (Figure 2).

Overview   The remainder of this paper is structured as follows. Section 2 describes related work. It is followed by an overview of the system architecture in Section 3. Section 4 describes the cellular particle system, and includes examples of cell programs that implement various behaviors. In Section 5 we discuss the particle converter, which produces geometry from the cell positions, orientations and other parameters.

Results are presented in Section 6, which describes the examples shown in the figures. The final section presents a discussion of the approach and some directions for future work.

2   Related Work

This approach is a synthesis and extension of work ranging from morphological models to general texture mapping. In this section, we discuss our approach in the context of four related areas:

- Levels of Detail
- Biologically Motivated Morphogenesis
- Reaction-Diffusion Methods
- Particle Systems

Levels of Detail   Choosing the appropriate level of detail for image synthesis at a given viewing distance has long been recognized as an important topic in computer graphics [4, 14, 15]. At large scales, geometric models are necessary; intermediate scales, texture mapping and similar techniques may be sufficient; at the smallest scales, illumination models suffice to describe the microgeometry of the object [38].

The level of detail of the models addressed in this paper falls somewhere between the use of hand-crafted geometric models and bump- or texture-mapping. A range of geometric levels is available to us because of the modular nature of our technique.

Complex, oriented textures have been created and rendered in many ways, notably with texels [15]. The texel approach is intermediate between geometry and mapping techniques, but leaves open the question of how to arrange the texel elements appropriately. Our approach addresses this problem, and can produce models to be rendered using texels.

Displacement mapping is another technique for adding geometric detail to surfaces [3]. As with texels, the displacement mapping technique does not address the problem of determining which displacements are necessary to create a specific effect, such as a field of similarly oriented thorns. A possible application of our technique

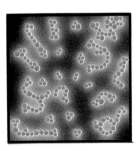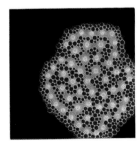

Figure 3: These images demonstrate the pattern formation capabilities of our 2-D cell simulator [8].

is to create such displacement maps, for example by creating flow fields [21].

Biologically Motivated Morphogenesis The cellular development system which forms the basis of this work [6, 7, 8] incorporates elements of several established biological models of morphogenesis: Turing's morphogens [35], Odell's mechanical models [20], and Lindenmayer-system cell lineage determinants [24], as well as our own model of cell contact and adhesion.

Much well-known computer graphics work is biologically based. The combination of developmental models with geometric constraints enables the creation of many organic patterns. It has been explored in work on plant growth [13, 23], plant organ placement [10], and seashell patterning [9].

Interacting geometric elements were used by [10] to model the placement of plant organs. Our cells are a generalization of these elements, with many additional capabilities, including independent movement, adhesion, and changes in size and orientation due to cell-cell interaction.

In [9], pigmentation patterns on seashells are modeled using reaction-diffusion equations on surfaces defined by sweeping a generating curve along a logarithmic spiral. This shares with our work the concept of applying pattern formation models on 3-D surfaces. Their use of continuous reaction-diffusion equations to generate the patterns differs from our use of discrete cells. For the types of cellular texture we are investigating, the choice of a discrete model seems appropriate.

Spatially-oriented models of plant growth are capable of generating attractive plant images [1, 13]. The placement of geometric objects in the environment of plants affects their growth. The importance of combining environmental and endogenous mechanisms in forming organic shapes in computer graphics has also been demonstrated using environmentally-sensitive L-systems [23], which allow interaction between the environment and the development of a structure defined by an L-system. In an application to synthetic topiary, elements sense their global position and orientation, and are pruned according to a bounding surface. Our work also combines geometric environmental factors with an endogenous developmental model to describe cell behavior. We differ from these plant models by the use of discrete motile cells that are able to move and rotate independently.

Reaction-Diffusion Methods Reaction-diffusion equations were first proposed as a model for morphogenesis by Turing [35]. They are a continuous approximation to a sheet of many discrete cells interacting over time. Our system models discrete cells explicitly, and can generate patterns similar to continuous reaction-diffusion equations since it is actually a more detailed model of the same biological system.

Reaction-diffusion equations have been successfully applied to the generation of texture maps [36, 40]. Because they are based on natural phenomena, they have an appealing organic quality. In addition, they avoid problems of parameterization and topology by creating the pattern directly on a surface. Our approach shares both of these benefits.

In our 2-D implementation (Figure 3), we include both discrete cells and a continuous reaction-diffusion computation. The two models are also able to interact, since the discrete cells can sense and emit the continuously diffusing chemicals. The 3-D implementation does not yet support continuously diffusing and reacting chemicals. However, we are able to reproduce some forms of reaction-diffusion behavior using cell-cell interaction in the discrete model.

Particle Systems Early particle systems [25, 28] had little or no interparticle interaction, unlike later work based on molecular models and other criteria [17, 34]. Our work includes elements of

Witkin and Heckbert's surface-constrained particles [41], and the orientation constraints of Szeliski and Tonneson [33]. Reynold's "boids" [27] introduced somewhat more sophisticated interacting particles with programmable behaviors. In addition, his boids, like our interacting cells, can sense and react to each other and to their environment.

3 Software Architecture

We arrange the process into three software modules (Figure 2).

cellular particle simulator with surface constraints: computes locations, orientations, sizes and other parameters of cells based on a behavioral specification. Allows particles to be constrained to a surface (implicit, polygon mesh, or volume dataset isosurface).

parameterized particle-to-geometry converter: converts cell positions, orientations and other parameters into shape and appearance parameters.

renderer: takes shape and appearance parameters plus a scene description and renders the scene. The images in this paper were generated with John Snyder's ray tracer [32], which was chosen primarily for its speed on large datasets.

The implementation of our framework involves the addition of cell-cell interactions, orientation constraints and surface constraints to a more traditional particle simulator. A simple version of a particle converter can be implemented using a geometric modeler to place a geometric object at each particle's location with the appropriate size and orientation. The cellular particle simulator and particle converter are described in further detail in the Sections 4 and 5.

4 Cellular Particle Simulator

The cellular particle system combines cell-cell interactions, cell-cell adhesion, oriented particles, and surface constraints into one unified framework. Additional discussion of the cell simulator and its implementation can be found in [7, 8].

Our system allows the user to specify cell behaviors such as 'go to a surface' and 'align with neighbors' by combining modular *cell programs*. Cell programs are first-order differential equation terms that modify the cell's state (see Table 1).

In Section 4.1 we discuss how to use the simulator, and then delve into a more detailed mathematical description of the cell programs in Section 4.2. Section 4.3 describes the cell programs used to create simulations like those shown in the figures. Section 4.4 presents methods for incorporating various types of surfaces into our surface constraint method.

4.1 Using the Simulator

For a particular simulation run, the user defines
- the cell state variables,
- the extracellular environment, and
- the cell programs.

The user also specifies initial placements and other initial conditions for the cells.

Users can control the simulation by writing cell programs to describe the behaviors of the cells, and by putting surfaces into the environment. More direct interaction is also possible during the simulation process. The user can halt the simulation, change the cell programs, and choose individual cells or groups of cells to modify or remove. The simulation is then restarted with the modifications. It is sometimes convenient to freeze certain cell values when they have reached a desirable state. Frozen values remain fixed while others continue to vary when the simulation is restarted. Particular seed cells can also be placed and frozen in situations where the user wishes to achieve a certain effect. For instance, frozen cells with a particular orientation could encourage fur to run in a particular direction on a surface.

4.2 Definitions

A *cell* is an entity that has position, orientation, shape, and an arbitrary length state vector for parameters such as chemical concentrations in a reaction-diffusion simulation. It is a generalization of a particle in a particle system.

Cell State Variables The state of a cell,

$$\mathbf{S} = (\quad \mathbf{p}, \mathbf{q}, r, S_{die}, S_{split}$$
$$S_{c0}, S_{c1}, S_{c2}, \cdots, S_{a0}, S_{a1}, S_{a2}, \cdots)$$

is a vector containing values representing position ($\mathbf{p}$), orientation ($\mathbf{q}$), size (r), and concentrations of chemicals within the cell (S_{ci}) or in the cell membrane (S_{ai}). The variable S_{split} is used to trigger an event, the cell splitting. This occurs when the value of this state variable exceeds a threshold, θ_{split}. S_{die} is defined similarly, with an associated threshold, θ_{die}.

In real cells, chemicals in the cell membranes of adjacent cells can bind together and enable cells to sense that they are in contact. The chemicals can also be adhesive. The binding of membrane chemicals is specific; some chemicals bind in complementary pairs, and others bind to themselves. Our model allows the user to specify the adhesive properties of the membrane chemicals, and provides the amount of each bound membrane chemical as an environmental parameter (described below).

To define a cell's motion, we specify cell programs that contribute to $\mathbf{p}'$, the viscous force on the cell. This is the *attempted* motion of the cell, which is further modified by the influence of collisions, adhesion, and viscous drag. We do not currently compute inertial dynamics, but instead use viscous dynamics ($F = mv$), which makes the cells easier to control and predict. Collision forces are computed using a polynomial penalty function (kx_o^n where x_o is the overlap between two cells).

We represent cell orientation in 3-D using a quaternion. In the exposition that follows, we sometimes refer to the cell's local coordinate frame using the three basis vectors: $\mathbf{e}_x, \mathbf{e}_y, \mathbf{e}_z$. This is the coordinate frame obtained by rotating from the lab frame using quaternion $\mathbf{q}$.

Extracellular Environment The cell's external environment is a vector of parameters that are provided as an input to the cell programs. These parameters describe everything the cell can sense from its current position:

$$\Lambda = (\quad \Lambda_{a0}, \Lambda_{a1}, \Lambda_{a2}, \cdots, \Lambda_{p0}, \nabla\Lambda_{p0}, \Lambda_{p1}, \nabla\Lambda_{p1}, \cdots,$$
$$\Lambda_{v0}, \Lambda_{v1}, \cdots,$$
$$\Lambda_{\omega x}, \Lambda_{\omega y}, \Lambda_{\omega z}, \Lambda_{u0}, \Lambda_{u1}, \cdots)$$

The Λ_{ai} values represent the amounts of membrane chemicals that are bound to membrane chemicals on neighboring cells. The value and gradient of a potential field, such as an implicit function or the concentration of a diffusing chemical, are provided in Λ_{pi} and $\nabla\Lambda_{pi}$. These fields are evaluated at the current location of the cell, and will generally have different values at different locations. Other scalar and vector fields can be provided in Λ_{ui} and Λ_{vi}, which can also be functions of position.

The orientation of a cell relative to its neighbors is made available to the cell programs in the vectors $\Lambda_{\omega i}$. This vector describes the rotation that would align this cell's $\mathbf{e}_i$ axis with the average orientation of the adjacent cells. This parameter is used to align the orientations of cells, as shown in Figure 8(a) and others. The direction $\Lambda_{\omega i}$ specifies the axis of rotation, and the magnitude specifies the rotation angle (similar to angular velocity). As an example, consider the computation of the average relative x-axis for a cell b, computed as a sum over neighboring cells c:

$$\Lambda_{\omega x} = \frac{1}{n} \sum_{c \in \text{ neighbors}} \frac{\mathbf{e}_x^b \times \mathbf{e}_x^c}{\|\mathbf{e}_x^b \times \mathbf{e}_x^c\|} \cos^{-1}(\mathbf{e}_x^b \cdot \mathbf{e}_x^c)$$

where $\mathbf{e}_x^c$ is the x-axis of the cell c, and cell b has n neighbors.

Cell Programs Each cell has several cell programs, which are first order differential equations describing how its state changes over time. Examples are given in Table 1 and Section 4.3. A cell program is a function of the cell's current state $\mathbf{S}$ and its environment as expressed by Λ. Different types of cells use different cell programs or different combinations of the same cell programs to define their behaviors. Even if two cells share the same set of cell programs, they will generally behave differently because they experience different local conditions depending on their position.

The entire system of differential equations to be solved is obtained by superposing ordinary differential equations from the cell programs for every cell. Additional equations arise from computation in the environment (e.g., diffusion of chemicals, although this is not in the current 3-D implementation). In order to handle discontinuous changes, such as when cells are created or die, we use a piecewise ordinary differential equation solver [2, App. C].

Mathematical Basis for Cell Programs Differential equations are a general tool for creating dynamic behavior. In our cell programs, we employ equations arising from physical models, as well as those arising from constraint solution techniques.

Higher order linear differential equations, such as those for mechanical or chemical systems, can be rewritten as multiple first order differential equations (i.e., cell programs) with the addition of state variables. In this case, the simulation dynamics reflect the dynamics of the equations.

In order to write constraints as cell programs, we formulate them as energy functions[1] to be minimized [39]. Each constraint is expressed as an energy function $E_i(\mathbf{S}, \Lambda)$ of the state of the system, $\mathbf{S}$, and the parameters describing the environment, Λ. Hard constraints could also fit into this framework using Lagrange multipliers [22].

Using relative constants k_i to weight the soft constraints, we express the overall energy to minimize as:

$$\hat{E}(\mathbf{S}, \Lambda) = k_1 E_1(\mathbf{S}, \Lambda) + \cdots + k_n E_N(\mathbf{S}, \Lambda)$$

We can minimize this energy according to gradient descent by modifying the state according to

$$\frac{dS_\ell}{dt} = -\sum_{i=1}^{N} k_i \frac{\partial E_i}{\partial S_\ell}$$

Superposition of Cell Programs Because the overall energy is expressed as a sum, the cell programs dS_ℓ/dt are also sums of terms, one for each constraint. We find it convenient to write cell programs as incremental collections of constraints. We write this as $dS_\ell/dt \mathrel{+}= \{\text{constraint term}\}$ in our example programs in Table 1. Multiple cell programs can thus be added together conveniently.

---

[1]Note that when we use constraint-based cell programs, the dynamics of our simulation depends upon the gradient descent algorithm, and is not necessarily physically meaningful.

Behavior	Environment Requirements	Cell Program
Go to a surface.	An implicit surface $f(\mathbf{x}) = 0$.	$\mathbf{p}' \mathrel{+}= -k\,f(\mathbf{p})\nabla f(\mathbf{p})$
Die if too far from surface.	An implicit surface $f(\mathbf{x}) = 0$.	$S'_{die} \mathrel{+}= \frac{1}{d} f(\mathbf{p})\,\theta_{die} - S_{die}$
Align an axis with a vector field.	A vector field, $\mathbf{v}(\mathbf{x})$. $\mathbf{e}_y$ is the cell's y-axis.	$\omega_v \equiv k\dfrac{\mathbf{e}_y \times \mathbf{v}(\mathbf{p})}{\|\mathbf{e}_y \times \mathbf{v}(\mathbf{p})\|}\cos^{-1}(\mathbf{e}_y \cdot \dfrac{\mathbf{v}(\mathbf{p})}{\|\mathbf{v}(\mathbf{p})\|})$ $\mathbf{q}' \mathrel{+}= (1/2)\,\omega_v\,\mathbf{q}$
Align x-axis with neighbors.	$\Lambda_{\omega x}$, x-axis orientation relative to neighbors.	$\mathbf{q}' \mathrel{+}= (1/2)\,\Lambda_{\omega x}\,\mathbf{q}$
Align z-axis with neighbors.	$\Lambda_{\omega z}$, z-axis orientation relative to neighbors.	$\mathbf{q}' \mathrel{+}= (1/2)\,\Lambda_{\omega z}\,\mathbf{q}$
Maintain unit quaternion.		$\mathbf{q}' \mathrel{+}= 4k(1 - \mathbf{q}\cdot\mathbf{q})\mathbf{q}$
Adhere to other cells	Membrane chemical $a2$ which binds to itself.	$S'_{a2} \mathrel{+}= 1.0 - S_{a2}$
Divide until surface is covered.	Λ_{a2}, amount of $a2$ which is bound.	$S'_{split} \mathrel{+}= \phi(\gamma, \Lambda_{a2})\,\theta_{split} - S_{split}$
Set size relative to surface feature size	Λ_{u0}, a value which reflects the size of the nearest feature on the surface.	$r' \mathrel{+}= \Lambda_{u0} - r$
Example of reaction-diffusion in discrete cells.	$\Lambda_{a0}, \Lambda_{a2}$ amounts of bound membrane chemicals. The user has specified that the membrane chemical $a0$ binds to $a1$, and that $a2$ binds to itself.	$S'_{c0} \mathrel{+}= -20\,\Lambda_{a0}/\Lambda_{a2} +$ $\qquad 10\,S^2_{c0}/(1 + S^2_{c0}) - 0.5\,S_{c0} + 13$ $S'_{a1} \mathrel{+}= 0.95\,\Lambda_{a0}/\Lambda_{a2}$ $S'_{a1} \mathrel{+}= \phi(3, S_{c0})\,S_{c0}$ $S'_{a1} \mathrel{+}= -S_{a1}$ $S'_{a0} \mathrel{+}= 5 - S_{a0}$ $S'_{a2} \mathrel{+}= 1 - S_{a2}$

Table 1: Example Cell Programs. Scalar or vector fields are given as a function of spatial location, $\mathbf{x}$, and are evaluated at the current location of the cell, $\mathbf{p}$. See cell program descriptions in Section 4.3.

4.3   Example Cell Programs

The cell programs listed in Table 1 exemplify the types of cell programs used to make the figures in this paper. We describe each briefly below.

Remember that the contributions from multiple terms are added together to make a single differential equation for each state variable (using the $\mathrel{+}=$ notation). Many of the cell programs shown here are of the form $S'_i(t) = dS_i/dt = \beta - S_i(t)$ for some constant β, which causes S_i to quickly approach the value β.

Go to a surface.   This cell program implements a constraint to keep a cell on the implicit surface $f(\mathbf{x}) = 0$. An approximation to the gradient, $\nabla f(\mathbf{x})$, is also available in the environment. As the simulation runs, a cell with this program will descend the gradient and come to rest on the surface. The parameter k determines the speed with which the particle approaches the surface.

Die if too far from surface.   Recall that when the variable S_{die} crosses the threshold θ_{die}, it triggers cell death (Section 4.2). In this cell program, we cause S_{die} to rise towards the threshold quickly if the cell is greater than a certain distance from the surface. Computing this requires a measure of the distance from the surface. For the implicit surfaces used in the figures, $f(\mathbf{x})$ is an approximation to the distance from the surface.

The equation in Table 1 causes cells at a distance greater than d to die. Similar cell programs can cause a cell to die if it becomes too large, its orientation strays too far from neighboring cells, or due to

any other condition that is a function of the cell's environment and internal state.

Align with a vector field.   In this example, we align the cell's y-axis, $\mathbf{e}_y$ with a given vector field $\mathbf{v}(\mathbf{x})$. The vector field is evaluated at the cell's current location, $\mathbf{p}$.

We first compute the vector ω_v, which represents the transformation required to rotate the $\mathbf{e}_y$ into $\mathbf{v}$. ω_v is the axis of rotation, and the length of ω_v specifies the angle through which to rotate. The formulation works with any of the cell's axes.

The form of the cell program comes from the equation

$$\mathbf{q}' = (1/2)\,\omega\,\mathbf{q},$$

which defines the rate of change of a quaternion, $\mathbf{q}$, for angular velocity ω [12].

If we have multiple cell programs of this form, the ω_i terms add, which allows us to constrain one, two, or all three axes of the cells. If the orientation constraints conflict, the cell's orientation will approach the average orientation. If they don't conflict, all constraints will become satisfied.

Align with neighbors.   The three orientation constraints on the cell's x-, y- and z-axes fully constrain its orientation. Constraining two axes would be sufficient in most cases, except where the vector field $\mathbf{v}(\mathbf{x})$ happened to be collinear with the x- or z-axis. Having the extra constraint keeps us from running into problems in that case, and also aids the convergence of the cell alignment process.

Maintain unit quaternion. It is wise to add a constraint to ensure that the quaternion does not stray too far from a unit quaternion during the integration of the differential equations. We can do this with another simple constraint. Table 1 shows a term for this constraint that comes from minimizing the energy expression $E = (1 - \mathbf{q} \cdot \mathbf{q})^2$, which describes the deviation of $\mathbf{q}$ from a unit quaternion.

Adhere to other cells. This equation causes the variable S_{a2} (representing the surface chemical *a2*) to approach and stay at the value 1.0. A pair of cells expressing *a2* will stick together once they come in contact, and a force is required to pull them apart. The environment vector for each cell will report the amount of chemical bound on each cell, Λ_{a2}, which may be used in other cell programs to determine if the cell has contacted another cell. The amount bound is computed from the contact area between the two cells, and the concentrations on each cell.

Divide until surface is covered. Divide until the amount of bound surface chemical *a2* reaches the level γ. Λ_{a2} reports the total amount bound from all cells that are in contact, which gives the cell a means of determining how many neighbors it has. Note that the mechanism has more general utility than just counting neighbors. For instance, a cell with twice the concentration of *a0* will contribute more to Λ_{a2}.

The auxiliary function $\phi(\gamma, \Lambda_{a0})$ is used in this cell program to compute a continuous version of the condition $(\Lambda_{a0} > \gamma)$. The function $\phi(a, b)$ computes a continuous version of the boolean condition $(b > a)$:

$$\phi(a, b) \equiv (tanh((b - a)) + 1)/2.$$

The value of this function will be near one for $(b >> a)$ and near zero for $(a << b)$.

Set size relative to surface feature size. In Figure 1, the cell sizes are related to the sizes of features in the polygonal database. This is achieved by providing the cells with a value Λ_{u0} that represents the area of the nearest triangle. The value Λ_{u0} could be used to pass information about local curvature or any other parameter that we wish to use to change the cell behavior.

Example of reaction-diffusion in discrete cells. The full derivation [7] of this set of equations is beyond the scope of this paper, however we will describe the equations briefly. The first equation in this set defines a genetic switch [18] that tends to drive S_{c0} towards one of two values, depending on the influence of the term $\Lambda_{a0}/\Lambda_{a2}$. In terms of Meinhardt's activator-inhibitor models [16], S_{c0} is the activator and S_{a1} is the inhibitor, which is propagated by the activity of membrane chemicals. The other equations determine interactions of membrane chemicals that lead to an effective diffusion of the value of S_{a1} among the cells. The value of S_{c0} can then be used to determine the final rendered shape of the cell, as illustrated in to Figures 2 and 7.

4.4 Surface Constraints

We have applied surface constraints to a variety of surface classes:
- polygonal mesh,
- implicit function, and
- isosurfaces of volume data.

The surface constraint cell program evaluates an implicit function to enable the cell to find and stay on the surface (Table 1).

Several of the surfaces used to create the figures are defined by triangular meshes. We create a rough approximation to an implicit function for these meshes. Any implicitization method will work, and in fact it doesn't have to be very exact. We implement this function by constructing an approximate *kd*-tree for the triangular mesh. In constructing a true *kd*-tree, each additional vertex may add several new partitions. Our approximation adds only the one necessary partition for each added vertex. This makes the tree smaller and faster to precompute, but no longer actually gives the closest point. To evaluate the function, we look up the triangle center in the *kd*-tree supposedly nearest to a given point. We then check adjacent triangles to see if they are closer, to improve the characteristics of the approximation. We then compute the direction and distance to that triangle, and use it as we would the gradient of an implicit function. We find the approximation, in conjunction with the local search, to be satisfactory for this application.

5 Particle Converter

The particle converter converts information about the particles and their environment into geometry and appearance parameters for rendering. It receives all of the results of the simulation, including the position, orientation and size of each cell, concentration of reaction-diffusion chemicals, and other arbitrary user-defined parameters, such as type or color. It also may have access to information about how far each cell is from the surface and properties of the surface near the cell (e.g, curvature) The converter also knows which cells contact each other.

The particle converter concept has proven to be extremely convenient. It enables us to do a variety of useful operations, including:
- choosing an appropriate representation for each cell based on its screen size (Figure 4);
- smoothly changing the appearance of a cell based on a continuously varying parameter (Figure 7);
- using the cell positions to generate a spatial subdivision (similar to [33, 37, 41]);
- using the cell orientations to compute a flow field on the surface (useful for displacement maps [21]); and
- experimenting with various colorations and geometries using the same simulation dataset.

The output of the particle converter is a collection of geometry and appearance information suitable for a particular renderer. This collection will generally include one or more geometric primitives for each cell, and the local texture, transparency, or bump information. The geometry can be simple, as in Figure 5, where each cell is rendered as a few polygons with a mottled-green texture map. Or it can be more complicated, as in the parameterized 3D thorn shape that curls based on cell state information (Figure 7 (c)).

The particle converter can also use contact information to calculate the size or shape of geometric primitives based on neighboring cell proximity, or to interpolate parameters such as orientation between cell centers.

We have implemented two particle converters. One provides options for choosing a particular geometry and texture for each cell. In addition, it considers information associated with the underlying polygons, such as which body part it represents in an anatomical model (lips, eyes, etc.) This can be used to change the rendering of cells in certain areas, as can be seen on the lips of the man in Figure 1.

Our second particle converter was implemented using a general purpose modeler [31]. Taking advantage of the flexibility of this modeler, we can create parameterized objects such as the bump-to-thorn shape shown in Figure 2. The modeler is used to create the

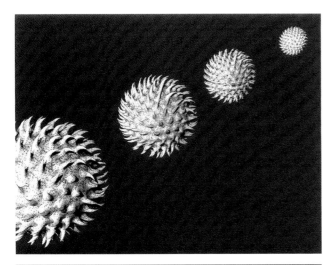

Figure 4: In the top image, the thorny spheres at further distances are rendered with fewer polygons. The bottom image shows a closeup of the nearest and furthest objects, so we can see the reduced number of polygons.

thorny spheres in Figure 7.

Rendering an appropriately scaled representation One of the drawbacks of data amplification techniques [30, 26] such as ours is their ability to generate a ridiculous amount of geometry to render. To ameliorate this, we use the particle converter to choose geometric primitives appropriate to the size of the object in the final image (Figure 4). This approach could be carried even further, for instance, by creating texture maps based on the cell positions.

6 Results

In this section we list a series of examples that highlight features of our system.

Scales Figure 5 shows four views of a spherical object with a uniform covering of similarly-oriented cells. The cell programs used here incorporate terms to divide until the surface is covered, to stay on the surface, and to die if pushed too far off of the surface. Initially, several cells were placed near the surface, and allowed to divide and wander. The cells were also given a soft constraint to align their y-axes with the gradient of the surface implicit function, and to align their x- and z-axes with their neighbors.

Note that two singularities in the orientations of cells arise naturally on the sphere, due to its topology. One is visible on the near

Figure 5: Scales: Four views of a spherical object uniformly covered with similarly oriented cells. Each cell is rendered as a group of four polygons with a texture and transparency map. The polygons are tilted slightly to give a layered appearance.

Figure 6: Cellular textures can handle unusual topologies.

side of the upper right sphere. Unlike standard texture mapping, this method introduces no particular parameterization problems, such as stretching or shrinking of the texture.

A Knotty Problem Figure 6 shows that the cellular texture approach is capable of creating textures for surfaces with unusual topologies. It is not necessary to have a parameterization for the surface. This surface was designed by John Hughes and John Snyder.

Thorny Head: Changing cell size to match surface features The examples described so far have used cells that are relatively uniform in size. Figure 1 shows an example where the cell size is related to the detail level in the underlying polygonal model. We achieve this by providing the cells with another environmental variable: the area of the nearest triangle in the underlying polygon mesh. Note the finer texture and geometry around the eyes and mouth.

Different rendering parameters were chosen according to properties of the underlying polygonal model. Each polygon in the underlying database is associated with a region of the body. The particle converter assigned different shading properties to the cells in the head and neck regions. At the eyes, the underlying polygonal representation shows through the cell texture.

Thorny Spheres: Differentiated cellular textures   This example shows several important capabilities of the system. It shows

- the creation of simple reaction-diffusion patterns on a surface,
- the use of the concentrations of cell chemicals to change parameters of the rendered geometry, and
- the ability to restart simulations from an previous state with new cell programs, causing new behaviors to occur.

These cells are using reaction-diffusion equations similar to those in Table 1 to create patterns of chemicals in the cells. The diffusion of chemicals occurs by contact between cell membranes, thus it can only occur between adjacent cells.

Using a geometric modeler, we created a parameterized geometric object that changes from a bump to a thorn based on a single parameter [31]. The particle converter sets this parameter to the value of a state variable representing the concentration of one of the reaction-diffusion chemicals.

We can see that there is a patch of cells on the front of the sphere with very little of the chemical (rendered as bumps), and a larger patch on the back with more of the chemical (rendered as thorns). In addition to the sharp boundary between the patches, note that the height of the thorns on the back patch varies continuously as they sweep around the sphere.

These simulations began where the earlier sphere simulation of Figure 5 left off, with new rules to cause the cells to differentiate. This is a common motif of user interaction with the system: halt a simulation, modify cell programs and parameters, and then continue simulating.

A Bear of a Surface   In Figure 8, we show a fur-covered model of a bear defined as an isosurface of sampled volume data. We would like for the bear's fur to have a natural-looking orientation [15]. The bear on the left, with the fully combed fur, started from a single cell and used a set of rules similar to those used for Figure 5 to distribute and orient the cells. Each cell on the bear is rendered with a group of geometric objects meant to roughly represent a hunk of thick hair.

The bear on the right, with the patchy fur, was the result of a serendipitous combination of unintentional cell programs. Rather than having each cell align with all of its neighbors, each cell chooses one neighbor to align with. Also, cells do not attempt to align with neighbors that are oriented in the directly opposing direction. This bear started from about 2000 arbitrarily chosen cells on the surface.

Additional, more specific, orientation constraints could cause the fur to run more naturally down the limbs. Other cell programs could be added to cause the fur to be shorter in the region of the face and longer on the haunches, or to change the coloration based on the orientation or curvature of the bear's features.

7   Discussion

The combination of particle constraint techniques with developmental models enables the generation of a variety of cellular textures, as shown in the figures. We have found the approach to be a powerful method of creating attractive computer graphics models of organic objects. In our experience with making cellular textures, we encountered some difficulties, which we describe below. Some of these limitations are associated with our current implementation, and can be remedied without changing the basic framework. The problems with simulation speed and data explosion are less easily finessed, and will require further research to address fully.

Some commercially produced computer graphics films and videos contain models that have textures that appear similar to ours. The techniques used to generate them are generally proprietary and unpublished, hence we cannot definitively compare them with our work. Software for orienting fur on a CG character has been developed at Industrial Light & Magic [5]. It is interesting to note that their discussion of the difficulties encountered closely parallels our own experience.

Shapes   The spherical shapes of cells in a simulation generally are not the shapes we want to render, and so the particle converter might make objects with undesirable intersections. This can be minimized by a careful choice of cell geometry, but a more robust solution is to use the desired geometric shape directly in the cellular particle simulation. This would allow cell programs to calculate collisions based on more accurate geometry.

Experience with Writing Cell Programs   Writing cell programs can be difficult. Programming independently moving cells by specifying differential equations has many desirable properties, but requires a different intuition than other types of programming, and often takes a while to get right. As with many tasks, it gets easier with practice. Here are some suggestions for using this programming paradigm:

- Copy and combine known cell programs from other researchers, such as surface or orientation constraints [41, 33].
- Think about the constraints in the energy formulation (Section 4, and [39]).
- Satisfy one constraint at a time; e.g., first get cell positions right, then modify other attributes.
- Force certain problem cells to be a certain way (through direct interaction, Section 4.1).
- Kill problem cells and regrow (Section 4.1).
- Apply artificial evolution [29], and be patient.

Simulation Speed   Simulations can be slow for some kinds of cell programs. We have some that run in seconds, and others, like the large datasets, that take many hours (e.g., the bear in Figure 8, and the head in Figure 1). Generally, performance degrades as the differential equations get stiff [11]. For some behaviors, clever cell programs like those described in [41] avoid creating stiff differential equations, and so run faster.

Data Explosion   The data produced both by the simulation and by the particle converter can get very large. We have partially addressed this by parameterizing the particle converter output by viewing distance (Figure 4). However, the simulation still has to compute enough cells to cover the surfaces, independent of viewing distance.

Figure 7: Varying Thorns. Reaction-diffusion-like equations determine the pattern of bumps and thorns on these spheres. Note the continuously varying thorn height and thorn curvature on the center and rightmost spheres.

Figure 8: The bear on the left is fully combed, with all cells oriented like their neighbors. The bear on the right has patches of similarly-oriented cells.

Future Work

There are several directions in which we would like to extend this work. First, we plan to continue extending and refining the cell programs to generate more complex cellular textures. We also are interested in running simulations on objects as they move and change shape. Modeling the motion of feathers on the wings of a flying bird, or hair on a running animal would be exciting. Initial experiments (not discussed in this paper) indicate that this will be feasible.

Implementing more sophisticated cell geometries in the particle simulator will give us more realistic placement of detail, and avoid self-intersections in the rendering. Finally, we would like to explore the possibilities of creating shapes directly from the fundamental interactions of the cells, without the surface constraint.

Acknowledgments

Many thanks to Erik Winfree for designing and implementing the *kd*-tree approximation, as well as for providing many helpful suggestions. We are grateful to Allen Corcorran, Matt Avalos, Cindy Ball, Dan Fain, Louise Foucher, Marcel Gavriliu, Barbara Meier, Mark Montague, Alf Mikula, Preston Pfarner, Ravi Ramamoorthi, Dian De Sha, and Denis Zorin for valuable discussions, support, code, and proofreading. MRI data was taken at the Huntington MRI center in Pasadena, CA.

This work was supported in part by grants from Apple, DEC,

Hewlett Packard, and IBM. Additional support was provided by NSF (ASC-89-20219) as part of the NSF/ARPA STC for Computer Graphics and Scientific Visualization, by the DOE (DE-FG03-92ER25134) as part of the Center for Research in Computational Biology, the Beckman Foundation, and by the National Institute on Drug Abuse and the National Institute of Mental Health as part of the Human Brain Project. All opinions, findings, conclusions, or recommendations expressed in this document are those of the authors and do not necessarily reflect the views of the sponsoring agencies.

REFERENCES

[1] James Arvo and David Kirk. Modeling plants with environment-sensitive automata. In *Proceedings of Ausgraph '88*, pages 27–33, 1988.

[2] Ronen Barzel. *Physically-Based Modeling: A Structured Approach.* Academic Press, Cambridge, MA, 1992.

[3] Robert L. Cook. Shade trees. In *Computer Graphics (SIGGRAPH '84 Proceedings)*, volume 18, pages 223–231, July 1984.

[4] F. C. Crow. A more flexible image generation environment. In *Computer Graphics (SIGGRAPH '82 Proceedings)*, volume 16, pages 9–18, July 1982.

[5] Jody Duncan. The making of a rockbuster. *Cinefex: the Journal of Cinematic Illusions*, 58:34–65, June 1994.

[6] Kurt Fleischer. Cells: Simulations of multicellular development. In *Siggraph Video Review*, 1994. *A video presented at Siggraph 94.*

[7] Kurt W. Fleischer. *A Multiple-Mechanism Developmental Model for Defining Self-Organizing Structures.* PhD dissertation, Caltech, Department of Computation and Neural Systems, June 1995.

[8] Kurt W. Fleischer and Alan H. Barr. A simulation testbed for the study of multicellular development: The multiple mechanisms of morphogenesis. In *Artificial Life III.* Addison-Wesley, 1994.

[9] Deborah R. Fowler, Hans Meinhardt, and Przemyslaw Prusinkiewicz. Modeling seashells. In *Computer Graphics (SIGGRAPH '92 Proceedings)*, volume 26, pages 379–388, July 1992.

[10] Deborah R. Fowler, Przemyslaw Prusinkiewicz, and Johannes Battjes. A collision-based model of spiral phyllotaxis. In *Computer Graphics (SIGGRAPH '92 Proceedings)*, volume 26, pages 361–368, July 1992.

[11] C. W. Gear. *Numerical Initial Value Problems in Ordinary Differential Equations.* Prentice-Hall, Englewood Cliffs, NJ, 1971.

[12] Goldstein. *Classical Mechanics.* Addison-Wesley, 1980.

[13] Ned Greene. Voxel space automata: Modeling with stochastic growth processes in voxel space. In *Computer Graphics (SIGGRAPH '89 Proceedings)*, volume 23, pages 175–184, July 1989.

[14] James T. Kajiya. Anisotropic reflection models. In *Computer Graphics (SIGGRAPH '85 Proceedings)*, volume 19, pages 15–21, July 1985.

[15] James T. Kajiya and Timothy L. Kay. Rendering fur with three dimensional textures. In *Computer Graphics (SIGGRAPH '89 Proceedings)*, volume 23, pages 271–280, July 1989.

[16] Hans Meinhardt. *Models of Biological Pattern Formation.* Academic Press, London, 1982.

[17] Gavin Miller and Andrew Pearce. Globular dynamics: A connected particle system for animating viscous fluids. *Computers and Graphics*, 13(3):305–309, 1989.

[18] J. D. Murray. *Mathematical Biology.* Springer-Verlag, New York, 2nd edition, 1993.

[19] B. N. Nagorcka, V. S. Manoranjan, and J. D. Murray. Complex spatial patterns from tissue interactions – an illustrative model. *Journal of Theoretical Biology*, 128:359–374, 1987.

[20] Garrett M. Odell, George Oster, P. Alberch, and B. Burnside. The mechanical basis of morphogenesis. *Developmental Biology*, 85, 1981.

[21] Hans Køhling Pedersen. Displacement mapping using flow fields. In *Proceedings of SIGGRAPH '94 (Orlando, Florida, July 24–29, 1994)*, pages 279–286. ACM Press, July 1994.

[22] John Platt. *Constraint Methods for Neural Networks and Computer Graphics.* PhD dissertation, Caltech, Department of Computer Science, Pasadena, CA, 91125, 1989.

[23] Przemyslaw Prusinkiewicz, Mark James, and Radomír Měch. Synthetic topiary. In *Proceedings of SIGGRAPH '94 (Orlando, Florida, July 24–29, 1994)*, pages 351–358. ACM Press, July 1994.

[24] Przemyslaw Prusinkiewicz and Aristid Lindenmayer. *The Algorithmic Beauty of Plants.* Springer-Verlag, New York, 1990.

[25] W. T. Reeves. Particle systems – a technique for modeling a class of fuzzy objects. *ACM Trans. Graphics*, 2:91–108, April 1983.

[26] William T. Reeves and Ricki Blau. Approximate and probabilistic algorithms for shading and rendering structured particle systems. In *Computer Graphics (SIGGRAPH '85 Proceedings)*, volume 19, pages 313–322, July 1985.

[27] Craig W. Reynolds. Flocks, herds, and schools: A distributed behavioral model. In *Computer Graphics (SIGGRAPH '87 Proceedings)*, volume 21, pages 25–34, July 1987.

[28] Karl Sims. Particle animation and rendering using data parallel computation. In *Computer Graphics (SIGGRAPH '90 Proceedings)*, volume 24, pages 405–413, August 1990.

[29] Karl Sims. Artificial evolution for computer graphics. In *Computer Graphics (SIGGRAPH '91 Proceedings)*, volume 25, pages 319–328, July 1991.

[30] Alvy Ray Smith. Plants, fractals and formal languages. In *Computer Graphics (SIGGRAPH '84 Proceedings)*, volume 18, pages 1–10, July 1984.

[31] John Snyder. *Generative Modeling for Computer Graphics and CAD: Symbolic Shape Design using Interval Analysis.* Academic Press, 1992.

[32] John M. Snyder and Alan H. Barr. Ray tracing complex models containing surface tessellations. In *Computer Graphics (SIGGRAPH '87 Proceedings)*, volume 21, pages 119–128, July 1987.

[33] Richard Szeliski and David Tonnesen. Surface modeling with oriented particle systems. In *Computer Graphics (SIGGRAPH '92 Proceedings)*, volume 26, pages 185–194, July 1992.

[34] Demetri Terzopoulos, John Platt, and Kurt Fleischer. From goop to glop: Heating and melting deformable models. In *Graphics Interface 89*, 1989.

[35] Alan Turing. The chemical basis of morphogenesis. *Phil. Trans. B.*, 237, 1952.

[36] Greg Turk. Generating textures for arbitrary surfaces using reaction-diffusion. In *Computer Graphics (SIGGRAPH '91 Proceedings)*, volume 25, pages 289–298, July 1991.

[37] Greg Turk. Re-tiling polygonal surfaces. In *Computer Graphics (SIGGRAPH '92 Proceedings)*, volume 26, pages 55–64, July 1992.

[38] Stephen H. Westin, James R. Arvo, and Kenneth E. Torrance. Predicting reflectance functions from complex surfaces. In *Computer Graphics (SIGGRAPH '92 Proceedings)*, volume 26, pages 255–264, July 1992.

[39] Andrew Witkin, Kurt Fleischer, and Alan Barr. Energy constraints on parameterized models. In *Computer Graphics (SIGGRAPH '87 Proceedings)*, volume 21, pages 225–232, July 1987.

[40] Andrew Witkin and Michael Kass. Reaction-diffusion textures. In *Computer Graphics (SIGGRAPH '91 Proceedings)*, volume 25, pages 299–308, July 1991.

[41] Andrew P. Witkin and Paul S. Heckbert. Using particles to sample and control implicit surfaces. In *Proceedings of SIGGRAPH '94 (Orlando, Florida, July 24–29, 1994)*, pages 269–278. ACM Press, July 1994.

Fast and Resolution Independent Line Integral Convolution

Detlev Stalling   Hans-Christian Hege

Konrad-Zuse-Zentrum für Informationstechnik Berlin (ZIB)[1]

Abstract

Line Integral Convolution (LIC) is a powerful technique for generating striking images and animations from vector data. Introduced in 1993, the method has rapidly found many application areas, ranging from computer arts to scientific visualization. Based upon locally filtering an input texture along a curved stream line segment in a vector field, it is able to depict directional information at high spatial resolutions.

We present a new method for computing LIC images. It employs simple box filter kernels only and minimizes the total number of stream lines to be computed. Thereby it reduces computational costs by an order of magnitude compared to the original algorithm. Our method utilizes fast, error-controlled numerical integrators. Decoupling the characteristic lengths in vector field grid, input texture and output image, it allows computation of filtered images at arbitrary resolution. This feature is of significance in computer animation as well as in scientific visualization, where it can be used to explore vector data by smoothly enlarging structure of details.

We also present methods for improved texture animation, again employing box filter kernels only. To obtain an optimal motion effect, spatial decay of correlation between intensities of distant pixels in the output image has to be controlled. This is achieved by blending different phase-shifted box filter animations and by adaptively rescaling the contrast of the output frames.

CR Categories: I.3.3 [Computer Graphics]: Picture/Image generation; I.3.6 [Computer Graphics]: Methodology and Techniques; I.4.3 [Image Processing]: Enhancement

Additional Keywords: vector field visualization, texture synthesis, periodic motion filtering

1 Introduction

Generation of textured images from various kinds of vector fields has become an important issue in scientific visualization as well as in animation and special effects. In 1993 Cabral and Leedom presented a powerful technique for imaging vector data called *line integral convolution* [1]. Their algorithm has been used as a general tool for visualizing vector fields. Additionally it has broad applications for image enhancement. A major drawback of the original algorithm, however, is its high computational expense and its restriction to a fixed spatial resolution.

In this paper we present an improved algorithm for line integral convolution, in which computation of streamlines is algorith-

mically separated from that of convolution. This allows us to exploit economies and to provide wider functionalism in each of the computational steps. The new algorithm

- is *about an order of magnitude faster* than original line integral convolution, making interactive data exploration possible
- is *more accurate* by employing an adaptive, error-controlled streamline integration technique
- is *resolution independent*, enabling the user to investigate image details by smooth detail enlargement (zooming)
- *improves texture animation* using shifted box filter kernels together with a simple blending technique.

In recent years a number of methods for artificially generating textures have been suggested. These methods cover a variety of applications. In the field of scientific visualization texture-based methods are of special interest because they allow the display of vector fields in an unrivaled spatial resolution. Traditionally, vector data has been represented by small arrows or other symbols indicating vector magnitude and direction. This approach is restricted to a rather coarse spatial resolution. More sophisticated methods include the display of stream lines [8], stream surfaces [10], flow volumes [14], as well as various particle tracing techniques [19, 9, 11]. These methods are well suited for revealing characteristic features of vector fields. However, they strongly depend on the proper choice of seed points. Experience shows that interesting details of the field may easily be missed.

Texture-based methods are not affected by such problems. They depict *all* parts of the vector field and thus are not susceptible to missing characteristic data features. In addition they achieve a much higher spatial resolution, which in some sense can be viewed as the *maximum possible* resolution since the minimum possible feature size of a textured image is a single pixel. In an early method introduced by van Wijk [18] a random texture is convolved along a straight line segment oriented parallel to the local vector direction. Line integral convolution (LIC) [1] modifies this method, so that convolution takes place along curved stream line segments. In this way field structure can be represented much more clearly. Forssell [5] describes another extension that allows her to map flat LIC images onto curvilinear surfaces in three dimensions.

Vector fields are not only of relevance in science and engineering. Many objects of our natural environment exhibit characteristic directional features which are naturally represented by vector data. Consequently algorithms for turning such data into pictorial information are of great importance for synthetic image generation, image post-processing, and computer arts [6, 16]. The variety of directional filters offered by commercial image processing software is just one evidence for this.

The remainder of the paper is organized as follows. Section 2 provides mathematical background and fixes notation. The basic ideas of the new algorithm are outlined in section 3. In the following three sections we present algorithms for fast and accurate streamline integration, discuss some optimization issues, and sketch strategies for fast texture map sampling. We then discuss periodic motion filtering and smooth detail enlargement. Finally we present some results and give an outlook concerning various aspects of LIC methods.

[1] Heilbronner Str. 10, D-10711 Berlin, Germany
E-mail: {stalling,hege}@zib-berlin.de

Permission to make digital/hard copy of part or all of this work for personal or classroom use is granted without fee provided that copies are not made or distributed for profit or commercial advantage, the copyright notice, the title of the publication and its date appear, and notice is given that copying is by permission of ACM, Inc. To copy otherwise, to republish, to post on servers, or to redistribute to lists, requires prior specific permission and/or a fee.

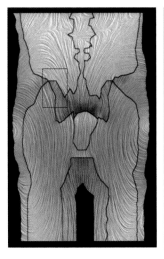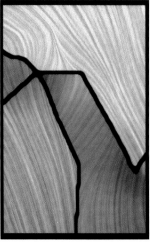

Figure 1: LIC image of a vector field (electrical field) containing discontinuities. Field strength $|v|$ is indicated by color.

2 Background

Before looking at line integral convolution, let us introduce vector fields formally, define some characteristic features and fix notation. For more detailed expositions on vector fields see standard texts on vector analysis, e.g. [13]. Restricting ourselves to the simplest case, we consider a stationary *vector field* defined by a map $v : \mathbb{R}^2 \to \mathbb{R}^2, x \mapsto v(x)$.

The directional structure of v can be graphically depicted by its *integral curves*, also denoted *flow lines* or *stream lines*[1]. An integral curve is a path $\sigma(u)$ whose tangent vectors coincide with the vector field:

$$\frac{d}{du}\,\sigma(u) = v(\sigma(u)) \qquad (1)$$

Like any path, $\sigma(u)$ can be reparametrized by a continous, strictly increasing function without changing its shape and orientation. For our purpose it is convenient to use arc-length s. Noting that $ds/du = |v(\sigma(u))|$ we have

$$\frac{d}{ds}\,\sigma(s) = \frac{d\sigma}{du}\frac{du}{ds} = \frac{v}{|v|} \equiv f(\sigma(s)). \qquad (2)$$

Of course, this reparametrization is only valid in regions of non-vanishing $|v|$, i.e. for non-degenerate curves σ. To find a stream line through x the ordinary differential equation (2) has to be solved with the initial condition $\sigma(0) = x$. It can be proved that there is a *unique* solution if the right hand side f locally obeys a Lipschitz-condition. In particular this condition is fulfilled for any function with continuous first derivative. Otherwise, there may exist *multiple* solutions at a single point x, i.e. multiple stream lines may start at that point. A typical example are point sources in an electrostatic field. Numerical integrators used in LIC have to be robust enough to handle such cases. Beside isolated singularities also discontinuities occur quite often in vector fields. Usually these are encountered across the boundaries of distinctly characterized field regions, e.g. regions with different electromagnetic properties. An example of this is shown in Fig. 1.

---

[1] The image of integral curves ("lines of force") and their graphical representation played a crucial role in Faradays development of the field concept during 1820-1850 [15].

Given a stream line σ, line integral convolution consists in calculating the intensity for a pixel located at $x_0 = \sigma(s_0)$ by

$$I(x_0) = \int_{s_0 - L}^{s_0 + L} k(s - s_0)\, T(\sigma(s))\, ds. \qquad (3)$$

Here T denotes an input texture, usually some sort of random image like white noise. The filter kernel k is assumed to be normalized to unity. The convolution operation (3) causes pixel intensities to be *highly correlated* along individual stream lines, but independent in directions perpendicular to them. In the resulting images the directional structure of the vector field is clearly visible. Usually good results are obtained by choosing filter length $2L$ to be 1/10th of the image width. It is possible to simultaneously visualize field strength $|v|$ by coloring or animating LIC images.

3 Making Line Integral Convolution Fast

In traditional LIC for each pixel in the output image a separate stream line segment and a separate convolution integral are computed. There are two types of redundancies in this approach. First, a single stream line usually covers lots of image pixels. Therefore in traditional LIC large parts of a stream line are recomputed very frequently. Second, for a *constant* filter kernel k very similar convolution integrals occur for pixels covered by the same stream line. This is not exploited by traditional LIC. Consider two points located on the same stream line, $x_1 = \sigma(s_1)$ and $x_2 = \sigma(s_2)$. Assume, both points are separated by a small distance $\Delta s = s_2 - s_1$. Then for a constant filter kernel k obviously

$$I(x_2) = I(x_1) - k \int_{s_1 - L}^{s_1 - L + \Delta s} T(\sigma(s))\, ds + k \int_{s_1 + L}^{s_1 + L + \Delta s} T(\sigma(s))\, ds. \qquad (4)$$

The intensities differ by only two small correction terms that are rapidly computed by a numerical integrator. By calculating long stream line segments that cover many pixels and by restricting to a constant filter kernel we avoid both types of redundancies being present in traditional LIC.

To design a fast LIC algorithm, we have taken an approach which relies on computing the convolution integral by sampling the input texture T at evenly spaced locations x_i along a pre-computed stream line $\sigma(s)$. For the moment we assume that input texture and output image are of the same size, like in traditional LIC. The distance between different sample points is denoted by h_t. We initiate stream line computation for some location $x_0 = \sigma(s_0)$ (see Fig. 2). The convolution integral for this location is approximated as

$$I(x_0) = k \sum_{i=-n}^{n} T(x_i), \text{ with } x_i = \sigma(s_0 + ih_t). \qquad (5)$$

To ensure normalization we take $k = 1/(2n + 1)$. The resulting intensity is added to the output image pixel containing x_0. Calculation of more accurate trapezoidal sums instead of Riemann sums is nearly as fast, but does not pay in terms of the visual effect. After having computed $I(x_0)$, we step in both directions along the current stream line, thereby updating the convolution integrals as follows

$$\begin{aligned} I(x_{m+1}) &= I(x_m) + k\,[T(x_{m+1+L}) - T(x_{m-L})] \\ I(x_{m-1}) &= I(x_m) + k\,[T(x_{m-1-L}) - T(x_{m+L})]. \end{aligned} \qquad (6)$$

For each sample point the corresponding output image pixel is determined and the current intensity is added to that pixel. In this way we efficiently obtain intensities for many pixels covered by the same

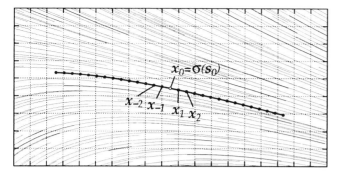

Figure 2: The input texture is sampled at evenly spaced locations $\boldsymbol{x}_i$ along a stream line $\boldsymbol{\sigma}$. For each location the convolution integral $I(\boldsymbol{x}_i)$ is added to the pixel containing $\boldsymbol{x}_i$. A new stream line is computed only for those pixels where the number of samples does not already exceed a user-defined limit.

stream line. The probability for an output image pixel to be hit by a sample point is proportional to the length of the line segment covering that pixel. This can be used to set up some sort of quality control. Running through all output image pixels, we require the total number of hits already occurred in each pixel to be larger than some minimum. If the number of hits is smaller than the minimum, a new stream line computation is initiated. Otherwise that pixel is skipped. At the end accumulated intensities for all pixels have to be normalized against the number of individual hits. Basically our algorithm (referenced as 'fast-LIC' hereafter) can be described by the following pseudocode:

```
for each pixel p
    if (numHits(p) < minNumHits) then
        initiate stream line computation with x₀ = center of p
        compute convolution I(x₀)
        add result to pixel p
        set m = 1
        while m < some limit M
            update convolution to obtain I(xₘ) and I(x₋ₘ)
            add results to pixels containing xₘ and x₋ₘ
            set m = m + 1
for each pixel p
    normalize intensity according to numHits(p)
```

There are a number of remarks necessary at this point. First, if stream line segments were computed for each pixel separately, the discrete sampling approach would be tainted with major aliasing problems, unless h_t is chosen much smaller than the width of a texture cell. However, if a single stream line is used for many pixels, correlation of pixel intensities along the stream line is guaranteed because exactly the same sampling points are used for convolution. We found a step size of $h_t = 0.5$ times the width of a texture cell to be completely sufficient. Although we have assumed input texture and output image to be of the same size, the fast-LIC algorithm can easily be generalized to set these sizes independently. This is necessary for smooth detail enlargement as discussed in Sect. 8.

The order in which all the output image pixels are processed is of some importance for the efficiency of the algorithm. The goal is to hit as many uncovered pixels with each new stream line as possible. Some optimization strategies are discussed in Sect. 5.

In our algorithm the computation of stream line segments can be performed without referencing input texture or output image. This allows us to utilize powerful, adaptive numerical integration methods. We have implemented several different integrators, which are discussed in Sect. 4. These methods not only accelerate stream line tracking significantly in homogeneous regions, but also ensure high accuracy necessary for resolving small details. Accuracy is especially important in fast-LIC because multiple stream lines determine

the intensity of a single pixel. If these lines are incorrectly computed, the LIC pattern gets disturbed. This is most evident near the center of a vortex in the vector field.

Accurate stream line integration also offers new opportunities for texture animation using shifted filter kernels, cf. Sect. 7. For animation we need a full sized convolution range. Therefore, when a stream line leaves the domain of $\boldsymbol{v}$, we continue the path in the current direction. For texture sampling all points are remapped to fall somewhere into the input texture. We continue stream lines in a similar way if $|\boldsymbol{v}|$ vanishes or if a singularity was encountered. Of course, artificially continued stream line segments can not be used to determine intensities of the underlying pixels.

4 Streamline Integration

Usually the vector field will not be available in functional form. For sake of simplicity we assume $\boldsymbol{v}$ to be given at discrete locations on an uniform grid. Vector values at intermediate locations have to be computed by interpolation. We use bilinear interpolation. Of course, better interpolation schemes can be employed if more information is available about the field. Sometimes global field properties are known, e.g. the existance of closed stream lines. In general these properties are not retained, when a local interpolation scheme like bilinear interpolation is used. In particular closed stream lines in the true vector field may no longer be closed in the interpolated field [12]. However, in practice errors due to interpolation are usually much smaller than errors caused by a poor numerical integrator, unless $\boldsymbol{v}$ is given on a very coarse grid.

Bilinear interpolation results in a representation of the field that is not differentiable across the boundaries of grid cells. Therefore, to integrate Eq. (2) in general we can't rely on sophisticated algorithms like extrapolation methods or predictor-corrector schemes, which require a very smooth right side. Instead we have employed traditional Runge-Kutta methods. Accompanied with modern error monitoring and adaptive step size control these methods are quite competitive [17, 7, 3]. We also have to take into account that in many applications vector fields arise that are very rough or even discontinuous. In such cases stream line integration is confronted with the potential risk of missing small details embedded in homogeneous regions. This problem can be tackled by delimiting the maximum allowed step size of an adaptive numerical integrator. At the extreme, a really safe method would require stepping from cell to cell in the $\boldsymbol{v}$-grid.

A fast and accurate general-purpose stream line integrator can be built up from the well-known classical fourth-order Runge-Kutta formula. This formula requires four evaluations of the right hand side to proceed from some point $\boldsymbol{x}$ to some other point $\hat{\phi}^h \boldsymbol{x}$ located a step size h ahead on the same stream line:

$$\begin{aligned} \boldsymbol{k}_1 &= h\boldsymbol{f}(\boldsymbol{x}) & \boldsymbol{k}_3 &= h\boldsymbol{f}(\boldsymbol{x} + \tfrac{1}{2}\boldsymbol{k}_2) \\ \boldsymbol{k}_2 &= h\boldsymbol{f}(\boldsymbol{x} + \tfrac{1}{2}\boldsymbol{k}_1) & \boldsymbol{k}_4 &= h\boldsymbol{f}(\boldsymbol{x} + \boldsymbol{k}_3) \end{aligned}$$

$$\hat{\phi}^h \boldsymbol{x} = \boldsymbol{x} + \frac{\boldsymbol{k}_1}{6} + \frac{\boldsymbol{k}_2}{3} + \frac{\boldsymbol{k}_3}{3} + \frac{\boldsymbol{k}_4}{6} + O(h^5) \tag{7}$$

The equation is called fourth-order because it resembles the true solution up to a power of h^4. However, an integration method is rather useless without any means for estimating the actual value of the error term. It turns out that an independent third-order approximation $\bar{\phi}^h \boldsymbol{x}$ can be computed by reusing some of the intermediate steps in (7), namely

$$\bar{\phi}^h \boldsymbol{x} = \boldsymbol{x} + \frac{\boldsymbol{k}_1}{6} + \frac{\boldsymbol{k}_2}{3} + \frac{\boldsymbol{k}_3}{3} + \frac{h\boldsymbol{f}(\hat{\phi}^h \boldsymbol{x})}{6} + O(h^4). \tag{8}$$

The difference between both methods simply equals to

$$\Delta = \hat{\phi}^h \boldsymbol{x} - \bar{\phi}^h \boldsymbol{x} = \frac{1}{6}(\boldsymbol{k}_4 - h\boldsymbol{f}(\hat{\phi}^h \boldsymbol{x})). \qquad (9)$$

This term is an estimate of the error of the less accurate formula. However, it can be shown [3] that in many cases this estimate can be safely used to control the step size of the more accurate method, too.

The idea of adaptive step size control is to choose h as large as possible while observing a user-defined error tolerance TOL. For p-th order integration methods the error term scales as h^{p+1}. Therefore if a step size h results in some error Δ, an optimized step size h^* can be obtained by

$$h^* = h \sqrt[p+1]{\rho \cdot \text{TOL}/\Delta}, \qquad (10)$$

with a safety factor $\rho < 1$. With this equation a control mechanism can be set up as follows. We ask the integrator to step forward by h and compute Δ from Eq. (9). If Δ is bigger than TOL, we repeat the current step with $h = h^*$. Otherwise, we proceed and take $h = \min(h^*, h_{\max})$ for the next iteration, where $h_{\max}$ is the maximum allowed step size. If h becomes much smaller than the grid spacing, we assume that a singularity was encountered and terminate stream line integration. The resulting adaptive numerical integrator, denoted as RK4(3) hereafter, turns out to be very robust and well suited for our application.

We have also implemented two fifth order methods with fourth order error estimation. The first method due to Dormand and Prince [4] requires five $\boldsymbol{f}$-evaluations per iteration. The other due to Cash and Karp [2] requires six. In our case, where the right hand side $\boldsymbol{f}$ is obtained by bilinearly interpolating between discrete grid points, the higher order methods usually will not be significantly superior to RK4(3), except for smooth vector fields sampled at high resolution. However, experience shows that they will never be significantly inferior either.

5 Selecting Streamlines

For the fast-LIC algorithm it is not only important to quickly compute single stream lines, but also to process the output image pixels in such an order that the total number of stream line computations is minimized. For instance it is not a good idea to process pixels in scanline order, because it would be quite probable that new stream lines hit pixels already being covered by other lines. Instead of looking for the optimal pixel to be processed next, we simply subdivide the image into smaller blocks, taking the first pixel of each block, then the second, and so on. With this method the number of computed stream lines is typically about 2% of the number of image pixels. It is possible to incorporate some more sophisticated schemes here like Sobol quasi-random sequences [17], which may be combined with methods for finding areas in the image not covered by stream lines so far.

To obtain an approximately equal stream line density in the image, we stop following an individual line after some distance Mh_t (cf. pseudocode in Sect. 3). Ideally, this length should be adjusted automatically. If lots of previously covered pixels are encountered, computation should be terminated. However, currently we are using a much simpler scheme which nevertheless works reasonably well. We use a fixed M until a certain percentage of pixels is hit. For the remaining pixels we simply compute a short stream line segment and the corresponding convolution integral, but do not traverse the stream line further. Usually a covering limit of 90% and a value Mh_t of about 50-100 pixel widths yield optimal run times, but these values are not that critical for overall performance.

A simple way to compensate for a non-optimal stream line selection strategy is to decrease the minimum number of hits required for

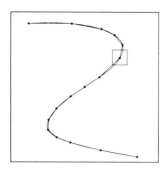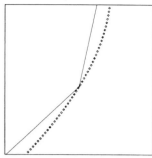

Figure 3: Distances between stream line points as returned by the adaptive numerical integrators are usually so large that cubic interpolation is necessary to track the path for texture sampling.

a pixel. Even with a low limit the total number of hits for each pixel may be large due to stream lines which are computed later. In fact, for all images in this paper we have taken a limit of only a single hit. Despite this low value, each pixel usually will be covered by several stream lines, as may be seen from Fig. 2.

6 Texture Map Convolution

The ODE solvers discussed in Sect. 4 are able to quickly compute long stream lines at guaranteed high accuracy. However, the actual step sizes used by these integrators are usually much bigger than the distance h_t needed for texture sampling. Therefore we have to interpolate between every two neighbouring locations returned by the ODE solver. The distance between these locations and the curvature of the stream line may easily take values that prohibit the use of a simple linear interpolation scheme. This is illustrated in Fig. 3. Average increments from 10 to 30 times the spacing of the $\boldsymbol{v}$-grid are quite common in practice.

A much better approximation of stream lines can be obtained using cubic Hermite-interpolation. This ensures that the first derivative at the boundaries of the interpolation interval is represented correctly. We need to evaluate the cubic interpolation polynomial at evenly spaced sample points only. Therefore forward differences can be employed for stream line tracking. After initialization, forward differences require just three additions per component to evaluate the polynomial, instead of three additions and three multiplications required by Horner's rule.

It should be noted that we do not necessarily need to keep interpolation separate from stream line integration. As an interesting alternative, so-called continous integration methods might be considered [7]. These methods use information gathered during integration to constitute an optimized interpolation polynomial, thereby providing dense output directly.

7 Periodic Motion Filters

LIC images can be animated by changing the shape and location of the filter kernel k over time. The apparent motion is well suited to envision vector field *direction* in addition to the pure tangential information contained in static images. In previous work [1] specially designed periodic filter kernels have been used to achieve a motion effect. On first sight it might appear difficult to combine texture animation with the fast-LIC algorithm, since the latter is restricted to constant filter kernels, i.e. box filters. However, this is not the case. In the following we will first introduce the notion of intensity correlation. We will then present a simple blending technique that keeps intensity correlation constant over time and thereby achieves high quality animations.

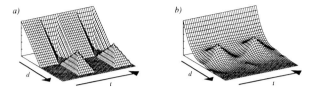

Figure 4: Intensity correlation between two points on a single stream line for different motion filter kernels: box filter (a) and Hanning filter (b). Two periods are shown in t-direction.

7.1 Intensity Correlation

Using box filters, an obvious method to animate LIC images is to cycle the boxes through some interval along the stream lines. If this is done with equal velocity for all pixels, a periodic sequence arises. Cycling a box filter can be easily accomplished with the fast-LIC algorithm. Essentially we just have to add some periodic offset function to the limits of the convolution sum in Eq. (5).

It turns out that this naive approach is not well suited for animation since noticeable artifacts are introduced when the boxes reenter the interval. To see this, consider two points p_1 and p_2 on a single stream line that are half a filter length apart. The corresponding pixel intensities initially have a 50% correlation because half of the texture cells being convolved are covered by both filter boxes. When the filter boxes reenter the interval, correlation suddenly drops to zero, as demonstrated in the following figure:

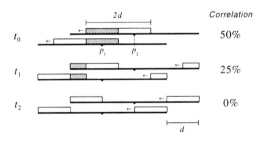

An intensity correlation function ξ measuring the amount of overlap between filter kernels k for two points separated by a distance d may be defined as

$$\xi(d, t) = \frac{\int \min(k(s, t), k(s + d, t)) \, ds}{\int k(s, t) \, ds} \qquad (11)$$

for each frame t. For a cycled box filter a plot of this function is shown in Fig. 4a. The length of the filter box was chosen to be 0.5 times the length of the interval. Reduced correlation results in a smaller feature size in the resulting LIC images. This is perceived as a disturbing artifact in animation. Note, that at the same time distant points temporarily become correlated.

To achieve a smoother motion Cabral and Leedom [1] suggested to employ a weighted filter kernel made up of two so-called Hanning filters. Correlation for their $n = 2$ filter is depicted in Fig. 4b. This function varies significantly less over time than the correlation for the cycled box filter. However, it cannot be used in conjunction with the fast-LIC algorithm. Fortunately, there is a simple method capable of generating periodic animation sequences that can be used in fast-LIC. With this method *no* artifacts at all occur due to reentering filter boxes.

7.2 Frame Blending

Consider an image sequence B_n, $n = 0, 1, ..., N-1$, with a filter box running along some stream line segment, but *not* reentering at the beginning. Obviously, such a sequence is not periodic anymore, but it will exhibit a constant intensity correlation over time. We have simply discarded all frames associated with the peaks in Fig. 4a. A periodic sequence A of length $N/2$ may be obtained by smoothly blending between phase-shifted B-frames, namely

$$A_n = w_1(n) \, B_{n \bmod N} + w_2(n) \, B_{(n + \frac{1}{2} N) \bmod N} \qquad (12)$$

with the weights w_1 and w_2 chosen as follows:

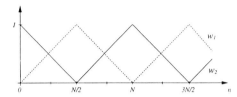

This means that frames get less and less weighted as their filter boxes get closer to the extreme positions. Whenever w_i equals one, the middle frame of B will be visible. For each pixel both intensity contributions are completely independent, provided that filter boxes do not overlap. In this case averaging multiple LIC images is statistically equivalent to computing the convolution integral from a modified input texture given as the weighted average of two textures distributed in the original way. While effective filter length L remains the same, averaging multiple frames causes the contrast of the resulting image to be reduced. This has to be compensated.

In raw LIC images intensity I of a single pixel usually is given by convolving a large number of independent texture cells. Therefore the central limit theorem of statistics applies and I can assumed to be gaussian distributed, that is

$$\psi(I) = \text{const.} \exp(-\frac{(I - \mu)^2}{2\sigma^2}). \qquad (13)$$

Here μ and σ^2 denote average and variance of the intensity distribution ψ, respectively. Any linear combination of independent gaussian distributed quantities will again be distributed gaussian. The resulting variance is given by $\sigma_{\text{res}}^2 = \sum w_i^2 \sigma_i^2$. Consequently, after averaging multiple LIC images of equal μ and σ^2, the original intensity distribution and therefore also contrast can be restored by a simple linear scaling,

$$I \leftarrow \frac{I - \mu}{\sqrt{w_1^2 + w_2^2}} + \mu. \qquad (14)$$

Figure 5 summarizes the process of frame blending and intensity rescaling. Note, that for Eq. (14) to be valid intensities need to be statistically independent. This is guaranteed if the filter boxes in the frames being averaged do not overlap, i.e. if filter length does not exceed 0.5 times the length of the interval. As an alternative we may also use two image sequences computed from completely different input textures. In this case a periodic sequence of length N would be obtained.

7.3 Variable Velocities

The simple blending technique described above comes to its real value when the texture is to be animated with *variable* velocities for each pixel. Such animations are useful to display not only vector direction and orientation, but also to give an impression of vector magnitude $|v|$.

For variable velocities the standard filter cycling approach will not yield periodic sequences anymore. Forsell [5] describes a technique for endlessly playing back a variable motion movie from a fixed number of pre-computed constant speed images. The final intensity for a pixel is computed by interpolating the pixel intensities

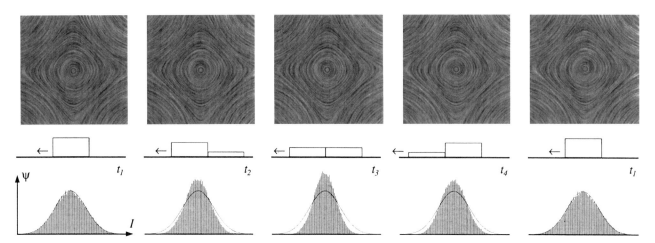

Figure 5: Snapshots from a periodic LIC animation obtained by frame blending. The first and the last image are identical. The figure contains a schematic view of the differently weighted filter boxes moving along the stream line. In the lower part intensity histograms of the blended images are shown. To keep contrast constant, intensity has to be rescaled to fit the original gaussian distribution.

from those two images, where the filter kernel phase approximately resembles the actual value. However, there still remains a major problem. With ongoing time, filter kernel phases for neighbouring pixels will lose any correlation. Drastic spatio-temporal aliasing effects are introduced. For example the texture may appear to move in the opposite direction in some areas.

To avoid these effects we build up a variable speed animation from only such frames, where the filter kernel phases are correlated. Correlated frames can be produced by letting filter boxes move some variable distance proportional to their velocity, as depicted in the following picture:

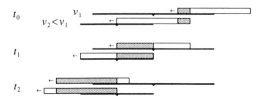

To generate a periodic sequence we would like to use the blending technique described above again. However, in general the intensities being averaged are not independent because filter boxes overlap in regions of low velocity. Therefore Eq. (14) is not valid anymore. It is also not a good idea to use two image sequences computed from different input textures. This would cause the LIC pattern to change over time in regions of low velocity. Although no flow would be perceived, blending between different patterns is somehow irritating. Instead, we have to rescale intensity *locally* according to the actual amount of filter box overlap. Overlap is inversely proportional to velocity and may be described by a number $u \in [0,1]$. An expression for the resulting local variance can be derived by splitting blended intensity into three independent contributions, one due to the overlapping part and two due to the non-overlapping parts of the individual boxes:

$$\sigma_{res}^2 = \left((w_1^2 + w_2^2)(1-u)^2 + u^2\right)\sigma^2. \qquad (15)$$

With this equation we are able to rescale intensity of every pixel so that the original σ^2 is restored. In this way a high quality animation sequence is obtained.

It should be noted that building up animation sequences from shifted box filter convolutions requires accurate stream line computation, because highly unsymmetric convolution ranges can occur. These will emphasize errors due to poor numerical integration.

For example, circular stream lines may be falsely depicted as spirals. Artifacts of this kind are usually disguised by a symmetric filter kernel [18, 1]. They do not occur if stream line integration is accurate.

8 Smooth Detail Enlargement

For many applications it is useful to adjust the size of a LIC input texture, so that a single texture cell is covered by lots of output image pixels. This can be easily accomplished with the fast-LIC algorithm. As before we are using Eq. (5) to compute the convolution integral for some initial point x_0. It is sufficient to sample the input texture at increments $h_t = 0.5$ times the width of a texture cell. However, when stepping along the stream line and updating the integral according to Eq. (6), we use a smaller step size in order to ensure that we hit as many pixels covered by the stream line as before. Of course, using a smaller step size means that the value of k in Eq. (6) has to be adjusted, too. The ability to choose the sizes of input texture and output image independently can be exploited in several ways.

First, in LIC images created from high frequency input textures, such as white noise, these high frequencies are retained in directions perpendicular to the field direction. This is caused by the one-dimensional nature of the filter kernel. The resulting images often look quite busy. Problems arise if the images are to be processed by lower bandwidth filters like video tape recorders or image compression algorithms. The usual remedy is to use a low-pass filtered input texture or to blur the final LIC images afterwards. With our algorithm convolutions over long distances L can easily be computed. Therefore a better approach is to simply scale up the size of a texture cell as well as convolution length L in terms of pixel width.

With traditional LIC it is hard to generate exactly the same image at different resolutions. It would require to use both a resampled input texture as well as a resampled vector field. This approach is tedious and will unnecessarily introduce errors. However, often it is important to create several versions of a single image at different resolutions, e.g. adopted to various output devices, or for use in animations that require distance dependent texture resolution. This can be easily accomplished with fast-LIC since the size of the output image can be chosen independently of vector field resolution and the input texture.

A slightly different utilization of this feature is the computation of smooth zooms into the vector data field to enlarge interesting details. As an example some close-ups of details in a vector field are

Figure 6: Details of a vector field displayed at different magnification factors (1, 3, 15, 100). For each frame a completely new LIC image has been computed. The data set had a resolution of 500^2. At the finest level only a few grid points are covered.

	L	LIC	RK	CK	DP
Hyperthermia 400 × 600	10	12.26	**3.36**	3.65	3.55
	20	21.93	**3.75**	4.15	3.99
	40	41.36	**4.60**	5.20	4.88
Dipole 500 × 500	10	18.35	4.35	4.41	**4.31**
	20	34.29	4.78	4.81	**4.60**
	40	71.14	5.61	5.61	**5.39**
Cylinder 600 × 200	10	7.76	**1.49**	1.54	1.57
	20	14.44	**1.62**	1.65	1.70
	40	27.01	**1.92**	1.99	2.00

Table 1: Performance of the original LIC algorithm compared to the new algorithm equipped with different numerical integrators: RK = adaptive Runge-Kutta scheme RK4(3), CK = Cash and Karp, DP = Dormand and Prince (cf. Sect. 4). The boldface entry gives the shortest time in each row.

shown in Fig. 6, where linear magnification extends up to a factor 100. If the zoom is to be played back in a sequence, care has to be taken for low magnification factors. If stream line integration is unconditionally started at the center of output image pixels, then in each frame slightly different stream lines are computed. This causes annoying variations in texture to occur from frame to frame. One solution would be to increase the minimal number of hits required for a pixel. Another more robust method is to try exactly the same stream lines used in the previous frame first. For these lines the starting point will not correspond to the center of an output image pixel anymore. Remaining pixels are treated as usual afterwards. This method yields smooth animation sequences, allowing one to compute striking trips into details.

9 Results

We have implemented the fast-LIC algorithm in the C++ programming language within the framework of the modular visualization environment *IRIS Explorer*. Within this system it is possible to pre-process the vector field as well as to post-process the resulting LIC images in various ways. We have found it especially useful to apply a directional gradient filter to the raw LIC images to further emphasize directional information. Another useful method is to multiply color into the images to simultaneously visualize a scalar quantity in addition to vector field orientation. The images in Fig. 1, 7, and 8 were post-processed in this way.

The data shown in Fig. 1 comes from so-called hyperthermia simulation, a form of cancer therapy based upon radiating radio waves into the human hip region. In Fig. 7 electrical field lines irradiated by a dipole antenna are depicted. This image has to be compared with Fig. 6a. In both cases the same vector field is shown. However, after gradient filtering and coloring, the image looks much more attractive. In Fig. 8 a snapshot from the simulation of an instationary fluid flow around a cylinder is shown. Finally, Fig. 9 presents an application of LIC in modern art.

Table 1 summarizes some execution times of fast-LIC compared to the original LIC algorithm of Cabral and Leedom. The numbers, obtained on a SGI Indigo[2] with 150 MHz MIPS R4400, are in seconds. They refer to the vector fields shown in Fig. 1, 7 and 8, but do not take into account computing time for gradient filtering and coloring. For better comparision with the original algorithm the dimensions of input texture, vector field, and resulting image were chosen to be equal. The actual sizes are indicated in the table. L is the extent of the convolution integral in one direction. The table contains different columns for various numerical integrators we have implemented. These integrators do not differ much in performance. Usually only about 25% of the time is spent in stream line integration. Most time is spent in texture sampling. For the hyperthermia data set, fast-LIC performs somewhat worse than in the other examples. This is caused by the discontinuities in the vector field, forcing the adaptive integrators to choose very small step sizes across the boundaries. The higher order methods are more affected by this than RK4(3).

10 Conclusion

We have introduced a new line integral convolution algorithm that performs an order of magnitude faster than previous methods. A feature of our method is the ability to compute images at arbitrary resolution. We presented methods for producing high quality texture animation sequences, employing constant filter kernels only.

The new techniques have particular significance for computer graphics. They are useful for fast procedural generation of textures with directional features and of texture sequences with continously variable spatial resolutions. The production of such sequences is of growing interest in computer animation, where several versions of a texture with different spatial resolutions are often needed for different views or output media.

There are a number of directions for future research. We intend to investigate the visualization of time varying and three-dimensional vector fields. The inclusion of visual representations of global and local vector field characteristics other than flow lines is also an interesting topic that deserves further investigation.

Finally there is room for considerable further research work with respect to computer animation, e.g. concerning the production of hierarchies of directional textures with different spatial resolutions, or new methods for synthesizing vector fields from images to autoconvolve them. This may lead to a new class of directional filters for image processing.

Acknowledgements

We would like to thank Charlie Gunn, Roland Wunderling, and Gerhard Zumbusch for reviewing the manuscript and for various helpful discussions. We are also grateful to the anonymous reviewers of this paper for their valueable remarks, and to Brian Cabral and Casey Leedom for making their code available on the net.

References

[1] Brian Cabral and Leith (Casey) Leedom. Imaging vector fields using line integral convolution. Proc. of SIGGRAPH '93 (Anaheim, California, August 1-6, 1993). In *Computer Graphics* 27, Annual Conference Series, 1993, ACM SIGGRAPH, pp. 263–272.

[2] J. R. Cash and Alan H. Karp. A variable order Runge-Kutta method for initial value problems with rapidly varying right-hand sides. *ACM transactions on Mathematical Software* 16, pp. 201–222, 1990.

[3] Peter Deuflhard and Folkmar Bornemann. *Numerische Mathematik II: Integration gewöhnlicher Differentialgleichungen.* Verlag de Gruyter, Berlin, 1994.

[4] J. R. Dormand and P. J. Prince. Higher order embedded Runge-Kutta formulae. *J. Comp. Appl. Math.*, 7, pp. 67–75, 1981.

[5] Lisa K. Forssell. Visualizing flow over curvilinear grid surfaces using line integral convolution. In Proc. of *Visualization '94*, (Washington, D.C., Oct. 17-21, 1994), pp. 240–247, IEEE Computer Society, 1994.

[6] Paul E. Haeberli. Paint by numbers: Abstract image representations. Proc. of SIGGRAPH '90 (Dallas, Texas, August 6-10, 1990). In *Computer Graphics*, 24(4) (August 1991), pp. 207–214.

[7] Ernst Hairer, Syvert Paul Nørsett, and Gerhard Wanner. *Solving Ordinary Differential Equations I, Nonstiff Problems.* Springer Verlag, Berlin, Heidelberg, New York, Tokyo, 1987.

[8] James L. Helman and Lambertus Hesselink. Visualizing vector field topology in fluid flows. *IEEE Computer Graphics and Applications*, 11(3), pp. 36–46, May 1991.

[9] Andrea J. S. Hin and Frits H. Post. Visualization of turbulent flow with particles. In Proc. of *Visualization '93* (San Jose, California, October 25-29, 1993), pp. 46–52, IEEE Computer Society, 1993.

[10] Jeff P. M. Hultquist. Interactive numerical flow visualization using stream Surfaces. *Computing Systems in Engineering*, 1(2-4), pp. 349–353, 1990.

[11] Kwan-Liu Ma and Philip J. Smith. Virtual smoke: An interactive 3d flow visualization technique. In Proc. of *Visualization '92* (Boston, MA, October 19-23, 1992), pp. 46–52, IEEE Computer Society, 1992.

[12] Gordon D. Mallinson. The calculation of the lines of a three-dimensional vector field. In Proc. of the International Symposium on *Computational Fluid Dynamics* (Sydney, Australia, August 1987), pp. 525–534, North-Holland, August 1988.

[13] Jerrold E. Marsden and Anthony J. Tromba. *Vector Calculus.* W. H. Freeman, New York, 3rd edition, 1988.

[14] Nelson Max, Barry Becker, and Roger Crawfis. Flow volumes for interactive vector field visualization. In Proc. of *Visualization '93* (San Jose, CA, Oct. 25-29, 1993), pp. 19–24, IEEE Computer Society, 1993.

[15] Nancy J. Nersessian. Faraday's field concept. In D. Gooding and F. A. J. L. James, eds., *Faraday Rediscovered: Essays on the Live and Work of Michael Faraday*, pp. 175–187. Stockton Press, New York, 1985.

[16] Ken Perlin. An image synthesizer. Proc. of SIGGRAPH '85 (San Francisco, California, July 22–26, 1985). In *Computer Graphics* 19, pp. 287–296, 1985.

[17] William H. Press, Saul A. Teukolsky, William T. Vetterling, and Brian P. Flannery. *Numerical Recipes in C: The Art of Scientific Computing.* Cambridge University Press, Cambridge, 2nd edition, 1992.

[18] Jarke J. van Wijk. Spot noise-texture synthesis for data visualization. Proc. of SIGGRAPH '91 (Las Vegas, Nevada, 28 July - 2 August, 1991). In *Computer Graphics*, 25, pp. 309–318, 1991.

[19] Jarke J. van Wijk. Rendering surface-particles. In Proc. of *Visualization '92* (Boston, Massachusetts, October 19-23, 1992), pp. 54–61, IEEE Computer Society, 1992.

Figure 7: Field of an irradiating dipole antenna. The same data as in Fig. 6 is shown. Field strength is indicated by color. Note, how gradient filtering and coloring emphasize the vector field structure.

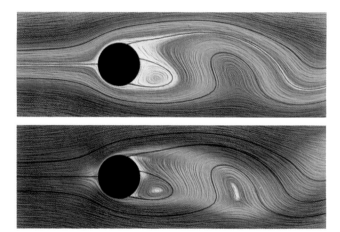

Figure 8: Flow around a cylinder. Color depicts the value of stream function (upper) and magnitude of velocity (lower). In the lower image directional information still is clearly visible, although color does not correspond to stream line shape.

Figure 9: LIC-based variations on a painting of Henri Matisse.

Correction of Geometric Perceptual Distortions in Pictures.

Denis Zorin, Alan H. Barr

California Institute of Technology, Pasadena, CA 91125

Abstract

We suggest an approach for correcting several types of perceived geometric distortions in computer-generated and photographic images. The approach is based on a mathematical formalization of desirable properties of pictures.

From a small set of simple assumptions we obtain perceptually preferable viewing transformations and show that these transformations can be decomposed into a perspective or parallel projection followed by a planar transformation. The decomposition is easily implemented and provides a convenient framework for further analysis of the image mapping.

We prove that two perceptually important properties are incompatible and cannot be satisfied simultaneously. It is impossible to construct a viewing transformation such that the images of all lines are straight and the images of all spheres are exact circles. Perceptually preferable tradeoffs between these two types of distortions can depend on the content of the picture. We construct parametric families of transformations with parameters representing the relative importance of the perceptual characteristics. By adjusting the settings of the parameters we can minimize the overall distortion of the picture.

It turns out that a simple family of transformations produces results that are sufficiently close to optimal. We implement the proposed transformations and apply them to computer-generated and photographic perspective projection images. Our transformations can considerably reduce distortion in wide-angle motion pictures and computer-generated animations.

Keywords: Perception, distortion, viewing transformations, perspective.

1 Introduction

The process of realistic image synthesis can be subdivided into two stages: modeling the physics of light propagation in three-dimensional environments and projecting the geometry of three-dimensional space into the picture plane (the "viewing transformation.") While the first stage is relatively independent of our understanding of visual perception, the viewing transformations are based on the fact that we are able to perceive two-dimensional patterns - pictures - as reasonably accurate representations of three-dimensional objects. We can evaluate the quality of modeling the propagation of light objectively, by comparing calculated photometric values with experimental measurements. For viewing transformations the quality is much more subjective.

Permission to make digital/hard copy of part or all of this work for personal or classroom use is granted without fee provided that copies are not made or distributed for profit or commercial advantage, the copyright notice, the title of the publication and its date appear, and notice is given that copying is by permission of ACM, Inc. To copy otherwise, to republish, to post on servers, or to redistribute to lists, requires prior specific permission and/or a fee.

a.

b.

Figure 1. a. Wide-angle pinhole photograph taken on the roof of the Church of St. Ignatzio in Rome, classical example of perspective distortions from [Pir70]; reprinted with the permission of Cambridge University Press. b. Corrected version of the picture with transformation applied.

The perspective projection [1] is the viewing transformation that has been primarily used for producing realistic images, in art, photography and in computer graphics.

One motivation for using perspective projection in computer

---

[1] By perspective projection or *linear perspective* we mean either central projection or parallel projection into a plane.

graphics is the idea of *photorealism*: since photographic images have one of the highest degrees of realism that we can achieve, perhaps realistic rendering should model the photographic process.

But the intuitive concept of realism in many cases differs from photorealism: photographic images, are often perceived as distorted (note the shape of the sphere in Fig. 1a.) On the other hand, some paintings, while using perspective projection, contain considerable deviations from it (Fig. 2). These paintings, however, are perceptually correct and realistic.

In this paper we derive viewing transformations from some basic principles of perception of pictures rather than by modeling a particular physical process of picture generation. Our approach is based on formalizations of desirable perceptual properties of pictures as mathematical restrictions on viewing transformations.

The main result (Section 5.1) allows us to construct usable families of transformations; it is a decomposition theorem which states that under some assumptions, any perceptually acceptable picture-independent viewing transformation can be decomposed into a perspective or parallel projection and a two-dimensional transformation.

Figure 2. "School of Athens" by Rafael. (©1994-95 Christus Rex, reproduced by permission) It is possible to reconstruct the center of projection from the architectural details. The calculated image of the sphere in the right part of the picture is an ellipse with aspect ratio 1:1.2, while the painting is a perfect circle.

Our approach allows us to achieve several goals:

- We construct new viewing transformations that reduce distortions that appear in perspective projection images. It turns out that some of these transformations can be implemented as a postprocessing stage (Equation 1 , pseudocode in Section 7) after perspective projection and can be applied to existing images and photos (Figs. 1,7,8,9,10.)
- We provide a basis for understanding limitations of two-dimensional images of three-dimensional space; certain perceptual distortions can be eliminated only at the expense of increasing other distortions.
- Our transformation works well in animations and movies.
- Our families of transformations can be modified or extended by adding or removing auxiliary perceptual requirements; this provides a general basis for constructing pictures with desirable perceptual properties.

The transformations that we propose may have a number of

applications: creation of computer-generated wide-angle pictures and wide-angle animations with reduced distortion, and correction of photographic images and movies.

Related Work Considerable data on picture perception have been accumulated by experimental psychologists; overviews can be found in [Kub86], [Hag80]. Computer graphics was influenced by the study of human vision in many ways: for example, RGB color representation is based on the trichromatic theory of color perception and anti-aliasing is based on various observations in visual perception.

Principles of the perception of color have been applied to computer graphics [TR93]. A curvilinear perspective system based on experimental data is described in [Rau86].

Limitations of perspective projection are well known in art and photography. [Gla94] mentions the limitations of linear perspective.

As far as we know, this paper is the first attempt to apply perceptual principles to the analysis and construction of viewing transformations in computer graphics.

Outline of the Paper. The paper is organized as follows:[2] In Section 2 we discuss the properties of linear perspective, in Section 3 we formulate our assumptions about perception of pictures and formulate some desirable properties. Section 4 describes some restrictions that we have to impose on the viewing transformation to make it practical. In Section 5.1 we discuss the decomposition theorem for viewing transformations. In Section 5.3 we discuss construction of the 2D component of decomposition,

Section 6 describes a perceptual basis for the choice of the projection component of the decomposition of viewing transformation.

In Section 7 we discuss the implementation issues and we propose some applications of our methods.

Sketches of mathematical proofs can be found in appendices in the CD-ROM version of the paper and in [Zor95].

2 Analysis of linear perspective.

The theory of linear perspective is based on the following construction (Fig. 3). Suppose the eye of an observer is located at the point O. Then, the image on the retina of his eye is created by the rays reflected from the objects in the direction of point O. If we put a plane between the observer and the scene, and paint each point on the plane with the color of the ray of light going into O and crossing the plane at this point, the image on the retina will be indistinguishable from the real scene.

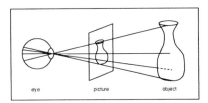

Figure 3. Pictures can produce the same retinal projection as a real object

The above argument contains some important assumptions:

- the observer looks at the scene with one eye, (or is located far enough from the image plane to consider the images in both eyes identical);
- when we look at the picture, the position of the eye coincides with the position of the eye or camera when the picture was made.

In fact, both assumptions for linear perspective are almost never true. We can look at a picture from various distances and directions

---

[2]The reader who is interested primarily in the implementation can go directly to Equation 1 in Section 5.3 and pseudocode in Section 7

with both eyes, but our perception of the picture doesn't change much in most cases [Hag76]. This property of pictures makes them different from illusions: while stereograms of all kinds should be observed from a particular point, traditional pictures are relatively insensitive to the changes in the viewing point. As the assumptions are not always true, it is not clear why perspective projection should be the preferred method of mapping the three-dimensional space into the plane.

In many cases we observe that perspective projection produces pictures with apparent distortions of shape and size of objects, such as distortions of shape in the margins (Figs. 1,7,8,9,10). These distortions are significantly amplified in animations and movies, resulting in shape changes of rigid bodies.

Leonardo's rule. The fact that linear perspective doesn't always produce pictures that look right was known to painters a long time ago. Leonardo da Vinci [dV70] formulated a rule which said that the best distance for depicting an object is about twenty times the size of the object. It is well-known in photography that in order to make a good portrait the camera should be placed far enough away from the object. In many paintings we can observe considerable deviations from linear perspective which in fact improve their appearance (Fig. 2.)

We conclude that there are a number of reasons to believe that linear perspective is not the only way to create realistic pictures.

3 Properties of pictures.

In this section we will describe our main assumptions about the nature of picture perception and specify the requirements that we will use in our constructions. A more detailed exposition can be found in [Zor95].

Structural features. We believe the that the features of images that are most essential for good representation are the *structural features* such as dimension (whether the image of an object is a point, a curve or an area) and presence or absence of holes or self-intersections in the image. The presence or absence of these features can be determined unambiguously.

Most of the visual information that is available to the brain is contained in the images formed on the retina. We will postulate the following general requirement, which will define our concept of realistic pictures: *The retinal projections of a two-dimensional image of an object should not contain any structural features that are not present in any retinal projection of the object itself.* Structural properties of retinal images are identical to the properties of the projections into an arbitrarily chosen plane [Zor95]; our requirement can be restated in more intuitive form:

> A two-dimensional image of an object should have only structural features that are present in some planar projection of the object.

We can identify many examples of structural requirements: the image of a convex object without holes should not have holes in it, the image of a connected object cannot be disconnected, images of two intersecting objects should intersect etc. We choose a set of three structural requirements that we will use to prove the decomposition theorem in Section 5.1.

Figure 4. Mappings forbidden by structural conditions 2 and 3

1. The image of a surface should not be a point.
2. The image of a part of a straight line either shouldn't have self-intersections ("loops") or else should be a point (Fig. 4).

3. The image of a plane shouldn't have "twists" in it. This means that either each point of the plane is projected to a different point in the image, or the whole plane is projected onto a curve (Fig. 4).

We will call these conditions *structural conditions 1, 2 and 3.* Note that these requirements are quite weak: we don't require that features of some particular planar projection are represented; we just don't want to see the features that are not present in *any* projection.

Desirable properties. Next, we formulate some requirements that are not as essential as the structural ones; the corresponding features of the images can be varied continuously and can be changed within some intervals of tolerance. Examples of such features include relative sizes of objects, angles between lines, verticality. We will refer to these properties as "desirable properties." We will use two of them which we consider to be the most important. One of the most restrictive desirable properties is the following one:

Zero-curvature condition. *Images of straight lines should be straight.*

Note that this is different from the structural requirement 2 above, which is weaker. However, as we can judge straightness of lines only with some finite precision, some deviations from this property can be tolerated.

Another requirement is based on the following observation: the images of objects in the center of the picture never look distorted, given that the distance to the center of projection is large compared to the size of the object (Leonardo's rule). We will call perspective projections into the plane perpendicular to the line connecting the center of projection with the object *direct view projections.* Then the requirement eliminating distortions of shape can be stated as follows:

Direct view condition *Objects in the image should look as if they are viewed directly – as they appear in the middle of a photograph.*

Unfortunately, as we will see later, the two properties formulated above cannot be satisfied exactly at the same time.

We found several other requirements (foreshortening of objects, relative size of objects, verticality) to be of importance, but having much larger tolerance intervals. We will discuss their significance in Section 7.

4 Technical requirements

To narrow down the area of search for perceptually acceptable viewing transformations we are going to specify several additional technical requirements. They don't have any perceptual basis and are quite restrictive; however, they make the task of constructing viewing transformations manageable and the resulting transformation can be applied to a wide class of images.

1. We need a parametric family of viewing transformations so that an appropriate one can be chosen for each image.
2. The number of parameters should be small, and they must have a clear intuitive meaning.
3. The mapping must be sufficiently universal and should not depend on the details of the scene too much.

5 Derivation of viewing transformations

In the following sections we formalize the perceptual and technical conditions that were stated above and use them to prove that any viewing transformation that satisfies the structural conditions and technical conditions for any image can be implemented as a perspective projection and subsequent transformation of the picture plane. We show that direct view and zero curvature properties cannot be exactly satisfied simultaneously. We introduce quantitative measures of corresponding distortions and describe a simple parametrized family of transformations (Equation 1) where values of parameters correspond to the tradeoff between the two types of distortion. This family of transformation is close to optimal in a sense described in Section 5.3 and is easy to implement (Section 7).

5.1 General structure of viewing transformations

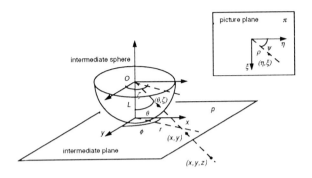

Figure 5. Coordinate systems

In this section we present a decomposition theorem derived from structural conditions 1 -3 (Section 3) and technical requirements of the previous section. The seemingly weak structural conditions 1-3 turn out to be quite restrictive if we want to construct image mappings that don't depend on the details of any particular picture, specifically, on the presence of lines or planes in any particular point of the depicted scene.

Applicaton of these requirements to *all* possible lines and planes allows us to prove that the viewing transformation with no "twists" in the images of planes and no "loops" or "folds" in the images of lines should be a composition of perspective or parallel projection and a one-to-one transformation of the plane.

In order to formulate the precise result let's introduce some definitions and notation:

We will use $x, y, ..$ for the points in the domain of a viewing transformation (a volume in 3D space), and $\xi, \psi...$ for the points in the range (a point in the picture plane).

By a *line segment* we mean any connected subset of a line.

A viewing transformation maps many points in space to the same point in the picture plane:

Definition 1 *The set of all points of the domain of a mapping that map to a fixed point ξ is called the* **fiber** *of the mapping at the point ξ.*

In our case, fibers typically are curves in space that are mapped into single points in the picture plane.

Consider a viewing transformation which is a continuous mapping P of a region of space to the picture plane, more particularly, of an open path-connected domain $V \subset \mathbf{R}^3$ to an open subset of $\mathbf{R}^2$, satisfying the following formalizations of structural conditions:

1. The mapping of any line l to its image $P(l)$ is one-to-one everywhere or it is a point.
   This condition prevents "loops" in the images of lines. It is more restrictive: it doesn't allow not only "loops" but also "folds", that is, situations when almost any point in $P(l)$ is the image of at least two points of l.
2. The dimension of the fiber dim $P^{-1}(\xi) = 1$ for all ξ in the range of P, and all the fibers are path-connected.
   This condition prevents mapping of regions of space to single points and continuous regions to discontinuous images.
3. the mapping of a subset of a plane m to the image $P(m)$ is one-to-one everywhere or nowhere.
   This condition prevents "twists" in the images of planes.

Then our theorem can be stated as follows:

Theorem 1 *For any viewing transformation P, satisfying the conditions above, there is a perspective projection Π such that the fibers of P are subsets of fibers of Π.*

An outline of the proof is given in Appendix A.

Our practical applications are based on the following corollary:

Corollary 1 *Let a viewing transformation P satisfy the assumptions of Theorem 1 and Π be the corresponding perspective projection. If Π is a central projection, assume, in addition, that the region V lies entirely in one half-space with respect to a plane going through the center of Π. Then P can be decomposed in two ways:*

– as a composition of a perspective projection Π_{plane} into a plane followed by a transformation T_{plane} of the plane ,

– as a projection into a sphere Π_{sphere} followed by one-to-one mapping T_{sphere} of the sphere into the picture plane .

It is not true that any picture satisfying only structural conditions (without additional technical requirements) should be generated with an image mapping which has this particular decomposition, because for a particular scene the structural conditions have to be satisfied only by the objects that are actually present in it. It also should be noted that our theorem is an example of a large number of statements that can be proven given some specific choice of structural conditions. We believe that our choice is reasonable for many situations, but it is quite possible that there are cases when least restrictive requirements are sufficient and larger families of transformations can be considered.

While the choice of possible viewing transformations is considerably restricted by this theorem, there are still several degrees of freedom left:

- 2D mappings T_{plane} and T_{sphere} can be any continuous mappings.
- We can choose the center of projection for the first part of the decomposition; it is important to note that the theorem places no restrictions on the position of this center. For example, in an office scene it can be located outside the room, which is impossible for physical cameras.
- If we can split our scene into several disconnected domains (for example, foreground and background), the viewing transformation can be chosen independently for each connected part of the scene. However, separation of the space into several path connected domains introduces dependence of the transformation on the scene.

In the next sections we will consider how we can use these degrees of freedom to minimize the perceptual distortions.

5.2 Formalization of desirable conditions

In this section we formalize the conditions listed in Section 5.1, to apply them to the construction of viewing transformations. We will find error functions for both conditions that can be used as a local measure of distortion and error functionals that measure the global distortion for the whole picture.

Let's establish some notation for the viewing transformations that satisfy the conditions of the theorem.

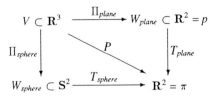

We will consider viewing transformations $P : V \subset \mathbf{R}^3 \to \mathbf{R}^2$, from an open connected domain V into the *picture plane* π, which are compositions of the projection Π_{plane} from the center O into the *intermediate plane p* and a mapping $T_{plane} : W_{plane} \subset \mathbf{R}^2 \rightarrow \mathbf{R}^2$, $W_{plane} = \Pi_{plane}(V)$, We can choose the plane p so that that the distance from O to the plane is L.

P can be also represented as a composition of central projection from O into the sphere of radius L with center at O (*intermediate sphere*) $\Pi_{sphere} : V \subset \mathbf{R}^3 \rightarrow \mathbf{S}^2$ and some mapping $T_{sphere} : W_{sphere} \subset \mathbf{S}^2 \rightarrow \mathbf{R}^2$, $W_{sphere} = \Pi_{sphere}(V)$, We will assume that the image of V in the sphere belongs to a hemisphere.

Let's introduce rectangular coordinates (x,y) and polar coordinates (r, ϕ) on the plane p; rectangular coordinates (η, ξ) and polar coordinates (ρ, ψ) in the plane π. On the sphere we will choose angular coordinate system (θ, ζ), and local coordinates in the neighborhood of a fixed point (θ_0, ζ_0): $u = L(\theta - \theta_0), v = L(\zeta - \zeta_0) \sin \theta_0$ (Fig. 5).

The correspondence between T_{plane} and T_{sphere} is given by the mapping $\mathbf{S}^2 \rightarrow \mathbf{R}^2$: $\phi = \zeta, r = \tan \theta$.

Curvature error function Formally the restriction on images of line segments from section 3 can be expressed as follows:

Images of line segments should have zero curvature at each point.

We will call this requirement the *zero-curvature condition*. Curvature of the image of a line at a fixed point gives us a measure of how well the viewing transformation satisfies the zero-curvature condition.

If we consider the decomposition of $P = T_{plane} \circ \Pi_{plane}$, we can observe that Π_{plane} satisfies the zero-curvature condition. Therefore, we have to consider only the mapping T_{plane}. We will denote components of $T_{plane}(x, y)$, which is a point in the picture plane, by $(\eta(x, y), \xi(x, y)$

The curvature depends not only on the point but also on the direction of the line, whose image we are considering. As an error function for the zero-curvature condition at a point x we will use an estimate of the maximum curvature of the image of a line going through x.

It can be shown (see Appendix B on CD-ROM, [Zor95]) that the curvature

$$|\kappa| \leq \frac{\sqrt{|\eta_{xx}|^2 + |\eta_{yy}|^2 + 2|\eta_{xy}|^2 + |\xi_{xx}|^2 + |\xi_{yy}|^2 + 2|\xi_{xy}|^2}}{\frac{1}{2}((A + C) - \sqrt{(A - C)^2 + 4B^2})}$$

where $A = (\eta_x)^2 + (\xi_x)^2$, $B = \eta_x \eta_y + \xi_x \xi_y$, $C = (\eta_y)^2 + (\xi_y)^2$. We use a characteristic size of $T_{plane}(W)$ (corresponding to the size of the picture for perspective projection) R_0 as a scaling coefficient to obtain a dimensionless error-function. We also use the square of the curvature estimate to make the expression simpler:

$$K(T_{plane}, x, y) = R_0^2 \frac{|\eta_{xx}|^2 + |\eta_{yy}|^2 + 2|\eta_{xy}|^2 + |\xi_{xx}|^2 + |\xi_{yy}|^2 + 2|\xi_{xy}|^2}{\frac{1}{4}\left((A + C) - \sqrt{(A - C)^2 + 4B^2}\right)^2}$$

If we set $K(T_{plane}, x, y) = 0$, we can see that the all the second derivatives of η and ξ should be equal to zero, therefore, T_{plane} should be a linear transformation. This coincides with the fundamental theorem of affine geometry which says that the only transformations of the plane which map lines into lines are linear transformations.

Direct view error function. In order to formalize the direct view condition we consider mappings which are locally equivalent to direct projection as defined in Section 3. We can observe that the projection onto the sphere is locally a direct projection. Therefore, if we use the decomposition $P = T_{sphere} \circ \Pi_{sphere}$ we have to construct the mapping T_{sphere} which is locally is as close to a similarity mapping as possible. Formally, it means that the differential of the mapping T_{sphere}, which maps the tangent plane of the sphere at each point x to the plane $T_{f(x)}\mathbf{R}^2 = \mathbf{R}^2$ coinciding with the picture plane π at the point $f(x)$, should be close to a similarity mapping. The differential $DT_{f(x)}$ can be represented by the Jacobian matrix J of the mapping T_{sphere} at the point x. A nondegenerate linear transforma-

tion J is a similarity transformation if and only if $|Jw|/|w|$ doesn't depend on w.

If this ratio depends on w, then we define the direct view error function to be

$$D(T_{sphere}, \theta, \zeta) = \left|\max\left(\frac{|Jw|^2}{|w|^2}\right) / \min\left(\frac{|Jw|^2}{|w|^2}\right) - 1\right|$$

can be used as the measure of "non-directness" of the transformation at the point (for more detailed discussion see [Zor95].).

It can be shown (see Appendix B on CD-ROM, [Zor95]) that

$$D(T_{sphere}, \theta, \zeta) = \frac{(E + G) - \sqrt{(E - G)^2 + 4F^2}}{(E + G) + \sqrt{(E - G)^2 + 4F^2}} - 1$$

where $E = (\eta_u)^2 + (\xi_u)^2$, $F = \eta_u \eta_v + \xi_u \xi_v$, $G = (\eta_v)^2 + (\xi_v)^2$.

Using the correspondence between intermediate sphere and plane we can write D as a function of T_{plane}, x and y.

Global Error functionals We want to be able to characterize the global error for each of the two perceptual requirements. We can use a norm of the error functions D and K as a measure of the global error. The choice of the norm can be different: the L^1-norm corresponds to the average error, the *sup*-norm corresponds to the maximal local error. In the first case, the error functionals are defined as

$$\mathcal{K}[T_{plane}] = \iint_W K(T_{plane}, x, y) dx dy,$$

$$\mathcal{D}[T_{plane}] = \iint_W D(T_{plane}, x, y) dx dy.$$

In the second case,

$$\mathcal{K}[T_{plane}] = \max_{(x,y) \in W} K(T_{plane}, x, y) \qquad \mathcal{D}[T_{plane}] = \max_{(x,y) \in W} D(T_{plane}, x, y)$$

5.3 2D Transformation

We are going to use the error functionals defined in Section 5.2 to construct families of transformations by solving an optimization problem. We consider only the 2D part of the decomposition of viewing transformation assuming that the perspective projection is fixed. Structural conditions suggest only that it be continuous and one-to-one.

Optimization problem. The error functionals defined above depend on the domain W_{plane} and the planar transformation T_{plane}. The first parameter is defined by the projection part of the viewing transformation, so we will assume it to be fixed now. In this case, functions satisfying $\mathcal{K}[T_{plane}] = 0$ are linear functions and the only functions satisfying $\mathcal{D}[T_{plane}] = 0$ are those derived from conformal mappings of the sphere onto the plane. Unfortunately, these two classes of functions don't intersect.

In this case for a given level μ for either error functional $\mathcal{K}$ or $\mathcal{D}$ we minimize the level of the other. The corresponding optimization problems are

$$\mathcal{K}[T_{plane}] = \min, \mathcal{D}[T_{plane}] = \mu \quad \text{or} \quad \mathcal{K}[T_{plane}] = \mu, \mathcal{D}[T_{plane}] = \min$$

These optimization problems are equivalent and can be reduced [Zor95]. to an unconstrained optimization problem for the functional $\mathcal{F}[T_{plane}] = \mu \mathcal{K}[T_{plane}] + (1 - \mu)\mathcal{D}[T_{plane}])$, where μ represents the desired tradeoff between two functionals: for $\mu = 0$ we completely ignore the zero-curvature condition, for $\mu = 1$ the direct view condition.

We also have to specify the boundary conditions in order to make the problem well-defined. This can be done by fixing the frame of the picture, that is, the values of T_{plane} on the boundary of W_{plane}.

We will consider solutions of this optimization problem in the next section.

Error functions for transformations with central symmetry From now on we will restrict our attention to transformations that also have central symmetry. This assumption allows distribution of the error evenly in all directions in the picture. The advantage of this additional restriction is a considerable simplification of the problem. The disadvantage is that real pictures seldom have this type of symmetry and, therefore, non-symmetric transformation might result in better images. We will discuss a way to create nonsymmetric transformations in Section 5.4.

In polar coordinates transformation T_{plane} can be written as $\rho = \rho(r)$ $\psi = \phi$. In this case we get the following simplified expressions for the error functions

$$K(\rho, r) = R_0^2 \frac{\frac{3}{r^2}\left(\frac{\rho}{r} - \rho'\right)^2 + \rho'^2}{\min\left(\frac{\rho^2}{r^2}, \rho'^2\right)^2}$$

$$D(\rho, r) = \frac{\max(\rho'^2(1 + r^2)^2, \rho^2(1 + \frac{1}{r^2}))}{\min(\rho'^2(1 + r^2)^2, \rho^2(1 + \frac{1}{r^2}))} - 1$$

We note that in both cases the dependence on the angular coordinate completely disappeared, so now the problem is one-dimensional. We did not use symmetry in our derivation for the general expression for $\mathcal{K}$; absence of dependence on the angle in the formulae above suggests that our bounds are quite tight.

In order for the problem to have a solution, the boundary conditions should have the same type of symmetry. We can take V to be the cone with angle at the apex θ_0. In this case $W = \Pi(V)$ will be a circle of radius $R = L \tan \theta_0$. The corresponding boundary conditions are $\rho(R) = 1$, $\rho(0) = 0$ (from continuity). Here we assume that the radius of the picture $P(V)$, corresponding to R_0 in Section 5.2, is 1.

Now there are unique functions ρ satisfying $K = 0$ or $D = 0$. For K it is obvious: $\rho_K = r/R$. For D it is $\rho_D(r) = \rho_{1D}(r)/\rho_{1D}(R)$, where $\rho_{1D}(r) = \sqrt{r^2 + 1} - 1/r$.

The solutions of the optimization problem will form a parametric family $\rho(\mu, r)$ and $\rho(0, r) = \rho_D(r)$, $\rho(1, r) = \rho_K(r)$.

We consider solutions for the *sup* norm, which is more appropriate from perceptual point of view: we are guaranteed that the distortion doesn't exceed a specified amount.

Now we can state the optimization problem that we have to solve:

Minimize the functional

$$\mathcal{F}[\rho] = \max_{[0 \, R]} F(\rho, r)$$

subject to boundary conditions $\rho(0) = 0$, $\rho(R) = 1$, $\rho''(0) = 0$, *where*

$$F(\rho, r) = \mu K(\rho, r) + (1 - \mu)D(\rho, r)$$

Solving a minimization problem of this type (Chebyshev minimax functional) is in general quite difficult. We found the lower estimate for the values of $\mathcal{F}$, and numerically approximated the optimal solution. It turns out that the values of $\mathcal{F}$ for linear interpolation between solutions for $\mathcal{K} = 0$ and $\mathcal{D} = 0$ are close to the optimal values.

It appears that for practical purposes linear interpolation can be used. The resulting transformations have the following form:

$$\rho(r) = \lambda r/R + (1 - \lambda)\frac{R(\sqrt{r^2 + 1} - 1)}{r(\sqrt{R^2 + 1} - 1)}; \quad \psi = \phi \quad (1)$$

where the original image is represented in polar coordinate system (r, ϕ), the transformed image in polar coordinate system (ρ, ψ).

5.4 Generalization to non-symmetric cases

We can use Equation 1 to construct more general transformations by replacing a constant λ with a λ depending on the angle. In this case we can choose the balance between direct view and zero curvature conditions to be different for different directions. First, an initial constant value of λ is chosen for the whole image. Then λ is specified for a set of important directions and then interpolated for the rest of the directions. (Figure 7c). Making λ dependent on the radius and angle is more difficult, but possible; we leave this as future work.

6 Choice of viewing transformation

In the previous section we obtained an analytical expression for a family of viewing transformations parameterized by L and λ. The distance L from the center of projection to the intermediate plane p determines Π_{plane}, and λ determines the tradeoff between the zero-curvature and direct-view conditions.

We need to choose both parameters for a particular scene or image. As we have mentioned before, in our approach the center of projection need not be the position of a hypothetical camera or observer; we are free to choose it using perceptual considerations. However, we are restricted in our choice by the content of the picture that we want to obtain. In many cases, the most important constraint is the amount of *foreshortening* that we want to have across the scene. By the amount of foreshortening we mean the desired ratio of sizes of identical objects placed in the closest and most remote part of the scene (for example, human figures in the foreground and background of Fig. 9a). This ratio can be small for scenes which contain only objects of comparable size placed close to each other, such as the office scene (Fig. 9), and should be large for scenes with landscape background (Fig. 10).

According to [HEJ78] people typically prefer pictures with a small amount of foreshortening in individual objects. The behavior of the error functionals is in agreement with this fact: as we move the center of projection away from the intermediate plane ($L \to \infty$), the size of the intermediate image W_{plane} goes to 0 and it is possible to show that both direct view and zero-curvature error functionals decrease. However, a total absence of foreshortening produces distortion (Fig. 9b). The best choice of the center of projection typically corresponds to the field of view in the range 10 to 50 degrees. When such a choice is possible, we can achieve reasonably good results simply by choosing a small field of view and taking λ to be equal to 1 (Fig. 9c).

There are some types of scenes, however, that don't allow us to choose small fields of view. If we try to decrease the field of view in some scenes, either parts of the scene are lost, or the amount foreshortening becomes too close to 1 and objects in the foreground become too small. (Fig. 10c,d).

In this case, we can choose the 2D transformation by varying λ to achieve the appropriate balance between two types of distortion that we described. We choose a "global" λ for the whole image; if parts of the image still look distorted, we can make additional corrections in various parts of the image by varying λ as described in Section 5.4. (Fig 10b, Fig. 7c).

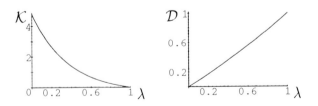

Figure 6. Functionals $\mathcal{K}$ and $\mathcal{D}$ for ρ given by Equation 1 as functions of λ for the field of view 90°. Note that when $\lambda = 1$, there is no curvature distortion. When $\lambda = 0$, then there is no distortion of shape. For a given μ, we can find λ that will approximately minimize the functional $\mathcal{F}$.

a   b   c

Figure 7. A wide-angle photograph of a room. a. Original image (approximately 100° angle. b.Transformation 1 applied with λ = 0. c. Generalization of transformation 1. (Section 5.4) applied. λ varies from 0 to 1.0 across the image. Note the correct shape of the head and straightness of the walls.

a   b

Figure 8. Photo from the article "Navigating Close to Shore" by Dave Dooling ("IEEE Spectrum". Dec. 1994). © 1994 IEEE. photo by Intergraph Corp. 92° viewing angle. a. Original image. b. Transformation 1 applied with λ = 0.

a   b   c

Figure 9. Shallow scene: model of an office (frames from the video). standard projections. a. 92° viewing angle. b. 3° viewing angle. c. 36° viewing angle. close to perceptually optimal for most people.

a   b

c   d

Figure 10. Deep scene. (frames from the video). If we want to have large images of men in the foreground while keeping the images of pyramids in the background. we have to make the angle of the picture wide enough. a. 90° viewing angle. Note the distorted form of the head of the men near the margins of the picture and differences in the shape of the bodies of the men in the middle and close to the margins. b. 90° viewing angle. transformation 1 applied. λ = 0. c. 60° viewing angle. keeping pyramids in the same position in the picture. d. 60° viewing angle. keeping people in the center in the same position.

7 Implementation and Applications

Implementation. The implementation of our viewing transformations is straightforward. The Π_{plane} projection practically coincides with the standard perspective/parallel projection. There is, however, an important implementation detail that is absent in some systems. As we mentioned before, our center of projection need not coincide with the position of the camera or the eye. It is chosen according to perceptual requirements. For instance, it can happen that the most appropriate center of projection for an office scene is outside the room. In these cases it is necessary to have a mechanism for making parts of the model invisible (these parts of the model should participate in lighting calculations but should be ignored by the viewing transformation). This can be done using clipping planes.

The 2D part of the viewing transformation T_{plane} can be implemented as a separate postprocessing stage. The advantage of such an implementation is that it allows us to apply it to any perspective image, computer-generated or photographic. The only additional information required is the position of the center of projection relative to the image. The basic structure of the implementation is very simple:

```
for all output pixels (i, j) do
    r := √(i² + j²)
    setpixel( i,j,
        interpolated_color( ρ⁻¹(r)i/r, ρ⁻¹(r)j/r ) )
end
```

The inverse function ρ^{-1} can be computed numerically with any of the standard root-finding methods, such as those found in *Numerical Recipes* [PFTV88]. The interpolated_color(x, y) function computes the color for any point (x, y) with real coordinates in the original image by interpolating the colors of the integer pixels.

The position of the center of projection is usually known for computer-generated images, but is more difficult to obtain for photos. For photos it can be calculated if we know the size of the film and focal distance of the lens used in the camera. Alternatively, it can be computed directly from the image if there is a rectangular object of known aspect ratio present in the picture [Zor95].

Applications. Examples of applications of our viewing transformations were mentioned throughout the paper. We can identify the following most important applications:

- Creation of wide-angle pictures with minimal distortions. (Figs. 9,10).
- Reduction of distortions in photographic images. (Figs 7,8).
- Creation of wide-angle animation with reduced distortion of shape.
- A better alternative to fisheye views. Fisheye views are used for making images with extremely wide angle (up to 180 for hemispherical fisheye), when the distortions in linear projection make it impossible to produce any reasonable picture. However, fisheye pictures have considerable distortions of their own. The pictures that we obtain using our transformations look significantly less distorted than fisheye views.
- Zooming of parts of a wide-angle picture: For example, we can cut out a portrait of one of the authors from the transformed image in Fig. 7b, while it would look quite distorted if we had used the original photo (Fig. 7a)

8 Conclusion and Future Work

We developed an approach for constructing viewing transformations on perceptual basis. We demonstrate that two important perceptually desirable requirements are incompatible and there is no unique viewing transformation producing perceptually correct images for any scene. We described a simple family of viewing transformations

suitable for reducing distortions in wide-angle images. These transformations are straightforward to implement as a postprocessing stage in a rendering system or for photographs and motion pictures.

As we have mentioned in Section 5.1, Theorem 1 applies only in cases when we consider all possible lines and planes in the scene, not only the ones present in it. Better results can be achieved by introducing direct dependence of the viewing transformation on the objects of the scene.

Possible extensions of this work include considering the dependence of λ in the Equation 1 on r, and conformal transformations of the plane preserving the direct-view property. We also can introduce new perceptually desirable properties and finding new families of transformations that produce optimal images with respect to these properties.

9 Acknowledgements

We wish to thank Bena Currin for her help with writing the software and Allen Concorran for the help with preparing the images. Many thanks to Greg Ward for his RADIANCE system that was used to render the image in the paper. We also thank the members of Caltech Computer Graphics Group for many useful discussions and suggestions.

This work was supported in part by grants from Apple, DEC, Hewlett Packard, and IBM. Additional support was provided by NSF (ASC-89-20219), as part of the NSF/DARPA STC for Computer Graphics and Scientific Visualization. All opinions, findings, conclusions, or recommendations expressed in this document are those of the author and do not necessarily reflect the views of the sponsoring agencies.

References

[dV70] Leonardo da Vinci. *Notebooks I, II*. Dover, New York, 1970.

[Gla94] G. Glaeser. *Fast Algorithms for 3-D Graphics*. Springer-Verlag, New York, 1994.

[Hag76] Margaret A. Hagen. Influence of picture surface and station point on the ability to compensate for oblique view in pictorial perception. *Developmental Psychology*, 12(1):57–63, January 1976.

[Hag80] Margaret A. Hagen, editor. *The Perception of pictures*. Academic Press series in cognition and perception. Academic Press, New York, 1980.

[HEJ78] Margaret A. Hagen, Harry B. Elliott, and Rebecca K. Jones. A distinctive characteristic of pictorial perception: The zoom effect. *Perception*, 7(6):625–633, 1978.

[Kub86] Michael. Kubovy. *The psychology of perspective and Renaissance art*. Cambridge University Press, Cambridge <Cambridgeshire>; New York, 1986.

[PFTV88] William H. Press, Brian P. Flannery, Saul A. Teukolsky, and William T. Vetterling. *Numerical Recipes in C: The Art of Scientific Computing*. Cambridge University Press, Cambridge, UK, 1988.

[Pir70] M. H. Pirenne. *Optics, painting and photography*. Cambridge University Press, New York, 1970.

[Pon62] L. S. Pontriagin. *The mathematical theory of optimal processes*. Interscience Publishers, New York, 1962.

[Rau86] B. V. Raushenbakh. *Sistemy perspektivy v izobrazitel'nom iskusstve : obshchaia teoriia perspektivy*. Nauka, Moskva, 1986. in Russian.

[TR93] Jack Tumblin and Holly E. Rushmeier. Tone reproduction for realistic images. *IEEE Computer Graphics and Applications*, 13(6):42–48, November 1993. also appeared as Tech. Report GIT-GVU-91-13, Graphics, Visualization & Usability Center, Coll. of Computing, Georgia Institute of Tech.

[Zor95] Denis Zorin. Perceptual distortions in images. Master's thesis, Caltech, 1995.

AutoKey: Human Assisted Key Extraction

*Tomoo Mitsunaga, Taku Yokoyama, Takashi Totsuka**

SONY Corporation

Abstract

Key extraction is an inverse problem of finding the foreground, the background, and the alpha from an image and some hints. Although the chromakey solves this for a limited case (single background color), this is often too restrictive in practical situations. When the extraction from arbitrary background is necessary, this is currently done by a time consuming manual task. In order to reduce the operator load, attempts have been made to assist operators using either color space or image space information. However, existing approaches have their limitations. Especially, they leave too much work to operators. In this paper, we present a key extraction algorithm which for the first time, addresses the problem quantitatively. We first derive a partial differential equation that relates the gradient of an image to the alpha values. We then describe an efficient algorithm that provides the alpha values as the solution of the equation. Along with our accurate motion estimation technique, it produces correct alpha values almost everywhere, leaving little work to operators. We also show that a careful design of the algorithm and the data representation greatly improves human interaction. At every step of the algorithm, human interaction is possible and it is intuitive.

CR Categories: I.3.3 [Computer Graphics]: Picture / Image Generation; I.4.6 [Image Processing]: Segmentation - *Edge and feature detection*; I.4.7 [Image Processing]: Feature Measurement; I.5.2 [Pattern Recognition]: Design Methodology - *Feature evaluation and selection*.

Additional Keywords: Key, alpha value, image composition, object extraction, block matching, edge detection, spline.

1 Introduction

In this paper, we consider the following problem; given a 2D image that consists of a foreground object and a background, determine the alpha value of the foreground object. Since

---

* Sony Corporation. 6-7-35 Kitashinagawa, Shinagawa Tokyo 141, Japan   e-mail: *mitsunag@av.crl.sony.co.jp*, *yokoyama@av.crl.sony.co.jp*, *totsuka@av.crl.sony.co.jp*

Permission to make digital/hard copy of part or all of this work for personal or classroom use is granted without fee provided that copies are not made or distributed for profit or commercial advantage, the copyright notice, the title of the publication and its date appear, and notice is given that copying is by permission of ACM, Inc. To copy otherwise, to republish, to post on servers, or to redistribute to lists, requires prior specific permission and/or a fee.

the alpha value is called *key* in the video/movie community, we call this key extraction problem.

Knowing the alpha (key) value is the first step in compositing images [12]. Unless the object shape is already known (e.g., rendered from a 3D model), alpha value is not available at hand. Therefore, usually it must be extracted from images that are taken by a camera or other input devices. Hence, key extraction is essential. Recent wide use of special effects increases the importance of key extraction.

For a limited special case – single constant background color, chromakey is the solution to key extraction. With the chromakey, objects such as actors are placed in front of a screen of a known color which is usually blue or green. By fixing the background color, the key extraction becomes much simpler (see section 2). Despite the limitation due to single background color, the chromakey is widely used since it is the only automated solution at this moment. However, due to the problems listed below, it is often inapplicable to high-end image works.

- Choice of foreground colors is limited. Usually, it must be different from the background color.

- In order to obtain a constant background color, shots are taken in a studio. Thus, for natural compositing, careful adjustment of the lights is necessary to mimic the condition of outside shots. Such adjustment often requires several trials, making indoor shots unattractive.

- Due to light reflection, the foreground color is affected by the background (called contamination). This is particularly noticeable near the object boundary.

When chromakey is insufficient or extraction from an arbitrary background is necessary, key extraction becomes a much harder problem. Although several techniques have been proposed, still much of the tedious pixel-by-pixel cleaning up job is left to human operators. We are told that this manual clean up can consume as much as 70% of operator's work, which is about a half of total production time[1]. This has been a major problem of image compositing works in the real world.

The key extraction from an image with arbitrary background is hard since this requires a high level image understanding that a human would do. However, it is still far beyond current capabilities of a machine vision. As a consequence, collaboration of a computer and an operator is necessary. In order to make such collaborative approach

---

[1]The numbers were obtained by our interviews at post-production studios working on TV commercials and movies. The operator work includes rendering, painting, image editing, and compositing.

satisfactory for an operator, the following requirements must be fulfilled.

- High accuracy. Even if perfect work is not expected, the algorithm must not leave more that a small acceptable amount of adjustment task to an operator.

- Hint directed. It must be easy to give hints to the algorithm. The algorithm should fully exploit the hints and work adaptively.

- Easy to fix problems. That is, the shape of the key must be easily modifiable. This suggests the use of a parameterized representation of the key (i.e., object shape) rather than a discrete (e.g., image) form. Also, such parameterization must be a local one to allow local modifications without changing the entire shape.

In this paper, we present a key extraction algorithm that satisfies these criteria. We first establish the relationship of the alpha value and the first derivative of the image. This relationship provides a quantitative foundation to our new key extraction scheme which consists of the three major components; (1) a color gradient computation algorithm, (2) a motion tracking algorithm, and (3) key (alpha) surface construction algorithm. Our color gradient computation yields significantly better SNR compared to existing edge detectors, contributing to the quality of the key signal. The motion tracking algorithm provides a reliable motion vector while minimizing perceptual artifacts due to errors. It is also robust against background color changes. The key surface construction makes shape modification easier by providing a parametric form of the key.

These techniques are developed by an interdisciplinary research of three related fields; graphics, image processing, and computer vision. Ideas in one field often helped development of a new algorithm in another field. Several examples are shown in our paper.

The rest of the paper is organized as follows. Section 2 reviews related works. Section 3 presents the relationship of the key and the derivative of the image, and section 4 describes the algorithm in detail. Section 5 show results from our implementation and section 6 gives conclusions and possible future directions.

2   Related Works

The color I of an image at a pixel (x, y) is defined as:

$$I = \alpha F + (1 - \alpha) B \qquad (1)$$

where F and B are the foreground and the background color, respectively. α is the alpha or key value. The key extraction problem is the inverse problem of equation 1; given I and some hint, compute α, F, and B. As shown in figure 1(a), in a color space, the key extraction can be viewed as a problem of defining a line segment FB which is divided by point I at the ratio of $(1 - \alpha) : \alpha$. Since the only constraint imposed by equation 1 is that the three points F, B and I lie on the same line, for any value for one of F, B, or α we can find other two that satisfy equation 1. Hence, we need more information in order to determine the three parameters. There are two approaches to add supplementary information; color space approach and image space approach.

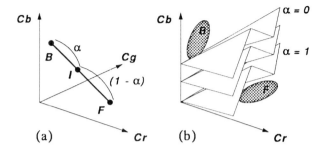

Figure 1: Key extraction in a color space. (a) relationship of the foreground, background, and observed colors, (b) an example of polygonal iso-surfaces of α.

Color Space Approach   The color space approaches provide some hints about the foreground and background colors. For example, the background color is given with the chromakey. Since both B and I are known, the range of search for F and α degenerates from 3D space to a line defined by B and I. α is estimated by the distance of B and I or some other metric.

As a generalization of the chromakey to the arbitrary background case, color distributions of the background, the foreground, or both can be given as a hint. Given a color distribution, α is assigned by some metric to each color (R,G,B) in the color space such that $\alpha = 0$ near the background and $\alpha = 1$ near the foreground. One can control this assignment by specifying one or more iso-surfaces of α (figure 1(b)). A popular chromakey system uses several triangular patches as the iso-surface [3][17]. A more general polyhedral slice approach was also proposed in[11].

Multivariate statistical analysis is another tool to assign α to RGB space [1]. For example, discriminant analysis[2] can separate colors into two groups and from the variance and distance of the groups, alpha values of the pixels in the intermediate region can be estimated.

These methods, however, do not work when the color distributions of the foreground and the background overlap. Not only due to multiple object colors, but also due to shading and reflection, the color distributions tend to spread, causing overlap of the distributions. Although subdivision of the image into small blocks improves the separation, as the block becomes smaller, the color distribution within such small block is statistically less reliable. We have encountered many examples in which a 16 by 16 block is still too large to separate the two regions. Since the boundary region is sometimes several pixels wide, any smaller block may not capture the entire fore to back transition.

Image Space Approach   Image space approaches exploit coherency; the fact that an object is a relatively large chunk, rather than a set of discrete dots. Under this assumption, the problem becomes a boundary detection and tracking problem which has been studied in computer vision.

The snake [9][16] is a popular technique for object tracking. An energy function is defined such that it is minimum when a polyline called snake correctly traces the object boundary. The object motion is tracked as an energy min-

---

[2]Given a set of points, find an axis along which the points are best separated into two groups.

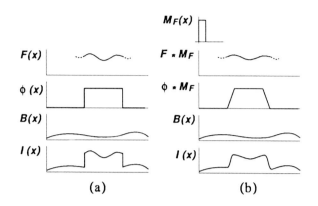

Figure 2: Alpha blending of 1D signals. (a) without motion blur, (b) with motion blur.

imization problem. Since the key shape usually is complex and changes quickly, initial placement of the control points may not be appropriate in later frames. Although it is possible to cope with it by providing more control points, increase in the number of points exponentially raises the computational cost of the search. The explosion of the search also occurs as the resolution of the search increases.

Clustering is another approach to tracking. With this approach, pixels are transformed to an appropriate space to find the similarity among them. For example, a five dimensional space (x,y and r,g,b) is used to find groups that represent the foreground object [4]. In the context of the key extraction, the problems of the clustering methods are that they do not provide a soft transition from the foreground to the background and that the clustering does not perform well under low color purity.

A different approach based on edge thinning and widening was also proposed [6] [7]. Edge detection is first performed and then a thinning process leaves pixels with high edge intensities which are treated as the object boundary. The boundary is then widened again to give a rough estimate of the location of the boundary on the next frame. Since such conventional edge detection responds to any transition of colors (e.g., textures, shadows), high edge intensity does not directly mean that the pixel is on the boundary. Although they mention a way of creating a soft key (smooth transition of the alpha value), it is rather empirical.

3 The Gradient of an Image

In this section, we establish an important relationship of the key (alpha) and the derivative of the image that our algorithm is based on. We also study conditions under which the relationship holds. For simplicity, we consider the key extraction of 1D scalar functions. The argument can be extended naturally to color images (3D vector field defined over a 2D space).

Consider placing a foreground object on top of a background. The foreground object is defined by its color $F(x)$ and the opacity $\phi(x)$. $B(x)$ is the background color. For an opaque object, $\phi(x)$ is a rectangle function which is 1 everywhere foreground object exists and 0 otherwise. $F(x)$ is undefined outside of the foreground region (figure 2(a)).

Clearly, the blended result $I(x)$ is given by

$$I(x) = \phi(x) F(x) + (1 - \phi(x)) B(x) \qquad (2)$$

Then the derivative of $I(x)$ is

$$I'(x) = \phi'(x) (F(x) - B(x)) + \phi(x) F'(x) + (1 - \phi(x)) B'(x) \qquad (3)$$

Near the boundary of the object where $\phi(x)$ changes quickly, we can assume that both F' and B' are relatively small compared to ϕ'. In this case, equation 3 can be approximated by

$$I'(x) \approx \phi'(x) (F(x) - B(x)) \qquad (4)$$

Since ϕ is the alpha value we want to determine, we can rewrite as

$$I'(x) \approx \alpha'(x) (F(x) - B(x)) \qquad (5)$$

under the condition that

$$\phi'(x) \gg F'(x), \quad \phi'(x) \gg B'(x) \qquad (6)$$

That is, the first derivative of the alpha value is proportional to the first derivative of the image. The ratio is given by the difference of the foreground and the background.

We now consider the effect of motion blur. The effect of blurring can be expressed by an operator $M_F(x)$. For example, suppose that the foreground object is moving at a constant velocity V and the shutter speed of the camera is T_s. Then $M_F(x)$ is a rectangle function of width VT_s as in figure 2(b). Using this function, the motion blurred object can be represented by its blurred color $(F * M_F)$ and the opacity $(\phi * M_F)$ where the operator $*$ denotes convolution.

By a similar derivation, we get

$$I'(x) \approx (\phi(x) * M_F(x))' ((F(x) * M_F(x)) - B(x)) \qquad (7)$$

With the motion blur, the alpha value we want is $(\phi * M_F)$. Hence,

$$I'(x) \approx \alpha'(x) ((F(x) * M_F(x)) - B(x)) \qquad (8)$$

Again, the derivatives are proportional. One of the condition in equation 6 is replaced by $(\phi(x) * M_F(x))' \gg (F(x) * M_F(x))'$. This condition is no stronger than the previous one, since the derivatives are equally attenuated by the blurring operator. Note that this relationship does not depend on types of blur (shape of M_F). By repeating the similar analysis, we can derive the same relationship, $I' \propto \alpha'$, under motion blur of both the foreground and the background.

In a real situation, we also have to consider the effect of the optical and electrical prefiltering before the sampling process. Since the prefiltering process can be expressed by a low-pass filter H, by replacing the M_F with $M_F * H^3$, we can make the same argument which leads to the same conclusion.

The above argument can be extended to the 2D image case. Since the image is a 2D function, relationship of the gradient vectors is obtained. That is, the gradient of the alpha and the image are parallel:

$$\nabla I(x, y) = c \nabla \alpha(x, y) \qquad (9)$$

where c is a scalar constant which represents the difference of the foreground and the background (see equation 5).

---

[3] The new operator includes the effect of both motion blur and the prefiltering

The alpha value is obtained by solving this partial differential equation. Given a path $P : \boldsymbol{p}(t)$, α at a point $\boldsymbol{p}(t)$ on P is given by

$$\alpha(\boldsymbol{p}(t)) \;=\; \frac{1}{c} \int_P \nabla I(x,y) \cdot d\boldsymbol{p}(t) \;+\; c_0 \qquad (10)$$

Since we have two obvious constraints – $\alpha = 0$ at background and $\alpha = 1$ at the foreground, c_0 can be easily determined.

Note that a color image has more information (i.e., three scalar values per pixel) than what is needed to solve the equation (single scalar value). As we see in section 4.3, this additional information can tolerate the condition that $\boldsymbol{F}$ and $\boldsymbol{B}$ be locally constant.

Using the relationship, we can obtain the alpha value or key from the first derivative of the image. This differential approach has the following advantages:

- Slope of the alpha value is given quantitatively.

- Unlike the chromakey, absolute values of B or F are not necessary. Local difference in the color provides enough information to determine the alpha.

- The requirement that F and B be constant is necessary only around small regions (e.g., a couple of pixels wide) on the boundary where the alpha changes quickly. The color space approaches discussed in section 2 require that the colors be constant over much larger area in order to assure the separation of the color distribution.

4 Key Extraction

4.1 Processing Cycle

We now describe our key extraction algorithm in detail. The flow or the algorithm is shown in figure 3. For each iteration, the algorithm takes an input frame as well as the previously processed frame which is used as a reference. At the end of the iteration, the key is output as a black and white image. A set of cubic spline segments is also produced which becomes another reference input during the next iteration.

Within the iteration, the following three steps are performed serially.

1. Boundary search. Estimate the boundary of the foreground object in the new frame.

2. Gradient computation. Along the boundary obtained in the previous step, compute the gradient of the image.

3. Key surface construction. Using the relationship described in section 3, compute a parametric surface whose Z coordinate represents the alpha value. The surface is then scan converted into a monochrome image of the alpha values, which is the output of the iteration.

4.2 Boundary Search

The purpose of this step is to provide the following gradient computation step with an accurate estimate of the object boundary. Accurate estimate of the boundary allows the gradient computation to work more precisely on the boundary, spatially eliminating the noise of the gradient vector field.

The estimate is computed by a block matching between the previous and the new frame. For our purpose, the following issues which existing block matching algorithms

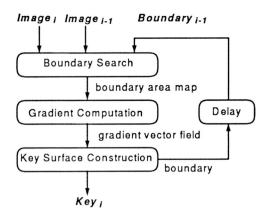

Figure 3: Flow of our key extraction algorithm.

(e.g. [14]) do not address must be considered: (1) Background color can change drastically as the foreground object moves. Hence, equally evaluating the foreground and the background pixels can cause matching errors. (2) Minimum difference of blocks does not necessarily mean that the two blocks correspond to each other. This is acceptable for image compression [20], but not for object tracking. (3) A poorly chosen block (e.g., a block that only contains a straight boundary) does not always exhibit a sharp peak in the autocorrelation, producing unreliable motion estimate depending on the motion direction. (4) Perceptual error must be minimized.

In consideration to the above issues, our block matching first searches high curvature points on the boundary which becomes the source block of the matching. It is well known in computer vision that human visual system responds strongly to high curvature [2], [5]. Hence, use of such points as the source block is desirable in order to minimize perceptual artifacts. Since such blocks contain curved portion of the boundary, the autocorrelation exhibits a sharp peak on any motion direction, which is also desirable. Figure 4(a) shows an example of source block placement. Yellow dots on the boundary indicates centers of the blocks. In this implementation, blocks are recursively placed till the difference of the orientation is within the predefined threshold.

For each of these blocks, its destination is searched in the new frame. In order to reduce the effect of the background color change, weighted mean square error MSE is computed as follows:

$$MSE \;=\; \frac{\sum_{i,j} w[i,j]\,(I_n[i,j] - I_{n-1}[i,j])^2}{\sum_{i,j} w[i,j]} \qquad (11)$$

where $I_n[i,j]$ and $I_{n-1}[i,j]$ are blocks of the new and the previous frames, respectively, and $w[i,j]$ is the weight. In order to emphasize the difference in the foreground region, the alpha value obtained in the previous frame is used as the weight.

Figure 4(b) and (c) show matching results of the blocks in figure 4(a) by conventional block matching (b) and by our method (c), respectively. Figures 4(d)~(f) repeat the same comparison using a different object. With the conventional method, color changes of the background near the boundary (c) and/or motion of the background (e) degrades the accuracy of the block matching.

  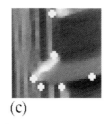 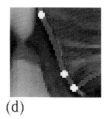 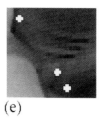 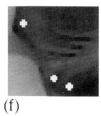

(a)　　　　　(b)　　　　　(c)　　　　　(d)　　　　　(e)　　　　　(f)

Figure 4: Block matching. (a) and (d): blocks (yellow dot) placed on along the object boundary (red line) in the previous frame, (b) and (e): results of the conventional block matching, and (c) and (f): results of our foreground weighted block matching.

Once the block matching is done, the destination blocks are connected to form a continuous boundary.

4.3 Gradient Computation

For pixels within the estimated boundary, gradient of the image is computed. Although the gradient is computed using the Sobel operator, a well known edge detector in image processing [8], its use is quite different in two ways. First, the Sobel operator is not applied to the RGB images. Instead, it is applied to the projection of the color image. Second, selectivity of the edge orientation is controlled by a non-linear post-processing.

As described in section 3, the gradient of the image and the alpha are proportional provided that F and B be constant near the boundary. This is usually true, but there are cases in which this condition no longer holds. Textures, shadows, strong shading, and reflections can sometimes cause non-negligible variation of the color, introducing turbulence to the gradient.

Figure 5(a) shows a typical color distribution of an object. Depending on the orientation of the surface, color changes from a dark color to the fully illuminated object color, and to a brighter color due to the specular reflection. This distribution corresponds to the local illumination model in graphics and it is called the dichromatic distribution in computer vision [10]. When the reflection is not negligible, the global illumination model must be introduced. In this case, the color of the object is shifted since a fraction of the background color, which is the product of the form-factor and the reflectivity, is added to the original color (figure 5(b)).

These observations suggest that we can tolerate the condition about F and B as long as the direction of the color variation described above is different from vector $F - B$, the direction of the color transition across the boundary. This is done by first choosing a color vector C such that it is approximately perpendicular to the distributions of the foreground and the background, and then projecting color I to the inner product I_p:

$$I_p(x,y) = (I(x,y) \cdot C) \qquad (12)$$

Since C is perpendicular to the main axis of the color distribution, color variations within the region do not cause much difference in I_p. Hence, the SNR of the gradient is considerably improved. Existing color edge detectors fails in this respect, for they try to detect *any* transition of the color [13] [15] [19].

Further improvement of the SNR is possible by weighting the gradient by the difference from the expected orientation which is obtained from the result of the previous frame.

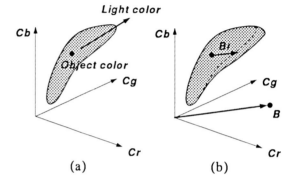

(a)　　　　　　　　　　(b)

Figure 5: Color distribution. (a) effect of local illumination, (b) effect of reflection (indirect light).

Strong textures and shadows can be eliminated as long as their orientation is different. A sharp selectivity which is not available by conventional linear filtering can be achieved by a classical technique in graphics as

$$G(x,y) = \nabla I_p(x,y) \left(\frac{\nabla I_p(x,y)}{|\nabla I_p(x,y)|} \cdot N \right)^s \qquad (13)$$

where G is the weighted gradient, N is the expected orientation (normalized), s is the selectivity index. The Phong shading uses the same technique to obtain a sharp selectivity.

Our implementation of the algorithm first subdivides the given object boundary into shorter regions such that both the color vector $F - B$ and the expected orientation N are similar within the region. Then, for each small region, the best color projection vector C is computed followed by calculations of equations 12 and 13. Finally, since each small region may choose different parameters such as C, the output G is rescaled such that the unit length has the same weight elsewhere.

An example is shown in figure 6. The original image (a) is processed by [19] which is claimed to be the best filter based color edge detector, and by our algorithm (c). Note that our algorithm is robust to color variations within the object even with strong shading and reflections.

  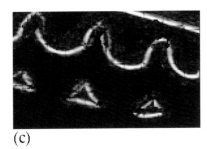

(a)　　　　　　　　　(b)　　　　　　　　　(c)

Figure 6: Edge detection. (a) original image, (b) gradient magnitude computed by a conventional edge detection algorithm, (c) gradient magnitude by our algorithm.

4.4 Key Surface Construction

The last step generates key image (monochrome image of the alpha value) as well as the parametric form of the key in order to ease modification of the shape when it is necessary. The parametric form is a surface whose Z coordinate represents the alpha value.

Given the gradient vector field from the previous step, the algorithm first generates the contour line of $\alpha = 0.5$ as cubic splines. We denote this curve as $C_M(t)$. The end points of each segment are selected from pixels with high gradient magnitudes. The tangent vectors are set orthogonal to the gradients at these points. Since adjacent segments share the same tangent vector, $C_M(t)$ has G^1 continuity. Finally, the velocities at the end points are chosen to satisfy the following two criteria: (1) the orientation is orthogonal to the gradient vector field, (2) the curve passes along peaks of the gradient magnitude (figure 7(a)). This is done by an exhaustive search. Some examples of the curve fitting are shown in figure 8. Both (a) and (c) are resulting cubic spline segments displayed on top of the gradient magnitude images, and (b) and (d) are the same splines but displayed on the original images. These closeups show that the fitting process can follow fine details of the boundary.

Construction of the surface is done as follows. First, examine pixels on both sides of $C_M(t)$ to determine the constant factor c in equation 9. Since the gradient of the image is already known, we get the gradient of the alpha from the equation. By a linear approximation, the endpoints of the contour lines of $\alpha = 0$ ($C_B(t)$) and $\alpha = 1$ ($C_F(t)$) are obtained. Their tangent vectors are set parallel to $C_M(t)$. The velocities are set such that the three segments share the same center of curvature (figure 7(a)). As a special case, if the distance between the endpoints (e.g., $P0$ and $Q0$) is longer than the curvature radius, the velocity of the inner curve is set to 0. Finally, the key surface $K(s,t)$ is defined by

$$K(s,t) = s\,C_F(t) + (1-s)\,C_B(t) \qquad (14)$$

Figure 7(b) shows an example of key surface $K(s,t)$. Clearly, the surface also has G^1 continuity. This surface is scan-converted to generate the key image, which is the other output of the step.

4.5 Human interaction

At each of above steps, human interaction can be easily done. At the boundary search step, human operator can specify

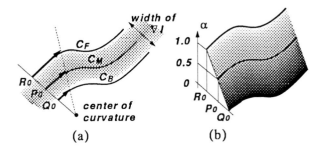

(a)　　　　　　　　　　(b)

Figure 7: Key surface construction. (a) fitting $C_M(\alpha = 0.5)$ on the gradient vector field and determining C_F ($\alpha = 1$) and C_B ($\alpha = 0$), (b) construction of the cubic spline surface.

additional characteristic points in order to improve the accuracy of the search.

The color vector C and the expected orientation used in the gradient computation step, can also be given interactively. Especially, the expected or preferred boundary orientation can be intuitively given by a brush movement.

At the key surface construction step, surface shape can be modified by known editors such as the one shown in figure 9.

With our algorithm, human interaction is easy because (1) the parameters are intuitive to a human operator, and (2) the parameters are local, affecting only the local behavior. If direct manipulation of images is necessary, such easy interaction is not possible.

Since our algorithm requires the result of the previous frame as a reference, initial solution must be given manually. We do this by providing a rough drawing of the boundary shape to the gradient computation step. The rough drawing provides an idea about the orientation of the boundary which helps the algorithm to selectively find the boundary.

5 Results

Figure 10 show some results of our key extraction algorithm. In this example, the trouser of the football player is chosen as the foreground object. For the initial frame shown in the first column, a rough drawing of the boundary was given as a hint. Successive frames are processed by the computer with operator's subtle correction where it is desired. The upper row is the output of the algorithm *before* human correction.

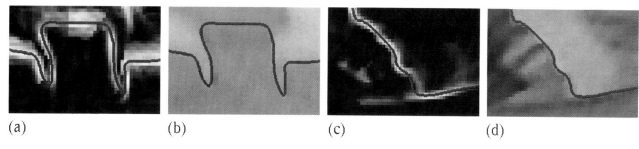

Figure 8: Results of curve fitting. (a) and (c): gradient magnitude and the spline segments, (b) and (d): the same spline segments placed on the original image.

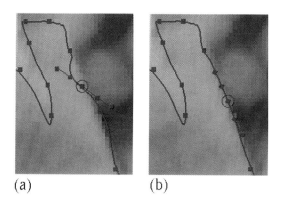

(a)　　　　　　(b)

Figure 9: Editing a boundary curve.

Figures (e), (f), (g), and (h) show that the algorithm can correctly work on such large change of the shape. Fine complex details such as waist-belt and around the left hand are well tracked across frames without human intervention. Despite the big change of the background color near the left knee, the left hand, and the right thigh, the algorithm follows the boundary and produces correct key images.

Figure 11 show some zoom-ups of the same image. (a) and (b) are part of the waist-belt and (c) and (d) are part of the hip. Due to the player's vertical motion, horizontal boundary (a) shows more blur than (c). Figure 11(b) and (d) show the quantitative correctness of our algorithm.

6 Conclusions

The key extraction from images with arbitrary backgrounds is a hard problem which cannot be totally automated. Hence, an algorithm for key extraction must be designed to allow easy human interaction.

By judicious choice of the parameters and the data representation, our algorithm allows human interaction at every step of the processing and it is intuitive to an operator. Because of the parametric form of the key shape, it is easy to incorporate other interactive techniques in graphics (e.g., morphing, key frames) that can further eliminate the need for human interaction.

Based on the relationship between the derivatives of the image and the alpha value, our algorithm provides a quantitative method for key extraction for the first time.

There are many areas that require further development. In the gradient computation, choice of a different color space and a projection should be considered since more compact projection of the color distribution yields yet better SNR.

Better estimate of the foreground color near the boundary is another area of study. Current assumption that the color is constant is not appropriate if there is a strong texture.

To improve the user interface and to improve the accuracy of the boundary estimate, the algorithm should be integrated with the key frame method or other morphing mechanisms.

References

[1] Anderson, T. W., *Introduction to Multivariate Statistical Analysis*, John Wiley & Sons, 1958.

[2] Attneave, F., "Some Informational Aspects of Visual Perception", *Psychological Review*, Vol.61, pp.183-193, 1954.

[3] Dadourian, A., "Compositor for Video Images", patent in U.S.A., US5343252-A, 1994.

[4] Etoh, M. and Shirai, Y., "Automatic Extraction of Complex Objects Using Region Segmentation", *NICOGRAPH'92*, pp.8-17, 1992.

[5] Inui, T., "A Model of Human Visual Memory", *6th Scandinavian Conference on Image Analysis*, pp.325-332, 1989.

[6] Inoue, S., "An Object Extraction Method for Image Synthesis", *IEICE Trans.*, Vol.J74-D-II, No.10, pp.1411-1418, 1991.

[7] Inoue, S. and Koyama, H., "An Extraction and Composing Method for Moving Image Synthesis", *Journal of ITEJ*, Vol.47, No.7, pp999.-1005, 1993.

[8] Jain, A. K., *Fundamentals of Digital Image Processing*, Prentice-Hall, 1989.

[9] Kass, M., Witikin, A. and Terzopoulos, D., "Snakes : Active Contour Models", *International Journal of Computer Vision*, Vol.1, No.3, pp.321-331, 1988.

[10] Klinker, G. J., Shafer, S. A. and Kanade, T., "The Measurement of Highlight in Color Images", *International Journal of Computer Vision*, Vol.2, pp.7-32, 1988.

[11] Mishima, Y., "A Software Chromakeyer Using Polyhedric Slice", *NICOGRAPH'92*, pp.44-52, 1992.

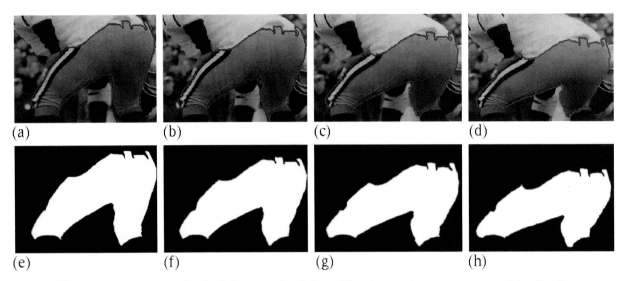

Figure 10: Key image sequence obtained by our algorithm. The four columns correspond to the four successive frames. The upper row shows result of the spline for $\alpha = 0.5$ before correction by an operator, the lower row shows the key image.

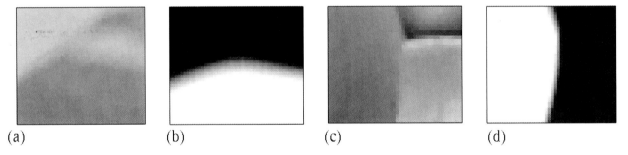

Figure 11: Magnified part of the original and key image by our algorithm. (a) and (b): a horizontal boundary part, (c) and (d): a vertical boundary part.

[12] Porter, T. and Duff, T., "Compositing Digital Images", *Computer Graphics*, Vol.18, No.3, pp.253-259, 1984.

[13] Robinson, G. S., "Color Edge Detection", *Optical Engineering*, Vol.16, No.5, pp.479-484, 1977.

[14] Sezan, M. I. and Lagendijk, R. L., *Motion Analysis and Image Sequence Processing*, Kluwer Academic Publishers, 1993.

[15] Trahanias, P. E. and Venetsanopoulos, A. N., "Color Edge Detection Using Vector Order Statistics", *IEEE Trans. Image Processing*, Vol.2, No.2, pp.259-264, 1993.

[16] Ueda, N., Mase, K. and Suenaga, Y., "A Contour Tracking Method Using Elastic Contour Model and Energy Minimization Approach", *IEICE Trans.*, Vol.J75-D-II, No.1, pp.111-120, 1992.

[17] Vlahos, P., "Combining Method for Colour Video Signals", patent in U.S.A., US4625231-A, 1986.

[18] Wong, R. Y. and Hall, E. L., "Sequential Hierarchical Scene Matching", *IEEE Trans. Comput.*, Vol.C-27, No.4, pp.359-366, 1978.

[19] Zenzo, S. D., "A Note on the Gradient of a Multi-Image", *Computer Vision, Graphics, and Image Processing*, Vol.33, pp.116-125, 1986.

[20] MPEG Video Committee, "Information Technology – Generic Coding of Moving Pictures and Associated Audio", ISO/IEC IS 13818-2, Nov. 1994.

Acknowledgements

The authors got comments from many movie and video engineers. We wish to thank all of them for their valuable comments and suggestions. Discussions with Norihisa Shirota and Tatsuo Shinbashi were helpful in developing the algorithm.

Stochastic Screening Dithering
with Adaptive Clustering

Luiz Velho

Jonas Gomes

IMPA – Instituto de Matemática Pura e Aplicada [1]

Abstract

We develop a clustered dithering method that uses stochastic screening and is able to perform an adaptive variation of the cluster size. This makes it possible to achieve optimal rendition of gray shades while preserving image details. The algorithm is an improvement to the dithering with space filling curves method, published in [3].

CR Descriptors: B.4.2 [**Input/Output and Data Communications**]: Input-Output Devices - *Image Display*; I.3.3 [**Computer Graphics**]: Picture/image generation - *Display algorithms*; I.3.6 [**Computer Graphics**]: Methodology and Techniques; I.4.3 [**Image Processing**]: Enhancement.
Additional Keywords: Digital Halftoning, Dithering Algorithms, Space Filling Curves, Adaptive Clustering.

1 INTRODUCTION

The reproduction of gray scale images in bilevel graphic display devices is achieved through a process called *halftoning*. Given a gray scale image it consists in generating a binary image which perceptually, approximates the original image. This process can be analog or digital. Digital halftoning is done using a technique called *dithering* to determine the binary state (black or white) of the elements of the output image. Dithering algorithms distribute the black and white pixels in such a way that the input and output images are perceptually as close as possible, within the physical limitations of the display device.

Dithering methods can be subdivided into two main groups according to the type of images they produce [2]. *Dispersed dot* dithering methods generate images in which black and white pixels are evenly distributed throughout the image area. *Clustered dot* dithering methods generate images in which black and white pixels are concentrated together forming clusters. These two approaches serve different purposes and are suitable for different classes of display devices.

Classical clustering dithering algorithms use regular, fixed size cluster, and the black and white dot patterns inside the cluster vary

[1] IMPA – Instituto de Matemática Pura e Aplicada, Estrada Dona Castorina, 110
22460-320 Rio de Janeiro, RJ, Brazil, **lvelho | jonas@visgraf.impa.br**

Permission to make digital/hard copy of part or all of this work for personal or classroom use is granted without fee provided that copies are not made or distributed for profit or commercial advantage, the copyright notice, the title of the publication and its date appear, and notice is given that copying is by permission of ACM, Inc. To copy otherwise, to republish, to post on servers, or to redistribute to lists, requires prior specific permission and/or a fee.

according to the image intensity values. These clusters are distributed periodically over the image domain. For this reason, these algorithms are known by the name of amplitude modulated (AM) dithering.

Stochastic dithering algorithms use a fixed size dot pattern and vary their spacing according to the image intensity values. For this reason, these algorithms are called frequency modulated (FM) dithering. Frequency modulated dithering techniques have been implemented recently on the raster image processors of high resolution phototypesetters.

The space filling curve dithering algorithm introduced in [3], contains characteristics of both AM and FM dithering: it is a clustered dithering technique, but the clusters are distributed stochastically over the image domain. Therefore the algorithm adapts well to a wide range of display devices.

Figure 1 describes the space of possibilities covered by the existing digital halftoning techniques: from periodic clustered dither, to periodic dispersed dot dither, and from this to aperiodic dispersed dot dithering techniques.

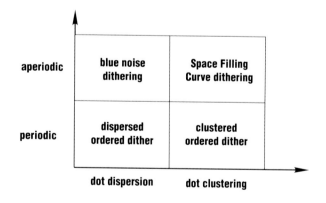

Figure 1: Range of existing dithering techniques.

In this paper we present an improvement to the cluster construction of the algorithm in [3] in order to get a better rendition of image details, without loosing tonal resolution. The major result though, is an extension of the algorithm to obtain a dispersed clustered dithering technique whose cluster size may vary adaptively according to image intensity characteristics. We should point out that this extension was suggested in [3].

An earlier report of the method presented in this paper containing some preliminary results and simple experiments appeared in [4]. Here, we formulate the problem from the point of view of

AM/FM dithering techniques and investigate the application of the algorithm to image reproduction on high resolution bilevel devices.

The remaining of the paper is organized as follows: Section 2 reviews the space filling curve dither algorithm. Section 3 describes the dither with adaptive clustering. Section 3.1 discusses implementation related issues. Section 4 shows results of experiments with the method.

2   SPACE FILLING CURVE DITHER

In this section we briefly review the dithering with space filling curves (SFC) introduced in [3]. The trace of a space filling curve approximation is used to scan the image, generating a parametrization of the image elements with many desirable properties.

The method consists of the following steps:

- Subdivision of the image into cells;

- Computation of the average intensities of each cell;

- Generation of corresponding black and white dot patterns for each cell;

- positioning of the dot pattern within the cell to generate the *cluster*.

The subdivision of the image is performed by following the path of the space filling curve until the number of elements visited is equal to the cluster size. This is illustrated in Figure 2(a), using a Hilbert space filling curve.

For each cell, the computation of the accumulated intensity is performed as each one of its elements is visited. Then, the corresponding dot pattern is generated by selecting a group of contiguous elements proportional in number to the total intensity. In this way, the cell is subdivided into subcells of black and white pixels such that its average intensity approximates the image average intensity within the cell. Figure 2(b), from [3], shows the configuration of dots corresponding to intensity levels 15/16 to 0 for a cluster of 4 × 4 pixels.

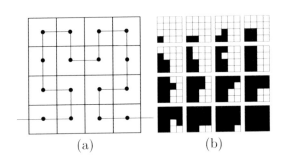

(a)   (b)

Figure 2: 4 × 4 cluster and dot patterns – from (Velho and Gomes, 1991).

There is a quantization error associated with each cell defined by the difference between the average intensity of the grayscale image and the intensity of the dot patterns. The quantization error in a region is diffused by the algorithm, propagating it to neighbor regions along the path of the space filling curve.

2.1   Cluster Generation

The last step of the algorithm creates the cluster by positioning the dot pattern within the cell. Here we introduce an improvement over the algorithm published in [3]. We position the central pixel of

the generated dot pattern at the pixel inside the cell which has the lowest intensity level (i.e. corresponding to the highest percentage of black ink). This is illustrated in Figure 3: (a) shows the image and a 4 × 4 cell; (b) shows (in gray) the lowest intensity pixel within the cell; (c) shows a dot pattern of 5 pixels; (d) shows the translation of the dot pattern center to the pixel of lowest intensity. This positioning method results in a much better rendition of the image details, without compromising tonal resolution.

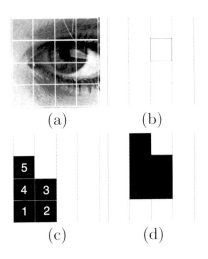

(a)   (b)

(c)   (d)

Figure 3: Dot pattern position.

We should observe that besides the non-directionality implied by the space filling curve traversal of the image pixels, the cluster generation method described introduces some randomness to the distribution of the dot patterns within the cell.

In brief, the dithering algorithm with space filling curves uses clustering similar to the traditional amplitude modulated (AM) algorithms, but at the same time it performs error diffusion. Therefore, it also incorporates characteristics of techniques that use frequency modulation (FM dithering).

3   SFC DITHER with ADAPTIVE CLUSTERING

From the results of the previous section we know that the dithering algorithm with space filling curves distributes stochastically the clusters and performs an error diffusion between neighbor cells. In this section we will show how to extend the method in order to have an adaptive control over the cluster size. This control will enable us to incorporate a variable size clustering, which along with the above mentioned properties, creates a dithering texture similar to the film grain found in photographic textures.

The space filling curve dithering algorithm subdivides the image domain into cells, and at each cell it approximates the image function $f(x, y)$ by some bi-level image function $\overline{f}(x, y)$. The approximation criteria is a perceptual one, based on pixel intensities. The adaptive clustering dithering consists of changing the size of each cell, based on some adaptive criteria, in order to get a better binary approximation $\overline{f}$ of the image function f.

The adaptiveness criteria to compute the cluster size depends on the desired effect to be obtained by the halftone method. In our case, the goal is to achieve the best rendition of image detail without compromising tonal reproduction. Therefore, we should use an adaptive criteria that varies the cluster size according to the rate of change of the image intensity. In order to accomplish for this, we need to measure the variation of image intensities as we scan the image.

Since we are scanning the image along the path of the space filling curve, the directional derivative along the curve provides a good measure ot the rate of change of the image intensities along the scanning direction. It is computed by modulating the gradient vector

$$\text{grad} f = (\frac{\partial f}{\partial x}, \frac{\partial f}{\partial y}),$$

of the image function f, by the unit vector u along the scanning direction defined by the space filling curve. That is,

$$\frac{\partial f}{\partial u} = \langle u, \text{grad} f \rangle,$$

where $\langle \, , \, \rangle$ is the usual euclidean inner product.

After deciding that the directional derivative will take care of the adaptiveness criteria, it remains to obtain the correct relationship between the cluster size and the derivative intensity. As the derivative magnitude gets bigger, image intensities change faster and, therefore, the cluster size should get smaller.

We need to find the correct relationship between the cluster size and the derivative values. For this, we first observe that the intensities distribution in a dithered image must follow a perceptual criteria. Also, the eye response to intensity changes obeys a logarithmic law (see [1]). Based on these two remarks, we conclude that we should vary the cluster size exponentially with the gradient magnitude. This rule maintains a linear relationship between the perceptual intensity inside each cluster and the directional slope of the image intensity.

3.1 Implementation Issues

It is possible to implement the space filling curve dithering with adaptive cluster in two stages:

1. Estimate the cluster size based on image characteristics;

2. Change the cluster size according to some function of (1).

The separation of these two mechanisms makes the algorithm more flexible and allows for experimentation with different sets of criteria in the specification of the cluster size. The latter procedure gives input to the former establishing a clean interface between them.

Although in this work we have experimented mainly with an adaptive criterium based on the variation of the directional derivative of the image intensity function, as explained in the previous section; there are other types of criteria that we believe are worth exploring. One example is the cluster adaptation based on the physical reproduction function of the imaging system in order to compensate for its deficiencies. Other example is an adaptation criterium based on a function of the image domain in order to create graphical effects. This opens up many other possibilities of use for the method.

In our implementation the cluster size control is done in the first pass through the cluster cells. At each point of the image, the maximum allowable cluster size is determined by the adaptation criteria. While image elements in the region are processed (to accumulate intensity), the current cluster size is compared with the maximum allowable cluster size at that point. If this maximum allowable size is smaller than the current size, it becomes the current cluster size. The algorithm terminates the first pass when the number of elements in the region exceeds the cluster size. Then, it moves on to generate the dot pattern configuration, as explained in the previous section.

To make the algorithm more versatile, the adaptation criteria can be passed as a parameter to the program. The default criterium is the rule described above using an exponential of base 2. The other options provided include: linear variation with the value of the directional derivative of the image function, or using a table supplied by the user.

4   RESULTS

In this section we show the results of applying the algorithm to various types of images. These test images reflect the main characteristics of images encountered in digital printing situations.

The figures below compare the output of the space filling curve dithering algorithm with and without adaptive clustering. All input images are gray-scale with 8 bits of intensity resolution and spatial resolution varying from 80 to 400 ppi (pixels per inch). The output images are halftoned and printed at 1200 dpi (dots per inch). The images in Figures 4 and 5 are scaled using pixel replication in order to show more clearly the halftone screen dots.

Figure 4 is a test pattern of intensity gradations using linear ramps. The gradient increases in steps such that the rate of change in intensity is almost constant for each rectangle. As the slope of the ramp doubles, the cluster size also decreases by a factor of two. The maximum cluster size is 31 pixels.

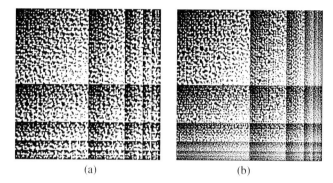

(a)   (b)

Figure 4: Linear intensity gradations (a) constant cluster size of 31 pixels (b) variable cluster size.

Figure 5 is a cartoon image consisting of line drawings and areas of constant gray level. The shadow on the wall in the background is rendered as regular pattern of dots simulating a standard halftone screen. The effect of the adaptive method is striking. The improvement obtained is mainly due to the high frequencies of the image. It needs dithering only in the areas of intermediate intensity. In this case, the algorithm was capable of matching exactly the edges of the drawings and at the same time reproducing with uniform dot patterns the different gray shades. We should remark that printing this image with the traditional AM clustering algorithm would certainly result in moirée patterns on the gray regions of the original image, because of the dot patterns used to produce the gray shade.

Figure 6 shows a comparison of the adaptive dithering (right) with the space filling curve dithering algorithm using fixed cluster size (left), as we increase the cluster size. The fixed cluster sizes in this figure are, from top to bottom, 30, 15 and 3 pixels. Also, these are the maximum cluster sizes used to process the corresponding image with the adaptive algorithm.

Finally, we show the application of the algorithm for high resolution printing. In order to do this, we made several tests to find the optimal cluster size for the phototypesetter used to print this paper. The image in Figure 7(b) is printed at 1200 dpi with a maximum cluster size of 7 pixels, as determined by the experiments. The image in Figure 7(a) is printed at the same resolution with a dispersed-dot dither (cluster size of 1 pixel). This comparison demonstrates the effectiveness of the method to match the characteristics of the output device.

5   CONCLUSIONS

An adaptive digital halftoning method with variable size clustering was presented. It extends the space filling curve dithering algorithm

Figure 5: Line drawing cartoon (a) constant cluster size of 27 pixels (b) variable cluster size

to change the size of pixel clusters according to local characteristics of the image. This makes possible to achieve an optimal rendition of gray shades while preserving image detail.

The dithering techniques described in this paper can also be applied with great effectiveness to color images. We developed a color halftoning algorithm that employs adaptive dot clustering with error diffusion on multiple image channels [5]. These features make the algorithm particularly suited for color reproduction using any number of process colors.

ACKNOWLEDGEMENTS

This work was done during the period the authors visited the Hewlett-Packard Labs in Palo Alto. We wish to thank Ricardo Motta who provided us with the working environment necessary for doing this research. The visit to HP was sponsored by the RHAE project from MCT/CNPq in Brazil.

REFERENCES

[1] A. Rosenfeld and A. C. Kak. *Digital Picture Processing*. Academic Press, 1976.

[2] R. Ulichney. *Digital Halftoning*. MIT Press, Cambridge, Ma, 1987.

[3] L. Velho and J. de M. Gomes. Digital halftoning with space filling curves. *Computer Graphics (Proceedings SIGGRAPH '91)*, 25(4):81–90, 1991.

[4] L. Velho and J. de M. Gomes. Space filling curve dithering with adaptive clustering. In *Proceedings of SIBGRAPI'92, V Brazilian Simposium of Computer Graphics and Image Processing*, pages 1–9. SBC – Sociedade Brasileira de Computação, 1992.

[5] L. Velho and J. de M. Gomes. Color halftoning with stochastic screening and adaptive clustering. Preprint, 1995. IMPA – Instituto de Matemática Pura e Aplicada.

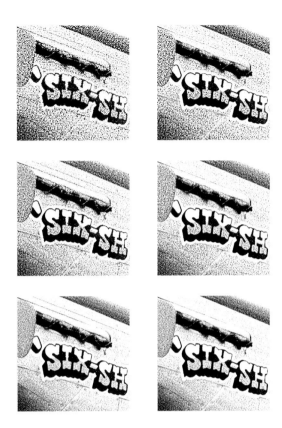

Figure 6: Comparison of adaptive (right) and non-adaptive (left) clustering. From top to bottom, cluster sizes of 30, 15, and 3 pixels.

(a)

(b)

Figure 7: Images printed at a resolution of 1200 dpi: (a) dispersed-dot dither, (b) adaptive dither with maximum cluster size of 7 pixels.

Fast Multiresolution Image Querying

Charles E. Jacobs   *Adam Finkelstein*   *David H. Salesin*

Department of Computer Science and Engineering
University of Washington
Seattle, Washington 98195

Abstract

We present a method for searching in an image database using a query image that is similar to the intended target. The query image may be a hand-drawn sketch or a (potentially low-quality) scan of the image to be retrieved. Our searching algorithm makes use of multiresolution wavelet decompositions of the query and database images. The coefficients of these decompositions are distilled into small "signatures" for each image. We introduce an "image querying metric" that operates on these signatures. This metric essentially compares how many significant wavelet coefficients the query has in common with potential targets. The metric includes parameters that can be tuned, using a statistical analysis, to accommodate the kinds of image distortions found in different types of image queries. The resulting algorithm is simple, requires very little storage overhead for the database of signatures, and is fast enough to be performed on a database of 20,000 images at interactive rates (on standard desktop machines) as a query is sketched. Our experiments with hundreds of queries in databases of 1000 and 20,000 images show dramatic improvement, in both speed and success rate, over using a conventional L^1, L^2, or color histogram norm.

CR Categories and Subject Descriptors: I.4.0 [Image Processing]: General — Image processing software; I.3.6 [Computer Graphics]: Methodology and Techniques — Interaction Techniques.

Additional Key Words: content-based retrieval, image databases, image indexing, image metrics, query by content, query by example, similarity retrieval, sketch retrieval, wavelets.

1   Introduction

With the explosion of desktop publishing, the ubiquity of color scanners and digital media, and the advent of the World Wide Web, people now have easy access to tens of thousands of digital images. This trend is likely to continue, providing more and more people with access to increasingly large image databases.

As the size of these databases grows, traditional methods of interaction break down. For example, while it is relatively easy for a person to quickly look over a few hundred "thumbnail" images to find a specific image query, it is much harder to locate that query among several thousand. Exhaustive search quickly breaks down as an effective strategy when the database becomes sufficiently large.

One commonly-employed searching strategy is to index the image database with keywords. However, such an approach is also fraught with difficulties. First, it requires a person to manually tag all the images with keys, a time-consuming task. Second, as Niblack *et al.* point out [20], this keyword approach has the problem that some visual aspects are inherently difficult to describe, while others are equally well described in many different ways. In addition, it may be difficult for the user to guess which visual aspects have been indexed.

In this paper, we explore an alternative strategy for searching an image database, in which the query is expressed either as a low-resolution image from a scanner or video camera, or as a rough sketch of the image painted by the user. This basic approach to image querying has been referred to in a variety of ways, including "query by content" [1, 4, 20], "query by example" [10, 13, 14], "similarity retrieval" [6, 16, 17, 21, 35] and "sketch retrieval" [14]. Note that this type of content-based querying can also be applied in conjunction with keyword-based querying or any other existing approach.

Several factors make this problem difficult to solve. The "query" image is typically very different from the "target" image, so the retrieval method must allow for some distortions. If the query is scanned, it may suffer artifacts such as color shift, poor resolution, dithering effects, and misregistration. If the query is painted, it is limited by perceptual error in both shape and color, as well as by the artistic prowess and patience of the user. For these reasons, straightforward approaches such as L^1 or L^2 image metrics are not very effective in discriminating the target image from the rest of the database. In order to match such imperfect queries more effectively, a kind of "image querying metric" must be developed that accommodates these distortions and yet distinguishes the target image from the rest of the database. In addition, the retrieval should ideally be fast enough to handle databases with tens of thousands of images at interactive rates.

In this paper, we describe how a Haar wavelet decomposition of the query and database images can be used to match a content-based query both quickly and effectively. The input to our retrieval method is a sketched or scanned image, intended to be an approximation to the image being retrieved. Since the input is only approximate, the approach we have taken is to present the user with a small set of the most promising target images as output, rather than with a single "correct" match. We have found that 20 images (the number of slides on a slide sheet) are about the most that can be scanned quickly and reliably by a user in search of the target.

In order to perform this ranking, we define an *image querying metric* that makes use of truncated, quantized versions of the wavelet decompositions, which we call *signatures*. The signatures contain only the most significant information about each image. The image querying metric essentially compares how many significant wavelet coefficients the query has in common with potential targets. We show how the metric can be tuned, using statistical techniques, to discriminate most effectively for different types of content-based image querying, such as scanned or hand-painted images. We also present a novel database organization for computing this metric ex-

Permission to make digital/hard copy of part or all of this work for personal or classroom use is granted without fee provided that copies are not made or distributed for profit or commercial advantage, the copyright notice, the title of the publication and its date appear, and notice is given that copying is by permission of ACM, Inc. To copy otherwise, to republish, to post on servers, or to redistribute to lists, requires prior specific permission and/or a fee.

© 1995   ACM-0-89791-701-4/95/008 $3.50

tremely fast. (Our system processes a 128×128 image query on a database of 20,000 images in under 1/2 second on an SGI Indy R4400; by contrast, searching the same database using an L^1 metric takes over 14 minutes.) Finally, we evaluate the results of applying our tuned image querying metric on hundreds of queries in databases of 1000 and 20,000 images.

The content-based querying method we describe has applications in many different domains, including graphic design, architecture [30], TV production [27], multimedia [29], ubiquitous computing [36], art history [13], geology [26], satellite image databases [16], and medical imaging [15]. For example, a graphic designer may want to find an image that is stored on her own system using a painted query. She may also want to find out if a supplier of ultra-high-resolution digital images has a particular image in its database, using a low-resolution scanned query. In the realm of ubiquitous computing, a computer may need to find a given document in its database, given a video image of a page of that document, scanned in from the real-world environment. In all of these applications, improving the technology for content-based querying is an important and acknowledged challenge [8].

1.1 Related work

Previous approaches to content-based image querying have applied such properties as color histograms [33], texture analysis [12], and shape features like circularity and major-axis orientation of regions in the image [7], as well as combinations of these techniques.

One of the most notable systems for querying by image content, called "QBIC," was developed at IBM [20] and is now available commercially. The emphasis in QBIC is in allowing a user to compose a query based on a variety of different visual attributes; for example, the user might specify a particular color composition ($x\%$ of color 1, $y\%$ of color 2, etc.), a particular texture, some shape features, and a rough sketch of dominant edges in the target image, along with relative weights for all of these attributes. The QBIC system also allows users to annotate database images by outlining key features to search on. By contrast, the emphasis in our work is in searching directly from a query image, without any further specifications from the user — either about the database images or about the particulars of the search itself.

The work of Hirata and Kato [10] is perhaps the most like our own in its style of user interaction. In their system, called "query by visual example" (QVE), edge extraction is performed on user queries. These edges are matched against those of the database images in a fairly complex process that allows for corresponding edges to be shifted or deformed with respect to each other.

It is difficult to directly compare our results with these previous methods, since running times are rarely reported, and since the number of tests reported and the size of the databases being searched have generally been quite small. From the little information that has been provided, it appears that the success rate of our method is at least as good as that of other systems that work from a simple user sketch.

To our knowledge, we are the first to use a multiresolution approach for solving this problem. Among other advantages, our approach allows queries to be specified at any resolution (potentially different from that of the target); moreover, the running time and storage of our method are independent of the resolutions of the database images. In addition, the signature information required by our algorithm can be extracted from a wavelet-compressed version of the image directly, allowing the signature database to be created conveniently from a set of compressed images. Finally, our algorithm is much simpler to implement and to use than most previous approaches.

1.2 Overview of paper

In the next section, we discuss our approach to image querying in more detail and define an "image querying metric" that can be used for searching with imprecise queries. Section 3 describes the image querying algorithm in detail; the algorithm is simple enough that almost all of the code is included here. Section 4 describes the application we have built on top of this algorithm, and gives some examples of its use. Section 5 describes the results of our tests, and Section 6 outlines some areas for future research. Finally, the appendix discusses the statistical technique, "logit," that we used to tune the weights of our metric.

2 Developing a metric for image querying

Consider the problem of computing the distance between a query image Q and a potential target image T. The most obvious metrics to consider are the L^1 or L^2 norms:

$$||Q,T||_1 \quad = \quad \sum_{i,j} |Q[i,j] - T[i,j]| \qquad (1)$$

$$||Q,T||_2 \quad = \quad \left(\sum_{i,j} (Q[i,j] - T[i,j])^2 \right)^{1/2} \qquad (2)$$

However, these metrics are not only expensive to compute, but they are also fairly ineffective when it comes to matching an inexact query image in a large database of potential targets. For example, in our experience with scanned queries (described in Section 5), the L^1 and L^2 error metrics rank their intended target image in the highest 1% of the database only 3% of the time. (This rank is computed by sorting the database according to its L^1 or L^2 distance from the query, and evaluating the intended target's position in the sorted list.)

On the other hand, the target of the query image is almost always readily discernible to the human eye, despite such potential artifacts as color shifts, misregistration, dithering effects, and distortion (which, taken together, account for the relatively poor performance of the L^1 and L^2 metrics). The solution, it would seem, is to try to find an image metric that is "tuned" for the kind of errors present in image querying; that is, we would like a metric that counts primarily those types of differences that a human would use for discriminating images, but that gives much less weight to the types of errors that a human would ignore for this task. This problem is related to that of finding a good perceptual error metric for images, although, to our knowledge, most previous work in this area has been devoted primarily to minimizing image artifacts, for example, in image compression [11, 24, 34].

Since there is no obvious "correct" metric to use for image querying, we are faced with the problem of constructing one from scratch, using (informed) trial and error. The rest of this section describes the issues we addressed in developing our image querying metric.

2.1 A multiresolution approach

Our goal was to construct an image metric that is fast to compute, that requires little storage for each database image, and that improves significantly upon the L^1 or L^2 metrics in discriminating the targets of inexact queries. For several reasons, we hypothesized that a two-dimensional wavelet decomposition of the images [31, 32] would provide a good foundation on which to build such a metric:

- Wavelet decompositions allow for very good image approximation with just a few coefficients. This property has been exploited for lossy image compression [3]. Typically, in these schemes, just the wavelet coefficients with the largest magnitude are used.

- Wavelet decompositions can be used to extract and encode edge information [19]. Edges are likely to be among the key features of a user-painted query.

- The coefficients of a wavelet decomposition provide information that is independent of the original image resolution. Thus, a wavelet-based scheme allows the resolutions of the query and the target to be effectively decoupled.

- Wavelet decompositions are fast and easy to compute, requiring linear time in the size of the image and very little code.

2.2 Components of the metric

Given that we wish to use a wavelet approach, there are a number of issues that still need to be addressed:

1. **Color space.** We need to choose a color space in which to represent the images and perform the decomposition. (The same issue arises for L^1 and L^2 image metrics.) We decided to try a number of different color spaces: RGB, HSV, and YIQ. Ultimately, YIQ turned out to be the most effective of the three for our data, as reported in Figure 4 of Section 5.

2. **Wavelet type.** We chose Haar wavelets, both because they are fastest to compute and simplest to implement. In addition, user-painted queries (at least with our simple interface) tend to have large constant-colored regions, which are well represented by this basis. One drawback of the Haar basis for lossy compression is that it tends to produce blocky image artifacts for high compression rates. In our application, however, the results of the decomposition are never viewed, so these artifacts are of no concern. We have not experimented with other wavelet bases; others may work as well as or better than Haar (although will undoubtedly be slower).

3. **Decomposition type.** We need to choose either a "standard" or "non-standard" type of two-dimensional wavelet decomposition [2, 31]. In the Haar basis the non-standard basis functions are square, whereas the standard basis functions are rectangular. We would therefore expect the non-standard basis to be better at identifying features that are about as wide as they are high, and the standard basis to work best for images containing lines and other rectangular features. As reported in Figure 4 of Section 5, we tried both types of decomposition with all three color spaces, and found that the standard basis works best on our data, for both scanned and painted queries.

4. **Truncation.** For a 128×128 image, there are $128^2 = 16,384$ different wavelet coefficients for each color channel. Rather than using all of these coefficients in the metric, it is preferable to "truncate" the sequence, keeping only the coefficients with largest magnitude. This truncation both accelerates the search for a query and reduces storage for the database. Surprisingly, truncating the coefficients also appears to *improve* the discriminatory power of the metric, probably because it allows the metric to consider only the most significant features — which are the ones most likely to match a user's painted query — and to ignore any mismatches in the fine detail, which the user, most likely, would have been unable to accurately re-create. We experimented with different levels of truncation and found that storing the 60 largest-magnitude coefficients in each channel worked best for our painted queries, while 40 coefficients worked best for our scanned queries.

5. **Quantization.** Like truncation, the quantization of each wavelet coefficient can serve several purposes: speeding the search, reducing the storage, and actually improving the discriminatory power of the metric. The quantized coefficients retain little or no data about the precise magnitudes of major features in the images; however, the mere presence or absence of such features appears to have more discriminatory power for image querying than the features' precise magnitudes. We found that quantizing each significant coefficient to just two levels — +1, representing large positive coefficients; or −1, representing large negative coefficients — works remarkably well. This simple classification scheme also allows for a very fast comparison algorithm, as discussed in Section 3.

6. **Normalization.** The normalization of the wavelet basis functions is related to the magnitude of the computed wavelet coefficients: as the amplitude of each basis function increases, the size of that basis function's corresponding coefficient decreases accordingly. We chose a normalization factor that makes all wavelets orthonormal to each other. This normalization factor has the effect of emphasizing differences mostly at coarser scales. Because changing the normalization factor requires rebuilding the entire database of signatures, we have not experimented further with this degree of freedom.

2.3 The "image querying metric"

In order to write down the resulting metric, we must introduce some notation. First, let us now think of Q and T as representing just a single color channel of the wavelet decomposition of the query and target images. Let $Q[0,0]$ and $T[0,0]$ be the *scaling function coefficients* corresponding to the overall average intensity of that color channel. Further, let $\tilde{Q}[i,j]$ and $\tilde{T}[i,j]$ represent the $[i,j]$-th *truncated, quantized wavelet coefficients* of Q and T; these values are either −1, 0, or +1. For convenience, we will define $\tilde{Q}[0,0]$ and $\tilde{T}[0,0]$, which do not correspond to any wavelet coefficient, to be 0.

A suitable metric for image querying can then be written as

$$||Q,T|| = w_{0,0}|Q[0,0] - T[0,0]| + \sum_{i,j} w_{i,j} |\tilde{Q}[i,j] - \tilde{T}[i,j]|$$

We can simplify this metric in a number of ways.

First, we have found the metric to be just as effective if the difference between the wavelet coefficients $|\tilde{Q}[i,j] - \tilde{T}[i,j]|$ is replaced by $(\tilde{Q}[i,j] \neq \tilde{T}[i,j])$, where the expression $(a \neq b)$ is interpreted as 1 if $a \neq b$, and 0 otherwise. This expression will be faster to compute in our algorithm.

Second, we would like to group terms together into "buckets" so that only a small number of weights $w_{i,j}$ need to be determined experimentally. We group the terms according to the scale of the wavelet functions to which they correspond, using a simple bucketing function $bin(i, j)$, described in detail in Section 3.

Finally, in order to make the metric even faster to evaluate over many different target images, we only consider terms in which the *query* has a non-zero wavelet coefficient $\tilde{Q}[i,j]$. A potential benefit of this approach is that it allows for a query without much detail to match a very detailed target image quite closely; however, it does not allow a detailed query to match a target that does not contain that same detail. We felt that this asymmetry might better capture the form of most painted image queries. (Note that this last modification technically disqualifies our "metric" from being a metric at all, since metrics, by definition, are symmetric. Nevertheless, for lack of a better term, we will continue to use the word "metric" in the rest of this paper.)

Thus, the final "L^q" *image querying metric* $||Q,T||_q$ is given by

$$w_0 |Q[0,0] - T[0,0]| + \sum_{i,j:\tilde{Q}[i,j]\neq 0} w_{bin(i,j)} \left(\tilde{Q}[i,j] \neq \tilde{T}[i,j] \right) \quad (3)$$

The weights w_b in equation (3) provide a convenient mechanism for tuning the metric to different databases and styles of image querying. The actual weights we use are given in Section 3, while the method we use for their computation is described in the appendix.

2.4   Fast computation of the image querying metric

To actually compute the L^q metric over a database of images, it is generally quicker to count the number of *matching* $\tilde{Q}$ and $\tilde{T}$ coefficients, rather than *mismatching* coefficients, since we expect the vast majority of database images not to match the query image well at all. It is therefore convenient to rewrite the summation in (3) in terms of an "equality" operator ($a = b$), which evaluates to 1 when $a = b$, and 0 otherwise. Using this operator, the summation

$$\sum_{i,j:\tilde{Q}[i,j]\neq 0} w_k \left(\tilde{Q} \neq \tilde{T} \right)$$

in equation (3) can be rewritten as

$$\sum_{i,j:\tilde{Q}[i,j]\neq 0} w_k - \sum_{i,j:\tilde{Q}[i,j]\neq 0} w_k \left(\tilde{Q} = \tilde{T} \right)$$

Since the first part of this expression $\sum w_k$ is independent of $\tilde{T}$, we can ignore it for the purposes of ranking the different target images in L^q. It therefore suffices to compute the expression

$$w_0 |Q[0,0] - T[0,0]| - \sum_{i,j:\tilde{Q}[i,j]\neq 0} w_{bin(i,j)} \left(\tilde{Q}[i,j] = \tilde{T}[i,j] \right) \quad (4)$$

This expression is just a weighted sum of the difference in the average color between Q and T, and the number of stored wavelet coefficients of T whose indices and signs match those of Q.

3   The algorithm

The final algorithm is a straightforward embodiment of the L^q metric as given in equation (4), applied to the problem of finding a given query in a large database of images. The complexity of the algorithm is linear in the number of database images. The constant factor in front of this linear term is small, as discussed in Section 5.

At a high level, the algorithm can be described as follows: In a preprocessing step, we perform a standard two-dimensional Haar wavelet decomposition [2, 31] of every image in the database, and store just the overall average color and the indices and signs of the m largest-magnitude wavelet coefficients. The indices for all of the database images are then organized into a single data structure in the program that optimizes searching. Then, for each query image, we perform the same wavelet decomposition, and again throw away all but the average color and the largest m coefficients. The score for each target image T is then computed by evaluating expression (4).

The rest of the section describes this algorithm in more detail.

3.1   Preprocessing step

A standard two-dimensional Haar wavelet decomposition of an image is very simple to code. It involves a one-dimensional decomposition on each row of the image, followed by a one-dimensional decomposition on each column of the result.

The following pseudocode performs this one-dimensional decomposition on an array A of h elements, with h a power of two:

```
proc DecomposeArray(A : array[0..h − 1] of color):
    A ← A/√h
    while h > 1 do:
        h ← h/2
        for i ← 0 to h − 1 do:
            A′[i] ← (A[2i] + A[2i + 1])/√2
            A′[h + i] ← (A[2i] − A[2i + 1])/√2
        end for
        A ← A′
    end while
end proc
```

In the pseudocode above, the entries of A are assumed to be 3-dimensional color components, each in the range $[0,1]$. The various arithmetic operations are performed on the separate color components individually.

An entire $r \times r$ image T can thus be decomposed as follows:

```
proc DecomposeImage(T : array[0..r − 1, 0..r − 1] of color):
    for row ← 1 to r do:
        DecomposeArray(T[row, 0..r − 1])
    end for
    for col ← 1 to r do:
        DecomposeArray(T[0..r − 1, col])
    end for
end proc
```

(In practice, the *DecomposeImage* routine is best implemented by decomposing each row, then transposing the matrix, decomposing each row again, and transposing back.)

After the decomposition process, the entry $T[0,0]$ is proportional to the average color of the overall image, while the other entries of T contain the *wavelet coefficients*. (These coefficients are sufficient for reconstructing the original image T, although we will have no need to do so in this application.)

Finally, we store only $T[0,0]$ and the indices and signs of the largest m wavelet coefficients of T. To optimize the search process, the remaining m wavelet coefficients for *all* of the database images are organized into a set of six arrays, called the *search arrays*, with one array for every combination of sign ($+$ or $-$) and color channel (such as R, G, and B).

For example, let $\mathcal{D}_+^c$ denote the "positive" search array for the color channel c. Each element $\mathcal{D}_+^c[i,j]$ of this array contains a list of all images T having a large positive wavelet coefficient $T[i,j]$ in color channel c. Similarly, each element $\mathcal{D}_-^c[i,j]$ of the "negative" search array points to a list of images with large negative coefficients in c.

These six arrays are used to speed the search for a particular query, as described in the next section. In our implementation, the search arrays are created as a preprocess for a given database and stored on disk. We use a small stand-alone program to add new images to the database incrementally. This program performs the wavelet decomposition for each new image, finds the largest m coefficients, and augments the database search arrays accordingly.

3.2   Querying

The querying step is straightforward. For a given query image Q, we perform the same wavelet decomposition described in the previous section. Again, we keep just the overall average color and the indices and signs of the largest m coefficients in each color channel.

To compute a score, we loop through each color channel c. We first

Figure 1: The image querying application. The user paints a query in the large rectangular window, and the 20 highest-ranked targets appear in the small windows on the right. To avoid copyright infringements, the database for this example contains only 96 images (all created by artists who have been dead more than 75 years). Because the database is so limited, only the intended target (in the upper-left small window) appears to match the query very closely.

compute the differences between the query's average intensity in that channel $Q^c[0,0]$ and those of the database images. Next, for each of the m non-zero, truncated wavelet coefficients $\tilde{Q}^c[i,j]$, we search through the list corresponding to those database images containing the same large-magnitude coefficient and sign, and update each of those image's scores accordingly:

```
func ScoreQuery(Q : array[0..r − 1, 0..r − 1] of color; m : int):
    DecomposeImage(Q)
    Initialize scores[i] ← 0 for all i
    for each color channel c do:
        for each database image T do:
            scores[index(T)] += wᶜ[0] ∗ |Qᶜ[0,0] − Tᶜ[0,0]|
        end for
        Q̃ ← TruncateCoefficients(Q, m)
        for each non-zero coefficient Q̃ᶜ[i,j] do
            if Q̃ᶜ[i,j] > 0 then
                list ← 𝒟ᶜ₊[i,j]
            else
                list ← 𝒟ᶜ₋[i,j]
            end if
            for each element ℓ of list do
                scores[index(ℓ)] −= wᶜ[bin(i,j)]
            end for
        end for
    end for
    return scores
end func
```

The function $bin(i,j)$ provides a way of grouping different coefficients into a small number of bins, with each bin weighted by some constant $w[b]$. For a given set of bins, the best weights $w[b]$ can be found experimentally, as discussed in the appendix. The larger the training set, the more weights that can be used. The size of our training set was sufficient for 18 weights: 6 per color channel.

In our implementation, we use the function

$$bin(i,j) := \min\{\max\{i,j\}, 5\}.$$

For our database of images, a good set of weights, using the YIQ color space and standard decomposition, was found to be:

	Painted			Scanned		
b	$w^Y[b]$	$w^I[b]$	$w^Q[b]$	$w^Y[b]$	$w^I[b]$	$w^Q[b]$
0	4.04	15.14	22.62	5.00	19.21	34.37
1	0.78	0.92	0.40	0.83	1.26	0.36
2	0.46	0.53	0.63	1.01	0.44	0.45
3	0.42	0.26	0.25	0.52	0.53	0.14
4	0.41	0.14	0.15	0.47	0.28	0.18
5	0.32	0.07	0.38	0.30	0.14	0.27

(All scaling function coefficients in our implementation are reals in the range $[0,1]$, so their differences tend to be smaller than the differences of the truncated, quantized wavelet coefficients. Thus, the weights on the scaling functions $w[0]$ have relatively large magnitudes because they generally multiply smaller quantities.)

As a final step, our algorithm examines the list of scores, which may be positive or negative. The smallest (typically, the most negative) scores are considered to be the closest matches. We use a "Heap-Select" algorithm [23] to find the 20 closest matches in linear time.

4 The application

We have built a simple interactive application that incorporates our image querying algorithm. The program is written in C++, using OpenGL and Motif. It runs on SGI workstations.

A screen dump of the running application is shown in Figure 1. The user paints an image query in the large rectangular area on the left side of the application window. When the query is complete, the user presses the "Match" button. The system then tests the query against all the images in the database and displays the 20 top-ranked targets in the small windows on the right. (The highest-ranked target is displayed in the upper left, the second-highest target to its right, and so on, in row-major order.)

For convenience, the user may paint on a "canvas" of any aspect ratio. However, our application does not currently use this information in performing the match. Instead, the painted query is internally rescaled to a square aspect ratio and searched against a database in which all images have been similarly rescaled as a preprocess. We discuss how a user-specified aspect ratio might also be used to improve the match in Section 6.

Figure 2(a) shows an example of a painted query, along with the L^q rank of its intended target (c) in databases of 1093 and 20,558 images.

(a) Painted	(b) Scanned	(c) Target

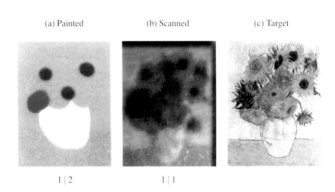

| 1 \| 2 | 1 \| 1 | |

Figure 2: Queries and their target: (a) a query painted from memory; (b) a scanned query; and (c) their intended target. Below the queries, the L^q ranks of the intended target are shown for two databases of sizes 1093 \| 20,558.

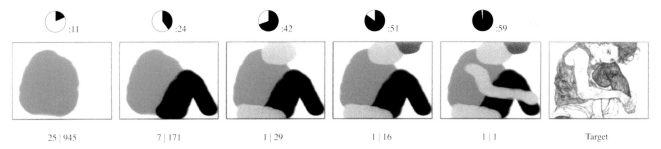

Figure 3: *Progression of an interactive query. Above each partially-formed query is the actual time (in seconds) at which the snapshot was taken. Below each query are the L^q ranks of the intended target for databases of sizes 1093 | 20,558.*

Rather than painting a query, the user may also click on any of the displayed target images to serve as a subsequent query, or use any stored image file as a query. Figure 2(b) shows an example of using a low-quality scanned image as a query, again with its L^q rank in the two databases.

Because the retrieval time is so fast (under 1/2 second in a database of 20,000 images), we have also implemented an "interactive" mode, in which the 20 top-ranked target images are updated whenever the user pauses for a half-second or more. Figure 3 shows the progression of an interactive query, along with the actual time at which each snapshot was taken and the L^q rank of the intended target at that moment in the two different databases.

5 Results

To evaluate our image querying algorithm, we collected three types of query data.

The first set, called "scanned queries," were obtained by printing out small $1/2" \times 1/2"$ thumbnails of our database images, using a full-color Tektronix Phaser IISDX printer at 300dpi, and then scanning them back into the system using a Hewlett-Packard ScanJet IIc scanner. As a result of these steps, the scanned images became somewhat altered; in our case, the scanned images generally appeared fuzzier, darker, and slightly misregistered from the originals. An example of a scanned query is shown in Figure 2(b). We gathered 270 such queries, of which 100 were reserved for evaluating our metric, and the other 170 were used as a training set.

The second set, called "painted queries," were obtained by asking 20 subjects, most of whom were first-time users of the system, to paint complete image queries, in the non-interactive mode, while looking at thumbnail-sized versions of the images they were attempting to retrieve. We also gathered 270 of these queries and divided them into evaluation and training sets in the same fashion.

The third set, called "memory queries," were gathered in order to see how well this style of querying might work if users were not looking at small versions of the images they wanted to retrieve, but instead were attempting to retrieve images from memory. To obtain these queries, we asked each subject to initially examine two targets T_1 and T_2, and paint a query for T_1, which we threw away. The subject was then asked to iteratively examine a target T_{i+1} (starting with $i = 2$) and paint query T_i, which had not been viewed since before query T_{i-1} was painted. In this way, we hoped to get a more accurate idea of how well a user might do if attempting to retrieve a familiar image from memory, without being able to see the image directly. An example of a memory query is shown in Figure 2(a). We gathered 100 of these queries, which were used for evaluation only.

5.1 Training

Each training set was subdivided into 2 equal sets. The first training set of 85 queries was used to determine the weights of the image querying metric, as described in the appendix. The second training set of 85 queries was used to find the optimal color space, decomposition type, and number m of coefficients to store for each image. We performed an exhaustive search over all three dimensions, using color spaces RGB, HSV, and YIQ; standard and non-standard wavelet decompositions; and $m = 10, 20, 30, \ldots, 100$. For each combination, we found weights using the first set of images, and then tested these weights on the second set of images, using "the percentage of intended targets that were ranked among the top 1% in our database of 1093 images" as the evaluation function.

The results of these tests for scanned and painted queries are reported in Figure 4. For scanned queries, 40 coefficients with a standard decomposition and YIQ worked best. The same configuration, except with 60 coefficients, worked best for painted queries. This latter configuration was used for testing the success of memory queries as well.

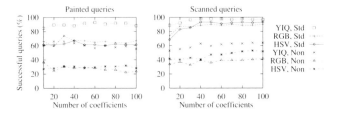

Figure 4: *Choosing among color spaces (RGB, HSV, or YIQ), wavelet decomposition type (standard or non-standard), and number of coefficients.*

5.2 Performance on actual queries

Using the weights obtained from the training set, we then evaluated the performance using the remaining 100 queries of each type. The graphs in Figure 5 compare our L^q metric to the L^1 and L^2 metrics and to a color histogram metric L^c, for a database of 1093 images. The three graphs show, from left to right: scanned queries (using 40 coefficients), painted queries (using 60 coefficients), and memory queries (using 60 coefficients).

The L^1 and L^2 metrics in these graphs were computed on both the full-resolution images (128×128 pixels) and on averaged-down versions (8×8 pixels), which have roughly the same amount of data as the 60-coefficient L^q metric. The color histogram metric L^c was computed by quantizing the pixel colors into a set of $6 \times 6 \times 6$ bins in RGB space, and then computing an L^1 metric over the number of pixels falling in each bin for the query versus the target.

Results for all six methods are reported by giving the percentage of queries y that were ranked among the top $x\%$ of the database images,

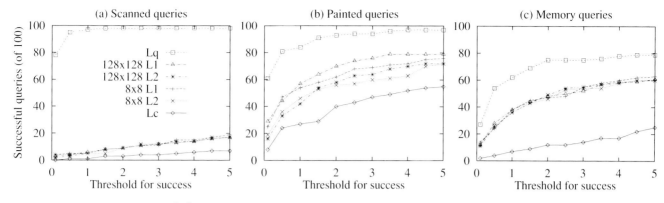

Figure 5: Comparison of L^q metric against L^1, L^2, and a color histogram metric L^c. The percentage of queries y ranked in the top x% of the database are plotted on the x and y axes.

with x and y plotted on the x- and y-axes. For example, the leftmost data point of each curve, at $x = 1/1093 \approx 0.09\%$, reports the percentage of queries whose intended targets were ranked in first place for each of the six methods; the data points at $x = 1\%$ report the percentage of queries whose intended targets were ranked among the top $\lfloor 0.01 * 1093 \rfloor = 10$ images; and so on.

Note that the scanned queries perform remarkably poorly under the L^1, L^2 and L^c metrics. These poor scores are probably due to the fact that the scanned queries were generally darker than their intended targets, and so matched many incorrect (darker) images in the database more closely.

5.3 Robustness with respect to distortions

In order to test more precisely how robust the different metrics are with respect to some of the distortions one might find in image querying, we devised the following suite of tests. In the first test, 100 randomly chosen color images from the database were scaled by a factor s ranging from 1 to 2 and used as a query. In the second test, the same images were rotated by a factor r between $0°$ and $45°$. In the third test, the same images were translated in a random direction by a distance t between 0 and 0.5 times the width of the query. In the fourth test, the colors of these images were uniformly shifted in normalized RGB space in a random direction by a distance c between 0 and 1. In the final test, all four of these transformations were applied for each test, in the order scale/rotate/translate/color-shift, with s, r, t, and c ranging as in the other tests. For all five tests, in cases where a border of the distorted image was undefined by the transformation (which occurs for rotations and translations), the image was padded with its overall average color. In cases where the color shift would lie outside the RGB cube, the color was clamped to $[0,1]^3$.

The top row of Figure 6 shows the results of these five tests. The curves in these graphs report the percentage of queries whose intended targets were ranked in the top 1% of the 1093-image database. Note that the L^q metric performs as well as or better than all other methods, except for L^c. However, as expected, the L^c metric does very poorly for color shifts, severely reducing this metric's utility in situations where a query's color is not always true. The bottom row shows the same five tests, but applied to each of our 100 scanned, painted, and memory queries — all with the L^q metric.

5.4 Effect of database size

We also wanted to test how well our method would perform as the size of the database was increased. We therefore gathered 19,465 images from the World Wide Web, using the WebCrawler [22] to find files on the Web with a ".gif" extension. We computed a signature and thumbnail for each image and stored the resulting database

locally, along with a "URL" for each image — a pointer back to the original Web site. The resulting application is a kind of graphical "Web browser," in which a user can paint a query and very quickly see the images on the Web that match it most closely. Clicking on one of these thumbnail images calls up the full-resolution original from the Web.

In order to check how well our metric performed, we created a set of 20 nested databases, with each database containing our original 1093 images plus increasingly large subsets of the Web database. The largest such database had 20,558 images. For each of the three sets of 100 queries, we then evaluated how many of those queries would find their intended target in the top 1% of the different nested databases. We found that the number of queries matching their correct targets by this criterion remained almost perfectly constant in all three cases, with the number of correctly matching queries varying by at most 2% across the different database sizes.

5.5 Speed of evaluation

We measured the speed of our program by running 68 queries 100 times each, with databases ranging in size from $n = 1093$ to $n = 20,558$, and with the number of coefficients ranging from $m = 20$ to $m = 1000$. A regression analysis indicates that the running time is linear in both m and n, with each query requiring approximately $190 + 0.11m + 0.012n$ milliseconds to process on an SGI Indy R4400. This running time includes the time to decompose a 128×128-pixel query, score all n images in the database according to the L^q metric, and find the 20 top-ranked targets.

As two points of comparison, Table 1 reports the average running time of our algorithm to that of the other methods surveyed for finding a query using $m = 20$ coefficients per channel in databases of size $n = 1093$ and $n = 20,558$ images. In all cases, the times reported do not include any preprocessing that can be performed on the database images alone.

Metric	Time	
	$n = 1093$	$n = 20,558$
L^q	0.19	0.44
L^1 (8×8)	0.66	7.46
L^2 (8×8)	0.68	6.39
L^1 (128×128)	47.46	892.60 (est.)
L^2 (128×128)	42.04	790.80 (est.)
L^c	0.47	5.03

Table 1: Average times (in seconds) to match a single query in databases of 1093 and 20,558 images under different metrics.

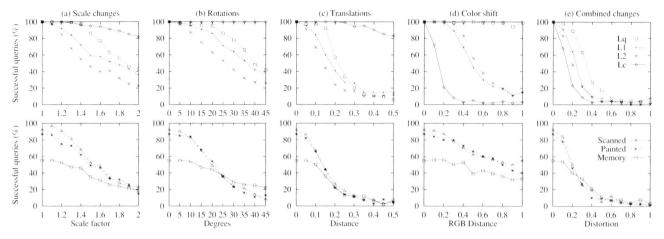

Figure 6: Robustness of various querying metrics with respect to different types of image distortions: (a) Scale changes; (b) Rotations; (c) Translations; (d) Color shifts; (e) All four effects combined. The top row (legend at upper right) compares the L^q metric to L^1, L^2 and L^c, using the target itself as the original undistorted query. The bottom row (legend at lower right) shows the same five tests applied to each of our 100 scanned, painted, and memory queries, using the L^q metric.

5.6 Interactive queries

To test the speed of interactive queries, we asked users to paint in the interactive mode, and we kept track of how long it took for the intended target to appear among the top 20 images in the database. For these tests, we used just $m = 20$ significant coefficients.

For the first such test, we had 5 users paint a total of 106 interactive queries, allowing them to look at thumbnails of the intended targets. The overall median time to retrieve the target images was 20 seconds.

Next, in order to see how this median query time might vary with database size, we asked 2 users to paint a total of 21 interactive queries in our database of 20,558 images. For each query, the application kept a log of each paint stroke and the time at which it was drawn. We then used these logs to simulate how quickly the same query would bring up the intended target among the top 20 images in databases of various sizes. The results are shown in Figure 7.

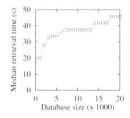

Figure 7: The effect of database size on median interactive query time.

To see if painting from memory would affect retrieval time, we selected 20 target images and, for each subject, we randomly divided these targets into two equal sets. Each subject was then asked to paint the 10 images from the first set while looking at a thumbnail of the image, and the 10 images from the second set from memory, in the style described for "memory queries" above. We used 3 subjects in this experiment. We found that the median query time increased from 18 seconds when the subjects were looking at the thumbnails, to 22 seconds when the queries were painted from memory.

In our experience with interactive querying, we have observed that users will typically be able to sketch all the information they know about an image in a minute or less, whether they are looking at a thumbnail or painting from memory. In most cases, the query succeeds within this short time. If the query fails to bring up the intended target within a minute or so, users will typically try adding some random details, which sometimes help in bringing up the image. If this tactic fails, users will simply give up and, in a real system, would presumably fall back on some other method of searching for the image. (In this case, we report an "infinite" query time.)

We have observed two benefits of painting queries interactively. First, the time to retrieve an image is generally reduced because the user simply paints until the target image appears, rather than painting until the query image seems finished. Second, the interactive mode subtly helps "train" the user to find images more efficiently, because the application is always providing feedback about the relative effectiveness of an unfinished query while it is being painted.

6 Discussion and future work

The algorithm we have described is extremely fast, requires only a small amount of data to be stored for each target image, and is remarkably effective. It is also fairly easy to understand and implement. Finally, it has parameters that can be tuned for a given database or type of query image.

Although this new image searching method has substantial advantages over previous approaches, its ultimate utility may depend to a large extent on the size of the image database being searched. Our tests suggest that, for the majority of non-interactive queries, our method will be able to pinpoint the correct target to within a 1%-sized subset of the overall database, regardless of the database's size. Thus, for a database of 100 images, it is easy to pull up the correct image precisely. However, for a database of 20,000 images, the user is still left with a list of 200 potential matches that must be searched visually, or by some other means. On the other hand, with interactive querying, even for a 20,000-image database it is still possible to place the target into the top 20 images the majority of the time. Nonetheless, creating a good query becomes increasingly difficult as the database grows. For a large enough database, even this interactive style of querying would begin to require more precision than most users can provide.

We have tried to perform a number of different tests to measure the success and robustness of our image querying metric. However, it is easy to envision many more tests that would be interesting to perform. One interesting test would be to try to quantify the degree to which different training sets affect our metric's sensitivity to various image distortions. For example, in querying images from memory, colors are less likely to be accurate. Presumably, a training set of "memory queries" would therefore reduce the metric's sensitivity to color accuracy. How significant is this effect? In addition, it would be interesting to examine whether providing separate training sets for individual users or for particular databases would make a significant difference in the metric's discriminatory power.

Our method also has some limitations, which we hope to address in future work. For example, while it is fairly robust with respect to a large degree of distortion in the query image, our metric does not currently allow for general pattern matching of a small query, such as an icon or company logo, inside some larger database image.

Here are some other areas for future research:

Aspect ratio. Currently, we allow users to choose an aspect ratio for their query; however, this aspect ratio is not used in the search itself. It would be straightforward to add an extra term to our image querying metric for the similarity of aspect ratio. The weight for this term could be found experimentally at the same time as the other weights are computed.

Perceptually-based spaces. It would be interesting to try using a perceptually uniform color space, such as CIE LUV or TekHVC [5], to see if it improves the effectiveness of our metric. In the same vein, it may help to compute differences on logarithmically-scaled intensities, which is closer to the way intensity is perceived [9].

Image clusters. Images in a large database appear to be "clustered" in terms of their proximity under our image querying metric. For example, using a portrait as a query image in our Web database selects portraits almost exclusively as targets. By contrast, using a "planet" image pulls up other planets. It would be interesting to perform some statistical clustering on the database and then show the user some representative images from the center of each cluster. These could be used either as querying keys, or merely as a way of providing an overview of the contents of the database.

Multiple metrics. In our experience with the system, we have noticed that a good query will bring up the target image, no matter which color space and decomposition method (standard or nonstandard) is used; however, the false matches found in these different spaces all tend to be very different. This observation leads us to wonder whether it is possible to develop a more effective method by combining the results of searching in different color spaces and decomposition types, perhaps taking the average of the ranks in the different spaces (or, alternately, the worst of the ranks), as the rank chosen by the overall metric.

Affine transformation and partial queries. As discussed above, a very interesting (and more difficult) direction for future research is to begin exploring methods for handling general affine transformations of the query image or for searching on partial queries. The "shiftable transforms," described by Simoncelli *et al.* [28], which allow for multiresolution transforms with translational, rotational, and scale invariance, may be helpful in these respects. Another idea for specifying partial queries would be to make use of the alpha channel of the query for specifying the portions of the query and target images over which the L^q metric should be computed.

Video querying. We would like to extend our method to the problem of searching for a given frame in a video sequence. The simplest solution would be to consider each frame of the video as a separate image in the database and to apply our method directly. A more interesting solution would be to explore using a three-dimensional multiresolution decomposition of the video sequence, combined perhaps with some form of motion compensation, in order to take better advantage of the extra coherence among the video frames.

Acknowledgements

We would like to thank Leo Guibas, Dan Huttenlocher, and Eric Saund for many useful discussions during the initial phase of this project; Jutta Joesch and Werner Stuetzle for guiding us to the logit statistical model; Jack Tumblin and Matthew Turk for informative background on perception and matching; Karin Scholz for advice on the user interface; Ronen Barzel and Maureen Stone for advice on the paper; and Michael Cohen for helpful discussions along the way. We would also like to thank Anh Phan for help in scanning images; Brian Pinkerton for help in using the WebCrawler to find still more; and Piotr Brzezicki, Dennis Dean, Stuart Denman, Glenn Fleishman, George Forman, James Gunterman, Li-Wei He, Greg Heil, David Keppel, Diane King, Andrea Lingenfelter, Gene Morgan, Jonathan Shakes, Taweewan Siwadune, Christina Tonitto, Connie Wellnitz, Erin Wilson, Michael Wong, and Mikala Woodward for trying out their artistic talents as subjects in our tests.

This work was supported by an Alfred P. Sloan Research Fellowship (BR-3495), an NSF Young Investigator award (CCR-9357790), an ONR Young Investigator award (N00014-95-1-0728), a grant from the University of Washington Royalty Research Fund (65-9731), and industrial gifts from Adobe, Microsoft, and Xerox.

References

[1] R. Barber, W. Equitz, W. Niblack, D. Petkovic, and P. Yanker. Efficient query by image content for very large image databases. In *Digest of Papers. COMPCON Spring '93*, pages 17–19, San Francisco, CA, USA, 1993.

[2] G. Beylkin, R. Coifman, and V. Rokhlin. Fast wavelet transforms and numerical algorithms I. *Communications on Pure and Applied Mathematics*, 44:141–183, 1991.

[3] R. DeVore, B. Jawerth, and B. Lucier. Image compression through wavelet transform coding. *IEEE Transactions on Information Theory*, 38(2):719–746, March 1992.

[4] C. Faloutsos, R. Barber, M. Flickner, J. Hafner, W. Niblack, D. Petkovic, and W. Equitz. Efficient and effective querying by image content. *Journal of Intelligent Information Systems: Integrating Artificial Intelligence and Database Technologies*, 3(3-4):231–262, 1994.

[5] James D. Foley, Andries van Dam, Steven K. Feiner, and John F. Hughes. *Computer Graphics: Principles and Practice*. Prentice-Hall, 1990.

[6] T. Gevers and A. W. M. Smuelders. An approach to image retrieval for image databases. In V. Marik, J. Lazansky, and R. R. Wagner, editors, *Database and Expert Systems Applicatons (DEXA '93)*, pages 615–626, Prague, Czechoslovakia, 1993.

[7] Yihong Gong, Hongjiang Zhang, H. C. Chuan, and M. Sakauchi. An image database system with content capturing and fast image indexing abilities. In *Proceedings of the International Conference on Multimedia Computing and Systems*, pages 121–130. IEEE, 1994.

[8] William I. Grosky, Rajiv Mehrotra, F. Golshani, H. V. Jagadish, Ramesh Jain, and Wayne Niblack. Research directions in image database management. In *Eighth International Conference on Data Engineering*, pages 146–148. IEEE, 1992.

[9] Donald Hearn and M. Pauline Baker. *Computer Graphics*. Addison-Wesley Publishing Company, Inc., 1994.

[10] K. Hirata and T. Kato. Query by visual example — content based image retrieval. In A. Pirotte, C. Delobel, and G. Gottlob, editors, *Advances in Database Technology (EDBT '92)*, pages 56–71, Vienna, Austria, 1992.

[11] N. Jayant, J. Johnston, and R. Safranek. Perceptual coding of images. In *Proceedings of the SPIE — The International Society for Optical Engineering*, volume 1913, pages 168–178, 1993.

[12] Atreyi Kankanhalli, Hong Jiang Zhang, and Chien Yong Low. Using texture for image retrieval. In *International Conference on Automation, Robotics and Computer Vision*. IEE, 1994.

[13] T. Kato. Database architecture for content-based image retrieval. In *Proceedings of the SPIE — The International Society for Optical Engineering*, volume 1662, pages 112–123, San Jose, CA, USA, 1992.

[14] T. Kato, T. Kurita, N. Otsu, and K. Hirata. A sketch retrieval method for full color image database — query by visual example. In *Proceedings of the 11th IAPR International Conference on Pattern Recognition*, pages 530–533, Los Alamitos, CA, USA, 1992.

[15] Patrick M. Kelly and T. Michael Cannon. CANDID: Comparison Algorithm for Navigating Digital Image Databases. In *Proceedings of the Seventh International Working Conference on Scientific and Statistical Database Management Storage and Retrieval for Image and Video Databases*. IEEE, 1994.

[16] A. Kitamoto, C. Zhou, and M. Takagi. Similarity retrieval of NOAA satellite imagery by graph matching. In *Storage and Retrieval for Image and Video Databases*, pages 60–73, San Jose, CA, USA, 1993.

[17] J. Liang and C. C. Chang. Similarity retrieval on pictorial databases based upon module operation. In S. Moon and H. Ikeda, editors, *Database Systems for Advanced Applications*, pages 19–26, Taejon, South Korea, 1993.

[18] G. S. Maddala. *Introduction to Econometrics*. Macmillan Publishing Company, second edition, 1992.

[19] Stephane Mallat and Sifen Zhong. Wavelet transform maxima and multiscale edges. In Ruskai, et al, editor, *Wavelets and Their Applications*, pages 67–104. Jones and Bartlett Publishers, Inc., Boston, 1992.

[20] W. Niblack, R. Barber, W. Equitz, M. Flickner, E. Glasman, D. Petkovic, P. Yanker, C. Faloutsos, and G. Taubin. The QBIC project: Querying images by content using color, texture, and shape. In *Storage and Retrieval for Image and Video Databases*, pages 173–187. SPIE, 1993.

[21] G. Petraglia, M. Sebillo, M. Tucci, and G. Tortora. Rotation invariant iconic indexing for image database retrieval. In S. Impedovo, editor, *Proceedings of the 7th International Conference on Image Analysis and Processing*, pages 271–278, Monopoli, Italy, 1993.

[22] Brian Pinkerton. Finding what people want: Experiences with the WebCrawler. In *The Second International WWW Conference '94: Mosaic and the Web*, October 1994.

[23] William H. Press, Brian P. Flannery, Saul A. Teukolsky, and William T. Fetterling. *Numerical Recipes*. Cambridge University Press, second edition, 1992.

[24] T. R. Reed, V. R. Algazi, G. E. Forrd, and I. Hussain. Perceptually-based coding of monochrome and color still images. In *DCC '92 — Data Compression Conference*, pages 142–51, 1992.

[25] SAS Institute Inc. *SAS/STAT User's Guide, Version 6, Fourth Edition, Volume 2*. SAS Institute Inc., 1989.

[26] R. Shann, D. Davis, J. Oakley, and F. White. Detection and characterisation of Carboniferous Foraminifera for content-based retrieval from an image database. In *Storage and Retrieval for Image and Video Databases*, volume 1908, pages 188–197. SPIE, 1993.

[27] M. Shibata and S. Inoue. Associative retrieval method for image database. *Transactions of the Institute of Electronics, Information and Communication Engineers D-II*, J73D-II:526–34, 1990.

[28] E. P. Simoncelli, W. T. Freeman, E. H. Adelson, and D. J. Heeger. Shiftable multiscale transforms. *IEEE Transactions on Information Theory*, 38:587–607, 1992.

[29] Stephen W. Smoliar and Hong Jiang Zhang. Content-based video indexing and retrieval. *IEEE Multimedia*, 1(2):62–72, 1994.

[30] P. L. Stanchev, A. W. M. Smeulders, and F. C. A. Groen. An approach to image indexing of documents. *IFIP Transactions A (Computer Science and Technology)*, A-7:63–77, 1992.

[31] Eric J. Stollnitz, Tony D. DeRose, and David H. Salesin. Wavelets for computer graphics: A primer, Part I. *IEEE Computer Graphics and Applications*, 15(3):76–84, May 1995.

[32] Eric J. Stollnitz, Tony D. DeRose, and David H. Salesin. Wavelets for computer graphics: A primer, Part II. *IEEE Computer Graphics and Applications*, 15(4), July 1995. In press.

[33] Michael J. Swain. Interactive indexing into image databases. In *Storage and Retrieval for Image and Video Databases*, volume 1908, pages 95–103. SPIE, 1993.

[34] Patrick C. Teo and David J. Heeger. Perceptual image distortion. In *Human Vision, Visual Processing and Digital Display V, IS&T/SPIE's Symposium on Electronic Imaging: Science & Technology*, 1994. In press.

[35] Chen Wu Tzong and Chin Chen Chang. Application of geometric hashing to iconic database retrieval. *Pattern Recognition Letters*, 15(9):871–876, 1994.

[36] M. Weiser. Some computer science issues in ubiquitous computing. *Communications of the ACM*, 36(7):74–84, 1993.

A   Tuning the weights of the metric

Recall that our L^q metric (3) involves a linear combination of terms. In this section, we discuss how a good set of weights w_k for these terms can be found.

The most straightforward approach for finding these weights is to use some form of multidimensional continuous optimization over these variables, such as Powell's method [23], using an evaluation function like "the number of queries that ranked their intended target in the upper 1% of the database." The difficulty is that this kind of evaluation function is fairly slow to compute (on the order of many seconds), since we would like to perform the evaluation over a large number of queries.

An alternative approach is to assume a regression model and to perform a kind of least-squares fit to the data [23]. For each pair ℓ of query and target images, we record an equation of the form:

$$r_\ell \;=\; v + \sum_k w_k t_{k,\ell} + u_\ell$$

where r_ℓ is either 1 or 0, depending on whether or not the query and target are intended to match; $t_{k,\ell}$ is the sum of the terms of equation (3) in bucket k; variables v and w_k are the unknowns to be found by the least-square fit; and u_ℓ is an error term to make the equality hold.

However, there are a number of problems with this method. The first problem is primarily an aesthetic one: once we have computed the weights v and w_k, they will give results that are in general neither 0 nor 1 — and in fact, may not even lie in the interval $[0, 1]$. In that case, we are left with the problem of interpreting what these other values should mean. The second problem is even more serious. The difficulty is that when collecting the data for tuning the weights, it is much easier to create data for mismatches than for matches, since in a database of 1000 images, every query corresponds to 999 mismatches and only a single match. If we use all of this data, however, the least-squares fit will tend to give weights that are skewed toward finding mismatches, since the best least-squares fit to the data will be to make every query–target pair score very close to 0. The alternative, using equal-sized sets of matched and mismatched image pairs, means throwing out a lot of perfectly useful and inexpensive data.

For these reasons, we use an approach from statistics called the *logit* model [18]. In the logit model, we assume a regression model of the form:

$$r_\ell^* \;=\; v + \sum_k w_k t_{k,\ell} + u_\ell$$

where r_ℓ^* is called a "latent variable," which is not observed directly. Observed instead is a dummy variable r_ℓ, defined by

$$r_\ell \;=\; \begin{cases} 1 & \text{if } r_\ell^* > 0 \\ 0 & \text{otherwise} \end{cases}$$

The idea behind the logit model is that there exists some underlying continuous variable r_ℓ^* (such as the "perceptual closeness" of two images Q and T) that is difficult to measure directly. The continuous variable r_ℓ^* determines a binary outcome r_ℓ (such as "image T is the intended target of the query Q"), which is easily measured. The logit model provides weights w_k, which can be used to compute the *probability* that a given r_ℓ^* produces a positive outcome r_ℓ.

Indeed, under the assumptions of the logit model, the probability P_ℓ that the query–target pair ℓ is indeed a match, is given by

$$P_\ell \;=\; F\left(v + \sum_k w_k t_{k,\ell}\right) \qquad \text{where} \qquad F(x) = \frac{e^x}{1 + e^x}$$

Once the weights are found, since $F(x)$ is monotonic and v is constant for all query–target pairs ℓ, it suffices to compute the expression

$$\sum_k w_k t_{k,\ell}$$

in order to rank the targets in order of decreasing probability of a match.

To compute the weights, we use the logit procedure in SAS [25]. It takes SAS about 30 seconds on an IBM RS/6000 to find appropriate weights for an input of 85 matches and 8500 (randomly chosen) mismatches. While these weights are not necessarily optimal with respect to our preferred evaluation function, they appear to give very good results, and they can be computed much more quickly than performing a multidimensional continuous optimization directly.

Animating Soft Substances with Implicit Surfaces

Mathieu Desbrun   Marie-Paule Gascuel
iMAGIS*/ IMAG

Abstract

This paper presents a hybrid model for animation of soft inelastic substance which undergo topological changes, e.g. separation and fusion and which fit with the objects they are in contact with. The model uses a particle system coated with a smooth iso-surface that is used for performing collision detection, precise contact modeling and integration of response forces. The animation technique solves three problems inherent in implicit modeling. Firstly, local volume controllers are defined to insure constant volume deformation, even during highly inelastic processes such as splitting or fusion. Secondly, we avoid unwanted distance blending between disconnected pieces of the same substance. Finally, we simulate both collisions and progressive merging under compression between implicit surfaces that do not blend together. Parameter tuning is facilitated by the layered model and animation is generated at interactive rates.

Keywords: implicit surface, physics-based animation, inelasticity.

1 Introduction

Most deformable models in Computer Graphics are dedicated to visco-elastic deformation: objects deform under an external force field and then progressively come back to their rest shape. Animating highly deformable inelastic substances, such as clay, dough or mud, is a more challenging problem. These substances are characterized by a smooth surface that fits with the objects it is in contact with and can undergo any topological change. One can make a hole in it, split a block of substance into several pieces and even merge two pieces together by compressing them strongly against each other. During all these deformations the total volume remains approximately constant. This paper presents an integrated set of methods for simulating these behaviors.

1.1 Previous inelastic models

Contrary to elastic objects, the shape of inelastic bodies depends on the entire history of applied forces. Terzopoulos et al. [10] use two layers to simulate this behavior: an inelastic reference component, that computes motion and absorbs large scale deformations, and an elastic layer that represents the difference between the current and reference shapes. The model handles visco-elasticity, plasticity and fractures. However, since the lattice used for discretizing equations has a fixed topology, the model is restricted to very structured inelastic objects.

Other models [5, 11, 12] use physically-based particle systems for modeling a wide range of behaviors, including visco-elasticity,

*iMAGIS is a joint project of CNRS, INRIA, Institut National Polytechnique de Grenoble and Université Joseph Fourier.
Address: BP 53, F-38041 Grenoble cedex 09, France
Email: [Mathieu.Desbrun|Marie-Paule.Gascuel]@imag.fr.

Permission to make digital/hard copy of part or all of this work for personal or classroom use is granted without fee provided that copies are not made or distributed for profit or commercial advantage, the copyright notice, the title of the publication and its date appear, and notice is given that copying is by permission of ACM, Inc. To copy otherwise, to republish, to post on servers, or to redistribute to lists, requires prior specific permission and/or a fee.

plasticity, collisions, separation and fusion. The change from stiff material to the quasi-liquid state is achieved by adapting the interaction laws between particles. However, visualizing the surface of a substance during animation is difficult since particles can change their positions during deformations. Therefore, a fixed set of "boundary particles" cannot be used for surface representation. One solution is to display an iso-surface generated by the set of particles [11, 12]. Nevertheless, since this surface is only introduced for rendering and is not considered for collision detection, visual anomalies such as local inter-penetrations with obstacles or bouncing before contact may occur.

1.2 Overview

This paper presents a new model for interactive animation of smooth soft substances which fit with other objects during contact, can be split into pieces and may merge when disconnected components are compressed against each other. The model ensures volume preservation, performs collision detection and models precise contact surface and local deformation during collisions. A precise description of the surface of an object is maintained throughout the animation and can be used for final high quality rendering.

Implicit surfaces seem to be the best surface representation for smooth bodies that deform over time and may change their topology [13]. Our basic idea, introduced in [2], is to combine particle systems and implicit surfaces during the animation. Controlled by the particles as in [11, 12], the implicit surface is animated according to the implicit elastic model of [4] that gives it the ability to detect collisions, to deform locally for exact contact modeling, and to compute precise integration of response forces. These forces are transmitted to the particles to be subsequently integrated.

However, the direct use of this model generates a number of anomalies. This paper presents novel and general methods for controlling volume variation, avoiding unwanted blending effects, and simulation of both collisions and progressive fusion under compression of disconnected pieces of the same substance.

Section 2 reviews the hybrid model for soft substances introduced in [2], and discusses its limitations. Section 3 presents our new method for generating constant-volume deformations. An algorithm for performing separation without subsequent distance blending is detailed in Section 4. Section 5 explains how to process either collision or progressive fusion between surfaces that do not blend, according to the amount of compression forces.

2 A Hybrid Model for Soft Substances

2.1 Combining particles and implicit surfaces

The hybrid model we use for modeling soft inelastic bodies is composed of two layers (see [2]). Motion and large scale deformations are governed by an inelastic reference component made of particles, while an elastic implicit layer gives the current shape of an object and is used to compute local deformation during collisions.

Reference component: As in [5, 12], we model inelasticity with a particle system, i.e. a set of mass points P_i subject to both attraction/repulsion forces F_{int} and fluid friction forces F_{fr} depending on local particle density. In our system, the forces applied by particle P_1 on particle P_2 are:

$$F_{int}(P_1 \to P_2) = \lambda \left(\left(\frac{r_0}{r} \right)^8 - \left(\frac{r_0}{r} \right)^4 \right) \frac{P_2 - P_1}{r^2} \quad (1)$$

$$F_{fr}(P_1 \to P_2) = \mu(r) \, ||\dot{P}_1 - \dot{P}_2|| \, (\dot{P}_1 - \dot{P}_2) \quad (2)$$

where $r = ||P_2 - P_1||$, λ is a parameter for regulating the stiffness of a material, $\dot{P}_i$ is the speed vector of particle P_i, and μ is a decreasing continuous function with a restricted scope of influence.

External elastic layer: Implicit surfaces such as distance surfaces [1, 13] are particularly suitable for animating deformable bodies capable of splitting and fusion. We use them as a coating over a particle system: each particle generates a field f_i, a smooth decreasing function of the distance with a restricted scope of influence, and the surface of an object is defined as the set of points P such as $f(P) = \sum f_i(P) = s$, s being a given isovalue.

The implicit elastic model of [4] is used to animate the implicit surface and for collision detection and response. This model defines a simple correspondence between applied forces and deformation, the force at a particular point being given by the local variation of the field value. Exact contact modeling is performed during collisions by adding deformation terms to the fields defining objects: for objects defined by $f_1 = s$ and $f_2 = s$, the respective values of these terms are $s - f_2$ and $s - f_1$. This generates an exact contact surface of equation $f_1 = f_2$ where opposite normal compression forces $F_{1 \to 2} = -F_{2 \to 1} = (s - f_1)N_2$ are applied.

At each time step, animation is computed as follows:

1. Compute the new position of each particle by integrating the associated equation of motion from the set of applied forces.

2. After a pre-detection with bounding boxes, use the implicit surface generated by the particles for detecting collisions (test the sample points of an object against the field of another one).

3. Avoid inter-penetration by generating exact contact surfaces between colliding objects, and compute response forces.

4. Distribute response forces between particles that contribute to surface generation in contact area. These forces will be used at the next time step.

2.2 Problems to be solved

Despite its capability of defining smooth substances that fit with other objects during contact, this hybrid model generates several anomalies.

Due to the implicit coating, a piece of substance may undergo very significant volume variation during deformations, especially during separation and fusion. The partial solution proposed in [2] is far from sufficient. Firstly, it is based on the choice of a specific field function[2], which is very restrictive since both the shape of an object and its stiffness are controlled by this function. Moreover, it gives good results near equilibrium states only, so it is of no use for animating large scale deformations and topological changes.

The second problem concerns the irreversibility of soft substance splitting. Two pieces coming back close to each other should not produce the same intermediate shapes than when they were disconnected, i.e. they should not blend before contact [9]. Unfortunately, since they are components of the same implicit body, their surfaces locally inflate and merge. This artifact is related to the well-known "unwanted blending problem" [6, 14], but the difficulty is intensified in this case, since the desired blending properties for a soft substance are changing with its topology.

---

[2]This function is $f_i(P) = (r_0/r)^3$, where r is the distance $d(P, P_i)$ and where r_0, introduced in equation (1), is the rest distance between particles.

Finally, both collision and progressive fusion between soft bodies are to be produced, depending on their physical properties and on the amount of compression forces that press them against each other.

The following sections present solutions to these three problems.

3 Constant Volume Deformation

Constant volume deformation of flexible models have already drawn some attention [7, 8]. In the case of objects discretized into lattices of fixed topology, the problem can be solved by using constrained optimization techniques based on Lagrange multipliers. To the authors knowledge, no solution has been proposed in the case of soft substances, although volume variations may increase due to topological changes such as separation or fusion.

This section presents a general method for controlling volume of objects defined using implicit surfaces. This method is well adapted to the soft substances we are modeling, but can also be applied to any other way of animating implicit surfaces.

3.1 Basic ideas

Our aim was to develop a general method for controlling the volume of an implicit object that does not set any restriction on the choice of the field function, thus allowing for a wide range of shapes and stiffness to be modeled.

First of all, a good way of detecting volume variation must be defined. An implicit volume defined by $V = \int \int \int_{f(P) >= s} dx dy dz$ where $P = (x, y, z)$, cannot be computed analytically for arbitrary field functions. Discretizing space into voxels can be used for finding an approximate value. However, this way of detecting volume variation would not give us any chance of solving the problem. As illustrated by the example in Figure 1, reducing the strength of field contributions at step 2 in order to avoid volume variation should only be done in the area where the object has been deformed. Thus, volume should be controlled locally.

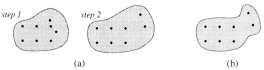

Figure 1: (a) Volume variation. (b) Local volume control in step 2.

Our basic idea is to detect the area where the volume is changing, and then adjust the strength of local fields in this area. Thus, a notion of local volume needs to be defined.

- We call the *territory* Ti of a particle P_i the part of the implicit object where its field contribution is the highest. Territories form a partition of the implicit volume ($f(P) \geq s$).

  $$T_i = \{P \in \mathbb{R} \ / \ (f(P) \geq s) \text{ and } (\forall j \ f_i(P) \geq f_j(P))\}$$

- The *local volume* V_i associated with P_i is the volume of T_i.

3.2 Detecting local volume variation

We are looking for an efficient way of approximating local volume. Since deformation is continuous over time, we can take advantage of temporal coherence. This is achieved by maintaining a sampling of territory boundaries throughout the animation.

Each particle sends a fixed number of points called "seeds" to sample its territory boundary, in a set of distributed directions called "seed-axes" that are defined in the particle local coordinates system (see Figure 2). At each animation step, seeds migrate to the surface from their previous position along their axis. They stop either when

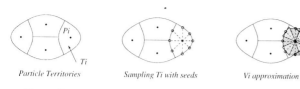

Figure 2: Particle territories and seeds used for volume approximation.

they have reached the isosurface or when the preponderant field f_i becomes smaller than another one.

We approximate V_i by the sum of the volumes of small pyramids defined by seeds (see Figure 2):

$$V_i = \sum_{s \in S_i} K_i \, d(s, P_i)^3$$

where S_i is the set of seeds sent by P_i, and where the factor K_i only depends on the seed repartition chosen for P_i. In practice, K_i can be left out in volume computations, since it is sufficient to maintain $\sum_{s \in S_i} d(s, P_i)^3$ at a constant level.

3.3 Local volume control

We control local volume variation by associating a proportional-derivative controller with each particle. Given the current local volume V_i and the initial value $V_{i,0}$ to maintain, this controller outputs an adequate adjustment of the field function f_i.

For our application, the way of modifying f_i must be chosen carefully since the norm of its gradient gives the local stiffness of an object [4]. In order to adjust the volume of particle territories without modifying the physical properties of the object, we combine the original field function with a translation $\epsilon_{i,t}$. At each time step, the field, originally defined by the decreasing function of the distance $f_i(P) = h_i(d(P, P_i))$, is replaced by: $f_{i,t} = h_i(d(P, P_i) - \epsilon_{i,t})$.

In order to produce steady shape variation, we control the time derivative $\dot{\epsilon}_{i,t}$ of the translation parameter rather than its value. The input of the proportional-derivative controller consists of the normalized volume variation $\Delta_{i,t}$ and its time derivative $\dot{\Delta}_{i,t}$:

$$\Delta_{i,t} = \frac{V_{i,t} - V_{i,0}}{V_{i,0}} \qquad \dot{\Delta}_{i,t} = \frac{V_{i,t} - V_{i,t-dt}}{V_{i,0} \, dt}$$

and its output is: $\quad \dot{\epsilon}_{i,t} = \alpha \Delta_{i,t} + \beta \dot{\Delta}_{i,t}$

A simple example of volume control is given in Figure 3. Figures 5 and 6 show the results obtained during fusion, where volume control is essential. Otherwise, very significant and sudden increases of volume would be produced when two soft bodies merge.

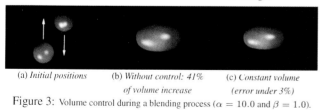

(a) *Initial positions*   (b) *Without control: 41%*   (c) *Constant volume*
of volume increase   *(error under 3%)*

Figure 3: Volume control during a blending process ($\alpha = 10.0$ and $\beta = 1.0$).

4 Avoiding Unwanted Blending

One of the main difficulties raised by the animation of implicit surfaces is the avoidance of undesirable blending effects between objects. This problem is well known in the case of character animation: arms and legs of a character should not blend together, although both blend with the body. The solution suggested in [14] pre-defines a blending graph where a connection between two skeletons indicates that their field contributions are to be added. Then, the field value at a point P is computed by first finding the skeleton with

the highest field contribution at P, and then adding the contributions of neighboring skeletons in the graph[3].

The unwanted blending problem is more difficult in the case of a soft substance splitting into pieces. If two disconnected pieces come back close to each other, they will blend at some distance as in Figure 3 rather than colliding because they are considered to be parts of the same object. Moreover, since the topology of the substance varies over time, a pre-defined blending graph cannot be used: the blending properties of the particles change according to the surface decomposition into connected components.

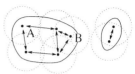

Figure 4: The influence graph and its connected components. Particles A and B lie in the same component, so their fields will blend if they come close to each other.

Therefore, we compute a time-varying blending graph, represented by lists of neighbors called a "blending list" associated with each particle. Processing unwanted blending is achieved by reducing blending lists each time the implicit surface breaks into disconnected components that no longer blend. Before the animation, the blending graph is initialized as a complete graph, where each particle is connected to all others. Then, at each animation step:

1. For each pair of particles, look if their spheres of influence, defined by the radius of influence of their field, intersect. Transitive closure of this relation, that defines an "influence graph", gives the "influence connected components" (see Figure 4).

2. For each particle, remove from its blending list those of the neighbors that are no longer in the same influence component.

3. Use the blending graph and the field function it defines for computing seeds migration. Since seeds sample the territory boundary of a particle, fields can be evaluated very efficiently: we already know which field contribution is the highest, so we just have to add the contributions from the neighbors.

The soft substances animated with this method split into components that no longer blend, as shown in the three first frames in Figure 5. The next section explains how to handle collisions between these components, and to enable fusions according to the amount of compression forces and to the properties of the substance.

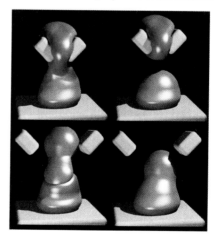

Figure 5: Soft substance made of 9 particles grabbed away by pliers and released.

---

[3]The blending graph must be defined with care, otherwise surface discontinuities may appear between areas where a given skeleton's contribution is still considered, and zones where it is not a neighbor anymore.

Figure 6: Progressive fusion under compression of two colliding bodies.

5 From Collision to Progressive Fusion

5.1 Collision processing

Instead of processing collisions between pairs of objects as in [2, 4], the collision processing algorithm computes collisions between *each pair of particle territories* such that the fields of the particles do not blend together. As a result, if a soft substance splits into pieces, subsequent collisions will be detected between the pieces. The main problem is to enable collision detection between particle territories. The methods for modeling contact and computing collision response, reviewed in Section 2, do not need to be modified.

The data needed for detecting collisions between implicit surfaces are a bounding box around each of these surfaces and a set of points that sample them. These sample points will be tested against the field function of another object. In our implementation, we use the seeds introduced in Section 3 for both sampling the portion of the surface associated with a particle territory T_i and computing a local bounding box around it:

- A seed is said to be "valid" if it reaches the iso-surface during migration. At each time step, the set of valid seeds associated with T_i gives the sample points needed for collision detection.

- The axis-parallel bounding box associated with T_i is computed from the positions of the valid seeds, and enlarged by the maximum distance between neighboring seeds.

- Local bounding boxes are grouped into connected component boxes to optimize collision detection.

Valid seeds can also be used for the interactive opaque display of the substance during the animation [3].

5.2 Fusion under compression

Blocks of soft substance such as clay or dough merge under compression forces that exceed a specified threshold. This behavior can be easily simulated with our model.

The fusion threshold is added as a new parameter in a substance description. Then, each time a collision is computed between two bodies made of the same substance, compression forces computed along the contact surface between two particle territories are compared with the fusion threshold. If the compression exceeds it, each particle adds the other one to its blending list. At the next time step, fields from the two bodies will locally blend in this area, while collisions will still be computed elsewhere (see Figure 6).

As mentioned in Section 4, the use of a blending graph that is not fully connected may produce discontinuities in the implicit surface. A solution, introduced in [6], defines the field value at a point P as the maximum field from groups of particles that blend together. In our current implementation we obtain the same effect by rendering a substance as a set of implicit components representing these groups. Each component includes the area where the groups merge and a union of all components gives the final isosurface. However, neither of these methods avoids tangent discontinuities in the final shape.

6 Conclusions

We have presented a hybrid model for animation of smooth soft substances that maintain their volume, collide and can undergo separa-

tion and fusion during animation. Control is facilitated by the layered nature of the model. It combines a particle system that models large scale inelastic deformations, an implicit surface that generates local deformations during contact and a control module that performs local volume preservation. Animation is computed and visualized at interactive rates. The implicit surface parameters are stored at each animation step providing a compact storage of the animation and enabling the direct use of surface/ray intersection algorithms for computing final high-quality images.

The solution developed for local control of implicit volumes offers a general contribution to the field of animation using implicit surfaces. For instance, it can be used in character animation, for setting user-defined volume variation that imitate the contraction and dilatation of muscles. We are currently experimenting with a solution to avoid tangent discontinuities in the implicit surface when an object is modeled using a blending graph.

Acknowledgements

Many thanks to Jean-Dominique Gascuel for his efficient ray-tracing software, to the reviewers for their helpful comments, and to Agata Opalach for carefully re-reading this paper.

References

[1] Jules Bloomenthal and Brian Wyvill. Interactive techniques for implicit modeling. *Computer Graphics*, 24(2):109–116, March 1990.

[2] Mathieu Desbrun and Marie-Paule Gascuel. Highly deformable material for animation and collision processing. In *5th Eurographics Workshop on Animation and Simulation*, Oslo, Norway, September 1994.

[3] Mathieu Desbrun, Nicolas Tsingos, and Marie-Paule Gascuel. Adaptive sampling of implicit surfaces for interactive modeling and animation. In *First International Workshop on Implicit Surfaces*, Grenoble, France, April 1995.

[4] Marie-Paule Gascuel. An implicit formulation for precise contact modeling between flexible solids. *Computer Graphics*, pages 313–320, August 1993. Proceedings of SIGGRAPH'93 (Anaheim, CA).

[5] Annie Luciani, Stéphane Jimenez, Olivier Raoult, Claude Cadoz, and Jean-Loup Florens. An unified view of multitude behaviour, flexibility, plasticity, and fractures: balls, bubbles and agglomerates. In *IFIP WG 5.10 Working Conference*, Tokyo, Japan, April 1991.

[6] Agata Opalach and Steve Maddock. Implicit surfaces: Appearance, blending and consistency. In *Fourth Eurographics Workshop on Animation and Simulation*, Barcelona, Spain, September 1993.

[7] John Platt and Alan Barr. Constraint methods for flexible models. *Computer Graphics*, 22(4):279–288, August 1988. Proceedings of SIGGRAPH'88 (Atlanta, Georgia).

[8] Ari Rappoport, Alla Sheffer, Daniel Youlus, and Michel Bercovier. Volume-preserving free-form deformations. In *ACM Solid Modeling'95*, Salt Lake City, Utah, May 1995.

[9] Jean-Paul Smets-Solanes. Surfacic textures for animated implicit surfaces: the 2d case. In *Fourth Eurographics Workshop on Animation and Simulation*, Barcelona, Spain, September 1993.

[10] Demetri Terzopoulos and Kurt Fleischer. Modeling inelastic deformations: Viscoelasticity, plasticity, fracture. *Computer Graphics*, 22(4):269–278, August 1988. Proceedings of SIGGRAPH'88 (Atlanta, Georgia).

[11] Demetri Terzopoulos, John Platt, and Kurt Fleisher. Heating and melting deformable models (from goop to glop). In *Graphics Interface'89*, pages 219–226, London, Ontario, June 1989.

[12] David Tonnesen. Modeling liquids and solids using thermal particles. In *Graphics Interface'91*, pages 255–262, Calgary, AL, June 1991.

[13] Brian Wyvill, Craig McPheeters, and Geoff Wyvill. Animating soft objects. *The Visual Computer*, 2(4):235–242, August 1986.

[14] Brian Wyvill and Geoff Wyvill. Field functions for implicit surfaces. *The Visual Computer*, 5:75–82, December 1989.

Decorating Implicit Surfaces

Hans Køhling Pedersen
Department of Computer Science
University of North Carolina at Chapel Hill*

Abstract

This work presents a new general approach for applying textures onto implicit surfaces. Its main contributions are:

- An improved set of interactive tools for subdividing implicit surfaces into convenient patches.

- An efficient and reliable algorithm for deriving parameterizations for these patches.

- A new set of useful texturing operations.

These results provide a unified representation scheme for a variety of texturing techniques that were previously incompatible, allowing more efficient manipulation, storage, and rendering of textured objects and a fuller use of current texture mapping hardware.

1 Introduction.

While the class of implicit surfaces often referred to as "soft objects", "blobs" or "meta-balls" historically has played a prominent role in the computer graphics literature, these models have only experienced limited practical use in the entertainment industry to date. This unfulfilled promise can largely be attributed to two weaknesses that have plagued implicits compared to the more widely used spline-based models.

First, difficulties in visualizing changing implicit surfaces in real-time have made interactive modeling awkward, and second, because implicits have no natural material coordinates, they are not as flexible with respect to texture mapping as parametric surfaces. Existing techniques for texturing implicit surfaces [1, 2, 3] are predominantly based on solid textures [4, 5], as these do not require material coordinates; solid textures are excellent for simulating objects carved out of wood, marble, and similar materials, but not a natural choice for patterns related to the intrinsic surface geometry.

While Witkin & Heckbert's recent progress in implicit surface modeling [6], based on visualizing implicits as a set of particles (see figure 4), provides a promising new approach to the first problem, the texturing problems continue to compromise the practical applicability of implicit surfaces in computer graphics imaging. This paper addresses that lack.

1.1 Related work.

For the purposes of our analysis, it will be convenient to divide existing work on interactive texturing of 3D surfaces into two categories: *painting* methods, in which texture detail is applied or manipulated locally on the object, and *patch based* methods, where the surface is covered with an atlas of charts, each of which defines a separate texture mapping.

---

*The author can be reached at Center for Integrated Systems, Stanford University, Stanford, CA 94305-4070 (e-mail: hkp@daimi.aau.dk).

Permission to make digital/hard copy of part or all of this work for personal or classroom use is granted without fee provided that copies are not made or distributed for profit or commercial advantage, the copyright notice, the title of the publication and its date appear, and notice is given that copying is by permission of ACM, Inc. To copy otherwise, to republish, to post on servers, or to redistribute to lists, requires prior specific permission and/or a fee.

© 1995   ACM-0-89791-701-4/95/008 $3.50

1.1.1 Painting methods.

Hanrahan and Haeberli presented the first systematic approach for painting 3D surfaces in [7], sparking the evolution of a new and thriving subfield in computer graphics software. Their method, which assumes that a suitable uv-parameterization for the surface is available, uses the parameter space to store texture information, and forms the basis for all currently available commercial 3D texturing applications [8]. The main shortcoming of this approach is that it relies entirely on user-intensive brush painting operations that require a substantial amount of patience and artistic skills in order to obtain good results in practice.

Motivated by the need for supplementary high-level texturing tools, Litwinowicz and Miller [9] presented an interactive strategy for compensating for the distortion of texture mappings, allowing the original parameterization to be replaced with a more suitable mapping of the texture. However, they did not develop a general mechanism for specifying the boundaries of the texture on the destination surface.

To eliminate the need for a parameterization of the surface, Agrawala et al. [10] developed an interactive system for painting scanned polyhedral meshes using a 3D input device. This alternative approach could also be applied in the case of implicit surfaces, but requires very densely sampled meshes and is not well suited for detailed high-frequency textures.

1.1.2 Patch based methods.

In this category, the common thread in the references ([11, 12, 13]) is to subdivide the surface into a set of charts and then introduce a bivariate uv-mapping for each chart while trying to minimize distortion within the parameterized regions.

Bennis et al. [11] presented an incremental algorithm for reducing distortion of C^2 continuous texture mappings in which the user first partitions the surface into suitable patches interactively, and these patches are then reparameterized (*"flattened"*) in a relaxation process. In [12], a different optimization scheme for improving an existing texture mapping was presented by Maillot et al. In addition, this paper discussed different *unfolding* methods for deriving parameterizations for general polygonal meshes. A comparison between an automatic and an interactive parameterization scheme produced the conclusion that the best results were obtained by letting the user specify the charts interactively and using the automated technique as a supplementary tool for complex surfaces. This observation is supported by the fact that animators like control over patch placement, so the model's surface and textures look correct when motion is added.

Unfortunately, these unfolding/flattening techniques suffer from several limitations. First, minimizing distortion within each chart is performed at the expense of introducing seams at the borders between the parameterized regions, and this type of zero-order discontinuities is a severe detraction for applications depending on visual appeal, no matter how much distortion is reduced (as an example of these artifacts, there would be half dots at the edges of a dotted region). Second, the methods offer little control over boundary conditions, resulting in difficulties in matching texels at borders between charts (see figure 1). Most importantly, however, the textures have to be aligned with the borders between the charts, and if, for example, a photo-texture is to be applied across a border, it is necessary to make changes in the underlying parameterization. Combined with the fact that existing tools for defining the charts are user-intensive, these problems make unfolding/flattening methods difficult to apply in practice and limit the range of texturing operations that can be applied.

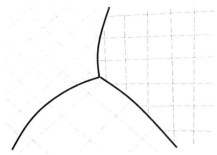

Figure 1: *Matching texels at borders between charts: existing parameterization techniques offer little control over boundary conditions, making the application of many texturing operations unnecessarily complex.*

1.2 Synthesis and outline of contents.

The historical distinction between painting and patch based texturing techniques is artificial and unfortunate: The patches produced by existing parameterization methods are not well suited for interactive painting, and existing painting methods could benefit from new high-level texturing operations based on flexible parameterization techniques. Furthermore, because existing techniques have focused on parametric and polyhedral surfaces, they have not taken advantage of the attractive mathematical representation offered by implicit models.

Motivated by these two observations, the remainder of this document will describe a new approach for parameterizing implicit surfaces that is specifically designed for 3D painting.

Although several of the quoted patch based references advocated the use of user specified curves in the surface subdivision step, none of them elaborated on how this interaction was performed, and we will therefore start with a coherent solution to this problem in section 2. Section 3 and 4 will deal with the problem of finding material coordinates for the patches, and these results will then lead to the design of new texturing algorithms in section 5. Finally, section 6 will discuss ideas for future work.

2 Curves on implicit surfaces.

While the theory of interpolating curves in the plane is well studied, its generalization to 3D surfaces remains an active area of research, and existing work can conveniently be categorized into parametric [14, 15, 16] and implicit/algebraic approaches. Our interest is in the latter category, which unfortunately is the least explored in the computer graphics literature.

Dietz et al. [17] derived and implemented analytical tools for fitting Bezier curves onto general quadratic surfaces, and related work is described in [18, 19, 20]. However, the non-polynomial nature of soft objects lends itself poorly to existing mathematical tools and has left their theory of interpolating curves largely unexplored. One solution is to polygonize the surface and thereby reduce the problem into the *discrete geodesics* problem, which is currently an active area of research in computational geometry [21, 22]. Unfortunately, this theory currently does not at allow such curves to be computed and manipulated interactively on general 3D surfaces, and its generalization to spline curves is yet to be explored.

Instead, we will use an optimization approach similar to the one employed in by Barr et al. in [23] for smoothly interpolating quaternions in 4-space. However, as the robustness of any optimization technique relies on the quality of the initial guess to the solution, and as the linear interpolation between the key nodes employed in [23] does not work in the case of soft objects, section 2.1 will derive an efficient algorithm for computing a better guess for the shortest geodesic between two points on the implicit surface. This initial approximation will subsequently be optimized

to a geodesic curve in section 2.2. Section 2.3 describes a generalization of this curve drawing algorithm from geodesics to smooth interpolating curves, and section 2.4 concludes with a discussion of implementation issues.

2.1 Estimating geodesics.

Given two arbitrary points on the implicit surface, the problem is to compute the shortest path between them that is embedded in the surface. Furthermore, these curves should be computed at interactive speed, and the interface for drawing them should be convenient (in our system, the user selects the two endpoints by pointing at arbitrary locations on the surface, and the algorithm described below then creates the geodesic on-line). As this is an overwhelming task for non-polynomial surfaces, we choose to make the following simplifying assumptions:

1. The surface does not deviate excessively from its tangent plane within a given distance 4σ of any point[1].

2. If, for two arbitrary points p and q on the surface, $|p - q| \leq 4\sigma$, then $\langle n_p, n_q \rangle \geq 0$, where n_p and n_q denote the local normal, n, at p and q.

3. The curve will be approximated by a piecewise polynomial interpolant.

The first two assumptions effectively set an upper bound for the Nyquist limit of the surface, allowing it to be sampled without missing any sharp spikes or violating the topology. These assumptions are reasonable as soft objects are characterized by their smoothness and rarely contain sharp corners or discontinuities, and are made in some formulation by virtually all existing algorithms involving implicit surfaces (for example [6, 24, 25]).

The last assumption is necessary as no practical mathematical tools for representing this kind of curves exist, and it makes sense as the implicit surface itself will eventually be replaced with a piecewise linear approximation in order to facilitate efficient scanline rendering.

2.1.1 Surface discretization.

The first task is to replace the continuous surface representation with a suitable discretization that is easier to work with. Fortunately, recent results [6] present an efficient interactive solution to this problem: the implicit surface is sampled by a uniformly distributed collection of particles that repel each other subject to the constraint that they lie on the surface. Although this algorithm does not automatically determine an appropriate sampling frequency (cf. assumption 1 above), it is so intuitive and easy to use that we will assume that the user sets the parameter σ manually.

The sampling distribution arising from [6] has the attractive property that the samples form a locally hexagonal pattern almost everywhere that maximizes the minimum distance between each sample and its closest neighbor. This coherence can be exploited for computing a guess for the shortest path between two points on the surface.

2.1.2 Approximating geodesics.

Given an appropriate set of samples, the idea is to use the observation that geodesics locally minimize the distance between two points on a surface [26] (prop. 4, p. 292) (the surface equivalent of the shortest curve between two points in a plane being a straight line). More specifically, the shortest path between the points in a graph faithfully representing the surface geometry is likely to be a good approximation to a geodesic, and computing such paths is a standard problem in graph theory. In particular, Dijkstra's algorithm for the single-source-all-nearest-neighbors problem has complexity $O(N \cdot \log N)$ if the graph is sparse [27] (pp. 527-532). We therefore proceed by constructing a sparse graph that represents the surface with sufficient accuracy. This graph then provides a rough approximation to a distance metric for the surface.

---

[1]Consistent with [6], σ denotes half the average distance between each sample and its closest neighbor, and 4σ is thus a reasonable estimate of the diameter of largest "disk" extending from a sample that does not contain other samples.

A possible solution could be to compute a suitable triangulation of the sampled surface [28], but as this problem is difficult to solve robustly, and as an exact triangulation is not needed for our purpose, we choose a simpler approach that produces an equally acceptable result:

The graph is constructed by computing the M nearest neighbors to each sample with the restriction that all edges longer than 4σ are discarded. Due to the aforementioned hexagonal sampling pattern, $M = 8$ works well, as all important edges are included while those violating assumption 1 are ignored. Using a simple *spatial subdivision* [29] (p. 294), the graph can be constructed in a time which is theoretically $O(N^2)$, but essentially linear for realistic problems, up to at least 10,000 points. As the surface is assumed to be modeled in advance, the graph can be computed in a pre-processing step and subsequently reused for computing arbitrary geodesics.

The resulting path will be a good guess to a short geodesic curve between the two points, and although this may not necessarily be the shortest solution globally, it is fully adequate for our interactive drawing application. It is important to note that this strategy relies on the regularity of the sampling, that characterizes the *point repulsion* technique [29], and does not necessarily generalize to more random sampling populations.

2.2 Optimizing geodesics.

The above algorithm produces a good guess for the geodesic, which is then refined using constrained optimization. For efficiency, we choose to minimize the length of the curve:

$$\int_T \left|\alpha'(t)\right| dt,$$

where $\alpha : T \subseteq R \mapsto R^3$ denotes some parameterization of the curve. As the curve has to be embedded in the implicit surface, this optimization must be performed subject to the following constraint:

$$F(\alpha(t)) = 0, t \in T,$$

where F is the scalar function defining the implicit surface. Simple discretization approximating by the difference quotient:

$$\alpha'(t_i) \approx \frac{p_{i+1} - p_i}{h}$$

with h being the average distance between the samples, works well, and the constraints are enforced using the feedback term, $\phi \frac{F(p)\nabla F(p)}{|\nabla F(p)|^2}$ (ϕ is some constant and ∇F denotes the gradient of F), derived in [6] (p. 271).

The complete algorithm for computing an approximation to the shortest geodesic between two points p and q looks like this:

```
class Curve
    integer size
    point samples[MAX_SIZE]

procedure Surface: Attract_Point(p)
    return p − φ F(p)∇F(p)/|∇F(p)|²

procedure Surface: Compute_Geodesic(p, q)
    Curve geodesic = graph.Estimate_Geodesic(p, q)
    while (geodesic.Stable() == FALSE)
        for pᵢ ∈ geodesic.samples do
            p_tmp = (p_{i−1}+p_{i+1})/2
            p_tmp' = pᵢ.Project_To_Tangent_Plane(p_tmp)
            pᵢ' = Attract_Point(p_tmp')
    return geodesic
```

What actually happens in the optimization process is quite simple: for each sample, p_i, along the curve, the midpoint between the two adjacent samples is first projected to the tangent plane through p_i and then pulled back towards to the implicit surface using the feedback formula. (See Kimmel and Kiryati's recent vision paper [30] for an alternative and more mathematical two-step approach to computing geodesics).

2.3 Smooth interpolating curves.

In addition to geodesics, it will be convenient to operate with smooth interpolating curves on the surfaces, similar to splines in the plane. Fortunately, this is easily accomplished: Given N points on the surface, a piecewise geodesic interpolating curve is first computed as already described, and then subjected to optimization. Again, this approach works because the piecewise geodesic serves as a good initial guess for optimization. Just as traditional splines minimize curvature subject to specified constraints, our problem is to find an interpolating curve with minimal curvature "as seen from the surface", or more formally to minimize the covariant derivative, $\frac{D\alpha'}{dt}$, along the curve.

Motivated by

$$\frac{D\alpha'}{dt}(t) = \alpha''(t) - \langle \alpha''(t), n(t) \rangle n(t),$$

where n denotes the local surface normal (the normalized gradient at $\alpha(t)$), and by

$$\alpha''(t) \approx \frac{1}{h^2} \left(\alpha(t+h) - \alpha(t) + \alpha(t-h) - \alpha(t) \right)$$

the following discretization was chosen empirically:

$$E = \sum_i |p_{i+1} - p_i - \langle p_{i+1} - p_i, n_i \rangle n_i|^2 + |p_{i-1} - p_i - \langle p_{i-1} - p_i, n_i \rangle n_i|^2$$

This functional can be minimized in the N p_i-s subject to the N "tangent plane" constraints:

$$\langle p_i - p_{i_{old}}, n_i \rangle = 0,$$

using the *Lagrange multiplier method* [31] (pp. 355-356) in each iteration. The complete algorithm for computing a smooth curve, connecting the fixed points $p_1, \ldots p_N$ on the surface, looks like this:

```
procedure Surface: Compute_Closed_Spline(p₁, . . . , p_N)
    Curve geodesics[N], spline
    for i = 1 to N do
        geodesics[i] = Compute_Geodesic(pᵢ, p_{i+1})
    spline = Concatenate_Curves(geodesics, N)
    while (spline.Stable() == FALSE)
        spline.Optimize_Lagrange()
        for pᵢ ∈ spline.samples do
            pᵢ' = Attract_Point(pᵢ)
    return spline
```

This optimization algorithm is a compromise between speed and mathematical accuracy that makes several simplifying assumptions in order to be applicable in our interactive system. However, it has proven to be efficient and reliable in practical use and produces smooth and visually attractive curves (see figure 6 and 11). (An alternative and more elaborate approach to constrained minimization of the geodesic curvature along a curve can be found in [23] (pp. 316-317)).

2.4 Implementation.

The algorithms presented in this section can be applied interactively: for surfaces represented by a few thousand samples, the shortest path is typically computed in the order of 5-15 seconds on an SGI Indy, and the subsequent optimization takes a similar amount of time. The practical performance is dramatically improved using a divide and conquer approach, allowing the user to interactively double or halve the sampling rate along the curve: reducing the number of samples and optimizing the curve at a lower resolution yields a much more rapid convergence to a coarse solution, which can then be refined at a higher sampling frequency (i.e. a multigrid method). For further efficiency, the curve optimizer is continuously running on-line, allowing the user to draw and manipulate curves while previously defined ones are still converging.

In conclusion, the new approach to interactive curve-drawing presented in this section provides a high-level alternative to previous brute-force methods. Instead of having to specify every sample point along the curve explicitly, the user simply clicks on a number of arbitrary key points on the implicit surface and selects the "geodesic" or "spline" operation. As the curves are sampled on a continuous surface and thus not limited to follow the edges of a polygonal mesh, they are more flexible and can, for example, be dragged continuously across the surface. Finally, due to the good initial approximation and the simplicity of the optimization procedure, the algorithms are reliable and robust.

3 Patch design.

The interactive tools described in the previous section provide a practical solution to the problem of subdividing an implicit surface. However, as the resulting charts are to be used for storing textures, a good design strategy should support simple and efficient manipulation of texture maps. For this reason, it will be useful to impose certain restrictions on the charts.

For many texturing and image processing algorithms (flood fills, anti-aliasing, etc.), it is desirable to avoid continuity problems at borders between charts (see figure 1), and this can be accomplished by imposing suitable boundary conditions. Furthermore, as current texture mapping hardware allow only a restricted amount of memory to be devoted to texture maps, the texture representation should be compact. Finally, parametric distortion (stretching/compression and shear) should be minimized inside each patch to avoid wasting resolution to an inhomogeneous sampling rate.

Aside from these purely technical aspects, perceptual concerns regarding the ease-of-use of the interface should be considered. It is a well know result in differential geometry that any regular surface can be decomposed into triangular or rectangular patches [26] (p. 272), but we have found that the interactive workload is greatly reduced if both types of patches are supported. Further improvement was gained by supplementing the geodesic curve tool with the smooth interpolating curves described in section 2.3.

Based on these observations, the following rules were adopted for defining the charts:

1. The charts are represented as polynomial tensor product patches with parameter space corresponding exactly to the unit square (for triangular patches: the triangle $u, v \geq 0, u + v \leq 1$).

2. A patch is defined by three or four non-intersecting boundary curves (any combination of geodesics or splines) connected in a cycle.

3. For any interior angle, θ, between two adjoining boundary curves of a patch, $0 < \theta < \pi$.

4. The interior of a rectangular patch is homeomorphic to the unit square such that the four edges of the square map onto to the boundaries of the patch (a similar condition holds for triangular patches).

To understand the significance of the third condition, imagine that the user has drawn four curves outlining a small rectangular patch on a large sphere and now wants to parameterize it before drawing additional patches. However, the small rectangle actually defines *two* patches on the surface: a small one, and a very large one. To be able to discard "uninteresting" patches automatically, our system enforces the third restriction so that only the small patch is considered when the "parameterize patches" operation is selected. As the idea of adding curves and patches incrementally is essential in our approach (see figure 5), this feature has proven to be very convenient.

The last condition rules out certain contrived cases, assuring that the interior of a patch does not have loops etc. As it is of marginal practical concern, the details are beyond the scope of this paper.

4 Deriving material coordinates.

Once the surface has been partitioned according to the guidelines in section 3, the next step is to construct a uv-parameterization for each patch. The general idea in the new parameterization algorithm, which will be presented in this section, is to start by identifying two families of *iso-parametric curves*, corresponding to fixed u and v parameters, and subsequently reconstruct a parameterization from these.

More specifically, given 3 or 4 piecewise linear curves, C_{u_i}, C_{v_i}, bounding some region R of the surface (see figure 2), the problem is to construct a mesh of iso-parametric curves that faithfully represents the geometry of R and minimizes parametric distortion. As the u and v curves are first estimated independently, and as the algorithm for rectangular patches can also be applied for the triangular case, it will be convenient to start by considering the subproblem of deriving the set of curves corresponding to fixed u values for a rectangular patch in section 4.1. Section 4.2 will describe how to combine the two sets of curves into a mesh and how to derive convenient (u, v) coordinates at each sample of this mesh. Section 4.3 discusses the modifications needed in the case of triangular patches, and section 4.4 how a continuous parameterization can be reconstructed from the discrete mesh. Finally, section 4.5 describes how the parameterizations can be used to store textures.

4.1 Computing iso-parametric (u) curves.

First, the bounding curves C_{v_0} and C_{v_1} (see figure 2) are resampled using the tools described in section 2, until a stable configuration with the average sample distance equal to 2σ (within some tolerance) is reached.

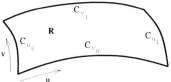

Figure 2: *A patch outlined by bounding curves.*

As the distances between adjacent iso-parametrics are to be less than 4σ everywhere to sample the surface properly, the initial guess for the required number of iso-parametrics is set to

$$dim_u = \max\left(\frac{Length(C_{v_0})}{4\sigma}, \frac{Length(C_{v_1})}{4\sigma}\right).$$

Next, dim_u samples are positioned uniformly along C_{v_0} and C_{v_1} respectively, and the idea is now to find a curve connecting each pair of samples.

4.1.1 Inside-outside test for efficiency.

Although the geodesic curve algorithm could be used directly for this purpose, it is convenient to consider only the subset of surface samples interior to the specific patch in the discrete shortest-path algorithm from section 2.1.2. Therefore, an equivalence relation is imposed on the set of samples, assigning each sample to the patch to which it belongs. We use the following algorithm:

```
stack = ∅
for p ∈ P do
    p.state = UNDETERMINED
    find closest point q to p on bounding curves
    if (|q − p| ≤ 4σ)
        if (p is on interior side of q)
            stack.Push(p,INSIDE)
        else
            stack.Push(p,OUTSIDE)
while (stack ≠ ∅)
    p = stack.Pop()
    for q ∈ p.neighbors do
        if (q.state == UNDETERMINED)
            stack.Push(q,p.state)
```

First, all samples within a distance of 4σ of any curve are marked. As no edge in the graph is longer than 4σ, this assures that no edge with an UNDETERMINED end point crosses a patch boundary, and the equivalence classes can then be computed using the last traversal. In the actual implementation, it is necessary to compensate for curvature of the surface and replace σ in the above algorithm by a slightly smaller number, depending on the approximation error introduced by assumption 1 in section 2.1. The algorithm has proven to work well in practice, on average reducing the number of samples to be considered in the shortest path algorithm to $\frac{N}{M}$, where N and M denote the number of samples and patches respectively, yielding a significant speed-up.

When the initial approximations for the u and v geodesics are computed, these are optimized to give a qualified guess for the iso-parametric curves.

4.1.2 Estimating u and v curves using 2D flows.

Using geodesics as the initial guess for the iso-parametrics works well if the boundary curves are geodesics and the patch is not too "bumpy". However, in order to be able to work with more irregular patches, it is sometimes desirable to compute a more accurate initial approximation (as an example, irregular patches are useful for warping photo-textures onto patches outlined by non-geodesic boundaries, such as the spline curves from section 2.3, see figure 8a). To get an intuitive understanding of the problem, consider a patch with a big bump in the middle: because the geodesic curves used to compute the iso-parametrics try to minimize distance, they will cluster together near the boundary curves and never reach the top of the bump. Therefore, a supplementary technique, capable of producing better approximations at the tradeoff of increased computing time, was developed.

The idea is to use two homogeneous *flows* (one for each parametric direction), parallel with each set of boundary curves, to align the approximated iso-parametrics with the boundaries and thus distribute the curves more evenly within the patch. This can be accomplished using simple vector field theory to find an optimal flow subject to appropriate boundary conditions and subsequently aligning the curves with the flow using optimization.

In order to work efficiently with continuous flows on a computer, a suitable discretization is needed. Fortunately, the discrete graph representing the surface (section 2.1.2) can be reused for this purpose. We use the following algorithm for computing the flows:

1. Each sample inside the patch and along the boundary curves is assigned an arbitrary unit reference vector in the tangent plane and two random angles, ϕ_u and ϕ_v. The reference vector induces a local polar coordinate system in a neighborhood around each sample, in which the angles, one for each parametric direction, represent the orientations of the flows (as we are only interested in directions, it is most convenient to perform the optimization in polar coordinates).

2. Impose boundary conditions: For each sample along the curves, ϕ_u and ϕ_v are initialized so each field is tangential to the corresponding pair of curves, and orthogonal to the other field along the remaining two curves (see figure 3a).

3. Align the orientations of the fields using simple optimization based on the energy function

$$E = \sum_i \sum_{j \; near \; i} \left| \phi_{u_i} - \phi_{u_{ij}} \right|^2 + \left| \phi_{v_i} - \phi_{v_{ij}} \right|^2,$$

where ϕ_{u_i} and ϕ_{v_i} denote the angles at the i'th vertex in the graph (relative to the fixed reference vector at this vertex), and $\phi_{u_{ij}}$ is the angle ϕ_u at the j'th neighbor to the i'th vertex measured relative to the reference vector at the i'th vertex (similar for $\phi_{v_{ij}}$).

4. When the system is stable, the set of boundary constraints requiring the fields to be orthogonal is removed, while the tangent constraints are still enforced. Repeat the optimization until the system converges again.

Given the flows, the idea is now to optimize the curves produced by the geodesic curve algorithm so that the *work* done by the fields along each curve is minimal. This make the interior curves align themselves with the flows and thus with the boundary curves, producing a better guess to the iso-parametric curves. We minimize the following functional:

$$\int_T \langle G(\alpha(t)), \alpha'(t) \rangle dt,$$

where G denotes the vector field, using a straightforward discretization.

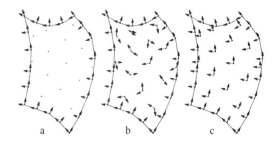

Figure 3: *a) Boundary conditions of the flows. b) Initial state. c) After optimization.*

As it is necessary to evaluate the vector fields at each sample point along the interior curves, an efficient mechanism for reconstructing a continuous vector function from the discretely sampled fields is needed. We use a *Gaussian filter* and a spatial subdivision provided by the surface graph: each sample, p, along the interior curves, continuously tracks the closest vertex, w, in the graph, and ϕ_u and ϕ_v at p are then reconstructed as a weighted average of the corresponding angles at w and its neighbors (in practice, it is only necessary to consider the immediately adjacent vertices in order to reconstruct the fields with sufficient accuracy).

Our experience is that the simple geodesic approximation of the iso-parametric curves is fully adequate for almost all the parameterization problems that occur in practice (figure 4a illustrates the robustness of this method), as the optimization procedures to be described below have proved to be reliable and forgiving. The vector field technique is more general, but slower and should only be applied in pathological cases (see figure 4b).

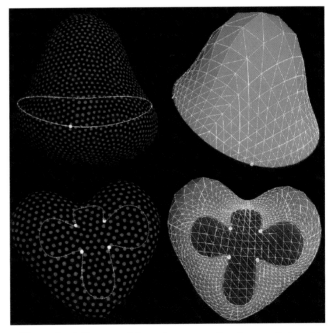

Figure 4: a) Parameterizing a bumpy patch using geodesics. b) An esoteric patch has been parameterized using curves aligned with vector fields.

4.1.3 Optimizing the iso-parametric curves.

The techniques described so far have computed the curve approximations independently, because the initial guess provided by the discrete geodesic algorithm was too inaccurate to exploit coherence between neighboring curves in the optimization. In order to take advantage of this coherence to further improve the approximations, it is necessary to assure that no two adjacent u- or v-curves are farther apart than approximately 4σ, as this is the requirement

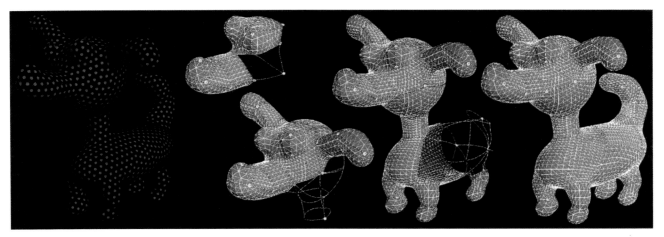

Figure 5: *Parameterizing an implicit surface (106 patches). Total time for entire session: 75 minutes using an SGI Onyx.*

for locally approximating distances on the surface by their Euclidean counterpart. Therefore, the number of iso-parametrics in each direction is increased if necessary:

$$dim'_u = \max(dim_u, \max_{0 \le i < dim_v} (\frac{Length(C_{v_i})}{4\sigma}))$$

$$dim'_v = \max(dim_v, \max_{0 \le i < dim_u} (\frac{Length(C_{u_i})}{4\sigma}))$$

If additional curves are needed in order to fulfill the sampling requirements, they are computed and optimized as described earlier in this section and added incrementally to the existing curves.

Figure 6: *Parameterized implicit surface. Each "mandrill" image corresponds to the texture space of one patch.*

To recap, we now have a set of dim_u independent curves, running from one side of the patch to the opposite, and from these we want to construct a regular grid in order to be able to apply standard finite difference methods for minimizing parametric distortion (in order to improve the modularization of our system, the distortion minimizing techniques have been implemented as a separate "black box"). However, although the curves were constructed to represent the patch faithfully, there is no guarantee that they do so. In order to supply the best possible mesh to the distortion reducing algorithms, we therefore choose to apply an additional optimization step dedicated to reducing irregularities in the distribution of

the curves that might cause more general optimization techniques to fail. This intermediate optimization step explores the fact that although some segments of adjacent curves may be more distant than 4σ, the curves are generally homogeneously distributed, and, moreover, the samples along each curve are uniformly spaced.

To explore this coherence, each curve is sampled uniformly so that the distance between any two samples is less than 2σ and all curves have the same number of samples (at this point, the set of v curves is discarded, as only one set of curves will be needed in the remaining steps; the v curves were only used to assure that a sufficient number of u curves was selected). The resulting samples define a regular grid, which is then refined using simple optimization in order to maximize the distance between adjacent curves subject to the (stronger) condition that the structural integrity of each curve is preserved. The implementation boils down to updating each interior point in the grid with an appropriately weighted average of its eight neighbors until a stable configuration is reached. The resulting mesh can now be passed on to the "minimize distortion"-module.

Figure 7: *Matching texels at patch boundaries.*

4.2 Minimizing distortion.

All our efforts have been devoted to ensuring that the mesh is regular and represents the patch accurately. Given such a mesh, standard optimization techniques for reducing parametric distortion can be applied, for example using the *Green-Lagrange deformation tensor* [12]. Because the mesh is represented as a regular grid rather than a more general graph, this final optimization step is particularly simple and robust (figure 6 shows an example of texture coordinates computed in this process).

4.3 Triangular patches.

The algorithm for parameterizing rectangular patches can also be applied for triangular patches, the only difference being slightly different boundary conditions when the flow technique from section 4.1.2 is utilized. The initial boundary conditions along the side corresponding to the hypotenuse can conveniently be set so both fields are orthogonal to this curve. It is convenient to orient the parameter space of a triangular patch so its origin coincides with the vertex corresponding to the widest dihedral angle in order to minimize distortion.

4.4 Reconstruction.

The parameterization algorithm produces a sampling of the surface with corresponding material coordinates. As each patch is represented by a regular grid of samples, the surface could now be reconstructed as spline patches [32, 33], but as existing hardware favors polyhedral representations, and as implicit surfaces typically are scan-line rendered as a set of polygons, we choose to reconstruct the surface as a triangulation (see figure 5). The patches were constructed so the maximum distance between any two adjacent samples was less than 4σ, but the sampling may be unnecessarily high in some low-curvature regions. Recent progress in polygonal and algebraic surface modeling [34, 35, 36] provides efficient tools for retiling polygonal representations of implicit surfaces. At present, only edge flipping [34] and adaptive sampling has been implemented in our experimental system, as this has produced satisfactory results, but we plan to enhance the system with more elaborate mesh optimization features in the near future.

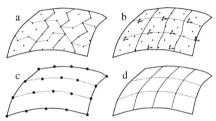

Figure 8: *Summary of the patch parameterization step: a) User supplies boundary curves, and discrete geodesics are used as an initial guess for iso-parametric curves. b) The approximations are refined using either simple geodesics or vector fields. Optimization based on coherence between neighboring curves improves the approximation further. c) One set of curves is sampled uniformly to define a mesh. d) The mesh is optimized to reduce parametric distortion and a continuous parameterization is extrapolated.*

4.5 Storing textures.

The patch parameterizations provide natural material coordinates for the surface, but we still need an effecient strategy for representing textures. It is emphasized that our goal is *not* to map a separate image onto each patch, but in lieu of developing more sophisticated texturing techniques in section 5, we need a way of storing the texture information. Eventually, our goal will be to make the network of patches and their corresponding texture mappings completely invisible to the artist.

There are several factors to consider regarding the texture representation. First, the sampling rate should be sufficiently high to avoid loss of high-frequency detail or visible rastering artifacts. Second, the sampling rate should be no higher than necessary to reduce overhead in memory consumption. Third, reconstruction should be simple and hardware supported, and fourth, matching texels at patch borders should be straightforward. Based on these observations and trade-offs, the following strategy was chosen:

The textures are represented as 2D tables for easy reconstruction and for compatibility with existing renderers and graphics hardware. The sampling rate in each parametric direction is chosen to be a power of 2 to make texel matching trivial at patch borders (see figure 7 and compare with figure 1):

$$res_u = 2^{log_2 \lfloor dim_u \cdot \frac{4\sigma}{\epsilon} \rfloor}$$
$$res_v = 2^{log_2 \lfloor dim_v \cdot \frac{4\sigma}{\epsilon} \rfloor}$$

where ϵ represents the desired maximum sample separation, and dim_u and dim_v are the number of iso-parametrics for the patch. For triangular patches, res_u and res_v are chosen to be equal for simplicity. This design supports both efficient texture representation and efficient texturing operations. Another nice property is

that the resolution need not be the same across the surface, but can easily be adapted if certain regions require a higher sampling frequency.

Given such a set of disjoint texture mappings covering the entire implicit surface (or whatever part of it has been parameterized), we can now move on to our original goal of designing new texturing algorithms.

5 Decorating Implicit Surfaces.

Our analysis of existing 3D painting techniques in section 1.1.1 produced the following results:

1. New high-level texturing operations with less dependence on the users artistic talent and patience would be useful.

2. These operations should be performed at interactive speed, while the user is free to view the texture from any angle and distance.

3. A general mechanism for specifying the global position and extent of a texture on a surface would be convenient.

4. Texture distortion should be minimal, but not at the expense of introducing discontinuities, which should be be avoided at all costs.

The remainder of this section will describe how these objectives can be met.

We propose four supplementary methods for decorating objects easily and without introducing seams: curve drawing (see figure 6), flood fill operations (figure 11), tiling (figure 9), and positioning of smaller images onto the object (figure 10). Common to these operations is that the resulting textures are not being mapped in the traditional sense, but are applied directly onto the surface while the texture mappings only serve to store the texture signal. This is a subtle but important difference from the traditional texture mapping paradigm, as the artist does not have to worry about the underlying mapping functions. We believe that "texture mapping" is an unfortunate term when it comes to decorating complex 3D shapes, as the mathematical details of how the textures are represented are irrelevant for the artist. Instead, we use the term "decoration", as it is a less technocratic and more friendly metaphor for the artistic process, our tools are aimed at. Flood- and pattern-fill operations are useful for quickly and accurately covering larger regions of a surface with a color or high frequency texture. Tiling is useful for covering a surface with a more complex pattern, and positioning of smaller images is useful for unique local patterns. The last two features require the derivation of a *change of coordinates* from the source image to the destination texture coordinates, and these tools will be developed in section 5.2, while section 5.3 and 5.4 will present our most recent results and discuss implementation issues.

To motivate these ideas, we note that none of the currently available high-end 3D brush-painting applications (i.e. in the price range $15,000+ [8]) offer a consistent solution to even basic geodesic curve-drawing operations, that simple flood fills therefore have to be accomplished through user-intensive brush painting operations, and that these systems do not provide any of the aforementioned change-of-coordinates based texture placement features.

5.1 Lines and curves.

The curve drawing algorithms from section 2 can be applied immediately for drawing geodesics and splines onto the surface. The remaining problem is how to convert these curves into texels in the texture representation. As the curves are sampled on the actual implicit surface and not on the corresponding triangulation, it is convenient to start by projecting each curve onto the triangulation. This approximation makes sense if the triangulation is a good approximation to the surface, and is valid as the polygonization was specifically designed to meet this criterion (cf. section 2.1).

First, the sample points along the curve are projected onto the triangulation by computing its intersection with the line defined by each sample and its corresponding normal vector (the exact surface normal at the sample computed from the gradient to the implicit function).

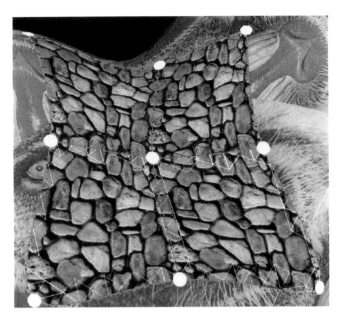

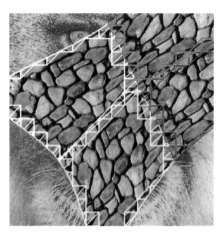

Figure 8: *a) Image textures. Four tiles were outlined and parameterized, and the corresponding change-of-coordinates to the destination surface patches was computed. b) The source texture was then drawn directly into the texture space of each destination patch using Reality Engine hardware. "Border polygons" (see section 5.2) are highlighted in both figures.*

These points form a series of line segments, not necessarily on the triangulation. Each segment is then projected onto the triangulation along the plane defined by the two end points and the average of the corresponding normal vectors, forming a connected chain of points completely embedded in the triangulation while preserving the structural integrity of the curve.

5.2 Patches.

As in the case of lines and curves, the previously described patch parameterization algorithm can be reused for positioning images onto the surface. Similar to the surface subdivision process, the user specifies the extent of the image using the curve-drawing tools. When the patch is defined and parameterized, the remaining problem is here to compute a change of coordinates from the source patch texture coordinates to the texture space of the surface. Again, this can be accomplished by a projection, transforming the source texture patch into a set of polygons aligned with the surface triangulation (see figure 8).

First, the bounding curves are projected onto the surface as described in section 5.1, and the destination coordinates of each

Figure 9: *Tiling.*

sample along the projected curve are computed using, for example, *barycentric coordinates*, [37] (remember that the destination texture coordinates are stored at each vertex of the surface triangulation). The resulting closed projected curve defines a set of interior polygons on the triangulation, which can conveniently be categorized into *border polygons* and *interior triangles*. Border

polygons (highlighted in figure 8) denote polygons directly adjacent to a border segment, and can theoretically have any number of vertices. However, border polygons are always planar, as they are each contained in a single triangle of the surface triangulation. Per definition, interior triangles are not divided by a border and thus always remain triangles.

5.2.1 Texture transformation.

Given these two sets of polygons and the destination texture coordinates at each of their vertices, the final step is to compute the corresponding source coordinates at each vertex. Just as the destination coordinates for vertices along the boundary curves of the source patch were derived by projecting these points onto the destination triangulation, the source coordinates for the interior vertices can be computed by projecting these onto the triangulation of the source patch. Because the normal vectors at each vertex on both source and destination triangulations are those of the actual implicit surface rather than estimates computed from the polyhedral approximations, the projections can be performed safely both ways with minimal loss of precision.

The final representation of the change of coordinates is thus a set of polygons embedded in the surface, where both source and destination coordinates are known at each vertex. Under the reasonable assumption that the coordinate change is linear within each polygon, an assumption shared by all existing scan-line rendering algorithms for polygonal surfaces, the actual transformation of the source texture information into the surface texture representation can now be accomplished through a series of linear transformations, one for each polygon. However, if Silicon Graphics hardware is available, this step can be performed particularly elegantly:

Because the polygons were designed to match the boundaries of the texture representation patches, no polygon crosses a patch border. Therefore, it is convenient to introduce an equivalence relation on the polygons with classes corresponding to the destination patches. The actual transformation algorithm now looks like this (see figure 8b):

```
set texture pointer to source texture
for each destination patch M do
    draw one rectangular polygon covering the entire
        texture space of M into a frame buffer
    for p ∈ M.polygons do
        for w ∈ p.vertices do
            set texture parameters to (w.source_u, w.source_v)
            set geometric parameters to (w.dest_u, w.dest_v)
        draw p
    read frame buffer back into texture space of M
```

All instructions used in this algorithm are provided by the Reality Engine texture mapping hardware, allowing it to be implemented efficiently in less than 20 lines of code. For anti-aliasing, we use 16 times super-sampling by drawing into a frame buffer 4 times the number of pixels in the texture representation in each parametric direction and subsequently reconstructing with an appropriate filter [38] (chapter 14).

Figure 8 shows an application of the change-of-coordinates algorithm. Destination texture coordinates are indicated by a "mandrill" image for every patch, and the source texture coordinates by a stone tiling. Notice the perfect match at the curved tile borders. Curves and images can be positioned arbitrarily on the surface and the underlying texture representation is completely invisible to the user. The total computing time for the four coordinate changes and subsequent transformation of the texture information was 18 seconds on an SGI Onyx.

5.3 Epilogue: dragging textures.

As a further extension of the interactive curve drawing and image positioning techniques described in section 5.1 and 5.2, a feature allowing textures to be selected, dragged, rotated, and scaled freely across the surface has been implemented. When the texture is first positioned on the surface, a mesh of springs representing its geometry is computed, and as the element deforms as it moves across the surface, an optimization process is used to restore it to its rest shape subject to the constraint that the entire texture remains embedded in the implicit surface. At any time, the user can paste the texture onto its current position on the surface.

Figure 10: *Cut and paste. An implicit surface has been decorated by dragging, rotating, and scaling a single patch across it. Total time for entire session: 8 minutes on an SGI Onyx.*

These facilities have proven to be useful for fine-tuning the position and extent of a texture. Unfortunately, space does not permit a detailed description of these algorithms.[2]

5.4 Implementation.

The new texturing operations presented in this section have been implemented on a Silicon Graphics Reality Engine, which is widely used in the industry that would benefit from this work.

---

[2]The work described in section 5.3 was done after the provisional acceptance of this paper.

Our experimental implementation runs at comfortably interactive speed for all operations, the most complex patch parameterization/change of coordinates step typically taking in the order of 5 to 30 seconds per patch, depending on the sampling density within the patch. As all operations are performed on-line, the user is free to, for example, rotate the objects and perform new operations while previously specified ones are still being computed. Although the texturing algorithms were developed specifically for the Reality Engine, the curve drawing and parameterization algorithms do not require the use of sophisticated graphics hardware. These techniques have performed well on a Silicon Graphics Indy and would probably also be applicable on a fast personal computer.

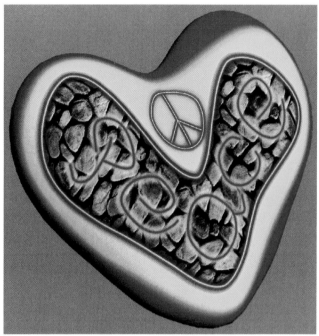

Figure 11: *Pattern fill, curve drawing, anti-aliasing.*

6 Future work.

The biggest limitation of our original implementation was that the parameter σ was specified globally, causing the sampling frequency to be unnecessarily high in low curvature regions. Therefore, a simple generalization of [6] to adaptive sampling has been implemented (see figure 6). Space does not permit a detailed account for these preliminary results, and although adaptive sampling has proven to be convenient, we emphasize that all algorithms presented in this paper are self-contained and have proven to perform well in practical use.

Generalization to splines and polyhedral surfaces. Although the algorithms in this paper lend themselves especially elegantly to implicit surfaces, we believe that they can be applied with spline patches and polyhedral meshes as well. [6] outlined how the point repulsion mechanism can be generalized to parametric surfaces, and an algorithm for curvature adaptive point repulsion on polyhedral meshes has already been published by Turk [35]. As these sampling results form the theoretical foundation for our curve-drawing and patch parameterization algorithms, the generalization to other models should be straightforward, and would, for example, allow the texture representation for spline surfaces to be specified independently of the patch parameterizations, and the new texturing algorithms to be applied directly in current spline based 3D painting applications.

Animation. Due to their flexibility, implicit surfaces have been used to simulate interesting visco-elastic effects in animations since the dawn of time [39], and this application of implicits is widely considered more important than their use in modeling. With simple extensions, it appears that the ideas in this paper could be generalized to animated skeletal models: The problem of making the textured patches follow the moving surface is straightforward and to some extent covered in [6], and feature alignment can be enforced by specifying *anchor points* at key positions on the textured surface. The anchors could, for example, be specified as the intersections between the implicit surface and line segments defined relative to specific limbs of the skeleton (imagine small "needles" sticking out from the skeleton). Given a skeletal model, an atlas of textured patches covering the surface, and a set of anchor points, the texture could be made to track the object using Witkin & Heckbert's ideas to keep the patches on the surface, and a generalization of Maillot et al. [12] to minimize parametric distortion subject to the constraint that the texture coordinates remain constant at each anchor point.

Texturing operations. There is a need for better high-level texturing operations for 3D objects; not only generalizations of existing 2D painting algorithms, but entirely new concepts specifically designed to meet the added challenges presented by complex shapes. As an example, we believe that the tiling operations outlined in section 5 could be useful in present texturing applications: in contrast to brush painting, tiling does not require particular artistic skills, and the interactive texture positioning tools in section 5.2 allows the borders of the tiles to be matched perfectly on curved surfaces (see figure 8). The mesh optimization algorithm (section 4.2) can easily be modified so parametric distortion is not only minimized within each patch, but also across patch borders. This is useful for avoiding first order discontinuities between adjacent tiles.

7   Conclusion.

The algorithms in this paper allow a new range of useful operations to be performed on implicit surfaces. In particular, they present a practical solution to the texturing problem, which has been one of the biggest limitations of soft objects. Paradoxally, as most of the texturing operations are new and currently have no counterparts in the case of parametric or polyhedral surfaces, it appears that implicits could have unexpected advantages in this respect.

In conclusion, abandoning the "editorial *we*" on a last note, I hope that this work will eventually provide artists and graphics programmers with better tools and that it will be used for the positive and creative purposes for which it was intended.

8   Acknowledgements.

Sebastian Grassia, Carnegie Mellon University, gave me the original inspiration for this work [40], but unfortunately was too busy taking classes to become co-author of a paper that would have greatly benefitted from his talent. I will always be indebted to Fred Brooks for a wonderful year in Chapel Hill and for giving me the freedom to pursue these ideas. Special thanks to Dinesh Manocha, Greg Turk and Peggy Wetzel for their hospitality and much appreciated help, to Paul Heckbert, Will Welch and Andy Witkin for immense amounts of inspiration while I was at CMU, to Pat Hanrahan, Stanford University, for an experience that I am very much looking forward to, and, not least, to the anonymous reviewers (#4: stop by any time for a free lunch!). Finally, thanks to the Fulbright Commission and USIA for sponsoring my studies in the United States.

References

[1]   E. A. Bier and K. R. Sloan, Jr. Two part texture mappings. *IEEE Computer Graphics and Applications*, 6(9):40–53, September 1986.

[2]   Nelson L. Max and Geoff Wyvill. Shapes and textures for rendering coral. In N. M. Patrikalakis, editor, *Scientific Visualization of Physical Phenomena (Proceedings of CG International '91)*, pages 333–343. Springer-Verlag, 1991.

[3]   Geoff Wyvill, Brian Wyvill, and Craig McPheeters. Solid texturing of soft objects. In *CG International '87*. Tokyo, May 1987.

[4]   Darwyn R. Peachey. Solid texturing of complex surfaces. In B. A. Barsky, editor, *Computer Graphics (SIGGRAPH '85 Proceedings)*, volume 19, pages 279–286, July 1985.

[5]   Ken Perlin. An image synthesizer. In B. A. Barsky, editor, *Computer Graphics (SIGGRAPH '85 Proceedings)*, volume 19, pages 287–296, July 1985.

[6]   Andrew P. Witkin and Paul S. Heckbert. Using particles to sample and control implicit surfaces. In Andrew Glassner, editor, *Proceedings of SIGGRAPH '94 (Orlando, Florida, July 24–29, 1994)*, Computer Graphics Proceedings, Annual Conference Series, pages 269–278. ACM SIGGRAPH, ACM Press, July 1994. ISBN 0-89791-667-0.

[7]   Pat Hanrahan and Paul E. Haeberli. Direct WYSIWYG painting and texturing on 3D shapes. In Forest Baskett, editor, *Computer Graphics (SIGGRAPH '90 Proceedings)*, volume 24, pages 215–223, August 1990.

[8]   Barbara Robertson. Fresh paint. *Computer Graphics World*, 17(12):28–37, December 1994.

[9]   Peter Litwinowicz and Gavin Miller. Efficient techniques for interactive texture placement. In Andrew Glassner, editor, *Proceedings of SIGGRAPH '94 (Orlando, Florida, July 24–29, 1994)*, Computer Graphics Proceedings, Annual Conference Series, pages 119–122. ACM SIGGRAPH, ACM Press, July 1994.

[10]   Maneesh Agrawala, Andrew C. Beers, and Marc Levoy. 3d painting on scanned surfaces. In *Proceedings 1995 Symposium on Interactive 3D Graphics (Monterey, California, April 9–12, 1995)*, pages 145–152.

[11]   Chakib Bennis, Jean-Marc Vézien, Gérard Iglésias, and André Gagalowicz. Piecewise surface flattening for non-distorted texture mapping. In Thomas W. Sederberg, editor, *Computer Graphics (SIGGRAPH '91 Proceedings)*, volume 25, pages 237–246, July 1991.

[12]   Jérôme Maillot, Hussein·Yahia, and Anne Verroust. Interactive texture mapping. In James T. Kajiya, editor, *Computer Graphics (SIGGRAPH '93 Proceedings)*, volume 27, pages 27–34, August 1993.

[13]   M. Samek. Texture mapping and distortion in digital graphics. *Visual Computer*, 2(5):313–20, 1986.

[14]   Richard Bartels, John Beatty, and Brian Barsky. *An Introduction to Splines for Use in Computer Graphics and Geometric Modeling*. Morgan Kaufmann Publishers, Palo Alto, CA, 1987.

[15]   S. Gabriel and James T. Kajiya. Spline interpolation in curved space. *State of the Art Image Synthesis, Course notes for SIGGRAPH '85*, 1985.

[16]   William Welch and Andrew Witkin. Variational surface modeling. In Edwin E. Catmull, editor, *Computer Graphics (SIGGRAPH '92 Proceedings)*, volume 26, pages 157–166, July 1992.

[17]   R. Dietz, J. Hoschek, and B. Jüttler. An algebraic approach to curves and surfaces on the sphere and on other quadrics. *Computer Aided Geometric Design*, 10(3):211–230, August 1993.

[18]   Ron Kimmel, A. Amir, and A. M. Bruckstein. Finding shortest paths on surfaces. In Pierre-Jean Laurent, editor, *Curves and Surfaces in Geometric Design*, pages 259–268. A. K. Peters, Wellesley, Massachusetts, August 1994.

[19]   Nicholas M. Patrikalakis and George A. Kriezis. Representation of piecewise continuous algebraic surfaces in terms of B-splines. *The Visual Computer*, 5(6):360–374, December 1989.

[20]   L. L. Schumaker and C. Traas. Fitting scattered data on spherelike surfaces using tensor products of trigonometric and polynomial splines. *Numerische Matematik*, 60(1):129–139, 1991.

[21]   J. S. B. Mitchell, D. M. Mount, and C. H. Papadimitriou. The discrete geodesic problem. *SIAM J. Comput.*, 16(4):647–668, 1987.

[22]   Karsten Opitz and Helmut Pottmann. Computing shortest paths on polyhedra: Applications in geometric modeling and scientific visualization. *Intl. Journal of Computational Geometry and Applications*, 4(2):165–178, June 1994.

[23]   Alan H. Barr, Bena Currin, Steven Gabriel, and John F. Hughes. Smooth interpolation of orientations with angular velocity constraints using quaternions. In Edwin E. Catmull, editor, *Computer Graphics (SIGGRAPH '92 Proceedings)*, volume 26, pages 313–320, July 1992.

[24]   J. Bloomenthal. Polygonization of implicit surfaces. *Computer Aided Geometric Design*, 5(4):341–356, 1988.

[25]   Brian Wyvill, Craig McPheeters, and Geoff Wyvill. Data structure for soft objects. *The Visual Computer*, 2(4):227–234, 1986.

[26]   Manfredo P. do Carmo. *Differential Geometry of Curves and Surfaces*. Prentice-Hall Inc., 1976. ISBN 0-13-212589-7.

[27]   Thomas H. Cohen, Charles E. Leiserson, and Ronald L. Rivest. *Introduction to Algorithms*. MIT Press, Cambridge, Massachusetts, 1990.

[28]   Hugues Hoppe, Tony DeRose, Tom Duchamp, John McDonald, and Werner Stuetzle. Surface reconstruction from unorganized points. In Edwin E. Catmull, editor, *Computer Graphics (SIGGRAPH '92 Proceedings)*, volume 26, pages 71–78, July 1992.

[29]   Greg Turk. Generating textures for arbitrary surfaces using reaction-diffusion. In Thomas W. Sederberg, editor, *Computer Graphics (SIGGRAPH '91 Proceedings)*, volume 25, pages 289–298, July 1991.

[30]   Ron Kimmel and Nahum Kiryati. Finding shortest paths on surfaces by fast global approximation and precise local refinement. In *SPIE Vision and Geometry III*, pages 198–209, November 1994.

[31]   Richard E. Williamson, Richard H. Crowell, and Hale F. Trotter. *Calculus of Vector Functions*. Prentice-Hall Inc., 1962 (first edition). ISBN 0-13-112367.

[32]   Charles Loop. A G^1 triangular spline surface of arbitrary topological type. *Computer Aided Geometric Design*, (11):303–330, 1994.

[33]   Jörg Peters. C^1 surface splines. *SIAM Journal on Numerical Analysis*, October 1993.

[34]   Paul Chew. Guaranteed quality mesh generation for curved surfaces. In *ACM Symposium on Computational Geometry*, 1993.

[35]   Greg Turk. Re-tiling polygonal surfaces. In Edwin E. Catmull, editor, *Computer Graphics (SIGGRAPH '92 Proceedings)*, volume 26, pages 55–64, July 1992.

[36]   William Welch and Andrew Witkin. Free-Form shape design using triangulated surfaces. In Andrew Glassner, editor, *Proceedings of SIGGRAPH '94 (Orlando, Florida, July 24–29, 1994)*, Computer Graphics Proceedings, Annual Conference Series, pages 247–256. ACM SIGGRAPH, ACM Press, July 1994. ISBN 0-89791-667-0.

[37]   Andrew J. Hanson. Geometry for N-dimensional graphics. In Paul Heckbert, editor, *Graphics Gems IV*, pages 149–170. Academic Press, Boston, 1994.

[38]   James D. Foley, Andries van Dam, Steven K. Feiner, and John F. Hughes. *Computer Graphics, Principles and Practice, Second Edition*. Addison-Wesley, Reading, Massachusetts, 1990. Overview of research to date.

[39]   James F. Blinn. A generalization of algebraic surface drawing. *ACM Transactions on Graphics*, 1(3):235–256, July 1982.

[40]   F. Sebastian Grassia. Using particles to texture implicit surfaces. *Assignment for Paul Heckbert's Rendering course at CMU, unpublished*, December 1993.

Implicitization using Moving Curves and Surfaces

Thomas W. Sederberg[1] and Falai Chen[2]
Brigham Young University

This paper presents a radically new approach to the century old problem of computing the implicit equation of a parametric surface. For surfaces without base points, the new method expresses the implicit equation in a determinant which is one fourth the size of the conventional expression based on Dixon's resultant. If base points do exist, previous implicitization methods either fail or become much more complicated, while the new method actually simplifies.

The new method is illustrated using the bicubic patches from Newell's teapot model. Dixon's method can successfully implicitize only 8 of those 32 patches, expressing the implicit equation as an 18×18 determinant. The new method successfully implicitizes *all* 32 of the patches. Four of the implicit equations can be written as 3×3 determinants, eight can be written as 4×4 determinants, and the remaining 20 implicit equations can be written using 9×9 determinants.

Categories and Subject Descriptors: I.3.5 [**Computer Graphics**]: Computational Geometry and Object Modeling.

General Terms: Algorithms

Additional Key Words and Phrases: Bézier patches, implicitization, base points.

1   INTRODUCTION

For any 2–D parametric curve $x = \frac{a(t)}{d(t)}$, $y = \frac{b(t)}{d(t)}$ where a, b, and d are polynomials, there exists an implicit equation $f(x, y) = 0$, where f is also a polynomial, which defines exactly the same curve. For example, a circle can be defined by the parametric equation $x = \frac{1-t^2}{1+t^2}$, $y = \frac{2t}{1+t^2}$ or by the implicit equation $x^2 + y^2 - 1 = 0$. The process of finding the implicit equation given the parametric equations is known as *implicitization*. Implicitization of 2–D curves leads to many practical algorithms. For example, a very fast algorithm for computing the intersection of two 2–D curves of low degree is based on implicitization [23]. Implicitization reduces the problem of curve intersection to one of finding the roots of a single polynomial.

Similarly, for any parametric surface $x = \frac{a(s,t)}{d(s,t)}$, $y = \frac{b(s,t)}{d(s,t)}$, $z = \frac{c(s,t)}{d(s,t)}$ where a, b, c, and d are polynomials in s, t, there exists a polynomial implicit equation $f(x, y, z) = 0$ which defines the same surface.

The general problem of surface implicitization has been studied for well over a century. In 1862, Salmon [18] noted that surface implicitization can be performed by eliminating the parameters from the parametric surface equations. Presumably he had in mind using Sylvester's "dialytic method" with which one could eliminate two variables from three polynomials, though the result generally needed to be "expressed as the quotient of one determinant divided by another" [17]. In 1908, Dixon published a more compact resultant for eliminating two variables from three polynomials which has become the standard method for surface implicitization, at least in the absence of base points. In 1983, Sederberg [19] resurrected Dixon's and Salmon's work in addressing the problem of how to implicitize surface patches. Other implicitization methods are surveyed in [10], and include ones based on Gröbner bases [1], numerical techniques [16], and multivariate resultants [4].

To implicitize a tensor product surface of degree $m \times n$, Dixon's resultant produces a $2mn \times 2mn$ matrix whose elements are linear in x, y, z. The determinant of that matrix is the implicit equation. For a biquadratic surface, the matrix is 8×8, and for a bicubic patch, the matrix is 18×18. (In this paper, any statement that a determinant is the implicit equation of a curve or surface should be taken as shorthand for "setting that determinant to zero gives the implicit equation".)

Surface implicitization has seen limited practical use partly because of the huge expressions involved, but also because in the event of base points (see section 4.1), things can get even more complicated. For example, if base points exist, Dixon's resultant is identically zero and hence fails to produce the implicit equation. Manocha has shown that in many cases the largest non-zero minor of Dixon's determinant is the implicit equation, but often it includes an extraneous factor [14]. Substantial further work is then needed to remove the unwanted factor. Implicitization using Gröbner bases [6] also usually fails when base points occur, since the implicit equation does not belong to the ideal generated by the parametric equations [15], although this problem can sometimes be circumvented by introducing some auxiliary polynomials into the Gröbner system [12, 10]. Nonetheless, Gröbner bases are known to be very slow in implicitizing bicubic patches.

Several other procedures have been devised to implicitize surfaces with base points [2, 9, 15, 16]. We don't review those methods here, but observe that those methods are generally more complicated than Dixon's method. Furthermore, base points are *not* a rare occurrence; most of the teapot patches have numerous base points.

This paper presents a fundamentally new procedure for implicitizing curves and surfaces in which the implicit equation can be written in much more compact form than before. Furthermore, in the presence of base points, the expressions actually *simplify*. In particular, the new method allows the implicit equation for a general bicubic patch to be written as a 9×9 determinant whose elements

[1]368 Clyde Building, Brigham Young University, Provo UT 84602-4014. tom@byu.edu

[2]Permanent Address: Dept. of Mathematics, University of Science and Technology of China, Hefei 230026, Anhui, P. R. China

Permission to make digital/hard copy of part or all of this work for personal or classroom use is granted without fee provided that copies are not made or distributed for profit or commercial advantage, the copyright notice, the title of the publication and its date appear, and notice is given that copying is by permission of ACM, Inc. To copy otherwise, to republish, to post on servers, or to redistribute to lists, requires prior specific permission and/or a fee.

© 1995   ACM-0-89791-701-4/95/008 $3.50

are all degree two in x, y, z. If a base point exists, one row of that determinant can in general be replaced by degree one elements. Section 2 introduces the new strategy as it applies to curve implicitization. We refer to this method as the *moving curve* method. Section 3 introduces the *moving surface* method for surface implicitization. Sections 4 and 5 discuss how to implicitize general tensor product and triangular patches using moving surfaces. Section 6 reports on what happens when those methods are used to implicitize the 32 bicubic patches of the teapot. It turns out that those patches show surprising diversity in the number of base points.

2 CURVE IMPLICITIZATION

The standard method for implicitizing a 2–D curve is to use Bezout's resultant [22]. For a degree n rational curve, Bezout's resultant is the determinant of an $n \times n$ matrix whose elements are linear in x, y. For example, the implicit equation of the curve

$$x = \frac{2t^2 + 4t + 5}{t^2 + 2t + 3}; \quad y = \frac{3t^2 + t + 4}{t^2 + 2t + 3} \tag{1}$$

can be found by taking the resultant of

$$t^2(x - 2) + t(2x - 4) + (3x - 5)$$

and

$$t^2(y - 3) + t(2y - 1) + (3y - 4).$$

Bezout's resultant for these two polynomials in t is:

$$\left| \begin{array}{cc} \left| \begin{array}{cc} x-2 & 2x-4 \\ y-3 & 2y-1 \end{array} \right| & \left| \begin{array}{cc} x-2 & 3x-5 \\ y-3 & 3y-4 \end{array} \right| \\ \left| \begin{array}{cc} x-2 & 3x-5 \\ y-3 & 3y-4 \end{array} \right| & \left| \begin{array}{cc} 2x-4 & 3x-5 \\ 2y-1 & 3y-4 \end{array} \right| \end{array} \right|$$

$$= \left| \begin{array}{cc} 5x-10 & 5x-y-7 \\ 5x-y-7 & -5x-2y+11 \end{array} \right|. \tag{2}$$

Setting (2) to zero gives the implicit equation for (1).

Bezout's resultant is purely an algebraic device. By studying the following geometric interpretation of Bezout's resultant, we are led to the new implicitization algorithm.

A pencil of lines can be described by the equation

$$(a_0 x + b_0 y + c_0)(1 - t) + (a_1 x + b_1 y + c_1)t = 0 \tag{3}$$

where the equations $a_0 x + b_0 y + c_0 = 0$ and $a_1 x + b_1 y + c_1 = 0$ define any two distinct lines.

Given two distinct pencils, $(a_{00} x + b_{00} y + c_{00})(1 - t) + (a_{10} x + b_{10} y + c_{10})t = 0$ and $(a_{01} x + b_{01} y + c_{01})(1 - t) + (a_{11} x + b_{11} y + c_{11})t = 0$, one line from each pencil corresponds to each value of t, and those two lines intersect in a point. The locus of points thus created for $-\infty \leq t \leq \infty$ is a conic section, as illustrated in Figure 1. This observation is attributed to Steiner and Chasles in the 1830's, though a roughly equivalent method for generating conic sections dates back to Newton [5].

It is easily shown that the implicit equation of this curve is

$$\left| \begin{array}{cc} a_{00} x + b_{00} y + c_{00} & a_{10} x + b_{10} y + c_{10} \\ a_{01} x + b_{01} y + c_{01} & a_{11} x + b_{11} y + c_{11} \end{array} \right| = 0. \tag{4}$$

This same curve can actually be defined using many different pairs of pencils of lines, and it turns out that Bezout's resultant for degree two curves is nothing more than one manifestation of this

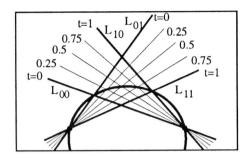

Figure 1: Intersection of Two Pencils of Lines

fact. For example, the two rows of the Bezout resultant (2) can be shown to define pencils of lines

$$(5x - 10)t + (5x - y - 7) = 0 \tag{5}$$

and

$$(5x - y - 7)t + (-5x - 2y + 11) = 0 \tag{6}$$

which intersect in the parametric curve (1).

The idea of defining a conic section as the intersection of two pencils of lines can be generalized to curves of any degree. One such generalization is given in [24]. This section presents some results similar to those in [24], but using a different approach. The approach taken here lays the foundation for the surface implicitization method presented in section 3.

Given a degree ν rational curve $\mathbf{Q}(t) = (x(t), y(t), w(t))$, define $g(t)$ to be the GCD of $x(t)$, $y(t)$, and $w(t)$. We can write

$$\mathbf{Q}(t) = g(t)\mathbf{P}(t) = g(t) \sum_{i=0}^{n} \mathbf{X}_i t^i, \tag{7}$$

where $\mathbf{X}_i \equiv (x_i, y_i, w_i)$. If β is the degree of $g(t)$, $n = \nu - \beta$, we will say that $\mathbf{Q}(t)$ has β base points.

A *moving line*

$$\mathbf{X} \cdot L(t) := \mathbf{X} \cdot \sum_{j=0}^{m} L_j t^j = 0; \quad L_j = (a_j, b_j, c_j), \quad \mathbf{X} \equiv (x, y, w) \tag{8}$$

is a parametric family of implicitly defined lines, with one line corresponding to each "time" t. For $m = 1$, the moving line is a pencil. A moving line is said to "follow" a rational curve if

$$\mathbf{Q}(t) \cdot L(t) \equiv 0, \tag{9}$$

which means that at any time t, point $\mathbf{Q}(t)$ lies on line $L(t)$.

A set of moving lines $L_i(t)$, $i = 0, \ldots, \lambda$ is linearly independent if there do not exist constants c_i, $i = 0, \ldots, \lambda$ (not all zero) such that $\sum_{i=0}^{\lambda} c_i L_i(t) \equiv 0$.

Theorem 1. *For a degree ν curve $\mathbf{Q}(t)$ with β base points, there exist at least $2m + 2 + \beta - \nu$ linearly independent moving lines of degree m which follow the curve.*

Proof:

$$\mathbf{Q}(t) \cdot L(t) \equiv g(t)\mathbf{P}(t) \cdot L(t) \equiv 0 \tag{10}$$

implies

$$\mathbf{P}(t) \cdot L(t) \equiv 0 \tag{11}$$

since $g(t) \not\equiv 0$. We define

$$\mathbf{P}(t) = \sum_{i=0}^{n} (x_i, y_i, w_i) t^i, \tag{12}$$

$$L(t) = \sum_{i=0}^{m} (a_i, b_i, c_i) t^i, \tag{13}$$

$$\mathbf{P}(t) \cdot L(t) = \sum_{k=0}^{n+m} \left\{ \sum_{i+j=k} (a_i x_j + b_i y_j + c_i w_j) \right\} t^k \tag{14}$$

The condition $\mathbf{P}(t) \cdot L(t) \equiv 0$ can be expressed $Mb = 0$ where M is the $(n+m+1) \times (3m+3)$ matrix

$$\begin{bmatrix} x_0 & y_0 & w_0 & 0 & \cdots & 0 & 0 & 0 \\ x_1 & y_1 & w_1 & x_0 & \cdots & 0 & 0 & 0 \\ x_2 & y_2 & w_2 & x_1 & \cdots & 0 & 0 & 0 \\ \vdots & \vdots & \vdots & \vdots & \vdots & \vdots & \vdots & \vdots \\ x_n & y_n & w_n & x_{n-1} & \cdots & . & . & . \\ \vdots & \vdots & \vdots & \vdots & \vdots & \vdots & \vdots & \vdots \\ 0 & 0 & 0 & 0 & \cdots & x_{n-1} & y_{n-1} & w_{n-1} \\ 0 & 0 & 0 & 0 & \cdots & x_n & y_n & w_n \end{bmatrix} \tag{15}$$

and

$$b = \begin{bmatrix} a_0 & b_0 & c_0 & \cdots & a_m & b_m & c_m \end{bmatrix}^T. \tag{16}$$

The dimension of the solution set is $3m + 3 - \mathrm{rank}(M)$. But $\mathrm{rank}(M) \leq n + m + 1$, so at least $2m + 2 - n = 2m + 2 + \beta - \nu$ linearly independent moving lines follow $\mathbf{Q}(t)$. ∎

If $m = n - 1$, we know from theorem 1 that there exist $m + 1$ linearly independent moving lines $L_i(t) \cdot \mathbf{X} = 0$ where

$$L_i(t) = \sum_{j=0}^{m} L_{ij} t^j; \quad L_{ij} = (a_{ij}, b_{ij}, c_{ij}); \quad i = 0, \ldots m \tag{17}$$

such that

$$\mathbf{Q}(t) \cdot L_i(t) \equiv 0, \quad i = 0, \ldots, m. \tag{18}$$

Theorem 2. *Select any set of $m + 1$ linearly independent moving lines that follow $\mathbf{Q}(t)$ and define*

$$f(\mathbf{X}) = \begin{vmatrix} L_{00} \cdot \mathbf{X} & \ldots & L_{0m} \cdot \mathbf{X} \\ . & \ldots & . \\ . & \ldots & . \\ . & \ldots & . \\ L_{m0} \cdot \mathbf{X} & \ldots & L_{mm} \cdot \mathbf{X} \end{vmatrix}. \tag{19}$$

Then $f(\mathbf{X}) = 0$ is the implicit equation of $\mathbf{Q}(t)$. (In the case of an improperly parametrized curve [20], $f(\mathbf{X}) = 0$ will actually be some power of the implicit equation, since we generally take the implicit equation to be an irreducible polynomial).

Proof: $f(\mathbf{X}) = 0$ is the implicit equation of $\mathbf{Q}(t)$ if the following conditions are met:
1. $f(\mathbf{Q}(t)) \equiv 0$.
2. For all $\mathbf{X}$ for which $f(\mathbf{X}) = 0$, there exists a value of t such that $\mathbf{X} = \kappa \mathbf{Q}(t)$ where κ is a scalar constant. Since we are dealing with homogeneous (projective) coordinates, this simply means that $\mathbf{X}$ and $\mathbf{Q}(t)$ map to the same point in 2–D Cartesian space.

As for requirement 1, (17) and (18) can be written

$$\begin{bmatrix} L_{00} & \ldots & L_{0m} \\ . & \ldots & . \\ . & \ldots & . \\ . & \ldots & . \\ L_{m0} & \ldots & L_{mm} \end{bmatrix} \begin{Bmatrix} 1 \\ t \\ \vdots \\ t^m \end{Bmatrix} \cdot \mathbf{Q}(t) \equiv \begin{Bmatrix} 0 \\ 0 \\ \vdots \\ 0 \end{Bmatrix}. \tag{20}$$

Specializing $t = \tau$ and letting $\mathbf{X} = \mathbf{Q}(\tau)$, (20) can be expressed

$$\begin{bmatrix} L_{00} \cdot \mathbf{X} & \ldots & L_{0m} \cdot \mathbf{X} \\ . & \ldots & . \\ . & \ldots & . \\ . & \ldots & . \\ L_{m0} \cdot \mathbf{X} & \ldots & L_{mm} \cdot \mathbf{X} \end{bmatrix} \begin{Bmatrix} 1 \\ \tau \\ \vdots \\ \tau^m \end{Bmatrix} = \begin{Bmatrix} 0 \\ 0 \\ \vdots \\ 0 \end{Bmatrix}. \tag{21}$$

For (21) to be valid, either

$$\begin{Bmatrix} 1 \\ \tau \\ \vdots \\ \tau^m \end{Bmatrix} = \begin{Bmatrix} 0 \\ 0 \\ \vdots \\ 0 \end{Bmatrix} \tag{22}$$

or

$$\begin{vmatrix} L_{00} \cdot \mathbf{X} & \ldots & L_{0m} \cdot \mathbf{X} \\ . & \ldots & . \\ . & \ldots & . \\ . & \ldots & . \\ L_{m0} \cdot \mathbf{X} & \ldots & L_{mm} \cdot \mathbf{X} \end{vmatrix} = 0. \tag{23}$$

Equation 22 never holds; hence (23) must be true, and condition 1 is satisfied.

Condition 2 requires that $f(\mathbf{X}) \not\equiv 0$. We can prove that this holds because the moving lines are linearly independent (see the appendix in the electronic version of this paper). Therefore $f(\mathbf{X})$ must be a non-zero polynomial of degree at most $n = m + 1$. Now consider a point $\mathbf{X}^*$ for which $f(\mathbf{X}^*) = 0$. Take an arbitrary line $ax + by + cw = 0$ that contains $\mathbf{X}^*$. There are ν roots of the equation $(a, b, c) \cdot \mathbf{Q}(t) = 0$, but β of those roots map to the undefined point $(0, 0, 0)$, leaving n values of t which map to actual intersection points between the line and $\mathbf{Q}(t)$. Each of those values of t satisfy condition 1, that is, they map to n points for which $f(\mathbf{Q}(t)) = 0$, and each of those points lies on the line $(a, b, c) \cdot \mathbf{X} = 0$.

The equation $f(\mathbf{X}) = 0$ defines an algebraic curve of degree n which intersects a general line in n points. Suppose $f(\mathbf{X}^*) = 0$, but there does not exist a value of t for which $\mathbf{Q}(t) = \kappa \mathbf{X}^*$. This means that we have found $n + 1$ points at which a degree n algebraic curve intersects a line, a violation of Bezout's theorem. ∎

So far, we have merely examined well known curve implicitization methods from a different angle, but yielding no significant computational advantage. We are now prepared to venture into profitable new territory. We define a 2–D *moving curve* as

$$C(\mathbf{X}; t) := \sum_{j=0}^{m} f_j(\mathbf{X}) t^j = 0 \tag{24}$$

where $\mathbf{X} = (x, y, w)$ and $f_j(\mathbf{X})$ is a polynomial of degree d. Thus $C(\mathbf{X}; t) = 0$ is a family of algebraic curves that vary with t. A moving curve is said to "follow" a rational curve $\mathbf{P}(t) = (x(t), y(t), w(t))$ if for all values of t, the point $\mathbf{P}(t)$ lies on the moving curve:

$$C(\mathbf{P}(t); t) = \sum_{j=0}^{m} f_j(x(t), y(t), w(t)) t^j \equiv 0. \tag{25}$$

For a degree n curve $\mathbf{P}(t)$, there are at least $\frac{d(d+3)(m+1)}{2} - nd$ linearly independent moving curves of degree d in $\mathbf{X}$ and degree m in t that follow the curve $\mathbf{P}(t)$. This can be shown as follows. Since $C(\mathbf{P}(t); t)$ is a degree $nd + m$ polynomial in t and the total number of coefficients in the polynomials $f_j(\mathbf{X})$ ($j = 0, 1, \ldots, m$) is $\frac{(d+1)(d+2)(m+1)}{2}$, condition (25) is equivalent to a system of $nd + m + 1$ linear equations with $\frac{(d+1)(d+2)(m+1)}{2}$ unknowns.

Hence there are at least $\frac{(d+1)(d+2)(m+1)}{2} - (nd + m + 1) = \frac{d(d+3)(m+1)}{2} - nd$ linearly independent moving curves that follow $\mathbf{P}(t)$. If $(m+1)(d^2 + 3d - 2) \geq 2nd$, there exist at least $m + 1$ linearly independent moving curves that follow $\mathbf{P}(t)$. For example, $d = 1$ and $m = n - 1$ is the case in theorems 1 and 2.

Theorem 3. *Given* $m + 1$ *moving curves*

$$C_i(\mathbf{X}; t) := \sum_{j=0}^{m} f_{ij}(\mathbf{X})t^j = 0, \quad i = 0, \ldots, m \quad (26)$$

which follow $\mathbf{P}(t)$, *we define*

$$f(\mathbf{X}) = \begin{vmatrix} f_{00}(\mathbf{X}) & \ldots & f_{0m}(\mathbf{X}) \\ \cdot & \ldots & \cdot \\ \cdot & \ldots & \cdot \\ \cdot & \ldots & \cdot \\ f_{m0}(\mathbf{X}) & \ldots & f_{mm}(\mathbf{X}) \end{vmatrix} \quad (27)$$

If the degree of $f(\mathbf{X})$ *is* $n - \beta$ *(which implies that* $f(\mathbf{X}) \not\equiv 0$*), then* $f(\mathbf{X}) = 0$ *is the implicit equation of* $\mathbf{P}(t)$.

Proof: Essentially the same as the proof for theorem 2. ∎

We now explore the possible degrees for moving curves which follow $\mathbf{P}(t)$. Letting $d = 2$ and $m = \lceil \frac{n-1}{2} \rceil$, we find that there exist at least $m + 1$ linearly independent curves of degree 2 in $\mathbf{X}$ and degree m in t that follow the curve $\mathbf{P}(t)$. In the case where n is odd, theorem 1 assures that there will also be one moving line of degree m which follows $\mathbf{P}(t)$. Thus, from theorem 3, a rational curve with no base points, and of even degree, can *generally* be implicitized as the determinant of a $\frac{n}{2} \times \frac{n}{2}$ matrix whose elements are degree 2 in x, y, w. Likewise, a rational curve of odd degree and no base points can *generally* be implicitized as the determinant of an $\frac{n+1}{2} \times \frac{n+1}{2}$ matrix with one linear row, and the remaining rows quadratic.

We emphasize the word *generally* because theorem 3 requires $f(\mathbf{X}) \not\equiv 0$. Under certain conditions, the determinant in (27) *will* vanish, even though the rows are linearly independent. The reason is that the rows might be linearly independent, but *polynomially* dependent. The following theorem shows that high order singularities can create such a condition. A thorough description of the geometric properties of curves for which this condition occurs remains an open question, though it appears at present that singularities are not the complete answer.

Theorem 4. *The implicit equation of a quartic curve with no base points can be written as a* 2×2 *determinant. If the curve doesn't have a triple point, then each element of the determinant is a quadratic; otherwise one row is linear and one row is cubic.*

The rather tedious proof includes showing that if $f(\mathbf{X})$ is formed by a 2×2 determinant with quadratic elements, the following four statements are equivalent:

1. $f(\mathbf{X}) \equiv 0$.

2. There exists a degree one moving line that follows $\mathbf{P}(t)$.

3. $\mathbf{P}(t)$ has a triple point.

4.
$$\begin{vmatrix} x_0 & y_0 & w_0 & 0 & 0 & 0 \\ x_1 & y_1 & w_1 & x_0 & y_0 & w_0 \\ x_2 & y_2 & w_2 & x_1 & y_1 & w_1 \\ x_3 & y_3 & w_3 & x_2 & y_2 & w_2 \\ x_4 & y_4 & w_4 & x_3 & y_3 & w_3 \\ 0 & 0 & 0 & x_4 & y_4 & w_4 \end{vmatrix} = 0. \quad (28)$$

The details of the proof are omitted here (see the appendix of the electronic version of the paper). However, this discussion is important because similar phenomena can occur with surfaces.

3 SURFACES

It is convenient to define a rational surface in homogeneous form:

$$\mathbf{X}(s, t) = (X(s, t), Y(s, t), Z(s, t), W(s, t)) \quad (29)$$

where $X(s, t), Y(s, t), Z(s, t), W(s, t)$ are polynomials in s, t. The Cartesian coordinates of points on the surface are given by

$$x = \frac{X(s, t)}{W(s, t)}, \quad y = \frac{Y(s, t)}{W(s, t)}, \quad z = \frac{Z(s, t)}{W(s, t)}. \quad (30)$$

Among the most common rational surfaces used in computer graphics are the tensor product patches for which, in power basis,

$$\mathbf{X}(s, t) = \sum_{i=0}^{d_1} \sum_{j=0}^{d_2} \mathbf{X}_{ij} s^i t^j, \quad \mathbf{X}_{ij} = (x_{ij}, y_{ij}, z_{ij}, w_{ij}). \quad (31)$$

3.1 Base Points

A base point is a value of (s, t) for which $\mathbf{X}(s, t) = (0, 0, 0, 0)$. In the absence of base points, the implicit equation of a tensor product surface can be expressed using Dixon's resultant [8], which is the determinant of a $2d_1d_2 \times 2d_1d_2$ matrix whose elements are linear in (x, y, z). For example, a biquadratic surface requires an 8×8 determinant, and a bicubic surface an 18×18 determinant. The method presented in this section expressed the implicit equation of a bicubic patch with no base points as a 9×9 determinant whose elements are degree two in (x, y, z). (It is well known that all tensor product surfaces have multiple base points at $s = \infty$ and $t = \infty$. Here we mean no *additional* base points.)

Base points are of interest for two reasons. First, each simple base point decreases the degree of the implicit equation of the rational surface by one. The full story on the relationship between base points and degree becomes more complicated when considering base points with higher multiplicity [3, 13].

Second, if base points exist, Dixon's resultant vanishes identically. To implicitize surfaces which contain base points, more complicated methods have been devised [2, 9, 15, 16] such as the method of undetermined coefficients, successive elimination, perturbations, and customized resultants. In general, these methods are much more complicated in the presence of base points.

By contrast, the implicitization approach in this paper simplifies in the case of base points. In general, for each base point on a bicubic patch, one of the rows of the 9×9 determinant can be converted from degree two to degree one in (x, y, z).

3.2 Moving Surfaces

We define a *moving surface* as

$$g(\mathbf{X}, s, t) := \sum_{i=1}^{\sigma} h_i(\mathbf{X})\gamma_i(s, t) = 0 \quad (32)$$

where the equations $h_i(\mathbf{X}) = 0$, $i = 1, \ldots, \sigma$ define a collection of implicit surfaces and where the $\gamma_i(s, t)$, $i = 1, \ldots, \sigma$ are a collection of polynomials in s and t. We will refer to the $\gamma_i(s, t)$ as the blending functions for the moving surface. We require the blending functions to be linearly independent and to have no non-constant factor common to all of them. A moving surface is said to follow a rational surface $\mathbf{X}(s, t)$ (29) if

$$g(\mathbf{X}(s, t), s, t) \equiv 0. \quad (33)$$

When we make a statement such as "so many moving surfaces exist", it is implied that those moving surfaces follow the parametric surface under discussion, even though we may not explicitly say so.

Theorem 5. *Given a set of σ moving surfaces*

$$g_j(\mathbf{X}, s, t) = \sum_{i=1}^{\sigma} h_{ji}(\mathbf{X})\gamma_i(s, t) = 0, \quad j = 1, \ldots, \sigma, \quad (34)$$

each of which follows a given rational surface $\mathbf{X}(s, t)$ (29). Define

$$f(\mathbf{X}) = \begin{vmatrix} h_{11}(\mathbf{X}) & \ldots & h_{1\sigma}(\mathbf{X}) \\ \vdots & \vdots & \vdots \\ h_{\sigma 1}(\mathbf{X}) & \ldots & h_{\sigma\sigma}(\mathbf{X}) \end{vmatrix}. \quad (35)$$

If the degree d of $f(\mathbf{X})$ is equal to the degree of the implicit equation of the rational surface $\mathbf{X}(s, t)$, then $f(\mathbf{X}) = 0$ is the implicit equation of $\mathbf{X}(s, t)$.

Proof: $f(\mathbf{X}) = 0$ is the implicit equation of $\mathbf{X}(s, t)$ if the following conditions are met:
1. $f(\mathbf{X}) \not\equiv 0$.
2. $f(\mathbf{X}(s, t)) \equiv 0$.
3. For all $\mathbf{X}$ for which $f(\mathbf{X}) = 0$, there exists a parameter pair s, t such that $\mathbf{X} = \kappa\mathbf{X}(s, t)$ where κ is a scalar constant.

Condition 1 is satisfied by the requirement in the theorem that the degree of $f(\mathbf{X})$ is equal to the degree of the implicit equation.

The fact that each of the σ moving surfaces follow $\mathbf{X}(s, t)$ means that the set of equations

$$\begin{bmatrix} h_{11}(\mathbf{X}) & \ldots & h_{1\sigma}(\mathbf{X}) \\ \vdots & \vdots & \vdots \\ h_{\sigma 1}(\mathbf{X}) & \ldots & h_{\sigma\sigma}(\mathbf{X}) \end{bmatrix} \left\{ \begin{array}{c} \gamma_1(s, t) \\ \vdots \\ \gamma_\sigma(s, t) \end{array} \right\} = 0 \quad (36)$$

is satisfied for $\mathbf{X} = \mathbf{X}(s, t)$. If for some (s, t) $f(\mathbf{X}(s, t)) \neq 0$, then $\gamma_1(s, t) = \ldots = \gamma_\sigma(s, t) = 0$. But since $\gamma_1(s, t), \ldots, \gamma_\sigma(s, t)$ have no common factor, there are at most a finite number of (s, t) values for which $\gamma_1(s, t) = \ldots = \gamma_\sigma(s, t) = 0$. Consequently if there are any (s, t) pairs such that $f(\mathbf{X}(s, t)) \neq 0$, the number of such pairs is finite. But since $f(\mathbf{X}(s, t))$ is a polynomial in (s, t), it is therefore identically zero and condition 2 is met.

Base points map ("blow up") to entire curves on the surface known as seam curves [15]. Some authors had argued that these curves can be interpreted as lying on the implicit surface but not on the parametric surface since there is not a parameter value for which $\mathbf{X} = \kappa\mathbf{X}(s, t)$ if $\mathbf{X}$ lies on a seam curve [3]. We avoid that debate here, and are content to prove that condition 3 holds at least for points not on seam curves. Suppose then that there exists a point $\mathbf{X}^*$ such that $f(\mathbf{X}) = 0$ but $\mathbf{X}^* \neq k\mathbf{X}(s, t)$ for any (s, t). Choose a line through $\mathbf{X}^*$ which does not intersect any seam curves and which is not tangent to the surface. Take any two planes containing that line and compute their intersection with the parametric surface $\mathbf{X}(s, t)$, yielding two curves in parameter space $g_1(s, t) = 0$ and $g_2(s, t) = 0$. Those two curves will intersect at all base points of the surface, and at d other (s, t) parameter pairs where d is the degree of the implicit equation of the surface [13]. But from condition 2, those d parameter pairs map to points for which $f(\mathbf{X}) = 0$, making a total of $d + 1$ points lying on a line for which $f(\mathbf{X}) = 0$, a contradiction of Bezout's theorem. ∎

Sections 4 and 5 will prove that it is *always* possible to find a square matrix of moving surfaces that follow any given tensor product or triangular surface patch, and they present a systematic way of finding such matrices. It is very difficult to give a rigorous proof that for any given $\mathbf{X}(s, t)$ a matrix (35) can always be found so that the degree of $f(\mathbf{X})$ is equal to the degree of the implicit equation of the rational surface $\mathbf{X}(s, t)$ (and hence the determinant is not identically zero). However, in scores of example cases, we have never failed to find such a matrix.

3.3 Examples

Theorem 5 proposes a method for implicitizing rational surfaces by finding sets of moving surfaces which follow it. We here illustrate that concept with a few simple cases. These may seem somewhat ad hoc, but they have the advantage of being concrete numerical examples which are small enough to verify by hand. No explanation is given in these examples of how to find the moving surfaces; sections 4 and 5 outline a procedure for that.

3.3.1 Explicit Surface

The simplest parametric surface to implicitize is the explicit surface

$$x = s; \quad y = t; \quad z = q(s, t) \quad (37)$$

for which the implicit equation is merely $q(x, y) - z = 0$. This case is so trivial, that it actually becomes a little more complicated to implicitize it using moving surfaces than to merely write $q(x, y) - z = 0$. However, it serves as a simple introduction to moving surfaces. In this case, we can take as blending functions $\gamma_1(s, t) = s$, $\gamma_2(s, t) = t$, $\gamma_3(s, t) = 1$. The three moving surfaces, in matrix form, are

$$\begin{bmatrix} 1 & 0 & -x \\ 0 & 1 & -y \\ a(x, y) & b(x, y) & -z + q(0, 0) \end{bmatrix} \left\{ \begin{array}{c} s \\ t \\ 1 \end{array} \right\} = 0 \quad (38)$$

where $a(x, y)$ and $b(x, y)$ are chosen to satisfy $a(x, y)x + b(x, y)y + q(0, 0) = q(x, y)$. These three moving surfaces clearly follow the parametric surface, and the determinant of the 3×3 matrix in (38) is clearly the implicit equation.

3.3.2 Cubic Surface

As far as the authors are aware, the closest hint in the literature to anything like moving surfaces is the observation, dating back at least to Salmon in 1862 [18], that a degree three algebraic surface can be defined as the intersection of three "bundles" of planes (the classical term for what we here would call a moving plane with blending functions 1, s, and t). Salmon began with those three bundles of planes, and computed the parametric and implicit equations of the surface from them (see [21] for a more recent presentation).

For implicitization, we work in reverse, finding the moving planes given the parametric equations. Here are a set of parametric equations for a surface that we know in advance to have a degree three implicit equation. The parametric equations have six base points.

$$x = 2 + 2t^3 + s^2 + 4t^2 + 4ts + 2t + ts^2 + 3s$$
$$y = -2t^2s - ts - 2s^2 + s - s^3 - 2t + 2$$
$$z = -3t^2s + 2t^2 - 2ts^2 - 3ts - 2t - s^3 - 3s^2 - 2s$$
$$w = -t + ts^2 + s^2 - s + s^3 + t^3 - 1 + t^2$$

Once again, the moving surface blending functions are 1, s, and t. The three moving surfaces, in matrix form, are

$$\begin{bmatrix} x & y & z \\ y + w & 2y - z & y + 2w \\ z - y & -x + 2w & x - y \end{bmatrix} \left\{ \begin{array}{c} s \\ t \\ 1 \end{array} \right\} = 0 \quad (39)$$

and the implicit equation is the determinant of the matrix.

3.3.3 Steiner Surface

The canonical Steiner surface is given by parametric equations

$$x = 2st; \quad y = 2t; \quad z = 2s; \quad w = s^2 + t^2 + 1.$$

This is a special case of a triangular surface patch, a general implicitization procedure for which is given in section 5. We can again take $\gamma_1(s,t) = s$, $\gamma_2(s,t) = t$, $\gamma_3(s,t) = 1$. The three moving surfaces, in matrix form, are

$$\begin{bmatrix} y & -2z & x \\ y & -z & 0 \\ xz & xy - xz - 2zw & x^2 + yz \end{bmatrix} \begin{Bmatrix} s \\ t \\ 1 \end{Bmatrix} = 0 \quad (40)$$

The determinant of the matrix, $x^2 y^2 + x^2 z^2 + y^2 z^2 - 2xyzw$ is indeed the implicit equation of the canonical Steiner surface.

3.3.4 Surface of Revolution

When Newell reverse-engineered his teapot in 1975 [7], rational Bézier patches were not in wide use and so the surfaces of revolution were approximated using polynomial patches. While that approximation is well within graphical tolerance, there are advantages to reformulating the teapot using rational Bézier patches. First, the rational case can exactly represent surfaces of revolution. Second, a rational bicubic patch can model 180° of a surface of revolution, thus cutting in half the number of patches used to model the rim, body, lid, and bottom. Third, and most importantly for current needs, an exact surface of revolution can be implicitized in a much more compact form than can the polynomial approximation in [7].

In this section, we implicitize a patch from the lower body of the teapot which has been modified to exactly represent a surface of revolution. As discussed in section 6, without that modification, the implicit equation takes the form of a 9×9 determinant whereas the implicit equation of the modified patch can be expressed in a 2×2 determinant.

The teapot lower body is defined by rotating around the z axis the cubic polynomial Bézier curve with control points $(2, 0, .9)$, $(2, 0, .45)$, $(1.5, 0, .225)$, and $(1.5, 0, .15)$. The exact surface of revolution can be represented in rational Bézier form by

$$\mathbf{X}(s,t) = [(1-t)^3 \; 3t(1-t)^2 \; 3t^2(1-t) \; t^3] M \begin{Bmatrix} (1-s)^3 \\ 3s(1-s)^2 \\ 3s^2(1-s) \\ s^3 \end{Bmatrix}$$

where $M =$

$$\begin{bmatrix} (2, 0, .9, 1) & (\frac{2,4,.9,1}{3}) & (\frac{-2,4,.9,1}{3}) & (-2, 0, .9, 1) \\ (2, 0, .45, 1) & (\frac{2,4,.45,1}{3}) & (\frac{-2,4,.45,1}{3}) & (-2, 0, .45, 1) \\ (1.5, 0, .225, 1) & (\frac{1.5,3,.225,1}{3}) & (\frac{-1.5,3,.225,1}{3}) & (-1.5, 0, .225, 1) \\ (1.5, 0, .15, 1) & (\frac{1.5,3,.15,1}{3}) & (\frac{-1.5,3,.15,1}{3}) & (-1.5, 0, .15, 1) \end{bmatrix}$$

The implicit equation of this surface can be expressed in a 2×2 determinant. In this case, we can take $\gamma_1(s,t) = 1$, $\gamma_2(s,t) = s$ and the two moving surfaces are

$$\begin{bmatrix} (x+y)C - B & -2xC \\ -yC & (x+y)C + B \end{bmatrix} \begin{Bmatrix} 1 \\ s \end{Bmatrix} = 0 \quad (41)$$

where

$$B = 618 \;\; + \;\; 6720z + 17000z^2 - 64000/9z^3$$
$$+ \;\; 1305/2y^2 - 120y^2z + 1305/2x^2 - 120x^2z$$
$$C = 3x^2 + 3y^2 + 1600z^2 + 6900z + 1197$$

The determinant then gives the implicit equation of the surface of revolution — a degree 6 polynomial.

4 TENSOR PRODUCT PATCHES

We now present a systematic method for computing moving surfaces which follow a tensor product patch (31). It is most convenient to work in power basis. As we will see, a good choice for the $\gamma_i(s,t)$ in (32) is simply the tensor product basis:

$$\gamma_i(s,t) = s^j t^k; \quad (42)$$
$$j = 0, \ldots, b_1; \; k = 0, \ldots, b_2; \; i = k(b_1 + 1) + j + 1,$$

so $\sigma = (b_1 + 1)(b_2 + 1)$.

A degree n polynomial in three variables has $(n+1)(n+2)(n+3)/6$ coefficients. Thus, if all σ polynomials $h_i(\mathbf{X})$ are degree n, there are a total of $\sigma(n+1)(n+2)(n+3)/6$ coefficients. We can determine η, a lower bound on the number of linearly independent families of moving surfaces $g(\mathbf{X}, s, t)$ that follow $\mathbf{X}(s, t)$ by generating a set of linear equations as we did for the curve case in (15). For the surface case, the identity in (33) can be satisfied by solving a set of $(nd_1 + b_1 + 1) \times (nd_2 + b_2 + 1)$ linear homogeneous equations in $\sigma(n+1)(n+2)(n+3)/6$ unknowns. Thus,

$$\eta = \frac{(b_1 + 1)(b_2 + 1)(n+1)(n+2)(n+3)}{6}$$
$$- (nd_1 + b_1 + 1)(nd_2 + b_2 + 1). \quad (43)$$

If we can find values of n, b_1, and b_2 so that $\eta \geq \sigma$, there will be enough $h_{ji}(\mathbf{X})$ to fill a square matrix and, if the conditions in theorem 5 are met, the determinant of that matrix will be the implicit equation of $\mathbf{P}(s,t)$. Two cases turn out to exactly give $\eta = \sigma$: moving planes, and moving quadrics. Choosing $n = 1$ (moving planes), $b_1 = 2d_1 - 1$ and $b_2 = d_2 - 1$ yields $\eta = \sigma = 2d_1 d_2$. With this choice, the implicit equation of a bicubic patch with no base points occurs as the determinant of an 18×18 matrix. It can be shown that Dixon's resultant is a special case of this implicitization method using moving planes.

If we choose $n = 2$ (the moving algebraic surfaces are quadrics), $b_1 = d_1 - 1$ and $b_2 = d_2 - 1$, we then have at least $\eta = \gamma = d_1 d_2$ linearly independent moving surfaces. This means, for example, that a bicubic patch with no base points can generally be implicitized in the form of a 9×9 determinant whose elements are quadratic in x, y, z. A biquadratic patch with no base points can generally be implicitized using a 4×4 matrix with quadratic elements.

We stress the word *generally*. For arbitrarily chosen control points, experience has shown that the conditions in theorem 5 are always satisfied. As will be seen in the teapot patches, however, when control points are placed in some coherent fashion, the likelihood of singularities increases and the conditions in theorem 5 may no longer be met. Section 7 comments on this in more detail.

4.1 Base Points

For $n = 1$, $b_1 = d_1 - 1$ and $b_2 = d_2 - 1$, we find that $\eta = 0$. Note that η in (43) is a lower bound on the number of linearly independent moving surfaces; the actual number might be higher, depending on the rank of the $(nd_1 + b_1 + 1) \times (nd_2 + b_2 + 1)$ matrix. Here we show that in the presence of base points, the rank does indeed drop.

Theorem 6. *If $\mathbf{P}(s,t)$ has ρ distinct base points in general position (as defined in the proof found in the appendix of the electronic version), there exist at least ρ linearly independent moving planes whose blending functions are given by (42) with $b_1 = d_1 - 1$ and $b_2 = d_2 - 1$.*

Proof: This is a brief sketch of the proof. The complete proof can be found in the appendix of the electronic version of the paper.

As noted, the identity in (33) can be satisfied by solving a set of $4d_1 d_2$ homogeneous linear equations in $4d_1 d_2$ unknowns. The way we generated those equations before was to simply expand (33), producing a polynomial of degree $2d_1 - 1$ in s and degree $2d_2 - 1$ in t. This polynomial has $4d_1 d_2$ terms, and the $4d_1 d_2$ equations are created by setting the coefficient of each of those terms equal to zero.

We could create an equally valid set of $4d_1 d_2$ equations by choosing $4d_1 d_2$ different parameter pairs $(s_j, t_j), j = 1, \ldots, 4d_1 d_2$ and taking the equations to be

$$\sum_{i=1}^{d_1 d_2} h_i(\mathbf{X}((s_j, t_j)))\gamma_i(s_j, t_j) = 0, \quad j = 1, \ldots, 4d_1 d_2.$$

However, if we take ρ of those (s_j, t_j) to be base points, those ρ equations will be identically zero and the rank of the matrix will diminish by ρ. Hence, it is possible to find at least ρ moving planes. ∎

This means that for $b_1 = d_1 - 1$ and $b_2 = d_2 - 1$, we can find ρ moving planes and (at least) $d_1 d_2 - \rho$ moving quadrics that follow $\mathbf{P}(s, t)$. If the determinant of the $d_1 d_2 \times d_1 d_2$ matrix containing those ρ moving planes and $d_1 d_2 - \rho$ moving quadrics is not identically zero, it is the implicit equation.

This discussion on base points has dealt with *distinct* base points. One might be tempted to postulate that base points with multiplicity greater than one [13] would always free up moving planes equal in number to the total base point multiplicity. While this happens in many cases (such as with the teapot), it is not always so. A more detailed analysis of this question must await a future paper.

What if more than $d_1 d_2$ base points occur, since then there are no more quadratic rows left to convert to linear rows? Again, a complete answer to this question will be left for later. However, preliminary tests suggest that the size of the matrix can continue to shrink, usually allowing blending functions with $b_1 \leq d_1 - 2$, and/or $b_2 \leq d_2 - 2$. The example in section 3.3.4 is such a case, involving 12 base points. We note that the surface of revolution can also be implicitized as a 4×4 determinant with two linear rows and two quadratic rows. In that case, $b_1 = b_2 = 1$.

5   TRIANGULAR PATCHES

By a triangular surface patch, we mean one whose parametric equations are of pure degree d:

$$\mathbf{X}(s, t) = \sum_{i+j \leq d} \mathbf{X}_{ij} s^i t^j. \tag{44}$$

In this case, the right choice for moving surface blending functions are the $\sigma = d(d + 1)/2$ monomials in s, t of total degree $< d$:

$$\gamma_i(s, t) = s^j t^k, \quad j = 0, \ldots, d-1; \quad k = 0, \ldots, d-j-1; \tag{45}$$

with $i = j(d - \frac{j-1}{2}) + k + 1$.

As in the tensor product case, if all σ polynomials $h_i(\mathbf{X})$ are degree n, there are a total of $\sigma(n+1)(n+2)(n+3)/6$ coefficients. The identity in (33) can be satisfied by solving a set of $(nd+d)(nd+d+1)/2$ linear homogeneous equations in $\sigma(n+1)(n+2)(n+3)/6$ unknowns. Thus, the number of degree n moving surfaces is at least

$$\eta = d(d+1)(n+1)(n+2)(n+3)/12$$
$$- (nd+d)(nd+d+1)/2. \tag{46}$$

Letting $n = 1$, we find that there are at least d moving planes. Letting $n = 2$, there are at least $(d^2 + 7d)/2$ moving quadrics. However, $4d$ of those moving quadrics can be created from the moving planes as follows. Let a moving plane be given by (32). Then

$$(c_1 x + c_2 y + c_3 z + c_4 w) \sum_{i=1}^{\sigma} h_i(\mathbf{X})\gamma_i(s, t) = 0$$

gives a moving quadric that also follows the surface. Hence, for each moving plane, there exists four moving quadrics, and there are only $(d^2 + 7d)/2 - 4d = (d^2 - d)/2$ moving quadrics which cannot be created from moving planes. Hence, the matrix in (35) can just exactly be filled with d linear rows and $(d^2 - d)/2$ quadratic rows. If the determinant does not vanish, $f(\mathbf{X})$ is degree d^2 as expected.

The Steiner surface example in section 3.3.3 is an application of this method, for $d = 2$.

The base point discussion in section 4.1 applies also to triangular patches; each simple base point will generally allow a quadratic row to be converted to a linear row.

The cubic surface example in section 3.3.2 illustrates what can happen when several (6 in this case) base points occur.

6   THE TEAPOT

The 32 bicubic patches defining Newells' teapot [7] provide a surprisingly diverse set of tests for moving surface implicitization.

The teapot patches fall into ten groups: rim, upper body, lower body, upper handle, lower handle, upper spout, lower spout, upper lid, lower lid, and bottom. All patches in a given group are simple linear transformations of one another, so their implicit equations are similar.

In every case, it is possible to implicitize these patches using 9×9 determinants with tensor product blending functions (42) for which $b_1 = b_2 = 2$. The 16 patches in the rim, lower lid, upper body and lower body all have degree nine implicit equations (all having nine base points), and their implicit equations can each be expressed as 9×9 determinants with nine linear rows. Those nine moving planes can be found by solving a set of linear equations as discussed in section 4.

The four patches in the upper lid have five base points (degree 13 implicit equations). The determinant has five moving planes and four moving quadrics. The four bottom patches have three base points (degree 15 implicit equations), and their determinant has three moving planes and six moving quadrics.

All four spout patches have no base points (degree 18 implicit equations), and their determinant has nine moving quadrics.

The four handle patches provided a surprise. These patches have no base points (degree 18 implicit equations). However, the determinant has three moving planes, three moving quadrics, and three moving cubics! This phenomenon is reminiscent of the degree four planar curve with a triple point.

It turns out that the rim's implicit equation can also be expressed as a 3×3 determinant using $\sigma_1 = 1$, $\sigma_2 = s$, $\sigma_3 = s^2$. In this case, there are two moving quartics and one moving plane. This discovery was made purely by trial and error, but the search was motivated by the fact that for this surface, z is a quadratic function of s only, so we immediately knew there exists a moving plane with $\sigma_1 = 1$, $\sigma_2 = s$, $\sigma_3 = s^2$. The two moving quartics were pure serendipity.

Similarly, the upper lid's implicit equation can be written as a 4×4 determinant with three moving quartics and one moving plane. The blending functions are $\sigma_1 = 1$, $\sigma_2 = s$, $\sigma_3 = s^2$, $\sigma_4 = s^3$. Finally, the four bottom patches can be implicitized using a 4×4 determinant with one moving plane, one moving quartic, and two moving quintics. The blending functions are $\sigma_1 = 1$, $\sigma_2 = s$, $\sigma_3 = s^2$, $\sigma_4 = s^3$.

7 DISCUSSION

This paper has proven several theorems and provided empirical support which suggests that the method of moving surfaces is a comprehensive solution to the problem of surface implicitization, and the resulting expressions for the implicit equation are much more compact than those obtained with previous methods.

This work has largely been an adventure in experimental mathematics. The basic notion of moving surfaces was arrived at using pencil and paper, as was the realization that σ moving surfaces can always be found for tensor product and triangular patches such that, if the determinant formed by them (35) does not vanish, it must be the implicit equation. While we have not yet succeeded in theoretically showing that a non-vanishing determinant always exists, empirical substantiation has been provided using computer algebra. We have tried numerous examples with randomly chosen control points (assuring that the surface has no base points or high order singularities), and the blending functions in sections 4.1 and 5 have always worked. Thus, we conjecture that for randomly chosen control points, the methods in sections 4.1 and 5 are robust.

We have also run numerous test cases in which we generated surfaces with randomly chosen simple base points, and have found no counterexample to the conjecture that in randomly chosen cases it always works to trade one quadratic row for a linear row (until there are more base points than quadratic rows), thereby reducing the degree of the surface by one.

Based on our experience, an automatic algorithm for implicitizing bicubic patches (for example) would begin by determining the degree of the implicit equation. This can be done very quickly by firing two skew rays into it [11] and checking at how many unique (s, t) pairs they each intersect the surface. This is the degree. If the degree is 18, compute how many moving quadrics exist. If there are exactly nine, they will fill a 9×9 determinant which defines the implicit equation. If there are more than nine, search for moving planes and moving cubics to fill the determinant. If the degree is between 9 and 18, search for r moving planes and s moving quadrics such that $r + 2s =$ degree. If the degree is less than 9, try blending functions (42) with $b_1 = b_2 = 1$

Whether or not a non-zero determinant can always be found which satisfies the conditions in theorem 5 remains an open question. All of the hundreds of cases we have studied thus far have yielded a non-zero determinant, though at present we have no proof that this is always so. We have observed that base points with multiplicity greater than one can produce surprising results. In one example, a case was studied involving a base point that was a common double point on the curves $x(s, t) = y(s, t) = z(s, t) = w(s, t) = 0$ (thus a base point of multiplicity four [13]). The anticipation was that four of the rows on the standard 9×9 determinant could convert from quadratic to linear. In fact, only three moving planes exist! Nonetheless, we succeeded in finding a solution involving an 8×8 determinant with six moving quadrics and two moving planes.

We note that moving surfaces can also solve the inversion problem (given a point on the surface, compute the corresponding parameter values).

Acknowledgements The first author formulated the central idea in this paper while driving to SIGGRAPH '91. The following year, Takafumi Saito and Wang Guojin provided helpful discussions while working as visiting scholars at Brigham Young University. Ron Goldman contributed much valuable feedback, and painstakingly edited several drafts of the manuscript. Thanks also to Malcolm Sabin, Dinesh Manocha and David Cox, along with five conscientious reviewers, for their very careful readings and helpful suggestions.

REFERENCES

[1] Buchberger, Bruno. Applications of Gröbner Bases in Nonlinear Computational Geometry. In D. Kapur and J. L. Mundy, editors, *Geometric Reasoning*, pages 413–446. Elsevier Science Publisher, MIT Press, 1989.

[2] Chionh, Eng Wee. *Base Points, Resultants, and the Implicit Representation of Rational Surfaces*. PhD thesis, University of Waterloo, 1990.

[3] Chionh, Eng Wee and Ronald N. Goldman. Degree, Multiplicity, and Inversion Formulas for Rational Surfaces using U-resultants. *Computer Aided Geometric Design*, 9:93–108, 1992.

[4] Chionh, Eng Wee and Ronald N. Goldman. Using Multivariate Resultants to Find the Implicit Equation of a Rational Surface. *The Visual Computer*, 8(3):171–180, 1992.

[5] Coolidge, Julian. *A History of the Conic Sections and Quadric Surfaces*. Oxford, 1945.

[6] Cox, David, John Little and Donal O'Shea. *Ideals, Varieties, and Algorithms*. Undergraduate Texts in Mathematics. Springer-Verlag, 1992.

[7] Crow, Frank. The Origins of the Teapot. *IEEE Computer Graphics and Applications*, 7(1):8–19, 1987.

[8] Dixon, A. L. The Eliminant of Three Quantics in Two Independent Variables. *Proceedings of London Mathematical Society*, 6:46–49, 473–492, 1908.

[9] Hoffmann, Christoph. *Geometric and Solid Modeling: An Introduction*. Morgan Kaufmann, 1989.

[10] Hoffmann, Christoph. Implicit Curves and Surfaces in CAGD. *IEEE Computer Graphics & Applications*, 13(1):79–88, 1993.

[11] Kajiya, James. Ray Tracing Parametric Patches. Proceedings of SIGGRAPH 82 (Boston, July 26–30, 1982). In *Computer Graphics*, 16,3 (July 1982), 245–254.

[12] Kalkbrener, Michael. *Three Contributions to Elimination Theory*. PhD thesis, Johannes Kepler Universitat, Linz, Austria, 1991.

[13] Katz, Sheldon and Thomas W. Sederberg. Genus of the Intersection Curve of Two Parametric Surface Patches. *Computer Aided Geometric Design*, 5:253–258, 1988.

[14] Krishnan, S. and Dinesh Manocha. An Efficient Surface Intersection Algorithm Based on the Lower Dimensional Formulation. Technical Report TR94-062, Department of Computer Science, University of North Carolina, 1994.

[15] Manocha, Dinesh and John F. Canny. Algorithms for Implicitizing Rational Parametric Surfaces. *Computer-Aided Geometric Design*, 9:25–50, 1992.

[16] Manocha, Dinesh and John F. Canny. The Implicit Representation of Rational Parametric Surfaces. *Journal of Symbolic Computation*, 13:485–510, 1992.

[17] Salmon, George. *Modern Higher Algebra*. Chelsea, New York, 5th edition, pp. 83–86, 1885.

[18] Salmon, George. *A Treatise on the Analytic Geometry of Three Dimensions*. Longmans, Green and Co., London, 5th edition, p. 264, 1915.

[19] Sederberg, Thomas W. *Implicit and Parametric Curves and Surfaces for Computer Aided Geometric Design*. PhD thesis, Purdue University, 1983.

[20] Sederberg, Thomas W. Improperly Parametrized Rational Curves. *Computer Aided Geometric Design*, 3:67–75, 1986.

[21] Sederberg, Thomas W. Techniques for Cubic Algebraic Surfaces. *IEEE Computer Graphics and Applications*, 10(4):14–26, 1990.

[22] Sederberg, Thomas W., David C. Anderson, and Ronald N. Goldman. Implicit Representation of Parametric Curves and Surfaces. *Computer Vision, Graphics and Image Processing*, 28:72–84, 1984.

[23] Sederberg, Thomas W. and Scott R. Parry. A Comparison of Curve-Curve Intersection Algorithms. *Computer-Aided Design*, 18:58–63, 1986.

[24] Sederberg, Thomas W., Takafumi Saito, Dongxu Qi, and Krzysztof S. Klimaszewski. Curve Implicitization using Moving Lines. *Computer Aided Geometric Design*, 11:687–706, 1994.

Polygonization of Non-Manifold Implicit Surfaces

Jules Bloomenthal and Keith Ferguson

Department of Computer Science

The University of Calgary

Abstract

A method is presented to broaden implicit surface modeling. The implicit surfaces usually employed in computer graphics are two dimensional manifolds because they are defined by real-valued functions that impose a binary regionalization of space (*i.e.*, an inside and an outside). When tiled, these surfaces yield edges of degree two. The new method allows the definition of implicit surfaces with boundaries (*i.e.*, edges of degree one) and intersections (*i.e.*, edges of degree three or more). These *non-manifold implicit surfaces* are defined by a multiple regionalization of space. The definition includes a list of those pairs of regions whose separating surface is of interest.

Also presented is an implementation that converts a non-manifold implicit surface definition into a collection of polygons. Although following conventional implicit surface polygonization, there are significant differences that are described in detail. Several example surfaces are defined and polygonized.

CR Categories and Subject Descriptors: I.3.5 [Computer Graphics]: Computational Geometry and Object Modeling - Curve, Surface, Solid, and Object Representations.

Additional Keywords and Phrases: Implicit Surface, Non-Manifold, Polygonization.

1 Introduction

In this paper we wish to broaden the scope of implicit surface modeling to include combinations of volumes and surfaces. Traditionally, implicit surfaces are two-dimensional manifolds. A manifold surface is, everywhere, locally homomorphic (that is, of comparable structure) to a two-dimensional disk.

Any tessellation of a manifold surface, such as the polygonization of a finite (*i.e.*, bounded) implicit surface, produces edges that are of degree two; that is, all edges are shared by exactly two faces. Uncommon to implicitly defined surfaces are manifolds *with boundaries*, which yield tessellations with edges of degree one, and non-manifold surfaces consisting of trimmed pieces whose tessellation yields edges of degree three or more.

The combination of finite three-dimensional volumes and two-dimensional surfaces is sometimes called mixed dimensional modeling and its surface is characteristically non-manifold. Such models are unusual in computer graphics. Although considerable study has been devoted to the smooth join of parametric surfaces [Farin 1988] and to blends of implicit volumes [Rockwood 1989], the representation of a combined surface and volume has received relatively little attention.

2 Related Work

There have been several efforts to extend conventional solid modeling [Mäntylä 1988] to non-manifold surfaces and manifolds with boundary. Solid modeling is often specified by a binary construction tree; if the leaf nodes are solid primitives, the process is known as *constructive solid geometry* and may be represented internally by three-dimensional half spaces. If the leaf nodes include two-dimensional surfaces, the half-space is unsatisfactory as an internal representation [Miller 1986]. In these cases, the *boundary representation*, or a variation [Weiler 1986], is often employed.

In [Muuss and Butler 1990] a non-manifold boundary representation is constructed in pairwise order from simpler solid and surface primitives. It appears the topology of the resulting surface must, however, be pre-established. In [Rossignac and Requicha 1991] and [Rossignac and O'Connor 1989] a *simplicial complex* is used to specify and internally represent a mixed dimensional model. A calculus is developed that permits the application of standard Boolean set operations upon the mixed dimensional primitives. This approach is examined further in [Paoluzzi *et al.* 1993].

Permission to make digital/hard copy of part or all of this work for personal or classroom use is granted without fee provided that copies are not made or distributed for profit or commercial advantage, the copyright notice, the title of the publication and its date appear, and notice is given that copying is by permission of ACM, Inc. To copy otherwise, to republish, to post on servers, or to redistribute to lists, requires prior specific permission and/or a fee.

© 1995   ACM-0-89791-701-4/95/008 $3.50

As observed in [Mäntylä 1988], the construction of intermediate structures during constructive solid modeling requires both considerable attention to numerical accuracy and significant case analysis of edge/edge and edge/surface intersections. These issues also receive considerable attention in the studies of mixed dimensional modeling.

Concrete examples are not presented in [Rossignac and O'Connor 1989] and [Muuss and Butler 1990] and are limited in scope in [Paoluzzi *et al.* 1993]. In this paper we provide several definitions for and renderings of mixed dimensional models. This paper describes the conversion of a non-manifold definition to a concrete representation. As in [Muuss and Butler 1990], we produce a polygonal tessellation to approximate a model. Unlike constructive geometry, however, we utilize an implicit representation for non-manifold surfaces, extending conventional implicit surface polygonization to accommodate these surfaces.

3 Implicit Representations

Let us consider a closed cylinder embedded in a sheet. Such an object poses a dilemma as to its implicit representation. As shown below, left to right, the object (truncated for illustration) can be represented as *surface only*, *surface and volume*, *thin volume*, and *volume and trimmed surface*. We regard the first representation as insufficiently faithful. The second representation is incorrect insofar as its physical usefulness (in terms of manufacturing) or its imaging (if, for example, the surfaces are semi-transparent).

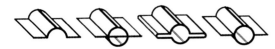

Figure 1. Possible Combinations of Cylinder and Sheet

The third representation offers difficulty for the sampling process commonly employed with implicit surfaces. The sampling rates for a ray-tracer and for a polygonizer must both be high (below left), when compared with those for the 'surface only' (below right).

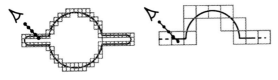

Figure 2. Sampling Rates for Polygonization and Ray-Tracing

Therefore, we conclude that the 'volume and trimmed surface' representation, which contains edges of degree one, two, and three, is the only accurate, compact, and unified representation of a volume embedded in a sheet. Unfortunately, this representation is not readily expressed as an implicit surface, *i.e.*, as a set of points p: $f(p) = 0$. An implicit surface separates regions for which $f(p) < 0$ from regions for which $f(p) > 0$. This binary partitioning of space provides a definition for the 'volume only' shape, below left. It can also, below middle and right, define the 'surface only' and 'surface and volume' shapes, if the surface bounds are

ignored. But it cannot define the 'volume and trimmed surface.' Conventional polygonizers assume that f is continuous and that points on opposite sides of the surface have oppositely signed values; therefore, they require a binary partitioning of space. For finite objects, they produce manifold tessellations but cannot produce a boundary, *i.e.*, an edge with only one face. Nor can they produce an intersection, *i.e.*, an edge with three or more faces. In contrast, any tessellation of a volume embedded in a surface requires edges of degree one, two and three.

Figure 3. Possible Implicit Definitions (cross-sections)

In this paper we describe a new method to define and polygonize implicit surfaces that are non-manifold or manifold with boundary. The method differs from conventional polygonization in that it permits multiple, rather than binary, regions of space. This multiple regionalization is noted in [Rossignac and Requicha 1991]. As an example, we employ four regions, shown below, to define a sphere embedded within a square.

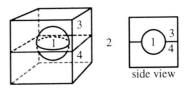

Figure 4. Multiple Regions define the Sphere-Square

Here, a cube bounds a plane, creating the square; the surface of the cube, however, is not of interest. Accordingly, our surface definition consists of two parts: an integer-valued *region function*, f_{reg}, that returns the *region value* of a point, and a set of *region-pairs of interest*. For the example above, the region pairs are {(1, 3), (1, 4), (3, 4)}, and $f_{reg}(p)$ is: 1 for $|p| < r$, 2 for $max\ (|p_x|, |p_y|, |p_z|) > s$, 3 for $p_z > 0$, and 4 otherwise, with r the sphere radius and s the half-length of the square. An approximation to this object, produced by our non-manifold polygonizer, is shown below. The use of multiple regions is conceptually simple, and may be implemented along the lines of conventional polygonization. There are, however, significant differences.

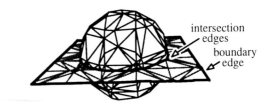

intersection edges

boundary edge

Figure 5. Tessellation of a Non-Manifold

4 Comparison to Conventional Polygonization

Conventional polygonizers of continuous functions partition space into adjoining cells that enclose the implicit surface [Ning and Bloomenthal 1993]. In a process known as *continuation* [Allgower and Georg], cells propagate across faces that contain both positively and negatively valued corners. With the non-manifold polygonizer, however, a face must contain a region pair of interest. This prevents unwanted propagation along uninteresting surfaces (such as the cube above).

As with many conventional polygonizers, we utilize the cube as the propagating cell and decompose it into tetrahedra. The tetrahedra serve as polygonizing cells, producing one or more polygons to approximate that portion of the surface contained in the cell. The fundamental steps of polygonization are diagrammed below As described in section 5, *surface vertices*, which control the direction of propagation, are produced during polygonization. Therefore, tetrahedra are polygonized concurrently with cube propagation.

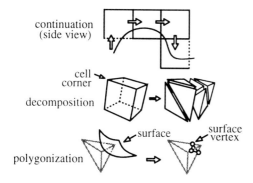

Figure 6. Overview of a Polygonizer

Conventional polygonizers assume that a surface passes through a polygonizing cell at most once. Thus, only a single surface vertex, or *edge vertex*, is produced along a cell edge that connects differently signed cell corners. This results in zero, three, or four edge vertices within a tetrahedron, and, at most, a single polygon edge, or *face line*, across a tetrahedral face. Traversing from one face line to the next, around the faces of the tetrahedron, produces a single three or four-sided polygon. The non-manifold polygonizer performs these steps of edge vertex computation and polygon creation, but, as we will now show, must also accommodate *face vertices*, multiple edge vertices along a single tetrahedral edge, and multiple face lines within a single tetrahedral face.

As a consequence of multiple regions, more than two regions can occur within a tetrahedral face. This yields more than two edge intersections on the face as well as an intersection internal to the face. For example, consider the three regions that meet along the circular intersection of sphere and square. In the illustration below (left), all three regions are spanned by a single tetrahedron; indeed, three regions are spanned by a single tetrahedral face (middle). This suggests the computation of three edge vertices, a face vertex, and their connection by three face lines (right).

Figure 7. The Face Vertex

Face vertices complicate implementation, but alternatives either produce a topological inconsistency (below, left) or are geometrically inaccurate (below, middle and right). These inaccuracies cause undesirable visual artifacts along intersections and boundaries of an object, unless the tetrahedra are very small. Unfortunately, uniformly small tetrahedra yield an excessive number of polygons, and adaptively sized tetrahedra appear difficult to implement for this application.

Figure 8. Alternatives to the Face Vertex

Regions can divide a face other than as shown in figure 7. Two common cases, below, left, suggest a need for multiple edge vertices, shown below, right. In one case, multiple edge vertices occur along an edge connecting equi-valued corners. Thus, unlike conventional polygonizers, the non-manifold polygonizer inspects all edges, not simply those that connect differently valued corners.

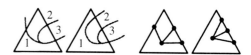

Figure 9. Multiple Vertices along an Edge

Let us consider the left face, above, its containing tetrahedron, and an adjoining tetrahedron. The face is repeated below, left, and the two tetrahedra are shown, right, separated for clarity. The front face of the right tetrahedron is shown, middle. The polygonal set produced by these tetrahedra are more complex than produced by conventional polygonizers. In particular, the left tetrahedron contains a 3, a 4, and a 5-sided polygon, each sharing the edge connecting the two face vertices. The right tetrahedron contains *disjoint surfaces*. Thus, in addition to a face vertex, a tetrahedral face must accommodate disjoint face lines, each connecting edge vertices that separate the same region pair.

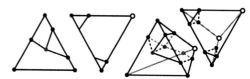

Figure 10. Disjoint Face Lines and Polygonal Surfaces

Because the tetrahedral corners may all differ in value, one tetrahedron may contain four face vertices, as shown below, left. To facilitate the connection of face vertices so that the four regions are properly separated, our polygonizer supports an *inner vertex* within the tetrahedron that connects face and edge vertices, as shown below, right (for clarity, the far bottom edge vertex is not shown). Complex arrangements of face, edge, and inner vertices can occur regardless of cell size. These complexities are more readily accommodated by evaluating tetrahedra independently; adaptive subdivision would likely complicate this process.

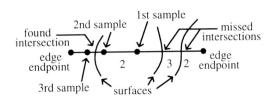

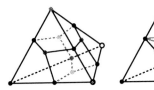

Figure 11. Disjoint Face Lines and Polygonal Surfaces

A sufficiently complex object can require an arbitrary number of face and edge vertices within a tetrahedron. For example, a face might contain any of the arrangements below, regardless of cell size. A robust polygonizer should handle these cases. We have, however, restricted our implementation to one face vertex per face or a collection of disjoint face lines per edge, and one inner vertex per tetrahedron. Nonetheless, our implementation produces reasonable results for the examples we present later.

Figure 12. Complex Face Topologies

5 Implementation

In this section we provide details for cell propagation, cell polygonization, and post-process vertex modification. Throughout, the polygonizer attempts to produce surface vertices whose location is independent of the region-pairs of interest. Pseudo-code detailing these algorithms is given in [Bloomenthal and Ferguson 1994].

We use the cube as the propagating cell, centering the first cube at a start point, usually given, whose distance to a surface of interest is less than half the size of the cube. To prevent cyclic propagation, each visited cube location is stored in a hash table, as described in [Wyvill *et al.*]. To simplify the polygonization step, each cube is decomposed into six tetrahedra [Koide *et al.* 1986]. For each tetrahedron intersected by a surface of interest, a) each tetrahedral edge is examined for edge vertices, b) each face is examined for a face vertex, c) any necessary inner vertex is calculated, and d) polygon(s) are produced.

As described in section 4, an edge vertex is placed at all edge intersections along a cell edge. A hash table associates the vertex with its tetrahedral edge and stored with each vertex is the region-pair it separates. The binary subdivision often used in conventional polygonizers is unsatisfactory because in the first subdivision step half of the edge is ignored and intervening intersections may be missed, as shown below.

Figure 13. Sampling by Binary Subdivision

Therefore, each tetrahedral edge is divided into equally sized sections, as shown below, left. Binary subdivision is applied to those sections whose endpoints have different region values, below, right. If, during this binary subdivision, a 'foreign' region (*i.e.*, a region not equal to either of the endpoint regions) is encountered, the subdivision continues recursively in both halves, detecting two (or more) intersections in the given section. Edge vertices are placed at the midpoint of the final interval(s) yielded by subdivision. To guard against a narrow region crossing a final interval, we test that the region value at the interval midpoint is one of the two endpoint region values of the interval; if not, the subdivision is continued. We choose n, the number of initial sections, and m, the minimum number of subdivision steps, such that each vertex will be within ε of an actual intersection, *i.e.*, $edgeLength/(2^{(m+1)}n) \leq \varepsilon$. We have employed $\varepsilon = 1/256$ of the propagating cell size.

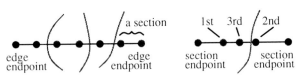

Figure 14. Two-Stage Edge Division

As explained shortly, it is important to order edge vertices during their storage; we use the location of the edge endpoints to compute an edge direction, and order the vertices accordingly. The region-pair for each vertex also is ordered according to this direction. We store all edge vertices, whether or not they belong to a surface of interest. This allows the polygonizer to produce geometry that is insensitive to changes in the region-pair interest set. Storing all edge vertices also permits computation of the region-set for a face vertex, as described below. Edge vertices are shared between adjoining tetrahedra; the presence of a previously computed edge vertex can be determined from the edge and the hash table.

As with edge vertices, face vertices are shared between adjoining tetrahedra. Therefore, we first test if a face has been previously processed; if not, we test if it contains an intersection. A face contains no face intersection if it contains only disjoint lines. To determine this, we traverse the edge vertices of a face, in order, adding and removing vertex region-value pairs from a stack, as shown below. If there are only disjoint lines in the face, then, beginning with a vertex *startV*, the stack will empty when the partner of *startV* is reached, fill again, and will empty a second time upon the return to *startV*.

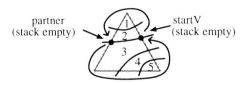

Figure 15. Determining if a Face Contains only Disjoint Lines

Our implementation accommodates any number of disjoint lines within a face, provided there is no face intersection. If an intersection exists, a face vertex is allocated and stored. Because it is computationally expensive to locate the intersection, we compute the location only if the face vertex is an intersection of surfaces of interest. We follow the face contour from an edge vertex *v*, continuing until a foreign region is found. This is similar to other local methods [Mortensen 1985], [Bajaj *et al.* 1988]. As shown below, left, the face contour is surrounded by small triangles until region 3 (in this example) is encountered.

The small triangles enclosing the contour are each specified by a directed edge, below, middle, that crosses the contour. A directed edge implies a new triangle apex, whose region value determines which of the new triangle sides becomes the next directed edge. The initial directed edge spans the start vertex. The contour follower terminates with a final triangle, below, right, whose apex belongs to a foreign region; the face vertex is located at the center of this triangle. So that this be within ϵ of the actual intersection, the length of a small triangle side (exaggerated below for illustration) should not exceed $(2\sqrt{3})\epsilon$, assuming the final triangle contains the actual intersection. A recursive contour follower, in which triangles become increasingly smaller, may prove more accurate.

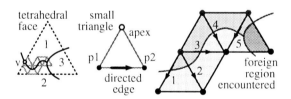

Figure 16. Following a Face Contour

For simple face topologies, as above, the choice of start vertex is immaterial. For complex topologies, as below, some vertices (*e.g.*, *v1* and *v2*) do not yield a face intersection. The contour follower must recognize when it fails, and begin again at a different edge vertex. Also, some vertices (*v3* and *v4*, for example) will yield different intersections; therefore searches begin first from edge vertices that separate regions of interest. This compromises our goal of a geometry independent of the region-pair set, but, because we are limited to a single face vertex, we prefer it be on a surface of interest.

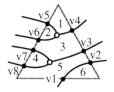

Figure 17. A Complex Face Topology

If the tetrahedron contains only disjoint face lines, as shown below, left, the lines are connected to form one or more disjoint polygons. As established in [Bloomenthal and Ferguson 1994], each polygon is of three or four sides. So that a polygon is properly associated with two regions (to provide, for example, polygon color), the polygons must be consistently oriented. We order each polygon so that, when viewed from the lesser of the two regions it separates, its vertices appear in clockwise order. The ordering begins with an edge vertex that separates a region of interest and a tetrahedral face that contains the edge vertex such that, if traversed in a clockwise direction, the edge traverses from lesser to greater region. We now proceed to the partner of this vertex, with respect to the given face (see figure 15). The partner becomes the 'current' vertex, and the face on the other side of the edge containing the new current vertex becomes the 'current' face. This step, similar to one described in [Bloomenthal 1988], is iterated until the current vertex becomes the start vertex. The process is repeated for those edge vertices not yet assigned to polygons. An optimized procedure could process those common cases typical of conventional tetrahedral polygonization.

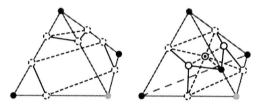

Figure 18. Polygon Formation

In the case of *non-disjoint* surfaces, there must be at least two face vertices that separate regions of interest. We create an inner vertex whose location is the average location of those face vertices that separate regions of interest. Each face line, together with this inner vertex, creates one triangle, as shown above, right. Each triangle is ordered clockwise when viewed from the lesser-valued of the two regions it separates.

A problem concerning face contours, which also affects propagation, is the 'loop.' A face contour is looped if it enters and exits the face along the same edge, as shown below, left. As shown below, middle and right, looped intersections may occur on edges of equal or differently valued corners, and may be nested.

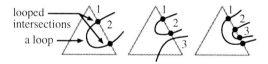

Figure 19. Looped Intersections

Looped intersections are problematic because there is no face vertex with which they can connect. They could be joined together, yielding a line coincident with the cell edge; this can duplicate polygons or align polygons with tetrahedral edges or faces, resulting in a staircased tessellation. They could be connected to a point on the face contour, preferably one that is maximally distant from the cell edge; this is an implementation complication we chose to avoid. Therefore, we ignore looped intersections, effectively truncating the surface, as illustrated below. Conventional polygonizers also truncate loops if they occur between equi-valued corners. Truncation can be arbitrarily large; when significant, truncation is best mitigated by a smaller cell size.

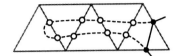

Figure 20. Truncation of Large Loop

There are two problems whose remedy we postpone until all cells are polygonized. The first concerns thin or small triangles. Thin triangles are produced when a polygonizing cell face is nearly tangential to the implicit surface; small triangles are produced if a polygonizing cell corner is close to the surface. Either triangle can occur when an inner vertex is close to a face vertex or a face vertex is close to an edge vertex. These triangles also occur in conventional polygonization and can cause visualization artifacts. They can yield orientation errors (*i.e.*, the normal of the triangle can vary significantly from the actual surface normal) if the triangle width is comparable to ε, the accuracy of edge and face vertices. In a post-polygonization step, each pair of connected vertices whose distance is less than ε is replaced by the average of the two vertices. Resulting degenerate triangles are removed. Perturbation of cell corners, as suggested in [Moore and Warren 1991], is another method to eliminate problematic triangles.

The second problem concerns vertices on intersection edges. Consider triangles t_1, t_2, and t_3, which share an edge along the intersection circle of the sphere-square, as shown below. For smooth shading, each vertex requires a surface normal, but, in this example, it is not possible to compute a single normal for v because t_1 and t_2 require a right-facing normal, whereas t_3 requires an upward-facing normal. To accommodate these competing requirements, we produce coincident vertices located at v, one for each different region-pair of the triangles sharing v.

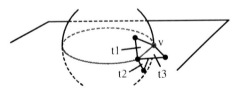

Figure 21. Duplicated Vertices

6 Results

We first compare the performance of the non-manifold polygonizer with a conventional polygonizer. For non-trivial objects, both polygonizers devote the vast majority of their time in evaluating the implicit surface function. Thus, we compare the two polygonizers according to the number of function evaluations. The non-manifold polygonizer performs many more evaluations along a surface border,

where it must locate a face intersection. Because a conventional polygonizer does not attempt to locate such intersections, we compare the frequency of evaluations for solid models only. This limits our consideration to the typical cases of three and four edge intersections per tetrahedron.

We assume the non-manifold polygonizer uses n (the number of edge sections, as described in section 5) = 16 and m (the number of binary subdivisions) = 4, and that the conventional polygonizer uses $m = 8$, so that their vertex accuracies are equal. We ignore function evaluations for corners of the tetrahedra. which should be the same for both polygonizers. For three edge vertices per tetrahedron, the conventional polygonizer requires (3×8) = 24 evaluations of f, whereas the non-manifold polygonizer requires $3\times16+3(16+4) = 108$ evaluations of f_{reg}. For four edge vertices, the conventional polygonizer requires (4×8) = 32 evaluations, and the non-manifold polygonizer requires $2\times16+4(16+4) = 112$ evaluations. Thus, the non-manifold polygonizer requires about four times as many function evaluations as does the conventional polygonizer.

Our first example blends a sphere and a square. Pseudo-code for the region value and the surface interest are given below.

Sigmoid *(d)* {
    if *abs* (*d*) > 1
        then return 0
        else return $1-(4d^6-17d^4+22d^2)/9$
        (a blend function from [Wyvill *et al.* 1986])
Saucer *(p)* { return *Sigmoid* $(\sqrt{p_x{}^2+p_y{}^2}/7)/3$ }
Region *(p)*
    if not *InsideCube* (*p*) then return 0
    if *Saucer* (*p*) > *abs* (p_z) then return 1
    if $p_z > 0$ then return 2 else return 3

Interest *(region-pair)*
    if **regionPair** = (1, 2) then return (true, red)
    if **regionPair** = (1, 3) then return (true, blue)
    if **regionPair** = (2, 3) then return (true, green)
    return (false)

Conventional polygonizers calculate surface normals by approximating the gradient, ∇f, of the implicit surface function. Our region function is integer valued, however, and cannot yield a gradient. Hence, we allow the software client to provide a real-valued function g from which the gradient can be calculated. For non-manifold polygonization, the normal depends not only on vertex location but also on the region-pair being separated. For a fixed region-pair, g should be a continuous function in the neighborhood of the surface separating that region-pair. Usually g can be defined in terms of those functions that underlie f_{reg}, as shown below:

g *(p,* **regionPair***)*
    if **regionPair** = (1, 2) then return $-p_z$-*Saucer* (*p*)
    if **regionPair** = (1, 3) then return p_z-*Saucer* (*p*)
    if **regionPair** = (2, 3) then return $-p_z$

The surfaces are rendered transparently to demonstrate that surfaces internal to the volume have been trimmed.

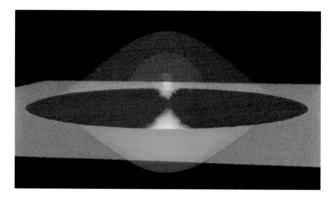

Figure 22. Saucer

The second example is a sphere embedded in a square, as in figure 4, with a smaller sphere removed. We observe that, whereas two adjacent regions of space define a surface, three adjacent regions define a curve. For example, in figure 4 the equator of the sphere is the intersection of regions 1, 3, and 4, and the boundary of the square is the intersection of regions 2, 3, and 4. These curves intersect polygonizing cells at cell faces, and are readily approximated simply by connecting face vertices. The boundary and intersection curves below are shown as thin (blue, yellow, cyan, and magenta) lines.

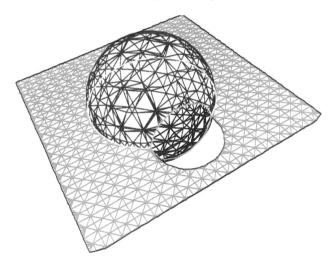

Figure 23. Object with Boundary and Intersection Curves

Our last example blends a sphere to a bicubic patch according to the following definition.

Region (p)
    if *Beyond* (***p, patch***) then return 0
    if *Sigmoid* (***p***) > abs (*DistanceToPatch* (***p, patch***)) return 1
    if *DistanceToPatch* (***p, patch***) > 0 return 2 else return 3

The distance between ***p*** and the closest point on the patch, $P(s, t)$, is computed numerically. s and t are initialized from an approximating triangle mesh and are refined by projecting the vector from $P(s, t)$ to ***p*** onto the tangent plane at $P(s, t)$, as shown below. If the closest point belongs to the patch border, ***p*** is regarded as 'beyond' the patch. Otherwise, the signed distance indicates whether ***p*** is above or below the patch.

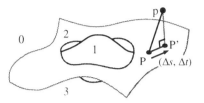

Figure 24. Region Definition for Blend to Patch

The shaded images are produced with transparency.

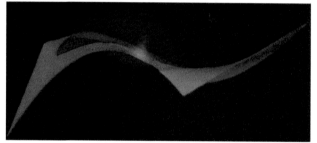

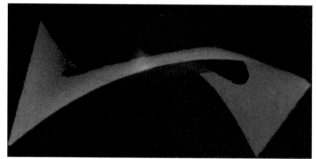

Figure 25. Blend to Patch

7 Conclusions

We have presented a new method to express and polygonize non-manifold implicit surfaces. This method permits a simple expression and evaluation for parametric surfaces combined with and trimmed against implicit volumes. These non-manifold implicit surfaces are defined by multiple regions of space, unlike the binary regions that typically define implicit surfaces. Included with the object definition is a list of region pairs whose separating surfaces are of interest. When polygonized, non-manifold surfaces may have borders and intersections.

The use of multiple regions significantly complicates the polygonizer. In particular, the accurate polygonization of surface borders requires vertices internal to faces of the polygonizing cell, which in turn require multiple intersections per cell edge. This leads to the need for multiple, disjoint surfaces. The accurate polygonization of surface intersections requires vertices fully internal to the polygonizing cell. This additional complexity, however, is exercised only in the relatively few cells that contain borders or intersections.

The formula used to define non-manifold implicit surfaces do not require extraordinary numerical stability because, unlike constructive geometric methods, the non-manifold implicit surface is not computed as a series of intermediate surfaces, nor are primitive intersections explicitly calculated.

The present polygonizer cannot accommodate arbitrary complexity per tetrahedron, although it does accommodate an arbitrary number of disjoint surfaces. Non-disjoint surfaces are limited to a single intersection per face and a single internal vertex per polygonizing cell. Future work might include the accommodation, within a single polygonizing cell, of disjoint surfaces and multiple face and multiple internal intersections. Other future work might include improved boundary accuracy and reduced truncation, as well as additional consideration of adaptive methods.

Ray-tracing can render non-manifold, implicitly defined shapes; indeed, many ray-tracers return an integer identifier for a particular object or region of space, usually to accelerate performance or invoke anti-aliasing. We prefer, however, a concrete representation of the object. We have yet to determine the power of the present method with respect to shape specification and editing. Considering the flexibility of non-manifold surfaces, continued work on the present method seems warranted.

Acknowledgements

We thank Przemek Prusinkiewicz for his insight and guidance. We also thank Dennis Arnon, Debbie Brooks, Tony DeRose, Adam Finkelstein, Pat Hanrahan, Paul Heckbert, Ken Shoemake, and Joe Warren for their comments. We are indebted to the University of Calgary and to Xerox Corporation for their support of this research.

References

E. Allgower and K. Georg, *Numerical Continuation Methods, an Introduction*, Springer-Verlag, 1990.

C. Bajaj, *Surface Fitting with Implicit Algebraic Surface Patches*, in Topics in Surface Modeling, H. Hagen. ed., SIAM Publications, 1992.

J. Bloomenthal, *Polygonization of Implicit Surfaces*, Computer Aided Geometric Design, Nov. 1988.

J. Bloomenthal and K. Ferguson, *Polygonization of Non-Manifold Surfaces*, Research Rep. 94-541-10, Dept. of Computer Science, The University of Calgary, June 1994.

G. Farin, *Curves and Surfaces for Computer Aided Geometric Design, a Practical Guide*, Academic Press, New York 1988.

A. Koide, A. Doi, and K. Kajioka, *Polyhedral Approximation Approach to Molecular Orbital Graphics*, Journal of Molecular Graphics 4, 1986.

M. Mäntylä, *An Introduction to Solid Modeling*, Computer Science Press, Md., 1988.

J. Miller, *Sculptured Surfaces in Solid Models: Issues and Alternative Approaches*, IEEE Computer Graphics and Applications, Dec. 1986.

D. Moore and J. Warren, *Mesh Displacement: An Improved Contouring Method for Trivariate Data*, Rice University Technical Rep. TR91-166, Sept. 1991.

M.E. Mortensen, *Geometric Modeling*. Wiley and Sons, New York, 1985.

M. Muuss and L. Butler, *Combinatorial Solid Geometry, B-Reps, and n-Manifold Geometry*, in Computer Graphics Techniques: Theory and Practice, D. Rogers and R. Earnshaw, eds., Springer Verlag, New York, 1990.

P. Ning and J. Bloomenthal, *An Evaluation of Implicit Surface Tilers*, IEEE Computer Graphics and Applications, Nov. 1993.

A. Paoluzzi, F. Bernardini, C. Cattani, and V. Ferrucci, *Dimension-Independent Modeling with Simplicial Complexes*, ACM Trans. on Graphics 12, Jan. 1993.

A. Rockwood and J.C. Owen, *Blending Surfaces in Solid Modeling*, Proc. of SIAM Conf. on Geometric Modeling and Robotics, G. Farin, ed., Albany New York, 1985.

J. Rossignac and M. O'Connor, *SGC: a Dimension-Independent Model for Pointsets with Internal Structures and Incomplete Boundaries*, Geometric Modeling for Product Engineering, Elsevier Science, 1990.

J. Rossignac and A. Requicha, *Constructive Non-Regularized Geometry*, in Beyond Solid Modeling, special ed. of Computer Aided Design, 1991.

K. Weiler, *Topological Structures for Geometric Modeling*, Ph.D. dissertation, Dept. of Computer and Systems Engineering, Rensselaer Polytechnic Institute, Aug. 1986.

G. Wyvill, C. McPheeters, and B. Wyvill, *Data Structure for Soft Objects*. Visual Computer 2, 4, Aug. 1986.

A Realistic Camera Model for Computer Graphics

Craig Kolb

Computer Science Department
Princeton University

Don Mitchell

Advanced Technology Division
Microsoft

Pat Hanrahan

Computer Science Department
Stanford University

Abstract

Most recent rendering research has concentrated on two subproblems: modeling the reflection of light from materials, and calculating the direct and indirect illumination from light sources and other surfaces. Another key component of a rendering system is the camera model. Unfortunately, current camera models are not geometrically or radiometrically correct and thus are not sufficient for synthesizing images from physically-based rendering programs.

In this paper we describe a physically-based camera model for computer graphics. More precisely, a physically-based camera model accurately computes the irradiance on the film given the incoming radiance from the scene. In our model a camera is described as a lens system and film backplane. The lens system consists of a sequence of simple lens elements, stops and apertures. The camera simulation module computes the irradiance on the backplane from the scene radiances using distributed ray tracing. This is accomplished by a detailed simulation of the geometry of ray paths through the lens system, and by sampling the lens system such that the radiometry is computed accurately and efficiently. Because even the most complicated lenses have a relatively small number of elements, the simulation only increases the total rendering time slightly.

CR Categories and Subject Descriptors: I.3.3 [Computer Graphics]: Picture/Image Generation; I.3.7 [Computer Graphics]: Three-Dimensional Graphics and Realism.

Additional Key Words and Phrases: ray tracing, camera modeling, lens simulation, sampling.

1 Introduction

The challenge of producing realistic images of 3d scenes is often broken into three subproblems: modeling reflection to account for the interaction of light with different materials, deriving illumination algorithms to simulate the transport of light throughout the environment, and modeling a camera that simulates the process of image formation and recording. In the last several years the majority of the research in image synthesis has been concentrated on reflection models and illumination algorithms. Since the pioneering work by Cook *et al.*[2] on simulating depth of field and motion blur, there has been very little work on camera simulation.

Although current camera models are usually adequate for producing an image containing photographic-like effects, in general they are not suitable for approximating the behavior of a particular physical camera and lens system. For instance, current models usually do not correctly simulate the geometry of image formation, do not properly model the changes in geometry that occur during focusing, use an improper aperture in depth of field calculations, and assume ideal lens behavior. Current techniques also do not compute exposure correctly; in particular, exposure levels and variation of irradiance across the backplane are not accounted for.

There are many situations where accurate camera models are important:

- One trend in realistic computer graphics is towards physically-based rendering algorithms that quantitatively model the transport of light. The output of these programs is typically the radiance on each surface. A physically-based camera model is needed to simulate the process of image formation if accurate comparisons with empirical data are to be made.

- In many applications (special effects, augmented reality) it is necessary to seamlessly merge acquired imagery with synthetic imagery. In these situations it is important that the synthetic imagery be computed using a camera model similar to the real camera.

- In some machine vision and scientific applications it is necessary to simulate cameras and sensors accurately. For example, a vision system may want to test whether its internal model of the world matches what is being observed.

- Many users of 3d graphics systems are very familiar with cameras and how to use them. By using a camera metaphor the graphics system may be easier to use. Also, pedagogically it is helpful when explaining the principles of 3d graphics to be able to relate them to real cameras.

Perhaps the earliest introduction of a camera model in computer graphics was the *synthetic camera model* proposed in the CORE system[3]. This and later work used a camera metaphor to describe the process of synthesizing an image, but did not intend to reproduce photographic effects or provide photographic-like control over image formation. The next major breakthrough in camera modeling was the simulation of depth of field and motion blur[10][2][12]. Current methods for simulating these effects use idealized lens systems and thus cannot be used to simulate the behavior of a particular physical system. A number of researchers have shown how to perform non-linear camera projections, such as those for fisheye or OMNIMAX lenses[7][5]. These methods derive a transformation that maps image points to directions in 3D, and have the disadvantage that effects such as depth of field cannot be combined with these special-purpose projections.

Permission to make digital/hard copy of part or all of this work for personal or classroom use is granted without fee provided that copies are not made or distributed for profit or commercial advantage, the copyright notice, the title of the publication and its date appear, and notice is given that copying is by permission of ACM, Inc. To copy otherwise, to republish, to post on servers, or to redistribute to lists, requires prior specific permission and/or a fee.

© 1995   ACM-0-89791-701-4/95/008 $3.50

radius	thick	n_d	V-no	ap
58.950	7.520	1.670	47.1	50.4
169.660	0.240			50.4
38.550	8.050	1.670	47.1	46.0
81.540	6.550	1.699	30.1	46.0
25.500	11.410			36.0
	9.000			34.2
-28.990	2.360	1.603	38.0	34.0
81.540	12.130	1.658	57.3	40.0
-40.770	0.380			40.0
874.130	6.440	1.717	48.0	40.0
-79.460	72.228			40.0

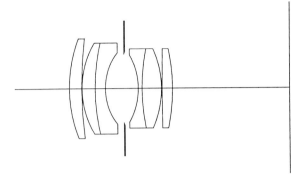

Figure 1: A tabular description and profile view of a double-Gauss lens. [14, page 312]. Each row in the table describes a surface of a lens element. Surfaces are listed in order from the front (nearest object space) to rear (nearest image space), with linear measurements given in millimeters. The first column gives the signed radius of curvature of a spherical element; if none is given, the surface is planar. A positive radius of curvature indicates a surface that is convex when viewed from the front of the lens, while a negative radius of curvature is concave. The next entry is thickness, which measures the distance from this surface to the next surface along the central axis. Following that is the index of refraction at the sodium d line (587.6 nm) of the material on the far side of the surface (if none is given, the material is assumed to be air). Next is the V-number of the material, characterizing the change of index of refraction with wavelength. The last entry is the diameter, or aperture, of each lens element. The row with a missing radius signifies an adjustable diaphragm; the diameter gives the size of the diaphragm when fully open. Note that if a surface separates two materials other than air, this indicates that two lenses have been cemented together as part of a "group." The lens as given has a focal length of approximately 100mm. The design may be changed to have any desired focal length by scaling each of the linear dimensions by the desired focal length divided by 100. The profile view on the right shows a 50mm version of this lens in relation to the diagonal of a piece of 35mm film.

This paper describes a physically-based camera model for computer graphics. The model is capable of simulating the image formation of a particular physical lens system described by the arrangement of simple lenses as specified by the manufacturer. Image formation is simulated by a modified distributed ray tracing algorithm that traces rays through the lens system in order to compute the exposure on the film plane. This algorithm is a hybrid of rendering techniques used by the computer graphics community and techniques used by lens makers to design camera lenses. Tracing rays through the lens system has the advantage that both the geometry and the radiometry of image formation can be accurately modeled. Moreover, we show that this simulation costs little more than previous algorithms.

For the purposes of this paper, our emphasis is on simulating the lens system, and as such the important effects caused by film response, shutter shape and movement, filters, and other parts of the camera will not be addressed here. We will further assume that the system is "aberration-limited," and so the effects of diffraction can be ignored.

The paper begins with a discussion of the construction of lenses and how they are modeled in our system. We then consider the various geometrical factors that effect image formation and how those factors can be accurately accounted for. The radiometry of image formation and its computation are then presented. Finally, results of an implementation of our model are shown and discussed.

2 Lens Systems

Lens systems are typically constructed from a series of individual spherical glass or plastic lenses and stops centered on a common axis. A stop is an opaque element with a roughly circular opening to permit the passage of light. The element that most limits the angular spread of the bundle of rays that will pass unobstructed through the system from the axial point on the image plane is termed the *aperture stop*. The size of the aperture stop in a camera is typically set by the photographer through the use of an adjustable diaphragm, and serves to provide control over the quantity of light striking the film plane and the depth of field in the image.

As shown in Figure 1, the construction of a lens is traditionally presented in a tabular format[1]. Our system reads tables like these and uses the information to model the behavior of the lenses they describe. Lens manufacturers are reluctant to release lens design data, but it is possible to find tables in patents that might cover a particular lens, or in collections of lens designs such as those given in the book by Smith[14].

There are two challenges to simulating a real lens system:

- *The geometry of image formation must be correctly computed.*

  Ideally, a lens will cause a point in object space to be imaged as a single point in image space, and will have constant magnification over the entire field of view. This is the assumption that is made in most rendering systems that use the pin-hole camera model or projective transformations. Unfortunately, no physical system is capable of ideal image formation. Real lenses exhibit deviations from the ideal in the form of *aberrations* such as coma or pin-cushion distortion[15].

- *The radiometry of image formation must be correctly computed.*

  The correct exposure must be computed given the lighting in the scene. In most rendering systems this computation is arbitrary, with little attention paid to units and their physical magnitudes. In a real camera, the exposure is controlled by a variety of factors and these must be correctly simulated if a physically-based rendering system is to produce realistic output. Moreover, while ideal lenses focus light energy evenly at

---

[1] In our figures, we follow the convention of drawing object space to the left of the lens system, image space to the right, with coordinates along the axis increasing from left to right. Distances in the lens system are signed quantities, with a distance measured from left to right being positive, and right to left negative. Unprimed variables are in object space, primed are in image space.

all points on the image plane, real lenses suffer from an uneven exposure across the backplane. Accurate computation is therefore more than a matter of simply computing a correct overall scale factor.

Abstractly, the purpose of our camera module is to transform the scene radiances computed by the lighting and shading modules into the response at a pixel. This may be modeled by the *measurement equation*[9] (in computer graphics sometimes called the *pixel equation*)

$$R = \iiiint L(T(x', \omega', \lambda); \lambda) S(x', t) P(x', \lambda) dx' \cdot d\omega' \, dt \, d\lambda$$

(1)

In this equation, x' represents a position vector on the backplane, ω' is a direction vector towards the lens system, t is time and λ is wavelength. L is the scene spectral radiance defined in object space. The function T models the geometry of image formation, in effect transforming from image space to object space (for generality, we assume this is a function of wavelength). S models the behavior of the shutter and is a function of time (more generally, the response of real shutters may also depend on position). P describes the sensor response characteristics and is a function of position within a pixel and wavelength.

The measurement equation provides the basis for quantifying the effects of the lens and other camera components on image formation. The rest of the paper discusses how we model the lens and evaluate the measurement equation.

3 Lens Geometry and Image Formation

In this section, we discuss the geometrical properties of lens systems. We describe how to trace rays through a lens system, how to derive a projective transformation that approximates the action of the lens system, how to accurately model the geometry of focusing, and finally how to derive the effective size of the aperture. These techniques allow us to use actual lens descriptions in rendering systems that use ray tracing, as well as those that use linear viewing transformations. They also allow us to model the depth of field and exposure due to real lens systems.

3.1 Tracing Rays Through Lens Systems

One robust and accurate method to predict how a lens will form an image is to trace rays of light through the system. Lens and optical system designers have employed ray tracing techniques to evaluate designs for more than a century, and thus the process is now quite well-understood. Typically, a random set of rays are traced from object space to image space and their positions on the film plane are recorded to form a spot diagram. Various statistics are derived from these diagrams to evaluate the quality of the lens. Surprisingly, to our knowledge, ray tracing is not used by lens designers to create synthetic imagery because of the perceived high cost of doing these calculations.

R = Ray(point on film plane, point on rear-most element)
For each lens element E_i, from rear to front,
    p = intersection of R and E_i
    If p is outside clear aperture of E_i
        ray is blocked
    Else if medium on far side of $E_i \neq$ medium on near side
        compute new direction for R using Snell's law

Figure 2: Basic algorithm for tracing a ray through a lens system.

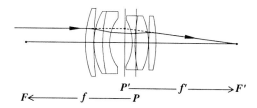

Figure 3: Finding a thick approximation to the lens in Figure 1. The actual path of an axis-parallel ray from object space is drawn as a solid line, and its idealized path is drawn as a dashed line.

The standard algorithm for tracing a ray through the lens is given in Figure 2. The propagation of a ray through a lens surface involves both finding the point of intersection between the ray and the surface and the refraction of the ray as it crosses the interface between the two media. The vast majority of lenses have spherical or planar surfaces, and therefore these computations are quite simple [16][17]. Although spherical surfaces are by far the most common, an object-oriented design of the lens software makes it possible to include elements of any shape for which intersection and normal-finding routines can be written.

Tracing rays through a lens system described in the tabular format is considerably faster than it would be if the lens were modeled as a collection of general objects for the ray tracer to render. This is because the exact visibility ordering of the surfaces is known *a priori*, and thus there is no search required to find the closest surface in a given direction. The main computational cost of tracing rays through spherical systems is two square roots per surface. This cost is fixed relative to scene complexity, and is usually small compared to the total cost of object intersection tests and other lighting calculations.

3.2 Thick Lens Approximation

In some situations the geometry of image formation may be approximated by treating the lens as an ideal *thick lens*. A thick lens forms perfect images; that is, each point in object space is imaged onto a single point in image space and all points in the plane of focus map onto the image plane with uniform magnification. We use thick lenses in our model to determine the exit pupil, as discussed in Section 3.4.

The behavior of a thick lens can be characterized by its focal points and principal planes, which are illustrated in Figure 3. Axis-parallel rays from a point at infinity in object space will enter the lens, be refracted through it, and emerge with a new direction and intersect the axis at the secondary focal point, F'. The point at which the incident ray and the emergent ray would intersect defines the secondary principal plane P'. P' is an imaginary surface normal to the axis at which we assume refraction to have occurred. Similarly, axis-parallel rays from image space intersect the axis at F, the primary focal point, and the intersection of the original and refracted rays define P, the primary principal plane. The signed distance from P' to F' is the effective focal length of the lens, f', and is equal to $-f$ when both object and image space are in the same medium.

The thick lens derives its name from the fact that, unlike the thin lens model usually used in computer graphics, the principal planes are not assumed to coincide. The distance from P to P' is the the lens' effective thickness, and may be negative, as for the lens in Figure 3. This additional parameter allows for a more general model of image formation. Although a thin lens approximation can be valid if the thickness is negligible, the thickness of photographic lenses is usually significant. The utility of both approximations is that their imaging properties can be modeled by a simple transformation.

To find a thick approximation to a given lens system, we apply the above definitions of focal points and principal planes directly. We trace rays through the lens system from each side and find the appropriate points of intersection to define P, F, P', and F'. An alternative way to find these values is by using the various thick lens formulas, which provide an analytical means for deriving a thick lens from a collection of simple lenses. The advantage of the first method is that it yields a more accurate approximation to the lens because typical lens systems are designed to exhibit ideal image formation even though the individual elements are less than ideal.

The geometry of image formation by a thick lens may be realized by a projective transformation defined by the focal points and principal planes[1]. Given a point in object space at a signed distance z along the axis from P, the conjugate equation holds that

$$\frac{1}{z'} - \frac{1}{z} = \frac{1}{f'} \qquad (2)$$

where z' is the axial distance from P' to the point's image in image space. This equation and some simple geometry can be used to find the image of a point on either side of the lens. However, the resulting equations are inconvenient in that z and z' are measured from different origins. If the origin is assumed to be at P and both distances are measured from it, the same equations apply, except that z' must then be translated by $t = P' - P$, the thickness of the lens. The total transformation can be written as a 4x4 matrix:

$$\begin{bmatrix} X' \\ Y' \\ Z' \\ W' \end{bmatrix} = \begin{bmatrix} 1 & 0 & 0 & 0 \\ 0 & 1 & 0 & 0 \\ 0 & 0 & 1+\frac{t}{f'} & t \\ 0 & 0 & \frac{1}{f'} & 1 \end{bmatrix} \begin{bmatrix} x \\ y \\ z \\ 1 \end{bmatrix}$$

Thus the thick lens approximation may be used in conventional rendering systems that use 4x4 projective transformations to model the camera. Note that when t is zero, the above transformation is identical to the usual thin lens transformation used in computer graphics[11].

3.3 Focusing

In order to make the camera model easy to control, it should be possible to specify the distance from the film plane at which the camera is focused. Focusing physical systems involves moving one or more lens elements along the axis in order to change the distance at which points are focused. For simple lenses, the housing and all of the elements are moved together, while in more complicated internal focusing lenses, only a few elements move while the lens housing itself remains stationary.

Given a point located at an axial distance z from the film plane, we can use (2) to determine how far the lens must be moved in order to bring the point into focus. If the lens is focused at infinity, refocusing at z can be done by moving the lens a distance T away from the film plane, where T satisfies:

$$T^2 + T(2f' + t - z) + f'^2 = 0 \qquad (3)$$

One solution to (3) corresponds to the lens being near the film and far from the object, the other to the lens being near the object and far from the film. In most situations, physical constraints on the distance the lens can move will make the latter solution unrealizable.

Moving the lens relative to the film plane has the additional effect of changing the field of view. As the distance at which the camera is focused is decreased, the distance of the lens from the film plane is increased and the field of view shrinks. This effect is not modeled in the standard camera model, which assumes that the film plane is always located at the focal point and that the lens can be focused at any arbitrary distance without any change of configuration.

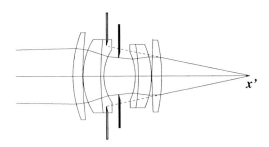

Figure 4: Illustration of the exit pupil for the double-Gauss lens of Figure 1. The diaphragm, drawn in solid black, acts as the aperture stop for the point x' on the axis at the film plane. The extent of the bundle of rays from x' that pass unobstructed through the lens is represented by the pair of solid lines on either side of the axis. The exit pupil, the image of the aperture stop through the rear-most two groups of elements, is drawn in outline. The exit pupil defines the cone of rays from x that pass unobstructed through the lens, as shown by the dashed lines.

3.4 The Exit Pupil

Recall that when looking through a lens system from a point on the backplane, there is a cone of rays within which the environment is visible, and that the aperture stop is the element limiting the extent of this cone. The *exit pupil* is defined to be the image of the aperture stop as viewed from image space (see Figure 4). Only rays directed from the film plane at the interior of the exit pupil will pass through the physical aperture stop, and so it is only these rays that we need consider when tracing rays through the system. Note the difference between this and directing rays at the aperture stop itself; this can produce incorrect results, because the image of the aperture may be larger than the aperture itself (as shown in Figure 4), and some rays that would pass through the system would not be generated. Note also the difference between this and firing rays at the lens element closest to the film plane. While this will produce correct results in the limit, it is wasteful because some of these rays may be blocked by the aperture stop. Using the correct exit pupil is critical if the depth of field and the exposure are to be computed consistently.

We find the exit pupil as follows: For each potential stop, we determine its apparent size and position from the axial point on the image plane. This is done by imaging the stop through those lens elements that fall between the stop and image space. We then determine which image disk subtends the smallest angle from the axial point on the image plane. This image is the exit pupil, and the stop corresponding to it is the aperture stop.

If we assume that each group of lens elements exhibits ideal image formation, the image of a given stop can be computed using a thick lens approximation to the appropriate subsystem of elements. In physical lenses, this is accurate only to the extent that the circular exit pupil is a reasonable approximation to the actual image of the aperture stop as viewed from off-axis points. In particular, some lenses distort the shape and position of the exit pupil when viewed from off-axis in order to increase or decrease exposure at points near the edge of the film[6]. We cannot validly use a thick approximation to find the exit pupil for such lenses in these cases. However, we can always ensure correct simulation by using the rear-most lens element as the exit pupil, at the cost of some loss of efficiency.

The exit pupil, rather than the aperture, should also be considered when using a thick lens in a ray tracer. Cook *et al.* described an algorithm for tracing rays through a thin lens by selecting a point on the aperture stop and tracing a ray from that point through the image of the current image plane point. As noted above, using the aperture stop rather than the exit pupil can lead to errors. The process of tracing a ray through a thick lens and exit pupil is shown in Figure 5.

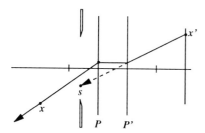

Figure 5: To trace a ray from x' through a thick lens, a point s on the exit pupil is chosen. The point of intersection of the ray from x' to s with P' is found, and is then translated parallel to the axis to P. The ray from this point through x, the image of x', is then used to sample the scene.

4 Radiometry and Sampling

In this section we describe how we compute exposure on the film plane.

4.1 Exposure

Sensor response is a function of exposure, the integral of the irradiance at a point x' on the film plane over the time that the shutter is open. If we assume that irradiance is constant over the exposure period, and that exposure time is fixed,

$$H(x') = E(x')T \qquad (4)$$

where $E(x')$ is the irradiance at x', T is the exposure duration, and $H(x')$ is the exposure at x'. This model is a simplification of the exposure process in physical systems, where the exposure at a point is dependent upon the shape and movement of the shutter.

In order to compute $E(x')$, we integrate the radiance at x' over the solid angle subtended by the exit pupil, which is represented as a disk, as shown in Figure 6.

$$E(x') = \int_{x'' \in D} L(x'', x') \frac{\cos \theta' \cos \theta''}{\|x'' - x'\|^2} dA'' \qquad (5)$$

If the film plane is parallel to the disk, this can be rewritten as

$$E(x') = \frac{1}{Z^2} \int_{x'' \in D} L(x'', x') \cos^4 \theta' dA'' \qquad (6)$$

where Z is the axial distance from the film plane to the disk. This formula differs from that described by Cook *et al.*, which assumed each ray has the same weight. It is also important to perform the integral using a disc-shaped exit pupil, rather than a rectangular one. Using a rectangular pupil causes the depth of field to be computed incorrectly, since points not in focus will then have rectangular "circles" of confusion on the film plane.

The weighting in the irradiance integral leads to variation in irradiance across the film plane due to the lens system. There are two simple analytical ways to estimate this effect: the $\cos^4$ law and the differential form factor to a disk.

1. If the exit pupil subtends a small solid angle from x', θ' can be assumed to be constant and equal to the angle between x' and the center of the disk. This allows us to simplify (5) to:

$$E(x') = L \frac{A}{Z^2} \cos^4 \theta' \qquad (7)$$

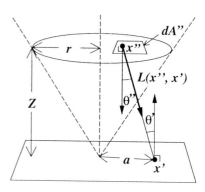

Figure 6: Geometry for computing the irradiance at a point on the film plane and the exact form factor.

where Z is the axial distance from the film plane to the disk, and A is the area of the disk. If Z is assumed to be the focal length, (7) can be written

$$E(x') = L \frac{\pi}{4} \frac{\cos^4 \theta'}{n^2} \qquad (8)$$

where n is the *f-number* of the lens. Equation (7) is the one most often found in optics texts, while (8) appears in many photographic texts. Note that both assume a small solid angle.

2. For larger solid angles, a more accurate way to estimate the variation in irradiance is to compute the differential form factor from a point on the film plane to a disk. This correctly accounts for the finite size of the disk, and the variation in angle as we integrate over the disk. This integral may be computed analytically[4] (an elegant derivation may be found in [8]).

$$F = \frac{1}{2} \left(1 - \frac{a^2 + Z^2 - r^2}{\sqrt{(a^2 + Z^2 + r^2)^2 - 4r^2 a^2}} \right) \qquad (9)$$

In real lens systems these analytical formulas overestimate the exposure. This is due to *vignetting*, the blocking of light by lens elements other than the aperture stop when a ray passes through the system at a large angle to the axis. Vignetting can be a significant effect in wide-angle lenses and when using a lens at full aperture. Fortunately, the ray tracing algorithm described in the last section accounts for this blockage, and hence computes the exposure correctly.

Figure 7 compares the irradiance computed by tracing rays through the lens system pointed at a uniform radiance field with

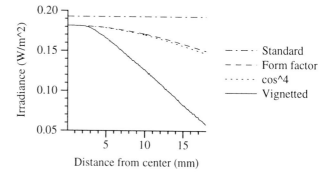

Figure 7: Irradiance on the film plane resulting from a uniform unit radiance field imaged through the double-Gauss lens at full aperture, as a function of distance from the center of the film.

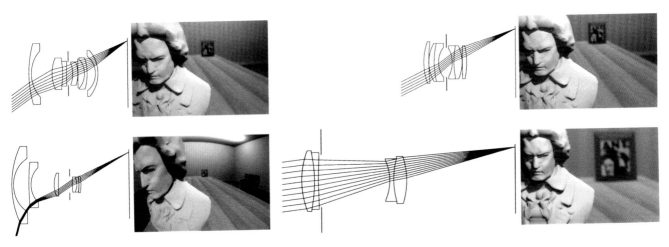

Figure 8: Four views of the same scene taken with a 16mm fisheye lens (bottom left), 35mm wide-angle lens (top left), 50mm double-Gauss lens (top right), and a 200mm telephoto lens (bottom right). A profile view of the lens system used to take each image is shown on the left. As with physical lenses, perspective is compressed with long focal lengths and expanded with short focal lengths. The fisheye image shows the lens' signature barrel distortion.

values computed using the usual computer graphics camera model (no weighting), the form factor, the $\cos^4$ approximation, and the full lens simulation. For this particular lens, the $\cos^4$ law and the form factor approximations do not differ significantly. However, vignetting reduces the true exposure near the edge of the film to nearly one third of its approximated value.

4.2 Sampling

In our model, a pixel's value is proportional to the radiant power falling on a hypothetical pixel-sized sensor in the image plane. The radiant power is given by the radiance integrated over the four-dimensional domain of pixel area and solid angle of incoming directions. This is estimated by sampling radiance over this domain (i.e., by casting rays from the pixel area toward the lens).

There are several ways to improve the efficiency of this calculation. First, we sample within the solid angle subtended by the exit pupil rather than sampling radiance over the entire hemisphere. Additional noise reduction might also be obtained by importance sampling, folding the factor of $\frac{\cos\theta' \cos\theta''}{\|x''-x'\|^2}$ into the distribution of rays over solid angle. Finally, efficiency can be improved by the use of good sampling patterns, which can reduce the amount of error in a pixel as well as affecting the overall distribution of noise in the final image. We have used stratified and quasirandom sampling patterns in our experiments.

Sampling without importance distribution is straightforward. Rays are cast from points in the pixel area toward points on the disk of the exit pupil, and the resulting values are weighted by $\frac{\cos\theta' \cos\theta''}{\|x''-x'\|^2}$. We can think of these pairs of points on the pixel area and exit pupil as being single points in the four-dimensional domain of integration.

Rather than generating uniformly distributed points on the lens and weighting them, we can perform importance sampling by generating rays with a cosine-weighted distribution in solid angle and averaging the unweighted radiance values. We implemented an importance version of the third square-to-disk mapping described below. In the 35mm camera lenses that we tested, importance sampling reduced noise by only about one percent, because the $\cos^4 \theta'$ weighting factor only varied by approximately twenty percent (see Figure 7). Since importance sampling adds a great deal of complexity and expense to the sampling operation, we believe it is not worth the effort in this particular application.

To generate these sample locations, it is usually necessary to start with some pattern of points defined in the hypercube $[0,1]^4$. Two of the dimensions are translated and scaled to the pixel area, and the other two dimensions are mapped to the disk of the exit pupil. The mapping from unit square to disk must be *measure preserving* (have a constant Jacobian) in order to avoid introducing a sampling bias. Thus, uniformly distributed points in the square map to uniformly distributed points on the disk. There are a number of such mappings. However, when mapping special sampling patterns such as stratified patterns it is good to choose a mapping that does not severely distort the shape of the strata. The obvious mapping,

$$r = \sqrt{u}, \ \theta = 2\pi v \tag{10}$$

is actually rather poor in this respect. A better mapping, used by Shirley[13], takes concentric squares to concentric circles. For example, in one wedge of the square, we have:

$$x' = 2x - 1, \ y' = 2y - 1$$
$$r = y', \ \theta = \frac{x'}{y'} \tag{11}$$

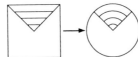

A third mapping we have implemented takes subrectangles $[0,x] \times [0,1]$ to a chord with area proportional to x, as illustrated below.

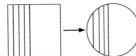

We have used two schemes to generate good sampling patterns in the hypercube. One is stratified sampling, dividing the dimensions of the hypercube into blocks and placing a sample randomly within each block. Given N samples, we could divide the hypercube into $N^{\frac{1}{4}}$ strata along each dimension. For typical values of N (it is unusual for a distributed ray tracer to cast more than a few hundred rays per pixel), this does not amount to many divisions of each dimension, and the benefits of stratification would be small. Instead, the pixel-area dimensions and the aperture-disk dimensions are strati-

Figure 9: Images synthesized with a 35mm wide-angle lens using, in order of decreasing accuracy, the full lens simulation (left), thick approximation (center), and the standard model (right). The top left arrow indicates the location of the scanline used in Figure 11.

fied separately as $\sqrt{N}$ by $\sqrt{N}$ grids on subsquares. To avoid systematic noise, the correlation of strata between pixel area and disk are randomly permuted.

We have found that the choice of square-to-disk mapping and stratification scheme strongly affect sampling efficiency and image quality. Using Shirley's mapping (11) yielded significantly lower RMS error (15 percent lower than (10) in typical experiments) as well as visibly improved image quality. Using the stratification method described above gives reasonable pixel antialiasing where edges are in sharp focus, and good distribution of noise in regions where depth of field causes blur.

5 Results

We have implemented our camera model as part of a ray tracer. The system supports rendering scenes using cameras constructed with different lenses and film formats. Figure 8 shows four images generated by the renderer and the lenses used in taking each of them. For each image, the camera was positioned in the scene so that the bust was imaged at approximately the same place and magnification on the film. As the focal length of the lens is increased, the relative size of the picture frame in the background grows, as expected. Darkening near the edge of the image due to vignetting is also apparent when using the fisheye and double-Gauss lens. These images typically required 90 minutes of CPU time to compute on a Silicon Graphics Indigo2 workstation at 16 rays per pixel. Approximately 10% of that time was spent tracing rays through the lens system, and thus the use of the full lens simulation is quite practical.

Figure 9 illustrates the differences in image geometry resulting from the use of different camera models. The standard camera model produces an image with too large a field of view, with both the bust and picture frame appearing smaller than in the full simulation image. The similarity of the full simulation and thick lens images illustrates the fact that using a thick lens can result in a good

Figure 10: Camera focused on picture frame.

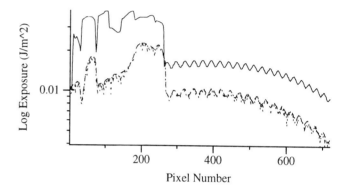

Figure 11: Comparison of exposure computed by the standard model (solid line), full simulation (dotted line), and thick approximation (dashed line), recorded at pixels along the indicated scanline of each image of Figure 9.

approximation if the actual lens forms nearly ideal images.

Figure 10 illustrates the change in field of view that occurs when the focus of a lens is changed. The figure shows the same scene as that in Figure 9, but with the lens focused on the picture frame in the background. Note that more of the front of the bust can be seen in the lower-left corner compared to the full simulation image in Figure 9. This increased field of view is caused by the movement of the lens towards the film plane when the lens is focused on a more distant object.

The new camera model also produces significant differences in exposure compared to the standard model. The exposure computed for a typical scene by the full simulation and the two approximations is shown in Figure 11. Exposure is generally overestimated in the standard model, and, as expected, the error tends to grow near the edge of the film.

An image taken with the fisheye lens is shown in Figure 12. Again, barrel distortion and darkening caused by vignetting are evident.

6 Summary and Discussion

The physically-based camera model that we have described draws upon techniques from both the lens design and computer graphics literature in order to simulate the geometry and radiometry of image formation. The lens system is described using standard lens construction information, and its behavior is characterized by tracing light rays through its various elements and weighting them properly. The primary added cost of using the model is finding the intersection with and refraction caused by each lens surface; for reasonably complex scenes the increase in rendering time is small, and the full

Figure 12:

simulation is very practical. Further, we show how the behavior of well-corrected lens systems can be approximated using a projective transformation derived from a thick lens approximation.

The new model is an improvement over standard models in a number of ways:

- The geometric relationships between the lens, object, and film plane are modeled properly by precise placement and movement of lens elements. This is necessary for accurate field of view and depth of field calculations.

- Image geometry is computed correctly by tracing the path of light through the system. The model is capable of simulating non-linear geometric transformations such as those produced by fisheye and anamorphic lenses, while simultaneously computing the correct exposure and depth of field.

- The image irradiance, or exposure, is computed properly because the model applies the correct weighting to rays traced through the lens system, and derives the correct exit pupil to control the limits of the integration. The model also correctly accounts for vignetting due to the blockage of rays.

Although our model is more accurate than previous camera models, there are many aspects of cameras and lens systems that we have not simulated. For example, our model assumes the shutter opens and closes instantaneously, which is not true. Our model also assumes that the lens transmittance is perfect, and that the properties of lens surfaces do not vary with position or time. We have also ignored many wavelength-dependent effects, in particular sensor sensitivity and response, and chromatic aberration due to the variation of index of refraction with wavelength. In the future we intend to experimentally verify our model by simulating particular lens systems and comparing the results with captured images. The goal of these experiments will be to find what level of detail of the camera must be simulated to match computer-generated and photographic images.

7 Acknowledgements

Thanks to Matt Pharr and Reid Gershbein for help with the figures and the rendering system, Viewpoint DataLabs for the Beethoven and Pentax models, and to the anonymous reviewers for their suggestions. This research was supported by equipment grants from Apple and Silicon Graphics Computer Systems, and a research grant from the National Science Foundation (CCR-9207966).

References

[1] Max Born and Emil Wolf. *Principles of Optics*. MacMillan, New York, second edition, 1964.

[2] Robert L. Cook, Thomas Porter, and Loren Carpenter. Distributed ray tracing. In *Computer Graphics (SIGGRAPH '84 Proceedings)*, volume 18, pages 137–145, July 1984.

[3] Status report of the graphics standards planning committee of the ACM/SIGGRAPH. *Computer Graphics*, 11:19+117, Fall 1977.

[4] P. Foote. Scientific paper 263. *Bulletin of the Bureau of Standards*, 12, 1915.

[5] Ned Greene and Paul S. Heckbert. Creating raster Omnimax images from multiple perspective views using the elliptical weighted average filter. *IEEE Computer Graphics and Applications*, 6(6):21–27, June 1986.

[6] Rudolph Kingslake. *Optics in Photography*. SPIE Optical Engineering Press, Bellingham, Washington, 1992.

[7] Nelson L. Max. Computer graphics distortion for IMAX and OMNIMAX projection. In *Nicograph '83 Proceedings*, pages 137–159, December 1983.

[8] Parry Moon and Domina Eberle Spencer. *The Photic Field*. The MIT Press, Cambridge, Massachusetts, 1981.

[9] F. E. Nicodemus, J. C. Richmond, J. J. Hsia, I. W. Ginsberg, and T. Limperis. Geometric considerations and nomenclature for reflectance. Monograph 161, National Bureau of Standards (US), October 1977.

[10] M. Potmesil and I. Chakravarty. A lens and aperture camera model for synthetic image generation. *Computer Graphics (SIGGRAPH '81 Proceedings)*, 15(3):297–305, August 1981.

[11] David F. Rogers and J. Alan Adams. *Mathematical Elements for Computer Graphics*. McGraw Hill, New York, second edition, 1990.

[12] Mikio Shinya. Post-filter for depth of field simulation with ray distribution buffer. In *Proceedings of Graphics Interface '94*, pages 59–66. Candian Human-Computer Communications Society, 1994.

[13] Peter Shirley. Discrepancy as a quality measure for sample distributions. *Eurographics '91 Proceedings*, pages 183–193, June 1991.

[14] Warren J. Smith. *Modern Lens Design*. McGraw Hill, New York, 1992.

[15] W. T. Welford. *Aberrations of the Symmetrical Optical System*. Academic Press, London, 1974.

[16] Turner Whitted. An improved illumination model for shaded display. *Communications of the ACM*, 23(6):343–349, June 1980.

[17] Charles S. Williams and Orville A. Becklund. *Optics: A Short Course for Engineers and Scientists*. Wiley-Interscience, New York, 1972.

Physically-Based Glare Effects for Digital Images

Greg Spencer*
Taligent, Inc.

Peter Shirley[†]
Cornell University

Kurt Zimmerman[‡]
Indiana University

Donald P. Greenberg[§]
Cornell University

Abstract

The physical mechanisms and physiological causes of glare in
human vision are reviewed. These mechanisms are scattering
in the cornea, lens, and retina, and diffraction in the coherent
cell structures on the outer radial areas of the lens. This scattering and diffraction are responsible for the "bloom" and
"flare lines" seen around very bright objects. The diffraction effects cause the "lenticular halo". The quantitative
models of these glare effects are reviewed, and an algorithm
for using these models to add glare effects to digital images
is presented. The resulting digital point-spread function is
thus psychophysically based and can substantially increase
the "perceived" dynamic range of computer simulations containing light sources. Finally, a perceptual test is presented
that indicates these added glare effects increase the apparent
brightness of light sources in digital images.

CR Categories and Subject Descriptors: I.3.0
[Computer Graphics]: General; I.3.6 [Computer Graphics]:
Methodology and Techniques.
Additional Key Words and Phrases: bloom, flare,
glare, lenticular halo, vision.

1 Introduction

There is a continual quest for photorealistic simulations, not
only by accurately modeling the physical behavior of light
reflection, propagation and transport, but by the creation of
images that are "perceived" to be realistic. Unfortunately,
a digital image can only be as realistic as the limited color
gamut, dynamic range, spatial resolution, field-of-view, and
stereo-capacity that the display medium will allow. If we had
a display medium which could produce the high luminances
of real scenes, we would calculate the radiometric quantities for each pixel in the two dimensional image lattice, and
send the resulting lattice to the display. However, digital
images are displayed on devices with from 256 to 1024 luminance levels and a maximum luminance of approximately
50 cd/m^2.

To illustrate why this lack of intensity can hamper realism,
consider the difference between the perception of a displayed

*10201 N. De Anza Blvd., Cupertino, CA 95014.
Greg_Spencer@Taligent.COM.
[†]580 ETC, Ithaca, NY 14850. shirley@graphics.cornell.edu.
[‡]Lindley Hall, Bloomington, IN 47405.
kuzimmer@cs.indiana.edu.
[§]580 ETC, Ithaca, NY 14850. dpg@graphics.cornell.edu.

Permission to make digital/hard copy of part or all of this work
for personal or classroom use is granted without fee provided
that copies are not made or distributed for profit or commercial
advantage, the copyright notice, the title of the publication and
its date appear, and notice is given that copying is by permission
of ACM, Inc. To copy otherwise, to republish, to post on
servers, or to redistribute to lists, requires prior specific
permission and/or a fee.

Figure 1: Carl Saltzmann, *Erste elektrische Straßenbeleuchtung in Berlin, Potsdamer Platz*, 1884.

digital image of a single white pixel on a black background,
and the real experience of looking at a small incandescent
bulb. The real bulb differs from the digital image in two
important ways. The first difference is a qualitative "brightness" that the bulb possesses. The second difference is the
hazy glow that can be seen around the bulb. This glow not
only gives an impression of greater brightness, but it can
also interfere with the visibility of objects near the bulb.

We can improve the realism of simulated images by adding
effects which perceptually expand and enhance the perceived
dynamic range. These effects are most pronounced where
bright light sources are visible within the scene. Perceptual
effects which exaggerate the brightness of objects in an image
have long been used in artistic expression. The impression-
ists, in the late 19th century depicted the brightness of illuminating sources by adding tell-tale radial lines (Figure 1).
Cinematographers often add etched lenses to create special
effects around lights, starbursts, or explosions to make them
appear brighter than otherwise. Although these techniques
are not psychophysically accurate, each produces the desired
impression by exaggerating the luminance of the sources.

The idea of adding glare effects to a digital image is not
new. Nakamae et al. [20] pointed out that the limited dynamic range of CRTs prevents the display of luminaires at
their actual luminance values, and that adding streaking and
blooming around the luminaires helps give the appearance of
glare. While Nakamae et al.'s glare algorithm is extremely
effective in conveying an impression of luminaire intensity,
it does not account for the visual masking effects of glare,
which is needed for object-visibility prediction.

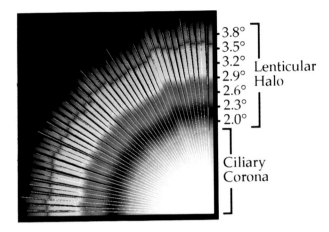

Figure 2: The ciliary corona and lenticular halo for a small white light source (after [29]).

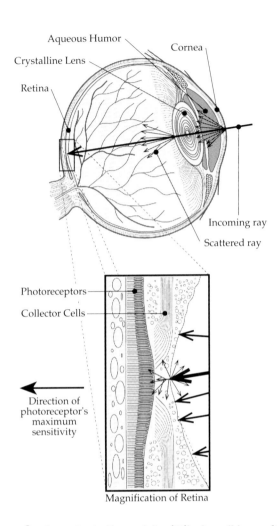

Figure 3: Scattering in the eye (after [28]). A small beam of light entering the eye is partially scattered in the cornea, the lens, and in the first layer of the retina.

Our approach has been to model the physical effects, primarily caused by the interaction of light rays and the physiology of the human eye. For many years, researchers in optics, psychophysics, and illumination engineering have attempted to determine the mechanisms behind glare, and to quantify the effects of glare on viewers. A camera lens filter that mimics the underlying mechanisms of glare in human vision has recently been developed, and had better results than conventional glare filters for some effects [1].

Glare effects can be subdivided into two major components: *flare* and *bloom*. Flare is composed of a *lenticular halo* and a *ciliary corona* (Figure 2), and is primarily caused by the lens [29]. Bloom is caused by scattering from three parts of the visual system: the cornea, lens and retina (Figure 3). The lenticular halo, ciliary corona, and bloom are the dominant contributing factors to glare effects and greatly affect our perception of the brightnesses of light sources.

Rays of the ciliary corona appear as radial streaks emanating from the center of the source. Similar ray patterns associated with other coronas have been studied by physicists and are caused by random fluctuations in refractive index of the ocular media [15].

The lenticular halo is observed as a set of colored, concentric rings, surrounding the light source and distal to the ciliary corona. The somewhat irregular rings are composed of radial segments, where the color of each segment of the ray varies with its distance from the source. The apparent size of the halo is constant and independent of the distance between the observer and the source. This phenomenon is caused by the radial fibers of the crystalline structure of the lens [29, 15].

Bloom, frequently referred to as "veiling luminance" is the "glow" around bright objects. Bloom causes a reduction in contrast that interferes with the visibility of nearby objects, such as the night-time view of the grill between two car headlamps. Bloom is caused by stray light attributed to scatter from three portions of the eye: the cornea, the crystalline lens, and the retina, all with approximately equal contributions [33].

The physiology of the eye and the resultant physical effects are explained in greater detail in the following section. In Section 3 we develop the quantitative aspects of this glare in terms of the *point-spread function* of the human eye and present an algorithm for generating the digital flare filter that approximates the point spread function. In Section 4 we describe a brief perceptual experiment which verified

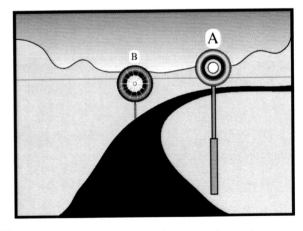

Figure 4: Glare around a nearby source **A** and distant source **B**. Since the halo subtends the same angle for each source, the halo around **B** has the illusion of being larger than the halo around **A**.

the increase in perceived brightness. We conclude the paper showing several vivid examples and recommendations for future work.

2 Physiology and Physical Effects

The physical mechanisms behind glare have been studied since the late 19th century [29] and have been a matter of debate until quite recently [15]. In this section we present the physical origins of glare, drawing mainly on Simpson's work on lenticular haloes [29], and Vos [33] and Hemenger's [15] work on scattering in the eye.

2.1 Lenticular Halo

When one observes a point source of light in a dark surround, there appears to be a series of concentric colored rings around the source. This is known as the lenticular halo (Figure 2). No matter how far away the source is from the observer, the haloes always subtend the same angle at the eye. As shown in Figure 4, this creates an illusion that haloes around distant light sources appear larger than haloes around nearby sources. The intensity of the halo decreases with distance, and streaks are seen if the source subtends a sufficiently small solid angle.

The lenticular halo is caused by the circular optical grating formed by the radial fibers at the periphery of the crystalline lens. This was first explained by Drualt in 1897 [29], and experimentally verified by the Emsley-Fincham tests in 1922 [29]. A clear explanation, first presented by Simpson in 1953 is illustrated below.

Figure 5(a) shows a biconvex lens with a circular grating etched into the outer portion of the lens. The axis of the lens is through the center, perpendicular to the plane of the paper, and meets the focal plane at point F. If we consider a small segment of the circular grating at G, where the lines of the segment are nearly parallel, we have a typical parallel diffraction grating.

Light is refracted according to the following equation:

$$\sin\theta = \frac{\lambda}{e},$$

where θ is the angular deviation of the light path, λ is the wavelength, and e is the distance between adjacent grating spaces. Thus, when white light is passed through the region G, and focused on the focal plane, the violet components appear at V, F, and V', and the red components appear at R, F, and R'. Thus two lines are formed, each one radiating outward and containing the full range of spectral colors. As we circumferentially traverse the circular grating, two overlapping haloes are produced.

The biconvex lens with the circular optical grating is actually a simplified model of the crystalline lens of the human eye (Figure 5(b)). This is composed of fibers which are relatively large strips of transparent material having a cross-section of roughly hexagonal shape [10]. Although the central part of the lens is optically homogeneous, the exterior portions act as an optical grating with a spacing of e, the width of the fibers.

A beam of light which is less than $3mm$ in diameter can pass through the clear portion of the lens, but subtending larger angles will always pass through the grating, thus creating the lenticular halo. This means that haloes are not seen in daylight levels of illumination (when the pupil is $2mm$ across) but is seen in darker conditions.

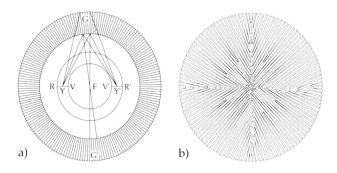

Figure 5: a) Diagram of the etched biconvex lens (after [29]). b) Cell structure of the Crystalline Lens (cell size exaggerated).

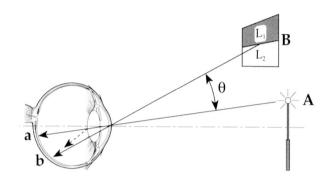

Figure 6: A reduction in contrast that results from scattered light in the eye causes a reduction in contrast that depends on θ, the angle of separation.

2.2 The Ciliary Corona

The ciliary corona is depicted in Figure 2 and consists of rays emanating from a point light source. These radial rays may extend beyond the lenticular halo, and are brighter and more pronounced as the angle subtended by the source decreases (Figure 4). The ciliary corona is caused by semi-random density fluctuation in the nucleus of the lens which causes forward scattering that is independent of wavelength [15]. As the size of the source increases, it appears that the ciliary corona blurs and contributes to the bloom effect. This is because superimposing the fine flare lines coming from each part of an areal source eliminates the crisp pattern of any given set of radial flare lines. Simpson observed that sources much larger than 20 minutes of arc did not have significant flare lines.

2.3 Bloom

Bloom, frequently referred to as "disability glare" or "veiling luminance" is best illustrated by the reduced visibility which occurs in the presence of bright light sources. This effect is attributed to the scattering of light in the ocular media, where the scatter contributions from the cornea, crystalline lens, and retina occur in roughly equal portions.

This effect is illustrated in Figure 6 where light from source **A** scatters inside the eye and is added to light coming from object **B**. This scattered light adds an effective luminance s that does not originate at **B**. Because light is added to both the light and dark parts of object **B**, the contrast ratio L_2/L_1 is reduced. In addition, since sensitivity to absolute luminance difference decreases as the base luminance increases, the difference between L_1 and L_2 might be discernible, while the difference between $s + L_1$ and $s + L_2$ is not. The magnitude of s depends on the angle of separation θ, and the luminance and solid angle of the source. The quantitative details of this dependence will be discussed in Section 3.

Veiling luminance has been the subject of investigations for almost two centuries, and there is still some controversy surrounding some of the details of the mechanisms for glare. It is evident that the stray or scattered light plays a dominant role [15], but neural inhibitory effects may also be present at very small angles of incidence [33].

It is not feasible to document the large number of psychophysical studies performed on this subject, and the reader is referred to the annotated bibliography of Ronci and Stefanacci [24], as well as the more recent studies of Owsley et al. [22], Ross et al. [25], and Ijspeert et al. [17]. Investigations by Stiles [31], Cornsweet and Teller [9], Blackwell and Blackwell [3], Hemenger [15] and others all corroborate that the masking effect of glare is caused primarily by stray light. Direct evidence has also been obtained by observing the interior of the eye, revealing that the light scattering comes primarily from the cornea, crystalline lens, and retina (Figure 2). These cellular structures, many microns in diameter, scatter light independent of wavelength, much like a rough reflecting surface.

For the cornea and the lens, the light is scattered in a narrow forward cone with approximately a Gaussian distribution [5]. The corneal scattering can be differentiated from the lenticular scattering since it casts a shadow of the iris on the retina. The retina to retina scattering, although physically in all directions is only important in the same forward directions due to the drastically reduced directional sensitivity of the cone system to obliquely incident light (the "Crawford-Stiles" effect). Because the rod sensitivity does not have as high a directional sensitivity as the cones, the magnitude of glare is greater in dark (scotopic) conditions.

For these reasons, the light scattering is somewhat like a "blurring" or "blooming" effect with a sharp drop-off, and can be approximated with empirical formulae to match the experimental results.

3   Algorithm

Although at a high level we understand the physical mechanisms behind scattering in the eye, the exact structure of the cells in the eye is not known to the extent that we can simulate the scattering from first principles. In fact, current knowledge about the cell structure in the eye comes from inversion of observed scattering behavior [2, 15]. For this reason, we use psychophysical and phenomenological results in addition to physical modeling.

If the eye is focused on a "point source", then ideally a small discrete area of non-zero irradiance would fall on the retina. Because the eye is a real optical system, there will be some blurring of this signal on the retina. This blurring can be described by a "point source function" (PSF) for the eye. In Section 3.1 we describe quantitative glare models in terms of the PSF of the eye, and in Section 3.2 we show how this model can be simulated by convolving a radiometric image with a particular digital filter kernel.

3.1   Quantitative Model of Glare

There is approximate agreement on the exact perceptual contribution of the bloom for a "normal" viewer. Several researchers [16, 31, 11] have studied the magnitude of the glare effect by examining the threshold of visibility of an object near a source that produces illuminance E_0 at the front of the eye. By turning the source off, and adding a background luminance L_v that makes the object barely visible, the "equivalent veiling luminance" L_v can be found. This has led to empirical equations taking the general form:

$$L_v(\theta) = \frac{kE_0}{f(\theta)}, \qquad (1)$$

where L_v is the equivalent veiling luminance in cd/m^2, E_0 is the illuminance from the glare source at the eye in lx, k is a constant depending on the experimental conditions, θ is the angle between the primary object and the glare source in degrees, and f is an experimentally determined function. Various values for k between 3 and 50 have been used, and $f(\theta)$ is usually set to be θ^N or $(\theta+\theta_0)^N$ with N ranging from 1.5 to 3. Since the bloom is viewer-dependent, all of these values for k and f can be considered to be in some sense reasonable, but recently an approximate consensus has been reached on the details of these parameters.

The form of Equation 1 is somewhat confusing because it involves both luminance and illuminance. Vos has presented the equation in a less intimidating form by rewriting it as a *point spread function* (PSF). A PSF is a density (unit volume) function defined on the visual field that describes how a unit volume point source (a delta function) is "spread" onto other points of the visual field. If we assume that the unscattered component of Equation 1 is unchanged (appears as an exact point source), then the PSF $P(\theta)$ is:

$$P(\theta) = a\delta(\theta) + \frac{k}{f(\theta)}, \qquad (2)$$

where $\delta(\theta)$ is an "ideal" PSF and a is the fraction of light that is not scattered.

The form of Equation 2 assumes that there is no energy loss in the system. This is not the case, and has been the cause of some debate in the glare literature. The perceived fraction of light scattered in Equation 2 (i.e. $\int k/f(\theta)$) is roughly 10% for normal viewers. However, physical experiments suggest that as much as 40% of the light is actually scattered [26, 4]. Researchers have investigated this apparent contradiction. The most common explanation is that angular dependence of the sensitivity of the cones in the retina (the Crawford-Stiles effect [36]) effectively absorbs some of the stray light, particularly for θ more than a few degrees. This same effect causes light transmitted by the outer edge of a fully dilated pupil to be 5-10 times less effective than light through the center of the pupil [33]. This implies that we should trust the ten percent figure for our purposes because it is the perceptual quality of the light that we need to account for. Thus, we should realize that Equation 2 represents a normalized perceptual PSF and does not measure the spread of retinal illuminance.

Recently, Vos has attempted to unify the large number of PSF models for the eye [33]. In this section we review Vos' work, and add two effects studied by Hemenger [15] not accounted for in Vos' model.

If the point spread function is defined on the hemisphere of directions entering the eye, where α is the angle from the gaze direction and ϕ is the angle around the gaze direction, then

$$\int_0^{2\pi} \int_0^{\frac{\pi}{2}} P(\theta) \sin\theta \, d\theta \, d\phi = 1, \qquad (3)$$

where the angles are measured in radians. This normalization condition asserts that the PSF P redistributes energy,

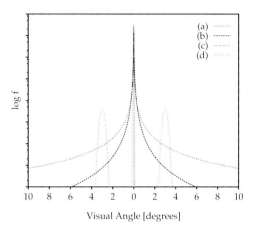

Figure 7: The PSF components (a) f_0, (b) f_1, (c) f_2, and (d) f_3.

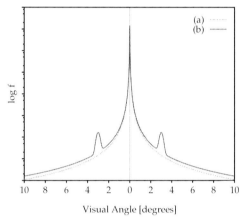

Figure 8: (a) The photopic PSF P_p. (b) The scotopic PSF P_s.

but does not emit or absorb energy. If the optical system does absorb energy, this is accounted for by a constant separate from the PSF.

Because the glare literature reports its results in degrees, we can rewrite the PSF normalization condition for a $P(\theta)$, where θ is in degrees:

$$\frac{\pi^2}{90} \int_0^{90°} P(\theta) \sin \theta d\theta = 1. \qquad (4)$$

Any non-negative function of θ that satisfies Equation 4 is a candidate for a point spread function. This means that any weighted average of functions that each satisfy Equation 4 is also a candidate. Vos [33] has reviewed the various models for glare and noted that there are three different empirical components in the PSF for an eye. The first is a narrow Gaussian that represents the unscattered component. The second is a function that is roughly proportional to θ^{-3} that is dominant for non-zero θ less than one or two degrees. The third is a term proportional to θ^{-2} for θ more than a degree. Because both the θ^{-3} and θ^{-2} terms would blow up near $\theta = 0$, Vos replaces them with $(\theta + a)^{-2}$ and $(\theta + a)^{-3}$ for some empirical constant a, and suggests the following three normalized components:

$$f_0(\theta) = 2.61 \times 10^6 e^{-\left(\frac{\theta}{0.02}\right)^2},$$

for the central Gaussian,

$$f_1(\theta) = \frac{20.91}{(\theta + 0.02)^3},$$

for the θ^{-3} component, and

$$f_2(\theta) = \frac{72.37}{(\theta + 0.02)^2},$$

for the θ^{-2} component. These functions are shown in Figure 7. The function f_0 represents the unscattered component of the light, It shows the typical Gaussian shape expected for an real-world imaging system. This term should vary slightly with pupil size [5] but for our purposes could be replaced by a delta function because the angular size of the Gaussian will be much smaller than a pixel width.

Finally, Vos suggests the following combination for the PSF of a normal viewer:

$$\begin{aligned} P_p(\theta) = \ & 0.384 f_0(\theta) + \\ & 0.478 f_1(\theta) + \\ & 0.138 f_2(\theta). \end{aligned} \qquad (5)$$

This PSF is subscripted with a "p" because it is appropriate for observers in a *photopic* (light adapted) state. The light adaptation of a viewer is described by one of three basic states [23]: less than 0.01 cd/m^2 is the *scotopic region* (night vision); the range 0.01-3 cd/m^2 is the *mesopic region* (mixed night and day vision); more than 3 cd/m^2 is the *photopic region* (day vision) The graph of Equation 5 is shown in Figure 8.

3.1.1 Adding the lenticular halo

For pupil diameters less than three millimeters, Simpson reports that the coherent fibers in the lens are blocked by the iris. The pupil diameter is influenced by many factors such as age, mood, and the spectral distribution of incoming light, but it is primarily related to the field luminance of the scene. Moon and Spencer (1944) [36] relate average pupil diameter D (in mm) to field luminance L (in cd/m^2):

$$D = 4.9 - 3 \tanh\left(0.4(\log_{10} L + 1)\right).$$

This yields a pupil diameter of about $3mm$ for $L = 10 cd/m^2$, which is the field luminance of a dimly lit interior. We should expect no lenticular halo in daylight conditions, a mild lenticular halo in dimly lit rooms, and prominent lenticular haloes for dark scenes.

It was observed by Mallero and Palmer [18] that light at $568nm$ caused a lenticular halo of approximately $3°$ radius with an angular width of $0.35°$. Based on this observation, Hemenger [15] used the following empirical formula to model the lenticular halo with these properties produced by light at 568nm:

$$C(t) = B e^{-19.75(\theta - \theta_0)^2}, \qquad (6)$$

where B is a constant and $\theta_0 = 3°$.

Since the angle of a diffraction pattern peak is proportional to wavelength, we can establish the formula:

$$\theta_0(\lambda) = \frac{\lambda}{568}.$$

Since we expect the same fraction of incident energy to be diffracted for each wavelength, we can construct a unit volume PSF for the lenticular halo:

$$f_3(\theta, \lambda) = 436.9 \frac{568}{\lambda} e^{-(\theta - 3\frac{\lambda}{568})^2}. \qquad (7)$$

Mallero and Palmer also observed that in dark conditions the halo at 568nm had about ten times the luminance of the ciliary corona. From this fact, and from Equation 5 and Equation 7 we see that $P_p(3°) = 1.462$ and $f_3(3°, 568) = 436.9$, so a reasonable coefficient for f_3 will make the ring appear ten times as bright as P_P, so the coefficient we use is $10 \times 1.462/436.9 = 0.033$. However, this assumes a fully dilated pupil, which is only true for scotopic conditions. So we assume that about half of the radial fibers of the lens are exposed, calling for a coefficient for f_3 of 0.016, resulting in the equation:

$$
\begin{aligned}
P_m(\theta, \lambda) = \quad & 0.368 f_0(\theta) + \\
& 0.478 f_1(\theta) + \\
& 0.138 f_2(\theta) + \\
& 0.016 f_3(\theta, \lambda). \quad (8)
\end{aligned}
$$

This assumes the lenticular halo is diverted from the central peak. The subscript m refers to a *mesopic* observer, whose pupil is large, but whose cones are still active.

For darker conditions the amount of glare may be higher. At $0.15 cd/m^2$ there is 50% more straylight than at $100 cd/m^2$ [22]. This suggests an alternative form for the darkest point-spread function:

$$
\begin{aligned}
P_s(\theta, \lambda) = \quad & 0.282 f_0(\theta) + \\
& 0.478 f_1(\theta) + \\
& 0.207 f_2(\theta) + \\
& 0.033 f_3(\theta, \lambda). \quad (9)
\end{aligned}
$$

The graph of P_s is shown in Figure 8.

3.1.2 Viewer-Specific Variation in PSF

There is an increase in glare with age, although the shape of the PSF stays the same [13]. If there are no cataracts, Vos [33] has established a rough age relation:

$$
\begin{aligned}
P_p(\theta) = \quad & (0.384 - 6.9 \times 10^{-9} A^4) f_0(\theta) + \\
& 0.478 f_1(\theta) + \\
& (0.138 + 6.9 \times 10^{-9} A^4) f_2(\theta), \quad (10)
\end{aligned}
$$

where A is the age of the viewer in years. This change in vision is caused primarily by optical changes in the eye [12], but there is some loss due to neural changes as well [21]. Equation 10 implies that the fraction of light scattered more than $0.05°$ increases from 0.36 at age 20 to 0.45 at age 60. The ratio of this light to unscattered light approximately doubles between the ages of 20 and 70. The situation can be even worse for viewers with cataracts, where the fraction of light that is scattered can be close to one [14]. There are no sex differences in the PSF [22], and only minor differences for viewers with different pigmentation [17]. The formulas for P_m and P_s will have similar behavior to P_p, but the coefficient for f_3 may remain relatively constant because the pupil diameter becomes more static with age. This may result in mild lenticular haloes in photopic conditions for old viewers.

There is also an age-related color shift toward the yellow in the light transmitted by the lens. This, as well as increased fluorescence of the lens, can cause an additional reduction in visibility for elderly viewers in some viewing conditions such as twilight [6] and scotopic conditions [21]. The yellowing of the lens also causes metamerism to vary with age [8]. Since age-related changes vary widely from viewer to viewer, these studies are primarily useful for establishing guidelines for the design of environments that are safe for "typical" elderly viewers.

3.2 Digital Glare Filter Generation

The glare formulae of Section 3.1 can be applied directly to digital images by using a digital point spread function to spread energy in high-intensity pixels to nearby pixels. This basic strategy has been used by Nakamae et al. [20] and Chiu et al. [7]. Unlike these previous approaches, we use different flare filters based on the adaptation state of the viewer.

To develop a filter for a particular image, we first construct digital versions of $f_0(\theta)$, $f_1(\theta)$, $f_2(\theta)$, and $f_3(\theta)$. Since each of these filters must have unit volume, we can calculate each filter proportional to a given function, and then renormalize the filter so that all pixels sum to one. These filters and the images they are applied to are stored in Ward's floating point file format [35], so that the small values in the off-center filter pixels are not lost. We compute the filter for an $N \times N$ image, where $N = 2n + 1$ so there is guaranteed to be a single central pixel. We number these pixels $(0, 0)$ through $(N - 1, N - 1)$ and we calculate the angle $\Delta\theta$ subtended by the pixels of the image that we will add glare to. This assumes a relatively small field of view so that $\Delta\theta$ can be approximated by a constant for all pixels. To calculate the value $d(i, j)$ for a particular flare component $f(\theta)$ we evaluate the integral

$$
p(i,j) = \int_{i-0.5}^{i+0.5} \int_{j-0.5}^{j+0.5} f\left(\Delta\theta \sqrt{(u-n)^2 + (v-n)^2}\right) dv\, du.
$$

We use the trapezoidal rule to evaluate this integral. For f_0, f_1, and f_2 we use 10000 sample points in the central part of the filter where there is rapid change in the function, and 100 sample points elsewhere. To construct the colors in the lenticular halo, $f_3(\theta, \lambda)$, we process Equation 7 for 50 wavelengths from $400nm$ to $700nm$ and then convert to a trichromatic transform as described by Meyer [19]. This halo is not a classic "pure" spectrum because each wavelength bleeds into its neighbors, so it is not on the boundary of the visible part of the CIE diagram and is thus easier to display on a monitor gamut. The resulting pattern is shown in Figure 9 and is consistent with Simpson's observations (Figure 2).

Unfortunately, the filters calculated in this manner will lack the flare lines we expect (Figure 2), because they are spatial averages over areas that cover many flare lines. We need to add these flare lines without disturbing the macroscopic structure suggested by Equations 5, 8, and 9. We add flare detail to our digital filter by drawing random antialiased radial lines of random intensity in the range $[0, 1]$ on a digital image the same size as our filter. We draw a number of lines to visually match Simpson's observations (Figure 2). We assume that the ciliary corona (represented by $f_1(\theta)$ and $f_2(\theta)$) is composed of one set of flare lines, and that the lenticular halo (represented by $f_3(\theta)$) is composed of a different set of flare lines. This separation is consistent with the fact that there is a different physical mechanism for the two components, as was discussed in Section 2.

We take the random pattern of flare lines and adjust it so that it has an average pixel value of 1.0, and that each small neighborhood also has an average value of 1.0. This has the effect of increasing the pixel intensity radially because the fraction of pixels in a streak decreases radially from the

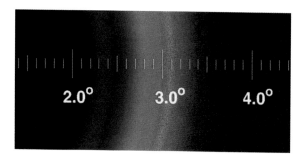

Figure 9: Algorithmically generated lenticular halo. Compare to Simpson's observed values in Figure 2.

center. This new pattern is then multiplied by the original flare functions, which gives them the appropriate detail without changing their carefully calculated macroscopic behavior. This process is shown in Figure 10, for the particular case of $P_m(\theta)$ (Equation 8), where the filter is built up in stages.

The filter is independent of a particular image, but must be recomputed for a new field-of-view because the angular size of a pixel changes. Thus only one filter is computed for an animation sequence that uses one set of camera parameters. The width and height of the filter is double the width and height of the target image. Because the values in the filter decrease away from the center (except for the lenticular halo which is approximately a factor of ten larger than its nearby interior neighbors), we can use only a central portion of the filter when processing dim pixels. This enormously decreases the execution time (approximately a factor of 100 in our implementation on the images in Section 5). Because the viewer will experience *actual* glare for the displayed pixels, we only need add glare to pixels whose full intensity is not displayed. So if the maximum displayable intensity is I_m, and the computed intensity for a given pixel is I, where $I > I_m$, the filter is applied to the value $I - I_m$. Note that the filter is applied at each of these bright pixels in the source image, which is spread to the appropriate regions of the destination image.

4 Perceptual Tests

Once the techniques are developed to simulate flare and bloom, simple experiments can be conducted to determine the perceptual effects.

In one simple experiment, two stimuli, one with a ciliary corona, and one without, were compared to see which one was perceived to be brighter. Each greyscale image was presented in a window with a short presentation time, $400ms$ or $700ms$. Colormap manipulation was implemented to control the presentation time to within $\pm 10ms$. Each image window was 300 by 300 pixels on the 1280 by 1024 display monitor. The presentation window was the only item visible on a screen with a black background.

The basic "staircase" method was utilized in the experiment with a three-way forced choice (choices were "Image A Brighter", "Image B Brighter" and "Neither Image Brighter"). The staircase method refers to a method of decreasing the adjustment to a stimulus to converge on a threshold while virtually eliminating predictive bias [36]. Images were presented on a Sony Trinitron 19 inch display connected to a Hewlett-Packard 9000/750 with a VGRX Graphics card.

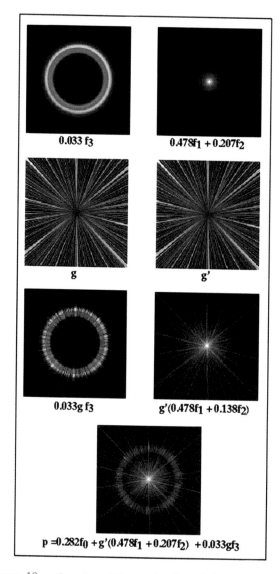

Figure 10: Overview of the construction of the scotopic point-spread filter P_s.

One window contained an image with the ciliary corona flare filter applied, and the other contained an identical image, except that the light source was replaced with a hardware-drawn disc surrounded by an annulus of one-third the intensity of the central disc (Figure 11(a)). The maximum intensity of the source with the corona flare was 75% of the maximum value displayable by the display device. The intensity of the disc varied from 0 to 100% of the maximum value.

Trials were arranged into two groups, with and without context for the source. In one group, the light source was presented by itself, in the center of a black field (Figure 11(b)). In the other group, the light source was placed into the context of a light bulb at the end of a desk lamp on a desk (Figure 11(c)). The order in which these groups of trials was run was randomized – half of the subjects performed the experiment with the context set first, and the other half observed the context free environments first. The glare images were also randomly swapped with the disc images so that one type of image did not always appear in the

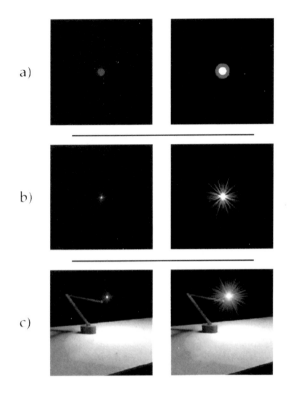

a)

b)

c)

Figure 11: Sample stimuli showing the lowest and highest flare intensity.

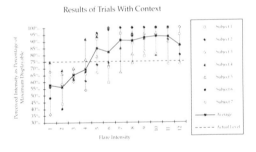

Results of Trials With Context

Figure 12: Stimulus with context.

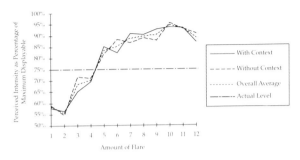

Comparison of With and Without Context

Figure 13: Overall results of experiment.

The results indicate a fairly strong effect due to glare. This observation implies that applying a glare filter improves the apparent dynamic range of an image.

same side of the display. In both groups of trials, there were 12 glare images, ranging from a simple slightly blurry dot to a light source which had too much glare to be believable. The entire experiment took place in a darkened room, so that the intensity of the test images would appear brighter overall, and enhance the glare effect.

4.1 Experimental Results

The experiment was conducted with a group of seven subjects, generating a statistically significant sample, given the small deviation usually present in brightness perception experiments.

The results, shown in Figures 12, and 13, show the expected response to the glare increase. If the glare had no effect, then the perceived intensity would be constant, as shown by the horizontal line at the 75% level.

The presence of a context (a lamp on a table) had no significant influence on the user's perception, but subjects did report having more confidence about the absolute brightness of the light source when the context was present.

5 Examples

The digital filters of Section 4 were applied to several digital images. By contracting the filter radius for dim pixels, we were able to run the filters in approximately one to three minutes per image on a HP9000/755. All of the images are shown before and after application of the flare filter.

The scotopic PSF P_s was applied to a night scene (Figure 14). Note that the haloes stay the same size for sources at different distances. The cars in two filtered images are at different angles, so only the car on the bottom shows appreciable glare. Also notice that the brightness of the headlights at different angles can only be detected once the glare is added. The images in Figure 14 we desaturated so that the saturation in HSV space was reduced by 70% to simulate scotopic (rod) vision. The image was not completely desaturated because color vision degrades gradually and is still partially active even under moonlight (about 0.03 cd/m^2) [30].

Figure 15 shows an application of the mesopic PSF P_m to a rendered image. Note that the lenticular halo is prominent.

Figure 16 shows an application of the photopic PSF P_p to a digital photo of a tree composited over a sky with luminance $4.0 \times 10^3 cd/m^2$ and a sun disk of $7.5 \times 10^8 cd/m^2$. The sun pokes through just a few holes in the leaves of the tree. Note that, as expected when viewing a bright scene, the lenticular halo is missing from Figure 16.

All of these images have some burn-out, where the value of the pixel goes above one. Ultimately, a more sophisticated tone mapping algorithm should be used [32, 7, 34, 27], so that the images will have the appropriate degree of object visibility, and qualitative lightness or darkness. This issue is not addressed in this work.

6 Conclusion

We have presented the mechanisms of glare in the human visual system, and have provided quantitative formulae used by the vision community that describe its magnitude. These mechanisms are scattering in the cornea, lens, and retina, and diffraction in the coherent cell structures on the outer radial areas of the lens. The scattering and diffraction are responsible for the "bloom" and "flare" lines seen around

Figure 15: An indoor simulation before and after the mesopic glare algorithm..

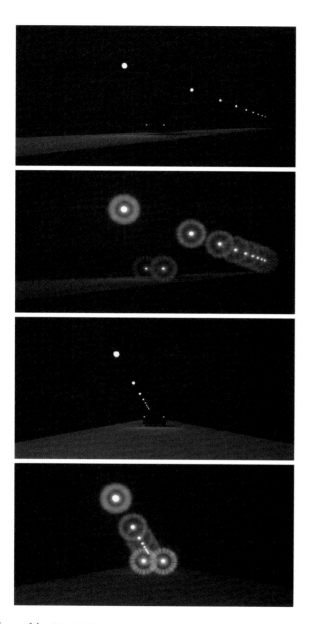

Figure 14: Two highway scenes before and after the scotopic glare algorithm. The orientation of the headlights is made obvious by the degree of glare.

Figure 16: The Sun showing through leaves before and after the photopic glare algorithm. The location of the Sun is obvious only after the glare is added. Note that there is no lenticular halo because the pupil of the viewer is contracted.

very bright objects. The diffraction effects are responsible for the "lenticular halo".

We have used these glare formulae to develop a digital point-spread function to add glare effects to digital images, and have run a perceptual experiment that indicates that the added glare increases the effective dynamic range in a digital image. Because the physically-based glare effects are expensive to compute, future work should focus on developing efficient methods that yield the same perceptual effects as the physically-based glare.

Acknowledgements

Thanks to Dan Kartch for help with the content and format of the paper, Andrew Kunz for help on image of the tree, Brian Smits for providing the theater image, Ben Trumbore and Bruce Walter for detailed comments on the paper, Alireza Esmailpour and Georgios Sakas for help obtaining a good reproduction of the Saltzmann painting, to Ken Torrance for proving important pointers into the optics literature, and to Jim Ferwerda for help understanding the methodology of psychophysics. This work was supported by the NSF/ARPA Science and Technology Center for Computer Graphics and Scientific Visualization (ASC-8920219) and by NSF CCR-9401961 and performed on workstations generously provided by the Hewlett-Packard Corporation.

References

[1] BECKMAN, C., NILSSON, O., AND PAULSSON, L.-E. Intraocular scatterinng in vision, artistic painting, and photography. *Applied Optics 33*, 21 (1994), 4749–4753.

[2] BETTELHEIM, F. A., AND PAUNOVIC, M. Light scattering of normal human lens 1. *Biophysical Journal 26*, 3 (April 1979), 85–99.

[3] BLACKWELL, O. M., AND BLACKWELL, H. R. Individual responses to lighting parameters for a population of 235 observers of varying ages. *Journal of the IES 2* (July 1980), 205–232.

[4] BOETTNER, E., AND WOLTER, J. Transmission of the ocular media. *Investigative Ophthalmology 1* (1962), 776.

[5] CAMPBELL, F., AND GUBISCH, R. Optical quality of the human eye. *Journal of Physiology 186* (1966), 558–578.

[6] CARTER, J. H. The effects of aging on selected visual functions: Color vision, glare sensitivity, field of vision, and accomodation. In *Aging and Human Visual Function*, R. Sekular, D. Kline, and K. Dismukes, Eds., vol. 2 of *Modern Aging Research*. Alan R. Liss, Inc., 1982, pp. 121–130.

[7] CHIU, K., HERF, M., SHIRLEY, P., SWAMY, S., WANG, C., AND ZIMMERMAN, K. Spatially nonuniform scaling functions for high contrast images. In *Graphics Interface '93* (May 1993), pp. 245–244.

[8] COREN, S., AND GIRGUS, J. Density of human lens pigmentation in vivo measures over an extended age range. *Vision Research 12*, 2 (1972), 343–346.

[9] CORNSWEET, T. N., AND TELLER, D. Y. Relation of increment thresholds to brightness and luminance. *Journal of the Optical Society of America 55* (1975), 1303–1308.

[10] DAVSON, H., Ed. *The Eye*, third ed., vol. 1a. Academic Press, inc. ltd., London, 1984.

[11] FRY, G. A re-evaluation of the scattering theory of glare. *Illuminating Engineering 49*, 2 (1954), 98–102.

[12] HEMENGER, R. P. Intraocular light scatter in normal vision loss with age. *Applied Optics 23*, 12 (1984), 1972–1974.

[13] HEMENGER, R. P. Small-angle intraocular light scatter: a hypothesis concerning its source. *Journal of the Optical Society of America A 5*, 4 (1987), 577–582.

[14] HEMENGER, R. P. Light scatter in cataractous lenses. *Opthalmological Phyisiological Optics 10* (October 1990), 394–397.

[15] HEMENGER, R. P. Sources of intraocular light scatter from inversion of an empirical glare function. *Applied Optics 31*, 19 (1992), 3687–3693.

[16] HOLLADAY, L. Action of a light source in the field of view on lowering visibility. *Journal of the Optical Society of America 14*, 1 (1927), 1–15.

[17] IJSPEERT, J. K., DE WAARD, P. W. T., VAN DEN BERG, T., AND DE JONG, P. The intraocular straylight function in 129 healthy volunteers; dependence on angle, age, and pigmentation. *Vision Research 30*, 5 (1990), 699–707.

[18] MELLERIO, J., AND PALMER, D. A. Entopic halos and glare. *Vision Research 12* (1972), 141–143.

[19] MEYER, G. W. Wavelength selection for synthetic image generation. *Computer Vision, Graphics, and Image Processing 41* (1988), 57–79.

[20] NAKAMAE, E., KANEDA, K., OKAMOTO, T., AND NISHITA, T. A lighting model aiming at drive simulators. *Computer Graphics 24*, 3 (August 1990), 395–404. ACM Siggraph '90 Conference Proceedings.

[21] ORDY, J. M., BRIZZEE, K. R., AND JOHNSON, H. A. Cellular alterations in visual pathways and the limbic system: Implications for vision and short-term memory. In *Aging and Human Visual Function*, R. Sekular, D. Kline, and K. Dismukes, Eds., vol. 2 of *Modern Aging Research*. Alan R. Liss, Inc., 1982, pp. 79–114.

[22] OWSLEY, C., SEKULER, R., AND SIEMSEN, D. Contrast sensitivity throughout adulthood. *Vision Research 23*, 7 (1983), 689–699.

[23] REA, M. S., Ed. *The Illumination Engineering Society Lighting Handbook*, 8th ed. Illumination Engineering Society, New York, NY, 1993.

[24] RONCI, C., AND STEFANACCI, S. An annotated bibliography on some aspected of glare. *Att. Fond. Ronci 30* (1975), 277–317.

[25] ROSS, J. E., CLARKE, D. D., AND BRON, A. J. Effect of age on contrast sensitivity function: uniocular and binocular findings. *British Journal of Opthalmology 69* (1985), 51–56.

[26] SAID, F., AND WEALE, R. The variation with age of the spectral transmissivity of the living human crystaline lens. *Gerontologia 3*, 4 (1959), 213.

[27] SCHLICK, C. Quantization techniques for visualization of high dynamic range imagess. In *Proceedings of the Fifth Eurographics Workshop on Rendering* (June 1994), pp. 7–18.

[28] SEKULER, R., AND BLAKE, R. *Perception*, second ed. McGraw-Hill, New York, 1990.

[29] SIMPSON, G. Ocular halos and coronas. *British Journal of Opthalmology 37* (1953), 450–486.

[30] SMITH, G., VINGRYS, A. J., MADDOCKS, J. D., AND HELY, C. P. Color recognition and discrimination under full-moon light. *Applied Optics 33*, 21 (1994), 4741–4748.

[31] STILES, W. The effect of glare on the brightness difference threshold. *Proceedings of the Royal Society of London 104* (1929), 322–351.

[32] TUMBLIN, J., AND RUSHMEIER, H. Tone reproduction for realistic computer generated images. *IEEE Computer Graphics & Applications 13*, 7 (1993).

[33] VOS, J. Disability glare- a state of the art report. *C.I.E. Journal 3*, 2 (1984), 39–53.

[34] WARD, G. A contrast-based scalefactor for luminance display. In *Graphics Gems IV*, P. Heckbert, Ed. Academic Press, Boston, 1994, pp. 415–421.

[35] WARD, G. J. The radiance lighting simulation and rendering system. *Computer Graphics 28*, 2 (July 1994), 459–472. ACM Siggraph '94 Conference Proceedings.

[36] WYSZECKI, G., AND STILES, W. *Color Science: Concepts and Methods, Quantitative Data and Formulae*, second ed. Wiley, New York, N.Y., 1992.

Applications of Irradiance Tensors to the Simulation of Non-Lambertian Phenomena

James Arvo

Program of Computer Graphics*
Cornell University

Abstract

We present new techniques for computing illumination from non-diffuse luminaires and scattering from non-diffuse surfaces. The methods are based on new closed-form expressions derived using a generalization of irradiance known as *irradiance tensors*. The elements of these tensors are *angular moments*, weighted integrals of the radiation field that are useful in simulating a variety of non-diffuse phenomena. Applications include the computation of irradiance due to directionally-varying area light sources, reflections from glossy surfaces, and transmission through glossy surfaces. The principles apply to any emission, reflection, or transmission distribution expressed as a polynomial over the unit sphere. We derive expressions for a simple but versatile subclass of these functions, called *axial moments*, and present complete algorithms their exact evaluation in polyhedral environments. The algorithms are demonstrated by simulating Phong-like emission and scattering effects.

CR Categories and Subject Descriptors: I.3.7 [Computer Graphics]: Three-Dimensional Graphics and Realism.

Additional Key Words and Phrases: angular moment, axial moment, directional luminaire, double-axis moment, glossy reflection, glossy transmission, irradiance tensor.

1 Introduction

Rendering algorithms are frequently quite limited in the surface reflectance functions and luminaires they can accommodate, particularly when they are based on purely deterministic methods. To a large extent, this limitation stems from the difficulty of computing multi-dimensional integrals associated with non-diffuse phenomena, such as reflections from surfaces with directional scattering. While numerous closed-form expressions exist for computing the radiative exchange among uniform Lambertian (diffuse) surfaces with simple geometries [7, 12, 17], these expressions rarely apply in more general settings. Currently, the only approaches capable of simulating non-diffuse phenomena are those based on Monte Carlo [6, 20, 25, 26], hierarchical subdivision [3], or numerical quadrature [5, 18].

*580 Engineering and Theory Center Building, Ithaca, New York 14853, http://www.graphics.cornell.edu

Permission to make digital/hard copy of part or all of this work for personal or classroom use is granted without fee provided that copies are not made or distributed for profit or commercial advantage, the copyright notice, the title of the publication and its date appear, and notice is given that copying is by permission of ACM, Inc. To copy otherwise, to republish, to post on servers, or to redistribute to lists, requires prior specific permission and/or a fee.

Currently, few methods exist for computing semi-coherent reflections of a scene in a nearly-specular or *glossy* surface. The earliest examples of glossy reflection in computer graphics are due to Amanatides [1] and Cook [6]. Amanatides used cone tracing to simulate glossy reflections for simple scene geometries and reflectance functions. Cook introduced a general Monte Carlo method for simulating such effects that was later extended to path tracing by Kajiya [8] and applied to realistic surfaces by Ward [25]. Wallace et al. [24] approximated Phong-like directional scattering by rendering through a narrow viewing aperture using a z-buffer. Aupperle et al. [3] devised the first general deterministic method using three-point transfers coupled with view-dependent hierarchical subdivision.

This paper offers the first analytic method for computing direct lighting effects involving area light sources and a wide range of surfaces from diffuse to highly directional: such effects include illumination from directional luminaires and view-dependent glossy reflection and transmission. The method greatly extends the repertoire of effects that can be computed in closed form.

The present work begins with a tensor representation of irradiance comprised of *angular moments*, or weighted integrals of radiance with respect to direction [14]. Methods based on angular moments have a long history in the field of radiative transfer [9, 19], but are applied here in a fundamentally different way. In classical radiative transfer problems only low-order moments are relevant since detailed surface reflections can generally be ignored [19]. For image synthesis, where surface reflection is paramount, high-order moments can be used to capture the appearance of a non-diffuse surface or the distribution of a directional luminaire.

The idea of using high-order angular moments is extremely general and applies to all emission and reflectance functions that are polynomials over the sphere. The specific algorithms that we present, however, address only a limited class of polynomial functions; essentially the Phong distributions [13]. This class of polynomials has a representation that is simply related to irradiance tensors, and this leads to convenient closed-form expressions in polyhedral environments. The expressions are not much more difficult to evaluate than Lamabert's formula for irradiance [12, 17]; however, this does entail finding the visible contours of luminaires when occlusions are present.

The remainder of the paper is organized as follows. Section 2 introduces basic definitions and motivates the concept of irradiance tensors, which is further developed in section 3. These tensors apply to a much larger class of functions than those explored in this paper. Using irradiance tensors, we derive expressions for *axial moments* in section 4; these are a simple but convenient form of moment with immediate applications. In section 5 we focus on polygonal luminaires and derive several closed-form expressions which are then applied to three related non-diffuse simulations in section 6.

2 Radiometric Concepts

In this section we introduce the fundamental radiometric concepts used in the following sections as well as several concepts that motivate the notion of irradiance tensors.

Let $f(\mathbf{r}, \mathbf{u})$ denote a monochromatic radiance function [watts/m²sr] defined at all points $\mathbf{r} \in \mathbb{R}^3$ and directions $\mathbf{u} \in \mathcal{S}^2$, where $\mathcal{S}^2$ is the set of all unit vectors in $\mathbb{R}^3$. The function f completely specifies the radiation field at large scales for a single wavelength. For fixed $\mathbf{r} \in \mathbb{R}^3$, the function $f(\mathbf{r}, \cdot)$ is known as the *directional distribution function*[1] [15, p. 29]. The goals of this paper are simply to obtain a useful characterization of $f(\mathbf{r}, \cdot)$ and apply it to the simulation of various direct lighting effects.

Most radiometric quantities can be defined in terms of weighted integrals of radiance. We shall examine three such quantities that lead naturally to irradiance tensors. First, the *monochromatic radiation energy density* [15] at the point $\mathbf{r} \in \mathbb{R}^3$ is defined by

$$u(\mathbf{r}) \equiv \frac{1}{c} \int_{\mathcal{S}^2} f(\mathbf{r}, \mathbf{u}) \, d\sigma(\mathbf{u}), \qquad (1)$$

where c is the speed of light in the medium and σ denotes the canonical measure on the sphere [4, p. 276]; that is, $\sigma(A)$ is the surface area of any measurable subset $A \subset \mathcal{S}^2$. The function $u(\mathbf{r})$ is then the radiant energy per unit volume at $\mathbf{r}$, with units [joules/m³]. Similarly, the *vector irradiance* [15] at $\mathbf{r}$ is defined by the vector integral

$$\Phi(\mathbf{r}) \equiv \int_{\mathcal{S}^2} \mathbf{u} \, f(\mathbf{r}, \mathbf{u}) \, d\sigma(\mathbf{u}), \qquad (2)$$

which has the units [watts/m²]. The scalar quantity $\Phi(\mathbf{r}) \cdot \mathbf{v}$ is the net flux of radiant energy through a surface at $\mathbf{r}$ with normal $\mathbf{v}$ [15]. Finally, the *radiation pressure tensor* [14] at $\mathbf{r}$ is a symmetric 3×3 matrix defined by

$$\Psi(\mathbf{r}) \equiv \frac{1}{c} \int_{\mathcal{S}^2} \mathbf{u} \, \mathbf{u}^{\mathrm{T}} \, f(\mathbf{r}, \mathbf{u}) \, d\sigma(\mathbf{u}), \qquad (3)$$

where $\mathbf{u}\mathbf{u}^{\mathrm{T}}$ denotes an outer product; this function has the units [joules/m³]. The bilinear form $\mathbf{w}^{\mathrm{T}}\Psi(\mathbf{r})\mathbf{v}$ is the rate at which photon momentum in the direction $\mathbf{w}$ flows across a surface at $\mathbf{r}$ with normal $\mathbf{v}$. Thus, each of the above integrals has a distinct interpretation and provides different information about the radiance distribution function at the point $\mathbf{r}$.

Note that in equations (2) and (3), the integral is in effect distributed across the elements of the vector or matrix. In equation (2) each element of the vector is a weighted integral of $f(\mathbf{r}, \cdot)$ where the weighting functions are first-order monomials on the sphere; that is, the direction cosines x, y, and z where $(x, y, z) \equiv \mathbf{u} \in \mathcal{S}^2$. Similarly, in equation (3) the weighting functions are the second-order monomials, $x^2, y^2, z^2, xy, xz,$ and yz. These scalar-valued integrals respectively correspond to first- and second-order angular moments of the radiance distribution function.

3 Irradiance Tensors

The ideas of the previous section can be extended to higher orders using the formalism of tensors. Aside from the con-

---

[1]Note that this function is distinct from a *radiant intensity distribution*, with the units of [watts/sr], which can be used to characterize a point light source.

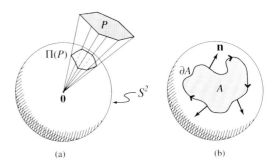

Figure 1: *(a) The surface P and its spherical projection $\Pi(P)$ onto the unit sphere $\mathcal{S}^2$. (b) For any region $A \subset \mathcal{S}^2$, the unit vector $\mathbf{n}$ is normal to the boundary ∂A and tangent to the sphere.*

stant $1/c$, all of the integrals described in section 2 are multilinear functionals of the form

$$\int_{\mathcal{S}^2} \mathbf{u} \otimes \cdots \otimes \mathbf{u} \, f(\mathbf{r}, \mathbf{u}) \, d\sigma(\mathbf{u}), \qquad (4)$$

where $\otimes$ denotes a tensor product. In this view, radiation energy density, vector irradiance, and the radiation pressure tensor are tensors of order 0, 1, and 2 respectively, with equation (4) providing the natural extension to tensors of all higher orders. Given that f is a radiance function, this family of tensors generalizes the notion of vector irradiance, with each member possessing the units of irradiance [watts/m²]. Consequently, these new expressions are called *irradiance tensors* [2]. Although high-order irradiance tensors lack direct physical interpretations [14, p. 5], they are nevertheless useful vehicles for integrating polynomial functions over the sphere, as we demonstrate in this paper.

In this work we restrict $f(\mathbf{r}, \cdot)$ to be piecewise constant or piecewise polynomial over the sphere. Angular moments of f then reduce to polynomials integrated over regions of the sphere. To concisely represent these integrals we introduce a simplified form of irradiance tensor given by

$$\mathbf{T}^n(A) \equiv \int_A \underbrace{\mathbf{u} \otimes \cdots \otimes \mathbf{u}}_{n \text{ factors}} \, d\sigma(\mathbf{u}), \qquad (5)$$

where $A \subset \mathcal{S}^2$ and $n \geq 0$ is an integer. The integrand of such a tensor contains all monomials of the form $x^i y^j z^k$ where $(x, y, z) \in \mathcal{S}^2$, and $i + j + k = n$; thus, $\mathbf{T}^n(A)$ consists of nth-order monomials integrated over A.

In what follows, the region $A \subset \mathcal{S}^2$ will represent the spherical projection of a luminaire $P \subset \mathbb{R}^3$, which we denote by $\Pi(P)$. Without loss of generality, we may assume that the sphere is centered at the origin, as shown in Figure 1a. The tensors $\mathbf{T}^n(A)$ allow us to perform several useful computations; for example, we may compute angular moments of the illumination due to uniform Lambertian luminaires, or irradiance due to directionally varying luminaires.

Irradiance tensors of all orders are defined by surface integrals, and in some cases may be reduced to one-dimensional integrals by means of the generalized Stokes' theorem [22]. The resulting boundary integrals can be evaluated analytically for certain patch geometries, such as polygons. The foregoing approach extends the classical derivation of Lambert's formula for irradiance [10, 21], yielding more complex boundary integrals in the case of higher-order tensors.

To express the fundamental formula for $\mathbf{T}^n(A)$, we require some special notation. To conveniently index tensors of all orders, we shall use the n-index $\mathrm{I} \equiv (i_1, i_2, \ldots, i_n)$, where $i_k \in \{1, 2, 3\}$ for $1 \leq k \leq n$. We then define I_k to be the kth sub-index, and I/k to be the $(n-1)$-index obtained by deleting the kth sub-index. That is,

$$\mathrm{I}/k \equiv (i_1, i_2, \ldots, i_{k-1}, i_{k+1}, \ldots, i_n).$$

Using this notation, we may concisely express the formula for irradiance tensors that will serve as our starting point. For all integers $n \geq 0$ and $A \subset \mathcal{S}^2$, the tensor $\mathbf{T}^n(A)$ satisfies the recurrence relation

$$
\begin{aligned}
(n+1)\, \mathbf{T}_{\mathrm{I}j}^n(A) \;=\; & \sum_{k=1}^{n-1} \delta(\mathrm{I}_k, j)\, \mathbf{T}_{\mathrm{I}/k}^{n-2}(A) \\
& - \int_{\partial A} (\mathbf{u} \otimes \cdots \otimes \mathbf{u})_{\mathrm{I}}\, \mathbf{n}_j\, ds,
\end{aligned}
\tag{6}
$$

where I is an $(n-1)$-index, and $\mathrm{I}j$ is the n-index formed by appending j to I. Here $\mathbf{n}$ denotes the outward normal to the boundary curve ∂A as shown in Figure 1b, ds denotes integration with respect to arclength, and $\delta(i, j)$ is the Kronecker delta, which is one if $i = j$ and zero otherwise.

Equation (6) follows from the generalized Stoke's theorem [2] and states that each tensor of the form defined in equation (5) can be reduced to a boundary integral and a term constructed from the tensor of two orders lower. The base cases $\mathbf{T}^{-1}(A) \equiv 0$ and $\mathbf{T}^0(A) \equiv \sigma(A)$ complete the recurrence relation.

It follows from equation (6) that $\mathbf{T}^n(A)$ can be computed analytically whenever the boundary integrals and base case can be. In particular, when A is the spherical projection of a k-sided polygon and $n = 1$, equation (6) yields

$$\mathbf{T}_j^1(A) \;=\; -\frac{1}{2} \int_{\partial A} \mathbf{n}_j\, ds \;=\; -\frac{1}{2} \sum_{i=1}^{k} \Theta_i\, \mathbf{n}_j^i, \tag{7}$$

where Θ_i is the length of the arc corresponding to the ith edge of the polygon, and $\mathbf{n}^i$ is its outward normal. This is a well-known formula with numerous applications in computer graphics [12] originally derived by Lambert more than two centuries ago [17]. Although equation (6) is impractical computationally for moments of high order, it succinctly expresses the relationship among all the tensors. For instance, it is apparent that all even-order tensors incorporate solid angle $\mathbf{T}^0(A)$, while the odd-order tensors do not. We now derive several useful formulas from this equation.

4 Axial Moments

From equation (6) we may obtain expressions for individual moments or sums of moments without explicitly constructing the tensors. This is of great practical importance since the size of $\mathbf{T}^n(A)$ grows exponentially with n, yet only $\mathrm{O}(n^2)$ of its elements are distinct. We first consider the special case of moments about an axis, which defines a simple class of polynomials over the sphere. Given an arbitrary subset $A \subset \mathcal{S}^2$ and a unit vector $\mathbf{w}$, we define the nth *axial moment* of A about $\mathbf{w}$ by

$$\bar{\tau}^n(A, \mathbf{w}) \equiv \int_A (\mathbf{w} \cdot \mathbf{u})^n\, d\sigma(\mathbf{u}). \tag{8}$$

As a cosine to a power, the polynomial weighting function within $\bar{\tau}^n$ is essentially a Phong distribution centered around

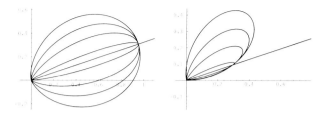

Figure 2: *Cross-sections of the weighting functions* $(\mathbf{w} \cdot \mathbf{u})^n$ *and* $(\mathbf{w} \cdot \mathbf{u})^n (\mathbf{v} \cdot \mathbf{u})$ *where* $\mathbf{v}$ *is the vertical axis; moment orders are 2, 4, 10, and 100, starting from the outer curves.*

the direction $\mathbf{w}$, as shown in Figure 2a. These functions are *steerable* in the sense that they can be re-oriented without raising their order [11]. The ease of controlling the shape and direction of the lobe makes this polynomial function useful in approximating reflectance functions, as Ward did with Gaussians [25], or an exact representation of simple Phong-like functions. To obtain a closed-form expression for $\bar{\tau}^n$, we begin by expressing the integrand of equation (8) as a composition of tensors:

$$(\mathbf{w} \cdot \mathbf{u})^n = (\mathbf{u} \otimes \cdots \otimes \mathbf{u})_{\mathrm{I}}\, (\mathbf{w} \otimes \cdots \otimes \mathbf{w})_{\mathrm{I}}. \tag{9}$$

Here we have adopted the summation convention, where summation is implicit over all repeated pairs of indices; in equation (9) this means all sub-indices of I. It follows that

$$\bar{\tau}^n(A, \mathbf{w}) = \mathbf{T}_{\mathrm{I}}^n(A)(\mathbf{w} \otimes \cdots \otimes \mathbf{w})_{\mathrm{I}}, \tag{10}$$

which associates the nth axial moment with the nth-order tensor. Using equation (6) to expand equation (10), and noting that $\delta(i, j)\mathbf{w}_i \mathbf{w}_j = \mathbf{w} \cdot \mathbf{w}$, we obtain

$$
\begin{aligned}
(n+1)\, \bar{\tau}^n \;=\; & (n-1)\, (\mathbf{w} \cdot \mathbf{w})\, \bar{\tau}^{n-2} \\
& - \int_{\partial A} (\mathbf{w} \cdot \mathbf{u})^{n-1}\, \mathbf{w} \cdot \mathbf{n}\, ds,
\end{aligned}
\tag{11}
$$

where the function arguments have been omitted for brevity. Equation (11) is a recurrence relation for $\bar{\tau}^n$ with base cases $\bar{\tau}^{-1}(A) = 0$ and $\bar{\tau}^0(A) = \sigma(A)$. When $n > 0$ the recurrence relation reduces to a single boundary integral involving a polynomial in $\mathbf{w} \cdot \mathbf{u}$. Since $\mathbf{w}$ is a unit vector, we have

$$
\begin{aligned}
(n+1)\, \bar{\tau}^n \;=\; \bar{\tau}^q - \int_{\partial A} & \big[(\mathbf{w} \cdot \mathbf{u})^{n-1} + (\mathbf{w} \cdot \mathbf{u})^{n-3} + \cdots \\
& + (\mathbf{w} \cdot \mathbf{u})^{q+1}\big]\, \mathbf{w} \cdot \mathbf{n}\, ds,
\end{aligned}
\tag{12}
$$

where $q = 0$ if n is even, and $q = -1$ if n is odd. This expression is useful as a component of more general expressions, such as double-axis moments.

4.1 Double-Axis Moments

An important generalization of equation (8) is to allow for moments with respect to multiple axes simultaneously; this will prove useful for handling radiant exchanges involving pairs of surfaces. We define the *double-axis moment* of A with respect to $\mathbf{w}$ and $\mathbf{v}$ by

$$\bar{\bar{\tau}}^{n,m}(A, \mathbf{w}, \mathbf{v}) \equiv \int_A (\mathbf{w} \cdot \mathbf{u})^n\, (\mathbf{v} \cdot \mathbf{u})^m\, d\sigma(\mathbf{u}). \tag{13}$$

A recurrence relation for $\bar{\bar{\tau}}^{n,m}$ can also be obtained from equation (6) by expressing the integrand as a tensor composition with n copies of $\mathbf{w}$ and m copies of the vector $\mathbf{v}$. We

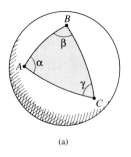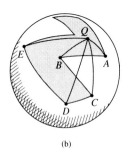

Figure 3: *(a) The solid angle of a spherical triangle is easily obtained from the internal angles. (b) Non-convex polygons can be handled by spoking into triangles from an arbitrary point Q.*

shall only consider the case where $m = 1$, which corresponds to $\mathbf{T}^{n+1}(A)(\mathbf{w} \otimes \cdots \otimes \mathbf{w} \otimes \mathbf{v})$ and yields the formula

$$(n+2)\, \bar{\bar{\tau}}^{n,1}(A, \mathbf{w}, \mathbf{v}) = n\, (\mathbf{w} \cdot \mathbf{v})\, \bar{\tau}^{n-1}(A, \mathbf{w}) \\ - \int_{\partial A} (\mathbf{w} \cdot \mathbf{u})^n\, \mathbf{v} \cdot \mathbf{n}\, ds. \qquad (14)$$

Figure 2a shows how an additional axis can change the shape of the weighting function. Note that when $\mathbf{v} = \mathbf{w}$, equation (14) reduces to the $(n+1)$-order axial moment given by equation (11). Recurrence relations for $\bar{\bar{\tau}}^{n,m}$ with $m > 1$ can be obtained in a similar manner, although the resulting boundary integrals are more difficult to evaluate.

Evaluating equations (12) and (14) in closed form is the topic of the next section. In section 6 we show how these moments apply to non-diffuse phenomena.

5   Exact Evaluation

Equations (6) and (12) reduce tensors and moments to one-dimensional integrals and (in the case of even orders) solid angle. This section describes how both of these components can be evaluated in closed form. Thus far no restrictions have been placed on the region $A \subset \mathcal{S}^2$; however, we shall now assume that A is the spherical projection of a polygon $P \subset \mathbb{R}^3$, which may be non-convex. The resulting projection is a *geodesic* or *spherical* polygon, whose edges are great arcs; that is, segments of great circles.

When P is a polygon, the computation of solid angles and boundary integrals are both greatly simplified. Because the outward normal $\mathbf{n}$ is constant along each edge of a spherical polygon, the factors of $\mathbf{w} \cdot \mathbf{n}$ and $\mathbf{v} \cdot \mathbf{n}$ can be moved outside the integrals in equations (12) and (14) respectively. A second simplification emerges in parametrizing the boundary integrals, as shown below.

5.1   Solid Angle

The surface integral defining the solid angle subtended by P does not reduced to a boundary integral; this is because the corresponding differential 2-form is not exact [22, p. 131]. Fortunately, the solid angle subtended by a polygon can be computed directly in another way. If P is a triangle in $\mathbb{R}^3$ its projection $\mathbf{\Pi}(P)$ is a spherical triangle $\triangle ABC$. Girard's formula for spherical triangles [4, p. 278] states that

$$\sigma(\triangle ABC) = \alpha + \beta + \gamma - \pi, \qquad (15)$$

where α, β, and γ are the three internal angles, as shown in Figure 3a. The internal angles are the dihedral angles

between the planes containing the edges. For instance, the angle α in Figure 3a is given by

$$\alpha = \cos^{-1} \frac{(B \times A) \cdot (A \times C)}{\| B \times A \| \, \| A \times C \|}. \qquad (16)$$

Equation (15) generalizes immediately to arbitrary convex polygons [4, p. 279]. One way to compute the solid angle subtended by an arbitrary polygon is to cover its spherical projection with n triangles, all sharing an arbitrary vertex $Q \in \mathcal{S}^2$. See Figure 3b. The solid angle is then the sum of the triangle areas signed according to orientation. In the figure, $\triangle QAB$, $\triangle QCD$, and $\triangle QDE$ are all positive, while $\triangle QBC$ is negative, according to the clock-sense of the vertices. This method does not require $\mathbf{\Pi}(P)$ to be decomposed into triangles.

5.2   Boundary Integrals

The boundary integrals in equations (12) and (14) can be approximated by numerical quadrature, or evaluated analytically in terms of $O(n)$ elementary functions per edge. We shall only describe analytic evaluation and a related approximation, both based upon a sum of integrals of the form

$$F_n(x, y) \equiv \int_x^y \cos^n \theta \, d\theta. \qquad (17)$$

These integrals may be evaluated exactly using a recurrence relation given below. To express the integral in equation (12) in terms of $F_n(x, y)$ when A is a spherical polygon, we parametrize the great arc corresponding to each edge by

$$\mathbf{u}(\theta) = \mathbf{s} \cos \theta + \mathbf{t} \sin \theta,$$

where $\mathbf{s}$ and $\mathbf{t}$ are orthonormal vectors in the plane of the edge, with $\mathbf{s}$ directed toward the first vertex. To simplify the line integral over a great arc $\zeta \subset \mathcal{S}^2$, let ℓ be the length of the arc, and let $a \equiv \mathbf{w} \cdot \mathbf{s}$, $b \equiv \mathbf{w} \cdot \mathbf{t}$, and $c \equiv \sqrt{a^2 + b^2}$. Then by the above parametrization, we have

$$\int_\zeta (\mathbf{w} \cdot \mathbf{u})^n ds = \int_0^\ell [a \cos \theta + b \sin \theta]^n \, d\theta \\ = c^n \int_0^\ell \cos^n(\theta - \phi) \, d\theta, \\ = c^n F_n(-\phi, \ell - \phi), \qquad (18)$$

where ϕ is the angle satisfying $\cos \phi = a/c$ and $\sin \phi = b/c$. To evaluate equation (18), we integrate equation (17) by parts to obtain the recurrence relation

$$F_n(x, y) = \frac{1}{n} \Big[\cos^{n-1} y \sin y - \cos^{n-1} x \sin x \\ + (n-1) F_{n-2}(x, y) \Big], \qquad (19)$$

where $F_0(x, y) = y - x$ and $F_1(x, y) = \sin y - \sin x$. By means of this recurrence relation the function $F_n(x, y)$ may be evaluated in $\lfloor (n+1)/2 \rfloor$ steps. The complete integral in equation (12) is a weighted sum of these integrals for a sequence of different exponents, which are all even or all odd. The corresponding sequence of integrals can be computed incrementally, as demonstrated in the following section.

5.3 Algorithms for Efficient Evaluation

We now show that nth-order axial moments of k-sided polygons may be computed exactly (in the absence of roundoff error) in $O(nk)$ time. The algorithm evaluates equation (12) in $O(n)$ time for each of the k edges, using recurrence relation (19). The steps are broken into three procedures: *CosSumIntegral*, *LineIntegral*, and *BoundaryIntegral*. The first of these is the key to efficient evaluation; procedure *CosSumIntegral* computes the sum

$$c^k F_k(x,y) + c^{k+2} F_{k+2}(x,y) + \cdots + c^n F_n(x,y), \qquad (20)$$

where $k = m$ if $m + n$ is even, and $k = m + 1$ otherwise, for a given integer $m \geq 0$. The parameter m is included to accommodate both single- and double-axis moments. Because recurrence relation (19) generates integrals of cosine with increasing powers, all integrals in expression (20) may be generated as easily as the last term $c^n F_n(x,y)$. This strategy is embodied in the following procedure.

CosSumIntegral(**real** x, y, c; **int** m, n)
  $i \leftarrow$ **if even**(n) **then** 0 **else** 1;
  $F \leftarrow$ **if even**(n) **then** $y - x$ **else** $\sin y - \sin x$;
  $S \leftarrow 0$;
  while $i \leq n$ **do**
    if $i \geq m$ **then** $S \leftarrow S + c^i * F$;
    $T \leftarrow \cos^{i+1} y * \sin y - \cos^{i+1} x * \sin x$;
    $F \leftarrow [T + (i+1) * F] / (i+2)$;
    $i \leftarrow i + 2$;
  endwhile
  return S;
end

The next procedure computes the line integral corresponding to a polygon edge; the steps correspond to equation (18), summed over a sequence of exponents from m to n.

LineIntegral(**vec** $\mathbf{A}, \mathbf{B}, \mathbf{w}$; **int** m, n)
  if $(n < 0)$ **or** $(\mathbf{w} \perp \mathbf{A}$ **and** $\mathbf{w} \perp \mathbf{B})$ **then return** 0;
  $\mathbf{s} \leftarrow$ *Normalize* $[\, \mathbf{A} \,]$;
  $\mathbf{t} \leftarrow$ *Normalize* $[\, (\mathbf{I} - \mathbf{ss}^\mathsf{T}) \mathbf{B} \,]$;
  $a \leftarrow \mathbf{w} \cdot \mathbf{s}$;
  $b \leftarrow \mathbf{w} \cdot \mathbf{t}$;
  $c \leftarrow \sqrt{a^2 + b^2}$;
  $\ell \leftarrow$ angle between $\mathbf{A}$ and $\mathbf{B}$;
  $\phi \leftarrow$ sign$(\, b \,) * \cos^{-1}(a/c)$;
  return *CosSumIntegral*$(-\phi, \ell - \phi, c, m, n)$;
end

The next procedure, *BoundaryIntegral*, computes the complete boundary integral for a given k-sided polygon P by forming a weighted sum of k line integrals. The weight associated with each edge is the cosine of the angle between its outward normal and the second vector $\mathbf{v}$, which may coincide with $\mathbf{w}$.

BoundaryIntegral(**pgon** P; **vec** $\mathbf{w}, \mathbf{v}$; **int** m, n)
  $b \leftarrow 0$;
  for each edge $\mathbf{AB}$ **in** P **do**
    $\mathbf{n} \leftarrow$ *Normalize* $[\, \mathbf{A} \times \mathbf{B} \,]$;
    $b \leftarrow b + (\mathbf{n} \cdot \mathbf{v}) *$ *LineIntegral*$(\mathbf{A}, \mathbf{B}, \mathbf{w}, m, n)$;
  endfor
  return b;
end

With these three basic procedures we may now define the procedure *AxialMoment*, which computes the nth axial moment of a polygon P with respect to the axis $\mathbf{w}$. Even-order moments also require the computation of a "signed" solid angle, which is handled by this procedure. Equation (12) then corresponds to the following function.

AxialMoment(**pgon** P; **vec** $\mathbf{w}$; **int** n)
  $a \leftarrow -$*BoundaryIntegral*$(P, \mathbf{w}, \mathbf{w}, 0, n - 1)$;
  if even(n) **then** $a \leftarrow a +$ *SolidAngle*(P);
  return $a / (n + 1)$;
end

The function *SolidAngle* returns the solid angle subtended by the polygon P using the method described in section 5.1. Because the sign of the boundary integral depends on the orientation of the polygon, the solid angle must be similarly signed. Thus, *SolidAngle* is positive if ∂P is oriented counter-clockwise as seen from the origin, and negative otherwise.

Finally, the procedure *DoubleAxisMoment* computes the nth-order moment of a polygon P with respect to the $\mathbf{w}$ axis and the 1st-order moment with respect to the $\mathbf{v}$ axis. Equation (14) then corresponds to the procedure

DoubleAxisMoment(**pgon** P; **vec** $\mathbf{w}, \mathbf{v}$; **int** n)
  if $n = 0$ **then return** *AxialMoment*$(P, \mathbf{v}, n)$;
  $a \leftarrow$ *AxialMoment*$(P, \mathbf{w}, n - 1)$;
  $b \leftarrow$ *BoundaryIntegral*$(P, \mathbf{w}, \mathbf{v}, n, n)$;
  return $(n * a * \mathbf{w} \cdot \mathbf{v} - b) / (n + 2)$;
end

If we assume that trigonometric and other elementary functions are evaluated in constant time, then it is easy to see that procedures *AxialMoment* and *DoubleAxisMoment* both require $O(nk)$ time.

5.4 Optimizations

For clarity, the pseudo-code in the previous section does not depict a number of simple optimizations. For instance, the powers in procedure *CosSumIntegral* may be computed incrementally. Also, in computing double-axis moments, a great deal of redundant computation may be avoided by allowing procedure *CosSumIntegral* to return one additional term in the series. These optimizations do not change the time complexity of the algorithms, but can significantly reduce the constant.

Another means of speeding the computation is to settle for an approximation. Note that the terms in equation (12) decrease in magnitude monotonically because $|F_{k+2}| < |F_k|$ for all k, and $0 \leq c \leq 1$. When the terms approach zero rapidly we may obtain an accurate approximation with little work. Moreover, by bounding the tail of the series it is possible to guarantee any given tolerance. For example, to compute a double-axis moment to a relative accuracy of ϵ, the loop in *CosSumIntegral* may be terminated immediately upon updating S if the condition

$$\left| \frac{(\mathbf{v} \cdot \mathbf{n}) c^n F}{(\mathbf{u} \cdot \mathbf{v})(\mathbf{u} \cdot \mathbf{n})} \right| + \left| \frac{c^k F}{1 - c^2} \right| \leq \epsilon \, |S| \qquad (21)$$

is met. In this case the tail of the series and the final integral in equation (14) may be dropped. Early termination of the loop is particularly useful with high orders; however, the test is costly and therefore should not be performed at every iteration of the loop.

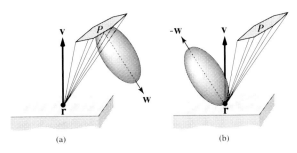

Figure 4: *(a) Computing the irradiance at the point* **r** *due to a directionally-varying area light source P is equivalent to (b) computing a double-axis moment of a uniform Lambertian source of the same shape.*

6 Applications

For ideal diffuse surfaces irradiance is sufficient to compute reflected radiance. The situation is dramatically different for non-diffuse surfaces, however. For surfaces that are neither ideal diffuse nor ideal specular, high-order moments can be used to quantify additional features of the incident illumination, in analogy with a power series expansion. For polygonal environments with emission and reflection distributions defined in terms of moments, the procedures given in the previous section may be used to simulate directional luminaires, glossy reflections, and glossy transmissions.

6.1 Directional Luminaires

Methods for simulating the illumination due to diffuse area sources [12] and directional point sources [23] are well known; however, directional area sources are problematic for deterministic algorithms. In this section we shall see how a class of directional luminaires can be handled using double-axis moments.

Let P be a polygonal luminaire whose emission distribution is spatially uniform but varies directionally according to a Phong distribution; that is, as a cosine to a power [13]. For instance, the direction of maximum radiance may be normal to the plane of the luminaire, falling off rapidly in other directions, as shown by the distribution in Figure 4a. The irradiance at the point $\mathbf{r}$ is then given by

$$\int_{\mathbf{\Pi}(P')} |\mathbf{u} \cdot \mathbf{w}|^n \cos \theta \, d\sigma(\mathbf{u}), \qquad (22)$$

where P' is the visible portion of the luminaire P translated by $-\mathbf{r}$, and θ is the angle of incidence of $\mathbf{u}$; thus $\cos \theta = \mathbf{v} \cdot \mathbf{u}$, where $\mathbf{v}$ is the surface normal. Observe that this computation is equivalent to a double-axis moment of a Lambertian source P, where the nth moment is taken with respect to $-\mathbf{w}$ and the factor of $\cos \theta$ is accounted for by the second axis $\mathbf{v}$. See Figure 4b. Therefore, procedure *DoubleAxisMoment* can be used to compute the irradiance due to directional luminaires of this type in closed form.

Figure 5 shows a simple scene illuminated by an area source with three different directional distributions. Note that the areas directly beneath the luminaire get brighter with higher orders, while the surrounding areas get darker. Polygonal occlusions are handled by clipping the luminaire against all blockers and computing the contribution from each remaining portion, precisely as Nishita and Nakamae [12] handled Lambertian sources.

Figure 5: *(Left column) Irradiance from a directional luminaire computed analytically at each pixel; moment orders are 1, 10, and 20. (Right column) Analytic glossy reflection of a window design by Elsa Schmid [16]; moment orders are 10, 45, and 400.*

6.2 Glossy Reflection

A similar strategy can be used to compute glossy reflections of polygonal Lambertian luminaires. Let $\mathbf{r}$ be a point on a reflective surface. Then the reflected radiance at $\mathbf{r}$ in the direction $\mathbf{u}$ due to luminaire P is given by

$$f(\mathbf{r}, \mathbf{u}) = \int_{\mathbf{\Pi}(P)} \rho(\mathbf{u}' \to \mathbf{u}) \, f(\mathbf{r}, \mathbf{u}') \cos \theta \, d\sigma(\mathbf{u}'), \qquad (23)$$

where ρ is the bidirectional reflectance distribution function (BRDF) and θ is the angle of incidence of $\mathbf{u}'$. Now consider a simple BRDF defined in terms a Phong exponent. Let

$$\rho(\mathbf{u}' \to \mathbf{u}) \equiv c \left[\mathbf{u}^{\mathrm{T}} \left(\mathbf{I} - 2\mathbf{v}\mathbf{v}^{\mathrm{T}} \right) \mathbf{u}' \right]^n, \qquad (24)$$

where c is a constant and $\mathbf{v}$ is the surface normal. Note that the Householder matrix $\mathbf{I} - 2\mathbf{v}\mathbf{v}^{\mathrm{T}}$ performs a reflection through the tangent plane at $\mathbf{r}$. This BRDF defines a cosine lobe about an axis in the direction of mirror reflection, as shown in Figure 6a. Because ρ obeys the reciprocity relation $\rho(\mathbf{u}' \to \mathbf{u}) = \rho(\mathbf{u} \to \mathbf{u}')$, the radiance reflected in the direction $-\mathbf{u}'$ is found by integrating over the distribution shown in the figure. To obey energy conservation the constant c must be bounded by $2\pi/(n+2)$.

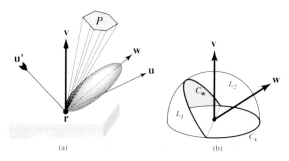

Figure 6: *(a) A simple BRDF defined by an axial moment around the mirror reflection $\mathbf{w}$ of $\mathbf{u}'$. By reciprocity, the radiance in the direction $-\mathbf{u}'$ due to P reduces to a double-axis moment of P with respect to $\mathbf{w}$ and $\mathbf{v}$. (b) The boundaries used for normalization.*

For a uniform Lambertian luminaire P, the function $f(\mathbf{r}, \cdot)$ is constant. In this case the integral in equation (23) reduces to a double-axis moment of P with respect to the vector

$$\mathbf{w} \equiv \left(\mathbf{I} - 2\mathbf{v}\mathbf{v}^{\mathsf{T}}\right)\mathbf{u}',$$

and the surface normal $\mathbf{v}$. Procedure *DoubleAxisMoment* may therefore be used in this context as well, to compute the glossy reflection of a diffuse luminaire. The technique is demonstrated in Figure 5 using a variety of moment orders to simulate surfaces with varying finishes.

More complex BRDFs may be formed by superposing lobes of different orders and/or different axes. Other effects such as anisotropic reflection and specular reflection near grazing can be simulated by allowing c and n to vary with the incident direction $\mathbf{u}'$; doing so does not alter the moment computations, however reciprocity is generally violated.

Figure 7: *A simple test scene with a glossy surface of order 300. The enlargemetns of the reflection were computed analytically (middle) and by Monte Carlo with 49 samples per pixel (right).*

In Figure 7 an exact solution is compared with a Monte Carlo estimate based on 49 samples per pixel; the samples were distributed according to the BRDF and stratified to reduce variance. Both methods operated directly on non-convex polygons in the scene. The run times were comparable: 6.5 seconds and 14.7 seconds respectively on an HP-755 workstation (100 MIPS). The analytic method eliminates the grainyness due to statistical noise and, in this instance, is also faster. The disparity in both time and quality is greater for lower moment orders and also for scenes with higher contrast.

6.3 Glossy Transmission

As a final example, we note that glossy transmission can be handled in much the same way as glossy reflection; the difference is in the choice of the axes $\mathbf{w}$ and $\mathbf{v}$, which must now exit from the far side of the transparent material. Figure 8 shows two images depicting "frosted glass", with different finishes

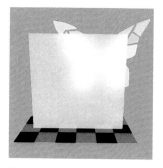 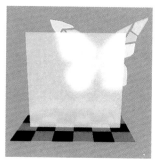

Figure 8: *A frosted glass simulation demonstrating glossy transmission. From left to right the moment orders are 10 and 65.*

corresponding to moments of different orders. This effect was first demonstrated by Wallace et al. [24] using a form of stochastic sampling; in Figure 8 a similar effect has been computed analytically using procedure *DoubleAxisMoment*.

6.4 Normalization

In applying the above methods, it is frequently useful to normalize the resulting distributions while ignoring negative lobes. We now show how this can be done for distributions defined in terms of double-axis moments.

The two planes orthogonal to the axes of a double-axis moment partition the sphere into four spherical *lunes* (also known as spherical *digons*); let L_1 and L_2 be the two lunes in the positive half-space defined by $\mathbf{v}$, as shown in Figure 6b. To normalize a BRDF, for example, we compute

$$N(\mathbf{w}, \mathbf{v}, n) \equiv \int_{L_2} (\mathbf{w} \cdot \mathbf{u})^n (\mathbf{v} \cdot \mathbf{u}) \, d\sigma(\mathbf{u}), \qquad (25)$$

where $\mathbf{v}$ is the surface normal; thus, the integrand of equation (25) is positive for all exponents n on the lune L_2. Typically, luminaires must be clipped by the planes defining this lune before computing the moments.

Integral (25) can be evaluated analytically using equation (14), which results in two boundary integrals corresponding to the arcs $C_\mathbf{w}$ and $C_\mathbf{v}$. The special nature of the boundaries greatly simplifies the computation. For instance, $\mathbf{w} \cdot \mathbf{u}$ is zero on $C_\mathbf{w}$ while $\mathbf{v} \cdot \mathbf{n}$ is one on $C_\mathbf{v}$. Incorporating these facts, and accounting for the minor differences due to parity, we obtain a very simple means of evaluating integral (25) for arbitrary unit vectors $\mathbf{w}$ and $\mathbf{v}$, and any integer $n \geq 0$. The optimized code, which runs in $O(n)$ time, is shown below.

```
N( vec w, v; int n )
    S ← 0;
    d ← w · v;
    c ← √(1 − d²);
    t ← if even(n) then π/2 else c;
    A ← if even(n) then π/2 else π − cos⁻¹ d;
    i ← if even(n) then 0 else 1;
    while i ≤ n − 2 do
        S ← S + T;
        T ← T * c² * (i + 1) / (i + 2);
        i ← i + 2;
    endwhile
    return 2 * (T + d * A + d² * S) / (n + 2);
end
```

7 Conclusions

We have presented a number of new closed-form expressions for computing the illumination from luminaires with directional distributions as well as reflections from and transmissions through surfaces with a wide range of non-diffuse finishes. The expressions can be evaluated exactly in $O(nk)$ time for arbitrary non-convex polygons, where n is related to the directionality of the luminaire or glossiness of the surface, and k is the number of edges in the polygon.

To derive the new expressions we examined several well-known physical quantities as well as a tensor generalization of irradiance. Irradiance tensors satisfy a recurrence relation that subsumes Lambert's formula for irradiance and leads to expressions for *axial moments* and *double-axis moments*, which are quantities with direct applications in simulating non-diffuse phenomena. The resulting formulas give rise to easily implemented algorithms.

8 Future Work

An important extension of this work is to accommodate more realistic emission and reflectance distributions by expanding the class of polynomials over the sphere; these may be constructed by superposing cosine lobes, by introducing additional axes, or by forming linear combinations from some appropriate set of polynomial basis functions.

Useful extensions of equation (12) include non-integer orders and non-planar luminaires. Since equation (6) places no restriction on the boundaries, surfaces such as spheres also admit closed-form solutions; perhaps more general surfaces do as well. Equation (6) can be extended to handle luminaires with spatially varying distributions, although the resulting expressions involve special functions such as dilogarithms or Clausen integrals [2]. These expressions may prove useful in collocation-based methods for global illumination.

Axial moments of with three or more axes and arbitrary orders are a more immediate extension of the present work. With this type of moment it is possible to combine the effects demonstrated here; for example, glossy reflections of directional luminaires. Another application would be the simulation of non-diffuse surfaces illuminated by skylight using the polynomial approximation of a skylight distribution proposed by Nimroff et al. [11]. It can be shown that all moments of this form admit closed-form expressions, however efficient algorithms for their evaluation do not yet exist.

Acknowledgments

The author wishes to thank Peter Shirley for many valuable discussions, Albert Dicruttalo and Ben Trumbore for their assistance in modeling the stained glass window, and the anonymous reviewers for helpful comments. This research was supported by the NSF/ARPA Science and Technology Center for Computer Graphics and Scientific Visualization (ASC-8920219) and performed on workstations generously provided by the Hewlett-Packard Corporation.

References

[1] AMANATIDES, J. Ray tracing with cones. *Computer Graphics 18*, 3 (July 1984), 129–135.

[2] ARVO, J. *Analytic Methods for Simulated Light Transport*. PhD thesis, Yale University, 1995.

[3] AUPPERLE, L., AND HANRAHAN, P. A hierarchical illumination algorithm for surfaces with glossy reflection. In *Computer Graphics* Proceedings (1993), Annual Conference Series, ACM SIGGRAPH, pp. 155–162.

[4] BERGER, M. *Geometry, Volume II*. Springer-Verlag, New York, 1987. Translated by M. Cole and S. Levy.

[5] CHRISTENSEN, P. H., STOLLNITZ, E. J., SALESIN, D. H., AND DEROSE, T. D. Wavelet radiance. In *Proceedings of the Fifth Eurographics Workshop on Rendering*, Darmstadt, Germany (1994), pp. 287–302.

[6] COOK, R. L. Distributed ray tracing. *Computer Graphics 18*, 3 (July 1984), 137–145.

[7] HOWELL, J. R. *A Catalog of Radiation Configuration Factors*. McGraw-Hill, New York, 1982.

[8] KAJIYA, J. T. The rendering equation. *Computer Graphics 20*, 4 (August 1986), 143–150.

[9] KROOK, M. On the solution of equations of transfer, I. *Astrophysical Journal 122*, 3 (November 1955), 488–497.

[10] MOON, P. *The Scientific Basis of Illuminating Engineering*. McGraw-Hill, New York, 1936.

[11] NIMROFF, J. S., SIMONCELLI, E., AND DORSEY, J. Efficient re-rendering of naturally illuminated environments. In *Proceedings of the Fifth Eurographics Workshop on Rendering*, Darmstadt, Germany (1994), pp. 359–373.

[12] NISHITA, T., AND NAKAMAE, E. Continuous tone representation of 3-D objects taking account of shadows and interreflection. *Computer Graphics 19*, 3 (July 1985), 23–30.

[13] PHONG, B. T. Illumination for computer generated pictures. *Communications of the ACM 18*, 6 (June 1975), 311–317.

[14] POMRANING, G. C. *The Equations of Radiation Hydrodynamics*. Pergamon Press, New York, 1973.

[15] PREISENDORFER, R. W. *Radiative Transfer on Discrete Spaces*. Pergamon Press, New York, 1965.

[16] SCHMID, E. *Beholding as in a Glass*. Herder and Herder, New York, 1969.

[17] SCHRÖDER, P., AND HANRAHAN, P. On the form factor between two polygons. In *Computer Graphics* Proceedings (1993), Annual Conference Series, ACM SIGGRAPH, pp. 163–164.

[18] SCHRÖDER, P., AND HANRAHAN, P. Wavelet methods for radiance computations. In *Proceedings of the Fifth Eurographics Workshop on Rendering*, Darmstadt, Germany (1994), pp. 303–311.

[19] SHERMAN, M. P. Moment methods in radiative transfer problems. *Journal of Quantitative Spectroscopy and Radiative Transfer 7*, 89–109 (1967).

[20] SHIRLEY, P., AND WANG, C. Distribution ray tracing: Theory and practice. In *Proceedings of the Third Eurographics Workshop on Rendering*, Bristol, United Kingdom (1992), pp. 33–43.

[21] SPARROW, E. M. A new and simpler formulation for radiative angle factors. *ASME Journal of Heat Transfer 85*, 2 (May 1963), 81–88.

[22] SPIVAK, M. *Calculus on Manifolds*. Benjamin/Cummings, Reading, Massachusetts, 1965.

[23] VERBECK, C. P., AND GREENBERG, D. P. A comprehensive light-source description for computer graphics. *IEEE Computer Graphics and Applications 4*, 7 (July 1984), 66–75.

[24] WALLACE, J., COHEN, M. F., AND GREENBERG, D. P. A two-pass solution to the rendering equation: A synthesis of ray tracing and radiosity methods. *Computer Graphics 21*, 3 (July 1987), 311–320.

[25] WARD, G. J. Measuring and modeling anisotropic reflection. *Computer Graphics 26*, 2 (July 1992), 265–272.

[26] WARD, G. J. The RADIANCE lighting simulation and rendering system. In *Computer Graphics* Proceedings (1994), Annual Conference Series, ACM SIGGRAPH, pp. 459–472.

Specializing Shaders

Brian Guenter, Todd B. Knoblock, Erik Ruf *

Microsoft Research

Abstract

We have developed a system for interactive manipulation of shading parameters for three dimensional rendering. The system takes as input user-defined shaders, written in a subset of C, which are then *specialized* for interactive use. Since users typically experiment with different values of a single shader parameter while leaving the others constant, we can benefit by automatically generating a specialized shader that performs only those computations depending on the parameter being varied; all other values needed by the shader can be precomputed and cached. The specialized shaders are as much as 95 times faster than the original user defined shader. This dramatic improvement in speed makes it possible to interactively view parameter changes for relatively complex shading models, such as procedural solid texturing.

1. Introduction

During the process of interactively producing a computer-rendered image, a user will typically experiment with various image parameters, such as the positions of objects and light sources, the optical characteristics of surfaces, and surface textures. We would like to display the results of such parameter changes as rapidly as possible. Some of these changes, such as moving an object, are likely to require significant recomputation, while others, such as changing the color of one object, should not.

This paper describes a mechanism for rapidly reacting to changes to shading parameters that control the *local* shading of objects in the scene. The local shading of an object is dependent only on object surface properties, such as the surface normal and surface position, and the geometric relationship of those properties with the illumination sources and the viewpoint. Global illumination effects, such as specular and diffuse interreflectance among objects, and shadows, are not part of the local shading model.

Consider the simple Phong-like shader in Figure 1. If the user changes control parameter ks, only the multiplication ks*specular_component and the enclosing addition and vector multiplication operations need be reperformed; all other computations are guaranteed to return the same values as before. If, on the other hand, the parameter specular is changed, we may either have to recompute specular_component (and all expressions referring to it), or nothing at all, depending on the value of n_dot_h for that particular pixel. In either case,

---

*Authors' address: Microsoft Research, One Microsoft Way, Redmond, WA 98052. Email: {briangu, toddk, erikruf}@microsoft.com.

Permission to make digital/hard copy of part or all of this work for personal or classroom use is granted without fee provided that copies are not made or distributed for profit or commercial advantage, the copyright notice, the title of the publication and its date appear, and notice is given that copying is by permission of ACM, Inc. To copy otherwise, to republish, to post on servers, or to redistribute to lists, requires prior specific permission and/or a fee.

© 1995 ACM-0-89791-701-4/95/008 $3.50

changing a parameter value invalidates only a small portion of the work already performed.

We take advantage of this observation as follows. Given an arbitrary user shading routine written in a subset of C and an indication of which parameter is to be altered, we perform an analysis to determine which of the shader's computations are invariant across changing values of the distinguished parameter. We then automatically generate

1. code to perform the non-varying computations and save an appropriate subset of the results into a per-pixel cache area, and

2. code to efficiently perform shading given the new parameter value and the cached information.

After executing (1) once, we need only execute the more efficient code in (2) each time the user alters the parameter. When the user selects a different parameter, we simply install new versions of (1) and (2). Figures 2 and 3 show the code resulting from the specialization of Phong on the parameter specular.

The remainder of this paper is divided into five sections. Section 2 outlines the general architecture of our system, while Section 3 describes the specialization process in more detail. In Section 4, we analyze the costs and benefits of our approach on several shaders. We conclude, in Sections 5 and 6, with descriptions of related and future work.

2. System Architecture

Our system consists of three main components: the geometric renderer, the specializer, and the user interface driver loop.

2.1 Geometric Renderer

We render geometric image information offline before the interactive manipulation stage. Each pixel of the geometric image contains an object identifier associated with the object visible at that pixel, and the depth and surface normal of the point on the object surface which is at the center of the pixel. Our prototype uses a modified version of the Vivid ray tracer [17] to compute this information.

During the interactive stage, the user loads a precomputed geometric image and then adjusts shading parameters on objects in the scene. Because the geometric image is rendered prior to the interactive stage, some image properties cannot be varied interactively. For example, the eyepoint is fixed, as are the position and orientation of all the objects in the scene. However, many scene characteristics, such as the position of lights, and the color and reflectance characteristics of objects, can be varied interactively.

```
void Phong(int i, int j, Vec eye_position, Vec surface_normal, Flt depth,
           Matrix view_inverse, Matrix model_inverse, Matrix shade_inverse,
           PImageStruct dib,
           /* the following are the control parameters for this shader */
           double red, double green, double blue, double specular,
           double ks, double kd, double ambient, double lx, double ly, double lz)
{
        Vec light = {lx, ly, lz};
        Vec world_position, light_vector, h_vector, eye_vector;
        double specular_component, diffuse_component, n_dot_h;
        Vec rgb = {red, green, blue};

        world_position = trans_vector(view_inverse, vec(i, j, depth));
        eye_vector = VecNormalize(VecSub(eye_position, world_position));
        light_vector = VecNormalize(VecSub(light, world_position));
        h_vector = VecNormalize(VecAdd(light_vector, eye_vector));
        n_dot_h = VecDot(surface_normal, h_vector);

        if (n_dot_h > 0)
                specular_component = pow(n_dot_h, specular);
        else
                specular_component = 0;

        diffuse_component = VecDot(surface_normal, light_vector);

        if (diffuse_component < 0)
                diffuse_component = 0;

        rgb = VecScalarMul(rgb,
                (kd*diffuse_component + ambient) + ks*specular_component);

        SetPixelColor(j, i, rgb, dib);
}
```

Figure 1: *Source for a simple Phong shader. The parts of the shader that are dependent upon the parameter specular are underlined.*

2.2 Specializer

The specializer takes a user shader function and a designation of the control parameter to be varied and produces shading code specialized for that parameter.

The user writes the shaders in a subset of C augmented with a library of useful graphics and mathematical functions. The framework is similar to that provided for writing shaders in *RenderMan* [7, 16]. The restricted subset of C excludes the following C features:

- struct, union, pointer, and array types other than limited support for primitive data types such as vectors and points,

- continue, break, and goto statements, and

- recursion in the shader functions (although subroutines may employ recursion).

In some cases (e.g., struct types and structured loop exits), these restrictions simplify the implementation; in other cases (e.g., pointers, goto), they serve to make the necessary analyses tractable.

The shader is responsible for calculating rgb values for each pixel based on image model information common to all shaders, and on shader-specific *control parameters*. Consider the sample shader, Phong, from Figure 1. The first 9 parameters of Phong, up through dib, are standard; they provide rendering data about each point and an output context. The remainder are the control parameters, and are associated with sliders in the user interface.

Given a shader and a designated parameter, the specializer produces C++ code for two new procedures: a *cache loader* that precomputes and caches intermediate values that are independent of the designated parameter, and a *cache reader* that performs shading using the cached information. Figures 2 and 3 show the generated loader and reader functions, respectively. We rely upon the compiler's optimizer to further improve the code by, e.g., eliminating dead code and hoisting loop-invariant computations.

We install a new shader into the system by calling the specializer on the shader and each of the shader's control parameters, generating a loader/reader pair for each parameter. These procedures are then compiled and dynamically linked into the system.

2.3 Driver Loop

The user interface driver loop allows the user to perform housekeeping tasks such as loading images, selecting shaders, and designating particular objects within the image for shading. It also allows the user to interactively modify the current shader's control parameters, and performs shading and image redisplay after each modification. Pseudocode for this portion of the driver is shown in Figure 4.

After the user has selected a parameter to modify, the driver executes the corresponding cache loader to precompute the shader

```
typedef struct {
  int c0;
  double c1;
  double c2;
} Cache;

world_position = trans_vector(view_inverse, vec(i, j, depth));
eye_vector = VecNormalize(VecSub(eye_position, world_position));
light_vector = VecNormalize(VecSub(light, world_position));
h_vector = VecNormalize(VecAdd(light_vector, eye_vector));
n_dot_h = VecDot(surface_normal, h_vector);
if (pcache->c0 = n_dot_h>0)
  pcache->c1 = n_dot_h;
else
  specular_component = 0;
diffuse_component = VecDot(surface_normal, light_vector);
if (diffuse_component<0)
  diffuse_component = 0;
pcache->c2 = kd*diffuse_component+ambient;
```

Figure 2: Body of the cache loader for the specialization with respect to specular.

```
if (pcache->c0)
  specular_component = pow(pcache->c1, specular);
else
  specular_component = 0;

rgb = VecScalarMul(rgb, pcache->c2+ks*specular_component);
SetPixelColor(j, i, rgb, dib);
```

Figure 3: Body of the cache reader for the specialization with respect to specular.

```
repeat until new image/object/shader
  user selects a parameter P
  for each pixel in current object
    invoke loader[P]
  repeat until new parameter P          (*)
    user supplies a value V for P
    for each pixel in current object
      invoke reader[P](V)
    redisplay all pixels in object
```

Figure 4: User interface driver loop.

values that will be needed by the cache reader. Then, each time the user supplies a value for the chosen parameter, the cache reader is executed to perform the actual shading and the image is redisplayed. This runs more quickly because we have hoisted the parameter-independent computations out of the inner repeat loop (marked with *) in Figure 4.

3. Specialization

The specializer begins by parsing and typechecking the shader function. The result is an abstract syntax tree (AST) annotated with type information. The core of the specialization process then proceeds in three steps.

- First, the dependence analysis determines which parts of the shader function are independent of the value of the designated control parameter.

- Second, the caching analysis determines which of the independent computations should be cached.

- Third, the splitting transformation separates the original shader function into cache loader and cache reader functions.

Space limitations prevent us from presenting the specializer in detail. The next three sections present a simplified description of the three specialization steps.

3.1 Dependence Analysis

Dependence analysis determines which parts of the computation are dependent or independent of the designated control parameter. The basic rule for dependence is that an expression is dependent on the designated parameter if one or more of its operands is. Although this basic rule would handle pure functional programs, the imperative assignment of variables in C requires a slightly more complicated analysis.

A reference to a variable is dependent (on the designated control parameter) if the value assigned to the variable is dependent. It is also dependent if the choice of which (independent) value to assign is dependent. For example, if an assignment statement is guarded by an if statement whose predicate is dependent, then a downstream reference to the variable is dependent.

In Figure 1, the parts of the function that are dependent upon the parameter specular are underlined. In this function, the first assignment to specular_component is dependent because it is assigned a value computed from the designated parameter, specular. This in turn forces the part of the calculation of rgb involving specular_component to be dependent. Finally, the call to SetPixelColor is dependent because it contains a reference to rgb, which is dependent because of the previous assignment.

Our solution to dependence analysis is a straightforward application of standard dataflow analysis/abstract interpretation techniques. It works by flowing a model of the dependence of every variable though the shader function along the control paths. The final result of the dependence analysis is an annotation on every node of the AST as to whether or not its value may be dependent upon the designated control parameter. These annotations are necessarily conservative; assuming that a computation is dependent upon the control parameter when in fact it is not may make the specializer miss an optimization opportunity, but will not make it produce the wrong result.

3.2 Caching Analysis

The caching analysis determines which of the independent values in the shader should be cached and which parts of the shader only need to occur in the cache reader. The results of the dependence analysis help to provide an upper bound on what might be cached. A priori, any independent computation is a candidate to be cached. However, independence is not sufficient to determine what *should* be cached. Consider the cache for the specialization of Phong on specular, represented in Figures 2 and 3. Since the value for kd*diffuse_component+ambient is cached, caching the either subexpression kd*diffuse_component, or the individual values of kd, diffuse_component, or ambient, would be inefficient.

The caching analysis classifies each shader expression as either *static, cache,* or *dynamic. Static* expressions are those that need only be evaluated at load time. For example, in the assignment

```
h_vector =
  VecNormalize(VecAdd(lightVector,
                      eye_vector));
```

even though the right hand side is independent of the designated parameter, it does not need to be cached because the only reference to h_vector is itself cached. *Cache* expressions are also evaluated at load time, but are consumed by dependent computations, so their results must be stored into the cache for later use by the cache reader. *Dynamic* expressions need to be computed during cache reading.

This classification is performed using simple heuristics. An expression is marked as cache if it is independent, is the maximal such expression, is governed only by independent control predicates, and is not within a dependent while statement. Independent, non-cached expressions that do not directly contribute to dependent computations are marked as static. The remaining expressions are marked as dynamic.

In the Phong shader, three expressions are selected for caching:[1]

- n_dot_h>0,

- n_dot_h, and

- kd*diffuse_component+ambient.

All of the assignment statements other than the assignments to specular_component and rgb are marked as static. The

---

[1]The reason that n_dot_h>0 and n_dot_h are both cached is that there are distinct (dependent) consumers of these values in the cache reader. One could choose to cache just n_dot_h and recalculate n_dot_h>0 in the cache reader.

```
AST MakeLoader(AST e) {
  switch on mark(e)
    case Static:
      return e

    case Cache:
      allocate a cache slot s for e
      return MakeAssignment(s,e)

    case Dynamic:
      switch on form of e
        case e is an expression e0⊕e1:
          return MakeExp(⊕, MakeLoader(e0),
                            MakeLoader(e1))

        case e is if (e0) e1 else e2:
          if (e0 is independent)
            return MakeIf(MakeLoader(e0),
                          MakeLoader(e1),
                          MakeLoader(e2))
          else
            return MakeLoader(e0)

        case e is while(e0) e1:
          if (e0 and e1 are independent)
            return MakeWhile(MakeLoader(e0),
                             MakeLoader(e1))
          else
            return ∅

        case ...
}
```

Figure 5: The cache loader transformation.

```
AST MakeReader(AST e) {
  switch mark(e)
    case Static:
      return ∅

    case Cache:
      find cache slot s allocated for e
      return s

    case Dynamic:
      switch on form of e
        case e is an expression e0⊕e1:
          return MakeExp(⊕, MakeReader(e0),
                            MakeReader(e1))

        case e is if (e0) e1 else e2:
          return MakeIf(MakeReader(e0),
                        MakeReader(e1),
                        MakeReader(e2))

        case e is while(e0) e1:
          return MakeWhile(MakeReader(e0),
                           MakeReader(e1))
        case ...
}
```

Figure 6: The cache reader transformation.

first `if` statement is dynamic because its then-part is dependent, but the second `if` is static.

3.3 Splitting Transformation

In its third and final phase, the specializer derives cache loader and cache reader functions from the AST, which has been annotated with the results of the dependence and cache analyses. Figures 5 and 6 present partial pseudo-code for the transformations that produce the cache loader and cache reader. The transformations are based solely upon the annotations and a case analysis on the form of the AST node *e*:

- If the node *e* is marked as static, then by definition it only needs to be included in the cache loader.

- If the node *e* is marked as cache, then the loader allocates a cache slot for it and generates an assignment statement in the cache loader function that assigns the slot the value of the expression. The corresponding piece of the reader simply reads the cache slot.

- If the node *e* is a dynamic `if` statement and it has a test that is independent of the designated parameters, then the loader may load cache values in the branches of the `if`. Such loading cannot be performed if the test is dependent, since the cached expressions will no longer be guarded by the test, possibly inducing a run-time exception that would not have occurred in the original program.

- If the node *e* is a dynamic `while` statement, we conservatively choose not to cache anything within it. This implementation misses some cases where an independent value could be cached: where (1) the independent value is loop invariant or (2) where the only dependent consumers are outside the loop.

Figures 2 and 3 contain the results of running the splitting transformation on the specialization of Phong for `specular`. The first five assignments of the shader are static, and are reproduced only in the loader. The first `if` statement is dynamic with an independent test; thus a version of the `if` appears in both the loader and the reader. Both the predicate and the reference to `n_dot_h` are cached, and are thus assigned in the loader and refernced in the cache reader. The assignment to identifier `specular_component` is actually dead in the loader--we would expect the compiler optimizer to remove it. The second `if` is static, and so is included only in the loader. The third and final cache element represents the maximally independent expression `kd*diffuse_component+ambient`.

3.4 Pragmatics

Cache space is a valuable resource. The pseudo-code in figure 5 implies that new space is allocated for each value that is cached, which would be correct but inefficient. For example, there are situations where two cached values may be correctly allocated to overlapping space in the cache, e.g., when only one of the values will be live on any given invocation of the cache loader. Our specializer employs some simple rules to more efficiently allocate cache slots.

Cache space is also a finite resource, as performance will suffer if the total space allocated for the cache exceeds the available physical memory. For the moderate-complexity shaders we have specialized thus far, cache size has not been an issue. In the specialization of more complex shaders, it will be necessary to explicitly limit the amount of cache space that is allocated. To do this effectively, we plan to introduce a cost metric that approximates the cost of each computation that is a candidate for caching. This would then be used to guide what should be cached and what should be recomputed in the cache reader by caching only the top-scoring candidates.

We can simultaneously improve cache size and reader efficiency by rewriting computations in the shader. One such opportunity is the associative rearrangement of arithmetic expressions.[2] For example, the expression `(x+y)+z` contains two computations that are independent of x, namely y and z. But if we reassociate it as `x+(y+z)`, this contains just one independent computation, `y+z`. The transformed code requires one less cache slot, and eliminates one "+" operation in the cache reader (Hanrahan and Lawson [7] describe a similar optimization).

Thus far, we have described specializing shaders on a single control parameter. The specializer, in fact, supports specializations on multiple parameters. So, for example, one could produce a specialization that would allow the fast manipulation of any of the red, green, or blue parameters without having to call the loader again. For combinations of control parameters, there are too many possible specializations for them all to be generated in advance. We plan to extend the system to dynamically call the specializer at run-time when a subset of the parameters is designated by the user.

4. Results

The specialization algorithm described above has been implemented in a prototype system consisting of approximately 20K lines of C++, Flex, and Bison code. The user interface driver loop is implemented in a small amount of Visual Basic. This section presents timing results for specialized shaders.

4.1 Timings

We show results of the specializations of two shaders: the Phong shader of Figure 1, which has 10 control parameters, and a procedural solid texture shader, Texture, having 18 control parameters. These shaders were tested on the 320 by 243 pixel image shown in Plate 1. This image consists of five objects, including the background plane. We chose to time our shaders on the background plane because it is the largest object in the image. The timings were performed on a Gateway 2000 P5-90 Pentium processor with 64 megabytes of physical memory. The performance of the specializer is not an issue; specialization is performed offline and typically requires less than one second per specialization generated. Thus, we present timings only for the shaders themselves.

Four statistics are of interest:

1. the time to execute the original shader,

2. the time to precompute the cached values,

---

[2]While floating point arithmetic does not obey the mathematical associativity laws, as long as the rewritten expression does not overflow, the effects are unlikely to be observable in a shading function.

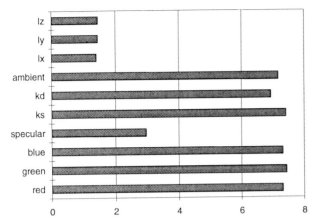

Figure 7: Relative speedup due to specialization for Phong for each control parameter.

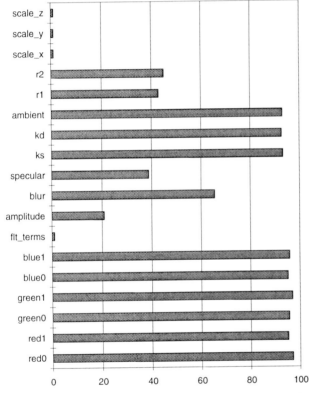

Figure 8: Relative speedup due to specialization for Texture for each control parameter

3 . the time to perform shading given the cached and the control parameter values, and

4 . the ratio of (1) and (3).

Figures 7 and 8 show the speedup ratio (4) for both shaders. These ratios vary from 1.4 through 7.4 for Phong, and 1.0 through 97.0 for Texture. Table 1 gives the absolute data for Texture; the table of absolute data for Phong is omitted to save space.

4.2 Discussion

The overhead of our two-phase shading approach is the time taken to run the cache loader. In our test cases, the sum of the loader and reader times is approximately equal to the time taken for a single invocation of the unspecialized shader. The cost of the additional memory operations to load the cache is balanced by the removal of statements that do not contribute to the cached values.

When the user first selects a new control parameter, the system must execute both the cache loader and reader; thus, the first shading may be slower than the original, unspecialized shader. Subsequent parameter changes only execute the cache reader; thus, our interactive speedup is the ratio of the original and reader times. The user will experience this speedup most of the time when interacting with the system.

The speedup ratio is highly dependent upon the particular control parameter chosen because we may only cache the results of computations that are independent of this parameter. In some cases, virtually all of the computations depend upon the chosen parameter, e.g., lx in Phong and flt_terms in Texture. Speedups for such cases are low, approaching 1, but never less than 1. In the majority of cases, however, the cache reader is much faster than the unspecialized shader, meaning that we achieve a net gain in processing speed when the user changes a parameter twice or more successively.

Figures 7 and 8 demonstrate that the majority of parameters are computed significantly faster in specialized form. For example, 7 of the 10 parameters in Phong were at least 3 times faster, and 6 parameters were at least 7 times faster, in specialized form. The speedup ratios are even more dramatic for the procedural solid texture shader. Of 18 parameters, 14 were at least 25 times faster and 9 were at least 90 times faster. The Texture shader contains several expensive computations that depend on only a few control parameters, allowing significant speedups in specializations on other parameters.

Parameter	User Shader	Cache Loader	Cache Reader	Ratio
scale_z	31.14	2.24	30.54	1.02
scale_y	31.15	2.43	30.46	1.02
scale_x	31.14	2.24	30.22	1.03
r2	31.27	32.25	0.70	44.95
r1	30.95	32.11	0.72	42.82
ambient	31.15	31.33	0.33	93.03
kd	31.15	31.22	0.34	92.69
ks	31.15	31.02	0.33	93.26
specular	31.11	30.70	0.80	38.80
blur	31.15	31.32	0.48	65.45
amplitude	31.15	32.43	1.50	20.83
flt_terms	44.81	2.23	43.08	1.04
blue1	31.15	31.25	0.32	95.87
blue0	31.15	31.47	0.33	95.17
green1	31.15	31.06	0.32	96.94
green0	31.15	31.03	0.33	95.64
red1	31.15	31.07	0.33	95.20
red0	31.15	31.24	0.32	97.05

Table 1: Execution time in seconds for the user shader, cache loader, and cache reader, and ratio of user shader time to reader time.

Color Plates 1 and 2 show a typical incremental control parameter change. In Plate 1, the amplitude parameter of the procedural texture shader for the tiled floor object is set to 12. In plate 2, it has been changed to 6. The time to reshade the image following this change was approximately 12 seconds for the original (unspecialized) shader and 0.5 seconds for the specialized shader.

5. Related Work

Relevant work includes the specialization of programs on partial input and the automatic construction of incremental versions of programs.

5.1 Partial Evaluation

The specialization of programs on partial input specifications is known as *partial evaluation* [9,13]. A partial evaluator takes a program and values for some of its inputs, and produces a new, specialized, program parameterized by the remaining inputs, while a *partial evaluator generator* takes a program and produces a transformer which, given some input values, generates the appropriate specialized program, eliminating the need to analyze the original program each time a specialization is needed. General-purpose partial evaluators for imperative languages include Andersen's C-Mix [1] and the system of Baier et al. [3], which process programs written in subsets of C and Fortran, respectively. Osgood [11] addresses the full C language, but the large time and space costs of his algorithm limit its applicability.

Our system can be viewed as a partial evaluator generator because it processes the original program only with respect to particular argument *positions*, generating a program (the cache loader) that later makes use of particular argument *values*. However, our approach differs from traditional partial evaluation strategies in that we are not limited to constructing specialized program text; we also construct specialized data values (such strategies are referred to as *mixed computation* in the literature). Applying a partial evaluator to our driver loop would yield a specialized shading procedure for each pixel in the image, whereas we limit ourselves to constructing specialized intermediate data values for each pixel, which are then processed by a single specialized shading procedure common to all pixels. The traditional approach might achieve better performance because of per-pixel code customization but is impractical due to the huge amount of specialized code that would be generated.

Several researchers have applied partial evaluation to ray-tracing by using a general-purpose partial evaluator to specialize a general intersection routine with respect to a scene, producing a specialized ray-tracer parameterized only by the viewpoint. Mogensen [10] partially evaluated a simple ray-tracer coded in Lisp and got a two-fold speedup; when shading was added to the ray-tracer, the speedup increased to 8 times. Andersen [2] performed a similar experiment in C, and achieved speedups of 1.8 with a code size blowup of 15-90 times. Other researchers used somewhat more application-specific specialization techniques. Hanrahan's "surface compiler" [6] symbolically simplifies input equations defining a general algebraic surface, then outputs a C program that uses numerical methods to find roots of the resulting polynomial. He reported a speedup of 1.3. Goad [5] proposed specializing a hidden surface elimination routine with respect to a fixed scene and variable viewpoint. In the area of mixed computation, Sequin [14] used ray tree caching

to significantly speed up shading computations for a ray traced image.

5.2 Incremental program execution

We know of two main approaches to efficiently handling incremental changes. One strategy encodes the program as a set of constraints, and explicitly reestablishes the constraints after each input change. Attribute grammars [4] are one example of a constraint system with an efficient incremental solver. Constraint systems are common in graphics; however, they are primarily used for their convenience and generality rather than as a foundation for efficient incremental execution.

Most other approaches are similar to ours in that they cache intermediate results of an existing batch program. Recent research on memoization for functional programs includes improved caching strategies [12] and methods for memoizing specialized functions instead of data values [15]. There is also research on adding dependence information to existing imperative code [8]. Incremental execution techniques are general, but suffer in performance due to the need to dynamically process arbitrary input changes. Our restricted application domain, in which the user performs a series of repeated modifications to individual scalar inputs, makes it practical for us to perform the dependence analysis and caching transformations statically, and to rebuild the intermediate value cache using batch rather than incremental methods.

6. Conclusion

We have described an automatic method for improving the performance of user-written shading routines by specializing them with respect to individual control parameters. By precomputing, caching, and reusing intermediate results that will remain constant as the user experiments with a single control parameter, the specialized shaders achieve up to a factor of 95 improvement in performance, allowing even complex shaders to be used in an interactive environment.

We plan to extend this work in several ways. The analyses and transformations will be extended to handle a larger subset of the C language, and to perform additional optimizations such as associative rearrangement of expressions and cost-based allocation of cache storage. Specializing the mathematical library routines (as opposed to only their user-level clients) may also achieve a significant gain in performance.

7. Acknowledgements

The authors would like to thank Stephen Coy for the use of his ray tracer and Greg Kusnick, Daniel Ling, Ellen Spertus, and the reviewers for helpful comments on previous drafts of this paper.

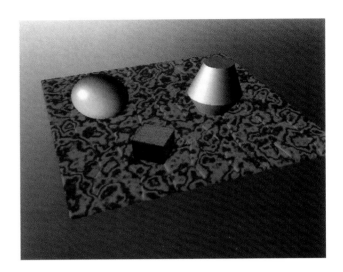

Plate 1: Test image.

Plate 2: Image obtained by reshading image of Plate 1. This took 12 seconds unspecialized, 0.5 seconds specialized.

Bibliography

[1] Andersen, Lars Ole. Self-applicable C Program Specialization. Proceedings of the ACM SIGPLAN Workshop on Partial Evaluation and Semantics-Based Program Manipulation (San Francisco, California, June 12-20, 1992). Yale University technical report YALEU/DCS/RR-909, 1992, 54-61.

[2] Andersen, Peter Holst. Partial Evaluation Applied to Ray Tracing. Unpublished manuscript, October 1994.

[3] Baier, Romana, Robert Glück, and Robert Zöchling. Partial Evaluation of Numerical Programs in Fortran. Proceedings of the ACM SIGPLAN Workshop on Partial Evaluation and Semantics-Based Program Manipulation (Orlando, Florida, June 25, 1994). University of Melbourne technical report 94/9, 1994, 119-132

[4] Demers, Alan J., Thomas Reps, and Tim Teitelbaum. Incremental Evaluation for Attribute Grammars with Application to Syntax-directed Editors. Proceedings of the Eighth Annual ACM Symposium on Principles of Programming Languages (Williamsburg, Virginia, January 1981), 105-116.

[5] Goad, Chris. Special Purpose Automatic Programming for Hidden Surface Elimination. Proceedings of SIGGRAPH 82 (Boston, Massachusetts, July 26-30, 1982). In Computer Graphics 16, 3 (July 1982), 167-178.

[6] Hanrahan, Pat. Ray Tracing Algebraic Surfaces. Proceedings of SIGGRAPH 83 (Detroit, Michigan, July 25-29, 1983). In Computer Graphics 17, 3 (July 1983), 83-90.

[7] Hanrahan, Pat and Jim Lawson. A Language for Shading and Lighting Calculations. Computer Graphics 24, 4 (August 1990), 289-298.

[8] Hoover, Roger. Alphonse: Incremental Computation as a Programming Abstraction. Proceedings of the SIGPLAN '92 Conference on Programming Language Design and Implementation (San Francisco, California, June 1992), 261-272.

[9] Jones, Neil D., Carsten K. Gomard, and Peter Sestoft. Partial Evaluation and Automatic Program Generation. Prentice-Hall, 1993.

[10] Mogensen, Torben. The Application of Partial Evaluation to Ray-Tracing. Master's thesis, DIKU, University of Copenhagen, Denmark, 1986.

[11] Osgood, Nathaniel David. PARTICLE: an Automatic Program Specialization System for Imperative and Low-level Languages. Master's thesis, MIT, September 1993.

[12] Pugh, William and Tim Teitelbaum. Incremental Computation Via Function Caching. Proceedings of the Sixteenth Annual ACM Symposium on Principles of Programming Languages (Austin, Texas, January 1989), 315-328.

[13] Ruf, Erik. Topics in Online Partial Evaluation. Ph.D. thesis, Stanford University, April 1993. Published as Stanford Computer Systems Laboratory technical report CSL-TR-93-563, March 1993.

[14] Sequin, Carlo H. and Eliot K. Smyrl. Parameterized Ray Tracing. Proceedings of SIGGRAPH 89 (Boston, Massachusetts, July 31-August 4, 1989). In Computer Graphics 23, 3 (July 1989), 307-314.

[15] Sundaresh, R.S. and Paul Hudak. A Theory of Incremental Computation and Its Application. Proceedings of the Eighteenth Annual ACM Symposium on Principles of Programming Languages (Orlando, Florida, January 1991), 1-13.

[16] Upstill, Steve. The RenderMan Companion. Addison-Wesley, 1989.

[17] Watkins, Christopher D., Stephen B. Coy, and Mark Finlay. Photorealism and Ray Tracing in C. M&T Books, 1992

[18] Watt, Alan and Mark Watt. Advanced Animation and Rendering Techniques. ACM Press, 1992.

A Signal Processing Approach To Fair Surface Design

Gabriel Taubin[1]
IBM T.J.Watson Research Center

ABSTRACT

In this paper we describe a new tool for interactive free-form fair surface design. By generalizing classical discrete Fourier analysis to two-dimensional *discrete surface signals* – functions defined on polyhedral surfaces of arbitrary topology –, we reduce the problem of surface smoothing, or fairing, to low-pass filtering. We describe a very simple surface signal low-pass filter algorithm that applies to surfaces of arbitrary topology. As opposed to other existing optimization-based fairing methods, which are computationally more expensive, this is a linear time and space complexity algorithm. With this algorithm, fairing very large surfaces, such as those obtained from volumetric medical data, becomes affordable. By combining this algorithm with surface subdivision methods we obtain a very effective fair surface design technique. We then extend the analysis, and modify the algorithm accordingly, to accommodate different types of constraints. Some constraints can be imposed without any modification of the algorithm, while others require the solution of a small associated linear system of equations. In particular, vertex location constraints, vertex normal constraints, and surface normal discontinuities across curves embedded in the surface, can be imposed with this technique.

CR Categories and Subject Descriptors: I.3.3 [**Computer Graphics**]: Picture/image generation - *display algorithms*; I.3.5 [**Computer Graphics**]: Computational Geometry and Object Modeling - *curve, surface, solid, and object representations*; J.6 [**Computer Applications**]: Computer-Aided Engineering - *computer-aided design*

General Terms: Algorithms, Graphics.

1 INTRODUCTION

The signal processing approach described in this paper was originally motivated by the problem of how to fair large polyhedral surfaces of arbitrary topology, such as those extracted from volumetric medical data by iso-surface construction algorithms [21, 2, 11, 15], or constructed by integration of multiple range images [36].

Since most existing algorithms based on fairness norm optimization [37, 24, 12, 38] are prohibitively expensive for very large surfaces – a million vertices is not unusual in medical images –, we decided to look for new algorithms with linear time and space complexity [31]. Unless these large surfaces are first simplified [29, 13, 11], or re-meshed using far fewer faces [35], methods based on patch technology, whether parametric [28, 22, 10, 20, 19] or implicit [1, 23], are not acceptable either. Although curvature

continuous, a patch-based surface interpolant is far more complex than the original surface, more expensive to render, and worst of all, does not remove the high curvature variation present in the original mesh.

As in the fairness norm optimization methods and physics-based deformable models [16, 34, 30, 26], our approach is to move the vertices of the polyhedral surface without changing the connectivity of the faces. The faired surface has exactly the same number of vertices and faces as the original one. However, our signal processing formulation results in much less expensive computations. In these variational formulations [5, 24, 38, 12], after finite element discretization, the problem is often reduced to the solution of a large sparse linear system, or a more expensive global optimization problem. Large sparse linear systems are solved using iterative methods [9], and usually result in quadratic time complexity algorithms. In our case, the problem of surface fairing is reduced to sparse matrix multiplication instead, a linear time complexity operation.

The paper is organized as follows. In section 2 we describe how to extend signal processing to signals defined on polyhedral surfaces of arbitrary topology, reducing the problem of surface smoothing to low-pass filtering, and we describe a particularly simple linear time and space complexity surface signal low-pass filter algorithm. Then we concentrate on the applications of this algorithm to interactive free-form fair surface design. As Welch and Witkin [38], in section 3 we design more detailed fair surfaces by combining our fairing algorithm with subdivision techniques. In section 4 we modify our fairing algorithm to accommodate different kinds of constraints. Finally, in section 5 we present some closing remarks.

2 THE SIGNAL PROCESSING APPROACH

Fourier analysis is a natural tool to solve the problem of signal smoothing. The space of signals – functions defined on certain domain – is decomposed into orthogonal subspaces associated with different frequencies, with the low frequency content of a signal regarded as subjacent data, and the high frequency content as noise.

2.1 CLOSED CURVE FAIRING

To smooth a closed curve it is sufficient to remove the noise from the coordinate signals, i.e., to project the coordinate signals onto the subspace of low frequencies. This is what the method of *Fourier descriptors*, which dates back to the early 60's, does [40]. Our approach to extend Fourier analysis to signals defined on polyhedral surfaces of arbitrary topology is based on the observation that the classical Fourier transform of a signal can be seen as the decomposition of the signal into a linear combination of the eigenvectors of the Laplacian operator. To extend Fourier analysis to surfaces of arbitrary topology we only have to define a new operator that takes the place of the Laplacian.

As a motivation, let us consider the simple case of a discrete time n-periodic signal – a function defined on a regular polygon of n vertices –, which we represent as a column vector $x = (x_1, \ldots, x_n)^t$. The components of this vector are the values of the signal at the

[1] IBM T.J.Watson Research Center, P.O.Box 704, Yorktown Heights, NY 10598, taubin@watson.ibm.com

Permission to make digital/hard copy of part or all of this work for personal or classroom use is granted without fee provided that copies are not made or distributed for profit or commercial advantage, the copyright notice, the title of the publication and its date appear, and notice is given that copying is by permission of ACM, Inc. To copy otherwise, to republish, to post on servers, or to redistribute to lists, requires prior specific permission and/or a fee.

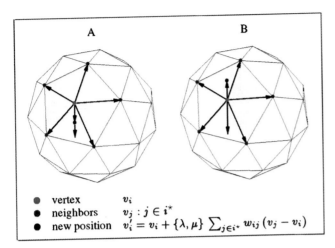

- ● vertex $\quad v_i$
- ● neighbors $\quad v_j : j \in i^\star$
- ● new position $\quad v_i' = v_i + \{\lambda, \mu\} \sum_{j \in i^\star} w_{ij}(v_j - v_i)$

Figure 1: The two weighted averaging steps of our fairing algorithm. (A) A first step with positive scale factor λ is applied to all the vertices. (B) Then a second step with negative scale factor μ is applied to all the vertices.

vertices of the polygon. The discrete Laplacian of x is defined as

$$\Delta x_i = \frac{1}{2}(x_{i-1} - x_i) + \frac{1}{2}(x_{i+1} - x_i) , \qquad (1)$$

where the indices are incremented and decremented modulo n. In matrix form it can be written as follows

$$\Delta x = -K x , \qquad (2)$$

where K is the circulant matrix

$$K = \frac{1}{2} \begin{pmatrix} 2 & -1 & & & -1 \\ -1 & 2 & -1 & & \\ & \ddots & \ddots & \ddots & \\ & & -1 & 2 & -1 \\ -1 & & & -1 & 2 \end{pmatrix} .$$

Since K is symmetric, it has real eigenvalues and eigenvectors. Explicitly, the real eigenvalues $k_1, \ldots, k_n$ of K, sorted in non-decreasing order, are

$$k_j = 1 - \cos(2\pi\lfloor j/2 \rfloor/n) ,$$

and the corresponding unit length real eigenvectors, $u_1, \ldots, u_n$, are

$$(u_j)_h = \begin{cases} \sqrt{1/n} & \text{if } j = 1 \\ \sqrt{2/n} \, \sin(2\pi h\lfloor j/2 \rfloor/n) & \text{if } j \text{ is even} \\ \sqrt{2/n} \, \cos(2\pi h\lfloor j/2 \rfloor/n) & \text{if } j \text{ is odd} . \end{cases}$$

Note that $0 \leq k_1 \leq \cdots \leq k_n \leq 2$, and as the frequency k_j increases, the corresponding eigenvector u_j, as a n-periodic signal, changes more rapidly from vertex to vertex.

To decompose the signal x as a linear combination of the real eigenvectors $u_1, \ldots, u_n$

$$x = \sum_{i=1}^{n} \xi_i u_i , \qquad (3)$$

is computationally equivalent to the evaluation of the Discrete Fourier Transform of x. To smooth the signal x with the method of Fourier descriptors, this decomposition has to be computed, and then the high frequency terms of the sum must be discarded. But

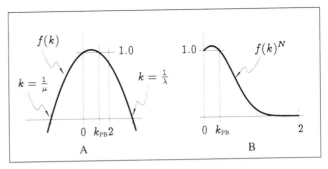

Figure 2: (A) Graph of transfer function $f(k) = (1 - \mu k)(1 - \lambda k)$ of non-shrinking smoothing algorithm.

this is computationally expensive. Even using the Fast Fourier Transform algorithm, the computational complexity is in the order of $n \log(n)$ operations.

An alternative is to do the projection onto the space of low frequencies only approximately. This is what a low-pass filter does. We will only consider here low-pass filters implemented as a convolution. A more detailed analysis of other filter methodologies is beyond the scope of this paper, and will be done elsewhere [33]. Perhaps the most popular convolution-based smoothing method for parameterized curves is the so-called *Gaussian filtering* method, associated with scale-space theory [39, 17]. In its simplest form, it can be described by the following formula

$$x_i' = x_i + \lambda \Delta x_i , \qquad (4)$$

where $0 < \lambda < 1$ is a scale factor (for $\lambda < 0$ and $\lambda \geq 1$ the algorithm enhances high frequencies instead of attenuating them). This can be written in matrix form as

$$x' = (I - \lambda K) x . \qquad (5)$$

It is well known though, that Gaussian filtering produces shrinkage, and this is so because the Gaussian kernel is not a low-pass filter kernel [25]. To define a low-pass filter, the matrix $I - \lambda K$ must be replaced by some other function $f(K)$ of the matrix K. Our non-shrinking fairing algorithm, described in the next section, is one particularly efficient choice.

We now extend this formulation to functions defined on surfaces of arbitrary topology.

2.2 SURFACE SIGNAL FAIRING

At this point we need a few definitions. We represent a polyhedral surface as a pair of lists $S = \{V, F\}$, a list of n vertices V, and a list of polygonal faces F. Although in our current implementation, only triangulated surfaces, and surfaces with quadrilateral faces are allowed, the algorithm is defined for any polyhedral surface.

Both for curves and for surfaces, a *neighborhood* of a vertex v_i is a set $i^\star$ of indices of vertices. If the index j belongs to the neighborhood $i^\star$, we say that v_j is a *neighbor* of v_i. The *neighborhood structure* of a polygonal curve or polyhedral surface is the family of all its neighborhoods $\{i^\star : i = 1, 2, \ldots, n\}$. A neighborhood structure is *symmetric* if every time that a vertex v_j is a neighbor of vertex v_i, also v_i is a neighbor of v_j. With non-symmetric neighborhoods certain constraints can be imposed. We discuss this issue in detail in section 4.

A particularly important neighborhood structure is the *first order* neighborhood structure, where for each pair of vertices v_i and v_j that share a face (edge for a curve), we make v_j a neighbor of v_i, and v_i a neighbor of v_j. For example, for a polygonal curve represented as a list of consecutive vertices, the first order neighborhood of a vertex v_i is $i^\star = \{i - 1, i + 1\}$. The first order neighborhood

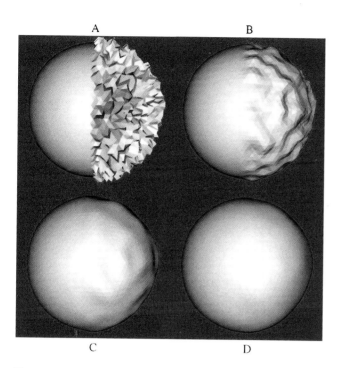

Figure 3: (A) Sphere partially corrupted by normal noise. (B) Sphere (A) after 10 non-shrinking smoothing steps. (C) Sphere (A) after 50 non-shrinking smoothing steps. (D) Sphere (A) after 200 non-shrinking smoothing steps. Surfaces are flat-shaded to enhance the faceting effect.

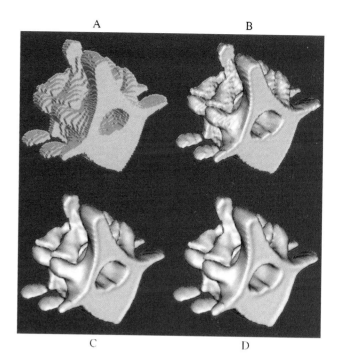

Figure 4: (A) Boundary surface of voxels from a CT scan. (B) Surface (A) after 10 non-shrinking smoothing steps. (C) Surface (A) after 50 non-shrinking smoothing steps. (D) Surface (A) after 100 non-shrinking smoothing steps. $k_{\text{PB}} = 0.1$ and $\lambda = 0.6307$ in (B), (C), and (D). Surfaces are flat-shaded to enhance the faceting effect.

structure is symmetric, and since it is implicitly given by the list of faces of the surface, no extra storage is required to represent it. This is the default neighborhood structure used in our current implementation.

A *discrete surface signal* is a function $x = (x_1, \ldots, x_n)^t$ defined on the vertices of a polyhedral surface. We define the discrete Laplacian of a discrete surface signal by weighted averages over the neighborhoods

$$\Delta x_i = \sum_{j \in i^\star} w_{ij} \left(x_j - x_i \right), \qquad (6)$$

where the weights w_{ij} are positive numbers that add up to one, $\sum_{j \in i^\star} w_{ij} = 1$, for each i. The weights can be chosen in many different ways taking into consideration the neighborhood structures. One particularly simple choice that produces good results is to set w_{ij} equal to the inverse of the number of neighbors $1/|i^\star|$ of vertex v_i, for each element j of $i^\star$. Note that the case of the Laplacian of a n-periodic signal (1) is a particular case of these definitions. A more general way of choosing weights for a surface with a first order neighborhood structure, is using a positive function $\phi(v_i, v_j) = \phi(v_j, v_i)$ defined on the edges of the surface

$$w_{ij} = \frac{\phi(v_i, v_j)}{\sum_{h \in i^\star} \phi(v_i, v_h)} .$$

For example, the function can be the surface area of the two faces that share the edge, or some power of the length of the edge $\phi(v_i, v_j) = \|v_i - v_j\|^\alpha$. In our implementation the user can choose any one of these weighting schemes. They produce similar results when the surface has faces of roughly uniform size. When using a power of the length of the edges as weighting function, the exponent $\alpha = -1$ produces good results.

If $W = (w_{ij})$ is the matrix of weights, with $w_{ij} = 0$ when j is not a neighbor of i, the matrix K can now be defined as

$K = I - W$. In the appendix we show that for a first order neighborhood structure, and for all the choices of weights described above, the matrix K has real eigenvalues $0 \le k_1 \le k_2 \le \cdots \le k_n \le 2$ with corresponding linearly independent real unit length right eigenvectors $u_1, \ldots, u_n$. Seen as discrete surface signals, these eigenvectors should be considered as the *natural vibration modes* of the surface, and the corresponding eigenvalues as the associated *natural frequencies*.

The decomposition of equation (3), of the signal x into a linear combination of the eigenvectors $u_1, \ldots, u_n$, is still valid with these definitions, but there is no extension of the Fast Fourier Transform algorithm to compute it. The method of Fourier descriptors – the exact projection onto the subspace of low frequencies – is just not longer feasible, particularly for very large surfaces. On the other hand, low-pass filtering – the approximate projection – can be formulated in exactly the same way as for n-periodic signals, as the multiplication of a function $f(K)$ of the matrix K by the original signal

$$x' = f(K)x ,$$

and this process can be iterated N times

$$x^N = f(K)^N x .$$

The function of one variable $f(k)$ is the *transfer function* of the filter. Although many functions of one variable can be evaluated in matrices [9], we will only consider polynomials here. For example, in the case of Gaussian smoothing the transfer function is $f(k) = 1 - \lambda k$. Since for any polynomial transfer function we have

$$x' = f(K)x = \sum_{i=1}^{n} \xi_i \, f(k_i) \, u_i ,$$

because $Ku_i = k_i u_i$, to define a low-pass filter we need to find a polynomial such that $f(k_i)^N \approx 1$ for low frequencies, and

$f(k_i)^N \approx 0$ for high frequencies in the region of interest $k \in [0, 2]$. Our choice is

$$f(k) = (1 - \lambda k)(1 - \mu k) \qquad (7)$$

where $0 < \lambda$, and μ is a new negative scale factor such that $\mu < -\lambda$. That is, after we perform the Gaussian smoothing step of equation (4) with positive scale factor λ for all the vertices – the shrinking step –, we then perform another similar step

$$x_i' = x_i + \mu\,\Delta x_i \qquad (8)$$

for all the vertices, but with negative scale factor μ instead of λ – the un-shrinking step –. These steps are illustrated in figure 1.

The graph of the transfer function of equation (7) is illustrated in figure 2-A. Figure 2-B shows the resulting transfer function after N iterations of the algorithm, the graph of the function $f(k)^N$. Since $f(0) = 1$ and $\mu + \lambda < 0$, there is a positive value of k, the *pass-band frequency* k_{PB}, such that $f(k_{PB}) = 1$. The value of k_{PB} is

$$k_{PB} = \frac{1}{\lambda} + \frac{1}{\mu} > 0 . \qquad (9)$$

The graph of the transfer function $f(k)^N$ displays a typical *low-pass filter* shape in the region of interest $k \in [0, 2]$. The *pass-band region* extends from $k = 0$ to $k = k_{PB}$, where $f(k)^N \approx 1$. As k increases from $k = k_{PB}$ to $k = 2$, the transfer function decreases to zero. The faster the transfer function decreases in this region, the better. The rate of decrease is controlled by the number of iterations N.

This algorithm is fast (linear both in time and space), extremely simple to implement, and produces smoothing without shrinkage. Faster algorithms can be achieved by choosing other polynomial transfer functions, but the analysis of the filter design problem is beyond the scope of this paper, and will be treated elsewhere [33]. However, as a rule of thumb, the filter based on the second degree polynomial transfer function of equation (7) can be designed by first choosing a values of k_{PB}. Values from 0.01 to 0.1 produce good results, and all the examples shown in the paper where computed with $k_{PB} \approx 0.1$. Once k_{PB} has been chosen, we have to choose λ and N (μ comes out of equation (9) afterwards). Of course we want to minimize N, the number of iterations. To do so, λ must be chosen as large as possible, while keeping $|f(k)| < 1$ for $k_{PB} < k \le 2$ (if $|f(k)| \ge 1$ in $[k_{PB}, 2]$, the filter will enhance high frequencies instead of attenuating them). In some of the examples, we have chosen λ so that $f(1) = -f(2)$. For $k_{PB} < 1$ this choice of λ ensures a stable and fast filter.

Figures 3 and 4 show examples of large surfaces faired with this algorithm. Figures 3 is a synthetic example, where noise has been added to one half of a polyhedral approximation of a sphere. Note that while the algorithm progresses the half without noise does not change significantly. Figure 4 was constructed from a CT scan of a spine. The boundary surface of the set of voxels with intensity value above a certain threshold is used as the input signal. Note that there is not much difference between the results after 50 and 100 iterations.

3 SUBDIVISION

A subdivision surface is a smooth surface defined as the limit of a sequence of polyhedral surfaces, where the next surface in the sequence is constructed from the previous one by a refinement process. In practice, since the number of faces grows very fast, only a few levels of subdivision are computed. Once the faces are smaller than the resolution of the display, it is not necessary to continue. As Welch and Witkin [38], we are not interested in the limit surfaces, but rather in using subdivision and smoothing steps as tools to design fair polyhedral surfaces in an interactive environment. The classical

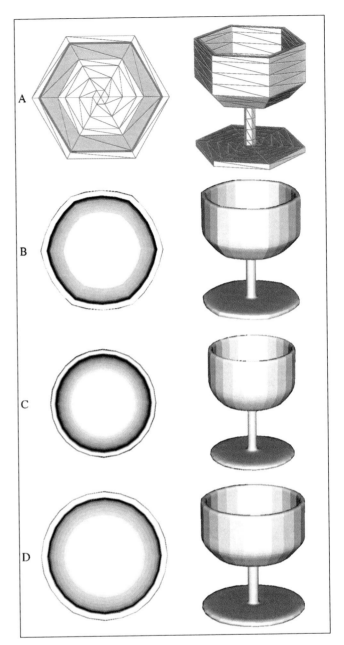

Figure 5: Surfaces created alternating subdivision and different smoothing steps. (A) Skeleton surface. (B) One Gaussian smoothing step ($\lambda = 0.5$). Note the hexagonal symmetry because of insufficient smoothing. (C) Five Gaussian smoothing steps ($\lambda = 0.5$). Note the shrinkage effect. (D) Five non-shrinking smoothing steps ($k_{PB} = 0.1$ and $\lambda = 0.6307$) of this paper. (B),(C), and (D) are the surfaces obtained after two levels of refinement and smoothing. Surfaces are flat-shaded to enhance the faceting effect.

subdivision schemes [8, 4, 12] are rigid, in the sense that they have no free parameters that influence the behavior of the algorithm as it progresses trough the subdivision process. By using our fairing algorithm in conjunction with subdivision steps, we achieve more flexibility in the design process. In this way our fairing algorithm can be seen as a complement of the existing subdivision strategies.

In the subdivision surfaces of Catmull and Clark [4, 12] and Loop [18, 6], the subdivision process involves two steps. A refinement step, where a new surface with more vertices and faces is created, and a smoothing step, where the vertices of the new surface are moved. The Catmull and Clark refinement process creates polyhedral surfaces with quadrilateral faces, and Loop refinement process subdivides each triangular face into four similar triangular faces. In both cases the smoothing step can be described by equation (4). The weights are chosen to ensure tangent or curvature continuity of the limit surface.

These subdivision surfaces have the problem of shrinkage, though. The limit surface is significantly smaller overall than the initial skeleton mesh – the first surface of the sequence –. This is so because the smoothing step is essentially Gaussian smoothing, and as we have pointed out, Gaussian smoothing produces shrinkage. Because of the refinement steps, the surfaces do not collapse to the centroid of the initial skeleton, but the shrinkage effect can be quite significant.

The problem of shrinkage can be solved by a global operation. If the amount of shrinkage can be predicted in closed form, the skeleton surface can be expanded before the subdivision process is applied. This is what Halstead, Kass, and DeRose [12] do. They show how to modify the skeleton mesh so that the subdivision surface associated with the modified skeleton interpolates the vertices of the original skeleton.

The subdivision surfaces of Halstead, Kass, and DeRose interpolate the vertices of the original skeleton, and are curvature continuous. However, they show a significant high curvature content, even when the original skeleton mesh does not have such undulations. The shrinkage problem is solved, but a new problem is introduced. Their solution to this second problem is to stop the subdivision process after a certain number of steps, and fair the resulting polyhedral surface based on a variational approach. Their fairness norm minimization procedure reduces to the solution of a large sparse linear system, and they report quadratic running times. The result of this modified algorithm is no longer a curvature continuous surface that interpolates the vertices of the skeleton, but a more detailed fair polyhedral surface that usually does not interpolate the vertices of the skeleton unless the interpolatory constraints are imposed during the fairing process.

We argue that the source of the unwanted undulations in the Catmull-Clark surface generated from the modified skeleton is the smoothing step of the subdivision process. Only one Gaussian smoothing step does not produce enough smoothing, i.e., it does not produce sufficient attenuation of the high frequency components of the surfaces, and these high frequency components persist during the subdivision process. Figure 5-B shows an example of a subdivision surface created with the triangular refinement step of Loop, and one Gaussian smoothing step of equation (4). The hexagonal symmetry of the skeleton remains during the subdivision process. Figure 5-C shows the same example, but where five Gaussian smoothing steps are performed after each refinement step. The hexagonal symmetry has been removed at the expense of significant shrinkage effect. Figure 5-D shows the same example where the five non-shrinking fairing steps are performed after each refinement step. Neither hexagonal symmetry nor shrinkage can be observed.

4 CONSTRAINTS

Although surfaces created by a sequence of subdivision and smoothing steps based on our fairing algorithm do not shrink much, they usually do not interpolate the vertices of the original skeleton. In this section we show that by modifying the neighborhood structure certain kind of constraints can be imposed without any modification of the algorithm. Then we study other constraints that require minor modifications.

4.1 INTERPOLATORY CONSTRAINTS

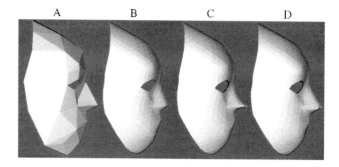

Figure 6: Example of surfaces designed using subdivision and smoothing steps with one interpolatory constraint. (A) Skeleton. (B) Surface (A) after two levels of subdivision and smoothing without constraints. (C) Same as (B) but with non-smooth interpolatory constraint. (D) Same as (B) but with smooth interpolatory constraint. Surfaces are flat-shaded to enhance the faceting effect.

As we mentioned in section 2.2, a simple way to introduce interpolatory constraints in our fairing algorithm is by using non-symmetric neighborhood structures. If no other vertex is a neighbor of a certain vertex v_1, i.e., if the neighborhood of v_1 is empty, then the value x_1 of any discrete surface signal x does not change during the fairing process, because the discrete Laplacian Δx_1 is equal to zero by definition of empty sum. Other vertices are allowed to have v_1 as a neighbor, though. Figure 6-A shows a skeleton surface. Figure 6-B shows the surface generated after two levels of refinement and smoothing using our fairing algorithm without constraints, i.e., with symmetric first-order neighborhoods. Although the surface has not shrunk overall, the nose has been flattened quite significantly. This is so because the nose is made of very few faces in the skeleton, and these faces meet at very sharp angles. Figure 6-C shows the result of applying the same steps, but defining the neighborhood of the vertex at the tip of the nose to be empty. The other neighborhoods are not modified. Now the vertex satisfies the constraint -- it has not moved at all during the fairing process –, but the surface has lost its smoothness at the vertex. This might be the desired effect, but if it is not, instead of the neighborhoods, we have to modify the algorithm.

4.2 SMOOTH INTERPOLATION

We look at the desired constrained smooth signal x_C^N as a sum of the corresponding unconstrained smooth signal $x^N = F x$ after N steps of our fairing algorithm (i.e. $F = f(K)^N$), plus a smooth deformation d_1

$$x_C^N = x^N + (x_1 - x_1^N) d_1 .$$

The deformation d_1 is itself another discrete surface signal, and the constraint $(x_C^N)_1 = x_1$ is satisfied if $(d_1)_1 = 1$. To construct such a smooth deformation we consider the signal δ_1, where

$$(\delta_i)_j = \begin{cases} 1 & j = i \\ 0 & j \neq i \end{cases} .$$

This is not a smooth signal, but we can apply the fairing algorithm to it. The result, let us denote it F_{n1}, the first column of the matrix F, is a smooth signal, but its value at the vertex v_1 is not equal to one. However, since the matrix F is diagonally dominated, F_{11}, the first element of its first column, must be non-zero. Therefore, we can scale the signal F_{n1} to make it satisfy the constraint, obtaining the desired smooth deformation

$$d_1 = F_{n1} F_{11}^{-1} .$$

Figure 7: Examples of using subdivision and smoothing with smooth interpolatory constraints as a design tool. All the surfaces have been obtained by applying two levels of subdivision and smoothing with various parameters to the skeleton surface of figure 5-A . Constrained vertices are marked with red dots. Surfaces are flat-shaded to enhance the faceting effect.

Figure 6-D shows the result of applying this process.

When more than one interpolatory constraint must be imposed, the problem is slightly more complicated. For simplicity, we will assume that the vertices have been reordered so that the interpolatory constraints are imposed on the first m vertices, i.e., $(x_C^N)_1 = x_1, \ldots, (x_C^N)_m = x_m$. We now look at the non-smooth signals $\delta_1, \ldots, \delta_m$, and at the corresponding faired signals, the first m columns of the matrix F. These signals are smooth, and so, any linear combination of them is also a smooth signal. Furthermore, since F is non-singular and diagonally dominated, these signals are linearly independent, and there exists a linear combination of them that satisfies the m desired constraints. Explicitly, the constrained smooth signal can be computed as follows

$$x_C^N = x^N + F_{nm}\, F_{mm}^{-1} \begin{pmatrix} x_1 - x_1^N \\ \vdots \\ x_m - x_m^N \end{pmatrix} , \qquad (10)$$

where F_{rs} denotes the sub-matrix of F determined by the first r rows and the first s columns. Figure 7 shows examples of surfaces constructed using subdivision and smoothing steps and interpolating some vertices of the skeleton using this method. The parameter of the fairing algorithm have been modified to achieve different effects, including shrinkage.

To minimize storage requirements, particularly when n is large, and assuming that m is much smaller than n, the computation can be structured as follows. The fairing algorithm is applied to δ_1 obtaining the first column $F\delta_1$ of the matrix F. The first m elements of this vector are stored as the first column of the matrix F_{mm}. The remaining $m - n$ elements of $F\delta_1$ are discarded. The same process is repeated for $\delta_2, \ldots, \delta_m$, obtaining the remaining

columns of F_{mm}. Then the following linear system

$$F_{mm} \begin{pmatrix} y_1 \\ \vdots \\ y_m \end{pmatrix} = \begin{pmatrix} x_1 - x_1^N \\ \vdots \\ x_m - x_m^N \end{pmatrix}$$

is solved. The matrix F_{mm} is no longer needed. Then the remaining components of the signal y are set to zero $y_{m+1} = \cdots = y_n = 0$. Now the fairing algorithm is applied to the signal y. The result is the smooth deformation that makes the unconstrained smooth signal x^N satisfy the constraints

$$x_C^N = x^N + F y .$$

4.3 SMOOTH DEFORMATIONS

Note that in the constrained fairing algorithm described above the fact that the values of the signal at the vertices of interest are constrained to remain constant can be trivially generalized to allow for arbitrary smooth deformations of a surface. To do so, the values $x_1, \ldots, x_m$ in equation (10) must be replaced by the desired final values of the faired signal at the corresponding vertices. As in in the Free-form deformation approaches of Hsu, Hughes, and Kaufman [14] and Borrel [3], instead of moving control points outside the surface, surfaces can be deformed here by pulling one or more vertices.

Also note that the scope of the deformation can be controlled by changing the number of smoothing steps applied while smoothing the signals $\delta_1, \ldots, \delta_n$. To make the resulting signal satisfy the constraint, the value of N in the definition of the matrix F must be the one used to smooth the deformations. We have observed that good results are obtained when the number of iterations used to smooth the deformations is about five times the number used to fair the original shape. The examples in figure 7 have been generated in this way.

4.4 HIERARCHICAL CONSTRAINTS

This is another application of non-symmetric neighborhoods. We start by assigning a numeric label l_i to each vertex of the surface. Then we define the neighborhood structure as follows. We make vertex v_j a neighbor of vertex v_i if v_i and v_j share an edge (or face), and if $l_i \leq l_j$. Note that if v_j is a neighbor of v_i and $l_i < l_j$, then v_i is not a neighbor of v_j. The symmetry applies only to vertices with the same label. For example, if we assign label $l_i = 1$ to all the boundary vertices of a surface with boundary, and label $l_i = 0$ to all the internal vertices, then the boundary is faired as a curve, independently of the interior vertices, but the interior vertices follow the boundary vertices. If we also assign label $l_i = 1$ to a closed curve composed of internal edges of the surface, then the resulting surface will be smooth along, and on both sides of the curve, but not necessarily across the curve. Figure 8-D shows examples of subdivision surface designed using this procedure. If we also assign label $l_i = 2$ to some isolated points along the curves, then those vertices will in fact not move, because they will have empty neighborhoods.

4.5 TANGENT PLANE CONSTRAINTS

Although the normal vector to a polyhedral surface is not defined at a vertex, it is customary to define it by averaging some local information, say for shading purposes. When the signal x in equation (6) is replaced by the coordinates of the vertices, the Laplacian becomes a vector

$$\Delta v_i = \sum_{j \in i^\star} w_{ij}\, (v_j - v_i) .$$

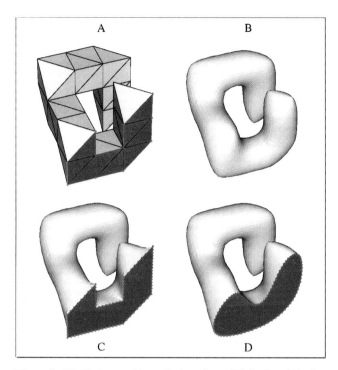

Figure 8: (A) Skeleton with marked vertices. (B) Surface (A) after three levels of subdivision and smoothing without constraints. (C) Same as (B) but with empty neighborhoods of marked vertices. (D) Same as (B) but with hierarchical neighborhoods, where marked vertices have label 1 and unmarked vertices have label 0. Surfaces are flat-shaded to enhance the faceting effect.

This vector average can be seen as a discrete approximation of the following curvilinear integral

$$\frac{1}{|\gamma|} \int_{v \in \gamma} (v - v_i) \, dl(v) \, ,$$

where γ is a closed curve embedded in the surface which encircles the vertex v_i, and $|\gamma|$ is the length of the curve. It is known that, for a curvature continuous surface, if the curve γ is let to shrink to to the point v_i, the integral converges to the mean curvature $\bar{\kappa}(v_i)$ of the surface at the point v_i times the normal vector N_i at the same point [7]

$$\lim_{\epsilon \to 0} \frac{1}{|\gamma_\epsilon|} \int_{v \in \gamma_\epsilon} (v - v_i) \, dl(v) = \bar{\kappa}(v_i) N_i \, .$$

Because of this fact, we can define the vector Δv_i as the normal vector to the polyhedral surface at v_i. If N_i is the desired normal direction at vertex v_i after the fairing process, and S_i and T_i are two linearly independent vectors tangent to N_i, The surface after N iterations of the fairing algorithm will satisfy the desired normal constraint at the vertex v_i it the following two linear constraints

$$S_i^t \Delta v_i^N = T_i^t \Delta v_i^N = 0$$

are satisfied. This leads us to the problem of fairing with general linear constraints.

4.6 GENERAL LINEAR CONSTRAINTS

We consider here the problem of fairing a discrete surface signal x under general linear constraints $C x_C^N = c$, where C is a $m \times n$ matrix of rank m (m independent constraints), and $c = (c_1, \dots, c_m)^t$

is a vector. The method described in section 4.1 to impose smooth interpolatory constraints, is a particular case of this problem, where the matrix C is equal the upper m rows of the $m \times m$ identity matrix. Our approach is to reduce the general case to this particular case.

We start by decomposing the matrix C into two blocks. A first $m \times m$ block denoted $C_{(1)}$, composed of m columns of C, and a second block denoted $C_{(2)}$, composed of the remaining columns. The columns that constitute $C_{(1)}$ must be chosen so that $C_{(1)}$ become non-singular, and as well conditioned as possible. In practice this can be done using Gauss elimination with full pivoting [9], but for the sake of simplicity, we will assume here that $C_{(1)}$ is composed of the first m columns of C. We decompose signals in the same way. $x_{(1)}$ denotes here the first m components, and $x_{(2)}$ the last $n - m$ components, of the signal x. We now define a change of basis in the vector space of discrete surface signals as follows

$$\begin{cases} x_{(1)} &= y_{(1)} - C_{(1)}^{-1} C_{(2)} \, y_{(2)} \\ x_{(2)} &= y_{(2)} \end{cases} \, .$$

If we apply this change of basis to the constraint equation $C_{(1)} x_{(1)} + C_{(2)} x_{(2)} = c$, we obtain $C_{(1)} y_{(1)} = c$, or equivalently

$$y_{(1)} = C_{(1)}^{-1} c \, ,$$

which is the problem solved in section 4.2.

5 CONCLUSIONS

We have presented a new approach to polyhedral surface fairing based on signal processing ideas, we have demonstrated how to use it as an interactive surface design tool. In our view, this new approach represents a significant improvement over the existing fairness-norm optimization approaches, because of the linear time and space complexity of the resulting fairing algorithm.

Our current implementation of these ideas is a surface modeler that runs at interactive speeds on a IBM RS/6000 class workstation under X-Windows. In this surface modeler we have integrated all the techniques described in this paper and many other popular polyhedral surface manipulation techniques. Among other things, the user can interactively define neighborhood structures, select vertices or edges to impose constraints, subdivide the surfaces, and apply the fairing algorithm with different parameter values. All the illustrations of this paper where generated with this software.

In terms of future work, we plan to investigate how this approach can be extended to provide alternatives solutions for other important graphics and modeling problems that are usually formulated as variational problems, such as surface reconstruction or surface fitting problems solved with physics-based deformable models.

Some related papers [31, 32] can be retrieved from the IBM web server (http://www.watson.ibm.com:8080).

REFERENCES

[1] C.L. Bajaj and Ihm. Smoothing polyhedra using implicit algebraic splines. *Computer Graphics*, pages 79–88, July 1992. (Proceedings SIGGRAPH'92).

[2] H. Baker. Building surfaces of evolution: The weaving wall. *International Journal of Computer Vision*, 3:51–71, 1989.

[3] P. Borrel. Simple constrained deformations for geometric modeling and interactive design. *ACM Transactions on Graphics*, 13(2):137–155, April 1994.

[4] E. Catmull and J. Clark. Recursively generated B-spline surfaces on arbitrary topological meshes. *Computer Aided Design*, 10:350–355, 1978.

[5] G. Celniker and D. Gossard. Deformable curve and surface finite-elements for free-form shape design. *Computer Graphics*, pages 257–266, July 1991. (Proceedings SIGGRAPH'91).

[6] T.D. DeRose, M. Lounsbery, and J. Warren. Multiresolution analysis for surfaces of arbitrary topological type. Technical Report 93-10-05, Department of Computer Science and Enginnering, University of Washington, Seattle, 1993.

[7] M. Do Carmo. *Differential Geometry of Curves and Surfaces*. Prentice Hall, 1976.

[8] D. Doo and M. Sabin. Behaviour of recursive division surfaces near extraordinary points. *Computer Aided Design*, 10:356–360, 1978.

[9] G. Golub and C.F. Van Loan. *Matrix Computations*. John Hopkins University Press, 2nd. edition, 1989.

[10] G. Greiner and H.P. Seidel. Modeling with triangular b-splines. *IEEE Computer Graphics and Applications*, 14(2):56–60, March 1994.

[11] A. Guéziec and R. Hummel. The wrapper algorithm: Surface extraction and simplification. In *IEEE Workshop on Biomedical Image Analysis*, pages 204–213, Seattle, WA, June 24–25 1994.

[12] M. Halstead, M. Kass, and T. DeRose. Efficient, fair interpolation using catmull-clark surface. *Computer Graphics*, pages 35–44, August 1993. (Proceedings SIGGRAPH'93).

[13] H. Hoppe, T. DeRose, T. Duchamp, J. McDonald, and W. Stuetzle. Mesh optimization. *Computer Graphics*, pages 19–26, August 1993. (Proceedings SIGGRAPH'93).

[14] W.M. Hsu, J.F. Hughes, and H. Kaufman. Direct manipulation of free-form deformations. *Computer Graphics*, pages 177–184, July 1992. (Proceedings SIGGRAPH'92).

[15] A.D. Kalvin. *Segmentation and Surface-Based Modeling of Objects in Three-Dimensional Biomedical Images*. PhD thesis, New York University, New York, March 1991.

[16] M. Kass, A. Witkin, and D. Terzopoulos. Snakes: active contour models. *International Journal of Computer Vision*, 1(4):321–331, 1988.

[17] T. Lindeberg. Scale-space for discrete signals. *IEEE Transactions on Pattern Analysis and Machine Intelligence*, 12(3):234–254, March 1990.

[18] C. Loop. Smooth subdivision surfaces based on triangles. Master's thesis, Dept. of Mathematics, University of Utah, August 1987.

[19] C. Loop. A G^1 triangular spline surface of arbitrary topological type. *Computer Aided Geometric Design*, 11:303–330, 1994.

[20] C. Loop. Smooth spline surfaces over irregular meshes. *Computer Graphics*, pages 303–310, July 1994. (Proceedings SIGGRAPH'94).

[21] W. Lorenson and H. Cline. Marching cubes: A high resolution 3d surface construction algorithm. *Computer Graphics*, pages 163–169, July 1987. (Proceedings SIGGRAPH).

[22] M. Lounsbery, S. Mann, and T. DeRose. Parametric surface interpolation. *IEEE Computer Graphics and Applications*, 12(5):45–52, September 1992.

[23] J. Menon. Constructive shell representations for freeform surfaces and solids. *IEEE Computer Graphics and Applications*, 14(2):24–36, March 1994.

[24] H.P. Moreton and C.H. Séquin. Functional optimization for fair surface design. *Computer Graphics*, pages 167–176, July 1992. (Proceedings SIGGRAPH'92).

[25] J. Oliensis. Local reproducible smoothing without shrinkage. *IEEE Transactions on Pattern Analysis and Machine Intelligence*, 15(3):307–312, March 1993.

[26] A. Pentland and S. Sclaroff. Closed-form solutions for physically based shape modeling and recognition. *IEEE Transactions on Pattern Analysis and Machine Intelligence*, 13(7):715–729, July 1991.

[27] E. Seneta. *Non-Negative Matrices, An Introduction to Theory and Applications*. John Wiley & Sons, New York, 1973.

[28] L.A. Shirman and C.H. Séquin. Local surface interpolation with bezier patches. *Computer Aided Geometric Design*, 4:279–295, 1987.

[29] W.J. Shroeder, A. Zarge, and W.E. Lorensen. Decimation of triangle meshes. *Computer Graphics*, pages 65–70, 1992. (Proceedings SIGGRAPH'92).

[30] R.S. Szeliski, D. Tonnesen, and D. Terzopoulos. Modeling surfaces of arbitrary topology with dynamic particles. In *Proceedings, IEEE Conference on Computer Vision and Pattern Recognition*, pages 82–87, New York, NY, June 15–17 1993.

[31] G. Taubin. Curve and surface smoothing without shrinkage. Technical Report RC-19536, IBM Research, April 1994. (also in Proceedings ICCV'95).

[32] G. Taubin. Estimating the tensor of curvature of a surface from a polyhedral approximation. Technical Report RC-19860, IBM Research, December 1994. (also in Proceedings ICCV'95).

[33] G. Taubin, T. Zhang, and G. Golub. Optimal polyhedral surface smoothing as filter design. (in preparation).

[34] D. Terzopoulos and K. Fleischer. Deformable models. *The Visual Computer*, 4:306–311, 1988.

[35] G. Turk. Re-tiling polygonal surfaces. *Computer Graphics*, pages 55–64, July 1992. (Proceedings SIGGRAPH'92).

[36] G. Turk and M. Levoy. Zippered polygon meshes from range data. *Computer Graphics*, pages 311–318, July 1994. (Proceedings SIGGRAPH'94).

[37] W. Welch and A. Witkin. Variational surface modeling. *Computer Graphics*, pages 157–166, July 1992. (Proceedings SIGGRAPH'92).

[38] W. Welch and A. Witkin. Free-form shape design using triangulated surfaces. *Computer Graphics*, pages 247–256, July 1994. (Proceedings SIGGRAPH'94).

[39] A.P. Witkin. Scale-space filtering. In *Proceedings, 8th. International Joint Conference on Artificial Intelligence (IJCAI)*, pages 1019–1022, Karlsruhe, Germany, August 1983.

[40] C.T. Zahn and R.Z. Roskies. Fourier descriptors for plane closed curves. *IEEE Transactions on Computers*, 21(3):269–281, March 1972.

APPENDIX

We first analyze those cases where the matrix W can be factorized as a product of a symmetric matrix E times a diagonal matrix D. Such is the case for the first order neighborhood of a shape with equal weights $w_{ij} = 1/|i^\star|$ in each neighborhood $i^\star$. In this case E is the matrix whose ij-th. element is equal to 1 if vertices v_i and v_j are neighbors, and 0 otherwise, and D is the diagonal matrix whose i-th. diagonal element is $1/|i^\star|$. Since in this case W is a *normal matrix* [9], because $D^{1/2}WD^{-1/2} = D^{1/2}ED^{1/2}$ is symmetric, W has all real eigenvalues, and sets of n left and right eigenvectors that form respective bases of n-dimensional space. Furthermore, by construction, W is also a *stochastic matrix*, a matrix with nonnegative elements and rows that add up to one [27]. The eigenvalues of a stochastic matrix are bounded above in magnitude by 1, which is the largest magnitude eigenvalue. It follows that the eigenvalues of the matrix K are real, bounded below by 0, and above by 2. Let $0 \leq k_1 \leq k_2 \leq \cdots \leq k_n \leq 2$ be the eigenvalues of the matrix K, and let $u_1, u_2, \ldots, u_n$ a set of linearly independent unit length right eigenvectors associated with them.

When the neighborhood structure is not symmetric, the eigenvalues and eigenvectors of W might not be real, but as long as the eigenvalues are not repeated, the decomposition of equation (3), and the analysis that follows, are still valid. However, the behavior of our fairing algorithm in this case will depend on the distribution of eigenvalues in the complex plane. The matrix W is still stochastic here, and so all the eigenvalues lie on a unit circle $|k_i - 1| < 1$. If all the eigenvalues of W are very close to the real line, the behavior of the fairing algorithm should be essentially the same as in the symmetric case. This seems to be the case when very few neighborhoods are made non-symmetric. But in general, the problem has to be analyzed on a case by case basis.

Modeling Surfaces of Arbitrary Topology using Manifolds[1]

Cindy M. Grimm

cmg@cs.brown.edu (401) 863-7693

John F. Hughes

jfh@cs.brown.edu (401) 863-7638

The Science and Technology Center
for Computer Graphics and Scientific Visualization

ABSTRACT

We describe an extension of B-splines to surfaces of arbitrary topology, including arbitrary boundaries. The technique inherits many of the properties of B-splines: local control, a compact representation, and guaranteed continuity of arbitrary degree. The surface is specified using a polyhedral control mesh instead of a rectangular one; the resulting surface approximates the polyhedral mesh much as a B-spline approximates its rectangular control mesh. Like a B-spline, the surface is a single, continuous object. This is achieved by modeling the domain of the surface with a manifold whose topology matches that of the polyhedral mesh, then embedding this domain into 3-space using a basis-function/control-point formulation. We provide a constructive approach to building a manifold.

CR Categories: I.3.5 [Computer Graphics]: Computational Geometry and Object Modeling, Curve, Surface, Solid, and Object Representations, Splines

1 Introduction

Surfaces of arbitrary topology are currently attracting a good deal of attention. While spline surfaces have proven a powerful modeling tool [BBB87] [Far88], modeling topologically arbitrary surfaces with them is hard, because they require a rectangular parameterization. To create complex surfaces, especially free-form ones such as Figure 17, we need a surface model which is computationally inexpensive and yet capable of modeling arbitrary topologies. Ideally, this surface model retains the power of spline surfaces: a compact representation, guaranteed continuity, and flexibility. This paper presents such a method of surface modeling.

Our approach differs from previous techniques in that the surface is constructed from pieces of surface which overlap substantially instead of abutting only along their edges. Mathematicians have studied such surfaces for many years [MS74] [ST67] using the technology of *manifolds*. Although the underlying mathematics is somewhat complicated, manifolds have advantages that make this complexity worthwhile.

[1] This work was supported in part by grants from NSF, ARPA, IBM, NCR, Sun Microsystems, DEC, HP, and ONR grant N00014-91-J-4052, ARPA order 8225.

Permission to make digital/hard copy of part or all of this work for personal or classroom use is granted without fee provided that copies are not made or distributed for profit or commercial advantage, the copyright notice, the title of the publication and its date appear, and notice is given that copying is by permission of ACM, Inc. To copy otherwise, to republish, to post on servers, or to redistribute to lists, requires prior specific permission and/or a fee.

Consider, for example, the problem of mapping textures onto two adjacent patches in a conventional spline surface. Matching the texture along the boundary between the patches may be difficult, since there is no common parameterization between the patches. With a manifold, however, the "edge" of one texture region is well within the adjacent texture region, so that the two textures can easily be blended.

Similarly, if one tries to make a smooth path on a surface, and the path crosses a patch boundary, maintaining smoothness of the path and its derivatives may be difficult. But there are no boundaries on a manifold because as a path gets near the edge of a patch, it has already entered the adjacent patch, and its derivatives can be computed in that new patch's coordinate system. This can be used to make various forms of user-interaction (sliding one object along another, for example) much smoother. Similarly, differential equations such as those used to generate reaction-diffusion textures can be solved by blending partial solutions across patch overlaps.

This paper begins with a survey of previous and related work, then sketches a high-level view of the surface construction technique. This is followed by a discussion of manifolds in general and how to build a manifold for a given surface. Next we discuss adding geometry to the manifold. Finally, we conclude with results and future work.

2 Previous work

Several different approaches to arbitrary-topology surface models have been suggested. Subdivision [CC78] [Loo87] produces a smooth surface by repeatedly subdividing a polyhedral mesh and in the limit yields a G^1 surface. This method is very general, but does not admit an analytical form (although recent work [HDK93] has made subdivision more tractable). Another approach is to "fill in" any non-rectangular parts of a mesh with n-sided patches [HM90] [LD89]. This is analogous to Bézier surfaces, in that it ensures continuity across the boundaries of patches by maintaining constraints on control points. A similar technique is to produce a collection of triangular (and possibly rectangular) elements from an initial mesh and stitch them together into a surface using the geometric information in the original mesh [Loo94]. In [WW94], the initial sketch is a set of contours over which a triangulated surface is stretched, using variational modeling techniques [WW92] to control the shape of the surface.

Unlike the previous methods, our approach produces a surface which is one continuous piece and hence does not require constraints to maintain continuity. Adding to (or removing from) the surface is similar to adding or removing a row of control points from a B-spline surface – continuity is automatically guaranteed.

Figure 1: Left: Gluing two patches together along their thin edge then bending the patches along the crease. Right: Gluing two patches together along a region then bending the patches together.

3 Overview

Spline patches are a powerful modeling tool but stitching them together into complex surfaces has proven difficult. As an analogy, consider building surfaces out of stretchy pieces of fabric that can be "glued" to each other. The pieces of fabric are spline patches, and the glue consists of mathematical operations such as control point constraints. Previous methods have focused on gluing these fabric pieces together by applying glue thinly along the abutting edges of the fabric pieces (see left of Figure 1). The problem with this technique is that a change to one of the fabric pieces is not reflected in the adjoining patch except along the glued edge. The smoothness of the joint is maintained by adjusting the adjoining patch afterwards.

Our approach is to apply glue to the top of one fabric piece and the bottom of another piece and then glue them together by *overlapping* the two pieces. Now, when the first piece is stretched or moved, the second, overlapping piece follows naturally with it (see right of Figure 1). This eliminates the need to re-establish the continuity of the join after every change to the surface. In the curve domain, this is the difference between Bézier curves and B-spline curves; Bézier curves are joined together into larger curves by constraining the control points at the end of one curve and at the beginning of the following curve. B-splines, on the other hand, are extended by adding in another overlapping curve segment. We prefer the B-spline approach because the domain is continuous and no constraints are required; to extend B-splines to arbitrary topologies, however, we first need a mechanism for adding overlapping pieces to a surface.

We begin by taking several pieces of fabric and gluing them together into a larger object by overlapping them. To describe the object, we need to describe the pieces of fabric and how they overlap. This is very similar to the familiar concept of an atlas of the world; each page of the atlas is rectangular (i.e., a piece of fabric) but the collection of pages describes a spherical object, the world. The pages of the atlas overlap enough to get from one page to the next. For example, the page for France contains part of Spain, and the page for Spain contains part of France. When traveling from France to Spain there is a time when one is located on both pages; the two maps may not be identical where they overlap but there is enough information to establish a correspondence between the two pages.

With an atlas we begin with an object, the world, and create a set of pages that cover the world, with each page overlapping with its neighbors. Suppose we did not have the world, but instead had just the pages of an atlas. We could put the pages onto stretchy pieces of fabric and glue them together using the information on the overlapping parts. This glued-together object is then a "world". This is a *constructive* approach to building a world as opposed to an analytical one. Because we do not have a world (i.e., the surface) *a priori*, we use this constructive approach to building a surface out of pieces of surface.

There is one more consideration: when we build our world from the pages of the atlas, how do we know what the world looks like?

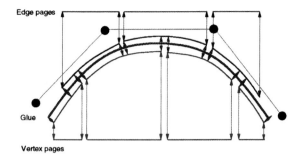

Figure 2: Stretching the pages of the atlas out to approximate the polygon, then gluing them together

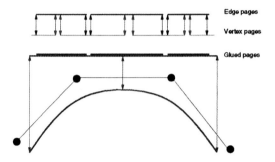

Figure 3: Glue the pages of the atlas together, then stretch them out to approximate the polygon.

The pages and their overlaps provide information on the *topology* of the object but no information on the *geometry* of it. With a real atlas we have some implicit knowledge of what the world looks like, but this knowledge is external to the atlas. There are two possible ways to add geometrical information into the atlas; consider the case of making an atlas for a curve. The rough shape of the desired curve is given by a control polygon. For each vertex and edge of the polygon we create have a page in the atlas. A page corresponding to an edge of the polygon overlaps with the two vertex pages corresponding to the vertices of the edge. The curve is built by gluing the vertex and edge pages together and adding geometrical information to describe what the curve looks like. This can be accomplished in two ways:

- First describe what each page looks like, then glue the pages together. This corresponds to taking the pages of the atlas, stretching them out to approximate the control polygon, then gluing them together (see Figure 2).

- First glue the pages together, then describe where they go. This corresponds to gluing the pages of the atlas together, then stretching them out to approximate the control polygon (see Figure 3).

We take the second approach because it is simpler. In the first approach, the gluing stage must be repeated every time the geometry of the surface changes, i.e., when the control polygon is moved. In the second approach, the gluing process is performed exactly once, and is independent of the particular geometry (but not topology) of the object.

Although this construction process is excessive for defining a curve, imagine constructing a surface from a polyhedron. Building an atlas provides us with a local description of the surface that is continuous and upon which we can navigate, i.e., perform operations such as calculating geodesics. The surface is relatively simple to describe locally but we can still perform global operations because the atlas pages overlap, allowing us to easily move from one area of the surface to another. In contrast, the traditional method of stitching patches together is to abut them, resulting in joins between the patches that must be dealt with separately.

4 Outline of the construction process

To build our surface we begin with a polyhedral mesh (created by the user) that describes the basic shape and topology of the surface. This is in analogy with a B-spline control mesh, except that the polyhedral mesh is not limited to a rectangular topology. We formally define this mesh in Section 5.

Next we define the pages of the atlas and how those pages overlap. We create one page for each *element* in the polyhedron, i.e., one page for each vertex, edge, and face. How the pages overlap is determined by the adjacency relationships in the polyhedron. For example, a face page overlaps with the pages for the vertices and edges of the face. Figure 20 shows a sample polyhedron and a surface colored by page type. In Section 6 we formally define an atlas and show how to construct an atlas using the polyhedron as a guide.

Finally, we add geometry ("shape") to the atlas. We do this in a manner similar to the one used for B-splines. On each page we build several basis functions and associate a control point with each function. This tells us where the middle part of each page goes; because the pages overlap, the location of the edges of the page will be influenced by the control points of the overlapping pages. This is covered in Section 8.

5 The polyhedron

Construction of a surface starts with a polyhedral "sketch." To simplify later steps, we require that every interior vertex have exactly four faces adjacent to it, i.e., vertices are of valence four. A polyhedron of this form can be constructed from an arbitrary polyhedron by taking the dual of the first subdivision [CC78][Kin77] (see Appendix D).

The polyhedral sketch must satisfy some technical restrictions that essentially say it "looks like" a surface: every vertex must be an end of some edge, every edge must be an edge of some face, at most two faces can meet at an edge, each *interior* vertex must have 4 edges and 4 faces adjacent to it, and each *boundary* vertex must have n edges and $n - 1$ faces adjacent to it. Furthermore, the polyhedron must be *orientable*, i.e., it must contain no embedded Mobius strips. These technical restrictions make the polyhedron an "oriented surface" in the sense of algebraic topology [Spa66]. Finally, we require that each face have 3, 4, 5, or 6 edges.

The polyhedral sketch contains three types of information: the *geometric* information given by the locations of the polyhedron vertices; the *local topological* information as given by the "incidence" relations—which vertices lie on which edges, which edges are in which faces; and the *global topological* information that can be derived from this local data: the number of components or pieces of the sketch, the number of boundary components, and the genus.

6 The atlas, or manifold

We have informally described an object consisting of pieces of fabric "glued together". This concept is called a *manifold*. Manifolds were introduced in the 1890s and formalized in the 1920s in order to describe objects whose topology was more complex than that of Euclidean space. The notion was that an object "locally like" Euclidean space could be studied in much the same way as Euclidean space. In one view, a manifold is a structure imposed on a set – a division of the set into overlapping regions, each of which is in correspondence with a portion of the Euclidean plane. Consider a

world atlas. Every point on the world can be found in at least one page in the atlas and sometimes in several. A path from one point to another can be found by tracing a line through the pages. Where the path must cross from one page to another, the two pages overlap enough that one can locate oneself on the second page. The individual pages are regions of $\Re^2$ but taken together they represent a sphere [MYV93]. There are also implicitly defined *transition functions* from one page to another. These are the "glue" we use to glue the pages together; they establish a correspondence between the region of one page and a region of another. Thus Brussels and its environs may appear on two different atlas pages: the page for Benelux countries, and also in the upper right corner of the page for France. The labels for Brussels and the surrounding towns, etc., establish a correspondence between the upper right corner of the France page and the lower left corner of the Benelux page.

6.1 Formal definition

In the traditional definition of a manifold the object exists and the manifold consists of *charts*, or mappings from the object to pieces of $\Re^n$. (The images of the charts are our atlas pages. From now on, we will refer to the atlas pages as charts.) This is an analytical view; because we do not have an object but are building it we depart from this view and define a *constructive* view of manifolds. Our constructive definition of a manifold starts with charts and information on how they overlap (the charts and the transition functions). We call this a *proto-manifold*. From the proto-manifold we build a manifold using an equivalence relation, i.e., we glue the charts together using "this place on this chart is the same as that place on that other chart." In [Gri] we show that this definition is equivalent to the traditional one.

Definition 1 A C^k differentiable proto-manifold K of dimension n consists of:

1. *A finite set A of connected open sets in $\Re^n$. A is called a* proto-atlas. *Each element $c \in A$ is called a* chart.

2. *A set of subsets $U_{ij} \subset c_i$, where c_i and c_j are charts in A and where $U_{ii} = c_i$.*

3. *A set of functions Ψ called* transition functions. *A transition function $\psi_{ij} \in \Psi$ is a map $\psi_{ij} : U_{ij} \to U_{ji}$ where $U_{ij} \subset c_i$ and $U_{ji} \subset c_j$. Note that U_{ij} and U_{ji} may well be empty. The following conditions on ψ_{ij} must hold:*

   (a) ψ_{ij} is $1 - 1$, onto, and C^k-differentiable

   (b) $\psi_{ij}^{-1} = \psi_{ji}$

   (c) $\psi_{ii}(x) = x, x \in c_i$

   (d) *The "cocycle condition": $(\psi_{ij} \circ \psi_{jk})(x) = \psi_{ik}(x)$ for $x \in U_{ik} \bigcap U_{ij}$ (see Figure 4)*

The charts $c \in A$ are the pages of the atlas. The subsets U_{ij} describe what part of chart i overlaps with chart j. The function ψ_{ij} defines the exact correspondence between points in U_{ij} and points in U_{ji}.

Next we build the manifold. If $K = (A, \Psi)$ is a proto-manifold then there is a relation $\sim$ defined on $\sqcup_{c \in A} c$ (where $\sqcup$ denotes disjoint union) such that if $x \in c_i, y \in c_j$, then $x \sim y$ iff $\psi_{ij}(x) = y$. Conditions (1)–(3) in Definition 1 ensure that $\sim$ is an equivalence relation [Gri].

Continuing the analogy, each chart c is a page of the world atlas, each transition function ψ_{ij} is a correspondence between parts of two charts, and the equivalence relation $\sim$ says that "the place labeled Brussels on page 93 is the same as the place labeled Brussels on page 24."

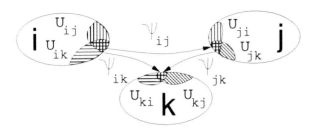

Figure 4: Three overlapping charts. The cocycle condition requires that $(\psi_{ij} \circ \psi_{jk})(x) = \psi_{ik}(x)$ for $x \in U_{ik} \bigcap U_{ij}$.

The relation $\sim$ lets us build a single object from the charts. If a point x in one chart is taken via ψ_{ij} to a point y in another chart $(\psi_{ij}(x) = y)$ then those two points are a single point on the final object.

Definition 2 *Let $\sim$ be the equivalence relation described above and K a proto-manifold as defined above. Define M as the quotient of $\sqcup_{c \in A} c$ by $\sim$. Let Π be the map taking $x \in \sqcup_{c \in A} c$ to $[x] \in M$, where $[x]$ is the equivalence class of x.*

In [Gri] we prove under weak conditions satisfied in the construction below that M is a Hausdorff space upon which we can construct a traditional manifold structure. The correspondence between our definition and the standard one is relatively simple: the image of a chart c under the map Π is a subset $\Pi(c) = D_c \subset M$; the restriction of Π to c defines a one-to-one correspondence

$$\gamma_c : c \to D_c \subset M, \qquad \gamma_c(x) = \Pi(x)$$

between c and D_c. The inverse of γ_c is a map α_c from a subset D_c of M to c which is a subset of $\Re^2$, i.e.,

$$\alpha_c : D_c \to c \subset \Re^2, \qquad \alpha_c(x) = \gamma_c^{-1}(x)$$

The maps α_c are the "coordinate charts" in the standard definition of a manifold structure on the set M [Spi70]. The map γ_c is called a *local parameterization* in [MS74] and a *coordinate system* in [Ste74].

Note that the name "chart" refers to one of our subsets of $\Re^2$ and that α and α^{-1} denote the correspondence between these charts and subsets of the manifold.

6.2 Building a manifold from a polyhedron

In the following discussion we construct a manifold without boundary, i.e., the polyhedron has no boundary vertices. Extending this construction to a manifold with boundary is straightforward, as explained in Section 7.

We use the topological structure of the polyhedron as a guide for building the manifold. We construct one chart for each element in the polyhedron and define the overlaps of the charts by the adjacency relationships in the polyhedron. This produces three sets of charts: the *vertex charts* — those charts corresponding to the vertices of the polyhedron — the *edge charts*, and the *face charts*. We denote these by $\mathbf{V} = \{$chart for $v\}_{v \in \mathcal{V}}$, $\mathbf{E}$, and $\mathbf{F}$, respectively. The entire proto-atlas A is then $\mathbf{V} \bigcup \mathbf{E} \bigcup \mathbf{F}$.

Figure 20 shows a polyhedron and the resulting surface, which has been colored according to chart type. The vertex charts ($\mathbf{V}$) are in red. Each vertex chart has eight other charts overlapping it: four edge charts (in green) and four face charts (in purple).

To keep the notation simple, henceforth V indicates the chart associated with a vertex v and V' the chart for a vertex named v', and similarly for edges and faces.

A chart in one set never overlaps with a different chart in that same set. A chart *does* overlap with those charts that are "nearby"

in the polyhedron. For example, a face chart only overlaps with the vertex and edge charts corresponding to the vertices and edges of the face. In summary:

1. $U_{VV'} = \emptyset$, $V \neq V'$ (and similarly for $U_{EE'}$ and $U_{FF'}$).

2. $U_{VE} \neq \emptyset$ iff $v \in e$.

3. $U_{VF} \neq \emptyset$ iff $v \in f$.

4. $U_{EF} \neq \emptyset$ iff e is an edge of f.

If we perform a similar construction in 2 dimensions then we have one chart for each vertex and one for each edge (see Figure 3). An edge chart E overlaps with two vertex charts V and V', where $e = \{v, v'\}$. In this case the charts are all segments of the real line; note how each edge chart is "nearly" covered by the two neighboring vertex charts. By "nearly" we mean the chart E is covered by the closure of U_{EV} and $U_{EV'}$, i.e.,

$$E = \overline{U_{EV} \bigcup U_{EV'}}.$$

To duplicate this in 3D we ensure that the edge and face charts are "nearly" covered by the overlapping vertex charts (see Figures 6 and 7).

In the 2D example, the interior vertex charts are also covered by the two overlapping edge charts, i.e.,

$$V = \overline{U_{VE} \bigcup U_{VE'}}.$$

We would also like to cover the vertex and face charts in this way but this turned out to be too restrictive. We do, however, require that the charts overlap as much as possible.

6.2.1 The charts

A chart is a connected, open subset of $\Re^2$. An overlap region is an open subset of the chart.

The vertex charts are unit squares centered at the origin. A vertex chart overlaps with four faces (the four quadrants) and four edges (Figure 5 shows the vertex chart and the overlap regions). A vertex-edge overlap region U_{VE} overlaps with the two regions U_{VF_0} and U_{VF_1} where f_0 and f_1 are the two faces adjacent to e.

The edge charts are diamonds with the left and right ends chopped off (see Figure 6). An edge chart overlaps with two vertex charts (the left and right half of the diamond) and two face charts (the upper and lower half of the diamond).

The face chart for an n-sided face is an n-sided regular polygon centered at the origin (slightly smaller then a unit polygon). The edge charts overlap the edges of the polygon, while the vertex charts overlap the corners. The region U_{FE} overlaps the two regions U_{FV_0} and U_{FV_1}, where v_0 and v_1 are the endpoints of e.

The details of the charts and their overlaps are given in Appendix B.

6.2.2 The transition functions

The transition functions are the glue that holds the charts together. We have described what parts of the charts to glue together but not the exact correspondence between them.

Transition functions must meet two requirements: they must be C^k, and the cocycle condition must hold (see Figure 4). Additionally, we would like the functions to be as close to the identity function as possible. By this we mean that a transformed (via $\psi_{cc'}$) image on $U_{c'c}$ should look as much like the original image on $U_{cc'}$ as possible.

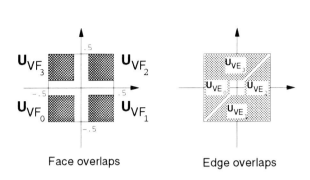

Figure 5: A vertex chart. Left: the four regions U_{VF_i} Right: the four regions U_{VE_i}

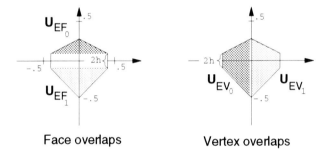

Figure 6: An edge chart. Left: the two regions U_{EF_i} (F_0 is 3-sided, F_1 is 4-sided). Right: the two regions U_{EV_i}

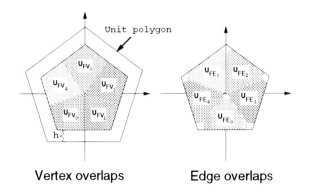

Figure 7: A face chart. Left: the n regions U_{FV_i} Right: the n regions U_{FE_i}

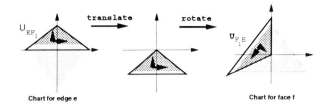

Figure 8: Mapping from an edge chart to a face chart by translating then rotating.

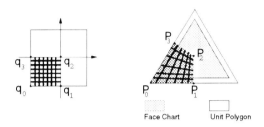

Figure 9: Mapping from a face chart to a vertex chart using a projective transformation.

Charts within the set $\mathbf{V}$ (and similarly $\mathbf{E}$ and $\mathbf{F}$) do not overlap. Thus the transition function $\psi_{VV'}$ is either the empty function (if $V \neq V'$) or the identity (if $V = V'$), and similarly for edge-edge and face-face transition functions.

This means we need only consider the transition functions between charts in distinct chart sets, e.g. vertex-to-face transitions. If we define the function $\psi_{CC'}$ then the function $\psi_{C'C}$ is defined as its inverse. Thus the transition functions we define can be divided into three categories: edge-to-face, vertex-to-face, and vertex-to-edge.

Satisfying the cocycle condition is a matter of ensuring that the function taking the edge chart to the vertex chart directly is the same as the combination of functions taking an edge chart to a face chart to a vertex chart (see Figure 10). We first define the edge-to-face and vertex-to-face functions, and then define the edge-to-vertex functions as compositions of the other two.

The edge-to-face transition function is a plane isometry; the region U_{EF} is simply translated and rotated (see Figure 8). The vertex-to-face transition function takes the quadrant U_{VF} and "stretches" it using a projective transformation to fit it into the corner of the face chart (see Figure 9).

The edge-to-vertex transition function is built as a blend of two functions which are compositions. Examining Figure 10, on the top half of the diamond the function must be the composition of the edge-to-face and face-to-vertex functions for the top face, while on the bottom half of the diamond the function must be the corresponding composition of the bottom face functions. These two composed functions will not, in general, agree along the x−axis. To fix this, we have left a *gap* between the two composed functions; this lets us *blend* between the two composed functions in the gap. (This is the reason the face charts are slightly smaller than the unit polygon – to give us room to do the blend.) Care must be taken to ensure that this function is 1-1, onto, and C^k; details of this (and the other functions) are given in Appendix C.

6.3 The manifold

A formal proof that these charts and transition functions form a proto-manifold (Definition 1) appears in [Gri]. Informally, the charts are defined to be open sets in $\Re^2$ and the transition functions are defined to be 1–1, onto, and C^k. The cocycle condition is satisfied because in the only non-trivial case, where three charts overlap (one each of

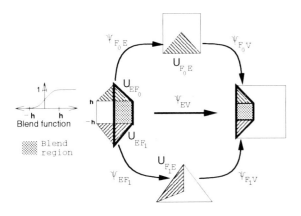

Figure 10: Mapping from an edge chart to a vertex chart using the upper and lower composition functions.

a vertex, edge, and face chart), we have defined the functions to be compositions of the others.

7 Manifolds with boundary

To extend our definition to a manifold with boundary we allow the charts of the proto-manifold to be half-balls in $\Re^n$. We use a manifold with boundary when the polyhedral sketch has a boundary, i.e., when an edge has a single adjacent face. Since a boundary never occurs in the middle of a face chart, we need only alter our descriptions of vertex and edge charts. An edge chart E corresponding to a boundary edge is simply a triangle joined with the $x-$axis. A vertex chart V corresponding to a boundary vertex is a contiguous subset of the quadrants of the unit square, with some part of the axes included (e.g., a vertex chart corresponding to a corner vertex would consist of a single quadrant).

The definitions of the transition functions remain unchanged except for the edge-vertex functions, since the overlap regions remain unchanged. The edge-vertex function becomes just the single composed function one one-half of the edge chart. The α_c functions also remain the same.

8 Adding geometry to the manifold

We now have a collection of stretchy fabric pieces glued together but with no geometric structure (they are just "collapsed on the floor in a pile"). Rather than describe what the entire object looks like all at once, we just describe what the middle of each chart looks like. Because of the way the charts overlap, this will determine the geometry of the entire manifold.

To define the geometry we use a basis-function control-point formulation. The basis functions $\{B_s : M \to \Re\}_{s \in S}$ are a finite collection S of local, C^k functions that sum to one everywhere; they are analogous to traditional B-spline basis functions. The basis function B_s determines how much the control point $G_s \in \Re^3$ influences the surface Q at a given point:

$$Q(p) = \sum_{s \in S} G_s B_s(p)$$

We next describe how to build the basis functions.

8.1 Basis functions

To build the basis functions we first define a set of *proto-basis functions* on the chart and associate a control point with each proto-basis

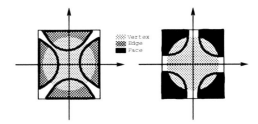

Figure 11: The center part of overlapping charts in a vertex chart.

function. Specifically, we have a set $\{\hat{b}_s\}_{s \in S}$ of C^k functions

$$\hat{b}_s : c \to \Re$$

where $s = \{c, i\}$, $c \in A$ and $i \in 1 \ldots n_c$. The number n_c is dependent upon the desired continuity k and the type of chart (vertex, edge, or face). We define these functions in Section 8.1.1; for now, suffice it to say they are C^k and go to 0 by the boundary of c and are similar to a tensor-product basis function.

The $\hat{b}$ functions are defined on the individual charts and hence do not interact with functions on other charts. We next extend the $\hat{b}$ functions to the manifold where they will interact. Imagine building piles of sand on each page of the atlas. When the pages of the atlas are glued together the piles of sand are no longer on a single page but possibly on several pages glued together, each page of which may have its own piles of sand. Formally these piles of sand are built by extending the proto-basis functions to the manifold by using the α_c functions where they are defined and 0 where they are not. Define $\hat{B}_s : M \to \Re$ by

$$\hat{B}_s(p) = \begin{cases} \hat{b}_s(\alpha_c(p)) & \text{if } p \in \alpha_c^{-1}(c) \\ 0 & \text{otherwise} \end{cases}$$

These functions are C^k and local. For the surface Q to behave like a spline surface, we require basis functions B_s that meet three properties that traditional basis functions satisfy:

- B_s is C^k for some k.

- B_s is local (its support lies in a single chart).

- $\sum_{s \in S} B_s(p) = 1$ for all $p \in M$.

The last step is to normalize the $\hat{B}_s$ functions to ensure that they sum to one. If for every point $p \in M$ we have $\sum_{s \in S} \hat{B}_s(p) \neq 0$ then the definition $B_s : M \to \Re$,

$$B_s(p) = \frac{\hat{B}_s(p)}{\sum_{s' \in S} \hat{B}_{s'}(p)}$$

is valid. Figure 11 shows how the center parts of edge and face charts overlap a vertex chart. Recall that the vertex charts "nearly" cover every chart and hence the manifold; to ensure that the above definition is valid, we make certain that the supports of the proto-basis functions cover the center area of the chart in which they are defined. As shown in Figure 11, this ensures that the vertex charts are covered by the supports of the $\{\hat{B}_s\}_{s \in S}$ functions and hence that the manifold is covered by them as well.

8.1.1 The proto-basis functions

We now show how to build the proto-basis functions using a tensor-product B-spline and a projective transformation. For each proto-basis function $\hat{b}_{c,i}(r)$ we start with a quadrilateral Q_i in its chart c

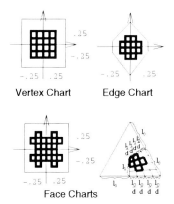

Figure 12: The quadrilaterals Q_i for the proto-basis functions with grid division 4.

(see Figure 12) and construct a projective transformation ϕ_{Q_i} (see Appendix A) from the quadrilateral to the unit square. Let $\beta : \Re^2 \to \Re$ be a C^k tensor-product B-spline whose support is from $0 - (k/2)$ to $1 + k/2$. Then the ith proto-basis function is

$$\hat{b}_i(r) = \beta(\phi_{Q_i}(r))$$

The quadrilaterals for the face chart are formed by mapping a subdivided unit square into U_{FV} via a projective transform. If ϕ_{FV} is a projective transform from U_{FV} to the unit square then the four corners of Q_0 are ϕ_{FV}^{-1} of $(0,0)$, $(0,1/d)$, $(1/d,1/d)$, and $(1/d,0)$.

The choice of d depends on k. The size and number of the quadrilaterals (and the size of the support of the tensor-product B-spline) are chosen so that the supports of the proto-basis functions cover as much of the chart as possible without falling out of it. For the C^2 pictures we used a grid division of 4.

8.2 The control points

The location of the control points is completely unconstrained; however, the user has already provided a rough sketch of the shape of the surface (the polyhedron). We provide an initial placement of the control points based on the subdivision surface of the polyhedron.

We describe how to assign values to the control points using the Catmull-Clark subdivision surface ($\mathcal{L}$) of the polyhedron. This produces a surface with the "feel" of a B-spline surface (note, though, that the choice of values does not affect the continuity). We define a mapping from the manifold to the subdivision surface $\mathcal{H} : M \to \mathcal{L}$ and assign the function G_s the value $\mathcal{H}(p_s)$, where p_s is the center of support for the basis function B_s.

To define $\mathcal{H}$, we first note that after one level of subdivision we have one subdivision point l_c for each chart c in M. We relate the origins of the charts to the subdivision points by $\mathcal{H}(\alpha_c(0,0)) = l_c$. This places the subdivision points in a chart V as shown on the left of Figure 13.

After one level of subdivision every face in the subdivision surface is 4-sided; these faces are mapped to the quadrants of the vertex charts. Further subdivisions "grids" the vertex chart as shown in the right of Figure 13. We define $\mathcal{H}$ by assigning the grid points $(\alpha_V^{-1}(\text{grid point}))$ to their corresponding points in the subdivision surface. Eventually, this relates a set of points that are dense in M to the subdivision points.[1] The function for $\mathcal{H}$ on this dense set can be extended to M in a natural way.

---

[1] We assign the points along the boundary of the vertex charts $\alpha_V(V)$ to their adjacent points in M.

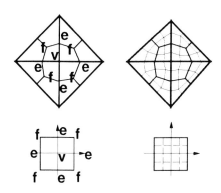

Figure 13: An abstraction of the subdivision process on a vertex chart. The polyhedron has been subdivided twice.

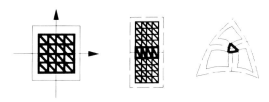

Figure 14: Left: Triangulating the interior of a vertex chart. Middle: Adjoining edges. Right: Filling in the corners.

8.3 Triangulating the embedding

There is a tradeoff between the number of triangles in the triangulation and how closely it approximates the surface. The triangulation presented here produces approximately $(2r)(2r)N_v$ triangles for a given resolution r. If the control points are evenly spaced then the resulting triangulation is also evenly spaced.

We triangulate the domain by first triangulating the vertex charts as shown on the left of Figure 14, where r determines the number of squares. To fill in the remaining gaps, we adjoin the triangles along the boundaries to the triangles of neighboring vertex charts using a strip of triangles. The corners are filled in with an appropriate n-sided triangulation (see Figure 14).

9 Remarks and future work

Images 17–22 show some example surfaces, most of which were created using an interactive editor. The coloring of Image 18 was determined by running a reaction-diffusion simulation on the manifold and using the resulting chemical concentrations to create the stripes [Tur91]. Because the embedding defines a metric on the manifold, we can use either that global metric or the local (chart) metric with the reaction-diffusion equations.

This surface technique produces aesthetically pleasing models fairly efficiently and easily. It is also suitable for data fitting because the topology of the surface can be made to fit the topology of the data, bringing the surface fairly close to the data initially. Additionally, continuity constraints need not be maintained while fitting the surface to the data.

Although this technique shares many of the properties of traditional splines, some techniques have yet to be developed, such as the equivalent of knot insertion and the Oslo algorithm. Although we can use subdivision to produce a more finely controllable surface similar in shape to the original surface, this surface is not necessarily identical to the original. Note that if the polyhedral mesh is rectangular then the resulting surface reduces to a B-spline surface.

10 Implementation

We have implemented a simple interactive polyhedral editor to create the surfaces shown here. The user builds an arbitrary polyhedron P by creating vertices and connecting them together into faces. The system automatically creates a second polyhedral model C which is the dual of the first subdivision surface of P. (Figure 16 shows both P and C for the flower model.) The user is free to move the vertices of C. The editor runs in real time on an HP-735 with surfaces of continuity C'^2 and a triangulation level of 4.

11 Acknowledgments

We would like to thank our sponsors for providing the support for this research, Dan Robbins for help with the video, Michael Kowalski for the model of Alexander's two-holed torus, and Tony DeRose, Jean Schweitzer, Marc Levoy, and Jules Bloomenthal for their helpful comments.

A Projective Transformations

Let $B_1 = (1, 0, 0)^t$, $B_2 = (0, 1, 0)^t$, $B_3 = (0, 0, 1)^t$, and $B_4 = (1, 1, 1)^t$ and let $P_1 \ldots P_4$ be the (column vectors of) homogeneous coordinates of four points of the plane, no three colinear. There is a matrix T_P such that $T_P(B_i)$ is a non-zero multiple of P_i. Here is the construction of T_P: Let M_P be the 3×3 matrix whose columns are P_1, P_2, and P_3. Let $\Lambda = M_P^{-1} P_4$. Letting λ_i ($i = 1, 2, 3$) denote the entries of Λ, T_P is the matrix whose columns are $\lambda_1 P_1$, $\lambda_2 P_2$ and $\lambda_3 P_3$.

To find a projective transformation on the plane taking any set of four points $\{P_i\}$, no three colinear, to any other such set $\{Q_i\}$, compute the matrix $K = T_Q T_P^{-1}$. Multiplying K by the vector $(x, y, 1)^t$ gives a vector $(X(x, y), Y(x, y), W(x, y))$. The projective transformation we seek is just $(x, y) \mapsto \left(\frac{X(x,y)}{W(x,y)}, \frac{Y(x,y)}{W(x,y)} \right)$.

B Charts

We describe the exact shape of each chart (a subset of $\Re^2$) and the overlap regions $U_{cc'}$.

Each vertex chart is a unit square centered at the origin (see Figure 5). A vertex chart overlaps four face charts (corresponding to the four faces having v as a vertex) and four edge charts (corresponding to the four edges having v as a vertex). The U_{Vc} are defined to be $\varphi_{cV}(U_{cV})$. If U_{VF_i} and U_{VE_j} overlap then e must be an edge of f.

The face chart for an n-sided face is an n-sided regular polygon centered at the origin. The size of the polygon is chosen so that the perpendicular distance from the edge of the face chart to the edge of the unit polygon containing it is a constant h (see Figure 7). Typically, h is small. For the figures in this paper a value of .1 was used. A *wedge* of a polygon is the triangle whose vertices are the center of the polygon and the two ends of one side of the polygon.

An n-sided face chart overlaps with n vertex charts (the n corners of F) and n edge charts (the n edges of F). The U_{FV_i} are bounded by lines drawn from the centroid of the polygon to the midpoints of the polygon edges. The U_{FE_i} are the parts of the chopped-off "wedges" mentioned above that actually lie in the chart F. If $U_{FV} \bigcap U_{FE} \neq \emptyset$ then v is a vertex of e.

The edge chart is a diamond with its left and right ends chopped off. The diamond consists of two triangles, one congruent to a wedge of a unit polygon with the same number of sides as each of the overlapping face charts. The triangles are joined along the sides that correspond to the edge, and that side is placed along the x-axis.

An edge chart overlaps two face charts and two vertex charts (the left and right sides of E). If $f_0 = \{\ldots, v, v', \ldots\}$ and $f_1 = \{\ldots, v', v, \ldots\}$ then U_{EF_0} is in the upper half plane. U_{EV} is on the left, and $U_{EV'}$ is on the right.

C Transition functions

The face-to-edge function is a rigid motion (see Figure 8). Let d_n be the height of the wedge and θ be the amount of rotation:

$$\varphi_{FE}(s, t) = \{s \cos\theta - t \sin\theta, t \cos\theta + s \sin\theta + d_n\}$$

The face-to-vertex transition function uses the unique projective transformation taking any four points in the plane, no three of which are collinear, to any other four such points (see Appendix A). Let ϕ_{PQ} denote the projective map that takes a corner of a unit polygon P containing a face chart F to a quadrant Q of a vertex chart V (see Figure 9). The function φ_{FV} is simply the restriction of ϕ_{PQ} to U_{FV} and φ_{VF} is ϕ_{PQ}^{-1} restricted to U_{VF}.

The edge-to-vertex transition is defined in terms of the other transition functions. We define φ_{EV} to be $\varphi_{F_0V} \circ \varphi_{EF_0}$ on U_{EF_0} and $\varphi_{F_1V} \circ \varphi_{EF_1}$ on U_{EF_1} so that the cocycle condition is satisfied (see Figure 10). To complete our definition, we need only define φ_{EV} on the no-man's land, i.e., we must produce a smooth blend between the two composite functions on the region $U_{EV} - (U_{EF_0} \bigcup U_{EF_1})$. Recall that the regions U_{EF_i} are each at a distance h from the x-axis (this displacement by h was included precisely to permit us do this blend). The choice of h will affect the embedding function defined in Section 8, but does not affect the discussion here.

To define φ_{EV} we first extend the domains of the functions φ_{EF_i} and φ_{F_iV}. φ_{EF_0} is linear, so it extends to all of $\Re^2$; similarly for φ_{EF_1}. Now we extend the domains of the functions φ_{F_iV} to the region $\varphi_{EF_0}(U_{EV} - U_{EF_1})$, i.e., the domain of the φ_{EF_0} plus the no-man's land. The singularities of φ_{VF_0} lie on a line that does not intersect $\varphi_{EF_0}(U_{EV} - U_{EF_1})$ [Gri]. Therefore the composite function can be extended to the region $U_{EV} - U_{EF_1}$. A similar argument holds for φ_{EF_1}. Using these extended functions, we define φ_{EV} by

$$\begin{aligned} \varphi_{EV}(x, y) &= \eta(y)\varphi_{EF_0} \circ \varphi_{F_0V}(x, y) \\ &\quad + (1 - \eta(y))\varphi_{EF_1} \circ \varphi_{F_1V}(x, y) \end{aligned}$$

where $\eta : \Re \to \Re$ is a blend function which is C^k, and is 1 to the right of h and 0 to the left of $-h$. In [Gri] we show that φ_{EV} is invertible and 1–1 on U_{VE}.

D Dual of first subdivision surface

Given a polyhedron P, the first subdivision surface P' of P contains a vertex for every vertex, edge, and face of P (see Figure 15). All of the faces of P' have exactly 4 sides [Kin77]. Taking the dual of this produces a polyhedron C with vertices of valence 4. Figure 16 shows the original polyhedron P in light blue, and the dual surface C in green. The vertices of C are initially placed at the centroids of the faces of P'.

REFERENCES

[BBB87]   R. Bartels, J. Beatty, and B. Barsky. *An Introduction to Splines for Use in Computer Graphics and Geometric Modeling*. Morgan Kaufmann, 1987.

[CC78]   E. Catmull and J. Clark. Recursively Generated B-spline Surfaces on Arbitrary Topological Meshes. *Computer Aided Design*, 10(6):350–355, November 1978.

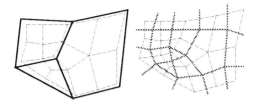

Figure 15: An example of taking the dual of the first subdivsion surface of an arbitrary polygon. The original polygon is shown in black, the first subdivision surface in dashed lines, and the dual in light grey.

[Far88]   G. Farin. *Curves and Surfaces for Computer Aided Geometric Design*. Academic Press, 1988.

[Gri]   C. Grimm. *Surfaces of Arbitrary Topology using Manifolds*. PhD thesis, Brown University (in progress).

[HDK93]   M. Halstead, T. DeRose, and M. Kass. Efficient, Fair Interpolation Using Catmull-Clark Surfaces. *Computer Graphics*, 27(2):35–44, July 1993. Proceedings of SIGGRAPH '93 (Los Angeles).

[HM90]   K. Hollig and H. Mogerle. G-splines. *Computer Aided Geometric Design*, 7:197–207, 1990.

[Kin77]   P. King. On Local Combinatorial Pontrjagin Numbers (I). *Topology*, 16:99–106, 1977.

[LD89]   C. Loop and T. DeRose. A Multisided Generalization of Bézier Surfaces. *ACM TOG*, 8(3):204–234, July 1989.

[Loo87]   C. Loop. Smooth Subdivision Surfaces Based on Triangles. Master's thesis, University of Utah, 1987.

[Loo94]   C. Loop. Smooth Spline Surfaces Over Irregular Meshes. *Computer Graphics*, 28(2):303–310, July 1994. Proceedings of SIGGRAPH '94.

[MS74]   J. Milnor and J. Stasheff. *Annals of Mathematical Studies*. Princeton University Press, Princeton, New Jersey, 1974.

[MYV93]   J. Maillot, H. Yahia, and A. Verroust. Interactive Texture Mapping. *Computer Graphics*, 27(4):27–35, July 1993. Proceedings of SIGGRAPH '93.

[Spa66]   E. H. Spanier. *Algebraic Topology*. McGraw-Hill Inc., New York, New York, 1966.

[Spi70]   M. Spivak. *Differential Geometry Volume 1*. Publish or Perish Inc., 1970.

[ST67]   I.M. Singer and J. A. Thorpe. *Lecture Notes on Elementary Topology and Geometry*. Scott, Foresman and Company, Glenview, Illinois, 1967.

[Ste74]   N. Steenrod. *The Topology of Fibre Bundles*. Princeton University Press, Princeton, New Jersey, 1974.

[Tur91]   G. Turk. Generating Textures on Arbitrary Surfaces Using Reaction-Diffusion. *Computer Graphics*, 25(2):289–298, July 1991. Proceedings of SIGGRAPH '91 (Las Vegas).

[WW92]   W. Welch and A. Witkin. Variational Surface Modeling. *Computer Graphics*, 22(2):157–166, July 1992. Proceedings of SIGGRAPH '92.

[WW94]   W. Welch and A. Witkin. Free Form Shape Design Using Triangulated Surfaces. *Computer Graphics*, 28(2):247–256, July 1994. Proceedings of SIGGRAPH '94.

Figure 16: The polyhedral sketch for the flower. The light blue polygon (drawn in wire-frame) is built by the user. The green polygon is the dual of the first subdivision surface of the light blue polygon and is constructed automatically. The locations of the vertices of the green polygon have been adjusted to produce finer detail.

Figure 17: A two-holed torus in the shape of a flower.

Figure 18: The coloring is achieved by running a reaction-diffusion system on the domain of the surface (the process was halted when partially finished for aesthetic reasons).

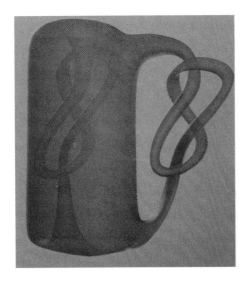

Figure 19: Alexander's two-holed torus (in the shape of a mug).

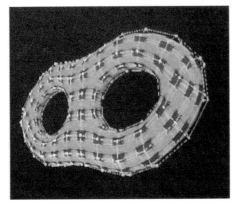

Figure 20: A two-holed torus colored by atlas page type (vertex, edge, or face).

Figure 21: A laser-scanned image of a ceramic bunny, courtesy of Stanford University.

Figure 22: An approximation of the laser-scanned bunny.

A General Construction Scheme for Unit Quaternion Curves with Simple High Order Derivatives[1]

Myoung-Jun Kim,[2] Myung-Soo Kim,[3] and Sung Yong Shin[2]

[2]Korea Advanced Institute of Science and Technology (KAIST)

[3]Pohang University of Science and Technology (POSTECH)

ABSTRACT

This paper proposes a new class of unit quaternion curves in $SO(3)$. A general method is developed that transforms a curve in R^3 (defined as a weighted sum of basis functions) into its unit quaternion analogue in $SO(3)$. Applying the method to well-known spline curves (such as Bézier, Hermite, and B-spline curves), we are able to construct various unit quaternion curves which share many important differential properties with their original curves.

Many of our naive common beliefs in geometry break down even in the simple non-Euclidean space S^3 or $SO(3)$. For example, the de Casteljau type construction of cubic B-spline quaternion curves does not preserve C^2-continuity [10]. Through the use of decomposition into simple primitive quaternion curves, our quaternion curves preserve most of the algebraic and differential properties of the original spline curves.

CR Descriptors: I.3.5 [**Computer Graphics**]: Computational Geometry and Object Modeling – Curve, surface, solid, and object representation, – Geometric algorithms. **Keywords**: Quaternion, rotation, orientation, $SO(3)$, Bézier, Hermite, B-spline

1 INTRODUCTION

In computer animation, it is very important to have appropriate tools to produce smooth and natural motions of a rigid body. A rigid motion in R^3 can be represented by a Cartesian product of two component curves: one in the Euclidean space R^3 and the other in the rotation group $SO(3)$ [3, 12]. The curve in R^3 represents the center position of the rigid body, and the other curve in $SO(3)$ represents its orientation. Often, techniques for specifying a rigid motion construct the two curves independently. It is relatively easy to produce smooth curves in the Euclidean space. B-spline, Hermite, and Bézier curves exemplify well-known techniques for constructing position curves in R^3. However, smooth orientation curves in $SO(3)$ are much more difficult to construct.

[1]This research was partially supported by the Korean Ministry of Science and Technology under the contract 94-S-05-A-03 of STEP 2000 and TGRC-KOSEF.

[2]Computer Science Department, KAIST, Taejeon 305-701, Korea.

[3]Dept. of Computer Science, POSTECH, Pohang 790-784, Korea.

E-mail: {mjkim, syshin}@jupiter.kaist.ac.kr and mskim@vision.postech.ac.kr.

Permission to make digital/hard copy of part or all of this work for personal or classroom use is granted without fee provided that copies are not made or distributed for profit or commercial advantage, the copyright notice, the title of the publication and its date appear, and notice is given that copying is by permission of ACM, Inc. To copy otherwise, to republish, to post on servers, or to redistribute to lists, requires prior specific permission and/or a fee.

The spline curves in R^3 are usually defined in two different but equivalent ways: i.e., either as an algebraic construction using basis functions or as a geometric construction based on recursive linear interpolations [2]. This paper proposes a general framework which extends the algebraic construction methods to $SO(3)$. Most of the previous methods are based on extending the linear interpolation in R^3 to the *slerp* (spherical linear interpolation) in $SO(3)$ [14, 16, 17, 18]. The two (i.e., algebraic and geometric) construction schemes generate identical curves in R^3; however, this is not the case in the non-Euclidean space $SO(3)$ [10]. Many of our commonplace beliefs in geometry break down in the non-Euclidean space $SO(3)$.

When the recursive curve construction is not based on a simple closed form algebraic equation, it becomes extremely difficult to do any extensive analysis on the constructed curve. For example, consider the problem of computing the first derivative of the cubic Bézier quaternion curve or the squad curve generated by a recursive slerp construction [17, 18]. Though Shoemake [17, 18] postulates correct first derivatives, the quaternion calculus employed there is incorrect (see [9] for more details). Kim, Kim, and Shin [9] developed a correct quaternion calculus for the first derivatives of unit quaternion curves; however, an extension to the second derivatives becomes much more complex (also see [11] for a related quaternion calculus on blending-type quaternion curves).

More seriously, the C^2-continuity of a spline curve in R^3 may not carry over to $SO(3)$. Furthermore, the curve conversion between two different spline curves, e.g., from a cubic Bézier curve to the corresponding cubic B-spline curve, may not work out in $SO(3)$ [10]. Kim, Kim, and Shin [10] show that there is no C^2-continuity guaranteed for the cubic B-spline quaternion curves which are generated by the recursive slerp construction of Schlag [16]. Similarly, the B-spline quaternion curve of Nielson and Heiland [13] also fails to have C^2-continuity (see [10] for more details).

In this paper, we take an important step toward generalizing the algebraic formulation of spline curves in R^3 to similar ones in $SO(3)$. In the new algebraic formulation, the computation of high order derivatives becomes almost as easy as that of the spline curves in R^3. We show that the quaternion curves generated in this way preserve many important differential properties of their original curves in R^3. They are defined in simple closed algebraic forms of quaternion equations, and they have the same degrees of geometric continuity as their counterparts in R^3.

As a demonstration of the feasibility of our proposed method, we first construct a Bézier quaternion curve with n control unit quaternions. Then, the cubic Bézier quaternion curve is used to construct a Hermite quaternion curve. We also construct a k-th order B-spline quaternion curve which is C^{k-2}-continuous and locally controllable. There are many other spline curves which can be defined by weighted sums of control points; our construction method is general in that all these spline curves are extendible to their corresponding quaternion curves. Since it is possible to manipulate the position curve as well as the corresponding orientation curve in a unified manner, the modeling and manipulation of rigid motions can be managed more conveniently.

The key to the success of our construction method is that the quaternion curve is formulated as a product of simple primitive quaternion curves: $q_i(t) = \exp(\omega_i f_i(t))$, $i = 1, \ldots, n$, for some fixed angular velocity $\omega_i \in R^3$ and real valued function $f_i(t)$, where $\exp : R^3 \rightarrow SO(3)$ is an exponential map [3]. Each primitive curve, $q_i(t)$, represents a rotation about a fixed axis, $\omega_i \in R^3$, for which the derivative formula has an extremely simple form: $q_i'(t) = \exp(\omega_i f_i(t))(\omega_i f_i'(t)) = q_i(t)(\omega_i f_i'(t))$. Since the chain rule can be applied to the quaternion product: $q(t) = q_1(t) \cdots q_n(t)$, the resulting differential formula has the simplest expression that one can expect for unit quaternion curves. Furthermore, a similar technique can be used to obtain high order derivatives of our quaternion curves. There have been many other methods suggested for the construction of quaternion curves, including the CAGD approaches based on constructing rational curves on the 3-sphere S^3 [8, 20]. Nevertheless, no method has provided such a simple derivative formula. The only exception is the method of Pobegailo [15] which constructs a C^k-continuous spherical curve as a product of $(k + 1)$ rotation matrices: $R_{k+1} R_k \ldots R_1$. The generated curve is, however, essentially restricted to the Bézier type quaternion curve of our method.

The development of closed form equations for the second order derivatives provides an important step toward solving the important problem of torque minimization for 3D rotations [1, 6, 7]. However, the torque minimization problem requires much more. The optimal solution is given as a critical path in the problem of calculus of variations among a set of quaternion paths which satisfy the given conditions. For this purpose, we may need to extend the quaternion curve construction scheme of this paper to that of quaternion surfaces and volumes. This is currently a difficult open problem. Therefore, the important problem of torque minimization for 3D rotations has not been solved in this paper. Nevertheless, the basic algebraic approach taken in this paper provides an important conceptual framework for future research toward this goal.

The rest of this paper is organized as follows. In Section 2, we briefly review some useful concepts and definitions related to unit quaternions. Section 3 describes the main motivation of this work. Section 4 outlines our basic idea for constructing unit quaternion curves. Section 5 constructs the Bézier, Hermite, and B-spline quaternion curves and discusses their differential properties. Section 6 shows some experimental results with discussions on possible further extensions. Finally, in Section 7, we conclude this paper.

2 PRELIMINARIES

2.1 Quaternion and Rotation

Given a unit quaternion $q \in S^3$, a 3D rotation $R_q \in SO(3)$ is defined as follows:

$$R_q(p) = qpq^{-1}, \quad \text{for } p \in R^3, \tag{1}$$

where $p = (x, y, z)$ is interpreted as a quaternion $(0, x, y, z)$ and the quaternion multiplication is assumed for the products [3, 17, 18]. Let $q = (\cos \theta, \hat{v} \sin \theta) \in S^3$, for some angle θ and unit vector $\hat{v} \in S^2$, then R_q is the rotation by angle 2θ about the axis $\hat{v}$. The multiplicative constant, 2, in the angle of rotation, 2θ, is due to the fact that q appears twice in Equation (1). Also note that $R_q \equiv R_{-q}$; that is, two antipodal points, q and $-q$ in S^3, represent the same rotation in $SO(3)$.

The two spaces S^3 and $SO(3)$ have the same local topology and geometry. The major difference is in the distance measures of the two spaces $SO(3)$ and S^3. A rotation curve $R_{q(t)} \in SO(3)$ is twice as long as the corresponding unit quaternion curve $q(t) \in S^3$. When a smooth rotation curve $R_{q(t)}$ has an angular velocity $2\omega(t) \in R^3$, the unit quaternion curve $q(t) \in S^3$ satisfies:

$$q'(t) = q(t)\omega(t). \tag{2}$$

In this paper, we construct the unit quaternion curves in S^3, instead of $SO(3)$; therefore, we interpret the velocity component $\omega(t)$ of $q'(t)$ as the angular velocity, instead of $2\omega(t)$.

The unit quaternion multiplication is not commutative; the order of multiplication is thus very important. Let $q_1, q_2, \cdots, q_n$ be a sequence of successive rotations. When each q_i is measured in the global frame, the product $q_n q_{n-1} \cdots q_1$ is the net rotation of successive rotations. However, when each q_i is measured in the local frame, the final product $q_1 q_2 \cdots q_n$ represents the net rotation. Note that the latter is the same as the successive rotations of $q_n, q_{n-1}, \cdots, q_2, q_1$ in the global frame. Here, we assume each rotation is specified in the local frame. This is simply for notational convenience; in the local frame, we can write the multiplications in the same order as the rotations. By reversing the order of quaternion multiplications, the same construction schemes can be applied to the quaternion curves defined in the global frame.

2.2 Exponential and Logarithmic Maps

Given a vector $v = \theta \hat{v} \in R^3$, with $\hat{v} \in S^2$, the exponential:

$$\exp(v) = \sum_{i=0}^{\infty} v^i = (\cos \theta, \hat{v} \sin \theta) \in S^3,$$

becomes the unit quaternion which represent the rotation by angle 2θ about the axis $\hat{v}$, where v^i is computed using the quaternion multiplication [3, 11, 18]. The exponential map $\exp$ can be interpreted as a mapping from the angular velocity vector (measured in S^3) into the unit quaternion which represents the rotation. When we limit the domain of $\exp$ so that $|\theta| < \pi$, the map $\exp$ becomes 1-to-1 and its inverse map $\log$ can be defined for unit quaternions. (See [9] for more details on $\exp$ and $\log$.) The power of a unit quaternion q with respect to a real valued exponent α is defined to be a unit quaternion: $q^{\alpha} = \exp(\alpha \log q)$.

Given two unit quaternions q_1 and q_2, the geodesic curve $\gamma_{q_1, q_2} \in S^3$ (which connects q_1 and q_2) has constant tangential velocity $\log(q_1^{-1} q_2)$. The geodesic curve equation is given by:

$$\gamma_{q_1, q_2}(t) = q_1 \exp(t \cdot \log(q_1^{-1} q_2)) = q_1 (q_1^{-1} q_2)^t. \tag{3}$$

The geodesic γ_{q_1, q_2} is also called the *slerp* (spherical linear interpolation) between q_1 and q_2.

3 MOTIVATION

For a translational motion in R^3, the position curve $p(t)$ is represented by:

$$p(t) = \int v(t)dt + p_0, \tag{4}$$

where $v(t)$ is the velocity and p_0 is the initial position. This relation can also be represented by the following linear differential equation:

$$p'(t) = v(t). \tag{5}$$

However, as shown in Equation (1), the relation between $q(t)$ and $\omega(t)$ is non-linear: $q'(t) = q(t)\omega(t)$.

One of the most important problems in aero-space engineering is how to find a torque optimal rotational path which connects the start and target orientations [7]. Many numerical methods have been suggested to find the optimal path, in which Equation (1) plays an important role as governing equation [6]. Barr et al. [1] also raised torque optimization as a significant problem in computer animation, and they constructed a torque optimal piecewise slerp quaternion path (i.e., as a sequence of discrete unit quaternions) by using a non-linear optimization technique. There still remains the important open problem of how to construct such a torque optimal path with piecewise spline quaternion curves which have simple closed form equations. An immediate open problem concerns the computation of high order derivatives of a unit quaternion curve. In this paper, we resolve the crucial problem of how to formulate the quaternion curves and their high order derivatives as closed form equations.

For a unit quaternion curve $q(t) \in S^3$, we may reformulate the curve in the following equivalent form:

$$q(t) = \exp(\log(q(t))).$$

By applying the chain rule to this equation, we obtain the first derivative formula:

$$q'(t) = d(\exp)_{\log(q(t))} \left(\frac{d}{dt} \log(q(t)) \right),$$

where $d(\exp)_{\log(q(t))}$ is the differential (i.e., Jacobian matrix) of exp. Kim, Kim, and Shin [9] used this formula to provide simple C^1-continuity proofs for various previous methods [11, 17, 18]. The second and high order derivative formulas, however, become extremely complex even with this representation. Moreover, for general quaternion curves $q(t)$, their logarithmic curves, $\log(q(t))$, also have very complex formulas. In this paper, we exploit simple primitive quaternion curves $q(t)$ which allow simple formulas for both the high order derivatives and the logarithmic curves.

Shoemake [18] used the formula:

$$dq^\alpha = q^\alpha \log(q) d\alpha + \alpha q^{\alpha-1} dq. \tag{6}$$

In general, this formula is incorrect. For example, Equation (6) claims that: $dq^2 = 2q \, dq$. However, we have:

$$dq^2 = d(qq) = dq \, q + q \, dq \neq 2q \, dq$$

since the quaternion multiplication is not commutative (also see [9] for more details). Nevertheless, there is a special case where this formula works. When the quaternion curve $q(t)$ is restricted to the rotation around a fixed axis $\omega \in R^3$: i.e.,

$$q(t) = \exp(\omega\alpha(t)),$$

for a real-valued function $\alpha(t)$, $q'(t)$ has a simple form:

$$q'(t) = \exp(\omega\alpha(t))(\omega\alpha'(t)) = q(t)(\omega\alpha'(t)),$$

which is equivalent to the formula of Equation (6) in this special case. Higher order derivatives of $q(t)$ are also easy to compute by the chain rule.

To make good use of this simple differential property, all the unit quaternion curves of this paper will be constructed as the products of primitive quaternion curves: $q_i(t) = \exp(\omega_i\alpha_i(t))$, $i = 1, \ldots, n$, for a fixed angular velocity $\omega_i \in R^3$ and a real valued function $\alpha_i(t)$. Since the chain rule can be applied to the quaternion product: $q(t) = q_1(t) \cdots q_n(t)$, the quaternion curve derivative can be obtained in an extremely simple form. Furthermore, applying a similar technique recursively, high order derivatives can also be obtained in simple forms. In this paper, we construct each component quaternion curve $q_i(t)$ to be C^k-continuous by choosing C^k-continuous basis function $\alpha_i(t)$. Therefore, their quaternion product $q(t) = q_1(t) \cdots q_n(t)$ becomes C^k-continuous.

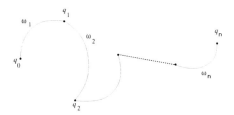

Figure 1: Piecewise Slerp Interpolation of $\{\omega_i\}$.

4 BASIC IDEA

4.1 Cumulative Form

Given a sequence of points $p_0, p_1, \cdots, p_n \in R^3$, the simplest C^0-continuous curve $p(t) \in R^3$, which interpolates each point p_i at $t = i$, is given by the following linear interpolation:

$$\begin{aligned} p(t) &= p_0 + \alpha_1(t)\Delta p_1 + \alpha_2(t)\Delta p_2 + \cdots + \alpha_n(t)\Delta p_n \\ &= p_0 + \sum_{i=1}^{n} \alpha_i(t)\Delta p_i, \end{aligned}$$

where

$$\Delta p_i = p_i - p_{i-1}$$

$$\alpha_i(t) = \begin{cases} 0 & \text{if } t < i \\ t - i & \text{if } i \leq t < i+1 \\ 1 & \text{if } t \geq i+1 \end{cases}$$

Similarly, given a sequence of unit quaternions $q_0, \cdots, q_n \in S^3$, we can construct a C^0-continuous unit quaternion curve $q(t) \in S^3$, which interpolates each unit quaternion q_i at $t = i$, as follows:

$$\begin{aligned} q(t) &= q_0 \exp(\omega_1\alpha_1(t)) \exp(\omega_2\alpha_2(t)) \cdots \exp(\omega_n\alpha_n(t)) \\ &= q_0 \prod_{i=1}^{n} \exp(\omega_i\alpha_i(t)), \end{aligned}$$

where

$$\omega_i = \log(q_{i-1}^{-1} q_i).$$

This is a piecewise *slerp* (spherical linear interpolation) of $\{q_i\}$ (see Figure 1). In the rotational space, a *slerp* implies a rotation with a constant angular velocity (around a fixed rotation axis). The slerp curve segment joining q_i and q_{i+1} is the geodesic interpolation, which is given by: $q_i \exp(\omega_i\alpha_i(t))$, based on Euler's theorem of principal rotation.

At this point, we may generalize $\{\alpha_i\}$ to other functions, rather than a piecewise linear function, so that the resulting quaternion curve becomes C^k-continuous while interpolating the given sequence of unit quaternions. The two sequences $\{\alpha_i\}$ and $\{\omega_i\}$ can be viewed as basis functions and their coefficients, respectively. We call $q_0 \prod \exp(\omega_i\alpha_i)$ the *cumulative form* of $q(t)$ with their coefficients $\{\omega_i\}$. The cumulative form has several advantages over other quaternion curve representations:

1. It has a simple closed form equation, which simplifies the evaluation of curve points and reduces the numerical errors.

2. It facilitates straight-forward computations of high order derivatives.

3. Using C^k-continuous basis functions $\{\alpha_i\}$, we can easily construct C^k-continuous quaternion curves, which are further controlled by the coefficients $\{\omega_i\}$.

4. A well-chosen set of basis functions makes the constructed quaternion curves locally controllable.

5. Since $\| \exp(\alpha\omega) \| = 1$, the quaternion curves are in S^3.

4.2 Cumulative Basis

In the Euclidean space R^3, there are many well-known spline curve construction schemes such as Bézier and B-spline curves. Most of the spline curves are represented as the sums of basis functions with their control points as the coefficients. Let $\{B_i\}$ be the basis functions and $\{p_i\}$ be the control points. Then, the spline curve $p(t)$, determined by $\{p_i\}$, is given by:

$$p(t) = \sum_{i=0}^{n} p_i B_i(t) \,,$$

which is called the *basis form* of $p(t)$. We present a general scheme that converts the basis form to the cumulative form of the quaternion curve. Using this method, we can easily construct various unit quaternion curves from their analogues in the Euclidean space R^3. The basis form can be first converted into the following form:

$$p(t) = p_0 \widetilde{B}_0(t) + \sum_{i=1}^{n} \Delta p_i \widetilde{B}_i(t) \,,$$

where

$$\Delta p_i = p_i - p_{i-1} \,,$$
$$\widetilde{B}_i(t) = \sum_{j=i}^{n} B_i(t) \,.$$

Then, the corresponding quaternion curve is obtained as follows:

$$q(t) = q_0^{\widetilde{B}_0(t)} \prod_{i=1}^{n} \exp(\omega_i \widetilde{B}_i(t)) \,, \tag{7}$$

by converting $p(t)$ to $q(t)$, p_0 to q_0, Δp_i to $\omega_i = \log(q_{i-1}^{-1} q_i)$, and vector addition to quaternion multiplication. Equation (7) is given in a cumulative form. One needs to be extremely careful in the order of multiplication: $q_{i-1}^{-1} q_i$. If the angular velocities are given in the global frame, the quaternion multiplication: $q_i q_{i-1}^{-1}$ should be used, instead of $q_{i-1}^{-1} q_i$. The new basis $\{\widetilde{B}_i\}$ is called the *cumulative basis* of $\{B_i\}$. The cumulative form is the basic tool for our quaternion curve construction in $SO(3)$. Simply by deriving a cumulative basis $\{\widetilde{B}_i\}$, we can easily obtain a quaternion curve which shares many important differential properties with its counterpart in the Euclidean space R^3.

5 A NEW CLASS OF QUATERNION CURVES

5.1 Bézier Quaternion Curve

We can represent an n-th order Bézier curve with Bernstein basis $\beta_{i,n}(t) = \binom{n}{i}(1-t)^{n-i} t^i$ as follows:

$$p(t) = \sum_{i=0}^{n} p_i \beta_{i,n}(t) \,, \tag{8}$$

where p_i's are the control points. For the Bézier curve given in a basis form, we can apply our quaternion curve construction method. We first reformulate Equation (8) as follows:

$$p(t) = p_0 \tilde{\beta}_{0,n}(t) + \sum_{i=1}^{n} \Delta p_i \tilde{\beta}_{i,n}(t) \,,$$

where the cumulative basis functions are given by:

$$\tilde{\beta}_{i,n}(t) = \sum_{j=i}^{n} \beta_{i,n}(t) \,. \tag{9}$$

Then, by converting it to the cumulative form, we can obtain the n-th order Bézier quaternion curve with control points $\{q_i\}$ as follows:

$$q(t) = q_0 \prod_{i=1}^{n} \exp(\omega_i \tilde{\beta}_{i,n}(t)) \,, \tag{10}$$

where

$$\omega_i = \log(q_{i-1}^{-1} q_i) \,.$$

Note that $\tilde{\beta}_{0,n}(t) = 1$. This Bézier quaternion curve has a different shape from the Bézier quaternion curve of Shoemake [17].

5.2 Hermite Quaternion Curve

A cubic Hermite curve is defined by two end points, p_a and p_b, and two end velocities, v_a and v_b. Alternatively, the Hermite curve can be represented by a cubic Bézier curve:

$$p(t) = \sum_{i=0}^{3} p_i \beta_i(t) \,, \tag{11}$$

with the condition:

$$p_0 = p_a, \; p_1 = p_a + v_a/3, \; p_2 = p_b - v_b/3, \; p_3 = p_b, \tag{12}$$

where $\beta_i(t) = \beta_{i,3}(t)$ for $i = 0, 1, 2, 3$.

Similarly, a cubic Bézier quaternion curve can be used to define a Hermite quaternion curve which interpolates two end unit quaternions, q_a and q_b, and two end angular velocities, ω_a and ω_b. From Equation (10), the cubic Bézier quaternion curve is given by:

$$q(t) = q_0 \prod_{i=1}^{3} \exp(\omega_i \tilde{\beta}_i(t)) \,, \tag{13}$$

where $\tilde{\beta}_i(t) = \tilde{\beta}_{i,3}(t)$ for $i = 1, 2, 3$. The quaternion counterpart of Equations (12) is given by:

$$q_0 = q_a, \; q_1 = q_a \exp(\omega_a/3), \; q_2 = q_b \exp(\omega_b/3)^{-1}, \; q_3 = q_b.$$

These four identities determine the three coefficients ω_i of the cubic Bézier quaternion curve in Equation (13) as follows:

$$\begin{aligned}
\omega_1 &= \log(q_0^{-1} q_1) = \log(q_a^{-1} q_a \exp(\omega_a/3)) = \omega_a/3 \\
\omega_2 &= \log(q_1^{-1} q_2) = \log(\exp(\omega_a/3)^{-1} q_a^{-1} q_b \exp(\omega_b/3)^{-1}) \\
\omega_3 &= \log(q_2^{-1} q_3) = \log(\exp(\omega_b/3) q_b^{-1} q_b) = \omega_b/3.
\end{aligned}$$

Using these three angular velocities, we can construct a cubic Hermite quaternion curve from Equation (13). Note that we can assign arbitrarily large angular velocities at the curve end points. The angular velocity ω_2 provides an extra degree of freedom in choosing the number n of revolutions while not losing the end point interpolation property. That is, instead of ω_2, we may use

$$\omega_2 + \widehat{\omega}_2 \cdot n\pi \quad \text{for an integer } n,$$

where $\widehat{\omega}_2 = \omega_2 / \|\omega_2\|$. The curve shape changes, depending on the number of revolutions. (Note that the angular velocity is measured here in S^3; therefore, the magnitude is half the rotation in the physical space.) Figure 2 shows the graphs of basis functions $\tilde{\beta}_i$'s. Figure 3 shows Hermite quaternion curves with the same control points, but with different angular velocities ω_b's. Since it is difficult to visualize the quaternion curves in S^3, they are projected onto a unit sphere in R^3.

Now, we will show that the cubic Hermite quaternion curve interpolates the two orientations, q_a and q_b, and the two angular

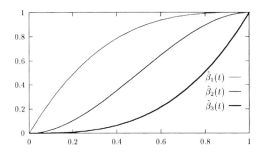

Figure 2: Graphs of $\tilde{\beta}_i$.

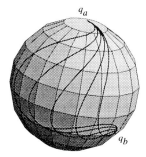

Figure 3: Examples of Hermite Quaternion Curves.

velocities, ω_a and ω_b, at the curve end points. It is easy to show that:

$$
\begin{aligned}
q(0) &= q_0 \exp(0)\exp(0)\exp(0) \\
&= q_0 = q_a, \\
q(1) &= q_0 \exp(\omega_1)\exp(\omega_2)\exp(\omega_3) \\
&= q_0(q_0^{-1}q_1)(q_1^{-1}q_2)(q_2^{-1}q_3) \\
&= q_3 = q_b.
\end{aligned}
$$

The first derivative of $q(t)$ is given by:

$$
\begin{aligned}
q'(t) &= q_0\exp(\omega_1\tilde{\beta}_1(t))(\omega_1\dot{\tilde{\beta}}_1(t))\exp(\omega_2\tilde{\beta}_2(t))\exp(\omega_3\tilde{\beta}_3(t)) \\
&+ q_0\exp(\omega_1\tilde{\beta}_1(t))\exp(\omega_2\tilde{\beta}_2(t))(\omega_2\dot{\tilde{\beta}}_2(t))\exp(\omega_3\tilde{\beta}_3(t)) \\
&+ q_0\exp(\omega_1\tilde{\beta}_1(t))\exp(\omega_2\tilde{\beta}_2(t))\exp(\omega_3\tilde{\beta}_3(t))(\omega_3\dot{\tilde{\beta}}_3(t))
\end{aligned}
$$

where

$$
\begin{aligned}
&\tilde{\beta}_1(t) = 1-(1-t)^3, \ \tilde{\beta}_2(t) = 3t^2-2t^3, \ \tilde{\beta}_3(t) = t^3, \\
&\dot{\tilde{\beta}}_1(t) = 3(1-t)^2, \dot{\tilde{\beta}}_2(t) = 6t(1-t), \dot{\tilde{\beta}}_3(t) = 3t^2.
\end{aligned}
$$

Thus, we have:

$$
\begin{aligned}
q'(0) &= q_0\exp(0)(\omega_1 3)\exp(0)\exp(0) \\
&+ q_0\exp(\omega_1\tilde{\beta}_1(t))\exp(0)(\omega_2 0)\exp(\omega_3\tilde{\beta}_3(t)) \\
&+ q_0\exp(\omega_1\tilde{\beta}_1(t))\exp(\omega_2\tilde{\beta}_2(t))\exp(0)(\omega_3 0) \\
&= q_0\omega_a = q_a\omega_a
\end{aligned}
$$

$$
\begin{aligned}
q'(1) &= q_0\exp(\omega_1)(\omega_1 0)\exp(\omega_2)\exp(\omega_3) \\
&+ q_0\exp(\omega_1)\exp(\omega_2)(\omega_2 0)\exp(\omega_3) \\
&+ q_0\exp(\omega_1)\exp(\omega_2)\exp(\omega_3)(\omega_3 3) \\
&= q_0q_0^{-1}q_1q_1^{-1}q_2q_2^{-1}q_3(3\omega_3) \\
&= q_3\omega_b = q_b\omega_b,
\end{aligned}
$$

which means that the quaternion curve $q(t)$ has its angular velocities $\omega_a = q_a^{-1}q'(0) = q(0)^{-1}q'(0)$ and $\omega_b = q_b^{-1}q'(1) = q(1)^{-1}q'(1)$ at the curve end points.

5.3 B-spline Quaternion Curve

The B-spline curve is very popular in computer graphics because of its extreme smoothness and local controllability. By moving a control point, we can selectively modify the B-spline curve without losing its geometric continuity. In this section, we consider how to convert a B-spline curve in R^3 into its quaternion analogue with a cumulative form. Then, we investigate the properties such as C^k-continuity and local controllability.

A B-spline curve is defined by a weighted sum of B-spline basis functions $B_{i,k}(t)$, which are C^{k-2}-continuous $(k-1)$-th order piecewise polynomials. Given a set of control points $\{p_i\}$, a B-spline curve $p(t)$ is given by:

$$
p(t) = \sum_{i=0}^{n} p_i B_{i,k}(t).
$$

The B-spline basis functions $B_{i,k}(t)$ are defined by the following recurrence relation [4]:

$$
B_{i,1}(t) = \begin{cases} 1 & \text{if } t_i < t < t_{i+1} \\ 0 & \text{otherwise} \end{cases}
$$

and

$$
B_{i,k}(t) = \frac{t-t_i}{t_{i+k-1}-t_i}B_{i,k-1}(t) + \frac{t_{i+k}-t}{t_{i+k}-t_{i+1}}B_{i+1,k-1}(t) .
$$

It is easy to show that $B_{i,k}$'s are C^{k-2}-continuous piecewise polynomials of degree $(k-1)$. They are C^{k-2}-continuous everywhere, and may not be C^{k-1}-continuous only at the knots $\{t_i\}$. Each $B_{i,k}(t)$ has a non-zero support on the interval $[t_i, t_{i+k}]$, i.e., $B_{i,k}(t) = 0$ for $t < t_i$ or $t > t_{i+k}$.

The B-spline curve may be reformulated in the following cumulative form:

$$
p(t) = p_0\widetilde{B}_{0,k}(t) + \sum_{i=1}^{n} \Delta p_i \widetilde{B}_{i,k}(t) ,
$$

where

$$
\Delta p_i = p_i - p_{i-1}
$$

and

$$
\begin{aligned}
\widetilde{B}_{i,k}(t) &= \sum_{j=i}^{n} B_{j,k}(t) \\
&= \begin{cases} \sum_{j=i}^{i+k} B_{j,k}(t) & \text{if } t_i < t < t_{i+k-1} \\ 1 & \text{if } t \ge t_{i+k-1} \\ 0 & \text{if } t \le t_i \end{cases}
\end{aligned}
$$

By converting $p(t)$ to $q(t)$, p_0 to q_0, Δp_i to ω_i, and summation to quaternion multiplication, the corresponding quaternion curve is obtained in a cumulative form as follows:

$$
q(t) = q_0^{\widetilde{B}_{0,k}(t)} \prod_{i=1}^{n} \exp(\omega_i\widetilde{B}_{i,k}(t)) ,
$$

where $\omega_i = \log(q_{i-1}^{-1}q_i)$. This gives our B-spline quaternion curve, which is C^{k-2}-continuous and locally controllable with the control points $\{q_i\}$ and the angular velocities $\{\omega_i\}$. The B-spline quaternion curve also allows arbitrarily large angular velocities between two consecutive control points $\{q_i\}$. Figures 4 and 5 show the graphs of basis functions $B_{i,4}(t)$ and $\widetilde{B}_{i,4}(t)$, respectively. Note that $\widetilde{B}_{i,k}(t)$ is non-constant only in the interval $[t_i, t_{i+k-1}]$, whereas $B_{i,k}(t)$ is non-constant in $[t_i, t_{i+k}]$. Figure 6 shows examples of B-spline quaternion curves. The local shape controllability is shown with dashed curves.

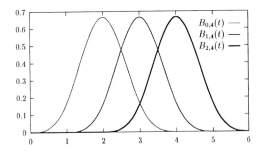

Figure 4: B-spline Basis Functions.

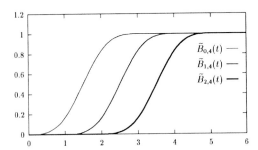

Figure 5: Cumulative B-spline Basis Functions.

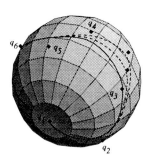

Figure 6: B-spline Quaternion Curve with Six Control Points.

6 EXPERIMENTAL RESULTS

6.1 Torque Computation

The spline interpolation in R^3 produces a path p which minimizes the energy:

$$\int \|\ddot{p}\|^2 dt,$$

while satisfying given constraints. Thus, the spline interpolation path does not generate unnecessary force (or acceleration). The energy minimization property makes the spline interpolation very useful. As far as rotational motion is concerned, it is important to minimize torque (or angular acceleration). Most of the previous results on quaternion interpolation have concentrated on improving the computational efficiency rather than attacking the more challenging problem of energy minimization.

Barr et al. [1] took an important step toward the energy minimization. The quaternion path is approximated by discrete unit quaternions and a time-consuming non-linear optimization is employed in the algorithm. There still remains an important open problem concerning how to construct an energy minimization quaternion path, ideally with a closed form equation and without using a time-consuming optimization technique. In this paper, we have provided a useful step toward the resolution of this problem by introducing a new class of spline quaternion curves for which high order derivatives can be obtained in simple closed form equations. Although the problem of how to deal with these closed form equations is still unsolved, our quaternion curves exhibit promising behaviors by generating relatively small torque compared with those generated by the previous methods.

Our cubic quaternion curves generate a similar amount of torque (in the range of $\pm 5\%$) to that of Shoemake [17] when the control unit quaternions have small angular variations. However, our curves perform much better when the variations are large. The methods based on recursive slerp constructions may generate twisted curves when the spherical control polygon on S^3 has edges of relatively large lengths. This effect can be explained as follows. The slerp-based methods generate a sequence of intermediate quaternion curves $q_{i,k}(t)$'s, and blend each pair of two consecutive curves $q_{i,k}(t)$ and $q_{i+1,k}(t)$ to generate another sequence of quaternion curves $q_{i,k+1}(t)$'s:

$$q_{i,k+1}(t) = q_{i,k}(t) \exp(f_i(t) \log(q_{i,k}(t)^{-1} q_{i+1,k}(t))),$$

for some blending function $f_i(t)$. When the variations of control quaternions are large, the two quaternion curves $q_{i,k}(t)$ and $q_{i+1,k}(t)$ have large curve lengths. They may have complex winding shapes in the compact space S^3. The difference quaternion curve

Now, we can investigate some interesting differential and geometric properties of the B-spline quaternion curve: i.e., C^k-continuity and local controllability. It is easy to show that $\widetilde{B}_{i,k}(t)$ is C^{k-2}-continuous since it is a weighted sum of C^{k-2}-continuous functions $\{B_{i,k}\}$. Therefore, the k-th order B-spline quaternion curve is C^{k-2}-continuous as well. Since the cumulative basis function $\widetilde{B}_{i,k}(t)$ is non-constant in the interval $[t_i, t_{i+k-1}]$, the quaternion curve $q(t)$ on the interval $t_l \leq t < t_{l+1}$ can be represented by:

$$
\begin{aligned}
q(t) &= q_0 \left(\prod_{i=1}^{l-k+1} \exp(\omega_i \cdot 1) \right) \left(\prod_{i=l-k+2}^{l} \exp(\omega_i \widetilde{B}_{i,k}(t)) \right) \\
&\quad \left(\prod_{i=l+1}^{n} \exp(\omega_i \cdot 0) \right) \\
&= q_{l-k+1} \prod_{i=l-k+2}^{l} \exp(\omega_i \widetilde{B}_{i,k}(t)).
\end{aligned}
$$

This equation shows that the quaternion curve $q(t)$ depends only on the quantities: $q_{l-k+1}, \omega_{l-k+1}, \cdots, \omega_l$, that is, only on the k control points: $q_{l-k+1}, q_{l-k}, \cdots, q_l$. In other words, by moving the control point q_l, the curve shape is influenced only on the interval $[t_l, t_{l+k}]$.

Furthermore, the derivation of $q'(t)$ is extremely simple due to the B-spline differentiation formula [4]:

$$\frac{d}{dt} \sum \alpha_i B_{i,k}(t) = \sum (k-1) \frac{\alpha_i - \alpha_{i-1}}{t_{i+k-1} - t_i} B_{i,k-1}(t),$$

where α_i's are constants. Therefore, we have:

$$\widetilde{B}'_{i,k}(t) = \frac{k-1}{t_{i+k-1} - t_i} B_{i,k-1}(t).$$

In the case of a uniform B-spline, there is a further reduction to: $\widetilde{B}'_{i,k}(t) = B_{i,k-1}(t).$

$q_{i,k}(t)^{-1}q_{i+1,k}(t)$ would also wind many times. However, the measure, $\log(q_{i,k}(t)^{-1}q_{i+1,k}(t))$, is always bounded by π, which totally ignores the large amount of winding. As a result, the blending curve $q_{i,k+1}(t)$ experiences large bending, which produces large torque. As the intermediate curves with bending shapes are blended recursively, the resulting quaternion curve has a twisting shape.

Our quaternion curves do not suffer from such a degeneracy. This is because our primitive quaternion curve $q_i(t) = \exp(\omega_i\alpha_i(t))$ may accommodate arbitrarily large angular velocity ω_i. The resulting curve has a large number of winding; however, the curve does not produce extraordinary bending and/or twisting. Therefore, our curves perform much better when the angular variations are large. Furthermore, our curves have C^2-continuity, which means that there is no torque jump at the curve joint. The piecewise cubic quaternion curves (based on the de Casteljau type construction) are not C^2-continuous; they have torque jump at each curve joint. High degree rational spherical curves have C^2-continuity [19]; however, their speeds are less uniform than the curves based on the de Casteljau type construction. Therefore, the rational curves generate redundant tangential accelerations, which has undesirable effect.

6.2 Animation Examples

We present some examples to demonstrate the feasibility of our quaternion curves. Figure 7 shows an animation of a flying boomerang. In this example, the motion path is composed of a Hermite curve for the translation and a Hermite quaternion curve for the rotation. Using the Hermite quaternion curve, we can specify arbitrary orientations and angular velocities of the boomerang at the start and end of the animated motion. Note that the boomerang experiences many revolutions. This effect is obtained by assigning large angular velocities at both ends.

Our cubic B-spline quaternion curve produces extremely smooth motions. Figure 8 shows a motion path, which is specified by a B-spline curve with six control points. A rigid motion path can be used to specify the sweeping of a 2D cross section. Figure 9 shows a sweep object generated from the same motion path given in Figure 8. Figure 10 shows an example of B-spline quaternion interpolation for a rigid body, where the position and orientation interpolation curves are constructed by the B-spline interpolation curves in R^3 and $SO(3)$, respectively. Six keyframes are used in this example, and they are shown in dark tints.

7 CONCLUSIONS

A general construction method is proposed for unit quaternion curves. Given a spline curve in R^3, the spline curve is reformulated in a cumulative basis form and the corresponding quaternion curve is constructed by converting each vector addition into the quaternion multiplication. The quaternion curve is formulated as a finite product of simple quaternion curves, which makes the evaluation of high order derivatives quite straightforward. The constructed quaternion curves preserve many important differential properties of their counterparts in R^3. Furthermore, the quaternion curves and their high order derivatives are given by simple closed form equations.

Experimental results are quite promising in that our quaternion curves use small torque compared with the previous quaternion curves, especially when the control quaternions have large variations. Although the important torque minimization problem has not been solved in this paper, our approach provides an important initial step toward this goal.

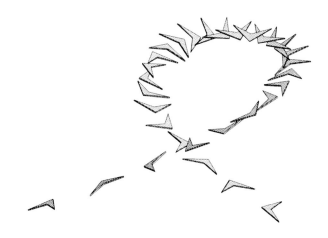

Figure 7: Boomerang Animation using one Hermite Quaternion Curve.

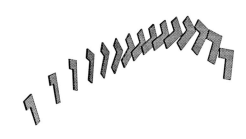

Figure 8: Rigid Motion by a Cubic B-spline Quaternion Curve.

Figure 9: Sweeping with Cubic B-spline Quaternion Curves.

Figure 10: Example of B-spline Quaternion Interpolation.

REFERENCES

[1] BARR, A., CURRIN, B., GABRIEL, S., AND HUGHES, J. Smooth interpolation of orientations with angular velocity constraints using quaternions. *Computer Graphics (Proc. of SIGGRAPH '92)* (1992), pp. 313–320.

[2] BARRY, P., AND GOLDMANN, R. A recursive evaluation algorithm for a class of Catmull-Rom splines. *Computer Graphics (Proc. of SIGGRAPH '88)* (1988), pp. 199–204.

[3] CURTIS, M. *Matrix Groups*, Springer-Verlag, 1972.

[4] DE BOOR, C. *A Practical Guide to Splines*, Springer-Verlag, 1978.

[5] HAMILTON, W. *Elements of Quaternions (Volume I, II)*, Chelsea Publishing Company, 1969.

[6] JUNKINS, J., AND TURNER, J. Optimal continuous torque attitude maneuvers. *J. Guidance and Control 3*, 3 (1980), pp. 210–217.

[7] JUNKINS, J., AND TURNER, J. *Optimal Spacecraft Rotational Maneuvers*, Elsevier, 1986.

[8] JUTTLER, B. Visualization of moving objects using dual quaternion curves. *Computers & Graphics 18*, 3 (1994), pp. 315–326.

[9] KIM, M.-J., KIM, M.-S., AND SHIN, S. A compact differential formula for the first derivative of a unit quaternion curve. To appear in *J. of Visualization and Computer Animation* (1995).

[10] KIM, M.-J., KIM, M.-S., AND SHIN, S. A C^2-continuous B-spline quaternion curve interpolating a given sequence of solid orientations. *Proc. of Computer Animation '95* (1995), pp. 72–81.

[11] KIM, M.-S., AND NAM, K.-W. Interpolating solid orientations with circular blending quaternion curves. To appear in *Computer-Aided Design* (1995).

[12] NIELSON, G. Smooth interpolation of orientation. *Models and Techniques in Computer Animation (Proc. of Computer Animation '93)* (1993), N. Thalmann and D. T. (Eds.), Eds., Springer-Verlag, pp. 75–93.

[13] NIELSON, G., AND HEILAND, R. Animated rotations using quaternions and splines on a 4D sphere. *Programmirovanie(Russia)* (July-August 1992), Springer-Verlag, pp. 17–27. English edition, *Programming and Computer Software*, Plenum Pub., New York.

[14] PLETINCKS, D. Quaternion calculus as a basic tool in computer graphics. *The Visual Computer 5*, 1 (1989), pp. 2–13.

[15] POBEGAILO, A. Modeling of C^n spherical and orientation splines. To appear in *Proc. of Pacific Graphics '95* (1995).

[16] SCHLAG, J. Using geometric constructions to interpolate orientation with quaternions. *Graphics GEMS II*, Academic Press, 1992, pp. 377–380.

[17] SHOEMAKE, K. Animating rotation with quaternion curves. *Computer Graphics (Proc. of SIGGRAPH '85)* (1985), pp. 245–254.

[18] SHOEMAKE, K. Quaternion calculus for animation. *Math for SIGGRAPH (ACM SIGGRAPH '91 Course Notes #2)* (1991).

[19] WANG, W. Rational spherical curves. Presented at Int'l. Conf. on CAGD, Penang, Malaysia (July 4-8, 1994).

[20] WANG, W., AND JOE, B. Orientation interpolation in quaternion space using spherical biarcs. *Proc. of Graphics Interface '93* (1993), pp. 24–32.

APPENDIX

In this appendix, we provide the pseudo codes for the construction of quaternion curves presented in Section 5.

Bézier Quaternion Curve

// $q_0, \ldots, q_n$: control points

double $\tilde{\beta}_{i,n}(t) = \sum_{j=i}^{n} \binom{n}{i}(1-t)^{n-i} t^i$

quaternion Bezier$(q_0, q_1, \ldots q_n)(t)$

    return $(q_0 \prod_{i=1}^{n} \exp(\log(q_{i-1}^{-1} q_i)\tilde{\beta}_{i,n}(t)))$;

end

Hermite Quaternion Curve

// q_a, q_b: the start and end orientations
// ω_a, ω_b: the start and end angular velocities

double $\tilde{\beta}_1(t) = 1 - (1-t)^3$, $\tilde{\beta}_2(t) = 3t^2 - 2t^3$, $\tilde{\beta}_3(t) = t^3$

quaternion Hermite$(q_a, q_b, \omega_a, \omega_b)(t)$

    $q_0 = q_a$;
    $\omega_1 = \omega_a/3$;
    $\omega_2 = \log(\exp(\omega_1)^{-1} q_a^{-1} q_b \exp(\omega_3))$;
    $\omega_3 = \omega_b/3$;
    return $(q_0 \exp(\omega_1 \tilde{\beta}_1(t)) \exp(\omega_2 \tilde{\beta}_2(t)) \exp(\omega_3 \tilde{\beta}_3(t)))$;

end

B-spline Quaternion Curve

// t_i : knot sequence

double $B_{i,k}(t)$ = B-spline basis of order k
double $\widetilde{B}_{i,k}(t) = \sum_{j=i}^{i+k} B_{j,k}(t)$

quaternion B-spline$(q_0, q_1, \ldots q_n)(t)$

    $l = \max\{ i \,|t_{i+k-1} \leq t\}$;
    if $(l < 0)$ **then**
        $\{l = 0; \; q = q_0^{\widetilde{B}_{0,k}(t)}\}$
    else
        $q = q_l$;
    for $(i = l + 1; i \leq n \,\&\& \, t_i < t; i{+}{+})$
        $q = q \exp(\log(q_{i-1}^{-1} q_i)\widetilde{B}_{i,k}(t))$;
    return (q);

end

Uniform B-spline Quaternion Curve

// $t_i = i - 2$: uniform knots
// $0 \leq t \leq n$
// uniform-B-spline$(0) = q_0$
// uniform-B-spline$(n) = q_n$
// uniform-B-spline$(i) \approx q_i$

quaternion uniform-B-spline$(q_0, q_1, \ldots q_n)(t)$

    $q_{-1} = q_0 q_1^{-1} q_0$;   //phantom
    $q_{n+1} = q_n q_{n-1}^{-1} q_n$;// control points
    $l = \lfloor t - 1 \rfloor$;
    $q = q_l$;
    for $(i = l + 1; i < t + 2; i{+}{+})$
        $q = q \exp(\log(q_{i-1}^{-1} q_i)\widetilde{B}_{i,k}(t))$;
    return (q);

end

X-Splines : A Spline Model Designed for the End-User

Carole Blanc   Christophe Schlick

LaBRI [*]

351 cours de la libération, 33405 Talence (France)

`[blanc|schlick]@labri.u-bordeaux.fr`

Abstract

This paper presents a new model of spline curves and surfaces. The main characteristic of this model is that it has been created from scratch by using a kind of mathematical engineering process. In a first step, a list of specifications was established. This list groups all the properties that a spline model should contain in order to appear intuitive to a non-mathematician end-user. In a second step, a new family of blending functions was derived, trying to fulfill as many items as possible of the previous list. Finally, the degrees of freedom offered by the model have been reduced to provide only shape parameters that have a visual interpretation on the screen. The resulting model includes many classical properties such as affine and perspective invariance, convex hull, variation diminution, local control and C^2/G^2 or C^2/G^0 continuity. But it also includes original features such as a continuum between B-splines and Catmull-Rom splines, or the ability to define approximation zones and interpolation zones in the same curve or surface.

1   Introduction

Since the ground work in CAD during the late sixties, many different models of splines have been introduced. One specific characteristic of CAD is that the mathematical models developped by researchers are later manipulated by non-mathematician end users (designers, architects, animators). Therefore, rather than its complete mathematical properties, a major criterion for the evaluation of a spline model may be the ability to understand intuitively the degrees of freedom that it provides. A full study of existing spline models on that particular point lies not within the scope of this short introduction, but let us just take one or two examples.

The popular NURBS model is a good example in which the user has to be familiar with the mathematical structure to obtain best results. For instance, the manipulation of the knot vector is really complex: first the geometrical effects generated by these manipulations can hardly be predicted, second these effects are not robust because further knot manipulations may move them along the curve, and third the effects are propagated along the whole isoparametric curves in the case of surfaces. Even the manipulation of the weights may sometimes be confusing: for instance, the modifications of two adjacent weights are mutually cancelled [11].

---

[*]Laboratoire Bordelais de Recherche en Informatique *(Université Bordeaux I* and *Centre National de la Recherche Scientifique).* The present work is also granted by the *Conseil Régional d'Aquitaine.*

Permission to make digital/hard copy of part or all of this work for personal or classroom use is granted without fee provided that copies are not made or distributed for profit or commercial advantage, the copyright notice, the title of the publication and its date appear, and notice is given that copying is by permission of ACM, Inc. To copy otherwise, to republish, to post on servers, or to redistribute to lists, requires prior specific permission and/or a fee.

The model that accounts the most for the ergonomics of the manipulation is undoubtedly the β-spline model [1] which includes intuitive shape parameters (tension and bias). Yet, if the behaviour of the model is really natural when using global tension and bias, the extended model [2] with local parameters is less convincing, mainly because these parameters are not directly related to the control points. Moreover, the C^0/G^2 continuity of the β-splines is lost by interpolation, this makes them inadequate for many applications [9].

This paper proposes a new spline model that has been designed to make user manipulations as intuitive as possible. Its formulation is presented in four steps: Section 2 presents the list of specifications for the new model, Section 3 explains the principle and the basic formulation, Section 4 derives a more complete expression including an original shape parameter, finally, Section 5 details the general formulation.

2   Background

2.1   Definition

In their most general definition, splines can be considered as a mathematical model that associates a continuous representation (curve or surface) with a discrete set of points of an affine space (usually $\mathbb{R}^2$ or $\mathbb{R}^3$). In the case of curves, this definition can be expressed as follows: let $P_k \in \mathbb{R}^3$ with $(k = 0..n)$ be a set of points called *control points*, and let $F_k : [0,1] \to \mathbb{R}$ (with $k = 0..n$) be a set of functions called *blending functions*, the spline curve generated by the couples (P_k, F_k) is the curve C defined by the parametric equation:

$$\forall t \in [0,1] \qquad C(t) = \sum_{k=0}^{n} F_k(t)\, P_k \qquad (1)$$

According to the shape of the blending functions, the resulting curve may either *approximate* the control points or *interpolate* them. Figure 1 and Figure 2 illustrate this distinction by showing two classical examples of spline curves (cubic uniform B-splines [12] in Figure 1, cubic Catmull-Rom [6] in Figure 2). Each figure is divided in two parts, the top shows the control lattice and the curve, the bottom shows the plots of the blending functions. The same graphical framework will be used throughout the paper.

2.2   Properties

The family of curves that obeys Equation 1 is extremely vast and thus many of its members are likely to be of little interest. In fact, the work done over the years in the literature has exhibited many properties that a spline model should include to become useful for geometric modelling. In a recent survey, we have shown that all these properties can be obtained by imposing specific constraints on the blending functions [3].

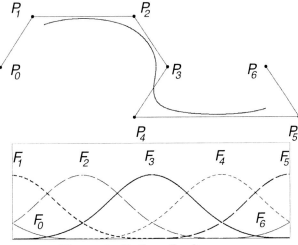

Figure 1: *Uniform B-spline curve*

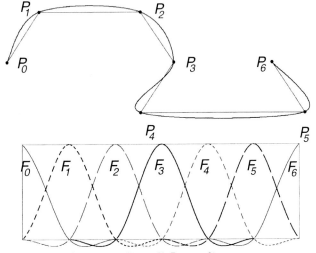

Figure 2: *Catmull-Rom spline curve*

Using that result, we are going to list now all the properties (as well as the corresponding constraints on the blending functions) that we have found vital or simply desirable to include in our user-oriented spline model:

• **Affine invariance**: The affine transformation of a spline should be obtained by applying the transformation to its control points. This is provided by the *normality constraint*:

$$\forall t \in [0,1] \qquad \sum_{k=0}^{n} F_k(t) = 1 \qquad (2)$$

• **Convex hull**: The spline should be entirely contained in the convex hull of its control lattice. This is provided by the normality constraint combined with the *positivity constraint*:

$$\forall k = 0..n \qquad \forall t \in [0,1] \qquad F_k(t) \geq 0 \qquad (3)$$

• **Variation diminution**: The number of intersections between the spline and a plane (or a line, for 2D splines) should be at most equal to the number of intersections between the plane and the control lattice, which means that the spline should have less oscillations than its control lattice. This property is provided by combining the normality, the positivity with the *regularity constraint*:

$$\forall k = 0..n \qquad \exists T_k \in [0,1] \ / \qquad (4)$$

$$\forall t < T_k \quad F_k'(t) \geq 0 \quad \text{and} \quad \forall k' = k+1..n \quad F_{k'}(t) \leq F_k(t)$$
$$\forall t > T_k \quad F_k'(t) \leq 0 \quad \text{and} \quad \forall k' = 0..k-1 \quad F_{k'}(t) \leq F_k(t)$$

This constraint may appear complex at a first glance, but it simply says that the blending functions are bell-shaped and that two functions cannot cross each other in the zone where they are simultaneously increasing or decreasing.

• **Local control**: Each control point should only influence the shape of the spline in a restricted zone. This property is provided by the *locality constraint*:

$$\forall k = 0..n \qquad \exists (T_k^-, T_k^+) \in [0,1]^2 \ / \qquad (5)$$

$$\forall t < T_k^- \quad F_k(t) = 0 \quad \text{and} \quad \forall t > T_k^+ \quad F_k(t) = 0$$

A spline may offer more or less local control according to the extent of the influence of a given control point. To quantify this aspect, the notion of L^p *locality* [3] can be used: a spline curve (resp. surface) has got L^p locality when each control point influences p segments (resp. patches) at most.

• **Smooth shapes/Sharp shapes**: The spline model should allow both smooth shapes and sharp shapes and more precisely mixing smooth zones and sharp ones in the same curve. It is well known that parametric continuity does not provided any information on the shape of the curve; therefore one has to use geometric continuity: smooth shapes are G^2 at least, sharp shapes are G^0 at most. On the other hand, parametric continuity is needed to provide smooth motion in animation; therefore the model should also provide C^2 continuity.

• **Intuitive shape parameters**: In addition to the control points, the spline should also provide other degrees of freedom, usually called *shape parameters*. But to be usable by a non-mathematician end user, the role of these parameters should be as intuitive as possible. Among all the shape parameters (knots, weights, tension, bias, curvature) that we can find in existing spline models, only the *local tension effect* (which allows the user to pull the curve locally toward one or several control points) appears totally intuitive.

• **Existence of refinement algorithms**: The spline model should allow the use of refinement or subdivision techniques which are powerful tools that increase the number of degrees of freedom for a spline (control points or shape parameters) without modifying its shape.

• **Representation of conics**: The spline model should be able to represent conic sections, and consequently a large set of curves and surfaces (circles, ellipses, spheres, cylinders, surfaces of revolution, etc) that are intensively used in CAD. The exact representation of conics is one reason for the popularity of the NURBS model [3]. Nevertheless, having only a close approximation (up to the resolution of the display, for instance) is sufficient for most applications.

• **Approximation/Interpolation**: For some applications or some users, approximation splines are preferable, whereas for others, interpolation splines are imperative. For that reason, the model should provide approximation splines and interpolation splines in a unified formulation. Among the existing models, only the general Catmull-Rom model [6] includes such a feature; but we would like to get a step further by allowing the creation of approximation zones and interpolation zones in the same curve.

In the following sections, we describe a new spline model which was designed to fulfill as many items as possible of the previous list. At the current stage in this development, all items but one (the existence of refinement techniques) are fulfilled by the model. The possibility of including the last item will be discussed in the conclusion.

3 Basic X-Splines

3.1 Principle

Building a new spline model from scratch implies defining a new family of blending functions. Among the constraints that have been listed in Section 2, the most difficult to fulfill is the normality constraint. Indeed, finding a family of functions $F_k(t)$ that sum to one whatever the value of t is a tricky task. For that reason, we have chosen to build our blending functions independently of the normality constraint, and then to apply in a final step, a normalization process which replaces $F_k(t)$ by $\overline{F}_k(t)$:

$$\forall t \in [0,1] \qquad \overline{F}_k(t) = \frac{F_k(t)}{\sum_{k=0}^{n} F_k(t)} \qquad (6)$$

Thus, the actual blending functions $\overline{F}_k(t)$ will be normalized rational polynomials which, as a side-effect, adds the projective invariance property to the resulting curves.

By combining the different properties recalled in Section 2, we can establish that for a normal, positive, regular and local spline, each blending function $F_k(t)$ is bell-shaped, starts to grow at a given value T_k^-, reaches its unique maximum at a second value T_k and drops to zero at a third value T_k^+ (see Figure 3). In classical spline models, $F_k(t)$ is defined by a piecewise polynomial or a rational piecewise polynomial, composed of as many segments as consecutive intervals between T_k^- and T_k^+ (e.g. four segments with cubic B-splines).

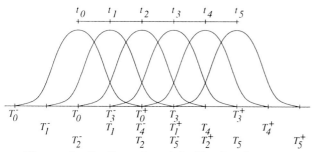

Figure 3: *Configuration of the blending functions*

The driving idea of the new model that we propose here is the following: the non-null part of the blending function should be composed of only two segments[1]. The first, called $F_k^-(t)$, is defined between T_k^- and T_k; the second, called $F_k^+(t)$, is defined between T_k and T_k^+. In order to make this idea clearer, let us take the case of a spline in which each control point P_k influences four segments of the curve (i.e. L^4 locality). This is a usual case (shared by every classical model of cubic splines, for instance) and is often considered [2] as the best trade-off between low degree splines on one hand (which are closely related to the control lattice and thus can hardly provide very smooth shapes) and high degree splines on the other hand (which can hardly provide very sharp shapes).

By definition, for an L^4 spline, each blending function is non-null over four consecutive intervals of the knot vector: $F_k(t)$ becomes non-null at knot t_{k-2}, is maximal at knot t_k and becomes null again at knot t_{k+2} (the knots are shown on the top of Figure 3). As $F_k(t)$ is composed only of two segments, it depends only on t_{k-2}, t_k and t_{k+2}. Thus there is a kind

of alternation in the way the knots are taken into account (even points use even knots and odd points use odd knots). Moreover, as we will see, the blending functions F_{k-2} and F_{k+2} cross each other at knot t_k and all the derivation of the model is based on this crossing. For that reason, we have called this new model, **cross-splines** or **X-splines**, for short.

3.2 Formulation

In fact, once the general principle has been established, the basic formulation of the new model can be derived quite naturally. Let us first take the case of a uniform knot vector:

$$\forall k = 1..n \qquad t_k - t_{k-1} = \Delta$$

If we apply the following reparametrization to the curve,

$$u(t) = \frac{t - t_{k-2}}{t_k - t_{k-2}} = \frac{t - t_{k-2}}{2\Delta} \qquad (7)$$

we are assured that $u = 0$ at knot t_{k-2} where $F_k(t)$ starts to grow and $u = 1$ at knot t_k where $F_k(t)$ reaches its maximum. Therefore, we have to find a polynomial $f(u)$ defined on the range $[0,1]$ which can be linked to the left part of $F_k(t)$ by:

$$F_k^-(t) = f\left(\frac{t - t_{k-2}}{2\Delta}\right) \qquad (8)$$

Because we want a C^2 continuous curve, the following constraints for the function $f(u)$ can be immediately derived:

$$f(0) = 0 \qquad f'(0) = 0 \qquad f''(0) = 0 \qquad (9)$$

As the maximum of the blending function is reached at $u = 1$, its first derivative is necessarily null. Moreover, we can set $f(1) = 1$ because the normalization step will reduce the maximum to its exact value anyway. Finally, the second derivative at $u = 1$ can be set to a given constant (we call this constant $-2p$ to simplify the formulation):

$$f(1) = 1 \qquad f'(1) = 0 \qquad f''(1) = -2p \qquad (10)$$

Thus we have derived a system of six constraints. As we search for a polynomial solution, it will necessarily be quintic, in order to get six degrees of freedom. By matching the constraints and the coefficients of the polynomial, we obtain:

$$f_p(u) = u^3 \left(10 - p + (2p - 15)\,u + (6 - p)\,u^2\right) \qquad (11)$$

Moreover, the property of regularity requires an increasing function on the range $[0,1]$ and thus a positive derivative. Therefore there is an additional condition on p:

$$0 \leq p \leq 10$$

The function $f_p(u)$ (see Figure 4) provides the left part of $F_k(t)$ according to Equation 8. By reversing the direction and the origin of the reparametrization, the right part of $F_k(t)$ is obtained similarly:

$$F_k^+(t) = f_p\left(\frac{t_{k+2} - t}{2\Delta}\right) \qquad (12)$$

The two functions F_k^- and F_k^+ join at knot t_k with C^2 continuity ($F_k'(t_k) = 0$ and $F_k''(t_k) = -p/2\Delta^2$) which means that the global blending function $F_k(t)$, and therefore the whole curve $C(t)$, are C^2 continuous.

---

[1] In fact, we have also tried the case where the non-null part is composed of only one segment. But this makes the model much more expensive (degree 8 rational polynomials) with no additional features.

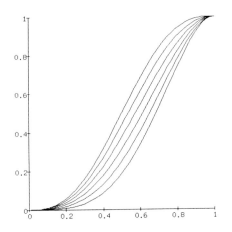

Figure 4: *Function $f_p(u)$ for $p = 0, 2, 4, 6, 8, 10$*

Finally, we get the formulation for a segment of the curve $C(t)$ on the parameter range $[t_{k+1}, t_{k+2}]$, defined by the four control points $P_k, P_{k+1}, P_{k+2}, P_{k+3}$:

$$C(t) = \frac{A_0(t)\ P_k + A_1(t)\ P_{k+1} + A_2(t)\ P_{k+2} + A_3(t)\ P_{k+3}}{A_0(t) + A_1(t) + A_2(t) + A_3(t)}$$

(13)

$$A_0(t) = f_p\left(\frac{t_{k+2} - t}{2\Delta}\right) \qquad A_1(t) = f_p\left(\frac{t_{k+3} - t}{2\Delta}\right)$$

$$A_2(t) = f_p\left(\frac{t - t_k}{2\Delta}\right) \qquad A_3(t) = f_p\left(\frac{t - t_{k+1}}{2\Delta}\right)$$

The process defined above has provided a *quintic rational approximation spline model* that includes the properties of normality, positivity, regularity, locality and C^2 continuity. Moreover, the curves contain a degree of freedom $p \in [0, 10]$ which allows a (slight) modification of their shapes. It should be noticed that a very interesting case is obtained for $p = 8$. Indeed, after the normalization step, the blending functions are very close to the cubic uniform B-splines basis functions (see Figure 6). It means that the resulting curves — call them *basic X-splines* — are almost identical to the uniform cubic B-splines (compare Figure 5 and Figure 1).

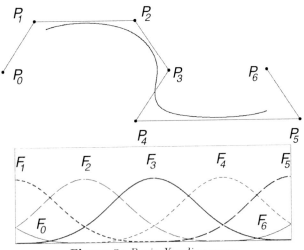

Figure 5: *Basic X-spline curve*

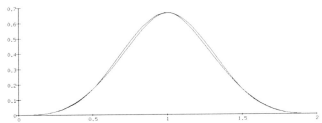

Figure 6: *Similarity of the cubic uniform B-splines and the basic X-splines blending functions (for $p = 8$)*

4 Extended X-Splines

4.1 Formulation

The degree of freedom p in Equation 11 does not offer enough variety in the shapes of the blending functions (see Figure 4) to provide interesting effects on the resulting curves. Therefore, it appears somewhat useless in the formulation of the new model. In fact, the existence of this degree of freedom will be hidden to the end user. As we will see below, this parameter p is needed to manage another parameter s, that we are going to introduce now and which is the actual degree of freedom accessible by the end user.

Among the items of our list of specifications, *tension* and *angular shapes* (G^0 continuity) can be included in our model by the same derivation. Indeed, the basic idea which has led to the concept of tension in the spline literature is to be able to strain the curve (or the surface) in order to pull it toward the control lattice. At its limit, this process forces the curve to interpolate one or several control points, and due to the convex hull property, this interpolation will create sharp edges.

To bring the curve closer to a given part of the control lattice, one has to increase the influence of the corresponding control points. A straightforward idea to realize this process is to add a specific weighting coefficient to each control points. But, as we have recalled in Section 1, this solution (which is used in every classical rational spline) does not work in a satisfying way, because the influences of neighbouring weights are mutually cancelled. Therefore, we propose here an original solution to include the concept of tension, which does not contain the drawback of the existing models.

To illustrate this new solution, let us take the blending functions F_2, F_3 and F_4 in Figure 3. We know that F_3 reaches its maximum at t_3. But, as F_2 and F_4 are not null at t_3, the normalization process has set the actual maximum to $F_3/(F_2 + F_3 + F_4)$. Therefore, a way to increase this maximum, in order to bring the curve closer to the control point P_3, is to decrease $F_2(t_3)$ and $F_4(t_3)$.

We know that in the area of interest, F_2 (respectively F_4) decreases (respectively increases) monotonically in the range $[t_2, t_4]$. Thus, to obtain smaller values for these functions at t_3, one has to speed up the decrease of the former and to slow down the increase of the latter. To realize these two operations symmetrically, we actually push the *crossing point of F_2 and F_4* down toward the horizontal axis. For that, we introduce a new degree of freedom $s_3 \in [0, 1]$ at point P_3. This parameter will be used, first to compute the value T_2^+ (where F_2 becomes null) by interpolation between t_4 and t_3:

$$T_2^+ = t_3 + s_3\ (t_4 - t_3) = t_3 + s_3\ \Delta$$

and second, to compute the value T_4^- (where F_4 becomes non null) by interpolation between t_3 and t_2:

$$T_4^- = t_3 + s_3\ (t_2 - t_3) = t_3 - s_3\ \Delta$$

In other words, it means that F_2 (respectively F_4) is null all over the range $[T_2^+, t_4]$ (respectively $[t_2, T_4^-]$). The same operation can be done for each k. The resulting values (T_k^-, T_k^+) have to be replaced in the reparametrization equations (Equation 8 and Equation 12) as follows:

$$F_k^-(t) = f_p\left(\frac{t - T_k^-}{t_k - T_k^-}\right) \qquad F_k^+(t) = f_p\left(\frac{t - T_k^+}{t_k - T_k^+}\right) \quad (14)$$

The two parts of $F_k(t)$ still join at t_k, their first derivatives are still null but their second derivatives are different:

$$F_k''(t_k^-) = \frac{-2p}{(t_k - T_k^-)^2} \qquad F_k''(t_k^+) = \frac{-2p}{(t_k - T_k^+)^2} \quad (15)$$

Here is the point where our parameter p will finally be used. Indeed, in order to equal the left and right expressions, the only thing to do is to use a specific value for p (noted p_{k-1}) in F_k^- and another one (noted p_{k+1}) in F_k^+. Taking

$$p_{k-1} = \frac{2\,(t_k - T_k^-)^2}{\Delta^2} \quad \text{and} \quad p_{k+1} = \frac{2\,(t_k - T_k^+)^2}{\Delta^2} \quad (16)$$

gives

$$F_k''(t_k^-) = F_k''(t_k^+) = -\frac{4}{\Delta^2}$$

which provides C^2 continuity but assures also that the parameters p_k are in the range $[0, 8]$ as needed to get the property of regularity and to obtain the cubic B-splines as a limit case.

Therefore we can derive a new formulation[2] for the segment of the curve $C(t)$ on the range $[t_{k+1}, t_{k+2}]$ defined by the four control points $P_k, P_{k+1}, P_{k+2}, P_{k+3}$:

$$C(t) = \frac{A_0(t)\,P_k + A_1(t)\,P_{k+1} + A_2(t)\,P_{k+2} + A_3(t)\,P_{k+3}}{A_0(t) + A_1(t) + A_2(t) + A_3(t)}$$
$$(17)$$

$$A_0(t) = t > T_k^+ \quad ? \quad 0 \quad : \quad f_{p_{k-1}}\left(\frac{t - T_k^+}{t_k - T_k^+}\right)$$

$$A_1(t) = t > T_{k+1}^+ \quad ? \quad 0 \quad : \quad f_{p_k}\left(\frac{t - T_{k+1}^+}{t_{k+1} - T_{k+1}^+}\right)$$

$$A_2(t) = t < T_{k+2}^- \quad ? \quad 0 \quad : \quad f_{p_{k+1}}\left(\frac{t - T_{k+2}^-}{t_{k+2} - T_{k+2}^-}\right)$$

$$A_3(t) = t < T_{k+3}^- \quad ? \quad 0 \quad : \quad f_{p_{k+2}}\left(\frac{t - T_{k+3}^-}{t_{k+3} - T_{k+3}^-}\right)$$

$$p_{k-1} = \frac{2}{\Delta^2}\,(t_k - T_k^+)^2 \qquad p_k = \frac{2}{\Delta^2}\,(t_{k+1} - T_{k+1}^+)^2$$

$$p_{k+1} = \frac{2}{\Delta^2}\,(t_{k+2} - T_{k+2}^-)^2 \qquad p_{k+2} = \frac{2}{\Delta^2}\,(t_{k+3} - T_{k+3}^-)^2$$

The expression of $C(t)$ seems complex but in fact it can be implemented very compactly and efficiently (12 lines of source code in C language).

So for the end user, an *extended X-spline* is totally defined by a set of quadruples (x_k, y_k, z_k, s_k) with $k = 0...n$. All these degrees of freedom have a very simple interpretation. The parameters $(x_k, y_k, z_k) \in \mathbb{R}^3$ are the coordinates of the control points P_k. The parameter $s_k \in [0, 1]$ symbolizes the *distance between the curve and the control lattice*: when $s_k = 1$, the curve passes relatively far away from point P_k; when s_k decreases, the curve comes closer and closer to P_k; finally when $s_k = 0$, the curve passes through P_k.

---

[2] We use here the (*test ? a : b*) operator borrowed from the C programming language which allows one to write multiple expressions in a compact way.

It should be noticed that the curve is always C^2 (due to the construction process that has been used), even when it interpolates a control point P_k. But in that case, the first and second derivatives drop to zero at t_k and therefore the curve is usually (when P_{k-1}, P_k and P_{k+1} are not aligned) only G^0 at P_k. In other words, it means that, even if it is always C^2, the model enables the creation of angular points or sharp edges.

4.2 Examples

This section demonstrates the role of the parameter s_k by showing its influence on the resulting shapes. The basic formulation defined in Section 3 is a particular case of the extended one, where all parameters s_k are set to one. As we have seen, basic X-splines are almost identical to uniform cubic B-splines.

A first variant consists in setting s_0 and s_n to zero in order to interpolate the end points of the control lattice and thus to enable better control of the curve boundaries. The resulting curves — call them extremal X-splines (see Figure 7)— are very close to the classical extremal cubic B-splines (also called non-periodic cubic B-splines).

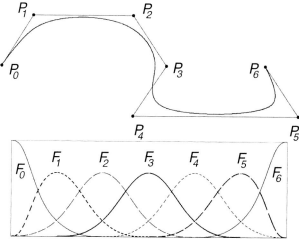

Figure 7: *Extremal X-spline curve*
$s_0 = 0, s_1 = 1, s_2 = 1, s_3 = 1, s_4 = 1, s_5 = 1, s_6 = 0$

Let us now decrease the value of one parameter s_k (say s_3). By comparing Figure 7 and Figure 8, one can see that the crossing point of F_2 and F_4 at knot t_3 has been pushed down.

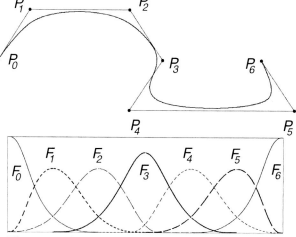

Figure 8: *Augmentation of the influence of point P_3*
$s_0 = 0, s_1 = 1, s_2 = 1, s_3 = 0.5, s_4 = 1, s_5 = 1, s_6 = 0$

Therefore, after the normalization step, the maximum of F_3 has been increased and the curve has been pulled toward P_3. Moreover, neither the maximum of F_2 nor the maximum of F_4 has been modified. This means that the curve has not changed near P_2 or P_4: all the modifications are localized in the neighbourhood of point P_3. More precisely, one can show that a shape parameter s_k influences only two segments of the curves which is half the extent of the other three coordinates (x_k, y_k, z_k) of point P_k (i.e. L^2 locality rather than L^4).

While s_3 decreases, the maximum of F_3 increases. Finally, for $s_3 = 0$, this maximum is set to one, which provides a "sharp" (G^0 continuous) interpolation of point P_3.

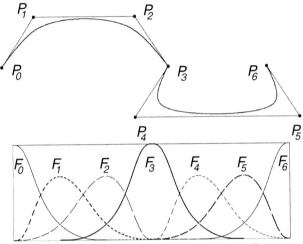

Figure 9: *Sharp interpolation of point P_3*
$s_0 = 0, s_1 = 1, s_2 = 1, s_3 = 0, s_4 = 1, s_5 = 1, s_6 = 0$

The L^2 locality of the influence of the parameters s_k allows the same kind of action on several adjacent control points. For instance, if we decrease s_2, s_3 and s_4, the curve is pulled simultaneously toward P_2, P_3 and P_4,

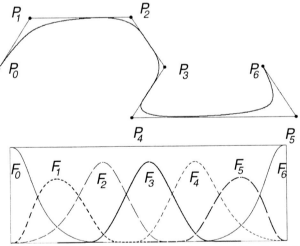

Figure 10: *Augmentation of the influence of P_2, P_3 et P_4*
$s_0 = 0, s_1 = 1, s_2 = 0.5, s_3 = 0.5, s_4 = 0.5, s_5 = 1, s_6 = 0$

and if we set the three parameters to zero, we obtain a sharp interpolation of P_2, P_3 and P_4 (see Figure 11). Finally, for the limit case where all the parameters s_k are set to zero, the curve merges with the control lattice (see Figure 12). But notice that the curve is *not* a linear spline because the parametrization is C^2 here, whereas it is only C^0 for linear splines.

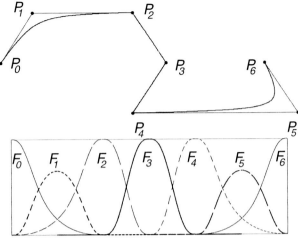

Figure 11: *Sharp interpolation of P_2, P_3 et P_4*
$s_0 = 0, s_1 = 1, s_2 = 0, s_3 = 0, s_4 = 0, s_5 = 1, s_6 = 0$

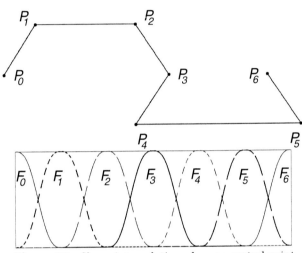

Figure 12: *Sharp interpolation of every control point*
$s_0 = 0, s_1 = 0, s_2 = 0, s_3 = 0, s_4 = 0, s_5 = 0, s_6 = 0$

This ability to mix smooth curves and sharp edges in an unrestricted way makes the extended X-spline model a candidate of choice for many applications. In vectorial font design, for instance, one switches frequenty between smoothness and sharpness. Therefore, the use of X-splines enables the design of characters with one single spline for the outline (plus eventually one spline for each hole) defined by a small number of control points (see left part of Figure 13)

To conclude this section, note that a very useful case is obtained when the control lattice forms a regular polygon and all the s_k are set to one: the resulting curve is a circle (see right part of Figure 13. In fact, this circle is only an approximated one but this approximation is so close (for 8 control points, the amplitude of the oscillations of the curve around the true circle represents less than a factor 10^{-3} of the radius, and for 12 control points, this variation is less than 10^{-6}) that it is sufficient for most of the applications[3]. Starting from that kernel case, other conics can be approximated as well with a similar accuracy [5].

---

[3]A similar result is obtained with B-splines [4], therefore it is not surprising that it holds also for X-splines which approximate B-splines in that particular configuration.

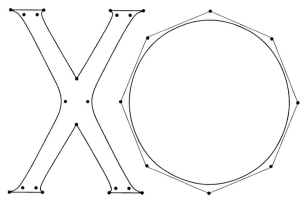

Figure 13: *Font design and representation of the circle*

5 General X-Splines

5.1 Formulation

As they have been formulated above, extended X-splines fulfill many of the properties listed in Section 2. Nevertheless, even if they allow interpolating one or several control points, extended X-splines are still approximation splines, because only sharp interpolations are provided. The last feature of our list was the ability to manipulate the same model either as an approximation spline or as an interpolation spline. The goal of this section is to show how this characteristic can be included in the X-spline model.

But, as recalled in Section 2, using interpolation splines implies forsaking the positivity of the blending functions and therefore the convex hull property. For some applications (and for some users), this is inconceivable. For that reason, we have purposely separated this extension from the previous section. So, the reader may choose between the formulation that fulfills the convex hull property and the formulation that provides the approximation/interpolation duality.

In Section 4, we saw that when the value of the parameter s_k is decreased, the blending function F_{k+1}^- (respectively F_{k-1}^+) becomes null between t_{k-1} and T_{k+1}^+ (respectively T_{k-1}^+ and t_{k+1}). At the limit case, when $s_k = 0$, F_{k+1}^- (respectively F_{k-1}^+) is null over the whole range $[t_{k-1}, t_k]$ (respectively $[t_k, t_{k+1}]$). Starting from that configuration of sharp interpolation, to get a "smooth" (G^2 continuity) interpolation of point P_k, we must allow F_{k+1}^- and F_{k-1}^+ to become negative over these ranges. Moreover, in the same manner as we have sought to approximate cubic B-splines with the basic formulation, we will try to approximate cubic Catmull-Rom splines with this general formulation.

If we apply the following reparametrization to the curve,

$$u(t) = \frac{t - t_k}{t_{k+1} - t_k} = \frac{t - t_k}{\Delta} \qquad (18)$$

we are assured that $u = -1$ at knot t_{k-1} where F_{k+1}^- gets negative, $u = 0$ at knot t_k where F_{k+1}^- gets positive, and $u = 1$ at knot t_{k+1} where F_{k+1}^- reaches its maximum. Therefore, we have to find two polynomials: $g(u)$ defined on $[0, 1]$ which represents the positive part of F_{k+1}^- and $h(u)$ defined on $[-1, 0]$ which represents its negative part. These two functions must join up at $u = 0$ with C^2 continuity. As in Section 3, we can derive a system of constraints but this time there are two functions, which means 12 constraints:

$$
\begin{aligned}
g(0) &= 0 & g'(0) &= q & g''(0) &= 4q \\
g(1) &= 1 & g'(1) &= 0 & g''(1) &= -2p \\
h(0) &= 0 & h'(0) &= q & h''(0) &= 4q \\
h(-1) &= 0 & h'(-1) &= 0 & h''(-1) &= 0
\end{aligned}
\qquad (19)
$$

where q is a degree of freedom that controls the value of the first derivative at $u = 0$ (the same degree of freedom has been used by Duff in his *tensed interpolation spline* model [8]. All these constraints can be fulfilled by two quintic polynomials:

$$
\begin{aligned}
g(u) &= q\,u + 2q\,u^2 + (10 - 12q - p)\,u^3 \\
&\quad + (2p + 14q - 15)\,u^4 + (6 - 5q - p)\,u^5 \\
h(u) &= q\,u + 2q\,u^2 - 2q\,u^4 + q\,u^5
\end{aligned}
\qquad (20)
$$

Starting from these equations, the same construction process detailed in Section 3 provides a rational quintic interpolation spline model that includes the properties of normality, locality and C^2 continuity. Moreover, the curves contain a degree of freedom q which allows modification of their shapes.

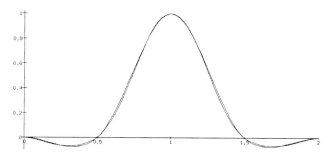

Figure 14: *Similarity of the cubic Catmull-Rom splines and the general X-splines blending functions (for $q = 1/2$)*

Two important remarks should be made about this model. First, as in every interpolation spline model, the regularity property is lost. thus the curve may have unwanted oscillations. We have observed experimentally that these oscillations can usually be avoided by limiting q to the range $[0, 1/2]$. Second, an interesting case is obtained for $q = 1/2$ because the blending functions are very close to the Catmull-Rom functions (see Figure 14). But it should be noticed that the new functions are C^2 continuous instead of C^1.

The final step of the construction of our new spline model will be to merge the parameter s of the approximation model and the parameter q of the interpolation one. Here again, the goal is to simplify the degrees of freedom manipulated by the end user. Practically, only one shape parameter s_k per control point P_k will be used. This is done with the following convention:

- When the user sets all s_k in the range $[0, 1]$, it means that he wants to manipulate approximation splines. In that case, s_k is the curve/lattice distance parameter defined in Section 4 (in particular, uniform cubic B-splines are approximated for $s_k = 1$).

- When the user sets all s_k in the range $[-1, 0]$, it means that he wants to manipulate interpolation splines. In that case, q_k is obtained from s_k by $q_k = -s_k/2$ (so, $s_k = -1$ provides $q = 1/2$ which approximates cubic Catmull-Rom splines).

The positive/negative distinction for s_k indicates clearly that there is a breaking point: for positive s_k, the convex hull property is fulfilled, for negative s_k, it is not the case anymore. On the other hand the intuitive notion of curve/lattice distance is preserved even for negative s_k. Indeed, as we will see below, the more s_k departs from zero, the more the curve departs from the control lattice.

5.2 Examples

We already know that a "sharp" (G^0 continuity) interpolation of the control lattice can be obtained by setting all s_k to zero (see Figure 12). If we want to realize a "smooth" (G^2 continuity) interpolation, the only thing to do is to set these parameters to negative values. For instance, by setting all s_k to -1, an interpolation spline almost identical to the Catmull-Rom spline is obtained (compare Figure 15 and Figure 2). As expected, the blending functions become partly negative, and thus the convex hull property is lost.

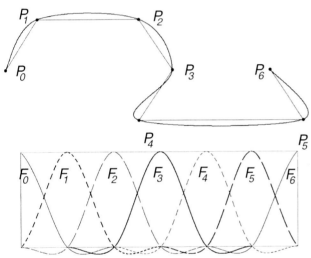

Figure 15: *Smooth interpolation of every control point*
$s_0 = s_1 = s_2 = s_3 = s_4 = s_5 = s_6 = -1$

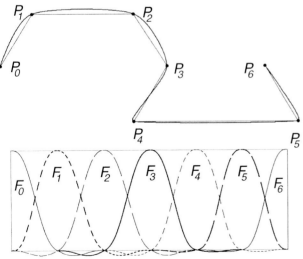

Figure 16: *Modification of the interpolation*
$s_0 = 0, s_1 = s_2 = s_3 = -1, s_4 = s_5 = -0.5, s_6 = 0$

By providing different values for the parameter s_k, the shape of the interpolation curve can be controlled precisely. For instance, one can enable very slack interpolation for a specific zone of the lattice and a much tighter interpolation for another zone (see Figure 16). And finally, what is perhaps the most interesting feature of the X-spline model, one can combine without any restriction, positive and negative shape parameters s_k in order to create approximation zones and interpolation ones in the same curve (see Figure 17).

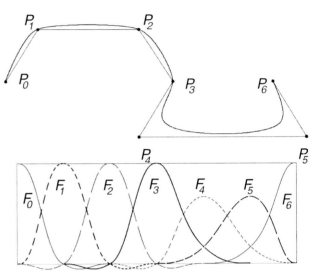

Figure 17: *Approximation zones and interpolation zones*
$s_0 = 0, s_1 = s_2 = s_3 = -1, s_4 = s_5 = 1, s_6 = 0$

6 Surfaces

The extension of the new model from curves to surfaces is straightforward. The only thing to do is to compute the tensor product of two non-normalized X-spline curves and then to apply the normalization step[4]. The characteristic of the X-splines to create all possible geometric effects by using only uniform knot vectors is vital here because, as we have recalled in Section 1, effects due to knot manipulations (e.g. sharp edges for B-splines) are propagated along the whole isoparametric curves. On the contrary, the shape parameters of the X-spline model are directly related to the control points and thus can be localized precisely on a given zone of the surface.

Because of the tensor product, two shape parameters r_k and s_k are provided for each control point P_k where r_k acts in the u direction of the surface and s_k acts in the v direction. A nice consequence is that non-isotropic manipulations are allowed (for instance, creating sharpness in one direction and smoothness in the other one). As a counterpart, the behaviour of these parameters is a bit more subtle than previously:

- $r_k > 0$, $s_k > 0$: P_k is a C^2/G^2 approximation point

- $r_k = 0$, $s_k = 0$: P_k is a C^2/G^0 interpolation point

- $r_k < 0$, $s_k < 0$: P_k is a C^2/G^2 interpolation point

- $r_k = 0$, $s_k > 0$: P_k is an approximation point providing C^2/G^0 continuity in u and C^2/G^2 continuity in v

- $r_k = 0$, $s_k < 0$: P_k is an interpolation point providing C^2/G^0 continuity in u and C^2/G^2 continuity in v

---

[4]This process is sometimes called *generalized tensor product* [11]

Figure 19 and Figure 18 shows some examples of X-spline surfaces. You should notice the ability to create interpolation of adjacent control points, localized sharp edges as well as soft transitions between sharp and smooth zones; three features that are impossible (or at best, only possible in specific cases) with any existing spline model.

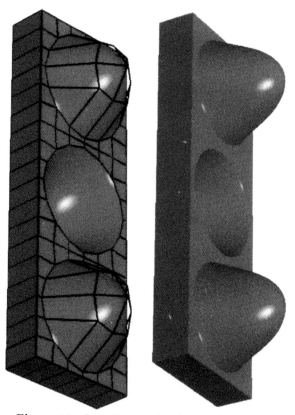

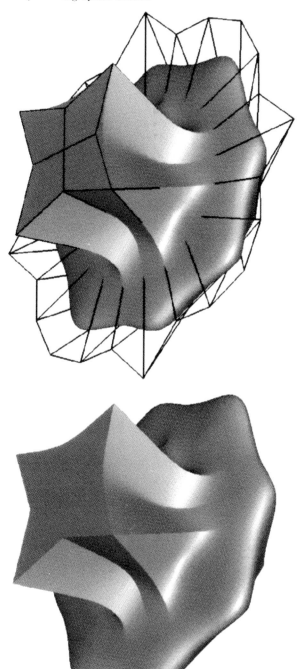

Figure 19: *Smooth extrusion from a sharp object*

7   Conclusion

In this paper, we have presented a new model of spline curves and surfaces. This model includes many classical properties such as affine and perpective invariance, convex hull, variation diminution, local control and C^2/G^2 or C^2/G^0 continuity, as well as some original features such as a continum between (an approximation of) B-splines and (an approximattion of) Catmull-Rom splines, or the ability to define approximation zones and interpolation zones in the same curve or surface. These properties have been obtained by defining a new family of blending functions that are quintic rational polynomials and introducing an original shape parameter that provides, for each control point, a smooth transition between approximation, sharp interpolation and smooth interpolation.

This paper is only intended as an initial presentation of X-splines. For space limitations, several topics could not be included here. We propose some additional results in [5] which should be considered as the companion paper of this one. More precisely, the following topics are discussed in it:

- *Some precisions on efficient implementation of X-splines:* For instance, one can show that even if they are quintic, rational and provide more geometrical effects, uniform X-splines are less expensive to compute than non-uniform cubic B-splines).

- *Lower order and higher order X-splines:* Quintic polynomials have been chosen here because we sought for C^2/G^2 continuity, but in fact a similar construction process can be used for any polynomial of degree $2k + 1$ providing splines with C^k/G^k continuity.

- *Extension to non-uniform knot vectors:* Geometrical effects generated by non-uniformity in classical splines can

Figure 18: *Sharp extrusion from a smooth object*
Note that the star-shaped flat face on the top of the object is composed of two sides with straight edges (left and bottom) and two sides with rounded edges (top and right). Straight sides create sharp edges that are propagated all along the extrusion whereas the sharp edges smoothly vanish when they come near the rounded sides of the top face.

be created by the shape parameters, so this extension is not that vital. Nevertheless, non-uniform knots may be useful for key-frame animation or data-fitting.

- *Refinement algorithms:* This is clearly a much harder task. For the moment, we propose only some preliminary results on a kind of De Casteljau subdivision algorithm.

Acknowledgements

We wish to thank all the anonymous reviewers for many helpful comments and suggestions. We also thank Brian Smith (from Lawrence Berkeley Laboratory), the maintainer of the xfig package, who gave us the permission to include the X-splines model in his software and to use it for public demonstration. Finally, special thanks to C. Feuille, S. Grobois, L. Mazière and L. Minihot who modified xfig for us and discovered the L^2 (rather than L^4) locality of the shape parameters.

8 References

[1] B. Barsky, *The Beta-Spline: a Local Representation based on Shape Parameters and Fundamental Geometric Measures*, PhD Thesis, University of Utah, 1981.

[2] R. Bartels, J. Beatty, B. Barsky, *An Introduction to Splines for Computer Graphics and Geometric Modeling*, Morgan Kaufmann, 1987.

[3] C. Blanc, *Techniques de Modélisation et de Déformation de Surfaces pour la Synthèse d'Images*, PhD Thesis, Université Bordeaux I, 1994 (in french).

[4] C. Blanc, C. Schlick, *More Accurate Representation of Conics by NURBS*, Technical Report, LaBRI, 1995 (submitted for publication).

[5] C. Blanc, C. Schlick, *X-Splines: Some Additional Results*, Technical Report, LaBRI, 1995 (available by HTTP at www.labri.u-bordeaux.fr/LaBRI/People/schlick).

[6] E. Catmull, R. Rom, *A Class of Interpolating Splines*, in Computer Aided Geometric Design, p317-326, Academic Press. 1974

[7] E. Cohen, T. Lyche, R. Riesenfeld, *Discrete B-Splines and Subdivision Techniques*, Computer Graphics & Image Processing, v14, p87-111, 1980.

[8] T. Duff, *Splines in Animation and Modelling*, SIGGRAPH Course Notes, 1986.

[9] G. Farin, *Curves and Surfaces for Computer Aided Geometric Design*, Academic Press, 1990.

[10] D. Forsey, R. Bartels, *Hierarchical B-Spline Refinement*, Computer Graphics, v22, n4, p205-212, 1988.

[11] L. Piegl, *On NURBS: a Survey*, Computer Graphics & Applications, v11, n1, p55-71, 1991.

[12] R. Riesenfeld, *Applications of B-Spline Approximation to Geometric Problems of Computer Aided Design*, PhD Thesis, University Syracuse, 1973.

Rendering Interactive Holographic Images

Mark Lucente   and   Tinsley A. Galyean

Massachusetts Institute of Technology

Media Laboratory*

ABSTRACT

We present a method for computing holographic patterns for the generation of three-dimensional (3-D) holographic images at interactive speeds. We used this method to render holograms on a conventional computer graphics workstation. The framebuffer system supplied signals directly to a real-time holographic ("holovideo") display. We developed an efficient algorithm for computing an image-plane stereogram, a type of hologram that allowed for several computational simplifications. The rendering algorithm generated the holographic pattern by compositing a sequence of view images that were rendered using a recentering shear-camera geometry. Computational efficiencies of our rendering method allowed the workstation to calculate a 6-megabyte holographic pattern in under 2 seconds, over 100 times faster than traditional computing methods. Data-transfer time was negligible. Holovideo displays are ideal for numerous 3-D visualization applications, and promise to provide 3-D images with extreme realism. Although the focus of this work was on fast computation for holovideo, the computed holograms can be displayed using other holographic media. We present our method for generating holographic patterns, preceded by a background section containing an introduction to optical and computational holography and holographic displays.

Keywords: Electro-Holography, Holovideo, Computer-Generated Holography, Accumulation Buffer.
CR Categories: I.3.1 [Computer Graphics]: Hardware Architecture - three-dimensional displays, graphics processors; **I.3.7** [Computer Graphics]: Three-Dimensional Graphics and Realism.

1. INTRODUCTION

The practical use of three-dimensional (3-D) displays has long been a goal in computer graphics. Three-dimensional displays are generally electronic devices that provide binocular depth cues, particularly binocular disparity and convergence. (See the Glossary on the next page.) Some 3-D displays provide additional depth cues such as motion parallax and ocular accommodation. The reference by McKenna[1] contains a good discussion of the visual depth cues and a detailed evaluation of 3-D display techniques.

Recently, some 3-D displays have been used interactively. A 3-D display allows the viewer to more efficiently and accurately sense both the 3-D shapes of objects and their relative spatial locations, particularly when monocular depth cues are not prevalent in a scene. When viewing complex or unfamiliar object scenes, the viewer can more quickly and accurately identify the scene contents. Therefore, 3-D displays are important in any application involving the visualization of 3-D data, including telepresence, education, medical imaging, computer-aided design, scientific visualization, and entertainment.

The merit of a 3-D display depends primarily on its ability to provide depth cues and high resolutions. The inclusion of depth cues - particularly binocular disparity, motion parallax, and occlusion - increases the realism of an image. Holography[2] is the only imaging technique that can provide all the depth cues[1]. All other 3-D display devices lack one or more of the visual depth cues. For example, stereoscopic displays do not provide ocular accommodation, and volume displays cannot provide occlusion. Image resolution and parallax resolution are also important considerations when displaying 3-D images. While most 3-D displays fail to provide acceptable image and parallax resolutions, holography can produce images with virtually unlimited resolutions.

In optical holography, a recorded interference pattern reconstructs an image with an extremely high degree of accuracy. A holographic pattern - called *fringes* - can be computed and used to generate a 3-D image, most recently in real time[3]. Both the computing process and the displaying process are significantly more difficult than in other 3-D display systems. Nevertheless, a real-time electro-holographic ("holovideo") display can produce dynamic 3-D images with all of the depth cues and image realism found in optical holography. Therefore, holovideo has the potential to produce the highest quality 3-D images. Also, to view holographic images, the viewer is unencumbered by equipment such as glasses or sensors. Figure 1 illustrates the basic functionality of holovideo.

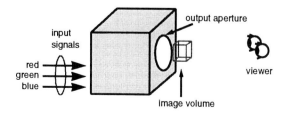

Figure 1: A typical real-time 3-D holographic (holovideo) display. When positioned in the viewing zone, viewers see a 3-D image in the vicinity of the output aperture. The input signals are generated by a computer.

*MIT Media Laboratory, Cambridge, MA 02139. (lucente I tag)@media.mit.edu
Mark Lucente is now at:
IBM T. J. Watson Research Center, P.O. Box 218, Yorktown Heights, NY 10598

Permission to make digital/hard copy of part or all of this work for personal or classroom use is granted without fee provided that copies are not made or distributed for profit or commercial advantage, the copyright notice, the title of the publication and its date appear, and notice is given that copying is by permission of ACM, Inc. To copy otherwise, to republish, to post on servers, or to redistribute to lists, requires prior specific permission and/or a fee.

© 1995   ACM-0-89791-701-4/95/008 $3.50

The size and complexity of holographic fringe patterns often precludes their computation at interactive rates. In the field of computational holography[4], a discretized holographic fringe pattern is generated by numerically simulating the propagation and interference of light. Typical sampling sizes are smaller than the wavelength of visible light. Therefore, a computer-generated hologram (CGH) must contain a huge number of samples. Furthermore, the cost of calculating each sample is high if a conventional approach is taken. Even with the power currently available in scientific workstations, researchers in the field of computational holography commonly report computation times in minutes or hours. In recent work[5], Lucente used a massively parallel supercomputer to calculate holographic fringes at interactive rates.

In this paper we describe the first use of a standard graphics workstation to render and display holograms at interactive rates. The graphics workstation provided both a platform for generating image information and the computing power for generating holographic fringes. Our use of a computer graphics workstation also eliminated data transfer bottlenecks that often prohibit interactive computation. We believe that new holographic displays will continue to emerge in the future, necessitating rapid rendering (computation) of holograms. Our work is an important first step toward practical computation systems for holovideo.

The following Background section gives a brief summary of the principles of holography. The computer generation of holograms and their display are reviewed, including a brief description of the real-time holographic display that we used in this research. In the section Method for Rendering Hologram we describe the hologram rendering algorithm, including the initial processing of object scene data to provide for realistic lighting, shading, occlusion, and other pictorial depth cues. Finally, we present results, future work, and a conclusion.

2. BACKGROUND

This section contains an introduction to holography, computational holography, holographic displays, and stereograms. The concepts discussed here were essential to the development of a faster method for hologram rendering.

2.1 Optical Holography

Optical holography[2] uses the physical phenomena of interference and diffraction to record and reconstruct a 3-D image. Holographic imaging became practical in the 1960's with the advent of coherent monochromatic laser light. To produce a hologram, light is scattered from the object to be recorded. A photosensitive medium records the intensity (irradiance) pattern that results when the light scattered from an object interferes with a spatially clean mutually coherent reference beam. The reference beam allows the medium to record both the magnitude and phase of the incident object wavefront, in essence recording variations in both the intensity and the direction of the light. The recording medium must have sufficient resolution to record spatial frequencies that are typically 1500 linepairs/millimeter or more.

To reconstruct an image, the recorded interference pattern modulates an illuminating beam of light. The modulated light diffracts (bends and focuses) and reconstructs a 3-D replica of the wavefront that was scattered from the object scene. Optical wavefront reconstruction makes the image appear to be physically present and tangible. The image possesses all of the depth cues exhibited by the original object, including continuous parallax (vertical and horizontal) and ocular accommodation. Both the image resolution and parallax resolution of an optical holographic image are virtually unlimited.

GLOSSARY

Visual Depth Cues

binocular disparity: the binocular depth cue effected by the slight differences between the two retinal images captured by each eye. The depth sensation caused by binocular disparity is called **stereopsis**.

convergence: a binocular depth cue effected when the eyes rotate to align the retinal images captured by each eye.

occlusion, overlap: monocular depth cue effected when one part of image is obstructed by another overlapping part.

ocular accommodation: a monocular depth cue in which the eye senses depth by focusing at different distances.

parallax, motion parallax: a (monocular) depth cue sensed from the apparent change in the lateral displacements among objects in a scene as the viewer moves. A display which provides parallax allows the viewer to move around the object scene.

pictorial depth cues: the monocular depth cues found in 2-D images, including occlusion, linear perspective, texture gradient, aerial perspective, shading, and relative sizes.

3-D Display Types

stereoscopic: a 3-D display type that presents a left view of the imaged scene to the left eye and a right view to the right eye. Examples include boom-mounted, head-mounted, and displays using polarizing glasses.

autostereoscopic: a 3-D display type that presents left and right views of the imaged scene without special viewing aids. Examples include lenticular, parallax barrier, slice stacking, and holography. Some provide motion parallax by presenting more than two views.

holovideo: a real-time 3-D electro-holographic display.

Additional Terms

basis fringe: an elemental fringe pattern computed to diffract light in a specific manner. The name "basis fringe" is an analogy to mathematical basis functions. Linear summations of basis fringes were used as holographic patterns.

computational holography, computer-generated holography: the numerical synthesis of holograms.

hololine: a horizontal line of samples of a holographic fringe pattern.

horizontal-parallax-only or **HPO**: possessing horizontal parallax but not vertical parallax. The viewer sees the same vertical perspective of the imaged scene regardless of the vertical location of the eyes.

image volume: the volume occupied by a 3-D image.

image resolution: the number of resolvable image features in the lateral dimensions of an image.

parallax resolution: the number of different perspective views available to the viewer.

2.2 Computational Holography

To produce dynamic holographic images, researchers can compute and display holographic fringe patterns. Computational holography[4] generally begins with a 3-D numerical description of the object or scene to be reproduced. Light is numerically scattered from the object scene and propagated to the plane of the hologram. The object wavefront is calculated, and a reference beam wavefront added, imitating optical interference. The resulting total intensity - the fringe pattern - is used by a holographic display to produce the 3-D image. Such a display spatially modulates a beam of light with the fringes, mimicking the reconstruction step in optical holography.

Computational holography produces 3-D imaging with a high degree of realism. Only recently have researchers achieved computational holography at interactive rates, impeded mainly by the enormous data content and by the computational complexity associated with holographic fringes[5]. A typical full-parallax hologram 100 mm × 100 mm in size has a space-bandwidth product (SBWP) of over 100 gigasamples of information. A larger image requires a proportionally larger number of samples. Several techniques have been used to reduce information content to a manageable size. The elimination of vertical parallax provides great savings in display complexity[3] and computational requirements[5] without greatly compromising the overall display performance. Other less desirable sacrifices include reducing the size of the object scene or the size of the viewing zone.

There are several methods of computing holographic fringes. Most imitate the interference that occurs when a hologram is produced optically using coherent light. Early methods made use of the Fourier transform to calculate the phase and amplitude of the object wavefront at the plane of the hologram[4]. At each sample point in the hologram plane, this object light wavefront was added to a reference beam wavefront, and the magnitude squared became the desired fringe pattern. This approach was used to create planar images. Multiple image planes were separately processed and combined to produce 3-D images. Consequently, the Fourier-transform approach was slow and inefficient for computing 3-D images.

A more straightforward approach to the computation of holographic fringes resembled 3-D computer graphics ray-tracing. Light from a given point or element of an object contributed a complex wavefront at the hologram plane[2]. Each of these complex wavefronts was summed to calculate the total object wavefront which was subsequently added to a reference wavefront. Black (non-scattering) regions of the image volume were ignored, enabling very rapid computations of simple object scenes. Again, for more complex images, computation was prohibitively slow.

In recent work[5], Lucente described a computational method that greatly simplified the ray-tracing approach. By computing fringes that diffracted light only to specific regions of the image volume, this approach had a number of advantages: (1) it enabled the real-valued linear superposition of fringe patterns; (2) it increased the speed of computation by a factor of 2.0; (3) it eliminated the need for an explicit reference beam wavefront; and (4) it eliminated certain imaging artifacts and noise that generally degrade the quality of holographic images. Real-valued summation enabled the efficient use of precomputed elemental fringe patterns (called *basis fringes*), an approach that achieved CGH computation at interactive rates when implemented on a supercomputer[5].

We chose to implement an approach similar to the Lucente approach - using an array of precomputed basis fringes - because it promised to provide the fastest holographic computation. We focused on further reducing computational complexity and on the implementation of holographic computation on hardware designed for computer graphics rendering.

2.3 Holographic Displays

A holographic fringe pattern is used to modulate a beam of monochromatic light to produce an image. In the earliest work in computational holography, the computed fringe pattern was recorded (permanently) in a piece of film[4]. The film provided the SBWP sufficient to represent the fringes. In some cases, the film also provided grayscale. Light passing through this film created a static holographic image.

To create dynamic holographic images, a dynamic spatial light modulator (SLM) must be used. The SBWP of a holographic SLM must be as high as that of holographic film. Ideally, a holographic SLM must display over 100 gigasamples. Current SLMs, however, can provide a maximum of 10 megasamples. Examples of SLMs include the flat-panel liquid-crystal display (LCD) and the magneto-optic SLM. These SLMs are capable of displaying a very small CGH pattern in real time. Early researchers employed a liquid-crystal SLM with an SBWP of 10,000 elements to produce a tiny planar image[6]. Most researchers reported images that were still quite small and essentially two-dimensional[7].

An ideal holographic SLM does not yet exist, but time-multiplexing of a very fast SLM provides a suitable substitute. The display system that we used in this research was similar to previously reported holovideo displays[3]. Our display used the combination of an acousto-optic modulator (AOM) and a series of lenses and scanning mirrors to assemble a small full-color 3-D holographic image at video frame rates. A partial schematic is shown in Figure 2. A general description follows, and a detailed description can be found in the reference by St. Hilaire et al.[3] It is important to note that the holographic rendering method described in this paper is not specific to one display. By incorporating the proper physical parameters, wavelengths and sample size, a hologram generated using this method can be viewed using other holographic displays.

In our holovideo display, as each line (*hololine*) of the fringe pattern was read out of a high-speed framebuffer, it passed through a radio-frequency (RF) signal processing circuit and into the AOM. At any instant, as one line of the holographic pattern traversed the aperture of the AOM in the form of an acoustic wave (at a speed of 617 m/s), a portion equal to roughly 2000 samples modulated the phase of the wavefront of laser light that passed through the AOM. Two lenses reconstructed the diffracted light at a plane in front of the viewer. By reflecting the light off of a synchronized horizontally scanning mirror, the apparent motion of the holographic pattern was cancelled. The scanning motion of the mirror also acted to angularly multiplex the image of the acoustic wave. It extended the apparent width of the imaged holographic pattern to 32768 samples, each sample representing a physical spacing of 1.0 micron.

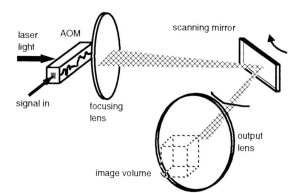

Figure 2: Partial schematic diagram of our holovideo display, shown from roughly the viewer's perspective. The scanning mirror angularly multiplexed the image of the modulated light. A vertical scanning mirror (not shown) positioned each hololine vertically. Electronic control circuits synchronized the scanners to the incoming holo-

The viewer saw a real 3-D image located just in front of the output lens of the system. The image occupied a volume that was 40 mm wide, 35 mm high and 50 mm deep. The size of the viewing zone - i.e., the range of eye locations from which the viewer can see the image - was 16 degrees horizontal. (Both viewing zone and image dimensions were minimized in order to reduce the required bandwidth of the display system.) The viewer experienced the depth cue of horizontal motion parallax. This was a horizontal-parallax-only (HPO) image. Vertical parallax was sacrificed to simplify the display. This restriction does not limit the display's usefulness in most applications. Because the holographic image possessed no vertical parallax, there was no need for diffraction in the vertical dimension. The vertical resolution of 64 lines over 35 mm was equivalent to that of a common 2-D display.

Because our display was a full-color system, the hologram was displayed as a vertical stack of 64 three-color hololines. The display modulated three parallel channels, one for each of the red, green and blue primary colors. The AOM had 3 separate but parallel channels, each modulating a separate beam of incident laser light (633 nm red, 514 nm green, 476 nm blue). Three separate fringe patterns were simultaneously read out of the 3-channel framebuffer.

To be displayed on our holovideo system, a fringe pattern must adhere to three specifications. First, for each of three color separations, the size of the fringe pattern must be 64 hololines of 32768 samples. Second, the sample size is 1.0 micron. Third, a separate fringe pattern must be computed at each of three wavelengths: 633 nm for red, 514 nm for green, and 476 nm for blue.

2.4 Stereograms

A stereogram is a type of hologram that is composed of a series of discrete 2-D perspective views of the object scene[8][9]. A stereogram has two essential characteristics: it has discretized parallax; and it creates an image at a single plane, the *image plane*. Parallax discretization simplifies fringe computation (and display). Computation is much faster than in the general case of a non-stereogram image. Provided that the number of discrete views is high enough, parallax appears to change smoothly, and the image appears to be 3-D.

An HPO stereogram produces a view-dependent image which presents in each horizontally displaced direction the corresponding perspective view of the object scene. The vertical perspective remains unchanged from any location in the viewing zone. In an image-plane stereogram, the image plane coincides with the physical plane of the hologram. As a result, the contribution to the object wavefront from each view-image pixel does not overlap with contributions from adjacent pixels. This reduces computational complexity. Specifically, discrete samples of the fringe pattern coinciding with a particular pixel are computed using only the view-dependent values of that pixel.

In a stereogram, the viewing zone is treated as an array of discretized subzones. An eye of the viewer, when moving from side to side, sees one discrete view of the scene after another. To compute a stereogram, a sequence of view images is rendered using a different camera geometry for each view image. These images are combined to calculate fringes for display. The only disadvantage of a stereogram is that it may not provide the depth cue of ocular accommodation. Ocular accommodation, however, is generally less important than binocular disparity, motion parallax and occlusion. A stereogram provides all other depth cues, and produces a realistic 3-D image.

The obvious advantage of a stereogram is that conventional computer graphics hardware can be used to render the sequence of view images. This makes pre-existing models and rendering methods applicable to holography.

Figure 3a: Three stereogram components. (Top view.) Light is diffracted from each in a specific direction.

Figure 3b: The composite hologram.

3. METHOD FOR HOLOGRAM RENDERING

The fast computation of a stereogram involved two parts: rendering different view images, and using them to create holographic fringes. Beginning with a finite number of views (in this case eight), our goal was to construct an HPO image-plane stereogram that showed the correctly rendered view image for each viewing angle.

The development of a computational approach began by considering how light should be diffracted (or scattered) by the fringes. Consider an image displayed on a CRT: the light from the 2-D image scatters over the entire (often wide) viewing angle. In contrast, a stereogram must diffract light selectively. A stereogram causes a particular view image to be visible only from a particular part of the viewing zone. Figure 3a shows light diffracting over only a part of the viewing zone for three different views. In Figure 3b, the composite holographic fringe pattern in a single pixel region diffracts specific amounts of light in three different viewing directions. The amount of light corresponds to the pixel brightness values at this particular pixel location for each view image.

This section describes each step of the computational algorithm that we implemented on a graphics workstation. We began by precomputing a set of basis fringes and storing them in memory. As described in the following subsection, each basis fringe controlled the specific directional behavior of diffracted light. The next three subsections describe the three steps used to compute the actual fringe pattern: rendering a set of views (using conventional computer graphics rendering methods), generating a component stereogram fringe pattern from each view using an array of precomputed basis fringes, and compositing these separate stereogram components into the final fringe pattern. The final subsection is a description of the implementation specifics of our research.

3.1 Precomputing the Set of Basis Fringes

The arrays of precomputed basis fringes were designed to diffract light in specific directions. One basis fringe was the holographic pattern that caused light to diffract from a particular view-image pixel location to a particular viewing subzone. An array of basis fringes - one for each view-image pixel - was computed for each viewing subzone. This entire set of basis fringe arrays - one for each viewing subzone - was computed for each of the three (primary color) wavelengths used to create the full-color holographic image.

The set of basis fringes can be computed in several ways. We used an iterative numerical approach to solve the common integral expression that describes the diffraction of optical wavefronts. We began by specifying the direction that light must be diffracted by each basis fringe. For an image-plane stereogram, each basis fringe was characterized by the diffraction from one view-image pixel region to one viewing subzone, as illustrated in Figure 4. The subzones, each of angular width Δ, divided the viewing zone into non-overlapping pieces across the horizontal range of the viewing zone. The horizontal parallax resolution was equal to the number of subzones. Each pixel region of width w coincided physically with a single rendered view-image pixel location. To make a view image visible from one of the viewing subzones, the basis fringe within each pixel region must be modulated by the pixel value of the rendered view image.

In the analysis that follows, we denoted the modulated light in the plane of the image (and hologram) as $u(x)$ in complex scalar notation. The light at the viewing zone distance z was represented by the complex scalar $v(\theta)$ expressed as a function of viewing angle θ. We defined each basis fringe through a set of constraints on the magnitudes of $u(x)$ and $v(\theta)$. Then, by relating related $u(x)$ and $v(\theta)$ through the law of diffraction, we calculated each basis fringe by numerically solving for the phase of $u(x)$.

For a single view-image pixel, the constraint on $|u(x)|$ was straightforward: within the pixel region, the diffracted intensity should be constant. Therefore, $|u(x)|$ must be virtually constant. For a single view, the modulated light $u(x)$ should diffract light only to a particular viewing subzone to avoid leakage or ghosting. Within the viewing subzone, $v(\theta)$ should be constant. Therefore, the constraint on $v(\theta)$ was that

$$|v(\theta)| = 1 \text{ for } |\theta - \theta_v| < \Delta/2,$$
$$|v(\theta)| = 0 \text{ elsewhere,}$$

where θ_v is the angle (from normal) connecting the center of a pixel region to the center of the viewing subzone. Finally, the phase of $v(\theta)$ was invisible and therefore was left unconstrained. When computed to satisfy these constraints, a basis fringe diffracts a unity brightness from a given pixel region to a specific viewing subzone.

The values of $u(x)$ and of $v(\theta)$ were related through the laws of optical diffraction[10].We invoked the far-field (Fraunhofer) diffraction approximation (expressed in complex time-harmonic notation):

$$v(\theta) = \frac{e^{ikz(1+\theta^2/2)}}{ikz} \int_{-w/2}^{w/2} u(x) e^{-ikx\theta} dx \qquad (1)$$

where $k \equiv 2\pi/\lambda$ and λ is the free-space wavelength of the light. The far-field approximation, valid for $z \gg w^2/\lambda$, was appropriate for the dimensions that we used: $w = 0.250$ mm and $z = 600$ mm.

The integral expression in Equation 1 is essentially a Fourier transform integral. The wavefront at the viewing zone, $v(\theta)$, is a Fourier transform of $u(x)$, with additional leading terms to account for phase curvature and for power conservation. Equation 1 reveals that while the constraints on $u(x)$ were spatial, the constraints on $v(\theta)$ determined the spectrum of $u(x)$. An appropriately band-limited $u(x)$ resulted in an angularly limited $v(\theta)$ that satisfies the constraints on $|v(\theta)|$.

For one pixel location and one viewing subzone, the unconstrained phase of $u(x)$ was numerically computed using an iterative constraint approach[11] that uses both the forward and the inverse Fourier transforms:

1. Generate a random fringe pattern of width w.
2. Apply the (spatial) constraints on $u(x)$.
3. Transform into the spatial frequency domain.
4. Apply the (spectral) constraints on $v(\theta)$.
5. Inverse transform back to the spatial domain.
6. Iterate starting at step 2.

The iteration continued until $u(x)$ converged. Satisfactory convergence resulted after typically 10 to 20 iterations. As in work by Lucente[5], the real part of $u(x)$ was used as the basis fringe. A selection of precomputed basis fringes is shown in Figure 5.

We computed the array of basis fringe patterns for each viewing subzone in the same way, with each basis fringe occupying different view-image pixel locations in the image plane. The array for each viewing subzone was computed using a unique viewing direction θ_v. Three different basis sets were computed - one for each color - at the correct red, green or blue wavelengths (633 nm, 514 nm, and 476 nm). These basis sets were stored in memory and used during actual hologram computation.

3.2 Generating the View Images

The first step during the actual computation of the CGH pattern was to render a series of perspective view images from left to right. Each discrete camera location had a unique angle with respect to the scene being rendered. The final hologram diffracted light in the directions corresponding to these camera view-angles. This section describes the recentering shear-camera geometry that we used to render the view images, as well as the bounding and discretization of the image volume.

To render each view image, the camera geometry was changed by moving the camera from left to right at a constant spacing along a straight line. (See Figure 6.) When lateral motion is the only

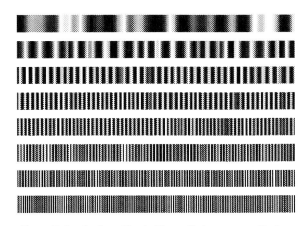

Figure 5: A selection of basis fringes that correspond to the center view-image pixel for each of the eight viewing subzones. Each is 256 samples long. The top fringe represents a mean diffraction angle of 1.8 degrees in red light, corresponding to the left-most viewing subzone. The bottom fringe represents a mean diffraction angle of 14.7 degrees in red light, corresponding to the right-most viewing subzone.

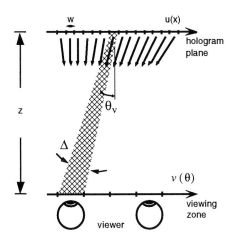

Figure 4: Diffraction caused by an array of basis fringes. Light diffracts from all pixel regions to a particular viewing subzone.

change in camera geometry, the object scene tends to walk out of the frame and becomes invisible in the far left or far right views. Therefore it was necessary to recenter the object scene in the frame of the camera as the camera moved from left to right.

The correct way to recenter the object scene for each camera location was to move the view window, as shown in Figure 6. For the center view (position A in Figure 6), where the camera was directly in front of the scene, the camera geometry was simple. The view normal faced the scene, and the view window was centered with respect to the view normal. For any other view, the view window was off center. As the camera was moved off center (Figure 6, position B), the view window was moved off center in the opposite direction. This is called a shear camera geometry. Note that the view normal does not change. This has the effect of keeping the objects in the center of the frame and in holography is called a recentering camera. If the recentering is done correctly, a point (in the 3-D object scene) that lies on the image plane renders to the same pixel location in each rendered view image.

When rendering the view images, we restricted the scene volume to match the size of the image volume achievable in our holovideo display. If an object crosses the frame, clipping occurs. This clipping (called image vignetting) is a window violation, which often hinders the feeling of depth. Therefore, we chose to confine objects to lie inside the restricted volume so that objects did not cross the frame boundaries.

We chose the resolution of the rendered view images to be 128 by 64. In the horizontal dimension, the CGH was capable of imaging to resolutions that were beyond the typical acuity of the human visual system. We chose a horizontal resolution of 128 to give an image pixel width of 0.25 mm, or roughly the smallest feature size that a human viewer can discern at typical viewing distances. We matched the vertical resolution of the view images to that of our holovideo display (64 lines).

3.3 Computing the Component for Each View

We chose to use the image-plane stereogram geometry because it ensured that a view-image pixel contributed only to the part of the fringe pattern that coincided with that pixel region. A given precomputed basis fringe was multiplied by its respective pixel value at each sample in the pixel region. When sent to the display, the resulting fringe pattern diffracted the correct amount of light to the correct viewing subzone. For one view, the fringe pattern in this pixel region was not a function of any other pixel values. In other words, in a given stereogram view component, the fringe contributions from each pixel did not overlap. Therefore, because of the image-plane stereogram geometry, each of the pixel values for one view image independently modulated each basis fringe in one array.

We designed the holovideo rendering algorithm to perform the multiplication of basis fringes by pixel values using a single tex-

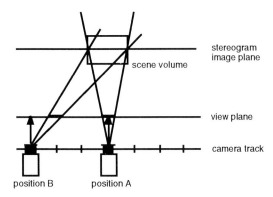

Figure 6: Camera geometry for rendering view images.

ture-mapping instruction, eliminating the need to multiply the basis fringe for each pixel one by one. The array of precomputed basis fringes for a particular view was multiplied by the appropriately resized pixel map of the rendered view image. The result, a single stereogram component, diffracted light to form the image for a given viewing subzone.

3.4 Compositing the View Components

After each stereogram component was generated, it was composited into the final CGH pattern. The approach that we use allowed for the linear superposition of computed fringe patterns[5]. Therefore, the components were simply summed. An array of basis fringes patterns were modulated by an array of weighting values (a view image) and accumulated in the accumulation buffer. The process is illustrated in Figure 7. Below is a piece of pseudocode that describes the process.

```
Set the accumulation buffer to zero.
For each view i {
        Load ith array of basis fringes.
        Generate ith view image.
        Modulate fringes with the view image.
        Add result to accumulation buffer.
}
Display sum contained in accumulation buffer.
```

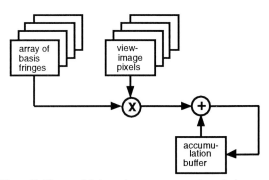

Figure 7: The modulate and sum process of rendering.

3.5 Implementation Specifics

Our algorithm for rendering holographic fringe patterns was implemented initially on an SGI Skywriter with a VGXT graphics subsystem and more recently on an Onyx with a RealityEngine2 (RE2). In both cases, the graphics hardware subsystems had two enabling features: an integrated accumulation buffer and a reconfigurable framebuffer. The accumulation buffer was an essential part of the fast algorithm. The reconfigurability of the framebuffer enabled the graphics subsystem to drive our holovideo display directly, but was not essential to the rendering algorithm.

We reconfigured the graphics framebuffers to provide three analog output signals in a format that was suited to our holovideo display. The active data array was set to 2048×1024 in each of the three 8-bit buffers. (The display system unfolds the 2048×1024 video signal to a 32768×64 pattern.) We adjusted the clock rate of the three 2-MB buffers to generate signals at a rate of 110 MB/-s/channel. We also adjusted blanking intervals to minimize the image noise caused by signal blanking that occurred within each hololine. We could not eliminate blanking, but the length of the blanking intervals was reduced to less than 4 percent of the active data line.

The following is a description of the algorithm illustrated in Figure 7 as we implemented it on the SGI graphics subsystems. The algorithm had three steps: render the view images, modulate the arrays of basis fringes using the rendered view images, and sum the results in the accumulation buffer. The view images were rendered using straightforward GL library calls. The camera geometry was adjusted for each view using the method described earlier in the section 3.2 Generating the View Images. Each of the 128×64-pixel view images was stored in memory. The framebuffer was loaded with the array of basis fringes for a particular view. The 32768×64 fringe pattern was folded into the 2048×1024 framebuffer. The 128×64 view image was mapped over the entire framebuffer and used to modulate the basis fringes. The graphics subsystem used the view image as a texture map on the surface of a polygon that covered the entire framebuffer. The "blending" feature of the graphics subsystem was set to multiply the current value in the framebuffer with the pixel value from the texture map. Effectively, the basis fringes were weighted by the view-image pixels. The resulting stereogram component was added to the accumulation buffer and the process was repeated for each view. The final holographic pattern was moved from the accumulation buffer to the framebuffer for viewing. All of these steps were performed in parallel for all three colors, generating a total of 6 MB of CGH.

4. RESULTS

Holographic fringes were computed on either SGI platform and used to generate 3-D images on our real-time holographic display. Figures 8, 9, and 10 are photographs of typical images, each generated using eight full-color view images at a resolution of 128 by 64. Figure 8 shows a human head and a car, both generated from polygonal models. Figure 9 shows a simple image of three cut cubes, photographed from different locations in the viewing zone. Figure 10 shows a time sequence of an object generated using an interactive modeling system.

The horizontal image resolution of 128 was sufficient to produce the appearance of continuous surfaces. Some noticeable image artifact was due to the 4-percent blanking, which produced the faint vertical stripes visible in Figures 8, 9, and 10. The vertical resolution, limited by the display system to 64, is also evident in these photographs. (We remark that photographing holographic images poses a challenge, and the quality of these illustrations suffers as a result.) As discussed in the Future Work section, image quality can be improved using a new approach that is more precise than the stereogram approach.

Image depth and color were very good. The images gave a good sensation of depth, though the limited viewing zone and lateral dimensions weakened the impact. Objects appeared to occupy a depth of over 50 mm. Color was superb. The three wavelengths used as primary colors spanned a very broad color space that was much larger than that of a typical high-quality 2-D display.

Computation time was 2 seconds (for the 6-MB fringe pattern) using the Onyx/RE2 platform (two-processor Onyx, 4-raster-manager RE2) and 5 seconds for the Skywriter/VGXT platform. (For comparison, the same hologram required over 8 minutes when implemented using a standard method on the SGI Skywriter.) Computation time comprised two parts: view-image rendering and fringe computation. The time spent rendering the view images was less than 10 percent of total hologram computation time. Fringe computation was $O(v*n)$, where v was the number of views (parallax resolution) and n was the total number of samples in the fringe pattern. The sample count n was essentially a measure of image volume. Fringe computation time was independent of view-image resolution, which only affected the rendering time. The precomputation of the basis fringes did not contribute to the computation time per CGH frame. The precomputed basis fringes were computed only once and stored in memory.

Transfer of the 6-MB fringe pattern from the accumulation buffer to the framebuffer required negligible time since these two buffers resided in the same hardware. Therefore, our implementation on either graphics subsystem avoided a common data transfer

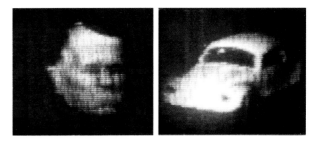

Figure 8: Two photographs of holographic images generated on our real-time holographic display. Left: polygonal model of head with texture-mapped face. Right: polygonal model of a car. View images for both objects were rendered in hardware at a resolution of 128×64.

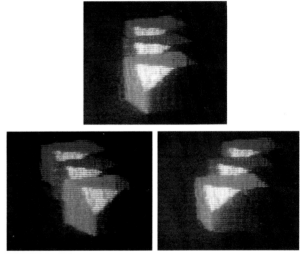

Figure 9: An image, composed of three cut cubes located at different depths, photographed from different locations in the viewing zone. Top: center. Left: left. Right: right.

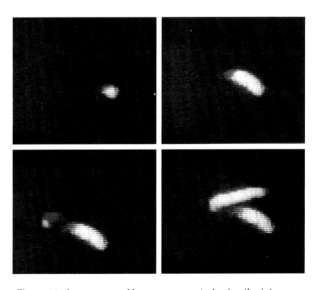

Figure 10: A sequence of images generated using the interactive "sculpt" system, showing the potential of holographic rendering and display for interactive applications.

bottleneck. For comparison, in past work by Lucente[5] using a data-parallel supercomputer, 0.4 s was spent transferring the 6-MB fringe pattern from the 16 K processors to the framebuffer.

The benchmark computation time of 2 s for our rendering method was fast enough to provide interactivity to a patient viewer. We anticipate that computation speeds will continue to increase as computational power increases and further computational efficiencies are obtained. In fact, the work using the Skywriter/VGXT platform was performed two years ago. Our recent upgrade to the Onyx/RE2 platform more than doubled speed, and new graphics hardware should continue to offer faster implementations of our hologram rendering algorithm.

5. FUTURE WORK

The holovideo rendering algorithm presented here is applicable not only to image-plane stereograms but to all types of synthetic holograms. Research is underway to adapt this rendering method to the computation of 3-D volume (non-stereogram) images using the newly developed method of "diffraction-specific" fringe computation that also allows for holographic bandwidth compression[12]. Such a 3-D volume image possesses more depth and tangibility because it produces an actual 3-D real image and provides the depth cue of ocular accommodation. Finally, the computation of full-parallax holographic images is possible, though no full-parallax holographic 3-D display yet exists.

We have generated holograms from live scenes. The simplest approach is to use an array of horizontally displaced video cameras to provide view images in our hologram rendering algorithm. Faster frame rates will enable the production of real-time holographic live video of actual scenes.

6. CONCLUSION

Three-dimensional displays are superior to 2-D displays in many applications of computer graphics. Holographic displays produce images with the greatest number of depth cues and therefore the greatest sensation of 3-D. With their ability to produce images in real time with high resolutions and full color, holographic displays promise the highest degree of image realism.

Our research has demonstrated that existing computer graphics workstation technology can be used to generate holographic fringe patterns at interactive rates for the real-time display of 3-D images. A workstation such as the SGI Onyx coupled with a specialized rendering engine is capable of driving a holovideo display directly. As holographic displays become larger and more practical, the computational method presented here can be scaled up to produce holographic fringes for images that occupy a larger volume and provide a larger viewing zone.

We have presented only a single case in a wide range of hologram types, computation techniques, display architectures, applications, and hardware and software support. Nevertheless, the importance of this work is that it breaks the deadlock that has impeded the development of methods for both the computing and the displaying of 3-D holographic images. We have reported the use of an existing computer graphics system to generate a high-bandwidth holographic signal for a holovideo display. Our research shows that a computer graphics workstation provides sufficient computational support for the development of real-time electronic holography. Furthermore, our work heralds the marriage of the two fields of computer graphics and electronic holography.

ACKNOWLEDGMENTS

We thank many: Stephen A. Benton for guidance in the holovideo project; Michael Halle for contributions to implementation issues; David Zeltzer; Pierre St. Hilaire and John D. Sutter for help with the holovideo display optics; Scott Pritchett, John Hallesy, Gregory Eitzmann, and Jim Foran at Silicon Graphics, Inc. for help with framebuffer reconfiguration; and Katherine Wrean for help in preparing this document.

Components of this research have been sponsored by Honda Research and Development Co., Ltd.; NEC Corporation; International Business Machines Corp.; the Advanced Research Projects Agency (ARPA) through the Naval Ordnance Station, Indian Head, Maryland (under contract No. N00174-91-C0117); the Television of Tomorrow research consortium of the Media Laboratory, MIT; Apple Computer Inc.; and NHK (Japanese Broadcasting Corp.).

Silicon Graphics, Inc. (Mountain View, CA, USA) are the creators of "Skywriter" and "Onyx" computer graphics workstations, the "VGXT" and "RealityEngine" graphics subsystems, and GL graphics software.

REFERENCES

[1] Michael McKenna and David Zeltzer. Three Dimensional Visual Display Systems For Virtual Environments. *Presence: Teleoperators and Virtual Environments.* Vol. 1 #4, 1992, pp. 421-458.

[2] P. Hariharan. *Optical Holography.* Cambridge: Cambridge University Press. 1984.

[3] Pierre St. Hilaire, Stephen A. Benton and Mark Lucente. Synthetic Aperture Holography: A Novel Approach To Three Dimensional Displays. *Journal of the Optical Society of America A*, Vol. 9, #11, Nov. 1992, pp. 1969 - 1977.

[4] William J. Dallas. Computer-Generated Holograms. Chapter 6 in *The Computer in Optical Research, Topics in Applied Physics*, Vol. 41, ed. B.R. Frieden. Berlin: Springer-Verlag. 1980, pp. 291-366.

[5] Mark Lucente. Interactive Computation Of Holograms Using A Look-up Table. *Journal of Electronic Imaging*, Vol. 2, #1, Jan 1993, pp. 28-34. Also: Mark Lucente. Optimization of hologram computation for real-time display. in *SPIE Proc. #1667 Practical Holography VI*, 1667-04 (SPIE, Bellingham, WA, 1992), pp. 32-43.

[6] F. Mok, J. Diep, H.-K. Liu and D. Psaltis. Real-time Computer-generated Hologram By Means Of Liquid-Crystal Television Spatial Light Modulator. *Optics Letters*, Vol. 11 #11, Nov. 1986, pp. 748-750.

[7] S. Fukushima, T. Kurokawa and M. Ohno. Real-time Hologram Construction And Reconstruction Using A High-resolution Spatial Light Modulator. *Applied Physics Letters*, Vol. 58 #8, Aug. 1991, pp. 787-789.

[8] Stephen A. Benton. Survey of Holographic Stereograms. In *Processing and Display of Three-Dimensional Data. Proceedings of the SPIE* 367, 1983, pp. 15-19.

[9] Michael Halle. *The Generalized Holographic Stereogram.* Master's thesis, Massachusetts Institute of Technology, 1991.

[10] Joseph W. Goodman. *Introduction to Fourier Optics.* New York: McGraw-Hill. 1968.

[11] J. R. Fienup. Iterative Method Applied to Image Reconstruction And to Computer-Generated Holograms. *Optical Engineering*, Vol. 19 #3, May/June 1980, pp.297-305.

[12] Mark Lucente. *Diffraction-Specific Fringe Computation for Electro-Holography.* Ph.D. Thesis, Massachusetts Institute of Technology, 1994.

An Integrated Environment to Visually Construct 3D Animations

Enrico Gobbetti and Jean-Francis Balaguer †

Center for Advanced Studies, Research and Development in Sardinia

ABSTRACT

In this paper, we present an expressive 3D animation environment that enables users to rapidly and visually prototype animated worlds with a fully 3D user-interface. A 3D device allows the specification of complex 3D motion, while virtual tools are visible mediators that live in the same 3D space as application objects and supply the interaction metaphors to control them. In our environment, there is no intrinsic difference between user-interface and application objects. Multi-way constraints provide the necessary tight coupling among components that makes it possible to seamlessly compose animated and interactive behaviors. By recording the effects of manipulations, all the expressive power of the 3D user interface is exploited to define animations. Effective editing of recorded manipulations is made possible by compacting all continuous parameter evolutions with an incremental data-reduction algorithm, designed to preserve both geometry and timing. The automatic generation of editable representations of interactive performances overcomes one of the major limitations of current performance animation systems. Novel interactive solutions to animation problems are made possible by the tight integration of all system components. In particular, animations can be synchronized by using constrained manipulation during playback. The accompanying video-tape illustrates our approach with interactive sequences showing the visual construction of 3D animated worlds. All the demonstrations in the video were recorded live and were not edited.

Keywords

3D Interaction, 3D Widgets, Virtual Tools, 3D Animation, Local Propagation Constraints, Data Reduction, Object-Oriented Graphics.

† CRS4, Scientific Visualization Group, Via Nazario Sauro 10, 09123 Cagliari, Italy.
E-mail: {gobbetti|balaguer}@crs4.it
WWW: http://www.crs4.it/~gobbetti
       http://www.crs4.it/~balaguer

Permission to make digital/hard copy of part or all of this work for personal or classroom use is granted without fee provided that copies are not made or distributed for profit or commercial advantage, the copyright notice, the title of the publication and its date appear, and notice is given that copying is by permission of ACM, Inc. To copy otherwise, to republish, to post on servers, or to redistribute to lists, requires prior specific permission and/or a fee.

1. INTRODUCTION

Modern 3D graphics systems allow a rapidly growing user community to create and animate increasingly sophisticated worlds. Despite their inherent three-dimensionality, these systems are still largely controlled by 2D WIMP user-interfaces. The lack of correlation between manipulation and effect and the high cognitive distance from users to edited models are the major drawbacks of this solution [13]. The inadequacy of user-interfaces based on 2D input devices and mindsets becomes particularly evident in the realm of interactive 3D animation. In this case, the low-bandwidth communication between user-interface and application and the restrictions in interactive 3D motion specification capabilities make it extremely difficult to define animations with straight-ahead actions. This inability to interactively specify the animation timing is a major obstacle in all cases where the spontaneity of the animated object's behavior is important [21; 35; 4].

In this paper, we present an expressive 3D animation environment that enables users to rapidly and visually prototype animated worlds with a fully 3D user-interface. A 3D device allows the specification of complex 3D motion, while virtual tools supply the interaction metaphors to control application objects. In our environment, there is no intrinsic difference between user-interface and application objects. Multi-way constraints provide the necessary tight coupling among components that makes it possible to compose animated and interactive behaviors. By recording the effects of manipulations, all the expressive power of the 3D user interface is exploited to define animations. Effective editing of recorded manipulations is made possible by compacting all continuous parameter evolutions with our data-reduction algorithm, designed to preserve both geometry and timing. Novel interactive solutions to animation problems are made possible by the tight integration of all system components. In particular, animations can be synchronized using constrained manipulation during playback.

In the following sections, we present an overview of the system, we make comparisons with related work, and we conclude with a view of future directions. The accompanying video-tape illustrates our approach with interactive sequences showing the visual construction of 3D animated worlds. All demonstrations in the video were recorded live and were not edited.

2. SYSTEM OVERVIEW

2.1 Dynamic Model

Our animation environment is built on top of *VB2* [17; 18], a graphics architecture based on objects and constraints. During interaction, the user is the source of a flow of information propagating from input device sensors to manipulated models.

VB2 applications are represented by a network of interrelated objects, and the maintenance of relationships is delegated to a constraint-based change propagation mechanism. Different primitive elements represent the various aspects of the system's state and behavior: *active variables* store the system's state, domain-independent *hierarchical constraints* [9] maintain multi-way relations between active variables, *daemons* provide support for discrete simulation tasks, and *indirect expressions* allow constraints and daemons to dynamically locate their variables. Constraints are maintained using an efficient local propagation algorithm based on *Skyblue* [27; 17; 18]. The solver is domain-independent and can maintain a hierarchy of multi-way, multi-output dataflow constraints. The fact that constraint solving consists in performing method selection on the basis of constraint priorities and graph structure, without considering the variables' values, allows an effective application of a lazy evaluation strategy [17; 18]. The main drawback of such a local propagation algorithm is the limitation to acyclic constraint graphs. However, as noted by Sannella et al. [28], cyclic constraint networks are seldom encountered in the construction of user interfaces, and limiting the constraint solver to graphs without cycles gives enough efficiency and flexibility to create highly responsive complex interactive systems. In *VB2*, the objects' internal constraint networks are designed so as to reduce the possibility of creating cyclic constraint graphs. Runtime introduction of a constraint that would create a cyclic graph causes an exception that can be handled to remove the offending constraint[1].

The state manager behavior and the constraint solving techniques are detailed in [17; 18].

2.2 Interaction

The system's desktop configuration uses keyboard commands to trigger mode changes and animation playback, a *Spaceball* for continuous specification of spatial transformations, and a mouse for picking. Both hands are thus used simultaneously to input information. LCD shutter glasses provide binocular perception of the synthetic world. Since our main research goal is to explore the potentialities of 3D interaction, we do not provide a two-dimensional graphical user interface. A 3D cursor, controlled by the *Spaceball*, is used to select and manipulate objects of the synthetic world.

Direct manipulation and virtual tools are the two techniques used to input information. Both techniques involve using mediator objects that transform the cursor's movements into modifications of manipulated objects. Virtual tools are visible first class objects that live in the same 3D space as application objects and offer the interaction metaphor to control them. Their visual appearance is determined by a modeling hierarchy, while their behavior is controlled by an internal constraint network [18].

As in the real world, users configure their workspaces by selecting tools, positioning and orienting them in space, and binding them to application objects. At the moment of binding, the tool decides whether to accept the connection by checking if the application object contains all the needed information and by verifying that the constraint graph obtained by connecting the tool to the model can be handled by the underlying solver (i.e. it is acyclic). The binding mechanism is defined in a declarative way by using indirect constraints [18].

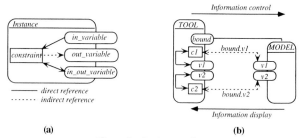

(a)   **(b)**

Figure 1a. Design notation
Figure 1b. Model and virtual tool

When bound, the tool changes its visual appearance to a shape that provides information about its behavior and offers semantic feedback. During manipulation, the tool's and the application object's constraint networks remain continuously connected, so as to ensure information propagation. Multiple tools can be active simultaneously in the same 3D environment in order to control all its aspects. The environment's consistency is continuously ensured by the underlying constraint solver. The bi-directionality of the relationships between user-interface and application objects makes it possible to use virtual tools to interact with a dynamic environment, opening the door to the integration of animation and interaction techniques.

2.3 Animation

By recording the effects of manipulations, animations can be sketched. In order to be able to edit the captured performance, a compact representation of continuous parameter evolution must be obtained. This representation must not only precisely approximate the shape of the initial parameter curves but also their timing. The data reduction algorithm must therefore treat the geometry and time components simultaneously in order to avoid the introduction of errors that would be difficult to control. We have developed an algorithm that incrementally builds, from the input sequence, a parametric B-spline preserving value and time of each input sample within a given tolerance. It is an incremental version of the Lyche and Mørken algorithm [22] that works in parallel with the interactive specification by considering only a small portion of the input curve at any time. Latency time and memory requirements for handling each portion of the curve are constant. Data reduction may therefore be performed concurrently with interactive parameter input, and the responsiveness of the application can be ensured when handling animations defined by any number of samples. The algorithm is presented in detail in [2; 4]. This performance-based approach complements key-framing by providing the ability to create animations with straight-ahead actions. It provides complete control over the animation shape and timing, while key-framing offers control only at a limited number of points.

The mediation of virtual tools makes it possible to sketch the evolution of non-geometric attributes, while constrained or free motion can be specified with 3D devices. Since these devices offer continuous control of spatial transformations, subtle synchronizations between position and orientation components can be directly specified. In our environment, straight-ahead animations are defined by expressing the desire to record parameter evolution during interaction. This is done simply by pressing a different mouse button when starting an interaction task. A controller object is connected to each animatable model and is responsible for monitoring model state changes. While recording, all changes are handled by the controller to feed the animation tracks. Continuous tracks apply the data reduction

---

[1]*VB2*'s current constraint solver [17; 28] is unable to find acyclic solutions of potentially cyclic constraint graphs. An algorithm that removes this limitation is presented in [36].

algorithm to the incoming information, while discrete tracks simply store a change value event. During playback, information propagates from the animation tracks through the controllers and down to the models. All connections are realized by bi-directional constraints. Since playback constraints are weaker than interaction constraints, the user can take control over animated models during playback. Animations involving synchronizations with the environment's evolution can thus be specified by interacting during playback [5].

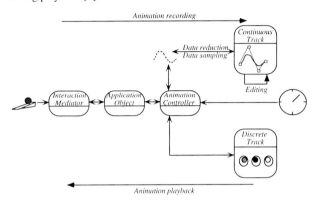

Figure 2. Interactive animation and playback

3. RELATED WORK

3.1 Constraint-based Architectures

Constraint-based architectures have long been used for 2D graphics systems (see [28] for a survey). In the 3D graphics world, one-way constraints are commonly employed to maintain dependencies between components [20; 34; 37; 38]. This type of constraint cannot easily model mutual relations between objects, thus hindering the tight coupling between user-interface and application objects [28]. Our system uses instead multi-way local propagation constraints, which offer support for two-way communication between objects while remaining efficient enough to ensure the responsiveness of the system [17; 18; 27]. *TBAG* [14] also uses multi-way constraints maintained by *Skyblue* [27], but its functional approach concentrates more on modeling time-varying behaviors than on creating interactive systems. Much effort has been spent in developing powerful numerical solvers for computer graphics (e.g. [7; 15; 16]). This work is complementary to ours, which focuses more on providing ways to interact with constrained environments. Such advanced solvers could replace local propagation in our system for the maintenance of numerical relationships.

3.2 Three-dimensional User Interfaces

Much recent research has focused on obtaining rich interaction with 3D environments by means of advanced devices and 3D interaction metaphors [8; 10; 11; 13; 16; 19; 26; 30; 32]. 3D widgets or manipulators, similar to our virtual tools, are presented in [13; 32]. These works focused on providing support for 3D widget construction, while we concentrate more on the integration of multiple tools in a single dynamic environment. We are not aware of any attempts to apply the results of 3D interaction research to enhance animation capabilities.

3.3 Performance Animation

A number of authors have proposed using live performances to drive computer animations (e.g. [1; 23; 33; 35]). We strive to bring the expressiveness of these approaches to general purpose animation systems running on graphics workstations. Instead of relying on advanced motion capture devices, we exploit our fully 3D user-interface to control the animated environment at a higher level of abstraction. The guiding approach proposed in [23] also seeks to provide better control of synthetic objects by raising the abstraction level of user interaction. That work concentrates on modeling complex behaviors in a discrete simulation framework, while we focus on providing intuitive user interfaces. A major limitation of current performance animation systems is the inability to build editable representations out of captured performances [35].

3.4 Data Reduction

Data reduction or curve fitting techniques have been successfully applied for the interactive specification of 2D or 3D curves or surfaces (e.g. [12; 24; 25; 29]). These techniques cannot be easily adapted to sketching animations of multi-dimensional parameters because they all exhibit one or more of the following problems: (i) restriction to 2D or 3D geometric constructions, (ii) lack of control on parameterization errors, and (iii) need to consider the entire input curve before reduction. An early attempt to use data-reduction for animation is described in [29]. In that system, path geometry and path timing specifications were decoupled, loosing thus the advantages of performance approaches. Banks and Cohen [6] proposed for their drafting tool an incremental version of the Lyche and Mørken algorithm [22] that does not have the aforementioned drawbacks and could be used in a performance animation context. Their method shares with ours the idea of processing successive portions of the input curve which are then spliced together, but is unable to ensure constant latency times and memory needs [4].

4. CONCLUSIONS AND FUTURE WORK

In this video-paper, we have presented an integrated environment for the rapid and visual prototyping of 3D animated worlds. Using our fully 3D user-interface, non-professional users can swiftly create complex animations with pose-to-pose and straight-ahead techniques. Thanks to automatic data-reduction, animations created by interactive performances can then be effectively edited.

In our future work, we intend to develop new virtual tools and visualizations that will improve our 3D user interface for discrete and continuous track manipulation. To allow the system to adhere to timing requirements, we are developing time-critical techniques for controlling rendering complexity and constraint evaluation.

ACKNOWLEDGMENTS

The authors would like to thank Ronan Boulic for providing the walking engine used in the interactive sequences, Sally Kleinfeldt as well as Dean Allaman for helpful comments and suggestions, Angelo Mangili for technical help, and Michele Müller for doing the voice on the video.

This research was conducted by the authors while at the Swiss Federal Institute of Technology in Lausanne.

REFERENCES

[1] Baecker RM (1969) Picture-driven Animation. *Proc. Spring Joint Computer Conference* 34: 273-288.

[2] Balaguer JF (1993) *Virtual Studio: Un système d'animation en environnement virtuel*. PhD Thesis, Swiss Federal Institute of Technology in Lausanne.

[3] Balaguer JF, Gobbetti E (1995) Animating Spaceland. To appear in *IEEE Computer Special Isssue on Real-world Virtual Environments* 28(7).

[4] Balaguer JF, Gobbetti E (1995) Sketching 3D Animations. To appear in *Proc. EUROGRAPHICS*.

[5] Balaguer JF, Gobbetti E (1995) Supporting Interactive Animation using Multi-way Constraints. Submitted for publication.

[6] Banks M, Cohen E (1990) Real-time Spline Curves from Interactively Sketched Data. *Proc. SIGGRAPH Symposium on Interactive 3D Graphics*: 99-107

[7] Barzel R, Barr A (1988) A Modeling System Based on Dynamic Constraints. *Proc. SIGGRAPH*: 179-188.

[8] Bier EA (1990) Snap-Dragging in Three Dimensions. *Proc. SIGGRAPH Symposium on Interactive 3D Graphics*: 193-204.

[9] Borning A, Freeman-Benson B, Wilson M (1992) Constraint Hierarchies. *Lisp and Symbolic Computation* 5(3): 221-268.

[10] Butterworth J, Davidson A, Hench S, Olano TM (1992) 3DM: A Three Dimensional Modeler Using a Head-Mounted Display. *Proc. SIGGRAPH Symposium on Interactive 3D Graphics*: 135-138.

[11] Card SK, Robertson GG, Mackinlay JD (1991) The Information Visualizer: An Information Workspace. *Proc. SIGCHI*: 181-188.

[12] Chou JJ, Piegl LA (1992) Data Reduction Using Cubic Rational Splines. *IEEE Computer Graphics and Applications* 12(3): 60-68.

[13] Conner DB, Snibbe SS, Herndon KP, Robbins DC, Zeleznik RC, Van Dam A (1992) Three-Dimensional Widgets. *SIGGRAPH Symposium on Interactive 3D Graphics*: 183-188.

[14] Elliott C, Schechter G, Yeung R, Abi-Ezzi S (1994) TBAG: A High Level Framework for Interactive, Animated 3D Graphics Applications. *Proc. SIGGRAPH*: 421-434.

[15] Gleicher M (1993) A Graphics Toolkit Based on Differential Constraints. *Proc. UIST*: 109-120.

[16] Gleicher M, Witkin A (1992) Through-the-Lens Camera Control. *Proc. SIGGRAPH*: 331-340.

[17] Gobbetti E (1993) *Virtuality Builder II: Vers une architecture pour l'interaction avec des modes sysnthétiques*. PhD Thesis, Swiss Federal Institute of Technology in Lausanne.

[18] Gobbetti E, Balaguer JF (1993) VB2: A Framework for Interaction in Synthetic Worlds. *Proc. UIST*: 167-178.

[19] Herndon KP, van Dam A, Gleicher M (1994) Report: Workshop on the Challenges of 3D Interaction, CHI Bulletin, October.

[20] Kass M (1992) CONDOR: Constraint-based Dataflow. *Proc. SIGGRAPH*: 321-330.

[21] Lasseter J (1987) Principles of Traditional Animation Applied to 3D Computer Animation. *Proc. SIGGRAPH*: 35-44.

[22] Lyche T, Mørken K (1987) Knot Removal for Parametric B-spline Curves and Surfaces. *Computer Aided Geometric Design* 4: 217-230.

[23] McKenna M, Pieper S, Zeltzer D (1990) Control of a Virtual Actor: The Roach. *Proc. SIGGRAPH Symposium on Interactive 3D Graphics*: 165-174.

[24] Plass M, Stone M (1983) Curve Fitting with Piecewise Parametric Cubics. *Proc. SIGGRAPH*: 229-239.

[25] Pudet T (1994) Real Time Fitting of Hand Sketched Pressure Brushstrokes. *Proc. EUROGRAPHICS*: 205-220.

[26] Sachs E, Roberts A, Stoops D (1990) 3-Draw: A Tool for Designing 3D Shapes. *IEEE Computer Graphics and Applications* 11(6): 18-26.

[27] Sannella M (1994) Skyblue: A Multi-Way Local Propagation Constraint Solver for User Interface Construction. *Proc. UIST*: 137-146.

[28] Sannella M, Maloney J, Freeman-Benson B, Borning A (1992) Multi-way versus One-way Constraints in User-Interfaces. *Software Practice and Experience* 23(5): 529-566.

[29] Schneider PJ (1988) *Phoenix: An Interactive Curve Design System Based on the Automatic Fitting of Hand-Sketched Curves*. Master's Thesis, University of Washington.

[30] Shaw C, Green M (1994) Two-Handed Polygonal Surface Design. *Proc. UIST*: 212-215.

[31] Shelley KL, Greenberg DP (1982) Path Specification and Path Coherence. *Proc. SIGGRAPH*: 157-166.

[32] Strauss PS, Carey R (1992) An Object-Oriented 3D Graphics Toolkit. *Proc. SIGGRAPH*: 341-347.

[33] Tice S (1993) VActor Animation Creation System. *SIGGRAPH Tutorial 1*.

[34] Upson C, Fulhauber T, Kamins D, Laidlaw D, Schlegel D, Vroom J, Gurwitz R, van Dam A (1989) The Application Visualization System: A Computational Environment for Scientific Visualization. IEEE CG&A 9(4): 30-42.

[35] Walters G (1993) Performance Animation at PDI. *SIGGRAPH Tutorial 1*.

[36] Vander Zanden B (1995) *An Incremental Algorithm for Satisfying Hierarchies of Multi-way, Dataflow Constraints*. Technical Report, University of Tennessee, Knoxville.

[37] Zeleznik RC, Conner DB, Wlocka MM, Aliaga DG, Wang NT, Hubbard PM, Knepp B, Kaufman H, Hughes JF, van Dam A (1991) An Object-Oriented Framework for the Integration of Interactive Animation Techniques. *Proc. SIGGRAPH*: 105-112.

[38] Zeltzer D, Pieper S, Sturman DJ (1989) An Integrated Graphical Simulation Platform. *Proc. Graphics Interface*: 266-274.

Navigation and Locomotion in Virtual Worlds via Flight into Hand-Held Miniatures

Randy Pausch & Tommy Burnette[a]

University of Virginia

Dan Brockway & Michael E. Weiblen[b]

Science Applications International Corporation

ABSTRACT

This paper describes the use of a World-in-Miniature (WIM) as a navigation and locomotion device in immersive virtual environments. The WIM is a hand-held miniature graphical representation of the virtual environment, similar to a map cube. When the user moves an object in the WIM, the object simultaneously moves in the surrounding virtual environment. When the user moves an iconic representation of himself, he moves (flies) in the virtual environment. Flying the user in the full scale virtual world is confusing, because the user's focus of attention is in the miniature, not in the full scale virtual world. We present the novel technique of flying the user into the miniature, providing perceptual and cognitive constancy when updating the viewpoint.

1 INTRODUCTION

A World-in-Miniature (WIM) [1], as shown in Figure 1, is a hand-held miniature 3D map [2]. When the user manipulates objects in the map, the corresponding objects simultaneously update in the full scale virtual reality (VR). This is useful because it gives the user a manipulable *God's eye view* [3] in addition to the surrounding immersive view. We have observed that naive users readily use the multiple views of the WIM for tasks like object placement.

2 NAVIGATION TECHNIQUES USING THE WIM

The camera icon in the WIM represents the user's current position and orientation in the VR. We find that when the user grasps the camera icon and moves it, simultaneous real-time update of the viewpoint is disorienting. An alternative is to defer viewpoint update until after the user releases the camera icon, and use slow-in-slow-out [4] animation of the viewpoint in the full scale virtual world. This is similar to specifying a flight trajectory and then executing that flight through the environment

[a]Thornton Hall, University of Virginia, Charlottesville, VA 22903, 804/982-2200, pausch@virginia.edu, tommy@virginia.edu
[b]4301 N. Fairfax Drive, Suite 200, Arlington, VA 22203, 703/908-4300, DBrockway@wb.com, mweiblen@wb.com

Permission to make digital/hard copy of part or all of this work for personal or classroom use is granted without fee provided that copies are not made or distributed for profit or commercial advantage, the copyright notice, the title of the publication and its date appear, and notice is given that copying is by permission of ACM, Inc. To copy otherwise, to republish, to post on servers, or to redistribute to lists, requires prior specific permission and/or a fee.

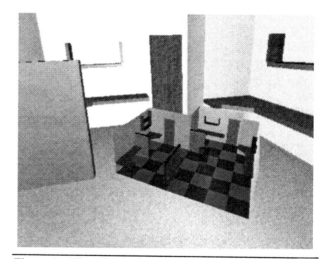

Figure 1: *The World In Miniature* (WIM) *viewed against the background of a life-sized virtual environment.*

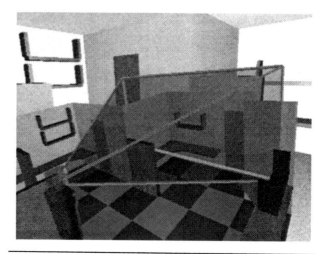

Figure 2: *A frustum which corresponds to the user's view.*

© 1995   ACM-0-89791-701-4/95/008 $3.50

This is still confusing to users, who react in one of two ways. Some users move the camera icon, and then "hunker down" during the animation; they keep their gaze fixed on the miniature world and wait until the animation around them stops, then look up to regain their bearings in the full scale virtual world. The second usage pattern is to move the camera icon and then lower the WIM quickly, attempting to reorient in the full scale virtual world before the flight begins. Some users requested addition of a delay, to allow them to re-assimilate their location in the full scale virtual world before the flight begins.

We speculate that when users focus on the camera icon, they *cognitively vest* themselves in the miniature. This theory is bolstered by the visceral positive reaction we received when changing the camera icon to an anthropomorphic doll icon. We speculate that users mentally envision themselves to be at the doll's vantage point, a much stronger association that merely using the miniature as a symbolic representation for viewpoint. Users also tend to align the WIM so that they are looking "over the shoulder" of the doll, similar to the way a automobile passenger might rotate a paper road map to align with the current direction of travel.

If the user is cognitively vested in the miniature, any animation between locations in the full scale virtual world requires the user to shift focus from the miniature back to full scale. Therefore, we now take a different approach: when the user releases the doll icon, the system animates the user *into* the miniature. The user *becomes* the doll. Geometrically, this operation involves either shrinking the user, or growing the WIM. In practice, users do not perceive a change in scale of either themselves or the WIM; they merely express a sense of *going to* the new location. As the animation completes, the user ends up in the new position and orientation in a full scale virtual world, which used to be the miniature. The graphics which formed the old full scale virtual world are then faded out, and a new WIM is presented to the user.

3 DISCUSSION

Instantaneously moving the viewpoint has many known disadvantages [5]. The use of smooth animation of viewpoint in the virtual world has two potential drawbacks:

1) the path to the new location may require planning to avoid obstacles, or in the worst case, traveling through obstacles

2) the distance to cover may be very large

When using a WIM-based doll icon, the user is very likely to have a clean line of sight to the doll icon, as he is currently manipulating it. The perceived distance to the new location is always at arm's length; changing scale during what is perceived as a fixed distance is an alternative to flying at great speed over what is perceived as a large distance.

Previous work [2,3,6] has implemented variations on allowing the user to scale the virtual world down to a miniature, select a new vantage point, and then re-scale the miniature world back up using the newly selected vantage point. Our work differs in that we deal with orientation, as well as position, and that our technique does not seem to be cognitively interpreted as scaling by our users.

There are numerous variations on how to display the doll icon in the WIM. One helpful variation is to show a view frustum which corresponds to the view possible from the doll's current location, as shown in Figure 2 We have also found it helpful to have the doll's head mirror the user's head motion in real time, especially when using the frustum.

Using a WIM as a locomotion tool becomes more powerful when using multiple WIMs in the same scene. With multiple WIMs, each WIM acts as a *portal* onto a different, perhaps distant, part of the surrounding immersive world, or to a different world altogether. By moving the doll icon from one WIM to another, the user can quickly transport his immersive viewpoint to another point in space, or to a completely different context.

As a final observation, consider the case where an external entity (e.g. the system or another user), aggressively forces a change in the user's viewpoint. The new location can first appear as a WIM in the current location, providing constancy for the forced navigation.

ACKNOWLEDGEMENTS

Our thanks to the many members of the University of Virginia User Interface Group. This and other work by the UVa User Interface Group is supported in part by ARPA, NSF, NASA, SAIC and the Commonwealth of Virginia.

4 CONCLUSIONS

Our early experiences with the world-in-miniature (WIM) paradigm led us to conclude that a WIM was useful for some common tasks in virtual environments. However, we found that manipulating the viewpoint and updating the viewpoint via smooth animation in the full scale virtual environment was confusing to many users. We claim that the perceptual and cognitive constancy provided by the technique of flying *into* a world-in-miniature is a useful alternative to smoothly animating the viewpoint in a 1-to-1 scale virtual environment.

We have presented an interaction technique that allows a user to navigate and travel via a miniature 3D map, but avoids the problem of shifting the user's cognitive focus back and forth from the map to the full scale VR. This effort is part of a larger research agenda that acknowledges that virtual reality (VR), like all new media, will eventually develop a set of standard idioms, much as film has evolved to use flashbacks, cross-cuts, dissolves, etc. We believe our technique of flying the user into the miniature may become one such idiom for VR.

REFERENCES

[1] R. Stoakley, M. Conway, R. Pausch *Virtual Reality on a WIM,* **Proceedings of the ACM SIGCHI Human Factors in Computer Systems Conference**, May, 1995, (to appear).

[2] S. Fisher, M. McGreevy, J. Humphries, W. Robinett, *Virtual Environment Display System,* **Proceedings on the 1986 Workshop on Interactive 3D Graphics**, October, 1986, pages 77-87.

[3] T. Furness, *Configuring Virtual Space for the Super Cockpit,* **Human Interface Technology (HIT) Laboratory of the Washington Technology Center,** Technical Report HITL-M-89-1, 1989.

[4] J. Lasseter, *Principles of Traditional Animation Applied to 3D Computer Animation,* **Proceedings of SIGGRAPH `87**, July 1987, pages 35-44.

[5] S. Card, G. Robertson, J Mackinlay, *The Information Visualizer, an Information Workspace,* **Proceedings of the ACM SIGCHI Human Factors in Computer Systems Conference**, May, 1991, pages 181-188.

[6] S. Bryson, C. Levit, *The Virtual Wind Tunnel,* **IEEE Computer Graphics and Applications,** pages 25-34, July 1992

A Frequency-Domain Analysis of Head-Motion Prediction

Ronald Azuma[§]

Hughes Research Laboratories

Gary Bishop[†]

University of North Carolina at Chapel Hill

Abstract

The use of prediction to eliminate or reduce the effects of system delays in Head-Mounted Display systems has been the subject of several recent papers. A variety of methods have been proposed but almost all the analysis has been empirical, making comparisons of results difficult and providing little direction to the designer of new systems. In this paper, we characterize the performance of two classes of head-motion predictors by analyzing them in the frequency domain. The first predictor is a polynomial extrapolation and the other is based on the Kalman filter. Our analysis shows that even with perfect, noise-free inputs, the error in predicted position grows rapidly with increasing prediction intervals and input signal frequencies. Given the spectra of the original head motion, this analysis estimates the spectra of the predicted motion, quantifying a predictor's performance on different systems and applications. Acceleration sensors are shown to be more useful to a predictor than velocity sensors. The methods described will enable designers to determine maximum acceptable system delay based on maximum tolerable error and the characteristics of user motions in the application.

CR Categories and Subject Descriptors: I.3.7 [**Computer Graphics**]: Three-Dimensional Graphics and Realism -- *virtual reality*
Additional Key Words and Phrases: Augmented Reality, delay compensation, spectral analysis, HMD

1 Motivation

A basic problem with systems that use Head-Mounted Displays (HMDs), for either Virtual Environment or Augmented Reality applications, is the end-to-end system delay. This delay exists because the head tracker, scene generator, and communication links require time to perform their tasks, causing a lag between the measurement of head location and the display of the corresponding images inside the HMD. Therefore, those images are displayed later than they should be, making the virtual objects appear to "lag behind" the user's head movements. This hurts the desired illusion of immersing a user inside a stable, compelling, 3-D virtual environment.

One way to compensate for the delay is to predict future head locations. If the system can somehow determine the future head position and orientation for the time when the images will be displayed, it can use that future location to generate the graphic im-

§ 3011 Malibu Canyon Road MS RL96; Malibu, CA 90265
(310) 317-5151   azuma@isl.hrl.hac.com
† CB 3175 Sitterson Hall; Chapel Hill, NC 27599-3175
(919) 962-1886   gb@cs.unc.edu

Permission to make digital/hard copy of part or all of this work for personal or classroom use is granted without fee provided that copies are not made or distributed for profit or commercial advantage, the copyright notice, the title of the publication and its date appear, and notice is given that copying is by permission of ACM, Inc. To copy otherwise, to republish, to post on servers, or to redistribute to lists, requires prior specific permission and/or a fee.

ages, instead of using the measured head location. Perfect predictions would eliminate the effects of system delay. Several predictors have been tried; examples include [2] [4] [5] [10] [11] [13] [17] [18] [19] [20].

Since prediction will not be perfect, evaluating how well predictors perform is important. Virtually all evaluation so far has been empirical, where the predictors were run in simulation or in real time to generate the error estimates. Therefore, no simple formulas exist to generate the values in the error tables or the curves in the error graphs. Without such formulas, it is difficult to tell how prediction errors are affected by changes in system parameters, such as the system delay or the input head motion. That makes it hard to compare one predictor against another or to evaluate how well a predictor will work in a different HMD system or with a different application.

2 Contribution

This paper begins to address this need by characterizing the theoretical behavior of two types of head-motion predictors. By analyzing them in the frequency domain, we derive formulas that express the characteristics of the predicted signal as a function of the system delay and the input motion. These can be used to compare predictors and explore their performance as system parameters change.

Frequency-domain analysis techniques are not new; Section 3 provides a quick introduction. The contribution here lies in the application of these techniques to this particular problem, the derivation of the formulas that characterize the behavior of the predictors, and the match between these frequency-domain results and equivalent time-domain results for collected motion data.

To our knowledge, only one previous work characterizes head-motion prediction in the frequency domain [18]. This paper builds upon that work by deriving formulas for two other types of predictors and exploring how their performance changes as system parameters are modified.

The two types of predictors were selected to cover most of the head-motion predictors that have been tried. Many predictors are based upon state variables: the current position x, velocity v, and sometimes acceleration a. Solving the differential equations under the assumption of constant velocity or acceleration during the entire prediction interval results in polynomial expressions familiar from introductory mechanics classes. Let the system delay (or prediction interval) be p. Then:

$$x_{predicted} = x + v\,p + \frac{1}{2}\,a\,p^2 \quad \text{or} \quad x_{predicted} = x + v\,p$$

The first type of predictor, covered in Section 4, uses the 2nd-order polynomial, under the assumption that position, velocity, and acceleration are perfectly measured.

In practice, real systems directly measure only a subset of position, velocity, and acceleration, so many predictors combine the polynomial expression with a Kalman filter to estimate the non-measured states. We know of no existing system that directly measures all three states for orientation, and linear rate sensors to measure translational velocity do not exist. The Kalman filter is an algorithm that estimates the non-measured states from the other measurements and smoothes the measured inputs. Section 5 derives formulas for three different combinations of Kalman filters and polynomial predictors. The combinations depend on which states are measured and which are estimated. These form the second class of predictor explored.

Section 6 uses the formulas from Sections 4 and 5 to provide three main results:

1) Quantifying error distribution and growth: The error in the predicted signal grows both with increasing frequency and prediction interval. For the 2nd-order polynomial, the rate of growth is roughly the square of the prediction interval and the frequency. This quantifies the "jitter" commonly seen in predicted outputs, which comes from the magnification of relatively high-frequency signals or noise. For the Kalman-based predictors, we compare the three combinations and identify the frequencies where one is more accurate than the others. Theoretically, the most accurate combination uses measured positions and accelerations.

2) Estimating spectrum of predicted signal: Multiplying the spectrum of an input signal by the magnitude ratio determined by the frequency-domain analysis provides a surprisingly good estimate of the spectrum of the predicted signal. By collecting motion spectra exhibited in a desired application, one can use this result to determine how a predictor will perform.

3) Estimating peak time-domain error in predicted signal: Multiplying the input signal spectrum by the error ratio function generates an estimate of the error signal spectrum. Adding the absolute value of all the magnitudes in the error spectrum generates a rough estimate of the peak time-domain error. A comparison of estimated and actual peak errors is provided. With this, a system designer can specify the maximum allowable time-domain error and then determine the system delays that will satisfy that requirement for a particular application.

This paper is a short version of chapter 6 of [1]. That chapter is included with the CD-ROM version of this paper.

3 Approach

The frequency-domain analysis draws upon linear systems theory, spectral analysis, and the Fourier and Z-transforms. This section provides a brief overview; for details please see [3] [9] [12] [14] [15] [16].

Functions and signals are often defined in the time domain. A function $f(t)$ returns its value based upon the time t. However, it is possible to represent the same function in the frequency domain with a different set of basis functions. Converting representations is performed by a transform. For example, the Fourier transform changes the representation so the basis functions are sinusoids of various frequencies. When all the sinusoids are added together, they result in the original time-domain function. The Z-transform, which is valid for evenly-spaced discrete functions, uses basis functions of the form z^k, where k is an integer and z is a complex number. Specific examples of equivalent functions in the time, Fourier, and Z domains are listed in Table 1. Note that j is the square root of —1 and ω is the angular frequency. A function in the Fourier domain is indexed by ω, which means the coefficients representing the energy in the signal are distributed by frequency instead of by time, hence the name "frequency domain."

The analysis in this paper makes three specific assumptions. First, the predictor must be linear. A basic result of linear systems theory states that any sinusoidal input into a linear system results in an output of another sinusoid of the same frequency, but with different magnitude and phase. If the input is the sum of many different sinusoids (e.g., a Fourier-domain signal), then it is possible to compute the output by taking each sinusoid, changing its magnitude and phase, then summing the resulting output sinusoids, due to the property of superposition. This makes it possible to completely characterize linear systems by describing how the

	Time domain	Fourier domain
Linearity	$A g(t) + B h(t)$	$A G(\omega) + B H(\omega)$
Time shift	$g(t + a)$	$e^{j\omega a} G(\omega)$
Differentiation	$\dfrac{\partial g(t)}{\partial t}$	$j\omega G(\omega)$
	Time domain	Z domain
Linearity	$A x(k) + B y(k)$	$A X(z) + B Y(z)$
Time shift	$x(k - a)$	$z^{-a} X(z)$

Table 1: Time, Fourier and Z domain equivalents

magnitude and phase of input sinusoids transform to the output as a function of frequency. This characterization is called a transfer function, and these are what we will derive in Sections 4 and 5.

The second assumption is that the predictor separates 6-D head motion into six 1-D signals, each using a separate predictor. This makes the analysis simpler. The assumptions of linearity and separability are generally reasonable for the translation terms, but not necessarily for the orientation terms. For example, quaternions are neither separable nor linear [2]. To use this analysis, we must locally linearize orientation around the current orientation before each prediction, assuming the changes across the prediction interval are small. By using the small angle assumption, rotations can be characterized by linear yaw, pitch, and roll operations where the order of the operations is unimportant. Another approach for linearizing orientation is described in [8].

Finally, the third assumption is that the input signal is measured at evenly-spaced discrete intervals. This is not always true in practice, but this assumption does not really change the properties of the predictor as long as the sampling is done significantly faster than the Nyquist rate, and it makes the analysis easier.

What does the ideal predictor look like as a transfer function? Ideal prediction is nothing more than shifting the original signal in time. If the original signal is $g(t)$ and the prediction interval is p, then the ideal predicted signal $h(t) = g(t+p)$. By the timeshift formula in Table 1, the magnitude is unchanged, so the magnitude ratio is one for all frequencies, but the phase difference is $p\omega$.

What do input head motion signals look like in the frequency domain? The power spectrum shows the averaged squared magnitudes of the coefficients to the basis sinusoids at every frequency. The square root of those values is the average absolute values of the magnitudes. Figure 1 shows such a spectrum for one translation axis. This data came from recording a user who had never been inside an HMD before, while the user walked through a virtual museum of objects. Note that the vast majority of energy is below 2 Hz, which is typical of most other data we have and corroborates data taken by [19]. This is one way to quantify how quickly or slowly people move their heads. These spectra are application dependent, but note that the equations derived in Sections 4 and 5 are independent of the specific input spectrum. Faster head motions have spectra with more energy at higher frequencies.

Estimating the power spectrum of a time-domain signal is an inherently imperfect operation. Careful estimates require the use of frequency windows to reduce leakage [6]. Even with such steps, the errors can be significant. What this means is that the theoretical results in Section 6 that use estimated power spectra do not always perfectly match time-domain results from simulated or actual data. Please see [7] and [16] for details.

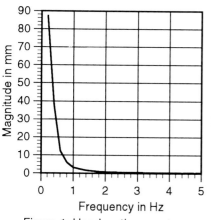

Figure 1: Head motion spectrum

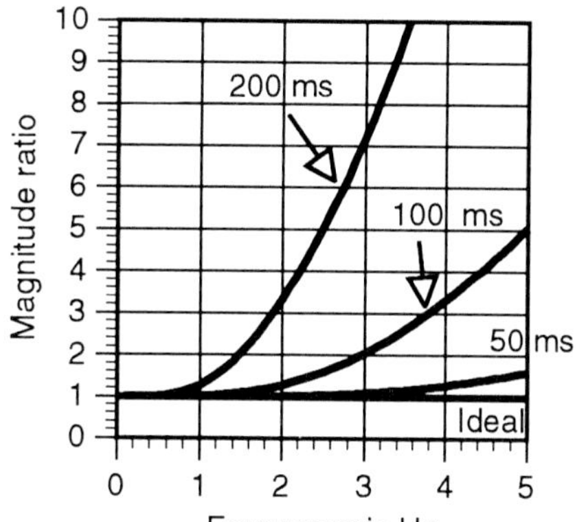

Figure 2: Polynomial predictor magnitude ratio

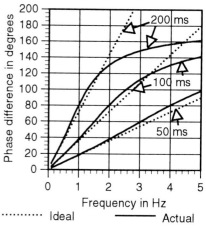

·········· Ideal ——— Actual

Figure 3: Polynomial predictor phase shift

4 Polynomial-based predictor

This section derives a transfer function that characterizes the frequency-domain behavior of a 2nd-order polynomial predictor. This analysis assumes that the current position, velocity, and acceleration are *perfectly* known, with no noise or other measurement errors. Even with perfect measurements, we will see that this predictor does not match the ideal predictor at long prediction intervals or high frequencies.

Let $g(t)$ be the original 1-D signal and $h(t)$ be the predicted signal, given prediction interval p. Then the 2nd-order polynomial predictor defines $h(t)$ as:

$$h(t) = g(t) + p\,g'(t) + \tfrac{1}{2}\,p^2 g''(t)$$

Convert this into the Fourier domain. $G(\omega)$ is the Fourier equivalent of $g(t)$. At any angular frequency ω, $G(\omega)$ is a single complex number, which we define as $G(\omega) = x + j\,y$. Then:

$$H(\omega) = \left(1 + j\,\omega\,p - \tfrac{1}{2}(\omega\,p)^2\right)(x + j\,y)$$

The transfer function specifies how the magnitude and phase change from the input signal, $G(\omega)$, to the output signal, $H(\omega)$. These changes are in the form of a magnitude ratio and a phase difference.

4.1 Magnitude ratio

We know the magnitude of the input signal. We need to derive the magnitude of the output signal. The squared magnitude of $H(\omega)$, after some simplification, is:

$$\|H(\omega)\|^2 = \left(x^2 + y^2\right)\left(1 + \tfrac{1}{4}(\omega\,p)^4\right)$$

Therefore, the magnitude ratio is:

$$\boxed{\frac{\|H(\omega)\|}{\|G(\omega)\|} = \sqrt{\left(1 + \tfrac{1}{4}(\omega\,p)^4\right)}} \qquad (1)$$

Figure 2 graphs equation (1) for three prediction intervals: 50 ms, 100 ms, and 200 ms. The ideal ratio is one at all frequencies, because the ideal predictor is simply a timeshift, but the actual predictor magnifies high frequency components, even with perfect measurements of position, velocity, and acceleration.

4.2 Phase difference

The phase α of the predicted signal $H(\omega)$ is:

$$\alpha = \tan^{-1}\left(\frac{\omega\,p\,x + y - \tfrac{1}{2}\,y\,p^2\,\omega^2}{x - y\,\omega\,p - \tfrac{1}{2}\,x\,p^2\,\omega^2}\right)$$

Let ϕ be the phase of original signal $G(\omega) = x + j\,y$. Apply the following trigonometric identity:

$$\tan(\alpha - \phi) = \frac{\tan(\alpha) - \tan(\phi)}{1 + \tan(\alpha)\tan(\phi)}$$

After simplification, the phase difference is:

$$\boxed{\alpha - \phi = \tan^{-1}\left(\frac{p\,\omega}{1 - \tfrac{1}{2}(p\,\omega)^2}\right)} \qquad (2)$$

Figure 3 graphs equation (2) for three prediction intervals: 50 ms, 100 ms, and 200 ms, with the phase differences plotted in degrees. Note that the ideal difference is a straight line, and that the ideal difference changes with different prediction intervals. The actual phase differences follow the ideal only at low frequencies, with the error getting bigger at large prediction intervals or large frequencies. The phase differences asymptotically approach 180 degrees.

Note the intimate relationship between p and ω in the formulas in Sections 4.1 and 4.2; they always occur together as $\omega\,p$. This suggests a relationship between input signal bandwidth and the prediction interval. Halving the prediction interval means that the signal can double in frequency while maintaining the same prediction performance. That is, bandwidth times the prediction interval yields a constant performance level.

5 Kalman-based predictors

Real systems directly measure only a subset of p, v, and a, and those measurements are corrupted by noise. Therefore, many predictors use the Kalman filter to provide estimates of the states p, v, and a in the presence of noise. These estimated states are then given to the polynomial-based predictor to extrapolate future locations.

This section provides a high-level introduction on how the Kalman filter works, then it derives the Kalman predictor transfer matrix. This transfer matrix is the product of three other matrices, modeling the measurements, the predictor, and the Kalman filter itself. These matrices depend upon the type of filter and predictor being used. We derive the transfer matrix for three cases:

- Case 1: Measured position. Predictor based on x and v.
- Case 2: Measured position and velocity. Predictor based on x, v, and a.
- Case 3: Measured position and acceleration. Predictor based on x, v, and a.

Case 1 is typical of most predictors that have been tried, being solely based on the measurements from the head tracker. This

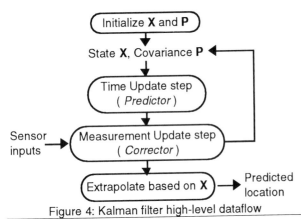

Figure 4: Kalman filter high-level dataflow

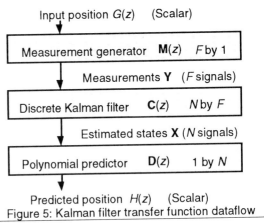

Figure 5: Kalman filter transfer function dataflow

predictor does not use acceleration because it is difficult to get a good estimate of acceleration from position in real time. Numerical differentiation accentuates noise, so performing two differentiation steps is generally impractical. A few predictors use inertial sensors to aid prediction, such as [2] [5] [11]. These sensors are used in Case 2 and Case 3. Section 6 will compare these three cases against each other, using the transfer functions derived in this section.

Throughout this section, x is position, v is velocity, a is acceleration, p is the prediction interval, T is the period separating the evenly-spaced inputs, and k is an integer representing the current discrete iteration index.

5.1 The Discrete Kalman filter

The Kalman filter is an optimal linear estimator that minimizes the expected mean-square error in the estimated state variables, provided certain conditions are met. It requires a model of how the state variables change with time in the absence of inputs, and the inaccuracies in both the measurements and the model must be characterizable by white noise processes. In practice, these conditions are seldom met, but the Kalman filter is commonly used anyway because it tends to perform well even with violated assumptions and because it has an efficient recursive formulation, suitable for computer implementation. Efficiency is important because the filter must operate in real time to be of any use to the head-motion prediction problem. This section outlines the basic operation of the filter; for details please see [3] [9]. Since the inputs are assumed to arrive at discrete, evenly-spaced intervals, the type of filter used is the Discrete Kalman filter.

Figure 4 shows the high-level operation of the Kalman filter. The Kalman filter maintains two matrices, $\mathbf{X}$ and $\mathbf{P}$. $\mathbf{X}$ is an N by 1 matrix that holds the state variables, like x, v, and a, where N is the number of state variables. $\mathbf{P}$ is an N by N covariance matrix that indicates how accurate the filter believes the state variables are. After initialization, the filter runs in a loop, updating $\mathbf{X}$ and $\mathbf{P}$ for each new set of sensor measurements. This update proceeds in two steps, similar in flavor to the predictor-corrector methods commonly used in numerical integrators. First, the time update step must estimate, or predict, the values of $\mathbf{X}$ and $\mathbf{P}$ at the time associated with the incoming sensor measurements. Then the measurement update step blends (or corrects) $\mathbf{X}$ and $\mathbf{P}$ based on the sensor measurements. Whenever a prediction is required, the polynomial extrapolation bases it on the x, v, and a from the current state $\mathbf{X}$.

5.2 Kalman-based predictor transfer matrix

The following discussion is terse due to space limitations; please read [1] for a more thorough explanation.

The goal is to derive a 1 by 1 transfer matrix $\mathbf{O}(z)$ relating input position $G(z)$ to predicted position $H(z)$. Figure 5 shows how this

is done by combining the Discrete Kalman filter with the polynomial predictor. $\mathbf{O}(z)$ is the product of three other transfer matrices:

$$H(z) = \mathbf{O}(z)G(z), \text{where } \mathbf{O}(z) = \mathbf{D}(z)\mathbf{C}(z)\mathbf{M}(z)$$

$\mathbf{O}(z)$ is different for each of the three cases. The matrices needed to compute $\mathbf{O}(z)$ for each case are listed in Sections 5.3 to 5.5. Once computed, a basic result from control theory states that one can plot $\mathbf{O}(z)$'s frequency response by substituting for z as follows [14]:

$$z = e^{(j\omega T)} = \cos(\omega T) + j\sin(\omega T)$$

Note that z is a complex number, so the matrix routines must be able to multiply and invert matrices with complex components. Now we describe how to derive the three component transfer matrices $\mathbf{M}(z)$, $\mathbf{D}(z)$, and $\mathbf{C}(z)$.

1) Measurement generator transfer matrix $\mathbf{M}(z)$: The transfer function developed in Section 4 does not apply here because the Kalman filter treats the estimated states and measurements as separate and distinct signals. Therefore, the predictor transfer function is now a 1 by N matrix that specifies how to combine the state variables to perform the polynomial-based prediction. If the predicted position is a function of more than one measurement, rather than just a measured position, the analysis becomes complicated. To simplify things, we force the measurements to be perfectly matched with each other so that everything can be characterized solely in terms of the input position. This is enforced by the measurement generator $\mathbf{M}(z)$, which generates v and a from x by applying the appropriate magnitude ratios and phase shifts to the input position. If an input position x sinusoid is defined as:

$$x = M\sin(\omega t + \phi)$$

Then the corresponding velocity and acceleration sinusoids are:

$$v = \omega M\cos(\omega t + \phi)$$

$$a = -\omega^2 M\sin(\omega t + \phi)$$

For example, a is derived from x simply by multiplying by $-\omega^2$, as listed in the $\mathbf{M}(z)$ in Section 5.5.

2) Polynomial predictor transfer matrix $\mathbf{D}(z)$: This expresses the behavior of the polynomial-based predictor, as described in Section 4. For example, if the state is based on x, v, and a, then the predictor multiplies those by 1, p, and $0.5p^2$ respectively, as listed in the $\mathbf{D}(z)$ in Section 5.4.

3) Discrete Kalman filter transfer matrix $\mathbf{C}(z)$: Deriving a transfer matrix that characterizes the frequency-domain behavior of the Discrete Kalman filter requires that the filter operate in steady-state mode. This will occur if the noise and model characteristics do not change with time. This is usually the case in the Kalman-based predictors that have been used for head-motion prediction. In our implementation, the filter converges to the steady-state condition with just one or two seconds of input data, depending on the noise and model parameters and the initial $\mathbf{P}$.

In the steady-state condition, $\mathbf{P}$ becomes a constant, so it is not necessary to keep updating it. This makes the equations for the time and measurement updates much simpler. The time update becomes:

$$\mathbf{X}^-(k+1) = \mathbf{A}\mathbf{X}(k)$$

and the measurement update becomes:

$$\mathbf{X}(k+1) = \mathbf{X}^-(k+1) + \mathbf{K}\left[\mathbf{Y}(k+1) - \mathbf{H}\mathbf{X}^-(k+1)\right]$$

where

- $\mathbf{Y}(k)$ is an F by 1 matrix holding F sensor measurements.
- $\mathbf{A}$ is an N by N matrix that specifies the model.
- $\mathbf{H}$ is an F by N matrix relating the measurements to the state variable $\mathbf{X}$.
- $\mathbf{K}$ is the N by F Kalman gain matrix that controls the blending in the measurement update.
- $\mathbf{X}^-(k+1)$ is the partially updated state variable.

Note that only the $\mathbf{X}(k)$ and $\mathbf{Y}(k)$ matrices change with time. Now combine the time and measurement update equations into one by solving for $\mathbf{X}(k+1)$:

$$\mathbf{X}(k+1) = \mathbf{A}\mathbf{X}(k) + \mathbf{K}\left[\mathbf{Y}(k+1) - \mathbf{H}\mathbf{A}\mathbf{X}(k)\right]$$

$$\mathbf{X}(k+1) = \left[\mathbf{A} - \mathbf{K}\mathbf{H}\mathbf{A}\right]\mathbf{X}(k) + \mathbf{K}\mathbf{Y}(k+1)$$

Convert this equation into the Z-domain and solve for $\mathbf{X}(z)$.

$$z\mathbf{X}(z) = \left[\mathbf{A} - \mathbf{K}\mathbf{H}\mathbf{A}\right]\mathbf{X}(z) + z\mathbf{K}\mathbf{Y}(z)$$

$$\mathbf{X}(z) = \left[z\mathbf{I} - \mathbf{A} + \mathbf{K}\mathbf{H}\mathbf{A}\right]^{-1} z\mathbf{K}\mathbf{Y}(z)$$

where $\mathbf{I}$ is the N by N identity matrix.

Define $\mathbf{C}(z)$ as the N by F transfer matrix for the Discrete Kalman filter. This specifies the relationship between the filter's inputs (measurement $\mathbf{Y}$) and the outputs (state $\mathbf{X}$):

$$\boxed{\mathbf{X}(z) = \mathbf{C}(z)\mathbf{Y}(z) \text{ where } \mathbf{C}(z) = \left[z\mathbf{I} - \mathbf{A} + \mathbf{K}\mathbf{H}\mathbf{A}\right]^{-1} z\mathbf{K}}$$

This equation shows how to compute $\mathbf{C}(z)$ from the $\mathbf{A}$, $\mathbf{K}$, and $\mathbf{H}$ matrices listed in Sections 5.3 to 5.5. The steady-state $\mathbf{K}$ matrices in those three sections depend on the noise parameters used to tune the Kalman filter. We adjusted those parameters to provide a small amount of lowpass filtering on the state variable corresponding to the last sensor input in the $\mathbf{Y}$ matrix. Then we ran each filter in simulation to determine the steady-state $\mathbf{K}$ matrices.

5.3 Case 1: Measured position

$$N = 2, F = 1$$

$$\mathbf{X} = \begin{bmatrix} x \\ v \end{bmatrix}, \ \mathbf{H} = \begin{bmatrix} 1 & 0 \end{bmatrix}, \ \mathbf{Y} = \begin{bmatrix} x_{measured} \end{bmatrix}$$

$$\mathbf{A} = \begin{bmatrix} 1 & T \\ 0 & 1 \end{bmatrix}, \ \mathbf{K} = \begin{bmatrix} 0.568 \\ 41.967 \end{bmatrix}, \ \mathbf{M}(z) = \begin{bmatrix} 1 \end{bmatrix}, \ \mathbf{D}(z) = \begin{bmatrix} 1 & p \end{bmatrix}$$

5.4 Case 2: Measured position and velocity

$$N = 3, F = 2$$

$$\mathbf{X} = \begin{bmatrix} x \\ v \\ a \end{bmatrix}, \ \mathbf{H} = \begin{bmatrix} 1 & 0 & 0 \\ 0 & 1 & 0 \end{bmatrix}, \ \mathbf{Y} = \begin{bmatrix} x_{measured} \\ v_{measured} \end{bmatrix}$$

$$\mathbf{A} = \begin{bmatrix} 1 & T & \frac{1}{2}T^2 \\ 0 & 1 & T \\ 0 & 0 & 1 \end{bmatrix}, \ \mathbf{K} = \begin{bmatrix} 0.0576 & 0.0032 \\ 0.0034 & 0.568 \\ -0.0528 & 41.967 \end{bmatrix}$$

$$\mathbf{M}(z) = \begin{bmatrix} 1 \\ j\omega \end{bmatrix}, \ \mathbf{D}(z) = \begin{bmatrix} 1 & p & \frac{1}{2}p^2 \end{bmatrix}$$

5.5 Case 3: Measured position and acceleration

$$N = 3, F = 2$$

$$\mathbf{X} = \begin{bmatrix} x \\ v \\ a \end{bmatrix}, \ \mathbf{H} = \begin{bmatrix} 1 & 0 & 0 \\ 0 & 0 & 1 \end{bmatrix}, \ \mathbf{Y} = \begin{bmatrix} x_{measured} \\ a_{measured} \end{bmatrix}$$

$$\mathbf{A} = \begin{bmatrix} 1 & T & \frac{1}{2}T^2 \\ 0 & 1 & T \\ 0 & 0 & 1 \end{bmatrix}, \ \mathbf{K} = \begin{bmatrix} 0.0807 & 0.000016 \\ 0.342 & 0.00345 \\ 0.0467 & 0.618 \end{bmatrix}$$

$$\mathbf{M}(z) = \begin{bmatrix} 1 \\ -\omega^2 \end{bmatrix}, \ \mathbf{D}(z) = \begin{bmatrix} 1 & p & \frac{1}{2}p^2 \end{bmatrix}$$

6 Results

This section takes the transfer functions derived in Sections 4 and 5 and uses them to determine three characteristics of the predictor: 1) the distribution of error in the predicted signal, 2) the spectrum of the predicted signal, and 3) the peak time-domain error. The frequency-domain results are checked against time-domain results, where appropriate.

6.1 Error distribution and growth

We can now plot the prediction error for both the polynomial predictor and the Kalman-based predictors.

1) Polynomial predictor: Figure 6 graphs the overall error behavior of the polynomial-based predictor, using the transfer functions derived in Section 4. The plot shows the errors at three different prediction intervals. The errors grow rapidly with increasing frequency or increasing prediction interval.

The overall error is a Root-Mean-Square (RMS) metric. A problem with showing the error of the predicted signal in the frequency domain is the fact that the transfer functions return *two* values, magnitude ratio and phase shift, rather than just one value. Both contribute to the error in the predicted signal. If the magnitude ratio is large, then that term dominates the error, but it is not wise to ignore phase at low magnitude ratios. An RMS error metric captures the contribution from both terms. Pick an angular frequency ω. Let M_r be the magnitude ratio at that frequency, ϕ be the difference between the transfer function's phase shift and the ideal predictor's phase shift, and T be the period of the frequency. Then define the RMS error at that frequency to be:

$$RMS_{error}(\omega, \phi, M_r) = \sqrt{\frac{1}{T}\int_0^T \left[M_r \sin(\omega t + \phi) - \sin(\omega t)\right]^2 dt}$$

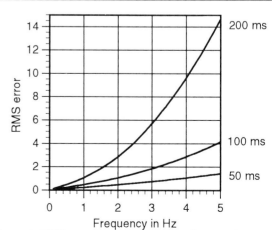

Figure 6: RMS error for polynomial predictor at three prediction intervals

#	Magnitude	Frequency (in Hz)	Phase (in radians)
1	5.0	1.0	0.5
2	3.0	2.0	-1.7
3	1.0	5.0	-0.3
4	0.01	60.0	0.2

Sinusoid = $M \sin(2\pi f t + \phi)$: Mag. M, Freq. f, Phase ϕ

Table 2: Four sinusoids

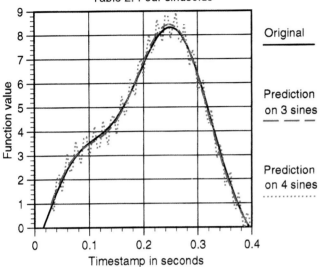

Figure 7: Polynomial prediction on 3 and 4 sinusoids, 30 ms prediction interval

The magnification of high-frequency components shown in Figure 6 appears as "jitter" to the user. Jitter makes the user's head location appear to "tremble" at a rapid rate. Because the magnification factor becomes large at high frequencies, even tiny amounts of noise at high frequencies can be a major problem.

We show this with a specific example of polynomial prediction on four sinusoids at a 30 ms prediction interval. Table 2 lists the four sinusoids. Figure 7 graphs these sinusoids and the predicted signals. The predicted signals are computed both by simulating the predictor in the time domain and by using the frequency-domain transfer functions to change the four sinusoids' magnitudes and phases: both approaches yield the same result. The "Original" curve is the sum of the sinusoids. The "Prediction on 3 sines"

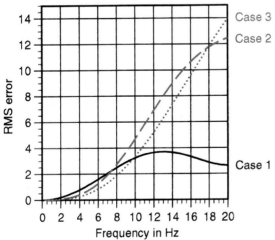

Figure 8: RMS error for Kalman predictors, 50 ms interval

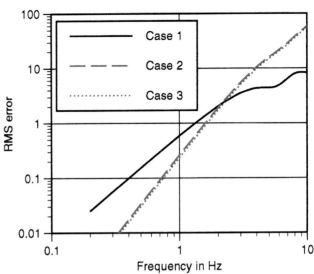

Figure 9: RMS error for Kalman predictors, 200 ms interval

shows what the predictor generates when the input signal is the sum of the first three sines in the table. That predicted signal follows the original fairly closely. However, if we also include the 4th sinusoid, then the predicted signal becomes jittery, as shown by the "Prediction on 4 sines" curve. The last sine has a tiny magnitude, but it is a 60 Hz signal. One can think of it as a 60 Hz noise source. This example should make clear the need to avoid high-frequency input signals.

2) Kalman-based predictors: We use the RMS error metric to compare the three Kalman cases and determine the frequency ranges where one is better than the others. These errors are computed using the transfer matrices described in Section 5.

Figure 8 graphs the RMS errors for the three cases at a 50 ms prediction interval. For frequencies under ~7 Hz, the inertial-based predictors Case 2 and Case 3 have lower errors than the non-inertial Case 1, and Case 3 is more accurate than Case 2 for frequencies under ~17 Hz. Figure 9 shows the errors for a 200 ms prediction interval. Both axes are plotted on a logarithmic scale. Now Case 2 and Case 3 have less error only at frequencies under ~2 Hz, instead of 7 Hz as in Figure 8.

These graphs provide a quantitative measurement of how much the inertial sensors help head-motion prediction. At high frequencies, Case 1 has less error than the other two because Case 1 does not make use of acceleration. Case 2 and Case 3 use acceleration to achieve smaller errors at low frequencies at the cost of larger errors at high frequencies. This tradeoff results in lower overall error for the inertial-based predictors because the vast majority of head-motion energy is under 2 Hz with today's HMD systems, as shown in Figure 1. The graphs also show that as the prediction interval increases, the range of frequencies where the prediction benefits from the use of inertial sensors decreases.

Case 3 is more accurate than Case 2 at low frequencies, because Case 3 has better estimates of acceleration. Case 2 directly measures velocity but must estimate acceleration through a numerical differentiation step. This results in estimated accelerations that are delayed in time or noisy. In contrast, Case 3 directly measures acceleration and estimates velocity given both measured position and acceleration, which is a much easier task. Case 3 is able to get nearly perfect estimates of velocity and acceleration. Since Case 2 represents using velocity sensors and Case 3 represents using accelerometers, this suggests that in theory, acceleration sensors are more valuable than velocity sensors for the prediction problem.

When the individual predictors are combined into a full 6-D predictor, the errors still increase dramatically with increasing

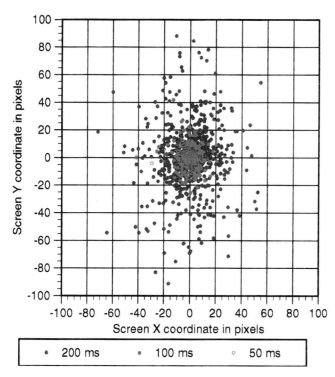

Figure 10: Scatterplots of screen-based error for simulated 6-D Kalman prediction, 30° FOV HMD, 512x512 screen

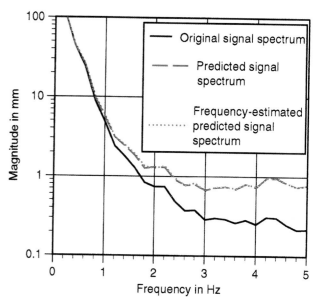

Figure 11: Kalman-predicted signal spectra

prediction intervals. This is shown by the scatterplot diagram in Figure 10. A *scatterplot* is a way of representing screen-based error as seen inside an HMD. Imagine a point one meter in front of the user's right eye. This point is rigidly attached to the user's head, so that no matter how the user turns and moves his head, that point is always one meter in front of his right eye. Ideally, the projection of this imaginary point should always lie in the center of the field-of-view. However, system delays and prediction errors will cause the projection to stray from the center, resulting in the dots seen in Figure 10. The wider the spread of dots, the larger the error. The motion sequence used to generate these scatterplots came from recording the head motion of a first-time user in our HMD system. The predictor used Case 2 for the orientation terms and Case 3 for the translation. The average errors at the 100 ms prediction interval are 2.3 times as large as the errors at the 50 ms prediction interval, but the factor jumps to 9 when comparing 200 ms against 50 ms.

6.2 Spectrum of predicted signal

The prediction transfer functions can generate an estimate of the spectrum of the predicted signal, given the spectrum of the original signal. Multiply the input spectrum by the magnitude ratio of the polynomial predictor in Section 4, or by the magnitude ratio of $\mathbf{O}(z)$ for the Kalman-based predictors in Section 5. An example would be multiplying Figure 1 by one of the curves in Figure 2. Since different applications generate different input motion spectra, and a particular spectrum can represent an entire class of inputs, this technique can specify how a particular predictor will perform with a different application.

Figure 11 shows a specific example for the Case 1 Kalman predictor, with a 100 ms prediction interval. The spectrum of the original signal was derived from actual motion data of a first-time user in our HMD system. The spectrum of the predicted signal was estimated in two ways. First, we ran the Case 1 predictor in simulation, reading the time-domain signal, generating the pre-

dicted time-domain signal, then performing spectral analysis on the predicted signal. This is the "Predicted signal spectrum" graph in Figure 11. Second, we used the frequency-domain technique described in the previous paragraph. This is the "Frequency-estimated predicted signal spectrum" graph. The two estimates are virtually identical.

The spectrum of the predicted signal demonstrates what jitter looks like in the frequency domain. At low frequencies, the predicted and original spectra coincide, but as the frequency increases, the predicted spectrum becomes larger than the original. These "humps" in the predicted spectrum represent jitter.

6.3 Maximum time-domain error

Deriving a theoretical expression for the maximum error in the time domain would be useful. Determining this requires estimating the spectrum of the error signal, which is briefly sketched here for the Kalman predictors; see [1] for details. Let $e(t)$ be the error signal, which is the difference between the predicted position $h(t)$ and the original position $g(t)$:

$$e(t) = h(t) - g(t+p)$$

where p is the prediction interval. The goal is to derive the 1 by 1 error transfer matrix $\mathbf{U}(z)$, where $E(z) = \mathbf{U}(z)\,G(z)$. Define:

$$g_p(t) = g(t+p)$$

It turns out that for sinusoidal inputs:

$$G_p(z) = e^{j\omega p}\,G(z)$$

Now convert things into the Z-domain:

$$E(z) = H(z) - G_p(z)$$

Substitute for $H(z)$ using the expression from Section 5.2:

$$E(z) = \mathbf{O}(z)G(z) - e^{j\omega p}G(z)$$

$$\boxed{\mathbf{U}(z) = \mathbf{O}(z) - \left[e^{j\omega p}\right], \text{ where } E(z) = \mathbf{U}(z)G(z)}$$

Multiplying the spectrum of the original signal by the magnitude ratio of the error transfer matrix $\mathbf{U}(z)$ yields an estimate of the spectrum of the error signal. We can compute an upper bound for the largest time-domain value of this signal. The spectrum estimates the average magnitude of the coefficient for each component sinusoid. The absolute value of the magnitude is the maximum value that each component sinusoid will ever reach. Therefore, summing the absolute values of all the magnitudes provides a maximum upper bound. That also turns out to be an

Name	Estimated maximum	Actual highest	Actual average
Tx	137.2 mm	100.1 mm	3.6 mm
Ty	153.7 mm	155.6 mm	3.4 mm
Tz	69.2 mm	54.2 mm	1.8 mm
Yaw	6.9 deg	2.6 deg	0.3 deg
Pitch	8.9 deg	5.2 deg	0.4 deg
Roll	13.1 deg	11.7 deg	0.4 deg

Table 3: Estimated vs. actual time-domain errors in a recorded head-motion sequence, 100 ms prediction interval

achievable upper bound because we cannot put enough restrictions on the phase to prevent that from being a possibility.

By using this procedure, a system designer could specify the maximum tolerable time-domain error, then determine the maximum acceptable system delay that keeps errors below the specification. Unfortunately, the estimate is not a guaranteed upper bound because of uncertainties in the power spectrum (as mentioned at the end of Section 3) and because the measured spectrum is an *average* of the entire signal, which may not represent what happens at a *particular* subsection of the signal. Therefore, how closely do the estimated maximum bounds match the actual peak errors, in practice?

Table 3 lists the estimated maximums against the actual for all six degrees of freedom in one recorded HMD motion sequence. The maximums are usually within a factor of two of each other, although for the *Ty* sequence the estimated peak is lower than the actual peak. Overall, the estimated maxima are reasonable ballpark approximations that may be useful to a system designer.

7 Conclusions and limitations

This paper provides methods for comparing a class of head-motion predictors against each other, through analysis rather than a purely empirical basis. The results presented here quantify the need for short prediction intervals, demonstrate that accelerometers may be the most valuable inertial sensors to use, and provide a system designer with analysis tools.

The approach presented here is limited to *linear* predictors. While many existing head-motion predictors are linear or linearized versions of nonlinear formulations, in the future more sophisticated predictors will be nonlinear. They will be adaptive and will account for correlations in the motion signals. Analyzing nonlinear predictors is more difficult and is an area for future work.

Future HMDs will be lighter, allowing faster head motion. That will not invalidate this analysis, which is independent of the input motion spectra. However, motion spectra of rapidly changing head motion will have more energy at higher frequencies, making the prediction problem much harder. Future systems must have better predictors or shorter system delays.

Section 6.3 estimates the peak time-domain error, but a more useful measurement may be the *average* time-domain error. Note that the peaks in Table 3 are much larger than the average errors. An expression to estimate the average error could be useful.

Acknowledgements

We thank Vern Chi, Fred Brooks and Henry Fuchs for encouraging us to explore this topic. Funding was provided by ARPA contract DABT63-93-C-C048, the NSF/ARPA Science and Technology Center for Computer Graphics and Visualization (NSF prime contract 8920219), and Hughes Electro-Optical Systems. We thank the anonymous reviewers for their constructive comments and criticisms. Approved by ARPA for public release -- distribution unlimited.

References

[1] Azuma, Ronald. Predictive Tracking for Augmented Reality. Ph.D. dissertation. UNC Chapel Hill Department of Computer Science technical report TR95-007 (February 1995).

[2] Azuma, Ronald, and Gary Bishop. Improving Static and Dynamic Registration in an Optical See-Through HMD. *Proceedings of SIGGRAPH '94* (Orlando, FL, 24-29 August 1994), 197-204.

[3] Brown, Robert Grover, and Patrick Y.C. Hwang. Introduction to Random Signal and Applied Kalman Filtering, 2nd edition. John Wiley & Sons. (1992).

[4] Deering, Michael. High Resolution Virtual Reality. *Proceedings of SIGGRAPH '92* (Chicago, IL, 26-31 July 1992), 195-202.

[5] Emura, Satoru and Susumu Tachi. Compensation of Time Lag Between Actual and Virtual Spaces by Multi-Sensor Integration. *Proceedings of the 1994 IEEE International Conference on Multisensor Fusion and Integration for Intelligent Systems* (Las Vegas, NV, 2-5 October 1994), 463-469.

[6] Harris, Frederic J. On the Use of Windows for Harmonic Analysis with the Discrete Fourier Transform. *Proceedings of the IEEE 66*, 1 (January 1978), 51-83.

[7] Jenkins, Gwilym M. and Donald G. Watts. Spectral Analysis and its Applications. Holden-Day. (1968).

[8] Lawton, W., T. Poston and L. Serra. Calibration and Coordination in a Medical Virtual Workbench. *Proceedings of Virtual Reality Applications* (Leeds, UK, 7-9 June 1994).

[9] Lewis, Frank L. Optimal Estimation. John Wiley & Sons, 1986.

[10] Liang, Jiandong, Chris Shaw, and Mark Green. On Temporal-Spatial Realism in the Virtual Reality Environment. *Proceedings of the 4th Annual ACM Symposium on User Interface Software & Technology* (Hilton Head, SC, 11-13 November 1991), 19-25.

[11] List, Uwe H. Nonlinear Prediction of Head Movements for Helmet-Mounted Displays. Technical report AFHRL-TP-83-45 [AD-A136590], Williams AFB, AZ: Operations Training Division (1984).

[12] Oppenheim, Alan V. and Alan S. Willsky. Signals and Systems. Prentice-Hall Inc. (1983).

[13] Paley, W. Bradford. Head-Tracking Stereo Display: Experiments and Applications. *SPIE Vol. 1669 Stereoscopic Displays and Applications III* (San Jose, CA, 12-13 February 1992), 84-89.

[14] Phillips, Charles L., and H. Troy Nagle. Digital Control System Analysis and Design, 2nd edition. Prentice-Hall, Inc. (1990).

[15] Press, William H., Brian P. Flannery, Saul A. Teukolsky, and William T. Vetterling. Numerical Recipes in C. Cambridge University Press (1988).

[16] Priestley, M.B. Spectral Analysis and Time Series, Vol. 1. Academic Press (1981).

[17] Rebo, Robert. A Helmet-Mounted Virtual Environment Display System. MS Thesis, Air Force Institute of Technology (December 1988).

[18] Riner, Bruce and Blair Browder. Design Guidelines for a Carrier-Based Training System. *Proceedings of IMAGE VI* (Scottsdale, AZ, 14-17 July 1992), 65-73.

[19] So, Richard H. Y. and Michael J. Griffin. Compensating Lags in Head-Coupled Displays Using Head Position Prediction and Image Deflection. *Journal of Aircraft 29*, 6 (November-December 1992), 1064-1068.

[20] Zikan, Karel, W. Dan Curtis, Henry A. Sowizral, and Adam L. Janin. A Note on Dynamics of Human Head Motions and on Predictive Filtering of Head-Set Orientations. *SPIE Proceedings volume 2351: Telemanipulator and Telepresence Technologies* (Boston, MA, 31 October - 4 November 1994).

A Frequency Based Ray Tracer

Mark R. Bolin   **Gary W. Meyer**

Department of Computer and Information Science

University of Oregon

Eugene, OR 97403

Abstract

A ray tracer has been developed that synthesizes images directly into the frequency domain. This makes it possible to use a simple vision model to control where rays are cast into a scene and to decide how rays should be spawned once an object is intersected. In this manner the most visible artifacts can be removed first and noise can be channeled into those areas of an image where it is least noticeable. The resulting image is produced in a format that is consistent with many image compression and transmission schemes.

CR Categories and Subject Descriptors: I.3.3 [Computer Graphics]: *Picture/Image Generation*; I.3.7 [Computer Graphics]: *Three-Dimensional Graphics and Realism*; I.4.2 [Image Processing]: *Compression (coding)*.

Additional Key Words and Phrases: visual perception, color, JPEG, DCT, Monte Carlo, ray tracing, adaptive sampling, reconstruction

1 Introduction

The fields of image science and image processing have long sought to exploit certain characteristics of the human visual system in the image representation schemes that they employ. The researchers in these fields have realized that there are limits to the sensitivity of the visual system in the intensity, spatial, and temporal domains. This has allowed them, among other things, to minimize the effects of noise in a picture and to decrease the amount of memory necessary to store an image. With only a few exceptions, the field of computer graphics has yet to exploit the limitations of the visual system in the realistic imaging algorithms that have been developed. In the meantime, the image compression and transmission techniques created by image scientists and image processors are routinely being applied after the fact to computer graphic pictures. This results in wasted effort as superfluous pictorial information is first synthesized, and then eliminated once the picture has been completed.

In this paper we present an image synthesis algorithm that takes advantage of three characteristics of the human visual system that are commonly exploited in image representation schemes:

---

[1] e-mail: mbolin | gary@cs.uoregon.edu

contrast sensitivity, spatial frequency response, and masking. It is well established that the contrast sensitivity response of the eye is nonlinear. This is shown in Figure 1 where it can be seen that an equal increment of light is not equally different from two backgrounds at two different intensities. This fact is used in image representation schemes to minimize the visibility of noise. The spatial frequency response of the human visual system is known to be less for patterns of pure color than for patterns that include luminance differences. This can be seen in Figure 2 where it is easier to resolve the leftmost achromatic wedge than either of the two color wedges. Image representation schemes make use of this fact to decrease the bandwidth used to transmit pictures. Finally, it is known that high spatial frequency detail in the field of view can mask the presence of other high frequency information. This is illustrated in Figure 3 where the quantization noise is more visible in the image of the low frequency mountain than in the

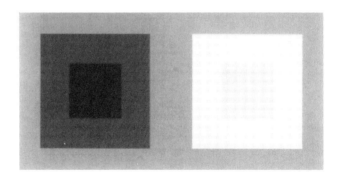

Figure 1: Light patches of equal luminance difference from the background but not equal brightness difference.

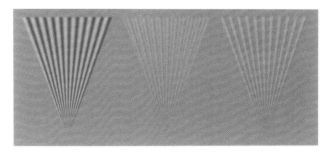

Figure 2: From left to right, spatial acuity wedges depicting variation in achromatic and two chromatic channels.

Permission to make digital/hard copy of part or all of this work for personal or classroom use is granted without fee provided that copies are not made or distributed for profit or commercial advantage, the copyright notice, the title of the publication and its date appear, and notice is given that copying is by permission of ACM, Inc. To copy otherwise, to republish, to post on servers, or to redistribute to lists, requires prior specific permission and/or a fee.

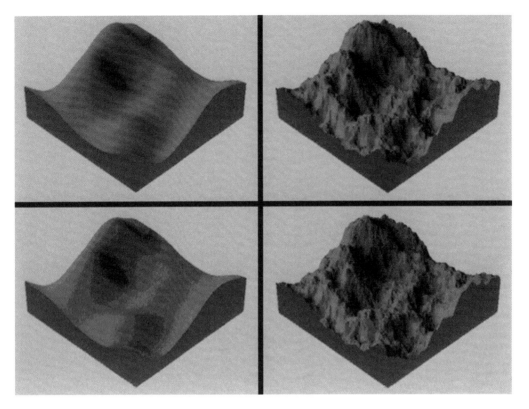

Figure 3: Visibility of noise when images with different spatial frequency content (top row) are quantized to 4 bits (bottom row).

picture of the mountain with high frequency detail. This fact is used in image compression algorithms to decrease the amount of memory necessary to store an image.

The ray tracing algorithm that will be presented in this paper is able to exploit the above characteristics of the visual system by synthesizing an image directly into the frequency domain. This makes it possible to decide how the synthesis should proceed by applying a simple vision model that has been developed by the image processing community. It also permits us to see the frequency representation for the image as it evolves and to use this information to control the sampling that is done to create the picture. This allows the algorithm to resolve the most apparent visual artifacts before those that are less visible. The iterative frequency representation that is employed is also able to interpolate between low density samples in order to provide the user with a useful early representation of the image as the ray tracing progresses.

To permit physically correct illumination calculations a Monte Carlo ray tracer is employed. This makes it possible to simulate global illumination effects, such as diffuse to diffuse interreflections, and local illumination effects that require the use of bidirectional reflection distribution functions (BRDF's). We will show how the interpolation properties of our approach allow us to take relatively few samples with high ray spawning to model low frequency features. Conversely, the quantization property of our method permits us to spawn few rays when many samples are necessary to capture high frequency detail. Finally, the frequency domain representation into which the image is synthesized has many similarities to the JPEG image compression scheme that is now widely used to store pictures. This has the practical advantage of decreasing the number of steps necessary to JPEG compress the final image.

Including this introduction, the paper is divided into seven major sections. In the second section we review related previous work in computer graphics. In the third and fourth sections we provide background information regarding vision models developed in the image processing field and discrete cosine based image compression schemes. The algorithm for synthesizing images directly into the frequency domain is presented in the fifth section followed by the sixth section which shows how the algorithm performs on several test cases. The paper concludes with a summary and conclusions.

2 Previous Work

Some attempts have already been made to incorporate what is known about the human visual system into the image synthesis process. The most successful examples of this work are the tone reproduction operators that have been developed by Tumblin and Rushmeier [32] and by Ward [33]. In both of these cases, a mapping function is provided between the radiances that are computed by the image synthesis algorithm and the light energy that is emitted from the cathode ray tube. These tone operators take into account the adaptive state of both the observer in the synthetic scene and the observer of the cathode ray tube. A spatially nonuniform mapping function has also been recently developed [6]. The limited color spatial frequency response of the human visual system was exploited in an image synthesis algorithm developed by Meyer and Liu [21]. In their work an adaptive spatial subdivision method [24] was used to cast more rays at luminance differences than at color differences.

While synthesis directly into the frequency domain has not been attempted, there has been work done on the use of nonlinear filters for image sampling. The most closely related research to that presented in this paper is that of Mitchell [22]. He used multistage filters to interpolate samples that were taken nonuniformly and at low density. To decide where these samples should be acquired, he used a contrast metric in RGB space and applied a differential weighting for each of the R, G, and B channels. While this work has the elements of a perceptual metric it is at best a crude model for the visual system. It also does not take into account the effect of masking and only provides for two levels of adaptivity in sampling. Other work with nonlinear filters includes the alpha trimmed filters of Lee and Redner [19] and the energy preserving nonlinear filters of Rushmeier and Ward [30].

Although synthesis of static images directly into a compressed format has not been attempted, information produced during the generation of animated sequences has been used to assist in the compression of these frames. Guenter *et al.* [12] has employed transformation information in the animation script to perform motion prediction computations. They also made use of identification information that was stored at each pixel to assist in this calculation. Wallach, Kunapalli, and Cohen [36] use workstation hardware to compute the optical flow for a scene. This information is then used in the MPEG compression of the generated sequence.

3 Image processing vision models

A simple three stage model of human vision has been developed by the digital image processing community. The model has been employed by image processors to solve a number of different image compression and transmission problems. It is similar, in many respects, to the NTSC encoding scheme that has been used for many years to broadcast commercial television programs. Because of the success which it has already enjoyed, we feel that this model is a good starting point from which to develop a perceptually based image synthesis technique. The model consists of a receptor first stage with logarithmic response to light, followed by a matrix to an opponent color space representation, and, finally, spatial frequency filtering which is applied to each of the color channels. There are a couple of different variations of the model that have been developed [28]. Our version, which is presented below, is most closely related to the model proposed by Faugeras [10]. It employs color spaces and spatial filters that were also used in [21].

The cones in the retina of the eye form the first stage of the model. The spectral sensitivities of the cones can be found from a linear transformation of the CIE XYZ color matching functions. Using the dichromatic confusion points suggested by Estevez [9] this transformation from CIE XYZ to SML space becomes [20]:

$$\begin{bmatrix} S \\ M \\ L \end{bmatrix} = \begin{bmatrix} 0.0000 & 0.0000 & 0.5609 \\ -0.4227 & 1.1723 & 0.0911 \\ 0.1150 & 0.9364 & -0.0203 \end{bmatrix} \begin{bmatrix} X \\ Y \\ Z \end{bmatrix} \quad (1)$$

Figure 4 shows the short (S), medium (M), and long (L) wavelength spectral sensitivity functions that result.

In the image processing vision models that have been developed, the contrast sensitivity of the eye is typically modeled as being a logarithmic response to light. This nonlinearity can be approximated by the use of a power law function [25]. We have chosen to do this for each of the fundamental sensitivity functions by using a power law with exponent of 2.2. In making this decision we assume that we are working within the dynamic range of a television monitor. (This does not preclude the use of more complicated tone reproduction operators [32,33] which could be applied to an initial low quality version of the image or to the key frames of an animated sequence in order to establish the mapping between the dynamic range of the environment and the dynamic range of the reproduction device.) We also acknowledge that this introduces a nonlinearity into the color matrixing and filtering that is done beyond this point. We accept this distortion because we are attempting to apply an existing model that has been used with some success. We also note that this same distortion is found in

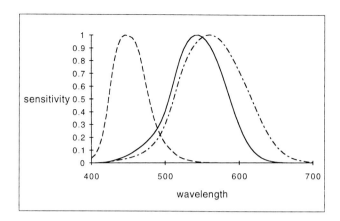

Figure 4: Spectral sensitivities for S (dashed), M (solid), and L (dot-dashed) components of SML space.

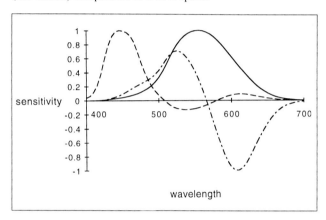

Figure 5: Spectral sensitivities for A (solid), C_1 (dot-dashed), and C_2 (dashed) components of AC_1C_2 space.

practical image transmission systems such as the NTSC encoding standard (see below).

In the second stage of the vision model, the cone signals are matrixed into an opponent representation. There is now abundant evidence from neurophysiological [8], psychophysical [15,17], and theoretical [4] studies that the SML signals produced by the cones undergo this type of transformation. Several different opponent representations have been proposed [13,16]. We have chosen to use a transformation developed by Buchsbaum and Gottschalk that is based upon the application of the discrete Karhunen-Loeve expansion to the SML fundamentals. This produces a representation that is optimal from the perspective of statistical communication theory and that is consistent with other opponent spaces that have been derived psychophysically. When this transformation is applied to the fundamentals defined above, the following opponent color space is defined:

$$\begin{bmatrix} A \\ C_1 \\ C_2 \end{bmatrix} = \begin{bmatrix} 0.0001 & 0.2499 & 0.7647 \\ 0.0018 & 2.9468 & -2.5336 \\ 1.0111 & -0.3877 & 0.2670 \end{bmatrix} \begin{bmatrix} S' \\ M' \\ L' \end{bmatrix} \quad (2)$$

where S', M', and L' represent the S, M, and L signals respectively after application of the power law transformation. Figure 5 shows the achromatic (A) and chromatic (C_1 and C_2) color channels that result (without the power law applied). This opponent representation has been used to select the wavelengths at which to perform synthetic image generation [20].

The third and final stage of the model applies a spatial filter to the achromatic and chromatic channels. As was mentioned

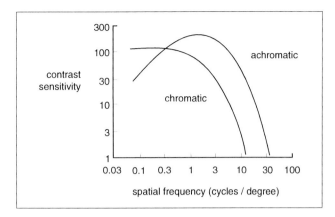

Figure 6: Achromatic versus chromatic (either red-green or yellow-blue) spatial frequency response (after Mullen, 1985).

above, the visual system is more sensitive to black and white spatial detail than it is to color spatial detail. This is partly the result of strong axial chromatic aberration in the eye [2] that causes shorter wavelengths of light to focus in front of the retina. The relative densities of the SML receptors also contributes to the difference in chromatic spatial frequency response. The ratio of L to M receptors has been shown to be approximately two to one [7] and Williams, MacLeod, and Hayhoe [37] have found that the spacing of the S receptors is very sparse (approximately one in every 10 minutes of arc). The combination of chromatic aberration and receptor spacing produces differences in the spatial frequency bandpass of the achromatic and chromatic channels. Mullen [23] has shown that cutoff for the luminance channel is 34 cycles/degree and for the red/green and yellow/blue channels it is 11 cycles/degree (Figure 6). Recent work by Poirson and Wandell [26] incorporates the effects of chromatic aberration and indicates that the cutoff for the yellow/blue channel may be as low as 4 cycles/degree. There is good correspondence between the dimensions of the AC_1C_2 system and the color space directions employed by Mullen and by Poirson and Wandell.

While this model has been developed by the image processing community from a first principles analysis of the human visual system, it has many similarities to the image representation scheme that is used in NTSC television encoding. The first stage of the NTSC system consists of the red, green, and blue taking sensitivities of the color television camera. These functions are different than the SML sensitivities used above, but they are colorimetrically related to them. Gamma correction for the display monitor is also done as part of the first stage of the NTSC system. Because there is a power law relationship between the voltage applied to the display primaries and the light emitted from the display screen, this gamma correction step is identical to the contrast sensitivity adjustment in the vision model. The second stage of the NTSC system consists of a matrixing of the camera signals into YIQ color space. This color representation scheme has been shown [5] to be very similar to the opponent representation that is used above. In the third and final stage of the NTSC system, the signals are band limited to 4.2 MHz (Y), 1.6 MHz (I), and .6 MHz (Q). It is interesting to note that the ratio between these bandwidths is similar to the ratio between the spatial frequency cutoffs used in the vision model.

4 DCT based compression algorithms

The Discrete Cosine Transform (DCT) is an integral part of several image compression schemes. The DCT works by decomposing the original image into a series of harmonic cosine waves

in a manner similar to the Discrete Fourier Transform (DFT). The original image can then be exactly reproduced by the sum of these cosine waves. The DCT provides a formula to determine the coefficients of these harmonically related cosine waves which sum to reproduce the original image [29].

$$F(u,v) = \frac{1}{4}\kappa(u)\kappa(v)\sum_{x=0}^{M-1}\sum_{y=0}^{M-1}f(x,y)C_{x,u}C_{y,v} \quad (3)$$

$$f(x,y) = \frac{1}{4}\sum_{u=0}^{M-1}\sum_{v=0}^{M-1}\kappa(u)\kappa(v)F(u,v)C_{x,u}C_{y,v} \quad (4)$$

where

$$C_{A,B} = \cos\left[\frac{(2A+1)B\pi}{16}\right]$$

and

$$\kappa(u),\kappa(v) = 1/\sqrt{2} \quad \text{for } u,v = 0$$
$$\kappa(u),\kappa(v) = 1 \quad \text{otherwise}$$

This transform also has the nice property that an M by M image may be exactly reproduced by M by M harmonically related cosine waves multiplied by the coefficients given by the transform. The image may therefore be completely represented by an M by M array of coefficients, the majority of which will tend to zero in the higher frequencies.

JPEG is a compression scheme that is based upon the DCT. JPEG first breaks the image into 8 by 8 pixel blocks. The values of the 8 by 8 block are then transformed into the frequency domain by means of the DCT. The new values take the form of an 8 by 8 block of frequency coefficients where each value is the amplitude of a harmonic cosine wave. These values are organized with the zero frequency (DC) value in the upper left corner of the block and increase in frequency to the highest frequency (AC) values in the lower right corner. These coefficients are then quantized by means of a scalar quantization table specified by the application. This step allows the algorithm to take advantage of masking and achieve further compression by discarding information that is not visually significant. This is accomplished by assigning less bits to the representation of the higher frequency elements.

In the JPEG scheme, additional encoding is done to the frequency coefficients. The DC values are handled separately from the AC values. The DC values are encoded as the difference from the DC term in the previous 8 by 8 block. This is known as Differential Pulse Code Modulation (DPCM). This is done because of the strong correlation between the average color of adjacent 8 by 8 blocks. The AC values are then read in zigzag order going from the upper left hand corner to the lower right. This helps to facilitate the following entropy encoding step, by placing the low frequency coefficients, which are more likely to be non-zero before the high frequency coefficients, which are more likely to be zero. This output is then encoded using either Huffman or Arithmetic encoding [35].

5 Synthesis into the Frequency Domain

We have chosen the initial frequency representation scheme that is used in JPEG as the format into which we synthesize our images. At this stage of the JPEG compression process, the image has been divided into 8 by 8 pixel blocks, the DCT has been applied to each of the blocks, and quantization has been performed on each of the terms in the resulting 8 by 8 array of frequency coefficients. We do not take account of the DPCM or Huffman encoding that is applied, in the JPEG approach, to this initial

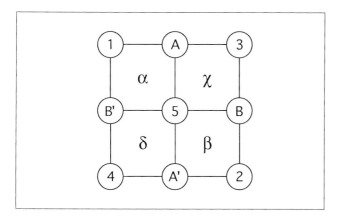

Figure 7: Ordering metric used to drive the selection of samples within the quad-tree subdivision method.

representation. However, as we construct the frequency representation, we do take advantage of the zigzag order in which the frequency coefficients are read out of the 8 by 8 array to be encoded. We represent the color for each block using the AC_1C_2 color space described in the previous section.

Our algorithm seeks to find the frequency representation for the A, C_1, and C_2 components of each 8 by 8 pixel block in the image. The order in which the blocks are processed is determined by a list that is sorted according to the level of refinement required by each block. The first block on the list is the next block that is worked on, and a special sampling scheme is used to determine where to cast new rays in this block. Once the samples have been taken, a least squares fit is used to find the cosine terms which interpolate the data. As more samples are generated in each block, additional frequency terms are added to the solution. To take advantage of masking, the precision with which the illumination model is evaluated decreases as higher frequency terms are included. The vision model described in the previous section is used to decide where to put the updated block back on the list of sorted blocks. When the desired level of refinement is achieved and the block is displayed, low pass filtering is used to minimize any aliasing that might remain.

The remainder of this section provides additional details regarding each of the steps in this algorithm.

5.1 Deciding Where to Take the Next Sample

After selecting the next block to be processed from the list of sorted blocks, a decision must be made about where to take the next sample within this block. The same sampling sequence is chosen for all blocks in order to minimize the expense of computing the cosine terms (see Section 5.2). The samples taken within each block are spread as wide as possible to enhance the speed and quality of the reconstructed function as the algorithm progresses. Spreading the samples out allows for the most accurate calculation of the cosine terms, provides even coverage of the sample space, and constrains the interpolation that is done between samples. The regular sampling pattern that results can give rise to bias [18] but we feel that this sampling approach is warranted due to the computational savings that it provides in our case.

The sampling positions within a block are chosen based on a quadtree subdivision method. The first four samples in the sequence are taken through the outermost four corners of the 8 by 8 block in the order given in Figure 7. The fifth sample, which marks the beginning of the repeated portion of the sequence, is taken through the center of the block. A random choice is then made between positions A and B to determine the sixth sample

position. This step is necessary to evenly distribute samples in both the horizontal and vertical directions. In the general case (which, as we will see below, is not the situation for this first block), the unselected A or B is chosen next, and the block is subdivided into sub-blocks α, β, χ, and δ which form the next four leaves on the quadtree.

The sequence then repeats with a breadth first search of the quadtree at the new level to take a sample at the center of each sub-block. This is followed by another breadth first search and a random sample at position A or B for each sub-block. After samples are taken at the unselected A or B for each sub-block, the sub-block subdivides and another new level of the quadtree is started. An exception to the repeated portion of this sequence occurs when either position A or B lies at the boundary of the 8 by 8 block at the top of the quadtree. In this case, position A' (see Figure 7) immediately follows position A and position B' immediately follows B. This means that all A' and B' positions will lie at the bottom-most and left-most edges respectively of the 8 by 8 block. In the case of the first block we see that the actual sampling sequence, for B chosen first, would be 1, 2, 3, 4, 5, B, B', A, and A'.

This method generates a list of sample positions which is shared and indexed into at varying positions by all blocks. The first block to exceed the number of samples contained within the list will calculate the position of the next sample. Otherwise the sample position is merely obtained from the current position within the list. Note should be taken that samples which border the 8 by 8 block may be used to refine the frequency representation of all blocks that they border. A sample cache is therefore employed at each block, to store bordering AC_1C_2 values returned by surrounding blocks. This is necessary since a strict ordering on samples has been imposed. To avoid casting redundant rays, these values are then used by the block when it reaches the corresponding position in its sampling sequence.

5.2 Computing the frequency representation

From the samples that have been taken in the block that is currently being refined, a least squares fit is used to determine the cosine terms that best interpolate the data. From Equation 4 we see that a block may be reconstructed from N cosine terms by the following equation

$$f(x, y) = \sum_{i=0}^{N-1} G(u_i, v_i) C_{x,u} C_{y,v} \qquad (5)$$

where the subscript i imposes a zig-zag ordering on the frequency terms u and v given by u_i and v_i and

$$G(u_i, v_i) = \frac{1}{4} \kappa(u_i) \kappa(v_i) F(u_i, v_i) \qquad (6)$$

The least squares solution for S monochromatic samples, taken at positions (x_s, y_s) within the block, is given when the following equation is at a minimum

$$\sum_{s=0}^{S} [f(x_s, y_s) - \alpha(x_s, y_s)]^2 \qquad (7)$$

where $\alpha(x_s, y_s)$ represents the sampled value for either the A, C_1 or C_2 color channel. The formula that solves this least squares problem is given by the following equation

$$[X] = [J]^{-1} [Y] \qquad (8)$$

where X and Y form $N \times 1$ column vectors, J is a $N \times N$ matrix, and

$$J_{ij} = \sum_{s=0}^{S} C_{x_s,u_i} C_{y_s,v_i} C_{x_s,u_j} C_{y_s,v_j}$$

$$Y_i = \sum_{s=0}^{S} \alpha(x_s, y_s) C_{x_s,u_i} C_{y_s,v_i}$$

$$X_i = G(u_i, v_i)$$

The actual frequency coefficients may then be obtained by inverting Equation 6.

This solution requires the inversion of a N by N matrix to be computed for each sampling position, where N is the number of frequency terms currently necessary to represent the portion of the image within the block. However, this operation is not as bad as it initially appears. Since this is an iterative solution we are able to reduce the time necessary to invert this matrix to $O(N^2)$ by using a rank one inverse matrix modification technique [27] which is tuned to suppress the accumulation of errors. In this technique the inverse matrix $(J')^{-1}$ which is used to solve the least squares problem for $(S+1)$ samples, may be obtained from the inverse matrix $(J)^{-1}$ which solves the problem for S samples, by the following equation

$$(J')^{-1} = (J + AA^T)^{-1} \qquad (9)$$

$$= J^{-1} + \frac{(A - J^{-1}\gamma)A^T J^{-1}}{(A^T J^{-1}\gamma)} \qquad (10)$$

where A forms a $N \times 1$ column vector and

$$\gamma = A(A^T A) + JA$$

$$A_i = C_{x_{S+1},u_i} C_{y_{S+1},v_i}$$

Since the matrix is dependent on only the sampling positions and not the sampled value, and, since we chose to use the same sampling sequence for all blocks, this matrix does not need to be inverted independently for all blocks. Instead a shared matrix inverse list is associated with a specific sampling position and ordering in the sampling sequence. This list is grown dynamically with the next matrix inverse being computed for the first block to reach the new sampling position. This inverse matrix may then be shared by all blocks that follow. The computation of the frequency description solution vector is then simply the result of finding the current sampling position from the sample list, sampling the image, and performing a matrix multiplication on the associated inverse matrix from the list for each of the A, C_1 and C_2 color channels.

5.3 Adding additional frequency terms

Within the block that is presently being modified, new frequency terms are added to the calculation as additional rays are cast. In a manner identical to how the frequency terms are read out of the 8 by 8 JPEG frequency block, a zig-zag pattern is used to select the next frequency term to be added. This sequence emphasizes horizontal and vertical frequencies over diagonal frequencies, and is therefore consistent with the anisotropic spatial frequency response of the human visual system. A new frequency term is added after each set of two to three samples that are taken in the block, up to the maximum of 64 frequency terms. Since the sampling theorem requires that sampling be done at twice the highest frequency present in the solution, this keeps us from admitting a frequency term into the solution until there have been enough samples taken to represent it. It also does not allow singularities to arise in the inverse matrices. Since the number of

frequency terms is limited, information will not be stored beyond the display resolution, even though the frequency coefficients will continue to be refined.

When the sampling progresses to a point at which a new frequency term should be added, it is necessary to expand the inverse matrix before placing it on the list. Use was made of the Frobenius' relation to do this expediently. As a result this can also be done in $O(N^2)$ time [3]. Frobenius' relation tells us that the inverse matrix $(J_{N+1})^{-1}$ that solves the least squares equation for $(N+1)$ terms may be computed from the inverse matrix $(J_N)^{-1}$ for N terms through the following equation

$$(J_{N+1})^{-1} = \begin{bmatrix} J_N & B \\ B^T & D \end{bmatrix}^{-1} = \begin{bmatrix} (J_N)^{-1} & 0 \\ 0 & 0 \end{bmatrix} +$$

$$\begin{bmatrix} (J_N)^{-1}B\Delta^{-1}B^T(J_N)^{-1} & -(J_N)^{-1}B\Delta^{-1} \\ -\Delta^{-1}B^T(J_N)^{-1} & \Delta^{-1} \end{bmatrix} \qquad (11)$$

where B forms a $N \times 1$ column vector and

$$\Delta = D - B^T (J_N)^{-1} B$$

$$B_i = \sum_{s=0}^{S} C_{x_s,u_i} C_{y_s,v_i} C_{x_s,u_{N+1}} C_{y_s,v_{N+1}}$$

$$D = \sum_{s=0}^{S} C_{x_s,u_{N+1}} C_{y_s,v_{N+1}}$$

The resulting inverse matrix may then be multiplied by the expanded Y vector to obtain the $(N+1)$ frequency terms given by X in Equation 8. The 64 term versions of J and Y are stored to yield B, D and Y_{N+1} in an expedient manner. This matrix is then stored on the shared inverse list for use by other blocks.

Because noise is less visible in the high frequency terms, the number of rays spawned from a surface by the Monte Carlo ray tracer decreases as more frequency terms are added to the solution. As was shown in Section 1, the masking property of the human visual system makes it difficult for high frequency noise to be seen. Therefore, as higher and higher frequency terms are added to the solution for the block that is currently being processed, the number of rays spawned from each surface by the Monte Carlo ray tracer decreases. The precision with which the local illumination model is evaluated at each ray/object intersection contributes to the accuracy of the final result for each ray cast. A bidirectional reflectance function is used to model local illumination, and this function is represented using a geodesic sphere and a novel data structure [11]. The decrease in rays spawned results in a less dense sampling of the bidirectional reflectance function and a poorer estimate of the light reaching the surface at the point where the ray intersects it. The rate at which the number of rays spawned decreases (from the number necessary to determine diffuse reflection) was modeled after the quantization table that is used in JPEG compression. Figure 8 shows a plot of the two dimensional function that was used to select a value for a particular frequency.

5.4 Choosing the next block to process

When the new frequency representation for the current block has been determined, the block must be placed back on the sorted list. Dividing the image into 8 by 8 blocks provides a certain amount of adaptive subdivision since the same level of detail (and therefore the same frequency representation) is not required to represent each region of the picture. Those blocks with the most visually

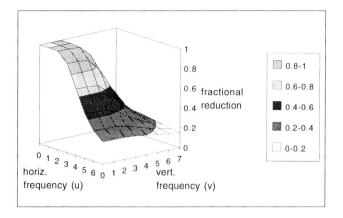

Figure 8: Rate at which the number of rays spawned decreases as higher frequency terms are added.

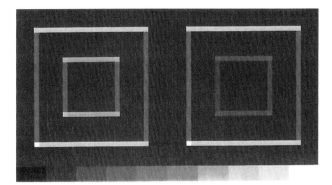

Figure 9: Sampling density for light patches in Figure 1.

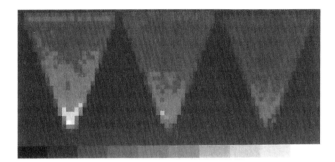

Figure 10: Sampling density for acuity wedges in Figure 2.

apparent artifacts should be scheduled for processing first. We employ the vision model described previously to decide where to put the current block back on the sorted list of blocks. First the frequency representation for each AC_1C_2 channel is filtered with rolloff set according to the cutoffs given in Section 3. This attaches more visual significance to the changes in the lower frequency terms. Next, the root mean squared change for each frequency term in the AC_1C_2 representation is computed as a result of the current sample. This value is taken as an approximate measure of the visually relevant aliasing that was removed. This is assumed to be an indicator that more refinement may or may not need to be done on this block. This is due to the assumption that blocks in which a large amount of aliasing has occurred tend to need refinement the most and blocks in which a small amount of aliasing has occurred tend to be well defined. This value is then combined with previous values and an initial uncertainty value to compute a gradient of change. The initial uncertainty value is introduced to insure that non-changing blocks still receive adequate sampling. These gradients form the sorted listed that is kept for all of the blocks in the image. The block at the head of this list is the one into which the next set of rays is to be cast.

5.5 Displaying the final result

Due to undersampling, there is aliasing as the solution for each block progresses. As more samples are taken, the aliasing decreases and the frequency representation for the block converges to the final solution. To control this aliasing, a low pass filter is applied to the frequency representation of each of the blocks. The frequency coefficients of the blocks are transformed back into a linear luminance RGB space before a simple 2-dimensional Butterworth filter is applied. The parameters of the Butterworth filter are set to roll the filter off as a ratio of the square root of the number of samples that have been taken. As the sampling rate grows larger and the final solution for the block is determined, the width of the filter grows large and its effect is greatly diminished.

6 Results

The scene depicted in Figure 1 was actually rendered using the frequency based ray tracing technique. Figure 9 shows the sampling densities that were employed. In this example, the two small squares are equally different in luminance from the backgrounds on which they are positioned. However, due to the nonlinear contrast sensitivity of the visual system, they are not perceived (in terms of brightness) to be equally different from the backgrounds.

The difference in brightness between the two darker squares is greater than the difference in brightness between the two lighter squares. It can be seen in Figure 9 that the darker pair of squares received more samples than the brighter pair. This result shows that the first stage of the vision model is correctly converting luminance differences into approximate brightness differences.

The resolution fans in Figure 2 were also rendered by the frequency based ray tracer and the sampling densities used are shown in Figure 10. The fan on the left represents a change in only the A channel, the fan in the middle a change in only the C_1 channel, and the fan on the right a change in only the C_2 channel. The amplitude of the oscillation in each fan is equal. The fact that it is more difficult to resolve the bottom of the color fans than it is for the monochromatic fan demonstrates that the visual system is able to resolve monochromatic differences more readily than chromatic differences. As can be seen in Figure 10, the monochrome resolution fan receives more samples at higher frequencies than the color resolution fans. This demonstrates that, in the vision model, the color is being properly transformed into an opponent space and that the correct spatial filtering is being performed.

The frequency based ray tracer has been used to render the fractal mountainsides in Figure 11. These mountains were created using a Fourier synthesis technique to produce two dimensional fractional Brownian motion. The $\frac{1}{f}$ frequency distribution has been cut off at a lower frequency for the mountain on the left than the mountain on the right. The lighting in the scene is very directional, with a small light placed in the foreground. This potentially creates a very noisy situation for the Monte Carlo ray tracer. In the top two images, 1000 rays were spawned to evaluate the BRDF for each ray that struck the mountain. In the bottom two images, the number of rays spawned was reduced to 100. Notice that the noise in the lower two images is visible on the low frequency mountainside but not on the high frequency mountain. This demonstrates the masking effect of the visual system and

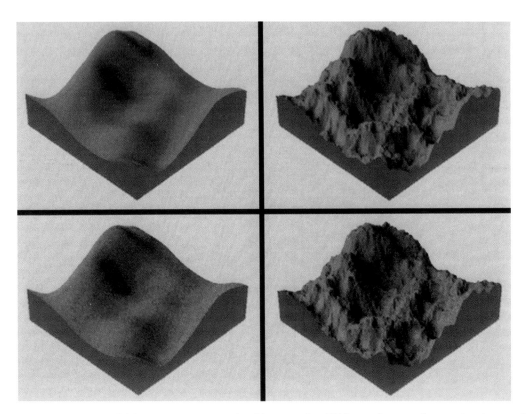

Figure 11: Images with different spatial frequency content rendered by spawning 1000 rays for every intersection (top row) and 100 rays for every intersection (bottom row).

shows that a smaller number of rays can be spawned when high frequency terms are being computed.

Figure 12 compares the result of using the frequency based ray tracer with a traditional ray tracer. The top two versions of the mountain were made by casting a ray through every pixel in the screen with a Monte Carlo ray tracer. In both cases, 1000 rays were spawned for each intersection with the mountain. Notice the noise that is evident in the low frequency mountain and the aliasing that is produced around the edges of the scene. The bottom two examples of the mountain were made by using the frequency based ray tracer. As frequency terms were added to the solution, the number of rays spawned was decreased as in Figure 8. In the bottom left image, on average, a half of a ray was cast through every pixel. In this case, the noise is reduced even though fewer rays were cast into the scene. This shows that the interpolation that is done by fitting the cosine terms reduces the number of samples required. For the low frequency mountain the effect is similar to the ray cache that was used by Ward, Rubinstein, and Clear [34]. In the bottom right image, on average, one ray was cast through every pixel. In this case, far fewer rays were spawned from all of the intersections as the algorithm attempted to resolve the higher frequencies present in the mountain. This shows that the masking effect allows us to severely quantize the quality of the shading model in high frequency regions without reducing the perceptual quality of the image.

7   Summary and Conclusions

A new frequency based approach to ray tracing has been presented in this paper. This method makes it possible to use a simple model of human vision developed by the image processing community to control where rays are cast into a scene. In this way, the contrast sensitivity, spatial frequency response, and masking properties of the visual system are taken advantage of. In deciding where to take samples, a specific luminance difference at low intensity is considered to be more important than the same difference at high intensity. Color spatial frequency variations are given fewer samples than spatial frequency variations in luminance. When used in conjunction with a Monte Carlo ray tracer, more rays are spawned when low frequency terms are being determined than when high frequency terms are being found.

The approach is also novel when considered simply as an image synthesis technique. The use of the frequency domain instead of the spatial domain to determine where additional rays should be cast is a new method of adaptively controlling a ray tracer. At low spatial frequencies, widely spaced samples, for which many rays are spawned to evaluate the BRDF, are interpolated in the image plane. This provides a result similar to a ray cache technique performed in object space [34]. The fact that high spatial frequencies cannot be added to the solution until many samples have been taken means that spurious high frequency artifacts cannot occur and eliminates the need for nonlinear filters [30].

The size of our implementation has not yet allowed us to refine each of its pieces as fully as we would have liked. Among the issues requiring further investigation are unbiased sampling patterns that permit efficient computation, the point at which to add new frequency terms to the calculation, the precise way in which ray spawning effects quantization, and how the solution is changed by the choice of priority metric. Nevertheless we feel that the architecture that we have outlined represents a first step on the path to an image synthesis technique that generates pictures directly in a compressed format. This is a topic that will continue to grow in importance as JPEG and MPEG become more widely used within the computer industry and digital high defini-

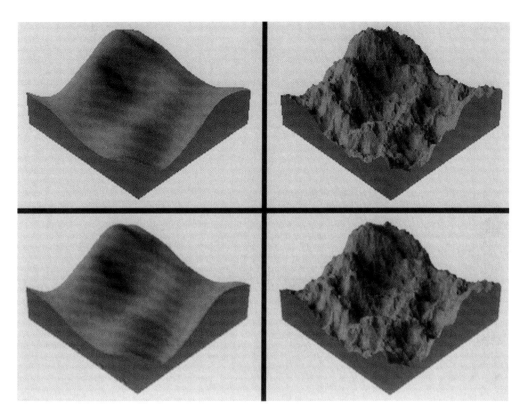

Figure 12: Images with different spatial frequency content rendered using a traditional Monte Carlo ray tracer and one ray per pixel (top row). Same images rendered using the frequency based ray tracer and one half ray per pixel (bottom left) and one ray per pixel (bottom right).

tion television eventually makes its appearance in the consumer marketplace.

8   Acknowledgments

The authors would like to thank Jon Newman for writing the Monte Carlo ray tracer that was used to perform part of this work and Jay Gondek for developing the software used to generate the fractal mountains. This research was funded by the National Science Foundation under grant number CCR 90-08445.

9   References

[1] Albert, A. E. and Gardner Jr., L. A., *Stochastic Approximation and Nonlinear Regression*, M.I.T. Press: Massachusetts, 1967.

[2] Bedford, R. E. and Wyszecki, G. "Axial Chromatic Aberration of the Human Eye," *Journal of the Optical Society of America*, Vol. 47, No. 6, pp. 564-565, 1957.

[3] Bodewig, E., *Matrix Calculus*, North Holland Publishing Company: Amsterdam, 1956.

[4] Buchsbaum, G. and Gottschalk, A. "Trichromacy, Opponent Colours Coding and Optimum Colour Information Transmission in the Retina," *Proceedings of the Royal Society of London, Series B*, Vol. 220, pp. 89-113, 1983.

[5] Buchsbaum, G. "Color Signal Coding: Color Vision and Color Television," *Color Research and Application*, Vol. 12, No. 5, pp. 266-269, 1987.

[6] Chiu, K., Herf, M., Shirley, P., Swamy, S., Wang, C., and Zimmerman, K., "Spatially Non-Uniform Scaling Functions for High Contrast Images," *Proceedings of Graphics Interface 1993*, pp. 245-253, 1993.

[7] Cicerone, C. M. and Nerger, J. L., "The Relative Numbers of Long-Wavelength-Sensitive to Middle-Wavelength-Sensitive Cones in the Human Fovea Centralis," *Vision Research*, Vol. 29, No. 1, pp. 115-128, 1989.

[8] DeValois, R. L., Smith, C. J., Karoly, A. J., and Kitai, S. T., "Electrical Responses of Primate Visual System, I. Different Layers of Macaque Lateral Geniculate Nucleus," *Journal of Comparative and Physiological Psychology*, Vol. 51, pp. 662-668, 1958.

[9] Estevez, O., "On the Fundamental Data-base of Normal and Dichromatic Color Vision," *Ph.D. Thesis, University of Amsterdam*, Krips Repro Meppel, Amsterdam 1979.

[10] Faugeras, O. D., "Digital Color Image Processing Within the Framework of a Human Visual Model," *IEEE Trans. Acoustics, Speech, and Signal Processing*, Vol. 27, No. 4, pp. 380-393, 1979.

[11] Gondek, J. S., Meyer, G. W., and Newman, J. G., "Wavelength Dependent Reflectance Functions," *Computer Graphics, Annual Conference Series*, ACM SIGGRAPH, pp. 213-220, 1994.

[12] Guenter, B. K., Yun, H. C., and Mersereau, R. M., "Motion Compensated Compression of Computer Animation Frames," *Computer Graphics, Annual Conference Series*, ACM SIGGRAPH, pp. 297-304, 1994.

[13] Guth, S. L., Massof, R. W., and Benzschawel, T., "Vector Model for Normal and Dichromatic Color Vision," *J. Opt. Soc. Am.*, Vol. 70, pp. 197-211, 1980.

[14] Hamming, R. W., *Digital Filters*, Prentice-Hall: New Jersey, 1977.

[15] Hurvich, L. M. and Jameson, D., "Some Quantitative Aspects of an Opponent-Colors Theory, II. Brightness, Saturation, and Hue in Normal and Dichromatic Vision," *Journal of the Optical Society of America*, Vol. 45, pp. 602-616, 1955.

[16] Ingling, C. R., "The Spectral Sensitivity of the Opponent-Colors Channels," *Vision Research*, Vol. 17 pp. 1083-1090, 1977.

[17] Jameson, D. and Hurvich, L. M., "Some Quantitative Aspects of an Opponent-Colors Theory, I. Chromatic Responses and Spectral Saturation," *Journal of the Optical Society of America*, Vol. 45, pp. 546-552, 1955.

[18] Kirk, D. and Arvo, J., "Unbiased Sampling Techniques for Image Synthesis," *Computer Graphics, Annual Conference Series*, ACM SIGGRAPH, pp. 153-156, 1991.

[19] Lee, M. E., and Redner, R. A., "A Note on the Use of Nonlinear Filtering in Computer Graphics," *IEEE Computer Graphics and Applications*, Vol. 10, No. 3, pp. 23-29, 1990.

[20] Meyer, Gary W., "Wavelength Selection for Synthetic Image Generation," *Computer Vision, Graphics, and Image Processing*, Vol. 41, pp. 57-79, 1988.

[21] Meyer, G. W., and Liu, A., "Color Spatial Acuity Control of a Screen Subdivision Image Synthesis Algorithm," *Human Vision, Visual Processing, and Digital Display III*, Bernice E. Rogowitz, Editor, Proc. SPIE 1666, pp. 387-399, 1992.

[22] Mitchell, D. P., "Generating Antialiased Images at Low Sampling Densities," *Computer Graphics, Annual Conference Series*, ACM SIGGRAPH, pp. 65-72, 1987.

[23] Mullen, K. T., "The Contrast Sensitivity of Human Colour Vision to Red-Green and Blue-Yellow Chromatic Gratings," *J. Physiol. (Lond.)*, Vol. 359, pp. 381-400, 1985.

[24] Painter, J. and Sloan, K. "Antialiased Ray Tracing by Adaptive Progressive Refinement," *Computer Graphics, Annual Conference Series*, ACM SIGGRAPH, pp. 281-288, 1989.

[25] Pearson, D. E., *Transmission and Display of Pictorial Information*, John Wiley and Sons, 1975.

[26] Poirson, A. B. and Wandell, B. A. "Pattern-Color Separable Pathways Predict Sensitivity to Simple Colored Patterns," to appear in *Vision Research*, 1996.

[27] Powell, M. J. D., "A Theorem on Rank One Modifications to a Matrix and its Inverse," *Computer Journal*, Vol. 12, pp. 288-290, 1969.

[28] Pratt, W. K., *Digital Image Processing*, Second Edition, John Wiley and Sons, 1991.

[29] Rao, K. R. and Yip, P., *Discrete Cosine Transform*, Academic Press: Boston, 1990.

[30] Rushmeier, H. E. and Ward, G. J., "Energy Preserving Non-Linear Filters," *Computer Graphics, Annual Conference Series*, ACM SIGGRAPH, pp. 131-138, 1994.

[31] Stark, P. A., *Introduction to Numerical Methods*, Macmillan Publishing Co.: New York, 1970.

[32] Tumblin J. and Rushmeier, H., "Tone Reproduction for Realistic Images," *IEEE Computer Graphics and Applications*, pp. 42-48, 1993.

[33] Ward, G., "The RADIANCE Lighting Simulation and Rendering System," *Computer Graphics, Annual Conference Series*, ACM SIGGRAPH, pp. 459-472, 1994.

[34] Ward, G., Rubinstein, F. M., and Clear, R. D., "A Ray Tracing Solution for Diffuse Interreflection," *Computer Graphics, Annual Conference Series*, ACM SIGGRAPH, pp. 85-92, 1988.

[35] Wallace, G. K., "The JPEG Still Picture Compression Standard," *Communications of the ACM*, Vol. 34, No. 4, pp. 30-44, 1991.

[36] Wallach, D. S., Kunapalli, S., and Cohen, M. F., "Accelerated MPEG Compression of Dynamic Polygonal Scenes," *Computer Graphics, Annual Conference Series*, ACM SIGGRAPH, pp. 193-196, 1994.

[37] Williams, D. R., MacLeod, D. I. A., and Hayhoe, M. M., "Punctuate Sensitivity of the Blue-Sensitive Mechanism," *Vision Research*, Vol. 21, pp. 1357-1375, 1981.

Optimally Combining Sampling Techniques
for Monte Carlo Rendering

Eric Veach   *Leonidas J. Guibas*

Computer Science Department
Stanford University

Abstract

Monte Carlo integration is a powerful technique for the evaluation of difficult integrals. Applications in rendering include distribution ray tracing, Monte Carlo path tracing, and form-factor computation for radiosity methods. In these cases variance can often be significantly reduced by drawing samples from several distributions, each designed to sample well some difficult aspect of the integrand. Normally this is done by explicitly partitioning the integration domain into regions that are sampled differently. We present a powerful alternative for constructing robust Monte Carlo estimators, by combining samples from several distributions in a way that is provably good. These estimators are unbiased, and can reduce variance significantly at little additional cost. We present experiments and measurements from several areas in rendering: calculation of glossy highlights from area light sources, the "final gather" pass of some radiosity algorithms, and direct solution of the rendering equation using bidirectional path tracing.

CR Categories: I.3.7 [Computer Graphics]: Three-Dimensional Graphics and Realism; I.3.3 [Computer Graphics]: Picture/Image Generation; G.1.9 [Numerical Analysis]: Integral Equations—Fredholm equations.

Additional Keywords: Monte Carlo, variance reduction, rendering, distribution ray tracing, global illumination, lighting simulation.

1 Introduction

Technically, rendering is all about clever ways to approximate integrals. For example, the pixel values in an "ideal" image usually involve integration over the image plane, lens position, and so on. Furthermore, the quality of a rendering algorithm is frequently measured by the accuracy and efficiency with which these integrals are approximated. In this paper, we focus on Monte Carlo (MC) methods for evaluating such integrals. These methods use random sampling to simplify the integration problem, by expressing the integral as the expected value of a random variable. The major drawback of MC integration is that the resulting estimates can have high variance; this is perceived as noise in a rendered image.

Address: Computer Science Department, Robotics Laboratory
 Stanford University, Stanford, CA 94305-2140
E-mail: ericv@cs.stanford.edu, guibas@cs.stanford.edu
Web: http://www–graphics.stanford.edu/

Permission to make digital/hard copy of part or all of this work for personal or classroom use is granted without fee provided that copies are not made or distributed for profit or commercial advantage, the copyright notice, the title of the publication and its date appear, and notice is given that copying is by permission of ACM, Inc. To copy otherwise, to republish, to post on servers, or to redistribute to lists, requires prior specific permission and/or a fee.

Unfortunately, the functions that we need to integrate in computer graphics are often ill-behaved. They are almost always discontinuous, and often have singularities or very large values over small portions of their domain. Because of this, we often need more than one sampling technique to estimate an integral with low variance. Normally this is accomplished by explicitly partitioning the domain of integration into several regions, and designing a sampling technique for each region. For example, a simple distribution ray tracer may use one technique to evaluate direct lighting, another to estimate glossy reflections, and a third for ideal specular contributions.

In this paper, we explore the general problem of constructing low-variance estimators by combining samples from several techniques. We do not construct new sampling methods—all the samples we use come from one of the given distributions. Instead, we look for better ways to combine the samples; in particular, strategies that compute *weighted combinations*. We show that there is a large class of unbiased estimators of this type, parameterized by a set of weighting functions. We then seek weighting functions within this class that minimize variance. In a sense, we are asking the inverse problem: given several sampling techniques, how should the domain be partitioned among them? (Or more generally, how should the samples be weighted?)

A good solution to this problem turns out to be surprisingly simple. We show how to combine samples from several distributions in a way that is provably good, both theoretically and practically. This allows us to construct MC estimators that have low variance for a broad class of integrands—we call such estimators *robust*. The significance of our methods is not that we can take several bad sampling techniques and concoct a good one out of them, but rather that we can take several potentially good techniques and combine them so that the strengths of each are preserved.

In Sec. 2, we review the fundamentals of MC integration for rendering, and give an example to motivate our variance reduction framework. Sec. 3 explains our ideas on combining samples from several distributions, and gives theoretical justification under several models (proofs can be found in App. A). In Sec. 4 we present computed images and numerical results for several application areas: glossy highlights from area light sources, the "final gather" pass of some radiosity algorithms, and direct solution of the rendering equation using bidirectional path tracing. Finally, Sec. 5 discusses of a number of tradeoffs and open issues related to our work.

2 Monte Carlo rendering

2.1 Integrals for radiance

We have chosen two basic problems in rendering to illustrate our techniques: evaluation of the radiance leaving a surface given a description of the incoming illumination (as in distribution ray tracing or some "final gather" approaches), and direct solution of the rendering equation[5]. For further details and background see [3].

Given the incident radiance distribution $L_i(\mathbf{x}', \vec{\omega}_i')$ at a point $\mathbf{x}'$,

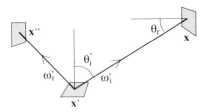

Figure 1: Geometry for the reflectance equation.

the reflected radiance $L_r(\mathbf{x}', \vec{\omega}_r')$ is given by the *reflectance equation*

$$L_r(\mathbf{x}', \vec{\omega}_r') = \int_{\mathcal{S}^2} f_r(\mathbf{x}', \vec{\omega}_i' \leftrightarrow \vec{\omega}_r') L_i(x, \vec{\omega}_i') \left|\cos(\theta_i')\right| d\sigma(\vec{\omega}_i') \quad (1)$$

where f_r is the bidirectional reflectance distribution function (BRDF), $\mathcal{S}^2$ is the set of all unit direction vectors, σ is the usual solid angle measure, and θ_i' is the angle between $\vec{\omega}_i'$ and the surface normal at $\mathbf{x}'$ (see Fig. 1). We allow f_r to model transmission as well (in this case f_r is the bidirectional scattering distribution function).

Sometimes it is preferable to express the reflectance equation as an integral over the domain $\mathcal{M}$ of scene surfaces (e.g. for direct lighting calculations). This form is given by

$$L_r(\mathbf{x}' \to \mathbf{x}'') = \int_{\mathcal{M}} f_r(\mathbf{x} \leftrightarrow \mathbf{x}' \leftrightarrow \mathbf{x}'') G(\mathbf{x} \leftrightarrow \mathbf{x}') L_i(\mathbf{x} \to \mathbf{x}') dA(\mathbf{x}) \quad (2)$$

$$\text{where} \quad G(\mathbf{x} \leftrightarrow \mathbf{x}') = V(\mathbf{x} \leftrightarrow \mathbf{x}') \cdot \frac{\cos(\theta_r)\cos(\theta_i')}{\|\mathbf{x} - \mathbf{x}'\|^2} \quad .$$

Here A is the usual measure of surface area, θ_r and θ_i' measure the angle between $\mathbf{x} \leftrightarrow \mathbf{x}'$ and the surface normals at $\mathbf{x}$ and $\mathbf{x}'$ respectively, while $V(\mathbf{x} \leftrightarrow \mathbf{x}')$ is 1 if $\mathbf{x}$ and $\mathbf{x}'$ are mutually visible and 0 otherwise. The term $G(\mathbf{x} \leftrightarrow \mathbf{x}')$ measures the *differential throughput of a beam*[3] from $\mathbf{x}$ to $\mathbf{x}'$.

Often the incident radiance distribution is unknown, and we must solve for it. This leads to the global illumination problem: given an emitted radiance distribution L_e, find the equilibrium radiance distribution L satisfying

$$L(\mathbf{x}' \to \mathbf{x}'') = L_e(\mathbf{x}' \to \mathbf{x}'') \quad (3)$$
$$+ \int_{\mathcal{M}} f_r(\mathbf{x} \leftrightarrow \mathbf{x}' \leftrightarrow \mathbf{x}'') G(\mathbf{x} \leftrightarrow \mathbf{x}') L(\mathbf{x} \to \mathbf{x}') dA(\mathbf{x}).$$

This is known as the three-point *rendering* or *light transport equation*[5]. Equation (3) can be written concisely in operator form as $L = L_e + \mathcal{T}L$, where $\mathcal{T}$ is the *light transport operator*. Under weak assumptions, the solution is given formally by the Neumann series

$$L = \sum_{i=0}^{\infty} \mathcal{T}^i L_e \quad . \quad (4)$$

This says that the equilibrium radiance L is the sum of emitted light, plus light that bounces once, twice, etc.

Our goal is to compute a finite set of measurements that approximately represent L. Each measurement I_p is expressed as an inner product or "weighted average" of the radiance distribution L, as modeled by the *measurement equation*:

$$I_p = \langle W_p, L \rangle = \int_{\mathcal{M} \times \mathcal{M}} W_p(\mathbf{x} \to \mathbf{x}') L(\mathbf{x} \to \mathbf{x}') G(\mathbf{x} \leftrightarrow \mathbf{x}') dA(\mathbf{x}) dA(\mathbf{x}')$$
$$(5)$$

where $W_p(\mathbf{x} \to \mathbf{x}')$ is the weighting function corresponding to a particular measurement I_p.

For example, the value of each pixel p in an image can be expressed in the form (5), using a weighting function W_p that is non-zero on the set of rays mapped to pixel p by the virtual lens. W_p can model arbitrary lens systems used to form the image, as well as any linear filters used for anti-aliasing.

2.2 Monte Carlo integration

We review the basic principle of MC integration, and establish some notation for the following sections. Our goal is to estimate

$$\mathcal{F} = \int_{\Omega} f(x) \, d\mu(x)$$

where $f : \Omega \to \mathcal{R}$ and μ is a measure function.

We define a *sampling technique* as an algorithm for choosing random points in the domain Ω. Let $p(x) \, d\mu(x)$ be the probability distribution of the points generated. The idea of MC integration is to generate a sample X, and then use $f(X)/p(X)$ as an estimate of $\mathcal{F}$. As long as the *sample value* $f(X)/p(X)$ is finite for all samples X, it is easy to show that this estimate is unbiased:

$$E\left[\frac{f(X)}{p(X)}\right] = \int_{\Omega} \frac{f(x)}{p(x)} p(x) \, d\mu(x) = \int_{\Omega} f(x) \, d\mu(x) = \mathcal{F} \quad (6)$$

where $E[Z]$ denotes the expected value of Z. In practice, we estimate $\mathcal{F}$ by taking several samples $X_1, \ldots, X_n$ distributed according to p, and computing

$$\mathcal{F} \approx \frac{1}{n} \sum_{i=1}^{n} \frac{f(X_i)}{p(X_i)} \quad . \quad (7)$$

MC integration has one inherent drawback, which manifests itself as a tradeoff between variance and running time. Letting F be the sample value $f(X)/p(X)$, the variance of F is

$$V[F] = E[F^2] - E[F]^2 = \int_{\Omega} \frac{f^2(x)}{p(x)} \, d\mu(x) - \mathcal{F}^2 \quad . \quad (8)$$

If we take n independent samples according to (7), variance is reduced by a factor of n, while running time is increased by a factor of n. This tradeoff is summarized by the *efficiency* [1, 6] of a Monte Carlo estimator,

$$\epsilon[F] = \frac{1}{V[F] \cdot T[F]}$$

where $T[F]$ is the time required to take a sample from F. The higher the efficiency, the less time required to achieve a given variance. The design of efficient estimators, often simply called *variance reduction*, is a fundamental goal of MC research.

Notice that the variance in (8) is strongly affected by the sampling distribution p—e.g. if p is proportional to f (assuming $f \geq 0$), the variance $V[F]$ is zero. Unfortunately the normalization $p = f/\mathcal{F}$ requires knowledge of $\mathcal{F}$, so this is not practical. However, by choosing a distribution p whose shape is similar to f, variance can be reduced. This idea is known as *importance sampling*[6].

On the other hand, suppose that we sample f inadequately in some region U where its value is large (i.e. $p \ll f/\mathcal{F}$). By (8) we see that samples from U can make a large contribution to the variance, even if U is relatively small. This effect is a major cause of noise in Monte Carlo images. Our primary goal is to show how this problem may be avoided, by combining samples from several distributions designed to sample well each significant region of f.

2.3 An example: glossy highlights

Consider how a distribution ray tracer might render the highlight produced by an area light source S on a nearby glossy surface (see Fig. 2). Given a viewing ray that strikes the glossy surface, there are two obvious strategies for MC evaluation of the reflected radiance, corresponding to forms (1) and (2) of the reflectance equation.

With *area* sampling, we randomly sample points on S to evaluate the integral (2). To compute the estimate (7), we must know the distribution $p(\mathbf{x}) \, dA(\mathbf{x})$ of the samples—for example, they may be chosen uniformly on S with respect to surface area or emitted power. Since there is considerable freedom in choosing p, area sampling

(a) Sampling the light sources

(b) Sampling the BRDF

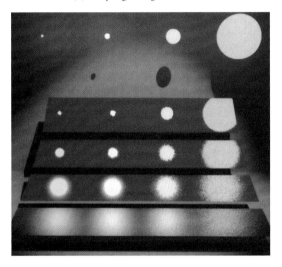

(c) A combination of samples from (a) and (b).

Figure 2: Sampling of glossy highlights from area light sources (Sec. 2.3, 4.1). There are four spherical light sources of varying radii and color, plus a spotlight overhead. All spherical light sources emit the same total power. There are also four shiny rectangular plates of varying surface roughness, each one tilted so that we see the reflected light sources.

Given a viewing ray that strikes a glossy surface, images (a), (b), (c) use different techniques for the highlight calculation. All images are 500 by 450 pixels.

(a) A sample direction $\vec{\omega}'_i$ is chosen uniformly (with respect to solid angle) within the cone of directions subtended by each light source, using $n_1 = 4$ samples per pixel.

(b) $\vec{\omega}'_i$ is chosen with probability proportional to the BRDF $f_r(\mathbf{x}', \vec{\omega}'_i \leftrightarrow \vec{\omega}'_r) \, d\sigma(\vec{\omega}'_i)$, using $n_2 = 4$ samples per pixel.

(c) A weighted combination of the samples from (a) and (b) is computed, using the power heuristic with $\beta = 2$.

The glossy BRDF is a symmetric, energy-conserving variation of the Phong model. The Phong exponent is $n = 1/r - 1$, where r is a surface roughness parameter, $0 < r < 1$. The glossy surfaces also have a small diffuse component. Similar results could be obtained with other glossy BRDF's.

is really a family of techniques. The glossy highlights in Fig. 2(a) were computed with an area sampling strategy.

With *directional* sampling, we estimate the integral (1) by random sampling of the incident direction $\vec{\omega}'_i$. Evaluation of L_i requires casting a ray; only the rays that strike S contribute to the highlight calculation. Typically the distribution $p(\vec{\omega}'_i) \, d\sigma(\vec{\omega}'_i)$ is chosen to be proportional to $f_r(\mathbf{x}', \vec{\omega}'_i \leftrightarrow \vec{\omega}'_r)$ or to $f_r(\mathbf{x}', \vec{\omega}'_i \leftrightarrow \vec{\omega}'_r)|\cos(\theta'_i)|$. Fig. 2(b) was computed with a directional sampling strategy.

One of these strategies can have a much lower variance than the other (see Fig. 2). For example, if the light source is very small, we are unlikely to hit it with rays chosen by randomly sampling the BRDF. On the other hand, if the BRDF is nearly specular, randomly chosen points on the light source will probably not contribute significantly to the radiance reflected along the viewing ray.

In both these cases, noise is caused by inadequate sampling where the integrand is large. To understand this, notice that the integrand in the reflectance equation (2) is the product of various unrelated factors—the BRDF, the emitted radiance L_e, and several geometric quantities. However, the area sampling distribution used in Fig. 2(a) does not take into account the BRDF for example, while the directional sampling in Fig. 2(b) does not depend on the emitted radiance. When an unconsidered factor is dominant (e.g. a small bright light, or a shiny surface), that sampling technique will do poorly.

It is important to realize that both strategies are importance sampling techniques aimed at generating sample points on the same domain (in this case, the light source S). Area sampling chooses a point $\mathbf{x} \in S$ directly, while directional sampling chooses $\mathbf{x}$ by casting a ray in the chosen direction $\vec{\omega}'_i$. Given a directional distribution $p(\vec{\omega}'_i) \, d\sigma(\vec{\omega}'_i)$, the corresponding area distribution $p(\mathbf{x}) \, dA(\mathbf{x})$ is

$$p(\mathbf{x}) = p(\vec{\omega}'_i) \cdot \frac{d\sigma(\vec{\omega}'_i)}{dA(\mathbf{x})} = p(\vec{\omega}'_i) \cdot \frac{\cos(\theta_r)}{\|\mathbf{x} - \mathbf{x}'\|^2} \; . \qquad (9)$$

(see Fig. 1)[1]. This lets us compute the probability densities assigned by area and directional methods to the same point $\mathbf{x}$.

2.4 Our framework for variance reduction

When choosing a Monte Carlo sampling technique, we rarely know exactly what the integrand is. Instead, we have some model for the integrand, defined by a set of parameters (e.g. the BRDF, the scene geometry, etc). Given several sampling techniques to choose from, the variance of each one can change dramatically as these parameters vary.

Our main goal is to show how Monte Carlo integration can be made more robust, by constructing estimators that have low variance for a broad class of integrands. To achieve this, we must avoid

---

[1] One could argue that $V(\mathbf{x} \leftrightarrow \mathbf{x}')$ should appear in (9). But if $V(\mathbf{x} \leftrightarrow \mathbf{x}') = 0$, the integrand (2) is also zero, which makes $p(\mathbf{x})$ irrelevant.

insufficient sampling of each candidate integrand f where its value is large. Our approach to this problem has three steps.

First, we design a set of importance sampling distributions $p_1, \ldots, p_n$. For each region where f has the potential to be large, we try to construct a sampling distribution that approximates f well over that portion of the domain. An excellent source of these distributions is the situation in the example above, where f is a product of several unrelated functions, and each p_i is proportional to the product of a subset of these.

Next, we determine how many samples to take from each p_i. We assume this is fixed in advance, based on knowledge of f and p_i.

Finally, the integral is estimated as a weighted combination of all the sample values. The main subject of this paper is how to do this, such that the estimate is unbiased and has low variance.

3 Combining sampling techniques

We are given an integrand $f : \Omega \to \mathcal{R}$, and several importance sampling distributions $p_1, \ldots, p_n$. Our goal is to estimate $\int_\Omega f(x) \, d\mu(x)$. We assume that only two operations are available: we can take a sample from any of the distributions p_i, and we can evaluate $f(x)$, and $p_i(x)$ for any $x \in \Omega$. Each sample is assumed to be independent, i.e. we generate new random bits to control its selection.

As mentioned above, we must also decide how many samples to take from each p_i. We define c_i as the relative number of samples taken from p_i, where $\sum_i c_i = 1$. In this paper, we assume that the c_i are fixed in advance, i.e. before any samples are taken. The choice of the c_i is an interesting problem that we discuss further in Sec. 5.2.

The key ideas in this section are simple. First, notice that by drawing a fraction c_i of the samples from each p_i, the resulting group of samples has the distribution $\bar{p}(x) = \sum_i c_i p_i(x)$. We propose that the natural way to combine importance sampling techniques is to consider this *combined sample distribution* when computing the unbiased estimate $f(X)/p(X)$.

Second, we show that this method of combining samples is provably good (compared to partitioning, simple weighted combinations, etc). To justify this claim, we explore a much larger class of unbiased combination strategies, parameterized by a set of weighting functions. We then look for weighting functions that minimize the variance of the combined estimator, and show that the combination strategy above is close to optimal. This gives us confidence that our methods compare favorably with other possible techniques.

Third, we use our framework of unbiased estimators to reduce variance further in an important special case. Specifically, it is common in practice that for the particular integrand f we are given, one of the given sampling distributions is far superior to the rest (e.g. a small bright light or shiny surface in Fig. 2). We study two families of weighting functions that perform significantly better in this situation, while retaining provably good behavior in general.

3.1 The combined sample distribution

Suppose that $n_i = c_i N$ independent samples $X_{i,j}$ are taken from distribution p_i, for a total of N samples. As a group, the samples have the distribution

$$\bar{p}(x) = \sum_{i=1}^n c_i p_i(x) \ .$$

More precisely, $\bar{p}(x)$ is the distribution of a random variable X which is equal to each $X_{i,j}$ with probability $1/N$. We call this the *combined sample distribution*. From this point of view, the standard estimator (7) gives

$$F = \frac{1}{N} \sum_{i=1}^n \sum_{j=1}^{n_i} \frac{f(X_{i,j})}{\bar{p}(X_{i,j})} \ . \tag{10}$$

As we will show, this is a provably good way to combine samples from several distributions. Within the framework described below, this strategy is called the *balance heuristic* (Sec. 3.3).

3.2 The multi-sample model

In this section we consider unbiased estimators that allow samples to be weighted differently, depending on which underlying distribution p_i they were chosen from. Each estimator is parameterized by a set of *weighting functions* $w_1, \ldots, w_n$, where $w_i(x)$ gives the weight associated with a sample x drawn from p_i. The *combined estimator* is given by

$$F = \sum_{i=1}^n \frac{1}{n_i} \sum_{j=1}^{n_i} w_i(X_{i,j}) \frac{f(X_{i,j})}{p_i(X_{i,j})} \tag{11}$$

where the $X_{i,j}$ are independent samples from distribution p_i, as before. For this estimator to be unbiased, we require that $\sum_i w_i(x) = 1$ for all x, since this gives

$$E[F] = \sum_{i=1}^n \frac{1}{n_i} n_i \int_\Omega \frac{w_i(x) f(x)}{p_i(x)} p_i(x) \, d\mu(x) = \int_\Omega f(x) \, d\mu(x) \ .$$

Think of this as a weighted sum of the estimators $f(X_{i,j})/p_i(X_{i,j})$. The weights are allowed to vary with position, but must always sum to one. For example, if at every point x all but one of the w_i are zero, we get a *simple partitioning* of the domain into n regions. This represents a heuristic such as dividing the visible hemisphere into light source regions and non-light-source regions, which are then sampled using different methods.

3.3 The balance heuristic

We now have a large parameter space over which to optimize (the space of allowable weighting functions w_i). Our goal is to minimize the variance of F by choosing the w_i appropriately. Consider the weighting functions

$$\hat{w}_i(x) = \frac{c_i p_i(x)}{\sum_j c_j p_j(x)} \ . \tag{12}$$

These $\hat{w}_i$ have the unique property that the sample value $\{\hat{w}_i(x) f(x)\} / \{n_i p_i(x)\}$ from (11) does not depend on i. Because the sample value at a particular x is the same for all underlying distributions, we call this strategy the *balance heuristic*. Substituting $\hat{w}_i$ into (11), this is simply a reformulation of the estimator (10) we obtained using the combined probability distribution.

The following theorem gives evidence that these weighting functions are good:

Theorem 1. *Let $w_1, \ldots, w_n$ be any non-negative functions with $\sum_i w_i = 1$, and let $\hat{w}_1, \ldots, \hat{w}_n$ be the weighting functions above (the balance heuristic). Let F and $\hat{F}$ be the corresponding combined estimators (11). Then*

$$V[\hat{F}] \leq V[F] + \left(\frac{1}{\min_i n_i} - \frac{1}{\sum_i n_i} \right) \mathcal{F}^2 \ .$$

See App. A for a proof. This theorem says that no choice of the w_i can improve upon the variance of the balance heuristic by more than $(1/\min_i n_i - 1/N)\mathcal{F}^2$ (recall that $\mathcal{F}$ is the quantity we are trying to estimate). This "variance gap" is very small relative to the variance caused by a poorly chosen sampling distribution, as we saw in Fig. 2. Also, the variance gap goes to zero as the number of samples increases (assuming all n_i are increased).

Furthermore, these weighting functions are practical to evaluate. The key requirement is that given a sample X_i from p_i, we must be able to evaluate $p_j(X_i)$ for all j. Any unbiased Monte Carlo algorithm must be able to evaluate $p_i(X_i)$, so this is often just a matter of reorganizing the routines that compute probabilities. The time to evaluate these probabilities is generally insignificant compared to other rendering calculations, as we show in Sec. 4.

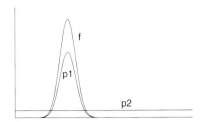

Figure 3: Two distributions for sampling the integrand.

3.4 Other weighting heuristics

Theorem 1 implies that although the balance heuristic is good, there is still room for improvement. In this section we discuss two families of heuristics that in practice often have lower variance than the balance heuristic. These heuristics satisfy $\sum_i w_i(x) = 1$ and thus give unbiased estimates.

We are motivated by the common situation where one of the p_i is an almost perfect match for f (e.g. BRDF sampling with the mirror-like surface in Fig. 2). To develop our ideas, consider the situation in Fig. 3, where f is a very peaked distribution, p_1 is proportional to f, and p_2 is the uniform distribution. Assume that we take an equal number of samples from both p_i, and form a weighted combination using the multi-sample model (11).

Since p_1 is a zero-variance importance sampling distribution ($f(X_1)/p_1(X_1) = \mathcal{F}$ is constant), the optimal weighting functions are obviously $w_1(x) \equiv 1$, $w_2(x) \equiv 0$. We cannot expect to guess this using only pointwise evaluation of the p_i and f; however, we would like to get as close to this ideal as possible.

How well does the balance heuristic perform in this situation, and how can we improve it? Consider the contributions of samples from p_1 and p_2 separately. Most samples from p_1 occur near the peak, where the weighted sample value (see (12)) is approximately equal to $\mathcal{F}$. Similarly, most samples from p_2 occur away from the peak, where their sample value is zero (because f is zero there).

So far, this is very close to optimal. However there are two effects that lead to additional variance. Occasionally a sample from p_1 occurs away from the peak (i.e. where $p_1 \gg p_2$ does not hold). In this case the weight $p_1/(p_1+p_2)$ produces a sample value smaller than $\mathcal{F}$; in an image, this shows up as dark spots. On the other hand, sometimes a sample X_2 from p_2 occurs near the peak of f. These have a weighted sample value slightly smaller than $\mathcal{F}$ (see Sec. 3.3). In an image, this shows up as occasional bright spots. However, these "spikes" are relatively small in magnitude, because a sample from p_2 contributes the same as an equivalent sample from p_1.

We present two families of heuristics that reduce variance in this important limiting case. They are variations on the balance heuristic, where the weighting functions have been "sharpened" by making large weights closer to one and small weights closer to zero. This is effective at reducing both types of noise above.

The *cutoff heuristic* modifies the weighting functions by discarding samples with low weight:[2]

$$w_i = \begin{cases} 0 & \text{if } p_i < \alpha\, p_{\max} \\ \dfrac{p_i}{\sum_j \{p_j \mid p_j \geq \alpha\, p_{\max}\}} & \text{otherwise} \end{cases} \quad (13)$$

where $p_{\max} = \max_j p_j$. The constant α determines how small p_i must be compared to $p_{\max}$ before we assign it a zero weight.

The *power heuristic* raises all weights to a power β, and then normalizes:

$$w_i = \frac{p_i^\beta}{\sum_j p_j^\beta} \quad . \quad (14)$$

Notice that when $\alpha = 0$ or $\beta = 1$, we get the balance heuristic. When $\alpha = 1$ or $\beta = \infty$, we get the *maximum heuristic*:

$$w_i = \begin{cases} 1 & \text{if } p_i = p_{\max} \\ 0 & \text{otherwise} \end{cases} \quad . \quad (15)$$

This heuristic simply partitions the domain according to which distribution p_i generates samples there with the highest probability.

The advantage of these heuristics is reduced variance when one of the p_i is much better than the rest. Their performance is otherwise similar to the balance heuristic; it is possible to show they are never much worse (we give bounds in App. A, measurements in Sec. 4.1).

3.5 The one-sample model: optimality

In this section, we consider a sampling model where we our combination methods are optimal. Under this *one-sample model*, each sample is taken from a randomly selected distribution p_i. Distribution p_i is chosen with probability c_i. This idea is used in path tracing for example, where at each bounce we choose randomly between the diffuse, specular, or transmitted distributions.

Again, each estimator is parameterized by a set of weighting functions $\{w_i(x)\}$. The process of choosing a distribution, taking a sample, and computing the weighted sample value is described mathematically by the combined estimator

$$F = \frac{w_I(X_I)f(X_I)}{c_I p_I(X_I)} \quad , \quad \text{where} \quad I = \min\{i \mid U < \sum_{j=1}^{i} c_j\} \quad . \quad (16)$$

Here U is a uniformly distributed random variable on $[0, 1)$, I is the index of the randomly chosen distribution, and X_I is a sample from distribution I. This estimator is unbiased as long as $\sum_i w_i = 1$.

In this case, the balance weighting strategy is optimal:

Theorem 2. *Let $w_1, \ldots, w_n$ be any non-negative functions with $\sum_i w_i = 1$, and let $\hat{w}_1, \ldots, \hat{w}_n$ be the weighting functions (12). Let F and $\hat{F}$ be the corresponding combined estimators (16). Then $V[\hat{F}] \leq V[F]$.*

4 Experiments

4.1 Distribution ray tracing

Our first test is the computation of glossy highlights from area light sources (see also Sec. 2.3 and Fig. 2). The area sampling technique[3] used in Fig. 2(a) works well for small light sources and rough surfaces. The directional sampling technique in (b) does well for large light sources and smooth surfaces. In (c), the power heuristic with $\beta = 2$ is used to combine both kinds of samples. This method works very well for all light source/surface combinations.

We have also measured variance numerically as a function of roughness. Fig. 4 shows the test setup, and the results are summarized in Fig. 5. Notice that all four weighting heuristics yield a variance that is close (on an absolute scale) to the minimum variance when either sampling technique is used alone. In particular, Thm. 1 guarantees that the variance σ^2 of the balance heuristic is within $\mu^2/2$ of the best input technique. The plots in Fig. 5(a) are well within that bound.

At the extremes of the roughness axis there are significant differences among the heuristics. As expected, the balance heuristic (a) performs worst at the extremes, since the other heuristics were specifically designed for the case when one sampling technique is much better than the rest. The power heuristic (c) with $\beta = 2$ works especially well over the whole range of roughness values.

---

[2] All p_i and w_i are implicitly functions of x. For simplicity we have assumed all n_i are equal; otherwise replace p_i by $n_i p_i$ everywhere.

[3] Direction $\vec{\omega}_i'$ is used to compute a point x on the light source directly, rather than casting a ray to find the first visible point. Thus form (2) of the reflectance equation is used, making this an area sampling technique.

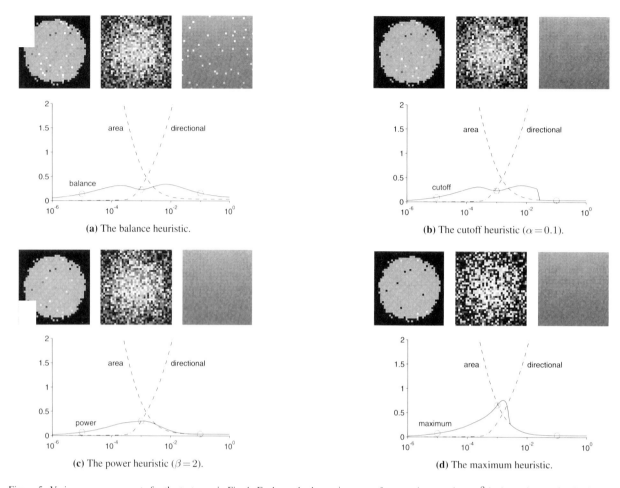

(a) The balance heuristic.

(b) The cutoff heuristic ($\alpha = 0.1$).

(c) The power heuristic ($\beta = 2$).

(d) The maximum heuristic.

Figure 5: Variance measurements for the test case in Fig. 4. Each graph plots σ/μ vs. surface roughness, where σ^2 is the variance of a single sample and μ is the mean. Three curves are shown, corresponding to the area sampling technique from Fig. 2(a), the directional sampling technique from Fig. 2(b), and a weighted combination of both sample types using the (a) balance, (b) cutoff, (c) power, and (d) maximum heuristics. The images above each graph are computed with the corresponding heuristic, for the three roughness values circled (one sample per pixel, box filter). The center pixel of these images corresponds to the viewing ray used for the variance measurements.

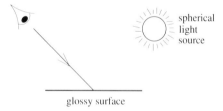

Figure 4: A scale diagram of the setup used to measure the variance of the highlight calculation. The light source occupies a solid angle of 0.063 radians. The variance for each roughness value was measured by taking 100,000 samples using the viewing ray shown.

Above the graphs we show how the variance of each method appears in an image, for three circled roughness values. Notice how the cutoff, power, and maximum heuristics reduce the "bright spot" and "dark spot" noise (Sec. 3.4) at the extremes.

Recall that to evaluate the weights at a point x, we must compute the probabilities with which *both* methods generate x. For example, if x is a point on the light source generated by (a), we find the probability $p_2(\vec{\omega}_i')\,d\sigma(\vec{\omega}_i')$ that (b) generates the direction $\vec{\omega}_i'$ pointing toward x, and convert this probability to the measure $p_2(x)\,dA(x)$ using (9). The total time spent evaluating probabilities and weighting functions in our tests was less than 5%.

4.2 Final gather

In this section we consider a simple test case motivated by *multipass global illumination algorithms*. These algorithms typically compute an approximate solution using the finite element method, followed by one or more ray tracing passes to replace parts of the solution that are poorly approximated or missing. For example, some radiosity algorithms use a *local pass* or *final gather* to recompute certain coefficients more accurately.

We examine a variation called *per-pixel final gather*. The idea is to compute an approximate radiosity solution, and then use it to illuminate the visible surfaces during a ray tracing pass[11, 2]. Essentially, this type of final gather is equivalent to ray tracing with many area light sources (one for each patch, or one for each link in a hierarchical solution). As with the glossy highlight example, there are two common sampling techniques. The brightest patches are classified as "light sources"[2], and are handled with an area sampling technique (e.g. samples are distributed on the light sources according to emitted power). The remaining patches are sampled by casting rays randomly into the scene (i.e. directional sampling from the point intersected by the viewing ray). If one of these rays hits a light source patch, the sample value is zero (to avoid counting those patches twice). Within our framework for combining sampling techniques, this is clearly a partitioning of the integration domain into two regions.

Given some classification of patches into light sources and non-

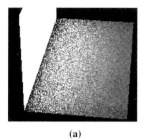  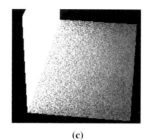 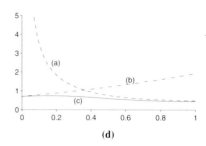

(a)   (b)   (c)   (d)

Figure 6: A simple test scene consisting of one area light source (i.e. a bright patch) and an adjacent diffuse surface. The images were computed by (a) sampling the light source according to emitted power, with $n_1 = 3$ samples per pixel, (b) sampling the hemisphere according to the *projected solid angle*[3] $\cos(\theta_i') \, d\sigma(\vec{\omega}_i')$ (see Fig. 1), with $n_2 = 6$ samples per pixel, and (c) a weighted combination of samples from (a) and (b) using the power heuristic with $\beta = 2$. (d) A plot of σ/μ (standard deviation divided by mean) as a function of distance from the light source, for $n_1 = 1$ and $n_2 = 2$.

light sources, we consider alternative ways of combining the two types of samples. To test our weighting strategies, we used the extremely simple test scene shown in Fig. 6. Twice as many samples are taken in (b) than (a); in practice this ratio would be substantially higher (i.e. the number of directional samples vs. the number of samples for any one light source).

Notice that Fig. 6(a) does poorly for points near the light source, because the sample distribution does not take into account the $1/r^2$ distance term of the reflectance equation (2). On the other hand (b) does poorly far away from the light source, when the light subtends a small solid angle. In Fig. 6(c), the power heuristic is used to combine samples from (a) and (b). As expected, this method performs well at all distances. Although (c) uses more samples (the sum of (a) and (b)), this is a valid comparison with the partitioning approach (which also uses both kinds of samples). Variance measurements are plotted in Fig. 6(d).

4.3 Bidirectional path tracing

The basic goal of Monte Carlo path tracing is to estimate the value of each pixel in an image by direct sampling of the rendering and measurement equations (Sec. 2.1). In this section, we show that by combining samples from several importance sampling techniques, this process can be made more efficient. As a source of sampling distributions, we use *bidirectional path tracing* (introduced independently in [14] and [8, 9]). We briefly overview the theory below.

To apply our methods, we must first express the value I_p of a pixel p in the standard form $\int_\Omega f(x) \, d\mu(x)$. To do this, we write out equations (3), (4), and (5) explicitly:

$$I_p = \langle W_p, L \rangle = \langle W_p, \sum_i \mathcal{T}^i L_e \rangle \tag{17}$$

$$= \int_{\mathcal{M}^2} L_e(\mathbf{x}_0 \to \mathbf{x}_1) G(\mathbf{x}_0 \leftrightarrow \mathbf{x}_1) W_p(\mathbf{x}_0 \to \mathbf{x}_1) \, dA(\mathbf{x}_0) \, dA(\mathbf{x}_1)$$

$$+ \int_{\mathcal{M}^3} L_e(\mathbf{x}_0 \to \mathbf{x}_1) G(\mathbf{x}_0 \leftrightarrow \mathbf{x}_1) f_r(\mathbf{x}_0 \leftrightarrow \mathbf{x}_1 \leftrightarrow \mathbf{x}_2)$$

$$G(\mathbf{x}_1 \leftrightarrow \mathbf{x}_2) W_p(\mathbf{x}_1 \to \mathbf{x}_2) \, dA(\mathbf{x}_0) \, dA(\mathbf{x}_1) \, dA(\mathbf{x}_2)$$

$$+ \cdots$$

To write this as a single integral $\int_\Omega f(x) \, d\mu(x)$, let Ω be the set of *transport paths* of all lengths. Each transport path π of length k is a sequence $\mathbf{x}_0 \mathbf{x}_1 \ldots \mathbf{x}_k$ of points $\mathbf{x}_i \in \mathcal{M}$. The measure $d\mu(\pi)$ on Ω is defined by $d\mu(\pi) = dA(\mathbf{x}_0) \ldots dA(\mathbf{x}_k)$.[4] Finally, the integrand $f(\pi)$ is simply the appropriate term from the expansion above, for example $f(\mathbf{x}_0 \mathbf{x}_1) = L_e(\mathbf{x}_0 \to \mathbf{x}_1) G(\mathbf{x}_0 \leftrightarrow \mathbf{x}_1) W_p(\mathbf{x}_0 \to \mathbf{x}_1)$.

Path tracing algorithms can be interpreted as methods for sampling this integral directly, by generating transport paths π randomly and using the standard estimate $f(\pi)/p(\pi)$. Observe that paths where $f(\pi)$ is large satisfy two conditions: they carry a relatively

---

[4] $d\mu(\pi) = dA(\mathbf{x}_0) G(\mathbf{x}_0 \leftrightarrow \mathbf{x}_1) dA(\mathbf{x}_1) \ldots G(\mathbf{x}_{k-1} \leftrightarrow \mathbf{x}_k) dA(\mathbf{x}_k)$ is another possibility—this measures the *differential throughput of a path*.

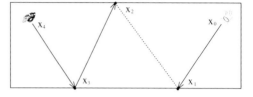

Figure 7: A transport path from a light source to the camera lens, created by concatenating two separately generated pieces.

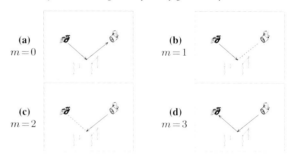

(a) $m = 0$ (b) $m = 1$

(c) $m = 2$ (d) $m = 3$

Figure 8: The four bidirectional sampling strategies for paths of length two (direct lighting). Intuitively, they can be described as (a) Monte Carlo path tracing with no special handling of light sources, (b) standard MC path tracing with direct lighting, (c) depositing (*splatting*) light on the image when a "photon" hits a visible surface, and (d) depositing light when a photon hits the camera lens.

large amount of light, and they have a relatively large weight in the measurement process that generates the final image. Bidirectional path tracing uses this idea to construct a family of importance-sampling techniques that trade off one property against the other.

Unlike standard path tracing, which generates transport paths by starting from the eye and following random bounces backward to the light sources, the bidirectional approach builds a path by connecting two independently generated pieces, one starting from the light sources and the other from the eye. For example, in Fig. 7 the *light subpath* $\mathbf{x}_0 \mathbf{x}_1$ is constructed by choosing a random point $\mathbf{x}_0$ on a light source (area sampling), followed by casting a random ray (directional sampling) to find $\mathbf{x}_1$. The *eye subpath* $\mathbf{x}_2 \mathbf{x}_3 \mathbf{x}_4$ is constructed by a similar process starting from a random point $\mathbf{x}_4$ on the camera lens. A complete transport path is formed by concatenating these two pieces. (This path may carry no light, for example if $\mathbf{x}_1$ and $\mathbf{x}_2$ are not mutually visible.)

This idea leads to a set of sampling techniques for transport paths. Each technique generates paths of a specific length k, by randomly generating a light subpath with m vertices, randomly generating an eye subpath with $k+1-m$ vertices, and concatenating them. In total there are $k+2$ distinct bidirectional sampling techniques for paths of length k (letting $m = 0, \ldots, k+1$, see Fig. 8). Each of these is really a framework for sampling rather than a specific technique,

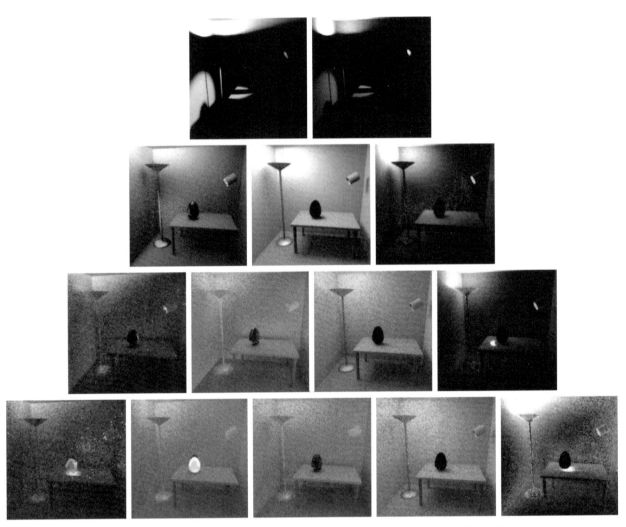

(a) The weighted contribution that each bidirectional sampling technique makes to image (b)

(b) Combines samples from all the bidirectional techniques

(c) Standard path tracing using the same amount of work

Figure 9: The scene contains a spot light, a floor lamp, a table, and a big glass egg. Image (b) uses the power heuristic (with $\beta = 2$) to combine samples from a family of bidirectional path tracing techniques, whose weighted contributions are shown in (a). Row i shows techniques that sample transport paths of length $i+1$; the m-th image uses the distribution $p_{i+1,m}$ (see Sec. 4.3). Images in row i have been over-exposed by i f-stops so that details can be seen.

since the paths generated depend on the distributions used to choose each vertex (area sampling for the first vertex of each subpath, usually directional sampling for the rest). These methods can be very diverse, e.g. sophisticated direct lighting techniques can be used to choose the first vertex of the light subpath.

Each technique defines a probability distribution $p_{k,m}(\pi)\,d\mu(\pi)$ on paths of length k. We can compute $p_{k,m}(\pi)$ explicitly by multiplying the probabilities $p(\mathbf{x}_i)\,dA(\mathbf{x}_i)$ with which the individual vertices were generated. Vertices that were chosen using a directional distribution $p(\vec{\omega})\,d\sigma(\vec{\omega})$ can be converted to the area measure using (9). To see why these distributions are good candidates for importance sampling, consider the integrand (17) for paths of length k. It is a product of many unrelated functions: L_{e}, W_p, k different G factors, and $k-1$ different f_{r} factors. Each bidirectional technique includes a different subset of these factors in its sampling distribution; among them, we are more likely to generate paths that contribute significantly to the image.

We now have all the tools to combine samples from these techniques using the methods of Sec. 3: we can take a sample from any of the distributions $p_{k,m}$, and given any path π of length k we can evaluate $f(\pi)$ and $p_{k,m}(\pi)$.

Fig. 9 shows a scene that we used to test these ideas. Diffuse, glossy, and pure specular surfaces are present. Transport paths of lengths up to $k=5$ were sampled using the bidirectional distributions $p_{k,m}$ described above. For efficiency, we randomly generate maximum-length eye and light subpaths in pairs. We then take samples from all $p_{k,m}$ by joining each prefix of the light subpath to each suffix of the eye subpath. For example, to sample $p_{2,1}$ we concatenate the first vertex of the light subpath and the last two vertices of the eye subpath. Each such group of samples is dependent, but this does not appear to significantly affect our results. Another important optimization reduces the number of visibility tests between the eye and light subpaths, by using Russian roulette [6] to randomly suppress small potential contributions without adding bias.

The final image in Fig. 9(b) was created by combining samples from all distributions using the power heuristic (with $\beta=2$). The image is 500 by 500 with 25 samples per pixel. The weighted contribution from each technique is shown in the pyramid in Fig. 9(a). The pyramid does not show the complete set of sampling techniques; paths of length one are not shown because the light sources are not directly visible, and one column has been stripped from the left and right sides of each row because these images are virtually black (i.e. the weighted contributions are very small).

Observe the caustics on the table, both directly from the spotlight and indirectly from reflected light on the ceiling. The unusual caustic pattern to the left is caused by the square shape of the spotlight's emitting surface. Notice that some effects, such as caustics and specular reflections, get their contributions almost entirely from one sampling technique. This says that the other techniques are very poor estimators of these contributions.

For comparison, Fig. 9(c) shows standard MC path tracing with 56 samples per pixel (the same computation time as Fig. 9(b)). Direct lighting was used on all paths except for caustics, which were rendered by following paths right back to the light sources (the caustics would otherwise not be visible).

5 Discussion

5.1 Conclusions

As we have shown, our methods for combining sampling techniques can substantially reduce the variance of Monte Carlo rendering calculations. These techniques are practical, and the additional cost is small—less than 10% of the time in our tests was spent evaluating probabilities and weighting functions. We also have strong bounds on their performance relative to other combination strategies.

Overall, we found that the power heuristic (with $\beta=2$) gave the best results. It is similar to the balance heuristic in general, but has significantly lower variance when one of the p_i is a good match for f. When none of the given sampling distributions is a good match for f (e.g. Fig. 6), the differences among the various weighting strategies are small.

5.2 Choosing the number of samples

First, observe that no strategy is greatly superior to that of simply setting all c_i equal. If we are allocating N samples among n sampling techniques, it is easy to show that

$$V[\hat{F}] \leq nV[F] + \frac{n-1}{N}\mathcal{F}^2$$

where $\hat{F}$ uses the balance heuristic with all c_i equal, and F uses any unbiased weighting functions and c_i (satisfying $\sum_i w_i = 1$ and $w_i \equiv 0$ if $c_i = 0$). Thus, changing the c_i can improve the variance by at most a factor of n, plus a small additive term. On the other hand, a poor choice of the w_i (e.g. a poor partitioning of the integration domain) can increase variance by an arbitrary amount.

Also, there are situations where the c_i are naturally constrained. For example, in bidirectional path tracing it is more efficient to take one sample from all distributions at once (Sec. 4.3). In the glossy highlights example, the c_i are constrained because the samples are used for other purposes (direct lighting samples for the diffuse component, and directional samples for glossy reflections of objects other than light sources). Often these other purposes will dictate the number of samples taken. In this case, by taking a weighted combination of both types of samples we can reduce the variance of the highlight calculation essentially for free.

5.3 Comments on direct lighting

The examples of Sec. 4.1, 4.2 are essentially direct lighting problems. They differ only in the terms of the reflectance equation that cause high variance—the BRDF, the $1/r^2$ distance term, or the emitted radiance distribution L_{e}.

In Sec. 4.2, we used a simple light source sampling technique. Although there are more sophisticated techniques for direct lighting[13], it can still be useful to combine several kinds of samples. Observe that *any* strategy for sampling a group of patches as light sources induces some probability distribution on the patch surfaces. Since these strategies are always approximations, some factors of the reflectance equation (2) will not be approximated well. In parts of the scene where these omitted factors become dominant, simple directional sampling can be more efficient. By combining both kinds of samples, we can make such strategies more robust.

Shirley and Wang[12] also compare directional and area sampling techniques for glossy highlights (Sec. 4.1). They analyze a specific Phong-like BRDF and light source sampling method, and derive an expression for when to switch from one to the other (as a function of surface roughness and light source solid angle). In contrast, our methods work for general BRDF's and sampling techniques, and can combine samples from any number of distributions.

5.4 Approximating the weighting functions

The models in Sec. 3 assume that given a sample X_i from distribution p_i, we can compute $p_j(x)$ exactly for all other j. Sometimes this is problematic—e.g. $p_j(x)$ may be expensive or complicated to evaluate. More difficulties arise when a sampling technique p_j uses random numbers that cannot be determined from the resulting sample point x. For example, some direct lighting strategies[13] generate several candidate sample points x_i, and then choose one randomly. Given an arbitrary point x, it is difficult to evaluate

$p_j(x)$ because this probability depends on information other than the sample location x itself.

The easiest way to handle these problems is to recall that the results are unbiased as long as $\sum_i w_i(x) = 1$. When computing the w_i, it is perfectly reasonable to use an approximation p'_j of the true probabilities p_j. This will give unbiased results even if the approximations p'_j are poor, as long as they are consistently used (i.e. $p'_j(X_i)$ does not depend on i). Of course, poor approximations may lead to increased variance. Note that $p_i(X_i)$ must always be evaluated exactly in (11) to avoid bias; however this is required of any unbiased Monte Carlo algorithm.

5.5 Future work

We would like to explore other applications where it makes sense to use several sampling distributions. Even within the framework of global illumination, there are many such problems. For example, bidirectional path tracing can be used to estimate the coefficients of basis functions defined on scene surfaces (let W_p in (5) be the dual basis function). This is an unexplored alternative to particle tracing models for Monte Carlo radiosity, and may be an effective solution to the problem of patches that do not receive enough particles.

We think that there is great potential for designing better sampling distributions—we hope that the existence of good methods to combine the samples will spur further work in this area. Again, global illumination provides a rich framework, because of the complexity of the domain and the integrand.

Another interesting problem is how to choose the c_i. One research area is the derivation of *a priori* rules for specific applications (similar to [12]). Another goal is to find strategies for the general case; adaptive methods seem promising here. Note that adaptive methods can introduce bias, unless two-stage sampling is used [7].

Acknowledgments

Thanks to Pat Hanrahan, Marc Levoy, Luanne Lemmer, and the anonymous reviewers for helpful comments that improved the presentation. Discussions with John Tukey were also useful. Thanks to Bill Kalsow for answering lots of questions about Modula-3 [10], the language we used for our rendering system. This research was supported by the National Science Foundation (CCR-9215219), the Digital Systems Research Center, and the Digital External Research Program.

References

[1] J. Arvo and D. Kirk. Particle transport and image synthesis. *Computer Graphics (SIGGRAPH '90 Proceedings)*, **24**, 63–66 (1990).

[2] S. Chen, H. Rushmeier, G. Miller, and D. Turner. A progressive multipass method for global illumination. *Computer Graphics (SIGGRAPH '91 Proceedings)*, **25**, 165–174 (1991).

[3] M. Cohen and J. Wallace. *Radiosity and Realistic Image Synthesis*. Academic Press, 1993.

[4] R. Cook, T. Porter, and L. Carpenter. Distributed ray tracing. *Computer Graphics (SIGGRAPH '84 Proceedings)*, **18**, 137–146 (1984).

[5] J. Kajiya. The rendering equation. *Computer Graphics (SIGGRAPH '86 Proceedings)*, **20**, 143–150 (1986).

[6] M. Kalos and P. Whitlock. *Monte Carlo Methods, Volume I: Basics*. J. Wiley, New York, 1986.

[7] D. Kirk and J. Arvo. Unbiased sampling techniques for image synthesis. *Computer Graphics (SIGGRAPH '91)*, **25**, 153–156 (1991).

[8] E. Lafortune and Y. Willems. Bi-directional path tracing. *Proceedings of CompuGraphics*, Alvor, Portugal, 145–153 (Dec. 1993).

[9] E. Lafortune, Y. Willems. A theoretical framework for physically based rendering. *Computer Graphics Forum*, **13**(2), 97–108 (1994).

[10] G. Nelson, editor. *Systems Programming with Modula-3*. Prentice Hall, 1991. An implementation of Modula-3 is available at http://www.research.digital.com/SRC/.

[11] H. Rushmeier. *Realistic Image Synthesis for Scenes with Radiatively Participating Media*. Doctoral Thesis, Cornell University, May 1988.

[12] P. Shirley and C. Wang. Distribution ray tracing: theory and practice. *Proceedings of the Third Eurographics Workshop on Rendering*, Bristol, England, 33–44 (1992).

[13] P. Shirley, C. Wang, and K. Zimmerman. Monte Carlo Techniques for Direct Lighting Calculations. *ACM Transactions on Graphics*, to appear.

[14] E. Veach and L. Guibas. Bidirectional estimators for light transport. *Proceedings of the Fifth Eurographics Workshop on Rendering*, Darmstadt, Germany, 147–162 (June 1994).

Appendix A   Proofs

Proof of Thm. 1:   The variance is

$$V[F] = V\left[\sum_{i=1}^{n}\frac{1}{n_i}\sum_{j=1}^{n_i}F_{i,j}\right] \text{ where } F_{i,j} = \frac{w_i(X_{i,j})f(X_{i,j})}{p_i(X_{i,j})}$$

$$= \sum_{i=1}^{n}\frac{1}{n_i^2}\sum_{j=1}^{n_i}E[F_{i,j}^2] - \sum_{i=1}^{n}\frac{1}{n_i^2}\sum_{j=1}^{n_i}E[F_{i,j}]^2$$

where the covariance terms are zero because the $X_{i,j}$ are sampled independently. We bound the two terms separately. For the first term, we get

$$\sum_{i=1}^{n}\frac{1}{n_i^2}\sum_{j=1}^{n_i}E[F_{i,j}^2] = \int_\Omega \sum_{i=1}^{n}\frac{w_i^2(x)f^2(x)}{n_i p_i(x)}\,d\mu(x) \ .$$

Using the method of Lagrange multipliers, we minimize the integrand independently at each point x subject to the condition $\sum_i w_i = 1$. Noting that $f^2(x)$ is a constant and dropping x from our notation, we must minimize

$$\sum_i \frac{w_i^2}{n_i p_i} + \lambda\left(\sum_i w_i - 1\right) \ .$$

Setting all $n+1$ partial derivatives to zero, we obtain $w_i = \hat{w}_i$ (12). Thus no other weighting strategy can reduce this term further.

The second term makes a negative contribution to the variance, so we will prove an upper bound $\mathcal{F}^2/\min_i n_i$ for the w_i and a lower bound $\mathcal{F}^2/\sum_i n_i$ for the $\hat{w}_i$. Letting $\mu_i = E[F_{i,j}]$ (this is independent of j), for the upper bound we have

$$\sum_{i=1}^{n}\frac{1}{n_i^2}\sum_{j=1}^{n_i}\mu_i^2 = \sum_{i=1}^{n}\frac{1}{n_i}\mu_i^2 \le \frac{1}{\min_i n_i}\sum_{i=1}^{n}\mu_i^2 \ .$$

Since $\sum_i \mu_i = \mathcal{F}$, we have $\max_i \mu_i \le \mathcal{F}$, and thus $\sum_i \mu_i^2 \le \mathcal{F}^2$ which proves the upper bound. The lower bound $\sum_i \hat{\mu}_i^2/n_i \ge \mathcal{F}^2/\sum_i n_i$ is easily proven with Lagrange multipliers. ∎

Proof of Thm. 2:   Because $\mathcal{F}^2$ is fixed in (8), it is enough to minimize the second moment $E[F^2]$. We have

$$E[F^2] = \int_\Omega \sum_{i=1}^{n}\frac{w_i^2(x)f^2(x)}{c_i p_i(x)}\,d\mu(x) \ ,$$

which is virtually identical to the second moment term that we minimized in the proof of Thm. 1. ∎

We also present worst-case bounds for the weighting heuristics from Sec. 3.4. The bounds have the form

$$V[\hat{F}] \le cV[F^*] + \left(\frac{1}{\min_i n_i} - \frac{1}{\sum_i n_i}\right)\mathcal{F}^2 \ ,$$

where $\hat{F}$ uses the indicated heuristic, and F^* uses the (unknown) optimal weighting functions. For the cutoff heuristic, we can show $c = 1 + \alpha(n-1)$, while for the power heuristic we can show

$$c = 1 + \frac{1}{\beta}((n-1)(\beta-1))^{1-1/\beta} \ .$$

When $\beta = 2$, we can prove the stronger bound $c = \frac{1}{2}(1 + \sqrt{n})$.

Analytic Antialiasing with Prism Splines

Michael D. McCool*
Computer Graphics Laboratory, University of Waterloo

ABSTRACT

The theory of the multivariate polyhedral splines is applied to analytic antialiasing: a triangular simplex spline is used to represent surface intensity, while a box spline is used as a filter. Their continuous convolution is a *prism spline* that can be evaluated exactly via recurrence. Evaluation performance can be maximized by exploiting the properties of the prism spline and its relationship to the sampling grid. After sampling, digital signal processing can be used to evaluate exactly and efficiently the sampled result of any analytic spline filter in the span of the box spline basis used as the original analytic filter.

1 INTRODUCTION

Splines are most often used in computer graphics as modelling primitives. However, their powerful approximation and signal processing properties can also be used to advantage in the representation and processing of image intensities.

A long-standing problem in computer graphics is aliasing: the appearance of jaggies, Moiré patterns, and other undesirable artifacts caused by undersampling. Under the assumptions of linear systems theory, aliasing can be eliminated by convolving the image with a low pass filter *before* sampling [16]. For images, doing such filtering exactly requires a multivariate integration, which is not only often analytically difficult but requires a representation of the image as a generalized function defined over the real plane. The multivariate *polyhedral splines* provide a mechanism for both the representation of the image and the exact analytic computation of the convolution.

Polyhedral splines are formed from sums of multivariate piecewise polynomial basis functions defined by the projection of n-dimensional convex polyhedra (or more correctly, polytopes) into m-dimensional space, with $m \leq n$. Some examples are given in Figure 1. Polyhedral spline basis functions are generalizations of the univariate B-spline basis functions; the latter can be viewed either as projections of simplices[†] or (in the uniform case) hypercubes. An important property of the polyhedral splines is the fact that convolving two polyhedral spline basis functions is equivalent to projecting the Cartesian product of the two defining polytopes.

---

*Department of Computer Science, University of Waterloo, Waterloo, Ontario, Canada N2L 3G1, (519) 888-4567 x4422,
mmccool@cgl.uwaterloo.ca
http://www.cgl.uwaterloo.ca/~mmccool/

[†]A *simplex* is a generalized triangle, defined as the convex hull of $n+1$ points in $\mathbb{R}^n$. See Grünbaum [10].

Permission to make digital/hard copy of part or all of this work for personal or classroom use is granted without fee provided that copies are not made or distributed for profit or commercial advantage, the copyright notice, the title of the publication and its date appear, and notice is given that copying is by permission of ACM, Inc. To copy otherwise, to republish, to post on servers, or to redistribute to lists, requires prior specific permission and/or a fee.

This elegant convolution property can be used to derive filtering algorithms for analytic antialiasing.

Our result advances the state of the art by providing not only high quality analytical antialiasing but also a connection to a variety of useful spline techniques. Polyhedral spline techniques can also potentially be extended to other rendering tasks that require multivariate integration.

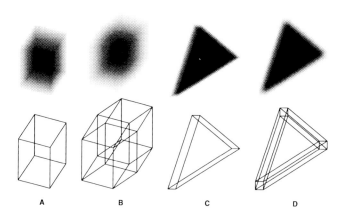

Figure 1: Some sample polyhedral spline basis functions and maps of their discontinuities. Multivariate generalizations of B-spline basis functions, polyhedral spline basis functions are projections of n-dimensional convex polytopes. On the left (A,B) we show two box splines, which are projections of hypercubes. The prism splines on the right are formed by (C) convolving a triangle with a segment (a degenerate 1D box spline) and (D) a square (a 2D box spline).

2 BACKGROUND AND PRIOR ART

Both antialiasing and polyhedral splines have had a long history of development in their respective subdisciplines. Here a short review of the relevant theory is given, along with some highlights of the literature.

2.1 Analytic Antialiasing

We review only analytic or near-analytic antialiasing techniques here, and assume the reader is familiar with the linear theory describing the causes of aliasing [16]. Approximate supersampling and subdivision techniques for antialiasing are also important, but are beyond the scope of this paper, as are specific techniques for texture antialiasing. We also only consider linear convolutional antialiasing, although other, nonlinear approaches are possible [12].

Feibush, Levoy and Cook [6] proposed a table based near-analytic antialiasing technique that could filter constant shaded polygons with radially symmetric filter functions. This approach was based on the precomputation of antialiased triangles and the decomposition of general polygons into summations of triangles.

Grant [9] generalized this technique to antialiased motion blur, using a tetrahedral decomposition of space-time.

Area sampling, as proposed by Catmull [2], was the first truly analytic antialiasing technique. Area sampling clips polygons to the extent of each pixel and weights the contribution of each polygon to the pixel by its clipped area. This technique can only support constant shaded polygons and box filtering, and is not entirely successful at removing aliasing artifacts. By scaling the filter, Catmull could approximate motion blur but without proper interpenetration or occlusion. Extensions of area sampling include beam [11] and cone sampling [1], which are generalizations of ray tracing.

Duff [5] extended Catmull's approach by replacing the area computation with a contour integral. He also describes several optimizations that exploit the coherence of scan-conversion. In theory, Duff's technique can handle any filter function and any intensity variation as long as the required integrals are computable. However, both Duff and Catmull's techniques require potentially expensive clips to the boundaries of each pixel.

Finally, Max [13] proposed a hybrid scanline technique which analytically antialiases one dimension and supersamples in the other.

2.2 Polyhedral Splines

Only a short sketch of the relevant polyhedral spline theory is possible here. The reader is referred to the references [4, 8, 14] for more information.

Polyhedral spline basis functions are based on projections of n-dimensional convex polytopes into n-dimensional space. Simplices lead to simplex splines, hypercubes lead to box splines, and infinite polyhedral cones lead to cone splines. The cone splines are a generalization of the truncated power functions $[\max(x, 0)]^n$ used in univariate B-spline theory.

If Ξ is an $m \times n$ projection matrix that maps $\mathbb{R}^n$ to $\mathbb{R}^m$ and $\mathcal{B}$ is a convex n-dimensional polytope, then at the point $\mathbf{x} \in \mathbb{R}^m$ the value of the polyhedral spline $M_{\mathcal{B}}(\mathbf{x}|\Xi)$ is given[‡] by

$$M_{\mathcal{B}}(\mathbf{x}|\Xi) = \mathrm{vol}_{n-m}\left(\Xi^{-1}\mathbf{x} \cap \mathcal{B}\right).$$

Here we use the set-valued inverse Ξ^{-1}, where $\Xi^{-1}\mathbf{x}$ is an $(n-m)$-dimensional affine subspace given by $\{\mathbf{z} : \mathbf{x} = \Xi\mathbf{z}\}$; thus the value of a polyhedral spline at a point is equal to the $(n-m)$-dimensional volume of the slice of the defining polytope that projects to that point.

Polyhedral splines satisfy the following recurrence [8] which is a generalization of the de Boor recurrence for univariate B-splines. Let the convex n-dimensional polytope $\mathcal{B}$ have s faces $\mathcal{B}_i$ each of dimension $n-1$. Let each face $\mathcal{B}_i$ have normal $\mathbf{n}_i$, and let $\mathbf{b}_i$ be any point in the plane of $\mathcal{B}_i$. Then $\mathcal{B}_i$ lies in the affine subspace given by all points $\mathbf{y}$ such that $\mathbf{n}_i \cdot (\mathbf{b}_i - \mathbf{y}) = 0$. Let $\mathbf{z} \in \mathbb{R}^n$ be any point that satisfies $\mathbf{x} = \Xi\mathbf{z}$ with $\mathbf{x} \in \mathbb{R}^m$. Then

$$(n - m)M_{\mathcal{B}}(\mathbf{x}|\Xi) = \sum_{i=1}^{s} \mathbf{n}_i \cdot (\mathbf{b}_i - \mathbf{z})M_{\mathcal{B}_i}(\mathbf{x}|\Xi_i').$$

Here Ξ_i' is a projection of Ξ to the plane of $\mathcal{B}_i$.

Box splines are projections of the unit hypercube $\square_n = \times_{i=1}^{n}[0, 1]$; they have the following property, which is reminiscent of the recursive convolutional definition of the uniform univariate

B-splines:

$$M_{\square_0}(\mathbf{x}) = \delta(\mathbf{x});$$
$$M_{\square_n}(\mathbf{x}|\Xi) = \int_0^1 M_{\square_{n-1}}(\mathbf{x} - \tau\boldsymbol{\xi}_n|\Xi\backslash\boldsymbol{\xi}_n)\, d\tau.$$

Here $\Xi\backslash\boldsymbol{\xi}_n$ refers to the removal of the column vector $\boldsymbol{\xi}_n$ from Ξ. The column vectors $\boldsymbol{\xi}_i$ of the projection matrix Ξ can be interpreted as the directions in which the spline is "smeared" during each step of the above recursion. Often, these *direction vectors* will be repeated, in which case we say $\boldsymbol{\xi}_i$ is of *multiplicity* μ_i. It should be noted that the m-dimensional uniform tensor product B-spline basis is a box spline with only m unique direction vectors; the multiplicity of each direction vector determines the order of the spline in that direction.

A simpler evaluation recurrence can be derived specifically for box splines. Assume that there are r unique vectors $\boldsymbol{\xi}_i \in \Xi$, each with multiplicity μ_i. Choose m vectors $\boldsymbol{\xi}_{j_1}, \ldots, \boldsymbol{\xi}_{j_m}$ from Ξ that form a basis of $\mathbb{R}^m$, and invert this basis to find $\mathbf{z}$ such that $\mathbf{x} = \Xi\mathbf{z}$, with $\mathbf{x} = \sum_{k=1}^{m} z_{j_k}\boldsymbol{\xi}_{j_k}$; set the remaining $n - m$ elements of $\mathbf{z}$ to zero and index them with $\{j_k\}_{m+1}^{n}$. Now the recurrence is given by

$$(n - m)M_{\square_n}(\mathbf{x}|\Xi)$$
$$= \sum_{k=1}^{m} z_{j_k} M_{\square_{n-1}}(\mathbf{x}|\Xi\backslash\boldsymbol{\xi}_{j_k})$$
$$+ \sum_{k=1}^{m} (\mu_{j_k} - z_{j_k})M_{\square_{n-1}}(\mathbf{x} - \boldsymbol{\xi}_{j_k}|\Xi\backslash\boldsymbol{\xi}_{j_k})$$
$$+ \sum_{k=m+1}^{n} \mu_{j_k} M_{\square_{n-1}}(\mathbf{x} - \boldsymbol{\xi}_{j_k}|\Xi\backslash\boldsymbol{\xi}_{j_k}).$$

The recursive convolution property satisfied by box splines is an instance of an important general theorem. If $M_{\mathcal{F}}(\mathbf{x}|F)$ and $M_{\mathcal{G}}(\mathbf{x}|G)$ are polyhedral splines, then their convolution is a polyhedral spline derived by forming the Cartesian product of the polytopes $\mathcal{F}$ and $\mathcal{G}$ and concatenating the projection matrices:

$$M_{\mathcal{F}}(\mathbf{x}|F) * M_{\mathcal{G}}(\mathbf{x}|G) = M_{\mathcal{F}\times\mathcal{G}}(\mathbf{x}|[F, G]).$$

When $\mathcal{F}$ is the interval $[0, 1]$ and $\mathcal{G}$ is a unit hypercube, the convolution property of the box splines given above develops. However, if the polytopes $\mathcal{F}$ and $\mathcal{G}$ are of different types, a hybrid is formed. A *prism spline* is a hybridization of a simplex spline and a box spline.

3 PRISM SPLINE EVALUATION

Simplex splines can support the approximation of functions defined on arbitrary triangular grids [3, 7]. Images that arise in rendering can be cast in this form by tessellation of curved objects, geometric hidden surface removal, and finally subdivision of any non-triangular polygons. Gouraud shading corresponds to the use of linear interpolation and can be evaluated with a sum of three linear simplex splines. A linear simplex spline is the projection of a tetrahedron into two dimensions. If two corners of the tetrahedron project to a single vertex of a triangle, a function results which has a triangular support, is zero at the corners corresponding to the projections of the single vertices of the tetrahedron, and ramps linearly up to the remaining double vertex corner. By mapping the extra vertex of the tetrahedron to each corner of a triangle in turn we derive the basis functions for linear interpolation. Gouraud shaded triangles will provide the examples we will use in our results. Other choices, including higher order simplex splines, are also possible.

Once the image function has been described as a summation of simplex spline basis functions, it can be filtered by convolving each

---

[‡]This is an informal definition. Formal definitions are based on a test function ϕ from a given continuity class and the distributional identity $\int_{\mathbb{R}^m} M_{\mathcal{B}}(\mathbf{x}|\Xi)\phi(\mathbf{x})\, d\mathbf{x} = \int_{\mathbb{R}^n} \phi(\Xi\mathbf{z})\, d\mathbf{z}.$

simplex spline with a box spline filter. The filtered image is thus a summation of prism splines.

An evaluation recurrence for a prism spline can be derived by slicing a higher-dimensional box spline [14]. This is convenient because the box spline already has a simple evaluation recurrence and we can avoid a derivation of the prism spline recurrence from first principles. However, the basic recurrence is too expensive, so in Section 3.2 we give several techniques for optimizing the recurrence statically and dynamically. Term reuse is particularly important, but we also give incremental algorithms which are especially useful in the context of a renderer.

3.1 Prism Spline Recurrence

We can evaluate a prism spline by slicing a box spline of one higher dimension by a hyperplane. Consider Figure 2. Let w be the last element of each three-dimensional direction vector $\boldsymbol{\theta}_i$; a three-dimensional box spline is described by a matrix Θ of n direction vectors $\boldsymbol{\theta}_i$ arranged as column vectors. Relative to the slice $w = 1$, direction vectors describing a simplex spline emanate from the origin to the plane $w = 1$, while direction vectors describing box spline filters are parallel to this plane and have $w = 0$.

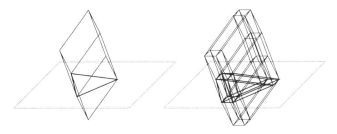

Figure 2: A prism spline can be interpreted as a slice of a box spline. Here the derivation for a constant triangle and a box filtered constant triangle are shown as particular slices of a box spline. Direction vectors from the origin to the plane define the triangle, while direction vectors parallel to the plane define the filter.

Given a matrix Ξ of n two-dimensional direction vectors $\boldsymbol{\xi}_i$ describing a box spline filter and a set V of $k + 1$ two-dimensional points $\mathbf{v}_j$ describing the vertices of a simplex spline, form the $m + 1 \times n + k + 1$ matrix Θ as follows:

$$\Theta = \left[\left[\begin{array}{c} \boldsymbol{\xi}_1 \\ 0 \end{array} \right] \cdots \left[\begin{array}{c} \boldsymbol{\xi}_n \\ 0 \end{array} \right] \left[\begin{array}{c} \mathbf{v}_1 \\ 1 \end{array} \right] \cdots \left[\begin{array}{c} \mathbf{v}_{k+1} \\ 1 \end{array} \right] \right].$$

Choose a basis Z of $m + 1$ linearly independent vectors from Θ, and compute $\mathbf{z} = Z^{-1}[\mathbf{x}, 1]^T$ for $\mathbf{x} \in \mathbb{R}^m$. Then a recurrence for the $(n + k)$th order prism spline $P_{n+k}(\mathbf{x}|\Xi, V)$ is given by

$$(n + k - m)P_{n+k}(\mathbf{x}|\Xi, V)$$
$$= \sum_{[\boldsymbol{\xi}_i, 0]^T \in Z} z_i P_{n-1+k}(\mathbf{x}|\Xi \backslash \boldsymbol{\xi}_i, V)$$
$$+ \sum_{[\boldsymbol{\xi}_i, 0]^T \in Z} (\mu_i - z_i) P_{n-1+k}(\mathbf{x} - \boldsymbol{\xi}_i|\Xi \backslash \boldsymbol{\xi}_i, V)$$
$$+ \sum_{[\boldsymbol{\xi}_i, 0]^T \notin Z} \mu_i P_{n-1+k}(\mathbf{x} - \boldsymbol{\xi}_i|\Xi \backslash \boldsymbol{\xi}_i, V)$$
$$+ \sum_{[\mathbf{v}_j, 1]^T \in Z} z_j P_{n+k-1}(\mathbf{x}|\Xi, V \backslash \mathbf{v}_j).$$

Suppose that we wish to render an image with antialiased Gouraud shaded, i.e. linearly interpolated, triangular primitives.

We will begin with constant triangles, filter them, and then generalize to triangular linear interpolation basis functions.

With $\Theta_{111} = [\boldsymbol{\theta}_1, \boldsymbol{\theta}_2, \boldsymbol{\theta}_3]$, let

$$M_{111}(x, y, w) = M_{\square_3}(x, y, w|\Theta_{111}).$$

The subscript 111 is used to indicate the unit multiplicity of each of the direction vectors $\boldsymbol{\theta}_i = [\mathbf{v}_i, 1]^T$. $P_{111}(x, y) = M_{111}(x, y, 1)$ defines an unfiltered constant triangle. Convolution of this triangle with a tensor product B-spline for the purposes of filtering is accomplished by adding the appropriate direction vectors with $w = 0$:

$$M_{111nn}(x, y, w)$$
$$= M_{111}(x, y, w) * M_{\square_{2n}} \left(\mathbf{x} \left| \left[\left[\begin{array}{c} \boldsymbol{\xi}_x \\ 0 \end{array} \right]^n \left[\begin{array}{c} \boldsymbol{\xi}_y \\ 0 \end{array} \right]^n \right] \right) \right.$$
$$= M_{\square_{3+2n}}(\mathbf{x}|[\Theta, \boldsymbol{\theta}_x^n, \boldsymbol{\theta}_y^n]),$$

where $\boldsymbol{\xi}_x = [1, 0]^T$ and $\boldsymbol{\xi}_y = [0, 1]^T$ are packed into $\boldsymbol{\theta}_x$ and $\boldsymbol{\theta}_y$ and each is repeated n times. Slice this filtered box spline to obtain a filtered triangle: $P_{111nn}(x, y) = M_{111nn}(x, y, 1)$. Finally, we repeat each of the vectors defining the corners of the triangle in turn to obtain symmetric basis functions for a filtered *linear* interpolant: $P_{211nn}(x, y)$, $P_{121nn}(x, y)$, and $P_{112nn}(x, y)$. A two-dimensional version of this process is shown in Figure 3.

Figure 3: In the upper row, the constant and linear interpolation basis functions in one dimension are derived by slicing a two dimensional box spline. By adding direction vectors parallel to the plane of the slice, we can filter these basis functions, as shown in the lower row.

The z_{j_k} factors used in the recurrence are coordinates relative to each of the possible choices of direction vectors. In order to compute the z_{j_k} needed in each term of the recurrence, we have to invert ten (5 choose 3) 3×3 matrices. However, most of these inverses are trivial as a consequence of the special form of $\boldsymbol{\theta}_y$ and $\boldsymbol{\theta}_x$. If only one of these vectors is chosen in a given basis, then the corresponding inverse computes coordinates of a point relative to an edge of the triangle. If two are chosen, coordinates are evaluated relative to the corner of a triangle, and the transformation amounts simply to a translation. The one non-trivial inverse involves $\boldsymbol{\theta}_1$, $\boldsymbol{\theta}_2$, and $\boldsymbol{\theta}_3$ but this is simply an evaluation of the barycentric coordinates of a point within the triangle $\mathbf{v}_1 \mathbf{v}_2 \mathbf{v}_3$, and can be evaluated through Gouraud interpolation.

As with Gouraud interpolation, the z_{j_k} coordinates for every choice of three basis vectors from Θ can be updated incrementally; in addition to the standard barycentric coordinates, six other coordinate systems defined relative to the edges need to be updated. The corner coordinates are so inexpensive to compute that incremental update is normally not advantageous.

A problem can arise if an edge of a triangle is perfectly (or nearly) horizontal or vertical; one of the edge coordinate systems will collapse. The theoretically justified solution is to set the offending term of the recurrence to zero, as the corresponding transformed polytope has zero volume. At polytope edges (which project to discontinuities in the spline) it is also important to evaluate only *one* of the incident faces. This can be accomplished by treating the supports of the lowest level constant box splines as semi-open.

3.2 Recurrence Optimization

Simply following the prism spline evaluation recurrence blindly will lead to a combinatoric-time algorithm unsuitable for a rendering system. Fortunately, because of the form of the vectors θ_x and θ_y the recurrence is redundant and the following optimizations can be made:

1. Terms can appear more than once in the evaluation tree. By sharing terms the tree can be converted into a directed acyclic graph (DAG), resulting in a polynomial-time algorithm.

2. Many terms in the recurrence are zero for any given evaluation point. This can be exploited dynamically by checking the current evaluation point against the convex support of the subspline.

3. If a prism spline is sampled on a grid defined by some of its direction vectors, terms in previous recurrence evaluations can be reused. This leads to incremental algorithms.

4. Only two of the basis functions P_{211nn}, P_{121nn}, and P_{112nn} need to be evaluated and combined with P_{111nn}, which would be part of either recurrence tree anyway.

5. The two remaining basis functions share many of the same recurrence terms, and can be evaluated simultaneously.

6. Recurrence terms and coordinate system evaluations from adjacent primitives can be reused, particularly along shared edges.

7. A decomposition of the underlying sliced box spline into a difference of truncated power functions (cone splines) leads to an incremental algorithm that eliminates the need to remember terms from previous recurrences. Unfortunately, this optimization risks some numerical instability and precludes most other optimizations.

8. Terms of the form $P_{001\ell k}$, $P_{010\ell k}$ and $P_{100\ell k}$ can be evaluated as tensor product B-splines. Likewise, terms of the form $P_{011\ell 0}$, $P_{101\ell 0}$, $P_{110\ell 0}$, P_{0110k}, P_{1010k}, and P_{1100k} can be evaluated using univariate B-splines. Unfortunately, for higher orders of filters both kinds of terms become relatively sparse.

9. Finally, recurrence terms can be evaluated and statically optimized offline. A code generator can be used to define the inner loop of the scan convertor.

Some of these optimizations are in conflict. For example, simultaneously applying both support culling (2) and the cone spline optimization (7) is not worthwhile, because cone splines have semi-infinite support. Likewise, not all these optimizations lead to the same increase in performance. Some attempt has been made to present the most useful optimizations first in the list above.

In the following sections some additional discussion is given to the most useful but less obvious optimizations: recurrence term reuse (1), support culling (2) and incremental algorithms (3).

3.2.1 Recurrence Term Reuse

The recurrence for the prism spline is similar to the de Boor recurrence for the univariate B-splines. The latter is an efficient evaluation technique because of the existence and reuse of repeated terms. Consider Figure 4, which shows an application of the de Boor recurrence to evaluate a segment of an order n B-spline curve. This algorithm is $O(n^2)$ because of the shared terms; without sharing, it would be $O(2^n)$.

Now consider Figure 5, which shows the recurrence for the prism spline P_{11111}. The recurrence graph is no longer planar, but we see that some sharing does occur. For higher orders of filter, the sharing becomes even more important.

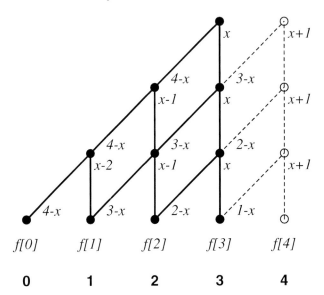

Figure 4: Points on B-spline curves can be evaluated using an $O(n^2)$ triangular algorithm. The evaluations shown are for the segment of a uniform cubic B-spline over $x \in [3, 4]$. Dashed lines show how a sample at the same joint-relative position, $x + 1 \in [4, 5)$, can be evaluated incrementally in only $O(n)$ time. The linear weights at each level of the recurrence are shown here without normalization factors.

The code generator implements term reuse by recording the existence and name of every term as it is generated during a postorder traversal of the recurrence tree. This record is called a *memo table*. When a term is needed, the table is first checked to see if it has already been computed. To implement sharing of terms between the recurrences for the prism splines P_{211nn} and P_{121nn} the memo table is simply not cleared between the generation of terms.

3.2.2 Support Culling

At a given point in the interior of the spline typically only a few terms in the recurrence are non-zero. In Figure 5, the non-zero terms for an evaluation point are emboldened. We can reduce the amount of work we have to do considerably if we can quickly determine which terms are non-zero.

The supports of all subsplines are convex, and are intersections of a finite number of halfspaces. The borders of these halfspaces, in turn, are translates of an even smaller number of lines. In the case of the tensor product prism spline, three lines are due to the edges of the triangle and two are the result of ξ_x and ξ_y.

Point-against-convex-support tests can be implemented efficiently with outcodes. First, the evaluation point is tested against each halfspace; the result (in or out) is stored as a bit in an integer.

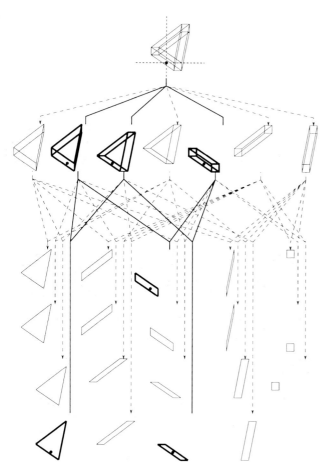

Figure 5: The recurrence tree of a prism spline evaluated at the point indicated with a dot is shown, with non-zero recurrence terms emboldened. Note that shared faces are evaluated twice and that any particular point in the support of the spline only involves a limited subgraph of the recurrence tree.

These tests can also take advantage of the redundancy that exists in the specification of the halfspaces. Halfspaces that are just translates of one another can reuse partial results from previous tests, perhaps even short-circuiting later evaluations. Before each recurrence term is evaluated, the outcode integer is masked and compared to a bit pattern unique to that term. If the bit pattern does not match, the evaluation point is not inside the support of the term, and evaluation can be avoided.

The interior of the triangle is a special case. Here we can drop back to simple linear interpolation (in the context of a linearly interpolated prism spline) because in the absence of edge effects a linear function is reproduced under convolution with a symmetric filter. Of course, the interior of the triangle vanishes if the minimum dimension of the triangle is smaller than the filter diameter.

3.2.3 Incremental Algorithms

Figure 4 shows another optimization in the evaluation of the uniform univariate B-spline: a new sample can be generated in $O(n)$ time if it is spaced at a unit distance from the last sample and a subset of the old recurrence terms are recalled.

Something similar can be done for the prism spline. The existence of ξ_x and ξ_y result in many recurrence terms shifted by 1 in x and y. Rather than regenerate these shifted values, the unshifted values can be recalled from the last recurrence evaluation. Initial-

ization requires setting recurrence terms outside the support of the spline to zero.

Terms can be recalled for both x and y. This requires storage for an entire scanline of partial results and the resulting data movement may degrade performance. *Scanline* incremental algorithms remember terms only from the very last evaluation. This limits the performance improvement, but results in much less memory use and fits in quite nicely with scanline rendering.

4 DIGITAL POSTPROCESSING

The prism splines only allow analytic filtering with box spline basis functions, including as a special case the tensor product B-spline basis functions. This is in fact sufficient to support all analytic filter functions that can be expressed as splines relative to these bases, because of the relationship

$$(f(x) * \phi(x))(i) = f[i] \star (B(x) * \phi(x))(i).$$

which depends only on the linearity and shift-invariance of convolution. Here $*$ is continuous convolution, $\star$ is discrete convolution, $\phi(x)$ is an input signal, and $f(x)$ is a filter function defined by $f(x) = \sum_i f[i]B(x - i)$ relative to a basis function $B(x)$.

No approximations are necessary. If we apply a digital filter with coefficients $f[i]$ to samples of $B(x) * \phi(x)$ at the integers, we will achieve exactly the same result as if we had originally applied the filter $f(x)$ analytically to $\phi(x)$ and *then* sampled the result at the integers. Since we have made no assumptions in the above regarding the dimension of the parameter space, this result also applies in multiple dimensions. The result actually applies to any shift-invariant basis function but is most useful in the context of a tensor product B-spline basis because of its separability.

Useful analytic filters with infinite support relative to the separable tensor product B-spline basis can be represented with efficient univariate recursive digital filters. Recursive filters reuse old output values to obtain infinite impulse responses with a finite amount of arithmetic. For example, the inner loop of a causal recursive filter with input sequence $g[i]$ and output sequence $f[i]$ is

$$f[i] \leftarrow \sum_{j=j_0}^{j_1} a_j g[i-j] + \sum_{k=1}^{m} b_k f[i-k] \text{ for } i \text{ increasing.}$$

An anticausal filter runs in the opposite direction:

$$f[i] \leftarrow \sum_{j=j_0}^{j_1} c_j g[i-j] + \sum_{k=1}^{m} d_k f[i+k] \text{ for } i \text{ decreasing.}$$

A *linear* filter has $m = 1$ and so recycles only one output value. A *quadratic* filter recycles two output values with $m = 2$.

The *fundamental spline* and the *smoothing spline* bases are useful alternative antialiasing filters and can be generated with cascaded causal and anticausal recursive filters [15] with $m = 1$ and $m = 2$ respectively.

Fundamental splines interpolate their control points. A recursive filter for converting the control points of a fundamental spline to those for an equivalent B-spline can be found by inverting the relationship $g[i] = f[i] \star b^{n,c}[i]$. Here the $g[i]$ are the samples to interpolate and the discrete centered B-spline basis $b^{n,c}[i] = B^{n,c}(i)$ with $B^{n,c}(x) = B^n(x + n/2)$. Let $b^{-n,c}[i]$ be the convolutional inverse of $b^{n,c}[i]$; it can be generated with a pair of linear causal/anticausal recursive digital filters applied to an impulse $\delta[i]$. Each of these recursive filters only needs to recall one past output value.

The sequence $b^{-n,c}[i]$ when used as the control points for an order n B-spline gives the order n *fundamental spline basis* function.

This function converges to the sinc function as the order n increases, and is an excellent approximation to the perfect low-pass filter. If we reconstruct the image with a tensor product B-spline as well and apply the fundamental spline filter twice, we in theory achieve a minimum least-squares representation of the geometric image. Unfortunately, this representation rings excessively.

Let $\phi(x)$ be a signal and $g(x)$ an order $2r$ spline approximation. The *smoothing splines* are defined as the spline functions that minimize the linear functional

$$\epsilon^2(g, \phi) = \int_{\mathbb{R}} (g(x) - \phi(x))^2 + \lambda \left(\frac{d^r g(x)}{dx^r} \right)^2 dx.$$

for any positive integer r and positive real parameter λ. Smoothing splines can be implemented with a pair of quadratic recursive filters that need only remember two past output values. The parameter λ controls the balance between the fit and the smoothness of the spline, thus providing some control over ringing. If we reconstruct $g(x)$ with a fundamental spline rather than a B-spline basis, then $\lambda = 0$ corresponds to the perfect least-squares reconstruction of $\phi(x)$.

These digital filters can be applied to the output of any antialiasing system that can compute an adequately accurate result relative to a spline basis filter kernel. However, these filters operate by enhancing high frequencies. Approximate techniques, i.e. stochastic sampling, often hide noise at high frequencies, so enhancement will decrease the signal-to-noise ratio. Images generated through analytic antialiasing will not suffer from this problem.

5 RESULTS

Our prototype implementation scan converts one primitive at a time and sums it into a frame buffer. This approach precludes sharing of recurrence terms along edges, and assumes that hidden surface removal has already been performed. The primitive scan convertor supports independent recurrence evaluation at each pixel as well as both scanline and xy incremental evaluation. Tensor product B-spline filters of orders one (box) through four (cubic) were implemented.

A finely striped sphere tessellated into triangles was used as a test model. Use of a sphere permits hidden-surface removal with only back-face culling. The sphere was shaded at the vertices of each triangle with a Phong lighting model, and each triangle was Gouraud shaded. A point-sampled rendering of this model is given in the right half of Figure 6 at a resolution of 200×200.§ On average, a triangle covers 2.54 pixels in this image over the support of the sphere. To control the reconstruction kernel and minimize postaliasing and halftone interference artifacts, all images have been enlarged with a cubic B-spline reconstruction kernel to the resolution of the device.¶

Several aliasing artifacts are obvious: Moiré patterns due to the stripes meeting the sampling grid at an angle, jaggies along the edges of the stripes, Moiré patterns at the silhouette due to foreshortening, and finally similar problems at the pole of the sphere.

In Figure 8 the test case has been rendered with first through fourth order tensor-product B-spline filtering. Even the first order box filter, corresponding to area sampling, is a significant improvement. The cubic filter essentially eliminates aliasing artifacts, but does result in some blurring of the image.

To resolve the blurring problem, digital postprocessing can be applied. In Figure 7, quadratic and cubic fundamental spline basis functions were used as the antialiasing filters. A double appli-

cation of the corresponding digital filter, in conjunction with the appropriate order of reconstruction kernel, results in a perfect least-squares fit of the output image to the geometric input. Unfortunately, this image (not shown) suffers from excessive ringing, occasionally going out of gamut. In Figure 9, the result of a regularized least-squares filter is shown for various values of λ and $r = 2$. This filter tends to the double cubic fundamental filter as λ tends to 0, but is controllable. At $\lambda = 0.05$, this filter results in a very high level of quality.

6 PERFORMANCE

The performance of the prism spline evaluation algorithm is proportional to the number of terms in the recurrence tree that need to be evaluated for each output pixel. The evaluation of each term is roughly proportional to one Gouraud interpolation, discounting data movement costs against overlap in the computation of the blending factors.

Table 1 compares the number of recurrence terms for unoptimized recurrences, scanline (x) incremental recurrences, xy incremental recurrences, recurrences with and without term reuse, and cone spline (truncated power function) recurrences. We did not implement zero term culling.

Our first observation is that unoptimized recurrences are completely unreasonable. Therefore any practical implementation must consider some form of optimization. Term reuse is the most straightforward and least complex optimization to implement, and results in major savings. We also note that the number of terms in the cone spline is the same as the number of terms in the xy incremental evaluation. This is to be expected, actually. Finally, we observe that the xy incremental evaluation uses about a third of the terms required by the scanline (x) incremental evaluation. This has to be balanced against the greater data movement in the xy incremental algorithm. In our implementation, the two variants of the incremental algorithm performed almost identically.

These numbers need to be taken in context. A non-adaptive supersampling algorithm on a jittered 8×8 grid would require (roughly) 64 times as much computation as point sampling, and would still only be an approximation. A 3rd order xy incremental prism spline algorithm requires 84 terms but would compute an exact, noise-free answer. We also need to emphasize that this is a prototype implementation; more optimizations remain to be exploited.

7 FUTURE WORK

The polyhedral spline framework can be extended in many directions:

- Other polyhedral spline filter functions . . .

- Better intensity approximants . . .

- Motion blur using tetrahedral decomposition [9] . . .

- Antialiased line and volume elements . . .

- Approximation of penumbra . . .

Efficient execution also needs to be further addressed. Implementation of the zero-cull optimization and sharing of terms between adjacent primitives should result in another order of magnitude improvement in performance. Implementation of the zero cull optimization should consider the hierarchical nesting of the supports of each of the subsplines. To implement interprimitive term sharing, hidden-surface removal needs to be closely tied to evaluation of the primitives so information about the relationships between primitives can be maintained.

---

§ An enlarged 50×50 rendering is also shown on the left.

¶ Unfortunately, space restricts us from enlarging these images as much as we would like. Please consider examining the electronic versions on the CD-ROM for a critical comparison.

Terms in Optimized Recurrences					
n	Optimization	Number of Terms			
		P_{211nn}	P_{121nn}	P_{112nn}	P_{111nn}
1	none	29	29	29	6
2	none	669	669	669	148
3	none	12875	12875	12875	2539
4	none	224961	224961	224961	39112
1	x incr	20	20	20	5
2	x incr	287	287	287	78
3	x incr	3020	3020	3020	712
4	x incr	28251	28251	28251	5750
1	xy incr	13	13	13	4
2	xy incr	101	101	101	34
3	xy incr	487	487	487	142
4	xy incr	2149	2149	2149	538
1	reuse	19	13	13	6
2	reuse	107	54	54	53
3	reuse	343	172	172	195
4	reuse	829	325	325	504
1	reuse, x incr	14	9	9	5
2	reuse, x incr	60	27	27	33
3	reuse, x incr	149	58	58	91
4	reuse, x incr	293	105	105	188
1	reuse, xy incr	10	6	6	4
2	reuse, xy incr	32	13	13	19
3	reuse, xy incr	62	22	22	40
4	reuse, xy incr	100	33	33	67
1	cone, no reuse	13	13	13	4
2	cone, no reuse	101	101	101	34
3	cone, no reuse	487	487	487	142
4	cone, no reuse	2149	2149	2149	538
1	cone, reuse	10	6	6	4
2	cone, reuse	32	13	13	19
3	cone, reuse	62	22	22	40
4	cone, reuse	100	33	33	67

Table 1: Number of terms in various optimized linear and constant prism spline recurrences. Also shown are the number of terms in the cone spline recurrence which could be used to evaluate the prism spline at some loss in stability. When reuse is enabled we merge the trees for the linear prism spline basis functions; the constant prism spline P_{111nn} tree is a subtree of the P_{211nn} tree. Since we only need the P_{211nn}, P_{121nn}, and P_{111nn} terms to form a basis for linear interpolation, add the number of terms under the P_{211nn} and P_{121nn} columns to determine the total number of recurrence terms required.

8 Conclusions

An analytical antialiasing technique based on the theory of polyhedral splines has been presented. Using the convolutional properties of the polyhedral splines, we can derive evaluation recurrences for triangular simplex splines convolved with box spline filters. We study and give results for a linearly interpolated triangle convolved with a tensor product B-spline filter. Several optimization techniques are given which are essential to an efficient implementation. Through digital signal postprocessing, the effect of any filter spanned by shifted linear combinations of the basic box spline filter can be evaluated. If the filter is a tensor product B-spline then univariate recursive filters can be used to evaluate a regularized least-squares fit of a spline reconstruction to the underlying geometrically defined image.

9 Acknowledgements

This research was conducted while I was a Ph.D. student under the capable supervision of Eugene Fiume at the Dynamic Graphics Project at the University of Toronto. I am indebted to Eugene and to all the people at DGP for providing such a stimulating and productive environment.

DGP is supported by the National Science and Engineering Research Council of Canada and by the Information Technology Research Centre. My Ph.D. work was supported by an NSERC Postgraduate Scholarship.

References

[1] Amanatides, John. Ray Tracing with Cones. *Computer Graphics (SIGGRAPH '84 Proceedings)*, 18(3):129–135, July 1984.

[2] Catmull, Edwin E. A Hidden-surface Algorithm with Antialiasing. *Computer Graphics (SIGGRAPH '78 Proceedings)*, 12(3):6–11, August 1978.

[3] Dahmen, Wolfgang, Charles A. Micchelli, and Hans-Peter Seidel. Blossoming Begets B-spline Bases Built Better by B-patches. *Math. of Comp.*, 59(199):97–115, July 1992.

[4] de Boor, Carl, Klaus Höllig, and Sherman Riemenschneider. *Box Splines*. Academic Press, 1994.

[5] Duff, Tom. Polygon Scan Conversion by Exact Convolution. In Jacques André and Roger D. Hersch, editors, *Raster Imaging and Digital Typography*, pages 154–168. Cambridge University Press, 1989.

[6] Feibush, Eliot A., Marc Levoy, and Robert L. Cook. Synthetic Texturing using Digital Filters. *Computer Graphics (SIGGRAPH '80 Proceedings)*, 14(3):294–301, July 1980.

[7] Fong, Philip and Hans-Peter Seidel. An Implementation of Multivariate B-spline Surfaces over Arbitrary Triangulations. In *Proceedings of Graphics Interface '92*, pages 1–10, May 1992.

[8] Goodman, T. N. T. Polyhedral Splines. In *Collection: Computation of Curves and Surfaces (Puerto de la Cruz, 1989)*, volume 307 of *NATO Adv. Sci. Inst. Ser. C: Math. Phys. Sci.*, pages 347–382. Kluwer Acad. Publ., Dordrecht, 1990.

[9] Grant, Charles W. Integrated Analytic Spatial and Temporal Anti-aliasing for Polyhedra in 4-space. *Computer Graphics (SIGGRAPH '85 Proceedings)*, 19(3):79–84, July 1985.

[10] Grünbaum, Branko. *Convex Polytopes*. John Wiley & Sons, 1967.

[11] Heckbert, Paul S. and Pat Hanrahan. Beam Tracing Polygonal Objects. *Computer Graphics (SIGGRAPH '84 Proceedings)*, 18(3):119–127, July 1984.

[12] Kajiya, James T. and Mike Ullner. Filtering High Quality Text for Display on Raster Scan Devices. *Computer Graphics (SIGGRAPH '81 Proceedings)*, 15(3):7–15, August 1981.

[13] Max, Nelson L. Antialiasing Scan-line Data. *IEEE Computer Graphics and Applications*, 10(1):18–30, January 1990.

[14] McCool, Michael D. *Analytic Signal Processing for Computer Graphics using Multivariate Polyhedral Splines*. PhD thesis, University of Toronto, Department of Computer Science, 1995. Also available as Technical Report CS-95-05 from the University of Waterloo, Department of Computer Science, or from ftp://dgp.utoronto.ca:/pub/mccool

[15] Unser, Michael, Akram Aldroubi, and M. Eden. *B*-spline Signal Processing. *IEEE Transactions on Signal Processing*, 41(2):821–848, February 1993.

[16] Watt, Alan and Mark Watt. *Advanced Animation and Rendering Techniques*. Addison-Wesley, 1992.

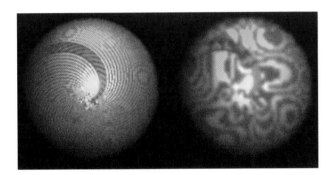

Figure 6: Point sampled 200×200 and 50×50 test images, reconstructed with a cubic B-spline kernel.

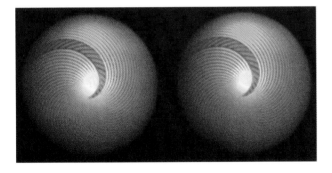

Figure 7: Test model analytically filtered with tensor product fundamental spline filters, orders three and four.

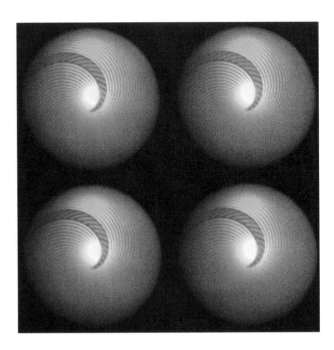

Figure 8: Test model analytically filtered with tensor product B-spline filters, orders one through four.

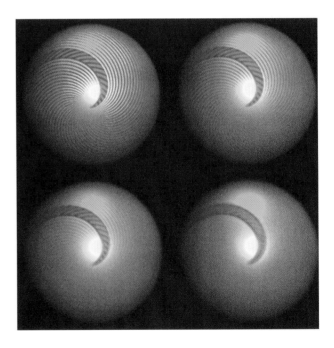

Figure 9: Test model analytically filtered with a tensor product smoothing spline, with $r = 2$ and $\lambda = 0.05$, 0.2, 0.8, and 3.2 from left to right, top to bottom. These images are reconstructed with a fundamental spline, which in tensor product form is somewhat anisotropic. As a consequence, some postaliasing is visible in these images.

Stratified Sampling of Spherical Triangles

James Arvo

Program of Computer Graphics*
Cornell University

Abstract

We present an algorithm for generating uniformly distributed random samples from arbitrary spherical triangles. The algorithm is based on a transformation of the unit square and easily accommodates *stratified* sampling, an effective means of reducing variance. With the new algorithm it is straightforward to perform stratified sampling of the solid angle subtended by an arbitrary polygon; this is a fundamental operation in image synthesis which has not been addressed in the Monte Carlo literature. We derive the required transformation using elementary spherical trigonometry and provide the complete sampling algorithm.

CR Categories and Subject Descriptors: I.3.5 [Computational Geometry and Object Modeling]: Geometric Algorithms.

Additional Key Words and Phrases: Monte Carlo, solid angle, spherical triangle, stratified sampling.

1 Introduction

Monte Carlo integration is used throughout computer graphics; examples include estimating form factors, visibility, and irradiance from complex or partially occluded luminaires [3, 5]. While many specialized sampling algorithms exist for various geometries, relatively few methods exist for sampling solid angles; that is, for regions on the unit sphere. The most common example that arises in computer graphics is the solid angle subtended by a polygon. We attack this problem by solving the sub-problem of sampling a spherical triangle.

The new sampling algorithm can be formulated using elementary spherical trigonometry. Let T be the spherical triangle with area $\mathcal{A}$ and vertices **A**, **B** and **C**. Let a, b, and c denote the edge lengths of T, and let α, β, and γ denote the three internal angles, which are the dihedral angles between the planes containing the edges. See Figure 1a. To generate uniformly distributed samples over T we seek a bijection $f : [0,1]^2 \to T$ with the following property: given any two subsets $\mathcal{S}_1$ and $\mathcal{S}_2$ of the unit square with equal areas, $f(\mathcal{S}_1)$ and $f(\mathcal{S}_2)$ will also have equal areas. The function f can be derived using standard Monte Carlo methods for sampling bivariate functions; for example, see Spanier and

*580 Engineering and Theory Center Building, Ithaca, New York 14853, http://www.graphics.cornell.edu

Permission to make digital/hard copy of part or all of this work for personal or classroom use is granted without fee provided that copies are not made or distributed for profit or commercial advantage, the copyright notice, the title of the publication and its date appear, and notice is given that copying is by permission of ACM, Inc. To copy otherwise, to republish, to post on servers, or to redistribute to lists, requires prior specific permission and/or a fee.

© 1995   ACM-0-89791-701-4/95/008 $3.50

Gelbard [6] or Rubinstein [4]. To apply these methods to sampling spherical triangles we require the following three identities:

$$\mathcal{A} = \alpha + \beta + \gamma - \pi \qquad (1)$$

$$\cos \beta = -\cos \gamma \cos \alpha \; + \; \sin \gamma \sin \alpha \cos b \qquad (2)$$

$$\cos \gamma = -\cos \beta \cos \alpha \; + \; \sin \beta \sin \alpha \cos c \qquad (3)$$

The first is known as Girard's formula and the other two are spherical cosine laws for angles [1].

2 The Sampling Algorithm

The algorithm proceeds in two stages. In the first stage we randomly select a sub-triangle $\widehat{\mathrm{T}} \subset \mathrm{T}$ whose area $\widehat{\mathcal{A}}$ is uniformly distributed between 0 and the original area $\mathcal{A}$. In the second stage we randomly select a point along an edge of the new triangle. Both stages require the inversion of a probability distribution function.

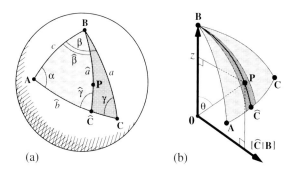

Figure 1: *(a) The vertex $\widehat{\mathbf{C}}$ is determined by specifying the area of the sub-triangle. (b) The point $\mathbf{P}$ is then chosen to lie along the arc between $\widehat{\mathbf{C}}$ and $\mathbf{B}$.*

Sub-triangle $\widehat{\mathrm{T}}$ is formed by choosing a new vertex $\widehat{\mathbf{C}}$ on the edge between **A** and **C**, as shown in Figure 1a. The sample point **P** is then chosen in the arc between **B** and $\widehat{\mathbf{C}}$. The point **P** is determined by its distance θ from **B** and by the length of the new edge $\widehat{b}$; these values are computed using the conditional distribution functions

$$F_1(\widehat{b}) \equiv \frac{\widehat{\mathcal{A}}}{\mathcal{A}} \qquad \text{and} \qquad F_2(\theta \,|\, \widehat{b}) \equiv \frac{1 - \cos \theta}{1 - \cos \widehat{a}},$$

where both $\widehat{\mathcal{A}}$ and $\widehat{a}$ are taken to be functions of $\widehat{b}$. Given two random variables ξ_1 and ξ_2 uniformly distributed in $[0, 1]$, we first find $\widehat{b}$ such that $F_1(\widehat{b}) = \xi_1$, and then find θ such that $F_2(\theta \,|\, \widehat{b}) = \xi_2$. Then $\widehat{b}$ will be distributed with a density proportional to the differential area of each edge $\widehat{a}$, and θ will be distributed along the edge with a density proportional to the differential area of the triangle with a vertex at $\mathbf{B}$ and base through $\mathbf{P}$, which is $(1 - \cos\theta)\,d\beta$. To find the edge length $\widehat{b}$ that attains the area $\widehat{\mathcal{A}} = \mathcal{A}\,\xi_1$, we use equations (1) and (2) to obtain

$$\cos\widehat{b} = \frac{\cos(\phi - \widehat{\beta})\,\cos\alpha \, - \, \cos\widehat{\beta}}{\sin(\phi - \widehat{\beta})\,\sin\alpha}, \qquad (4)$$

where $\phi \equiv \widehat{\mathcal{A}} - \alpha$. Then from equations (1) and (3) we have $u\cos\widehat{\beta} + v\sin\widehat{\beta} = 0$, where

$$u \equiv \cos(\phi) - \cos\alpha,$$
$$v \equiv \sin(\phi) + \sin\alpha\,\cos c.$$

It follows that

$$\sin\widehat{\beta} = \frac{\mp u}{\sqrt{u^2 + v^2}} \quad \text{and} \quad \cos\widehat{\beta} = \frac{\pm v}{\sqrt{u^2 + v^2}}.$$

The sign is determined by the constraint $0 < \widehat{\beta} < \pi$, but is immaterial in what follows. Simplifying equation (4) using the above expressions, we obtain

$$\cos\widehat{b} = \frac{[\,v\cos\phi - u\sin\phi\,]\,\cos\alpha \, - \, v}{[\,v\sin\phi + u\cos\phi\,]\,\sin\alpha}. \qquad (5)$$

Note that $\cos\widehat{b}$ determines $\widehat{b}$, since $0 < \widehat{b} < \pi$, and that $\widehat{b}$ in turn determines the vertex $\widehat{\mathbf{C}}$. Finally, we may easily solve for $z \equiv \cos\theta$ using $F_2(\theta\,|\,\widehat{b}) = \xi_2$ and $\cos\widehat{a} = \widehat{\mathbf{C}} \cdot \mathbf{B}$.

To succinctly express the sampling algorithm let $[\,\mathbf{x}\,|\,\mathbf{y}\,]$ denote the normalized component of the vector $\mathbf{x}$ that is orthogonal to the vector $\mathbf{y}$. That is,

$$[\,\mathbf{x}\,|\,\mathbf{y}\,] \equiv \text{Normalize}\,(\mathbf{x} - (\mathbf{x} \cdot \mathbf{y})\mathbf{y}). \qquad (6)$$

The algorithm for mapping the unit square onto the triangle T takes two variables ξ_1 and ξ_2, each in the unit interval, and returns a point $\mathbf{P} \in \text{T} \subset \mathbb{R}^3$.

---

point *SampleTriangle*(**real** ξ_1, **real** ξ_2)

Use one random variable to select the new area.
$\quad \widehat{\mathcal{A}} \leftarrow \xi_1 * \mathcal{A}$;

Save the sine and cosine of the angle ϕ.
$\quad s \leftarrow \sin(\widehat{\mathcal{A}} - \alpha)$;
$\quad t \leftarrow \cos(\widehat{\mathcal{A}} - \alpha)$;

Compute the pair (u, v) *that determines* $\widehat{\beta}$.
$\quad u \leftarrow t - \cos\alpha$;
$\quad v \leftarrow s + \sin\alpha * \cos c$;

Let q *be the cosine of the new edge length* $\widehat{b}$.
$\quad q \leftarrow \dfrac{[\,v * t \, - \, u * s\,] * \cos\alpha \, - \, v}{[\,v * s \, + \, u * t\,] * \sin\alpha}$;

Compute the third vertex of the sub-triangle.
$\quad \widehat{\mathbf{C}} \leftarrow q * \mathbf{A} + \sqrt{1 - q^2} * [\,\mathbf{C}\,|\,\mathbf{A}\,]$;

Use the other random variable to select $\cos\theta$.
$\quad z \leftarrow 1 - \xi_2 * (1 - \widehat{\mathbf{C}} \cdot \mathbf{B})$;

Construct the corresponding point on the sphere.
$\quad \mathbf{P} \leftarrow z * \mathbf{B} + \sqrt{1 - z^2} * [\,\widehat{\mathbf{C}}\,|\,\mathbf{B}\,]$;
$\quad$ **return** $\mathbf{P}$;
end

If ξ_1 and ξ_2 are independent random variables uniformly distributed in $[0, 1]$, as produced by most pseudo-random number generators, then $\mathbf{P}$ will be uniformly distributed in triangle T. Note that $\cos\alpha$, $\sin\alpha$, $\cos c$, and $[\,\mathbf{C}\,|\,\mathbf{A}\,]$ need only be computed once per triangle, not once per sample.

3 Results

Results of the algorithm are shown in Figure 2. On the left, the samples are identically distributed, which produces a pattern equivalent to that obtained by rejection sampling; however, each sample is guaranteed to fall within the triangle. The pattern on the right was generated by partitioning the unit square into a regular grid and choosing one pair (ξ_1, ξ_2) uniformly from each grid cell, which corresponds to *stratified* or *jittered* sampling [2]. The advantage of stratified sampling is evident in the resulting pattern; the samples are more evenly distributed, which generally reduces the variance of Monte Carlo estimates based on these samples.

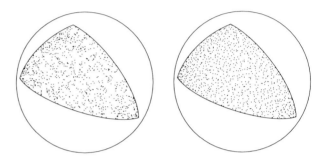

Figure 2: *Uniform and stratified sampling. The samples on the right were generated from stratified points in the unit square.*

The sampling algorithm can be applied to spherical polygons by decomposing them into triangles and performing stratified sampling on each component independently, which is analogous to the method for planar polygons [7]. This provides an effective means of sampling the solid angle subtended by a polygon.

Acknowledgments

Many thanks to Pete Shirley for his valuable suggestions and for urging the author to write this paper. This work was supported by the NSF/ARPA Science and Technology Center for Computer Graphics and Scientific Visualization (ASC-8920219) and performed on workstations generously provided by the Hewlett-Packard Corporation.

References

[1] BERGER, M. *Geometry, Volume II*. Springer-Verlag, New York, 1987. Translated by M. Cole and S. Levy.

[2] COOK, R. L. Stochastic sampling in computer graphics. *ACM Transactions on Graphics 5*, 1 (1986), 51–72.

[3] HANRAHAN, P., SALZMAN, D., AND AUPPERLE, L. A rapid hierarchical radiosity algorithm. *Computer Graphics 25*, 4 (July 1991), 197–206.

[4] RUBINSTEIN, R. Y. *Simulation and the Monte Carlo Method*. John Wiley & Sons, New York, 1981.

[5] SHIRLEY, P., WANG, C., AND ZIMMERMAN, K. Monte carlo methods for direct lighting calculations. *ACM Transactions on Graphics* (1995). To appear.

[6] SPANIER, J., AND GELBARD, E. M. *Monte Carlo Principles and Neutron Transport Problems*. Addison-Wesley, Reading, Massachusetts, 1969.

[7] TURK, G. Generating random points in triangles. In *Graphics Gems*, A. S. Glassner, Ed. Academic Press, New York, 1990, pp. 24–28.

Image Metamorphosis Using Snakes and Free-Form Deformations

Seung-Yong Lee[†], *Kyung-Yong Chwa, Sung Yong Shin*
Department of Computer Science
Korea Advanced Institute of Science and Technology
Taejon 305-701, Korea

George Wolberg
Department of Computer Science
City College of New York / CUNY
New York, NY 10031

Abstract

This paper presents new solutions to the following three problems in image morphing: feature specification, warp generation, and transition control. To reduce the burden of feature specification, we first adopt a computer vision technique called snakes. We next propose the use of multilevel free-form deformations (MFFD) to achieve C^2-continuous and one-to-one warps among feature point pairs. The resulting technique, based on B-spline approximation, is simpler and faster than previous warp generation methods. Finally, we simplify the MFFD method to construct C^2-continuous surfaces for deriving transition functions to control geometry and color blending.

Keywords: Image metamorphosis, morphing, snakes, multilevel free-form deformation, multilevel B-spline interpolation.

1. Introduction

Image metamorphosis deals with the fluid transformation from one digital image into another. This technique, commonly referred to as *morphing*, has found widespread use in the entertainment industry to achieve stunning visual effects. Smooth transformations are realized by coupling image warping with color interpolation. Image warping applies 2D geometric transformations on the images to retain geometric alignment between their features, while color interpolation blends their color.

Given two images, their correspondence is established by an animator with pairs of points or line segments. Each point or line segment specifies an image feature, or landmark. The feature correspondence is then used to compute warps to interpolate the positions of the features across the morph sequence. Once the source and destination images have been warped into alignment for intermediate feature positions, ordinary color interpolation (i.e., cross-dissolve) is performed to generate an inbetween image. Since color interpolation is straightforward, research in image morphing has concentrated on warp generation from the feature correspondence.

In mesh-based techniques, such as mesh warping [19] and the method of Nishita *et al.* [14], nonuniform meshes are used to specify the image features. Spline interpolation or Bézier clipping [15]

computes warps from the correspondence of mesh points. Though fast and intuitive, the mesh-based techniques have a drawback in specifying features. A control mesh is always required although the features on an image may have an arbitrary structure.

Field morphing [2] uses a set of line segments to effectively specify the features on an image. A pair of line segments on two images determines a warp from their local coordinate systems. When two or more pairs of line segments are specified, the influences of line segments are blended by their weighted average. This technique suffers from unexpected distortions, referred to as *ghosts*, which prevent an animator from realizing a precise warp in a complex metamorphosis.

If the features on an image are specified by a set of points, the x- and y-components of a warp can be derived by constructing the surfaces that interpolate scattered points. Warp generation by this approach was extensively surveyed in [16, 19], and recently two similar methods were independently proposed using the thin plate surface model [10, 12]. These techniques generate smooth warps that exactly reflect the feature correspondence.

When a warp is applied to an image, the one-to-one property of the warp guarantees that the distorted image does not fold back upon itself. An energy minimization method has been proposed which derives a C^1-continuous and one-to-one warp from a set of feature point pairs [11]. The performance of that method is hampered by its high computational cost. This paper presents a new multilevel free-form deformation (MFFD) technique to derive a C^2-continuous and one-to-one warp that exactly satisfies the feature correspondence. The proposed technique, based on 2D B-spline approximation, is much simpler and faster than the energy minimization method.

Another interesting problem in image morphing is transition control. If transition rates differ from part to part in inbetween images, more interesting animations are possible. In mesh warping [19], a transition curve is assigned to each point of the mesh to control the transition behavior. When complicated meshes are used to specify the features, it is tedious to assign a proper transition curve to every mesh point. Nishita *et al.* mentioned that the transition behavior can be controlled by a Bézier function defined on the mesh [14]. However, the details of the method were not provided.

An effective method for transition control has been proposed in [11]. Transition rates on an inbetween image are derived from transition curves by constructing a smooth surface. The surface represents the propagation of transition rates defined by the user at sparse positions across the image. In this paper, the MFFD technique for warp generation is simplified and applied to efficiently generate a C^2-continuous surface.

The most tedious aspect of image morphing is feature specification. Despite their usefulness, computer vision techniques remain only marginally utilized for this task [3]. In this paper, we adopt snakes [8], an active contour model made popular in computer vision, to reduce the burden of feature specification for animators.

[†] Current address: Dept. of Computer Science, City College of New York,
138th St. at Convent Ave., Rm. R8/206, New York, NY 10031.
[cssyl | wolberg]@cs-mail.engr.ccny.cuny.edu
[kychwa | syshin]@jupiter.kaist.ac.kr

Permission to make digital/hard copy of part or all of this work for personal or classroom use is granted without fee provided that copies are not made or distributed for profit or commercial advantage, the copyright notice, the title of the publication and its date appear, and notice is given that copying is by permission of ACM, Inc. To copy otherwise, to republish, to post on servers, or to redistribute to lists, requires prior specific permission and/or a fee.

2. Preliminaries

The authors have proposed a general framework for generating an inbetween image from two images, including transition behavior control [9, 11, 19]. The framework is also taken for the new image morphing technique given in this paper.

2.1 Metamorphosis framework

Let F_0 and F_1 be two sets of features specified by an animator on the source and destination images I_0 and I_1, respectively. For each feature f_0 in F_0, there exists a corresponding feature f_1 in F_1. Let W_0 and W_1 be the warp functions that specify the corresponding point in I_1 and I_0 for each point in I_0 and I_1, respectively. When it is applied to I_0, W_0 generates a distorted image so that the features in F_0 coincide with their corresponding features in F_1. The requirement for W_1 is to map features f_1 onto f_0 when it distorts I_1. Although W_1 is the inverse of W_0 at the features, this is not necessarily true at other positions across the image. Together, W_0 and W_1 serve to retain geometric alignment of the features during the morph.

Transition functions specify a transition rate for each point on the given images over time. Let T_0 be a transition function defined for source image I_0. For a given time t, $T_0(p; t)$ is a real-valued function that determines how fast each point p in I_0 moves towards the corresponding point q in destination image I_1. $T_0(p; t)$ also determines the color contribution of each point p in I_0 to the corresponding point in an inbetween image $I(t)$.

Let T_1 be the transition function for destination image I_1. For each point q in I_1, $T_1(q; t)$ is defined to have the same transition rate as $T_0(p; t)$ if q corresponds to p in I_0. Hence, $T_1(q; t)$ can be derived from $T_0(p; t)$ using warp function W_1. That is, $T_1(q; t) = T_0(W_1(q); t)$. For simplicity, we treat the transition functions for both geometry and color to be identical, although they may be different in practice.

Let $W \bullet I$ denote the application of warp function W to image I. The procedure for generating an inbetween image $I(t)$ can be described as follows.

$$\overline{W}_0(p; t) = (1 - T_0(p; t)) \cdot p + T_0(p; t) \cdot W_0(p)$$
$$\overline{W}_1(q; t) = T_1(q; t) \cdot q + (1 - T_1(q; t)) \cdot W_1(q)$$
$$I_0(p; t) = \overline{W}_0(p; t) \bullet ((1 - T_0(p; t)) \cdot I_0(p))$$
$$I_1(q; t) = \overline{W}_1(q; t) \bullet (T_1(q; t) \cdot I_1(q))$$
$$I(r; t) = I_0(r; t) + I_1(r; t).$$

Note that $0 \leq T_0, T_1 \leq 1$ and $0 \leq t \leq 1$. Transition rates 0 and 1 imply the source and destination images, respectively. To complete the procedure, a solution is needed to each of the following problems:

- how to specify feature sets F_0 and F_1,

- how to derive warp functions W_0 and W_1, and

- how to derive transition functions T_0 and T_1.

2.2 The energy minimization method

An energy minimization method has been proposed for deriving warp functions in [11]. That method allows extensive feature specification primitives such as points, polylines, and curves. Feature correspondence is established by converting non-point features to feature points using point sampling. A warp is interpreted as a 2D deformation of a rectangular plate. The feature correspondence assigns a new position to each feature point to derive a warp. A

deformation technique is provided to derive C^1-continuous and one-to-one warps from the positional constraints. The requirements for a warp are represented by energy terms and satisfied by minimizing their sum. The technique generates natural warps since it is based on physically meaningful energy terms. It is, however, a bit involved to implement.

Transition functions are obtained by selecting a set of points on a given image and specifying a transition curve for each point. The transition curves determine the transition behavior of the selected points over time. For a given time, transition functions must have the values assigned by the transition curves at the selected points. Considering a transition rate as the vertical distance from a plane, transition functions are reduced to smooth surfaces that interpolate a set of scattered points. The thin plate surface model [18] was employed to obtain C^1-continuous surfaces for transition functions.

2.3 Overview

With the metamorphosis framework described in Section 2.1, we present a more effective technique than the previous energy minimization method. To help an animator specify image features, we use snakes [8], a technique popularized in computer vision. Snakes make it possible to capture the exact position of a feature easily and precisely.

To derive warps from positional constraints, we propose the MFFD as an extension to free-form deformation (FFD) [17]. We take the bivariate cubic B-spline tensor product as the deformation function of FFD. A new direct manipulation technique for FFD, based on 2D B-spline approximation, is developed in this paper. We apply it to a hierarchy of control lattices to exactly satisfy the positional constraints. To guarantee the one-to-one property of a warp, we present a sufficient condition for a 2D cubic B-spline surface to be one-to-one. The MFFD generates C^2-continuous and one-to-one warps which yield fluid image distortions. It is much simpler and faster than the energy minimization method. We also present a hybrid approach that combines the two methods.

To obtain smooth surfaces for transition functions, we simplify the MFFD to obtain multilevel B-spline interpolation. This interpolation algorithm efficiently generates a C^2-continuous surface through a set of scattered points.

3. Feature Specification

Features consist of image landmarks, e.g., the profile, eyes, noise, and mouth of a facial image. The position of a feature is usually identified by a boundary curve at edges, where color values change abruptly. We adopt the use of snakes to assist us in the precise positioning of features.

3.1 Snakes

Snakes [8] are energy-minimizing splines under the influence of image and constraint forces. The spline energy serves to impose a piecewise smoothness constraint on a snake. The image forces push the snake toward salient image features such as lines, edges, and subjective contours. The constraint forces are used for pulling the snake to a desired image feature among the nearby ones. Snakes have proven to be useful for the interactive specification of image features.

Representing the position of a snake in parametric form, $v(s) = (x(s), y(s))$, its energy functional can be written as

$$E_{snake}(v) = \int_0^1 [E_{spline}(v) + E_{image}(v)] \, ds.$$

E_{spline} represents the spline energy due to bending, and E_{image} is the energy defined from the intensity distribution of an image. We have removed the term related to the constraint forces because it is not used in this paper. We also simplify the spline energy to $E_{spline} = \beta|\frac{d^2v}{ds^2}|^2$, which makes a snake act like a thin plate.

For a gray-scale image I, the gradient ∇I measures the local changes of image values and can be computed by a difference operator or the Sobel operator [1]. The image energy functional can be defined by $E_{image} = -\nabla^2 I = -|\nabla I(x,y)|^2$. It makes a snake precisely localize a feature at a boundary having large image gradients. While minimizing the energy functional E_{snake}, the snake slithers from its initial position to a nearby feature.

A feature is allowed to attract a distant snake if image gradients are convolved with a smoothing filter. For example, the convolution results in an image energy functional, $E_{image} = -(G_\sigma * \nabla^2 I)$, where G_σ is a Gaussian of standard deviation σ. Other image energy functionals and the details of the energy minimization procedure can be found in [8].

3.2 Feature specification primitives

In this paper, the feature specification primitives include points, polylines, and curves as in [11]. However, the positions of features can be derived more effectively by generating snakes from polylines and curves. To specify a feature having large image gradients, a snake is initialized by positioning a polyline or curve near the feature. We then uniformly sample a sequence of points on the polyline or curve, e.g., 20 points per segment. As the snake minimizes its energy, it slithers and finally locks onto the feature by the image force.

To tailor the response of the snake, the user may clamp any of the sampled points in place. Internally, this is achieved by assigning a large value to the parameter γ in [8] for the selected points. Since it is often tedious to select among the many sampled points, we provide an option for fixing those that lie on the control points of the user-specified primitive.

When a feature specification primitive f_0 is placed on image I_0, a primitive f_1 is also deposited on the other image I_1. We either move f_0 repeatedly or generate a snake from f_0 to identify a feature on I_0. f_1 is then moved to designate the corresponding feature on I_1, and a snake is initiated if necessary.

If f_0 and f_1 are polylines or curves, the correspondence between them is established by their vertices or control points, respectively. The correspondence between two snakes can be derived from the polylines or curves that provide their initial positions. The feature correspondence between two images is internally translated to a set of point pairs sampled on the specified feature primitives.

Fig. 7 shows an example. Fig. 7(a) is the input image. We convert it to a gray-scale image and apply the Sobel operator [1] to compute image gradients. Fig. 7(b) shows the image gradients convolved with a Gaussian filter, where bright intensities denote large gradients. In Fig. 7(c), we place a polyline near the profile of the image. The snake starting from the polyline exactly captures the profile, as in Fig. 7(d). Fig. 7(e) illustrates the specified feature primitives overlaid on the image. The cyan points in Fig. 7(f) represent internally sampled feature points on the primitives. We typically use a uniform sampling rate of 20 points per primitive segment, although only five points per segment are shown in the figure.

4. Warp Generation

Free-form deformation (FFD) was proposed by Sederberg and Parry as a powerful modeling tool for 3D deformable objects [17]. The basic idea of FFD is to deform an object by manipulating a 3D

parallelepiped lattice containing the object. The manipulated lattice determines a deformation function that specifies a new position for each point on the object. Coquillart extended the FFD method to handle non-parallelepiped lattices [4] and proposed a technique for animating objects modeled by FFD [5]. Hsu et al. employed the FFD method to directly control the shape of an object under complex deformations [7]. They took the trivariate cubic B-spline tensor product as the deformation function instead of the Bernstein polynomials used by Sederberg and Parry.

In this paper, we consider a 2D FFD to generate a C^2-continuous and one-to-one warp from positional constraints. A rectangular plate in the xy-plane is deformed by manipulating a parallelepiped lattice overlaid on it. We take the bivariate cubic B-spline tensor product as the deformation function of FFD because a B-spline has local control. This property makes it possible to locally manipulate the lattice when a point on the plate is moved to the specified position. Therefore, the new lattice producing this movement can be efficiently computed even for a large number of control points.

4.1 Free-form deformation and the 1-to-1 property

Let Ω be a rectangular plate placed on the xy-plane. We assume that Ω contains points $p = (u,v)$ where $1 \le u \le m$ and $1 \le v \le n$. When plate Ω is deformed in the xy-plane, its shape can be represented by a vector-valued function, $\mathbf{w}(p) = (x(p), y(p))$. Let Φ be an $(m+2) \times (n+2)$ lattice of control points overlaid on plate Ω. In the initial configuration of Φ, the ij-th control point lies at its initial position, $\phi_{ij}^0 = (i,j)$. With the FFD method, a desired deformation $\mathbf{w}$ of plate Ω is derived by displacing the control points on lattice Φ from their initial positions (Fig. 1).

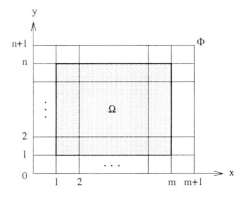

Figure 1: The initial arrangement of the plate and control lattice

Let ϕ_{ij} be the position of the ij-th control point on lattice Φ. The function $\mathbf{w}$ is defined in terms of ϕ_{ij} by

$$\mathbf{w}(u,v) = \sum_{k=0}^{3}\sum_{l=0}^{3} B_k(s)B_l(t)\phi_{(i+k)(j+l)}, \quad (1)$$

where $i = \lfloor u \rfloor - 1$, $j = \lfloor v \rfloor - 1$, $s = u - \lfloor u \rfloor$, and $t = v - \lfloor v \rfloor$. $B_k(s)$ and $B_l(t)$ are the uniform cubic B-spline basis functions evaluated at s and t, respectively. Since a B-spline curve through collinear control points is itself linear, the initial configuration of lattice Φ generates the undeformed shape of the plate. That is,

$$\mathbf{w}^0(u,v) = (u,v) = \sum_{k=0}^{3}\sum_{l=0}^{3} B_k(s)B_l(t)\phi_{(i+k)(j+l)}^0. \quad (2)$$

From Eq. (1), we know that the deformed position $\mathbf{w}(p)$ of point p on plate Ω relates to the sixteen control points in its neighborhood.

Now, we consider the one-to-one property of the function $\mathbf{w}$ defined in Eq. (1). Function $\mathbf{w}$ can be regarded as a 2D uniform cubic B-spline surface where plate Ω is the parameter space. The one-to-one property of a 2D B-spline surface has not been studied because B-spline surfaces are usually considered in three dimensions to model free-form surfaces.

Recently, Goodman and Unsworth presented a sufficient condition for a 2D Bézier surface to be one-to-one [6]. They commented that the condition can also be applied to a 2D B-spline surface. For an $m \times n$ lattice of control points, the condition contains $2m(m+1) + 2n(n+1)$ linear inequalities. If the number of control points is large, the time to check the condition becomes prohibitive. Moreover, if the condition does not hold, there is no simple way for manipulating the control lattice to satisfy the condition.

In this paper, we present a sufficient condition for the function $\mathbf{w}$ to be one-to-one in terms of the displacements of control points. With the following theorem, a 2D uniform cubic B-spline surface can be made one-to-one by limiting the displacements of control points.

Theorem 1 *The function $\mathbf{w}$ given in Equation (1) is one-to-one if* $(-0.48, -0.48) \leq \phi_{ij} - \phi_{ij}^0 \leq (0.48, 0.48)$ *for all i, j.*

Proof: See Appendix. $\square$

Theorem 1 provides a tight, sufficient, although not necessary, condition. There are examples in which the B-spline surface is not one-to-one even though all control points are displaced by amounts less than 0.5. This means that a B-spline surface may violate the one-to-one property even when control lattice gridlines do not intersect among themselves.

4.2 Manipulation of free-form deformation

Suppose that plate Ω should be deformed to place a point p at the specified position q, that is, $\mathbf{w}(p) = q$. Without loss of generality, we may assume that $p = (u, v)$, $1 \leq u, v < 2$. Then, the displacements of the kl-th control points, $k, l = 0, 1, 2, 3$, on lattice Φ determine the deformed position $\mathbf{w}(p)$ of point p. See Fig. 2(a). Let $\Delta q = \mathbf{w}(p) - \mathbf{w}^0(p) = q - p$ be the movement of the point p from its original position. Let $\Delta\phi_{kl} = \phi_{kl} - \phi_{kl}^0$ be the displacement of the kl-th control point from its initial position. From Eqs. (1) and (2), the displacements $\Delta\phi_{kl}$ must satisfy Eq. (3):

$$\Delta q = \sum_{k=0}^{3} \sum_{l=0}^{3} B_k(s) B_l(t) \Delta\phi_{kl}, \tag{3}$$

where $s = u - 1$ and $t = v - 1$.

There are many values of $\Delta\phi_{kl}$ that are solutions to Eq. (3). We choose one in the least-squared sense such that

$$\Delta\phi_{kl} = \frac{w_{kl}\Delta q}{\sum_{a=0}^{3} \sum_{b=0}^{3} w_{ab}^2}, \tag{4}$$

where $w_{ab} = B_a(s) B_b(t)$. Among all the solutions to Eq. (3), Hsu *et al.* showed that this minimizes the squared sum of control point displacements [7]. In this solution, the control points near point p get larger displacements than the others because w_{kl} depends on the distance between the kl-th control point and point p. Hence, it generates the deformation $\mathbf{w}$ whereby the effect of the movement of p tapers off smoothly.

Now, suppose that plate Ω should be deformed to place a set of points P at a set of positions Q. That is, $\mathbf{w}(p) = q$ for each point p in P and its position q in Q. A point p in P can be moved to the specified position q if its surrounding control points are displaced by the amount $\Delta\phi_{kl}$ given in Eq. (4). However, these displacements

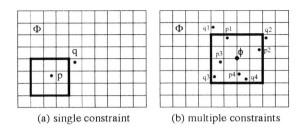

| (a) single constraint | (b) multiple constraints |

Figure 2: Examples of the positional constraints

may mislead another point in P to another position than the one specified in Q.

Let $P' = \{(u_c, v_c)\}$ be the set of points in P such that $i - 2 \leq u_c < i + 2$ and $j - 2 \leq v_c < j + 2$. Let ϕ be the ij-th control point on lattice Φ whose initial position is (i, j), as in Fig. 2(b). The displacement of control point ϕ influences the movement of points in P' when we evaluate the deformation function $\mathbf{w}$. For each point p_c in P', Eq. (4) gives the displacement $\Delta\phi_c$ of control point ϕ required for moving p_c to the specified position. Since the displacement $\Delta\phi_c$ may be different from point to point in P', the displacement $\Delta\phi$ of control point ϕ is chosen to minimize an error.

The error is defined as the squared sum of differences between $w_c\Delta\phi$ and $w_c\Delta\phi_c$, where $w_c = B_k(s)B_l(t)$, $k = (i+1) - \lfloor u_c \rfloor$, $l = (j+1) - \lfloor v_c \rfloor$, $s = u_c - \lfloor u_c \rfloor$, and $t = v_c - \lfloor v_c \rfloor$, for each point $p_c = (u_c, v_c)$ in P'. That is, the error is

$$\sum_c (w_c\Delta\phi - w_c\Delta\phi_c)^2.$$

$w_c\Delta\phi$ is the movement of point p_c due to the displacement $\Delta\phi$ of control point ϕ. $w_c\Delta\phi_c$ represents the contribution of control point ϕ, determined by Eq. (4), for moving p_c to its specified position. By differentiating the error with respect to $\Delta\phi$ and equating the derived formula to zero, we get

$$\Delta\phi = \frac{\sum_c w_c^2 \Delta\phi_c}{\sum_c w_c^2}. \tag{5}$$

When the displacements of the control points on lattice Φ are computed by Eq. (5), the resulting deformation function $\mathbf{w}$ is not guaranteed to be one-to-one. To make the function $\mathbf{w}$ one-to-one, we truncate the displacement $\Delta\phi$ of a control point ϕ so that $(-0.48, -0.48) \leq \Delta\phi \leq (0.48, 0.48)$. Then, the condition of Theorem 1 holds and the derived function $\mathbf{w}$ is one-to-one.

Hsu *et al.* presented a technique for manipulating control points so that the points on an object modeled by FFD may be moved to the specified positions [7]. That technique calculates the pseudoinverse of a matrix to derive the displacements of control points that minimize the squared sum of distances between the specified and actual positions. The matrix contains the values of B-spline basis functions and its size depends on the number of positional constraints. When a large number of points must be moved, the computation for calculating the pseudoinverse is prohibitive.

On the other hand, the technique proposed in this section runs very fast even when the number of moved points is large. The deformation of plate Ω nicely reflects the movements of points because the displacement of each control point minimizes a reasonable error. Fig. 3 shows examples. In the figures, black spots represent the positions of the selected points in the undeformed and deformed shapes. Thick curves show the control lattice Φ overlaid on plate Ω. The control lattice is a rectangular grid in its initial configuration. It is transformed when plate Ω is deformed.

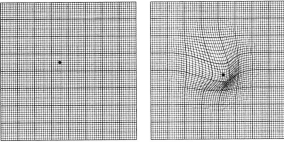

(a) single positional constraint

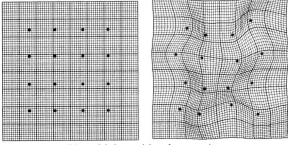

(b) multiple positional constraints

Figure 3: Examples of the FFD manipulation

4.3 Multilevel free-form deformation

Let P be a set of points on plate Ω and Q be a set of corresponding positions. An application of the FFD manipulation presented in Section 4.2 cannot always deform plate Ω to place each point in P at its specified position in Q. One reason is that the displacement of a control point on lattice Φ is the weighted average of the displacements required for moving its neighboring points in P. The other reason is that we limit the maximum displacement of a control point to approximately a half of the spacing between control points in order to make the deformation function one-to-one.

We may circumvent the first problem if we make the control lattice finer until every point in P can be moved by its surrounding control points without interfering with other points in P. The second can be overcome if we repeatedly apply the FFD manipulation to plate Ω so that the accumulated movement of a point in P can be sufficiently large. Hence, an obvious method for deriving a one-to-one deformation function from the positional constraints is to overlay a sufficiently fine control lattice over plate Ω and iterate the FFD manipulation. However, in this case, the resulting shape of plate Ω will show only sharp local deformations near the points in P. Moreover, a large number of FFD manipulations may be required to satisfy the positional constraints because a point in P can only move a short distance by the FFD manipulation when a fine control lattice is used. In this section, we present the multilevel free-form deformation (MFFD) technique that overcomes the drawbacks of the simple method.

In MFFD, a hierarchy of control lattices, $\Phi_0, \Phi_1, ..., \Phi_m$, is used to derive a sequence of deformation functions with the FFD manipulation. Let h_k be the spacing between control points on the initial configuration of lattice Φ_k. We assume that h_0 and h_m are given and that $h_k = 2h_{k+1}$. When plate Ω is deformed with a coarse control lattice, the positional constraints merge with each other and result in a smooth deformation, although they are not exactly satisfied. The remaining deviations between the deformed and specified positions will be handled by subsequent deformations with finer control lattices.

Let $\mathbf{w}_0, \mathbf{w}_1, ..., \mathbf{w}_n$ be the sequence of deformation functions derived in the MFFD. Then, the deformation of plate Ω is defined by the composite function $\mathbf{w} = \mathbf{w}_n \circ \mathbf{w}_{n-1} \circ ... \circ \mathbf{w}_0$. That is, $\mathbf{w}(\Omega) = \mathbf{w}_n(\Omega_n)$, where $\Omega_0 = \Omega$ and $\Omega_{i+1} = \mathbf{w}_i(\Omega_i)$. $\mathbf{w}(\Omega)$ and $\mathbf{w}_i(\Omega_i)$ denote the resulting shapes when the deformation functions $\mathbf{w}$ and $\mathbf{w}_i$ are applied to the plate Ω and deformed plate Ω_i, respectively. Let $P_{i+1} = \mathbf{w}_i(P_i)$, where $P_0 = P$. P_i is the set of points on the deformed plate Ω_i that lie at the deformed positions of the points in P. The deformation function $\mathbf{w}_i$ is computed to move the points in P_i to their specified positions in Q. When the deformation function $\mathbf{w}$ is applied to plate Ω, we define the error as

$$\max_c \| \mathbf{w}(p_c) - q_c \|^2,$$

where q_c is the position in Q specified for the point p_c in P.

When we deform a plate Ω_i with a control lattice Φ_k, a point in P_i can move at most $(0.48h_k, 0.48h_k)$ if and only if all 16 surrounding control points are displaced by $(0.48h_k, 0.48h_k)$. Note that this maximum movement follows from Theorem 1 whereby the displacements of control points must be truncated to keep the one-to-one property of the deformation function. If each point in P_i moves by $(0.48h_k, 0.48h_k)$, the error decreases by at least $(0.48h_k)^2$. In this case, more FFD manipulations with the control lattice Φ_k may be helpful for moving the points in P_i to their specified positions.

In MFFD, the FFD manipulation starts with the coarsest control lattice Φ_0. With a control lattice Φ_k, the FFD manipulation iterates until the change in error falls below $\alpha(0.48h_k)^2$. Then, the next finer control lattice Φ_{k+1} is used for the successive FFD manipulation, as long as Φ_k is not the finest control lattice. This process continues while the error exceeds a user-specified threshold. The parameter α is a real value between 0 and 1. A small α generates a smooth deformation of plate Ω because FFD manipulations tends to be performed on coarser control lattices. We usually use 0.5 as the value of α.

The FFD manipulation generates a C^2-continuous and one-to-one deformation function. In the MFFD, a deformation function is the composition of several functions derived by FFD manipulations. Hence, the resulting deformation of plate Ω is C^2-continuous and one-to-one. Furthermore, the result is guaranteed to remain one-to-one even when the positional constraints are prone to foldovers. This is achieved by relaxing the requirement to exactly satisfy the positional constraints in order to retain the one-to-one property.

Fig. 4 gives an example in which the MFFD is applied to generate a deformation of plate Ω from positional constraints. Fig. 4(a) shows the selected points in the undeformed shape of the plate. Figs. 4(b) through (e) show a sequence of deformations in which the deformed positions of the selected points gradually approach the specified positions. Fig. 4(f) shows the resulting deformation with the specified positions. In this example, the FFD manipulations are performed no more than twice at each level of the control lattice.

Most of the computation for the MFFD is consumed in evaluating the deformation function $\mathbf{w}$ on plate Ω. When the function $\mathbf{w}$ is evaluated on a 64×64 grid, it takes 0.2 seconds for an SGI Crimson to generate the deformation in Fig. 4(f). When the size of the grid is 512×512, the computation time is 9.2 seconds.

4.4 A hybrid approach

An energy minimization method has been proposed to derive C^1-continuous and one-to-one warps from positional constraints [11]. It generates natural warps but requires much computation if warps are evaluated on large grids. The MFFD can be combined with that method to derive warps more effectively.

Suppose that warps are to be evaluated on an $m \times n$ grid. First, the energy minimization method is used to obtain a warp $\mathbf{w}_e$ on a coarse $(m/k) \times (n/k)$ grid using positional constraints derived

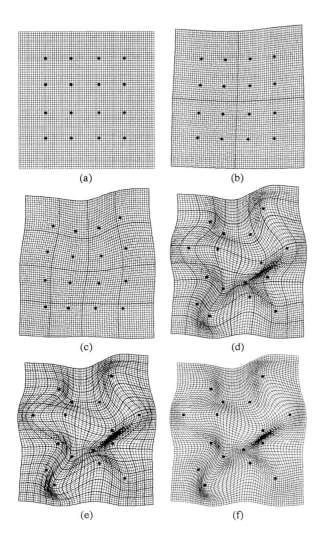

Figure 4: An example of the MFFD

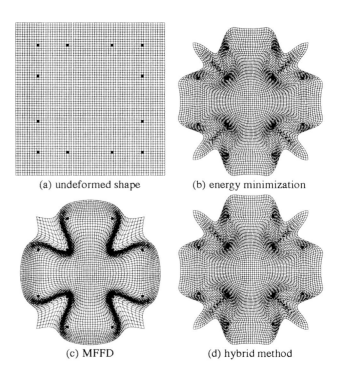

(a) undeformed shape   (b) energy minimization

(c) MFFD   (d) hybrid method

Figure 5: Comparison of the deformed shapes of a plate

from the original grid by weighted averaging. Then, a warp $\mathbf{w}_0$ is derived on the $m \times n$ grid by constructing a 2D uniform cubic B-spline surface that interpolates the values of the function $\mathbf{w}_e$. The function $\mathbf{w}_0$ is C^2-continuous and one-to-one but does not satisfy the given positional constraints exactly. Finally, the MFFD is applied to handle the remainder of the positional constraints, where $(m/k) \times (n/k)$ is the size of the coarsest control lattice.

In the hybrid approach, the energy minimization method determines the global shape of the generated warp on a coarse grid in a short time. The MFFD on the original grid makes it possible to avoid the excessive computation required for energy minimization on a fine grid. Hence, the hybrid approach generates a nice warp similar to the energy minimization method in a computation time comparable to the MFFD.

Fig. 5 gives an example. Fig. 5(a) shows the selected points in the undeformed shape of the plate. Figs. 5(b), (c), and (d) show the deformations of the plate derived by energy minimization, MFFD, and the hybrid method, respectively. In the figures, warps are evaluated on a 512×512 grid. For the hybrid approach, the energy minimization method is applied to a 128×128 grid. The computation times for Figs. 5(b), (c), and (d) on an SGI Crimson are 26.7, 6.4, and 7.5 seconds, respectively.

5. Transition Control

B-spline surfaces are widely used to model free-form surfaces because they offer nice properties such as continuity and local control. In this section, we consider uniform cubic B-splines to generate a surface that interpolates a scattered set of 3D height field points. The purpose of deriving this surface is to propagate the transition control information specified at only sparse positions. This information is given by the user with transition curves specified along primitives. Note that these primitives do not necessarily relate to feature primitives. That is, a different set of points, polylines, or curves may be defined to specify transition behavior.

5.1 Manipulation of B-spline surfaces

Let Ω be a rectangular region in the uv-plane which contains points $p = (u, v)$ such that $1 \leq u \leq m$ and $1 \leq v \leq n$. Let Φ be a $(m + 2) \times (n + 2)$ lattice of control points overlaid on the region Ω. In the initial configuration of Φ, the ij-th control point lies at its initial position (i, j) in the uv-plane. When the control points on lattice Φ are displaced only in the direction perpendicular to the uv-plane, the resulting B-spline surface can be represented by a real-valued function f. The function value $f(p)$ for a point $p = (u, v)$ on Ω implies that the point p is placed at the position $(u, v, f(p))$ when the surface is generated.

Let ϕ_{ij} be the height of the ij-th control point from the uv-plane. Then, the function f is given by

$$f(u, v) = \sum_{k=0}^{3} \sum_{l=0}^{3} B_k(s) B_l(t) \phi_{(i+k)(j+l)},$$

where $i = \lfloor u \rfloor - 1$, $j = \lfloor v \rfloor - 1$, $s = u - \lfloor u \rfloor$, and $t = v - \lfloor v \rfloor$. $B_k(s)$ and $B_l(t)$ are the uniform cubic B-spline basis functions evaluated at s and t, respectively. The above formula for f is in the same form as Eq. (1) for the deformation function $\mathbf{w}$ in Section 4.1.

Suppose that a B-spline surface is required to interpolate a set of scattered points (u_c, v_c, t_c), where (u_c, v_c) is a point in the region Ω. That is, $f(u_c, v_c) = t_c$ for each point in the set. A surface that approximately satisfies the positional constraints can be obtained by following the same approach for FFD manipulation described in Section 4.2. The required heights of control points from the uv-plane are derived by Eqs. (4) and (5), replacing Δq with t_c. The computed heights of control points are not truncated in this case because it is not necessary to consider the one-to-one property.

5.2 Multilevel B-spline interpolation

Let P be a set of points (u_c, v_c, t_c) in 3D space, where (u_c, v_c) is a point in the region Ω. As in the case for a warp, the B-spline surface derived by Eqs. (4) and (5) does not necessarily interpolate the points in P. A straightforward solution is to use a sufficiently fine control lattice so that every point in P can be interpolated without interfering with other points. However, the resulting surface will show only sharp local deformations near the points in P. Thus, we introduce multilevel B-spline interpolation to overcome this drawback.

In multilevel B-spline interpolation, a hierarchy of control lattices, $\Phi_0, \Phi_1, ..., \Phi_m$, is overlaid over the region Ω to derive a sequence of functions, $f_0, f_1, ..., f_m$. Let h_i be the spacing between control points in the initial configuration of lattice Φ_i. We assume that h_0 and h_m are given and that $h_i = 2h_{i+1}$. The final function f is defined by the sum of the functions f_i, that is, $f(p) = \sum_i f_i(p)$, for each point p on Ω. The coarsest spacing h_0 determines the area of the resulting surface on which an interpolated point has effect. The finest spacing h_m controls the precision to which the resulting surface interpolates the given points.

The manipulation of a B-spline surface starts with the coarsest control lattice Φ_0. The heights of control points on lattice Φ_0 are derived to generate the surface f_0 that interpolates the points in P. Sometimes, however, surface f_0 only passes near the points in P, leaving the deviation $\Delta^0 t_c = t_c - f_0(u_c, v_c)$ for each point (u_c, v_c, t_c) in P. Then, the next finer control lattice Φ_1 is used to obtain the B-spline surface f_1 that interpolates the set of points $(u_c, v_c, \Delta^0 t_c)$. In general, we manipulate the control points on lattice Φ_{k+1} to derive the B-spline surface f_{k+1} that interpolates the set of points $(u_c, v_c, \Delta^k t_c)$, where $\Delta^k t_c = t_c - \sum_{i=0}^k f_i(u_c, v_c)$. This process continues to the finest control lattice Φ_m until the maximum difference between the points in P and the final surface f falls below a given threshold. Unlike the MFFD case, the B-spline surface manipulation is applied only once on each control lattice because the heights of the control points are not truncated.

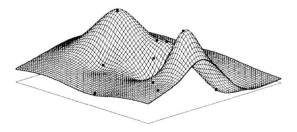

Figure 6: An example of multilevel B-spline interpolation

A surface generated by multilevel B-spline interpolation is C^2-continuous because it is the sum of C^2-continuous B-spline surfaces. Fig. 6 shows an example. Black spots in the figure represent the interpolated points. Most of the computation time is spent by evaluating function f in the region Ω. For a 64×64 grid, it takes 0.1 seconds for an SGI Crimson to generate the surface given in Fig. 6. For a 512×512 grid, the surface is generated in 1.5 seconds.

6. Metamorphosis examples

Fig. 10 gives metamorphosis examples. Figs. 10(a) and (b) show selected frames from a morph sequence between Seung-Yong and George (two of the authors), and Linda. All the images in Fig. 10(a) were generated using the same transition rate everywhere. The transition rates were allowed to vary to generate the images in Fig. 10(b). Fig. 10(c) shows the specified features overlaid on the input images. The bottom two inbetween images in that column demonstrate the effect of a procedural transition function. Fig. 10(d) shows the frames of a morph sequence between Linda and Seung-Yong. Note that transition control is applied to overcome the considerable differences between the hairlines.

One set of transition curves for the source image is sufficient to relate the transition behavior in a morph sequence. Figs. 8(a) and (b) show the primitives upon which transition curves are defined for the inbetween images given in Figs. 10(b) and (d), respectively. Each primitive may have a different transition curve, with all points along a primitive sharing the same transition rate. Figs. 8(c) and (d) depict the transition curves for the respective outer and inner primitives of Figs. 8(a) and (b). For the inbetween images shown in Fig. 10(c), linear functions in y are applied to vary the transformation between the source and destination images. In the first inbetween image, Seung-Yong is changed into George from top to bottom. Similarly, George is transformed into Seung-Yong in the second image.

Fig. 9(a) illustrates the warp function generated for transforming Seung-Yong to George in Fig. 10(a). Dark lines represent the new positions of feature points that have been internally sampled on the source image. Fig. 9(b) shows the surface interpolating through the transition rates that are evaluated from the transition curves along the primitives in Fig. 8.

All images shown in Fig. 10 are 468×480 and were generated on a SUN SPARCsystem 10. We used the hybrid method to derive the warp functions and multilevel B-spline interpolation to compute the surfaces for transition control. It took 22.0 and 1.0 seconds, respectively, to generate the warp function and surface in Fig. 9.

7. Conclusions

This paper has presented new solutions to the following three problems in image morphing: feature specification, warp generation, and surface generation for transition control. The features in an image can be specified with snakes [8], a popular computer vision technique. Snakes help an animator to easily and precisely capture the exact position of a feature. They also may reduce the work of an animator in establishing the feature correspondence between two image sequences. We introduced a new deformation technique, the MFFD, which derives C^2-continuous and one-to-one warps from feature point pairs. The technique is fast, even when the number of features is large. The resulting warps provide visually pleasing image distortions. We also presented multilevel B-spline interpolation to construct smooth surfaces that are used to control geometry and color blending. The method efficiently generates a C^2-continuous surface that interpolates a set of scattered points.

The warp and surface generation techniques in this paper may be applied to other areas of computer graphics. The MFFD can be readily extended to 3D and used to directly manipulate the shape of deformable objects. Multilevel B-spline interpolation can be used to rapidly generate free-form surfaces from positional constraints.

8. Acknowledgements

This work was supported in part by the Korean Ministry of Science and Technology (contract 94-S-05-A-03 of STEP 2000), NSF PYI award IRI-9157260, and PSC-CUNY grant RF-665313.

References

[1] Ballard, Dana H., and Christopher M. Brown. *Computer Vision*. Prentice-Hall, 1982.

[2] Beier, Thaddeus, and Shawn Neely. Feature-Based Image Metamorphosis. *Computer Graphics 26*, 2 (1992), 35–42.

[3] Benson, Philip J. Morph Transformation of the Facial Image. *Image and Vision Computing 12*, 10 (1994), 691–696.

[4] Coquillart, Sabine. Extended Free-Form Deformation: A Sculpturing Tool for 3D Geometric Modeling. *Computer Graphics 24*, 4 (1990), 187–196.

[5] Coquillart, Sabine, and Pierre Jancene. Animated Free-Form Deformation: An Interactive Animation Technique. *Computer Graphics 25*, 4 (1991), 23–26.

[6] Goodman, Tim, and Keith Unsworth. Injective Bivariate Maps. Tech. Rep. CS94/02, Dundee University, U.K., 1994.

[7] Hsu, William M., John F. Hughes, and Henry Kaufman. Direct Manipulation of Free-Form Deformations. *Computer Graphics 26*, 2 (1992), 177–184.

[8] Kass, Michael, Andrew Witkin, and Demetri Terzopoulos. Snakes: Active Contour Models. *International Journal of Computer Vision* (1988), 321–331.

[9] Lee, Seung-Yong. *Image Morphing Using Scattered Feature Interpolations*. PhD thesis, KAIST, Taejon, Korea, February 1995.

[10] Lee, Seung-Yong, Kyung-Yong Chwa, James Hahn, and Sung Yong Shin. Image Morphing Using Deformable Surfaces. In *Proceedings of Computer Animation '94* (Geneva, Switzerland, 1994), IEEE Computer Society Press, pp. 31–39.

[11] Lee, Seung-Yong, Kyung-Yong Chwa, James Hahn, and Sung Yong Shin. Image Morphing Using Deformation Techniques. *The Journal of Visualization and Computer Animation 6*, 3 (1995).

[12] Litwinowicz, Peter, and Lance Williams. Animating Images with Drawings. In *SIGGRAPH 94 Conference Proceedings* (1994), ACM Press, pp. 409–412.

[13] Meisters, G.H., and C. Olech. Locally One-to-one Mappings and a Classical Theorem on Schlicht Functions. *Duke Mathematical Journal 30* (1963), 63–80.

[14] Nishita, Tomoyuki, Toshihisa Fujii, and Eihachiro Nakamae. Metamorphosis Using Bézier Clipping. In *Proceedings of the First Pacific Conference on Computer Graphics and Applications* (Seoul, Korea, 1993), World Scientific Publishing Co., pp. 162–173.

[15] Nishita, Tomoyuki, Thomas Sederberg, and Masanori Kakimoto. Ray Tracing Trimmed Rational Surface Patches. *Computer Graphics 24*, 4 (1990), 337–345.

[16] Ruprecht, Detlef, and Heinrich Müller. Image Warping with Scattered Data Interpolation. *IEEE Computer Graphics and Applications 15*, 2 (1995), 37–43.

[17] Sederberg, Thomas W., and Scott R. Parry. Free-Form Deformation of Solid Geometric Models. *Computer Graphics 20*, 4 (1986), 151–160.

[18] Terzopoulos, Demetri. Multilevel Computational Processes for Visual Surface Reconstruction. *Computer Vision, Graphics, and Image Processing 24* (1983), 52–96.

[19] Wolberg, George. *Digital Image Warping*. IEEE Computer Society Press, Los Alamitos, CA, 1990.

Appendix: Proof of Theorem 1

Let $\Delta\phi_{ij} = \phi_{ij} - \phi_{ij}^0$ and $\mathbf{w} = (x, y)$. Suppose that $\frac{\partial x}{\partial u} > |\frac{\partial x}{\partial v}|$ and $\frac{\partial y}{\partial v} > |\frac{\partial y}{\partial u}|$ at each point on the domain Ω when $(-0.48, -0.48) \leq \Delta\phi_{ij} \leq (0.48, 0.48)$ for all i, j. Then, the Jacobian, $J = \frac{\partial x}{\partial u}\frac{\partial y}{\partial v} - \frac{\partial x}{\partial v}\frac{\partial y}{\partial u}$, is greater than zero at all points in Ω including the boundary, which implies that function $\mathbf{w}$ is one-to-one [13]. Let $\phi_{ij} = (x_{ij}, y_{ij})$, $\phi_{ij}^0 = (x_{ij}^0, y_{ij}^0)$, and $\Delta y_{ij} = y_{ij} - y_{ij}^0$. $\frac{\partial y}{\partial v} > |\frac{\partial y}{\partial u}|$ if and only if $\frac{\partial y}{\partial v} > \frac{\partial y}{\partial u}$ and $\frac{\partial y}{\partial v} > -\frac{\partial y}{\partial u}$. In what follows, we only show that $\frac{\partial y}{\partial v} > \frac{\partial y}{\partial u}$ if $-0.48 \leq \Delta y_{ij} \leq 0.48$. A symmetrical argument can be applied to the case when $\frac{\partial y}{\partial v} > -\frac{\partial y}{\partial u}$. Similarly, we can prove the remaining case, $\frac{\partial x}{\partial u} > |\frac{\partial x}{\partial v}|$.

From Eqs. (1) and (2), we have

$$
\begin{aligned}
y &= \sum_{k=0}^{3}\sum_{l=0}^{3} B_k(s)B_l(t)y_{(i+k)(j+l)} \\
&= v + \sum_{k=0}^{3}\sum_{l=0}^{3} B_k(s)B_l(t)\Delta y_{(i+k)(j+l)},
\end{aligned}
$$

and hence,

$$
\begin{aligned}
\frac{\partial y}{\partial v} - \frac{\partial y}{\partial u} \\
= 1 + \sum_{k=0}^{3}\sum_{l=0}^{3}(B_k(s)B_l'(t) - B_k'(s)B_l(t))\Delta y_{(i+k)(j+l)}.
\end{aligned}
$$

Let $c_{kl} = B_k(s)B_l'(t) - B_k'(s)B_l(t)$. From the formulae of B-spline basis functions, it holds that $B_k(t) \geq 0$, for $i = 0, 1, 2, 3$, $B_0'(t) \leq 0$, $B_1'(t) \leq 0$, $B_2'(t) \geq 0$, and $B_3'(t) \geq 0$ when $0 \leq t \leq 1$. Therefore, it immediately follows that $c_{20}, c_{30}, c_{21}, c_{31} \leq 0$ and $c_{02}, c_{12}, c_{03}, c_{13} \geq 0$. If we let $t = s + \Delta t$, then $c_{10} = -(s + \Delta t - 1)^2((s-2)^2 + (4s - 3s^2)\Delta t)/12$. Since $\Delta t \geq -s$ and $(4s - 3s^2) \geq 0$ when $0 \leq s \leq 1$, we get $(4s - 3s^2)\Delta t \geq -s(4s - 3s^2) \geq -1$, which implies $c_{10} \leq 0$. Similarly, it can be proved that $c_{32} \leq 0$, $c_{01} \geq 0$, and $c_{23} \geq 0$ when $0 \leq s, t \leq 1$.

From the fact that $c_{00} = (s - t)(s - 1)^2(t - 1)^2/12$ and $c_{33} = (s - t)s^2t^2/12$, it follows that if $s \geq t$, then $c_{00}, c_{33} \geq 0$ and if $s < t$, then $c_{00}, c_{33} \leq 0$. By manipulating the formula of c_{11}, we get $c_{11} = (s - t)(3(st + 1)(3st - 4s - 4t + 5) + 1)/12$. Let $f(s, t) = 3st - 4s - 4t + 5$. Then, $\frac{\partial f}{\partial s} = 3t - 4 < 0$ and $\frac{\partial f}{\partial t} = 3s - 4 < 0$ when $0 \leq s, t \leq 1$, which implies that f has a global minimum at $(1, 1)$. Because $f(1, 1) = 0$, $c_{11} \geq 0$ if $s \geq t$ and $c_{11} < 0$ if $s < t$. Similarly, it can be shown that $c_{22} \geq 0$ if $s \geq t$ and $c_{22} < 0$ if $s < t$.

In summary, $c_{kl} \geq 0$ if $k < l$ and $c_{kl} \leq 0$ if $k > l$ when $0 \leq s, t \leq 1$. Also, if $s \geq t$, then $c_{kk} \geq 0$, and if $s < t$, then $c_{kk} \leq 0$. We consider the case when $s \geq t$. Let

$$
C = \sum_{k=0}^{3}\sum_{l=0}^{k-1} c_{kl} - \sum_{k=0}^{3}\sum_{l=k}^{3} c_{kl}.
$$

C is a function of s and t defined on $0 \leq s, t \leq 1$. From the condition that $-0.48 \leq \Delta y_{ij} \leq 0.48$ and the properties of the values of c_{kl}, it holds that

$$
\begin{aligned}
&\frac{\partial y}{\partial v} - \frac{\partial y}{\partial u} \\
&= 1 + \left(\sum_{k=0}^{3}\sum_{l=0}^{k-1} c_{kl}\Delta y_{(i+k)(j+l)} + \sum_{k=0}^{3}\sum_{l=k}^{3} c_{kl}\Delta y_{(i+k)(j+l)}\right)
\end{aligned}
$$

$$\geq \quad 1 + 0.48 \left(\sum_{k=0}^{3} \sum_{l=0}^{k-1} c_{kl} - \sum_{k=0}^{3} \sum_{l=k}^{3} c_{kl} \right)$$
$$= \quad 1 + 0.48C.$$

To derive a lower bound of C, we partition the domain $0 \leq s, t \leq 1$ to the grid in which the internode distance Δd is 0.0001. When C is evaluated at each grid point by 64 bits double-precision arithmetic, the minimum value is -2.0463927 at $(s_0, t_0) = (0.7552, 0.2448)$. Let (s_g, t_g) be a grid point and $D = C(s_g + \Delta s, t_g + \Delta t) - C(s_g, t_g)$, where $0 \leq \Delta s, \Delta t < \Delta d$. D consists of terms $s_g^\alpha t_g^\beta \Delta s^\gamma \Delta t^\delta$, where $\alpha, \beta, \gamma, \delta = 0, 1, 2, 3$. To simplify the formula of D, we assign $s_g = t_g = 0$ and $s_g = t_g = 1$ to the terms in D having positive and negative coefficients, respectively. Then, from that $\Delta d > (\Delta s)^\gamma$ and $\Delta d > (\Delta t)^\delta$, it holds that $D > -\varepsilon \Delta d$ for $\varepsilon = \frac{4230}{36}$.

Let (s, t) be a point on the domain $0 \leq s, t \leq 1$. Let $s_g = \Delta d \lfloor s/\Delta d \rfloor$ and $t_g = \Delta d \lfloor t/\Delta d \rfloor$. Let $\Delta s = s - s_g$ and $\Delta t = t - t_g$. Then, $C(s, t) = C(s_g + \Delta s, t_g + \Delta t) > C(s_g, t_g) - \varepsilon \Delta d \geq C(s_0, t_0) - \varepsilon \Delta d \geq -2.0581427$. Hence, $1 + 0.48C > 0$ on the domain $0 \leq s, t \leq 1$, which implies that $\frac{\partial y}{\partial v} > \frac{\partial y}{\partial u}$. The case when $s < t$ can be treated similarly. $\square$

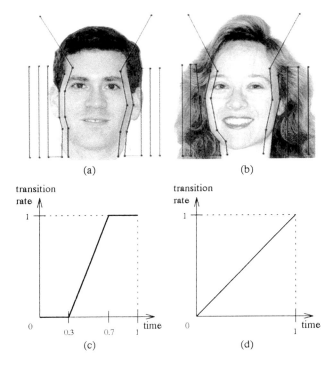

(a)   (b)

transition rate   transition rate

(c)   (d)

Figure 8: Primitives with transition curves

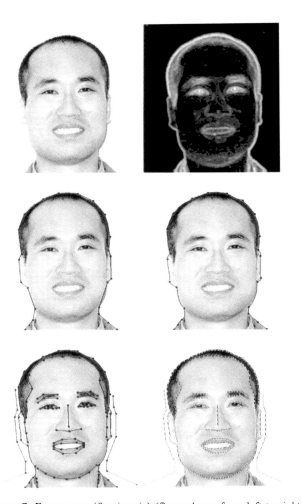

Figure 7: Feature specification; (a)-(f) are shown from left-to-right and top-to-bottom.

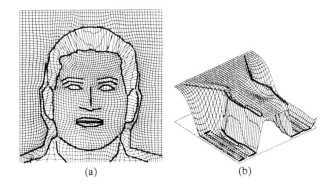

(a)   (b)

Figure 9: Warp function and surface

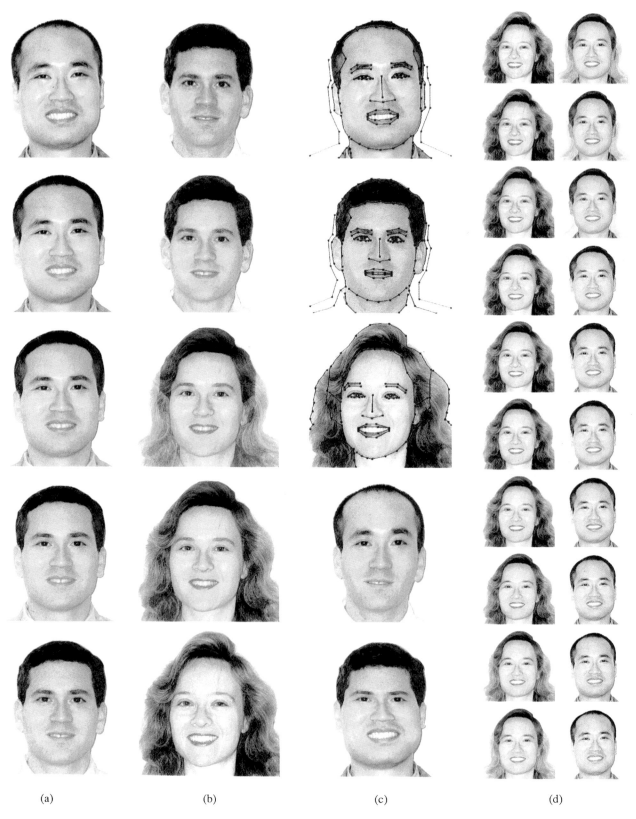

(a)   (b)   (c)   (d)

Figure 10: Metamorphosis examples

Feature-Based Volume Metamorphosis

Apostolos Lerios, Chase D. Garfinkle, Marc Levoy *

Computer Science Department
Stanford University

Abstract

Image metamorphosis, or image *morphing*, is a popular technique for creating a smooth transition between two images. For synthetic images, transforming and rendering the underlying three-dimensional (3D) models has a number of advantages over morphing between two pre-rendered images. In this paper we consider 3D metamorphosis applied to volume-based representations of objects. We discuss the issues which arise in volume morphing and present a method for creating morphs. Our morphing method has two components: first a warping of the two input volumes, then a blending of the resulting warped volumes. The warping component, an extension of Beier and Neely's image warping technique to 3D, is feature-based and allows fine user control, thus ensuring realistic looking intermediate objects. In addition, our warping method is amenable to an efficient approximation which gives a 50 times speedup and is computable to arbitrary accuracy. Also, our technique corrects the ghosting problem present in Beier and Neely's technique. The second component of the morphing process, blending, is also under user control; this guarantees smooth transitions in the renderings.

CR Categories: I.3.5 [Computer Graphics]: Computational Geometry and Object Modeling; I.3.7 [Computer Graphics]: Three-Dimensional Graphics and Realism.

Additional Keywords: Volume morphing, warping, rendering; sculpting; shape interpolation, transformation, blending; computer animation.

1 Introduction

1.1 Image Morphing versus 3D Morphing

Image morphing, the construction of an image sequence depicting a gradual transition between two images, has been extensively investigated [21] [2] [6] [16]. For images generated from 3D models, there is an alternative to morphing the images themselves: *3D morphing* generates intermediate 3D models, the morphs, directly from the given models; the morphs are then rendered to produce an image sequence depicting the transformation. 3D morphing overcomes the

following shortcomings of 2D morphing as applied to images generated from 3D models:

- In 3D morphing, creating the morphs is independent of the viewing and lighting parameters. Hence, we can create a morph sequence once, and then experiment with various camera angles and lighting conditions during rendering. In 2D morphing, a new morph must be recomputed every time we wish to alter our viewpoint or the illumination of the 3D model.

- 2D techniques, lacking information on the model's spatial configuration, are unable to correctly handle changes in illumination and visibility. Two examples of this type of artifact are: (i) Shadows and highlights fail to match shape changes occuring in the morph. (ii) When a feature of the 3D object is not visible in the original 2D image, this feature cannot be made to appear during the morph; for example, when a singing actor needs to open her mouth during a morph, pulling her lips apart thickens the lips instead of revealing her teeth.

1.2 Geometric versus Volumetric 3D Models

The models subjected to 3D morphing can be described either by geometric primitives or by volumes (volumetric data sets). Each representation requires different morphing algorithms. This dichotomy parallels the separation of 2D morphing techniques into those that operate on raster images [21] [2] [6], and those that assume vector-based image representations [16]. We believe that volume-based descriptions are more appropriate for 3D morphing for the following reasons:

- The quality and applicability of geometric 3D morphing techniques [12] is highly dependent on the models' geometric primitives and their topological properties. Volume morphing is independent of object geometries and topologies, and thus imposes no such restrictions on the objects which can be successfully morphed.

- Volume morphing may be applied to objects represented either by geometric primitives or by volumes. Geometric descriptions can be easily converted to high-quality volume representations, as we will see in section 2. The reverse process produces topologically complex objects, usually inappropriate for geometric morphing.

1.3 Volume Morphing

The 3D volume morphing problem can be stated as follows. Given two volumes $\mathcal{S}$ and $\mathcal{T}$, henceforth called the *source* and *target* volumes, we must produce a sequence of intermediate volumes, the *morphs*, meeting the following two conditions:

---

* Center for Integrated Systems, Stanford University, Stanford, CA 94305
{lerios,cgar,levoy}@cs.stanford.edu
http://www-graphics.stanford.edu/

Permission to make digital/hard copy of part or all of this work for personal or classroom use is granted without fee provided that copies are not made or distributed for profit or commercial advantage, the copyright notice, the title of the publication and its date appear, and notice is given that copying is by permission of ACM, Inc. To copy otherwise, to republish, to post on servers, or to redistribute to lists, requires prior specific permission and/or a fee.

© 1995   ACM-0-89791-701-4/95/008 $3.50

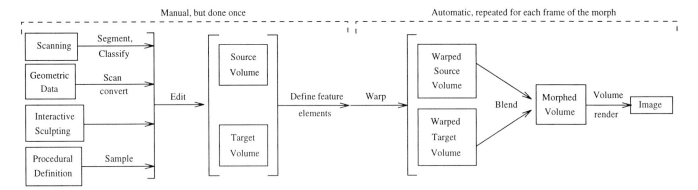

Figure 1: Data flow in a morphing system. Editing comprises retouching and aligning the volumes for cosmetic reasons.

Realism: The morphs should be realistic objects which have plausible 3D geometry and which retain the essential features of the source and target.

Smoothness: The renderings of the morphs must depict a smooth transition from S to T.

From the former condition stems the major challenge in designing a 3D morphing system: as automatic feature recognition and matching have yet to equal human perception, user input is crucial in defining the transformation of the objects. The challenge for the designer of a 3D morphing technique is two-fold: the morphing algorithm must permit fine user control and the accompanying user interface (UI) should be intuitive.

Our solution to 3D morphing attempts to meet both conditions of the morphing problem, while allowing a simple, yet powerful UI. To this end, we create each morph in two steps (see figure 1):

Warping: S and T are warped to obtain volumes S' and T'. Our warping technique allows the animator to define quickly the exact shape of objects represented in S' and T', thus meeting the realism condition.

Blending: S' and T' are combined into one volume, the morph. Our blending technique provides the user with sufficient control to create a smooth morph.

1.4 Prior Work

Prior work on feature-based 2D morphing [2] will be discussed in section 3.

Prior work in volume morphing comprises [9], [8], and [5]. These approaches can be summarized in terms of our warping/blending framework.

[5] and [8] have both presented warping techniques. [5] examined the theory of extending selected 2D warping techniques into 3D. A UI was not presented, however, and only morphs of simple objects were shown. [8] presents an algorithm which attempts to automatically identify correspondences between the volumes, without the aid of user input.

[9] and [8] have suggested using a frequency or wavelet representation of the volumes to perform the blending, allowing different interpolation schedules across subbands. In addition, they have observed that isosurfaces of the morphs may move abruptly, or even completely disappear and reappear as the morph progresses, destroying its continuity. This suggests that volume rendering may be superior to isosurface extraction for rendering the morphs.

Our paper is partitioned into the following sections: Section 2 covers volume acquisition methods. Sections 3 and 4

present the warping and blending steps of our morphing algorithm. Section 5 describes an efficient implementation of our warping method and section 6 discusses our results. We conclude with suggestions for future work and applications in section 7.

2 Volume Acquisition

Volume data may be acquired in several ways, the most common of which are listed below.

Scanned volumes: Some scanning technologies, such as Computerized Tomography (CT) or Magnetic Resonance Imaging (MRI) generate volume data. Figures 5(a) and 5(c) show CT scans of a human and an orangutan head, respectively.

Scan converted geometric models: A geometric model can be *voxelized* [10], preferably with antialiasing [20], generating a volume-based representation of the model. Figures 6(a), 6(b), 7(a), and 7(b) show examples of scan-converted volumes.

Interactive sculpting: Interactive modeling, or *sculpting* [19] [7], can generate volume data directly.

Procedural definition: Hypertexture volumes [15] can be defined procedurally by functions over 3D space.

3 Warping

The first step in the volume morphing pipeline is warping the source and target volumes S and T. Volume warping has been the subject of several investigations in computer graphics, computer vision, and medicine. Warping techniques can be coarsely classified into two groups: (i) Techniques that allow only minimal user control, consisting of at most a few scalar parameters. These algorithms automatically determine similarities between two volumes, and then seek the warp which transforms the first volume to the second one [18]. (ii) Techniques in which user control consists of manually specifying the warp for a collection of points in the volume. The rest of the volume is then warped by interpolating the warping function. This group of algorithms includes free-form deformations [17], as well as semi-automatic medical data alignment [18].

As stated in section 1.3, user control over the warps is crucial in designing good morphs. Point-to-point mapping methods [21], in the form of either regular lattices or scattered points [13], have worked in 2D. However, regular grids provide a cumbersome interface in 2D; in 3D they would likely become unmanageable. Also, prohibitively many scattered points are needed to adequately specify a 3D warp.

Our solution is a feature-based approach extending the work of [2] into the 3D domain. The next two sections will introduce our feature-based 3D warping and discuss the UI to feature specification.

3.1 Feature-Based 3D Warping using Fields

The purpose of a *feature element* is to identify a feature of an object. For example, consider the X-29 plane of figure 6(b); an element can be used to delineate the nose of the plane. In feature-based morphing, elements come in *pairs*, one element in the source volume $\mathcal{S}$, and its counterpart in the target volume $\mathcal{T}$. A pair of elements identifies corresponding features in the two volumes, i.e. features that should be transformed to one another during the morph. For instance, when morphing the dart of figure 6(a) to the X-29 plane, the tip of the dart should turn into the nose of the plane. In order to obtain good morphs, we need to specify a *collection* of element pairs which define the overall correspondence of the two objects. These element pairs interact like magnets shaping a pliable volume: while a single magnet can only move, turn, and stretch the volume, multiple magnets generate interacting fields, termed *influence fields*, which combine to shape the volume in complex ways. Sculpting with multiple magnets becomes easier if we have magnets of various kinds in our toolbox, each magnet generating a differently shaped influence field. The elements in our toolkit are points, line segments, rectangles, and boxes.

In the following presentation, we first describe individual elements, and discuss how they identify features. We then show how a pair of elements guarantees that corresponding features are transformed to one another during the morph. Finally, we discuss how multiple element pairs interact.

Individual Feature Elements

Individual feature elements should be designed in a manner such that they can delineate any feature an object may possess. However, expressiveness should not sacrifice simplicity, as complex features can still be matched by a group of simple elements. Hence, the defining *attributes* of our elements encode only the essential characteristics of features:

Spatial configuration: The feature's position and orientation are encoded in an element's *local coordinate system,* comprising four vectors. These are the position vector of its origin $\mathbf{c}$, and three mutually perpendicular unit vectors $\mathbf{x}$, $\mathbf{y}$ and $\mathbf{z}$, defining the directions of the coordinate axes. The element's *scaling factors* s_x, s_y, and s_z define a feature's extent along each of the principal axes.

Dimensionality: The dimensionality of a feature depends on the subjective perception of a feature's relative size in each dimension: the tip of the plane's nose is perceived as a point, the edge of the plane's wing as a line, the dart's fin as a surface, and the dart's shaft as a volume. Accordingly, our simplified elements have a *type*, which can be a point, segment, rectangle, or box. In our magnetic sculpting analogy, the element type determines the shape of its influence field. For example, a box magnet defines the path of points within and near the box; points further from the box are influenced less as their distance increases.

The reader familiar with the 2D technique of [2] will notice two differences between our 3D elements and a direct extention of 2D feature lines into 3D; in fact, these are the only differences as far as the warping algorithm is concerned.

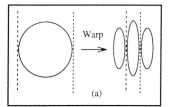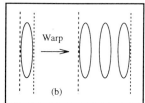

Figure 2: 2D warp artifacts (not to scale). (a) shows the result of squeezing a circle using two feature lines placed on opposite sides of the circle. The warped circle spills outside the corresponding, closely spaced, lines. Similarly, in (b), the narrow ellipsoid with two lines on either side does not expand to a circle when the lines are drawn apart; we get instead three copies of the ellipsoid.

First, in the 2D technique, the shape of a feature line's influence field is controlled by two manually specified parameters. Instead, we provide four simple types of influence fields — point, segment, rectangle, and box — thus allowing for a more intuitive, yet equally powerful, UI.

Second, our feature elements encode the 3D extent of a 3D feature via the scaling factors s_x, s_y, and s_z; by contrast, feature lines in [2] capture only the 1D extent of a 2D feature, in the direction of each feature line. These scaling factors introduce additional degrees of freedom for each feature element. In the majority of situations, these extra degrees have a minor effect on the warp and may thus be ignored. However, under extreme warps, they permit the user to solve the *ghosting* problem, documented in [2] and illustrated in figure 2. For instance, in part (b) of this example, the ellipsoid is replicated because each feature line requires that an unscaled ellipsoid appear by its side: the feature lines in [2] cannot specify any stretching in the perpendicular direction. However, in a 2D analogue of our technique, the user would use the lines' scaling factors to stretch the ellipsoid. First, the user would encode the ellipsoid's width in the scaling factors of the original feature lines. Then, in order to stretch the ellipsoid into a circle, the user would not only move the feature lines apart, but will also make the lines' scaling factors encode the desired new width of the ellipsoid. In fact, using our technique, a single feature line suffices to turn the ellipsoid into a circle.

Element Pairs

As in the 2D morphing system of [2], the animator identifies two corresponding features in $\mathcal{S}$ and $\mathcal{T}$, by defining a pair of elements (e_s, e_t). These features should be transformed to one another during the morph. Such a transformation requires that the feature of $\mathcal{S}$ be moved, turned, and stretched to match respectively the position, orientation, and size of the corresponding feature of $\mathcal{T}$. Consequently, for each frame of the morph, our warp should generate a volume $\mathcal{S}'$ from $\mathcal{S}$ with the following property: the feature of $\mathcal{S}$ should possess an intermediate position, orientation and size in $\mathcal{S}'$. This is achieved by computing the warp in two steps:

Interpolation: We interpolate the local coordinate systems[1] and scaling factors of elements e_s and e_t to produce an *interpolated element* e'. This element encodes the spatial configuration of the feature in $\mathcal{S}'$.

Inverse mapping: For every point in $\mathbf{p}'$ of $\mathcal{S}'$, we find the corresponding point $\mathbf{p}$ in $\mathcal{S}$ in two simple steps (see

---

[1]The axes directions $\mathbf{x}$, $\mathbf{y}$, and $\mathbf{z}$ are interpolated in spherical coordinates to ensure smooth rotations.

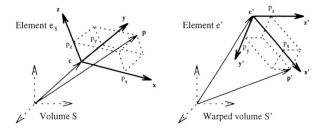

Figure 3: Single element warp. In order to find the point **p** in volume $\mathcal{S}$ that corresponds to **p**′ in $\mathcal{S}'$, we first find the coordinates (p_x, p_y, p_z) of **p**′ in the scaled local system of element e'; **p** is then the point with coordinates (p_x, p_y, p_z) in the scaled local system of element e_s. To simplify the figure, we have assumed unity scaling factors for all elements.

figure 3): (i) We find the coordinates of **p**′ in the scaled local system of element e' by

$$
\begin{aligned}
p_x &= (\mathbf{p}' - \mathbf{c}') \cdot \mathbf{x}'/s'_x \\
p_y &= (\mathbf{p}' - \mathbf{c}') \cdot \mathbf{y}'/s'_y \\
p_z &= (\mathbf{p}' - \mathbf{c}') \cdot \mathbf{z}'/s'_z.
\end{aligned}
$$

(ii) **p** is the point with coordinates p_x, p_y and p_z in the scaled local system of element e_s, i.e. the point $\mathbf{c} + p_x s_x \mathbf{x} + p_y s_y \mathbf{y} + p_z s_z \mathbf{z}$.[2]

Collections of Element Pairs

In extending the warping algorithm of the previous paragraph to multiple element pairs, we adhere to the intuitive mental model of magnetic sculpting used in [2]. Each pair of elements defines a field that extends throughout the volume. A collection of element pairs defines a collection of fields, all of which influence each point in the volume. We therefore use a weighted averaging scheme to determine the point **p** in $\mathcal{S}$ that corresponds to each point **p**′ of $\mathcal{S}'$. That is, we first compute to what point $\mathbf{p}_i$ each element pair would map **p**′ in the absence of all other pairs; then, we average the $\mathbf{p}_i$'s using a weighting function that depends on the distance of **p**′ to the interpolated elements e'_i.

Our weighting scheme uses an inverse square law: $\mathbf{p}_i$ is weighted by $(d + \epsilon)^{-2}$ where d is the distance of **p**′ from the element e'_i; ϵ is a small constant used to avoid division by zero.[3] The type of element e'_i determines how d is calculated:

Points: d is the distance between **p**′ and the origin **c** of the local coordinate system of element e'_i. This definition is identical to [21].

Segments: The element is treated as a line segment centered at the origin **c**, aligned with the local x-axis and having length s_x; d is the distance of **p**′ from this line segment. This definition is identical to [2].

Rectangles: Rectangles have the same center and x extent as segments, but also extend into a second dimension, having width s_y along the local y-axis. d is zero if **p**′ is on the rectangle, otherwise it is the distance of **p**′ from the rectangle. This definition extends segments to area elements.

Boxes: Boxes add depth to rectangles, thus extending for s_z units along the local z-axis. d is zero if **p**′ is within the box, otherwise it is the distance of **p**′ from the box's surface.

The reader will notice that the point, segment, and rectangle element types are redundant, as far as the mathematical formulation of our warp is concerned. However, a variety of element types maintains best the intuitive conceptual analogy to magnetic sculpting.

3.2 User Interface

The UI to the warping algorithm has to depict the source and target volumes, in conjunction with the feature elements. Hardware-assisted volume rendering [4] makes possible a UI solely based on direct visualization of the volumes, with the embedded elements interactively scan-converted. Using a low-end rendering pipeline, however, the UI has to resort to geometric representations of the models embedded in the volumes. These geometric representations can be obtained in either of two ways:

- Pre-existing volumes are visualized by isosurface extraction via marching cubes [14]. Several different isosurfaces can be extracted to visualize all prominent features of the volume, a volume rendering guiding the extraction process.

- For volumes that were obtained by scan converting geometric models, the original model can be used.

Once geometric representations of the models are available, the animator can use the commercial modeler of his/her choice to specify the elements. Our system, shown in figure 6(d), is based on Inventor, the Silicon Graphics (SGI) 3D programming environment. Models are drawn in user-defined materials, usually translucent, in order to distinguish them from the feature elements. These, in turn, are drawn in such a way that their attributes — local coordinate system, scaling factors, and dimensionality — are graphically depicted and altered using a minimal set of widgets.

4 Blending

The warping step has produced two warped volumes $\mathcal{S}'$ and $\mathcal{T}'$ from the source and target volumes $\mathcal{S}$ and $\mathcal{T}$. Any practical warp is likely to misalign some features of $\mathcal{S}$ and $\mathcal{T}$, possibly because these were not specifically delineated by feature elements. Even if perfectly aligned, matching features may have different opacities. These areas of the morph, collectively called *mismatches*, will have to be smoothly faded in/out in the rendered sequence, in order to maintain the illusion of a smooth transformation. This is the goal of blending.

We have two alternatives for performing this blending step. It may either be done by cross-dissolving images rendered from $\mathcal{S}'$ and $\mathcal{T}'$, which we call 2.5D morphing, or by cross-dissolving the volumes themselves, and rendering the result, i.e. a full 3D morph. The 2.5D approach produces smooth image sequences and provides the view and lighting independence of 3D morphing discussed in section 1.1; however, some disadvantages of 2D morphing are reintroduced, such as incorrect lighting and occlusions. Consequently, 2.5D morphs do not look as realistic as 3D morphs. For example, the "missing link" of figure 5(f) lacks distinct teeth, and the base of the skull appears unrealistically transparent.

---

[2]$\mathcal{T}$ is warped into $\mathcal{T}'$ in a similar way, the only difference being that e_t is used in this last step in place of e_s.

[3]Distance measurements postulate cubical volumes of unit side length. Also, we always set ϵ to 0.001.

For this reason, we decided to investigate full 3D morphing, whereby we blend the warped volumes by interpolating their voxel values. The interpolation weight $w(t)$ is a function that varies over time, where "time" is the normalized frame number[4]. We have the option of using either a linear or non-linear $w(t)$.

4.1 Linear Cross-Dissolving

The pixel cross-dissolving of 2D morphing suggests a linear $w(t)$. Indeed, it works well for blending the color information of $\mathcal{S}'$ and $\mathcal{T}'$. However, it fails to interpolate opacities in a manner such that the rendered morph sequence appears smooth. This is due to the exponential dependence of the color of a ray cast through the volume on the opacities of the voxels it encounters. This phenomenon is illustrated in the morph of figure 5. In particular, the morph abruptly snaps into the source and target volumes if a linear $w(t)$ is used: figure 5(g) shows that at time 0.06, very early in the morph, the empty space towards the front of the human head has already been filled in by the warped orangutan volume.

4.2 Non-Linear Cross-Dissolving

In order to obtain smoothly progressing renderings, we would like to compensate for the exponential dependence of rendered color on opacity as we blend $\mathcal{S}'$ and $\mathcal{T}'$. This can be done by devising an appropriate $w(t)$.

In principle, there cannot exist an ideal compensating $w(t)$. The exact relationship between rendered color and opacity depends on the distance the ray travels through voxels with this opacity. Hence a globally applied $w(t)$ cannot compensate at once for all mismatches since they have different thickness. Even a locally chosen $w(t)$ cannot work, as different viewpoints cast different rays through the morph.

In practice, the mismatches between $\mathcal{S}'$ and $\mathcal{T}'$ are small in number and extent. Hence, the above theoretical objections do not prevent us from empirically deriving a successful $w(t)$. Our design goal is to compensate for the exponential relation of rendered color to opacity by interpolating opacities at the rate of an inverse exponential. The sigmoid curve given by

$$\frac{\tan^{-1}(2s(t - 0.5))}{2\tan^{-1}s} + \frac{1}{2}$$

satisfies this requirement. It suppresses the contribution of $\mathcal{T}'$'s opacity in the early part of the morph, the degree of suppression controlled by the *blending parameter s*. Similarly, the contribution of $\mathcal{T}'$'s opacity is enhanced in the latter part of the morph. Figure 5(h), illustrates the application of compensated interpolation to the morph of figure 5: in contrast to figure 5(g), figure 5(h) looks very much like the human head, as an early frame in the morph sequence should.

5 Performance and Optimization

A performance drawback of our feature-based warping technique is that each point in the warped volume is influenced by all elements, since the influence fields never decay to zero. It follows that the time to warp a volume is proportional to the number of element pairs. An efficient C++ implementation, using incremental calculations, needs 160 minutes to warp a single 300^3 volume with 30 element pairs on an SGI Indigo 2.

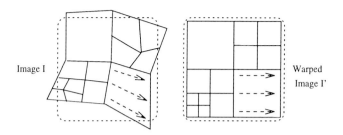

Figure 4: 2D analogue of piecewise linear warping. A warped image $\mathcal{I}'$ is first subdivided by an adaptive grid of squares, here marked by solid lines. Then, each square vertex is warped into $\mathcal{I}$. Finally, pixels in the interior of each grid cell are warped by bilinearly interpolating the warped positions of the vertices. The dashed arrows demonstrate how the interior of the bottom right square is warped. The dotted rectangles mark image buffer borders.

We have implemented two optimizations which greatly accelerate the computation of the warped volume $\mathcal{V}'$, where we henceforth use $\mathcal{V}$ to denote either $\mathcal{S}$ or $\mathcal{T}$. First, we approximate the spatially non-linear warping function with a *piecewise linear warp* [13]. Second, we introduce an *octree subdivision* over $\mathcal{V}$.

5.1 Piecewise Linear Approximation

The 2D form of this optimization, shown in figure 4, illustrates its key steps within the familiar framework of image warping. In 3D, piecewise linear warping begins by subdividing $\mathcal{V}'$ into a coarse, 3D, regular grid, and warping the grid vertices into $\mathcal{V}$, using the algorithm of section 3.1. The voxels in the interior of each cubic grid cell are then warped by trilinearly interpolating the warped positions of the cube's vertices. Using this method, $\mathcal{V}'$ can be computed by scan-converting each cube in turn. Essentially, we treat $\mathcal{V}$ as a solid texture, with the warped grid specifying the mapping into texture space. The expensive computation of section 3.1 is now performed only for a small fraction of the voxels, and scan-conversion dominates the warping time.

This piecewise linear approximation will not accurately capture the warp in highly non-linear regions, unless we use a very fine grid. However, computing a uniformly fine sampling of the warp defeats the efficiency gain of this approach. Hence, we use an adaptive grid which is subdivided more finely in regions where the warp is highly non-linear. To determine whether a grid cell requires subdivision, we compare the exact and approximated warped positions of several points within the cell. If the error is above a user-specified threshold, the cell is subdivided further. In order to reduce computation, we use the vertices of the next-higher resolution grid as the points at which to measure the error. Using this technique, the non-linear warp can be approximated to arbitrary accuracy.[5]

Since we are subsampling the warping function, it is possible that this algorithm will fail to subdivide non-linear regions. Analytically bounding the variance of the warping function would guarantee conservative subdivision. However, this is unnecessary in practice, as the warps used in generating morphs generally do not possess large high-frequency components.

This optimization has been applied to 2D morphing systems, as well; by using common texture-mapping hardware

---

[4]In other words, "time" is a real number linearly increasing from 0 to 1 as the morph unfolds.

[5]We always use an error tolerance of a single voxel width and an initial subdivision of 15^3 cells.

to warp the images, 2D morphs can be generated at interactive rates [1].

5.2 Octree Subdivision

V usually contains large "empty" regions, that is, regions which are completely transparent. The warp will map these parts of V into empty regions of V'. Scan conversion, as described above, need not take place when a warped grid cell is wholly contained within such a region. By constructing an octree over V, we can identify many such cells, and thus avoid scan converting them.

5.3 Implementation

Our optimized warping method warps a 300^3 volume in approximately 3 minutes per frame on an SGI Indigo 2. This represents a speedup of 50 over the unoptimized algorithm, without noticeable loss of quality. The running time is still dominated by scan-conversion and resampling, both of which can be accelerated by the use of 3D texture-mapping hardware.

6 Results and Conclusions

Our color figures show the source volumes, target volumes, and halfway morphs for three morph sequences we have created.

The human and orangutan volumes shown in figures 5(a) and 5(c) were warped using 26 element pairs to produce the volumes of figures 5(b) and 5(d) at the midpoint of the morph. The blended middle morph appears in figure 5(e).

Figures 6 and 7 show two examples of color morphs, requiring 37 and 29 element pairs, respectively. The UI, displaying the elements used to control the morph of figure 6, is shown in 6(d).

The total time it takes to compose a 50-frame morph sequence for 300^3 volumes comprises all the steps shown on figure 1. Our experience is that about 24 hours are necessary to turn design into reality on an SGI Indigo 2:

Hours	Task
10	CT scan segmentation, classification, retouching
1	Scan conversion of geometric model
8	Feature element definition (novice)
3	Feature element definition (expert)
5	Warping
3	Blending: 1 hour for each s: 2, 4, 6; retain best
4	Hi-res volume rendering (monochrome)
12	Hi-res volume rendering (color)

We have presented a two step feature-based technique for realistic and smooth metamorphosis between two 3D models represented by volumes. In the first step, our feature-based warping algorithm allows fine user control, and thus ensures realistic morphs. In addition, our warping method is amenable to an efficient, adaptive approximation which gives a 50 times speedup. Also, our technique corrects the ghosting problem of [2]. In the second step, our user-controlled blending ensures that the rendered morph sequence appears smooth.

7 Future Work and Applications

We see the potential for improving 3D morphing in three primary aspects:

Warping Techniques: Improved warping methods could allow for finer user control, as well as smoother, possibly spline-based, interpolation of the warping function across the volume. More complex, but more expressive feature elements [11] may also be designed.

User Interface: We envision improving our UI by adding computer-assisted feature identification: the computer suggesting features by landmark data extraction [18], 3D edge identification, or, as in 2D morphing, by motion estimation [6]. Also, we are considering giving the user more flexible control over the movement of feature elements during the morph, i.e. the rule by which interpolated elements are constructed, perhaps by keyframed or spline-path motion.

Blending: Blending can be improved by allowing local definition of the blending rate, associating an interpolation schedule with each feature element.

Morphing's primary application has been in the entertainment industry. However, it can also be used as a general visualization tool for illustration and teaching purposes [3]; for example, our orangutan to human morph could be used as a means of visualizing Darwinian evolution. Finally, our feature-based warping technique can be used in modeling and sculpting.

Acknowledgments

Philippe Lacroute helped render our morphs, and designed part of the dart to X-29 fly-by movie shown on our video. We used the horse mesh courtesy of Rhythm & Hues, the color added by Greg Turk. John W. Rick provided the plastic cast of the orangutan head and Paul F. Hemler arranged the CT scan. Jonathan J. Chew and David Ofelt helped keep our computer resources in operation.

References

[1] T. Beier and S. Neely. Pacific Data Images. Personal communication.

[2] T. Beier and S. Neely. Feature-based image metamorphosis. In *Computer Graphics*, vol 26(2), pp 35–42, New York, NY, July 1992. Proceedings of SIGGRAPH '92.

[3] B. P. Bergeron. Morphing as a means of generating variation in visual medical teaching materials. *Computers in Biology and Medicine*, 24(1):11–18, Jan. 1994.

[4] B. Cabral, N. Cam, and J. Foran. Accelerated volume rendering and tomographic reconstruction using texture mapping hardware. In A. Kaufman and W. Krueger, editors, *Proceedings of the 1994 Symposium on Volume Visualization*, pp 91–98, New York, NY, Oct. 1994. ACM SIGGRAPH and IEEE Computer Society.

[5] M. Chen, M. W. Jones, and P. Townsend. Methods for volume metamorphosis. To appear in *Image Processing for Broadcast and Video Production*, Y. Paker and S. Wilbur editors, Springer-Verlag, London, 1995.

[6] M. Covell and M. Withgott. Spanning the gap between motion estimation and morphing. In *Proceedings of IEEE International Conference on Acoustics, Speech and Signal Processing*, vol 5, pp 213–216, New York, NY, 1994. IEEE.

[7] T. A. Galyean and J. F. Hughes. Sculpting: An interactive volumetric modeling technique. In *Computer Graphics*, vol 25(4), pp 267–274, New York, NY, July 1991. Proceedings of SIGGRAPH '91.

[8] T. He, S. Wang, and A. Kaufman. Wavelet-based volume morphing. In D. Bergeron and A. Kaufman, editors, *Proceedings of Visualization '94*, pp 85–91, Los Alamitos, CA, Oct. 1994. IEEE Computer Society and ACM SIGGRAPH.

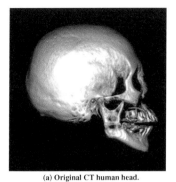
(a) Original CT human head.

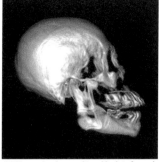
(b) Human head warped to midpoint of morph.

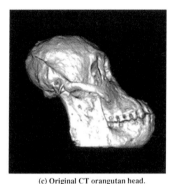
(c) Original CT orangutan head.

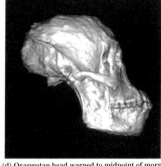
(d) Orangutan head warped to midpoint of morph.

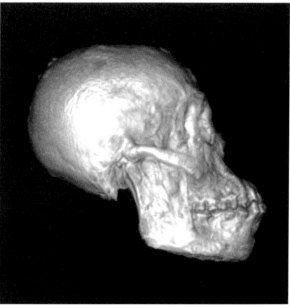
(e) 3D volume morph halfway between human head and orangutan head.

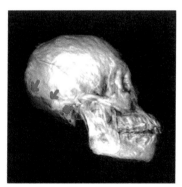
(f) Cross–dissolve of figures 5(b) and 5(d) illustrating a drawback of 2.5 D morphing. The base of the skull (indicated by red arrows) appears unrealistically transparent, and the teeth are indistinct, compared to the full 3D morph shown in figure 5(e).

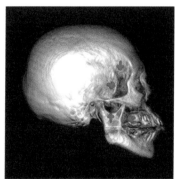
(g) Volume morph at time 0.06 using linear interpolation of warped volumes. Due to the exponential dependence of rendered color on opacity, the empty space towards the front of the human head has already been filled in by the warped orangutan volume (red arrows).

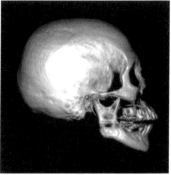
(h) Volume morph at time 0.06 using non–linear interpolation of warped volumes to correct for the exponential dependence of color on opacity. The result is now nearly identical to the human (see section 4.2).

Figure 5: Human to orangutan morph.

[9] J. F. Hughes. Scheduled Fourier volume morphing. In *Computer Graphics*, vol 26(2), pp 43–46, New York, NY, July 1992. Proceedings of SIGGRAPH '92.

[10] A. Kaufman, D. Cohen, and R. Yagel. Volume graphics. *Computer*, 26(7):51–64, July 1993.

[11] A. Kaul and J. Rossignac. Solid-interpolating deformations: Construction and animation of PIPs. In F. H. Post and W. Barth, editors, *Eurographics '91*, pp 493–505, Amsterdam, The Netherlands, Sept. 1991. Eurographics Association, North-Holland.

[12] J. R. Kent, W. E. Carlson, and R. E. Parent. Shape transformation for polyhedral objects. In *Computer Graphics*, vol 26(2), pp 47–54, New York, NY, July 1992. Proceedings of SIGGRAPH '92.

[13] P. Litwinowicz. Efficient techniques for interactive texture placement. In *Computer Graphics Proceedings*, Annual Conference Series, pp 119–122, New York, NY, July 1994. Conference Proceedings of SIGGRAPH '94.

[14] W. E. Lorensen and H. E. Cline. Marching cubes: A high resolution 3-D surface construction algorithm. In *Computer Graphics*, vol 21(4), pp 163–169, New York, NY, July 1987. Proceedings of SIGGRAPH '87.

[15] K. Perlin and E. M. Hoffert. Hypertexture. In *Computer Graphics*, vol 23(3), pp 253–262, New York, NY, July 1989. Proceedings of SIGGRAPH '89.

[16] T. W. Sedeberg, P. Gao, G. Wang, and H. Mu. 2-D shape blending: An intrinsic solution to the vertex path problem. In *Computer Graphics Proceedings*, Annual Conference Series, pp 15–18, New York, NY, Aug. 1993. Conference Proceedings of SIGGRAPH '93.

[17] T. W. Sederberg and S. R. Parry. Free-form deformations of

(a) Dart volume from scan–converted polygon mesh.

(b) X–29 volume from scan–converted polygon mesh.

(c) Volume morph halfway between dart and X–29.

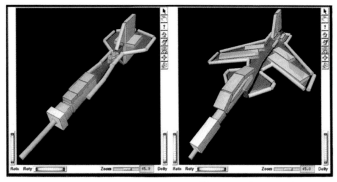

(d) User interface showing elements used to establish correspondences between models. Points (not shown), segments, rectangles, and boxes are respectively drawn as pink spheres, green cylinders, narrow blue slabs, and yellow boxes. The x, y, and z axes of each element are shown only when the user clicks on an element in order to change its attributes; otherwise, they remain invisible to prevent cluttering the work area (see section 3.2).

Figure 6: Dart to X-29 morph.

(a) Lion volume from scan–converted polygon mesh.

(b) Leopard–horse volume from scan–converted polygon mesh.

(c) Volume morph halfway between lion and leopard–horse.

Figure 7: Lion to leopard-horse morph.

solid geometric models. In *Computer Graphics*, vol 20(4), pp 151–160, New York, NY, Aug. 1986. Proceedings of SIGGRAPH '86.

[18] P. A. van den Elsen, E.-J. D. Pol, and M. A. Viergever. Medical image matching — a review with classification. *IEEE Engineering in Medicine and Biology Magazine*, 12(1):26–39, Mar. 1993.

[19] S. W. Wang and A. Kaufman. Volume sculpting. In *Proceedings of 1995 Symposium on Interactive 3D Graphics*, pp 151–156,

214, New York, NY, Apr. 1995. ACM SIGGRAPH.

[20] S. W. Wang and A. E. Kaufman. Volume sampled voxelization of geometric primitives. In G. M. Nielson and D. Bergeron, editors, *Proceedings of Visualization '93*, pp 78–84, Los Alamitos, CA, Oct. 1993. IEEE Computer Society and ACM SIGGRAPH.

[21] G. Wolberg. *Digital Image Warping*. IEEE Computer Society P., Los Alamitos, CA, 1990.

Time-Dependent Three-Dimensional Intravascular Ultrasound

Jed Lengyel*
Cornell University

Donald P. Greenberg†
Cornell University

Richard Popp‡
Stanford University

Abstract

Intravascular ultrasonography and x-ray angiography provide two complimentary techniques for imaging the moving coronary arteries. We present a technique that combines the strengths of both, by recovering the moving three-dimensional arterial tree from a stereo pair of angiograms through the use of compound-energy "snakes", placing the intravascular ultrasound slices at their proper positions in time and space, and dynamically displaying the combined data.

Past techniques have assumed that the ultrasound slices are parallel and that the vessel being imaged is straight.

For the first time, by applying simple but effective techniques from computer graphics, the *moving* geometry of the artery from the angiogram and the *time-dependent* images of the interior of the vessel wall from the intravascular ultrasound can be viewed simultaneously, showing the proper geometric and temporal relations of the slice data and the angiogram projections. By using texture-mapped rectangles the combined ultrasound slice/angiogram display technique is well suited to run in real time on current graphics workstations.

CR Categories and Subject Descriptors: I.3.0 [Computer Graphics]: General; I.3.8 [Computer Graphics]: Applications. J.3 [Life and Medical Sciences].

1 Introduction

Although the current trend in medical imaging is towards non-invasive and low-radiation techniques such as MRI (magnetic resonance imaging), for cardiac patients there is still a need for high-resolution, high-detail information particularly for planning coronary treatments such as by-pass surgery, balloon angioplasty, and atherectomy. No current non-invasive imaging technique can provide the accurate high-resolution data required for these decisions at the present time.

Intravascular ultrasound imaging is a relatively new technique for imaging the interior structure of arteries and provides one method for obtaining such high-detail images.[14][15] Unlike traditional cardiac ultrasound that uses an exterior probe and is limited to imaging between the patient's ribs or a transesophageal probe, intravascular

ultrasound uses a miniature ultrasound transducer mounted on the tip of a catheter. (Figure 1(a))

To image the coronary arteries, both intravascular ultrasound and standard contrast angiograms use the same catheter placement technique. The catheter is threaded inside the patient's arterial system through an artery in the thigh, and then maneuvered through the descending aorta, around the aortic arch, and into the coronary arteries. For contrast angiograms, radio-opaque dye is injected at the catheter's tip so that the blood flow in the lumen of the vessel appears in fluoroscopic x-ray images. For intravascular ultrasound, the transducer at the tip of the catheter is rotated by a drive shaft that runs the length of the catheter. The rotating transducer can then image cross-sections by emitting pulses of ultrasound (currently in the 20-50 MHz range) and then receiving time-delayed echos. (Figure 1(b))

The main advantage of intravascular ultrasound over the standard contrast angiogram is that intravascular ultrasound can make images of the interior structure of the artery wall. Although the resolution of ultrasound devices is generally lower than other imaging methods, because of the small field of view and lack of any obstructing tissue, and the reduction of noise with intravascular positioning, fine detail structure can be obtained. The standard angiogram shows only a two-dimensional projection of the lumen of the vessel. (Figure 1(c) and Figure 1(d)) Recently it has been shown that intravascular ultrasound can both reveal disease that does not appear in the standard contrast angiogram and accurately measure the vessel lumen.[10][9] (Figure 1(e) and Figure 1(f))

Previous work on three-dimensional reconstruction of two-dimensional ultrasound slices has been limited to static geometries and has assumed that the vessel being imaged was straight. Visualizations were composed of stacked slices to form three dimensional cylindrical images. [8] [4] [2] The images produced in this way show the three-dimensional relations of vessel structures, but distort the geometry.[7] Furthermore, slices collected from different times in the heart cycle are shown together. Previous research by the authors has extended these procedures to handle a static but curved arterial tree.[5]

This paper describes a prototypical system which uses advanced computer graphics techniques to:

- Accurately reconstruct the three-dimensional geometry of the coronary arterial tree from two-dimensional angiograms through the use of compound-energy "snakes."

- Precisely position time-dependent, two-dimensional ultrasound slices on the dynamic arterial tree.

- Dynamically display the combined data for medical diagnosis.

The interactive system can run on an advanced graphics workstation and provide immediate feedback to the cardiac surgeon/cardiologist.

* *Current address:* One Microsoft Way,
Redmond WA 98052-6399, jedl@microsoft.com.
† 580 ETC, Ithaca, NY 14850. dpg@graphics.cornell.edu.
‡ School of Medicine, Stanford, CA 94305.

Permission to make digital/hard copy of part or all of this work for personal or classroom use is granted without fee provided that copies are not made or distributed for profit or commercial advantage, the copyright notice, the title of the publication and its date appear, and notice is given that copying is by permission of ACM, Inc. To copy otherwise, to republish, to post on servers, or to redistribute to lists, requires prior specific permission and/or a fee.

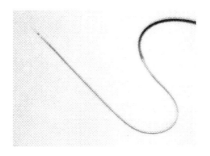

(a) Catheter for Intravascular Imaging

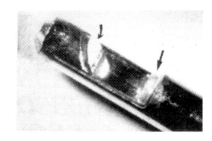

(b) Detail of Transducer

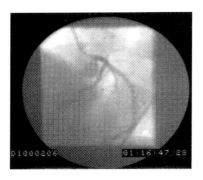

(c) Standard Angiogram — Left Anterior Oblique

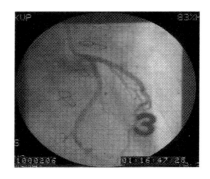

(d) Standard Angiogram — Right Anterior Oblique

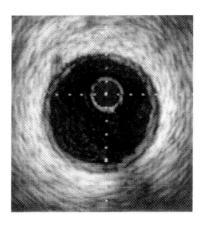

(e) Typical Intravascular Ultrasound Cross-Section of a Normal Adult Coronary Atery

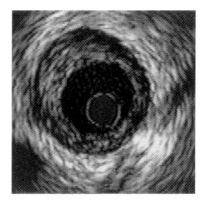

(f) Cross-Section of a Diseased Coronary Artery — The eccentric plaque (soft gray echoes) surrounds the blood-filled vessel lumen (black).

Figure 1: Data Input Devices and Examples

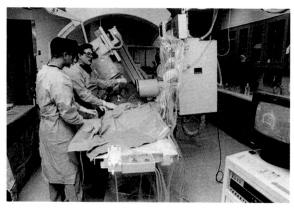

Figure 2: Hospital with patient being imaged by a biplane angiogram.

2 Geometry of the Arterial Centerline

Determining the centerline of a dynamic three-dimensional arterial tree is non-trivial. Standard angiograms have poor contrast, poor signal to noise ratios, and, most importantly, changing points of discontinuity caused by the overlapping projections of the branches of the arterial tree. Standard edge-tracking methods easily get confused, requiring frequent user intervention.

Our initial technique for reconstructing a segment of the arterial tree was an interactive one in which the stereo angiograms were presented to the user who then positioned points along the length of the artery segment in both images. Standard stereo inverse techniques were then used to calculate the three-dimensional points.[6] This technique was far too labor intensive to be useful, especially when considering the goal of capturing the *moving* geometry of the arterial tree. The goal of automatic tracking motivated the use of the technique described below.

Since arteries are made of elastic material, the model we use to fit to the arteries should capture this behavior. One such model used in computer vision is energy-based splines, or "snakes". Snakes have been used to track edges, to follow moving features, and to perform stereo matching—all of which are needed for tracking a moving artery. [3][1] Our work differs from the previous work by the use of compound snakes with offset energy functions. The use of a centerline and symmetric offsets is similar to the more general three-dimensional symmetry-seeking models found in [11].

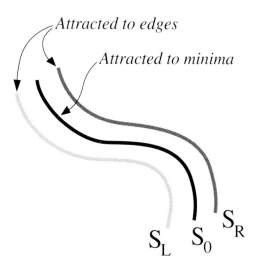

Figure 3: Snake — Physically-based spline attracted to image features specified in energy functions.

2.1 Energy-Minimizing Splines

Snakes are modeled with an internal elastic energy, E_{internal}, and external energy functions, E_{external}. The internal energy gives the snake its elastic character. The external energy functions are important for getting a desired behavior. For example, if one uses an energy such as $E_{\text{external}}(x, y) = I(x, y)$ where I is the image intensity, by minimizing the energy function, the snake will seek dark areas in the image.

To make a good artery tracker, we use a combination snake with a center and two offset sides and the following energies (Figure 3):

- Minima-seeking, $E_{\text{minima}} = I(x, y)$

- Edge-tracking, $E_{\text{edge}} = -|\nabla I(x, y)|^2$

Let $s_C(u)$ be the centerline of the snake. We will define $s_L(u)$ and $s_R(u)$ to be perpendicularly offset from $s_C(u)$ at each u by r_{width}. Let

$$s_L(u) = s_C(u) + r_{\text{width}} n(u)$$
$$s_R(u) = s_C(u) - r_{\text{width}} n(u)$$

where $n(u)$ is the normal to the curve of $s_C(u)$. Using these curves, we can define the following energy to minimize:

$$E_{\text{external}}(u) = k_{\text{minima}} E_{\text{minima}}(s_C(u)) + \\ k_{\text{edge}}(E_{\text{edge}}(s_L(u)) + E_{\text{edge}}(s_R(u)))$$

The center of the combination snake seeks minima and is intended to find the center of an artery, where the image is most opaque. The offset parts of the combination snake seek edges. The combination of the two energies is more effective than the individual energies alone.

There are several free parameters to set.

- k_{minima}, the strength of the minima-seeking energy

- k_{edge}, the strength of the edge-seeking energy

- r_{width}, radius to seek

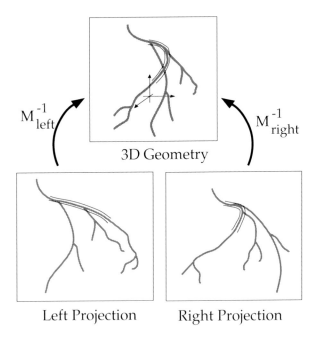

3D Geometry

M^{-1}_{left} M^{-1}_{right}

Left Projection   Right Projection

Figure 4: Stereo Matching

For the work described here, the constants were set with initial rough estimates and then tuned interactively for good performance. Ideally, these parameters should be assigned from measurements of the physical properties of the actual catheter and actual vessels. This might eliminate the need for a tuning step.

Note that for this particular formulation, r_{width} is an input parameter specifying the desired size of the matching artery. To make the combination snake more general, the radius could be made a function of u.

2.2 Stereo Matching

We require at least two views to reconstruct the centerlines of the arteries (Figures 3 and 4). We use two of the compound snakes as described above, with an additional energy that tries to minimize the distance between the two snakes in three-dimensions:[3]

$$E_{stereo}(u) = |M^{-1}_{left}(S_{0_{left}}(u)) - M^{-1}_{right}(S_{0_{right}}(u))|^2$$

where M^{-1} is the inverse of the projection transformation and the subscripts $left$ and $right$ refer to the two projected views. M^{-1} is usually taken as a 4×4 perspective matrix, but the snake energy based method can also include nonlinear warping corrections for distorted camera images. Although we have not yet incorporated this, the warping function can be calculated by imaging a regular grid and calculating the inverse warping function.

2.3 Snakes in 3D

Since we are reconstructing a three-dimensional geometric structure, it makes sense to use a three-dimensional model. The technique we use is similar to the two-dimensional energy functionals described previously, but we use one snake in three dimensions and project to two dimensions to express the energy functionals (Figure 2.3) This is similar to other work by the original snake authors[12].

We use the two two-dimensional snakes as above to get an initial position for the three-dimensional snake. Once we have a single snake, we no longer have the parametrization problems that occur when using two different snakes.

As described in the original paper by Kass [3], the internal energy is given by

$$E_{internal} \quad = \quad (\alpha(s)|v_s(s)|^2 + \beta(s)|v_{ss}(s)|^2)/2$$

which works in two and three dimensions, but with a slightly different interpretation of the terms (there is no torsion in two dimensions).

Let $s_C(u)$ be the centerline of the snake in three dimensions. We will define $s^0_C(u)$ and $s^1_C(u)$ to be $s_C(u)$ transformed by the projections M^{left} and M^{right}, respectively.

$$s^0_C(u) \quad = \quad M^{left}s_C(u)$$
$$s^1_C(u) \quad = \quad M^{right}s_C(u)$$

Then as above we define s^i_L and s^i_R to be perpendicularly offset from $s^i_C(u)$ at each u by r_{width}. Let

$$s^i_L(u) \quad = \quad s^i_C(u) + r_{width}n^i(u)$$
$$s^i_R(u) \quad = \quad s^i_C(u) - r_{width}n^i(u)$$

where $n^i(u)$ is the normal to the curve of $s^i_C(u)$ in the projected plane. Since s^i_C is a projection, it is possible that non-zero segments of the original curve s_C will project onto a single point. For such cases, n^i will have degeneracies. To handle these degenerate cases and to prevent sudden sign flips, the discretized version of n^i is constrained to be positive and on just one side of s^i_C. This is accomplished by sequentially testing the dot product of the candidate normal with the previous discretized point's normal. If the dot product is close to or equal to zero, the previous point's normal is used. If less than zero, then the new normal is flipped.

Once we have the two offset curves and centerlines in both projections, we use the same formulation for the energies as in the previous section—the centerline seek minima and the offset curves seek edges.

The energy equation is solved by taking a variational derivative which gives rise to a set of Euler equations. The solution technique as described in [3] requires the partial derivatives of the external energy function. Since the snake is now 3D, we need derivatives in the x, y, and z coordinates of the artery.

But the energy terms are described in the coordinates of the plane of the projections. Thus, we must multiply the vector of partial derivatives by the inverse jacobian matrix of the transformation. If we consider the two projection transformations as 4×4 matrices, then the inverse jacobian matrices are just the inverses of the matrices. If we include the de-warping grid, then we also need a local inverse jacobian of the de-warping function.

Once we have the partial derivatives f_x, f_y, and f_z in the artery coordinates, we can use the same solution technique as for the two-dimensional snakes, using the LU-decomposition inverse of a pentadiagonal banded matrix that handles the implicit step for the internal energy and an explicit Euler step for the external energy.

Figure 5 shows the two-dimensional snakes in each of the angiograms tracking the same section of artery and the reconstructed result. The three-dimensional display of the angiograms along with the computed three-dimensional artery centerline clearly shows the geometric relation of the two projections with the result.

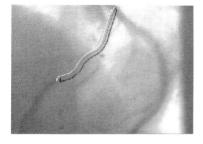

(a) Left Snake

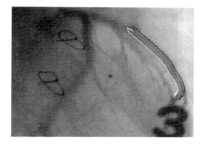

(b) Right Snake

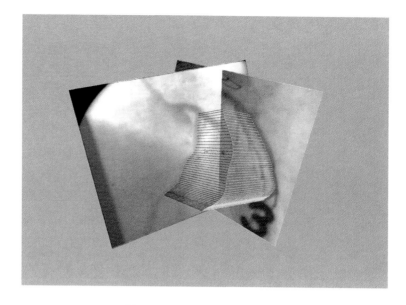

(c) Computed 3D artery centerline.

Figure 5: Left and right projections with snakes and the resulting 3D snake

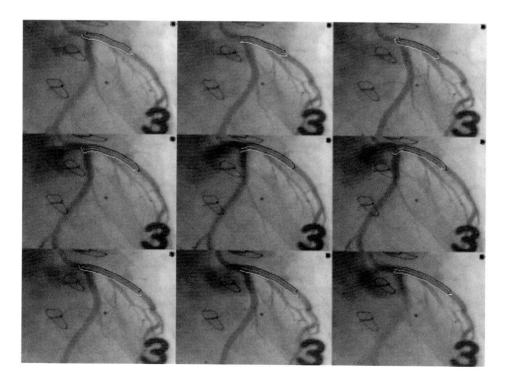

Figure 6: Motion Tracking — Sequence of frames showing inter-frame tracking of arteries by composite snake.

3 Motion Tracking

The computation for the snakes involves a simulated elastic system that is evolved forward in time. Since time is built into the calculation, it is straightforward to let the images change with time. The snakes will track the local minima (Figure 6) as long as the jumps in the motion between successive frames are not too large.[3] We worked with angiogram data sets from heart-transplant patients whose heart rates were elevated up to 120 beats per minute. This made the jumps between frames more pronounced, and our snakes tended to jump out of the proper local minima. Since arteries have mass and a smoothly changing velocity, we added a mass term to the snake which helped to predict where the artery would be.[3][1] This mass term is calculated by keeping track of the previous two time steps for the snake and estimating acceleration. The mass term only became effective when the weighting term and the number of relaxation steps were tuned.

Since the snakes seek local minima in the energy functions, it is important to start them with the proper initial conditions, or they will find the wrong local minima. For the first frame, we set the initial position of the snake in both of the stereo images by interactively sketching a series of line segments over the desired artery segment. The snake was then activated and allowed to relax into the local minimum in each frame. Then the stereo energy weight was ramped from 0 to 1, allowing the two snakes to find a good stereo match. The above steps were all done on a single stereo-pair angiogram. The rest of the motion was tracked automatically, using the previous frames to estimate the starting location of subsequent frames. Certain highly curved sections of the artery needed interactive adjustment to make the snake track properly.

4 Positioning of Time-Dependent 2D Ultrasound Slices

Landmark sites, located at branching points in the ultrasound sequence, are used to orient the slices (Figure 7). Each landmark shows a correspondence between a sidebranching vessel in the ultrasound data and in the angiographic data. These sidebranches are used to orient the slice data around the centerline of the artery. The current arclength of the catheter, as measured relative to a landmark site (or by a linear encoder on the shaft), is used to get the slice's distal location along the arterial tree. The distal location maps directly to a 3D location, since we have already calculated the 3D geometry of the arterial tree and catheter path.

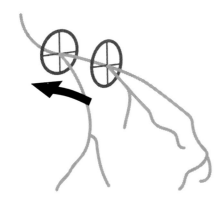

Figure 7: Landmark Sites

This calculation is complicated by the time-dependence of both the arterial tree and the catheter arclength as it is pulled back. Assume that the arterial tree motion is cyclic (regular heartbeat) and that either the catheter arclength versus time is linear or measurable with a linear encoder. Also assume that the distortion of the vessel due to the catheter is negligible. Then for a given time, we know both the phase of the arterial tree (point in the cardiac cycle) and the distal location and thus the geometric position of the ultrasound slice relative to the current arterial tree geometry. Future testing with physical phantoms will be needed to get error bounds on these assumptions.

Figure 8 plots the spacetime path of one coordinate (x, y, or z) of the moving arterial tree and shows the path of the transducer moving in the surface that results. The difficulty is that sequential slices represent not only different positions along the artery centerline, but are taken at different phases of the cardiac cycle. The slices active at a given cycle phase are the slices from transducer distal locations whose times modulo the cycle period T correspond to the same phase. Thus slices $t_0, t_0 + T, t_0 + 2T, \ldots$ are all active slices of the same cycle. Thus the problem is reduced to one of retrieving the appropriate ultrasound slice for each specific space-time position.

To dynamically display the cross-sectional images, the complete set of ultrasound slices must be assembled for each phase of the cardiac cycle.

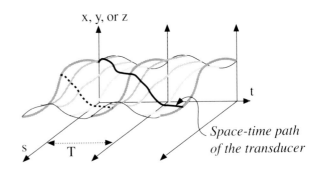

Figure 8: Path of transducer relative to heart cycle. The slices are reorganized so that for each frame the only slices shown are those that match the artery centerline's phase of the heart cycle.

5 Examples

Figure 9(a) shows a static image of the ultrasound slices placed along the artery centerline, with a sagittal split applied to each slice to reveal the internal structure of the arterial wall. Figure 9(b) shows a coronal split applied to each slice.

The dark semi-circle in the very center of each ultrasound frame is the ring-down region in which no data is received. The larger dark circular region is the lumen of the vessel through which the blood flows. The white region beyond the lumen in each of the slices shows the interior structure of the vessel wall. Since the x-ray contrast dye flows in the blood, the lumen is all that appears in the two projected angiograms. Note how the positioning of the slices with the reference of the two projected angiograms clearly shows the relation of the slices to the curved geometry of the artery.

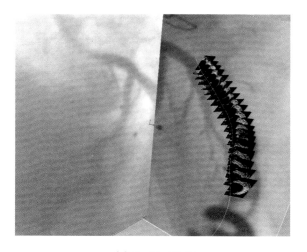
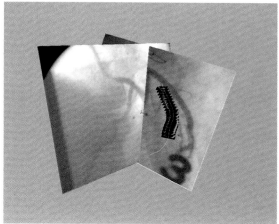

(a) Sagittal Split

(b) Coronal Split

Figure 9: Slices Positioned Along the Transducer Path

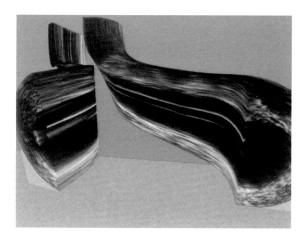
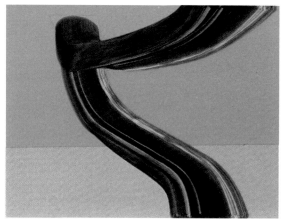

(a) Sagittal Split

(b) Coronal Split

Figure 10: Volume-Rendered Images

6 Volume Rendering

Originally we attempted to use a parametric interpolation volume imaging technique to portray the three-dimensional information.[5] Unfortunately, with the pullback rates used, the sample spacing between slices was an order of magnitude larger than the in-slice resolution, yielding interpolated volumes which were too smooth to be useful for diagnosis (Figure 10). We are currently try to obtain images at slower pullback rates providing more closely packed slices.

Another drawback to volume rendering is the long time typically needed to render a frame (approximately one hour with the current testbed.)

7 Conclusion

By recovering the moving three-dimensional arterial tree and placing the slices at their proper positions in time and space, we are able to combine the strengths of both intravascular ultrasound and x-ray angiograms. For the first time, the moving geometry of the artery from the angiogram and the time-dependent images of the interior of the vessel wall from the intravascular ultrasound can be viewed simultaneously, with proper geometric relations.

There are several limitations to the technique described here which should be the subject for future work. First, the use of the centerline of the artery to place the slices is an approximation, since the catheter is, in general, off-center and tilted with respect to the artery. This may be corrected by recovering the path of the catheter and transducer relative to the artery centerline — we are pursuing a technique that uses the offset and elliptical shape of the lumen in the ultrasound slices.

Second, the correlation of ultrasound slice and angiogram timing is inexact, but this is easily corrected by using digital data marked with the current heart cycle from an electro-cardiogram.

Third, there is a substantial tuning step required to find the proper parameters for the artery-seeking snakes. One possible approach to avoid this tuning step would be to use a three-dimensional snake with the internal elastic energy constants corresponding to the measured elastic properties of actual arteries and catheters. The image-seeking energy weights could then be set relative to the resulting physically-based snake.

Other future work includes using a slow pullback to obtain a dataset with more closely spaced slice data, and applying the techniques described here to experimentally reconstruct, render, and compare a physical phantom with known geometry.

Ultimately, with greatly increased machine speed and closely spaced slice data, volume rendering the dynamic data may prove to be more effective than showing just the slice data, particularly for views that are nearly parallel to a slice.

By using texture-mapped rectangles the combined ultrasound slice/angiogram display technique is well suited to run in real time on current graphics workstations. Accurate knowledge of the dynamic interior anatomy of the diseased vessel will permit improved diagnostic techniques for the physician attempting angioplasty or atherectomy. We hope that this kind of display will move into the interventional catheter laboratory.

Acknowledgements

Thanks to Jon Blocksom without whom the paper would not have been completed. Thanks to Peter Shirley and Dan Kartch for help with the document preparation, to Alan Yeung, Edwin Alderman, and Peter Fitzgerald for providing datasets and insight. Thanks to Allison Hart. This work was supported by the NSF/ARPA Science and Technology Center for Computer Graphics and Scientific Visualization (ASC-8920219) and performed on workstations generously provided by the Hewlett-Packard Corporation.

References

[1] HYCHE, M., EZQUERRA, N., AND MULLICK, R. Spatiotemporal detection of arterial structure using active contours. *Proceedings of Visualization in Biomedical Computing 1808* (1992), 52–62.

[2] ISNER, J. M., ROSENFIELD, K., LOSORDO, D. W., AND KRISHNASWAMY, C. Clinical experience with intravascular ultrasound as an adjunct to percutaneous revascularization. In Tobis and Yock [13], part 16, pp. 186–197.

[3] KASS, M., WITKIN, A., AND TERZOPOULOS, D. Snakes: Active contour models. *International Journal of Computer Vision* (1988), 321–331.

[4] KRISHNASWAMY, C., D'ADAMO, A. J., AND SEHGAL, C. M. Three-dimensional reconstruction of intravascular ultrasound images. In Tobis and Yock [13], part 13, pp. 141–147.

[5] LENGYEL, J., GREENBERG, D. P., YEUNG, A., ALDERMAN, E., AND POPP, R. Three-dimensional reconstruction and volume rendering of intravascular ultrasound slices imaged on a curved arterial path. In *Proceedings of CVRMed'95* (Apr. 1995).

[6] MACKAY, S. A., SAYRE, R. E., AND POTEL, M. J. 3d galatea: Entry of three-dimensional moving points from multiple perspective views. *Proceedings of SIGGRAPH'82 (Boston, Massachusetts, July 26–30, 1982) 16*, 3 (July 1982), 213–222.

[7] ROELANDT, J. R., DI MARIO, C., PANDIAN, N. G., WENGUANG, L., KEANE, D., SLAGER, C. J., DE FEYTER, P. J., AND SERRUYS, P. W. Three-dimensional reconstruction of intracoronary ultrasound images. *Circulation 90* (1994), 1044–1055.

[8] ROSENFIELD, K., LOSORDO, D. W., RAMASWAMY, K., PASTORE, J. O., LANGEVIN, E., RAZVI, S., KOSOWSKY, B. D., AND ISNER, J. M. Three-dimensional reconstruction of human coronary and peripheral arteries from images recorded during two-dimensional intravascular ultrasound examination. *Circulation 84* (1991), 1938–1956.

[9] ST. GOAR, F., PINTO, F. J., ALDERMAN, E. L., FITZGERALD, P. J., STADIUS, M. L., AND POPP, R. L. Intravascular ultrasound imaging of angiographically normal coronary arteries: An in vivo comparison with quantitative angiography. *Journal of the American College of Cardiology 18* (1991), 952–958.

[10] ST. GOAR, F., PINTO, F. J., ALDERMAN, E. L., VALANTINE, H. A., SCHROEDER, J. S., GAO, S.-Z., STINSON, E. B., AND POPP, R. L. Intracoronary ultrasound in cardiac transplant recipients—in vivo evidence of "angiographically silent" intimal thickening. *Circulation 85* (1992), 979–987.

[11] TERZOPOULOS, D., WITKIN, A., AND KASS, M. Symmetry-seeking models and 3d object reconstruction. *International Journal of Computer Vision 1* (1987), 211–221.

[12] TERZOPOULOS, D., WITKIN, A., AND KASS, M. Contraints on deformable models : Recovering 3d shape and nonrigid motion. *Artificial Intelligence 35* (1988), 91–123.

[13] TOBIS, J. M., AND YOCK, P. G., Eds. *Intravascular Ultrasound Imaging.* Churchill Livingstone Inc., New York, 1992.

[14] YOCK, P., JOHNSON, E., AND DAVID, D. Intravascular ultrasound: Development and clinical potential. *American Journal of Cardiac Imaging 2* (1988), 185–193.

[15] YOCK, P., LINKER, D., AND ANGELSON, A. Two-dimensional intravascular ultrasound: Technical development and initial clinical experience. *Journal of the American Society of Echocardiography 2* (1989), 296–304.

Extracting Surfaces from Fuzzy 3D-Ultrasound Data

Georgios Sakas, Stefan Walter
Fraunhofer Institute for Computer Graphics[1]

Abstract

Rendering 3D models from 3D-ultrasonic data is a complicated task due to the noisy, fuzzy nature of ultrasound imaging containing a lot of artifacts, speckle etc. In the method presented in this paper we first apply several filtering techniques (low-pass, mathematical morphology, multi-resolution analysis) to separate the areas of low coherency containing mostly noise and speckle from those of useful information. Our novel BLTP filtering can be applied at interactive times on-the-fly under user control & feed-back. Goal of this processing is to create a 'region-of-interest' (ROI) mask, whereas the data itself remains unaltered. Secondly, we examine several alternatives to the original Levoy contouring method. Finally we introduce an improved surface-extraction volume rendering procedure, applied on the original data within the ROI areas for visualizing high quality images within a few seconds on a normal workstation, or even on a PC, thus making the complete system suitable for routine clinical applications.

CR Descriptors: General Terms: **Algorithms**. I.3.3 [**Computer Graphics**]: Picture/image generation; I.3.8 [**Computer Graphics**]: Applications; I.4.3 [**Image Processing**]: Enhancement, Smoothing, Filtering; I.4.6 [**Image Processing**]: Segmentation, Edge and Feature Detection, Pixel Classification; J.3 [**Life and Medical Sciences**]. Additional Keywords: 3D ultrasound, multi-resolution analysis, morphology, volume rendering

1 Introduction

3D ultrasound is a very new and most interesting application in the area of 'tomographic' medical imaging, able to become a fast, non-radiative, non-invasive, and inexpensive volumetric data acquisition technique with unique advantages for the localisation of vessels and tumours in soft tissue (spleen, kidneys, liver, breast etc.). In general, tomographic techniques (CT, MR, PET etc.) allow for a high anatomical clarity when inspecting the interior of the human body. In addition, they enable a 3D reconstruction and examination

[1]Fraunhofer Institute for Computer Graphics
Wilhelminenstr. 7, 64283 Darmstadt, Germany
fax: +49/6151/155-199, email: {gsakas,walter}@igd.fhg.de

Permission to make digital/hard copy of part or all of this work for personal or classroom use is granted without fee provided that copies are not made or distributed for profit or commercial advantage, the copyright notice, the title of the publication and its date appear, and notice is given that copying is by permission of ACM, Inc. To copy otherwise, to republish, to post on servers, or to redistribute to lists, requires prior specific permission and/or a fee.

of regions of interest, offering obvious benefits (reviewing from any desired angle, isolation of crucial locations, visualization of internal structures, 'fly-by', accurate measurements of distances, angles, volumes etc.).

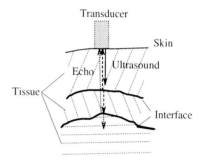

Figure 1: The principal function of ultrasound

The physical principle of ultrasound is as following [11]: sound waves of high frequency (1–15 MHz) emanate from a row of sources that are located on the surface of a transducer which is in direct contact with the skin. The sound waves penetrate the human tissue travelling with a speed of 1450–1580 m/s, depending upon the type of tissue. The sound waves are reflected partially if they hit an interface between two different types of tissue (e.g. muscle and bone). The reflected wavefronts are detected by sensors (microphones) located next to the sources on the transducer. The intensity of reflected energy is proportional to the sound impedance difference of the two corresponding types of tissue and depends on the difference of the sound impedances Z_1 and Z_2:

$$I_r = I_e \cdot \frac{\left(1 - \frac{Z_2}{Z_1}\right)}{\left(1 + \frac{Z_2}{Z_1}\right)} \qquad (1)$$

An image of the interior structure can be reconstructed based upon the total travelling time, the (average) speed, and the energy intensity of the reflected waves. The resulting 3D images essentially represent hidden internal "surfaces". The principle is similar to radar with the difference being that it uses mechanical instead of electromagnetic waves.

In contrast to the common 2D case where a single image slice is acquired, 3D ultrasonic techniques cover a volume within the body with a series of subsequent image slices. The acquisition of these slices can be achieved by means of various scan and tracking techniques and will be not discussed further in this paper; please refer to [12], [19], and [21] for more details.

2 Previous Works & Drawbacks

One of the major reasons for the limited acceptance of 3D ultrasound to date is the complete lack of an appropriate visualisation technique, able to display clear surfaces out of the acquired data. Our very first approach was to use well known techniques, used for MRI and CT data to extract surfaces. Such techniques include binarization [7], iso-surfacing [4], contour connecting [3], marching cubes [9], and volume rendering either as semi-transparent cloud [13], or as fuzzy gradient shading [8]. Manual contouring [19] is too slow and impractical for real-life applications. Unfortunately, ultrasound images posses several features causing all these techniques to fail totally. The most important of these features as reported in [16] are:

1. significant amount of noise and speckle
2. much lower dynamic range as compared to CT or MR
3. high variations in the intensity of neighbouring voxels, even within homogeneous tissue areas
4. boundaries with varying grey level caused by the variation of surface curvature and orientation to the sound source
5. partially or completely shadowed surfaces from objects closer and within the direction of the sound source (e.g. a hand shadows the face)
6. the regions representing boundaries are not sharp but show a width of several pixels
7. poor alignment between subsequent images (parallel–scan devices only)
8. pixels representing varying geometric resolutions depending on the distance from the sound source (fan–scanning devices only)

The general appearance of a volume rendered 3D ultrasound dataset is that of a solid block covered with 'noise snow' (fig. 13 right). A closer analysis proved that noise and speckle contained in the image caused so many obstacles (blobs) around the objects, that rays usually fail to penetrate deep enough to reach the crucial internal surfaces. The low dynamic range makes a straight-forward discrimination between speckle and information (e.g. by means of thresholding) impossible. Even when a surface is reached, methods based on a single threshold value ([4], [7], [9] etc.) fail to detect a continuous surface due to the features 3, 4, & 5 listed above. Lastly, the nature of gradient shading employed, e.g. in [8], is very sensitive to high frequency noise and speckle and therefore it is not suitable to generate a smooth surface because of reasons 3, 6, 7, & 8 (see fig. 2 upper left). However, Levoy's continuous opacity classificator (eq. 2) has been found to give good estimations of the presence of a surface contour (a and r are scaling factors and S a threshold value):

$$opacity = a \cdot \begin{cases} 1 & : g(u,v,w) = S \\ 1 - \frac{1}{r} \cdot \frac{|g(u,v,w)-S|}{|\nabla g(u,v,w)|} & : |\nabla g(u,v,w)| > 0 \\ 0 & : otherwise \end{cases}$$

(2)

Some time ago we started to search for ways of discriminating the tissue of interest from the lerge amount of apparently noisy signal. Initially we filtered the original voxels with an approximation of a Gaussian kernel with discrete binomial coefficients due to its separability, normality and symmetry [6]:

$$G(x, \sigma) = \frac{1}{2 \cdot \pi \sigma^2} \cdot e^{\left(\frac{x^2}{2 \cdot \sigma^2} \right)}$$

(3)

In a discrete implementation the factors of this kernel are usually calculated by the binomial coefficients:

$$\binom{n}{k} = \frac{n!}{k! \, (n-k)!} \qquad 0 \le k \le n$$

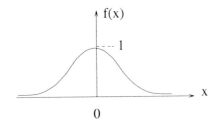

Filtering a function g with a filter F is a convolution [6]:

$$g'(x) = g(x) * F(x) = \int_{-\infty}^{+\infty} g(x) \cdot F(x - x_1) \cdot dx_1 \qquad (4)$$

In the discrete case,, a convolution is expressed as a weighted sum of the signal g over the $(2n + 1)$ size of the filter kernel F:

$$g'(u) = \sum_{i=-n}^{n} g(u) \cdot F(u - i) \qquad (5)$$

An extension to higher dimensions is straightforward by convoluting the filter function by itself. The main effect of such a low-pass filtering is a smoothing of sharp details together with a reduction of noise and speckle. The separability enables a filtering of a 256^3 dataset by a Gaussian kernel of 3^3 within 6.51 seconds, see also tab. 2. On the other hand, the intermediate results must be buffered, which temporally requires a duplication of memory space.

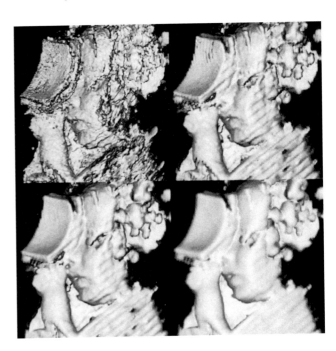

Figure 2: Filtering and volume rendering of an original 256^3 dataset with Gaussian kernels of 3^3, 5^3, and 7^3

Fig. 2 presents a 256^3 dataset after filtering with Gaussian kernels of increasing size and volume rendering using Levoy's method [8]. Although noise and speckle artifacts are reduced, the surfaces gradually appear over-smoothed, non-sharp, unnatural, and do not show much details.

In an earlier study [16] we tested the processing of the original data by the combination of three different filters: Gaussian for noise/speckle reduction, speckle removal for contour smoothing, and median for both noise/speckle reduction and closing of small gaps caused by misalignments and differences in the average luminosity between subsequent images. The filters had been implemented in 3D and applied to the acquired data during a pre-processing stage. Although the results have been very encouraging, such filters require significant computing times and therefore they remain pre-processing stages. Further, the large pre-processing times do not allow interactive control of the filtering level by the user, thus making this approach inflexible, non-interactive and not suitable for clinical applications. Finally filtering also changes the original nature of the data and is therefore not generally accepted in the medical community.

3 Multi-Resolution Surface Identification

The aim of this paper is to develop a fast, intuitive and effective method for rendering clear contours from fuzzy data. All techniques must allow for a user-defined, interactive, on-line processing on average computers in order to be used under routine clinical conditions. This goal has been achieved through a combination of multi-resolution analysis [2], [18], [10], filtering [6], and volume rendering [8], and consists of three subsequent tasks:

1. identify and separate noisy areas carrying effectively no information (segmentation), discussed in section 4
2. process the data within the remaining areas (filtering), discussed in section 5
3. use adequate visualization methods (volume rendering), discussed in section 6.

The first task is used to allow the rays to penetrate up to the internal surfaces of interest. In addition, it accounts for significant speed-up, since the following computer intensive tasks can be performed only within the remaining areas. The second task enables the reconstruction of a well-defined surface and the third task is necessary to create a smooth-looking surface meaningful to the human eye. All three tasks are performed in a multi-resolution framework. After reading the original data, a Gaussian pyramid of levels-of-detail (fig. 3) is initially generated [14]. Such a pyramid requires only 14% additional memory space and is computed within 0.27 additional seconds for a 128^3 and 0.88 additional seconds for a 256^3 field for a kernel of 3^3 on a SUN Sparc20 due to the separability of the Gaussian kernel (see tab. 2).

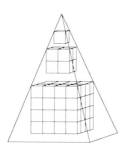

Figure 3: The Gaussian pyramid

4 Segmentation

The main idea for the multi-resolution feature identification and segmentation is that 'real' surfaces posses a higher coherency as compared to speckle or noise. This means that when filtering the data to successive lower levels of detail(corresponding to higher pyramid levels with lower voxel resolution), noise, speckle and minor

structures could be expected to disappear faster than useful surfaces due to their lower coherency, whereas 'larger' surfaces should still remain detectable even on lower resolutions. By inverting this idea, after generating a level-of-detail representation of the original data, we first try to identify crucial regions on higher pyramid levels where little or no noise/speckle is expected. Information carrying areas are then propagated (mapped) to higher resolution levels and the process is repeated until the original data level is reached. Regions 'masked out' by this processing are not further examined by any of the subsequent levels. The result of the segmentation processing is a *binary mask defining a region of interest* ROI (since we operate in voxel space, we generate a 3D mask defining a volume of interest VOI). Only within this VOI region are valid contours expected and therefore only these are accessed during volume rendering. The remaining non-valid areas are regarded to be empty.

In a multi-resolution framework, the process theoretically starts with the first node (the root) of the pyramid. In practice, however, only 1 to 3 levels over the highest resolution (pyramid basement) are used. Starting on a certain level n, regions of interest are identified: we tested two different selection methods discussed in the following sections 4.1 and 4.2. Then each valid voxel is projected on the next higher resolution level. Due to the multi-resolution framework, one voxel of level n projects onto 8 voxels of the level $n - 1$. Changing the levels, the same procedure is repeated with levels $n - 1$ and $n - 2$ and so on until the highest resolution level 0 is reached. However, after leaving the starting level n, only voxels falling within the already selected areas are considered, reducing the amount of computing time, a crucial fact with increasing volume resolution.

An implication of each voxel projecting on 8 successors is that the selection procedure is a crucial decision for the success of the method. A voxel misclassified as empty on level n will introduce a gap of 8 voxels on level $n-1$, 64 voxels on level $n-2$ etc. Such gaps introduce serious visible artifacts similar to those shown in fig. 7 left. On the other hand, if the selection criterion is rather relaxed, the effect of noise/speckle reduction will be missed. A possible solution is to start with a rather relaxed criterion and become gradually more restrictive when propagating to higher resolutions.

Instead of filtering the grey values of the voxels $V_n[u, v, w]$, we decided to process the opacity volume $O_n[u, v, w]$ and leave the data itself unchanged. Thus, for every level of the data pyramid we allocate a second opacity field of equal size thereby creating an opacity pyramid and assigning to each element the corresponding opacity value as calculated by Levoy's classificator (eq. 2).

4.1 Mathematical Morphology

Mathematical morphology can be used to implement a wide spectrum of operations on binary images or datasets. The fundamental morphological operations on a binary image P with an element E are *erosion* and *dilation*, as well as their combination *opening*.

$$\text{EROSION}(P, E) := \{p | E_p \text{ included in} P\}$$
$$\text{DILATION}(P, E) := \{p | E_p \cap P \neq \{\}\}$$
$$\text{OPENING}(P, E) := \text{DILATION}(\text{EROSION}(P, E), E)$$

The theoretical details are given in [5] and will not be repeated here. In simple words, depending on the shape and size of E, erosion removes structures smaller than a certain size and can be used for removing noise or speckle blobs. Dilation enlarges details larger than a minimum size and can be used to fill up small contour gaps. Opening is an erosion followed by a dilation. All operations can be used in an iterative way, i.e. an already eroded volume can be eroded again etc.

The element for the morphology can have several shapes. The most common candidates are a small cube of 3^3 voxels or a 3D cross

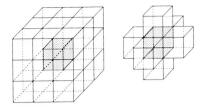

Figure 4: Two possible morphological elements E_{27} and E_7

containing the central voxel and its 6 face-connected neighbours (see fig. 4). An additional degree of freedom is to decide how many voxels of E should be occupied in order to select the central voxel as to be valid. For reasons of computational efficiency, we choose to use the cross with 3 occupied voxels on higher and 4 on lower pyramid levels. This means that our selection criterion is more relaxed in the beginning and becomes more restrictive on higher resolution levels.

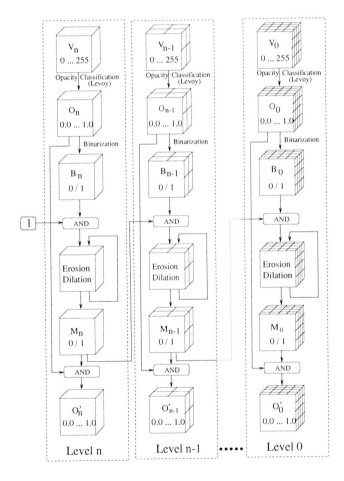

Figure 5: The morphological pipeline

The first action is to calculate for each voxel field $V_n[u, v, w]$ on pyramid level n the corresponding opacity field $O_n[u, v, w]$. For each opacity field we calculate a binary volume $B_n[u, v, w]$ by setting all elements with a non-zero opacity to 1. This binary field is then morphologically processed and the result is the mask $M_n[u, v, w]$, which is then used to mask the local level opacities by means of the AND operation and is propagated to the higher resolutions as shown schematically in fig. 5.

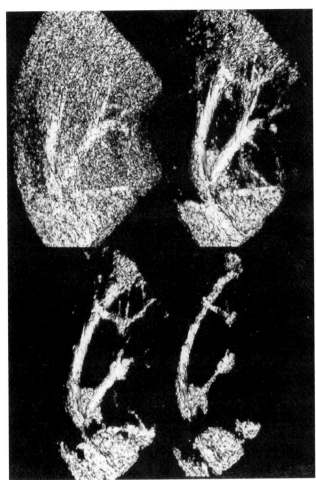

Figure 6: From upper left to lower right: 256^3 dataset showing liver vessels before filtering and processed with erosion after 20, 30 and 40 iterations

Fig. 6 demonstrates the effect of erosion after several iterations The example shows and erosion performed with one level and an element E_6 size of 3. Small and isolated noise/speckle areas have been successfully suppressed but the surface of the objects has also been eroded, producing image artifacts clearly visible on the magnification shown in fig. 7 left. To suppress aliasing of the surfaces we apply the opening operation, i.e. a dilation after the erosion in order to 'fill the surface gaps' created by the erosion. Opening successfully suppresses the surface artifacts, preserving the shape of major structures. A comparison of erosion and opening can be seen in fig. 7. However, more than 20–30 iterations are necessary in order to obtain a good image, resulting in a very time intensive procedure as shown on tab. 2.

To conclude, applying erosion alone is not sufficient, since it removes parts of the useful surface together with speckle and noise, whereas opening gives better results. Both filters require several iterations before providing an acceptable image quality. An additional drawback of using morphological filters lies in the large number of parameters to be adjusted, i.e. Levoy threshold and tolerance, shape & order of E, and number of iterations for erosion and dilation. This gives a total of over 6 degrees of freedom, making the whole process non-intuitive and impractical for clinical applications.

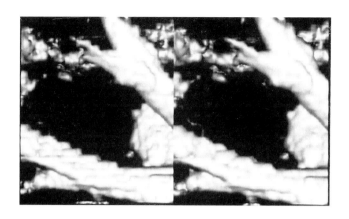

Figure 7: Left a magnification of fig. 6 after 30 erosion iterations showing visible artifacts. Right the same data after 30 opening operations.

4.2 BLTP-Method

In order to overcome the drawbacks of the morphological filters in intuiton and computational efficiency, we developed a method we called BLTP meaning *binarize, low-pass, threshold & propagate*. The principle of the filter is better explained in a 1D example shown in fig. 8 and 9, an extension to 3D is straightforward.

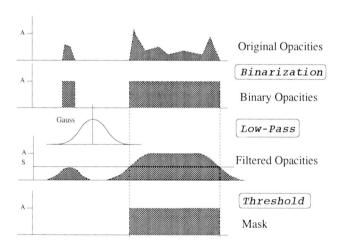

Figure 8: The principle of extracting a VOI mask using BLTP filtering in 1D

Again, the first action is to create for each opacity field $O_n[u, v, w]$ a two-valued *real numbers* volume $D_n[u, v, w]$ by setting all voxels with an non-zero opacity to 1.0, see fig. 10. Small details, speckle and isolated noisy voxels will be converted to small unity steps, whereas large occupied areas will generate more extended structures as demonstrated in fig. 8. Due to the usage of discrete unity steps, the convolution (low-pass filtering) of $D_n[u, v, w]$ with a Gaussian kernel is represented by a discrete sum of Gaussian kernels, symmetrical to the position of the occupied voxel and accordingly shifted in relation to each other:

$$g'(u) = \sum_{i=-n}^{n} g(u) \cdot \frac{1}{2 \cdot \pi \sigma^2} \cdot e^{\frac{(u-\imath)^2}{2 \cdot \sigma^2}}$$

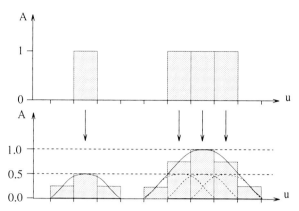

Figure 9: Result of the convolution of unity steps (upper) with a Gaussian kernel of size 3 (lower)

where g represents the original grey values, g' the filtered function, and $2n + 1$ the size of the Gaussian kernel. The graphical representation of such a convolution applied on structures of different size is shown in fig. 9.

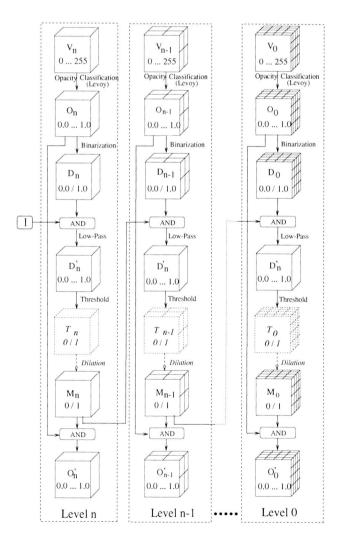

Figure 10: The principle of the BLTP pipeline

The numerical result of such a filtering for the 1D case can be seen on tab. 1. The structures are symmetrical over the corresponding maximum value; Due to lack of space some 'overflowing' values have been omitted in tab. 1. We call the low-pass filtered field $LP_n[u, v, w]$.

Kernel		3				5				
1 Vox.		.25	**.5**	.25		.0625	.25	**.375**	.25	.0625
2 Vox.		.25	**.75**	.75	.25	.0625	.3125	**.625**	.625	.3125
3 Vox.	.25	.75	**1.0**	.75	.25	.0625	.3125	.6875	**.875**	.6875
4 Vox.	.25	.75	**1.0**	1.0	.75	.0625	.3125	.6875	**.9375**	.9375
5 Vox.	.25	.75	**1.0**	1.0	1.0	.0625	.3125	.6875	.9375	**1.0**

Table 1: 1D low-pass filtering discrete unit jumps of varying size with different Gaussian kernels. The structures are symmetrical over the corresponding maximum value; Due to lack of space some values have been omitted

In simple words, low-pass filtering will change the sharp edges of the unity steps to smoother slopes and change the maximum of small structures to a lower value. The shape of a structure after filtering (inclination of the slope, value of maximum) depends on both the order of the kernel and the size of the initial structure. From tab. 1 one can easily see that filtering a structure of k unit steps width with a kernel of $2n + 1$ results in a structure with an extend of $k + 2n$ pixels. In addition, if $k \leq 2n$, all values of the result will be below 1.0, and when $k \geq 2n + 1$, there will be $k - 2n$ coefficients having the value 1.0. This allows filtering of structures up to a given size as explained below.

There are two different possibilities to process the field $LP_n[u, v, w]$. The first arises from the above observation that structures smaller than the kernel size will have all their coefficients smaller than 1.0. Therefore, in order to eliminate structures up to a given structure size k, one has to select a filter with the next greater odd size $2n + 1 \geq k$ and threshold the resulting field LP_n, setting all opacities below 1.0 to zero. The binary mask $M_n[u, v, w]$ is calculated by dilating the result field after thresholding $T_n[u, v, w]$ by an element E of the size k in order to expand again the remaining 1.0–coefficients to the original extend of the structures[1]. After dilation the resulting mask $M_n[u, v, w]$ is used for masking the opacities of the current level (AND operation) as well as propagating to the next level as shown in fig. 10. The method can effectively and accurately suppress noise and speckle blobs. Due to the fact that thresholding with 1.0 is a trivial operation and dilation is performed only in regions where 1.0–coefficients are presented, this processing is completed quick even with large datasets.

A simplified and faster version of the above algorithm avoids dilation. After choosing the appropriate kernel size and filtering the binary field $D_n[u, v, w]$ in a way similar as above, $LP_n[u, v, w]$ is subsequently filtered to a binary field $T_n[u, v, w]$ by means of a free definable threshold th_s, i.e. values below th_s are mapped to 0 and above th_s to 1. By varying the width k of the kernel and the threshold value of th_s one can easily control the degree of blob suppression. As an example, one can see on tab. 1 that when using a kernel of size 5, a threshold just above 0.375 will eliminate structures of unit size and leave larger ones unchanged, a threshold just above 0.625 will eliminate structures with a size of one or two voxels etc. A graphical representation of this effect can also be seen in fig. 8. The result after thresholding is the binary field $M_n[u, v, w]$ which is used to mask the opacities of level n and propagated to level $n + 1$ as shown schematically[2] in fig. 10.

Thus this variant is an approximation of the previous one, using a free adjustable threshold and avoiding the dilation after calculating $T_n[u, v, w]$.

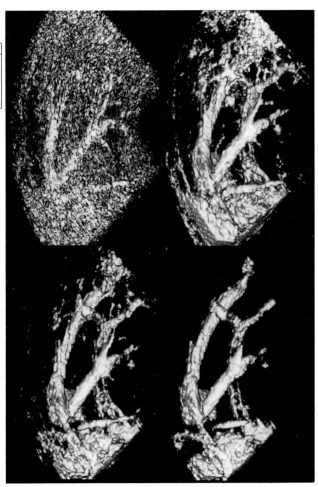

Figure 11: BLTP filtering of a 256^3 liver dataset without dilation with a Gaussian kernel of 5^3 and thresholds increasing from upper left to lower right

The advantage of this variant of the BLTP method as compared with morphological operation lies in its simplicity and computational efficiency. A BLTP re-calculation including thresholding, mask calculation and propagation without low-pass re-calculation requires only 24.8 seconds for a 256^3 pyramid and 8.78 seconds for a 128^3 one (see tab. 2), making the process suitable for interactive purposes. Although the exact size of the eliminated structures is only approximately known, the interactive adjustment of the threshold th_n and the quick feed-back allows a comfortable and intuitive processing of the dataset. The effects of using the BLTP filter can be shown in fig. 11. By varying the threshold th_n, a significant amount of speckle and noise could be reduced whereas the liver vessels remained effectively unchanged. To date, this BLTP variant is the one most frequently used.

All three examined methods suppress only blobs of noise or speckle. Other obstacles, such as the ultrasound field near the transducer or the hand of the fetus obscuring the face, show the same characteristics as the 'real surfaces' and therefore must be removed semi-automatically using methods reported in [16].

---

[1] To eliminate structures with size 1 and 2 one has to use an appropriately scaled kernel of size 3

[2] Fig. 10 demonstrates only the principle of the method. For reasons of computational efficiency the C-code implementation includes several differences, e.g. buffering stages are omitted or merged together with filter stages etc.

Volume resolution	Kernel size	Lowpass level 0	Pyramid level 1...n	Opacity field	Dilation 1 iteration	Opening 1 iteration	Threshold, Mask, Project	BLTP pipeline	Morphology 20 iterations
128^3	3^3	1.0	0.27	3.38	3.15	6.54	8.78	10.05	139.53
	5^3	1.2	0.38					10.36	
256^3	3^3	6.51	0.88	20.36	28.21	54.78	24.8	32.19	1099.6
	5^3	12.17	1.24					38.21	

Table 2: CPU times on SUN Sparc 20 for various filtering operations with two different kernel sizes and volume resolutions. Lowpass & pyramid are computed once per dataset, opacity only when changing Levoy's iso-value; these three stages are regaded as offset times since they change very rarily. Morphological operations given for an element $E = 3$. On the right the total processing time for BLTP with variable threshold and opening after 20 iterations.

5 Contour Filtering

After segmenting the regions of interest, our second task was to improve the appearance of the contours within these VOIs. Levoy's opacity formula (eq. 2), being essentially a combination of an iso-surfacing weighted by the local grey level gradient, has been used as starting point for further experiments. We examined two additional edge detectors more closely as an alternative to the gradient proposed by Levoy (see [1] for an excellent survey). In the first case we employed a 3D version of the Sobel-operator instead of the gradient in the denominator of eq. 2. The 2D kernel is:

$$S_x = \frac{1}{8} \cdot \begin{bmatrix} -1 & 0 & 1 \\ -2 & 0 & 2 \\ -1 & 0 & 1 \end{bmatrix} \quad S_y = \frac{1}{8} \cdot \begin{bmatrix} -1 & -2 & -1 \\ 0 & 0 & 0 \\ 1 & 2 & 1 \end{bmatrix}$$

$$opacity = a \cdot \begin{cases} 1 & : \ g(u,v,w) = S \\ 1 - \frac{1}{r} \cdot \frac{|g(u,v,w)-S|}{\sqrt{S_x^2+S_y^2+S_z^2}} & : \ \sqrt{S_x^2 + S_y^2 + S_z^2} > 0 \\ 0 & : \ otherwise \end{cases}$$

The result can be seen in fig. 12. The differences in the quality as compared to Levoy's original method are rather small, however, the computation time has been almost doubled. In the second case we used a Laplacian-of-Gaussian (LOG) operator. Again, the 2D kernel is:

$$L_{u,v} = \frac{1}{16} \cdot \begin{bmatrix} 0 & 0 & 0 \\ 0 & 16 & 0 \\ 0 & 0 & 0 \end{bmatrix} - \frac{1}{16} \cdot \begin{bmatrix} 1 & 2 & 1 \\ 2 & 4 & 2 \\ 1 & 2 & 1 \end{bmatrix}$$

$$= \begin{bmatrix} -1 & -2 & -1 \\ -2 & 12 & -2 \\ -1 & -2 & -1 \end{bmatrix}$$

$$opacity = a \cdot \begin{cases} 1 & : \ g(u,v,w) = S \\ 1 - \frac{1}{r} \cdot \frac{|g(u,v,w)-S|}{|L_{u,v,w}|} & : \ |L_{u,v,w}| > 0 \\ 0 & : \ otherwise \end{cases}$$

This filter is a combination of a low-pass followed by an edge detector and is expected to give good results even with noisy images. Although the computing time has been doubled again, the result shown on fig. 12 has not been significantly improved as compared to Levoy's original method.

We implemented several other experiments with the goal to improve the selectivity of Levoy's formula, e.g. by using information for contours and/or grey values from neighbouring resolution levels. All these experiments failed to provide significant improvements and therefore are not reported here. As a result, the original Levoy formula has so far provided the best trade-off between quality and speed.

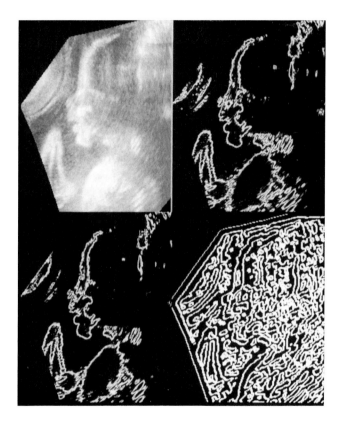

Figure 12: Testing alternative edge detection methods for estimating the opacity. From upper left to lower right: grey image, Levoy, Sobel and LOG edge detection

6 Volume Rendering

In order to volume render the processed datasets we had to apply three modifications to the standard volume rendering pipeline [15]. The first modification is due to the nature of ultrasonic data as is shown in fig. 13. The ultrasound cone shown on the left is surrounded by empty space, i.e. voxels with zero value. Due to the opacity formula (eq. 2) this causes a very high gradient and thus a high opacity value along the interface to the empty space, which is manifested as a solid 'curtain' obscuring the volume interior. This effect can be totally suppressed by turning every opacity neighbouring an empty voxel to zero: Due to the nature of ultrasonic imaging, voxels with a zero value may occur only in the empty space and not within the data itself. The size of this neighbourhood must be adjusted in accordance with the size of the Gaussian kernel for the higher pyramid levels. For a kernel with a size of $2n + 1$ the suppression neighbourhood is:

$$opacity(u, v, w) = \begin{cases} opacity & : & g(u + i, v + j, w + k) \neq 0 \\ & & \forall \ (i, j, k) \ \in (-n \dots n) \\ 0 & : & otherwise \end{cases}$$

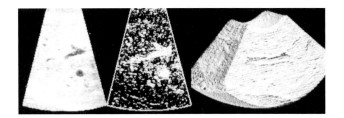

Figure 13: Left a grey image of the liver, middle the corresponding opacity values, right a volume rendered dataset. Note the high opacity values along the interface between data and empty space (middle) causing a solid 'curtain' obscuring the volume interior (right)

The second modification deals with the visual appearance of the reconstructed surface. As mentioned in section 2, Levoy's method used the local gradient as the surface normal, thus being very sensitive to intensity fluctuations typically apparent in ultrasonic data, thereby creating an extremely rough surface. Fig. 14 upper left shows how rough such a surface can be after removing almost 100% of the noise and speckle using BLTP filtering. It is important to remember that all filtering operations only mask out regions not containing coherent edges leaving thereby the original data unchanged. Thus, the small intensity fluctuations remain on the surface and cause large normal vector perturbations resulting in an unrecognisably rough surface. Our solution is to accumulate the opacity values as originally proposed but *to use a normal vector from higher pyramid levels*. These levels contain low-pass filtered data, so that the normal vectors are also less perturbed and change more smoothly. Similarly, one can use normal vectors from a lower level to add 'sharpness' to a smooth surface. By means of a slider the degree of smoothness or sharpness can be changed continuously through (linearly) interpolating the normal vectors from the corresponding pyramid levels.

$$N(u, v, w) = N_n(u, v, w) \cdot (1 - |t|) + N_{n+\lceil t \rceil}(u, v, w) \cdot |t|$$
$$-1.0 \leq t \leq 1.0 \quad (6)$$

This effect is shown in fig. 14. It is important to note that for all images *exactly the same opacities* have been used; the different visual appearance is caused only by the modification of the normal vector.

The last feature is that we extract both surface as well as volumetric information during a single traversing. Extracted features are depth-sorted and stored together with their individual depth in a 2D structure similar to a ZZ-buffer [17]. After traversing and during visualisation one can select the type of desired visual representation interactively. Also mixed values (e.g. 40% surface, 60% X-ray) can be displayed as shown in fig. 15. The visualisation evaluates the values of the ZZ-buffer and since it requires no new ray-traversing, it can be performed at rates of several frames per second. The $O(n^2)$ requirements of space allow the pre-calculation and storage of a complete rotation sequence in the main memory. The visual representation can be selected interactively during the play-back of a pre-recorded loop.

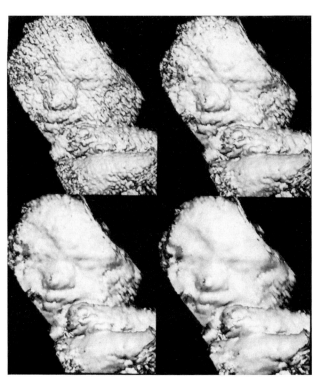

Figure 14: Fetus after removing almost all blobs, before (upper left) and after normal vector smoothing with $t = 0.3, 0.7, 1.0$

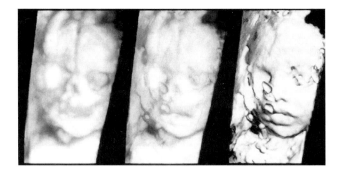

Figure 15: Continuous transition between MIP and surface rendering

7 Results & Further Works

For our tests we used datasets from different devices showing either fetuses around the 25th week of pregnancy (3–4 months before birth, fig. 16) or scans of the liver (fig. 5, 11). More than a dozen datasets like those presented in fig. 16 have been acquired under routine clinical conditions in the Heidelberg University Hospital, using a 'Kretz Voluson 530' device. The typical resolution in a Cartesian coordinate system is 10 Mvoxels, the maximum resolution 16 Mvoxels (256^3). Using the methods reported here and in [16], we succeeded in visualizing *all* of the provided datasets. The time required for the complete processing of each set was less than five minutes and included loading from the disc, filtering, segmenting, smoothing, visualization and loop generation. The first results from the clinical routine have been very encouraging indicating clinical evidence at least in the area of the fetal diagnosis [20]. Fig. 17 compares an image reconstructed from data acquired in the 25th pregnancy week with a photo of the baby 24 hours after birth. The time for volume rendering one image with resolution of 512^2 pixels is about 10 seconds on an IBM R6000, a rotation sequence required only 3 minutes. Diagnosis of abnormal cases can be definitely improved. Tab. 3 presents the results for volume rendering a field of 4 MVoxels in a resolution of 300^2 pixels using various hardware platforms.

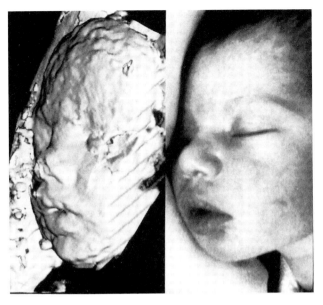

Figure 17: Left data of the 25th pregnancy week, right a photograph 24 hours after birth

- Understanding the content of 3D ultrasound images has been significantly improved. Our visualisation methods provide a true 'added value' for diagnosis.
- Noise and speckle included in the 3D ultrasound data has been significantly reduced without altering the original data.
- The type and degree of noise/speckle reduction, surface smoothing, visual representation, etc., can be interactively selected. The original data remains thereby unchanged and can be referred to at all times. This allows the user (physician) to control the degree of altering the original data.
- The speed of visualisation enables an immediate evaluation of the acquired data during examination of the patient.
- The system runs on common commercial workstations including PCs and needs no special hardware.

In addition, the BLTP filtering is clearly the method of choice because it provides results similar to mathematical morphology but runs at least one order of magnitude faster, is more intuitive and easy-to-use and allows interactive manipulation.

After several years of research we recognise that the work just started. The most important conclusion from this work is that we showed that global filtering provides good results but is unacceptably slow for practical applications. On the other hand, VOI identification and local, possibly adaptive, filtering provides even better results within interactive times. Advanced filtering that adapts to the local data features in a multi-resolution framework is the most important goal for future work.

First of all, the BLTP method should be further extended. Instead of using a Gaussian low-pass filter, we should consider the possibility of employing more suitable band-limiting filters, enabling an elimination of structures of a specific size. A rich amount of literature exists on this topic. As a very promising avenue of research we are currently investigating the possibility of using wavelets as an alternative for BLTP filtering. Wavelets offer very attractive possibilities, because they combine highly desired signal processing features with the multi-resolution framework employed here. Furthermore, one could also investigate the usage of 3D-correlation functions, most likely implemented in the frequency domain, for identification of surfaces. Both these methods require substantial computing power and have therefore not been considered yet for the

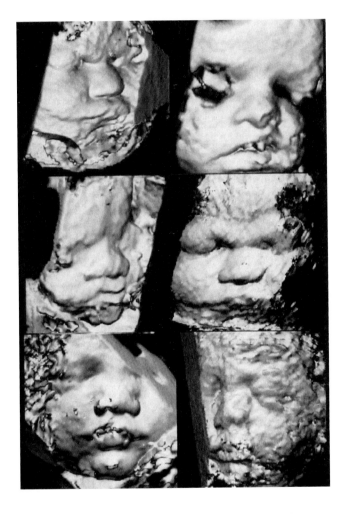

Figure 16: Different fetal faces 3–4 months before birth

Hardware	Surface Vol. Rendering			Surface & MIP Vol. Rendering		
Platform	Standard	High	Highest	Standard	High	Highest
SUN Sparc10	5.1	11.7	13.6	5.3	12.2	22
SUN Sparc20	2.3	7.8	9.6	3.6	6.8	14.2
SGI Indigo	2.5	7.7	8.4	2.9	5.9	11.0
IBM R6000	1.9	5.3	5.5	2.5	4.9	9.1
486 40 MHz	10.9	27.5	44.6	16,5	42.4	68.9
586 90 MHz	1.8	4.4	5.9	3.1	5.4	11.0

Table 3: Runtimes in CPU seconds for volume rendering a dataset of $256^3 \times 64$ voxels creating both surface and transparent (MIP) images at a resolution of 300^2 pixels at three different image quality levels

The major advantages of our method in visualizing ultrasonic data are:

desired interactive low-cost system. However, processing times can be reduced when working in the frequency domain by using signal processors, which makes the additional hardware costs rather reasonable. Different possibilities employ filters for edge-preserving resolution reduction, possibly combined with local speckle removal. We expect that such filters may provide better results than the Gaussian kernels employed here.

A remarkable piece of work is presented in [18] claiming excellent results in both precision and robustness for extracting edges from noisy images. The author also uses a pyramid of Gaussian filtered 2D images to recognise edges in a multi-resolution framework. In addition he provides a very good review of the theory and mathematics proofing of the applicability and superior performance of his method. The main idea there is to calculate edges on different scales using the LOG operator and then multiply the corresponding magnitudes. Major edges will thereby be amplified whereas minor edges will be attenuated below a given threshold. This shows similarities to our concept of mask propagation along resolution levels. An additional step eliminates 'false positives', i.e. points not surrounded by edges of similar strength along the direction perpendicular to the local gradient. This reflects the idea that edges must show a continuity perpendicular to their surface and shows similarities to morphological operators. Although the principle ideas are similar, the two approaches also show substantial differences. Schunck's method works without resolution reduction, a fact introducing a memory space explosion not tractable in 3D imaging. Secondly, he detects edges whereas we identify areas (VOI). Thirdly, the calculation and multiplication of edge magnitudes at different scales is extremely computation intensive whereas we restrict the calculations within the areas masked from the lower resolution. Nevertheless, a combination of our approach with his advanced and robust edge estimators seems possible and promising.

Acknowledgements Thanks to Dr. Meindl from the DKD, W. Duda and K. Holle from Kretz Ultrasound for providing clinical data, as well as to Prof. Wischnik and Dr. Hiltmann from the Universitäts-Frauenklinik Heidelberg for medical advice and for being the first users of the system.

REFERENCES

[1] Antoniu, E: *Trends in Edge Detection Techniques*, EUROGRAPHICS'91 State of the Art Report, pp. 111-162, Vol. EG 91 STAR, ISSN 1017-4656, 1991

[2] Burt, P.: *The Pyramid as a Structure for Efficient Computation*, A. Rosenfeld (Ed.), Multi-Resolution Image Processing and Analysis, Springer Verlag, New York, 1984

[3] Fuchs, H., Kedem, Z., Uselton, S.: *Optimal Surface reconstruction from Planar Contours*, Comm. of the ACM, Vol. 20, No. 10, pp. 693-702, 1977

[4] Gallagher, R., Nagtegaal, J.: *An Efficient 3D Visualization Technique for Finite Elements*, Computer Graphics, Vol. 23, No. 3, pp. 185-194, July 1989

[5] C.R. Giardina, E.R. Dougherty: *Morphological Methods in Image and Signal Processing*, Prentice Hall, Englewood Cliffs, New Jersey, 1988

[6] Gonzalez, R. C., Wintz, P.: *Digital Image Processing*, Second Edition, Addison Wesley Publishing Company, 1987

[7] Herman, G., Liu, H.: *3D Display of Human Organs from Computer Tomograms*, Computer Graphics and Image Processing, Vol. 9, No. 1, pp. 1-21, January 1991

[8] Levoy, M.: *Display of Surfaces from Volume Data*, IEEE Computer Graphics & Applications, Vol. 8, No. 3, pp. 29-37, May 1988

[9] Lorensen, W., Cline, H.: *Marching Cubes: A High Resolution 3D Surface Construction Algorithm*, ACM Computer Graphics, SIGGRAPH-87, Vol. 21, No. 4, pp. 163-169, July 1987

[10] S. Mallat and S. Zhong, *Characterization of Signals from Multiscale Edges*, IEEE Transactions on Pattern Analysis and Machine Inteligence, Vol. 14, pp. 710-732, 1992

[11] Millner, R.: *Ultraschalltechnik, Grundlagen und Anwendungen*, Physik Verlag, Weinheim, ISBN 3-87664-106-3, 1987

[12] Nelson, T., Elvis, T.: *Visualization of 3D Ultrasound Data* IEEE Computer Graphics & Applications, Vol. 13, No. 6, pp. 50-57, November 1993

[13] Sabella, P.: *A Rendering Algorithm for Visualizing 3D Scalar Fields*, ACM Computer Graphics, Vol. 22, No. 4, pp. 51-58, August 1988

[14] Sakas, G., Gerth, M.: *Sampling and Anti-Aliasing Discrete 3D Volume Density Textures*, EUROGRAPHICS'91 Award Paper, Computer and Graphics, Vol. 16, No. 1, pp. 121-134, Pergamon Press, 1992

[15] Sakas, G.: *Interactive Volume Rendering of Large Fields*, 'The Visual Computer, Vol. 9, No. 8, pp. 425-438, August 1993

[16] Sakas, G., Schreyer, L., Grimm, M.: *Pre-Processing, Segmenting and Volume Rendering 3D Ultrasonic Data*, IEEE CG & A, Special Issue, Vol. 15, No. 4, July 1995. Revised version of *Case Study: Visualization of 3D Ultrasonic Data*, "Outstanding Case Study Award", Proceedings Visualization'94, pp. 369-373

[17] Salesin, D., Stolfi, J.: *The ZZ-Buffer: A Simple and Efficient Rendering Algorithm with Reliable Antialiazing*, Proceedings 'PIXIM'89 Conference', pp. 451-466, Hermes Editions, Paris, September 1989

[18] B. G. Schunk : *Edge detection with Gaussian Filters at Multiple Scales of Resolution*, in: 'Advances in Image Analysis', Y. Mahdavieh and R. C. Gonzales (Eds.), McGraw Hill 1987

[19] Stata, A., Chen, D., Tector, C., Brandl, A., Chen, H., Ohbuchi, R., Bajura, M., Fuchs, A.: *Case Study: Observing a Volume Rendered Fetus within a Pregnant Patient*, Proceedings Visualization'94, pp. 364-368, 1994

[20] Sakas, G., Walter, S., Hiltmann, W., Wischnik, A.: *Foetal Visualization Using 3D Ultrasonic Data*, Proceedings CAR'94, Berlin/Germany, 21-24 June 1995

[21] Sohn, C., Zoller, W. (Eds.): *Proceedings II Symposium 3D Ultraschalldiagnostik*, Munich, 25-26 June 1993, 'Imaging - Application & Results', Vol. 61, No. 2, pp. 81-135, Karger Pub., June 1994

David vs Goliath or Mice vs Men?
Production Studio Size in the Entertainment Industry

Chair
Pauline Ts'o, Rhythm & Hues

Panelists
Theresa Ellis, In-Sight Pix
Ralph Guggenheim, Pixar
Brad Lewis, Pacific Data Images
Ron Thornton, Foundation Imaging

The panelists come from a variety of backgrounds - some have helped small companies grow large, others have left large studios to form small ones. They all have senior management experience in markets that span the entire spectrum - feature films effects, television commercials, motion-based simulator rides, animated features, television series, animated shorts, broadcast graphics, special venue films, and interactive multi-media. The panel will draw upon this diverse history to discuss one strategic aspect of surviving in the entertainment industry.

Introduction

The appetite for digital content has grown enormously over the past eight years. The entertainment industry seems finally convinced that computer animation and digital effects are viable tools for many of its markets including feature films, television, theme parks and interactive multi-media. As with any increase in demand, there has been a corresponding increase in supply and, of course, a proliferation of approaches to cornering market share.

The size of a production studio affects every aspect of its competitive edge including hardware capacity, software capability, the depth of its creative environment, the types of services it can provide its clients, and which clients it can reach. Does a studio choose its size or is it chosen by the marketplace? And are the stereotypes associated with company size valid?

For example, one of the biggest problems facing studios today is finding qualified 3D computer animators. There are typically three major points that become the crux of an applicant's decision - career opportunity, standard of living, and salary. Studio size can have a drastic effect on each of these factors - for instance, a small studio typically asks an individual to perform in many different areas while a large one often allows an individual to perfect a particular skill. Which set of advantages and disadvantages is more appealing to more animators is becoming increasingly crucial. A studio that has work, but not enough animators, is in as much trouble as a studio in the opposite situation.

Financial stability may also depend on strategic diversification. Each market has its own particular financial cycles, such as television's fall premiere of new shows or the Thanksgiving release of major feature films. To smooth the rigors of boom-or-bust cash flow, most studios look for a balance between several markets. Large studios tend to pursue projects that take advantage of, and therefore justify, their inherently larger capacity. This has historically meant that certain markets are dominated by larger studios and other markets, by smaller studios. But technology for entertainment is extremely fluid. Will the small studios be the small, adaptive mammals of the future or will the large studios be the 800-lb gorillas?

Some believe that the technology is beside the point and what will really determine the long-term success or failure of individual computer animation studios is their ability to own creative content. But this development of creative property can be an expensive and risky endeavor, dependent upon just the right combination of talent, resources, and timing. Again, size can play a crucial role in the ability of studio to seize opportunities today for the future.

It will certainly be interesting to look at this issue again in another eight years. Given changes in commercial software, the rapid decline in hardware costs and the even faster expansion of communication and information flow, it may be that size won't matter at all.

Theresa Ellis

In comparing large CGI production companies with the smaller "boutique" streamlined companies such as In-Sight Pix, one may find that while the overall approach is very different, basically, they are much the same. We use the same high-end equipment and software as the larger companies. We work on effects and CGI elements with live action for commercial and film projects, with quality and creativity being the ultimate goal. Our client base and reputation is also world wide. On the other hand, having worked for several large and small companies, I would say the big difference between them is the company philosophy. In-Sight Pix is a small studio that, well, thinks globally and acts locally.

What makes us unique from the larger companies is that we have more control over the creative process of realizing the director's vision. All people involved are key. We provide and work with people who are very excited about what they do and are knowledgeable about every aspect of how to best see the project through. These qualities are evident in our work. As a whole, the ability and necessity to continually learn the latest is encouraged. Our work is respected by many repeat clients who constantly challenge our abilities with new ideas, as well as with young software companies who want to hear our new ideas to incorporate into their software.

Naturally, there is always the option of growing into a larger company or allowing one large project to take over the company. However, to do either of these would give up the control and personal relationships we have developed with our clients. For now, as a small company, being small is what keeps us strong and our work innovative.

Ralph Guggenheim

Pixar's unique environment houses a feature film animation studio side-by-side with a small TV commercial production unit. Toy Story, the first ever full-length computer animated feature film employs the talents of 100+ animators, technical directors, editors, artists, illustrators and production management staff.

Simultaneously, Pixar Shorts, our short-form animation group, has won two Clios in as many years for its TV commercial work with a small team of 15. These two groups produce highly creative work, though with very different markets and working styles. Is Pixar a large studio or a small boutique? How can these two diverse groups foster creativity and produce high-quality work with such different agendas?

Brad Lewis

Digital effects and computer animation production companies large or small are faced with similar challenges. We have to create and produce compelling and challenging visuals. We need to recruit and attract talented computer artists and animators, while maintaining a creative and challenging environment. We must also possess strong management skills and run viable businesses.

The entertainment industry is largely a traditional field that has existing production models that don't work for our industry. We are a different breed that combines a variety of disciplines that mesh into a new configuration: art, animation, computer science, software development, r&d, film and video, business and management. Many companies are pursuing these issues along very different paths that are based upon individual experience, strength, opportunity and various degrees of planning.

There are no exact answers, but there are practical examples of how our industry is currently approaching the challenges. There has been explosive growth over the past two years in which many companies have desperately responded in ways that are not sustainable. There is the major challenge of determining what our industry will be, what it could be, and ultimately, what should we be?

Ron Thornton

By using digital technology to create visual effects, we are continually faced with a constantly changing technology base and are forced to make decisions now which will effect our capabilities in the near future. Given this climate, we feel a smaller company is better able to adapt to quickly changing technologies than a larger company, because a smaller company doesn't have to invest in the volume of technology that a larger studio requires. Therefore, we can make both major and minor changes in the technology we use, with very little loss of time or revenue.

However, regardless of the size of the company and the equipment its artists use, the real focus is on the artist, not the technology. A computer, by itself, is not creative - it is the artist who creates the visual effect. The technology gives us more creative choices and increases our output, but it is important to remember to utilize the proper tool for the job. As our company tends to work mainly in the television arena, we can tailor our investment in digital equipment to suit our output. This doesn't have any effect on the quality of the visual - it would still be as spectacular on the big screen - but it does allow us to maintain great quality and meet a deadline.

In addition, because we don't have a huge overhead to support (in terms of equipment and software), we can take on work that large companies cannot afford to, or, conversely, decline to participate in projects which we feel are ill-conceived, regardless of the amount of money involved, which is something a big studio may not be able to afford to do. We feel it is important to promote our company's strengths and not attempt to service all areas of the marketplace.

Regardless of the size of the visual effects company, we are still governed by 3 variables: schedule, economy, quality - pick two.

A National Research Agenda for Virtual Reality: Report by the National Research Council Committee on VR R&D

Chair
Randy Pausch, University of Virginia

Panelists
Walter Aviles, Massachusetts Institute of Technology
Nathaniel Durlach, Massachusetts Institute of Technology
Warren Robinett, Virtual Reality Games, Inc
Michael Zyda, Naval Postgraduate School

In 1992, at the request of a consortium of federal agencies, the National Research Council established a committee to "recommend a national research and development agenda in the area of virtual reality" to set U.S. government R&D funding priorities for virtual reality (VR) for the next decade. The committee spent two years studying the current state of VR, speculating on where likely breakthroughs might happen, and deciding where funding could have the greatest impact. The result is a 500-page report that will have tremendous effect on what does and does not get funded in Virtual Reality research by agencies such as ARPA, the Air Force Office of Scientific Research, the Army Research Laboratory, Armstrong Laboratory, the Army Natrick RD&E Center, NASA, NSF, NSA, and Sandia National Lab.

The committee's report tries to "describe the current state of research and technology that is relevant to the development of synthetic environment systems, provide a summary of the application domains in which such systems are likely to make major contributions, and outline a series of recommendations that we believe are crucial to rational and systematic development of the synthetic environment field."

The purpose of this panel is to report the (often surprising) recommendations in the committee's report. Few researchers will have time to read this very influential document, but this forum will disseminate the basic highlights, and attempt to explain some of the more fractious points that the committee dealt with. For example, the report recommends "no aggressive federal involvement in computer hardware development in the [virtual reality] area at this time."

Based on last year's SIGGRAPH, Virtual Reality is one of the hottest areas for the computer graphics community, and funding is clearly needed from the federal government. Industrial sources are not viewed as having sufficiently long-term strategies to advance the field in many necessary areas. Therefore, the funding priorities and strategies discussed in this report may have a direct impact on the future directions of the SIGGRAPH community.

The report itself is Virtual Reality, Scientific and Technological Challenges, copyright 1995 National Academy of Sciences; ISBN 0-309-05135-5, Nathaniel I. Durlach and Anne S. Mavor, editors.

The purpose of the panel is to disseminate the report, the various panelists will be covering the following areas of the report and its recommendations:

Durlach: explanation of the committee's charge, government policy implications, and a high-level overview of the anticipated impact.

Pausch: description of the recommendations regarding the need for psychologists and evaluation criteria, and the recommendations in the area of education.

Aviles: discussion of recommendations regarding teleoperation and haptic/force feedback.

Robinett: discussion of human-machine interface recommendations, augmented reality, and sensory extension via VR.

Zyda: discussion of networking and hardware recommendations.

PANELISTS

Randy Pausch, University of Virginia (panel organizer) is an Associate Professor of Computer Science at the University of Virginia. He received a B.S. in Computer Science from Brown University in 1982 and a Ph.D. in Computer Science from Carnegie Mellon in 1988. He is a National Science Foundation Presidential Young Investigator and a Lilly Foundation Teaching Fellow. He currently leads the University of Virginia User Interface Group, which is developing the Alice VR system. His primary interests are human-computer interaction and undergraduate education.

Nathaniel Durlach, MIT, (chair of the NRC committee) is a senior scientist in the Department of Electrical Engineering and Computer Science at the Massachusetts Institute of Technology and has been co-director of the Sensory Communication Group in the Research Laboratory of Electronics there for over 20 years. He has also been a visiting scientist in the Biomedical Engineering Department of Boston University for five years. He received an M.A. degree from Columbia University in mathematics and an M.A. degree from Harvard University in psychology and biology. He is the author (or coauthor) of numerous book chapters and refereed articles in such journals as Perception and Psychophysics and the Journal of the Acoustical Society of America; he continues to review articles, proposals, and research programs in the field of pschophysics; and he has recently been selected to receive the silver medal award for outstanding work in psychoacoustics by the Acoustical Society of America. Recently, his research interests have focused on teleoperator and virtual environment systems, with special emphasis on the human-machine interfaces used in such systems. He is cofounder and director of the MIT Virtual Environment and Teleoperator Research Consortium, as well as cofounder and managing editor of the new MIT Press journal Presence: Teleoperators and Virtual Environments.

Walter Aviles, MIT, has over a decade of experience in the design and development of advanced human/machine interfaces and robotic systems. His technical-emphasis areas include real-time control and integration architectures for distributed robotic and sensor systems and multi-modal, spatially-oriented, interactive human /machine interfaces. He is one of the founding members of the Virtual Environment and Teleoperator Research Consortium (VETREC) and is an Associate Editor of the MIT Press journal Presence. Currently a Ph.D. candidate at MIT, Walter is responsible for the day to day management of the Virtual Environment Technology for Training Research Testbed. His current research involves exploring the efficacy of multi-modal user interfaces (MMUIs) in training applications After graduating from Stanford University in 1982, Walter spent the next 11 years at the Naval Ocean Systems Center (NOSC), a US Navy research and development laboratory.

Warren Robinett, Virtual Reality Games, Inc., is a designer of interactive computer graphics software and hardware and president and founder of Virtual Reality Games, Inc., a developer of virtual reality video games for the home market. In 1978, he designed the Atari video game Adventure, the first graphical adventure game. In 1980, he was cofounder and chief software engineer at The Learning Company, a publisher of educational software. There he designed Rocky's Boots, a computer game that teaches digital logic design to 11-year-old children. Rocky's Boots won software of the year awards from three magazines in 1983. In 1986 Robinett worked as a research scientist at the NASA-Ames Research Center, where he designed the software for the Virtual Environment Workstation, NASA's pioneering virtual reality project. From 1989 to 1992 at the University of North Carolina, he directed the virtual reality and nanomanipulator projects. He is an associate editor for the journal Presence.

Michael Zyda, Naval Postgraduate School, is a professor in the Department of Computer Science at the Naval Postgraduate School. He is also the academic associate and associate chair for academic affairs in that department. His main focus in research is in the area of computer graphics, specifically the development of large-scale, networked, three-dimensional virtual environments and visual simulation systems. He is the senior editor for virtual environments for the quarterly Presence; for that journal, he has coedited special issues on Pacific Rim virtual reality and telepresence.

Set-Top Boxes - The Next Platform

Chair
Jonathan Steinhart, Jonathan Steinhart Consulting, Incorporated

Panelists
Derrick Burns, Silicon Graphics, Inc.
James Gosling, Sun Microsystems, Inc.
Steve McGeady, Intel, Inc.
Rob Short, Microsoft, Inc.

Successive price/performance iterations in computer and computer graphics technology have increased the penetration of this technology into everyday life. Access to early computer graphics technology, based on large computers and specialized displays, was limited to computer professionals. A larger portion of the population had access to high performance computer graphics technology as prices dropped and performance increased through successive generations of mini-supercomputers, workstations, and personal computers. However, this population is still primarily limited to the workplace. Set-top boxes are poised as the next big price/performance step. With this step, computer graphics and high performance computing technology are expected to achieve significant penetration into the home market.

How's all this going to happen? What hardware is being built for set-top boxes? What software is going to run on them, both at the systems level and the application level? What communications technologies are going to support all this? What's the market?

Who is going to use services provided via set-top boxes? We're already running out of hours in the day to watch television. Are set-top boxes just for entertainment or are they going to facilitate telecommuting, shopping, school homework, etc? Will the television become a household bottleneck?

Will set-top boxes succeed in the home market or will elements of the technology be absorbed into the business environment?

There is considerable disagreement as to the answers to these questions. Many companies have joined into partnerships to try to grab a portion of the projected market. There's a lot of hype, as there are no real product offerings today.

Derrick Burns

Interactive television is much more than video on demand. It is a new medium by which the consumer is both educated and entertained. The settop box provides access to this medium. It serves both as a gateway to a vast repository of stored multimedia information and as a tool that can navigate through this store, creating for the each individual viewer a presentation tailored to his/her desires. Personalization demands substantial processing power. To meet my vision of interactive television, the settop must offer not just playback of audio and video, but it must synthesize sound and imagery as well. The settop box will provide synthetic spatial (3D) audio and texture-mapped 3D graphics, and it will provide these features at very low cost. This settop box is a true SYNTHESIS ENGINE. The synergy of synthesis and access to a broadband network will enable new services whose markets will eventually dwarf that of simple video-on-demand.

James Gosling

It's madness out there. Every vendor is doing something different, usually proprietary. They all dream of controlling the universe and being the next MicroSoft. But even MicroSoft is having problems because few want to be dominated by the current Master Of The Universe. (The other Master Of The Universe, Nintendo, is similarly hemmed in by its success) Settop boxes are caught in the usual cost trap: features that lead to Nirvana are promised, but when the cost is examined, enthusiasm drops. Some try to get around this by making the settops very cheap, and putting the intelligence in downstream servers, but all they succeed in doing is shifting the cost.

My personal guess is that there never will be "intelligent set top boxes": intelligence will continue to be in personal computers, whose multimedia capabilities will continue to grow. People are used to spending a few thousand dollars for them, while they expect set tops to be free. I don't think any of the high-function set top experiments will achieve the volume necessary to attract a significant developer community. The actual features available on the box are almost inconsequential to a developer relative to the market size.

Steve McGeady

We have been bombarded lately with breathless reports about an 'Information Superhighway,' coming soon to your home. But experts can't seem to agree on what devices will connect your home or office to the Infobahn, what services will be offered on it, or what business and technical form this information revolution will take. Intel is at the heart of an industry that has delivered a 1000-fold increase in computing power over the last 15 years. Intel's Communications Technology Lab is now charting a course to integrate the personal computer with the rapidly-increasing communication bandwidth that is being made available to enable new applications in the office and home. In order to deliver a rich and truly interactive experience, the device in your home needs computing power and memory, high-resolution display, mass storage, and multiple high-bandwidth two-way communication channels. It needs to be programmable by others than the broadcast industry, and it needs to offer the user interactivity beyond simple yes/no answers and selections. Over 30 Million homes already have a device that begins to meet these criteria - the personal computer.

Rob Short

The key to gaining consumer acceptance of interactive TV is ease of use. If the average consumer can't find their way through the tens of thousands of services offered to them interactive TV will flop. Microsoft is concentrating on developing intuitive and fun interfaces for TV users. The challenge is that these interfaces must be much more powerful than those on todays PC's while at the same time being much easier to learn and use. High quality computer graphics are the enabling technology for these new user interface paradigms. How will these systems evolve?, we don't know. We do know that there are 20 million PC's in U.S. homes today, and that these PC's have capabilities that will not appear in set-tops for several years. Many of the concepts and services will appear on the PC earlier than on the set-top, perhaps in a different form. As technology advances we expect to see a convergence of the services provided through PC's and set-tops although the user interface paradigm may need to be totally different.

Museums Without Walls: New Media for New Museums

Chair
Alonzo C. Addison, University of California at Berkeley

Panelists
Douglas MacLeod, The Banff Centre for the Arts
Gerald Margolis, Simon Wiesenthal Center
Beit Hashoah Museum of Tolerance
Michael Naimark, Interval Research Corporation
Hans-Peter Schwarz, MediaMuseum, ZKM (Center for Arts and Media Technology)

What role should computer graphics, multimedia, virtual reality, and networks play in the 'Museum of the Future' and what effect will these technologies have upon it?

This panel is focused on the evolving nature of the museum in the information age. Society's traditional methods of presenting and exhibiting cultural, social, and historic artifacts and information are being profoundly affected by the proliferation of computers, multimedia, and networks. Museum directors and designers around the world are rapidly discovering that older passive and static presentation models are increasingly inappropriate in an 'instant gratification' society raised on television and accustomed to computers and other new media. Can and should museums attempt to keep pace with the media of the 'Nintendo' generation? A proliferation of World Wide Web "museum" sites on the Internet begs the question of what makes a museum today-is physical presence still a defining criteria? Is an interactive, networked 'virtual museum' a viable substitute for a physical place, or do we need both? How can and should traditional museum facilities work with and link to virtual ones? Just as a good novel can be more powerful than an interactive, multimedia CD-ROM story, technology alone does not necessarily make a better museum. How much media is appropriate? How interactive should it and does it need to be? When does media begin to overpower the message of the museum itself? How do we overcome (or should we even care about) problems of graphic realism 'brainwashing' visitors who may come to museums to see 'truths' about their society and history? With technology providing the potential to customize the museum to the visitor's interests, new dilemmas arise, and old debates resurface. Do the curatorial advantages of being able to present multiple 'tours' through a virtual site outweigh the losses of not being able to physically see an artifact itself? And how does a museum fund high technology with computer power and features advancing at a dizzying pace? These and similar questions are among those the panelists are grappling with in their own work, have previously discussed, and are looking forward to debating with each other and the SIGGRAPH audience. The panelists bring a multitude of perspectives to the discussion. From roles as museum directors and designers, to educators and artists, they have all dealt with the issues surrounding the museum of the future. They have similarly faced the challenges of being at the technologic forefront-from the difficulties of synchronizing and ensuring nonstop operation of a multitude of electronics for days on end, to the problems of creating and maintaining a state-of-the-art showplace in the era of rapid media obsolescence. Although many of the experiences of the panelists are in many respects similar, different museums, artifacts, and ideas require different types and levels of technology-what works at the Museum of Tolerance may not be appropriate at the Getty or the Exploratorium.

Douglas MacLeod
New media that simply mimics a walkthrough of the paintings and sculptures of a museum is a waste of time and effort. The possibilities of real-time, interactive graphics and sound demand much more. Coupled with emerging high-speed, high bandwidth networks, engaging and evocative exhibits are possible that question the idea of a static collection inhabiting a single space. Converging new media are already undermining the traditional idea of a museum. Art pieces produced at the Banff Centre through its Art and Virtual Environments Project demonstrate the potential of new cultural experiences; and testbed networks such as WURCNet (Western Universities Research Consortium) in Western Canada demonstrate new delivery systems and content. Together the two trends of real-time interactions and high-speed networks will revolutionize our experience of culture and radically transform the institution of the museum.

Gerald Margolis
The Museum of Tolerance is a media-rich facility that reflects and comments on social problems in the United States and reprises the watershed event of the 20th century, the Holocaust. Since its opening in February 1993, the Museum has garnered significant attention and become a regular stop for adults, school groups, and professional organizations interested in diversity-training. As the first Museum to discuss the Holocaust within the context of prejudice and aggression in our society, it employs diverse multimedia, from low tech physical props and sets to state-of-the-art interactive computer displays, to help visitors confront personal feelings and beliefs and thus convey a powerful, if sometimes unpleasant, message. Ultimately, the Museum is interested in communicating values and ideas which are of greater importance than the vehicle-multimedia-of delivery. The Museum is interested in presentation and interpretation as these strategies surround and reflect issues of social justice and inter-ethnic relations.

Michael Naimark
Museums WITH walls will offer experiences very different from-but symbiotic with-museums without walls. As public spaces, new media can be used for unique immersive environments on a scale much larger than for homes, with high resolution, panoramic, stereoscopic visuals, and high quality multi-channel audio, haptic feedback, and novel input. Museums with walls will always collect and display original art and artifacts. Representations of such work, while convenient and economical, will never completely replace the originals. Museums of the future can take advantage of a powerful symbiosis by planning to be both a node on the global network and a place for unique sensory rich experiences.

Hans-Peter Schwarz

The Museum of the Future will be an interactive art gallery on the data highway. However, we still need physical museums as bases, or buildings, to link individual places across the world together. Because the museum is more than a storage room or repository for artwork, it has to be a meeting place as well as a forum for discussions, experimentations, and education. The main outlet for this ongoing dialogue will be "Salon Digital"-an interactive electronic Cafe which encourages social and theoretical discourse. The MediaMuseum, planned in the Center for Art and Media Technology in Karlsruhe, will be such a forum. A combination of the virtual museum and the real sensual museum, it will be a place to confront the visitor with a new view of history as well as to talk about the presence and the future of media art and media technology. Its primary focus is to make a critical use of the unbelievable possibilities of new media technology.

Afterword

This panel is an outgrowth of the discussions of an interdisciplinary group of computer graphic and multimedia specialists, museum directors, designers, artists, and educators with a common interest in 'The Museum of the Future'. This international museum group was first brought together by the University of California at Berkeley and the University of Ferrara, Italy for several days of meetings during 1994 to think about and debate issues of museums with and without walls. It is our hope that through this panel some of what has been learned by our group can be shared with the greater SIGGRAPH community.

Interactive MultiMedia: A New Creative Frontier or Just a New Commodity?

Chair
Ruth E. Iskin, Head, Visual Arts & New Media, UCLA Extension

Panelists
Mikki Halpin
Michael Nash
George Legrady
Rodney Alan Greenblat

The last one hundred and fifty years have generated an avalanche of visual technologies through which an ever expanding visual culture has been marketed to mass audiences. From the invention of photography in 1839 to film in the 1890's and the marketing of television in the 1940's-50's, our steady diet of images has increased our voracious appetite by quantum leaps. In the 1990's we are faced with another invention of great potential, much hype and as yet unforseen repercussions—interactive multimedia. "Employing these new media requires inventiveness as well as overcoming the double jeopardy of techno-phobias and the strictures of a paper/print design mentality; it calls upon practitioners operating in a new electronic paradigm whose parameters are still forming to recreate the roles of designer, artist and entertainer.." It remains to be seen to what extent this new communication commodity truly represents a new artistic frontier. A multi-sensory dynamic form of communication, multimedia enables a new unprecedented level of intermediality between the previously relatively separate forms of writing, voice, music, still images, motion pictures and video. It promises innovative intermedia relationships between these in non-linear, user-driven options incorporating the interactive game format along with more passive reception and unlimited playback options. To be sure, it recycles older communication products from photography, film and books to museum art collections.

Is multimedia as yet more than the sum of its recycled parts? Michael Nash states that "The promise of the new media lies in its ability to intertextualize the elements that constitute our tele-visual systems of meaning with a depth and richness that will enable artists to more fully mirror the activities of consciousness, and to engineer new dialogues between its reflection and articulation, between reading and writing."

Interactive multimedia are a genre of culture commodities that stimulate consumer interest with the promise of repeated and engaged usage. Yet "the significance of interactivity extends far beyond an emergence of a more enticing set of commodities, though that they certainly are. Interactivity is also not reducible to a new art genre, though that too, it certainly is becoming. Rather, we intuit interactivity as a fundamental change in socialized patterns of intersubjectivity, forms of knowledge and communication and relationship to objects. In the process, notions of self, agency, art and commodity are reconfigured...It should come as no surprise then that art... is claiming interactivity as its arena along-side with inert objecthood." Artists and users/consumers alike have a heightened sense that multimedia plays a crucial role in the tidal wave of changes sweeping the late twentieth century world of communications. The questions that arise are vast. This panel will begin to tackle some of them.

Panel Goals and Issues

This roundtable of artists and producers share brief segments from their most recent work and address a range of questions: What makes for successful interactivity and multi-sensory communication? The highs and lows of making multimedia for the mass market: Can artistic innovation flourish in a fiercely competitive market, corporate climate and bottom-line driven business plans? Are we entering a Renaissance or an electronic sweatshop? What is the potential of digital cash for Internet distribution by artists? And what are the realities of selling creative work to multimedia companies: How are artists' rights and copyrights effected?

Panel participants' Statements

Mikki Halpin: Independent Multimedia Producer, columnist on new technologies for Filmmaker, Computer Player, CD-ROM Player, Hun, and an instructor of "The Culture of Multimedia," at UCLA Extension brings a rich perspective as a writer and multimedia producer. Her past encompasses both Hollywood development and Ivy League theory; her roots and connections span the fringes of the art world and the mainstream multimedia publishing world.

Statement

A friend of mine who runs a media art program recently confided in me a fear she has about the future, a future in which, she said, all the artists she knows and respects end up working for CD-ROM companies. She envisioned the artists as virtual slaves to their given employer, a commodity to be traded or secreted away, like Hollywood stars of old. She may not be far off.

Faced with dwindling government and community resources, and excited by the possibilities of interactive media, many artist are forming new alliances with industry. But, unlike corporate patronage of the arts evidenced in corporate art collections and sponsorship of exhibitions, multimedia companies tend to expect more from an artist than just their work. It is not unusual for a company to demand ownership of such things as character rights, amusement or even theme park rights in perpetuity from an artist before agreeing to produce or distribute the artist's work. In return for this complete abandonment of his or her rights, the artist receives a small advance against the royalties. Demands which would be scoffed at in negotiations for literary or theatrical rights are de rigueur in multimedia. The internet, with its growing consumer base and increasing multimedia capabilities, offers many possibilities to artists. As remuneration engines such as "digital cash" and other protocols emerge, perhaps artists will be able to take hold of their own destiny without selling their souls."

Michael Nash: President and Creative Director of Inscape, a multimedia company he formed in partnership with Home Box Office and the Warner Music Group brings both art world expertise as a former museum curator of video art and as producer of CD-Rom titles at The Voyager.

Statement

Cultural coups like the emergence of San Francisco cult bands The Residents as CD-ROM stars demonstrate opportunities presented by the new media to establish new relationships between artists and their constituencies. As business-plan driven multimedia product developments efforts fall embarrassingly short of not just artist expectations but also economic projections, successes like Myst make it increasingly clear that the inception of new artistic forms is a visionary enterprise driven by the exigencies of personal creative expression.

The articulation of transformative new versions changes what we expect of new technology or any property of new technology. But in order for artists to extend their impact beyond formal innovations and truly change cultural dialogue, it is necessary to engage in marketing. Marketplace dynamics and creative strategies offer opportunities to develop a new audience for art in the digital culture of the future.

George Legrady: Associate Professor, Information Arts in the Art Department at San Francisco State University and Winner of the 1994 "New Voices, New Visions," competition by the Voyager, Wired, and Interval Research, brings the perspective of a fine artist. His two decades of producing work in photography and conceptual art have recently culminated in a new synthesis by pioneering fine art interactive multimedia work. Paying close attention to aesthetic issues, the construction of meaning, ideology and the interweaving of personal and historical circumstances, his work constitutes a true breakthrough in the fine art of interactive multimedia.

Statement

Metaphor-based interfaces form organizational models that situate the viewer of multimedia works and provide a way of accessing and understanding data. By knowing "the story" or metaphor, the viewer can successfully navigate inside the interactive program. These environments promise to be the key site for innovative developments of linguistic, symbolic, aesthetic, sensory and conceptual nature.

Rodney Alan Greenblat: Artist, The Center for Advanced Whimsy, brings extensive dual experience in the New York art world (from the 1980s off-beat Village scene to the prestigious Whitney Biennial) coupled with popular success as a multimedia artist who has broken through to the mass market.

Statement

It is ridiculous to talk about "multimedia" being new. Artists have been creating multimedia since cromagnon man first scratched an image of his grandmother being trampled by a mammoth and then sang a song about it. The hype really seems to be about some kind of viewer-controlled experience, or possibly it is just peoples preoccupation with technology. Whatever it is, the digital medium seems to be a great way to make money in the late 20th century. Unfortunately, few have really profited from this fad.

Making computer art is a high challenge that calls for multiple talents, extreme patience and total devotion. A degree in law or an MBA is an advantage if you wish to actually publish what you make. Nevertheless, I really love my computers. They are like brilliant little parrots waiting for idea crackers to digitize and spit out as a colorful animated show. They regularly fuss and refuse, and constantly ask "OK?" When one of them is sick I am filled with frustration and concern. When everything finally works, and the creation is finished, I have an art work that is part magical part math. It glows at night, fits on a small disk, and can travel around the world in a few minutes. It is part audio recording, part movie, part novel, and part painting. It is a medium for building worlds, and the kids really like it.

Integrating Interactive Graphics Techniques with Future Technologies

Chair
Theresa Marie Rhyne, Lockheed Martin / U.S. EPA Scientific Visualization Center

Panelists
Eric Gidney, College of Fine Arts/University of New South Wales, Australia
Tomasz Imielinski, Rutgers University
Pattie Maes, MIT Media Laboratory
Ronald Vetter, North Dakota State University

This panel examines the need to integrate computer graphics techniques with other methodologies and technologies such as mobile and wireless personal assistants, intelligent agents, cartography, human perception, voice recognition, interactive television, cooperative computing, and high speed networking. The need to develop new interfaces and displays which reflect the social changes associated with the way people will interact with integrated computer systems and the information highway is addressed.

Theresa Marie Rhyne: Cartography, Visualization, & Decision Support

Interactive computer graphics techniques are just one component of integrated decision support systems. For comprehensive interpretation of geographically referenced data, visualization environments need to be merged with large remotely distributed and networked spatial data bases. Three dimensional isosurface and volume rendered images must be referenced against cartographic, statistical and plotting displays for effective interpretation of scientific results. The requirements of research, policy analysis, and science education are not necessarily the same. Therefore, user interfaces need to be flexible in their design to support these different viewpoints and interpretations of data. Decision making is rarely done in a vacuum but rather is a collaborative process. To support these collaborative efforts, interactive computer graphics techniques will need to merge with multi-media tools for desktop and wireless videoconferencing, cooperative computing technologies, mobile ways for collecting and accessing data, and high speed networking.

A geographic decision support system which is comprehensively integrated will alter the perceptual thinking of individuals and communities. This will result in differing interpretations of information and the need to build computing tools which visually display these discerning viewpoints and the paths taken for arriving at the results.

Tomasz Imielinski: The Challenge — User Interfaces for Mobile Users

Palmtops such as the Newton or HP 100LX are equipped with very small screens. Keyboards with these machines will likely be of little use. This requires a new approach to user interface design. There will be a growing role for pens and speech recognition. Additionally a few companies are exploring "magnifying technology." This allows the user to magnify the size of the screen with little effect on resolution through some form of headmounted display. Voice activated input will be very useful in the car, while less likely in public places where visual interfaces will still remain dominant.

What is the nature of applications which will be run on palmtop computers? Many such applications will be location dependent and deal with the area immediately surrounding the user such as a local supermarket (shopping), restaurant and movie theater (entertainment), and local yellow pages (business). Thus, we define the metaphor of a map centric interface. At any location, the user sees a local map, as a background on his mobile computer screen. This display plays the role of a "magnified eye" which sees further than the real eye and provides labels and interpretations of "whats around." Additionally, the interface will allow rotation and repositioning of images on the screen to reflect the current location of the user. A user standing in front of a building will readjust the mobile computer image to his own unique position, This feature will use information positioning devices such as global positioning systems (GPS).

Summarizing: new hardware restrictions and developments as well as new applications call for revolutionary approaches to user interfaces on small battery powered terminals. Due to battery power limitations and bandwidth restrictions, especially outdoors, CPU intensive visual interfaces will have to be ruled out. There is a need for new solutions, which are attractive to the naive users, while not overly resource consuming.

Ronald Vetter: High Speed Networking

Recent advances in communication networks, computer hardware, software, and visualization are generating interest in the cross- fertilization of application areas . Interaction with massive amounts of three dimensional images, generated in real-time, requires communication networks with high data rates and low latency. The sheer volume of data that must be transmitted in these short periods of time requires networks running at multimegabit speeds. The deployment of high speed networks will allow the integration of computer-generated and real-world imagery to finally reach the desktop.

An example of this kind of interaction is exemplified by an application called TerraVision. In TerraVision, the integration of remote databases, including massive amounts of heterogeneous data (e.g., aerial photography, satellite imagery, digital elevation models) on mass-storage systems, and temporal data from a real-time global positioning satellite system were transmitted over a high speed network. This enabled a U.S. Army commander to "drive through" and "see the battlefield" from a remote workstation. Global positioning sensors were used to track vehicles which were then integrated as 3-D objects in real-time into the terrain image display. TerraVision was developed over a wide-area, switched asynchronous transfer mode (ATM) network of supercomputer systems, gigabit LANs, graphics workstations, mass storage systems, and multimedia facilities.

The impact of network and display technology is also seen by the rapid growth of graphical-based browsing tools on the Internet. NCSA Mosaic type browsers allow wide-area distributed asynchronous collaboration and hypermedia-based information discovery and retrieval. One concern users have with existing Internet browser tools involves the overwhelming number of possible links (choices) to select from. It is also difficult to recall where a particular piece of information is located. In the future, intelligent interface agents will be able to learn particular interests, habits, and preferences of individual users and help them obtain information when they need it. This will add much more flexibility to many of today's closed hypermedia- based systems.

Eric Gidney - Collaboration in Media & Design Pre-Production

Real-time communications presents a different, more urgent and more sociable paradigm then the human-computer interaction we normally associate with computing. Asynchronous collaboration does not provide the benefits of rapid contextualisation and decision- making that are achievable in real time.

Distributed work environments are now common, but the technology of sharing favourite applications in real time is not readily accessible. Companies need to be able to integrate application sharing into their current work and social contexts. This includes requirements for mobile computing, which may impose constraints on what can be shared.

Media and design companies that work visually need to share images over distance in real time. However, they will have to rationalise bandwidth utilisation versus cost. It may be better, for example, to provide good, fast shared graphics rather than poor videoconferencing.

Pattie Maes: Intelligent Agents & Personal Assistants

Computers are becoming the vehicle for an increasing range of everyday activities. Acquisition of news, information, and mail, as well as social interactions and entertainment, are becoming more computer-based. Simultaneously, more untrained users are interacting with computers. This number will rise as technologies like hand-held computers and interactive TV increase in popularity. Unfortunately, these technological developments are not going hand in hand with changes in the way people interact with computers. The currently dominant interaction metaphor of direct manipulation requires the user to initiate all tasks explicitly and to monitor all events. This metaphor will need to change if untrained users are to make effective use of the computers and networks of tomorrow.

Techniques from the field of Artificial Intelligence, in particular "autonomous agents," can be used to implement a complementary style of interaction. Instead of user-initiated interaction via commands and/or direct manipulation, the user is engaged in a cooperative process in which human and computer agents both initiate communication, monitor events and perform tasks. The metaphor used is that of a "personal assistant" who is collaborating with the user in the same work environment. The assistant becomes gradually more effective as it learns the user's interests, habits and preferences (as well as those of his or her community). Notice that the agent is not necessarily an interface between the computer and the user. In fact, the most successful software agents are those that do not prohibit the user from taking actions and fulfilling tasks personally.

The premise of the talk is that the ideal interface for agent-human collaboration consists of a virtual graphical world in which the agents are depicted as life-like computer characters. I will demonstrate such a system, called ALIVE, which allows a user and an agent (or agents) to co-inhabit a semi-real, semi-virtual 3D environment. In contrast with traditional virtual reality systems (goggles and gloves systems), the ALIVE system allows wireless, full-body interaction. We use a single CCD camera to obtain a color image of a person, which we composite into a 3D graphical world. The resulting image is projected onto a large screen which faces the user and acts as a type of "magic mirror": the user sees herself surrounded by objects and agents (real as well as virtual ones). Computer vision techniques are used to extract information about the person, such as her 3D location, the position of various body parts as well as simple gestures performed. In addition, simple audio and speech processing allows the user to complement the communication with verbal and sound- based cues. Because of the presence of agents, the system does more than the obvious direct-manipulation style of interaction. It provides for a powerful, indirect style of interaction in which gestures can have more complex meanings, which may vary according to the situation the agents and user find themselves in.

Selected References:

Gidney, C.E., Chandler, A. and McFarlane, G., CSCW for Film and TV Preproduction, IEEE Multimedia, Summer 94, 16 - 26.

Gidney, C.E. and Robertson, T., Remote Collaborative Drawing for Visual Designers, workshop notes, Computational Support for Distributed Collaborative Design workshop, Key Centre of Design Computing, University of Sydney, Sept. 1993, 53 - 66.

Imielinski, Tomasz and B.R. Badrinath, Mobile Wireless Computing, Communications of the ACM, October 1994.

Maes, Pattie "Agents that reduce work and information overload", Communications of the ACM, July 1994

Maes, Pattie "Animated Agents: Artificial Life meets Interactive Entertainment", Communications of the ACM, March 1995

Rhyne, Theresa Marie, GIS and Visualization Integration - An Unresolved Computing Challenge for the Environmental Sciences, Proceedings of the International Specialty Conference on Computing in Environmental Management (Dec. 1994), Air & Waste Management Association (A&WMA), 1995, pp. 133 - 144.

Rhyne, Theresa Marie, "Collaborative modeling and visualization: An EPA HPCC initiative", Hot Topics (R. Williams, editor), IEEE Computer, Vol. 27, No. 7, July 1994.

Vetter, R., Juell, P., Brekke, D., and Wasson, J., "Storage and Network Requirements of a Low-Cost, Computer-Based Virtual Classroom", Journal of Computing and Information Technology, Vol. 2, No. 4, December 1994.

Vetter, R., Tong, S., and Du, D., "Design Principles for Multi-Hop Wavelength and Time Division Multiplexed Optical Passive Star Networks", Journal of High Speed Networks, Vol.4, No. 2, March 1995.

Vetter, R., Spell, C., and Ward, C., "Mosaic and the World Wide Web", IEEE Computer, Vol. 27, No. 10, October 1994.

Videogame Industry Overview: Technology, Markets, Content, Future

Chair
Jane Veeder, Time Warner Interactive

Panelists
Mark Stephen Pierce, Time Warner Interactive
Eugene Jarvis, Williams/Bally/Midway
John N. Latta, 4th Wave, Inc.
Heidi Therese Dangelmaier, Hi*D
Jez San, Argonaut Software, Ltd.

Description

While innovative (but secretive) early on, the videogame industry is now rejoining the computer graphics mainstream. In production, we see a rapid move from 2D to 3D animation, low-end to high-end production technologies, limited in-house tools to cutting-edge animation production techniques such as motion capture and 3D character animation. In game formats, we see experimentation with multi-player games, cooperative strategies, and virtual reality. Interactive entertainment overall is a rapidly expanding area with a great requirement for creative intervention and sophisticated computer graphics. The videogame industry has only very recently come into focus for many people in the computer graphics field, yet this industry is now driving much of the technology development in computer animation.

Videogame development is being drawn deeper into the media mainstream. We have entered the age of the "commercial transmedia supersystem" where entertainment content is proliferated across multiple marketing opportunities: the game, the movie, the music CD, the book, the doll. Application developers have recently focused on an "author once, deploy many" imperative for cost effective production. As a new generation tackles the problem of interactive content production, their tools apply contemporary technical solutions to a process done with graph paper and assembler code not so many years ago.

Videogame content may evolve as well, driven by the new delivery systems which underly market growth. For example, the corporate dreams of interactive television list the two largest consumer revenue areas as shopping and (then) games. Ubiquitous interactive television would certainly leverage today's limited multi-user games. New audiences means designing for new cognitive models of fun and taking advantage of recent research in how media products relate to gender and childhood development. Electronic gaming could evolve to encompass nationwide social events such as elections, celebrity trials, virtual participation in natural disasters, and so forth.

All these new products, applications, and markets require technical, design, and artistic contributions for development, yet our skills, knowledge sets, and innovation must be translated into the new forms. To make this translation we must develop a coherent picture of how this industry is currently constituted and how it may evolve in the future. This panel will focus on a number of topics including platform hardware, delivery systems and their markets, the move into 3D computer graphics, virtuality in videogame design, overlapping areas of interactive entertainment, e.g. multimedia and theme parks, markets and content, and projected future developments.

Mark Stephen Pierce: Evolution of Game Content

The history of videogames spans less than a quarter century.

Technology, design processes, and content have all been forced to evolve quickly and haphazardly over this period. Technological evolution has been the most consistently rapid, keeping production techniques unsettled. Content has evolved at the slowest pace.

In relation to the rest of the high-tech world, the videogame industry has been something of a paradox. Due to a broad consumer base, videogames enabled the personal computer age to get an early start with lower cost monitors, processors, and memory, making affordable PCs a reality in the 80's. But, at the same time videogames has been a major enabler of this technological revolution, it has also been considered a backwater fit only for hackers and bold, technologically capable artists who tolerated "jaggies" and tight content and performance restrictions.

Now, as we start the second quarter century, we in our backwater find everyone from Hollywood agents, large communications conglomerates, and high-end hardware producers at our doorstep telling us that our industry is about to go through a content revolution. Increased capabilities of delivery technology and dreams of large profits have convinced many newcomers that undiscovered territories of audience and content lie hidden in the uncharted interior of the games continent. We stand on the shore and wave "Hello" to the many newcomers rushing headlong into this entertainment arena armed with venture capital and buzzwords like VR, LBE's, HMD's, FMV, CD-ROM, "Doom Engines" and "Infotainment." While we hope they find the treasure they seek (More fun for us too!), they are in danger of ignoring the core issues of what has historically made for successful interactive entertainment product.

How will this drama play out? Will we indeed see the light, change our content and design for perhaps mythical markets or will they learn to love lucrative fighting games? Must we give up our drums and pagan idols and take up the new religion? Will they convert us or we them?

As an industry veteran, I would like to make these newcomers aware of the rich and humorous history of the medium they seek to conquer and change. And remember: Television ALSO could be a constructive societal enablement, but Oprah and her ilk still seem to be going strong. Perhaps Drive-and-Kill IS all we really want to do as an interactive entertainment consuming species!

Eugene P. Jarvis: Video Game Platform Technology from PONG to PHONG

The conflict between the quest for cool graphics vs. the lust for $$ has created the strange alchemy that drives video game platform technology. The early '70s saw the birth of the video game before the advent of the microprocessor or RAM or ROM. The platforms of this "Kill the Blip" era such as the immoral

"PONG" were based on hardwired SSI TTL logic. Colors were strictly black and white, and blips were any shape as long as it was square.

In the late 70's and early 80's the microprocessor came of age. Video game platforms sprouted MPU's and sprites, and bitmaps. "Space Invaders" in 16 colors on the Atari VCS was king in the "Kill the Martian" era. You could design anything you wanted as long as it fit in 256 bytes of RAM. The late 80's and early 90's brought 2D graphics technology to its greatest refinements in the "Kill the Human" era. Digitized 64 color graphics and multilayered backgrounds brought Mortal Kombat to full glory.

Today, the super nova of 3D, RISC, networking technologies and the prospect of Nintendo sized profits has created a feeding frenzy of corporate hype to stake out the new frontiers in interactive cyberspace. The merciless laws of consumer economics have crowned CD-ROM the winner, but which format? and where? PC (den), settop console (living room), arcade, or themed location (LBE)?

On the video technology front the battle is between full motion video (FMV) and real time rendering (RTR). FMV offers Oh, Wow! graphics with little or no interactivity for couch potatoes. RTR delivers incredible realism while demanding unlimited computing power. This is the classic confrontation between the Studio Weenies (content without interaction) and the Techies (interaction without content). When the vaporware clears, the Hollywood FMV scam will be left in the dust by hyper-reality based designs. Phong rules!

The golden age of On-Line Gaming is dawning as the richness of human-human interaction surmounts physical limitations. Networked multiplayer games with real-time audio and video links for interplayer communication are coming as technical barriers fall in the age of the Internet. The promise of VR will finally be realized as headset and rendering technology advances beyond the current barf-bag stage. VR peripherals will become ubiquitous plug-ins to consumer CD-ROM systems.

The only thing that remains constant is game theme in this new "Kill everything in 3D" era.

John N. Latta: Video Game Market Dynamics

The coin operated video game business is seen by many as a testing ground for new content, technology and the delivery of entertainment to the consumer. However, the market dynamics are racked with economic uncertainty, competition and a fickle customer. Increasingly, the consumer does not see the out-of-home video game as an isolated experience but as part of a continuum of where fun can be experienced. The market for video games can only be examined in the context of home video games, theme parks, urban entertainment centers, and personal computer games. This presentation will examine the forces which are shaping these markets both in terms of technology, the consumer and the business models. With this foundation, a wide range of issues will be explored which will shape the market in the future. These include: diversity of participation; cost of equipment and play; role of content development on multiple platforms; expenditure patterns for in-home and out-of-home entertainment; the development of new out-of-home play venues and the role of 3D technology in leveling the playing field.

Heidi Therese Dangelmaier: New Markets and New Game Paradigms

The existing types of video games were not born out of sterile market studies. They came to us in a more organic manner. Designer created types of play activities which allowed them to participate in their fantasies, activities which met their needs, or simply provided them a fun time. For those genres which have

sustained, the needs and desires these genres addressed resonated meaning in many, and hence became archetype.

If we are to facilitate the development of new markets, we must recognize that the are many different types of fun, and what is a meaningful experience for one, may not hold any bearing in the value system of another. WE must eliminate the artistic exclusivity of this industry and allow room and opportunity for new artists, people intrinsically driven by different motives. We must not fool ourselves by believing that commercially market-driven projections will be our guiding light.

Only then, through an organic start, can we achieve the fundamental impact and attraction necessary to spawn a new movement of audiences. Only through a natural process will we identify the new archetypal interactive activities of the future... those activities which have the capacity to speak to the hearts, souls and desires of new audiences.

Jez San: Consumer Videogames Move into 3D Graphics

The early 2D consumer machines had the CPU do most of the pixel pushing, followed by sprite based machines moving hand-drawn 2D graphic objects with lightning speed and accuracy. Later, the 16-bit consoles from Nintendo and Sega had more colours, sprites, and backgrounds but games were still of the happy scrolly jumpy variety. Some were cute 3D hacks, but there was no real 3D capability until aftermarket rendering chips arrived. The 3D games around were highly playable but looked quite basic compared to regular scrolly games with hand-drawn artwork.

Then came the big PC guns, with their bags of CPU power, wads of memory, and correspondingly astronomical price tags. They did a pretty decent job rendering 3D graphics on the fly using software algorithms but now the new 3D games consoles have arrived in abundance with more to follow. These do fast texture mapping and shading in hardware allowing incredible 3D games to cover both food groups (look great, and play well) but the console companies are trying to keep them proprietary and incompatible.

What with 3D capability on both PCs and gameboxes the norm, it is time for games developers to bolster their 3D content creation capabilities by both learning new tools, and finding innovative ways to create content. All those hundreds of thousands of polygons per second need to be consumed by 3D games with interesting and curvy looking shapes that animate fluidly, and it is for this new market that the animation tool companies are now re-focussing their efforts (we assume their sales in the movie biz have flattened). In case you haven't already noticed, 3D Games are BIG BUSINESS.

Where does the new talent pool come from? Animators who can think in 3D are worth their weight in Onyxs. Any trick in the book to make the animators more productive should be considered, like Motion Capture allowing you to use real actors and stunt-dudes as reference animation, the way that people in the cartoon biz use rotoscoping only digital and in 3D.

3D games open up huge opportunities that were difficult to represent in those old fangled flat games, like having networked multi-players online at once with sophisticated character interaction, surrogate travel, virtual reality, you name it. All these things rely heavily on 3D real-time rendering and simulated worlds together with novel forms of input, like head tracking, pressure sensitive joysticks, more axes of freedom.

It's been said that there are really only four types of game, yet every traditional 2D game, from Pac-Man, Space Invaders, Donkey Kong, Pole Positon, Street Fighter can be revisited in 3D with new twists, concepts and imagination. It's about time we showed those developers of happy jumpy scrolly games a thing or two!

New Developments in Animation Production for Video Games

Chair
Jane Veeder, Time Warner Interactive

Panelists
Paul D. Lewis, Time Warner Interactive
Bob Zigado, Inter-Multi Studios
Robert Stein III, Trilobyte, Inc.
Craig Upson, Silicon Studio

Abstract

The booming videogame industry is currently making a dramatic move from modest, low end production techniques to state-of-the-art computer animation frontiers such as 3D character animation. Videogames is driving the development of new animation techniques such as motion capture and adapting cinematic production techniques as Hollywood and Silicon Valley merge. Through presentations and demonstrations by the midwives of these dramatic developments, animators, producers, and directors will gain practical insight about the special demands of videogames animation and how new production techniques are being developed and adapted.

Description

Interactive entertainment overall is a rapidly expanding area with a great requirement for creative intervention and sophisticated computer graphics: a good target for SIGGRAPH conference focus. Videogame development is the largest and most established component of the interactive entertainment field. The videogame industry has only very recently come into focus for many people in the computer graphics field and has certainly not figured much at all in SIGGRAPH venues and events. Yet, this industry is driving much of the technology development in computer animation.

The production segment of the SIGGRAPH audience will benefit from information about new animation production techniques being applied to this large job market. Why this special panel focusing on videogames and not just generic production show-and-tell on these topics? Because a) the application of existing techniques in videogames development requires major adaptations and b) videogames are driving the development of many new techniques and technologies.

Videogame production has all the complexity of linear-media animation production, but the animation must then interface with interactive software and be displayed in real-time on low cost platform hardware. Non-linear content presents different challenges than linear content. Platform hardware, whether arcade, consumer cartridge, or PC/CDROM, changes regularly and frequently. All these factors introduce additional and demanding requirements to animation design and execution which must be discussed within the context of videogame animation production to be understood. Here are some of the primary topics to be considered:

3D Graphics, 3D Character Animation, and Motion Capture - Videogame development is moving quickly from exclusively 2D into 3D computer graphics, from low-end to high end technologies, and from proprietary to production standard software. Low-end and limited only a couple of years ago, the videogames industry is emerging as a primary developer and user of motion capture and 3D character animation, both state-of-the-art computer animation techniques.

Evolution of Production Techniques and Animator Roles - How exactly were videogame graphics designed and produced in the past? As we work to define and master new production techniques and adapt them to videogames, how does the role of the animator change?

Adaptation of Cinematic and Special Effects Production Techniques - Inspired by market scale and encouraged by advances in data compression, Hollywood has turned to videogames as another publishing dimension and now, cinematic production techniques are now being adapted to videogames development.

Future of Interactive Entertainment Authoring - The demands of interactive entertainment media authoring and an increasingly competitive market are stimulating innovations in HOW such games designers and animators work. Reminiscent of the introduction in the 1980's of user interface toolkits and management systems, digital media development is embarking on an era of high level authoring environments, sophisticated assets management, and game prototyping environments.

Paul D. Lewis: Applying and Adapting High-End Computer FX Production Techniques to Videogames

Our current videogame projects have all the content development complexity of a high-end film FX facility, with a considerably reduced schedule and with the additional requirement to interface with interactive software in real-time display. The subject of my talk will be the problems and opportunities of combining these domains.

The videogame development process is different from that of conventional special effects in many ways and comparing the two is instructive. The development process for conventional media such as movies mirrors the resulting linear product. In the same way, the videogame development process mirrors the dynamic, non-linear, interactive resulting product. In film, you carve out a plan of what you want and fill it with work, but in coin-op videogame development someone (the market) is digging a trench that constantly changes depth and direction.

Film aims for a finely tuned product presented to a passive audience. The audience response may vary but the film is predictable. The character of a videogame changes based upon the player's participation. Content development for games requires producing not just the artwork for one path, but all of the possible paths allowed and how to transition smoothly between them all arbitrarily. The content development process for film is relatively well understood and established while game format and interaction, not to mention production techniques and platform capabilities, may change with each new product.

Content volume and schedule are other areas of contrast. A film action sequence might have 30 FX shots, where a typical fighting game will have 1200-1500 moves, or shots. Film production from concept to delivery might be 4 years or more, where game development cycles need to be 16 months or less to be cost effective and stay in tune with audience trends.

As different as film FX and videogame graphics production are, one of the primary challenges of the expanding field of "interactive entertainment" is to successfully combine them. There are many motivating factors. Videogames are subject to the movie and television trained audience expectations of photorealism, character expressiveness, and overall graphics sophistication and complexity. Production and delivery technologies as well as professional expertise are now migrating freely across all these linear and non-linear realms in response to market opportunities.

We embarked upon applying state-of-the art animation technology to videogame projects, only to discover that it needed to be expanded and extended yet further to meet our requirements. Some requirements were in the areas of shared databases and work practices, computer supported cooperative work, parallel distributed processing, prototyping pipelines, production tracking, and assets management.

Development flexibility is a key component. Building on the high-end to deliver to many different low-end platforms is one obvious but essential production translation. Equally essential, but perhaps not so obvious is the ability to make radical design changes during actual content creation. For example, a character may be largely redesigned based upon a weekends field test. Not planning for such flexibility can expand production schedules unexpectedly and miss market opportunities.

I will discuss and illustrate a number of the practical issues encountered in moving videogame animation into high-end 3D technologies. I will also contrast the design and production methodologies for 3D for 2D versus 3D for 3D character animation for videogame projects.

In addition to improving existing production techniques, the competitive nature of the videogame industry compels us to develop new animation and production technology as well. Designing flexible systems that can respond to future needs in a demanding market will contribute valuable tools to the interactive entertainment industry as a whole.

Bob Zigado: Breaking from Tradition in 3D Character Design for Videogames

The incorporation of 3D computer animated characters into videogames present opportunities for breaking with two burdensome traditions of character animation: the elastically exaggerated 2D cartoon character and the coldly perfect 3D computer animated character from the (by now) old rigid-body days. This opportunity is being afforded by the convergence of 3D computer animation, real-time polygon display platform technology, and the initial emergence of inverse kinematics in production-standard software – all fueled by a flurry of risk oriented, venture capital driven development of videogame titles. This much awaited opportunity is giving wings to the visions of many, heretofore marginalized, character animators.

Historically, my character designs were controversial when considered within the context of traditional, Disney-dominated character animation. Yet, the capabilities of rigid body 3D computer animation could only hint at the psychological interiority that my characters needed to communicate graphically. The new digital expressiveness combined with the Oedipal underpinnings of the lucrative electronic fighting game is providing the perfect theatre for a previously unavailable depth and intensity of game character-as-self.

Real-time polygon display hardware will, for the next 2-3 years, force us to display-what-we-mean using the minimum "physical" form of expression, i.e. minimal geometry. Making every polygon work for the visual message will not allow the squandering of real-time computational power upon gratuitous photorealistic effects that, while providing eye candy for the viewer, generally contribute nothing to meaning and frequently distract from it.

Robert Stein III: Case Histories in Developing Interactive Adventure Games

I will be presenting a brief history of the production tools and techniques from Trilobyte's adventure games, "The 7th Guest,"and how they varied through the "11th Hour" to today with emphasis on surmounting file format incompatibilities, training 3D artists, beta testing tools, cross media integration and in-house compression.

In tandem with developing "The 7th Guest" and "11th Hour," Trilobyte developed an in-house compression and authoring environment. Previous to this, our artists and designers were using mid-range 3D graphics and animation software for development but were limited in their ability to quickly prototype the final results - no control over playback speed except using scaled down or lower resolution images which then distorted that aspect of the product.

Our authoring environment, "groovie," gives the artists and designers the ability to see the final sequences at either real-time playback speed and full color OR a frame playback speed and resolution emulating any of various game platforms, PC/CDROM or consumer, without having to wait for integration with final game programming. This authoring environment also produces final output by compositing graphics overlay with incoming video, embedding sound, and creating an executable file targeted for the platform hardware. I will be describing and illustrating how these new authoring tools have impacted design and production.

Craig Upson: Authoring Tools Futures

There are several factors shaping the development of media authoring tools for video games, among them are the following:

1. Console platform proliferation and confusion. Since several new consoles come to the market over the next year, the game developer is left with some risky decisions that can have enormous financial impact. Choosing which platform to author for is not obvious. Game developers desire to minimize their risk by authoring the same or similar game for several platforms at once. Frequently called the "holy grail of authoring," multi-mastering of the same content and game logic is key to the strategy of several authoring tool efforts currently underway. How can multi-mastering work when the platforms are so different?

2. New Console hardware capabilities. Each console platform under development contains substantial 3D graphics functionality. Currently there are few authoring tools that address real time 3D graphics in any capacity. The new generation tools must treat real-time 3D as a first class citizen along with audio, images, sprites and movies - a goal that is difficult to achieve.

3. The emerging use of characters in interactive stories. This factor coupled with the next generation console's ability to render is enabling a transition from indexing into precomputed media (movies) to on-the-fly rendering. While this leads to much more realistic visual representations, it causes tremendous complexities for the author - as well as the authoring tool developer.

4. Life-Like behavioral models. Consumers are beginning to expect characters with life-like behaviors. These characters require more than believable motion and articulation: they require complex inter-character relationships, autonomous actions and goal directed behavioral models. The repetitive, predictable characters' days are numbered. How is it possible to breath life into a computer modeled character and how can the authoring system help?

5. Performance, Performance, Performance. Authoring tools have traditionally produced sluggish runtimes. Is it possible to use a higher level tool and still get acceptable performance?

These factors among others are defining the baseline functionality of authoring systems. In this talk we will present out perspective on the foundations of tools for game developers of the future.

Aesthetics & Tools in the Virtual Environment

Chair
Christian Greuel, Fakespace, Inc.

Panelists
Patrice Caire, Virtual Reality and Multimedia
Janine Cirincione, Cirincione + Ferraro
Perry Hoberman, Telepresence Research
Michael Scroggins, California Institute of the Arts

Christian Greuel

We hear the talk of endless technological revolutions. We are surrounded by high-tech gadgetry that does our bidding. Yet what does all of this magnificent machinery really offer us? Does progress in fact exist? And if so, what is it actually worth without substantial content?

This discussion panel is addressing the current state of aesthetics in the virtual environment by focusing on the roles that tools have played in artistic communities of the past and how virtual technologies will undoubtedly affect their future.

The beginning of history shows human beings using naturally-made pigments to draw images on cave walls, allowing them to represent their experiences to others. Through tomorrow's technology, we may find ourselves projecting our very thoughts into the space around us in order to do exactly the same. The purpose of the aesthetic action has and always will be to visualize ideas and to explore our environments using whatever devices are available.

Today we have increasingly powerful instruments, such as personal computer workstations, stereoscopic video displays and interactive software, to present artificially fabricated environments, popularly known as Virtual Reality. The technological elements are in place and we have begun our investigation into the latest and greatest form of artistic communication.

Virtual Reality promises artists the most exciting breakthrough for the creative process since the invention of motion pictures. Now at the dawn of an era of virtual arts, the first generations of tools wait patiently to tell us something that we don't already know.

But what message do they bring? Is there any passion here? High-end technology is not an end in itself. It merely represents the latest in a long list of tools that can be used for human expression. We have not come this far just to do cool computer tricks or sell vacant office space. There has been an unfortunate lack of artistic activity in cyberspace. We must focus on this cultural deficit and breathe life into the cold silicon void that we have created.

By considering the tools of Virtual Reality in a historical context of art and technology as they relate to the fabrication of simulated experience, this panel of active artists intends to provoke constructive thought amongst the virtual arts community, promote active exploration of experience as an art form and unlock doors to possible roads for our artistic travels throughout this age of cybernetics.

Patrice Caire

The type of work I am pursuing can be explained by example with a description of project called Cyberhead that I designed and managed. Caire's Cyberhead, a Virtual Reality installation, is a fully immersed interactive fly through a head reconstructed

from Magnetic Resonance Imaging (MRI) data. This Virtual Reality journey runs on a Silicon Graphics Onyx Reality Engine2 in real time with texture maps using a Fakespace BOOM 2C as high-resolution stereoscopic viewing and navigating device. To build the world the Sense8 WorldToolKit software was used. 3D sound is generated in real-time by two Beachtrons from Crystal River.

Cyberhead was developed in the Virtual Reality Laboratory and the Artificial Intelligence Center of SRI International in collaboration with the Lucas MRS Center at Stanford University. Additional 3-D CAD models and animation were created at Colossal Pictures; Spectrum HoloByte; and by Cyberware. My principal collaborators included Harlyn Baker, Nat Bletter, Aron Bonar, Tamar Cohen, Gina Faber, Mark Ferneau, Paul Hemler, Lee Iverson, Andy Kopra, Lance Norskog, Tom Piantanida, Marc Scaparro, Pierre Vasseur.

My primary goals with Cyberhead were to create a rich, detailed virtual environment with convincing, high quality, real time, reality-based (MRI) visual images that were properly lit, smoothed, shaded, textured, and anti-aliased. Directional sound was an equally important part of this world and experience. The human interface was designed to be simple, non-intrusive, and suitable for use by the general public. In relation to the audience, the goal was to create an entertaining experience that would make users think about such issues as how we interpret and associate the information we receive from our environment.

My motivation in doing this work was to explore new presentation paradigms made possible by this technology. This work also had to address the problem of how to represent data which is not easy to represent; how to be immersed in, interact with, and navigate through, this kind of data; and finally make the process esthetically engaging and educational.

Janine Cirincione

From the Futurists to the Bauhaus, artists of the 20th C. have embraced new ideas and new technologies in an attempt to reach beyond mere aesthetic aims, and to help create the future. For one reason or another these movements have been superseded by other, more promising visions of the future. How do we keep interactivity from turning into yesterday's news as opposed to the important, rich, aesthetic medium it can be?

One way of doing this is to incorporate a healthy level of self-awareness and criticality into the artistic process. What can the medium do? By what standards should the new medium be judged? Is the work's essential meaning best expressed in this medium? Does the work fully exploit the medium's potential? My collaborative work in virtual reality addresses these and other questions.

The Imperial Message, designed in collaboration with Michael Ferraro and Brian D'Amato was created as part of the

1993-94 Artist-in-Residency Award at The Wexner Center for the Arts, at the Ohio State University in Columbus, Ohio. The work is a prototype for an interactive virtual-reality game—a new medium somewhere between architecture, film and game. The piece is loosely based on the Kafka parable of the same name which deals with the vast distance between the Emperor and the Individual. The Imperial Message attempts to extend this sense of scale to present inherent conflicts between the individual and the state and between the unspoken, secret "Law" and its corrupted representation.

Kafka's probing vision of bureaucracy, communications, authoritarian, legal and social structures in the formative stages of Imperial China relate directly to issues that we face today as we examine the "Utopia" of cyberspace.

Perry Hoberman

We live in an age in which technological paradigms shift about every half year. Almost every month seems to offer radically new media. Overnight, new standards are created and, suddenly, what was once exotic becomes merely commonplace (if it isn't totally forgotten).

This brings up many profound questions for working artists. Is this relentless change a permanent state of affairs, or are we witnessing the infancy of some new constellation of interactive media, one that will eventually (like the cinema) coalesce into something more lasting? Until then, how can we (and should we) keep up? Do we spend all our time learning to operate new hardware and software? How can we keep any critical distance at all when we are so close to our tools? And what happens to our work when the currently state-of-the-art hardware and software that it depends on have become obsolete? (Perhaps obsolescence itself has become a key category, one that needs to have its pejorative connotations reconsidered.)

For most of the recent history of technology, interactions between people and machines have been overwhelmingly monogamous - one user, one interface. Even the fantasy of total interconnectedness that drives the current mushrooming of the global network posits each and every user at home or work with their own terminal; and networked virtual reality is usually understood as requiring a head-mounted viewer for each participant. What implications does this have for the public display of artworks? And what happens when this one-to-one correspondence between person and machine is disrupted? Are there more robust models for interactive art, arrangements that allow for a simultaneous, fully realized experience for an unspecified number of people?

The twin dreams of immersion and interactivity have been with us for some time, but we have recently seen their possibilities vastly enriched with the advent of ever more powerful computer hardware and software. Concepts and ideas that could previously be only described can now be fully visualized and inhabited. What new kinds of artworks (if any) are made possible by these unprecedented capabilities? Will artists be put in the position of merely supplying content for this emerging medium? Or will they play an active role in actually defining the medium itself?

Michael Scroggins

VR technology offers many possibilities for transforming the practice of art; however, I would like to concentrate here on addressing a potential of great personal interest. The ability to shape temporal experience through the manipulation of a set of simultaneous and successive acoustic events is a power which sound producing instruments have afforded the aural composer/performer since pre-history. The development during the last decade of videographic devices capable of instantaneous

generation and manipulation of absolute (or abstract) images has given the visual artist a similar power. In this decade, the rapid advancements being made in real-time computer graphics technology promise even more powerful visual instruments. My work in videographic animation extends a cinematic tradition which began in the twenties with visionary artists such as Oskar Fischinger, Viking Eggeling, and Walter Ruttmann. Like those pioneers of absolute cinema, I have aspired to the creation of a visual experience of purely formal means which —like absolute music— achieves affect through the architectonic structuring of basic elements. Aside from obvious disparities in how the organs of seeing and hearing are mapped onto the brain (and thus consciousness), absolute animation has differed from musical experience because of the isolating boundary of the frame. VR technology offers a means to dissolve that boundary. For the first time in history we may become as totally immersed in the field of visible radiation constituting synthetic image as in the ocean of air pressure constituting musical sound. Immersive VR will prove to be a great advance in the age-old search for an engaging art of pure movement.

Visualizing the Internet: Putting the User in the Driver's Seat

Chair
Nahum D. Gershon, The MITRE Corporation

Panelists
Bran Ferren, Walt Disney Imagineering
James Foley, Georgia Institute of Technology
Joseph Hardin, National Center for Supercomputing Applications
Frank Kappe, Graz University of Technology, Austria
William A. Ruh, The MITRE Corporation

Summary Description

Information is dispersed over many Internet resources and quite frequently, users feel lost, confused, and overwhelmed. The panel and the audience will discuss how advances in interactive computer graphics and visualization methods, software, and hardware could make the information distributed over the Internet more intuitively searchable, accessible, and easier to use by people from all walks of life and interests. This will enable the us to make full use of the Internet's information universe from our computers.

The audience and the public have been encouraged to submit samples of slides and video material illustrating effective, valuable, and user-oriented approaches to visualize the Internet.

Visualizing the Internet: Putting the User in the Driver's Seat

We live in an exciting time. Connecting numerous information-stuffed computers dispersed around the world has created an exciting universe of information. This information revolution has enabled us to explore this universe from our computers. However captivating, we still have a long way before the use of this information universe is easy and intuitive.

Information is dispersed in many sources over the Internet and at times users feel lost, confused, and overwhelmed (justifiably so). To find required information or to browse through information, users need nowadays to confront frustrating searches through arrays of user-debilitating menus and belligerent computer systems. Some of the remote sources are massive and once the user has got the information, he or she needs to browse through large amounts of text, data tables, and images. How should the user know where the sources of the relevant information reside, how to get them, and, once the sources are retrieved, how to get the relevant information from them?

The World Wide Web (WWW), developed at CERN, Switzerland, and Hyper-G, developed at Graz Univ. of Technology, allow the user through a set of menus to roam through information spaces of documents or images. Captivating browsers, such as NCSA Mosaic and also Harmony have transformed the process of getting information off these Internet distributed information systems. However, some major difficulties still remain.

Advances and experience in interactive computer graphics hardware and mass storage have created new possibilities for information navigation, retrieval, and access in which visualization and user interface (UI) could play a central role. The question is how to utilize these advances and experience to reduce these frustrations and lower the time and cost of navigating through the information dispersed over the Internet, finding specific information, and accessing it once found.

If we do not involve the users in designing the information highway and its interfaces, we will create useless information systems. As long as there is a human being sitting in the front of the screen, the user interface of the information highway needs to be user-oriented (UO), taking the user needs into account. To be able to do so, we need to understand

• How human beings perceive information visually

• How the human mind works when searching for unknown or known information. How it is similar to visual processes

• The medium of the computer and its associated visual display.

Additional difficulties and issues confronting the design of human interfaces to the Internet and other distributed information systems of the future are:

• Users come in many flavors. How do we create user interface, navigation, and search methods that will cater to users of many different kinds, levels of understanding, capabilities, and cultures

• Information representation has many views. Information representation is multifaceted and flexible and could be used to suit the user's needs.

• Information is abstract. There is not always a straightforward mapping between an abstract information space and the display physical space. This is a problem that graphic designers have been struggling with for generations. Appropriate visual organization could make the understanding of the processes contained in the information easier.

• How could information visualization transform the traditional methods of information navigation, retrieval, and access beyond the automation of a library process?

• Is there is a way to browse through information using a better interface than sequential menus?

• How to facilitate information organizations that are flexible and changeable (e.g., changing the links among documents, providing global and detailed views of the information)?

• What are efficient visual abstractions that speed visual perception and understanding? What is the role of experience and training?

• How to incorporate use semiautonomous agents with visualization processes to reduce the work load?

• How to maximize the user interaction with the system?

• What are the users' needs?

Nahum Gershon: Putting the User in Charge of the Information Space Using Visual Skills

One of the major problems of current information systems distributed over the Internet is that the information is rigidly put in place. Pieces of information are linked together in a rigid structure - no changes are allowed. However, these pieces of information could be related to each other in various ways depending on the application, problem, personal way of thinking and perception, or culture. For distributed information systems to be effective, they should allow each user to construct his or her own information space with links and associations (among pieces of information and whole documents and images) that fit the problem, application, or ways of thinking and perception.

Another major problem facing systems of today is that while surfing over the Internet, users often do not know where they are in information space and do not remember how they got there. In short, users are lost. One solution is to provide users with visual views of the information space promoting quick perception and understanding. The user can "jump" from one document to another by clicking the mouse button without the necessity to go back resource by resource.

Enabling the user to modify interactively the links among the documents and images using a visual display and to (visually) view the information space globally and locally have been implemented over the World Wide Web in a MITRE enhancement to NCSA Mosaic.

Bran Ferren: Who Cares About the Internet?

To succeed with the new wideband networks, we will have to deliver a spectrum of experiences that add value to our lives. This is a significant challenge in a world where the competition for one's time and attention is fierce. This promise of a unique and rich experience will not be fulfilled by movie rental, games, or "I Love Lucy" reruns. It will require the invention of entirely new communications and art forms that to date have eluded definition. When these creative and technical challenges can be met, it *will* change our lives. Perhaps even for the better.

Jim Foley: Visual Navigation Through the Internet

Navigating the Internet, AKA cruising the infobahn, bears almost no resemblance to navigating the real world. The Internet is a linguistic world; the real world is visual. When I drive from city to city, I have a visual tool, the road map, to help me find my way, aided by linguistic aids (road signs) along the way. The objective of our research is to make the information highway system more like the interstate highway system.

The panel presentation will draw both from work at Georgia Tech on visualization tools for the WWW [3] and for text retrieval, as well as on insights from a recent NSF-sponsored workshop on 'Research Issues for the WWW' which I organized and chaired.

The WWW is especially difficult to visualize in a meaningful way because there is essentially no meaningful metadata. Nevertheless, we have developed several ways of viewing and searching collections of web pages which deal with the "lost in hyperspace problem." Similarly, we have been developing new ways to visualize the results of free-text queries to better understand how well-formulated the query is, and to assist in its reformulation, if necessary.

More generally, a broad research agenda to facilitate visualizing the Internet will be described. It includes developing 'information road maps' based on what we know about how people navigate through spaces; incorporating more meaningful semantics into the WWW to drive the information road maps; improving information authoring tools so that the metadata needed to provide information road maps is more readily provided; and developing means to adapt Internet information for presentation on a variety of information appliances, ranging from video-enabled phones to personal digital assistants to set-top boxes to workstations.

Joseph Hardin: Navigation on the Web

In the last 18 months, hundreds of thousands of people have been introduced to hypermedia through World Wide Web browsers like NCSA Mosaic. These tools provide users with the ability to easily browse through the global online information mass by simply clicking on hyperlinks. An early addition to the textual hyperlink was the ability to map links to images or portions of images. Anything that could be placed in an image with a format like GIF could be made into a link or set of links. This resulted in a rapid blossoming of methods on the Web to provide people with visual signposts to online resources. Maps, pictures of buildings, images of floor plans, aerial views of cities all were put up on the Web and used as guides to a variety of subject domains. This portion of the panel will tour some of these examples of visual navigation on the Web, discussing the ways authors have utilized graphic navigation, and the advantages and limitations of current practices.

Frank Kappe: Browsing and Navigation Through Deep Hyperspace

One of the big issues in finding information in the Internet is what is known as the "lost in hyperspace" syndrome: users cannot get an overview, cannot find specific information, stumble over the same information again and again, cannot identify new and outdated information, cannot find out how much information there is on a given topic and how much of it has been seen, etc.

I can see three counter measures to deal with this problem: reasonable a-priori organization of information, advanced search facilities, and visual navigation aids. Based on my experience with Hyper-G, the distributed information system developed at Graz University of Technology, I have the strong feeling that a combination of the three approaches can significantly reduce the "lost in hyperspace" syndrome, and I propose to explore the usefulness of graphical navigation aids to the extent possible.

As in Hyper-G browsers, information could be displayed in overview and local maps showing the position of the current document with respect to a collection hierarchy. Users can "fly" over a 3-D hyperspace landscape of local map and search results (encoding numerous features of the objects matched, rather than just a one- dimensional list sorted by match score) looking for salient features, select interesting documents, etc. Usability tests will have to reveal whether these visualizations are really useful for end users or just gimmicks.

William A. Ruh: The Role of Graphics in Future Information Delivery Systems

Next generation information systems will be very different than those fielded today. The stimulus for change is the need for organizations to improve the exploitation of their corporate information assets as well as to effectively exploit the massive amounts of information available from external sources and integrate these two. This information is inherently different than the information around which today's systems are built. Current information systems are developed around the management of reasonably sized, highly structured, record information. New information systems will be built around the management of massive, un- and semi-structured, multimedia information.

One of the four major issues that need to be addressed is the organization, retrieval and exploitation of this massive information base. Is current technology adequate for providing integrated retrieval tools on the user's desktop and organized access to large volumes of data? Can the system search a massive collection in a reasonable time and identify precisely the items of interest to the user?

Graphical, tailorable display of information will be critical to this next generation. Access devices will include hand held computers where there will be no keyboard and maybe even no visual display, only audio. Mapping between mediums and modes, understanding what is appropriate and when are all critical issues. This will require a multi-disciplinary approach for development of graphical applications and interfaces.

Afterword

Internet technology would not transform applications areas if users cannot use it easily and efficiently. Advances in methods, software, and hardware of computer graphics and visualization together with understanding of the needs of the users and application areas could enable us to make fuller use of the Internet's information universe.

References

1. Andrews, K. and F. Kappe, Soaring through Hyper Space: A Snapshot of Hyper-G and its Harmony Client, in Proc. of Eurographics Symposium of multimedia/Hypermedia in Open Distributed Environments, Graz, Austria, W. Hezner and F. Kappe, (editors), pages 181-191, Springer Verlag, June 1994.

2. Gershon, N.D., and W.A. Ruh, The Information Highway: Putting the User in the Driver's Seat (If we do not balance user needs with technical innovation, we will create useless information systems), IEEE Spectrum, to be published

3. Mukherjea, S., and J. Foley, Navigational View Builder: A Tool for Building Navigational Views of Information Spaces, CHI '94 Conference Companion, p. 289-290.

4. Schatz, B.R, and J.B. Hardin, NCSA Mosaic and the World-Wide Web: Global Hypermedia Protocols for the Internet, Science, 265, 895-901 (1994).

Algorithms and the Artist

Chair
Peter Beyls, St Lukas Art Institute, Brussels

Panelists
Stephen Bell, Bournemouth University
Brian Evans, Vanderbilt University
Jean-Pierre Hebert, independent artist
Ken Musgrave, George Washington University
Roman Verostko, Minneapolis College of Art and Design

Introduction

We address a number of problems related to viewing algorithms as the formulation of artistic statements. We analyze the nature of the algorithmic approach as opposed to direct physical action. Here are some of the basic questions that will be raised. Why do artists choose to express themselves indirectly, by way of formal descriptions of their ideas and what are the sources of inspiration for algorithmic activity. How does current algorithmic work relate to formal methods in an art-historical context. What is the relationship between paint systems and a pure algorithmic approach and is there a way to integrate both. What determines the beauty and effectiveness of an algorithm. What is the relationship between an algorithm and the nature of the physical results it produces i.e. how to externalize (materialize) algorithmic processes. What is the role of interaction in the development of algorithms. Do algorithms allow for progressive optimization or do they require fully preconceived ideas? Finally, and most pertinent, does computer programming force a focus on the surface component i.e. perceivable structure, or does it allow for the manipulation of deeper components such as meaning and emotion? We shall confront the algorithmic practice of the panelists and hope for strong audience interaction.

Stephen Bell: Algorithm

I am interested in producing work which is realized through engaging the audience in active physical participation. In a general sense it can be said that I have been producing work by proposing rules for the generation of images but leaving significant parameters open to change. The form of the work is defined by the limits imposed by the rules and the degree and manner of control over the parameters afforded to participants. An algorithm can perform a role in creative activity similar to that of any other constraint used in art practice; the self-imposed limits within which one works in order to free oneself to indulge in creative play and experiment and yet at the same time ensure our focussed and hence enhanced attention. It is in this way that I use algorithms in my work. As I have been using computer graphic workstations the rules are encapsulated in an appropriate computer programming language. Computers are very useful control devices and the programming languages which have been developed to determine how they behave are effective, if somewhat limited, in enabling one to describe rules for the interactive real-time generation of the kind of graphic images which I am interested in; Representations of the interactions of programmed automata with each other and the audience-participants. I would like to hope that we can interpret the word ALGORITHM in a relaxed way. It is our prerogative as humans, particularly as artists, to interpret language fuzzily, not to define the meaning of a word for eternity but to exploit its value in passing, in a dynamic interchange of ideas and notions with

fellow humans in which it plays a significant yet ephemeral part. The word ALGORITHM in the context of the panel will, I hope, be as a catalyst for lively and diverse discussion rather than a straight-jacket. That is, after all, the value that I have found in using algorithms in art practice.

Brian Evans: The Catalytic Algorithm

With technology it is possible to manifest mathematical ideas as images, sounds, sculpture and even poetry. Artists in all media have found mathematical processes of value in their creative enterprise. These processes are often described using algorithms. An algorithm is nothing more than a recipe, a finite list of instructions. This recipe will have precise steps to follow, perhaps requiring some initial input (i.e. ingredients). The algorithm will have a desired outcome, and be considered effective if the outcome is achieved. A tasty apple pie is the result of one algorithm, an image or piece of music derived from a mathematical process, generated from a computer program, is another. In describing mathematical processes with algorithms, beauty and meaning can be discovered. Numbers are mapped into light and/or sound, and perceived through the senses as objects. It is the mathematical source of these works that has aesthetic worth. Algorithms, implemented on computers, make it possible for us to see and hear the beauty of mathematical processes. We can explore the inherent beauty of these abstract processes, logical, human-made constructs that initially seem to have meaning only because they can be used to predict natural phenomena. These are processes our culture exploits to myriad purposes, from predicting tomorrow's weather, to navigating and landing a jumbo jet. When we see a mathematical model visualized, perhaps a model of water resistance over the hull of a racing yacht, a chart of planetary motion, or even the abstract image of a Mandelbrot Set, are we looking at something that, in some metaphysical way exists? Or is the mathematics describing nothing more than an intellectual construct, and the images simply pretty, and sometimes inexplicably useful? Is meaning culturally attributed, or is mathematics meaningful and effective because it describes "grand truths?" We trust our lives on a daily basis to the effectiveness of these mathematical models. What is the basis of our faith? Why do we trust them? The algorithmic image or composition gives us something to see or hear and begin to ponder. Aesthetic experience isn't in the viewing or the listening, it's in the pondering. For me it reduces to a question of divine presence, a point of irresistible curiosity and a source of infinite wonder.

Jean-Pierre Hebert

I explore the creative power of algorithms.

Under the keen control of wit and taste algorithms can reveal order, beauty and truth to surprise our minds, please our eyes and inspire our souls.

Without restraint, they can also mass-produce ugly and boring vulgarity as any other medium, only much faster and cheaper.

Thanks to GA and GP, algorithms themselves can be mass-produced too. Integrating wit and taste into fitness functions is an interesting project, raising myriads of sensitive issues.

Another interesting idea in line with 'Algorithms and the artist': why not establish 'the art of the art algorithm' as a new form of 'conceptual art'.

When will a flow chart, or ASCII code on paper or any other form of code be exhibited as art without showing what it can produce ? Then of course, Donald Knuth will run the show.

Obviously, computer generated art is rejected by the commercial art world. Why is algorithmic art similarly rejected by most computer artists?

Ken Musgrave: Formal Logic and Self-Expression
Determinism precludes free will. Artistic expression is perhaps the highest manifestation of free will. Yet artistic expression can be obtained strictly through the digital computer, which operates precisely in the real of formal logic, which in turn is the epitomy of deterministic reasoning. The creative act of self-expression directly through a computer program places in unique juxtaposition these mutually contradictory philosophical extrema. My own work entails mapping scientific models, based on the formal logic of mathematics, into the formal logic of computer programs, and using these programs to generate images which (I claim) represent artistic self-expression of a spiritual nature. This bizarre new creative process marks, I further claim, a greater discontinuity in the creative process than any other new medium or process in the history of the visual arts. It's deep and well-developed roots in the formal disciplines of math, science, and logic give it unprecedented conceptual depth. I propose to present, fortify, and defend these claims in this panel. In the process, I will highlight the serendipitous character of proceduralism in the process, the use of random fractal models in reproducing the kind of visual complexity typical of natural scenes, and the ramifications of the computer's returning representationalism to the "open problems" category in visual art.

Roman Verostko: Notes on algorithm and art
Almost as if by magic - whatever procedure you dream of - you can probably extend the power of your dream to the computer and let it develop the dream beyond your wildest expectations. You may identify procedures for improvising with color, scale, and position - which is what artists have always done. Given sufficient definition you could develop a form generator and from your new vantage point see new possibilities for further elaboration on your routine. Through trial and error - interacting with the algorithm itself you proceed further into the new frontier. So what can we learn from this? We learn what artists have always known - that "CAD" programs, paint brush programs, paint brushes and drawing paraphernalia do not make art. Neither do artists or designers simply "make art". The one over-riding essential element to the process, "a developed artistic procedure", is necessarily unique for each artist and for each work of art. The procedure addresses a singular conjunction of elements for which there is no "universal" rule. The "calculus of form" may be placed in the service of such procedures but should not be confused with the art-making procedure. For the artist who writes the code the artistic procedure is the act of "writing the code", pretty much like the creative work of the composer when the composer writes a musical score. Making art does indeed require a "calculus of form". But the artist's

instructions on how to employ the "calculus of form" precede the "calculus". One needs an "artistic procedure" which addresses the entire complex of elements for each specific work. The final form, unique and specific to each work, embraces more than the "calculus". While it embraces and grows from a "calculus" it might employ any of an infinite number of approaches to deliver the form. These may include metaphor, improvisations of the form phenomenon in and of itself, or reference to some other phenomenon or idea - historical, literary, political, mathematical or philosophic. Can an artist write an algorithm then for an artistic procedure? Emphatically yes! Such algorithms provide the artist with self-organizing form generators which manifest his or her own artistic concerns and interests. We are looking to an interesting time ahead of us when artists will be able to exchange and interact with each other's form-generating tools in ways we never dreamed. There are procedures yet to be developed to make this kind of interactive expression accessible - a time ahead when we will literally see an evolution of form including a genealogy associated with its creators.

Peter Beyls: Algorithms for conceptual navigation
I have always thought of computers as dynamic tools for introspection, exploration and discovery. Computer programming is instrumental in the externalization of ideas and algorithms are formal descriptions of ones hypothesis of what constitutes the production of creative statements. The computer is a playground to speculate on the generative potential of ideas. As a matter of fact, the physical, tangible management of purely conceptual constructs becomes possible. However, the paradox is that while algorithmic specification allows the artist to touch the essence of his ideas it also creates a distance since all specification is indirect and seems to exclude spontaneous action. The idea is to view computers as partners in the process of creative decision making. By way of algorithms we can explore various man- machine relations in this partnership: from studying total autonomy in computer programs to systems designed for explicit interaction. The development of personal algorithms is the key to exploration and the gradual specification of objectives from incomplete knowledge, in sharp contrast to view the computer as a slave; as a medium for deterministic visualization. We have characterized the interactive method where man and machine collaborate in a common effort and with common objectives as conceptual navigation; the artist-programmer gets feedback, his expectations are confirmed or contradicted by the program's behavior. Eventually, unexpected results may signal new and promising routes exposing unknown territories. Thus, man and machine contribute both to the creation of a computational climate that favours invention and to the development of a critical attitude towards the often complex relationships between programmed intention and actual result. Writing algorithms has also forced us to evaluate experience vs. speculation. If one relies on models that have proven to be successful in the past, one confirms what is already known. Algorithms that use rules reflecting this knowledge produce predictable results. Otherwise, designing processes with the greatest possible freedom in pure speculation is like working outside of any known context, making evaluation very hard indeed. The creation of new contexts for growing algorithmic activity mixing memories of the past and an open imagination is, I think, perhaps the most interesting challenge to algorithmic art.

Performing Work within Virtual Environments

Chair
Henry Sowizral, Boeing Information and Support Services

Panelists
Ian G. Angus, Boeing Information and Support Services
Steven Bryson, CSC/NASA Ames Research Center
Stefan Haas, Fraunhofer Center of Research in Graphics
Mark R. Mine, University of North Carolina
Randy Pausch, University of Virginia

We can now use virtual environments to visualize fairly complex structures, to move around within those structures, and even grab objects and move them around. Now we need to discover how to work effectively within immersive environments. Experience to date indicates that we need to:

- Access or change environmental/system/meta parameters
  - Who designed this part?
  - Where am I?
  - Load the electrical system.
  - How do I change the lighting condition?
  - Make a notation.
  - Show me the isosurface originating at this point.

- Find or manipulate particular objects
  - Place me in front of the electrical panel
  - Change the couch's upholstery to a different fabric

- Perform analyses
  - Can I remove this part?
  - Do the wingtip vortices collide with the main body?

- Export changes to permanent storage

Ian G. Angus Boeing Information and Support Services
VR will remain inferior to the desktop as a serious work environment until users of VR can access the same data as available on the desktop.

VR promises users the ability to visualize and manipulate data in ways different or even more natural than possible on a flat screen display. However, unless users have access to all the data they need to make intelligent decisions, VR interfaces will only provide a partial solution, one that may in the end hamper rather than enhance users' ability to perform work.

The design and analysis process needs more information than just geometry. Design engineers need to access information such as text descriptions and 2D schematic graphics, and even programmatic information such as machine checkable design rules. Without access to such mundane information sources, a designer may find it difficult to perform a required task within VR.

Realistically, VR will not replace the workstation in the immediate future. Most VR users and especially those located in a design setting will spend a limited amount of time per day, perhaps only a few tens of minutes, in a VR environment. Most of the time these users will use a flat screen application to access the data they need. Requiring a whole new mode of data access just for use within the VR environment does not make sense, especially if the data more naturally fits within a flat screen paradigm.

We believe that one of the crucial challenges for virtual environments is allowing immersed users to access and manipulate all of their non-geometric data in a familiar manner.

To meet this challenge, we have a developed a mechanism for inserting new and even some existing flat screen applications into virtual environments. We display their window on a "virtual clipboard." Users hold the clipboard in their hand and control the application by any of several mechanisms, for example, by touching the application's virtual screen. To demonstrate the effectiveness of this capability we inserted the familiar "Mosaic" browser into our VR environment. Users can now access the entire World Wide Web from within VR in the same way as on they do from the desktop.

The virtual clipboard can also allow users to control the virtual environment's parameters, parameters not easily changed using physical metaphors, such as a user's location within the environment. While not a complete solution to the problems of performing work in a virtual environment, we believe the virtual clipboard or tools similar to it will provide critical support to future users of virtual environments.

Steven Bryson CSC/NASA Ames Research Center
Interaction between the user and objects in a virtual environment is a key to useful application. Little is understood, however, about how to usefully interact in three dimensions in ways that really help perform tasks. This problem is further compounded by the marginal accuracy of the tracking systems typically used to allow interaction. There are times when real-world metaphors are helpful and there are times when they are hinderances. Using the virtual windtunnel as an example, we will examine the various ways of approaching this problem. Various interaction options will be surveyed. We will stress the use of user studies in the determination of useful interaction techniques.

Stefan Haas: Fraunhofer Center of Research in Graphics
The feeling of being immersed distinguishes working in virtual environments from desktop-oriented working. New interaction techniques help exploring all three dimensions and enable a free orientation. Using virtual environments will change the way of using computers at least as much as graphical user interfaces did, as they enabled thousands of applications to be used easily in the last decade. But will virtual environments be able to run 2-D applications and make their usage as easy as it has been up to now.

Taking the complexity of some systems, e.g., CAD systems, which are sometimes still FORTRAN based (not quite ready to jump into the VR age). Even if the technical problem of embedding non-VR applications into VR environments can be solved it is still the question of how user will be able to work efficiently in button and text input environments.

Another approach for bringing the benefits of virtual environments to regular mouse-and-keyboard-users is to introduce collaborative working between text, gui and VR applications by transmitting what-is-done instead of how-it-is-done. By this way, immersed users can grab and objects which leads to the selection the associated CAD and FEM system of the other partners. Fraunhofer has several years of experience of working with real-time collaborative tools even across the atlantic. In the Virtual Prototyping project of Fraunhofer CRCG, these new way of working is applied to virtual environments as well as gui tools.

Practical experiences show the bilateral benefits for both users of virtual environments as well as gui-/text-based systems. The latter become experts, which can be contacted for specific questions, in which the standard work tools available in the virtual environment are not sufficient, e.g. in modeling, simulation or data conversion. This enhances the working in the virtual environment. Most of the standard tasks can be solved by few tools. Toolchests or personal servants can be metaphors for this out-of-few selection. Only in the case of dedicated tasks, e.g., changing the tangent vector of a NURBS surface in the dimension of the associated tolerances, another expert has to be contacted and can use his dedicated tools, no matter if text-, gui- or VR-based.

Mark R. Mine: University of North Carolina
Virtual Environments: Nice Place To Visit, But Would You Want To Work There?

Despite considerable promise there has been a surprising lack of real-world applications in the virtual world. Why? What is so hard about working in a virtual environment? While a great deal of research has been focused on technological limitations such as low resolution displays, limited tracking systems and end-to-end delays, some of the greatest difficulties facing virtual-environment application developers are conceptual rather than technological in nature. We are unfamiliar with this new medium we work in, unable to utilize its power and to compensate for its limitations.

Before the promise of virtual environments can be fully realized, we must endeavor to understand the benefits and limitations of working in the immersive domain. We must characterize the inherent differences between working immersed and working through-the-window. We must determine which tasks are helped by implementation in a virtual environment and which tasks are not. We must realize that many of the characteristics which give a virtual environment its power are also the source of its problems.

Direct manipulation, for example, allows people to naturally interact with objects by reaching out and grabbing them. The lack of haptic feedback and physical work surfaces in a virtual world, however, make it impossible to perform precise positioning tasks using direct manipulation. Furthermore, virtual environment systems lack alphanumeric input, the mechanism typically used for precise manipulation in through-the-window systems.

As another example, immersion within a virtual world means we can distribute controls (and other information) about the user. It also means, however, that these controls can be difficult to find in the virtual world. Even if visible, controls may obscure your view of the virtual environment or you may have to traverse the environment to reach them.

Does this mean there is no hope for virtual environments applications? No! We must, however, realize that not all applications are suited for the virtual world. We must be careful how we choose applications to migrate to the virtual world, focusing on applications which depend on the display of and interaction with three-dimensional, geometric information. We must avoid converting these applications into two-dimensions applications floating in three-space with no value added. To do this we must develop virtual environment interaction techniques such as Orbital mode or Worlds-in-Miniature which take into account the limitations of the virtual world; techniques which take advantage of the naturalness of virtual worlds interaction while at the same time extending this interaction in ways not possible in the real world.

Randy Pausch: University of Virginia
Our recent efforts has been in areas involving

- use of physical input prop devices
- use to two-handed input
- analysis of tasks where immersion via HMD makes a difference
- general purpose interaction techniques

We believe that the use of two hands, controlling physical input devices with mass and some small number of buttons (combined with voice input) will provide a large number of break-through interaction techniques. We have already produced novel interaction techniques for volume data visualization and navigation/locomotion using two-handed prop-based interfaces. To this end, we feel that the utility of formless (i.e. glove/gesture) input has been highly over-rated.

We have had moderate success in finding tasks where immersion via HMD can be shown to quantitatively improve task performance. However, we have had much greater success establishing that even when measured (timed) task performance is comparable, the user's confidence level in the result achieved is much higher in an immersive interface.

Standardisation – Opportunity or Constraint?

Chair
David Arnold, UEA, Norwich, UK

Panelists
Jack Bresenham, Winthrop University
Ken Brodlie, University of Leeds, UK and Rapporteur GKS-94
George S. Carson, President, GSC Associates, Inc. and Chairman, SC24
Jan "Yon" Hardenbergh, Oki Advanced Products
Paul van Binst, University of Brussels and President, EWOS
Andries van Dam, Brown University

Panel Summary

Who and what are standards for? Are standards there to protect users' investments and ease the design of working, integrated solutions or are they there to generate product opportunities for suppliers? Given enough confusion in the market place the effect is to turn standards into supplier's opportunity, at the expense of users' protection. Extensions, registrations, revisions, profiles, and levels of certification all conspire to confuse the situation. The pressure to adopt Publicly Available Specifications and the perceived advantages of "de facto" standards can undermine the protective intent of "de jure" standards.

This panel debates different attitudes to standards, often associated with different sides of the Atlantic, but also between standardiser, politician, supplier and user.

Concern over slow progress in ISO growing, but even concern is slow to take effect! Political pressure for change has never been stronger (for example at the recent CEC workshop on choosing standardisation policy - attended by 350+ delegates.

Proposed methods of standardisation often assume that fast-tracking PASs will produce a better result, more speedily, but ignore the lack of success of fast-tracking to date in the graphics area.

Related topics for discussion include:
1) Is conformance certification worth the cost?
2) Portability v Extensibility?
3) Upwards compatibility - how is/should existing investment in products be protected.
4) Should registered items be allowed as a way of bypassing standards?
5) How should profiling be used.
6) De facto v de jure standardisation.
7) Can/should fast-tracking PASs be made to work?

David B. Arnold

With extensive experience in ISO projects cited as successes (e.g. CGM) and as failures (e.g. CGI) I feel well able to comment upon the issues of timeliness and effectiveness of the ISO standards process. Whilst CGI has not been taken up as the foundation of a range of device independent graphics products, neither did X11 protocol achieve the status of formal standard. A great deal of expense and energy was expended upon both so why did both fail? CGI was produced almost exactly to the original timescales defined when the project first entered the ISO arena - but there were then too many stages to go through. X11 Protocol, I believe, failed as a project, since the de facto route had failed to pay sufficient attention to how it would fit the other standards around at the time and how it could be phrased in unambiguous language. There are lessons from both failures.

These lessons will require both the de facto and the de jure camps to recognise the potential for getting things wrong.

I believe that as panel chair it would be my role to explain some pitfalls and to outline the trends and pressures which seem to be driving the mechanisms for standardisation in particular directions. Many of these pressures are derived from historical failings; some are political pressures which are justified to an extent, but where the expectations of the solutions seem to be based on the false premise that standardisers are getting in the way of standardisation. In fact the reverse is normally true - standardisers are normally trying to get genuinely standard definitions - but the brief to find an unambiguous definition by consensus often means being asked to solve the wrong problem! The standardisers are frequently as frustrated by this as the critics.

Dr. Jack Bresenham

Like many things in life, standards can be helpful, hurtful, or even neutral & indifferent. Time & circumstance play a part. Quality and completeness play a part. Economic realities & jockeying for competitive position must always be recognised. Entrepreneurs, academicians, and corporate minions each have egos mixed with personal & business interests they pursue. People make standards so it is essential to see up-front who's playing and what is the pay-off coin each seeks.

IEEE 803 for Ethernet & Token Ring in the early 1980's helped consolidate LAN protocols and brought to the fore the physical layer abstraction. By contrast, CGI as the ISO 9636 Computer Graphics Interface (formerly known as VDI in its initial stage of a lengthy gestation) took so long and wandered so far that its final approval was viewed by many as a non-event. CGM the Computer Graphics Metafile and GKS the Graphics Kernel System have enjoyed some degree of success as has PHIGS. CORE & GINO never made it to an internationally approved status but did exert significant influence in graphics development. PostScript, GL, RENDERMAN, GOCA, PLOT10 and the like have been proprietary pseudo-standards or de facto specifications of major consequence. Large bodies deliberating at length, especially large committees of 'professional' standards setters or lobbyists known as consultants or system architects, can muddy most any useful technical endeavour. Active, front line practitioners who have real problems to solve are more likely to agree in a timely manner and come up with something practical than are those far removed from the development process or those with no actual product to deliver on deadline. The so-called Green Pages in the Design Summary Book for S/360, Token Ring in IEEE 803, ISO 9636 CGI, and spanned variable-length records in MFT/MVT support do offer some instructive examples as attempts to promulgate de facto & de jure standards. It really boils down to timing, knowledge, motivation, economics, and a goodly measure of common sense.

Ken Brodlie: Should we standardise and if so how?

Enthusiasm for graphics standards was high in the early 80s, with GKS and CGM defined, and a 3D standard in prospect. Now the ISO process is in competition with faster ways of creating "standards"- for example OpenGL, created as a proprietary specification, and later made available to a consortium.

It is now a good time to evaluate the two approaches. The ISO process has a number of positive characteristics; international; consensus; publication only when mature; but some negative ones; voluntary effort and staccato progress.

The proprietary approach has two flavours: in one, control of the specification is handed over to a consortium including the originator who does not have a veto; in the other, the originator retains control - "open" with a small "o"!

Both are valid approaches, but what sort of standard world do you wish to live in? I am for the democratic ISO process, so that the user voice can be heard. Some specifics:

(1) Conformance. Creating a test suite is fine, but running a certification process something else. Test suites should be made available for self-testing; governments should decide if they want a certification service, and, if so, need to back it up with legislation.

(2) Extensibility. Originally I felt that extensibility should be forbidden (as only sure way of ensuring portability) but this has mellowed to "the system should flag any extensions, in a health warning".

(3) Upwards compatibility. In recent revision of GKS to GKS-95, the twin aims have been to protect the legacy code, but also to go forward in a way which will bring back its old following amongst the user community, attract new users, and persuade suppliers there is a market for implementations.

Dr. George S. Carson

Standards have a time and place in the cycle of technology. This can be explained using a familiar bell-shaped curve showing the stages in the evolution of a technology. This explains where standards belong and the pitfalls of standardising too early or too late.

There are historical problems with formal standards. These include: standards that take too long (CGI); standards that ignore the marketplace, producing solutions that are not sufficiently differentiated from competitive ones to survive (OSI vs Internet); and standards that try to drive the market to a point solution where greater diversity is better (contrast LAN standards (diverse) with graphics standards (point solutions)). Diversity can be understood in the context of graphical file exchange formats, where the single ISO computer graphics standard is little used, while several platform-dependent formats predominate. Both the length of a development effort and diversity of solutions may be understood in terms of the consensus-building process.

Vendors and users have different attitudes about standards. Vendors desire rubber stamping of their technologies. The abortive attempt to standardize the X Window System is a good example. Users want openness (the ability to influence the content of standards) and long term stability (especially to influence the evolution of the standard.)

A new process being used by ISO/IEC JTC1 ISO PAS will make it far easier to adopt de-facto solutions (now called "Publically Available Specifications") as ISO standards without traditional consensus or technical review. This new process may significantly affect the quality of some future ISO standards.

I believe that better management of the standards development process, and not a set of totally new procedures that bypass traditional standards development, is the answer to the problems I have described.

Jan "Yon" Hardenbergh

Standards for computer graphics and multimedia come in three flavors: APIs (Application Programming Interfaces), file formats, and protocols. Each of these have direct beneficiaries and downstream beneficiaries. Standards influence everyone, willingly or not. The question is how to judge the success of a standard, and how to make standards more successful.

A successful standard makes it easier for many people to get better work done faster. Good APIs make it easier to create richer tools. Good file formats proliferate of high quality documents.

A good standard combines politics, religion and even a little bit of technology. It should target a constituency and focus to please them. A successful standard also needs financial support to make it easy to use and easy to notice. PHIGS, PEX, OpenGL have each had a measure of success in the 3D graphics market. Each had a very different process.

A good standard comes with a sample implementation and a test suite. It is critical that a software API have common header files across implementations, better if the actual API library code is common. This was a severe problem with PHIGS; each vendor had a different version of the API - sometimes based on different drafts of the emerging standard. The ideal standard needs to emerge early enough in the technology curve to shape everyone's opinion on what the "right" way to do things is. This gives it a religious component (based on quality technology). There is a brief time when the definition of the technology is still malleable and could become formal standard. The industry should treat a new technology like a crisis and iterate through periods of definition and prototyping.

Paul van Binst

The standardisation process in the field of Information and Communication Technology (ICT) has definitely been in need of reassessment for a little while. ISO, IEC and ITU at world level, CEN, CENELEC and ETSI in Europe are not "what they used to be" anymore in front of the waves of "de facto" standards or "publicly available specifications". The role of Governments and of the European Commission in the standardisation process is also often questioned.

Being the chairman of the Steering Committee of EWOS (the European Workshop for Open Systems) puts me in the particular position of playing simultaneously inside and outside the standardisation process; indeed, as a University Professor heading a department of "Telematics and Communication" I am by no means a professional standardiser while chairing EWOS definitely puts me in the middle of the standardisation process.

EWOS, a workshop originally associated with CEN to do the profiling of OSI standards, has seen its role and scope considerably enlarged over the years. Today, it is one of the very few standards related institutions addressing directly the hot issues such as interoperability between de jure and Internet standards for instance, and doing this on a global scale by our relations with our American and Asian counterparts.

A profound analysis of the ICT standardisation process is presently going on in Europe and it is expected that EWOS will play an expanded - and more market oriented - role in the future. This panel will be a chance to review the situation in the European and worldwide contexts.

Andries van Dam, Brown University

Graphics standards efforts started with de facto standards in the sixties and early seventies (Calcomp, PLOT-10, GINO from the Cambridge CAD Center, GPGS from Nijmegen, Delft, and Cambridge Universities), then committee standards in the mid-seventies (SIGGRAPH Core, Germany's GKS) and then "official" standards (ANSI/ISO GKS, PHIGS, PHIGS+). Today we have de facto standards (e.g., Adobe PostScript, Apple QuickDraw, AutoDesk/Ithaca Software HOOPS, SGI Open GL and Open Inventor, Microsoft GDI and DDI, X Consortium Xlib/Xt/PEX, and Pixar RenderMan) which are commercially far more important and influential than official standards. Contrast this to the impact of, say, the IEEE floating point standard. Meanwhile, hot new 3D graphics libraries specialized for games are appearing (e.g., Microsoft/RenderMorphics Reality Lab, Canon/Criterion RenderWare) and will be rapidly disseminated in the personal computer space.

Given this situation, is it still relevant and useful to have cumbersome, multi-year standards efforts engaged in by committees whose members belong to competing techno-political-national factions? I will try to answer this rhetorical question in my role as cynic, i.e., as a frustrated idealist who believed in the value of standards bodies and efforts, despite all their built-in handicaps.

Some Background Material and Reference Lists

[1] IBM 3270 Personal Computer/G or GX Reference Information for Picture Interchange Format, SC33-0244, IBM Corporation, Armonk, NY

[2] Arnold, D.B. and Bono, P.R. CGM and CGI: Metafile and Interface Standards for Computer Graphics. Springer-Verlag. 1988.

[3] Henderson, L.R. and Mumford, A.M. The Computer Graphics Metafile. Butterworths. 1990.

[4] Bresenham, J.E. Computer Graphic Attributes and Reference Model Alternatives. Proceedings Ausgraph'90, Australasian Computer Graphics Association. 1990. pp413-424.

[5] Bresenham, J.E. Attribute Considerations in Raster Graphics. Computer Graphics Techniques: Theory and Practice edited by D.F. Rogers and R.A. Earnshaw. Springer-Verlag. 1990. pp9-41.

[6] ISO, Information processing systems - Computer graphics - Interfacing techniques for dialogues with graphical devices, Pts 1-6 IS9636 (1991)

[7] Arnold, D.B. and D.A.Duce, ISO Standards for Computer Graphics: The First Generation, Vol. 1 in Computer Graphics Standards Reference Series, Butterworth's Scientific. ISBN 0-408-04017-3, pp264 (March 1990)

[8] How to choose the right ICT Standardization Policy? Report of and commentary on the CEC workshop. Submitted to Standard View, ACM Perspectives on Standardization (1995)

Cross-Media Authoring

Chair
Jeff Martin, Apple Computer, Inc.

Panelists
Allejandro Villarroel, Cole and Weber
Chris Gulker, Hearst Newspapers
Rick Capps, Capps Studios Ltd.
Rick Smolan, Against All Odds Productions

Abstract
Today's world has become very media-centric: multimedia, print media, and now, of course, new media. However, with this panel of authors, entertainers, and publishers, it becomes clear that the message does indeed come before the medium, so content comes before context. The panlists show how messages should not be created for media vehicles in isolation, but rather should "cross the media" from video to print, and CD to online, delivering a core or graphics message in concert. The panel examines several questions: What is this new expertise of cross-media authoring? What is the creative and career proposition for its authors? What are the tools or transfer agents for crossing media without compromising quality? How do authors implement a unified design strategy while realizing the unique opportunities of each medium?

Grids, Guys and Gals: Are you oppressed by the Cartesian Coordinate System?

Chair
Greg Garvey

Panelists
Brenda Laurel, Interval Research
Rob Tow, Interval Research
Joan Staveley
Allucquere Rosanne Stone (a.k.a Sandy Stone), The University of Texas at Austin

Summary
This panel will address issues of gender differences regarding computer technology in general and computer graphics in particular by examining and debating the question first raised at SIGGRAPH 93: is the Cartesian Coordinate System oppressive?

Panel Topic Description
Grids, Guys and Gals: Are you oppressed by the Cartesian Coordinate System? examined the very real and palpable issues of gender differences regarding computer technology in general and computer graphics in particular. This panel brought to the SIGGRAPH audience the ongoing debate in the classroom, academic journals, and the popular press regarding significant differences between men and women especially in learning, using, and designing technology. Research points to measurable gender differences involving spatial cognition that may well contribute to the formation of social and cultural norms. Issues of gender and technology linked even to a discussion of identity are no longer seen as irrelevant to such practical concerns as the design of the user interface, input devices and visualization tools.

Many of the women and men who utilize computer technology are legitimately engaged in a critical appraisal of their role in the technological and scientific order. There is much to be gained by challenging certain assumptions, examining and critiquing gendered constructions of space or the interface and proposing alternatives (a feminist computer?, non-Euclidean computer graphics?). It reflects the will to transform and remake technology that is responsive to the range of human capabilities, limitations, needs and desires.

In many ways, Joan Staveley, artist and agent provocateur is responsible for the existence of this panel. At SIGGRAPH 93 during the NANOSEX Panel her remark encapsulated the issues at hand. The statement that the Cartesian Coordinate System is oppressive refers directly to the constraints of the tools and is of utmost importance because only by criticizing our current tools and seeing the limitations then can better models of the user interface can be developed. Her statement of course reaches much further in daring to suggest there are shortcomings to Cartesian rationalism.

However it would be a mistake to reject this view as that of a 20th-century Luddite. As an artist she is demanding more of the tools and seeking to reveal the barriers and biases that are only reluctantly acknowledged in what was a previously male dominated field. The near future promises a continuing transformation of this field as women increasingly play a more prominent role.

OSMOSE is a new work by Montreal based artist Char Davies, supported by SOFTIMAGE-Microsoft that confronts the limitations of Cartesian Rationalism. Davies, formerly a painter, is well-known for her series of large-scale lightboxes of still images created on SOFTIMAGE which explored metaphorical aspects of Nature with an aesthetic which was rich, multi-layered and ambiguous. OSMOSE continues this research, bringing it into fully-immersive and interactive virtual space. As in Davies' previous work, OSMOSE's visual aesthetic deliberately circumvents the Cartesian coordinate system (i.e. static, solid, hard-edged objects in empty space) to create spatially-complex and ambiguous relationships whereby distinctions between figure and ground, interior and exterior are dissolved. Similarly, the project's interactive aesthetic seeks to subvert the Cartesian privileging of mind over matter by grounding the immersive experience in the participant's own interior bodily processes thereby re-affirming the presence of the body in virtual space. In addition, interaction is designed to transcend the Cartesian dualism of subject and object by emphasizing mutual inter-relationship between self and "others", and encouraging behaviour based on gentleness and sensitivity rather than domination and control. At the direction of the artist, programmers at SOFTIMAGE are developing tools to achieve these goals and liberate the medium of VR from the cultural values of the Cartesian grid. Phase one of the project will be exhibited at the Montreal Museum of Contemporary Art for six weeks this summer in conjunction with the Sixth International Symposium on Electronic Arts, and will be exhibited in New York City later in the fall of 1995.

Other contributors to this panel examine the importance of spatial representation and links to cognition. Brenda Laurel: Artist, Author, and Researcher at Interval Research, Palo Alto, CA writes:

> "How space is represented in art, science, religion, and other cultural domains reveals much about the nature of a culture and transmits a variety of loaded understandings to its individual members. In turn, differences in experience and interpretation among individuals and subcultural groups reciprocally influence the larger cultural constructions of spatiality as both metaphor and practice. How we shape and employ spatial representations, metaphors and narratives in the construction of interactive media has enormous influence on who will experience our work, how it will be integrated and interpreted, and what its political ramifications might be. These considerations are especially relevant as regards both cultural and biological aspects of gender."

Brenda's colleague Rob Tow research scientist at Interval Research adds: "There are many representations of spatial relationships in human culture, art, and science, both now and through history. All are abstracted tools of knowing embedded in particular situations, and all work better for some people than for others. Rectilinear coordinate systems, and their close cousin Renaissance perspective, are examples. Recognizing these differences, we should NOT strive for the mediocre ideal of some sort of androgyny of geometry, but must instead build instrumentalities and interfaces that are richly multimodal in the way they empower people who are differently endowed."

Allucquere Rosanne Stone a.k.a Sandy Stone: Professor, author, at the University of Texas at Austin joins the fray with:

"PUTTING DESCARTES BEFORE DESHORSES...:Or, is the Cartesian system's relation-ship to gender a cause or an effect? The Cartesian coordinate system didn't spring intact from the brow of Rene; it arose in complex interaction with its social contexts. Other changes were in the wind too, and a lopsided gender binarism was just one of them. Stay tuned for a quick trip down mammary lane..."

This panel is also informed by the ongoing debate regarding significant differences between men and women especially in learning, using, and designing technology as part of a more general discussion of what is sometimes termed "cultural studies." One such view is that the edifice of western science and technology is but only a 'constructed' artifact of the dominant white male patriarchy driven by the imperatives of expansionist monopoly capitalism.

Examining this view in some detail reveals how moral and ethical concerns are extracted from a seemingly innocent and innocuous coordinate system. The Cartesian Co-ordinate System is seen to be a construct that paves over, subdues and silences the natural but raucous, unruly, diversity with the steamroller of reason. The Panoptic Cartesian Grid extended by projective geometry casts its net of domination over all that is observed, surveyed and measured. The convention of perspective at the service of the male gaze is a phallic instrument that penetrates the visible world of nature. Today many of us, male and female would recoil from the words of Francis Bacon, a white male and father of the enlightenment when he recommends that nature(female) is to be "hounded in her wanderings" "put into constraint," "bound into service," and made a "slave." [1]

In spite of claims of objectivity modern science is appar-ently not so innocent. In "The Science Question in Feminism," Sandra Harding [2] writes:

"...science today serves primarily regressive social tendencies; and that the social structure of science, many of its applications and technologies, its modes of defining research problems and designing experiments, its ways of constructing and conferring meanings are not only sexist but also racist, classist, and culturally coercive."

Similar lines of argument assert that the rise of modern science founded on domination and possession is coupled with the development of capital and private property. From this perspective Descartes' Coordinate System is seen as a tool that merely facilitated for example mapping the globe at the service of colonial exploitation.

However Marshall McLuhan puts the blame on Gutenburg:

"The same Gutenburg fact of uniform, continuous, and indefinitely repeatable bits inspired also the related concept of the infinitesimal calculus, by which it became possible to translate any kind of tricky space into the straight the flat the uniform and the 'rational'.

This concept of infinity was not imposed upon us by logic. It was a gift of Gutenburg. So, also later on, was the industrial assembly line. The power to translate knowledge into mechanical production by the breaking up of any process into fragmented aspects to be place in a lineal sequence, yet uniform, parts was the formal essence of the printing press." [3]

McLuhan continues by connecting Gutenburg to the exploitation of both humans, animals and the environment that follows from the admonitions of Bacon: "The breaking up of every kind of experience into uniform units in order to produce faster action and change of form (applied knowledge) has been the secret of western power over man and nature alike." [4]

We should give credit where credit is due because one of Descartes' primary contributions is his analytical method of breaking a problem down into pieces and putting them into a logical order. This method is at the service of the familiar imperative of the enlightenment project: the domination and transformation of unruly nature by reason. The opposition of man alienated from nature also happens to be the classic Marxist dialectic – Man must appropriate and dominate nature through analysis and praxis in order to realize his humanness. This inevitably leads to moral judgement and revolutionary self righteousness. From a completely different direction John Ralston Saul in his turgid sweeping indictment, "Voltaire's Bastards" convicts the enlightenment faith in unbridled rational-ism by condemning it for training a generation of amoral, irresponsible, and all too often destructive rational elites. [5]

At this point it may be appropriate to heed Foucault's admonishment: "In any case, I think that, just as we must free ourselves from the intellectual blackmail of 'being for or against the Enlightenment,' we must escape from the historical and moral confusionism that mixes the theme of humanism with the question of the Enlightenment." [6]

Descartes' search for a method of analytical doubt led to his partition of mind and matter. God Himself is seen to have created nature as a mathematical machine and was the necessary source of the light of reason that enabled the human mind to perceive this order. The 19th century mathematician Leopold Kronechker held to this with the declaration that "God made the integers; all else is the work of man." [7] Yet God's position as the guarantor of reason was not eternal. The reductionism of Descartes drove Bertrand Russell to this inevitable conclusion:

"I shared with Frege a belief in the Platonic reality of numbers which, in my imagination, peopled the timeless realm of Being. It was a comforting faith, which I later abandoned with regret. In the end it seemed to result that none of the raw material of the world has smooth logical properties, but that whatever appears to have such properties is constructed artificially in order to half them." [8]

Russell clearly acknowledges that the net of reason constructs its own artificial reality by attempting to ensnare the natural world. Even Albert Einstein remarked that the integers are "obviously an invention of the Human Mind, a self-created tool which simplifies the ordering of certain sensory experi-ence." [9] So in the words of an arbitrary selection of major male architects of the edifice of the math and science-it's all an artificial reality. But as Chomsky might ask: "Who benefits?"

The answer to this question may be found in the artificiality of internet cross dressing or gender/identity aliasing. Kevin Kelly points out the peculiar phenomenon of gender bias of player's of on-line interactive games. "So many female presenting characters are actually males" "Players now assume all players to be male unless proven otherwise. This has led to a weird prejudice against true female players who are subject to the harassment of proving their gender." [10]   Alan Turing anticipated the contemporary gender clash on the net with the imitation game-the so-called Turing Test for artificial intelligence where: "The object of the game for the interrogator is to determine which of the other two is the man and which is the woman." [11]

In her article "The Men's Club Is Now Closed" available through Gopher, Stacy Horn writes passionately on what it's like for a woman on-line. Some relevant excerpts follow:

> "There are gender differences on the net, of course, regardless of the proliferation of bad metaphors. The on-line world is often touted as a bodiless medium. As The New Yorker magazine put it, in a drawing of a dog typing at a computer: "On the Internet no one knows you're a dog." Nonsense. The illusion of free and unbiased communication can only be maintained, and then only briefly, as long as people hide. It's a trick. If no one knows you are a woman, until that is discovered then you will not be treated like a woman." The only way to be treated equally is by going under cover? No, thanks. I want to be in your face, I don't want to be a man on-line or otherwise."

> Is the men's club sustained by a grid of innate and/or learned behavioral norms? Do male occipital lobes incorporate a wetware coding of the ready-to-wear Cartesian coordinate system maintained by a steady influx of testosterone? As the Wall Street Journal reports is the popularity of Tetris among women explicable by a drive for (Cartesian?) order based on the nesting instinct and rewarded with a flood of endorphins? Is it the case that (male?) metaphors such as the electronic frontier or information superhighway simply do not capture the true nature of the on-line experience? Stacy Horn suggests "the word 'infrastructure' invokes the idea of a web or a tapestry, a metaphor which allows for infinite color, texture and variety."

Ada Lovelace is credited with being Charles Babbage's Muse and with providing inspiration for his analytical engine of punched cards. If the Jacquard Loom is seen as the progenitor of mechanical computation marking the beginning of the age of computing, could not La Dentellerie or lace making be a more apt metaphor for the net? Was weaving itself – a woman's task – the unacknowledged inspiration for Descartes' grid?

In spite of the rants, raves, and the loss of the thread of meaning through a welter of deconstructed text, the seemingly neutered grid remains indifferent, implacable and maintains a periodic refresh and panoptic sway over mind and raster graphics.

Footnotes

1. Quoted by Fritjof Capra, The Turing Point, New York, A Bantam Book, (1982), p. 56

2. Harding, Sandra, The Science Question in Feminism, Cornell University Press, Ithaca and London, 1986, p. 9

3. McLuhan, Marshall, Understanding Media-The Extensions of Man, A Mentor Book, New York, 1964, p. 112

4. McLuhan, Marshall, Understanding Media-The Extensions of Man, p. 88

5. Saul, John Ralston, Voltaire's Bastards, Toronto, London, New York, etc, 1992

6. Rabinow, Paul, The Foucault Reader, Panopticism (from Truth and Method)., Pantheon Books, New York, 1984, p.45

7. Quoted by George Johnson in the New York Times, The Week in Review, 1994

8. Russell, Bertrand, Principles of Mathematics, New York, W. W. Norton & Company, (Originally published 1903 revised in 1938), p. XI

9. Quoted by George Johnson in the New York Times

10. Kelly, Kevin, Out of Control-The Rise of Neo-Biological Civilization, Addison Wesley, Redding, MA, 1994.

11. Turing, Alan, Mind-A Quarterly Review of Psychology and Philosophy, Vol. LIX. No. 236., Oct. 1950.

Visual Effects Technology – Do We Have Any?

Chair
Derek Spears, Cinesite Digital Film Center

Panelists
Scott Dyer, Windlight Studios, Inc.
George Joblove, R/GA-LA
Charlie Gibson, Rhythm & Hues Studios
Lincoln Hu, Industrial Light & Magic

Introduction

Derek Spears

This panel is focused on taking a look at what key technologies we need to push visual effects father into the realms of realism. We will start by examining what tools we have used so far in order to provide a firm reference to understand where we are going. Tools in the areas of Input/Output (Scanning/Recording/Data Transfer), Image Processing, and Animation/Motion Capture will be covered. These are not only major concerns for the visual effects industry, but cover large areas of interest for mainstream computer graphics.

Why is this important? The visual effects industry as a whole has become in and of itself a proving ground for cutting edge digital technologies. Morphing, Motion Capture and Digital Compositing were largely born out of the needs of the Visual Effects industry and Visual Effects has benefited enormously from advances in Computer Graphics. This is partially due to the Visual Effects Industry's willingness to embrace new technologies, riding the bleeding edge. These technologies have enabled us to do things never before imaginable.

While we all think that the quality of visual effects has been stunning in the past, we need to stop and look at how we really achieve these images. The tools obviously work, we have produced breathtaking imagery with them. But we have to ask the questions "Are they good enough? What more do we need?" These questions relate not only to the search for solutions to previously impossible problems, but also the search to do things we already understand better, faster and cheaper. The search for new technology includes advances in algorithms, totally new approaches, and even solving more basic and historically ignored problems, such as user interfaces and artist interaction. We will take a look at our present and a glimpse into our future of where our tools are (and more importantly, should be) headed.

Panelists Summaries

Scott Dyer

The technology behind the creation of convincing computer animation is changing on an almost daily basis. While the early days were dominated by purely technical achievements that often lacked sophistication, today's achievements are visually stunning as well as being grounded in good stories, characters, and situations. Technology is no longer an end unto itself; it is often used invisibly to aid the story without undue attention. It is this new emphasis, I think, that has allowed computer animation to move into the mainstream without fanfare (or objection).

While computer animation technology continues to move forward on a variety of fronts, Windlight has chosen to concentrate on motion capture as a mechanism to enable inexpensive high quality long format production. Now that the novelty of motion capture has worn off, and many of the myths have been debunked, we believe the industry will gradually apply motion capture increasingly but only where it is appropriate. Motion capture isn't a solution to animation; it is simply another tool.

How motion capture data is mapped from an actor to an arbitrary character is of great interest to Windlight; the use of this technology on non-human figures has been significantly less successful than its use in human animation. There is also a lot of interest in the joining of motion capture sequences (using some underlying biomechanical model) so that the promise of "clip" animation could be realized. The impact of these developments on the highest end animation isn't clear, but they are of great importance in the television and video games markets.

The larger question, though, is not just about motion capture but about how "performance" animation can be better used as a timing and animation tool. Computer animation has generally been a slow, quiet process done in private and performance capabilities can open new doors on providing interactivity and participation in the process. Windlight is actively pursuing these areas as ways to increase the quality of our animation and to take better advantage of the experience of our animators.

George Joblove

The presentation will discuss the use of image processing and compositing as visual-effects tools. We will begin with a brief introduction to the problem: how compositing is the basic operator of visual effects, and why it is so important. For perspective, we will review how it was done before computers, and why it continued to be done that way for so long after computers, and look at the fundamental technology that digital manipulation requires. The kinds of capabilities that currently form the basis for such systems will be discussed, such as color correction, framing, filtering, matte extraction, compositing, and others. Then we will discuss the importance of this technology, the need for more development in this area, and some ideas for new tools. The importance of tools that provide the effects artist with power without impeding his creative input, and the need for keeping the artist in the loop, will be stressed.

Charlie Gibson

We have seen amazing growth in the digital imagery market in combination with feature films. With respect to Feature Visual Effects, our studio chooses to focus on two trendy and highly visible forms of digital technology. The first is compositing and image manipulation, in which digitized imagery is mixed together, manipulated or cut-and-pasted with other digitized imagery. The second is photorealistic image synthesis, which involves creating "realistic"-looking imagery from scratch in the computer (usually characters, environments or vehicles). This process is simply not yet easy enough. The technology and algorithms for creating the basic imagery are there, but the user interface paradigms are just not keeping up.

The talent pool in this industry is very nearly drained. There is more work out there than there are qualified people. Rather than training people to perform under unnecessarily arcane and complex UI systema, I would like to see a complete rethink on the current user interfaces for 2-D and 3-D computer graphics. Computers are going to get even faster and cheaper in the future. With the promise of complex image analysis, procedural and physical simulation tools coming into the realtime relm, we should really think about the way that we work with computers when producing visuals of any kind. We will also need a clever way to wrangle scenes of very high complexity! In the case of photorealism, complex detail is the most important component of the mix. We still bump up against hardware and software limitations every single day in production.

Lincoln Hu

Successful visual effects often depend on the careful manipulation and seamless integration of elements with live action background environments. Over the last few years, many practitioners in this field have developed interesting techniques to help produce these visual effects. We will take a look at some of the underlying technologies that were developed, including the work in imaging, computing hardware, network, I/O, and user interfaces. In addition, we can also take a brief look at some of the developments in 2D and 3D computer graphics tools in painting, image warping, digital compositing, image processing, modeling, animation and rendering, and examine how these tools have been used in the production of feature film visual effects at Industrial Light & Magic. We will also discuss some possible directions for future development in these areas.

3D Graphics through the Internet – a "Shoot-Out"

Honorary Chair
Carl Machover, Machover Associates Corporation

Panelists
Gavin Bell, Silicon Graphics
Tamara Munzner, Geometry Center, University of Minnesota
Fabio Pettinati, Apple Computer
Val Watson (organizer), NASA Ames Research Center

3D graphics through the Internet needs to move beyond the current lowest common denominator of pre-computed movies because these movies excessively consume bandwidth and are non-interactive. Panelists will demonstrate and compare new approaches for accessing, analyzing, and collaborating on 3D graphical information through the Internet and World-Wide Web. This "shoot-out" will illustrate which tools are likely to be the best for the various types of 3D graphical information, including dynamic scientific data, 3D objects, and virtual environments.

The computer graphics community (and especially SIGGRAPH) can provide a major service to mankind by promoting the use of graphical tools that improve the effectiveness of the Information Superhighway. A significant step in this process is an open comparison, evaluation, and discussion of the graphical tools being proposed. The panel provides this step by having demonstrations and open discussions of the proposed tools.

The issue is much larger than just the issue of data formats for Internet. The tools should provide for efficient access of the information, effective analysis, and effective collaboration with others over the Internet.

The organizer has selected tools for demonstration that he believes have the greatest potential at this time. The selected tools for 3D objects and virtual environments are QuickTime VR and QuickDraw 3D by Apple Computer [1, 2], WebSpace by Silicon Graphics [3], and a public domain 3D browser from the Geometry Center of the University of Minnesota [4]. QuickTime VR is based on images. QuickDraw 3D is a cross platform 3D graphics API. WebSpace and the Geometry Center's public domain browser are based on the Virtual Reality Modeling Language (VRML) described in [5]. The selected tool for 3D scientific data is the FASTexpedition described in [6]. (It is not expected that one tool will be the best for all applications.)

Gavin Bell

The VRML 1.0 draft specification defines a general, powerful, extensible language for describing objects and scenes. It is a subset of Open Inventor's ASCII file format, plus two extensions for reading objects from across the internet. Open Inventor's file format was chosen as the basis for VRML because it has repeatedly proven itself to be useful for exchanging information between applications, it is stable and very well supported, and there are already a large and growing number of tools written which work with the Inventor file format.

The challenge when designing VRML was to make it as simple as possible, so that it was fairly easy to implement, but to make it general enough so that it could be THE standard for exchanging resolution-independent, three-dimensional graphical information. At the same time, it had to be bandwidth-efficient

and scalable to allow potentially infinite virtual worlds. I believe those goals have been met.

Extensibility is almost as crucial as simplicity and generality when defining a widely useful product. VRML retains the extensibility features of the Open Inventor file format. It defines the syntax for new types of objects, allowing tools that don't understand the new objects to read and write them properly. VRML will never be finished; however, it provides the solid foundation of a common language upon which a rich set of tools will be built.

The ultimate goal of networked, distributed 3D graphics is a full-fledged cyberspace; a collaborative, distributed, interactive virtual meeting place, where people can get together to become educated, create something new, entertain each other, or conduct business. The VRML 1.0 draft specification is really only a small (but very important) step towards that goal. VRML defines static, non-shared, distributed 3D objects and scenes. However, I'm confident that VRML will be extended to describe animated objects, interactive objects, simulations, and objects with complex behaviors. And I'm confident that technologies for collaborative information environments will be developed, and that they will be combined with VRML to produce the kind of infinitely scalable shared cyberspaces that science fiction authors have been writing about.

Tamara Munzner

Three dimensional graphics can be integrated into the World Wide Web at many levels. Currently, most authors of hypertext documents can rely on the availability of external viewers for 2D images. The next step is to encourage authors to routinely include 3D scenes in documents, which depends on widespread availability of 3D browsers on all common platforms and agreement on a 3D object format. VRML provides a standard for 3D world interchange, and additionally the capability of embedding hyperlinks in the 3D objects.

For some applications, the most appropriate use of the Internet is simply to download 3D data and interact with that data locally. For other situations, further interaction through the Internet is reasonable, and the netlag incurred is an acceptable price to pay for distributed capabilities. I will demonstrate applications that explore the potential of incorporating hyperlinks into interactive 3D graphics, including visualizing the connectivity of Web itself.

Although ideally every user would like to run interactive 3D browsers locally, the reality of hardware and software often falls short of the dream. Even though machine speed is rapidly increasing, there is a large base of users with older slow machines, particularly in the schools. Organizations are moreover often unwilling or unable to devote resources to porting software to every possible platform. I will demonstrate "quasi-interactive" 3D applications that run directly through conventional and widely available Web browsers without any additional local software installation. The threshold of interactivity is much lower than conventional interactive 3D graphics viewers: an update can take minutes rather than a fraction of a second, since a new image created in response to local user interaction is computed on the fly at the server end. While these applications are bandwidth-intensive since pixels are being sent through Internet, they are a step up from precomputed movies since the user controls what is seen. The toolkit for creating such applications allows application writers to sidestep issues of porting, distribution, and hardware speed.

Fabio Pettinati

The Web and 3D graphics have always been on a collision course; it was just a matter of time for it to happen. The recent VRML proposal is just the beginning of an encompassing collaborative environment, where people can learn new concepts, travel to distant places, explore new business opportunities, or just entertain themselves. The concept of using 3D graphics technology to help create the illusion of a virtual space has been received with enthusiasm by researchers, the press, and end users.

The concept of a well-defined and standardized virtual reality modeling language (in its current VRML instantiation, or any other future form) is critical to establishing the foundation for a successful cyberspace. More critical, perhaps, is the need to accommodate additional data types that can convey the illusion of three-dimensional spaces. A very good example is Apple's QuickTime VR technology. QuickTime VR immerses users in a three-dimensional environment represented by panoramas. The illusion of movement can be further enhanced by linking panoramas together, and using hot spots for navigation. One of the advantages of this technology is the ability to convey a rich visual experience with very low bandwidth requirements: exactly one of the limitations in today's Web. For those users who would prefer the freedom to explore virtual worlds beyond what is possible with panoramas, traditional 3D rendering environments are the natural choice. On Macintosh and other personal computer environments, always popular among Web users, Apple's new 3D graphics API, QuickDraw 3D, can render VRML models with great efficiency and speed.

The ability to move virtual space scenes to a client computer, and to render them seems trivial when compared to the issues of offering users a rewarding experience. This makes the Web the ideal laboratory environment. By virtue of its large-scale distributed environment, and the speed with which it disseminates information, the Web lets researchers explore new rendering algorithms, and fine tune new interaction paradigms, in ways never previously imagined. At the same time, the Web places a tremendous responsibility in the hands of these researchers: the Web's user base is constantly evolving and becoming predominantly composed of non-computer literate users who crave for interesting content, and the opportunity to explore exciting sites. These same users will flatly reject Web sites they perceive as unattractive, regardless of their technical merits.

Offering users rich content and enticing interaction metaphors are two important areas that often are not seen as research topics, but that are critical to the Web's future.

Val Watson

Scientists, teachers, and students can now obtain information about dynamic scientific phenomena from the Internet — however, the format is usually a pixel file to be shown with a movie player. Movies show only one unchangeable sequence of views of the phenomena, and no "what if" analysis can be performed.

For phenomena that can be represented by vector and scalar fields, a much more effective tool than the movie player should be used. The demonstration of the FASTexpeditions will show that, with "clicks of a mouse" on a Mosaic page, one can obtain all of the following: (1)the vector and scalar data representing the phenomena; (2) a rich variety of guided expeditions through the data; (3) the ability to branch off from the guided expeditions for independent "what if" analyses with a sophisticated analysis tool; (4) the ability to explore the data in a truly 3D space; (5) the ability to interactively collaborate on the exploration of the data with fellow scientists, teachers, or students at remote sites.

I would like to see the computer graphics community work with agencies such as the National Science Foundation to: (1) select some of the best graphical tools for use with Internet; (2) promote the use of these tools by Internet information suppliers and users; and (3) bring these tools into the schools as quickly as possible

REFERENCES

1. http://www.info.apple.com/dev/
   appledirections/apr95/editornote.html
2. http://www.info.apple.com/cgi-bin/
   read.wais.doc.pl?/wais/
   TIL/Macintosh!Software/QuickDraw!3D/
   QuickDraw!3D!!Q-A
3. http://www.sgi.com/Products/WebFORCE/WebSpace/
4. http://www.geom.umn.edu/docs/weboogl/
   weboogl.html
5. http://vrml.wired.com/
6. http://www.nas.nasa.gov/FAST/Nationalgoals/

Conference Committee

CONFERENCE CO-CHAIRS
Brian Herzog (Sun Microsystems)
Peter Meechan (Wavefront Technologies)

CONFERENCE COMMITTEE CHAIRS
Kenneth O'Connell (University of Oregon), *Art Gallery*
Tom Hutton (San Diego Supercomputer Center), *Computer Systems*
Wayne Carlson (The Ohio State University), *Courses*
Jamie Thompson (Tivoli Systems, Inc.), *Electronic Media*
John Dill (Simon Fraser University), *Exhibits Development*
Coco Conn (Digital Circus Productions), *Interactive Communities*
Andy Goodrich (Parallax Graphics), *Interactive Communities*
Rob Hennigar (Art Center College of Design), *Interactive Communities*
Isaac Victor Kerlow (Pratt Institute), *Interactive Entertainment*
Midori Kitagawa De Leon (The Ohio State University), *International*
Carolyn Williams (Williams/Keeler), *Marketing/Public Relations*
Marke Clinger (FORE Systems, Inc.), *Networking*
Leo Hourvitz (Pixar), *Panels*
Rob Cook (Light Source, Inc.), *Papers*
Walt Bransford, *Space Planning*
Amit Parghi (The Banff Centre for the Arts), *Student Volunteer*

CONFERENCE PLANNING COMMITTEE
Adele Newton (Newton Associates)
Robert Judd (Los Alamos National Laboratory)
Mark Resch (Xerox Business Services)
Dino Schweitzer (US Air Force Academy)
Patti Harrison
Brian Herzog (Sun Microsystems)
Peter Meechan (Wavefront Technologies)
Betsy Johnsmiller
John Fujii (Hewlett-Packard)
Molly Morgan

PAPERS COMMITTEE
Rob Cook (Light Source, Inc.)
Kurt Akeley (Silicon Graphics Inc.)
Jules Bloomenthal (George Mason University)
Kellogg S. Booth (The University of British Columbia)
Ed Catmull (Pixar)
Michael Cohen (Microsoft)
Frank Crow (Interval Research)
Tony deRose (University of Washington)
Steven Feiner (Columbia University)
Kurt Fleischer (California Institute of Technology)
Andrew Glassner (Microsoft Corporation)
Pat Hanrahan (Stanford University)
John Hughes (Brown University)
Dave Kirk (Crystal Dynamics)
Wolfgang Krueger (German National Research Center for Computer Science)
Marc Levoy (Stanford University)
Nelson Max (Lawrence Livermore National Lab)
Dimitri Metaxas (University of Pennsylvania)
Don Mitchell (Microsoft Corporation)
Randy Pausch (University of Virginia)
Holly Rushmeier (NIST)
David Salesin (University of Washington)
Robert Sproull (Sun Microsystems)
Maureen Stone (Xerox PARC)

Turner Whitted (Numerical Design Limited)
Andrew Witkin (Carnegie Mellon University)

PANELS COMMITTEE AND JURY
Leo Hourvitz (Pixar)
Mark Bolas (Fakespace, Inc.)
Jamie Dixon (Pacific Data Images)
Beth Gerber
Alyce Kaprow (The New Studio)
Mike Keeler (Silicon Studio, Inc.)
F. Kenton Musgrave (George Washington University)
Theresa-Marie Rhyne (Martin Marietts Technical Services)
Linda Stone (Microsoft)

COURSES COMMITTEE
Wayne Carlson (The Ohio State University)
Bob McCarthy (The Ohio State University)
Nan Schaller (Rochester Institute of Technology)
Scott Sentfen (Shell Oil)
Barb Helfer (Ohio Supercomputer Center)
Jeff McConnell (Canisius College)
Mike Bailey (San Diego Supercomputer Center)
Stephan Keith (Sterling Software)

INTERNATIONAL COMMITTEE
Midori Kitagawa De Leon (The Ohio State University)
Jean Ippolito (Savannah College of Art and Design)
Igor S. Alexandrov
Len Breen
Paul Brown (Griffith University)
Felipe Gonzalez Carrasco
Thierry Frey
Masa Inakage (Media Studio)
Myeong Won Lee (Korea Telecom)
Maria Grazia Mattei
Joachim Rix (Fraunhofer-Institut für Graphische Datenverarbeitung)
Hung-Chuan Teh (National University of Singapore)
Wim van der Plas
Steve Shi-Nine Yang (National Tsing Hua University)
Marcelo Knorich Zuffo

COMPUTER SYSTEMS
Tom Hutton (San Diego Supercomputer Center)
Ralph Orlick (The University of Chicago)

ELECTRONIC MEDIA
Jamie Thompson (Tivoli Systems, Inc.)

FUNDAMENTALS SEMINAR
Dino Schweitzer (U.S. Air Force Academy)
G. Scott Owen (Georgia State University)

PUBLICATIONS PRODUCTION
Steve Cunningham (California State University Stanislaus)
Stephan Keith (Sterling Software)
Stephen Spencer (The Ohio State University)
Rosalee Nerheim-Wolfe (DePaul University)

TECHNICAL SLIDE SET JURY
Steve Cunningham (California State University Stanislaus)
Robert Cook (Light Source, Inc.)
Clark Dodsworth
Brian Herzog (Sun Microsystems)
Rosalee Nerheim-Wolfe (DePaul University)

COURSES REVIEWERS
Roni Yagel
Bret (Bump) Verde
Mark E. Lee
Raghu Machiraju
David Reed
Peter Carswell
Steven May
Lawson Wade
Ferdi Scheepers
Nathan Loofbourow

PAPERS REVIEWERS
Salim Abi-Ezzi
Greg Abram
Debra Adams
Ted Adelson
Dov Adelstein
John M. Airey
John Amanatides
Tony Apodaca
Jim Arvo
Ian Ashdown
Dan Asimov
Larry Aupperle
Norm Badler
Chandrajit L. Bajaj
Ruzena K. Bajcsy
Harlyn Baker
Thomas Banchoff
David C. Banks
David Baraff
Al Barr
Bill Barrett
Brian Barsky
Richard Bartels
Ronen Barzel
Carl Bass

Joseph Bates
Dan Baum
Rick Beach
Ben Bederson
Andrew Beers
Thad Beier
David Benson
Stephen A. Benton
Reinhard Bernstein
Neeta Bhate
Eric Bier
Gary Bishop
Avi Bleiweis
Jim Blinn
Rod Bogart
Kadi Bouatouch
David Brainard
David Breen
Chris Bremser
Jack Bresenham
Fred Brooks
Marc Brown
Peter F. Brown
Armin Bruderlin
Steve Bryson
John Buchanan
Richard Bukowski
Peter Burt
Brian Cabral
Tom Calvert
A. T. Campbell
Rikk Carey
Loren Carpenter
Andrew Certain
David Chen
Eric Chen
Jim Chen
Fuhua Cheng

Diane Chi
Per Christensen
Richard Chuang
Harvey Cline
James Coggins
Elaine Cohen
Matt Conway
Michael Cox
Roger Crawfis
Jim Cremer
Brian Curless
Bena Currin
Wolfgang Dahmen
Glorianna Davenport
Leila De Floriani
Jonas de Miranda Gomes
Van de Pann
Doug DeCarlo
Michael Deering
Tom DeFanti
Gary Demos
Sam Dicker
John Dill
Doug Dixon
David Dobkin
Steve Dollins
Julie Dorsey
Bob Drebin
George Drettakis
Steve Drucker
Tom Duchamp
Tom Duff
David Ebert
Matthias Eck
Steve Eick
T. Todd Elvins
Nick England
John Eyles
Kim Fairchild
Adam Finkelstein
Eugene Fiume
Robin Forrest
D. Forsey
David Forsey
Nick Foster
Farhad Fouladi
Alain Fournier
Geoffrey Fox
Bernd Froehlich
Tom Funkhouser
George Furnas
Don Fussell
Steve Gabriel
Andre Gagalowicz
Geoffrey Gardner
Marie-Paule Gascuel
Robert Geist
Guido Gerig
Ziv Gigus
Bernd Girod
Michael Gleicher
Ronald N. Goldman
Kevin Goldsmith
Eli Goldstein
Steven Gortler
Chuck Grant
Sebastian Grassia
Mark Green
Dan Greene
Ned Greene
Cindy Grimm
Larry Gritz
Markus Gross
Brian Guenter
Paul Haeberli
James Hahn

Tom Hahn
Eric Haines
Roy Hall
Mark Halstead
Blake Hannaford
Jonathan Hardis
Steve Harrington
John C. Hart
Alejo Hausner
Chris Healey
Paul Heckbert
David Heeger
Christian Hege
Ken Herndon
Roger Hersch
Ken Hinckley
Jessica Hodgins
Christoph Hoffmann
Jim Hollan
John Hollerbach
Hugues Hoppe
John Horn
Jack Hsia
Phillip Hubbard
Robert J. K. Jacob
Adam Janin
Zoran Kacic-Alesic
Jim Kajiya
Michael Kallay
Jeff Kallman
Peter Karp
Dan Karron
Michael Kass
Arie Kaufman
Tim Kay
Jonathan Kaye
Erwin Keeve
Mike Kelley
Victor Klassen
Brian Knep
Hyeongseok Ko
Jeff Koechling
Yotto Koga
Evangelos Kokkevis
Craig Kolb
Jeffrey H. Kulick
Tosiyasu L. Kunii
Jim Lackner
Philippe Lacroute
David Laidlaw
Anslemo Lastra
Olin Lathrop
Mike Lavelle
Mark Leather
Jed Lengyel
Apostolos Lerios
Ming Lin
Andy Lippman
Dani Lischinski
Pete Litwinowicz
Bart Locanthi
Jack Loomis
Charles Loop
Bill Lorensen
Tom Lyche
Dick Lyon
Jock Mackinlay
Bruce Madsen
Nadia Magnenat-Thalmann
Tom Malzbender
Dinesh Manocha
Dave Marimont
Joe Marks
Greg Marques
Paul Martin
Leonard McMillan

Clyde McQueen
Barbara Meier
Gary Meyer
Tom Meyer
Gavin Miller
Steven Molnar
Gary Monheit
John Montrym
Henry Moreton
Mike Moshell
Ken Musgrave
Eihachiro Nakamae
Sandy Napel
Reuel Nash
Bruce Naylor
Tom Ngo
Gregory Nielson
Paul Ning
Tomoyuki Nishita
Duane Northcutt
Chris Odgers
Peter Oppenheimer
Victor Ostromoukhov
Rick Parent
Sumant Pattanaik
Richard Patterson
Theo Pavlidis
Darwyn Peachey
Alex Pentland
Sandy Pentland
Ken Perlin
Jorg Peters
Thomas J. Peters
Cary Phillips
John Platt
Tomaso Poggio
Michael Potmesil
Pierre Poulin
John Poulton
Vaughan Pratt
Dennis Proffitt
Przemyslaw Prusinkiewicz
Pearl Pu
Claude Puech
Marc Raibert
Lyle Ramshaw
Arun Rao
Ari Rappoport
Ulrich Reif
Steve Reiss
Earl Rennison
Craig Reynolds
Dan Robbins
George Robertson
Alyn Rockwood
David Rogers
John Rohlf
Jarek Rossignac
Elisha Sacks
Robert Safranek
Georgios Sakas
Daniel Sandin
Lori Scarlatos
Peter Schroder
William J. Schroeder
Tom Sederberg
Mark Segal
Hans-Peter Seidel
Carlo H. Sequin
Steve Shafer
Shaun Shariff
Alan Shaw
Chris Shaw
Doron Sherman
Mikio Shinya
Pete Shirley

Ken Shoemake
Richard Shoup
H.B. Siegel
Francois Sillion
Ken Sloan
Philipp Slusallek
David Small
Alvy Ray Smith
Brian Smith
Brian Smits
John Snyder
Henry Sowizral
Dave Springer
Jos Stam
John Stasko
Eric Stollnitz
Ing. W. Strasser
Steve Strassmann
Paul Strauss
R. Szeliski
Fillipo Tampieri
Brice Tebbs
Seth Teller
Demetri Terzopoulous
Daniel Thalmann
Nadia Thalmann
Larry Thayer
Bond-Jay Ting
Carlo Tomasi
Ken Torrance
Greg Turk
Greg Turk
Matthew Turk
Ken Turkowski
Robert Ulichney
Sam Uselton
Jerry Van Aken
Michael Van De Panne
Mark Van de Wettering
Jack van Wijk
Amitabh Varshney
Eric Veach
Luiz Velho
Sean Vikoren
Doug Voorhies
John Wallace
Dan Wallach
Bruce Walter
Greg Ward
Colin Ware
Joe Warren
Keith Waters
Kevin Weiler
Will Welch
Steve Westin
Scott Whitman
Jane Wilhelms
Lance Williams
Tom Williams
James M. Winget
Stephanie Winner
Matthias Wloka
George Wolberg
Adam Woodbury
Brian Wyvill
Geoff Wyvill
Roni Yagel
Hussein Yahia
Paul Yanover
Hiroshi Yoshikawa
Jeff Yost
Jovan Zagajac
Ellen Scher Zagier
Harold Zatz
Bob Zeleznik
David Zeltzer

Mark Zimmer
Denis Zorin
Michael Zyda

PROFESSIONAL SUPPORT

ACM SIGGRAPH Conference Coordinators
Betsy Johnsmiller
Robin Myran

ACM SIGGRAPH Program Director
Patrick McCarren

Audio-Visual Support
AVW Audio Visual, Inc.
Gary Clark
Ed Goodman

Conference Accounting
Smith, Bucklin & Associates
Nicholas Chibucos
Jesse Del Toro

Conference Management
Smith, Bucklin & Associates
Brenda Dreier
Jackie Groszek
Peggy Sloyan
Cindy Stark
Julie Walker

Conference Travel Agency
ATI Travel Management, Inc.
Susan Neal
Lynda Shellist

Service Contractor
GES Exposition Services
Bob Borsz
John Loveless
John Patronski

Exhibition Management
Hall-Erickson, Inc.
Pete Erickson
Barbara Voss
Mike Weil

Graphic Design/Editing
Quorum, Inc.
Jeff Callender
Tom Rieke

Copy Coordination/Merchandise
Smith, Bucklin & Associates
Leona Caffey

Electronic Theater Directors
Joan Collins
Frank Foster

Public Relations/Marketing
Carolyn Williams
Hi-Tech Communications
Cassie Roduner
Cheryl Stumbo
Gary Thompson

Exhibitors

(As of 25 March 1995)
3D Construction Company
3Name3D/Yglesias Wallock Divekar, Inc.
5D
Abekas Video Systems
Academic Press, Inc.
Accom, Inc.
Acuris, Inc.
Adaptive Optics Associates, Inc.
ADCOM Electronics, Ltd.
Addison-Wesley Publishing Company
Adjile Systems
Adobe Systems Inc.
Advanced Digital Imaging
Advanced Imaging
Advanced Media Production
Advanced Visual Systems Inc.
AK Peters, Ltd.
Alias Research Inc.
All Effects Company
American Showcase, Inc.
Ampex Corporation
Anacapa Micro Products
Animation Magazine
AP Professional
Apple Computer, Inc.
Apunix Computer Services
Ariel Corporation
(Art)n Laboratory
Ascension Technology Corporation
AT&T Multimedia Software Solutions
auto.des.sys, Inc.
Autodesk, Inc.
Autometric, Inc.
AVID Technology, Inc.
AV Video/Montage Publishing
Balboa
Barco
Bit 3 Computer Corporation
CAD Institute, Inc.
CADalyst Magazine
Calcomp
Caligari Corporation
Camaleon Graphics Software
Cambridge Animation Systems Limited
Cambridge University Press
Canon U.S.A., Inc.
CGSD Corporation
Chemical Design Company
Chyron Group Corporation
Ciprico, Inc.
CIRAD
Cirrus Logic, Inc.
Cogswell Polytechnical College
Computer Artist
Computer Graphics World
Computer Video
Coryphaeus Software, Inc.
Criterion Software, A Canon Company
Crystal River Engineering
Cyberware
Cymbolic Sciences International
Data Translation
Desktop Images
Diaquest, Inc.
Digital Compositing Systems, Inc.
Digital Equipment Corporation
Digital Imaging
Digital Imaging Systems, Inc./Computrend
Digital Processing Systems
Digital Video
Digital Wisdom Inc.
Discreet Logic
Division Inc.
Eastman Kodak Company
Elastic Reality, Inc.
Electric Image, Inc.
ElectroGIG USA, Inc.
ENCAD, Inc.
ENEL
Engineering Animation, Inc.

Ensemble Designs
Epson America, Inc.
Eptron, S.A.
Equilibrium
Eurographics
Evans & Sutherland Computer Corporation
Extron Electronics
FARO Technologies Inc.
Fast Electronic U.S., Inc.
Film & Video
Folsom Research, Inc.
FOR-A Corporation
Fractal Design Corporation
Fraunhofer Center for Research in Computer Graphics, Inc.
Fujitsu Microelectronics Inc.
FWB, Inc.
Genesis Microchip Inc.
Gil Bruvel by Image Station
GMS Ltd.
Grand Junction Networks
Hash Inc.
Helios Systems
Hewlett-Packard Company
High Techsplanations, Inc.
HSC Software
Hyperspeed Technologies, Inc.
IBM Corporation
ICARI Inc.
I.D. Magazine
IEEE Computer Society
Imagica Corporation of America
Imagina - INA
Immersion Corporation
Infogrip, Inc.
in:sync corporation
Integrated Research
Intelligent Resources Integrated Systems
Interactive Effects
Intergraph Corporation
International Memory Products of IL, Inc.
IRIS Graphics, Inc.
Ithaca Software
James Grunder & Associates, Inc.
JVC Professional Products Company
Kingston Technology Corporation
KUB Systems
Kurta Corporation
Laser InSpeck inc.
LegaSys International
Leitch Incorporated
Lightscape Technologies, Inc.
Lightwave Communications, Inc.
Linker Systems, Inc.
logitech
Macromedia
Management Graphics, Inc.
Martin Marietta
Maximum Strategy, Inc.
Mediascape Corporation
Micropolis Corporation
Millimeter Magazine
Minicomputer Exchange
Mirus Industries Corporation
Mitsubishi Electronics America
MMS GmbH
Morgan Kaufmann Publishers
Motion Analysis Corporation
MultiGen Inc.
NEC Electronics Inc.
NewMedia Magazine
NewTek, Inc.
Nippon Computer Graphics Association (NICOGRAPH)
Numerical Algorithms Group, Inc.
Odyssey Visual Design
Oki Advanced Products Division
On Production Magazine
Onyx Computing, Inc.
Optical Disc Corporation
Oxberry, Division of Cybernetics Products, Inc.

Panasonic Broadcast & Television Systems Company
Paradigm Simulation, Inc.
Parallax Graphics, Inc.
Parallax Software Limited
Parity Systems Inc.
PC Graphics & Video
PHI Enterprises, Inc.
Pioneer New Media Technologies, Inc.
Pixar
PIXEL (Japan)
Pixibox
Pixo Arts
Polhemus Incorporated
Portable Graphics, Inc.
Precision Equipment Photron
Prentice Hall - PTR
Proxima Corporation
Quantel
Radius Inc.
RasterOps Corporation
Ray Dream, Inc.
Reality Simulation Systems, Inc.
Research Triangle Institute
RFX Inc.
RGB Spectrum
Sanyo Industrial Video
Scientific Computing
Seek Systems, Inc.
Seiko Instruments USA Inc.
SensAble Devices, Inc.
Sense 8 Corporation
Shoot
Side Effects
Sigma Electronics, Inc.
Silicon Graphics, Inc.
Silicon Graphics World
Silicon Solutions
SimGraphics Engineering Corporation
S-MOS Systems, Inc.
SMPTE
SOFTIMAGE, Inc.
Solsource Computers
Sony Electronics Inc.
Springer-Verlag New York, Inc.
StereoGraphics Corporation
Storagepath by SWS Corporation
Storage Technology Corporation
Strata, Inc.
Sun Microsystems Computer Company
Supercomputing T95
Superscape, Inc.
Syndesis Corporation
Synthonics Incorporated
Techexport, Inc.
Tech-Source Inc.
Tektronix, Inc.
Template Graphics Software, Inc.
Texas Memory Systems, Inc.
UNIX Review Magazine
Van Nostrand Reinhold
Vangard Technology
V.A.S. Group-Video Authoring Systems Group, Inc.
Vertigo Technology Inc.
Video Systems Magazine
Videomedia, Inc.
Viewpoint DataLabs
Virtual I/O
Visual Numerics Inc.
Visual Software, Inc.
Volumetric Imaging, Inc.
Wacom Technology Corporation
Wavefront Technologies, Inc.
Western Scientific, Inc.
John Wiley & Sons, Inc.
WideCom Group Inc.
Winsted Corporation
Wright Line

Index

Cover Image Credits

Front Cover

"Spike"
Copyright © 1995, Kurt W. Fleischer, David H. Laidlaw, Bena L. Currin, Alan H. Barr, and the Caltech Graphics Group.
To create this image of a thorn-covered bust, we used thousands of interacting geometric elements constrained to lie on a surface defined by a polygonal dataset. Each element tries to match the orientation of its neighbors, creating a flow field. The elements are then rendered as thorns (on the head) or patches (on the neck and chest). Note that the size of each thorn is relative to the local feature size on the dataset. Smaller thorns appear around the mouth and nose.
Cindy Ball helped with modeling this object, and Erik Winfree wrote some important sections of the code. The image was rendered using John Snyder's ray-tracer, with parallel extensions written by Mark Montague. Many thanks to Barbara Meier for textures, and to members of the Caltech Graphics Group for software and support.
Reference: "Cellular Texture Generation," Kurt W. Fleischer, David H. Laidlaw, Bena L. Currin, and Alan H. Barr, p. 239.

Title Page

"Artistic Screening"
Copyright (c) 1995 Victor Ostromoukhov and Roger D. Hersch, Ecole Polytechnique Féde´rale de Lausanne
This picture shows the image of 10-year old Bella, daughter of Victor Ostromoukhov, and her favorite parakeet Gosha, halftoned with artistic screen elements created with the lettershapes "SIGGRAPH95." It illustrates how one can incorporate a logo or a message such as "SIGGRAPH95" into the screening layer of a halftone image. A rectangular screen tile made up of a large number of replications of the "SIGGRAPH95" character outline descriptions was created. A smooth transform was found, which maps the rectangular screen tile into a deformed screen tile incorporating many different screen element orientations and periods. The smoothly deformed screen tile offers a highly esthetic appearance and gives protection against forgery due to the fact that at high resolution, the artistically halftoned picture can hardly be rescanned without producing significant Moiré effects. Please note that while the screen tile underwent a strong non-linear transformation, the image was left untouched.
Reference: "Artistic Screening," Victor Ostromoukhov and R.D. Hersch, p. 219.

Back Cover, top left

"Glossy Reflection and Transmission"
Copyright © 1995, James Arvo, Cornell University
These Phong-like glossy reflections and transmissions were computed analytically at each pixel. The new closed-form expressions were derived using a general recurrence relation for irradiance tensors. Albert Dicruttalo and Ben Trumbore assisted in modeling the stained glass window design by Elsa Schmid.
Reference: "Applications of Irradiance Tensors to the Simulation of Non-Lambertian Phenomena," James Arvo, p. 335.

Back Cover, top right

"3 1/2 Months Before Birth"
Copyright © 1995 Georgios Sakas, Fraunhofer Institute of Computer Graphics
The image on the left shows a reconstruction of the face of a fetus. The data used for the reconstruction have been acquired 3 1/2 months before birth by means of 3D ultrasound. To the right, one can see a photograph of the baby 24 hours after birth. The comparison shows a significant similarity in appearance and facial expression. Several new techniques have been used for filtering and extracting a valid surface from the noisy, "fuzzy" ultrasonic data. The developed algorithms are implemented entirely in software (no special boards, graphics engine etc.) and allow a complete processing, filtering, reconstruction, smoothing and volume rendering of similar images within less than a minute on a Pentium PC or other similar platform.
Reference: "Extracting Surfaces From Fuzzy 3D-Ultrasound Data," Georgios Sakas and Stefan Walter, p. 465.

Back Cover, middle left

"Human to Orangutan Volume Morph"
Copyright © 1994, Apostolos Lerios, Stanford University.
Three frames from a 3D volume morph, depicting the transformation of a human head on the left into an orangutan head on the right; the middle stage of the transformation is shown in the center. All three images are volume renderings of opacity volumes. The human and orangutan opacity volumes originated from CT scans. Using an interactive program, we manually specified corresponding features of these two volumes. Given this input, our software generated a sequence of opacity volumes which, when volume rendered, depict a smooth and realistic transformation of the human into the orangutan.
Acknowledgments: We used Philippe Lacroute's VolPack package for volume classification and rendering. The plastic cast of the orangutan head was lent to us by John W. Rick and was CT scanned with the help of Paul F. Hemler.
Reference: "Feature-Based Volume Metamorphosis," Apostolos Lerios, Chase D. Garfinkle, and Marc Levoy, p. 449.

Back Cover, middle right

"Weeping Willow"
Jason Weber and Joseph Penn, Teletronics Intl. Inc. and Army Research Lab.
The tree is created using a set of parameters such as lengths, angles, curvatures, and variations at different recursive levels of growth. The model relies on basic geometric principles that the general user can easily measure and visualize. The willow pictured uses downward attraction and pruning to conform to the characteristic shape.
The original 3300x4500 image was created with the CREATION software (in-house) using IrisGL on a SGI workstation. At common resolutions, most trees can be rendered in real-time.
Reference: "Creation and Rendering of Realistic Trees," Jason Weber and Joseph Penn, p. 119.

Back Cover, bottom left

"Bonfire with Smoke"
Copyright © 1995, Jos Stam, University of Toronto.
This image shows four frames from an animation of a fire with smoke. The creation of the flame and the smoke are governed by simple Arrhenius type reactions. The smoke and the flame are modelled as a superposition of 'warped blobs.' These blobs are moved using a superposition of smooth and turbulent wind fields. The interchange of light of the flame and the smoke with the rest of the environment is computed using a global illumination algorithm that includes gaseous blobs. Motion created using an interactive gas/fire modeller written by the author. The images were rendered using a modified ray-tracer with a blob tracer and global illumination preprocess. Hardware: Iris Indigo with RS4000 processor.
Reference: "Depicting Fire and other Gaseous Phenomena Using Diffusion Processes," Jos Stam and Eugene Fiume, p. 129.

Back Cover, bottom right

"Interior With Intraocular Glare Simulation"
Copyright © 1995, Cornell University
Optical effects are added which mimic the glare perceived by viewers in interior lighting. The model is of the Center for Cultural Arts, San Francisco, Polshek & Partners Associates. It was created by Jason Ardizzone, and the radiosity solution was created by Brian Smits.
Reference: "Physically-Based Glare Effects for Digital Images," Greg Spencer, Peter Shirley, Kurt Zimmerman, and Donald P. Greenberg, p. 325.

SIGGRAPH Professional Chapters

California

Los Angeles
Brian Bowman and Aliza Corson
PO Box 90698
Worldway Postal Center
Los Angeles, CA 90009-0698
Phone: +1 (310) 450-9991 Chapter Info
Phone: +1 (310) 450-4494
FAX: +1 (818) 997-6585
Los_Angeles_Chapter@siggraph.org

San Diego
Kathie LePage (acting)
Garden Graphics
9534 Wintergarden Blvd., Suite D-146
Lakeside, CA 92040
Phone: +1 (619) 297-1233
FAX: +1 (619) 390-1459
GardnGrafx@aol.com
HIProd@aol.com

San Francisco
Connie W. Siu
310 Richland Avenue
San Francisco, CA 941110
Phone: +1 (415) 642-9605
73052.624@compuserve.com

Silicon Valley
Domenic Allen
PO Box 1205
Mountain View, CA 94042-1205
Phone: +1 (408) 435-9100 x 288
Silicon_Valley_Chapter@siggraph.org
http://www.best.com/~siggraph

Colorado

Denver/Boulder
Dave Miller
Denver/Boulder ACM/SIGGRAPH
PO Box 440785
Aurora, CO 80041
Phone: +1 (303) 696-6863
Denver_Boulder_Chapter@siggraph.org

Florida

Ft. Lauderdale
Garry Paxinos
Metro Link Inc.
4711 N Powerline Road.
Fort Lauderdale, FL
Phone: +1 (305) 938-0283 x 414
FAX: +1 (305) 938-1982
FortLauderdale_Chapters@siggraph.org
http://flsig.org/chapter/chapter.html

Orlando
Dave Levinson
PO Box 2208
Winter Park, FL 32790-2208
Phone: +1 (407) 672-3654
        +1 (407) 356-9711
FAX: +1 (407) 356-9798
Orlando_Chapter@siggraph.org
http://flsig.org/os/

North Central Florida
Millard Pate
Micron / Green
1240 N. W. 21st Ave.
Gainesville, FL USA 32609
Phone: +1 (904) 376-1529
Fax: +1 (904) 376-0466
Florida_Chapter@siggraph.org

Tampa Bay
Steve Pidgeon
PO Box 6402
Clearwater, FL 34618-6402
Phone: +1 (813) 977-8414
pidgeon@pulseprod.com
TampaBay_Chapter@siggraph.org
http://www.gate.net/~pidgeon

Georgia

Atlanta
D. Alan Stewart
PO Box 250382
Atlanta, GA 30325
Phone: +1 (404) 785-2911
dastewart@aol.com

Illinois

Chicago
Dennis James
P.O. Box 578365
Chicago, IL 60657-8365
Phone: +1 (708) 387-2149
Fax: +1 (708) 387-2159
Chicago_Chapter@siggraph.org

Massachusetts

Greater Boston
Michael Silton
PO Box 194
Bedford, MA 01730
Phone: +1 (508) 881-9911
Fax: +1 (508) 881-8818
msilton@mcimail.com
New_England_Chapter@siggraph.org

Minnesota

Minneapolis/St. Paul
Stan Bissinger
School of Communication Arts
2526 27th Avenue South
Minneapolis, MN 55406
Phone: +1 (612) 721-5357
dickm3@aol.com

New Jersey

Princeton
Douglas Dixon
David Sarnoff Research Center
CN 5300
Princeton, NJ 08543-5300
609-734-3176
Fax: 609-734-2259
ddixon@vaxserv.sarnoff.com
Princeton_Chapter@siggraph.org

New Mexico

Rio Grande
David Callahan
PO Box 8352
Albuquerque, NM, USA 87198-8352
Phone: +1 (505) 667-1449
Fax: +1 (505) 575-6442 (fax)
Rio_Grande_Chapter@siggraph.org

New York

New York City
Deborah Herschmann
c/o Scott Lang (Treasurer)
United Nations Intl. School
24-50 FDR Drive
New York, NY 10010
Phone: +1 (212) 684-7400, Ext. 3270
Fax: +1 (212) 889 - 8959
New_York_Chapter@siggraph.org

North Carolina

Research Triangle
Randy Brown
3407 Carriage Trail
Hillsborough, NC 27278
Phone: +1 919-677-8000
randy@unx.sas.com
Research_Triangle_Chapter@siggraph.org

Texas

Dallas
Wade Smith
PO Box 800691
Dallas, TX, USA 75380-0691
Dallas_Area_Chapter@siggraph.org
wsmith@convex.com
Dallas_SIGGRAPH_Chapter@siggraph.org

Houston
Jim Maida
Houston ACM/SIGGRAPH
NASA JSC, SP34
Nasa Rd. 1
Houston, TX 77058
Phone: +1 (713) 483-1113
maida@graf6.jsc.nasa.gov
Houston_Area_Chapter@siggraph.org

SIGGRAPH Professional Chapters

Washington
Tri Cities Washington
Don Jones
Battelle Pacific Northwest Labs
Box 999
MS K1-87
Richland, WA 99352
Phone: +1 509 375 2913
djones@carbon.pnl.gov
Washington_Tri_Cities_Chapter@siggraph.org

Washington, D.C.
Washington, D.C.
P.O. Box 32254
Washington, DC 20007
Phone: +1 (703) 968-3313
Washington_DC_Chapter@siggraph.org

Brazil
Sao Paulo
Sergio Martinelli
Digital Group
Rua Bairi 294
05059 San Paulo, SP1 Brazil
sigrapsp@lsi.usp.br

Bulgaria
Sofia
Stoyan Maleshkov
Technical Univ of Sofia
Dept of Prog & Computer Appl
1756 Sofia, Bulgaria

Canada
Montreal (forming)
contact: Kaveh Kardan
Phone: +1 (514) 842-6172
kardank@ede.umontreal.ca

Toronto
Greg Blair
8 Corley Ave
Toronto, Ontario M4E 1T4
Phone: +1 (416) 691-7273 (home)
Phone: +1 (905) 513-3024 (work)
blair_greg@tandem.com
siggraph@dgp.utoronto.ca
Toronto_Chapter@siggraph.org

Vancouver
Brian D. McMillan
PO Box 33986 Postal Station D
Vancouver, B.C., Canada V6J-4L7
Phone: +1 (604) 822-2466
Fax: +1 (604) 822-3808
Vancouver_BC_Chapter@siggraph.org
http://fas.sfu.ca/0/cs/research/groups/
  GMRL/ACM-SIGGRAPH/main.html

France
Paris
Alain Chesnais
#2 Rue Henre Matisse
59300 Aulnoy-les-Valenciennes
France
Phone: +33 27-28-42-42
Paris_Chapter@siggraph.org

Israel
Central Israel
Craig Gotsman
Department of Computer Science
Technion
Haifa 32000
Israel
gotsman@cs.technion.ac.il
Central_Israel_Chapter@siggraph.org

Mexico
Mexico City
Arnulfo Zepeda
Barranca del Muerto #24, Piso 3 Norte
Mexico DF, CP 01020
MEXICO
zepeda@siggraph.org
Mexico_City_Chapter@siggraph.org
http://www.spin.com.mx/sigmex/sighome.htm

Spain
Madrid
Felix Berges Munoz
Postdata
c/o Breton de los Herreros
35 3 Izqda.
Madrid, 28003 Spain
ruy@asterix.fi.upm.es

Russia
Moscow
Yuri Bayakouski
Keldysh Institute of Appl. Maths
Miusskaya Sq., 4
Moscow, 125047 Russia
Phone: +095 250-7817
Moscow_Chapter@siggraph.org

United Kingdom
London
Dr. Gregg Moore
27 Sinclair House
Sandwish Street
London, WC1H 9PT
Phone: +44 (81) 362-5000 X7475
London_Chapter@siggraph.org

**Professional Chapters
Steering Committee**

Ed Council, Member at Large
Timberfield Systems
650 Worcester Road
PO Box 2345
Framingham, MA 01701
Phone: +1 (508) 872-5522
FAX: +1 (508) 875-0521
council@siggraph.org

Alain Chesnais, Member at Large
Wavefront Technologies S.A.
22 ave Hegesippe Moreau
75018 Paris
France
Phone: +33 1 44 90 11 49
FAX: +33 1 44 90 11 31
chesnais@siggraph.org

Len Breen, Member at Large, Startups
31 Old Gloucester Street
Bloomsbury, London WC1N 3AF
England
Phone: +44 71 242 0551
FAX: +44 71 831 9377
breen@siggraph.org

Scott Lang, Member at Large, Startups
United Nations Intl. School
24-50 FDR Drive
New York, NY 10010
Phone: +1 (212) 684-7400, Ext. 3270
FAX: +1 (212) 889 - 8959
lang@siggraph.org

Jeff Jortner, Director for Local Groups &
PCSC Chair
Sandia National Laboratories
Department 8920, MS 9012
Livermore, CA 94551-0969
Phone: +1 (510) 294-3846
FAX: +1 (510) 294-1225
jortner@siggraph.org

**Mailing to leaders in all SIGGRAPH
professional chapters:**
professionalchapterschairs@siggraph.org

**Mailing to members of the Professional
Chapters Steering Committee:**
pcsc@siggraph.org

**Email contact to get more information
about professional chapters:**
localgroupinfo@siggraph.org